Microsoft®

Office 2010
IN DEPTH

Joe Habraken

800 East 96th Street
Indianapolis, Indiana 46240

MICROSOFT® OFFICE 2010 IN DEPTH

ISBN-13: 978-0-7897-4309-1

ISBN-10: 0-7897-4309-4

Library of Congress Cataloging-in-Publication data is on file.

Printed in the United States of America

First Printing: October 2010

Trademarks

All terms mentioned in this book that are known to be trademarks or service marks have been appropriately capitalized. Que Publishing cannot attest to the accuracy of this information. Use of a term in this book should not be regarded as affecting the validity of any trademark or service mark.

Microsoft is a registered trademark of Microsoft Corporation.

Warning and Disclaimer

Every effort has been made to make this book as complete and as accurate as possible, but no warranty or fitness is implied. The information provided is on an "as is" basis. The authors and the publisher shall have neither liability nor responsibility to any person or entity with respect to any loss or damages arising from the information contained in this book.

Bulk Sales

Que Publishing offers excellent discounts on this book when ordered in quantity for bulk purchases or special sales. For more information, please contact

    U.S. Corporate and Government Sales

    1-800-382-3419

    corpsales@pearsontechgroup.com

For sales outside the United States, please contact

    International Sales

    international@pearsoned.com

Associate Publisher
Greg Wiegand

Senior Acquisitions Editor
Loretta Yates

Development Editor
Charlotte Kughen

Technical Editor
Doug Holland

Managing Editor
Sandra Schroeder

Project Editor
Seth Kerney

Indexer
Heather McNeill

Proofreader
Leslie Joseph

Publishing Coordinator
Cindy Teeters

Interior Designer
Anne Jones

Cover Designer
Anne Jones

Page Layout
Bronkella Publishing, Inc.

CONTENTS AT A GLANCE

CONTENTS

ABOUT THE AUTHOR

Joe Habraken is a computer technology professional, educator, and best-selling author with more than 20 years of experience in the information technology and digital media production fields. His books include numerous titles on the Microsoft Office application suite, computer networking, and Microsoft's Windows Server network platform. His books include Que's *Microsoft Office 2003 All in One* and *Sams Teach Yourself Windows Server 2008 in 24 Hours*. Joe is an associate professor and department chair at the University of New England in Biddeford, Maine, where he teaches a variety of desktop application, information technology, and digital media courses.

Dedication

I would like to dedicate this book to my wonderful wife, Kim. She has put up with me and my home office filled with computers, technology junk, and stacks of books for more than 28 years; thanks honey, I love you!

Acknowledgments

Creating a large and comprehensive book like this "takes a village" (as Hillary Clinton once said). It has been a real privilege for me to work with the team of professionals at Que who have helped make this project a reality and a success. I would like to thank Loretta Yates, our acquisitions editor, who worked very hard to assemble the project team for this book, helped determine the content coverage for the text, and showed the patience of a saint during the actual writing process. I would also like to thank Charlotte Kughen, who served as the development editor for this book and who waded through first draft text and came up with many great ideas for improving its content. Our technical editor, Doug Holland, did a fantastic job making sure that everything in the book was correct and suggested a number of additions that made the book even more technically sound. I would also like to thank our other team members: managing editor Sandra Schroeder; proofreader Leslie Joseph; indexer Heather McNeill; publishing coordinator Cindy Teeters; interior and cover designer Anne Jones, who made everything look great; and our page layout guru Tricia Bronkella. Finally a great big thanks to our project editor Seth Kerney, who ran the last leg of the race and made sure the book made it to press on time—what a fantastic group of publishing professionals!

WE WANT TO HEAR FROM YOU!

As the reader of this book, *you* are our most important critic and commentator. We value your opinion and want to know what we're doing right, what we could do better, what areas you'd like to see us publish in, and any other words of wisdom you're willing to pass our way.

As an associate publisher for Que, I welcome your comments. You can email or write me directly to let me know what you did or didn't like about this book—as well as what we can do to make our books better.

Please note that I cannot help you with technical problems related to the topic of this book. We do have a User Services group, however, where I will forward specific technical questions related to the book.

When you write, please be sure to include this book's title and author as well as your name, email address, and phone number. I will carefully review your comments and share them with the author and editors who worked on the book.

Email: feedback@quepublishing.com

Mail: Greg Wiegand
Associate Publisher
Que Publishing
800 East 96th Street
Indianapolis, IN 46240 USA

For more information about this book or another Que Publishing title, visit our website at www.quepublishing.com. Type the ISBN (excluding hyphens) or the title of a book in the Search field to find the page you're looking for.

INTRODUCTION

Congratulations! You are about to harness the incredible capabilities of the latest version of Microsoft Office: Office 2010. Microsoft Office has been the gold standard for application suites for many years and provides all the applications that you need for a wide variety of tasks. Whether you are writing a novel, balancing your budget, managing your emails and contacts, or creating an important sales presentation, you will find all the features and tools that you need to get the job done.

If you have used Microsoft Office in the past but have not upgraded in the last few years, you will find that the Office applications have undergone a substantial makeover that enables you to work even more quickly and efficiently. All the Office applications embrace the Ribbon-based Office Fluent interface, providing an intuitive interface that enables you to get up and running in Office applications that you might not have used in the past.

As personal computing moved from a somewhat solitary environment to a new world of connectivity and collaboration, Microsoft enriched the Microsoft Office applications to make it easier for you to communicate and collaborate with other users on your business or home network and via the Internet. Office collaboration tools make it easier for you to share files and to review documents edited by colleagues.

This latest version of Office also takes into account the fact that we all now work in a much more graphically rich computing environment and typically create files that include images, diagrams, and other graphics. Office 2010 provides greatly improved tools for working with digital images, and makes it easy for you to create a variety of graphics that greatly enhanced the visual impact of your documents, worksheets, and presentations.

Who Should Buy This Book

If you are thumbing through the table of contents of this book, trying to make a determination as to whether you should take the leap and buy it; let me give you some concrete reasons why this would be a good purchase. First, this book is part of Que's *In Depth* series, which is dedicated to providing you with a series of comprehensive guides for a variety of software applications and operating systems. The highly skilled publishing team at Que Publishing works hard to provide you with the very best computer reference books.

This particular book is designed for a range of Microsoft Office users—from the novice to the well-seasoned veteran. New users will find it an excellent hands-on tool for learning the basics of the various Office applications. More experienced users will find it a resource that allows them to go well beyond the basic capabilities of powerful application software packages such as Word, Excel, Outlook, PowerPoint, Publisher, and OneNote.

This book's approach is simple: It provides in-depth coverage of Microsoft Office 2010 application features and software tools, and also provides you with the context in which that particular feature or tool will be used as you edit documents, create email messages, or fine-tune complex worksheets. This book serves you as a reference for specific application features, but can also serve as a resource for learning how to best take advantage of the capabilities provided by each of the individual Office applications and to leverage the capabilities of Office as an integrated suite of software tools. As someone whose job it is to teach students to understand the practical application of software in the real world, I have made sure that this book embraces that ideal and will enable you to use the various Office applications more completely and effectively whatever your endeavors.

The book is written in an easy-to-read, conversational style that allows you to concentrate on learning and understanding. Although you will find that each of the Office applications provides multiple ways to tackle nearly every task, this book stresses best practices in using applications such as Word, Excel, and PowerPoint to enable you to realize better results when using these software tools.

How This Book Is Organized

Microsoft Office 2010 In Depth is organized into seven parts and also includes two appendices. Each Office application covered in this book is discussed in detail in its own part or section. This makes it possible for you to quickly access information related to a specific Office application: Word, Excel, PowerPoint, Outlook, Publisher, or OneNote. All the most important and useful features and tasks are covered in the application-specific sections of this book. The book also includes an introductory section (Part I) that enables you to quickly get up to speed with the Office 2010 interface and new features and tools found in this version of the powerful Microsoft Office application suite. Two appendices are included; one provides insight into using the Office applications in an integrated fashion and the other is a primer on Office macros.

Part I, "Office 2010 Interface and Common Features," gets you oriented to the Office application interface and geography stressing Microsoft's Office Fluent user interface approach and also looks at improvements and new features found in the Office applications. This section also discusses managing and sharing your Office application files and working with graphics and images in the various Office applications. An introduction to the new Office Web apps is also provided in this section.

Part II, "Word," takes an in-depth look at the Office suite's powerful word processor and desktop publishing application. This section begins with an overview of the Word application environment and how to access essential Word features and tools. Each subsequent chapter in this section builds your Word knowledge base from commonly used features and commands to advanced subject matter that will allow you to create more complex and specialized Word documents using styles, tables, and sections. This section also provides you with complete coverage of advanced features, such as Word's mail merge and forms, and it details approaches for creating larger documents requiring a table of contents, footnotes, and cross-references.

Part III, "Excel," quickly orients you to this powerful spreadsheet application so that you can immediately begin to work with worksheets, text labels, values, formulas, and cell ranges. This section then focuses on worksheet management and advanced formatting and provides an in-depth discussion of the use of formulas and functions in your Excel worksheets. The use of charts, pivot tables, and tools for sorting and filtering data are also covered in this section, which culminates in coverage of Excel's advanced features for validating and analyzing your worksheet data.

Part IV, "PowerPoint," provides you with a detailed discussion of this powerful presentation tool. Beginning with an overview of the PowerPoint application environment and basic presentation tools and concepts, this section provides you with all the information you will require to build complex and compelling PowerPoint presentations. Chapters in this section include information on how to build better PowerPoint slides using themes, slide transitions, and special animations. The options and best practices for presenting PowerPoint presentations are also provided with particular insight into how printed materials such as handouts and notes can be used to make a presentation even more effective.

Part V, "Outlook," covers how to use this powerful information manager in both small office/home office environments and on corporate networks. The chapters in this section provide you with an overview of the Outlook interface and common features, and then concentrates on the diverse abilities that Outlook provides as an email client, contact information manager, calendar manager, and organizer of tasks, notes, and other personal information. Coverage is also provided to help you secure the information in Outlook and protect your Outlook Inbox from spam, viruses, and other security threats.

Part VI, "Publisher," discusses the Office suite's dedicated desktop publishing application. Publisher has slowly evolved from a home office–oriented application into an extremely useful and robust design application that enables you to quickly create a variety of visually appealing and professional documents. This section orients you to the basics of creating special documents in Publisher and then builds your knowledge base in the application so that you can create more complex items, including online content.

Part VII, "OneNote," covers the capabilities of this information manager, which enables you to gather, organize, and share information. This section begins with an overview of the OneNote interface and the creation of OneNote notebooks. Chapters in this section walk you through the use of tabs, pages, and tables in your notebooks to store and organize information. This section concludes with a look at how OneNote can be integrated with other Office applications such as Word and Excel.

This book completes its discussion of the Office applications with Appendices A and B, which provide information on integrating the Office applications and Office macros, respectively. Each appendix is designed to provide you with additional information related to the Office applications that can be used to leverage your capabilities when using Office suite members such as Word, Excel, and PowerPoint. In my mind, the appendices provide information that is over and above the in-depth coverage provided for each Office application in the seven sections of the book. It would make sense to have a very strong working knowledge of the Office applications before you tackle the information provided in the appendices.

Conventions Used in This Book

Special conventions are used throughout this book to help you get the most out of each and every page as you ramp up your knowledge of Microsoft Office 2010.

Key Combinations

Much of what we do in the various Office applications is typically a matter of mouse clicks (if we aren't typing text); however, some commands are a result of key combinations on the keyboard. Key combinations are respresented with a plus sign. For example, if you the text calls on you to bold text using the Ctrl+B key, the plus symbol denotes that the keys are to be pressed at the same time.

Special Elements

Special elements in this book provide you with additional information that will help you better understand the text in a particular chapter section or warn you about a potential problem with a particular software feature. These elements are to help you better navigate the features and tools discussed in this book. These special elements consist of Notes, Tips, Cautions, and Cross-References. The name of each special element provides you with insight into how you could use the information provided by an element.

 note

Notes provide information that expands on information in a chapter. The extra information in Notes isn't essential as you work through a chapter, so you can take advantage of the Notes provided as time allows.

 tip

Tips provide you with best practices and shortcuts as you work with the various Office features and tools. Tips are designed to help you get the most out of a particular software feature and increase your overall efficiency and ability with the application.

caution

Cautions are designed to warn you about potential pitfalls with an application feature or tool. Heeding the warning provided by a caution can save you both time and frustration as you navigate a tricky or confusing concept, feature, or tool in an Office application.

Cross References

Cross references are designed to point you to other locations in this book or other books in the Que family. Cross references make it easy for you to jump to another part of the book for supplemental information related to the topic in the chapter you are currently reading. Cross references appear as follows:

 For information on configuring an Outlook profile and email account the first time you run Outlook, see Chapter 22, "Requisite Outlook: Configuration and Essential Features," on page 597.

GETTING ORIENTED TO THE OFFICE 2010 APPLICATIONS

Microsoft Office 2010 is the latest version of Microsoft's powerful application suite. Office 2010 provides you with a number of versatile and impressive applications, including Word, Excel, PowerPoint, and Outlook, which enable you to tackle a large variety of business and personal tasks. Whether you are creating reports, crunching budget numbers, organizing a presentation, or managing your email and contacts, Office 2010 provides you with all the tools and features that you will need to get the job done.

This chapter provides an introduction to the Office 2010 application suite, including a look at the different versions of Office 2010 available. New features and tools available in Office 2010 are also discussed. Installing Office 2010 is also covered, as is getting help and support when using the various Office applications.

Introducing Office 2010

On first inspection, the Office 2010 suite members, such as Word, Excel, and PowerPoint, look very similar to their predecessors. The Office 2010 applications use the same Microsoft Office Fluent user interface introduced in Office 2007. This application interface uses the Ribbon as the primary location for accessing application-specific commands and features.

Although the Office 2010 suite members might look somewhat like their predecessors, there have been a lot of changes to each of the applications. Extremely obvious improvements include the adoption of the Office Fluent user interface by

 note

The Office 2010 Ribbon is customizable. You can add your own tabs to the Ribbon with commands you use frequently.

Outlook, Publisher, and OneNote. All three applications now use the Ribbon as their command center. Figure 1.1 shows the Outlook 2010 application window and the Outlook Ribbon. The inclusion of the Ribbon in these applications also means that the Quick Access Toolbar will be available. The Quick Access Toolbar can include many commonly used commands such as Undo, Redo, Save, and Print. You can also customize the Quick Access Toolbar to hold any commands you want.

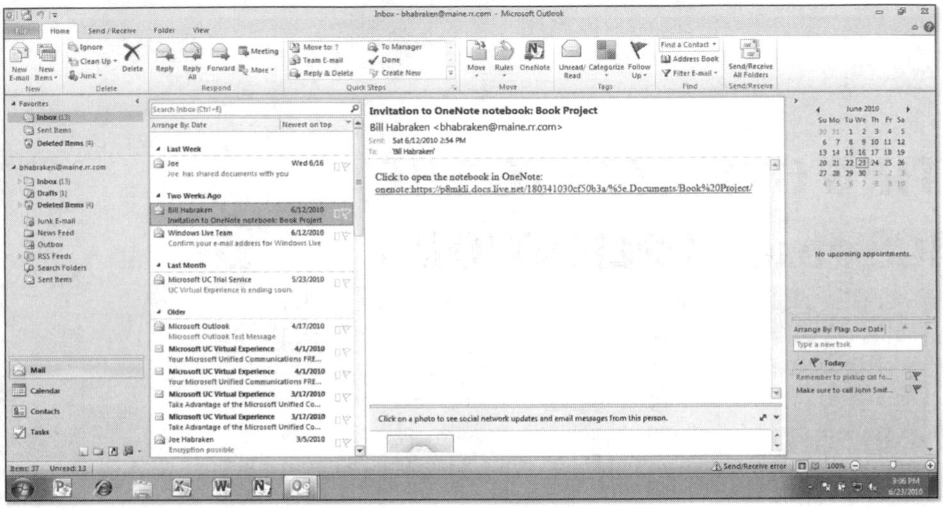

Figure 1.1
Outlook 2010 adopts the Office Fluent user interface.

Not only does the Outlook 2010 application window provide the Ribbon, but you will find that when you create a new mail message, new contact, or new appointment, the Ribbon will also be available and provide a specific set of commands related to the new item that you are creating. The adoption of the Office Fluent user interface and the Ribbon in applications such as Outlook and OneNote provides you with a completely consistent look for all the Office 2010 applications. This makes it easier for you to quickly become familiar with the commands and features of Office suite members that you use less frequently.

New Features and Tools in Office 2010

The Office 2010 applications boast a number of new features and capabilities. Some of the new features provided in Office 2010 will affect all the Office suite members or a subset of the Office member applications. Many other changes and improvements will be application specific.

For example, the Office Backstage is available in all the Office applications and provides you with a number of tools for managing and working with your Office files, including sharing and printing files. A new feature that is specific to Excel is the inclusion of sparklines. Sparklines are mini-charts that appear inline with worksheet data and enable you to visually summarize the data.

We will introduce some of the more global changes to the Office applications in this chapter. Some of the new features specific to the individual Office 2010 applications will also be discussed, with more coverage on these changes provided within the chapters that discuss the individual applications such as Word, Excel, PowerPoint, or Outlook.

The Office Backstage

The Office Backstage view is one of the biggest changes to the Office application interface. The Office Backstage is accessed via the File tab included on each of the applications' Ribbon. The Backstage provides commands such as Save, Save As, Open, and Close in applications such as Word, Excel, PowerPoint, and Publisher. Figure 1.2 shows the Excel Backstage with Save & Send selected.

Figure 1.2
The Excel
Backstage.

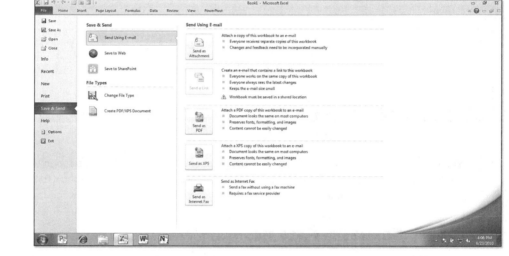

The Save & Send options shown in Figure 1.2 are new to Office 2010 and make it easy for you to share your files with other users. You can email a file as an attachment, save the file to the Windows Live SkyDrive (Save to Web), and share files on a SharePoint Server site using the Save to SharePoint command. Office 2010 is designed for better file sharing and taking advantage of different platforms such as SharePoint Server that enable you to easily share files with your coworkers and colleagues.

The Backstage also gives you access to information related to the current file via the Info window. Files recently opened in the application are listed when you select Recent, and you can create a new file in an application by selecting New.

> *For more information about preparing an Office file for sharing, see page 71 in Chapter 3, "Managing and Sharing Office Files."*

The Backstage is also home to one of the biggest changes in Office 2010, which makes previewing and printing of your document easier to manage: The print commands are integrated into the Backstage. Selecting Print in the Backstage opens the Print window. The Print Preview pane is built right into the Print window, so you can preview the printout as you select your printer and adjust your print settings. Figure 1.3 shows the Word Print window.

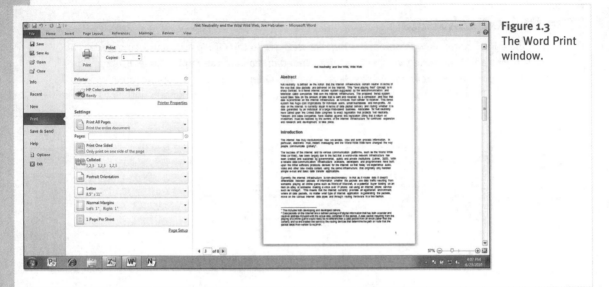

Figure 1.3
The Word Print window.

You can use the Print window to set the number of copies, specify the page range to print, and adjust page orientation, size, and margins. You can also easily navigate through the pages of the preview provided and zoom in and out on the preview using the Zoom slider.

Enhanced Smart Art Graphics

If you add diagrams to your Word, Excel, or PowerPoint files, you will find that Office 2010 makes it easy to create visually informative SmartArt that takes advantage of both pictures and text. You can now easily rearrange content, such as text, in a diagram and the capabilities for inserting and changing pictures in a diagram are much improved. Figure 1.4 shows a PowerPoint slide containing a picture strip SmartArt graphic.

The text pane on the right of the SmartArt graphic makes it easy to add and edit text. Pictures can be added to the graphic by double-clicking placeholders provided in the text pane.

When you work with SmartArt graphics in Excel, Word, and PowerPoint, the SmartArt Tools become available when you select a SmartArt graphic. The SmartArt Tools consist of a Design and Format tab. The Design tab enables you to modify the SmartArt layout, apply SmartArt styles to your graphic, and manage the elements in the graphic.

For more information about SmartArt, see page 79 in Chapter 4, "Using and Creating Graphics."

Figure 1.4
Office 2010 provides enhanced SmartArt graphics.

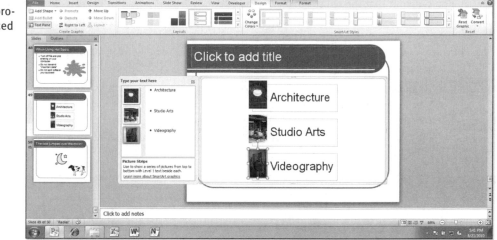

New Screen Capture Tool

A Screenshot command has been added to the Ribbon's Insert tab in Word, Excel, PowerPoint, and Outlook. This new tool makes it easy to include visual information in a document, worksheet, presentation, or email by enabling you to include a capture of another application's screen. Figure 1.5 shows the Screenshot gallery, which is opened when you select the Screenshot command on the Ribbon's Insert tab.

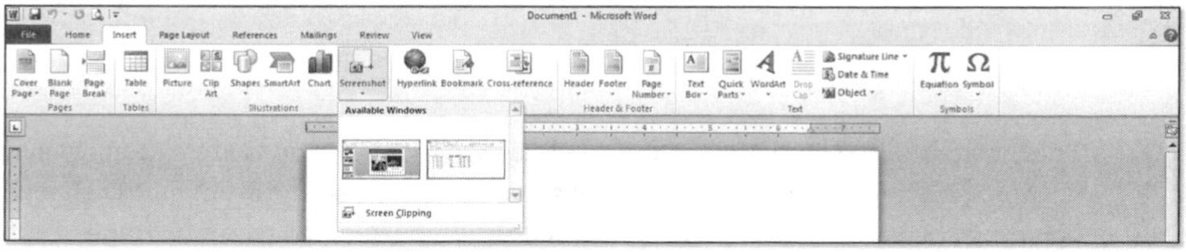

Figure 1.5
Capture application screens using the Screenshot command.

The Screenshot command enables you to capture an entire application window or you can use the Screen Clipping option to capture a portion of an application screen using the mouse. Captured screenshots can then be manipulated as you would any other picture that has been inserted into a document. The contextual Picture Tools become available whenever you select a picture (or screenshot) in the Office applications. This enables you to adjust the picture, format the picture with a picture style, and crop the picture if needed.

➡ *For more information about using the Screenshot command, see page 97 in Chapter 4.*

New Background Removal Tool

You will find that the Office 2010 versions of Word, PowerPoint, and Excel have really been stepped up a notch (perhaps even several notches) in terms of manipulating pictures. The Picture Tools provide you with the ability to correct brightness and contrast issues and modify other aspects of a picture including color and artistic effects. The Picture Tools Format tab also includes the Remove Background command.

The Remove Background command enables you to remove the background elements of a picture (such as a digital photo) while leaving the foreground elements untouched. Figure 1.6 shows the Remove Background command at work and the Background Removal commands that are provided to help you fine-tune the removal of background elements from a photo.

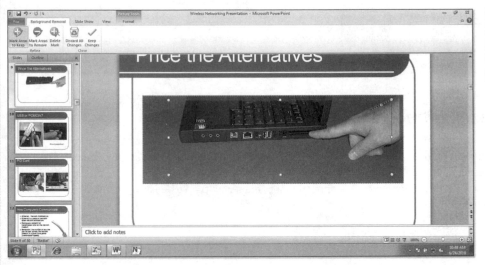

Figure 1.6
Remove the background from a digital photo.

The Background Removal tool and the commands that it provides are extremely simple to use. This new tool will provide you with the ability to quickly create interesting photo effects that can be difficult to achieve even in some high-end photo manipulation software packages.

➡ *For more information on using the Remove Background command, see page 91 in Chapter 4.*

Other Office 2010 Improvements and Updates

As our discussion thus far proves, the Office 2010 applications provide a number of new possibilities for working with graphics. Even if you don't use a lot of visuals in your Office documents, you will find that there are a number of other changes in the Office 2010 application suite that will improve your productivity and just make it easier to do high-quality work. Some of these updates are as follows:

- **Paste Preview:** You can now preview the various paste options for text or other items that you have cut or copied. This makes it easy for you to determine what paste option will give you the desired results before you paste.

- **Recover Versions of Office Files:** The Office 2010 applications such as Word, PowerPoint, and Excel now keep track of different versions of your Office documents that are autosaved as you work. You can view a list of the different file versions and open a specific version by using the Manage Versions command available in the Info window of the application's Backstage view.

- **Improved Conversation View in Outlook:** Outlook now provides a new conversation view of your emails that enables you to easily work with associated email messages whether they are messages that you sent or received. You also now have the ability to ignore conversations, which helps cut down on the clutter as you work with your important emails.

- **WordArt Improvements:** WordArt now provides you with the ability to apply text effects directly to text in your document. You don't have to create a separate WordArt object to take advantage of eye-catching fonts and exciting text effects. Word, Excel, and PowerPoint share this text-formatting update.

- **Embed and Edit Videos in PowerPoint:** Microsoft PowerPoint now provides support for embedded video objects. Not only can you insert video into PowerPoint, including your own videos and videos streamed from the Web, but you can also adjust video settings and crop the video window.

- **OneNote Linked Notes:** Microsoft OneNote, an information organizer, has been greatly improved. One of its great new features is that you can take notes while working in Word, PowerPoint, or Internet Explorer. OneNote inhabits a docked window on the desktop as you work in the other application. Any notes that you take in OneNote are automatically linked to the application and file that you are using as you take the notes.

Although this is certainly not an exhaustive list of changes to the Office 2010 applications, I hope you get the feeling that Office 2010 is a truly exciting upgrade to Microsoft's powerful application suite. You can now do more in the applications and do it more effectively.

➥ *For more information on inserting video into PowerPoint slides, see page 571 in Chapter 20, "Enhancing Slides with Animation, Transitions, and Multimedia."*

➥ *For more information on creating linked notes, see page 851 in Chapter 32, "Integrating OneNote with the Office Suite Applications."*

Introducing the Office Web Apps

One of the biggest and most exciting changes related to Office 2010 isn't an update or change to the Office applications; it is a major addition: the Office web apps. The Office web apps consist of versions of Word, Excel, PowerPoint, and OneNote that you can run in your web browser. A web app provides you with a scaled-down version of an Office 2010 application that enables you to work with

Office documents when you aren't able to get to a computer that has the Office 2010 application suite installed.

Figure 1.7 shows the PowerPoint web app with a PowerPoint presentation loaded. You can create new files using the web apps and you can open files that have been saved to a Microsoft SharePoint Server site or Microsoft's SkyDrive.

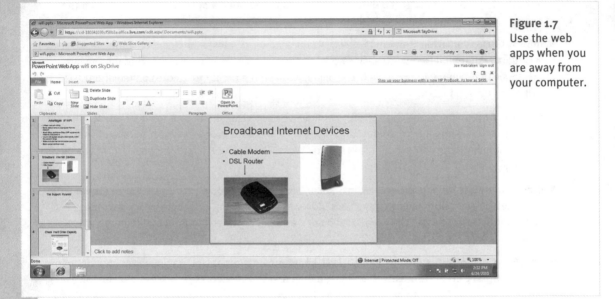

Figure 1.7
Use the web apps when you are away from your computer.

Using the web apps on a SharePoint Server corporate intranet enables you to open, modify, and change Office files directly from your browser window. Microsoft Live's SkyDrive is available to anyone with a Microsoft Live ID. You can save files from your installed Office 2010 applications to the SkyDrive and open files on SkyDrive in the web Apps. The new web apps are discussed in detail in Chapter 5, "Working with the Microsoft Office Web Apps."

➡ *For an overview of the Office web Apps, see page 105 in Chapter 5.*

The Office 2010 Suite Applications

The Office 2010 suite applications available to you will depend on the version of Office 2010 that you or your company purchases. We look at the different versions and their application mix in the next section. In terms of coverage of the Office 2010 applications in this book, we will concentrate on the following applications:

- **The Web Apps:** Although each web app has an Office 2010 suite member counterpart, we cover the web apps in their own chapter (Chapter 5) in Part I of this book: "Office 2010 Interface and Common Features."

- **Word:** The standard for word processing in the Windows environment for many years, Word 2010 provides you with a number of new features and possibilities. Whether you use Word to create letters, short reports, or lengthy documents that include footnotes, table of contents, and cross-references, you will find in-depth coverage of Word in Part II of this book.

- **Excel:** This powerful number cruncher provides a number of new features such as sparklines and PivotTable slicers and has a new add-on for data analysis called PowerPivot. Excel in-depth coverage can be found in Part III of this book.

- **PowerPoint:** Your PowerPoint presentations can even be more exciting with the addition of new transitions and animation effects. You can now also organize slides in a presentation into sections, making it easier to organize a lengthy and complex slide show. PowerPoint's in-depth coverage is located in Part IV of this book.

- **Outlook:** This versatile personal information manager and email client enables you to communicate with coworkers and friends and manage all your messages, contacts, and appointments. New views for managing emails and Quick Steps, which are a new way to execute multiple commands with a single click, make it even easier to manage information in Outlook. Outlook is covered in depth in Part V of this book.

- **Publisher:** With the adoption of the Office Fluent user interface and the inclusion of new improvements for working with pictures and saving your publications in multiple file formats, Publisher has become an excellent desktop publishing platform. Publisher can be used to create a number of different publication types from the simple to the complex. Part VI of this book provides coverage of this newest version of Publisher.

- **OneNote:** OneNote was introduced in the Office 2007 suite. This organizational tool enables you to store information in electronic notebooks, which can easily be shared with other users. OneNote 2010 boasts a number of new features, including the adoption of the Office Fluent user interface. Coverage of OneNote is provided in Part VII of this book.

The Office 2010 suite that you purchase can also include other applications (as already mentioned) such as Microsoft Access, the powerful database application, Microsoft InfoPath, Microsoft Communicator, and Microsoft SharePoint Workspace. SharePoint Workspace basics are discussed in Chapter 3, "Managing and Sharing Office Files."

One thing to keep in mind as you use the various Office applications is that they are designed as an integrated group of software tools. You can easily share information between the applications and use multiple applications to build powerful reports, presentations, and shared content.

For an introduction to SharePoint Workspace, see page 72 in Chapter 3.

The Different Versions of the Office 2010 Suite

Office 2010 comes in a number of different flavors or versions. Some of these versions are only available via volume licensing. Other versions are designed for the student or home office user. Each of the versions provides a different set of Office member applications.

The Office 2010 available versions and the applications that they include are

- **Microsoft Office Professional Plus 2010 (volume licensing only):** This high-end version includes Excel, Outlook (with the Business Contact Manager), PowerPoint, Word, Access, InfoPath, Office Communicator (2007), Publisher, OneNote, SharePoint Workspace, and the Microsoft Office web apps (for SharePoint Server environments).

- **Microsoft Office Professional 2010:** This version (which is available as a retail product) includes Excel, Outlook, PowerPoint, Word, Access, Publisher, and OneNote.

- **Microsoft Office Home and Business 2010:** This version (available retail) includes Excel, Outlook, PowerPoint, Word, and OneNote. A noncommercial version of this Office version (for use in academic settings with volume licensing) also is available and includes the applications listed here with the exception of Outlook, which is omitted from the version.

- **Microsoft Office Standard 2010:** This version (volume licensing only) includes Excel, Outlook, PowerPoint, Word, OneNote, Publisher, and the web apps (for deployment via a SharePoint Server environment).

All the available versions of Office 2010 provide you with Office core applications that include Excel, PowerPoint, and Word. Even home and small business users can also take advantage of Outlook 2010 as their email client and personal information manager and can use OneNote to organize and share information.

Hardware and Software Requirements for Office 2010

Office 2010 provides a number of new features and all these bells and whistles do come with hardware requirements. It is always better to have a computer that exceeds the minimum hardware requirements for a software application. The more memory that your computer has, and the faster its processor, the more enjoyable your experience will be as you use the Office 2010 member applications. The minimum hardware requirements for Office 2010 and some realistic recommendations are as follows:

- **Processor:** 500MHz processor; 1GHz (at least) is suggested and is the minimum required if you use Business Contact Manager with Outlook. I would suggest at least 2GHz or better to really take advantage of what Office 2010 has to offer—the faster the better. Any new computer with a dual-core processor (or better) would run the Office applications at peak performance.

- **Memory (RAM):** 256MB with 512MB recommended for graphics and other advanced features. I would suggest a bare minimum of 1GB. Memory is relatively inexpensive. RAM in the 2GB to 4GB range will make your life a lot easier when you are running multiple applications.

- **Hard Drive Space:** The minimum amount required for installation of the Office suite is 3GB. If you are running low on the hard drive that also contains your Windows installation, get an external drive such as a USB drive and clean up your files and move them off the main drive. You can then install Office.

- **Graphics Card:** You need a DirectX 9.0–compatible graphics card that provides at least 64MB of memory. Again, as with everything else, the more video memory you have, the better graphic-intensive Office features will run.

In terms of the Windows operating system and Office 2010 compatibility, you can run the 32-bit version of Office 2010 on a computer that is running Windows XP with Service Pack 3 installed. You can also use Windows Vista (SP1 installed) and Windows 7. If you are running the 64-bit version of Windows (XP, Vista, or 7), you can also take advantage of the 64-bit version of Office 2010. In terms of operating system recommendations, I would have to say that Office 2010 runs fine on Windows XP and Vista but seems to run best on Windows 7. Even though the operating system might make a difference, it is probably more important to have a fast processor and a lot of memory.

Although it is not a hardware or software requirement, I suggest that you get a Windows Live ID if you do not currently have one. A Windows Live ID enables you to take advantage of a lot of different Web-based tools provided by Microsoft such as Hotmail. More importantly, a Windows Live ID will provide you with access to Microsoft's SkyDrive. You can store files on the SkyDrive and you can also share files with other users using it. More importantly, you can take advantage of the new Office 2010 web apps from SkyDrive and can open files that you have stored there via your installed Office applications. In addition, you can create new files and save them to SkyDrive using the web apps.

Installing Office 2010

The environment that you work in will more than likely dictate how you install Office 2010. Corporate networks might provide a method to upgrade or install your Office applications over the network. Your network administrator might also take care of the upgrade so that you need to do nothing. In the case of retail purchases of Office 2010, you will need the DVD that you purchase and the license key that accompanies it.

Office 2010 uses a similar scheme for validation and activation as that used by Windows 7. When you enter your product key, it will be validated before you can continue with the installation. After you install the Office 2010 suite, you will also need to activate the software. This can be attempted automatically as discussed in a moment. It you want to use automatic activation, you need to make sure that you are connected to the Internet.

When you insert the DVD, it should automatically open on the Windows desktop, In Windows 7, click the run SETUP.EXE option to begin the installation process. The first thing that the

> **tip**
>
> The installation process discussed here is for a new Office installation. If you have a previous version of Office installed on your computer, you will be provided the option of upgrading and the previous version will be removed. You can choose not to have your previous version upgraded, which will enable you to run both versions of the Office applications. This can get weird sometimes because of the way the applications share resources, so why not just take the attitude of "out with the old and in with the new" and do an upgrade.

Setup Wizard will request is your 25-character product key. It should be in the Office product box. Enter the product key. It might take a moment but the key will be validated. At the bottom of the Enter Your Product Key window is the Attempt to Automatically Activate My Product Online check box. This should be enabled. This will allow the Office suite to attempt activation online at the completion of the installation.

tip

If the DVD does not automatically run, open the Windows Explorer via the Start menu (click Computer) and then you can access the Setup file on the DVD.

After your product key has been validated, you can click Continue. A Software License Terms window will open. Read the software license terms and then click the I Accept the Terms of This Agreement check box. You can then click Continue.

You have the option of installing all the Office products on your DVD using the Install Now button or you can click Customize and select the applications that you do not want to install. If you select Install Now, the installation process begins immediately.

If you select the Customize option, a window will open that enables you to select the applications that you do not want to install. Select the drop-down arrow to the left of an application and select Not Available as shown in Figure 1.8 if you do not want to install the application. If you don't install a particular application, you can always add it later by reinserting your installation media (that is, the DVD).

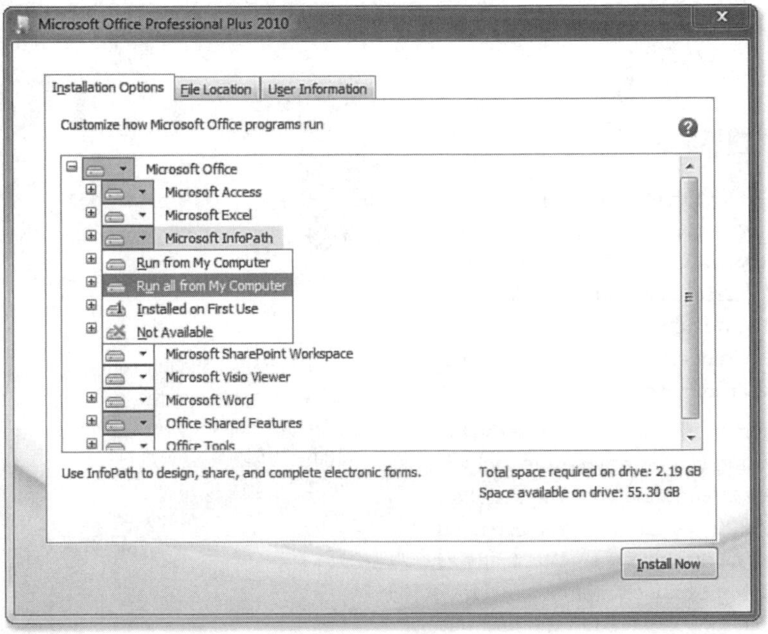

Figure 1.8
You can choose not to install some of the Office suite members.

The installation window that provides you with the ability to remove some of the Office applications from the installed list also enables you to specify a different path for the Office installation. The File Location tab can be used to browse to a different location for the installation. If you want to enter your user information such as your name, initials, and organization, you can do so on the User Information tab. When you are ready to install your selected subset of Office applications, select Install Now.

Whether you selected to install the Office suite immediately or you chose to remove some products from the installation, you will be provided with the installation progress. After the installation is complete, you can click Close to close the installation window.

Launching the Office applications is accomplished via the Start menu. Select Start, All Programs, and then Microsoft Office. Icons for all your installed Office applications will be provided in the Microsoft Office folder. Select an icon to start a particular application. The first time you start an application, the Welcome to Microsoft Office 2010 window will open. It provides you with different options for how Microsoft Office will be updated and how problems with Office will be diagnosed. Figure 1.9 shows the Welcome to Microsoft Office 2010 window.

Figure 1.9
The Welcome to Microsoft Office 2010 window.

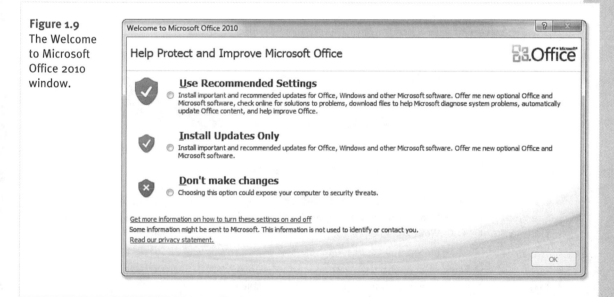

You can choose to have updates installed automatically and to enable Microsoft to offer you optional software and check for problem solutions online by selecting the Use Recommended Settings option button. If you want only updates installed and want new optional software to be offered, select Install Updates Only. This will negate the options related to only problem solutions and problem diagnoses from being included. If you don't want any changes made, you can select Don't Make Changes; however, it makes sense to at least have Office updated periodically. Hackers can exploit holes in the Office coding, so at least go with the Install Updates Only option. After you have selected an option, click OK. Now you can start working with your Office applications.

Getting Help and Support for Office Applications

There are different ways to get help in the Office 2010 applications. As already mentioned, the Backstage, which is common to all the Office 2010 members, provides commands for saving, opening, and printing your Office files. It also provides you with access to help. When you select Help in the Backstage, you are provided with a Support window. This window is shown in Figure 1.10.

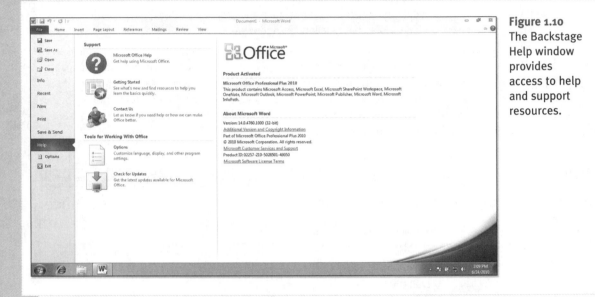

Figure 1.10
The Backstage Help window provides access to help and support resources.

You can select the big question mark to open the Help window for the application you are currently using. For example, if I am in Microsoft Word and I select Microsoft Office Help, the Word Help window will open and provide me with the Getting Started with Word 2010 help screen.

A Getting Started link in the Backstage Help window will open your web browser and load the "getting started" web page for the application you are currently using. This enables you to access additional help for a particular application and search the Microsoft Office.com website for more information related to the application or the entire Office suite.

The Help window can also help you get support for Microsoft Office. When you select the Contact Us link provided in the Help window, your web browser will open and load the Microsoft Support web page. This web page provides you with the ability to contact Microsoft via email, online chat, or telephone. It also provides support for other information related to technical support and other inquires.

 **note**

The Help window also provides your application version, product ID, and information on whether the product has been activated.

tip

You can access help at any time in the Office applications by pressing the F1 key.

You can also get help when you need it as you work in the Office applications. A Help button is provided on the far right of the Ribbon in all the Office 2010 applications. Click it to open the Help window and get help in the current application. Figure 1.11 shows the Word Help window.

Figure 1.11
Help is only a click away.

Links are provided on the various help screens that enable you to quickly jump to various information topics. You can use the Search box provided at the top of the Help window to search for specific information. Dialog boxes provided by the various applications also provide a Help button at the top right of the dialog box. When you select a Help button in a dialog box, the Help system will provide you with help related to that dialog box. Click the recommended links provided for more information on the feature you are actually using. Because the Help system is really an online tool, you will need to be connected to the Internet to take full advantage of the Office help system.

NAVIGATING AND CUSTOMIZING THE OFFICE INTERFACE

Navigating the Office 2010 applications and quickly accessing important commands has never been easier in a version of Microsoft's popular application suite. In this chapter we take a look at the Office interface and how to work with the various command elements that you will interact with in the Office 2010 suite members including dialog boxes, task panes, and even the status bar.

We will look at new options for customizing the Ribbon and also take a look at the new Backstage view. We will also explore the Trust Center, which enables you to specify trusted locations for opening files and other security settings.

Getting Familiar with the Office Interface

The Office 2010 applications employ much of the same "application geography" first introduced in Office 2007. The Microsoft Office Fluent user interface (a term coined by Microsoft) replaces all the menus and toolbars found in earlier versions of Office and replaces them (primarily) with a Ribbon containing a series of tabs. Each tab consists of several command groups, and each group contains related commands.

This user interface is designed to keep related commands together, making it easier for you to complete specific tasks. The Ribbon tabs to tab group to individual commands hierarchy allows you to drill down to a specific result faster and in a more intuitive manner than the menu to submenu to dialog box structure provided by the menu-driven interface of the pre-2007 Office applications.

The Ribbon-dominated user interface uses each tab for grouping commands into somewhat broad yet related categories. For example, in Word 2010 the Review tab (shown in Figure 2.1) provides groups of commands related to reviewing and finalizing a document.

These groups include the Proofing group, the Tracking group, the Changes group, and the Protect group. All these groups provide commands related to reviewing the document, such as the Spelling & Grammar command in the Proofing group and the Track Changes command in the Tracking group.

> **note**
>
> If you are upgrading to Office 2010 from Office 2003 or earlier, you will find the Office Fluent user interface a big change but also a great improvement. For Office 2007 users who are upgrading there have been some changes and refinements to the user interface (such as the Backstage) that I think you will appreciate.

Figure 2.1
Ribbon tabs house related command groups.

The Microsoft Office Fluent user interface also provides consistency across the Office applications. The Home tab in the Word, Excel, PowerPoint, or Publisher application window contains the Clipboard group and other groups related to font formatting, text alignment, and styles. Considering the different purposes of the Office applications, the Ribbon tabs and accompanying command groups obviously vary from application to application in the Office suite.

Galleries

When you work with specific commands on the Ribbons, there will be occasions when you need to select from a list of options. Some commands will provide a list of available choices (not unlike what was typically found in a dialog box), whereas others will provide you with options in the form of a gallery.

> **note**
>
> The tooltips in Office 2010 have been enhanced and provide you with more information about a particular command when you place the mouse on it.

A gallery is different from a list of options in that a gallery supplies actual results related to a command. For example, if you want to apply a theme to a PowerPoint presentation, you would access the Design tab and select from the available theme choices as shown in Figure 2.2.

Figure 2.2
Galleries
provide result-
driven options.

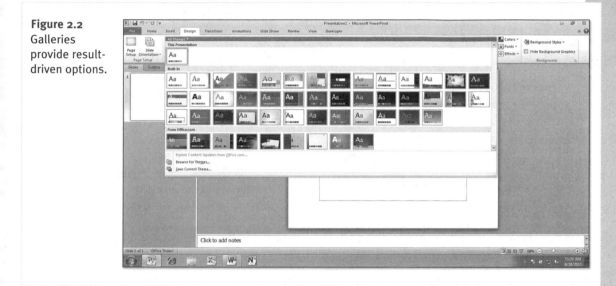

Because many of the galleries are related to the visual appearance or formatting of objects (such as tables or charts), documents, slides, and worksheets, you will find that moving the mouse over the different gallery options actually provides a live preview of how that particular option would be applied to your application's content. Being able to immediately preview and then apply a particular gallery option provides you with both greater flexibility and efficiency as you work with gallery-driven commands on the various Ribbon tabs.

Contextual Tabs

As you work in an Office application, you will find that the Ribbon tabs that are available do not remain static. Contextual tabs become available when you are working with a particular object or feature.

For example, if you insert a table into a Word document or PowerPoint slide and then place the insertion point inside that table or select a row or column in the table, two Table Tools tabs appear: Design and Layout. Figure 2.3 shows the Design and Layout tabs of the Table Tools tab with the Layout tab selected.

> **🔍 note**
>
> Office 2010 also provides Paste Preview, which allows you to view different options for pasting an object into a file before you actually commit to the paste.

You can use the commands on these contextual tabs related to tables as long as the table object is active. As soon as you click outside the table, the contextual tabs disappear and you return to the Ribbon with only the core tabs available. The core tabs include Home, Insert, and so forth; the specific tabs available depends on the application you are using.

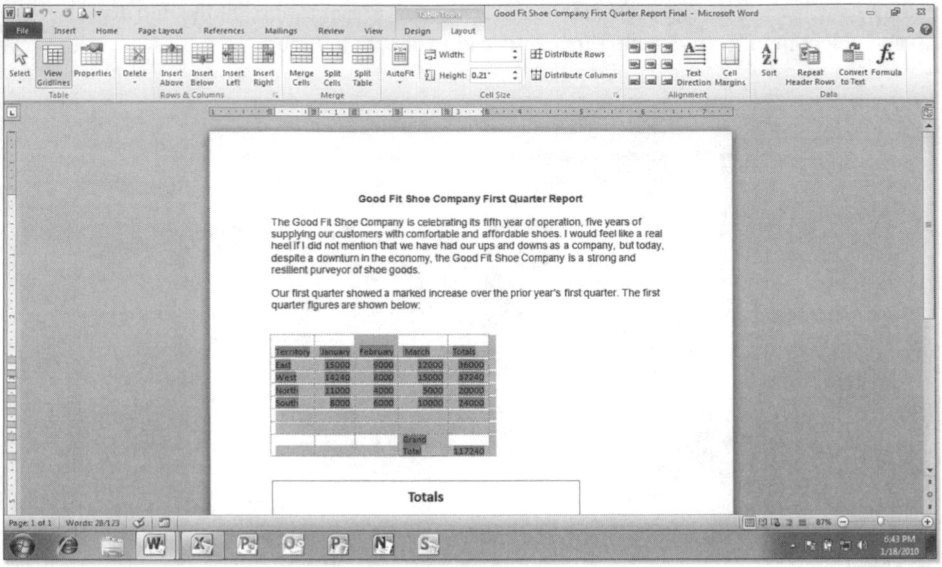

Figure 2.3
Contextual tabs
provide tools
for the task at
hand.

Changes in the Office 2010 User Interface

Changes in the Office 2010 user interface relate to a fine-tuning of the Office Fluent user interface introduced in the Office 2007 suite of applications. Although not an actual change in the interface itself, all the applications discussed in this book take full advantage of the Ribbon-centric Office Fluent user interface. Applications such as Outlook, OneNote, and Publisher did not employ (or fully employ) the Microsoft Office Fluent user interface in their Office 2007 versions, but they do in Office 2010. So, the Office 2010 applications are more consistent in terms of the user interface itself.

A big change to the user interface in Office 2010 is the replacement of the Office button with the File tab. In Office 2007, applications had with an Office button that provided access to commands related to saving, printing, and distributing a file created in the application. The Office button also provided access to the option settings for that application and allowed you to exit an application.

The File tab, the leftmost tab on the default Ribbon for an Office application, opens a new entity called the Backstage. The Backstage (or Backstage view as it is sometimes referred to) is new to the Office 2010 user interface. Figure 2.4 shows the Word Backstage with the Info command selected.

As you can see in Figure 2.4, the Backstage isn't like any of the other tabs that you find on the Ribbon. It contains commands such as Save, Open, New, Print, and Info that are common to all the Office applications. However, the commands available in Backstage vary depending on the Office 2010 application you are using; this is really due to the fact that each application has a primary purpose, making it impossible to make the Backstage's commands the same for the Office suite members.

More about the changes found in the Office 2010 applications is discussed in Chapter 1, "Getting Oriented to the Office 2010 Applications," on page 6.

Figure 2.4
The Backstage.

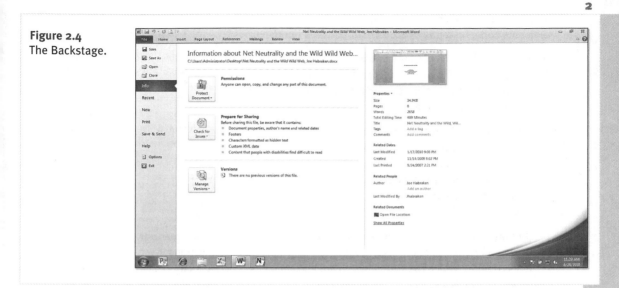

Overview of the Office Application Window

If you are new to the Office Fluent user interface, it makes sense to take some time and gain familiarity with its various parts. Some of these application window elements have been around as long
as Windows applications have. Others are additions to either Office 2007 (which launched the Office
Fluent user interface) or new additions provided by Office 2010. Figure 2.5 shows the Excel application window with callouts for a number of the application window elements.

Figure 2.5
The Excel
application
window.

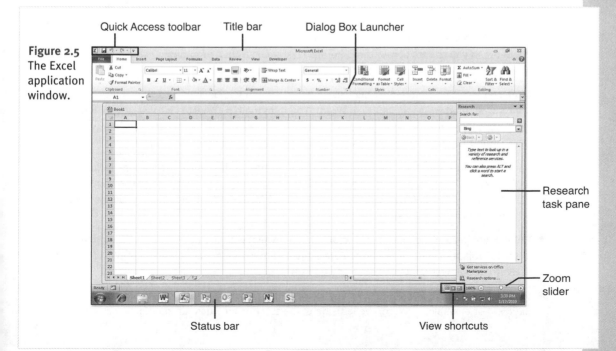

The list that follows provides a short overview of a number of elements common to the Office 2010 application interface:

- **Title Bar:** The title bar provides the application name and the name of your file (after you have saved it). The title bar also includes the Minimize, Maximize/Restore, and Close buttons on the far right.

- **Quick Access Toolbar:** The Quick Access Toolbar is nestled into the left side of the title bar. The Quick Access Toolbar provides the Save, Undo, and Redo buttons by default. You can customize it to include a number of other commands by using the Customize Quick Access Toolbar button.

> 🔍 **note**
>
> Although they call it a dialog box launcher, you will find that some of the items that are opened by a launcher are more a task pane than a dialog box. The Styles window in Word, which is opened with the launcher on the Styles group, is a good example.

- **Ribbon:** The Ribbon is the primary tool for accessing commands and features in Office applications. It contains a set of default tabs for each of the Office applications. Each tab includes command groups, which then contain individual commands. The Microsoft Office Help button resides on the far right.

- **Dialog Box Launcher:** Some command groups on the Ribbon tabs provide a dialog box launcher to the right of the group's name. The launcher enables you to open a dialog box that contains options related to that particular group. For example, the Font group on Excel's Home tab provides a dialog box launcher that opens the Format Cells dialog box with the Font tab selected.

- **Task Panes:** The number of task panes in Office 2010 is minimal when compared to the number of task panes that were in Office 2003. A task pane is a multipurpose, feature-related window. A good example of a task pane is the Research task pane, which opens via the Research command on the Ribbon's Review tab. You can actually open multiple task panes in the application window if needed. The individual task panes in the Office 2010 applications are completely independent, so you cannot access the different task panes from a drop-down list at the top of a task pane as was the case in Office 2003.

- **Mini Toolbar:** The mini toolbar becomes available when you have selected an object in your application window (such as text in Word). The mini toolbar "ghosts" into view, and when you place the mouse pointer on it, you can access its options via the toolbar buttons, many of which relate to various formatting options such as bold, italics, alignment, and font size.

- **Shortcut Menus:** Shortcut menus have been a mainstay of the Office applications for many years. Right-click on a selected object and you will be provided options related to that object. The shortcut menus are often referred to as contextual menus because they provide commands that are within the context of the selected object.

- **Ruler:** Both vertical and horizontal scrollbars are available in the applications. This provides you with the ability to align objects more precisely and to set tabs and indents in applications such as Word and PowerPoint.

- **Status Bar:** The status bar provides application information, feature indicators, and view commands. For example, in Word, the left side of the taskbar provides information such as the page number and other application-specific information, such as word count and section number. The far right of the status bar provides the View shortcuts and the Zoom Slider by default.

It goes without saying that the individual Office application windows vary depending on the application you are using. Word, Excel, and PowerPoint share the most elements of the Office applications; whereas Outlook is the odd man out—primarily due to its function as a personal information manager. Figure 2.6 shows the Outlook application window.

Figure 2.6
The Outlook application window.

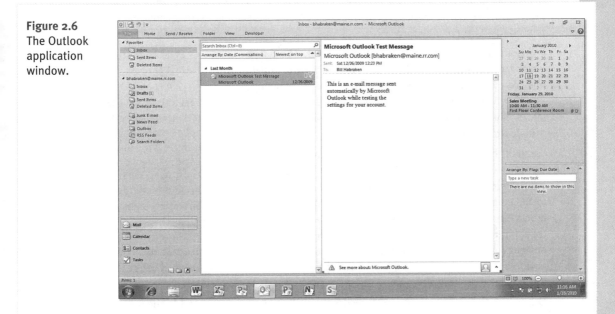

Outlook's application windows provide specialized elements that allow you to access its various features and tools. This is because Outlook manages a variety of information for you, such as email, calendar, tasks, and contacts. For example, you can quickly access appointments and tasks in the To-Do Bar on the right side of the Outlook window.

➡ *Outlook is discussed in depth in this book in Part V, beginning on page 597.*

Navigating the Office Applications

Because the Office 2010 applications take advantage of the same basic user interface, there are some universal procedures for navigating and using the individual applications. However, because each Office application creates different things (say worksheets versus documents, versus calendars, versus contacts lists), the nuances that make up the more detailed command structures of the individual applications require that you develop some specific knowledge for each application.

As already mentioned earlier in this chapter, at the center of the Office Fluent user interface is the Ribbon. So, the Ribbon is a good place to start an investigation of common features and tools in the Office 2010 applications.

Working with the Ribbon

The Ribbon tabs provide a results-driven grouping of application commands that divide closely related commands into groups. Accessing Ribbon commands is just a matter of selecting the appropriate tab and then accessing the command that you want from the group containing the commands related to a particular feature.

For example, in Excel, you might want to insert a Sum function into a selected worksheet cell to total a column of values. You would select the Ribbon's Formulas tab, look in the Function Library group, and then select the AutoSum command. The Ribbon's structure makes it very easy to quickly drill down to a specific command or feature.

Some of the individual commands in the command groups include a drop-down arrow. Selecting this arrow on some commands provides you with a simple list of options related to the command, which might also open dialog boxes associated with that particular feature. For example, selecting the Insert command on the Excel Ribbon's Home tab provides the options Insert Cells, Insert Sheet Rows, Insert Sheet Columns, and Insert Sheet. The Insert Cells option opens the Insert dialog box allowing you to specify how the inserted cells should affect existing cells or whether Excel should insert an entire row or column.

> **tip**
>
> Some Ribbon tabs you find in Office applications actually relate directly to a menu that existed in the Office 2003 release. For example, the Data menu in Office 2003 contained commands related to sorting, filtering, and working with subtotals. The Data tab on the Excel Ribbon contains many of the same commands.

Other commands provide you with access to a gallery of choices related to the command. For example, if you have selected text in a Word document and want to select a new style for the selected text, you can select from the Style gallery, which is available in the Style group on the Ribbon's Home tab.

When you place the mouse pointer on one of the styles provided in the Style gallery, the style is previewed on the selected text (see Figure 2.7). This feature, Live Preview, allows you to test various options as you work in an Office application and apply only the option that works best. This saves you from having to apply a certain option to see how it looks and then using the Undo command to start over when you don't like the results.

You will find that the Live Preview feature is most prevalent in Office applications such as Word, Excel, PowerPoint, and Publisher. For example, a number of Word commands provide you with Live Preview, including the Line and Paragraph Spacing command in the Paragraph group on the Home tab and the Header, Footer, and Page Number commands on the Ribbon's Insert tab (in the Header & Footer group).

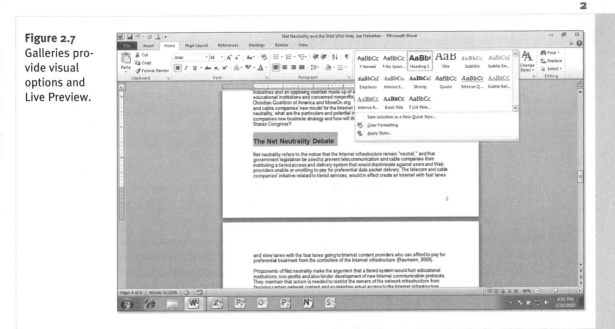

Figure 2.7
Galleries provide visual options and Live Preview.

Minimizing the Ribbon

The ribbon takes up a big chunk of the application window, particularly because it provides a number of visual cues for accessing commands and actually contains some galleries directly on Ribbon tabs. You can minimize the Ribbon to temporarily gain space in the application window.

To minimize the Ribbon, select the Minimize the Ribbon button on the far right of the Ribbon (next to the Help button). The Ribbon itself hides, but the individual Ribbon tabs still appear at the top of the application window. You can access any Ribbon tab as needed and the Ribbon temporarily appears. When you click in your application workspace, the Ribbon hides again.

To expand the Ribbon, click the Expand Ribbon button (it is the same button as the Minimize Ribbon button). The Ribbon commands return to the application window.

Accessing the Ribbon with the Keyboard

You can also access some Ribbon commands using the keyboard. The actual keystrokes aren't really your typical keyboard shortcuts, such as Ctrl+B for bold, but they can work for you in situations where you would prefer to keep your hands on the keyboard.

Press (and release) the Alt key and individual shortcut keys appear for the tabs on the Ribbon. For example, the Home tab is assigned the H shortcut key, the Insert tab is assigned N, and so on. Select one of the Ribbon tabs using the appropriate shortcut key.

> **note**
>
> When you press Alt to access the Ribbon using keyboard shortcuts, the Quick Access Toolbar buttons are assigned numerical shortcuts.

The Ribbon tab opens and keyboard shortcuts are assigned to the commands on the tab. Figure 2.8 shows the keyboard shortcuts assigned to the Word Ruler's Home tab.

Figure 2.8
Access Ribbon commands from the keyboard.

Individual alphanumeric keystrokes and multiple alphanumeric keystrokes define the commands on the Ribbon tab. To access a particular command, press the key or key combination for that command. For example, you press the H key to access the Theme Colors in Word using the shortcut key (refer to Figure 2.8). Some commands, such as the Font Color command, require that you press two keys simultaneously—in this case, F and C.

When you select a keyboard shortcut, the command activates and the keyboard shortcuts on the Ribbon disappear. To exit the current command and go back to the Ribbon with keyboard shortcuts, press Esc. You can toggle off the keyboard shortcuts by pressing Alt or by clicking inside the application workspace.

Working in the Backstage

On first examination you might see the Office Backstage as merely a collection of commands such as Save, Open, and Print. The Backstage, however, provides access to the tools that determine the final form and properties of your Office files, particularly in situations where you will share those files with other users.

To access the Backstage, select the File tab on the Ribbon. When you are in the Backstage, you still can see and access the other Ribbon tabs. This is different from the Office Button menu in Office 2007, which supplied a menu environment that opened different dialog boxes or windows when you selected a particular command. The Office 2010 Backstage provides you with options related to the particular command you have selected in an attached Backstage window. You don't actually leave the Backstage to access the information or the associated commands.

> **note**
>
> The fact that the Backstage allows you to "hop" from command to command is a marked improvement over the Office button menu, which in many cases required that you close a window or dialog box and then return to the Office button menu by selecting the Office button again.

This makes it very easy for you to view the information related to a file (such as a Word document or Excel workbook) via the Info command. You can then quickly access the Share command's options without having left the Backstage.

The commands available in the Word, Excel, PowerPoint, and Publisher Backstage are the same. This makes sense because these applications all create files as their products. The Backstage in Outlook and SharePoint Workspace differ by virtue of the fact that they are primarily information management tools rather than applications used to create a particular item such as a Word document or Excel workbook.

Let's concentrate for a moment on the Backstage commands provided by Office application members such as Word and Excel. A list of the commands on the Backstage is as follows:

- **Save:** Saves changes to the current file. Opens the Save As dialog box if the file has not been previously saved.

- **Save As:** Opens the Save As dialog box.

- **Open:** Provides access to the Open dialog box.

- **Close:** Closes the current document (workbook or presentation).

- **Info:** Provides access to permission settings for the file and allows you to check the file for any issues that might cause problems if you share the file with other users. The Info command also provides access to versions of the file automatically saved during your application settings. This command also provides a thumbnail preview of the file and provides access to the file's properties.

- **Recent:** This command provides a list of recent files that you have worked with. You can click a filename in the Recent list to open that file.

- **New:** Opens the Available Templates window and allows you to choose from templates available on your computer and Office.com.

- **Print:** The Print window provides access to print and page setup commands. It also provides the Print Preview pane.

- **Save and Send:** Provides options for sharing the file with other users. Options include sending the file using an email and saving the file to Microsoft SkyDrive. This window also provides options for changing the file type and creating Adobe Acrobat (PDF) and XPS documents.

- **Help:** Provides access to the Support window, which allows you to access the Office Help system and contact Microsoft for additional help. This window also lets you know whether your Office products have been activated and provides the version number of the application. This window also provides a link for checking updates available for Microsoft Office.

- **Options:** This command provides access to the configuration options for the application. We discuss how to change application options later in this chapter.

- **Exit:** This command exits the application.

In terms of actually using the commands accessed via the Backstage, commands such as Save, Open, New, and Help probably don't require a lot of additional comment. The three most intriguing Backstage commands are Info, Print, and Share, and require a little more discussion.

The Info Window

The Info command, as already mentioned, provides access to permission settings and allows you to check a file for any problems that might make it difficult to share the file with other users. These problems can be in the form of inadvertently sharing personal information contained in the document or attempting to share a file that contains Office 2010 features incompatible with users of earlier versions of Office. Chapter 3, "Managing and Sharing Office Files," discusses the details of using the tools found in the Info window.

 For more details related to permissions and the sharing of files see Chapter 3, "Managing and Sharing Office Files," beginning on page 51.

The Print Window

When you select Print in the Backstage, you will find one of the big changes that the Backstage provides when compared to the Office button in Office 2007. The Print window provides a coupling of the print-related commands with layout commands and Print Preview. Figure 2.9 shows the Word Backstage Print window.

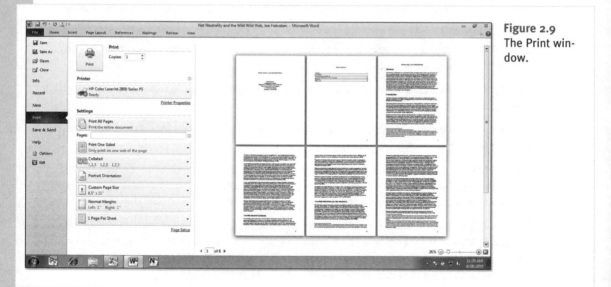

Figure 2.9
The Print window.

The Print window provides access to printer control settings and print settings. Other options are available related to page setup, such as page orientation and the page margins. Note also the integration of the Print Preview pane into the Print window. You can use the Zoom slider to zoom in and out on a single page or zoom to view multiple pages. Providing all the print-related options and print preview in the same window makes it easier for you to adjust print or page setup options and immediately view those changes using print preview.

Share

When you select Save & Send in the Backstage, the Save & Send window provides you with a number of options for sharing your current file with other users. It allows you to send the file via email, save it to Microsoft SkyDrive (Save to Web), or save it to a SharePoint site provided by a SharePoint server.

 Working with Microsoft SkyDrive is discussed in Chapter 5, "Working with the Microsoft Office Web Apps," on page 110.

The Send Using E-mail command in the Share window is particularly useful in terms of quickly sharing a file. You have the option of sending the file as an attachment, link, PDF, or XPS file. Figure 2.10 shows the Share window open in the Excel Backstage with the Send Using E-mail command selected.

Figure 2.10
The Save &
Send window.

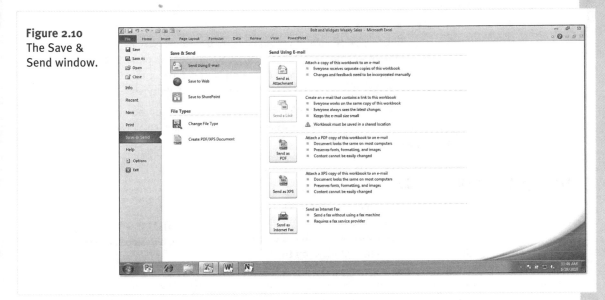

The Share window also provides you with the ability to change the file type of the current file or save it as a PDF or XPS file. When you select the Change File Type command, you are provided with a Change File Type pane that provides a listing of all the file types that you could use to save the file. When you select one of the possibilities, the Save As dialog box opens with the file type you selected in the Share window selected in the Save as Type box of the Save As dialog box.

When you select Create PDF/XPS Document in the Share window, you are provided with a Create a PDF/XPS command button and a short explanation of what the PDF and XPS file formats provide in document formatting and the availability of free viewers to view the document in the PDF or XPS file formats.

When you select the Create a PDF/XPS command button, the Publish as a PDF or XPS dialog box opens with the XPS file format selected (by default) in the Save as Type dialog box. You can change the Save as Type format selection to PDF as needed. When you save the file in the XPS or PDF format, the new document will open in the appropriate viewer for your inspection.

Dialog Boxes and Task Panes

When a command requires more information to complete a particular task or you want more control over a particular feature, you must deal with a dialog box or, in some cases, a task pane. Dialog boxes have been around as long as graphical user interfaces, so you are probably aware that they contain different options related to a feature. Task panes were important in Office 2003 (there were at least 14 task panes), but are deemphasized in the Office Fluent interface.

When working with a dialog box, the options provided are presented to you in a variety of ways, including text boxes, check boxes, drop-down lists, and option buttons. After selecting the options in the dialog box, you typically select OK to verify your selections.

 tip

You can access different views via the Ribbon's view tab.

Task panes (which aren't even necessarily called task panes in Office 2010) typically provide you with a list of possibilities, and in some cases you are provided with the ability to search or filter the list of possibilities provided by the task pane. A good example of a task pane is the Clip Art task pane. It allows you to search your computer and Office.com for clip art by keyword search. You can also filter the search by different media types.

Although a task pane typically opens as a nested element on the right side of the application window, you can drag the task pane within the application window as needed. Click the Close button at the top right of a task pane to close it.

Using the Status Bar

The status bar is an application window element that has primarily served as an information feature. For example, in the past, the Word status bar provided you with the current page number, line number, and other information related to the current document, such as the section number where the insertion point was currently parked. The status bar also let you know when the Caps Lock was on or Overtype mode had been enabled by using the Insert key on the keyboard. The Office 2010 application status bar plays a much more important part of your navigation of the application interface than just letting you know where you are in a document or whether you have turned on Overtype mode.

note

The big difference between dialog boxes and task panes is that dialog boxes are closed (via OK) when you confirm your choices. Task panes allow you to continue working in the task pane even after making choices or manipulating the possibilities provided. For example, the Research task pane will stay open until you close it.

By default the status bar houses the View shortcuts, the Zoom level, and the Zoom slider. You can use the View shortcuts to quickly change from your current view to another available view. For example, if you are in Word and currently using the Print Layout view, you can switch to the Draft view by selecting the Draft button.

The Zoom level button shows the current zoom percentage, but you can also use it (click the Zoom level button) to open the Zoom dialog box. The Zoom dialog box provides you with different zoom level option buttons and other tools for changing the current view in terms of the zoom percentage and the number of pages or items shown. The options available in the Zoom dialog box vary depending on the application you are using.

The status bar also provides access to the Zoom Slider, which makes it very easy for you to zoom in or out on your current document. Drag the slider to a new position to change the zoom percentage, or use the Zoom Out or Zoom in buttons (on the left and right of the slider, respectively) as needed.

Customizing an Application Interface

You can customize the Office 2010 application interfaces to suit your own needs. These customization options include customizing the Ribbon, Quick Access Toolbar, and the status bar.

Before we look at customizing the Ribbon and the Quick Access Toolbar, which really allows you to be selective about the commands and features available to you, we should briefly discuss the fact that customizing the application interface also relates to whether certain elements or tools are shown in the application window. For example, we have already discussed ways to show or hide the Ribbon. We have also discussed that a task pane, such as the Research task pane, can be opened and left in the application window until you finish using that particular tool.

 note

The status bar can be customized in terms of what appears on the status bar. Customizing the status bar is discussed in the next section.

Depending on the application you are using, you might also find it advantageous to have the ruler available in the application window, particularly if you are aligning objects on a page or are working in Word or PowerPoint and would like to set tab stops or indents using the ruler. To place the vertical and horizontal rulers in the application workspace, select the Ribbon's View tab and then select the Ruler checkbox. In an application such as Publisher, the ruler is particularly important in aligning objects in your publications, and you can drag guides from the rulers to help you position items on the page.

➥ *Publisher is discussed in depth in this book in Part VI, beginning on page 759.*

Customizing the Ribbon

Because the Ribbon is really the command center for the Office applications, it makes sense that you might want to customize it. You have control over the tabs available on the Ribbon as well as the commands available on those tabs. The capability to customize the Ribbon is a new feature provided in Office 2010.

 tip

You open the Research task pane by using the Research command on the Ribbon's Review tab.

Each Office application has an Options window. One of the options available relates to tailoring the Ribbon to your needs. You access the application options, such as Word Options, via the Backstage. Select File to open the Backstage and then select Options. The Options window for that application opens.

Each Options window provides an options list on the left side of the window. To work with the Ribbon, select Customize Ribbon. Figure 2.11 shows the Customize Ribbon settings in the Word Options window.

Let's start our discussion on the right side of the Customize Ribbon window. The list box on the right lists available tabs for the Ribbon. By default the Customize the Ribbon drop-down box is set to Main Tabs (which will be explained in a moment). You will find that some of the tabs are enabled and the check box for the tab is selected. Other tabs are not enabled or checked, and these tabs are not available on the application's Ribbon.

Figure 2.11
The Word Options window with Customize Ribbon selected.

You can use the Customize the Ribbon drop-down list to view different lists of the tabs available in an application; to see all the tabs available, select All Tabs. As already mentioned, the main tabs are listed by default. The main tabs are those tabs that remain available on the Ribbon no matter what you are working on in the application. The main tabs include the default tabs, such as Home, Insert, and so forth, and other tabs that are not available by default, such as the Developer tab. The tool tabs are a different story; these tabs are the contextual tabs that appear when you are working on a specific application object or element. For example, in Word, Table Tools is a set of contextual tabs (Design and Layout) that appear when you are working on a table. You can enable (show) or disable (hide) either main tabs or tool tabs. Just remember that you don't normally see the tool tabs until they activate when you perform a particular task in the application.

You can expand a particular tab in the Tabs list to view the groups available on that tab. You can then expand a group on the tab to view the commands available in a group. You can enable a tab in the tabs list if you want. For example, if you would like to create macros in a particular application, you need to have access to the Developer tab. To include the Developer tab on the application's Ribbon, select the Developer tab check box.

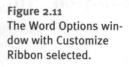

tip

If you want to rearrange the order of the tabs on the application's Ribbon, you can use the Move Up and Move Down buttons to the right of the Tabs list. Select a tab and then use either button to move the tab.

Below the Tabs list is a set of buttons that will be useful if you are going to create new tabs and groups (with the intention that these groups will contain commands). A brief description of each command button follows:

- **New Tab:** This button creates a new tab below the currently selected tab in the Tabs list. When you create a new tab, a new group is automatically created for the new tab.

- **New Group:** This button creates a new group below the currently selected group.

- **Rename:** This button enables you to rename a tab or group in the Tabs list.

- **Reset:** This button enables you to reset the selected ribbon tab or reset all the customizations that you have made to an application's Ribbon. This is useful when you have been overzealous in your creation of tabs and groups.

- **Import/Export:** This button enables you to import a customization file or create a new customization file based on the changes that you have made to the application's Ribbon. After you have created a customization file for an application's Ribbon, you can import it on other computers running Office 2010. This allows you to have access to your custom Ribbon at home or the office.

> **⊙ tip**
>
> You can also access the New Tab, New Group, Rename, Move Up, and Move Down commands by right-clicking on the Tabs list.

Creating custom tabs with custom groups requires that you use the New Tab, New Group, and Rename commands. After you create your custom tabs and groups, you will want to add commands to them.

You can add commands to the groups on the existing Ribbon tabs. You can also add commands to a group or groups contained in any new tabs you have created. On the left of the Ribbon settings windows is a list of available commands. By default, popular commands are shown. You can use the Choose commands from drop-down list at the top left of the window to select the type of commands listed. You can select from command lists such as Commands Not in the Ribbon, All Commands, and commands by tab such as File Tab, All Tabs, and so forth. If you want to see all the commands available in an application, select the All Commands option.

> **⊙ tip**
>
> You can customize (or add) keyboard shortcuts for the various Ribbon commands. Select Customize (below the Command list). Use the Customize Keyboard dialog box to locate a particular command, and then set the new shortcut key for that command.

Adding a command or commands to a Ribbon tab's group is very straightforward. Select the group in the Tabs list. Then select the command that you want to add to the group in the Command list. Select the Add button to add the command to the group. You can repeat this procedure as needed to add commands that you use frequently to existing groups on the main or tools tabs. You can also populate the custom groups that you have created for any custom tabs.

Removing a command from a group requires only that you locate the command (in the group and on the tab) in the Tabs list. Select the command and then select Remove to remove the command.

When you finish modifying the Ribbon, you can close the application's Options window. The changes you made to the Ribbon become available as soon as you return to the application's workspace.

Customizing the Quick Access Toolbar

The Quick Access Toolbar is located in the upper-left corner of the application window. By design, it provides you with a toolbar where you can quickly find commands that you use often. The Quick Access Toolbar provides the Save, Undo, and Redo commands by default.

You can add commands to the Quick Access Toolbar using the list provided on the Customize Quick Access Toolbar menu. Click the Customize Quick Access Toolbar button to the right of the Quick Access Toolbar to access the menu. Figure 2.12 shows the Excel Quick Access Toolbar menu.

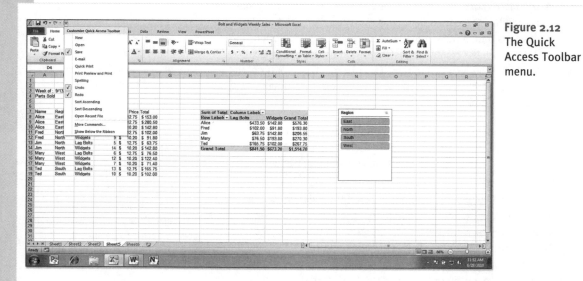

Figure 2.12
The Quick Access Toolbar menu.

When you want add a command button to the toolbar, select a command on the menu. A check mark will appear to the left of the command and the command button will be placed on the Quick Access Toolbar. You can also remove any command button from the toolbar by deselecting it on the menu.

The Customize Quick Access Toolbar menu provides only a short list of commands to add to the toolbar. If you want to add a command not listed, you need to access the Customize the Quick Access Toolbar window. This window provides you with a complete listing of all the commands available in the application.

On the Customize Quick Access Toolbar menu, select More Commands. Doing so opens the application's Options window with the Quick Access Toolbar options selected. Figure 2.13 shows the Excel Options window with Quick Access Toolbar selected.

> **tip**
>
> To place the Quick Access Toolbar below the Ribbon in the application window, select Show Below the Ribbon on the Customize Quick Access Toolbar menu.

Figure 2.13
Customize the Quick Access Toolbar in the Options window.

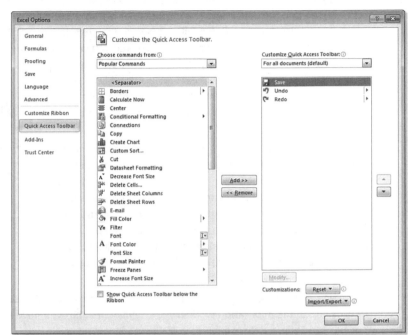

On the right of the Quick Access Toolbar options is a list the commands currently on the Quick Access Toolbar. On the left side of the Options window is a list of the popular commands. You can use the Choose commands from the drop-down List to list other command sets such as Commands Not in the Ribbon and All Commands. You can also select a particular Ribbon tab in this list to view the commands on that tab.

To add a command from the Command list, select the command and then click the Add button. The command appears in the Quick Access Toolbar list on the right side of the window. To rearrange the commands in the Quick Access Toolbar list, you can use the Move Up and Move Down buttons as needed. The list order determines the order in which the commands appear on the Quick Access Toolbar. If you decide you don't want a command on the toolbar, select the command and then click Remove.

You can also create a secondary Quick Access Toolbar for the current file (be it a Word document, Excel workbook, and so forth). Note the Customize Quick Access Toolbar drop-down list above the Quick Access Toolbar command list (on the right side of the window). By default you are customizing the Quick Access Toolbar for all the documents that you create in the application, such as all the workbooks you create in Excel or all the presentations you create in PowerPoint. So, any changes that you make to the Quick Access Toolbar will be available whenever you use the application.

note
You can also add macros that you create to the Quick Access Toolbar and the Ribbon. For a primer on creating Office 2010 macros, see Appendix B, "Office Macros."

If you are creating a template or a document where you want a secondary Quick Access Toolbar particular to that document and is available in only that document, you can use the Customize Quick Access Toolbar drop-down list to select the current document. This empties the Command list (on the right side of the Options window), and you can select commands in the Command list (on the left side of the window) and then use the Add button to populate the special Quick Access Toolbar for that document. This new Quick Access Toolbar appears to the right of the default Quick Access Toolbar above the Ribbon in the application window after you close the Customize the Quick Access Toolbar Options window.

A couple more things about the Quick Access Toolbar options: If you decide that you don't like the changes that you have made to Quick Access Toolbar, you can click the Reset button at the bottom right of the window. As with custom Ribbons, you can use the Import/Export button to import custom Quick Access Toolbars that you have created on other computers running Office 2010. You can also export your Quick Access Toolbar configuration to an exported Office UI file that can be used on any computer with Office 2010 installed.

 tip

The type of work that you do in an application influences the commands that you add to that application's Quick Access Toolbar. However, in terms of good additions to the toolbar in any Office application, I'm partial to the Open, Open Recent File, Paste Special, Save As, and Quick Print commands.

When you have finished working in the options window, click OK. This closes the window and returns you to the application workspace. The changes that you have made to the Quick Access Toolbar are immediately available.

Customizing the Status Bar

The Office applications' status bar has, at least historically, served as an informational tool at the bottom of the application window. It provided you with information related to file that you were working and let you know whether certain features (such as overtype) were enabled. The Office 2010 applications' status bar is customizable, as it was in the Office 2007 release of the application suite.

We have already discussed the fact that the View shortcuts, Zoom, and Zoom slider tools are on the right side of the status bar and let you control your view of your document in the application window. This is a big departure from earlier versions of the Office suite that provided a static status bar.

tip

Each of the Office applications provides a different list of status bar options. For example, Excel includes a Num Lock option (which the other applications do not) because the numerical keypad on the keyboard is often used to enter values into Excel worksheets.

You can customize the status bar to show additional information related to your current document (or worksheet or slide). Other informational additions to the status bar, such as Caps Lock, allow you to see from the status bar whether the Caps Lock has been enabled, for example.

You can also place options on the status bar that actually perform an action when you click on them. For example, in Word you can add Word Count to the status bar and use it to quickly open the Word Count dialog box and view the statistics for the document. Another useful status bar option is

Overtype, which allows you to toggle between Insert and Overtype by clicking the currently enabled option (Overtype or Insert) on the status bar.

To customize the status bar, right-click anywhere on it and the Customize Status Bar menu appears. Figure 2.14 shows the Word Customize Status Bar menu.

To add an item to the status bar, click on the item. You can also remove items from the status bar by deselecting them (remove the check mark) on the Customize Status Bar menu as needed.

Figure 2.14
Customize the
Status Bar.

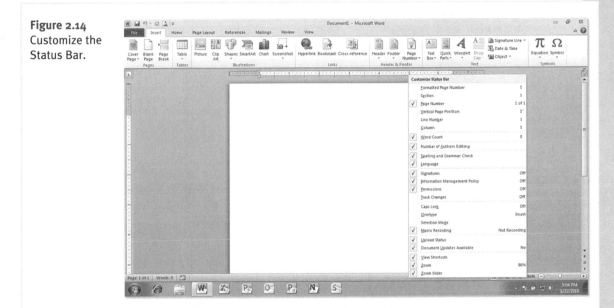

Configuring Application Options

Microsoft has done a very good job of making the tools for configuring the various Office 2010 members extremely consistent across the applications. Excel, Word, PowerPoint, and Publisher use many of the same option categories such as General, Customize Ribbon, and Add-Ins. Even Outlook and OneNote provide the same overall approach to configuring the application using the Options window.

We have already looked at options related to configuring the Ribbon and Quick Access Toolbar in this chapter and these options are consistent across all the Office applications. There are obviously some differences in the configuration options provided for the Office applications because each application serves a different function. In Excel, for example, there is a Formulas option category, which makes sense because of Excel's capability to do calculations. In Outlook, there are configuration options for the calendar, contacts, and mail, which again makes sense because of the type of work you do in Outlook.

All the applications in Office 2010 suite provide an Options button in the Backstage. Select File, and then Options in an application to open its Options window. Figure 2.15 shows the Excel Options window with the General category selected.

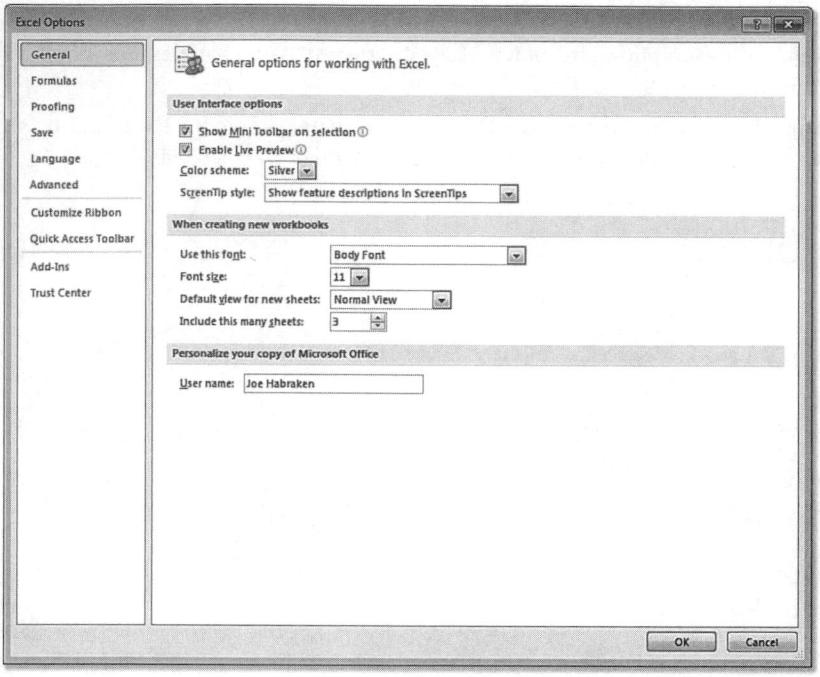

Figure 2.15
Excel General Options
window.

The Options window breaks down the various application configuration possibilities into a series of categories. Each category provides a set of tools for configuring a set of associated features. In Figure 2.15, the General category is selected and provides user interface options such as enabling the Mini Toolbar and enabling Live Preview. An option such as the User Name option available under the Personalize Your Copy of Microsoft Office is a universal setting, and any change to the username in Excel ports over to other applications such as Word and PowerPoint.

Two other option categories contain settings that can affect multiple Office applications: Proofing and Language. The Proofing options enable you to set the AutoCorrect settings specifically for an application such as Excel, Word, or PowerPoint. However, when you select options related to how spelling is corrected in the application or the default dictionary language, these settings are also used by other applications. Figure 2.16 shows the Excel Proofing options.

Note that a number of the spelling options are controlled using check boxes, and drop-down lists provide options for different language modes and the main dictionary language. The Proofing category provides very similar options when accessed in Word or PowerPoint. You need to change Proofing options in only one application, however, for them to be in force in the other applications.

The settings available in the Language options are also Office preferences rather than individual application preferences. Changing settings such as the editing, display, and help languages affects the other Office applications. Think of the Proofing and Language options as universal options that are applied to all the applications.

Figure 2.16
Excel Proofing options.

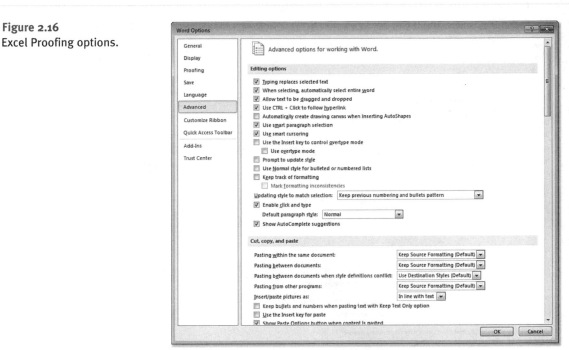

In terms of options specific to an application (other than the Ribbon and Quick Access Toolbar settings that we have already discussed), most of these are housed in the Advanced category. Advanced options are divided into subcategories such as Editing, Print, Display, and a catch-all General subcategory. Figure 2.17 shows the Advanced option window for Word with the Editing options and the Cut, Copy, and Paste options visible.

The Advanced options available for each application vary; however, the subcategories (such as Editing and Print) are consistent across the applications, particularly Word, Excel, PowerPoint, and Publisher. Outlook is a good example of the odd man out, and has a number of configuration options that you don't have to deal with in the other applications. These relate to the different types of information that you create and manage in Outlook such as emails, calendars, and contacts. Outlook's use and configuration is discussed in detail in the Outlook section of this book.

➧ *Outlook's configuration is discussed in Chapter 22, "Requisite Outlook: Configuration and Essential Features," beginning on page 604.*

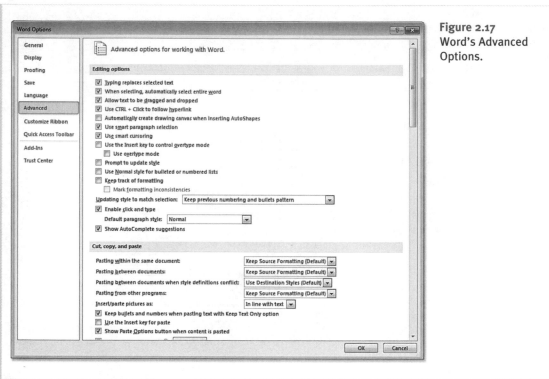

Figure 2.17
Word's Advanced
Options.

Advanced Option Settings

So, you will find the most application-specific settings in the Advanced options category no matter which Office application you are configuring. Advanced option subcategories that you will use in applications such as Word, Excel and PowerPoint, are as follows:

- **Editing Options:** These options relate to editing and selecting items in the application. For example, Word provides an Editing option related to whether selected text is replaced when you type. Excel provides an Editing option that enables or disables Auto-Complete. Look for features in this subcategory that make it easier for you to select and edit information in the applications.

- **Cut, Copy, and Paste:** True to their names, these options relate to settings such as whether the Paste Options button is enabled when you paste an item. They also include settings in Word for setting formatting options related to pasting within the same document, between documents, or between programs.

- **Display:** This set of options provides settings for the number of recent files that should be displayed in the Backstage, and contains other settings related to whether screen elements such as ScreenTips and the ruler should be shown in the application window.

- **Print:** These options relate to the quality of certain objects when they are printed. For example, in Excel, you can set a high-quality mode for graphics. In PowerPoint, you can specify that all printing is high quality. Word and PowerPoint also provide options for background printing so that you can continue to use the application as you are printing.

You will find that many of the Advanced options available for Office applications are easy to work with. Most are enabled or disabled via check boxes. This makes it simple for you to try out a particular setting by enabling it with a click of the mouse. If it isn't particularly useful, you can return to the Advanced options and easily disable the option with another click.

Add-Ins

One other category of application options that you should be aware of is the Add-Ins. Add-Ins are additions to an application that increase the application's functionality. Each Office application has add-ins available. Some are added to the application by default when you install the application. For example, in Word, the Instant Message Contacts Add-in is active in Word by default. This add-in recognizes names and addresses of contacts that can be identified by your instant message application (such as Microsoft Instant Messenger).

Other add-ins are copied to your computer when you install Office 2010, but are not added to the application by default. This means that they are inactive add-ins. For example, Excel has a number of add-ins available such as the Solver, Analysis ToolPak, and the Euro Currency Tools. To use these add-ins, you must add them to your Excel configuration.

When you select the Add-Ins category in the application Options window, you can view the active and inactive add-ins. Figure 2.18 shows the Add-Ins options for Excel. By default, Excel has no active add-ins.

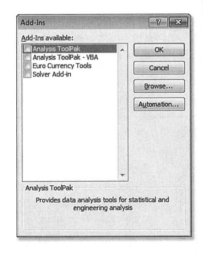

Figure 2.18
Excel's Add-Ins Options window.

You can view specific information related to a particular add-in by selecting the add-in in either the Active or Inactive list. Each add-in typically provides a description, which allows you to get at least a general idea of what the add-in provides when you add it to the application.

As already mentioned, there are inactive add-ins supplied as part of the Office installation are available for your Office applications. Add-ins also periodically become available from Microsoft to address the functionality of a particular application. There are also many third-party add-ins typically available for the Office applications that are specific to particular tasks or application functions. These can be acquired and added to your Office applications as needed.

You can activate an add-in in an application from the Add-Ins Options window. Follow these steps:

1. Select File on the Ribbon to access the Backstage.

2. Select Options to open the Options window.

3. Select Add-Ins in the Options window.

4. At the bottom of the Options window, make sure that Add-ins is selected in the Manage drop-down list and then click Go.

5. An Add-Ins dialog box appears that is specific to the application (such as Excel or Word). The dialog box lists the available add-ins. Figure 2.19 shows the Excel Add-Ins dialog box.

 tip

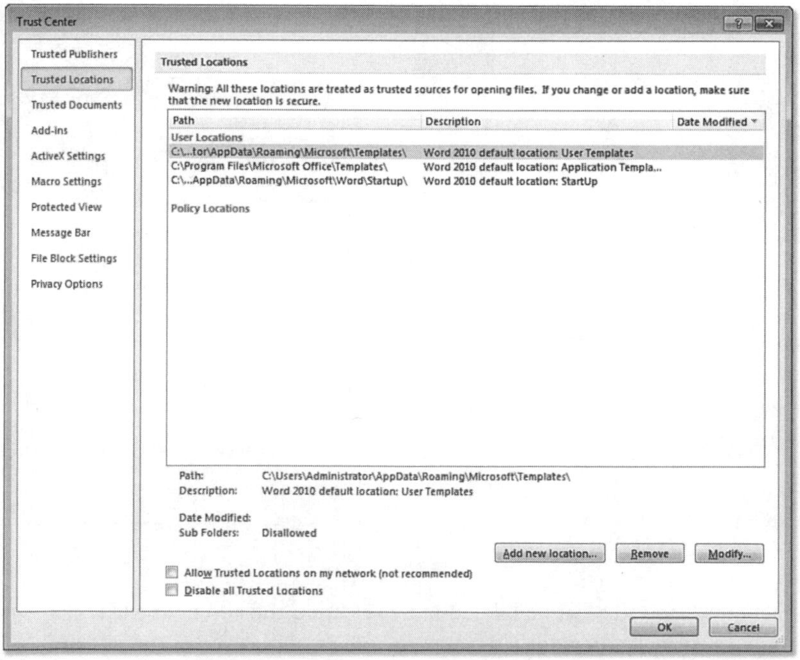

The Office add-ins are also referred to as COM (Component Object Model) add-ins. Office add-ins can be written in different object-oriented languages such as C++ and Visual Basic. It doesn't take long after the release of a new Microsoft product for programmers to come up with a lot of interesting add-ins that you can use. Of course, user beware; don't download and activate add-ins not from Microsoft or a source that you trust.

Figure 2.19
Excel's Add-Ins dialog box.

6. Select an add-in. If you have downloaded an add-in, you can use the Browse button to locate it.

7. After selecting an add-in (or add-ins) to activate, click OK. The Add-Ins dialog box closes.

When you return to the Options window for the application and select Add-Ins, you will find that the Active Application Add-ins list includes the add-ins that you activated. You can now use the add-in as needed in the application.

Using the Trust Center

Keeping your computer secure from attack and protecting personal information on your computer has become a greater challenge as connectivity to the somewhat untrustworthy networking infrastructure of the Internet has become commonplace. We use the Internet in many instances for private communication and the sharing of files (both by email and other means) without necessarily considering that we are opening up our files and computer to a public global network. Even extremely secure corporate networks that protect users from the risks of having a persistence connection with the Internet can have problems with security and privacy issues.

Microsoft has worked hard to build security and privacy protections into the Office applications themselves and this is where the Trust Center comes in. Each Office applications has its own Trust Center, which provides access to security and privacy settings for the application. You access the Trust Center settings via the Options window of the specific application. To open the Trust Center for an Office application, follow these steps:

> **⚠ caution**
>
> If you work on a corporate network, or are a small office or home user and don't have an actual need that requires changes to the Trust Center, don't change the settings. A compelling reason might be that you are working with macros or you are considering using add-ins from a source other than Microsoft and you want the add-ins to be signed by a trusted publisher.

1. Select File on the Ribbon to access the Backstage.

2. Select Options to open the Options window.

3. In the Options window, select Trust Center. Because the Trust Center is related to privacy and security settings, the Options window provides a series of links that include access to Microsoft's privacy statement for the current application and Office and a link for Microsoft Trustworthy Computing. Microsoft recommends not changing the settings in the Trust Center if you want to keep your computer secure. Unless you have a compelling reason to change these settings, it makes sense to go with the defaults. Changing the security settings could potentially open up your computer to attack, particularly if you use macros from a source unknown to you.

4. Select Trust Center Settings to open the application's Trust Center. Figure 2.20 shows the Word Trust Center with the Trusted Locations options selected.

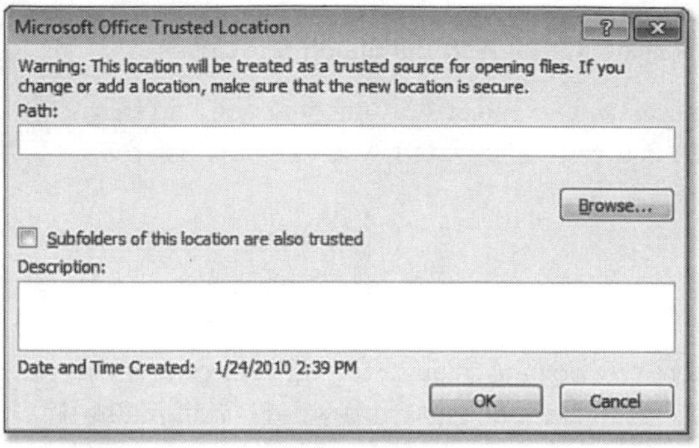

Figure 2.20
The Trust Center.

The Trust Center for each of the Office applications differs in the options available. For example, Outlook also provides E-Mail Security settings and Automatic Download options (related to pictures in HTML emails). Outlook does not have Trusted Documents or Add-ins options as Word does. Word, PowerPoint, and Excel have very similar options available in their Trust Centers. Outlook, OneNote, and Publisher provide only a subset of the options you will find in the other applications (such as Word and Excel), but include some special options related to the actual function of the application such as the Trust Center options found in Outlook as we've already mentioned.

> **tip**
>
> Remove publishers from the list only in cases when the digital signature has expired or you no longer use content from that publisher.

Because Microsoft sees the Trust Center as a way to make your application environment more secure, make changes to these settings only if a change actually provides you with greater security or privacy as you work. Although it is very easy to select a Trust Center option category and begin to make what seems like good choices, Trust Center options are really "if it isn't broke, don't fix it" settings; don't change them unless you have a compelling reason to do so.

Two options related to the Trust Center that make it easier for you to take advantage of files containing active content, such as macros or ActiveX controls, are the Trusted Publishers and Trusted Documents settings. You will find both these settings available in the Word, Excel, and PowerPoint Security Centers. This makes sense because Word documents, Excel worksheets, and PowerPoint presentations are most likely to use active content such as macros. The information that follows looks more closely at trusted publishers and trusted locations.

Trusted Publishers

If you use macros, add-ins, or ActiveX controls to enhance the capabilities of your Microsoft Office applications and you acquire these application additions from a legitimate developer, you can add the publisher to the Trusted Publishers list. For you to add a publisher to the list, the developer's add-in or ActiveX control must be digitally signed using a digital certificate that has been acquired by the developer or publisher. The certificate must be from a reputable certificate authority. A number of certificate authorities are available online, such as A-Trust (http://www.a-trust.at), CertPlus (http://certplus.com), and VeriSign (http://digitalid.verisign.com).

You don't actually add the publisher to the Trusted Publishers list in the Trust Center. You can use the Trust Center only to view details related to a trusted publisher or to remove a publisher from the list. To remove a publisher, select the publisher in the Trusted Publishers list and then click Remove.

When you attempt to run a macro or ActiveX control that you have acquired, it is disabled by default. A message bar appears below the Ribbon in the application window, letting you know that the macro or ActiveX control is disabled. When you click the Options button in the message bar, the Security Options dialog box for that item opens. In the dialog box, you will be able to see whether the developer/publisher digitally signed the item. You can view details related to the digital signature by selecting the Show Signature Details link.

> **note**
>
> If you create your own macros or use macros created by co-workers, changes to Trust Center options related to macros might come into play. Macros are discussed in Appendix B.

If you are satisfied that the signed item is using a legitimate digital certificate and you want to add the publisher to the Trusted Publishers list, select the Trust All Documents from This Publisher option in the Security dialog box. Then click OK; doing so adds the publisher to the list in that application.

Trusted Locations

In Word, Excel, and PowerPoint, the Trusted Locations list contains the default paths for documents, templates, startup files, and other items such as add-ins (in Excel). If you are a user on a sophisticated network (other than a home network), some of these locations might be local paths on your computer or might have been edited by your network administrator to use network paths.

The whole purpose of trusted locations is that these folders are used to store files that you trust; meaning you do not want the Trust Center to raise a fuss when you open a file stored in a trusted location. This allows you to place files that contain macros or other content, such as add-ins, in a trusted folder and not have the Trust Center disable any of the content when you open the file.

You can edit the default trusted location path if you want. Select a user location in the list and then click the Modify button in the Trusted Locations pane. The Microsoft Office Trusted Location dialog box opens. Change the path in the Path box and then click OK to close the dialog box.

In most cases, it is probably advisable not to change any of the default trusted locations, particularly if your Office applications were configured specifically to run on your corporate network. This doesn't mean that you can't create your own trusted locations and use them as depots for files that contain content that must be trusted in order to run correctly (such as macros, ActiveX controls, and so forth).

To create a new trusted location, select the Add New Location button. The Microsoft Office Trusted Location dialog box opens as shown in Figure 2.21.

Type the path for the new location in the Path text box or use the Browse button to locate the folder on your computer or your network. If you want to have all the subfolders in the new trusted folder also be trusted, select the Subfolders of This Location Are Also Trusted check box.

You can add an optional description for the new trusted location in the Description box. When you have completed entering the information for the new trusted source, click the OK button.

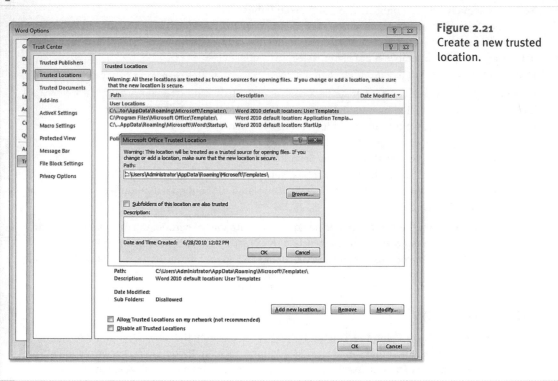

Figure 2.21
Create a new trusted location.

The new trusted location is added to the Trusted Locations list. If you need to remove a location that you no longer use or need, select the location in the list. You can then click the Remove button to remove the trusted location.

3

MANAGING AND SHARING OFFICE FILES

The Microsoft Office 2010 applications provide you with all the tools that you need to create documents, presentations, workbooks, and publications. After you create your various files using the Office applications, it is up to you to manage your files and also to share files with colleagues and coworkers.

In this chapter we take a look at the Office file formats used in each of the Office applications. We also take a look at your options for managing and sharing your files including using Microsoft SharePoint Workspace.

Understanding Office File Formats

With a great deal of fanfare (and not a little suffering by Office application users) Office 2007 rolled out new default file formats for each of the core Office applications—Word, Excel, and PowerPoint—that used the open XML (eXtensible Markup Language) file standards. Office 2010 also embraces these file formats, which actually do provide benefits in terms of file compaction, improved damage recovery, better detection of files containing macros, and better compatibility with other vendor software.

Most of the backward-compatibility issues involved with these new file formats has been ironed out. Users still working with earlier versions of the Office applications (including versions of Microsoft Office running in the Mac OS environment) can take advantage of various conversion utilities and software updates. You can also save your files in file formats that offer backward compatibility for coworkers still using older versions of the Office applications.

However, in addition to the benefits already listed related to the open XML file standard there is another fairly compelling reason to use the open XML file formats if possible. A number of useful Office features, such as previewing formatting options (from Ribbon commands related to tables, line spacing, or columns) and using themes (in Word, Excel, and PowerPoint), are not available if you are using one of the legacy file formats provided by the Office 2010 suite members (such as the .doc file type in Word).

Publisher 2010, on the other hand, saves publications by default in the .pub file type, which was introduced with the Office 2003 version of Publisher. The .pub file type is compatible with Publisher 2010 (and Publisher 2007); however, it is not part of the open XML file standards (as is the default for Word, Excel, and so forth). Publisher does, however, provide you with the ability to save files in the XPS file type, which is an XML file format for "electronic paper." Publisher also has file types available that you can use to make your publications backward compatible with collaborators who are using previous versions of Microsoft Publisher, such as Publisher 2000 and Publisher 98.

For more about Publisher file types, see Chapter 28, "Requisite Publisher: Essential Features," in the section "Creating a New Publication."

As already mentioned, Word, Excel, and PowerPoint use the open XML file formats by default when you save a file in these applications. And, as already mentioned, you have a number of other file format options in these applications if needed. Options are available for backward compatibility with earlier versions of these Office iapplications. The lists that follow provide an overview of some of the file types used in Word, Excel, and PowerPoint, respectively.

Word:

File Extension	Description
docx	XML file type—default file type for Word 2010 document
docm	XML file type—macro-enabled document
dotx	XML file type—Word template
dotm	XML file type—macro-enabled Word template
doc	Binary file type—document compatibility with Word 97–2003
dot	Binary file type—template compatibility with Word 97–2003

Excel:

File Extension	Description
xlsx	XML file type—default file type for Excel 2010 workbook
xlsm	XML file type—macro-enabled workbook
xltx	XML file type—Excel template
xltm	XML file type—macro-enabled Excel template
xls	Binary file type—document compatibility with Excel 97–2003
xlt	Binary file type—template compatibility with Excel 97–2003

PowerPoint:

File Extension	Description
pptx	XML file type—default file type for PowerPoint 2010 presentation
pptm	XML file type—macro-enabled presentation
potx	XML file type—PowerPoint template
potm	XML file type—macro-enabled PowerPoint template
ppsx	XML file type—PowerPoint show
ppsm	XML file type—macro-enabled PowerPoint show
ppt	Binary file type—presentation compatibility with PowerPoint 97–2003
pot	Binary file type—template compatibility with PowerPoint 97–2003

The Office 2010 applications also provide other file formats that make it simple for you to share your documents or workbooks in a format designed for easy viewing. For example, you can use the PDF file format (created by Adobe Systems), which allows users who have the free Adobe Reader software installed on their computer to view your file. The XML electronic paper file format—XPS—can also be used to make it easy for others to view your work. Windows 7 supplies an XPS viewer that allows any Windows user to open and view files in the XPS file type. Figure3.1 shows the Windows 7 XPS viewer containing a Word document converted to an XPS document.

Figure 3.1
A Word XPS document in the Microsoft XPS viewer.

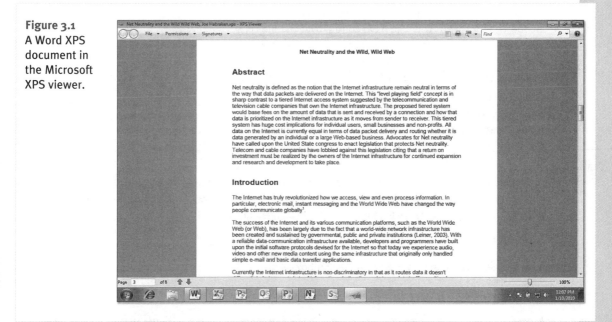

Both the PDF and the XPS file formats are primarily designed to enable you to share a view of a particular file without requiring that the Office applications themselves be installed on the computer of the user who will view the file. Although both the PDF and XPS file types require a particular viewer type to actually view the file, viewers such as Acrobat Reader and a number of XPS viewers (including Microsoft's XPS viewer) are available for free download on the Web.

 tip

To download Microsoft's free XPS viewer (for Windows XP and above), go to http://www.microsoft.com/whdc/xps/viewxps.mspx. To download the Acrobat Reader from Adobe Systems, go to http://get.adobe.com/reader/.

Saving Files to Different File Types

When you create a new Word document, Excel workbook, or PowerPoint presentation, a point will arrive when you want to save your work to a file. Each of these applications uses the open XML file format by default. For example, if you save a new Word document and do not change the Save as Type setting, you are going to get a file with the extension .docx. This file type is compatible with Word 2007 and Word 2010, but you might have some issues if you share the file with someone using a legacy version of Word, such as Word 97.

tip

Outlook isn't addressed in this particular chapter because how it stores and works with different items such as emails and contacts is different from applications where you create specific files such as Word or Excel. Outlook is covered in depth in Part V, "Outlook," beginning on page 597.

When you save a file for the first time, the Save As dialog box opens. At minimum you must provide a filename for the new file and you have the option of specifying the location where the file will be saved. You also have control over the file type used when the file is saved. The file type can be selected in Save as Type drop-down list. Figure 3.2 shows Word's Save As dialog box with the Save as Type drop-down list selected.

After selecting the file type, click Save to save the file. When you have saved the file for the first time, the Save button on the application's Quick Access Toolbar saves the changes that you make to the file as you add and edit information to the file.

tip

Office files such as Word documents, Excel worksheets, and PowerPoint presentations can also be saved in various web page formats, making it easy to include the content on a website.

You can also convert an existing file to another file type by using the Save As dialog box. After you save a file, the only route to the Save As dialog box is via the application's Backstage. Follow these steps to open the Save As dialog box for a previously saved file:

1. Select File to access the Backstage.

2. Select Save As to open the Save As dialog box.

3. Use the Save as Type drop-down list to specify the file type for the file.

4. You also have the option of changing the name and location for the new file that will be created.

5. Click Save.

Figure 3.2
Selecting the file type for a
Word document file.

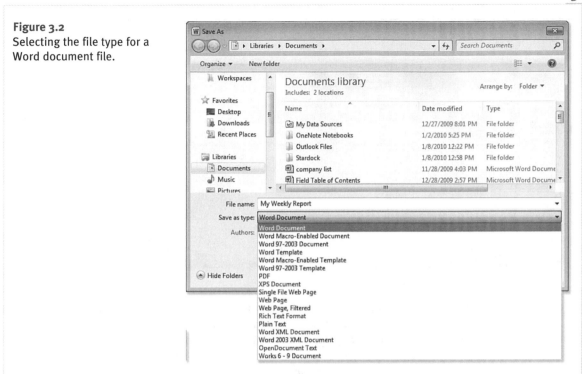

The Save As dialog box closes. The file is saved using the new file format that you selected. The file
has a new name and save location if you chose to change these settings in the Save As dialog box.

Converting Files to Different File Types

Another option for converting a particular file to a different file type is to take advantage of the
Change File Type pane, which you access via the Backstage's Save & Send window. The Change
File Type pane actually makes changing a file's file type less confusing than just picking a file type
from the Save as Type drop-down list in the Save As dialog box. File types are visually represented
in the Change File Type pane and short descriptions of each file type are provided. Figure 3.3 shows
the Excel Change File Type pane in the Backstage.

To create a copy of the current file in a new file type, select one of the alternative file types provided
in the Change File Type pane. For example, you might want to save an Excel workbook that is currently in the Excel .xlsx file format (the default) to the Excel 97–2003 workbook file type (.xls) so that
you can share the file with a colleague who uses an earlier version of Excel.

Select the new file type in the Change File Type pane and the Save As dialog box opens. The file
type that you chose in the Change File Type pane will be selected in the Save as Type drop-down
list. You can change the filename or the file location as needed. Then select Save to save a copy of
the original file in the file type.

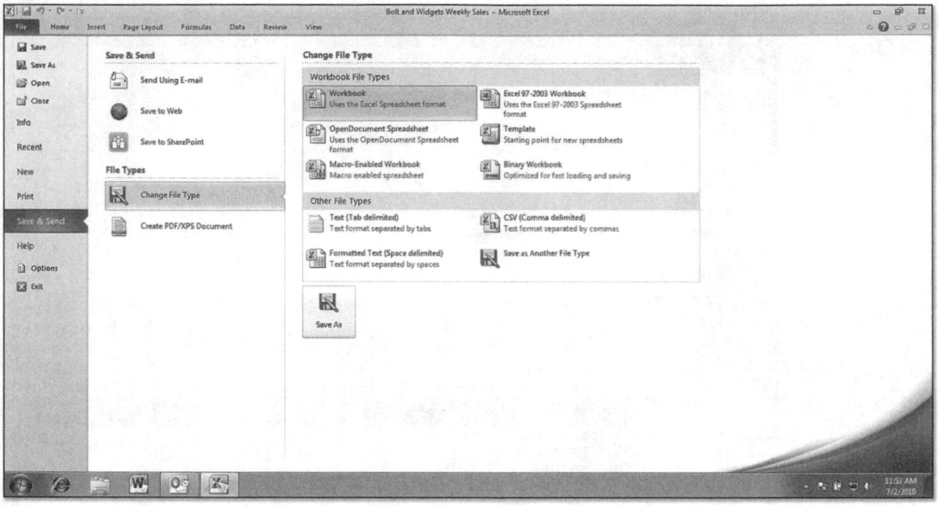

Figure 3.3
The Excel Change File Type pane.

Although going directly to the Save As dialog box via the Backstage Save As command might seem to be a faster option than getting to the Save As dialog box via the Change File Type pane, the latter option does a better job of laying out the possibilities. Until you have a good feel for which file type is which on the Save as Type drop-down list in the Save As dialog box, use the Change File Type pane as an aid to selecting the appropriate file type for the file. Obviously, "appropriate" depends on what you are actually going to do with the file in its alternative file type.

Configuring Save File Options

When you save a file in one of the Office applications, you have the option of specifying the location where the file will be saved. By default, files saved in Office applications are saved to your Documents folder. So, if you don't provide an alternative location, the files end up in the default folder.

The previous paragraph is true if you installed Microsoft Office 2010 on your own computer or if a network administrator installed your Office applications and did not change the default location for saved files. If you work on a corporate or other business network, you might find that your default folder for files created in the Office applications is actually a network folder and not the Documents folder on your own computer that most home office users would use for saved files.

Knowing where your files are saved and the file format that they are saved in is essential to using the Microsoft applications in a productive way. You do, in most cases, have control

> **⚠ caution**
>
> If you work in a networked environment other than a home or small office environment, you might drive your network administrator completely insane if you change the default Save settings for your Office applications. So, check with your administrator before you attempt to change these settings.

over the default file location and the default file format used to save files in a particular Office application. The settings for these options are found on the Save pane of an Office application's Options window.

To open the Options window for an Office application, select File to open the Backstage. Then select the Options command. The Options window for the application opens. Select Save to view the save settings for the application. Figure 3.4 shows the Save pane for PowerPoint. The Save options for PowerPoint, Word, and Excel are extremely similar. Publisher provides you with options related only to the AutoRecover feature on the Save pane.

Figure 3.4
The PowerPoint Save options.

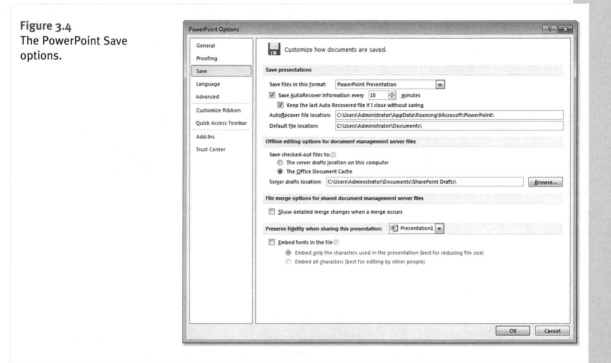

To change the default file format, use the Save Files in This Format drop-down list. Change the file format only if you have a good reason, such as the fact that you always work with people that are using a legacy version of an Office application and you want to match the file type that they use. You can also edit the default file location, which is the location where your files are stored by default. In PowerPoint, you have to actually type in the path for the folder in the Default File Location box. In Word and Excel, a Browse button allows you to browse for the new location.

note

Everything that you create in the Office applications is actually based on a template. Each application has a default template. For example, in Word the default template is called the Normal template and is used when you create a new blank document.

Other options provided by the Save pane relate to the AutoRecover feature and offline editing options when you work in an environment that uses network servers running SharePoint Server. Most of these options should be left at the defaults—particularly those related to offline editing in a server environment.

Creating and Managing Files

The Office applications provide you with different possibilities for creating your new files. When you start one of the Office applications, such as Word, Excel, and PowerPoint, a new blank document, workbook, or presentation opens automatically. All you have to do is enter information and then you can save the file. So, one option for creating a new file in one of the Office applications is to take advantage of the blank workspace provided and begin to enter your information.

Publisher operates a little differently from the "standard" Office applications in that you must select a template before you can begin to create your new publication. So, what is a template and how do templates interact with other Office applications, such as Word and Excel?

Templates are, by design, ready-made blueprints for documents, workbooks, or other Office application files. For example, you might want to create a monthly budget for your household. If you would like some help in creating the overall layout that would go into creating this budget in Excel, you can take advantage of a Household Monthly Budget template that is provided by Office Online and is easily opened via the Excel Backstage.

Templates often provide layout attributes, text formatting, and even placeholder text. The sophistication of the file created using a particular template depends on the actual template. For example, you might use a Word Memo template that creates a simple memo containing some placeholder text (that you replace) in the To, From, and Re areas of the memo. Or you might take advantage of the Household Monthly Budget template mentioned a moment ago. It provides individual tables in a worksheet for items such as projected costs and projected monthly income, and supplies ready-made charts for your monthly expenses and expenses by category. Figure 3.5 shows a new Excel worksheet opened using the Household Monthly Budget template.

Excel, Word, PowerPoint, and Publisher provide you with templates installed on your computer when you install the Office applications. Office Online provides a huge number of templates and the number seems to grow daily. You can preview and download any of these templates into your template library on your computer. To open a new file based on a template, follow these steps:

1. Select File to open the Backstage.

2. Select New in the Backstage. The Available Templates window opens.

3. Select a templates collection in the Available Templates window. You can select Sample Templates or Recent Templates to view templates on your computer or select any of the Template group icons available in the Office.com Templates area.

4. Select one of the templates available in a template collection. The template previews in the right pane of the Available Templates window. Figure 3.6 shows the selection of an Excel Sales Invoice template in the Office.com Invoice group.

Figure 3.5
Excel's
Household
Monthly
Budget tem-
plate.

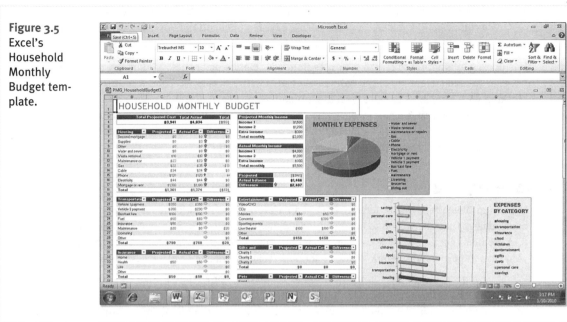

Figure 3.6
Create new
files from
the Available
Templates win-
dow.

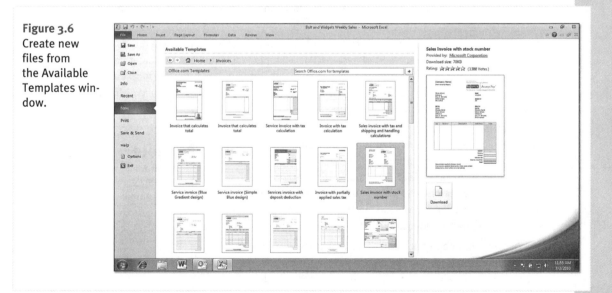

5. If you selected a template stored locally on your computer, click Create. If the template is on Office.com, click Download. In either case a new file opens in the application window based on the template.

It is up to you whether to create your files from new blank documents, workbooks, or presentations, or to take advantage of the various templates that you can access in the Office applications. Working with templates can help you determine how a special document, such as a newsletter, or a special worksheet, such as an invoice, should be laid out. So, rather than reinventing the wheel, particularly as you become more familiar with the capabilities and features of each Office application, why not take advantage of the benefits provided by templates?

Managing Files

Managing files effectively is actually a bit of an art form. You need to create some sort of structured environment that allows you to keep your saved files organized but also makes it easy for you to find the files that you work with often. Your particular situation might also require that you store your files in particular network shares (folders) so that others can easily access them.

Whether you store your files on your computer's hard drive or a shared drive on a network server, the same basic containers for file storage are available to you. The drive (local or on the network) is pretty much the equivalent of a filing cabinet. Each drawer in the filing cabinet would be equivalent to a folder on the drive. The hanging file folders that we like to stick in filing cabinet drawers would be equivalent to the subfolders that we place inside the main folders that reside on our computer's hard drive.

The naming conventions that you use for the folders and subfolders that you create are really up to you, but should reflect some sort of system. For example, you could have a folder named Projects that contains subfolders named for each of the specific projects that you are working on. So, take some time to figure out your folder taxonomy. If you end up with a folder named Miscellaneous, I suggest you rethink your naming system.

This method of organizing files in folders and subfolders works no matter what version of Windows (Windows 7, Vista, or Windows XP) you are currently running. However, before you get too far along in your planning, you might want to take a look at a new option—the library—that can be used to help you organize and access files no matter where they are stored on your computer (or your network).

In Windows 7, a library is a container that gathers files from different locations on your computer and your network and displays them as a collection that you can access. By default, Windows 7 provides the Documents, Music, Pictures, and Videos libraries.

note

You might want to use your Documents folder as the parent container for the subfolders that you create for your various projects. This allows you to create the necessary folder structure without cluttering the C: drive with a lot of new folders.

So, you can go "old school" and create folders and subfolders on your computer's hard drive or you can take advantage of libraries to provide you with easy access to the Office files that you use. Whether you are creating new folders on your computer or on a network share assigned to you, you can use Windows Explorer as your primary tool. The same goes if you want to create new libraries—you will use Windows Explorer.

Creating a New Folder

In Windows 7, select Start and then Computer to open Windows Explorer. The Explorer window (shown in Figure 3.7) provides links on the left side of the window, such as various links to the Desktop or your current libraries such as Documents and Music. In its main pane it provides a listing of the hard drives, DVD drives, CD drives, and so forth on your computer and any network shares (in the Network Location area) configured for your use.

Figure 3.7
Create new libraries or folders in Windows Explorer.

To view the folders on a particular drive, such as the C: drive (which is typically the default drive on most PCs), double-click the drive. You can create new folders on any drive or in existing folders such as the Documents folder. Navigate to the drive or folder that will serve as the parent container and then click the New Folder link on Windows Explorer's toolbar. Type a new name for the folder and you are good to go. You can drag existing files and folders into the new folder (using Windows Explorer) and specify the new folder when you save an Office file in the Save As dialog box.

tip

You can also create new folders in an Office application's Save As dialog box. Navigate to where you want to create the new folder and then Select New Folder on the toolbar in the Save As Dialog box. Provide a name for the folder. You can now use the folder as a location to save the current file.

Creating a New Library

As already mentioned, a Windows 7 library allows you to view and access files from different locations on your computer and your network. A library isn't really a container because a library doesn't store the actual files. A library is a kind of virtual container that can point to different folder locations and enable you to access related files (such as all the files related to a particular project).

To create a new Library in Windows Explorer, select Libraries in the links pane (on the left). On the Windows Explorer toolbar, select New Library. The new library will appear in Windows Explorer. Type a name for the new library. After you create the new library, you can select folders to be included in it. This inclusion of folders is what actually provides you access to the various files included in the folders.

Double-click on the new library in the Windows Explorer to open it. Click the Include a Folder button. The Include Folder dialog box opens for the current library. Navigate to a folder that you want to include in the library. Select the folder and then click Include Folder. This closes the Include Folder dialog box. Notice that the subfolders and files included in the folder that you included in the library are now listed in the library.

You can add additional folders to the library as needed. Use Windows Explorer to navigate to any folder on your computer or on your network. Right-click the folder and then point at Include in Library. A list of available libraries appears. Select the library.

When you are working in one of the Office applications and want to open a particular file from one of your libraries from the Open dialog box, select the library in the Location list and then locate the file you want to open. You can also save your Office application files to folders in a library when you are in the Save As dialog box.

Viewing File Versions in an Application

When you are working in an Office application, such as Word or Excel, the application is using the autosave feature to create different versions of the file that you are working on. By default, the Office applications save AutoRecover information for your current file every 10 minutes. If you accidentally close a document or workbook in Word or Excel without saving, the last AutoRecovered version of your file is saved so that you can access it (this is also a default setting in the application's Save options).

When you save a file and close it, all the AutoRecovered versions of the file are deleted. But you can peruse the different versions of your file saved by the AutoRecover feature as you work on the document. This includes any autosaved versions of the document that exist because you did not save changes that you made to the file before you closed it.

To view any autosaved versions of the current file, such as a Word document, select File to open the Backstage and then click on Info. Figure 3.8 shows the Info window for Microsoft Word. The area of interest in this window is the Versions area.

> **note**
>
> You can include a maximum of 50 folders in a library.

Figure 3.8
The Word Info
window.

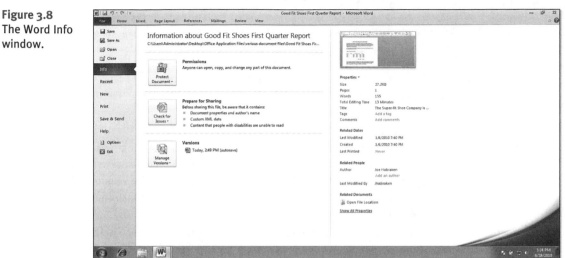

You can also browse for autosaved versions of files by clicking the Manage Versions button and then selecting Recover Draft Versions. This allows you to browse for any draft versions saved on your computer.

Any versions of the current document that have been autosaved are listed in the Versions area of the window. This includes any autosaved versions saved because you did not save the current file before closing it.

You can open a version of the file from the list by selecting it. When you open the autosaved version of the file, a message bar appears at the top of the document window below the Ribbon. It states that the current document is an AutoSaved Version. It provides you with two options: Compare and Restore. You can select Compare to compare this version of the file with the current version of the file. Any differences between the two files are detailed using the Track Changes feature and are displayed in the document and the Reviewing Pane. You can go through each of the changes marked in the document and accept or reject them as needed.

 **note**

You can delete all draft versions of unsaved files. Select Manage Versions and then Delete All Draft Versions.

You also have the option of selecting Restore. This option saves the autosaved version of the file over the current copy of the file. A message box opens, letting you know that the current version will be overwritten by the autosaved version. Click OK to overwrite the current version.

Searching for Office Files

If you haven't done a good job of keeping your files organized and can't seem to locate the file that you need, you can search for files a couple of different ways. First, you can use the Search box on the Windows 7 Start menu. Just type the name or part of the filename into the Search box and the search results will appear in the Search pane.

> **note**
> You can see all the results from your Windows search by clicking the See More Results link in the Search pane. The search results open in Windows Explorer.

The files or other items found will be categorized. For example, if you searched by a company name, you might have documents listed that contain the company name in the filename or you may have Outlook items such as appointments appear in the search results that have the company name somewhere in the appointment. So, the Windows 7 search engine is looking for all occurrences of your search terms. To open an item that appears in the Search pane, click the item.

Another option for searching for your Office files is to do a search in an Office application's Open dialog box. This is particularly useful if you remember at least part of the filename but don't really remember what folder contains the actual file. To access the Open dialog box, select File to open the Backstage. Then select Open.

In the Open dialog box, navigate to the drive, folder, or library that you would like to search for the file. Type your keywords for the search in the Search box in the upper-right corner of the Open dialog. Files that match your search criteria will have the search keywords highlighted in both the document title and document content as shown in Figure 3.9.

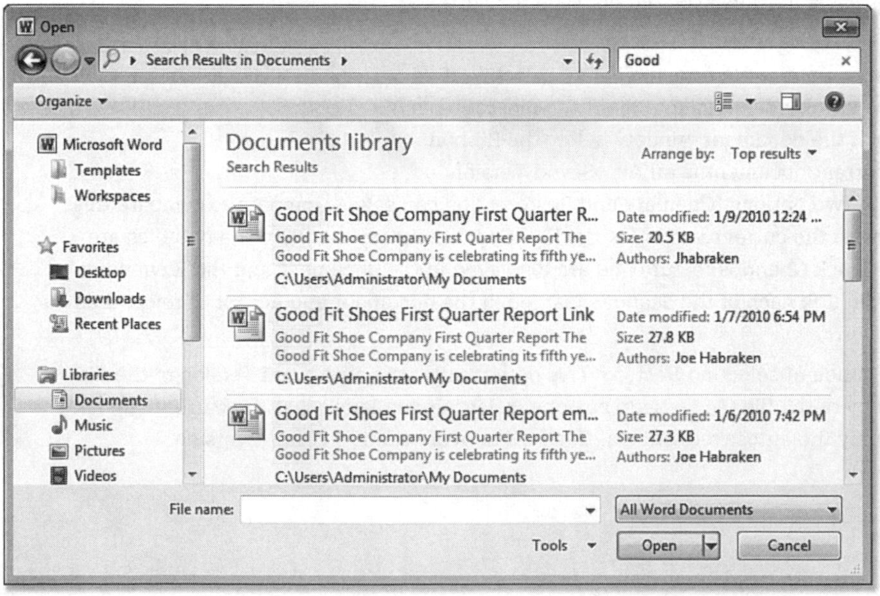

Figure 3.9
The Word Open dialog box as it appears after you have searched for a keyword in the document titles.

If you want to search a different folder using the search, select that folder and then click on the Search box to select your recently used keywords. When you want to open a file that has been identified by the search, double-click the filename to open it in the current application.

Sharing Files Using Windows 7 Homegroup

Files can be shared with other users in shared folders on your computer or network shares on your company's network servers. File permissions can be controlled on corporate networks using share and NTFS permissions. Access control is also used to protect shared resources, and only those who need access to a particular resource, such as a shared drive or printer, are given access by the network administrator.

> **🔍 note**
>
> If you need a complete reference to Windows 7, check out *Microsoft Windows 7 In Depth* by Robert Cowart and Brian Knittel.

In the small business or home office environment, the ability to share individual folders has been around as long as the Windows for Workgroups version of the Windows operating system. Even Windows 7 allows you to set up workgroups on your home or small business network to share resources. However, Windows 7 has also introduced a new way to share resources called homegroup. Although all the ins and outs of network file sharing using Windows 7 are beyond the scope of this book, we should look at the homegroup option because it provides some options for securing shared folders and files, and because doing so gels nicely with our earlier discussion related to organizing files in libraries.

When you install Windows 7, you have the option of joining an existing homegroup already on the network or creating a new homegroup. If you create a homegroup, Windows generates the password used by subsequent users who want to join the homegroup.

The homegroup shares resources on your computer by sharing libraries such as the Documents or Pictures libraries. We discussed libraries earlier in this chapter. Libraries allow you to share folders in place; a library is really a virtual container that lists the files in a folder that has been added to the library. The default access level assigned to libraries shared via the homegroup is read only, meaning other users cannot make changes to your shared files or delete them.

Other access levels can be set for libraries that you share via the homegroup. You can share the library as read only (as already mentioned) or as read/write, and you can share the library with specific people.

To access the homegroup settings, select Start, Control Panel, Network and Internet and then HomeGroup. Figure 3.10 shows the Control Panel's HomeGroup window. The settings are extremely straightforward. To add any of the listed libraries to the homegroup, select the library.

> **🔍 note**
>
> If you aren't part of a homegroup, click the Join Now button in the HomeGroup settings. You will need the homegroup password generated when the homegroup was first created on the network.

66 | Managing and Sharing Office Files

Obviously, only the default Windows libraries are listed in the HomeGroup settings. You can, however, add any libraries that you have created to the homegroup. When adding the libraries, you can also set the access level for each library. Follow these steps:

1. Select Start and then select your username on the Start menu. Your personal folder opens.

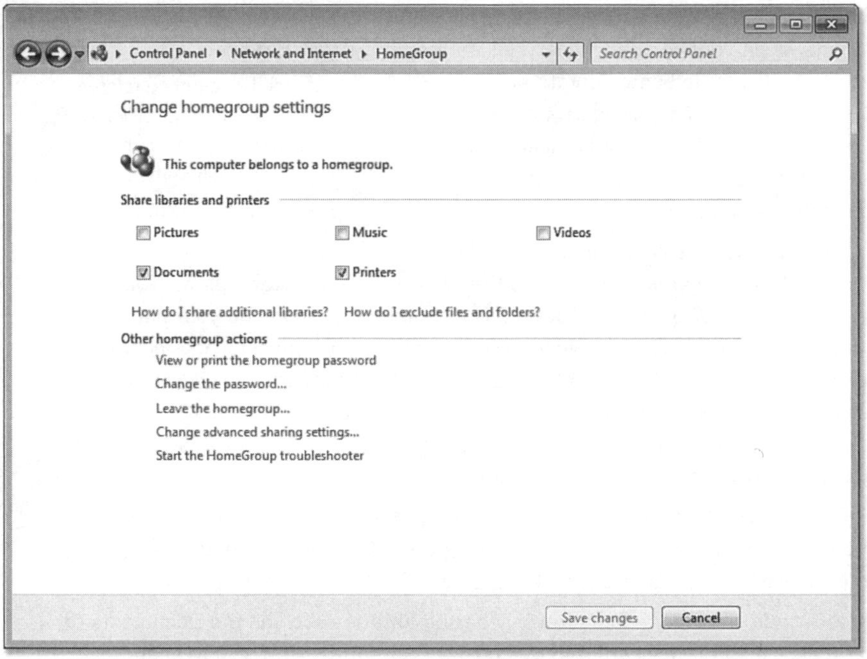

Figure 3.10
The Windows
HomeGroup settings.

2. Your libraries, including the libraries you have created, are listed on the left side of the windows. Right-click a library currently not shared in the homegroup.

3. Point at Share With on the shortcut menu that appears. The share settings for the library appear as shown in Figure 3.11.

4. Select the level of access you want to assign to the library: Nobody (the default), Homegroup (Read), or Homegroup (Read/Write).

Or, if you want to set access for specific people, select Specific People. Then use the File Sharing dialog box to specify the users and the permission level.

After you set the access level for the library, it is added to the homegroup. Obviously you can also use these steps to remove a library from the homegroup by selecting the Nobody access level for that particular library.

Figure 3.11
Sharing a library.

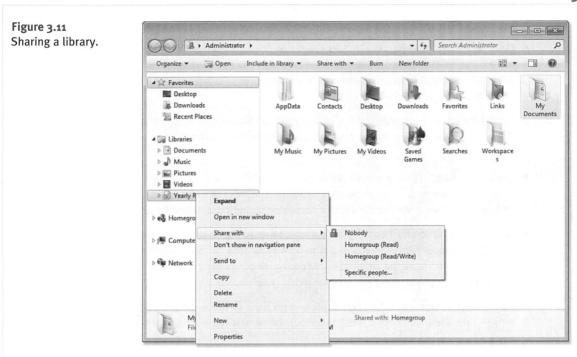

In terms of accessing shared resources in the homegroup, you can expand the HomeGroup link in Windows Explorer to view the computers currently available in the homegroup (these computers are considered "awake"). Select a computer to view the shared libraries provided by that particular member of the homegroup. The level of access afforded when you access a shared library in the homegroup depends on the access level assigned to that library by the owner. The same goes for other users on the network in terms of the access levels that you have assigned to your shared libraries in the homegroup.

Setting Office Permissions

If you are not taking advantage of Windows strategies for securing files that you share on a network, access to a file, such as a Word document, is pretty much completely wide open. Even if you do secure your shared files using Windows permissions, emailing a copy of a file to another user or sharing via a Web-based strategy such as Microsoft's SkyDrive negates the permissions that secure the file on your computer or the network. This means that if there is no protection set for the file, anyone can open, copy, and change the document as they want.

The Office applications enable you to set permissions related to a file (such as a document or workbook) that can help protect the content of the file, and can also potentially restrict what can be changed in the document and by whom. To view permissions options, click the Protect Document button in the Info window. The options available are as follows:

- **Mark as Final:** This command marks the file as final and makes the file read-only. All editing commands for the file are disabled. However, any user opening the document can remove the Mark as Final setting in the Backstage. This feature is primarily designed to keep users from inadvertently making changes to a file.

- **Encrypt with a Password:** The file is encrypted and protected with a password. When you select this option, you are required to enter a password for the file. Only users with the password can open the file.

- **Restrict Editing:** This command opens the Restrict Formatting and Editing task pane in the document, presentation, or worksheet window. You can restrict formatting to a selection of styles and specify editing restrictions for the document including making the document read only.

- **Restrict Permission by People:** This option allows you to take advantage of the Information Right Management Service. You can sign up for this free service from Microsoft using a Windows Live ID account. After the service is active on your computer via an installed certificate, you can assign users different permission levels using their email address for authentication.

- **Add a Digital Signature:** You can digitally sign a file to prove its authenticity. Signing a file digitally requires that you obtain a digital certificate. A certifying authority can provide digital certificates.

The first three options provided by Protect Document are self-explanatory. The Mark as Final option is useful in cases where you want your collaborators to know that the current version of the document is the final version. This setting also makes the file read-only but anyone wanting to change the file can remove the Mark as Final attribute and edit away. So, this option is not a strong security measure.

Encrypting the document with a password (the second option) definitely limits access to the file because the password is necessary to open it. This means that you also have to keep track of the password because it is the only way to open the encrypted file. This is a strong security measure, but it can backfire if you forget the password for the file.

The Restrict Editing setting allows you to be somewhat selective in what you allow other users to do to the file. You can specify both formatting and editing restrictions using the Restrict Formatting and Editing task pane. You can also choose parts of a document or worksheet and choose the actual users that can edit those portions of the file. This feature requires that you have user groups on your network, such as domain user groups on a Windows Server network.

The other two options for securing your files—Restrict Permission by People and Add a Digital Signature—are a little more complicated to take advantage of because they require that you do some special things on your computer before you take use them. Restrict Permission by People requires that you sign up for Microsoft's Information Right Management Service (IRMS). The Add a Digital Signature option requires that you have access to a digital certificate that you can sign the file with. Let's look at restricting permission by people using IRMS and then we can examine adding a digital signature to a file.

Restricting Permission by People

To restrict permissions to an Office document by people, you need to install Microsoft's Information Right Management Service. You will need a Microsoft Live ID to sign up for the service, which is free.

Select the Protect Document button and then point at Restrict Permission by People. Select Restricted Access. Because you don't have the IRMS installed on your computer to set the access levels for users by email address, the IRMS Service Sign-Up Wizard opens when you select the Restricted Access option.

Read all the information in the first wizard screen to make sure that you do want to take advantage of IRMS. If you decide to sign up for the service, select Yes, I Want to Sign Up for This Free Service from Microsoft. Then click Next.

On the next screen, select the Yes, I Have a Windows Live ID option button and then click Next. The next screen (shown in Figure 3.12) requires that you enter your Windows Live ID (which is typically a Hotmail account email address) and password.

Enter your email address and password. Then you can click Sign in.

On the next wizard screen, you must specify whether your computer is a private computer or a public/shared computer. You can use the IRMS in either situation, but you must remember to log off your Windows Live ID when you use a public or shared computer. Select the appropriate option for your computer and then click I Accept. Your computer has been configured for IRMS. You can click Finish to close the wizard.

Figure 3.12
Enter your
email address
and password.

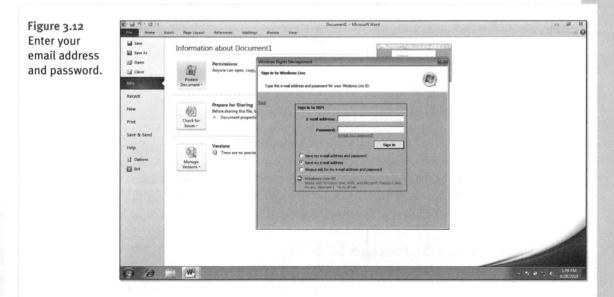

Now (and in the future when you select one of the restricted access settings via the Protect Document button) the Select User box opens. Select your Windows Live ID and then click OK. The Permission dialog box opens for the current file (such as a Word document). Select the Restrict Permission to This Document check box to begin assigning users at either the Read or Change permission levels.

For example, if I want to assign the read permission to a user or users, I type their email addresses into the Read box of the Permission dialog box as shown in Figure 3.13. I can also type the email addresses of users that I want to be able to edit and save changes to the document (but not print it) in the Change box.

> **note**
>
> If you want to give another user complete control over the file, click the More Options button in the Permission dialog box and then use the Access Level drop-down list to assign the Full Control permission level.

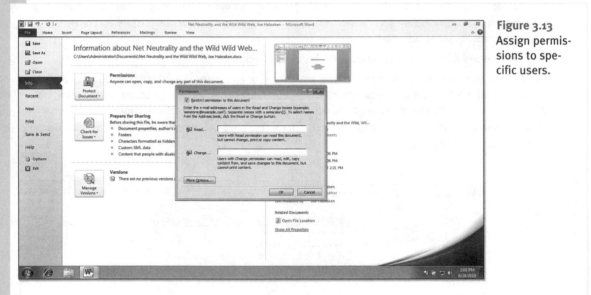

Figure 3.13
Assign permissions to specific users.

After you finish entering the email addresses into boxes on the Permission dialog box, click OK. This closes the Permission dialog box and assigns the permission levels as you dictated. You can reopen the Permissions dialog box as needed to adjust the permission level for a particular user or to delete a user from one of the permission boxes.

Adding a Digital Signature to a File

Digitally signing a file is a way to authenticate that a file is from a trusted source. So, adding a digital signature to a file is more about letting users who you will share the file with know that the file is authentic and does not contain any malicious code that might damage their computers or computer files. Adding a digital signature to a file provides protection to your collaborators—the people who will review the shared file—more than it protects you from a particular security problem.

To digitally sign an Office file, you need a digital certificate. A certifying authority can provide digital certificates. You can obtain digital certificates from online certifying authorities such CertPlus (http://certplus.com) and VeriSign (http://digitalid.verisign.com). You can also create your own digital certificate using the Digital Certificate for VBA Projects utility that you access in the Microsoft Office 2010 group on the Windows Start menu. A complete walkthrough of how you use this utility is provided in Appendix B, "Office Macros," in the section, "Digitally Signing Macros."

You should digitally sign a file only when you are providing a final draft to your collaborators. Signing the file marks the file as final, which makes it read-only. So, when you have a final file and the certificate is on your computer, you are ready to go.

Click Protect Document and then Add a Digital Signature. A message box opens, containing a disclaimer from Microsoft related to the use of digital signing as a way to verify a document's integrity. Read the fine print and then click OK. The Sign dialog box will open. Enter your purpose for signing the file. Your default signing certificate will be listed in the dialog box in the Signing As pane. You can use the Change button to locate a different certificate if you have multiple certificates on your computer.

When you are ready to sign the document, click Sign. The Signature Confirmation box opens, letting you know that your signature has been saved with the document. However, if the document is changed, the signature becomes invalid.

Prepare a File for Sharing

The Microsoft Office applications also provide with tools that you can use to check a document before you share it. These features are primarily designed for both security and accessibility issues. For example, you can check the document for any personal information that might be contained in it; this would be a security check because you don't necessarily want to share personal information in the shared document. Or you might have text in the document that will be difficult for people with disabilities to read; this is an accessibility issue.

The Check for Issues button on the Info window in the Backstage provides three tools that check your file for possible issues related to sharing. These tools are

- **Document Inspector:** This tool inspects the document for specific content such as comments, annotations, document properties, and hidden text. The main purpose of the inspector is to help ferret out personal information that you might have inadvertently stored in the document.

- **Accessibility Checker:** This tool opens the Accessibility Checker task pane in the document and provides a list of warnings related to accessibility issues in your document. For example, several blank lines between paragraphs might signal to a person using a screen reader that the document has ended. As you select each warning in the task pane, you are presented with information on why you should fix the issue and suggestions on how to fix it.

- **Compatibility Checker:** This tool checks the file for items that are not supported by earlier versions of the application that you are using. For example, I might have used the citation and bibliography feature in Word 2010. But the Compatibility Checker tells me that earlier versions of Word (Word 97–2003) will have to convert these items to static text.

As already mentioned, you can run these tools from the Backstage in the Info window. The Document Inspector and the Compatibility Checker run in their own windows. The Accessibility Checker takes the form of a task pane.

Using these tools to check a document before sharing it helps you get an Office file in the proper shape for actually sharing it. For example, if you used features in Excel 2010 that are not compatible with a legacy version of Excel, such as Excel 97–2003, and you know that one of your collaborators uses this version of Excel, you can save the file in a compatible file format.

Sharing Files Using SharePoint Workspace

One other option for sharing files with other users is to take advantage of Microsoft SharePoint Workspace. This application is designed to share workspaces with other users. These workspaces, which can contain any number of associated files, are typically shared with other uses via Microsoft SharePoint servers. However, you can share workspaces with users on a home or small business network that does not have access to a SharePoint server. This very brief look at SharePoint Workspace is intended only as an introduction to one of the Office applications that has a great deal of possibilities for collaboration with others, but that we do not actually cover in depth in this book.

> **🔍 note**
>
> SharePoint Workspace is the Office 2010 successor to Microsoft Office Groove 2007. SharePoint Workspace is also backward compatible with Groove 2007, so you can share workspaces with Groove users.

SharePoint Workspace is installed as one of the standard Microsoft Office applications. SharePoint Workspace can be opened from the Microsoft Office folder on the Start menu by using the Microsoft SharePoint Workspace 2010 icon.

The first time that you start SharePoint Workspace, you will be required to create a new account using the Account Configuration Wizard. The wizard makes it very easy for you to create your new account. In network environments that use SharePoint servers to house workspaces, you create a new account using an account configuration code supplied to you by your network administrator. For those of you who want to use SharePoint Workspace in a small network environment (with no servers), you can create a new account using your email address. Figure 3.14 shows the wizard screen used to specify the type of new account that you will create.

After you create your account, you can then create workspaces and share them with other users. As already mentioned, each workspace can include files, making it easy for you to share a number of Microsoft Office application files associated with a particular project with any number of other users.

Creating a New Workspace

The Microsoft SharePoint Workspace Launchbar is the main platform for creating, managing, and accessing your workspaces. To create a new workspace, Select New on the Launchbar's Home tab Ribbon. The new command provides three different possibilities:

- **SharePoint Workspace:** This command creates a SharePoint site on your computer and synchronizes it with your network's SharePoint server.

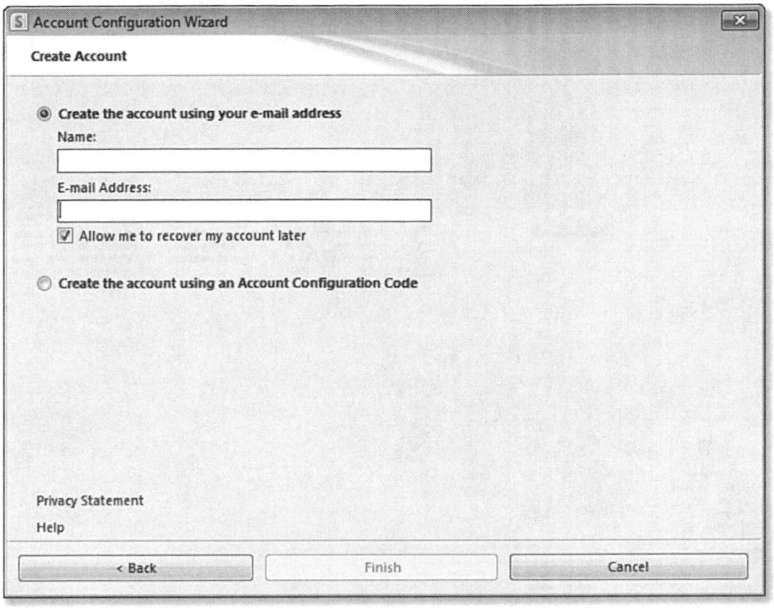

Figure 3.14
Create a new SharePoint
Workspace account.

- **Groove Workspace:** This command creates a workspace on your local computer that can then be shared and synchronized with other workspace members including those who are using Groove 2007.

- **Shared Folder:** You can also create a new folder on your computer and share it with other users.

Because we have been talking about using SharePoint Workspace in a networking environment that does not have a SharePoint server, you would select Groove Workspace to create a new workspace. The New Groove Workspace dialog box requires that you supply a new name for the new workspace and then click Create.

The new workspace is listed on the Launchbar. To open the workspace in the Microsoft SharePoint Workspace application window, double-click the workspace name.

Adding Files to the Workspace

After you have the workspace open in SharePoint Workspace, you can add documents to the workspace's root folder or you can create subfolders in the root and add documents to those folders as needed. The commands for creating new documents in the workspace, adding existing documents, or creating new folders are provided in the New group on the Home tab of the Ribbon.

To add existing files, click the Add Files command in the New group. The Add Files dialog box opens. Use the dialog box as needed to add files to the workspace. You can add any type of Office files (Excel, Word, PowerPoint, and so on) to be included in the workspace. Figure 3.15 shows a workspace that contains several files in the root folder.

Figure 3.15 The workspace window in SharePoint Workspace.

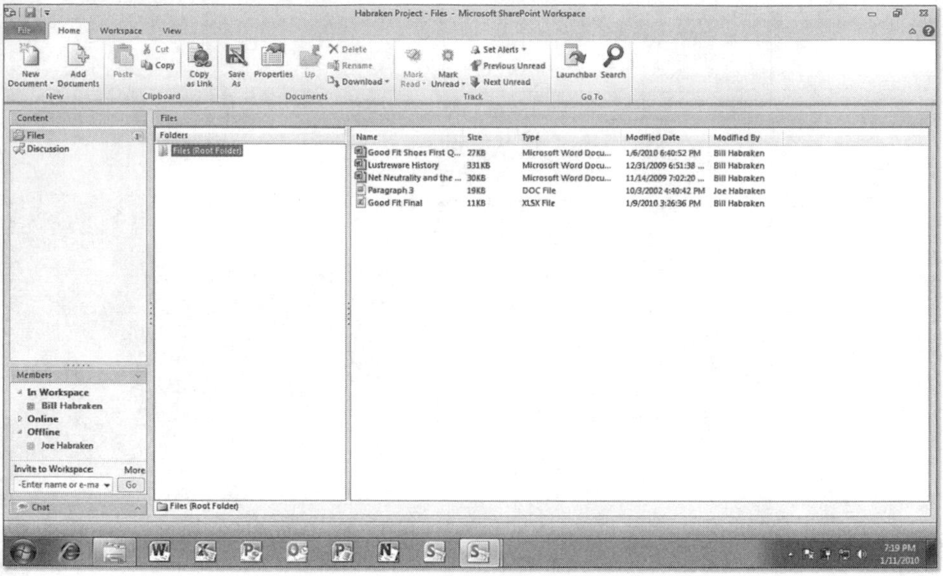

You can actually open the files from the workspace. Double-click any file to open it in its parent application. The workspace allows you to group together files that relate to the same project, or allows you to group files that you use often. There is no reason for the workspace to relate to a specific project; it can just relate to what you have to do on a daily basis as part of your job.

Inviting Members

After you have files in a workspace, you can invite members to participate in the workspace. This allows the workspace members to access any and all files that you place in the workspace. The other members can also add files to the workspace, making it an excellent environment for pulling together all the files involved in a multimember project.

To invite other members, select the Ribbon's Workspace tab. Select the Invite Members command in the Invite group and select one of the invitation options, such as Invite Members. The Send Invitation dialog box opens as shown in Figure 3.16.

Enter the invitee's email address on the To: box (in a SharePoint server environment, you enter the invitee's name). Use the Role drop-down list to specify the role for the new member: Participant, Manager, or Guest. Participants have access to all the files and can invite other participants. They cannot control the permissions assigned to other participants, however. The Manager permission level can change other member's roles (for example, change a Participant to a Guest). Guests can access information in the workspace, but have no workspace management permissions.

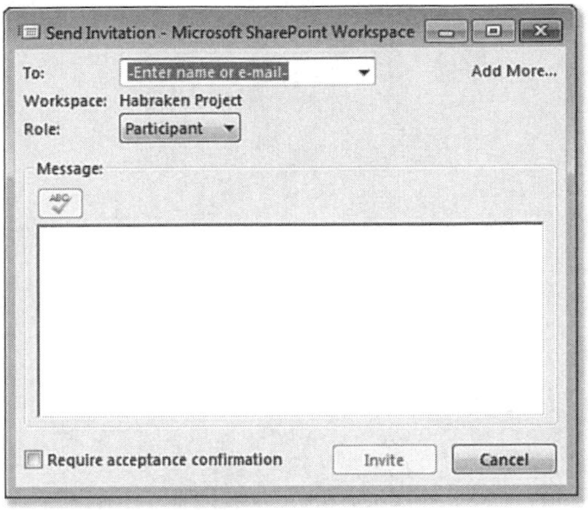

Figure 3.16
Invite a new member.

In the Message box, type the message to accompany your invitation for the workspace. You can require acceptance confirmation by selecting the Require Acceptance Confirmation check box. When you are ready to send the invitation, click Invite.

After the invited member (or members) receive the invitation in their email inbox, they can confirm acceptance of the invitation. You will receive notification of their acceptance (or refusal) via the SharePoint Workspace icon in your system tray. When you point at the icon, you will see an information link that says "so-and-so is accepting an invitation, please confirm." Select the link and a Confirm acceptance box opens. To authenticate the invitee's acceptance, click Confirm. The invitee is now a member of the workspace. The new member can work with files already in the workspace or add additional files as needed.

You will find that SharePoint Workspace also has the capability to send messages to members and include discussion threads in the workspace. SharePoint Workspace is certainly an excellent collaboration platform for sharing your Office files with other users.

4

USING AND CREATING GRAPHICS

Each of the Office applications is designed for a particular purpose. Excel is a number cruncher, Word is a powerful word processor, and PowerPoint is a presentation application extraordinaire. Although you use the different Office applications for different purposes, graphics—images, shapes, and clip art—are used for pretty much the same purpose in all the applications. Graphics enable you to enhance information and add interest to the spreadsheets, documents, and presentations that you create. In Office 2010, the commands and tools used to insert and modify images, shapes, SmartArt graphics, and clip art are very consistent across the different applications in the Office suite. So, if you know how to use graphics in Word, you can apply that knowledge to another Office application, such as PowerPoint.

This chapter provides an overview of the options for adding graphics to your Office application files. We will look at how to insert shapes, SmartArt graphics, images, and clip art. We will also look at some of the new features that Office 2010 provides for working with graphics in the applications, including the screen capture tool and the background removal tool.

The Office 2010 Options for Graphics and Pictures

The Office 2010 applications offer a number of different possibilities for adding graphics to the files that you create in each of the applications. Graphic options range from the drawing of shapes and the insertion of customizable SmartArt graphics to the ability to insert and enhance your own digital images.

How you use graphics in your Office documents (let's consider Office document to mean a Word document, Excel worksheet, PowerPoint slide, or any other file type used by the Office applications) is really as important as the type of graphic you use. Graphics are meant to enhance a Word document, Excel worksheet, or PowerPoint slide. Enhancing your work with a graphic can mean different things depending on the type file you a creating. For example, a neighborhood newsletter created in Word might benefit from the use of clip art as design elements or headlines formatted as graphics using WordArt. In another scenario, a PowerPoint slide detailing a particular business process could be greatly enhanced using a SmartArt graphic diagram that provides a visualization of the process described on the slide. It definitely makes sense to weigh the benefits of adding a graphic to an Office document; you should avoid graphics that make a document or slide too busy or do not enhance the information provided. Make sure that your graphic elements increase the impact of information being provided.

Charts, for example (which are discussed in the context of their use in particular Office applications such as Excel and PowerPoint) are extremely useful graphics used to provide a visualization of numeric data. Charts can be particularly useful when they accompany worksheet data in Excel or help explain numerical data provided on a PowerPoint slide. Consider the chart as your measuring stick in terms of weighing whether to use a particular graphic type in an Office application. We know how charts enhance the understanding of numerical values in tables, so try and apply the same measuring stick when you are going to use digital images, clip art, and diagrams; make sure that they add to document and don't just serve as a cute distraction. I realize that pictures of puppies will melt nearly anyone's heart, but using puppy pictures to mask bad sales trends shown on a PowerPoint slide is just plain wrong (although those puppies can be real cute).

 For information on creating charts in Excel, see page 381 in Chapter 14, "Enhancing Worksheets with Charts."

 For information on using charts in PowerPoint, see page 542 in Chapter 19, "Better Slides with Clip Art, Pictures, and SmartArt."

As already mentioned, the Office applications provide a number of different possibilities in terms of the different types of graphical elements available to you. The list that follows provides a brief description of each of the possibilities:

- **Picture:** You can insert your digital pictures into your Office documents. The Office applications support a number of different file formats including Windows Bitmap (.bmp), Graphics Interchange Format (.gif), Joint Photographic Experts Group (.jpg), Portable Network Graphics (.png), and Tagged Image File Format (.tif).

- **Clip Art:** Each Office application has access to an installed library of clip art images. Additional clip art can be downloaded from Microsoft.com as you work in a particular application. Microsoft.com provides you with a seemingly unending library of clip art images. Static clip art is referred to as an illustration. The Clip Art library also provides animated GIF images, which are referred to as videos; however, GIF images are just a layering of static images that provide the appearance of motion. The Clip Art gallery also includes photographs and audio files.

- **Shapes:** The ability to insert different drawn shapes into an Office application has been around nearly as long as the Office applications. A Shapes gallery provides a number of different shape

categories that make it easy to add lines, rectangles, stars, and even callouts to your Office documents. Shapes can also be edited and combined to provide you with all sorts of possibilities.

- **SmartArt:** This graphic type was a huge addition to the Office applications when it was introduced with the release of Office 2007. Office 2010 provides additional SmartArt diagrams and
makes it easier to edit SmartArt diagrams.

- **Screenshot:** This tool provides you with the ability to take a snapshot of the Windows desktop
and/or any windows open on the desktop. This can be particularly useful if you want to visually
document the steps required to use in a particular feature in one of the Office applications (or
any application open on the Windows desktop). You can also use it to capture the screen of messaging platforms such as Skype or the wall on your Facebook page.

- **WordArt:** WordArt was actually created using a separate WordArt application for a number of
the Office suite releases and was inserted into a document as an object such as clip art or a digital image. WordArt attributes can now be assigned to text in place, allowing you much greater
flexibility in converting text to WordArt using the WordArt gallery.

The commands used to insert the various graphic types such as pictures, clip art, or shapes are provided on the Ribbon's Insert tab in each of the Office applications such as Word or PowerPoint. You
can even insert pictures, clip art, and shapes into your Outlook emails; the Ribbon provided by the
message window provides the various commands for inserting graphics on the Insert tab.

In Word, Excel, Outlook, and Publisher (Publisher does not include SmartArt graphics or the
Screenshot command), the commands for inserting different graphic types are bundled into the
Illustrations command group. Figure 4.1 shows the Ribbon's Insert tab in Word.

Figure 4.1
The Insert tab
includes the
Illustrations
group.

In PowerPoint, these commands have been split into two groups. The Images group includes the
Picture, Clip Art, Screenshot, and Photo Album commands (which enables you to take a series of
digital images and quickly create slides for each image). The Illustrations group in PowerPoint
houses the Shapes, SmartArt, and Chart commands.

The WordArt command and associated gallery are found in the Text group on the Ribbon's Insert
tab in all the Office applications mentioned. WordArt can be inserted on a document page as a new
object. You can also convert existing text to WordArt.

Working with SmartArt Graphics

SmartArt provides a large gallery of all sorts of different graphics that can be used for creating eye-
catching lists and diagrams. You can create lists that use shapes to better define the relationship

between text entries in a list and you can create lists that combine text and pictures. Figure 4.2 shows a vertical picture list SmartArt graphic that includes thumbnail photos and text.

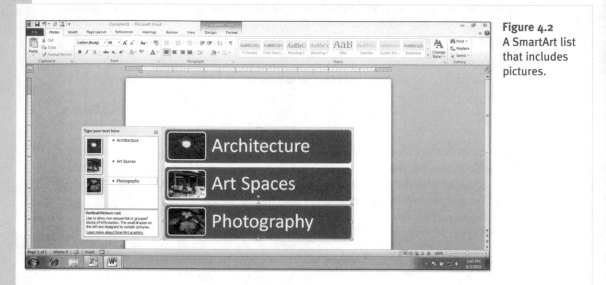

Figure 4.2
A SmartArt list that includes pictures.

SmartArt lists enable you to go beyond the possibilities normally associated with numbered and bulleted lists. SmartArt lists can be particularly useful in PowerPoint where you can replace bulleted lists on slides with SmartArt lists. SmartArt lists are actually better at showing how the different items in a list are related than the typical bulleted list found on a PowerPoint slide.

➥ *For information on converting text to SmartArt in PowerPoint, see page 540 in Chapter 19.*

The SmartArt gallery also provides a large number of different diagram types. There are process diagrams, relationship diagrams, and hierarchy diagrams just to name a few. For example, a hierarchy organization chart could be used in an Excel worksheet to provide information related to how different departments shown in a worksheet relate to each other in terms of the corporate structure. Figure 4.3 shows a half-circle organization chart in an Excel worksheet.

Each SmartArt diagram category provides you with a specific way to represent information visually in your Office documents. The list that follows provides a brief description of each of the SmartArt graphic categories:

- **List:** Enables you to place text in nonsequential vertical or horizontal lists.

- **Process:** Designed to show a logical progression or flow, this diagram type enables you to break down the steps in a process or cycle.

- **Cycle:** Enables you to show the steps in a continuous process.

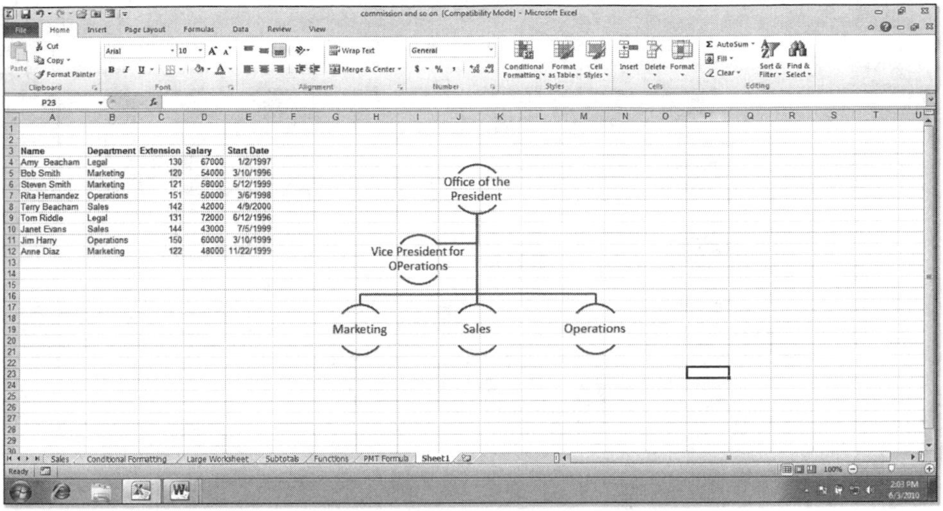

Figure 4.3 Organization charts can be inserted into Excel worksheets or other Office documents.

- **Hierarchy:** These diagrams show the hierarchical relationship between items shown in the diagram. A hierarchy diagram can also be used to show a decision tree.

- **Relationship:** Enables you to show how elements in the diagram are related or connected.

- **Matrix:** This diagram type shows how the parts relate to the whole.

- **Pyramid:** Used to show both hierarchical relationships and the proportional importance of items in the hierarchy.

- **Picture:** This group will list all the SmartArt lists and diagrams that enable you to incorporate images into the SmartArt structure.

- **Office.com:** This group provides additional SmartArt graphics provided online via the Office.com website.

SmartArt graphics are easy to create. They are also easy to edit and modify. Let's take a look at inserting SmartArt graphics into the Office applications and then look at the tools available for modifying and enhancing SmartArt lists and diagrams.

Inserting SmartArt Graphics

SmartArt graphics are inserted using the SmartArt command, which is housed in the Illustration group on the Ribbon's Insert tab. To insert SmartArt into an Office document, follow these steps:

1. On the Insert tab, select SmartArt. The Choose a SmartArt Graphic dialog box will open as shown in Figure 4.4.

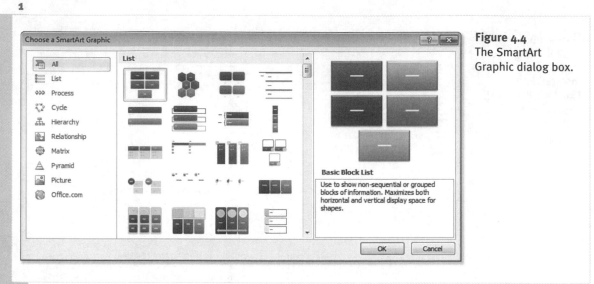

Figure 4.4
The SmartArt
Graphic dialog box.

2. Select a SmartArt category to view the individual diagrams provided by a particular category.

3. Select the list or diagram that you want to insert.

4. Click OK. The list or diagram will be inserted into your current Office document.

You can now enter the text that you want to place in the diagram. Figure 4.5 shows a Venn diagram SmartArt graphic that has been inserted into a Word document.

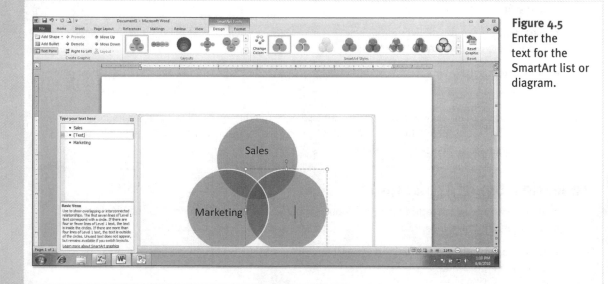

Figure 4.5
Enter the
text for the
SmartArt list or
diagram.

You can enter the text for the diagram directly onto the diagram parts by replacing any of the [TEXT] placeholders. You can also enter and edit text entries for the diagram in the Text pane that accompanies each SmartArt graphic (to the left of the SmartArt). The Text pane can be collapsed by clicking the pane's Close button. If you want the Text pane to reappear, click the Expand button on the left edge of the SmartArt frame.

Some SmartArt lists and diagrams enable you to include pictures as part of the list or diagram. After you insert a SmartArt graphic that includes placeholders for pictures, you will find that picture placeholders are provided in the different diagram parts as well as the Text pane for the SmartArt graphic. To replace a picture placeholder, click the placeholder in either the diagram or the Text pane. The Insert Picture dialog box will open. Navigate to the folder that houses the picture graphic and then select the file. Click Insert to place the picture in the SmartArt graphic.

> **⚠ caution**
>
> If you are going to use SmartArt graphics in an Office application, save the file that you are creating in an Office 2010 File format. For example, Word would use the file format .docx, whereas Excel would use .xlsx. Using an Office 2010 file extension will enable you to take advantage of all the SmartArt possibilities and tools. Some functionality and capability is lost when attempting to use SmartArt graphics in earlier Office file formats, particularly in files created in Office applications that predate the Office 2007 release.

The picture will be sized according to the space allotted for it in the list or diagram. For example, if you insert a picture into a circle that is part of a particular diagram type, the picture will be sized to fit in the shape, meaning the circle. This means that you do not have to size or crop images before you insert them into a SmartArt list or diagram. Even the largest digital photo will be sized to fit appropriately into the SmartArt graphic shape.

After you have completed entering the text and pictures (if applicable) for the SmartArt graphic, click outside the graphic's frame. You can now continue to work on the document, worksheet, or presentation that you are creating. The SmartArt graphic is like any other object in that it can be moved or sized as required.

Modifying SmartArt Graphics

When you select a SmartArt graphic in an Office document, the SmartArt Tools become available on the Ribbon. The SmartArt Tools consist of a Design and a Format tab.

The Design tab is primarily devoted to the selection of layouts and styles for the SmartArt graphic. Figure 4.6 shows the SmartArt Tools Design tab.

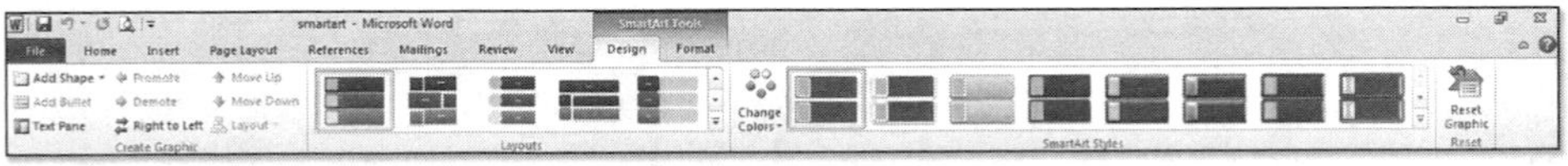

Figure 4.6
The SmartArt Tools Design tab.

When you work with the Design tab command groups, you will be affecting the entire SmartArt graphic. For example, the Layouts gallery enables you to choose from a number of different layouts for the particular type of SmartArt list or diagram that you inserted into your Office document. The Change Colors command in the SmartArt Styles group enables you to specify a color combination for the SmartArt graphic based on the current theme as well as a number of other color categories. After you have specified a color combination for SmartArt, you can use the SmartArt Styles gallery to fine-tune the use of the color scheme selected for the graphic and apply 3D styles to the SmartArt.

Two other command groups serve as the end caps for the Design tab. On the far left is the Create Graphic group and at the far right is the Reset group. In the Create Graphic group, you are provided the Add Shape command, which enables you to add additional shapes (the same shape that is used as the primary building block for the SmartArt graphic) to the graphic.

So, if you have inserted a SmartArt list that provides three list boxes, you can increase the number of boxes using the Add Shape command. The Create Graphic group also has other commands that enable you to promote or demote and move up or move down shapes in the SmartArt graphic. The availability of these commands will depend on the type of SmartArt graphic you have inserted into your Office document.

If you make design changes to your graphic using the Change Colors command or the SmartArt Styles gallery and just don't like the way things turned out, you can reset the graphic and start over (or leave things well enough alone). Click the Reset Graphic command in the Reset group. The Reset Graphic command does not reset changes that you make using the Layouts gallery or the commands in the Create Graphic group.

The other SmartArt Tools tab is the Format tab. The Format tab is shown in Figure 4.7. The Format tab commands are a little different from those provided on the Design tab, which were geared to making global changes to the SmartArt graphic.

> **tip**
>
> If you are working with a 3D SmartArt graphic, it might be easier to edit the shape settings in 2D. Select the Edit in 2-D command in the Shapes group.

> **tip**
>
> You can toggle the SmartArt graphic's Text Pane on or off using the Text Pane command in the Create Graphic group.

> **tip**
>
> If you are attempting to select a shape in a SmartArt graphic that is behind another shape, the easiest way to select it (rather than using Bring Forward) is to select the shape's text in the Text pane.

Figure 4.7
The SmartArt Tools Format tab.

Many of the command possibilities provided by the Format tab can be applied to the entire SmartArt graphic or the individual shapes (elements) that make up the graphic. This enables you to fine-tune the look of a SmartArt graphic and modify an existing graphic as you require.

For example, you might want to change the shape of a specific element (which is referred to as a shape, so this can be confusing) in the SmartArt graphic. You can select a specific shape and modify it or you can select a number of shapes (select the first shape or element and then hold down the Ctrl key when selecting the other shapes) and modify them collectively. The Shapes group on the Format tab enables you to change the shape of a selected element or elements using the Change Shape gallery. You can also change the size of a shape or shapes using the Larger and Smaller commands.

The Format tab also provides you with the ability to modify the style for a selected shape or shapes and modify shape fill, outline, and effects. The Shape Styles group provides access to the Shapes Styles gallery, which provides a number of different border fill and text styles. Shape Fill, Shape Outline, and Shape Effects enable you to modify these style elements individually.

The WordArt Styles gallery provides you with a number of different WordArt text styles that can be applied to the text in a shape. These styles include color, outline, shadow and text effects. If you want to fine-tune the WordArt style assigned to a particular shape or a number of selected shapes, you can use the Text Fill, Text Outline, and Text Effects commands as needed.

The Text command group provides commands used to specify the text direction in a shape or shapes that make up the SmartArt graphic. You can use the Text Direction command to change the direction of the text. The Align Text command enables you to specify whether the text should be aligned to the top, middle, or bottom of the graphic or shape.

The Arrange group commands are related to how a shape is layered with other shapes and how the text in a document such as a Word document deals with the SmartArt graphic. To layer shapes in a graphic, use the Bring Forward and Send Backward command as needed. You can change the alignment and rotation of an entire SmartArt graphic or entire shape by using the Align and Rotate commands, respectively.

Aligning Graphics and Text

In terms of a SmartArt graphic in a document that includes text, you can use the Position command to specify whether the graphic is to be inline with the text or will allow the text to wrap around it. You can also change how the text wraps around the graphic by using the Wrap Text command. When you insert a graphic such as a SmartArt graphic, you are, in effect, creating a new drawing layer that sits on top of the text, which lives in its own layer: the text layer. The choices available for wrapping text in relation to a SmartArt graphic also apply to other graphics that you might use, such as images, clip art, or shapes. The choices provided on the Wrap Text command's gallery are as follows:

- **In Line with Text:** The SmartArt graphic is placed in the text layer, enabling you to position the graphic in the text paragraphs in the document. The text will not wrap around the graphic.

- **Square:** The text wraps around the graphic in a square pattern, which is defined by the outside boundaries of the graphic's frame (not the graphic's shape).

- **Tight:** The text wraps around the graphic based on the graphic's shape.

- **Through:** The text wraps around the graphic as if the graphic was an inline element with the text. The text remains outside the graphic, however. This is very similar to the Tight setting.

- **Top and Bottom:** Text wraps on the top of the graphic and then continues below the graphic, placing the graphic between the text flow.

- **Behind Text:** The graphic is moved behind the text layer. This enables you to use a graphic as a frame or as a watermark on the page.

- **In Front of Text:** The graphic is placed in the drawing layer, which sits on top of the text layer. The text will be behind the graphic. This can be used in PowerPoint to unveil or hide a bullet point or bullet points when an animation effect is added to the graphic.

These different text-wrapping options become particularly important when you are working in Office applications such as Word and Publisher where the SmartArt graphic will cohabitate the page along with a potentially large amount of text. Remember that the text is in its own layer and the SmartArt graphic is in the drawing layer. This not only enables you to determine how the graphic will interact with the text but how graphics in the drawing layer interact with each other.

Adding and Manipulating Pictures

The Microsoft Office applications enable you to insert a number of different digital picture file formats into your Office documents. Because it is true that a picture is worth a thousand words, you can use pictures to enhance your Word documents, PowerPoint slides, Excel worksheets, and even your Outlook emails. Some of the commonly used digital picture file formats are as follows:

- Windows Bitmap (.bmp)

- Graphics Interchange Format (.gif)

- Joint Photographic Experts Group (.jpg)

- Portable Network Graphics (.png)

- Tagged Image File Format (.tif)

- Windows Metafile (.wmf)

Digital image files are compressed and the compression scheme used by a particular file format can have an effect on the overall quality of the image. Lossless compression schemes compress the file without discarding any of the file data; the lossy compression scheme actually discards some of the file's data to compress the image file. Image files also differ in the number of colors they can provide, so you will find that each file format definitely has its own plus and minuses. For example, GIF files provide for a total number of only 256 colors, but GIF files are often small (in terms of size) and can be used as pictures on websites. The PNG format provides millions of colors and uses a lossless compression scheme, so you get a fantastic-looking image but the file size can be quite large. A JPG image uses a lossy compression scheme and so might not look as good as a PNG file but it will definitely provide you with a smaller file size.

Most digital cameras shoot either JPG or PNG files by default. Most digital cameras also enable you to adjust the number of megapixels used in a shot, which relates to the resolution of the picture and the file size created.

In terms of using digital images in your Office applications, you don't really need to worry about file size, megapixels, or file type. The Office applications can deal with most of the common file types and will typically size the image to fit into the shape or frame that will hold the image.

Inserting Pictures

The Picture command is on the Ruler's Insert menu. To insert a picture, follow these steps:

1. Select the Picture command. The Insert Picture dialog box will open as shown in Figure 4.8.

 tip

You can also scan images directly into Office documents. Use the Object command on the Insert tab and in the Object dialog box to create a new image using your scanner's or other device's listing in the Object type list.

Figure 4.8
The Insert Picture dialog box.

2. Locate and select the picture file that you want to insert.

3. Select the Insert button. The Insert Picture dialog box will close and the picture will be inserted into the document.

After the image has been inserted in the document, you can size the document using the handles provided on the picture frame. The image size can also be modified using the Height and Width spinner boxes, which are provided in the Size group of the Pictures Tool Format tab. The Picture Tools are available on the Ribbon when the picture is selected.

Adjusting Pictures

The Picture Tools Format tab provides commands that modify different aspects of the picture. For example, the Picture Styles gallery enables you to change the border type and the shape, and to apply some 3D effects to the picture. The picture border and the effects applied to the picture such as settings for the shadow, glow, or 3D rotation can be accessed using the Picture Border and Picture Effects commands, respectively.

You will find that many of the commands provided on the Picture Tools Format tab are the same as those found on the SmartArt Tools Format tab. For example, the Position, Wrap Text, and other Arrange Group commands will be the same for a picture, SmartArt graphic, or shape. However, the Picture Tools tab does provide the Adjust group, which contains a number of extremely useful commands specific to digital pictures. The Adjust group commands are as follows:

 tip

To add a caption to a picture (or clip art), right-click on the selected picture and then select Insert Caption. You can then set up the caption in the Caption dialog box.

- **Remove Background:** This command enables you to remove the background from the picture. This is a new tool for the Microsoft Office applications. We look at using this tool later in the chapter.

- **Corrections:** With this command you can select from a gallery of choices that enables you to sharpen and soften the image or adjust the brightness and contrast. Thumbnails of your image are provided in this gallery with different correction settings applied to them. All you have to do is select one of the possibilities. To view the actual brightness and contrast settings for one of the gallery thumbnails, place the mouse on that thumbnail to view a screen tip that provides the percent brightness and contrast.

- **Color:** This command provides a gallery of different color saturations and tones as well as a number of recolor settings for your image. The Color Saturation gallery is shown in Figure 4.9. Color saturations are denoted by percent saturation such as 100%, 200%, and so on. The color tones are denoted by degrees Kelvin (lower numbers are "cooler" and tend toward the blues; higher numbers are "warmer" and tend toward yellow). To apply a setting from the gallery, select the thumbnail of your image that provides the color changes that you want to make to your picture.

- **Artistic Effects:** This command provides a gallery of different photo effects such as Pencil Sketch, Cement, and Plastic Wrap. You can preview any of the effects on your picture by placing the mouse on a particular effect in the gallery. Some of the possibilities are mind-blowing (of course I grew up in the 1960s).

Figure 4.9
The Color gallery for a picture.

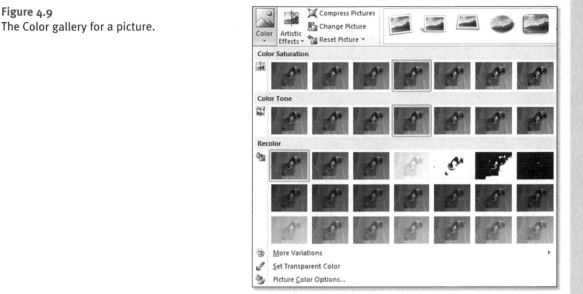

- **Compress Pictures:** This command enables you to compress the image so that its size (in terms of file size, not size in the document) is smaller and therefore your entire document file size will be smaller. When you select Compress Pictures, the Compress Pictures dialog box opens. It enables you to delete any cropped areas of the picture and to select a target output size such as 96 ppi pixels per inch) for emails and 150 ppi for web pages.

- **Change Picture:** Use this command to open the Insert Picture dialog box and select a picture to replace the current image.

- **Reset Picture:** This command will throw out all the formatting changes that you have made to the picture. This enables you to return to square one with no harm, no foul.

Although the galleries provided by a number of the Adjust group commands might be sufficient for your needs in terms of changing an image's attributes, you can fine-tune these settings using the Format Picture dialog box. You can access the dialog box by selecting the additional Options link provided at the bottom of the Corrections, Color, and Artistic Effects galleries. For example, if I select Picture Corrections Options at the bottom of the Corrections gallery, the Format Picture dialog box opens as shown in Figure 4.10 with Picture Corrections selected.

You can use the different settings provided in the Format Picture dialog box to specify the fill, line color, line style, and the 3D format and rotation for the image. You can also fine-tune changes that you have made to the picture, such as brightness and contrast corrections, color changes, and the addition of artistic effects. For example, the Picture Corrections settings (shown in Figure 4.10) can be adjusted using slider bars that can soften or sharpen an image or change the brightness and contrast of the image.

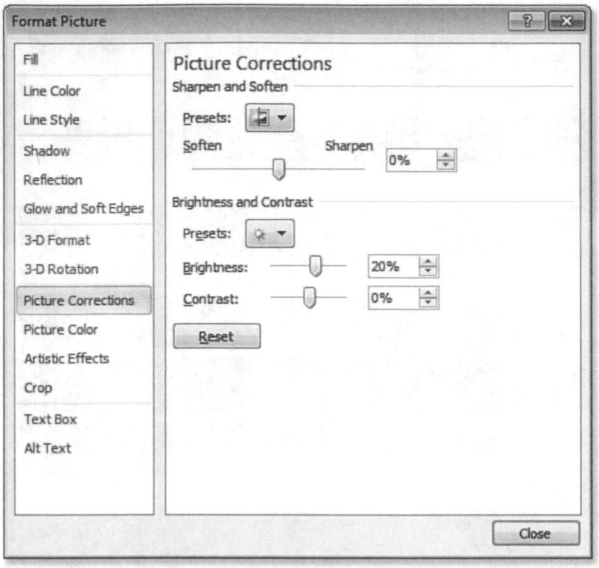

Figure 4.10
The Format Picture dialog box.

Cropping an Image

Another useful command for adjusting an image is the Crop command. Although this command isn't included in the Adjust group, the Crop command is very useful in cases where you want to trim unneeded parts of the image. It is located at the other end of the Format tab in the Size group.

The Crop command actually provides you with more than one possibility for cropping an image. When you select the Crop command the following options are provided:

- **Crop:** Select Crop to place the crop frame around the image. You can then adjust the cropping handles as needed. Select the Crop command again to apply your cropping settings.

- **Crop to Shape:** You can apply a shape to the image from the Shape gallery and have the image cropped to that specific shape.

- **Aspect Ratio:** You can have the image cropped using a specific aspect ratio such as 1:1 (square), 2:3 (portrait), or 3:2 (landscape).

- **Fill:** The image will be resized to fill the entire picture area (such as a picture box) and the portions of the image that fall outside the picture area will be cropped.

- **Fit:** The image will be resized to fit in the picture area, maintaining the original aspect ratio of the image (this is actually the opposite of cropping).

If you find that you have gone overboard on the cropping, you can remove the cropping by using the Undo command on the Quick Access Toolbar. The Reset Picture command will not undo cropping.

Using the Background Removal Tool

The Background Removal tool is probably one of the most intriguing additions to the Office application in terms of working with images. The Remove Background command does exactly what it claims to do: It enables you to remove the background from an image.

The great thing about this tool is that it is intuitively able to differentiate the background from the foreground elements in your photo and so will automatically select the background areas to be removed from the photo. How well this works will depend on the photo. Some photos contain color combinations or low contrast between the elements in the photo that make it difficult to easily separate the background from the foreground elements. However, after the Background Removal tool takes the first cut at selecting the background of the photo, you can step in and fine-tune the selection so that you can end up with some good results.

To use the Remove Background tool, select a photo in your Office application. Then click the Remove Background command. The Background Removal tab will appear on the Ribbon as shown in Figure 4.11.

Figure 4.11
The Background Removal tab and a selected picture.

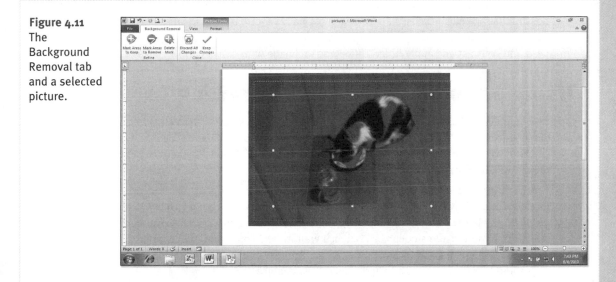

The commands provided on the Background Removal tab are self-explanatory. Two command groups are provided: Refine and Close. The Refine group provides commands that enable you to refine the initial selection of the background. The Close group provides you with two possibilities that enable you to either discard the changes or keep the changes.

On first inspection after selecting the Remove Background command, you will find that the background areas that have been designated in the photo for removal are designated by a magenta overlay. A marquee with sizing handles is also floated on your image to specify the area of the image that contains the foreground elements to keep. If the marquee has excluded foreground items that you want to keep, you can change the size of the marquee or move the marquee's position as required.

Adjusting the marquee isn't going to get you much, so for greater refinement, you will need to take advantage of the Refine group commands. Let's start with marking areas that you want to keep: Select the Mark Areas to Keep command. The mouse pointer will become a pencil. Use the pencil to outline each area that you want to keep that has been marked for removal. Click the pencil to place a mark point on an area and then continue to drag the mouse. Marking points makes it easier to connect the dots and get all of an area that you want to mark to keep. You might find that you enclose only a portion of an area to keep using the mouse when the Background Removal tool suddenly catches on and finishes the selection for you by removing the magenta overlay from that area.

You can also mark areas to remove. Select the Mark Areas to Remove command and use the pencil to mark areas that should be removed. When the area has been marked for removal, the magenta overlay is applied to that area of the image.

When you are ready to complete the process by keeping all the fine-tuning that you did with the Mark Areas to Keep and the Mark Areas to Remove commands, select the Keep Changes command. The background will be removed from the image. Now you can take advantage of the picture styles that provide background fill colors or shadow effects.

If you have ever attempted to manipulate digital photos, you are probably aware that many of the possibilities we have discussed here would normally require a sophisticated piece of digital image-editing software. It is pretty amazing that you can quickly correct such image parameters as brightness and contrast and apply artistic effects to an image with only a couple clicks of a mouse.

Using Shapes and the Office Drawing Tools

The Microsoft Office applications also provide you with the ability to add a variety of shapes to your Office documents. The Shapes gallery, which you access via the Shapes command on the Insert tab, provides a number of different shape categories. You can add lines, rectangles, block arrows, callouts, and a number of other different shape types.

One of the available shapes is a text box, which as advertised, is used to add a box containing text to a document. However, other shapes can also contain text; this means that you can use any shape as a design element and get double duty out of it as a text container. This can be very useful when you want to add text to a document but also want to add some visual interest at the same time, say in a Word document or a PowerPoint slide. The text in a shape can be formatted using WordArt styles and text fill, outline, and effects tools. This enables you to create shapes with text entries that are eye-catching and serves an informational purpose in your document.

When you add a shape to an Office document, the shape is placed on a drawing canvas. This is particularly important in Word and Publisher where a large amount of text might already exist on a page or will exist on the page when the document is complete. The drawing canvas floats on top of the document's text layer. This means that you don't have to worry about the text layer as you work with your shapes until you determine how the shapes will interact with the text

> **⚠ caution**
>
> You cannot select multiple shapes that are in different layers. For example, if one shape is in line with the text and the other shape is in front of the text, you will not be able to select both of them and then group them. It's best to place all the shapes on the same drawing canvas and then group them.

in terms of the text's alignment with respect to the shape or shapes (which is controlled using the Wrap Text command on the Drawing Tools Format tab).

You can insert multiple shapes on a drawing canvas and then arrange or layer the shapes as needed. This allows you to build your own custom graphics. Although the SmartArt graphics provide many different composite drawings that contain different shapes (and can be manipulated individually), you can use the shapes to create pretty much anything that you require. After you create the graphic using multiple shapes, you can then select the shapes (hold down the Ctrl key to select multiple shapes) and the select the Group command. Now when you move or size one shape in the group, all the shapes in the group will be moved or sized.

If you are going to insert a single shape as a graphic element in an Office document, you can insert it using the Shapes gallery, which you access via the Shapes command on the Ribbon's Insert tab. Figure 4.12 shows the Shapes gallery.

Figure 4.12
The Shapes gallery.

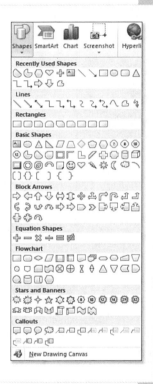

Select the shape you want to insert. The mouse pointer will become a drawing tool. Click and drag to draw the shape on the document, worksheet, or slide.

After the shape has been inserted, you can size the shape using the sizing handles provided when the shape is selected. You can also drag the shape in the document to position it. When the Shape is selected, the Drawing Tools Format tab becomes available on the Ribbon. It supplies a number of different commands for formatting the shape and text that appears in the shape.

Adding Multiple Shapes to a Drawing Canvas

In cases where you want to combine several shapes into a single graphic, you probably should insert a new drawing canvas and then insert all the shapes onto this canvas. The shapes will then be easier to arrange and group if necessary because they will all be in the same drawing canvas layer. You can insert a new drawing canvas (which looks like a blank graphic frame on the page or slide) by selecting the New Drawing Canvas command at the bottom of the Shapes gallery.

After you have the new drawing canvas in your document, you can size the canvas as needed. To insert shapes into the canvas, use the Shapes gallery provided in the Insert Shapes gallery, which is on the Drawing Tools Format tab. You can add shapes as needed to the canvas. Figure 4.13 shows a drawing canvas that includes multiple shapes.

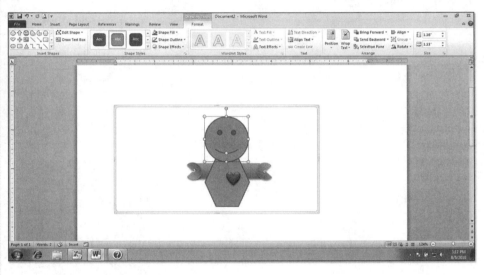

Figure 4.13
A drawing canvas containing multiple shapes.

As you work with the shapes, you can use the various tools in the Shape Styles group to modify fill color, outline, and effects for a selected shape or shapes. You can use the commands in the Arrange group to layer shapes in the canvas. The Bring Forward command and the Send Backward command each provide a menu with different possibilities for positioning shapes in layers.

> **tip**
> You can rotate and flip shapes by using the Rotate command in the Arrange group.

After you have placed the shapes in layers or arranged the shapes in the drawing canvas the way that you want them, drag the mouse to select all the shapes. You can then use the Group command to group the shapes into a single composite shape.

Adding Text to a Shape

You can add text to any shape. When the shape is selected, type the text that you want to appear in the shape. When you use certain styles available in the Shape Styles gallery to format the shape, the text color will also be changed.

If you want to format the text, select the text in the shape. You can use the commands in the WordArt Styles group to add WordArt styles to the text. You can also manipulate the text fill, outline, and effects using the Text Fill, Text Outline, and/or Text Effects commands, respectively.

 tip

You can also right-click on a shape and then select Add Text to add text to the shape.

For aligning the text within the shape, you can take advantage of the Text Direction command to rotate the text within the shape. The Align Text command enables you to align the text in the shape and provides the following options: Top, Middle, or Bottom.

Formatting a Shape with the Drawing Tools

All the tools that you need for formatting a shape are provided in the Drawing Tools Format tab. Some of the command groups on this tab are specific to the shape itself and others are related to the text in a shape and how a shape interacts with text in a document and other shapes. The Drawing Tools Format command groups are as follows:

- **Insert Shapes:** This group provides the Shapes gallery and the Edit Shape and Draw Text Box. The Edit Shape command enables you to replace a selected shape or view the edit points on a shape. The edit points enable you to manipulate different parts of a single shape. For instance, on a Smiley Face, the edit points would give you control over the placement of the eyes and mouth on the face.

- **Shape Styles:** This group enables you to apply shape styles to your shapes that include fill, outline, and text color formatting. You can fine-tune the style for a shape using the Shape Fill, Shape Outline, and Shape Effects commands. The Shape Effects command enables you to apply a number of different effects to the shape such as Shadow, Reflection, and Glow. You can also use the 3-D Rotation option to add 3D effects to the shape.

- **WordArt Styles:** This group becomes available when you have added text to the shape. You can apply WordArt styles to the text and manipulate the fill, outline, and effects for the text. The Text Effects command provides Shadow, Reflection, and Bevel effects as well as 3D rotation effects.

- **Text:** This group provides commands that are used to format the text in the shape. You can change the text direction and alignment within the shape. In cases where you have created multiple text boxes (which again, can be any shape), you can link the shapes containing text together using the Create Link command. This enables the text to flow through the linked text containing shapes.

- **Arrange:** This group enables you to position the shape (or multiple shapes on a canvas) with the text layer in a document. The Position command is used to specify whether the shape is inline with the text. The Wrap Text command is then used to specify how the text actually wraps around the shape. This group also provides the Bring Forward, Send Backward, and Group commands.

- **Size:** This group contains the height and width spinner boxes, which can be used to size the selected shape.

If you have layered a number of shapes, you might find it difficult to select a specific shape, particularly a shape that is at the back or behind another shape. You can view a list of shapes and the canvas that they are associated with using the Selection Pane. Figure 4.14 shows the Selection pane.

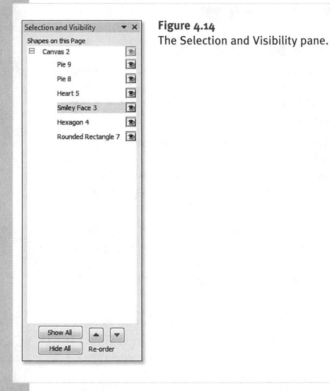

Figure 4.14
The Selection and Visibility pane.

To select a particular shape, select the shape (by name) in the Selection pane. You can then use the Drawing Tools to format that particular shape.

At the bottom of the Selection pane is a Reorder area, which contains a Bring Forward and a Send Backward button. You can use these buttons to rearrange how the shapes listed are layered.

Using the Screenshot Feature

The screenshot feature is new to the Office 2010 applications. It provides the ability to capture a screenshot of an open application or a specific area of an application window by using the screen clipping tool. This enables you to place screenshots of any application, utility, or web browser window into your Office application documents. For example, you could place a screenshot of an Excel worksheet in a Word document as part of a report or you could include a screenshot of a website page on a PowerPoint slide. The possible uses of the screenshot feature are really up to you and can be quite useful if you are writing a set of procedures on how to use a particular application for a particular purpose.

You can capture screenshots in Word, Excel, PowerPoint, and in Outlook when creating new email messages, appointments, tasks, and contacts. The Screenshot command is housed in the Illustrations group on the Ribbon's Insert tab, except for PowerPoint where it resides in the Images group on the Insert tab. As already mentioned, you can create a screenshot of an entire application window or specify an area to be captured. To capture an entire window, follow these steps:

1. Open the application window that you will capture in the screenshot.

2. Switch to the Office application that will serve as the destination for the screenshot. For example, you might insert the screenshot into a Word document or onto a PowerPoint slide.

3. Select the Screenshot command. An Available Windows gallery will appear as shown in Figure 4.15.

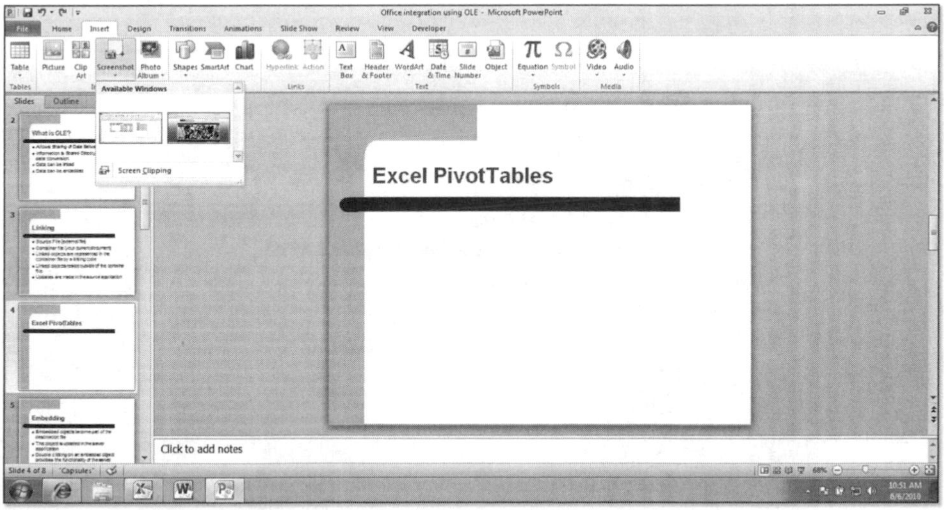

Figure 4.15
Specify a window for the screenshot.

4. Select the window that you want to capture. The entire application window will be pasted as a screenshot into the current Office application.

The inserted screenshot can be sized or moved as needed. It is no different from any other graphic object. In fact, when the screenshot is selected, the Picture Tools Format tab becomes available on the Ribbon. You can use the commands available to manipulate and format the screenshot as you would a digital image, which we discussed earlier in this chapter. For example, you can crop the screenshot or you can adjust brightness and contrast settings using the Correction command. Styles can also be added to the screenshot using the Picture Styles gallery.

You can also capture screenshots of specific areas of a window. The Screen Clipping tool provided by the Screenshot command makes it very easy for you to use the mouse to specify the area to be captured.

Before you use the Screen Clipping tool, you need to get the open windows cued up so that you have access to the correct application window when you select the Screen Clipping tool. This is particularly important if you have more than two windows open on the Windows desktop; select the application window that contains the area you want to capture using the appropriate icon on the Windows taskbar. This places that window at the top of the windows that are currently open. Switch back to the Office application that would serve as the destination for the screenshot using that application's icon on the taskbar.

Now you can capture the screenshot: Select Screenshot and then Screen Clipping. You will be switched to the application window where you will make the screen capture. The mouse pointer becomes a screen-clipping tool. Click and drag the mouse as needed to specify the area of the window that you want to capture. When you release the mouse, you will be returned to the screenshot destination application and the screen area you selected will be pasted into to the current Office document as a screenshot. Figure 4.16 shows a portion of an Excel window that has been clipped and captured as a screenshot and placed in a PowerPoint slide.

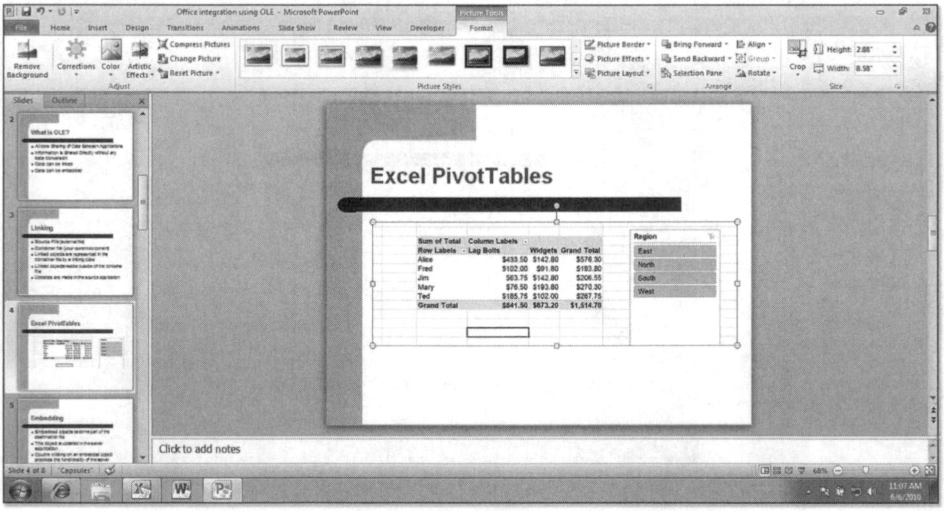

Figure 4.16
Capture a portion of an application window as a screenshot.

You can save your screenshots as image files for further use. Right-click on a selected screenshot and then select Save as Picture. The Save as Picture dialog box will appear. Provide a name for the screenshot and navigate to the folder that will serve as the destination for the file. By default the screenshot is saved as a PNG file. You can also save the file in other digital image formats such as GIF and JPEG and as a bitmap file.

Working with Clip Art

Clip art has been available in the Office applications for a very long time and has served as a way to add design elements and thematic images to Office documents. Clip art was at one time merely a collection of line drawings and cartoons. The clip art library provided by the Office 2010 applications, however, consists of photos in the JPEG format (.jpg), illustrations in the Windows Media File format (.wmf), and animated GIFs or videos in the GIF format (.gif). The clip art library also contains audio files in the WAV file format.

The Clip Art task pane provides you access to all the clip art provided that is placed on your computer when you install the Office applications. You are also provided access to Office.com, which houses an ever-growing collection of clip art files that will serve just about any clip art need you might have.

To insert clip art into an Office document, select the Clip Art command on the Ribbon's Insert tab. When you select the Clip Art command, the Clip Art task pane will open on the right side of the application window. Type a search string in the Search For box and then click Go. A collection of clip art that meets your search criteria will be listed in the Clip Art task pane. Figure 4.17 shows the Clip Art task pane after a search was conducted for the text string "hockey."

Figure 4.17
The Clip Art task pane.

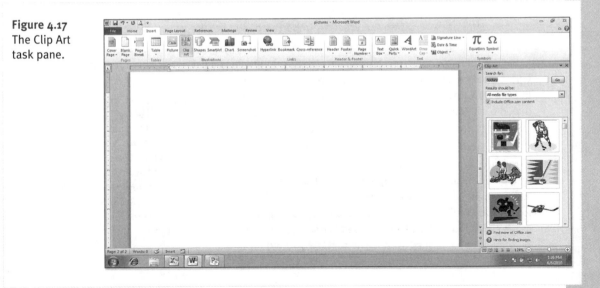

By default, the Clip Art task pane searches for all media file-types that meet your search criteria and includes files located on Office.com. You can fine-tune your search based on file type by selecting the Results Should Be drop-down list. On this list, you can select specific file type categories such as Illustrations, Photographs, or Videos. You can then rerun the search to filter the results.

After you have located a clip art file that you want to insert into your application document, such as a Word document or PowerPoint slide, you can do so by clicking on the thumbnail of the clip art provided in the task pane.

When the clip art is selected in the document, the Picture Tools Format tab becomes available on the Ribbon. This can be used to adjust the image settings, add picture styles to the image, and specify how text in the document should flow around the clip art frame. This is the same set of tools available when you are working with digital pictures such as JPEG files (which many of the clip art images are) and screenshots that you have added to your document. The Format tab tools were discussed earlier in the chapter in the section "Formatting Pictures."

Viewing Clip Art Properties

You can view the properties for a clip art file before you insert it into an Office application document. This enables you to view the file format and resolution for the clip art file and to preview clip art videos in the animated GIF file format.

Click the drop-down arrow on the right of a clip art thumbnail in the Clip Art task pane. Select Preview/Properties on the shortcut menu. The Preview/Properties dialog box will open for that clip art image. Figure 4.18 shows the Preview/Properties dialog box for a clip art WMF file.

The Preview/Properties dialog box provides all sort of information on the selected clip art file. It provides the filename, type, resolution, and size. It also provides a list of keywords that are associated with the clip art file. You can edit the keywords list by selecting the Edit Keywords button. This will open the Keywords dialog box. You can add keywords as needed and then click OK to return to the Preview/Properties dialog box.

The Preview/Properties dialog box can also be used as a way to quickly view the properties related to the other clip art that was found based on your original keyword search in the Clip Art task pane. Use the Next or Previous buttons at the bottom of the Preview/Properties dialog box to move to the next or previous clip art file shown in the task pane, respectively. When you have finished working with the Preview/Properties dialog box, select Close.

Figure 4.18
The Preview/Properties dialog box.

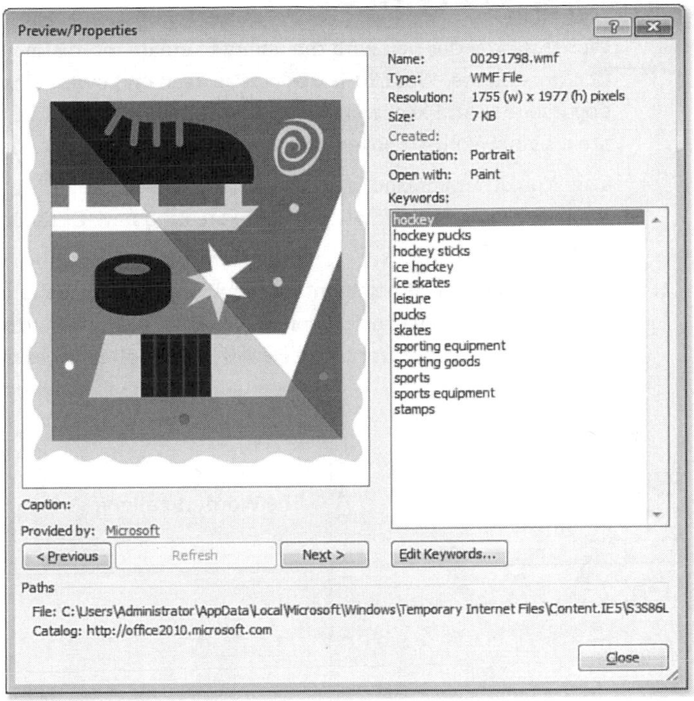

Adding Clip Art to Your Collection

A lot of the clip art available in the Office applications is actually on the Microsoft.com website. So, you might want to make certain clip art images available offline if you know you are going to be working on an Office document in a situation where you do not have an Internet connection.

You can copy clip art to your My Collections folder and you can also create subfolders, which enables you to keep similar clip art images in the same container. To open the Copy to Collection dialog box, click the drop-down arrow to the right of a clip art image in the Clip Art task pane and select Make Available Offline.

By default, the Copy to Collection dialog provides the My Collections folder, which contains a Favorites and Unclassified Clips folder. If you want to add a subfolder, select the New button. The New Collection dialog box will open. Type a name for the collection subfolder and then click OK. The new collection subfolder will appear in the Copy to Collection dialog box.

Select the collection folder that will serve as the destination for the copied clip art file. Then click OK. The file will be copied to your collection.

Using WordArt

WordArt provides you with the ability to create interesting text effects within your Office application documents. WordArt boxes can be used on PowerPoint slides or as graphic elements in a Word document or an Excel worksheet. A WordArt object can be created from existing text or you can create a blank WordArt object and then type the required text directly in the WordArt frame.

The WordArt command is on the Ribbon's Insert tab. It is available in Word, PowerPoint, Excel, Publisher, and Outlook when you are creating new Outlook items such as emails, contacts, and appointments.

Inserting a WordArt object into a document is really just a matter of selecting the WordArt command and then selecting one of the WordArt styles from the WordArt gallery. If you are formatting existing text as WordArt, select the text before accessing the gallery. Figure 4.19 shows the WordArt gallery.

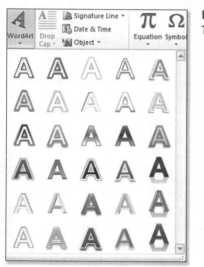

Figure 4.19
The WordArt gallery.

If you formatted selected text as WordArt, your existing text will appear in the WordArt frame and be formatted with the selected WordArt style. A new WordArt box will contain the placeholder text "Your text here," which you can replace with your own text.

You can move the WordArt in the document as needed and size the WordArt box if required. When the WordArt box is selected, the Drawing Tools Format tab appears on the Ribbon. You can change the style of the WordArt box (or frame) by using the shape styles and shape-related commands (such as Shape Fill and Shape Outline) in the Shape Styles group.

The commands that actually affect the way the WordArt text looks are found in the WordArt Styles group. You can change the WordArt style that you have assigned to the selected WordArt by using the WordArt Styles gallery. The gallery provides styles that incorporate interesting effects such as bevel and reflection.

The Text Fill and Text Outline commands enable you to control the fill for the WordArt text characters and the outline of the characters, respectively. The really cool part of using WordArt, however, lies in the different text effects that you can apply to the WordArt via the Text Effects command. Figure 4.20 shows the Text Effects gallery, including the Transform gallery.

Figure 4.20
The Text Effects gallery.

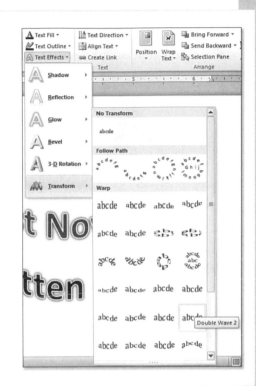

The Text Effects gallery enables you to apply a number of different effects to the WordArt text, including Show, Reflection, Glow, and 3-D Rotation. For those of you who lament the loss of the old WordArt utility that operated as a rather clunky add-on to the Office applications prior to the release of Office 2007, you will find that the Transform gallery provides you with all the different text-warping effects that were available in the original WordArt utility.

In terms of working with the WordArt object, the other Format tab command groups enable you to manipulate the text direction and alignment and how the object is positioned in relation to existing text in the Office document. Office 2010 (as did Office 2007) integrates WordArt into the Office applications themselves and enables you to edit and manipulate the WordArt object as you would any other graphic object such as pictures, SmartArt graphics, or clip art.

> **tip**
> For more control over the WordArt text effects, right-click on the WordArt and select Format Shape to open the Format Shape dialog box. It provides shape attributes such as fill and line color and also enables you to manipulate text effects such as 3-D format and rotation.

5

WORKING WITH THE OFFICE WEB APPS

We have all found ourselves in situations while we're on the road or just away from the office when we would like to be able to look at a Word document recently completed by a colleague or an Excel workbook that we prepared but didn't save to our laptop. Now Microsoft Office 2010 offers a solution to this problem with the Office Web Apps. Not only do the Excel, Word, and PowerPoint Web Apps enable you to view files created using your installed versions of the Office 2010 applications, but the Web Apps also provide you with the capability of editing Office files, creating new Office files, and sharing files with other users online (including yourself).

In this chapter, we look at what the Web Apps can actually do and how you access the Web Apps. We also look specifically at the Word, Excel, and PowerPoint Web Apps and how they can be used to complement the work that you do using your installed Office 2010 applications.

What the Web Apps Can Do

The Web Apps provide you with the ability to view, edit, and save Office files to an online workspace that can be accessed from any computer with an Internet connection and a supported web browser. The Web Apps are actually just one of the tools that are part of the online file storage and access that Microsoft has developed as a resource for users of Microsoft Office applications. Office files can be stored on the Microsoft Live SkyDrive website or on a SharePoint Server site provided on your company's or institution's intranet.

The Web Apps provide you with basic capabilities for working with files that you have created using the desktop versions of the Microsoft applications such as Word, Excel, PowerPoint, and OneNote. The Web Apps also provide you with the ability to create new files, but the Web Apps are certainly not as full-featured as the installed versions of the Office applications.

Although the Web Apps lack features and capabilities found in the installed versions of the Office applications, there is actually a lot that you can do with them. Figure 5.1 shows a PowerPoint presentation that was stored on the Windows Live SkyDrive.

Even though you are using the PowerPoint Web App, you can add new slides to the presentation, modify existing slides, and format text on the slides. You can even add a picture or SmartArt to a new slide, and then view the presentation as a slide show—all from the Web App.

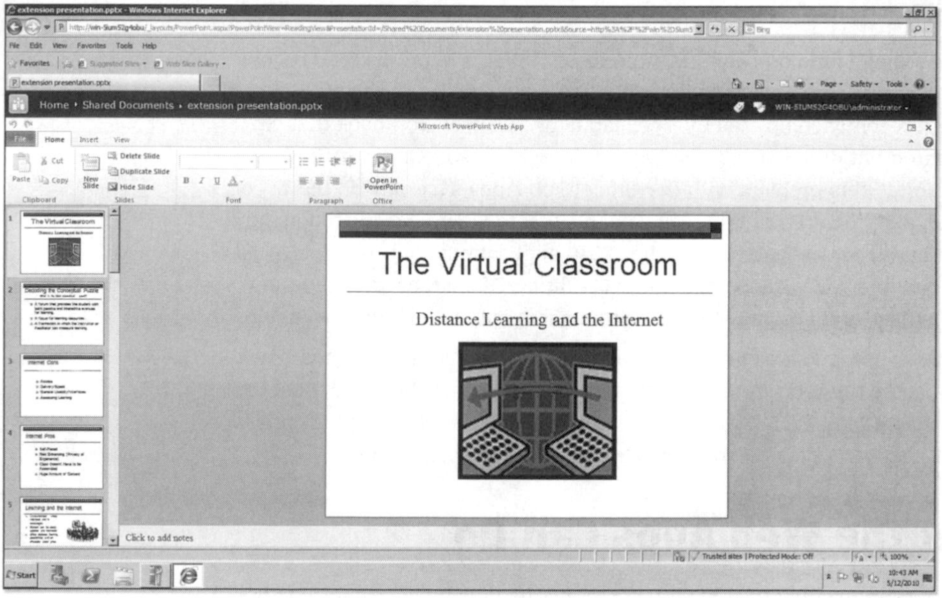

> **note**
>
> Whether you use the Web Apps via the Microsoft SkyDrive or a site provided using SharePoint Server technology, you will find that these two flavors of the Web Apps are the same and provide the same level of functionality and Ribbon command groups.

Figure 5.1
Files stored on SkyDrive or a Share- Point site can be opened in the Web Apps.

Note the PowerPoint Web App has a Ribbon just like the installed version of PowerPoint 2010. The PowerPoint Web App Ribbon, however, has only a subset of the tabs provided in the full-blown PowerPoint application. Figure 5.2 shows the same PowerPoint presentation open in the installed version of PowerPoint.

So, the Web Apps provide a subset of the commands that you would find in the installed versions of a Microsoft Office application such as PowerPoint or Excel. This is because the Web Apps are designed to be used when you are working on a computer that does not provide the installed Office applications and you just need to do some basic modifications or view a file that is available on a SharePoint site or the SkyDrive.

Figure 5.2
The same
PowerPoint
presentation
in the installed
PowerPoint
application.

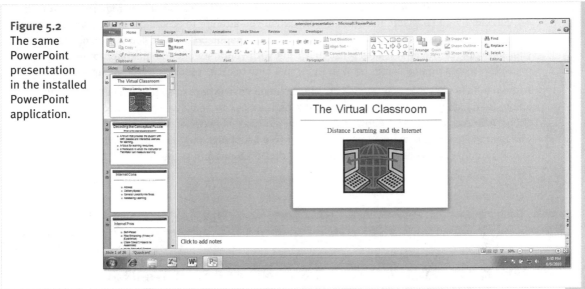

You don't get all the bells and whistles provided by the full-blown Office applications, but that wasn't Microsoft's intent in developing the Web Apps. The Web Apps provide you with a fallback plan when you just don't have access to the installed Office 2010 suite. And the fact that they are available from any computer with a web browser and an Internet connection means that the Web Apps provide you with a lot of portability and possibilities for accessing your own files from any computer and sharing files with co-workers or colleagues.

> **⚑ caution**
>
> The Web Apps can time out when you are working on SkyDrive, so keep this in mind when you step away from your computer for a coffee break. This is really an issue only with the Word Web App, which requires you to save changes that you make to your documents.

Where the Web Apps Live

As already mentioned, the Office Web Apps operate in your web browser whether you are using the Web Apps via the Microsoft SkyDrive website or by connecting to a SharePoint Server installation that provides the Web Apps on your business intranet. For the Web Apps to function, you need to be using a supported web browser. The following web browsers (at the time of the writing of this book) support the Office Web Apps:

- Internet Explorer 8.0

- Internet Explorer 7.0

- Firefox 3

- Safari 4 for the Macintosh

If you have access to a SharePoint site that provides the Web Apps, you will be required to provide a logon name and password to access the site when you attempt to access the site via your web browser. The username and password may be the same as the credentials you use to log on to your network. However, it makes sense to consult with your network administrator for information related to accessing and using the Web Apps on a network that provides a SharePoint site.

After you have accessed your SharePoint site, you will have access to shared files and have the ability to upload your own files. Files available on the site can be viewed and edited using the Office Web Apps. Figure 5.3 shows a SharePoint site that has been accessed via Internet Explorer. The Shared Documents window provides access to a list of files that have been added to the site. Additional files could be added using the Add Document link at the bottom of the Shared Documents pane.

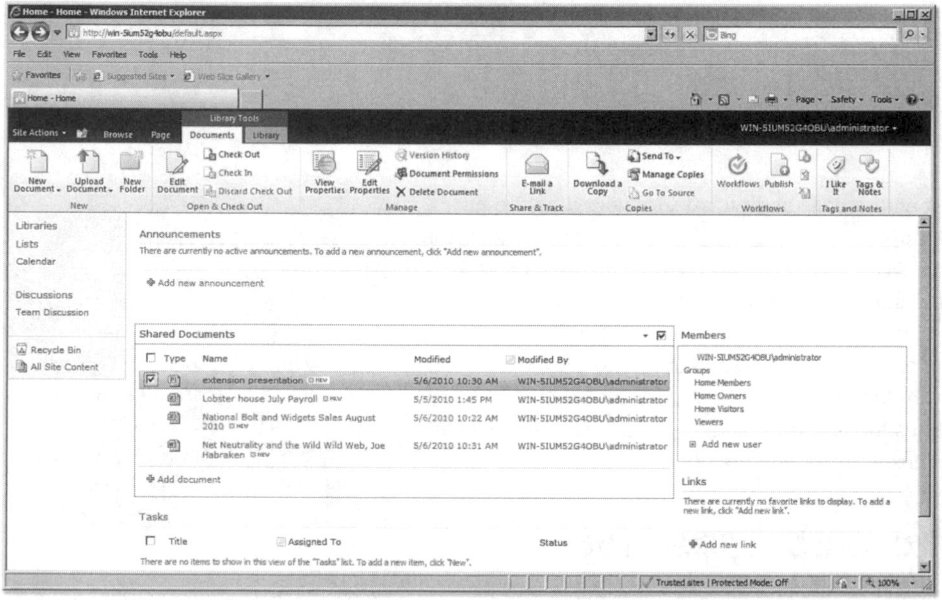

Figure 5.3
Files on a SharePoint site can be viewed and edited using the Web Apps.

When you are working with files on a SharePoint site, you can view the file in a Web App viewer or open the file in the associated Web App to edit the file. For example, if a Word document available on the SharePoint site was selected, the Word Web App viewer would open as shown in Figure 5.4.

The Web App View mode, such as the Word Web App View mode shown in Figure 5.4, enables you to quickly look at a particular Word document, Excel workbook, or PowerPoint presentation and then determine what you want to do next with the file. Options are provided to open the file in the installed version of the Office application that was used to create the file (Word, in the case of Figure 5.4) or to edit the file using the appropriate Web App.

In cases where you don't want to view a file on a SharePoint site but want to open the file in the associated Web App, you can do so with a couple of clicks. Select the file's check box in the Shared Documents pane and then click Edit Document.

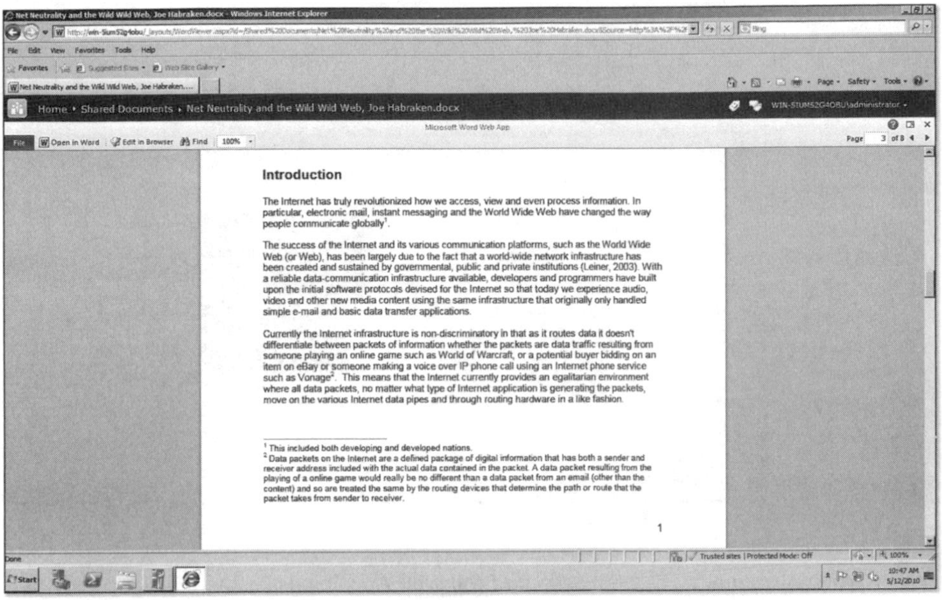

Figure 5.4
A Word file in
the Word Web
App viewer.

Even if you are a home or small business computer user and don't have access to a SharePoint site,
you can take advantage of the Web Apps via the Microsoft SkyDrive website, which is available
to anyone with a Windows Live ID. SkyDrive not only enables you to use the Web Apps, it also
provides you space to save your files online. This is extremely useful when you want to access a
file from anywhere and don't have your laptop. SkyDrive also makes it easy for you share files with
other users, which is also the case when you have access to a SharePoint site.

Working with the Web Apps in SkyDrive isn't all that different
from working with the Web Apps via a SharePoint site. You
can view files in a Web App viewer and you can open files
directly in the associated Web App. Figure 5.5 shows the My
Documents folder on SkyDrive, which lists the files available.

Not only does SkyDrive enable you to view or edit existing files,
you can also create new Word, Excel, PowerPoint, and OneNote
files by launching the appropriate Web App via the New command. A SharePoint site accessed via a web browser also
provides a New command that enables you to create new files
using the Web Apps.

> ### 🔍 note
> The OneNote Web App doesn't have
> a view mode. Selecting an OneNote
> file on SkyDrive or a SharePoint site
> (if the site provides the Web Apps),
> will open the file in the OneNote
> Web App.

So, don't think of SkyDrive or a SharePoint site as merely a means to an end, the end being the ability to access the Web Apps. The fact that both these platforms provide online file storage and sharing capabilities makes them extremely useful, even if they don't provide the bonus of access to the
Office Web Apps.

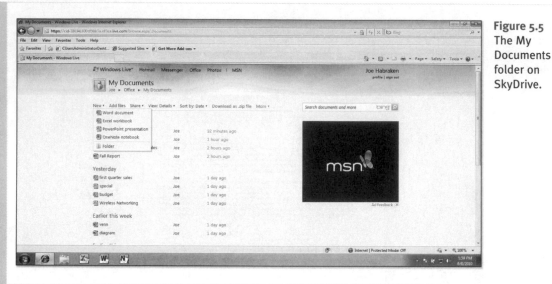

Figure 5.5
The My
Documents
folder on
SkyDrive.

You will actually get the most out of the Web Apps by using them in concert with the Office 2010 applications. The Office 2010 applications such as Word, Excel, and PowerPoint make it very easy for you to save your Office application files directly from your desktop to a SharePoint site or the folders you have created on SkyDrive.

Saving Office Application Files to SkyDrive and SharePoint Sites

The installed versions of the Office applications have the ability to save files to a Microsoft SkyDrive folder or to a SharePoint site workspace. This means that you can quickly add files to an online storage area directly from Excel, Word, PowerPoint, or OneNote. You can then access these files from any computer with a web browser and edit them using the Web Apps. You can also share files on both the SkyDrive and a SharePoint site, making the files available to other users.

The process for saving files from Word, Excel, and PowerPoint is the same for all three applications. The process for storing OneNote notebooks online is a little different, so we will discuss that process in a moment. Let's look at saving a Word document to SkyDrive. We can then examine saving a PowerPoint presentation to a SharePoint site.

Saving a File to SkyDrive

You can create a file in one of the installed Microsoft Office 2010 suite members such as Microsoft Word and take advantage of all the commands and utilities that the full-fledged ver-

> ### 🔍 note
>
> The Windows Live Sign-in Assistant enables you to open your documents in the Office Web Apps without having to repeatedly sign in to your Windows Live account. You can install the Windows Live Sign-in Assistant by selecting the link provided when you use SkyDrive or you can search for the Sign-in Assistant on Microsoft.com.

sion of the Office applications provide. As you work in Word, you will probably save the document to your computer's hard drive or local area network. When you have completed the file or have it in a draft version that you want to place online, you can save a copy to one of your SkyDrive folders. This is accomplished via the Save & Send window, which is accessed in the Word Backstage (or the Excel or PowerPoint Backstage).

Select File on the Ribbon to access the Backstage and then select Save & Send. The Save & Send window provides a number of different possibilities for sharing Word documents, including sending them using email or publishing them as a blog post. We want to save the document to the Web.

Select Save to Web in the Save & Send window. The Save to Windows Live SkyDrive pane will become available. Select the Sign In button to sign in to SkyDrive. You might have to provide your Windows Live ID (such as your Hotmail email address) and password if you have not previously logged on to SkyDrive using one of the Office applications.

After you have logged onto SkyDrive, a list of your folders will appear. Figure 5.6 shows the Save & Send window and folders available for a SkyDrive account.

> 🔍 **note**
>
> Think of the Windows Live SkyDrive as "SharePoint Lite." SkyDrive uses SharePoint technology to provide you with the Web Apps and file-sharing capabilities. However, the file-sharing environment it provides is not as secure as the environment provided by a SharePoint site.

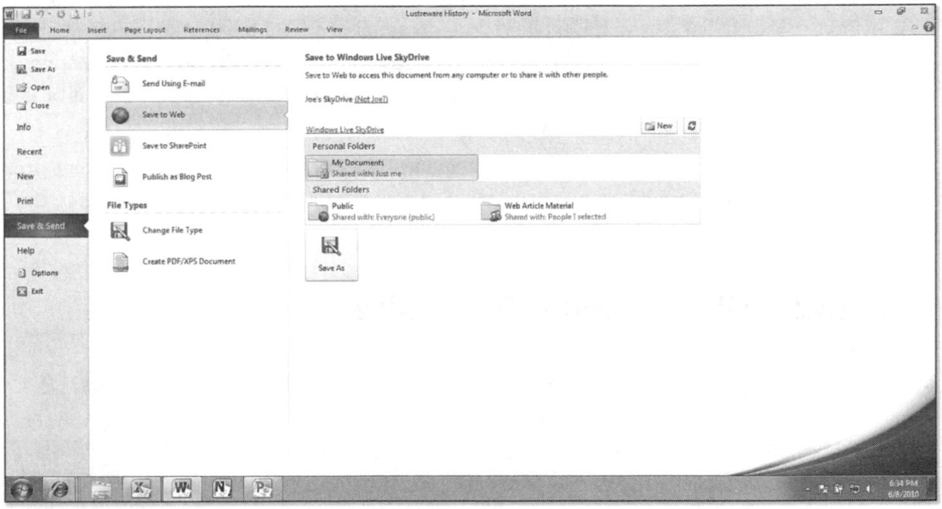

Figure 5.6
The Backstage Save & Send window.

Select an existing folder as the destination for the document. You can choose from Personal Folders or Shared Folders on SkyDrive. If you want to create a new folder, select the New button. This will take you to your SkyDrive page where you can select the New menu to create a new folder. After the folder has been created, return to the Word window (the Backstage Save & Send window will still be selected). You might have to click Refresh to update the list of Windows Live SkyDrive folders shown in the Save & Send window.

Select the folder destination for the document and then click Save As. It might take a moment (as Word connects to SkyDrive), but the Save As dialog box will open. The Save As dialog box will show the contents of the SkyDrive folder that you selected as the destination for the file. If that folder, such as your My Documents folder, contained subfolders, you can actually save the document to one of the subfolders. When you are ready to save the file, select Save. The Save As dialog box will close and you will be returned to your document in the Word window.

The document you saved to the SkyDrive folder is now the active document in the Word window. You have in effect used the Save As command to save your document to a new location. This means that any changes that you make to the current document in Word will be saved in the document on your SkyDrive page. If you saved the document to your local hard drive or network folder before you saved it to the SkyDrive, that file still exists. It is the SkyDrive-based file that is now the most up-to-date version of the file (as soon as you make any changes in the document and save them).

After the file is available on SkyDrive, there are all sorts of possibilities for opening and working with the file. You can quickly open the document on the computer that you used to create it by opening Microsoft Word 2010 and then selecting the file in the Recent window provided by Word. Documents that have been saved to SkyDrive will not have a location specified by a location name such as My Documents or Desktop, but will have their location specified by a URL that begins with https:// followed by the path to the SkyDrive folder you specified as the destination for the document.

The document can also be accessed via a web browser (on any computer) by logging on to your SkyDrive account. If you have placed the document in a folder that provides shared access to other users, they can also access the document. After you're on SkyDrive, you can open the file in the installed version of Word 2010 if the computer you are working on provides it or you can work with the document using the Word Web App.

As already mentioned, the process for saving Excel workbooks and PowerPoint presentations to the SkyDrive is the same. It is all accomplished using the Save to Web command in the Backstage Save & Send window.

Saving a File to a SharePoint Site

You can also save Office files directly from your Office 2010 desktop applications such as PowerPoint, Word, or Excel directly to a SharePoint site. You can then access the files from other computers and open or edit the files using either the installed versions of the Office applications or the Web Apps in cases where you are working on a computer that does not have Office 2010 installed.

 note

If you are saving the file to the SkyDrive so that other users can also access the file, make sure to save the file in the Public folder.

To save a file to a SharePoint site library from an Office application, such as PowerPoint, follow these steps:

1. Access the Backstage by selecting File on the Ribbon.

2. Select Save & Send to open the Save & Send window.

3. Select Save to SharePoint. Recent SharePoint site locations will be listed in the Save to SharePoint pane of the Save & Send window.

4. Select from one of the locations listed in the Recent Location list or select the Browse for a Location link under Locations.

5. Select Save As. The Save As dialog box will open. You might have the option of selecting from multiple workspaces on the SharePoint site.

6. You can specify a new name for the presentation if you choose.

7. Select Save to save the PowerPoint presentation to the current site and workspace.

The currently open PowerPoint presentation now resides on the SharePoint site that you designated. You can view the path to the SharePoint site by selecting File and then selecting Info. The SharePoint URL will be shown at the top of the Info window. You would use the same steps to save an Excel workbook or a Word document to a SharePoint site library.

Sharing a OneNote Notebook Online

The process for saving a OneNote notebook to SkyDrive or a SharePoint site is a little different from the scenario that we explored for Word, PowerPoint, and Excel. OneNote notebooks are really information containers. You can use a notebook to keep a project or any of your endeavors organized. OneNote notebooks are extremely useful, however, when they are shared with other users.

You can save a new OneNote notebook directly to a SkyDrive folder or SharePoint site library or you can share an existing notebook to either location. After the notebook has been shared, a copy is kept in a local cache on your computer and the changes made to the shared copy are synchronized with the local copy. This means you can work offline on the notebook and then synchronize it with the shared version when you connect to the Internet (for SkyDrive) or your intranet (for a SharePoint site).

New notebooks are created in OneNote in the Backstage, which is accessed by selecting File on the Ribbon. When you select New in the Backstage, the New Notebook window opens and provides you with the ability to save your new notebook to the Web (SkyDrive), the network (your local area network or a SharePoint site), or your computer. Figure 5.7 shows the options for storing the new notebook.

 tip

You can also create a OneNote notebook on SkyDrive or a SharePoint site library and then open the notebook using your installed OneNote 2010 application.

As already mentioned, notebooks that you store on your computer (when they are created) can be shared on SkyDrive or a SharePoint site after the fact. This enables you to access your notebook from other computers and potentially share the notebook with other users. Existing notebooks are shared via the Share window, which is accessed via the Share command in the Backstage.

For much more detail on creating OneNote notebooks and sharing notebooks on SkyDrive or a SharePoint site, see the information that begins on page 814 in Chapter 30, "Requisite OneNote: Essential Features."

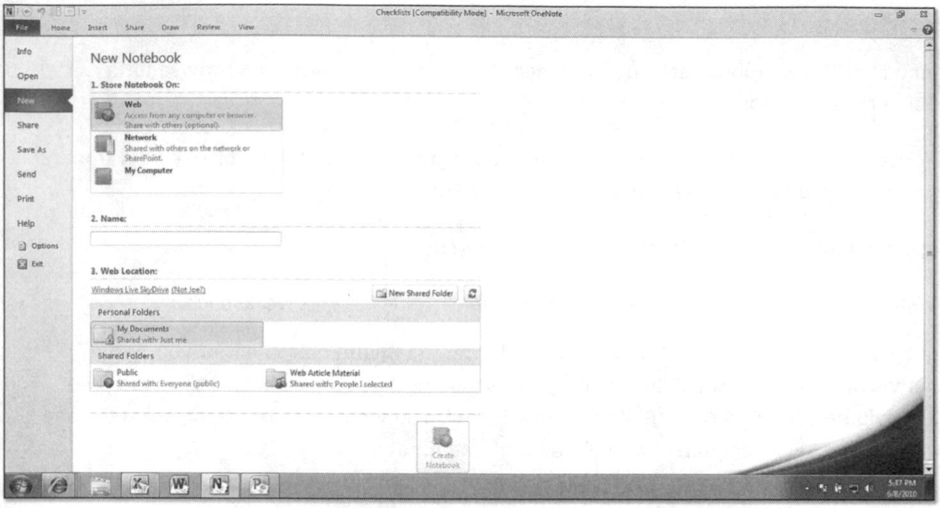

1

Figure 5.7
Store a new
notebook on
SkyDrive or a
SharePoint site.

Other Ways to Get Files Online

Obviously, the installed Microsoft Office 2010 applications—Word, Excel, PowerPoint, and OneNote offer very direct ways to quickly save the files that you create on online folders on SkyDrive or a SharePoint site. These applications also provide you with the most bells and whistles in terms of creating your Office documents.

You can also upload files to your SkyDrive folders or a SharePoint site directly from your web browser when you are logged on to SkyDrive or a SharePoint site. For example, you can quickly add files from your computer to your SkyDrive folders such as the My Documents folder. Figure 5.8 shows the Add Documents page provided by SkyDrive and Windows Explorer with the Documents library selected.

The SkyDrive upload page enables you to drag documents from Windows Explorer and drop them onto the web page to add a file or files to the current SkyDrive folder. You can click the Select Documents from Your Computer link to open Windows Explorer. When you have finished adding files to the folder, select Continue and you will be returned to the folder and a list of the files in the folder.

Adding files to a SharePoint site is just as easy. Access the SharePoint site in your web browser. You can then use the Upload Document command on the site Ribbon or use the Add Document link in the Shared Documents pane. The Upload Document dialog box will appear as shown in Figure 5.9.

Because you can access SkyDrive from practically any computer, and you might also be able to access your SharePoint site from multiple locations (depending on how your SharePoint administrator has configured site security settings and how the site can be accessed via Internet connections), uploading files to either location can be very handy when you are on the road.

Figure 5.8
Drag files from Windows Explorer to add them to a SkyDrive folder.

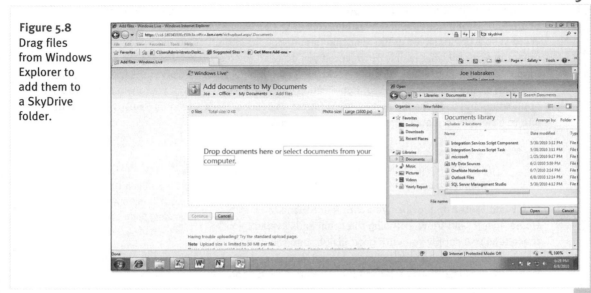

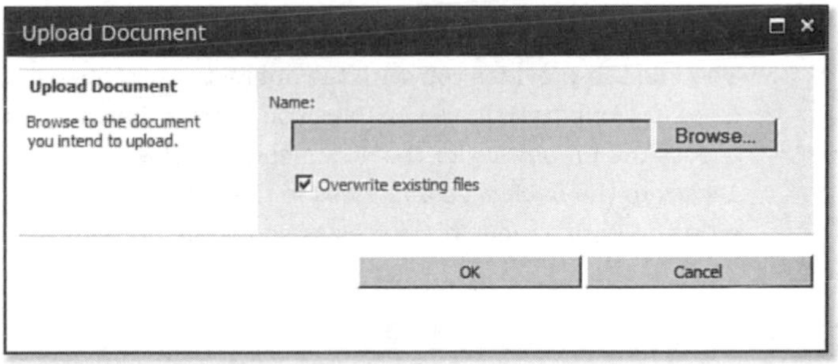

Figure 5.9
Browse for a file you want to upload to the SharePoint site.

For example, you might need to share a file with someone at your business or with a colleague who is halfway around the world and the only copy of the file is on a USB thumb drive in your suitcase. You can upload the file to SkyDrive in a shared folder and perhaps even add it to your SharePoint site for even more secure sharing.

Using the Word Web App

The Word Web App provides you with the ability to edit existing documents and create new documents. It supplies a number of commands for working with text, including character- and paragraph-formatting attributes. It also provides you with the ability to insert tables, pictures, and clip art into the document. The document views in the Word Web App are limited to the Editing view and the Reading view.

tip

When you are using SkyDrive to access the Web Apps, the Office folder list page provides icons for each of the Office Web Apps; click an icon to start a new document in that application.

When you create a new document, you are required to supply a filename (on SkyDrive and a SharePoint site) before the new document opens in the Word Web App. New files created in the Word Web App are saved in the .docx file format. You are not provided the option of saving the document in any other file format. However, if you do need to create a copy of the file in a different file format, such as .doc, which provides backward compatibility with co-workers or friends who are still using an earlier version of the Word application, you can open the file in your installed Word 2010 application and save the file in a different format as needed. Files stored on SkyDrive or a SharePoint site in other file formats might not open in the Web Apps, however.

➥ *For information on using saving Office 2010 application files in different file formats, see page 54 in Chapter 3, "Managing and Sharing Office Files."*

The Word Web App provides you with four Ribbon tabs: File, Home, Insert, and View. Perusing the commands available on these tabs will supply you with good insight into the overall capabilities that you're afforded by the Word Web App. Let's look at each of the Ribbon tabs and the command groups that they provide.

> **🔍 note**
>
> Microsoft SharePoint sites provide a much more robust system for assigning permissions to work-spaces, folders, and individual files. Consult with your SharePoint administrator for information on how to set permissions for file sharing.

The File Tab

The File tab provides you with the ability to open the current document in Word 2010 (installed on your computer). It also enables you to save the changes that you have made to the document, access the properties for the document, and close the document. The File tab does not provide access to the Backstage as it does in the full-blown versions of the Office applications; it does provide you with a menu of choices as shown in Figure 5.10.

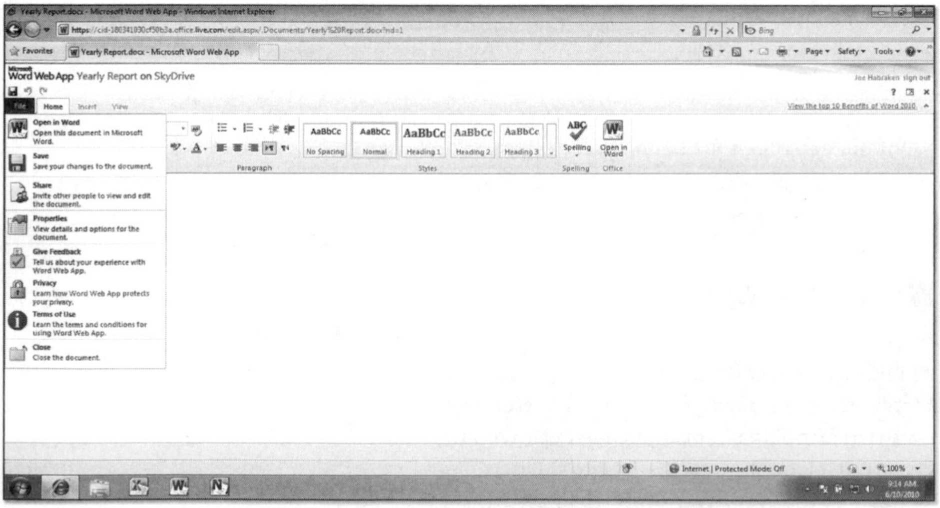

Figure 5.10
The File tab menu enables you to access save, share, and properties commands.

The Share command enables you to share the current Word document with other users. In SkyDrive, the share permissions for files are set at the folder level (in a SharePoint site, file-level permissions can be set for sharing). By default, you are provided with the My Documents and Public folder. You cannot edit the permissions for the Public folder. You can change the permissions for the My Documents folder and new folders that you create on SkyDrive.

It makes sense to leave the permission setting for your My Documents folder set to Just Me. This enables you to use the My Documents folder as a proprietary folder for saving the Office documents that you work with exclusively. Create new folders as needed and then set the folder permissions for those folders based on the access required by other users for files that you have stored in that folder. For example, if you create a new Word document in the Web App from a specific folder (this is the way that you get the file in the SkyDrive folder in the first place), or open an existing document in a SkyDrive folder that you have created, you can then select the Share command on the File tab to set the permissions for the folder that holds that file. Figure 5.11 shows the Edit permissions page for a SkyDrive folder.

> **note**
>
> Microsoft SharePoint sites provide a much more robust system for assigning permissions to workspaces, folders and individual files. Consult with your SharePoint administrator for information on how to set permissions for file sharing.

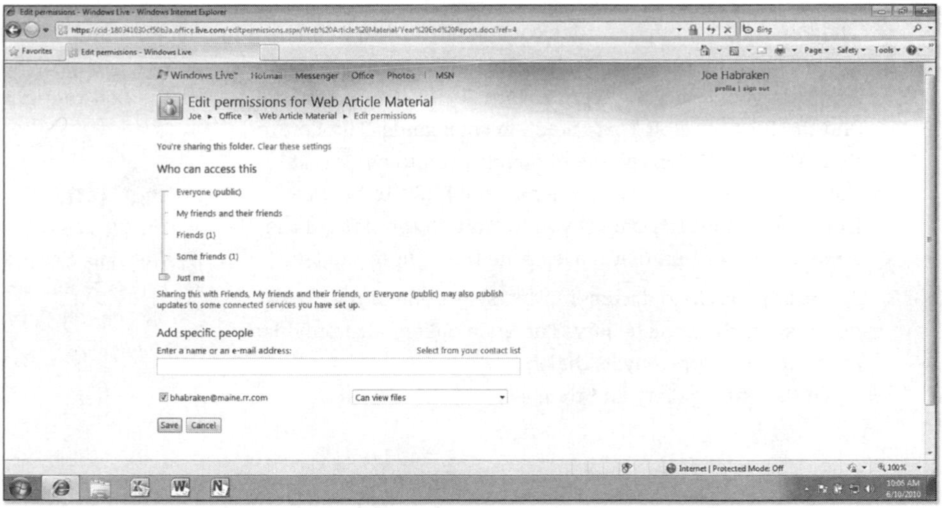

Figure 5.11
Setting permissions for a SkyDrive folder.

By default, the access level for the folder is set to Just Me. You can use the slider bar to set the access level to several different levels, including Some Friends, Friends, and Everyone. You can also add specific people to a list using the Enter a Name or an E-mail Address (or Select from Your Contact List) box. Each person that you add can then be assigned a specific access level for the folder using the drop-down list provided. The two access levels provided are Can View Files and Can Add, Edit Details, and Delete Files. Remember that these access levels are being assigned to the folder. So, any files that you place in the folder will inherit the same access settings that you have provided other users.

The Word Web App Home Tab

The Home tab in the Word Web App provides a subset of the commands that you would find on the Word 2010 Home tab. The Word Web App Home tab provides you with the ability to change font attributes, set paragraph alignment settings, and assign styles to your document text. Figure 5.12 shows the Word Web App Ribbon's Home tab. The default font and size for the Word Web App are Calibri, 11 point.

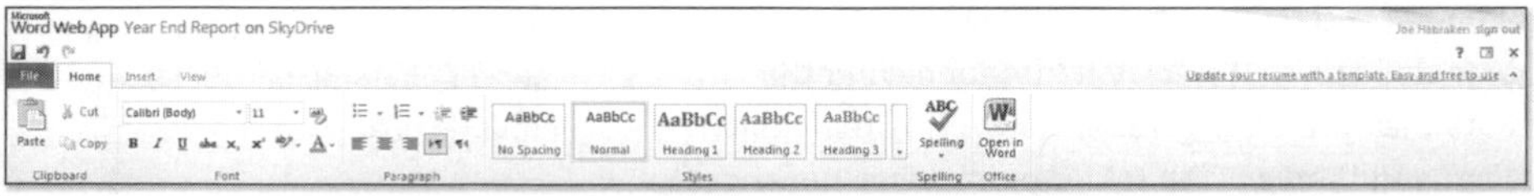

Figure 5.12
The Word Web App Ribbon's Home tab.

One of the first things that you will notice is that none of the Home tab command groups, such as Font or Paragraph, include dialog box launchers. So, the commands available in the groups are limited to those provided on the Ribbon.

The Font group provides you with the ability to change the font, font size, and assign font attributes to your text such as bold, italic, and underline. By default, the Font group also includes Subscript and Superscript commands.

The Paragraph group provides commands for text alignment and indents and enables you to create bulleted and numbered lists. Two commands supplied in the Paragraph group by the Word Web App that you won't find on the Word 2010 Home tab by default are the Left-to-Right Text Direction and the Right-to-Left Text Direction commands. The Left-to-Right Text Direction command enables you to enter text on the page from left to right, whereas the Right-to-Left Text Direction command enables you to start on the right of the page and enter text that moves from the right to the left.

To assign a style to document text, select one of the styles provided in the Style gallery. The Style gallery also provides access to the Apply Styles dialog box shown in Figure 5.13. Open the Style gallery and then select Apply Styles.

> **tip**
>
> The Web Apps, such as the Word Web App, also provide a Quick Access Toolbar above the Ribbon. It provides the Save, Undo, and Redo commands.

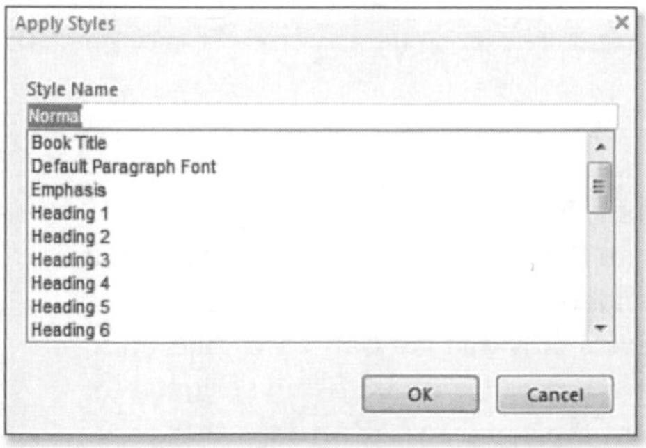

Figure 5.13
Apply Styles dialog box.

Select a style in the Apply Styles dialog box and then click OK. The style will be applied to the text.

The Home tab is rounded out by the Clipboard group that provides you with the ability to copy, cut, and paste text in the document. The Word Web App also provides access to the Spelling feature via the Home tab and enables you to set the proofing language used by the Spelling feature. If you want to open the current document in Word 2010, select the Open in Word command.

 For information on text and paragraph formatting in Word 2010, see page 149 in Chapter 6, "Requisite Word: Essential Features."

The Word Web App Insert Tab

The Word Web App Ribbon's Insert tab provides you with a number of possibilities for enhancing your document with a table, picture, or clip art image. The Insert tab also provides you with the ability to quickly insert a hyperlink into your document. You can insert a table and then add or delete columns and rows as needed. You can also upload pictures from your computer to the document and insert clip art from the Office.com library of clip art images.

The Table command provides a table grid that enables you to select the number of columns and rows in the new table. After the new table is inserted into the document, the Table Tools Layout tab becomes available on the Ribbon. The Table Tools Layout tab enables you to select the table or the current column row or cell. You can then use the commands in the Delete group to delete the table or selected column or row. You can also insert new columns or rows above, below, or to the left or right, respectively, of the currently selected column, row, or cell. Text in the table can be aligned using the commands provided in the Alignment group.

 For information on working with tables in Word 2010, see page 210 in Chapter 8, "Working with Tables, Columns, and Sections."

The Insert tab also enables you to add pictures to your document. Select the Picture command and the Choose File to Upload dialog box opens. Select the picture file you want to insert and then select Open.

When you insert a picture, the Picture Tools Format tab becomes available on the Ribbon. This tab enables you to specify alternative text for the image (in cases where the document is viewed on the Web and the picture cannot be loaded), and enables you to enlarge, shrink, or scale the image. You will find that large picture files will take a while to load when you insert them into the Web App. If you want to take advantage of a much more complete set of picture commands, you might want to insert pictures into your documents using Word 2010 rather than the Word Web App.

 For information on working with pictures in the Office 2010 applications, see page 86 in Chapter 4, "Using and Creating Graphics."

The Word Web App View Tab

The Word Web App view tab is definitely bare-bones when compared to the possibilities provided by the Word 2010 Ribbon's view tab. The Web App View tab provides two possibilities: Editing view and Reading view.

The Editing view is the view that you are using as you edit the document in the Word Web App. When you select the Reading view, as shown in Figure 5.14, you are taken to the Word Web App view. This is the same view provided when you select a file that is listed in a SkyDrive folder or in your SharePoint site library.

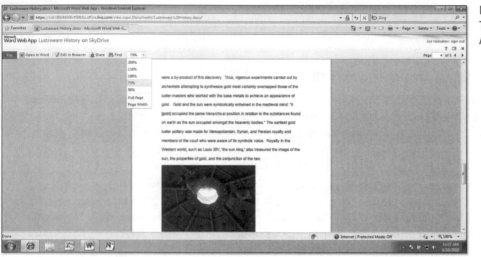

Figure 5.14
The Word Web App view.

This viewer does enable you to zoom in and out on the document and also to open the Find in Document pane. You can search for text in the document using the search box that this pane provides. You have the option of searching forward or backward in the document.

When you have finished viewing your document, you can then select Edit in Browser to reopen the document in the Word Web App. You also have the option of opening the document in Word 2010 by selecting Open in Word.

Using the Excel Web App

The Excel Web App provides you with the ability to create new Excel workbooks and to edit your existing workbooks that have been saved to a SkyDrive folder or a SharePoint site library. The Web App provides basic capabilities for formatting labels and values that you add to your worksheet and by default provides a new workbook with three worksheets. The Excel Web App does not provide you with the ability to add worksheets to a workbook, but it will enable you to edit a workbook created in Excel 2010 that contains more than three worksheets.

The Excel Web App is probably strongest in working with Excel tables, and provides you with the ability to specify a cell range as a table. You can then use the Sort/Filter drop-down lists provided for each field heading to sort and/or filter the table. The Excel Web App also enables you to update connections in a workbook if you are editing a workbook created in Excel 2010 that includes external data sources such as a SQL Server database or other data source accessed through Microsoft Query.

➡ *For information about Excel tables, PivotTables, and data sources, see the information that begins on page 415 in Chapter 15, "Using Excel Tables and PivotTables."*

The Excel Web App File Tab

The Excel Web App provides a Ribbon with three tabs: File, Home, and Insert. The File tab, which is really a menu, provides you with the ability to open the workbook in Excel 2010 and also to save the workbook under a new name and share the workbook with other users (the sharing possibilities are the same as those provided by the Word Web App). The Excel Web App File tab is shown in Figure 5.15.

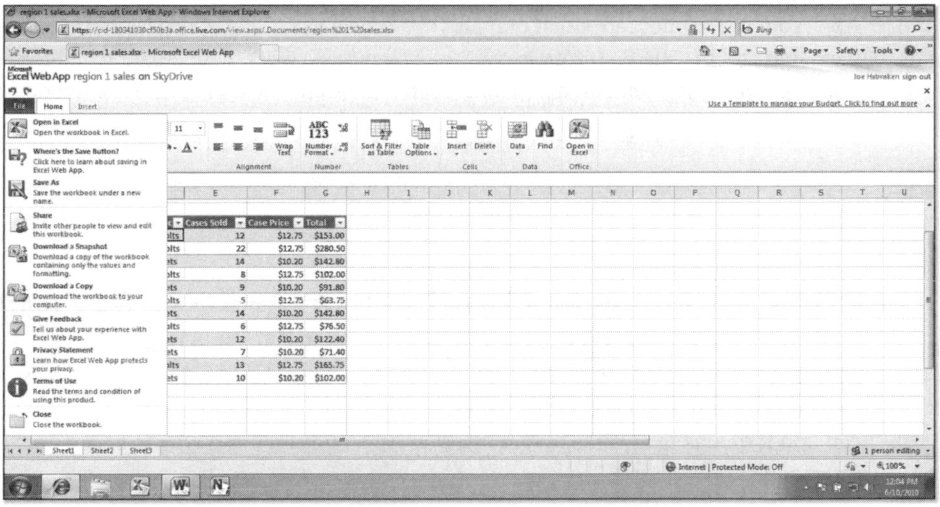

Figure 5.15
The Excel Web App File tab.

The File tab also provides you a couple of different possibilities for downloading the current workbook. You can download a copy of the workbook by selecting Download a Copy. This option will include all the formulas and functions and other objects in the sheets found in the workbook.

The Download a Snapshot option is a little different and will download a copy of the workbook containing only the values and formatting found in the worksheets in the workbook. This means that all formulas and functions contained in the worksheets will be converted to their resulting values. When you do download a snapshot, any objects that were contained in the chart will be included so the snapshot option affects only formulas and functions that were in the workbook.

Working in the Excel Web App

The Excel Web App is tailored to basic worksheet data entry and manipulation of table data. The Home tab of the Web App's Ribbon provides you with the command groups for the formatting and alignment of cell entries. It includes a Number group that enables you to format numbers (values) in a worksheet and also to increase or decrease the decimal places in value entries. The Cells group enables you to insert rows, columns, or cells and also provides you with the ability to delete rows, columns, or cells.

You can adjust row heights and column widths in a worksheet by using the mouse. The best fit column width function (double-clicking on a column border) is not available in the Web App, so you will need to drag a column's border to change the width for a column.

As already mentioned, you are provided three worksheets in a new workbook that you create using the Excel Web App. You cannot change the name of a worksheet, delete a worksheet, or rearrange the worksheets in a workbook via the Web App.

You can view graphics that you have added to a worksheet created in Excel 2010 such as pictures, clip art, SmartArt, or more importantly, charts, but you cannot edit or delete them in the Excel Web App. You also cannot reposition graphics in a worksheet in the Excel Web App or add new graphics, including charts. The Web App is really all about basic worksheet creation and table manipulation. It also provides you with an excellent resource in terms of viewing an Excel workbook when you do not have access to Excel 2010.

 For more information on creating charts in Excel 2010, see Chapter 14, "Enhancing Worksheets with Charts," which begins on page 381.

Inserting Formulas and Functions in the Excel Web App

If you have perused the Excel Web App, you have probably found that the Ribbon does not include a Formulas tab nor does the Home tab provide access to the AutoSum command. So, the possibilities for inserting a function into a worksheet that you create in the Web App might seem bleak. You can add formulas to a worksheet in the Web App, and there is a way to select from a list of available functions.

To add a formula, type the equal sign (=) and then specify the cell addresses and the operators required for the formula. You can use the mouse to specify the cell addresses that appear in the formula as you would in Excel 2010 when you create a formula. When the formula is complete, press the Enter key.

In terms of copying a formula in a worksheet, there is no Fill handle available on a selected cell, but you can use the Copy and Paste commands in the Clipboard group to copy and then paste the formula as needed. When you select the Copy command to copy a cell or range of cells in the Web App, an Internet Explorer web box will open asking if you will allow access to your Clipboard. The Web Apps use your Clipboard for the Copy, Cut, and Paste commands, so you will want to allow access.

After you have copied the formula (this will also work for an inserted function, which we discuss in a moment), you can select a cell or range of cells and then select Paste. The Paste command in the Excel Web App provides a menu that enables you to paste formulas, paste values, or paste formatting. Select Paste Formulas to paste the formula.

You can also add functions to a worksheet, but you will need to know the name of the function that you want to use. Select the cell that will contain the function and then type an equal sign (=). Type the first letter or first couple of letters in the function's name and the function list will appear as shown in Figure 5.16.

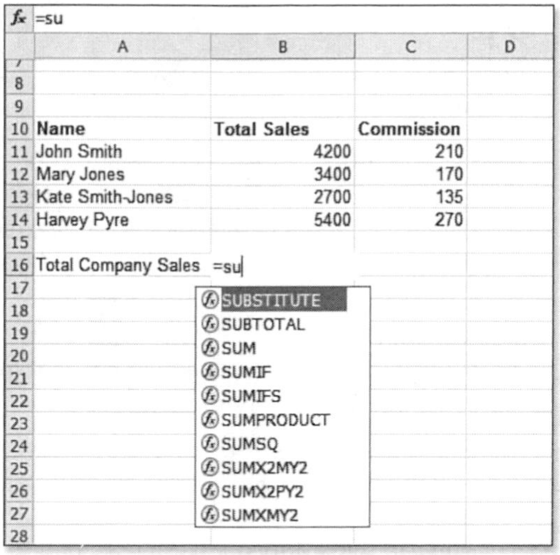

Figure 5.16
The Excel Web App's function list.

Double-click the function to insert it into the cell. You can then select the range of cells that you want the function to act on and they will be specified in the function. You need to remember to type the closing parenthesis for the function to complete it; you can then press Enter. The function will return a result. You can use the Copy and Paste commands as needed to copy the function to other cells.

➡ *For more information on Excel 2010 formulas and functions, see Chapter 13, "Getting the Most from Formulas and Functions," which begins on page 349.*

Using the PowerPoint Web App

The PowerPoint Web App provides you with a solid collection of commands for creating a new presentation or editing an existing presentation that you have saved to your SkyDrive or SharePoint site library. When you create a new presentation, you must provide a filename (as with the other Office Web Apps) and then the PowerPoint Web App will open in your browser window.

The first thing that the Web App requires when you create a new presentation is that you select a theme for the presentation. The Select Theme dialog box will open as shown in Figure 5.17. The fact that the PowerPoint Web App requires that you choose a theme from the get-go is actually an improvement over PowerPoint 2010. There is nothing worse than creating a number of slides and then selecting a theme only to have to backtrack and work with certain slides because of the way the theme has overlapped or otherwise positioned objects on crowded slides.

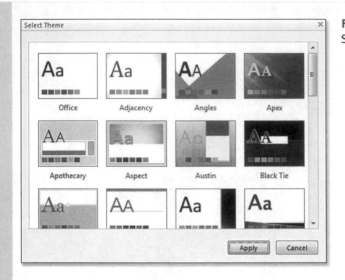

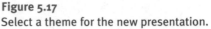

Figure 5.17
Select a theme for the new presentation.

You can scroll through the themes provided in the Select Theme dialog box. After you find the theme you want to use, select the theme, and then click the Apply button. You can't change the theme unless you open the presentation in PowerPoint 2010. The Web App doesn't provide the Theme gallery on the Ribbon.

The PowerPoint Web App Ribbon provides the File, Home, Insert, and View tabs. The File tab provides you with a menu that enables you to print, share, and view the properties of the current presentation.

The Home tab provides you with ability to insert and delete slides. It also provides you with commands that enable you to format font and paragraph attributes for the text on your slides, including bulleted and numbered lists.

The Insert tab enables you to insert objects such as pictures, SmartArt, and hyperlinks. However, to insert items such as pictures or SmartArt, the slide must have a content placeholder on it. You cannot add objects, including links, to blank or title-only slides in the PowerPoint Web App.

The Ribbon's View tab provides you with several different views. These views are as follows:

- **Editing View:** This view, which is the default view for the Web App, shows the current slide and provides the Slides pane, which provides a thumbnail of all the slides in the presentation. At the bottom of the current slide is the top edge of the Notes pane, which can be used to add speaker's notes to the presentation.

- **Reading View:** This command opens the Web App viewer, which is the same view that you get when you select a saved PowerPoint presentation in a SkyDrive folder or a SharePoint site library. This view enables you to open the presentation in PowerPoint 2010, return to the Web App (by selecting Edit in Browser), set share settings for the file, or view a slide show of the presentation.

- **Slide Show:** This command takes you to the PowerPoint Web App viewer. To view the presentation as a full-screen slide show, select the Start Slide Show command. When you have finished viewing the slide show, press Esc to return to the Web App viewer. You can then return to the Web App by selecting Edit in Browser.

- **Notes:** This command expands the Notes pane at the bottom of the current slide. You can add notes as needed. The Notes command functions as a toggle switch, so you can expand the Notes pane with one click and then minimize it with a second click.

You will find that the PowerPoint Web App views are limited when compared to PowerPoint 2010. The Web App neither provides access to the Slide Sorter nor provides you with any capabilities in terms of zooming in or out on the slide that you are editing.

 For more information on working in different PowerPoint 2010 views, see page 485 in Chapter 17, "Requisite PowerPoint: Essential Features."

Working with Slides

You can add, delete, and duplicate presentation slides. The slide-related commands are on the Ribbon's Home tab. Your new presentation is provided with a title slide by default. You can click on the title slide and enter the title slide text as needed.

To insert a new slide, select the New Slide command. The New Slide dialog box will open as shown in Figure 5.18.

Figure 5.18
Insert a new slide.

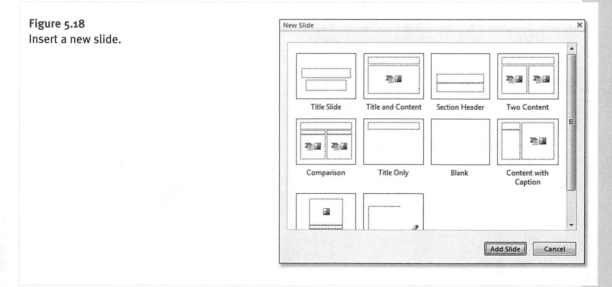

Select a layout for the new slide. If you are going to add an object such as a picture or SmartArt, select a slide layout that provides a content placeholder. Click Add Slide to insert the new slide.

After you have inserted the new slide, you can enter the text for that slide. You can format the text using the Font and Paragraph group commands provided on the Home tab. You can add other slides as needed. Changes that you make to the presentation are saved automatically.

You can delete elements on a slide; select a text box or content box and then press Delete. You cannot, however, rearrange elements on the slide or reposition objects.

You can actually use the Slides pane to rearrange the slides in a presentation in the Web App as you can in PowerPoint 2010. Drag a slide to a new position in the presentation as needed. To delete a slide, select the slide in the Slides pane and then click Delete Slide on the Home tab.

Adding Pictures and SmartArt

To add pictures, SmartArt, or links to a slide using the PowerPoint Web App, you need a slide that contains one or more content placeholders. You can then use the commands on the Ribbon's Insert tab as needed. For example, to insert a SmartArt graphic, select the SmartArt command on the Insert tab. The SmartArt gallery will open.

> **note**
>
> You can't change a slide's layout after the fact in the Web App as you can in PowerPoint 2010.

The gallery contains thumbnails of many different types of SmartArt lists and diagrams. Select a SmartArt list or diagram in the gallery to insert it into a content placeholder on the slide.

When a SmartArt graphic is selected on a slide, the SmartArt Tools become available on the Ribbon as shown in Figure 5.19. You can change the layout of the SmartArt graphic, colors, and also the style for the currently selected SmartArt graphic.

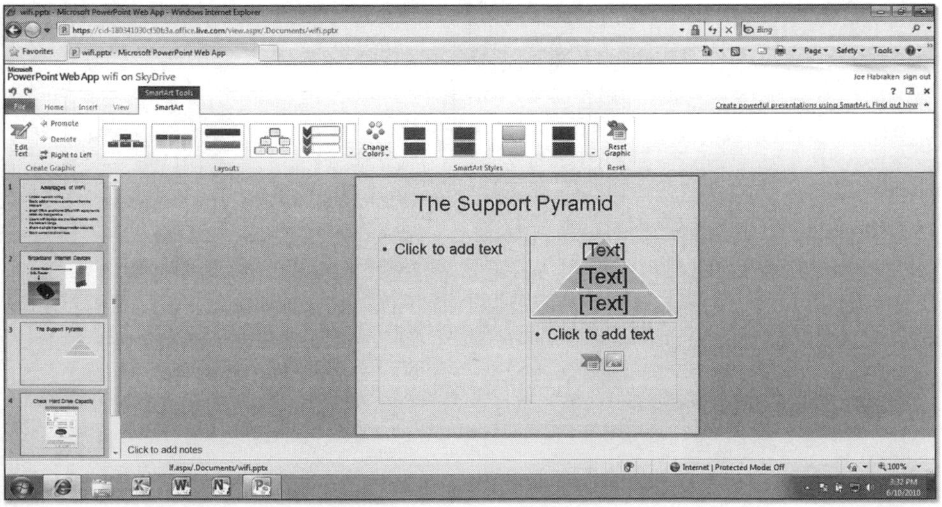

Figure 5.19
The SmartArt Tools.

To make text entries in a SmartArt graphic, click on one of the text placeholders on the graphic. You can then enter your text (or edit your text) as needed. When you have finished working with the text, click outside the graphic.

Pictures can also be added to your slides via the Insert tab when you are using the PowerPoint Web App. When an inserted picture is selected, the Picture Tools become available on the Ribbon. Assign a style to the selected picture or you can use the Change Picture command to specify that a different picture file be used in the slide.

 For information on working with pictures and SmartArt in the Office 2010 applications, see page 88 in Chapter 4, "Using and Creating Graphics."

Using the OneNote Web App

The OneNote Web App enables you to create OneNote notebooks. A notebook is basically an organizational container like a three-ring binder. A notebook consists of sections that you create to specify the organizational sections of the notebook. Pages can then be inserted into each section. Pages can contain all sorts of information such as text notes, tables, pictures, and a variety of other items.

The OneNote Web App does a pretty good job in enabling you to create a basic notebook that includes text tags, tables, and pictures. It does not provide a number of features provided by OneNote 2010, such as the drawing tools found on the Ribbon's Draw tab. The Web App also does not enable you to check the sync status for a shared notebook via the Sync icon in the Navigation pane or via the Info window in the OneNote 2010 Backstage.

OneNote notebooks that are shared provide an excellent platform for collaboration among a group of co-workers or colleagues. Shared notebooks on SkyDrive or a SharePoint site make it easy for multiple users to update information in a notebook, and users can work on the same notebook simultaneously.

You can create a new notebook using the OneNote Web App or you can edit existing notebooks that are stored in a SkyDrive folder or SharePoint library. As with the Other Office Web Apps, the OneNote Web App only provides a basic subset of the commands and features available in OneNote 2010.

The Ribbon's File tab provides you with commands that enable you to share the notebook or view the notebook's properties. You can also open the notebook in OneNote 2010 by selecting the Open in OneNote command.

The OneNote Ribbon also includes a Home tab that provides the Paste, Cut, and Copy commands and also basic formatting commands for text and the Styles gallery. The Home tab also provides access to note tags and the Spelling feature.

The OneNote Web app does not include a Save button on the Quick Access Toolbar or the File tab. Your notebook is saved automatically as you work on it. OneNote 2010 operates in the same manner; notebooks are saved automatically as you work on them.

Adding Sections and Pages

As already mentioned, a OneNote notebook is divided into different parts using sections. When you create a new notebook using the OneNote Web App, the notebook is created with one section and one page. You can rename the default untitled section by right-clicking on the section tab and selecting Rename from the shortcut menu. Type the new name in the Section Name dialog box and then click OK.

Each page, including the default page in the default section, contains a header area above a time stamp in which you click to enter a name for the page. The sections that you add to a notebook will appear in the Navigation pane on the left of the Web App workspace. Pages contained in a section will appear under the section name. The Navigation pane looks a lot like an outline after you have populated it with sections and pages.

To add a new section to the notebook, select the Ribbon's Insert tab and then select New Section. The Section Name dialog box will appear. Provide a name for the section and then click OK.

The new section will be added to the notebook. When you add a new section, a new untitled page is also added to the section. You can type a name for a new page in its header area.

You can also insert pages as needed into a particular section in the notebook. Select a section in the Navigation pane and then click the New Page icon on the right of the section tab. You can then type a name for the page in the page's header area. New pages can also be inserted from the Ribbon's Insert tab using the New Page command.

You can rearrange pages in a section by dragging a page to a new position in the Navigation pane. You can also drag a page from one section to another section. Sections in the notebook can also be rearranged by dragging them as needed in the Navigation pane.

 For information on working with sections and pages in OneNote 2010, see the information that begins on page 820 in Chapter 30, "Requisite OneNote: Essential Features."

Adding Notes and Note Tags to Pages

The real value of a notebook is the information included on the pages it contains. You can click below the time stamp on a page to add a text note to the page. To add the text note, just start typing at the insertion point. The OneNote Web App enables you to place notes along only the left margin of the page. To add blank lines between the notes on the page, use the Enter key.

Tags or note tags can take the form of preformatted notes such as to-do lists, contact note boxes, or idea boxes. Some note tags are just icons or text formatting that is applied to the text in a note. Note tags not only make it easy to enter a list or contact information, but also serve as special reminders and enable you to differentiate between the different types of notes that you have added to a page.

To insert a new note tag, select the Tag command on the Ribbon's Home tab. The Tag gallery will open as shown in Figure 5.20. To view additional tags, select the More Tags option at the bottom of the Tag gallery.

Figure 5.20
Insert a note tag.

Select a tag from the gallery. It will be inserted onto the page. Enter the appropriate text associated with the tag. For example, if you inserted a To Do note tag, type each item in the To Do list as needed. A check box will be provided for each item in the list.

You can remove the tag from a note that you have typed. Place the insertion point on the tagged note. Then access the Tag gallery and select Remove Tag from the gallery. The note will remain on the page; only the tag is removed.

 For information on working with notes and tags in OneNote 2010, see the information that begins on page 828 in Chapter 30.

Inserting Tables and Other Objects onto Pages

The OneNote Web App also provides you with the ability to insert table and other objects, such as pictures and clip art. Tables enable you to organize information in columns and rows. Pictures enable you to provide images that give visual support for notes that you have placed on your notebook pages.

To insert a table, select the Table command on the Insert menu. Use the table grid provided to specify the number of rows and columns for the table. Enter the required text in the table. You can move from cell to cell by pressing the Tab key. You can move backward in the table (from cell to cell) by using Shift+Tab.

You can format the text in the table by using the basic text commands and the styles provided in the Style gallery. When the insertion point is in the table, the Table Tools Layout tab is available on the Ribbon. You can use these commands to modify the table, such as deleting columns or rows or inserting columns and rows. You can also use the Align Left, Center, and Align Right commands, which can be used to align the text in a cell or a group of selected cells in the table.

You will find that the Table Tools Layout command groups found in OneNote 2010 are identical to those provided by the OneNote Web App. So, working with information in tables is one of the Web App's strong suites.

➡ *For information on inserting and formatting tables in OneNote 2010, see page 833 in Chapter 30.*

The OneNote Web App's Insert tab also enables you to insert pictures and clip art. When you insert a picture, you select from picture files that are stored on your computer. When you insert clip art, you are searching Microsoft.com for it, so any clip art on your computer will not be included in the search. Oddly enough, the OneNote Web App provides a command for inserting clip art. There is not an insert clip art command provided in the installed version of OneNote 2010, however.

To insert clip art, select the Clip Art command on the Insert menu. The Insert Clip Art dialog box will open as shown in Figure 5.21. Type a search string for the search and then click the Search icon.

Figure 5.21
Search for a clip art image.

Clip art matching your search string will appear in the Insert Clip Art dialog box. Select a clip art image in the dialog box and then click the Insert button. The clip art will be inserted onto the notebook page. When the picture is selected, you can take advantage of the Picture Tools Format commands that enable you to enlarge or shrink the image and to specify the image size by using the Scale spinner box. You cannot undo the insertion of clip art onto the page, but you can select the image and then press Delete to remove it.

➡ *For information on adding pictures to OneNote 2010 pages, see page 845 in Chapter 31, "Working with Notebook Pages."*

REQUISITE WORD: ESSENTIAL FEATURES

Word processing might not seem like the most exciting task to perform on your computer; however, Word 2010 can make the document creation process much more productive and creative. In this chapter we take a look at the Word application window and the basic features and tools of this powerful word processor provides.

We will cover your options for creating new Word documents and look at ways to navigate the Word application window and your documents. We will also look at document formatting including working with font and paragraph formatting. We will also work with tabs, margins and page orientation settings.

Introducing Word 2010

Microsoft Word has been the standard for word processing on Windows-based PCs for nearly two decades. And it is certainly safe to say that it is the most often used member of the Microsoft Office application suite—no matter what our job or personal computing endeavors, we all need to create documents. Some of us use Word to create lists, memos, and letters, whereas others create more complex documents such as reports, newsletters, and forms. No matter what you type of documents you create in Word, you will find that Word 2010 provides all the tools and word processing features that you require. In fact, Word has really evolved over the years from a word processor to a full-fledged desktop publishing application.

The Word 2010 Interface

For the most part, Microsoft Word 2010 employs the same application interface introduced in its predecessor, Word 2007 (and some of the other Office 2007 applications). The biggest change to the Word interface and the Office 2007 suite was the introduction of the Ribbon, which provides a quickly accessible logical grouping of commands and features. You will also find that you can quickly access commands and features via the Ribbon tabs; commands and features appear directly on the Ribbon, negating the need to work through a menu and potentially submenus.

As far as the Ribbon's geography is concerned, you will work with tabs, groups, and commands. For example, Figure 6.1 shows the Ribbon with the Home tab selected. The Home tab includes a number of command groups including Clipboard, Font, and Paragraph. Each group contains a number of commands. Take the Font group, for instance. It contains a number of font formatting commands, such as Bold, Italic, Font Size, and Font Color, to name just a few.

The Ribbon also provides a contextual approach to accessing the tools that you need as you work on a particular task or with a particular Word feature. For example, you can quickly create a table from the Insert tab of the Ribbon; select the Insert tab, and then Table, and then choose one of the methods of table creation. After the table is in the document, you will notice that when the insertion point is in the table, a contextual tab, Table Tools, appears over top of the Ribbon's Design and Layout tabs. Selecting either the Design or Layout tab provides tools specific to formatting the table. Figure 6.2 shows the Tables Tools that become available when a table is selected in a document.

Figure 6.1
The Word 2010 application window and Ribbon.

The Table Tools provide two different tabs: Design and Layout. The Design tab enables you to assign styles to the table and set style options. The Layout tab enables you to work with rows and columns and also merge cells and change the text alignment in cells.

➡ *For more information about customizing the Ribbon, see "Customizing an Application Interface," page 35.*

Word 2010 Improvements

Word 2010 builds on the decidedly different application interface of Word 2007 (which was definitely different to veteran Word users) and provides some important enhancements of its own. Some of the more exciting improvements to Word 2010 are as follows:

- **Print and Print Preview:** The Print command in the Backstage (which replaces the Office Button menu of Office 2007) opens the Print Settings window, which consolidates printing commands (such as printer selection and other print options) and print preview. A zoom slider and navigation buttons make it easy for you to preview your document and then quickly send it to a selected printer.

- **New SmartArt Graphics:** A number of new SmartArt graphics have been added to the existing SmartArt library, making it easy for you to create visually descriptive and interesting documents. A new category of SmartArt graphics, Picture, provides possibilities for image diagrams such as Bubble Picture List and Titled Picture Blocks.

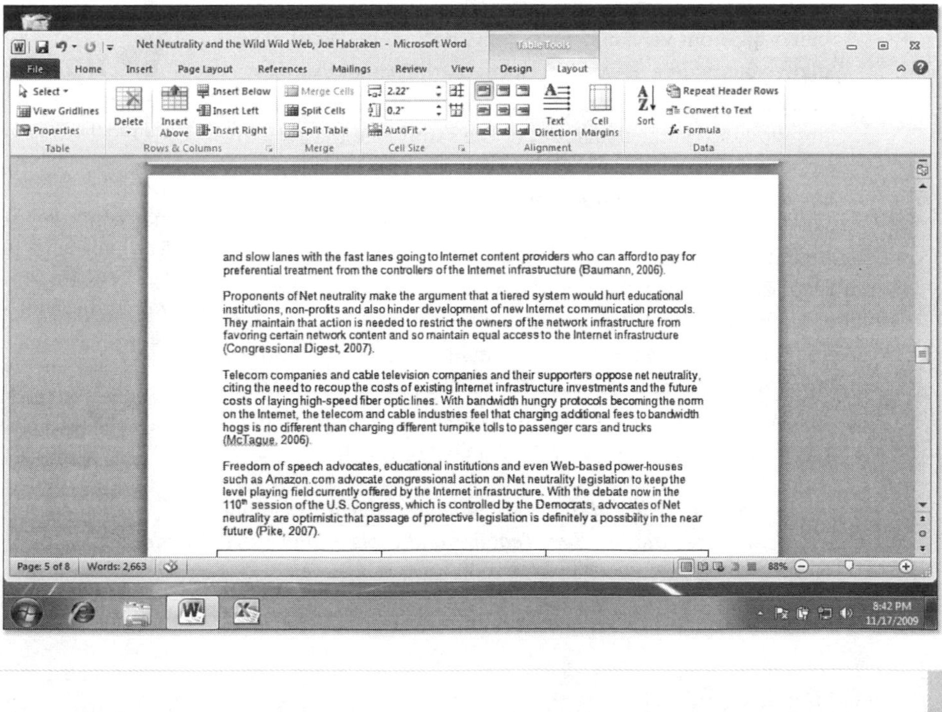

Figure 6.2
The contextual Table Tools tab become available on the Ribbon when you work with a table.

- **Paste Preview:** The Paste command now includes paste options that enable you to preview (when you place the mouse on one of the options) how the pasted text will look before it is actually inserted in the document. The options make it possible for you to keep the formatting of the pasted text, merge the formatting with the document text, or insert the pasted text without formatting (which in the past required the use of Paste Special).

- **Navigation Pane:** The new navigation pane replaces the document map. The navigation pane provides an outline view of your document (as did the document map). The navigation pane also enables you to access search capabilities (within the pane) and view where search results occur in the document and document sections if they exist.

- **New Text Effects:** Text effects have been added to the Format group on the Home tab of the Ribbon. These effect options can be quickly applied to selected text and include effects such as Glow, Shadow, Bevel, and Outline.

- **Better Picture Tools:** Word 2010 provides you with a more robust set of image-editing tools including more picture effects, picture styles, and the Background Removal tool. For a detailed overview of working with graphics and pictures in Microsoft Office, check out Chapter 4, "Using and Creating Graphics."

> **note**
>
> As with all software version upgrades, some of the improvements found in Word 2010 will be under the hood features that are not all that noticeable to most users but make the application perform better. Other changes to Word such as command changes and interface improvements will have an impact on how you navigate and use the application.

- **Co-Author a Document in Real Time:** Working on a document with colleagues always posed problems in reviewing changes to the document and reconciling different versions of the same document. Word now allows users on a network to work on the same document simultaneously. You can even view a list of the users who are working on the document at the same time that you are and view information about those users. This is a big step forward for the corporate Word user.

Although not an exhaustive list of all the new tweaks found in Word 2010, it does give you a preview of a number of the new features that you can take advantage of as you use Word. Coupled with the dramatic changes made to the user interface in Word 2007, you will find that Word 2010 provides you with all the functionality that you need to create both professional and personal documents that are visually appealing.

> **tip**
>
> You can pin the Word Start menu icon to the Windows 7 Taskbar or to the Start menu so that you can open Word without going through the start menu. Right-click on the Word icon and then select either of the "pin" options. If you want to place a Word icon on the Windows desktop, copy the Word icon from the menu (right-click on it and select copy) and the paste it on the desktop (right-click and then paste).

 For an overview of the new and improved features found in Office 2010 see "New Features and Tools in Office 2010," page 6.

Options for Creating a New Word Document

When you start Word, you are provided with a new blank document. Faced with a clean slate, most of us just begin typing away without really considering the best way to approach the creation of a new Word document.

Obviously, one way to create a new document is to use the blank document provided. This document will contain all your default page layout settings such as margins and page orientation and will use Word's default font and font attributes. Starting a document from scratch affords you complete control over how the document looks from the font to the paragraphs to the page. However, you might want to create some sort of specialized document (such as a newsletter) or you want some help with the overall design and look of a document. In some cases, you might even want to use all or part of an existing document (something you have already created and saved) in your new document, which will then require only some text editing and format fine-tuning.

When you open the Backstage view (click the File tab on the Ribbon), the New command provides you with all the possibilities for creating a new document. Figure 6.3 shows what happens when you select New in the Backstage view.

The Available Templates window, which includes a template preview pane on the right, provides all the options for creating a new document. As you can see from Figure 6.3, when

> **🔍 note**
>
> The File tab replaces the Office button found in Office 2007 (which replaced the File menu found in Office 2003 and its predecessors). The File tab menu, which is actually referred to as the Backstage view, is anchored on the application window (which was not the case for the Office Button menu), so when you select one of the backstage view options such as Info, New, or Print, you can still access all the other File tab menu choices with a single click. This makes it easier for you to choose one of the other menu options without having to close a window and return to the menu as you did in Office 2007.

you first open the Available Templates window, a Blank Document icon is selected in the Available Templates window and a preview of a blank document is provided in the Preview pane. It is also apparent that there are a lot of other options for creating a new document, many of them involving templates. For now, know that a template is basically a document blueprint that is described in more detail in the next section, "Using Templates." In terms of broader options for creating a new document, you really have three choices:

- Create a new blank document based on Word's default template

- Create a new document based on one of Word's numerous templates

- Create a document based on an existing document

Creating a particular kind of new document is really just a matter of choosing the appropriate option in the Available Templates window. For example, if I want to create a new blank document, I select the Blank Document option and then click Create. .

In cases where a document already exists, say a letter that you wrote a week ago, you could base a new document on that particular saved document. In effect, Word opens a copy of the document, so the original document remains untouched when you make your editing changes. When you save the document, you are required to provide a new filename and a new location (if desired) for the file.

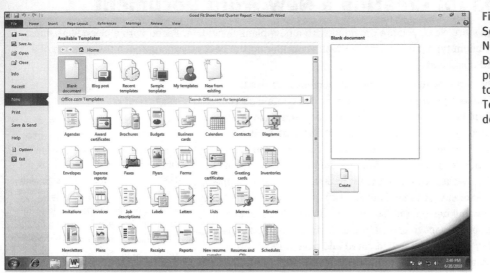

Figure 6.3
Selecting
New on the
Backstage view
provides access
to the Available
Templates win-
dow.

To create a new document based on an existing document, follow these steps:

1. Open the Backstage view (click the File tab on the Ribbon).

2. Select New on the Backstage list.

3. Select New from existing in the Available Templates window.

4. In the New from Existing Document dialog box, locate and select the document that you will base the new document on.

5. Click Open and a copy of the existing document opens in the Word application window.

So, the more mechanical aspect of creating a new document, which of the new document options you select, depends on whether you want to start a new document from scratch (a blank document), base the new document on an already existing document, or take advantage of one of Word's docu-ment templates. In the next section, we explore what templates actually are and how you can take advantage of them.

Using Templates

As already mentioned in the previous sections, one of your options for creating a new document is to select one of the templates provides in the Available Templates window. When you create a new document in Word, you always use a template. For example, the blank document that automatically opens when you start Word is based on the Normal template. The Normal template uses all your default settings such as the default font, margins, tabs, paragraph settings, and the other document layout attributes. If you haven't changed any of the default Word settings (something we talk about later in this chapter), the Normal template provides you with all the default settings that Word provides at installation.

For example, the default margins for the Normal template are 1 for left, right, top, and bottom (of the page). The default page orientation is portrait (meaning the page is taller than it is wide, based on the default page size in the U.S. of 8.5 by 11). The default font is Calibri with a default font size of 11 points (there are 72 points to an inch). The default line spacing (which is a paragraph setting) is set to Multiple, which is actually 1.15 spaces between each line. This is different than earlier versions of Word which used 1 as the default line spacing.. Obviously, if you were going to create a special document such as a resume, flyer, or restaurant menu, you would want to edit these and other default settings to provide you with the appropriate overall design and look for your special document.

Templates, by design, contain formatting and layout attributes particular to a certain special document type. So, if you need to create a restaurant menu, all you have to do is select one of the menu templates provided. The template will take care of the font, paragraph, and page formatting attributes; all you have to do is provide the content for the document such as text and possibly images such as your restaurant's logo. Then you can quickly print out your required number of menus. Figure 6.4 shows a menu template that provides you with a four-page traditional menu. It contains placeholder text that you replace with your text and has placeholders for images.

Templates also often contain sample text or text placeholders. You replace the sample text with your text or click on one of the text placeholders and insert the required text. Some templates will also contain borders, shading, and even graphics (some of the graphics might take the form of watermarks on the page). The whole point behind templates is to enable you to quickly and efficiently create a specialized document, which typically requires special formatting and layout attributes.

At this point in our discussion, you might not have a complete feel for all the different font, paragraph, and page layout formatting attributes that can be controlled by a Word template (although you will after you have perused through the Word section of this book). Suffice it to say that you can still take advantage of the templates to create special documents (I drive an automobile, but can't necessarily explain the science behind the gasoline combustion engine). Using a template does not, however, lock you into the formatting attributes provided by the template and you can fine-tune your new template-based document in terms of its settings just as readily as a simple document that you created from scratch (which as you now know is actually based on the Normal template).

If you decide you want to use a template, you have three options in terms of selecting a particular template:

- A number of templates are installed on your computer when you install Microsoft Office (or install Word as a standalone application).

- Office Online provides a huge number of templates that you can preview and then quickly download into your template library.

- You can create your own templates (as you would any Word document) and base new documents on that template.

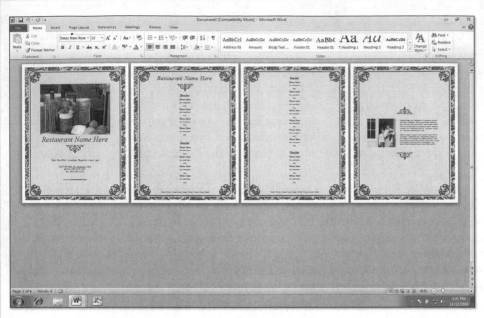

Figure 6.4
Templates, such as the menu template, enable you to quickly create specialized documents.

The actual steps for creating a new document based on a template are as follows:

1. Open the Backstage (click the File tab on the Ribbon).

2. Select New in the Backstage.

3. Select a templates collection in the Available Templates window. You can select Sample Templates to view templates on your computer or select any of the Template group icons available in the Office.com Templates area of the Available Templates window.

4. Select one of the templates available in a template collection and then click Create (if the template is on the local computer) or click Download. In both cases, a new document based on the template opens in the Word window.

After the new document is open in the Word window, you can edit the document as needed. Remember that your changes to the document are reflected in the document only; you are not editing the template itself. When you save the document, the Save As dialog box opens and you can specify a name and location for the document.

note

Templates take advantage of styles. Styles are a collection of font, paragraph, and other formatting attributes saved under a style name. Styles allow you to apply a number of formatting attributes to text just by assigning the style to the text (such as a heading or a paragraph). Styles are discussed in depth in Chapter 7, "Enhancing Word Documents."

tip

When you create a new document based on an existing document, you are in effect creating the new document based on the template of the existing document. All the layout and formatting attributes stored in the existing document (which you probably set yourself as you created the document) are carried over into the copy of the original document that you will be editing.

Creating a Template

As your knowledge of Word begins to parallel your creativity and need (in terms of creating specialized documents), you will find that it is extremely advantageous to create your own document templates. Although an incredible number of templates are available on Office.com, you might still want to create templates specific to the type of documents you need to create in Word.

Creating a template is very straightforward. First, open a new blank document (or an existing document) and configure the various document settings such as font attributes, paragraph attributes, and page layout settings. You can also create styles in the document that are then available in the template based on the document.

After the document is completed, you can save it as a template. Follow these steps:

1. Select the File tab and then select Save As in the Backstage

2. In the Save As dialog box, navigate to the folder that contains the Normal template and any templates that you have downloaded from Office.com (typically this folder is Users/your username/AppData/Roaming/Microsoft/Templates).

3. Type a name for your template and change the Save as Type box to Word Template (see Figure 6.5).

4. Click the Save button to save your new template.

Now when you want to base a new document on the saved template, click the My Templates icon in the Available Templates window. The New dialog box opens. Select your template (make sure that the Document option button is selected) and then click OK. A new document based on the template will open in the Word window.

Templates can provide both uniformity and efficiency in terms of creating new documents. If you repeatedly create documents that are extremely similar (such as a weekly report), it makes sense to use templates to create those documents.

> ## note
>
> As already mentioned, templates can also contain pictures, watermarks, and other graphics. They can also contain building blocks (one of the Quick Parts options covered in Chapter 7), which are blocks of text that are saved as part of the template and then can be quickly added to a document. Templates can also contain macros, which are small user-coded programs that enable you to automate tasks in Microsoft Office (macros are discussed in Appendix A). Anything that you add to a document that you save as a template is available when you base a new document on that saved template.

Attaching a Template

Because templates can include building blocks, styles, and macros, you might find it advantageous to change the template currently assigned to the document that you are working on. Attaching a template replaces the template currently assigned to the document.

tip

If you are having trouble finding the Templates folder (Users/your username/AppData/Roaming/Microsoft/Templates) that holds your downloaded templates and the Word Normal template so that you can save your own templates to the folder and access them later via Available Templates window, it might be because the Templates folder and its parent folders are typically hidden in Windows 7 by default. Open the Windows 7 Control Panel and select System and Security. Then select Appearance and Personalization. Under Folder Options, click the Show Hidden Files and Folders link. In the Folder Options dialog box, click the Show Hidden Files, Folders, and Drives option button and then click OK. Now you can save your own templates to the Templates folder. You will find that all templates saved in this folder will be listed in the New dialog box when you select My Templates.

To attach a template to a document, you will need access to the Developer tab on the Ribbon. It is not included by default. The Developer tab provides access to the Templates and Add-ins dialog box, which is where you actually attach the template.

Select the File tab on the Ribbon and then select Options. In the Word Options dialog box, select Customize Ribbon. On the right of the dialog box is a list of the Ribbon's main tabs. Select the Developer check box and then click OK.

The Developer tab appears on the Ribbon. Select Developer and then, on the Developer tab, click Add-Ins. The Templates and Add-ins dialog box opens as shown in Figure 6.6.

In the Templates and Add-in dialog box, click the Attach button. The Attach Template dialog box opens. The templates listed are the templates you have downloaded or saved to your Templates folder (Users/your username/AppData/Roaming/Microsoft/Templates). Select a template and click on Open.

The template that you selected appears in the Document Template box on the Templates and Add-ins dialog box. Click OK to close the Templates and Add-ins dialog box. The document now has access to any styles or other items, such as building blocks saved with the template.

Figure 6.5
Save any document
as a template.

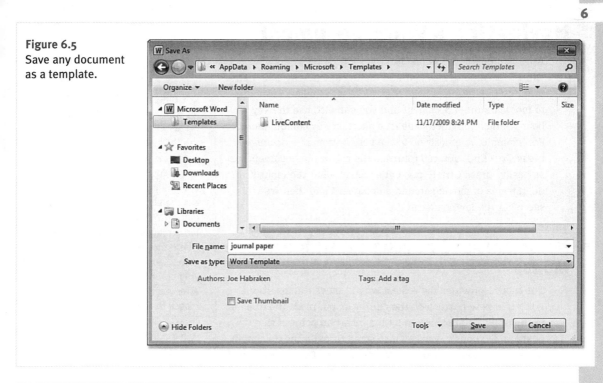

Figure 6.6
You can attach a different
template to your docu-
ment.

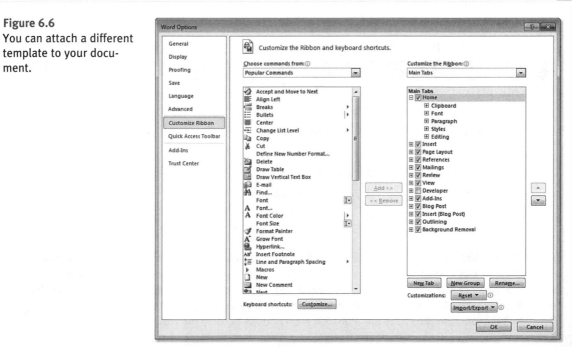

Navigating a Word Document

After you create a document in the Word application, you want to be able to move around the document (say from paragraph to paragraph or page to page). You can use the mouse to move around a document and you can also use the keyboard, which provides some nice shortcut key combinations. For example, to quickly go to the very bottom of a document, press Ctrl+End. You can return to the top of the document just as easily: press Ctrl+Home. Let's look at what the mouse can do in terms of moving around a document and then we will see what the keyboard can do.

Moving Around a Document with the Mouse

The mouse provides the easiest way to move the insertion point to a new position on the current page: place the I-beam in the text and then click to fix the insertion point at that position. Obviously, you can also scroll through the document pages using the scroll button on the mouse. The vertical scrollbar provides several different ways to move through the document, as listed in Table 6.1.

> ### 📡 caution
>
> One thing to remember in navigating a document with the keyboard versus the mouse is that when you use the keyboard shortcut keys or the arrow keys to move around a document, you are moving the insertion point to a new position. You can then immediately start typing or editing. When you use the mouse to move around a document (including when you use the mouse and the vertical scrollbar), you are changing your viewpoint of the document. After you locate the place using the mouse that you intend to go to, you need to click the I-beam in the text to place the insertion point.

Table 6.1 Using the Mouse and Vertical Scrollbar

Mouse Movement	Your View of the Document Will
Click up scroll arrow	Move up a line
Click down scroll arrow	Move down a line
Click Next Page	Move to next page
Click Previous Page	Move to previous page
Click below scroll box	Move to next screen
Click above scroll box	Move to previous screen
Drag scroll box	Moves to specific page

The vertical scrollbar also provides the Select Browse Object button, which is located between the Previous Page and Next Page buttons. When you click the Select Browse button, an icon box appears containing a number of icons including Go To, Find, Browse by Graphic, Browse by Footnote, and Browse by Page. When you select one of the Browse By options, such as Browse by Footnote, the Next Page and Previous Page buttons become the Next Footnote and Previous

Footnote buttons, respectively (meaning when you click the Next Footnote button, you are taken to the next footnote in the document).

When you click the Go To icon on the icon box, the Find and Replace dialog box opens with the Go To tab selected (see Figure 6.7). To go to a particular page, type the page number in the Enter page number box and then click Go To.

The horizontal scrollbar offers the capability to scroll to the left and the right of a document page. The horizontal scrollbar will not appear if the document window is wide enough to display the entire page from left to right. You will find that the horizontal scrollbar is useful when you zoom in on a document and need to pan left and right to view all the text and other items (such as graphics) in the document.

> **⟋ tip**
>
> You can also move a specified number of pages forward or backward in the document on the Go To tab. For example, type +3 and you will be taken 3 pages forward. You can use the minus (*) with a number to move backward in the document.

Moving Around a Document with the Keyboard

Word also embraces a number of keyboard shortcuts that allow you to move around your document. For example, everyone is familiar with the fact that the arrow keys on the keyboard can be used to move around in your document. The up arrow takes you up a line and the down arrow takes you down a line. By themselves, the arrow keys are not all that efficient in terms of quickly moving around your document. Table 6.2 shows some slightly more elegant keyboard shortcuts for moving around a document.

> **🔍 note**
>
> More complex documents that contain multiple sections can (and often will) have different page layout settings in each of the sections. For more about sections see Chapter 8, "Working with Tables, Columns, and Sections."

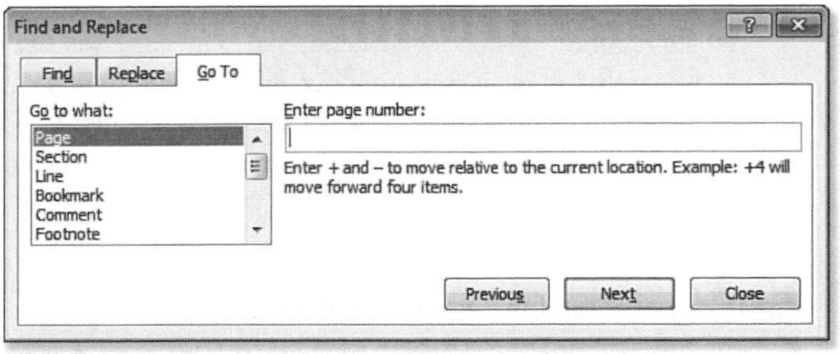

Figure 6.7
Use Go To to go to a specific page.

Table 6.2 Using the Keyboard to Move Through a Document

Key Combination	The Insertion Point Will
Home	Move to the beginning of a line
End	Move to the end of a line
Ctrl+Right arrow	Move one word to the right
Ctrl+Left arrow	Move one word to the left
Ctrl+Up arrow	Move to the previous paragraph
Ctrl+Down arrow	Move to the next paragraph
PgUp	Move up one window
PgDn	Move down one window
Ctrl+PgUp	Move up one page
Ctrl+PgDn	Move down one page
Ctrl+Home	Move to the top of a document
Ctrl+End	Move to the bottom of a document

Your use of the mouse or keyboard for moving around your document relies to a certain extent on personal preference. However, because we strive for maximum efficiency, it makes sense to consider (as you are initially typing your document), keeping your hands on the keyboard rather than constantly reaching for the mouse. Using the keyboard shortcuts should save you some time.

Selecting Text

When you use the mouse to select text, you actually have a number of options depending on whether the mouse pointer is in the document text itself or along the left margin of the document, which is referred to as the selection bar. The selection bar is the whitespace on the left edge of your document window, just in front of your text paragraphs. When you place the mouse in the selection bar, the mouse pointer becomes an arrow (in contrast to placing the mouse in the document, where the pointer appears as an I-beam). Table 6.3 provides the possibilities for selecting text using the mouse.

Table 6.3 Selecting Text with the Mouse

Text Selection	Mouse Action
Selects the word	Double-click a word
Selects text block	Click and drag Or Click at beginning of text, and then hold down Shift key and click at the end of text block
Selects line	Click in selection bar next to line

Text Selection	Mouse Action
Selects multiple lines	Click in selection bar and drag down through multiple lines
Selects the sentence	Hold Ctrl and click a sentence
Selects paragraph	Double-click in selection bar next to paragraph
	Or
	Triple-click in the paragraph
Selects entire document	Hold down Ctrl and click in selection bar

You can also select text using the keyboard. Hold down the Shift key and use the arrow keys to select text as needed. If you are old school, you can also use the Word Extend feature to select text using the keyboard. Position the insertion point before a word or sentence that you want to select. Press the F8 function key to turn on Extend. Press the spacebar to select a word (each time you press the spacebar the next word is selected. To select an entire sentence, turn on the extend feature, and then press the period (.) key. Entire paragraphs can be selected using this method by pressing the Enter key. To turn off the extend feature, press the Esc key.

Understanding Document Formatting

The overall look of your document actually depends on different types of attributes and layout settings, which many Word users lump together under the general term of formatting. However, you will find that text or character formatting relates to how the characters actually look (settings such as bold, 14 point, red), whereas paragraph formatting is concerned with things like line spacing, indents, borders, and alignment. Other document layout settings such as margins, columns, and page orientation fall under the Page Layout settings. So, it is important when you create documents in Word to understand that although they are distinctly different in how they are applied to the document and how they change the document, the character formatting, paragraph formatting, and document layout settings all work together to give the document its overall look.

In terms of simple documents (such as a two-page letter), I think we would agree that when changing a page layout setting such as the margins, we expect the margins on all the pages to change to our new settings. Page layout settings are pretty much all encompassing when we change them in a document. Character and paragraph formatting, on the other hand, are most specific in their application and are discussed in the next part of this chapter.

Character Formatting Versus Paragraph Formatting

We have all selected text and then clicked on the Bold command on the Home tab of the Ribbon. The selected text becomes bold; it's very simple. Character formatting relies on you to select the text that you want to format and then you are required to select a character attribute such as bold or red to actually format the selected text.

Paragraph formatting such as line spacing, indents, borders, and other paragraph-formatting attributes are a little different. For paragraph formatting to completely make sense, you need to understand what Word considers a paragraph.

When you click the Show/Hide command on the Ribbon's Home tab, Word shows you the paragraph marks and the spaces between words. In our discussion here, the paragraph marks are of extreme importance. Every time you press the Enter key, which creates a blank line, you are creating a paragraph (in terms of what Word sees as a paragraph).

So, when you click in a block of text preceded and followed by the paragraph mark symbol, you are in a paragraph (what Word considers as a separate paragraph). With the insertion point in that paragraph, all you have to do to center that text (all the text in the paragraph) is to click the Center command on the Ribbon's Home tab. You are not required to actually select the text (as you do when you want to change a character formatting attributes such as bold or italic). When you want to apply paragraph formatting to multiple paragraphs, you would have to select the paragraphs.

> **tip**
>
> By default, the Show/Hide command shows paragraph marks and spaces between words. You can view other hidden formatting marks on the screen by opening the Word Options dialog box (click the File Tab and then Options) and selecting the formatting marks on the Display Options screen.

Manual Formatting Versus Styles and Themes

Character formatting attributes can quickly and easily be applied to text in the document. It is very easy to make a heading bold and then 14 point. The same goes with paragraph formatting; click in a paragraph and change the line spacing using the Line Spacing command on the Home tab.

The problem with this manual formatting approach to changing the way text and paragraphs look is that building a consistent look throughout a document that consists of several pages can be a real chore.

If you desire a uniform look for a document, it makes sense to take advantage of styles and themes. A style can be a collection of character and paragraph formatting attributes saved under a style name. This style can be repeatedly applied to text in the document, providing consistent formatting. A theme, on the other hand, is an integrated set of formatting attributes that provides font, color, and effects settings.

In terms of a consistent look for a document, styles and themes provide you with a more controlled approach than manual formatting does. It makes sense to take advantage of styles and themes, particularly when you are working on special document types that require a greater amount of overall formatting.

➥ *Read more about styles in the "Understanding Styles" section, p. 195.*

➥ *To learn more about themes, see "Formatting with Themes," p. 171.*

Working with Fonts and Text Formatting

The basic look of the text in a Word document is controlled by the font that you are using. Each font set has a particular typeface, meaning the physical characteristic of the characters. And each font has a particular look that makes it unique. An example of a font set would be Calibri, which is the default Word font. A variety of other fonts exist, with names such as Arial, Courier, Times New Roman, Cooper Black, Bookman Old Style, and so on; the fonts you have access to when working in Word depend on the fonts installed on your computer. Most of the fonts you will work with are software fonts or "soft fonts" and are Microsoft Open Type fonts (formally called True Type fonts) provided by your Windows operating system.

Most of the fonts that we use on our computers are proportional fonts. This means that the characters can have varying widths. For example, the letter W would be wider than the letter I. Proportional fonts have a typeset look and are not only easier to read but also work better in columns and tables (as opposed to nonproportional fonts such as those found on a typewriter, which all have the same width). Figure 6.8 shows some of the proportional fonts available in Word.

Proportional fonts are measured in points, which refer to the character height. Each point is 1/72 of an inch. For example, a 12-point font would be 1/6 of an inch tall; a 36-point font would be 1/2 inch tall.

Figure 6.8
Proportional fonts in different point sizes.

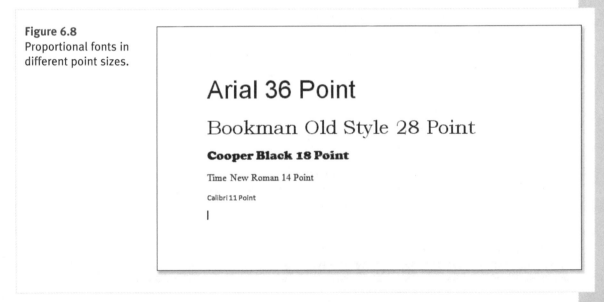

You can change the font attributes before you begin typing in a document or you can change the various text attributes after the fact and format existing text. If you want to change the font name or the font size in a new document before you begin typing, use the Font and Font Size drop-down boxes on the Home tab. Or if you are going to type a heading that you want in bold, you could press Ctrl+B to turn on the bold and then press Ctrl+B a second time to toggle off the bold. Let's take a look at using the various text formatting commands that Word provides.

Formatting Text

The easiest way to change a number of the commonly used font attributes (whether you are typing new text or working with selected text) is to take advantage of the formatting commands in the Font group of the Ribbon's Home tab. This group includes the Font, Font Size, Bold, Italic, Strikethrough, Subscript, Superscript, Text Highlight Color, and Font Color commands, which are very straightforward in how they are used. The great thing about drop-down lists such as Font, Font Size, Underline, and Font Color are that you can preview the formatting before you apply it to your selected text (this is called Live Preview). Just point at one of the choices, such as a particular size on the Font Size list, for example, and the size change will be previewed directly on the selected text.

Some of the Font group commands warrant additional discussion. The list that follows provides a brief description of these commands:

- **Text Effects:** This new addition to the Font group provides text effects such as Glow, Shadow, Bevel, and Outline (see Figure 6.9).

- **Grow Font:** This command grows the font by one increment (to the next preset). This means that if the font is currently 18 point and the next increment on the Font Size list is 20 point, you will increase the font size from 18 point to 20 point.

- **Shrink Font:** This command shrinks the font one increment (goes down one preset). It is the antithesis of the Grow Font command.

- **Change Case:** This command provides a drop-down list that allows you to change the selected text to sentence case, lowercase, or uppercase. It also provides you with the ability to capitalize each word in the selection or toggle the case of the text.

- **Clear Formatting:** This command clears all the formatting on the selected text. This includes font-formatting attributes and paragraph-formatting attributes. This command also removes a style from the selected text.

Obviously, these commands are easy to use when you are formatting text that already exists and has been selected. Using these commands as you type might slow you down quite a bit. Table 6.4 provides some of the most often used font-formatting shortcut key combinations.

Table 6.4 Font Formatting Keyboard Shortcuts

Attribute	Shortcut Keys
Bold	Ctrl+B
Italic	Ctrl+I
Underline	Ctrl+U
Double underline	Ctrl+Shift+D
Small Caps	Ctrl+ Shift+K
Subscript	Ctrl+equal sign (=)

Attribute	Shortcut Keys
Superscript	Ctrl+Shift+plus sign (+)
Increase Size	Ctrl+Shift+>
Decrease Size	Ctrl+Shift+<
Toggle Case	Shift+F3
Clear Formatting	Ctrl+spacebar

Figure 6.9
New Text Effects provide interest to your documents.

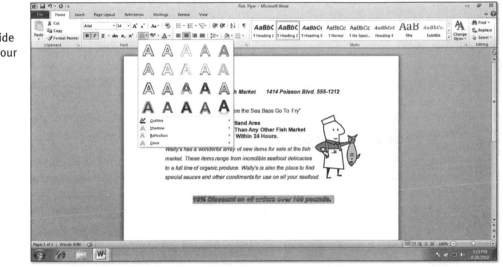

Although not all inclusive in terms of font-formatting options, these keyboard shortcuts provide you with the ability to quickly toggle a font format attribute on and off. For example, you can press Ctrl+I, type your italicized text, and then press Ctrl+I again to toggle italics off.

The Mini Toolbar

When you select text in a document, you will find that a transparent floating toolbar appears near the selected text. This is the Mini Toolbar. It provides quick access to a number of the font-formatting commands (and some paragraph-formatting commands such as Center and Indent). Figure 6.10 shows the Mini Toolbar with the Font Color list selected.

To use the Mini Toolbar, move the mouse onto it immediately upon its appearance near your selected text. You select commands from the Mini Toolbar as you do any of the commands that you work with on the Ribbon's Home tab.

tip

You can copy and then paste font and paragraph formatting attributes from one paragraph in a document to another (or to more than one paragraph). Select the text that has the formatting attributes you want to copy. Then click the Format Painter on the Clipboard group of the Ribbon's Home tab. You can click on a paragraph to paste the formatting or use the Format Painter mouse pointer to select text, which then has the formatting copied to it. To apply the copied formatting multiple times, double-click the Format Painter initially and use it as needed. When finished click the Format Painter again to turn the tool off.

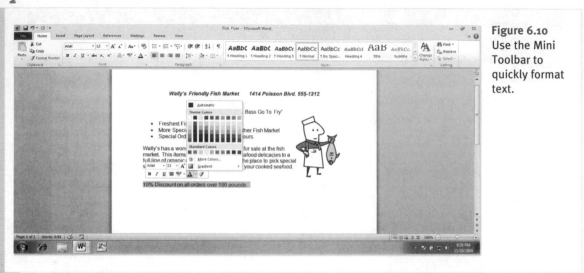

Figure 6.10
Use the Mini Toolbar to quickly format text.

The Font Dialog Box

Although the Font Group on the Ribbon's Home tab and the Mini Toolbar provide you with most of the font-formatting attributes that you will need, the one place that provides access to all the font attributes and a number of other advanced character settings is the Font dialog box. To open the Font Dialog box, click the dialog box launcher (on the right side of the Paragraph group on the Home tab).

The Font dialog box has two tabs: Font and Advanced. The Font tab provides access to the font, font style (bold, italic, and so forth) and font effects. Text effects can also be accessed from the Font tab. Select a font attribute and it will be applied to selected text in the document.

The Advanced tab of the Font dialog box allows you to control features related to text spacing and Open Type features. First the Character Spacing settings:

- **Scale:** This setting allows you to stretch or condense the text (horizontally). For example, a scale setting of 200% would stretch out the font characters making them larger. A scale setting of less than 100% would compress the characters.

- **Spacing:** This setting controls the distance between the characters. Expanded increases the space between the characters and condensed compresses the spacing.

- **Position:** This setting enables you to raise or lower the selected characters from the text's baseline position.

- **Kerning:** This setting allows you to compress the distance between characters (meaning the space between the characters). You specify a baseline font size and all fonts of that size (and above will be kerned.

The ligature-related features provided by the Advanced tab of the Font dialog box are new to Word 2010 (and the Open Type font family used by Microsoft products). A ligature is a combination of two adjacent characters by a common element. For example the letters f and i would be combined as a ligature as shown in Figure 6.11.

Figure 6.11
Word 2010 supports ligatures.

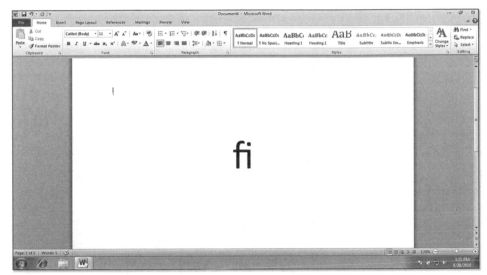

Not all font families support ligatures. So, although this feature shows improvement in how you can manipulate fonts in Word 2010, don't expect to get a lot of mileage out of it.

Working with Paragraph Formatting

Paragraph formatting encompasses a number of formatting attributes that we are all familiar with, including alignment (think of center and align text left), line spacing (single spaced versus double spaced), tabs, and indents. However, there are other settings related to how paragraphs are broken between lines and pages (such as widow/orphan control) that are often ignored but still need to play a part in this discussion of paragraph formatting.

As discussed earlier in this chapter, Word sees a paragraph as any text block (or blank line or lines) that is preceded and followed by a paragraph mark (meaning you pressed Enter before the paragraph and after the paragraph). Each paragraph can be assigned different paragraph attribute settings such as center or indent. Each paragraph can also have different tab settings.

You can access all the paragraph settings by using the Paragraph dialog box, which you can open via the Paragraph command in the Paragraph group (on the Home tab of the Ribbon). Settings such as alignment and indentation are available on the Indents and Spacing tab, as shown in Figure 6.12. Widow/Orphan control and other break and formatting options are available on the Line and Page Breaks tab.

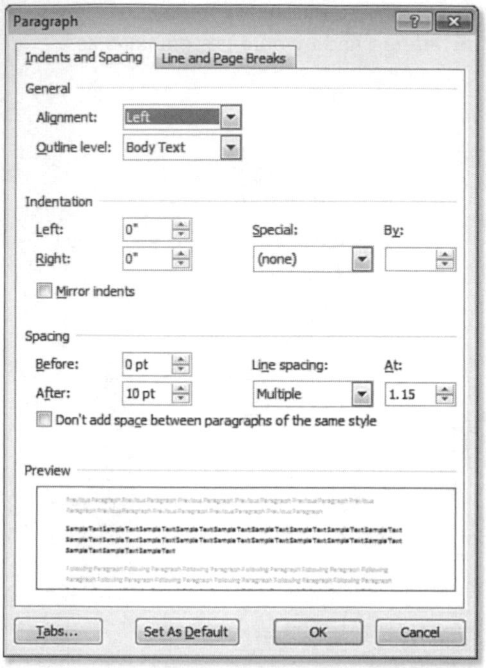

Figure 6.12
All paragraph-formatting options can be accessed in the Formatting dialog box.

All you need to do to apply paragraph formatting to a single paragraph is to make sure that the insertion point is in the paragraph. If you want to format multiple paragraphs, you must select those paragraphs. Let's look at the various formatting attributes related to paragraphs. We also look at how you can view the formatting present in a document, and how you can copy formatting attributes from paragraph to paragraph.

tip

You can change font settings in the Font dialog box and make them the default settings for Word (meaning you are changing the Normal template). After you select the various font attributes you want to use by default, click the Set as Default button.

Setting Paragraph Alignment

A basic formatting attribute of every paragraph, whether it is a 20-line paragraph or a single-line heading, relates to how that paragraph is aligned on the page in relation to the left and right margins. By default all text uses the Align Text Left setting, which is characterized by text that is straight or unvarying on the left margin but has a ragged right-edged margin.

Paragraph alignment that varies from the norm of left alignment can serve to set elements of a document apart from other document elements, such as a centered heading. You can also use alignment to provide a document page with a look of uniformity, such as a letter or resume that uses justification on all paragraphs. The list that follows provides a brief explanation of each of the paragraph alignment possibilities.

- **Align Text Left:** The default placement for normal text, aligned on the left.

- **Align Text Right:** Text is aligned at the right margin and text lines show a ragged left edge.

- **Center:** Text is centered between the left and right margins of the page (with both margins having irregular edges).

- **Justify:** Text is spaced across each line so that both the left and the right margins are straight-edged and uniform (often used in printed publications such as daily newspapers).

The fastest way to change the alignment of a single paragraph, or a number of selected paragraphs, is to use the alignment commands provided by the Paragraph group of the Ribbon's Home tab. For example, to center a heading, click on the heading and then click Center in the Paragraph group. Alignment can also be controlled using the Alignment drop-down box on the Indents and Spacing tab of the Paragraph dialog box.

 tip

You can also set the alignment for a new line of text using Word's Click and Type feature. As you move the mouse I-beam from left to right on the page, the I-beam becomes an indent pointer, and then a center point, and then a justify right pointer. Double-click the mouse to place the insertion point horizontally on the line based on the current mouse alignment pointer.

 tip

You can also set the spacing before and after a paragraph using the spinner boxes on the Spacing portion of the Paragraph group found on the Ribbon's Page Layout tab.

Changing Line Spacing

Line spacing is the vertical space between each line of text in the paragraph. The default line spacing is multiple 1.5 (the actual spacing depends on the height of the font you are using). Line spacing options can be controlled using the Line Spacing command, which is part of the Paragraph group on the Ribbon's Home tab. Click Line Spacing and then select one of the line-spacing options such as 1.0, 2.0, 3.0, and so forth.

If you want to set custom line-spacing settings, you can set those in the Paragraph dialog box in the Spacing pane of the Indents and Spacing tab. The Before and After spinner boxes enable you to set spacing before and after a particular paragraph or paragraphs. This is particularly useful for headings or other special text items. Be advised that the After setting of a paragraph is added to the paragraph that follows, and so if you have set a Before setting for the next paragraph the space between the paragraphs will actually be the same as the After setting for the current paragraph and any Before setting from the next paragraph.

You can also control the line spacing for paragraphs using the Line spacing drop-down list. It provides the following options:

- **Single**—Spacing accommodates the largest font size found on the lines and adds a small amount of whitespace (depending on the font used) between lines.

- **1.5**—The line spacing is 1 and 1/2 times greater than single spacing.

- **Double**—Twice the size of single-line spacing.

- **At Least**—(The default setting) Line spacing adjusts to accommodate the largest font on the line and special items, such as graphics.

- **Exactly**—All lines are equally spaced, and special font sizes or items such as graphics are not accommodated. These items, if larger than the setting used here, appear cut off in the text. You can still accommodate these items by using the Multiple box described next to shift all the text lines to a higher spacing percentage that accommodates special items.

- **Multiple**—You specify the line spacing by a particular percentage. This feature is used in conjunction with the Exactly option to set a line-spacing percentage that accommodates special font sizes or graphics found in the document. For example, if you want to decrease the line spacing by 20%, you enter the number 0.8. To increase the line spacing by 50%, you enter 1.5.

 tip

If you are using two different fonts in a document, you might find that setting line spacing to Exactly (and a specific point size) in the Paragraph dialog box provides you with a more uniform look in the document.

Some of the setting options that you select from the Line Spacing list are influenced by the point size you enter in the At box (this applies only when you have selected At Least, Exactly, or Multiple). Use the click arrows to increase or decrease the point size of the line spacing. The Preview pane provides you with an overview of how the line spacing that you set will actually look on the paragraph or paragraphs affected by the line settings.

Setting Line and Page Breaks

The Paragraph dialog box also provides you with control over how line and page breaks affect a paragraph or paragraphs. Figure 6.13 shows the Line and Page breaks tab of the Paragraph dialog box.

By default, Widow/Orphan control is set (note the selected check box for Widow/Orphan control in Figure 6.13). A widow is the last line of a paragraph that appears by itself at the top of a page and an orphan is the first line of a paragraph left by itself at the bottom of the page. Widow/Orphan control keeps the last line or first line of a paragraph from printing on the next or previous page, respectively. The Keep Line Together option keeps the entire paragraph together on a page, and the Page Break Before option forces Word to start the paragraph on a new page if it can't keep it all on the previous page.

The Line and Page Breaks also provide formatting exception settings that you can apply to your paragraphs. Word can assign line numbers to all the lines in a document (the line numbers setting is in the Page Setup group of the Ribbon's Page Layout tab). If you are using line numbering, you can use the Suppress Line Numbers formatting exception if you want to suppress line numbers for specific paragraphs in a document.

Word does not hyphenate words in paragraphs automatically; it actually wraps them to the next line. In cases where you have turned on hyphenation (the Hyphenation command is on the Page Setup group on the Ribbon's Page Layout tab), you can use the Don't Hyphenate check box on the Line Page Breaks tab to turn off the hyphenation on a paragraph or paragraphs.

Figure 6.13
The Line and Page Beaks tab.

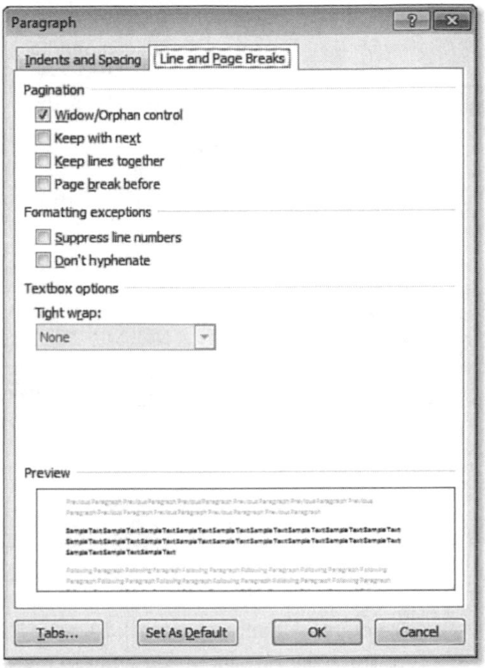

Setting Indents

You can use indents to offset paragraphs (including individual lines such as headings) from both the left and the right margins. By default, indents are set every half inch (.5). The Increase Indent command is in the Paragraph group of the Ribbon's Home tab. Each time you click Increase Indent, you are indenting the paragraph another half inch. To decrease the indent, use the Decrease Indent command.

You can also use the ruler to set the indent for a paragraph. The ruler has both a left indent and a right indent marker. It also has a first line indent marker and a hanging indent marker. These two markers are stacked on the top of the left indent marker, but you can move them independently. Figure 6.14 shows the different ruler indent markers.

You can drag the left indent marker or the right indent marker as needed to indent the left or right of a paragraph, respectively. You can also create hanging indents by using the indent markers. Hanging indents are created by separating the first line indent marker from the left indent marker on the ruler.

> **tip**
>
> To view the ruler (both the horizontal and vertical rulers) click the Ruler check box in the Show group of the Ribbon's View tab.

> **tip**
>
> You can also set the left and right indent for a paragraph using the Indent settings on the Paragraph group of the Ribbon's Page Layout tab.

First Line Indent marker

Left Indent marker

Right Indent marker

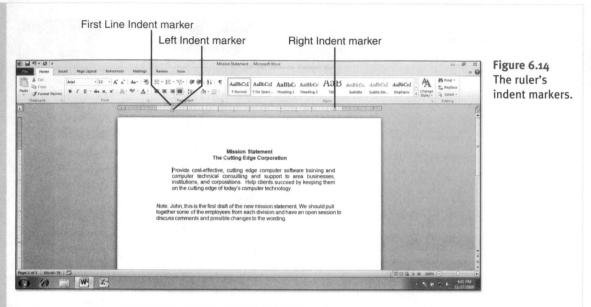

Figure 6.14
The ruler's indent markers.

To create a hanging indent, drag the left indent marker (using the square bottom of the marker) to the position where you want to indent the second and subsequent lines of the paragraph. Then drag the first line indent marker (drag it by the top of the marker) back to the position where you want the first line to begin. Hanging indents are useful in cases where you want to subordinate the remainder of a paragraph under the first line of the paragraph, such as job descriptions in resumes.

Working with Tabs

You can use tabs to align text in your documents. We typically think of the tab as a way to offset the first sentence of a paragraph (one tab stop from the left margin) from the rest of a paragraph. Word actually provides different types of tabs that you can use as a way to align items in much the same way (at least visually) that you align items in a table.

By default, Word provides a tab stop every half inch. Every time you press the Tab key on the keyboard, you offset the text line from the left margin one tab stop. You can set your own tab stops using the Tabs dialog box or the ruler. You open the Tabs dialog box from the Paragraph dialog box (click the Open Dialog Box button in the Paragraph group). Figure 6.15 shows the Tabs dialog box.

You can change the default tab stops from .5 to any increment using the Default Tab Stops spinner box. To create a new tab, enter a tab stop position (in inches) and then select the alignment for the new tab (Left, Center, Right, and so on). You can also select one of the Leader options for your tab, such as Dot Leader (2). When you have finished setting the tab's options, click Set to create the tab. You can then create the process as needed.

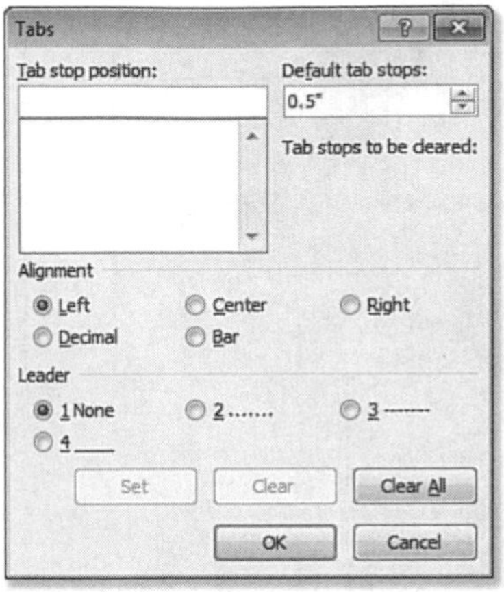

Figure 6.15
The Tabs dialog box.

Word actually provides different tab types and the following list provides a brief description of each:

- **Left Tab**: Aligns the beginning of the text line at the tab stop

- **Center Tab**: Enters the text line at the tab stop

- **Right Tab**: Right-aligns the text line at the tab stop

- **Decimal Tab**: Lines up numerical entries at their decimal point

- **Bar Tab**: Inserts a vertical bar at the tab stop (it doesn't actually align text)

Because it provides a more visual medium for setting tabs, the ruler is your best bet for quickly setting tabs and using the different types of tabs that Word offers. To set a tab on the ruler, click the Tab button on the far left of the ruler to select the tab type (Left, Center, Right, and so on). Each time you click the Tab button, you cycle to the next tab type. If you go past the type of tab you want to set, keep clicking until the tab type appears on the Tab button.

After you have the appropriate tab type selected on the Tab button, place the mouse pointer on the ruler where you want the tab and click to place it. If you need to adjust the position of a tab, drag it to a new position on the ruler. Figure 6.16 shows the different tab stop types and how they actually align text at the tab stop.

In cases where you want to remove a tab from the ruler, drag it off the ruler and it is cleared. You can also clear a tab or all your tab settings in the Tabs dialog box.

Revealing Format Settings

A feature that you will find useful when you are working with a lot of manually assigned font and paragraph formatting attributes is the Reveal Formatting task pane. This feature allows you to quickly review the font and paragraph formatting that you have assigned to your text.

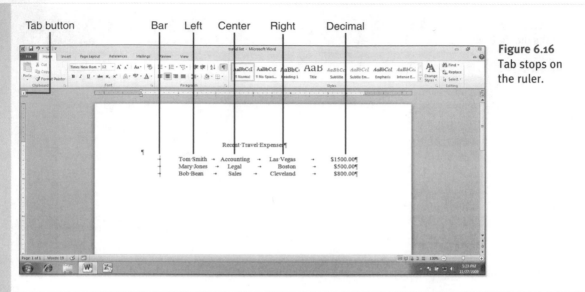

Figure 6.16
Tab stops on
the ruler.

To open the Reveal Formatting task pane, press Shift+F1. To view the font and paragraph formatting in a particular paragraph, click on that paragraph (or select text as needed).

For more detail about the source of the formatting that has been assigned to test, click the Distinguish Style Source check box in the Options area of the Reveal Formatting task pane (see Figure 6.17).

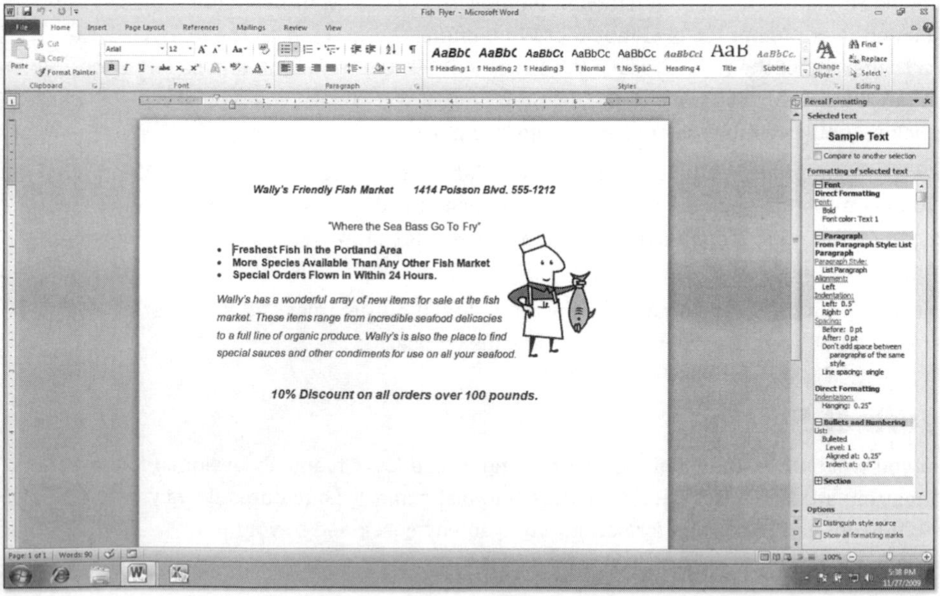

Figure 6.17
The Reveal
Formatting task
pane.

The Reveal Formatting task pane also has a Show All Formatting Marks check box. You can select it to view paragraph marks, spaces, and tabs in the document.

Page Layout: Margins and Page Options

The standard page layout options are primarily related to the document margins, page orientation, and paper size. There are other page setup options, such as the paper source settings, which are more closely associated with how you print your documents and so we will forgo that discussion until the next session. Layout settings are control issues related to sections and headers and footers, so we will discuss that layout options when we discuss these features in the book.

Margins control the amount of whitespace of the page. There are four margins: top, bottom, left, and right. By default each of these margins is set to one inch (1). You can change any of the margin settings for your document as needed. You can also change the margins for just a portion of a document. Select the text in the document and then change the margins. The changes will affect only the selected text.

> **◉ tip**
>
> You can have Word mark formatting inconsistencies the same way it marks spelling errors and grammar problems. On the File tab, open Options and then click Advanced. Under Editing Options, select the Keep Track of Formatting check box and the Mark Formatting Inconsistencies box. Now Word marks formatting inconsistencies with a wavy blue line.

Changing Margins

To change the margins for the document or selected text, use the Margins command in the Page Layout group of the Ribbon's Page Layout tab. You can select from one of the margin presets provided or you can select Custom Margins. This opens the Page Setup dialog box as shown in Figure 6.18.

The Page Setup dialog box enables you to set each of the margins. Use the appropriate spinner box or type a new margin setting.

> **◉ note**
>
> A document divided into sections can potentially have different margin settings for each section. Sections are discussed in Chapter 8.

In cases where you are creating a special document, such as a document with mirror margins or a book fold document, you can change the multiple pages setting in the Pages area of the Page Setup dialog box so that your margins accommodate that type of document. For example, if you select mirror margins (the margins on the facing pages will be mirrored) in the Multiple pages drop-down list, you have Top, Bottom, Inside, and Outside margins. You also set a gutter. The gutter provides extra space between the inside margin and the edge of the page. This will help accommodate binding or punch holes if you are going to bind your document in a three-ring notebook.

> **▲ caution**
>
> Be advised that your default printer defines the minimum (and the maximum) margins for a page. If you set margins less than the minimum, a dialog box appears when you close the Page Setup dialog box letting you know that your margins are outside the printable area of the page. Click Fix to return to the dialog box and fix the margins.

In cases where you want to change only the document margins forward in the document from where you parked the insertion point, you can select From This Point Forward in the Apply To drop down box (this actually creates a new section in the document). When you have completed your changes to the margin settings, click OK to return to the document.

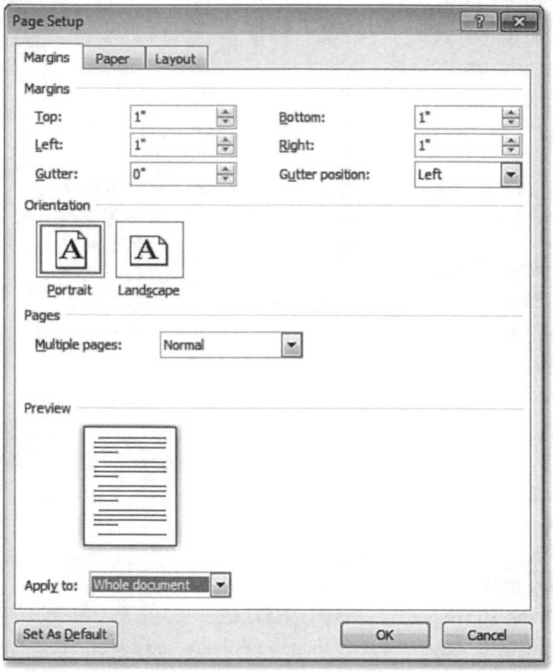

Figure 6.18
The Page Setup dialog box.

Changing Page Orientation and Paper Size

The default page orientation in Word is portrait. The default page size (in the U.S.) is Letter (8.5 by 11). You can change both the page orientation and the page size as needed.

To change the page orientation click Orientation in the Page Setup group of the Page Layout tab. Then select Portrait or Landscape as needed. You can also change the page orientation on the Margins tab of the Page Setup dialog box.

The Size command in the Page Setup group of the Page Layout tab provides a list of paper sizes such as Letter, Legal, Executive, and so on. You can select from the list or you can click More Paper Sizes. This opens the Paper tab of the Page Setup dialog box. This allows you to select from a list of preset paper sizes. More importantly it allows you to set the paper size to Custom Size and then set your width and height for the paper.

> **tip**
>
> You can view your document margins in the Print layout and Full Screen Reading views. You can also see the margins in Print Preview. To add Print Preview to the Quick Access Toolbar, select the drop-down menu on the right of the Quick Access Toolbar and select Print Preview.

Inserting Page Breaks

As you type your document, Word automatically starts a new page when you fill the current page with text or other document items (such as tables, clipart, and so on). You can insert a page break in your document as needed. Page breaks can be inserted from the Page Break command on the Insert tab of the Ribbon (in the Pages group). You can also insert page breaks from the Break list in the Page Setup group on the Page Layout tab).

When you want to be able to visually differentiate between the page breaks that Word has placed in the document and the page breaks you have inserted, select the Show/Hide command (on the Home tab) and then go to the Draft view using the view icons along the bottom right of the status bar.

Page breaks that you insert show a dotted line and the words Page Break. You can select your inserted page break and then delete them if needed.

> **tip**
> The quickest way to insert a new page break is from the keyboard: Ctrl+Enter.

> **tip**
> Type a range of page numbers (for example 1–4,6) below the Print All Pages box. This will change the setting to Print Custom Range and will only print the pages you have specified.

Printing Documents

Word 2010 provides a number of improvements in controlling what actually comes out of your printer when compared to the previous version of Word. The new Backstage View Print page allows you to quickly select a printer, specify what you want to print, and even change how pages are printed. You can even change page orientation, page size, and margins. The Print Backstage also provides a print preview of the page in the document, and if you use the Zoom slider to zoom out, you can view multiple pages. Figure 6.19 shows the Print Backstage.

Figure 6.19
The Print Backstage view.

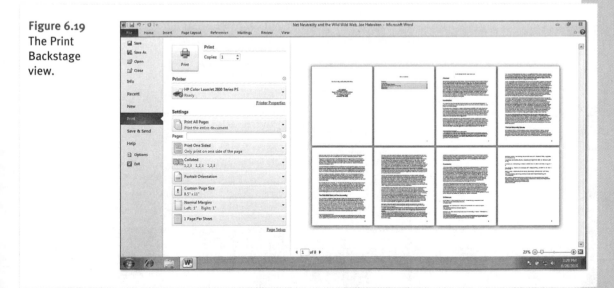

To send the document to the printer, you click the Print button. If you need to change the number of copies, you can use the Copies spinner box. Before printing, you might want to examine some of the possibilities that the new Print Backstage view provides. A number of print-related settings are listed under the Settings area. These options are as follows:

- **Selecting what to print:** By default, Print All Pages is selected and the entire document prints. You can select other options from the list such as Print Selection and Print Current Page. You can also choose to have certain lists related to the document's properties printed, such as styles, autotext entries, and a list of customized shortcut keys.

- **Printing One or Two Sided:** This option allows you to set up the print job to print one sided or print on both sides. You can also choose to manually print on both sides, which allows you to flip the paper over and reload it in the printer.

- **Collated or Uncollated:** You can choose to have your printout collated or uncollated using this setting.

- **Paper Size:** You can change the paper size before printing. Remember that this repaginates the document.

- **Margins:** You can change the margins before printing.

- **Pages per Sheet:** You can select how many pages are printed per page. You can also have the document pages scale to the paper size.

In previewing the document, you can use the Zoom slider on the right-lower portion of the screen. A Zoom to Page button will zoom you back to a single-page view if you have been previewing multiple pages.

7

ENHANCING WORD DOCUMENTS

Word provides a number of features that enable you to enhance your documents. In this chapter we take a look at a number of different possibilities for making your documents look more interesting and more professional. We begin with a look at bulleted and numbered lists and also take a look at formatting options such as themes and styles.

This chapter also explores the use of headers and footers in documents and discusses page numbering options. We also discuss enhancing your Word documents with pictures, clip art, and charts. This chapter includes a look at different ways to view a document and how to use building blocks and document review tools including the Spelling feature and the Thesaurus.

Creating Better Documents

When you have a good feel for the typical features used to create, save, and print documents, you will want to explore features that enable you to enhance your documents. You will also want to be able to enhance your approach to creating documents and find ways of making your overall use of Word more productive both in the kinds of documents that you create and the amount of time you expend creating those documents.

Word provides a number of features that enable you to create more interesting looking documents: features such as bulleted and numbered lists, borders, shading, and themes. There are also features and tools such as quick parts and styles that allow you to create documents more efficiently and help you create more uniform documents.

Additionally, there are tools that enable you to root out the errors in a document and there are tools that make it possible for you to enhance the actual content of the document. These tools include the review tools, such as spelling and grammar, which help you detect errors, and the Research pane and thesaurus, which enable you to improve the content of the document.

Creating Bulleted and Numbered Lists

Numbered and bulleted lists emphasize text and make it stand out from other text on a document page. Bulleted lists work best when you want to separate and highlight items from other text, but the items in the list don't have a particular order or hierarchy. Numbered lists work well in cases where you are detailing a procedure in which each step is important and the order of the steps is important in terms of accomplishing a particular task.

Both bullets and numbers can be quickly assigned to existing lists or you can toggle on bullets or numbering and create your list as you type. You have complete control over the bullet type (using special characters or other graphics) used in a bulleted list and the alignment of the text lines in the list. You can also format numbered lists by specifying the numbering format, including where the numbering starts, and the numbered items' text alignment.

You will find the commands for bullets, numbering, and multilevel lists in the Paragraph group of the Ribbon's Home tab. Each command also provides you with a drop-down list that enables you to fine-tune the formatting related to the particular list type (bullets versus numbers) that you select.

Bulleted Lists

Whether you are formatting an existing list that you have selected or are going to type the bulleted list on the fly, all you have to do is select Bullets in the Paragraph.

If you would like to select the bullet character used in the list, click the arrow next to the Bullet command to choose one of the bullet characters provided by either the Recently Used Bullets list or the Bullet library. When you are changing the bullet for a selected, existing bulleted list, place the mouse on any of the bullets to preview that bullet on the list. Figure 7.1 shows the Bullet library and the selected bullet is previewed in the document.

> **tip**
>
> You can also turn on bulleting using the Mini Toolbar, which appears when you select text (such as several lines of text in a list). Click the Bullets icon on the Mini Toolbar group of the Home tab. This formats the existing list as a bulleted list or turns on the bullets so that each paragraph you add to the list is bulleted.

In cases where you want to use a bullet type not provided in the library, select the Bullets command arrow and then click Define New Bullet. The Define New Bullet dialog box opens. It provides you with the ability to select a new bullet character from available symbols. You can also ramp up the look of your bullets by using bullet pictures (including many available on Office.com). You can also import your own pictures to use as bullets. Figure 7.2 shows the Define New Bullet dialog box.

To select a new bullet character from the various symbols installed on your computer as part of your available fonts, click the Symbol button in the Define New Bullet dialog box. The Symbol dialog box provides a Font drop-down box that allows you to select the font or character set from which you will select the new bullet character. After you select the new bullet, click OK to return to the Define New Bullet dialog box.

The Define New Bullet dialog box also enables you to select the alignment for the bullet (Left, Centered, Right) and makes it possible you to select the font family used to render the bullet (by default, the bullet uses your default font).

Figure 7.1
Change the
bullet for the
selected list.

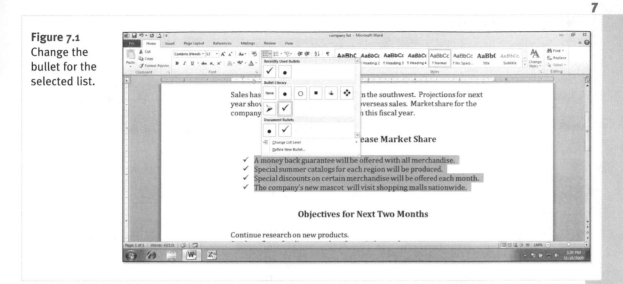

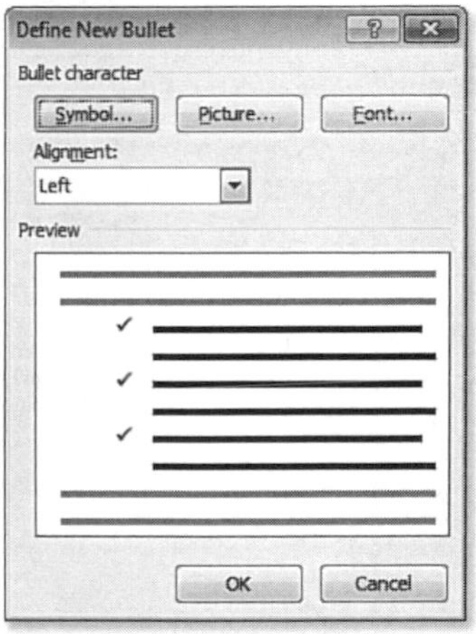

Figure 7.2
Define your own bullets for your lists.

Although we don't typically think of bulleted lists as having different levels, you can change the list level for a bulleted item (or items) in a list. To change the list level, click the Bullets command arrow, point at the Change List Level command, and then select a list level from the list level presets provided (nine list levels are provided).

Numbered Lists

Numbered lists can be created in your document as you type or you can format an existing list as numbered. You can also take advantage of a variety of different number formats. To start numbering or to format a selected list, click the Numbering command (in the Paragraph group on the Ribbon's Home tab). Doing so provides you with a list using the default numbering format (1,2,3) and starting at the number 1.

You can use the Numbering command arrow to access different number formats in the Numbering library (such as the Roman numeral format). It also provides you with the ability to change the list level for an item or items.

In situations where the number formats in the Numbering Library don't meet your needs, you can define your own number format. Use Define New Number Format (on the Numbering command arrow menu) to open the Define New Number Format dialog box (see Figure 7.3).

 tip

Some of the more interesting bullet characters are in the Wingdings and Webdings font groups. You can access these and other installed font groups from the Font drop-down box in the Symbol dialog box.

tip

You can quickly change a numbered list to a multilevel list by changing the list level for items in the numbered list.

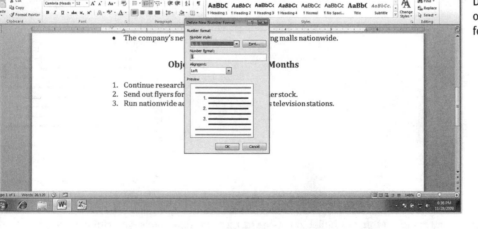

Figure 7.3
Define your own number formats.

In the Define New Number Format dialog box, you can set the number style, the number format, and the alignment of the number (Left, Centered, Right). You can also select the font used for the numbers.

If you want to change the starting number of the list, you can open the Set Numbering Value dialog box (click Set Numbering Value on the Numbering menu). This dialog box also provides you with the option of starting a new list (the default) or continuing the numbering from a previous list. You can also continue from a previous list but set an advance value, which allows you to skip numbers.

Multilevel Lists

You can create outlines or lists that require different levels by using the Multilevel List command in the Paragraph group on the Ribbon's Home tab. As with other lists, you can format selected existing text or start a new list. As you type a new list, use the tab to demote an item to the next lower level or Shift+Tab to demote an item. You can also change the level of a list item by using Change List Level command and selecting a level from the provided list. Click the Multilevel List command arrow to access this option.

> *For more information about Outline view, see "Changing the Document Display," page 185.*

> **note**
>
> Multilevel lists are fine for simple outlines. However, when you need to use outlining as a more advanced organizational tool in complex documents, you will want to use the Outline view. It provides tools for designating headings, promoting and demoting paragraphs, and expanding and collapsing levels.

To select the format for the multilevel list, click the Multilevel List command arrow and select a format from the List library. If you need a custom list format, select the Define New Multilevel List command. This opens the Define New Multilevel List dialog box as shown in Figure 7.4

Figure 7.4
Set the parameters for a new multilevel list.

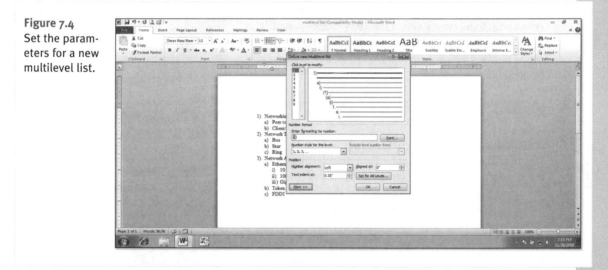

You can modify each level including the number formatting, number style, and the position for the level. If you click the More button, you can also select other options such as the start number for the level, the level to be shown in the gallery, and whether the number should be followed with a specific character such as a tab, space, or nothing (yes, nothing is a choice).

Working with Borders and Shading

Font-formatting attributes such as increasing the font size, and bold, italics, and underlining are often used to emphasize text in a document (as are changes in font size). In cases where you want draw attention to a certain paragraph or heading but don't want to rely on font or paragraph formatting attributes (such as paragraph alignment), you can take advantage of borders and shading. Borders and shading provide a simple way to add some color and graphical elements to a special document such as a flyer or newsletter.

You can place a border around any text paragraph or a number of selected paragraphs. To place a border around a single paragraph, make sure that the insertion point is in that paragraph. If you want to put a border around several paragraphs, select them.

To select one of the border options for the paragraph (or paragraphs), select the Borders and Shading command in the Paragraph group of the Ribbon's Home tab. The border list provides many border options, including Bottom Border, Left Border, and Outside Borders (designed for use on tables). Select an option and the borders are applied to your text.

Oddly enough, the Borders and Shading drop-down list does not directly provide any options for placing shading behind the text that you will place the border around. You apply the shading using the Shading command in the Paragraph group. When you click the Shading command arrow, a palette of theme colors will be provided (you can also choose from a list of standard colors). To custom select additional colors, select the More Colors option. This opens the Colors dialog box where you can select standard colors or mix your own custom colors (on the Standard and Custom tabs, respectively).

 To learn more about themes, read "Formatting with Themes," page 171.

If you want greater control over the borders (and shading) you assign to document paragraphs, including settings such as the border's line style, line width, and line color, you can open the Borders and Shading dialog box as shown in Figure 7.5. Select Borders and Shading on the Borders and Shading drop-down list (click the arrow next to Borders and Shading in the Paragraph group).

The Borders tab of the dialog box gives you control over the style and color of the line and provides settings that allow you to include a shadow or 3D effect on the border. The Page Border dialog box allows you to place a border around the entire page (or pages), which we discuss in a moment. The Shading tab provides you with the ability to select a fill color and an optional pattern style for the paragraph shading.

---

tip

When you are editing a multilevel list, you can use the Decrease Indent and Promote Indent commands on the Paragraph group to demote and promote items, respectively.

---

tip

The Borders and Shading drop-down list also provides you with the ability to insert a horizontal line at the insertion point or draw a table.

---

note

On the Custom tab of the Colors dialog box, you can actually specify a color by its RGB code. This is particularly useful if you want to make sure that you are consistently using the same color for different document elements (say paragraph shading and font color). For example, to make sure that I am using steel blue as my shading color, I would enter the Red Blue Green code of 70–130–180. A number of websites provide the RGB color codes; just do a Bing or Google search.

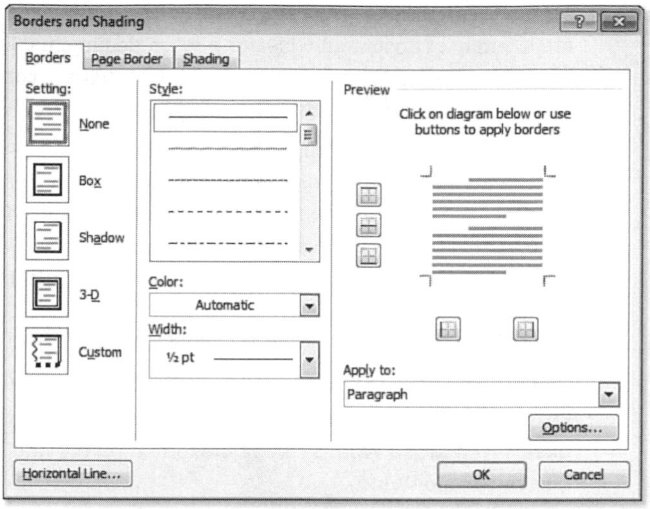

Figure 7.5
The Borders and Shading dialog box.

You can also place a border on the pages of your document. This can be accomplished using the Page Border tab of the Borders and Shading dialog box. It provides you with setting options that are very similar to those provided for paragraph borders such as shadow and 3D effects and the ability to control the line style, color, and width. Page borders can also include repeating art elements (such as repeating palm trees or gingerbread men). You select these border elements by using the Art drop-down list.

Word also provides you with the ability to assign a page background color to a page (or pages). Select the Page Color command arrow on the Page Background group of the Ribbon's Page Layout tab. This opens the color palette where you can choose from theme colors or standard colors, or open the Color dialog box to choose from the colors or mix your own. Fill effects such as gradients, textures, patterns, and pictures can be configured for your page background by selecting Fill Effects from the Page Color palette. This opens the Fill Effects dialog box.

> **tip**
> You can open the Page Border tab of the Borders and Shading dialog box directly from the Page Borders command on the Page Background group of the Ribbon's Page Layout tab.

Formatting with Themes

Providing a document with a uniform look when you are working with different colors (including font, border, and shading colors), different fonts, and text effects can be somewhat difficult. And there might be some situations where you want the color and font schemes used in a Word document to match an accompanying Excel worksheet or PowerPoint presentation. Keeping a document's appearance consistent, particularly in situations where you have used some special formatting attributes, is best done using themes. A theme is a collection of colors, fonts, and text effects. The Themes gallery provides many different themes, and you can modify existing themes to create your own themes.

Themes are consistent across the Microsoft Office applications such as Word, Excel, and PowerPoint. This allows you to create a family of documents (meaning Word documents, Excel worksheets, and PowerPoint presentations) that are consistent in terms of the overall look.

Each Word template (such as the Normal template) has a specific default theme. You can change that default theme to any of the built-in themes, and you can also browse for themes that you have created (they are typically saved to the Documents Themes folder: Microsoft/ Templates/Document Themes folder on your computer).

> **note**
>
> Office 2007 introduced themes in Word and Excel. Themes have actually been available in PowerPoint in versions prior to 2007.

➥ *See Chapter 6, "Using Templates," for more about templates.*

To take advantage of themes, you need to be working with a document in one of the Word 2007–2010 file XML-based file formats, such as .docx. Themes cannot be applied to documents that you have saved in the Word 972–003 file format (to provide backward compatibility with users of previous versions of Word).

To access the Theme settings, select the Ribbon's Page Layout tab. The commands for Theme selection and the selection of the theme settings, Color, Font, and Effects, reside in the Themes group. To change the current theme, select Themes and the Theme gallery opens (see Figure 7.6).

Figure 7.6
The Themes gallery.

Place the mouse pointer on a theme to preview how that theme will affect the text in your document. When you actually select a theme, the theme is applied to your document.

As already mentioned, the Themes group (on the Page Layout tab) includes three additional drop-down lists: Colors, Fonts, and Effects. These adjustable theme settings provide insight into how themes actually affect your document's text and overall look. Themes affect the color of text (headings and body text), the actual fonts used in the document, and the border lines and fill effects you might have used in the document (this is controlled by the Effects settings).

To modify the current theme, you use the Colors, Fonts, and Effects drop-down lists (as needed) to choose the theme settings for the current document. For example, to change the fonts used by the theme, click Fonts and then make a selection in the Fonts list as shown in Figure 7.7. As you move the mouse over the selections, they will be previewed in your document.

Figure 7.7
The Fonts list.

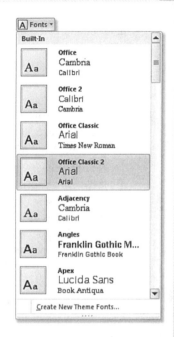

If you want to create your own theme, all you have to do is modify the existing document theme (or one of the themes provided in the Theme gallery). After you modify the theme, select the Themes command and then select Save Current Theme. The Save Current Theme dialog box opens. Supply a name for the new theme and then click the Save button. You can access your saved themes using the Browse for Themes command on the Themes gallery.

Themes will affect (actually override) the formatting attributes that make up styles used to format your document text, such as headings, titles, and the body text. A change in theme also affects styles that you have created for the document. Although we discuss how to create and manage styles later in this chapter, please be advised at this point that if you have spent a lot of time modifying built-in styles or have created your own styles in a document, changing the theme will affect these styles.

tip

You can also create your own theme color sets and font sets. Both the Colors list and Fonts list provide you with the option of naming and saving your color or font modifications. Use the Create New Theme Colors command or the Create New Theme Fonts command at the bottom of the Colors or Fonts list (respectively) to open a dialog box that allows you to set the color or font settings and then save the new set for use with your themes.

Creating Headers and Footers

It is common practice in business documents such as reports, manuals, or even some correspondences to place repeated text or even images (such as a company logo) at the top and/or bottom of each document page. And I'm probably safe in assuming that pretty much everyone has at one time or another had to create a multipage document that required page numbering on each page.

Headers and footers provide you with a way to include repeating information on each page of a document, such as a document title, the current date, or the page number. Headers and footers can also contain pictures, design elements, or even clip art. Text in a header or a footer can be formatted using the same formatting tools that you use for your text in the document itself.

note

Documents published either in print or online (such as journal articles, published essays, manuscripts, and so on) typically need to conform to a particular style manual (an example of an often used style manual is the *Chicago Manual of Style*). The manual provides guidelines on how headers and footers should be structured and what information should actually be placed in the headers and footer areas of the document.

The header resides at the top of a page and the footer resides at the bottom of a page. The header and footer areas are actually within the top and bottom margins of the document. Because the header and footer cannot grow beyond the limits of the margins (they can't be on unprintable portions of the page), larger headers and footers (meaning a header or footer with a number of text lines or a large image such as a logo) actually steal line space from the regular text portion of the page.

How you use headers and footers can depend greatly on the overall structure of your document. For example, let's say you have a report document with a title page. All the pages that follow the title page consist of the actual report details. It is common practice not to include on the title page of a report (or any document), headers and footers, things such as page numbers, the report title, or a draft number. So, you need different headers/footers on the first page (actually no header or footer) than those headers and footers that appear on the rest of the document pages. Word provides you with the ability to have different headers/footers on the first page of the document.

Another document structure issue that will affect headers and footers is a situation where you want to bind a document with facing pages (where you have printed on both sides of the pages). Bound documents often use different headers and footers on the odd and even pages of the document (take a look at this book as an example). Word has you covered when creating different odd and even page headers and footers.

One more point related to headers and footers: It is not uncommon, when working with more complex documents, to have different document parts that vary greatly in terms of layout, content, and purpose. For example, you could be working on a document that has a table of contents, the main body of the document, and then a bibliography or index. It would make sense to have different headers and footers for these very different parts of the document.

Documents can be divided into sections. Sections (which are discussed in the next chapter) provide you with the ability to set different page layout settings including headers and footers for each of the sections. So, because each section of the document can have its own set of headers and footers, you could provide the table of contents with its own headers/footers, the body of the document with its own headers/footers, and so on.

 See "Understanding Sections," in Chapter 8 for more about sections.

Creating Headers and Footers

The commands related to headers and footers are in the Header & Footer group on the Ribbon's Insert tab. The commands are Header, Footer, and Page Number. Let's look at headers and then footers.

To place a header in the header area, select the Header command. The Header gallery (shown in Figure 7.8) provides several different header styles, including a blank header. Header styles make it easy for you to insert your text into the header area. For example, the Annual Header style provides placeholder text for the document title and the year. It also provides a horizontal line, and the font and paragraph formatting for the header text. The Header gallery also provides the Edit Header and the Remove Header commands.

Figure 7.8
The Header gallery.

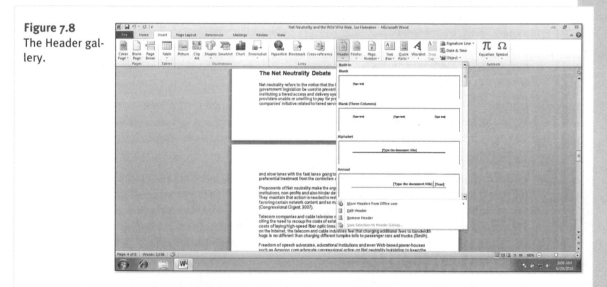

After you select one of the header options in the gallery, the Header area appears at the top of the current page. Replace the placeholder text with your own text. If you select the blank header, type and format your text as needed in the Header area.

Placing a footer in the Footer area is pretty much the same process as placing a header in the Header area. Select a footer style from the Footer gallery and once the insertion point appears in the Footer area, type and format your footer text as needed.

The Header and Footer Tools

When the insertion point is in the Header or the Footer area, the Ribbon takes on the form of the contextual Header & Footer Tools Design tab. This special Header and Footer toolkit contains the following command groups:

- **Header & Footer:** This group provides the Header, Footer, and Page Number commands. These are the same commands found in the Header & Footer group on the Ribbon's Insert tab. We have already discussed the Header and Footer commands (which place a header or footer). We will look at the Page Number command later in this section.

- **Insert:** This group enables you to insert items into the header and footer, including date and time information, quick parts, pictures, and clipart.

- **Navigation:** This group allows you to go to the header or the footer (in essence, switch between the header and footer); move to the previous or next header or footer; and control whether the current header or footer is linked to the previous header or footer in the document (in cases where you have multiple sections in the document and, therefore, multiple headers and footers).

- **Options:** This group provides the Different First Page, Different Odd & Even Pages, and the Show Document Text check boxes. To have different headers and footers on the first page of the document (different from the rest of the document), you would select the Different First Page check box.

- **Position:** This group allows you to set the distance for the header in relation to the top of the page and the footer from the bottom of the page (remember that this setting cannot place the header or footer into the unprintable portion of the margin, as dictated by your printer settings). This group also provides the Insert Alignment tab, which allows you to insert an alignment tab at the left, center, or right of the header or footer, and select a leader such as dot leader for the tab setting.

- **Close:** This group contains the Close Header and Footer command. It closes the Header or Footer area and returns the insertion point to your document text.

> ### 🌐 tip
> If you want to go old school with headers and footers, you can place the insertion point in the header or footer without using either the Header or Footer command (in the Header & Footer group). Make sure that you are in the Print Layout view and then double-click in the Header or Footer area (top or bottom margin of the page). You can then type the text for the header and footer and format the text as needed. Be advised that even the default header and footer settings include formatting: a center tab at 3.25 inches and a right tab at 6.5 inches.

When you are working with headers and footers, you will find that the use of these commands depends on the complexity of your document (such as the Different First Page and Different Odd & Even Pages commands), and the number of headers and footers in the document (such as a document with sections where you need to move from header to header or footer to footer using the Previous and Next commands).

In terms of what you actually place in your header and footer, you will find that the Insert group makes it easy for you to include information such as the current date or a picture such as a logo. This group also makes it extremely easy to create informational headers and footers quickly.

For example, if you need to insert your name, your company name, or other information that you have stored as an AutoText entry, you can click the Quick Parts command and then select from your AutoText entries. You can also use the Quick Parts command to access the Document Property list, which provides a list of the various document property fields available in the Document Property list. So, if you wanted to quickly insert the author name and the title of the document into the header or footer, you can select Author and then select Title from the Document Property list.

The Quick Parts command also opens the Building Blocks Organizer, which provides access to all default building blocks (which include added AutoText entries and added Quick Parts). The Building Blocks Organizer contains some building blocks specifically designed for headers, footers, and page numbering.

The Quick Parts command also provides access to the Field dialog box, which allows you to insert fields into your header or footer. We actually look more closely at fields (in relation to Word forms) in Chapter 9, "Managing Mailings and Forms." For now, I want to stress that some fields can be used to great effect in headers and footers. Figure 7.9 shows the Field dialog box.

Figure 7.9
The Field dialog box.

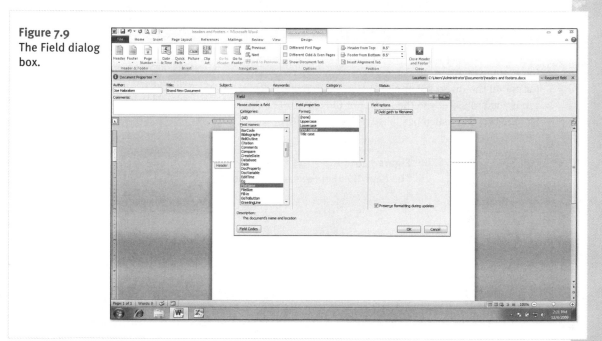

In terms of useful fields, you can insert the PrintDate and the SaveDate fields into a header or footer to add the date a file was last printed or saved. There are also fields that will insert the author, the create date, and even the edit time.

One of the most useful fields has to be the FileName field. It allows you to place the file's name in the header or the footer. When you select the FileName field in the Field names list, you must also select a format for the field information such as Uppercase, Lowercase, and so on. There is also a field option for FileName that allows you to add the path to the filename. This combination of the filename and the path makes this information in the header or the footer of a document invaluable. There is no easier way to find the actual file on your computer when you have a hard copy that details the name and path for the file.

Working with Page Numbering

Placing page numbers in the header or the footer of the document is just a matter of selecting the Page Number command (on the Ribbon's Insert tab) and then selecting a position for the page numbers. You can place the page numbering at the top of the page or the bottom of the page.

When you select Top of Page or Bottom of Page on the Page Number list, you are provided a gallery of different page-numbering formats. You can also access more page number formats from Office.com.

You can also change the number format for your header and footer page numbers. Select the Page Numbers command (either on the Insert tab or on the Headers &Footers Tools tab if you are already in the header or the footer). The Page Number Format dialog box, shown in Figure 7.10, opens.

> **🔍 note**
>
> You can also place page numbers in the page margin or at the current position (which is where you parked the Insertion point).

> **〰 tip**
>
> If you create your own page number format (using fields and paragraph and font formatting attributes), you can select it and then save it as a page number format via the Page Number gallery (look for the Save Selection command).

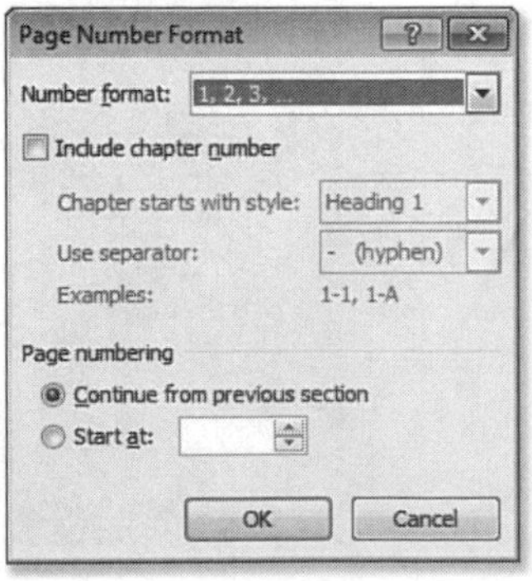

Figure 7.10
The Page Number Format dialog box.

Use the settings in the dialog box to change the number format using the Number Format drop-down list. If you have chapters in your document, you can also have chapter numbers included along with the page number (you specify the style used for your chapter titles to let Word know where the chapters actually start). You can also choose to continue the page numbering from the previous section or you can use the Start At box to specify a specific number for the start of the page numbering.

Inserting Pictures, Clip Art, and Charts

You can add pictures, clip art, and other graphics, such as charts and equations, to your documents. It is really just a matter of parking the insertion point in the document where you want to insert the graphic and then specifying the type of document you want to insert. You can use digital photographs, scanned images, and the extensive clip art gallery provided by Microsoft. If a specific kind of clip art has not been installed on your computer (when you installed Microsoft Office), you can search for it on Office.com. You can also insert shapes, SmartArt, and charts. You can even cut and paste graphics from other applications including your web browser.

 A detailed overview of working with pictures and other graphics in Microsoft Office 2010 is provided in Chapter 4, "Using and Creating Graphics."

A huge improvement in terms of working with pictures in Word 2010 is that the same set of picture tools is available to whether you are working with a document that is in compatibility mode (a document saved in the Word 97–2003 file format) or the Word 2010 file format (.docx). This differs from the Office 2007 applications, which did not provide the full set of tools when you were working on a document in compatibility mode.

Inserting Pictures

Picture files can be inserted using the Picture command in the Illustrations group, which resides on the Ribbon's Insert tab. You can take advantage of many different picture file formats in your Word documents. The possibilities are as follows:

- Portable Network Graphics (.png)
- CompuServe GIF (.gif)
- Encapsulated PostScript (.eps)
- Various paint programs (.pcx)
- Tagged Image File format (.tif)
- Windows bitmap (.bmp and .dib)
- JPEG file interchange format (.jpg)
- Microsoft meta files (.emf and .wmf)

To actually insert a picture that resides on your computer into the current document, place the insertion point where you want to insert the picture and then select Picture. The Insert Picture dialog box opens. It opens by default to the Picture folder (library). You can navigate to the folder that holds your picture file and then select the file. Click Insert to insert the image into the Word document.

The picture will be selected in the Word document after it is inserted. When a picture is selected on a page, the picture tools appear on the Ribbon. Figure 7.11 shows an inserted picture file and the picture tools.

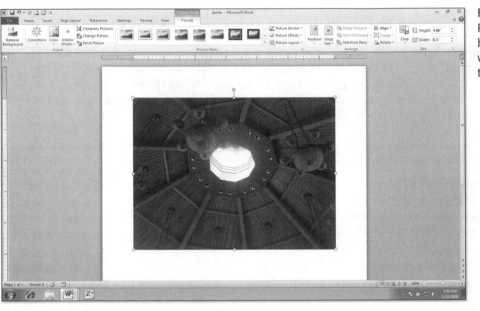

Figure 7.11
Pictures can be adjusted with the picture tools.

For more about manipulating pictures and other graphics in the Office applications, see Chapter 4, "Using and Creating Graphics."

The picture tools provide you with the ability to adjust the picture (such as brightness and contrast), select a picture style, arrange multiple pictures on the page, and crop and size the selected picture. The picture tools groups are as follows:

- **Adjust:** This group provides a number of tools that allow you to alter and fine-tune the picture settings. You can correct the contrast, make color corrections, add artistic effects, and even remove the portions of the photo's background. Options provided by tools in this group enable you to preview the adjustment before applying it to the picture. You can also compress a picture in a document (it is saved in the document as a .jpg file) so that the overall Word file size is more accommodating if you share the file online or via email.

- **Picture Styles:** Picture styles provide you with frame formats such as Metal Frame, Reflected Rounded Rectangle, and Double Frame Black. Place the mouse on a style to preview the style on the picture. This group also provides you with the ability to select the color of the picture border and add effects to the picture.

- **Arrange:** This group allows you to layer multiple images (using commands such as Bring Forward and Send Backward). It also allows you to group graphics, align images (left, center, right, top, middle, bottom) and provides you with the ability to rotate and flip pictures.

- **Size:** This group provides Height and Width spinner boxes for sizing a picture. You can also use the Crop command to crop the image as needed.

When you finish adjusting the various settings related to a picture in the document, click anywhere in the document to deselect the picture. This returns the Ribbon to its normal set of tabs and functionality.

Adding Clip Art

Microsoft Office and Office.com (the online resource for Microsoft Office) provides you with a seemingly unending supply of clip art images that you can use to enhance your documents. Whether or not you choose to use clip art is up to you; remember that you don't want professional documents to look too cute and you don't want to overshadow the actual text content of the document with too many images.

To insert clip art at the insertion point, use the Clip Art command in the Illustration group (on the Ribbon's Insert tab). The Clip Art task pane opens (see Figure 7.12).

You can use the Search For text box to enter search items for the type of clip art you want to locate. By default, the search will be conducted on your computer's storage devices and the Office.com collection. The search also looks for all supported media file types (including video and audio files). If you want to limit the search to a specific media type, such as illustrations or photographs, use the Results should be drop-down list to specify the media types for the search.

When the search is complete, click any of the clip art files provided in the Clip Art gallery and that image will be inserted at the insertion point. If used appropriately, clip art can definitely improve the overall look of certain documents, particularly special documents such as flyers, newsletters, and brochures.

Inserting a Chart

You can insert a number of other graphics into your Word documents including shapes, SmartArt (shapes and SmartArt are discussed in Chapter 4) and charts into your Word documents. The Chart types include column, line, pie, bar, doughnut, and radar charts.

 tip

You can remove all the picture-formatting changes that you have made to a picture using the various tools provided by the picture tools (except for Change Picture and Compress Picture). Click the Reset Picture command.

 note

You can preview and view the properties of a clip art file, which is particularly useful if you want to insert an animated clip art image into a document that you will provide online. Click the drop-down arrow on the right of any clip art image to access the Preview/Properties dialog box for a clip art file.

note

You can also insert charts and worksheets created in Microsoft Excel into your Word documents. See Appendix A, "Office Application Integration," for more about sharing information between Office applications such as Word and Excel.

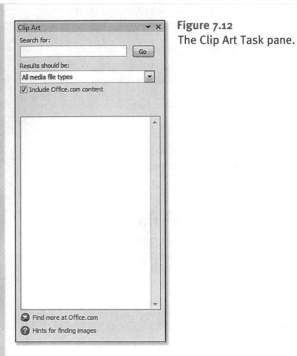

Figure 7.12
The Clip Art Task pane.

To insert a chart at the insertion point, select Chart (in the Illustrations group on the Insert tab). The Insert Chart dialog box opens as shown in Figure 7.13.

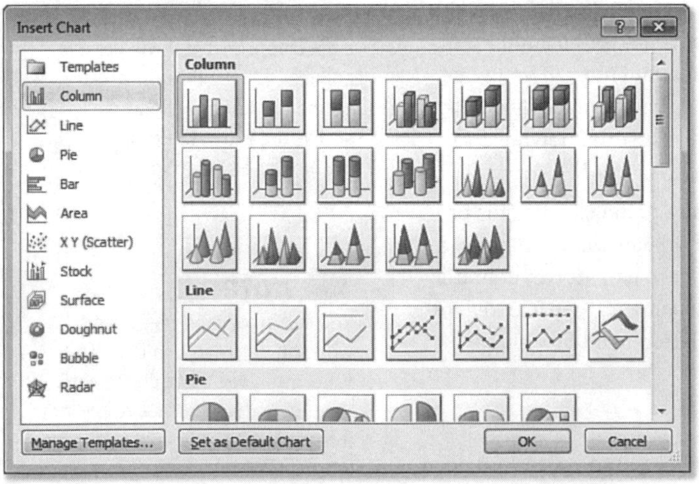

Figure 7.13
The Insert Chart dialog box.

Select a chart type in the Chart Type list. You can then select one of the specific chart types for that category of chart (such as Line or Pie). Click OK and chart of that type will be inserted into the Word document. An Excel worksheet also opens that provides a default table (see Figure 7.14). You can change the category and series names as well as the data on the worksheet until they contain the information required for your chart.

Best practices related to using and selecting charts and entering chart data are discussed in Chapter 14, "Enhancing Worksheets with Charts."

Figure 7.14
Edit the table data to create the chart.

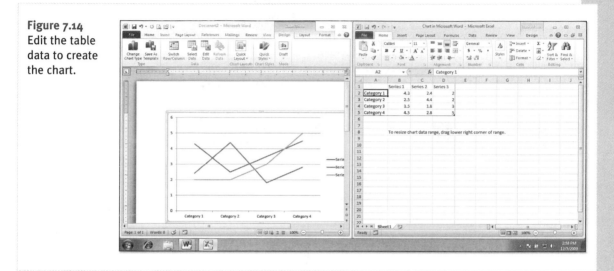

When you finish making your changes to the Excel table, you can close the Excel window (you don't need to save the table data). When the chart is selected, you will find in the Word document that the Ribbon provides the chart tools that contain a Design, Layout, and Format tab. The Design tab provides you with the ability to edit the data, change the chart type, and layout, and choose one of the chart styles.

The Layout tab of the chart tools allows you to edit chart labels such as the title, axes, and the legend. It also provides tools that enable you to enhance the background of the chart.

The Format tab of the chart tools allows you to change shape styles and select WordArt styles for the text labels in the chart. You can also use the Height and Width spinner boxes to set the size for the chart.

It is a straightforward process to create simple charts within Word. In cases where you are working with more complex sets of data, you might want to actually use Excel to create the chart. You can then copy and paste the chart into Word (see Appendix A for more about integrating Word and Excel).

Integrating Text and Images

One of the most important aspects of using pictures, clip art, or charts in Word is integrating the image with the text in the document. This primarily relates to sizing the picture or clip art file and determining how you want the text to wrap in relation to the image.

You can click on any image and use the sizing handles that appear on the image to change its size. To maintain the height/width ratio of the image (so that you don't stretch or distort the image), use the sizing handles on the corners of the image and drag diagonally. If you would rather change the size of the image more precisely, you can use the Height and Width spinner boxes on the Size group (you can find this group on the picture tools and the chart tools).

For complete control over the height and width of an image, and to lock the aspect ratio (the height/width) of an image, you have to take advantage of the Layout dialog box, particularly its Size tab. To open the Layout dialog box (with the Size tab selected), click the dialog box launcher (Advanced Layout: Size on the Size group. Figure 7.15 shows the Layout dialog box.

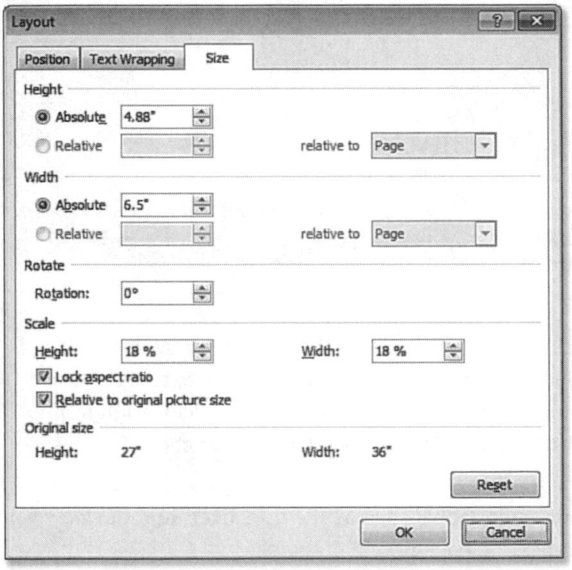

Figure 7.15
The Size tab of the Layout dialog box.

You can use the settings on the Size tab to adjust the height and width, and to rotate the image. When you select Lock Aspect Ratio, any change to the height or width results in a change to the other measurement; for example, if you change the height, the width changes based on the aspect ratio.

Another aspect of integrating the image with the text relates to the text wrapping you set. By default the wrapping style is set to In Line with Text. This means that the image will be placed between the margins and text will appear over and below the image. You can use the Wrap Text command on the Arrange tab of the picture tools and the chart tools to change how the text wraps in relation to the image. You can use the Square setting to have the text frame run along the top, bottom, left, and right of the image. You can also use Behind Text or In Front of Text to set the text to appear in front of the image or behind the image, respectively. These settings are also available on the Text Wrapping tab of the Layout dialog box.

Changing the Document Display

Word provides you with several different viewing possibilities as you work on your documents in the application window. All the viewing options are available on the Ribbon's View tab. The Document Views group provides commands for the different document views such as Print Layout and Draft. The Zoom group allows you to access the Zoom dialog box and quickly zoom to 100%. The Window group allows you to arrange the open document windows and view two documents side-by-side. Figure 7.16 shows the Ribbon's View tab and a document in the Print Layout view with Two Pages selected in the Zoom group.

Figure 7.16
The Ribbon's View tab.

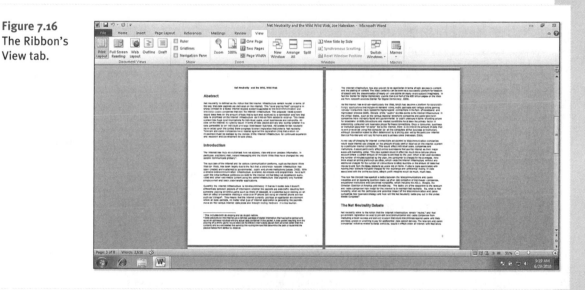

Using the different document views to your advantage can help you visualize and create great-looking Word documents. The list that follows provides an overview of the different document views provided in the Document Views group of the View tab.

■ **Print Layout:** Shows your document exactly as it will appear on the printed page. Working in this view allows you to view headers and footers, margins, and other page layout settings. It also allows you to fine-tune graphic placement because pictures and clip art appear as they will print in this view.

 tip

You can quickly change the document view using the View icons on the Word taskbar (on the far right). You can also use the Zoom slider on the taskbar to zoom in and out on the document.

- **Full Screen Reading:** This view is designed to allow you as much of the application window as possible to read the current document. Set up much like a book, document pages appear as facing pages. Previous and Next arrows are available on the bottom of each two-page set so that you can move forward and backward in the document. The Ribbon is not available in the Full Screen Reading view. Much like the Print Preview screen of past versions of Word, you use the Close button to return to the full application window.

- **Web Layout:** This view is designed for the creation of HTML documents for the Web. It does not show margins or other layout attributes. Rather it provides a workspace much like what is seen in a browser window when you view a web page.

- **Outline:** This view is designed so that you can see the document in an outline format. Headings appear as level 1 of the outline and text that follows each heading displays as secondary level body text. The Outline view can be used to rearrange text in a document by moving a heading and its associated body text. The Outline view is also designed for working with master documents, which are discussed in Chapter 10.

 tip

The View Options drop-down list in the Full Screen Reading view allows you to increase the text size for reading, show one or two pages, and access margin settings (as well as access other view settings).

- **Draft:** This view displays character and paragraph formatting that you place in the document; however, it does not display the document headers and footers or show graphics in the document as they will print. It is an excellent view for finding page breaks that you have placed in the document and for finding section breaks that you have assigned to a document.

Each view embraces a different way of looking at your document. Most users will actually create the initial draft of a document in the Print Layout or the Draft view. For organizing the document text, you might then switch to the Outline view, particularly if you are working with a larger document that contains headings and different document sections. Full Screen Reading is designed to allow you to read through a document although you can use the Allow Typing option on the View Options list so that you can edit your document as you read.

Using the Navigation Pane

Although it is not designated as a full-fledged view (as are Print Layout and Draft), the Navigation pane enables you to navigate through a document using the document headings and page thumbnails. The Navigation pane is somewhat similar to the Outline view in that the text that follows a heading is considered subordinate to the heading. This means that if you drag a heading to a new location in the Navigation pane, the text under that heading will be moved as well.

To open the Navigation pane, select the Navigation Pane check box in the Show group (of the Ribbon's View tab). The Navigation pane itself appears on the left side of the document window (see Figure 7.17).

Figure 7.17
The Navigation pane.

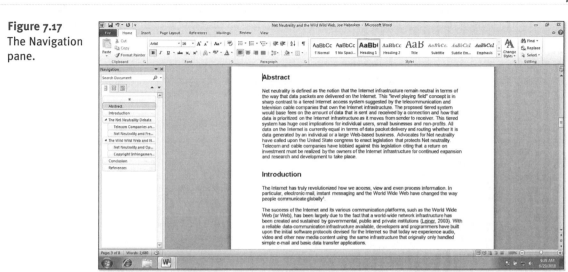

The Navigation pane allows you to view the document by heading (as shown in Figure 7.17), or you can click the Browse the Pages in Your Document button to browse the document by thumbnails. A search pane makes it easy for you to search the document using keywords. The search term that you use is highlighted in the document every time that it appears. When you click the Browse the Results from Your Current Search button, the Navigation pane displays individual text blocks that contain the search term. You can then navigate the document by selecting one of the text blocks provided. When you have completed working with the Navigation pane, click the Close button to remove it from the application window.

Splitting the Document Window

Another useful view-related tool is the ability to split the current document into two panes. This allows you to scroll to a different part of the same document in the different panes. You can then use two panes to drag and drop information from one part of a document into another. Remember that changes you make in either of the split panes affect the document.

To split the document screen into two panes, select the Split command (in the Zoom group of the View tab). Use the mouse to position the split in the document and then click the mouse to place the split.

 note

The Navigation pane is a slightly upscale version of the document map in previous versions of Word.

 tip

Another useful view-related tool is the View Side By Side command in the Window group. It allows you to view two different documents side-by-side. By default the two documents have their scrolling synchronized. You can click the Synchronous Scrolling command to scroll independently through each document. You can then drag and drop text between the documents and compare the documents as needed.

Each of the separate panes can be treated as a separate document. You can use Zoom to change the zoom level of each pane independently and you can use all the other Word tools as needed in each of the panes. Figure 7.18 shows a document split into two panes.

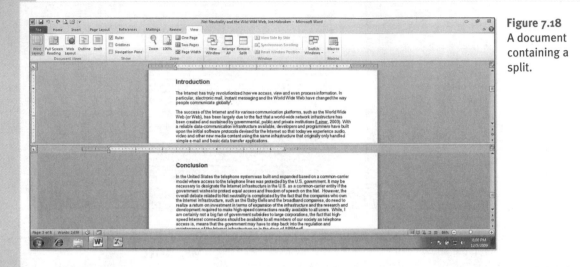

Figure 7.18
A document containing a split.

When you have finished working in the split document window, select Remove Split in the Window group. The splitter bar is removed from the document.

Using the Review Tools

An important part of enhancing your documents is to make them error-free. Word provides proofing tools such as the Spelling and Grammar features, which are designed to ferret out errors in your text. Word actually proofs your document as you type and automatically flags spelling and grammar errors as you enter text into your document. This enables you to quickly and immediately correct errors as you build your document.

Spelling errors are flagged with a red wavy underscore and grammar errors are flagged with a green wavy underscore. Right-click on spelling errors to access a shortcut menu providing suggested spellings. You can also right-click on grammar errors to view possible corrections. You can use this method to correct errors on the fly, or you might find it more efficient to correct them collectively by running the spelling and grammar checking features after you have finished entering all your text.

> **note**
>
> Some spelling errors are corrected automatically by the AutoCorrect feature. We discuss AutoCorrect in the next section of this chapter.

You can change the default settings associated with the automatic spelling and grammar checking features (meaning turn them off). Click File to go to the Backstage view and then select Options. In the Word Options dialog box, select Proofing. Clear the check boxes on Check Spelling as You Type and the Check Grammar Errors as you Type to turn these features off. Then click OK to return to the document window.

Running Spelling and Grammar

Waiting to correct spelling and grammar errors in a document until you have finished composing enables you to concentrate on getting your thoughts down without interruption. Then you can check the entire document on completion. The Ribbon's Review tab provides access to the Spelling and Grammar command and other proofing tools such as the thesaurus, Research pane, and the Word Count command.

To check the spelling and grammar in the document, click the Spelling & Grammar command. The Spelling and Grammar dialog box opens as shown in Figure 7.19.

Figure 7.19
Checking the spelling and grammar.

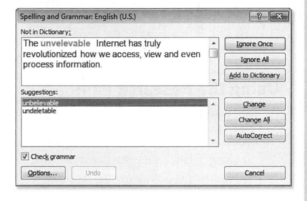

Words not found in the dictionary are flagged, and the text in which the word is contained in is displayed in the Not in Dictionary box. To change the misspelling to one of the suggestions, select that suggestion and then click Change. If you know you have misspelled the word consistently throughout the document, you can click Change All.

In terms of grammar errors, the suspected error appears in the text box at the top of the Spelling and Grammar dialog box with a heading that describes the type of error. Suggestions may also be provided in the Suggestions box. You can change the error using a suggestion or you can choose to ignore the entry (Ignore Once) or choose to ignore the rule (Ignore Rule) as you check the document.

> ### tip
> If the word is something you consistently misspell, select the correct replacement and then click AutoCorrect to add the misspelled/correctly spelled pair to the AutoCorrect list.

Using the Thesaurus

The Word thesaurus provides you with a tool that you can use to find synonyms for the words in your document. Synonyms are words that mean the same thing. Because the thesaurus can generate a list of synonyms for nearly any word in your document, you can avoid the repetitive use of a particular descriptive adjective (such as "excellent") and actually add some depth to the vocabulary that appears in your document.

Click on a word in your document and then click the Thesaurus command in the Proofing group. The Research task pane opens on the right side of the Word window. To replace the word with a synonym, place the mouse on the synonym in the synonym list, and then click on the drop-down arrow that appears to the right of the synonym. Click Insert from the menu that appears.

If you prefer to forgo the use of the Research pane for synonyms, you can view a short list of synonyms for a selected word by right-clicking. Point at the Synonyms command on the shortcut menu and a list of synonyms for the word appears. Click one of the words provided to replace the word in the document.

Using the Research Pane

The Research task pane provides a tool that you can use to access all sorts of information related to a selection in a document. As already discussed, one tool provided by the Research task pane is the thesaurus. You can also use the Research pane to search for information on text in your document or by typing a new term in the Search For box.

You can do a search using Bing (Microsoft's web search engine) or other Web-based reference books such as Encarta, MSN Money stock quotes, and Thomson Gale company files. Figure 7.20 shows a Bing search for the word "Internet."

You can add additional reference books to the Research task pane by selecting Research options at the bottom of the pane. Doing so opens the Research Options dialog box. You can select any of the services provided in the Services list. You can also add other services to the Research pane by using the Add Services command in the Research Options dialog box. This opens the Add Services dialog box. Provide the URL (the full web address) for a service provider (such as a search engine or an online reference site) and then click Add. You can add other services as needed.

Figure 7.20
The Research
task pane.

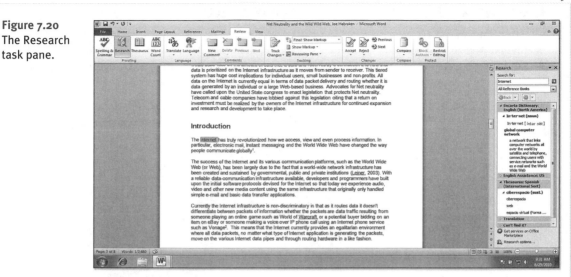

Working with Quick Parts

As we create documents, we are always looking for shortcuts and timesavers that allow us to work more efficiently. The Quick Parts features, which was added to Word 2007 and builds on the AutoText feature, provides a new way to build a library of words and text phrases you use often. In Word 2010, AutoText has actually resurfaced as part of the Quick Parts feature, which also includes the Building Block Organizer. So, let's sort out the differences between AutoText and building blocks and then we can explore how you actually create and use these Quick Parts options.

Let's look at the latter first: building blocks. Building blocks are any words, text lines, paragraphs, or even entire pages that you save as a building block. Building blocks by definition are meant to be used to help you quickly enter often-used text into your documents. Word actually provides a number of building blocks, such as different headers and footers, page-numbering formats, and even text boxes and watermarks. You can add building blocks as needed and then access your building blocks in the Building Blocks Organizer.

Building blocks are organized in galleries. These galleries include possibilities such as cover pages, headers, tables, and a number of others. Building blocks go far beyond the possibilities that the simple AutoText feature provided in earlier versions of Word (the versions before 2007).

AutoText in Word 2010 is actually pretty much the same thing as a building block in terms of how you create it. However, AutoText can be inserted more quickly (than a building block) into a document and are saved in an AutoText gallery. Think of the difference between AutoText entries and building blocks as being practical rather than technical. I suggest that you reserve AutoText for words and phrases such as company names, letter closings, and the like—short text entries that you use often. Save the more complex items that you insert occasionally as building blocks—items such as long paragraphs, a particular page type (such as a cover page), or a special table.

Creating and Inserting an AutoText Entry

To create an AutoText entry, select the text you want to save as the AutoText entry. Select the Ribbon's Insert tab and then select Quick Parts. On the Quick Parts menu, point at AutoText and then select Save Selection to AutoText Gallery. The Create New Building Block dialog box opens as shown in Figure 7.21.

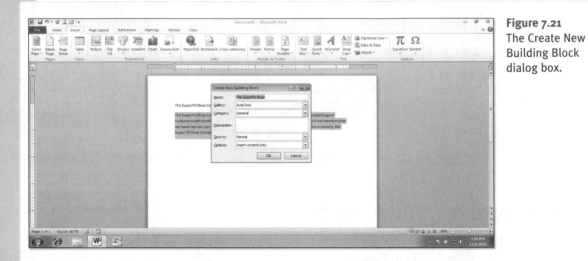

Figure 7.21
The Create New Building Block dialog box.

In the dialog box, provide a name for the new AutoText entry (a name based on the text content is provided by default). You can also choose options related to the entry, such as whether you should insert the content only or insert the content in a separate paragraph or on a separate page. Click OK to create the entry.

To insert an AutoText entry in your document, place the insertion point where you want to place the entry. Select the Quick Parts command and then point at AutoText. Select the entry you want to place in the document from the choices provided in the AutoText gallery.

Creating and Inserting Building Blocks

Creating a building block is very similar to creating an AutoText entry. Select the text, table, header, footer, or other object that will serve as the building block. Select the Ribbon's Insert tab and then select Quick Parts. On the Quick Parts menu, select Save Selection to Quick Part Gallery. The Create New Building Block dialog box opens (refer to Figure 7.21).

Provide a name for the new building block. You can also select the gallery and category for the building block. More importantly, you can control the options related to how the building block will be inserted into the document via the Options drop-down list.

tip

You can provide an optional description for the new entry in the Create New Building Block. This can be useful if you end up with a number of AutoText or building block entries that have similar names.

If the building block contains only text that you want to insert into other paragraphs (much like an AutoText entry) use the Insert Content Only option. The building block will then be formatted the same as the surrounding text.

If you are creating a building block with specific formatting or a special building block such as a table, use the Insert Content in Its Own Paragraph option. This maintains the formatting of the block. If you are creating a building block that consists of a page such as a cover page (or a number of pages, such as front matter for a book) select the Insert Content in Its Own Page option. This places the building block into the document as a new page or pages. When you have completed selecting the various options, click OK to create the building block.

When you want to insert a building block that you created into a document, you insert it from the Quick Parts menu (if you used the General category when you built the building block). Select Quick Parts and then select the building block from the menu.

In cases where you want to use building blocks that Word provides or want to peruse the various building blocks available (including AutoText and building blocks you created), you can open the Building Blocks Organizer from the Quick Parts menu. Figure 7.22 shows the Building Blocks Organizer.

Figure 7.22
The Building Blocks Organizer.

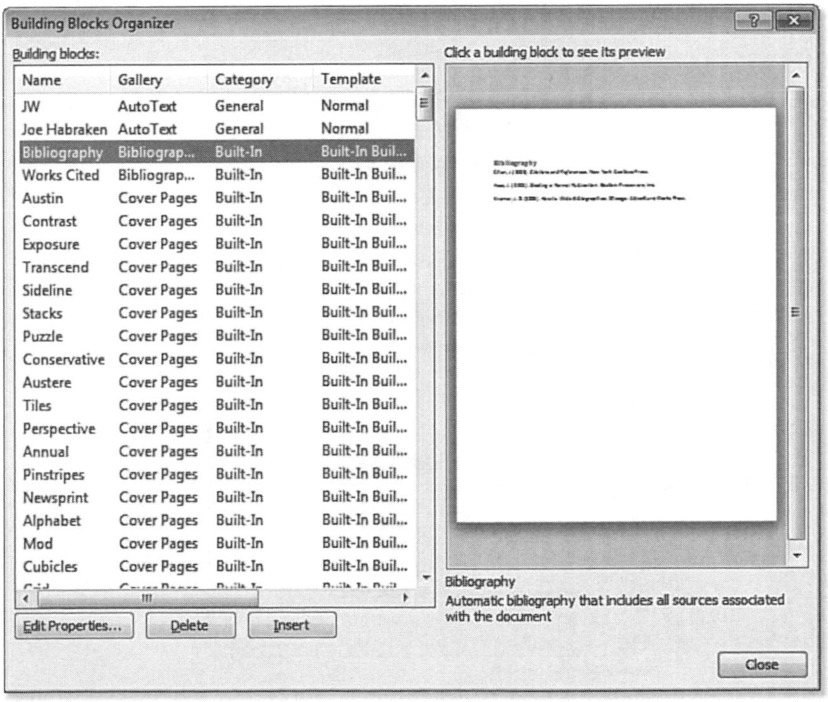

You can insert building blocks from the organizer (select the building block and then click Insert). You can also manage your building blocks by editing their properties and even deleting unwanted building blocks. To change the text or other objects in a building block, you can insert the building block into a document and then modify it as needed. You can then save it to the Building Block gallery using the same name and properties. You will then be asked whether you want to redefine the building block; click Yes and the building block is modified.

Obviously, building blocks can save you a lot of time and add consistency (in terms of content) to your Word documents. If you create a number of building blocks, remember to use the appropriate gallery and category for each building block to help you keep the library of text blocks organized.

Configuring AutoCorrect

AutoCorrect is one of the Word features that has remained fairly consistent in terms of its configuration from version to version of Microsoft Word. AutoCorrect can correct commonly misspelled words (and words that you add to it). It also corrects things such as initial caps, automatically capitalizes the first letter of sentences, and automatically capitalizes the names of days.

You can access the AutoCorrect dialog box (see Figure 7.23) from the Word Backstage. Select File, and then Options. In the Word Options dialog box, select Proofing and then click the AutoCorrect Options button.

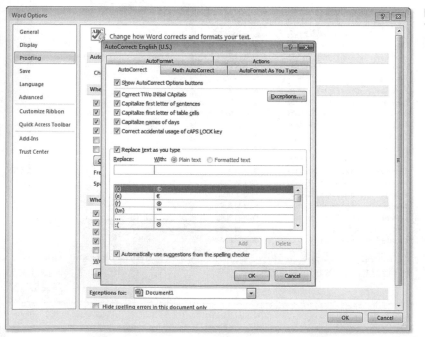

Figure 7.23
The AutoCorrect dialog box.

You can add entries to the Replace Text as You Type list. In the Replace box, enter a word as you misspell it. In the With box, enter the correct spelling of the word. Click Add to add the entry to the AutoCorrect list.

You can also access settings related to AutoFormat such as replacing straight quotes with smart quotes on the AutoFormat tab of the AutoCorrect dialog box. Other options, such as automatic bulleted lists and the formatting of a list item the same as the previous item, are accessed on the AutoFormat as You Type tab.

Understanding Styles

When you create Word documents that contain a great deal of formatting attributes for the various headings, special paragraphs and the like, it makes sense to take advantage of styles. A style is a grouping of formatting attributes identified by a style name. Styles can contain text formatting attributes such as bold and 14 point, and can also contain paragraph formatting attributes such as indents and other alignment settings (such as Center or Justify).

The great thing about using styles to format your text is that when you modify the style itself, the modifications apply to all the text that has been assigned that style. For example, if you have used a style for all the headings in your document and decide that you would like the headings to be in bold (along with the other formatting contained in the heading style), all you have to do is modify the style to include the bold attribute.

Word provides Quick Styles that are predesigned styles. Quick Styles come in families or sets of styles to provide consistency in look and formatting when you use them to format the various items in a document such as headings, titles, quotes, and other text items.

In cases where you want to create your own styles, you certainly have that option. Styles can be created, modified, and, of course, deleted. You can quickly inspect a style in a document with the Style Inspector and you can import and export styles from document to document (or to and from a Word template). Let's look at taking advantage of the Quick Styles provided by Word and then we can examine how best to create your own styles.

Using Quick Styles

Quick Styles can be applied to selected text or a paragraph (remember that even a single-line heading is considered a paragraph by Word). The Quick Styles reside in a style gallery in the Styles group of the Ribbon's Home tab.

After you specify the text that you will format with the Quick Style, place the mouse pointer on any of the available styles to preview the style's formatting (on your text). To view additional Quick Styles in the current set, use the arrows to the right of the Quick Style gallery. You can also click the More button (just below the arrows) to expand the gallery so that you can see more of the Quick Styles in one view.

> **⚠ caution**
>
> The Quick Styles that you have assigned to your document's text will be affected (in terms of their formatting attributes such as the fonts and font colors used) when you change the theme for your document. If you are going to use themes and Quick Styles, assign the theme to the document when you begin creating it and then select the appropriate Quick Styles for each text item as needed (such as headings and titles).

If you want to use a different set of Quick Styles in the current document, you can click the Change Styles command (in the Styles group) and point at Style Set. A Quick Style Set list opens as shown in Figure 7.24.

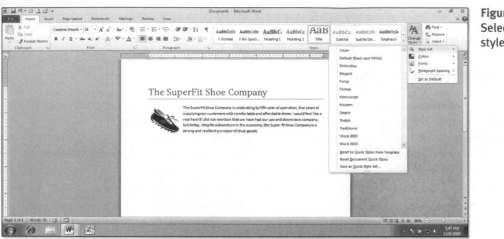

Figure 7.24
Select a new style set.

If you place the mouse pointer on any of the style sets listed, you get a preview of how the Quick Styles that you have used in your document will look when the new style set is applied. You can also use the Style Set to reset the Quick Styles for the current template (which in many cases is the Normal template), and reset the document's Quick Styles to their defaults if you have edited any of them.

The Change Styles menu also allows you to change the color scheme for the Quick Styles (via a Colors gallery), and you can change the fonts used by the Quick Styles and the paragraph spacing used in the document. Changing any of the style parameters, such as color scheme, font scheme, and paragraph spacing, affects all the Quick Styles in your document.

> **tip**
> The paragraph-spacing options accessed via the Change Styles command are a set of built-in spacing with names such as Compact, Open, Relaxed, and so on. If you would rather set your own custom paragraph spacing, click the Custom Paragraph Spacing command at the bottom of the Paragraph Spacing gallery. This opens the Paragraph dialog box where you can specify your own line-spacing settings for the current Style set.

Creating Styles

You can create your own styles quickly and easily by example. Apply font and paragraph formatting attributes to selected text. The text can be a single-line heading or consist of an entire paragraph of text. Any of the font-formatting attributes such as bold, italics, font color, font size, and even font type are fair game for your style, as are paragraph-formatting attributes related to alignment, line spacing, indents, borders, and shading.

When you have the text formatted, click the More command in the Styles group and select Save Selection as a New Quick Style (in the Quick Style gallery). The Create new Style from Formatting dialog box opens as shown in Figure 7.25.

Figure 7.25
Create a new
style by exam-
ple.

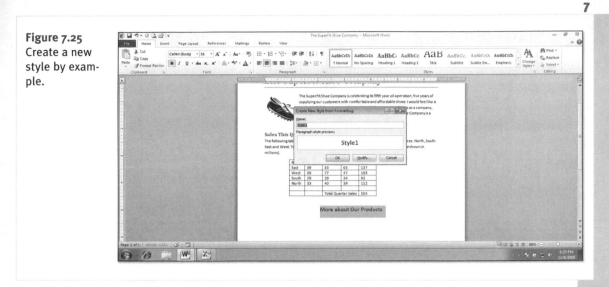

Provide a name for the new style in the Name box and then
click OK. The new style will appear in the Quick Style gallery.
You can apply it to your document text as needed.

Editing Styles

You can edit any style in the document, including the Quick
Styles provided by the current template and any styles that you
have created. A quick way to view all the styles in the current
document, and to access a particular style for editing, is to open
the Styles window (click the Styles command on the edge of the
Styles group).

The Style window lists all the styles in the document (see
Figure 7.26). If you want to see a preview of the style's formatting attributes, click the Show Preview check box at the bottom
of the Styles window.

There are two ways you can modify a style from the Style window. You can modify it by example or edit the style's formatting
attributes manually.

To modify the style by example, reformat text that has been
assigned the style so that it is formatted with the attributes you
want in the modified version of the style. Click the drop-down
arrow next to the style that you want to modify (in the Style
window) and select Update (*style name*) to Match Selection. The
style will be updated, as will all the text that has been assigned
that style.

 tip

If you decide that you wanted to
modify the new style before actually
saving it to the Quick Style gallery, click Modify in the Create New
Style from Formatting dialog box
and a larger Create New Style from
Formatting dialog box appears. The
larger dialog box provides you with
the ability to change the various formatting attributes of the style before
you save the style.

 tip

To quickly view the formatting attributes of a style in your document,
select text that has been applied
the style and then click the Style
Inspector button in the Styles window. The Style Inspector provides
paragraph- and text-level formatting
for the style. The Style Inspector can
actually be used to clear formatting
attributes used in the style.

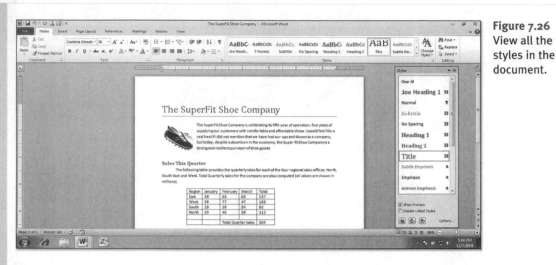

Figure 7.26
View all the styles in the document.

You can also modify a style using the Modify Style dialog box; click the drop-down arrow next to the style and select Modify. The Modify Style dialog box provides Formatting toolbars that you can use to change font-formatting attributes and paragraph attributes.

You can also access specific dialog boxes from the Modify Style dialog box, providing you even greater control over the formatting attributes contained in the style. Select the Format button at the bottom left of the dialog box and select Font, Paragraph, Tabs, Borders, or any of the other dialog boxes listed and that particular dialog box opens (such as the Font dialog box or the Paragraph dialog box).

After you have made changes to formatting attributes in one of the dialog boxes, closing the dialog box (clicking OK) returns you to the Modify Style dialog box. When you close the Modify Style dialog box, you are returned to your document and the Styles window.

> **tip**
>
> If you want to delete a style, click the drop-down arrow next to the style in the Style window and select Delete (*style name*) on the menu. Click Yes to confirm the deletion.

Managing Styles

The Styles window not only provides a comprehensive list of the styles in a document, but it also allows you to quickly modify and even delete styles from the document. The Styles window also provides access to the Manage Styles dialog box, which provides even greater capability to manage the styles in your document. It even gives you the ability to import and export styles into and from your current document.

> **tip**
>
> You can also create a new style from the Styles window by clicking the New Style button at the bottom of the window.

In the Styles window, select the Manage Styles button. This opens the Manage Styles dialog box (see Figure 7.27).

Figure 7.27
The Manage Styles dialog box.

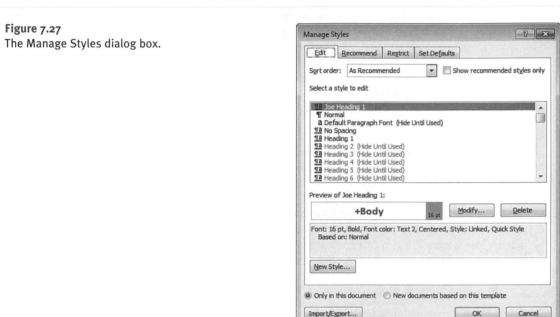

This dialog box enables you to modify any of the styles in your document (or template, if you are working on a template) including deleting them, and also to create new styles (directly from the dialog box). The Manage Styles dialog box also provides you with the ability to determine which styles appear in the Quick Style gallery and Styles window as well as the order in which the styles appear. It also provides options related to setting some of the font and paragraph formatting attributes for the document.

The Manage Styles dialog box provides four tabs. The following provides a brief description of each tab:

- **Edit:** This tab allows you to modify and delete styles. It also provides the ability to change how the list of styles is sorted on the tab. For example, you can change the sort order to Alphabetical using the Sort Order drop-down list. The default sort order, As Recommended, is based on a numerical system (a style assigned a 1 would appear at the top of the list), which you can set on the Recommend tab.

- **Recommend:** The Recommend list is determined on this tab by assigning a particular order number to a style (1 being the highest). The order determined by the Recommend list is basically the priority used to list the styles in the Quick Style gallery and the Styles windows. Use the Move Up, Move Down, and Assign Value buttons to assign the priority number to a style in the list. You can also choose to have certain styles hidden until you use them (via the Hide Until Used button) and you can actually hide styles. Any styles assigned the Hide Until Used or Hide status can be shown by selecting the style or styles and clicking Show.

- **Restrict:** You can actually limit access to formatting in the document. This is particularly useful if you are designing a template where you want users of the template to have restricted access to the formatting tools on the Ribbon and want only certain styles to be used for formatting (in lieu of direct formatting). Select a style or styles in the Styles list to permit or restrict the style. If you are going to limit formatting to the permitted styles, make sure to select the Limit Formatting to Permitted Styles check box. This feature actually grays out formatting commands on the Ribbon's Home tab, making them unavailable.

- **Set Defaults:** This tab allows you to specify some of the default formatting attributes for the current document or documents based on the template that you are creating and configuring. These attributes include Font and Font Size, Paragraph Position, and Paragraph Spacing.

Another tool that you can access via the Manage Styles dialog box is the Organizer. It enables you to copy styles from other documents and templates into your current document (and export them to other documents and templates). Think about it: There are definitely instances when you would like to have access to styles that you have created in other documents or that are contained in other Word templates (existing templates and templates that you have created).

➡️ *See Chapter 6, "Using Templates," for more about templates.*

To open the Organizer, click the Import/Export button at the bottom of the Manage Styles dialog box (the button is available on all the tabs of the Manage Styles dialog box). The Organizer (shown in Figure 7.28) provides two separate panes that list the styles in the current document (on the left of the dialog box) and the styles in the current document template, which in Figure 7.28 is the Normal template.

The trick here is to leave the current document and its styles in the Organizer (in the left pane) and use the right side of the Organizer window to open the document that you want to use when you import (or export) styles. To close the current template file on the right side of the dialog box, click the Close File button.

Now you need to open the document or template that will serve as the source for the styles you want to import or it will serve as the destination for the files you want to export from the current

document. Click Open File on the right side of the Organizer dialog box. The Open dialog box appears. Use it to locate and open the document or template from which you want to copy the styles (or export styles to). Double-click the file in the Open dialog box to open the file.

Now all you have to do is import or export the styles. Select a style or styles (use the Shift key to select multiple styles) in the document opened on the right side of the Organizer and then click Copy to import the styles into your current document. If you want to export styles from the current document, select them on the left and then copy them to the file on the right. The dialog box also allows you to select styles in either style list and delete them.

> **⊛ tip**
>
> If you want to import a style into a document (from a document or template) but that style has the same name as a style that already exists in the document that will receive the imported style, you will need to use the Rename command to rename the style before you can import it.

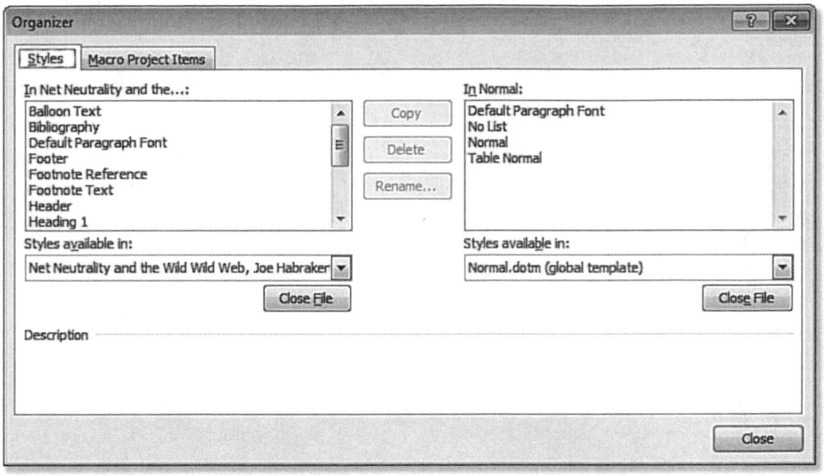

Figure 7.28
The Organizer dialog box.

WORKING WITH TABLES, COLUMNS, AND SECTIONS

Many of the documents that you create will probably require that you arrange information on the page in ways other than the typical paragraphs that you find in a simple business letter. You might, for example, need to show sales data best displayed in a table format or you might be creating a newsletter that requires your text and images to appear in columns.

Word makes it relatively simple to add tables to your documents. It also provides you with the ability to create columns on a document page or pages. However, you might run into a situation where you need to display a very large table (in terms of the number of columns) on a page in land-scape but need to have the other pages in the document remain in the portrait orientation. Or perhaps you might want a document to have regular single-column text in paragraphs, but then need to switch at a certain point in the document to a two-column layout.

These types of layout issues are handled by sections. Each section can have its own page layout settings such as the number of columns, the margins, even the headers and footers. Let's begin our discussion in this chapter with the table, and then columns, and finally end it with an in-depth discussion of Word sections.

Options for Adding a Table

When you think about the spatial arrangement of text on a Word document page, the actual positioning of the information is dictated primarily by the document margins and then any paragraph alignment or line-spacing settings that you choose (such as centered or double-spaced text). Tables, however, are a container that provides a way for you to arrange information on a page in a grid-like format. Tables consist of columns and rows and each intersection of a column and row is referred to as a cell. You enter your data (text or images) into the table cells.

Although you can arrange text on a page in a tabular (or table-like) format using tabs, tables are much more flexible, particularly in cases where the amount of text to be entered into each column is not uniform. The cell's height will grow as needed to accommodate your entered text and you can easily widen the columns when required. Tables can also contain pictures and other graphics and so provide you with layout possibilities that would be nearly impossible to achieve using tab stops.

Word actually provides multiple options for creating a table in your document. Figure 8.1 shows the possibilities when you select the Table command on the Ribbon's Insert tab. The table creation possibilities are as follows:

> **note**
>
> You might think that it would be best to use Excel for information that needs to be in a table format and then copy and paste the Excel sheet data into Word. In cases where the data is already in Excel, this makes sense. However, you will find that the Word table feature is extremely robust and flexible and provides you with a number of options in terms of the format and layout of the table. Word also allows you to insert formulas into the table so that you can do calculations (like Excel). So, if the data isn't already in Excel, and doesn't need to be in Excel just enter it into a Word table.

- **Quick Tables:** You can select a premade table from the Quick Tables gallery. You access the gallery via the Table command on the Ribbon's Insert tab (select Table, and then point at Quick Tables). Quick Tables provide different table layouts and formatting (see Figure 8.1). They also provide sample text, which you can then replace with your own text.

- **Table Grid:** You can insert a table by dragging the mouse on the table grid to select the number of columns and rows that will make up the table. You access the table grid by selecting the Table command in the Table group. When you insert a table using the table grid, you are initially limited to a maximum table size of 10 columns by 10 rows, although you can easily insert additional columns and rows after the fact.

- **Insert Table:** This old school table option uses the Insert Table dialog box and enables you to specify the number of columns and rows. To open the Insert Table dialog box, select Table on the Insert tab and then select Insert Table.

- **Draw Table:** You can draw your table in the document using a "pencil" mouse pointer. You can add columns and rows using the drawing tool as needed (you can distribute the rows and columns evenly after the fact via commands on the Table Tools Layout tab). To draw a table, select Table and then select Draw Table.

- **Convert Text to Table:** You can convert existing text to a table. This is useful when you have used tabs to place text in a tabular arrangement.

All of these options will place a table into the document at the insertion point. However, keep in mind that the differences between these different table creation methods provide you with a great deal of flexibility for actually creating a table. For example, if you want to quickly create a table such as a tabular list and are happy with the layout and formatting provided by the Quick Table Tabular List, it would make sense to go with a Quick Table and then replace the sample text provided with your own text.

Figure 8.1
Create a new
table via the
Table com-
mand.

If you are creating a table where you want to more precisely control the number of columns and rows, you may choose to use the Insert Table option. This option also allows you to work through the process of setting the design and layout options for the table and to format the cell contents (text) exactly as you see fit. Let's walk through each of the options for creating a table from scratch and then we can look at fine-tuning tables, including the use of the Design and Layout Table tools provided by Word 2010.

Inserting a Table

Inserting a table enables you to specify the initial number of rows and columns in the table. It also makes it possible for you to specify the position on the page where you would like to place the table; all you need to do is park the insertion point where you want to place the table. The insertion point marks the top-left starting point of the table.

Obviously, if you use the Insert Table grid on the Table command's menu, all you have to do is drag the mouse to specify the number of columns and rows. In terms of initial setting options, the Insert Table dialog box provides you with more options, so let's assume that you will go that route to insert the new table; follow these steps:

1. Place the insertion point in the document where you want to insert the table.

2. Select the Table command on the Ribbon's Insert tab and then select Insert Table. The Insert Table dialog box appears as shown in Figure 8.2.

3. Use the Number of Columns and Number of Rows spinner boxes to specify the number of columns and rows for the table (or type a number in either box).

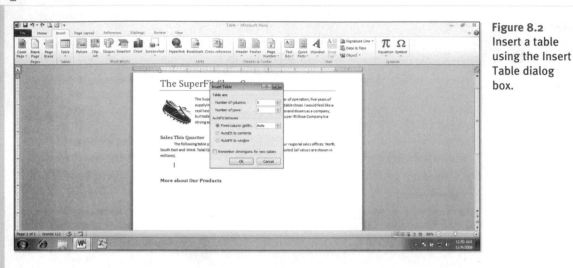

Figure 8.2
Insert a table
using the Insert
Table dialog
box.

4. The AutoFit options allow you to specify how the columns in the table behave in relation to the amount of text placed in each column. The options are as follows:

- **Fixed Column Width:** This setting enables you to set a fixed width (an actual number in inches) for all the columns in the table. When you use this option, you must manually resize columns in the table (using the sizing tool) to change any of the column widths.

- **AutoFit to Contents:** Column widths adjust to the amount of text in the column. So, a column grows in width (at the expense of the other columns in the table) as you enter text.

- **AutoFit to Window:** This option keeps the table aligned between the left and right margins. It is primarily designed for web pages so that the table adjusts its size based on the web browser window size.

5. (Optional) If you want the settings you selected to become the default for new tables, select the Remember Dimensions for New Tables check box.

tip

To access the AutoFit settings for the table (after you have created the table), use the AutoFit command in the Cell Size group on the Table Tools Layout tab.

6. When you have completed setting the options for the new table, click OK.

The table is inserted into the document. The Ribbon also switches to the table tools, which we will discuss later in this chapter.

You can also insert Excel spreadsheets into a Word document. For more about integrating Word and Excel, see Appendix A, "Office Application Integration."

Drawing a Table

An alternative to inserting a table into your document is to draw the table. When you draw the table, you can make the table any height and width instead of Word determining the height and width based on the number of columns and rows. You are actually creating the outside table borders without any rows or columns. Of course, you then must manually insert the rows and columns using the Table Drawing tool.

Although you can build a highly customized table using this method, it is not as fast as inserting a table with a prescribed number of rows and columns (like what happens when you insert a table). Follow these steps:

1. Select Table on the Insert tab and then select Draw Table. The mouse pointer becomes a "pencil" drawing tool.

2. Click and drag to create the table's outside borders (its "box" shape). Release the mouse when you have the outside perimeter of the table completed.

3. To add rows and columns to the table, use the pencil to draw (click and drag) the row and column lines.

4. When you have completed drawing the column and row borders (they do not have to be spaced evenly at this point), select Draw Table on the Design tab of the table tools. This turns off the pencil drawing tool.

5. To distribute the drawn rows and/or columns in the table evenly, select the Layout tab (of the Table Tools Ribbon) and then select Distribute Rows and/or Distribute Columns as needed.

If you click outside of the table (in the document's text), when using the table drawing tool, the Draw Table feature is toggled off. All you have to do is click inside the table and then click the Draw Table command on the table tools Design tab to reactivate the pencil drawing tool. You can then add tables or rows as needed. You can also use the Eraser tool to erase rows or columns that you have placed in the table. Select Eraser on the Design tab and then click and drag the Eraser to select a row or column border. When you release the mouse, the column or row border is erased. You can also use the Eraser to fine-tune borders and erase parts of a column or row to join cells.

> ## tip
> You can change the line style, line weight, and the pen color when you are using the Draw Table feature. Change any of the color or line settings in the Draw Borders group on the Design tab of the table tools.

Converting Text to a Table

Although I did not include this option in the original list of ways to create a new table, you can also convert existing text to a table. This is particularly useful in cases where you have used tabs to align text in a tabular format but find that you are better served by converting the text into a table.

To convert delimited text (there must be some sort of delimiter between each of the text entries), select the text. On the Ribbon's Insert tab, select Table and then select Convert Text to Table. The Convert Text to Table dialog box will open (see Figure 8.3).

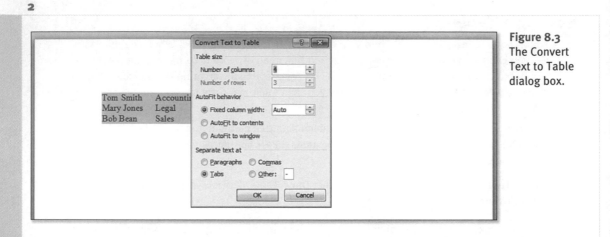

Figure 8.3
The Convert Text to Table dialog box.

Select the delimiter that separates the text in the list in the Separate Text At area of the dialog box. You can select from Paragraphs, Commas, Tabs, or designate a delimiter using the Other option. Based on the delimiter used, Word specifies a table size showing the number of columns and rows. You can also set the AutoFit behavior in the Convert Text to Table dialog box if warranted.

When you click OK, the text converts to a table. If the table isn't perfect in how it has arranged the data, you can insert columns and rows (if needed) and then drag and drop cell entries until you have the data appropriately placed in the table.

Entering Text and Navigating a Table

After you have the table in your document, you will want to add data, which in most cases will be text, although pictures and other graphics can be inserted into a cell. Entering text into the table is very straightforward. Click in the first cell of the table and enter the appropriate text. To move to the next cell, press the Tab key. You can continue to move through the cells in the tables by pressing Tab and entering your text. If you want to back up a cell, press Shift+Tab. This moves you to the cell to the left of the current cell. If you move to a cell that contains text, that text will be selected. If you type new text, it overwrites the original contents of the cell.

> **tip**
> You can also convert a table to text. Use the Convert to Text command on the Layout tab of the table tools.

Of course, you can use the mouse to click in any cell of the table at any time. However, if you are entering information into the table, it is quicker to use some of the other keyboard combinations available to navigate a table:

- **Alt+Home**—Takes you to the first cell in the current row

- **Alt+Page Up**—Takes you to the top cell in the current column

- **Alt+End**—Takes you to the last cell in the current row

- **Alt+Page Down**—Takes you to the last cell in the current column

Deleting text from the table is really no different from deleting text in your document. Select text in the table and press Delete to remove it. If you want to delete all the text in an entire row, place the mouse pointer at the left edge of the particular row. Click to select the entire row. When you press Delete, all the text in the selected row is deleted. You can also use a column pointer (a solid black arrow; place the mouse at the top of any column) to select an entire column and delete text in that column using the Delete key.

Selecting and Positioning a Table

To select a table, place the mouse just above the top-left corner of the table. The Table handle appears. Click on the handle and the entire table will be selected. You can also reposition a table using the Table handle. Use the handle as needed to drag the table to a new position in the document.

Because a table is basically seen by the text that surrounds it (the text in your paragraphs) as a graphic element, you can configure how the surrounding text wraps around the table (as you can a picture or clip art). Drag the table to position it within a paragraph of text. Right-click on the table and select Table Properties from the shortcut menu. The Table tab of the Table Properties dialog box is selected as shown in Figure 8.4.

In the Alignment area of the Table tab, select Left, Center, or Right to position the table in relation to the text in the paragraph. If you do not want the text to wrap around the table, select None in the Text Wrapping area. To return to the document, click OK.

tip

The contents of the cells in your table are not limited to text. You can place clip art, pictures, and other graphics in a cell. You can also nest a table in a table. For example, you could include a table of data (in a cell) that is beside a chart of that data (which is also in a cell).

tip

You can also select a cell, column, row, or the entire table from the shortcut menu. Click in the table and then right-click. On the shortcut menu, point at Select and then select Cell, Column, Row or Table.

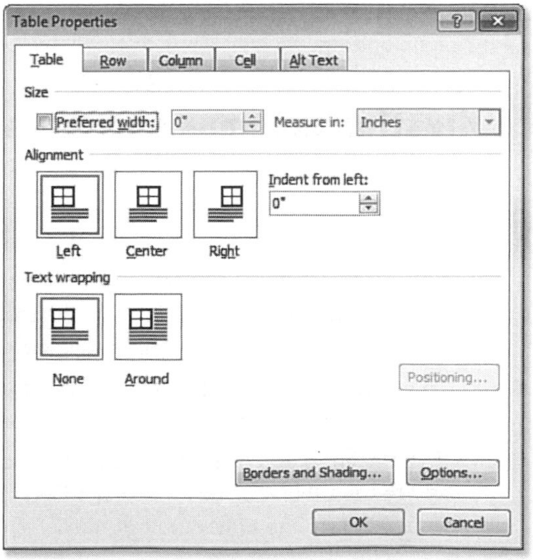

Figure 8.4
The Table Properties dialog box.

Formatting Tables

In terms of formatting tables, you will be working with two broad categories of tools: layout and design. The Layout commands appear on the table tools Layout tab. These tools include commands that enable you to insert columns and rows, merge and split cells, and change the text alignment in a cell or cells. Figure 8.5 shows the Layout tab.

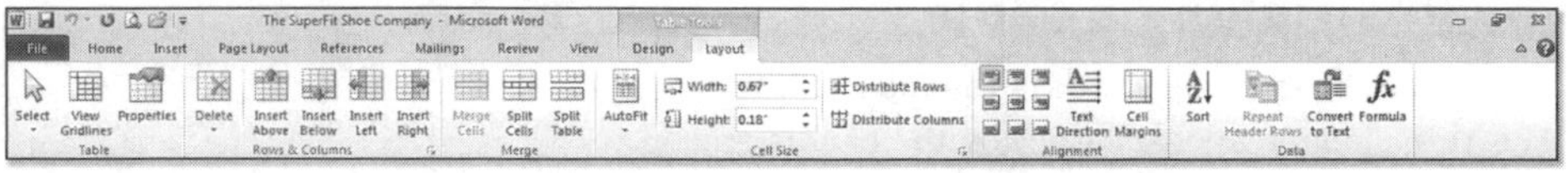

Figure 8.5
The table tools Layout tab.

In the design tools, you have commands related to the use of table styles (a number of table styles are built into Word) and shading and borders settings. The Draw Borders group is also part of the Design tab of the table tools and is shown in Figure 8.6.

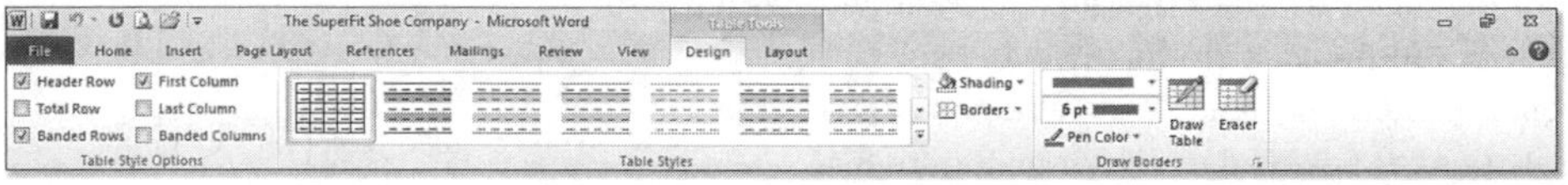

Figure 8.6
The table tools Design Tab.

In terms of providing a unified theme for the Layout commands versus the Design commands, think of the Layout commands as tools that allow you to manipulate the four basic building blocks of a table: columns, rows, cells, and text (within the cells). The Design commands control more of the overall "look" of the table by providing table styles and table style options.

> **tip**
>
> If you are working on a table that does not have borders, click the View Gridlines command on the table tools Layout tab. Seeing the nonprinting gridlines makes it easier to work with the table.

Adjusting Columns and Rows

The columns and rows provide the table's basic structure or "bones." You have complete control over the number of rows and columns in your table. You also control column widths and row heights.

To insert a column, place the insertion point in the column next to where you want to insert the new column. On the Layout tab of the table tools, use the Insert Left or Insert Right command to insert a new column to the left or right of the current column, respectively.

To insert a row, place the insertion in a row. Then use the Insert Above or Insert Below command to insert a new row above or below the current row.

If you need to add more than one column or row, select the number of columns or rows you want to add to the table. Then use the commands in the Rows & Columns group to insert columns or rows as needed (to the right or left of the selected columns or above or below the selected rows).

In terms of adjusting column widths and row heights, you can use the sizing tool to visually change the width of a column or the height of a row. To change the column width, place the mouse between two columns until the resizing pointer appears. Drag the mouse to increase or decrease the column width.

To set a more precise width for a column (or selected columns), you can use the Width Spinner box in the Cell Size group of the Layout tab. Use the arrows to increase or decrease the width or type a measurement (in inches) in the box to specify the width.

You can also increase the row height by using the resizing pointer to drag down (on the bottom) border of a row. To change the height for selected rows, use the Height command spinner box in the Cell Size group.

You can also set column widths and row heights in the Table Properties dialog box. Click in a column or row that you want to adjust. Select the Properties command in the Table group of the Layout tab. If you are adjusting the width of a column (or columns), select the Column tab of the Table Properties dialog box (see Figure 8.7).

Figure 8.7
The Column tab of the Table Properties dialog box.

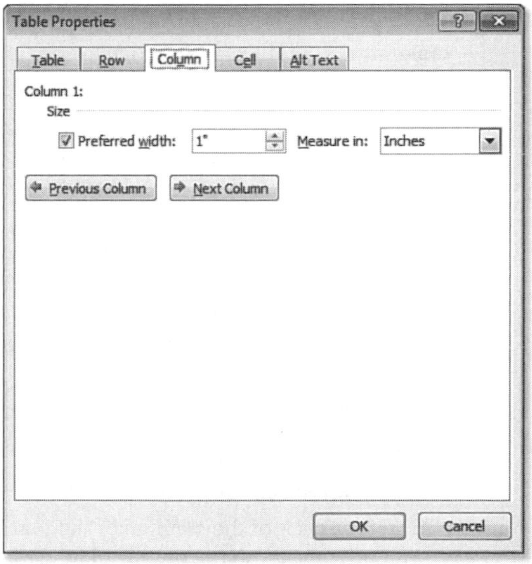

Use the Preferred Width spinner box to set the width for the column (the default measurement is inches). You can use Previous Column or Next Column to set the preferred width for columns adjacent to the current column.

For row height, use the Row tab. The Specify Height spinner box enables you to set the row height, and the Row Height spinner box makes it possible for you to specify that the specified height of the row is at least or exactly the height you have

tip

The Repeat as Header Row at the Top of Each Page check box on the Row tab enables you to specify that the current row is the header (top row of the table) and should be repeated when the table is broken over multiple pages.

entered. An option is also available that allows you to specify if the row should be allowed to break across pages.

Columns and rows can be selected and dragged to new positions in a table. You may also find it necessary to delete columns or rows in the table. Deleting columns or rows is very straightforward. Select a column (or columns) or a row (or rows). Select the Delete command on the Layout tab. Use the Delete Columns or Delete Rows command as needed. If you want to delete the entire table, select Delete Table.

Formatting Cells

Word provides formatting attributes to relate directly to the cells in a table. These formatting features include the ability to merge and split cells. You also have control over how text is aligned in the cell and the cell margins.

Merging cells gives you control over the internal space of the table. To merge cells, select the cells and then click the Merge Cells command in the Merge group of the Layout tab. You can also split a cell; use the Split Cells command to split the current cell into two cells.

There is also another split-related command available in the Merge group. If you want to split a table into two tables at a particular row, place the insertion point in that row and then click Split Table.

Several other cell-specific commands are in the Alignment group on the Layout tab. These commands control the following cell settings:

 tip

You can adjust the width of an individual cell. Select the cell and then drag the cell border as needed to change the width. Note that this takes the cell out of alignment (in terms of its borders) with the rest of the cells in that column.

- **Alignment Commands:** In the right of the Alignment group are nine alignment commands that control where the text is aligned in a cell (or selected cells); the specific commands are Align Top Left, Align Top Center, Align Top Right, Align Center Left, Align Center, Align Center Right, Align Bottom Left, Align Bottom Center, and Align Bottom Right.

- **Text Direction:** This command allows you to cycle through two text-direction possibilities: On the first click of the command, the text is rotated 90° and placed in the upper right of the cell; the next click rotates the text 180° (from the previous setting) and placed in the bottom left of the cell. The third time you click the Text Direction button, it returns the text to its normal text orientation and default alignment.

- **Cell Margins:** This command allows you to set the default cell margins for the table. This is particularly useful if you want to provide crowded cells with a little more breathing room and add some whitespace to the interior of the table. When you select the Cell Margins command, the Table Options dialog box opens (see Figure 8.8). You can specify the top, bottom, left, and right cell margins and also set the default cell spacing.

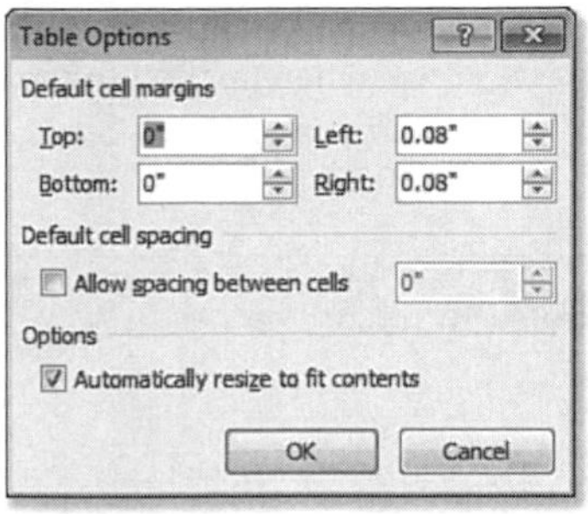

Figure 8.8
Table Options dialog box.

One thing to remember when working with the individual cell settings, such as the Alignment commands and the Cell Margins command, is that you should make these types of adjustment *after* you apply a style to the table. Table styles override any specific cell formatting attributes that you configure except for the Text Rotation setting, which is not affected by assigning a style to a table.

Using Table Styles

Table styles provide you with a unified design for your tables that include a number of table-formatting attributes, including fonts, borders, and shading. By default, all new tables created use the Table Grid style, which provides black borders for the table cells, uses the default font from the current template (in most cases Calibri and the Normal template), and applies no shading to the cells. The check boxes provided in the Table Style Options group on the table tools Design tab determine how the table styles affect the different parts of the table. The options are as follows:

- **Header Row:** The header row is the first row of the table and typically contains the column headings for the table. Because the header row differs from the rows that contain regular data, the table style formats it differently. This option is selected by default.

- **First Column:** The first column often contains the row headings for the table. If you select the First Column option, the table style formats the first column differently than the other columns in the table. This option is selected by default.

- **Total Row:** Totals are typically included in the last row of the table. This option requires the table style to format the last row differently.

- **Last Column:** This option indicates that you want the table style to format the last column differently than the other columns in the table.

- **Banded Rows:** When you select this option, the style formats the odd and even rows in the table differently. This option is selected by default.

- **Banded Columns:** This option allows the table style to format the odd and even columns in the table differently.

tip

You can access the Borders and Shading dialog box for more control over the border and shading options for your table; select Borders and Shading on the Borders drop-down list.

After you decide on the options for the table styles by selecting or deselecting options in the Table Style Options group, you can preview how the various styles provided in the Table Styles group will look when applied to the table (just point at a style to preview it). Figure 8.9 shows the Table Styles gallery (click the More button to view the gallery) and the Table Style Options group (on the left).

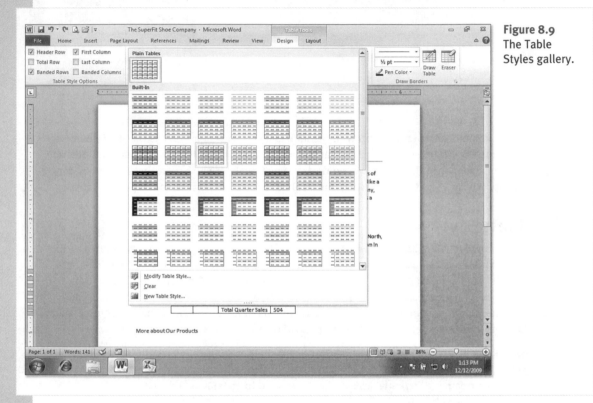

Figure 8.9
The Table Styles gallery.

After you apply a particular style to the table, you can actually change the Table Style options after the fact and apply them to the current style (and any change in style that you make). You can also use the Shading and Borders drop-down list to fine-tune any the shading or the borders for any and all the cells in the table. Select the cell or cells and then change the shading or border settings as needed.

Use the various formatting tools provided to select the formatting for the table. You can apply formatting changes to the whole table or to the header row, first column, odd banded rows, and so on by using the Apply Formatting To drop-down list.

You also can specify whether you want the style modification to be available only in the current document or all the new documents created using the current template: use the Only in This Document and the New Documents Based on This Template options buttons, respectively. When you finish configuring the style modifications, click OK to return to the document.

> **tip**
>
> You can modify any of the existing table styles as needed. Select the More command in the Table Styles group. From the Table Style gallery, select Modify Table Style. The Modify Style dialog box opens (see Figure 8.10).

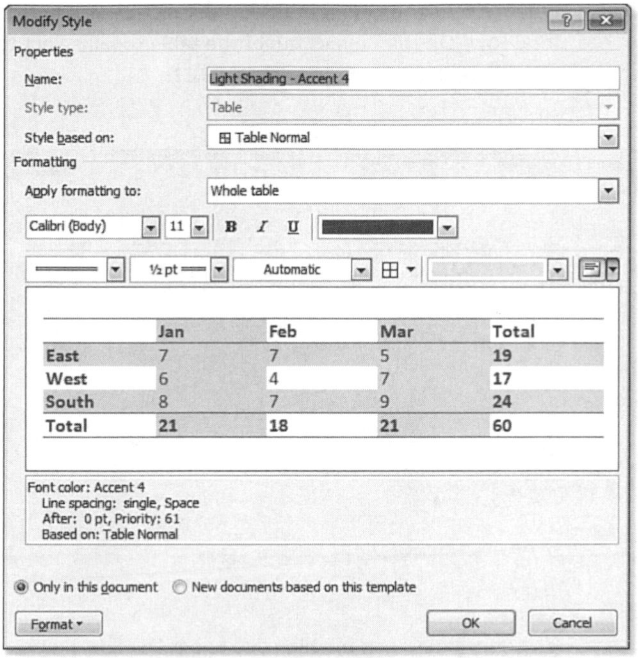

Figure 8.10
The Modify Style dialog box.

If you format a table from scratch (including borders, shading, and font changes), you can save the table's formatting as a new style. You can also create a new style to save modifications that you have made to one of the existing styles (rather than modifying it as discussed previously). To open the Create New Style from Formatting dialog box, open the Table Style gallery and then select Create New Style from Formatting. Provide a name for the style in the Name box (at the top of the dialog box). You can then use the various formatting tools provided in the dialog box to make any additional changes to the style's formatting attributes (the tools are the same as those provided by the Modify Style dialog box). When you are ready to save the style, click OK. The new table style will appear in the Table Styles gallery.

You can delete a table style if needed. Right-click on the style in the gallery and select Delete Table Style from the shortcut menu. You can also access the new Table Style and the Modify Table Style dialog boxes from this same menu.

Sorting Table Data

Word provides you with the ability to sort data within the table. You can select a group of cells and then sort the data in those cells, or you can sort all the data in the table based on the contents of a particular column in the table. To sort an entire table, your table layout must be consistent; so, if you have split or merged cells within the table, you must select specific groups of cells for the sort to work correctly.

To sort data in the table, select the cells to be included in the sort or click anywhere in the table when you are sorting a uniform table with no split or merged cells and no special rows such as a total row. On the Layout tab of the table tools, select the Sort command (it is in the Data group). The Sort dialog box opens (see Figure 8.11).

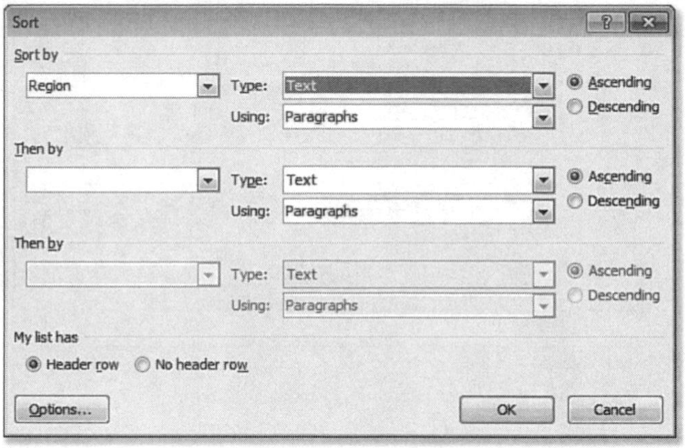

Figure 8.11
The Sort dialog box.

The Sort dialog box enables you to set the Sort by parameter (Region or a particular column) and makes it possible for you to specify the type of data (Text, Number, or Data). If you are sorting an entire table with uniform cells and the table has a header row, take advantage of the Header row option.

The Sort dialog box actually allows you to sort by three different sort conditions (for example, you could sort by last name and then first name in a table of clients or employees). After you set the various sort parameters, click OK to perform the sort and return to the table.

Using Formulas in Tables

Word provides you with the ability to do a number of different types of calculations in your tables. It certainly does not provide the large number of functions you find in Excel, but there are functions provided for averages, sums, maximum, and minimum among others.

Word (like Excel) does have the capability to take an educated guess in relation to the type of calculation you want to make in a table. For example, if you insert a formula at the bottom of a column of numbers, Word assumes that you want to sum the data above the current cell and suggests the formula =SUM(ABOVE).

In cases where you must specify the group of cells that will be acted on the function you insert into the table, you need to understand how cell addresses are determined and how they are expressed in the formula. Each column in the table receives a unique letter designation, starting with A. So, the first column is A, the second is B, and so on. The first row in

> **note**
>
> In situations where you need to do multiple calculations, you might want to copy and paste the table into Excel. Excel provides greater flexibility and ease of use when you are working with calculations.

the table is 1. The second row is 2, and so on. The first cell in a table, which is in column A and row 1, would be cell A1. Each cell's address is the column letter followed by the row number.

To specify a group of cells to be acted on by a formula, you have to specify the first cell in the group and then the last cell in the group. So, if you were adding cells B2, B3, B4, and B5, you would designate the cell group with B2:B5. This tells Word where the cells to act on begin and end.

To insert a formula into a table cell, click in the cell where you will place the formula. To open the Formula dialog box, select the Formula command in the Data group.

In the Formula dialog box, you need to specify the formula in the Formula box. As already mentioned, if you are inserting a formula at the bottom of a column of numbers or at the end of a row of numbers, Word provides a formula in the Formula box.

You can specify a formula for the Formula box by selecting a function from the Paste function list. After you paste in the function, you have to specify the cells that the formula will act on. To do so, type the cell range (which is the starting cell address and ending cell address) between the parentheses provided in the formula.

You can also use the Number format drop-down box to specify how the calculation result in the cell should be formatted (such as currency or a percentage). When you complete setting the formula options, click OK to insert the formula.

> **tip**
>
> You can specify the cell range for the formula to act on by using a bookmark. Select a group of cells in the table, select Bookmark on the Ribbon's Insert tab, and provide a name for the bookmark. You can now use the bookmark when you create your formula in the Formula dialog box.

> **caution**
>
> Word columns are not appropriate for arranging text in a tabular format (meaning side-by-side text). Use a table or tabs if you need to arrange text on the page in side-by-side columns.

Adding Columns to a Document

The columns that you work with in Word are called newspaper or "snaking" columns. This means that if you have two columns on a page and fill the first column, the text snakes over into the second column and continues to be inserted there. Word columns are perfect for newsletters and brochures.

You can format a blank document for columns, or you can select text and then apply column settings to the selected text. You can also have Word begin the column settings at the insertion point and place all the text from that point forward in the number of columns that you have selected. When you apply column settings to any selected text, Word automatically places the text (now in the number of columns you selected) into its own document section. We discuss sections in the next section of this chapter. For now, it is probably clear to you that the point of a section is to separate the new page layout settings from the rest of the document.

To insert columns into a document at the insertion point, select the Columns command on the Ribbon's Page Layout tab. You can select One, Two, or Three from the Columns list that appears. Selecting the option Two (or more) places columns of equal width on the page. You can also select Left or Right. These settings place two columns; however, the Left selection creates a narrower left column (1.8 and a wider right column (4.1) The Right selection does just the opposite. All of these selections separate the columns with a spacing of a half inch.

If you want more control over the column settings, select More Columns. This opens the Columns dialog box (see Figure 8.12).

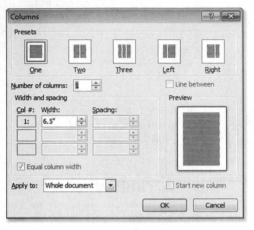

Figure 8.12
The Columns dialog box.

You can also select the presets from the Columns dialog box or specify your own number of columns using the Number of Columns spinner box. After you specify the number of columns, you can specify the width and spacing (between the columns) using the Width and Spacing boxes.

You can also specify whether you want the column settings to apply to the whole document or from this point forward in the document (from the insertion point). If you select This Point Forward in the Apply to drop-down list, a new section is created in the document. When you finish entering your settings for the columns, click OK.

 tip

If you want to place a line between the columns in your document, select the Line Between check box in the Columns dialog box.

You can edit the columns settings that you have applied to your document (or a section of the document). Make sure that you place the insertion point within a document section formatted for columns. Then click the Columns command in the Page Setup group and select More Columns. This opens the Columns dialog box and you can edit the current settings as needed.

Because you are working with continuous, newspaper-type column settings, at times you might want to force a column break in a column. This allows you to balance the text between columns or end the text in a column at a particular point and force the rest of the text into the next column. To place a column break at the insertion point, select the Breaks command on the Ribbon's Page Layout tab. Select Column on the Breaks list.

Understanding Sections

Most of the documents that we create (the smaller, less complex documents) typically consist of one section. All the page layout attributes such as the margins, page orientation, number of columns, even the headers and footers are the same for the entire document. More complex documents can be a little more challenging in terms of page layout settings; think of a report that has a cover page, a table of contents, and then the body text of the report.

Each of these different parts or sections of the document might require different page layout attributes. The section meets the need for different page layouts in a single document. A section is defined by a section break, and each section can have its own page layout settings as well as its own headers and footers.

> **tip**
>
> You can actually copy the formatting from one section to another in a document by copying the section break. In the Draft view, select and copy the section break. Then paste it into another part of the document. This creates a copy of the section, including all the page layout settings from the copied section.

Adding and Removing Section Breaks

When you are inserting new section breaks into a document, switch to the Draft view (Draft on the View tab). This enables you to view the section break and the type of section break that you insert. Then inserting the new section break is very straightforward.

Place the insertion point in the document where you want the new section to start. On the Ribbon's Page Layout tab, select Breaks (in the Page Setup group). Figure 8.13 shows the Break options.

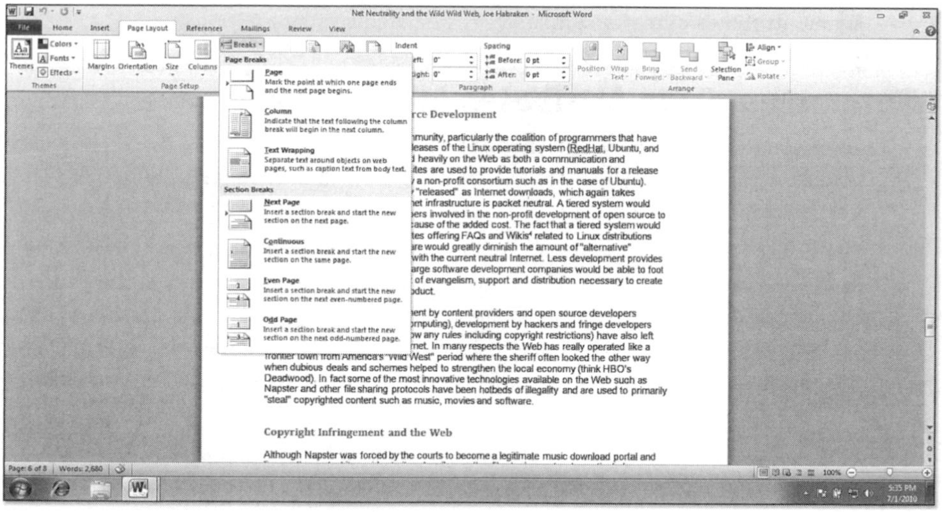

Figure 8.13
The Break list.

You will find that there are four different types of Section Breaks listed:

- **Next Page:** A page break is placed in the document, and the new section begins on this new page.

- **Continuous:** The new section starts at the insertion point and continues for the rest of the document (or until it comes to the next section break).

- **Even Page:** The new section starts on the next even-numbered page.

- **Odd Page:** The new section starts on the next odd-numbered page.

The type of section break you select will, obviously, depend on the type of document you are creating. If you have a document that has a table of contents followed by the body of the document, it makes sense to use a Next Page section (starting the body of the document on a new page). Even page and odd page sections are often used when you will create a document with facing pages. Different headers and footers are then created for the even pages and the odd pages.

➡ *For more about headers and footers, see "Working with Headers and Footers" in Chapter 7.*

After you select a type of section break, it is inserted into the document. As already mentioned, you can view the section break in the Draft view. This view doesn't provide you with any insight into the different page layout settings configured before and after the section break, but it provides the only way for you to see where the section break was actually inserted into the document.

To delete a section break in the Draft view, select the section break and then press Delete. This removes the section from the document. It also removes all the page layout formatting that was applied to the section. In effect, removing the section resets the text that was in that section to the layout attributes of the section above the deleted section.

Formatting Page Attributes in a Section

After you establish a new section in the document, you can specify the various page layout settings for that section. When you want to format a particular section, make sure that you have the insertion point in that section.

Some of the common page layout and other document attributes that differ from section to section in the document require the use of the Page Setup commands found on the Page Layout tab. These commands enable you to change margins, page orientation, and the number of columns for each section. Other settings that you might want to configure differently for document sections relate to headers, footers, and page numbering. These commands are located in the Header & Footer group on the Insert tab.

Remember that to view the actual location of a section break, use the Draft view. To view the effect of the page layout settings for a section, you can use the Print Layout view or the Print Preview pane in the Print window.

MANAGING MAILINGS AND FORMS

Creating form letters, mailing labels or envelopes might seem to be daunting tasks. Word, however, takes a very straightforward approach to creating all the printed materials necessary for a mass mailing to a group of customers, colleagues or friends. Word also makes it easy to gather information electronically by creating forms that can be circulated on your network or via email. This enables you to create questionnaires or other materials that make it very easy for the recipient of the form to provide you with the information you need.

In this chapter we take a look at how to create mail-related documents such as envelopes and labels. We will also perform a mail merge in which you merge names and addresses with a form letter or email message. We wrap up the chapter with a look at how you can create forms using form controls.

Options for Mail-Related Documents

Most of the tasks that we undertake in Word relate to communicating with others; we create documents such as letters, e-mails, and forms. Word definitely provides you with all the tools required for letters, envelopes, and mailing labels. You can quickly create any "snail mail" document that you require.

Word also provides you with the ability to take a data source, such as a list of names and addresses, and quickly merge it into a document such as a form letter. Merges can also be accomplished using data from Microsoft Outlook that is then merged into an email. So, Word definitely has you covered in terms of mass mailings.

For mail-related documents, Microsoft Word and Office Online provide a number of letter templates. You can use these templates to create a letter to send to an individual or a form letter that will play a part in a merge that produces a number of letters based on a list of names and addresses.

You can also create a single envelope in Word or you can merge to an envelope and create envelopes for your entire mailing list. The same goes for creating a sheet of labels that repeat a single address (such as your return address) or labels created for each person on your mailing list.

Word also provides you with the ability to build forms. The use of form controls on your forms provides a convenient way for you to share a network document with respondents, who can then quickly use the form to record their responses. Form controls even allow you to specify the actual responses that respondents can give to a particular form question.

Creating an Envelope

When you create a letter in Word, it (typically) contains the name and address of the individual who will receive your letter. Having the name and address available in the letter makes it very easy for you to then create an envelope for that letter.

So, it makes sense to create the letter before creating the envelope. As already mentioned, you can use one of Word's letter templates to create the actual letter.

> **tip**
>
> You can quickly insert the current date into the letter using the Date and Time command in the Text group of the Insert tab.

To create the envelope, select the Envelopes command on the Ribbon's Mailings tab. This opens the Envelopes and Labels dialog box as shown in Figure 9.1. Note that the Envelopes tab of the dialog box is selected.

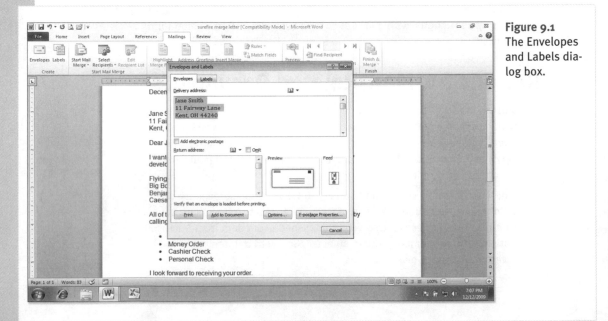

Figure 9.1
The Envelopes and Labels dialog box.

If a delivery address was present in your letter, it should appear in the Delivery address box (in the dialog box). You can type in the address if needed or you can use the Address Book icon to add the address from Outlook. You can type your address in the Return Address box or you can use the Address Book icon to add your address to the box using your Outlook profile.

The Envelopes and Labels dialog box also provides you with the ability to add electronic postage to the envelope. To specify envelope options such as the envelope size and the fonts used on the envelope, select the Options button in the Envelopes and Labels dialog box. This opens the Envelope Options dialog box (see Figure 9.2).

Figure 9.2
The Envelopes Options dialog box.

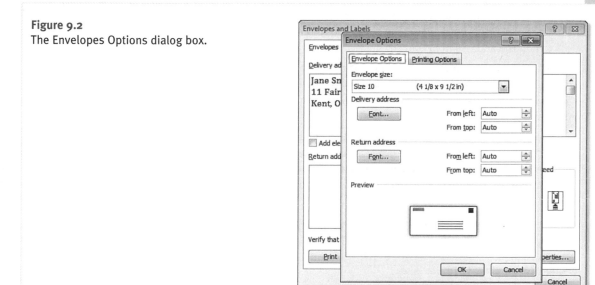

You can specify the envelope size and the fonts to use for both the delivery and return address. You can also specify the distance from the left and top of the envelope for the addresses. Click OK to return to the Envelopes and Labels dialog box.

You can now print the envelope if you want. Click the Print button in the Envelopes and Labels dialog box. If you want to add the envelope to the current document (your letter), click the Add to Document button. When you select this option, you are actually creating a new section in the document (remember that different sections can have different page layout settings). Having the envelope as part of the current document means that you can print the envelope and the letter during the same print job.

Creating a Sheet of Labels

Word also provides you with the ability to print a sheet of labels. This is particularly useful if you want to print a sheet of labels with your return address. Or if you send mail to a particular addressee frequently, it also wouldn't hurt to have ready-made labels on hand.

To create the labels, click the Envelopes command on the Ribbon's Mailings tab. The Envelopes and Labels dialog box opens with the Label tab selected. You can enter the address for the labels in the Address box or use the Address Book icon to add the address from Outlook.

The default setting for printing labels is to print a full page of the same label. You can print the labels via the Print button or save them as a new document (use the New Document button).

More important, you need to select the type of label that you are using before you print the labels or create the new document. Click on the current label type shown in the dialog box and the Label Options dialog box opens (see Figure 9.3).

 caution

You would think that creating labels in Word would be a pretty simple process. However, labels have always been a little problematic in Word. I suggest that you purchase labels made by a company on the Vendors list and also use labels that appear in the Product Number list. It will make your life a lot easier.

tip

If you have a letter open in Word that contains your return address, you can click the Use Return Address check box to have your address placed in the label's Address box.

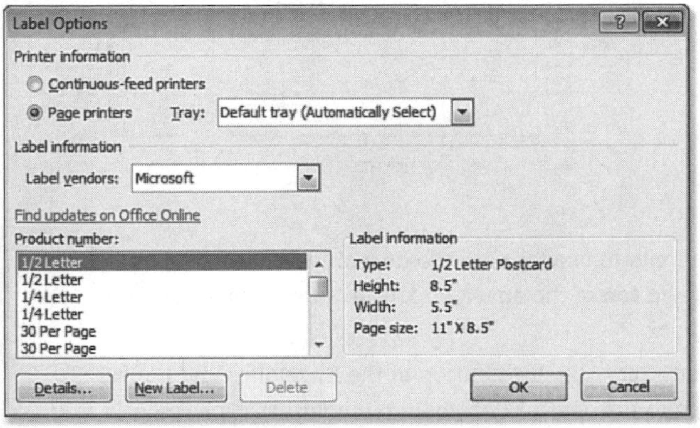

Figure 9.3
The Label Options dialog box.

The Label Options dialog box allows you to specify the label vendor and the product number of the labels you are using. Select the vendor in the Label Vendors list and then scroll through the Product Number list and identify your label.

You can access the details for a particular label by selecting the Details button. You can adjust the margins, pitch, height, and width for your label. This should not be necessary if you are using a standard label.

When you have selected your label vendor and type (of label) you can then choose to immediately print the labels (via the Print button). You also have the option of creating a new document (use the New Document button) for the labels. This allows you save the labels for future printing.

Understanding Word's Options for Mass Mailings

We normally equate mass or group mailings with form letters. And although Word's mail merge feature does enable you to create a variety of documents for group mailings such as letters, envelopes, and labels, you can use it to send email messages to a group or to create a directory of information.

To perform a mail merge you need two things: a merge document that will be mass produced (one will be created for each recipient) and the data that will go into the document. The document that will be merged with the data can really take any form; it is most often a letter or an envelope, but you can merge data into any type of Word document.

The other thing that you need for a mail merge is data. This can be names and addresses or it could be a list of email addresses. The data, such as the names and addresses, is stored in a file called a data source. So, the big question is how does the data in the data source know where to end up in a document such as the form letter?

The information in the data source is actually inserted into the form letter, envelope, or mailing label using placeholder codes called merge fields. Each merge field in the merge document relates to a piece of information in the data source document, such as first name, last name, or street address, and the merge field gets its name from that particular field in the data source.

Performing a Mail Merge

The commands that you will use to perform a mail merge are found in the Start Mail Merge group (on the Ribbon's Mailings tab). As already mentioned, the merge process requires that you have a document such as a form letter and that you also have a data source. The actual process of performing the mail merge really consists of four distinct parts: creating or opening the merge document, creating or specifying the data source, inserting the merge fields into the main document, and finally running the merge, which creates the form letters, envelopes, and so on.

Each of these four actions can and probably will require you to perform a subset of tasks. For example, to create merged letters during the merge process, you have to supply the initial form letter. This can be accomplished by creating the letter during the merge process or by opening an existing letter.

When you need to specify your list of recipients (the data source), you might create the recipient's list on the fly or you might already have the list available (and it might even be in another application such as Microsoft Outlook). And even if you have the list of recipients available, you might want to edit the list or specify that the merge use a subset of the available recipients. Obviously, what actually happens during each of the major phases of the merge will be dictated by your particular needs in relation to the merge document, the recipient list, and the merge fields you are going to use.

To actually perform the mail merge, you can use the Mail Merge Wizard, which will walk you step by step through the entire process. To invoke the Mail Merge Wizard, select the Start Mail Merge command and then select Step by Step Mail Merge Wizard. The Mail Merge task pane opens as shown in Figure 9.4.

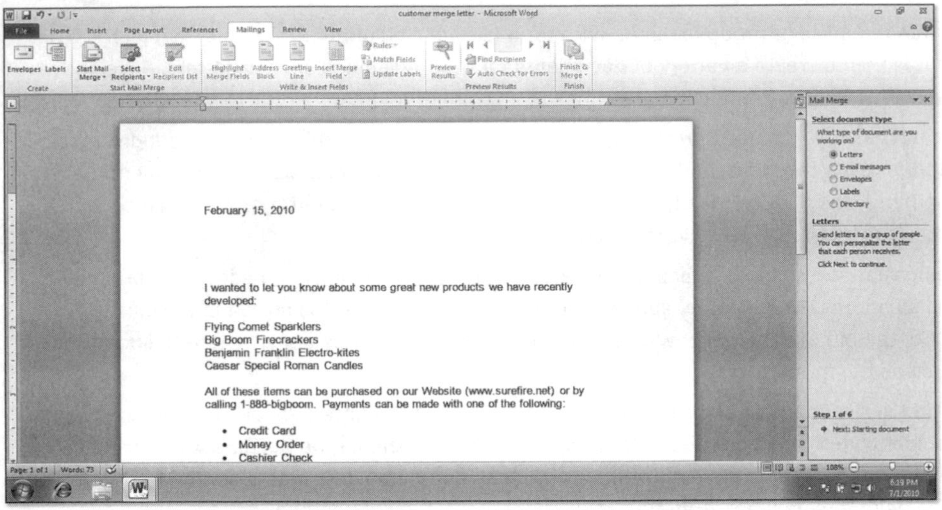

Figure 9.4
The Mail Merge task pane.

The wizard breaks the mail merge process into six distinct steps:

1. **Select Document Type**: This step provides option buttons allowing you to specify the type of merge document you wish to create: Letters, E-Mail Messages, Envelopes, Labels, or a Directory. A directory does not create a separate document for each of the recipients; an example would be a list of names and addresses created from your data source.

2. **Select Starting Document**: This step enables you to specify how you will set up the merge document. You can select from the following options: Use the Current Document, Start from Template, or Start from Existing Document.

3. **Select Recipients**: This step is important in that it not only provides the list of recipients for the merge but also determines the merge field codes (based on the data source's fields) that will be available to insert into the merge document. You can use an existing list, select from Outlook contacts, or type a new list.

4. **Write Your Letter**: This step allows you to type your merge document such as a letter or email or set up your envelope or labels (if you haven't already done it). This is also the step where you

> **⚠ caution**
> Although the Mail Merge Wizard makes sure that you complete all the steps necessary to perform the merge, you might find more flexibility in terms of completing the merge process if you forego the use of the wizard and use the various commands on the Mailings tab. Let's take a closer look at each of the major parts of the mail merge process and add some depth to your knowledge of the various commands on the Ribbon's Mailings tab.

insert merge fields into the document. Merge files included in the task pane are the Address Block, Greeting Line, and Electronic Postage.

> 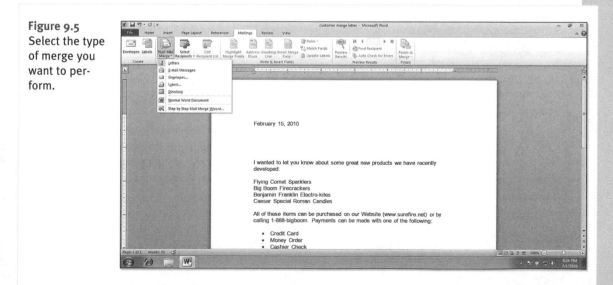 *We look more closely at merge fields in this chapter in the section "Using Merge Fields."*

> **tip**
>
> A form letter always contains the current date (typically at the top of the letter). To insert the date into your form letter so that it automatically updates, open the Date and Time dialog box using the Date & Time command on the Insert tab. Select a date format in the dialog box and then select the Update Automatically check box.

5. **Preview Your Letters**: This step allows you to preview your letters (or other merged document such as envelopes or labels). Use the Next and Previous buttons as required to preview the results of the merge.

6. **Complete the Merge**: This step allows you to either send the results of the merge to a printer or to edit each of the individual documents that have resulted from the merge (such as your letter, envelopes, and so on).

Using the Mail Merge Commands

Deciding not to use the Mail Merge Wizard doesn't really handicap you in terms of working with the mail merge feature; you are still going to go through the same overall process to create merged form letters, envelopes, or labels. You will be selecting your commands from left to right on the Mailings tab as you move through the mail merge process.

To begin the process, select the Start Mail Merge command in the Start Mail Merge group (see Figure 9.5). As you do when you use the wizard, you select the type of document you wish to create using the merge: Letters, E-mail Messages, Envelopes, Labels, or Directory. The Start Mail Merge command also provides an additional option: Normal Word Document.

Figure 9.5
Select the type of merge you want to perform.

For best practices, create your letter or email before you even think about the merge process. In the final analysis, the content of the letter or email is of primary importance (although you do want the merge to work correctly). Make sure that you spend the appropriate amount of thought and time on the correspondence itself.

The two most problematic parts of performing the merge relate to creating and manipulating the recipient list and then inserting (appropriately) the merge fields into your document. Let's look at some issues related to recipient lists and then work with merge fields.

Understanding Recipient Lists

The data source or recipient list (if you prefer) consists of the information that you will merge into your form letter, email, or envelope. As already mentioned, it is typically names and addresses, but it can also include other information such as email addresses and telephone numbers.

A couple of terms that will help you work with data sources should be introduced at this point: records and fields. A record is the information related to a particular person (or place or thing). So, each person in your recipient list has his or her own record.

More important (at least in terms of understanding the merge process), each piece of information in a record, such as the first name or street address, is called a field. The fields in the data source relate directly to the merge field codes available to you to insert into your form letter or envelope. Each field code, then, directly relates to information (a field) in each record in your recipient list.

> **note**
>
> If you are using the Mail Merge Wizard, the recipient list is created or specified in step 3 of the wizard's merge process provided in the Mail Merge task pane.

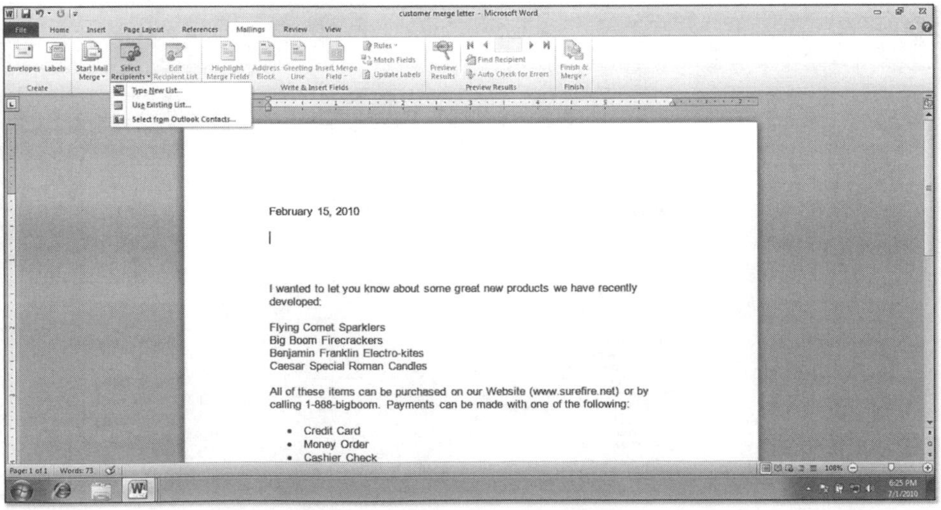

For specifying a recipient list for a particular merge, you have options. You can access these options via the Select Recipients command in the Start Mail Merge group (see Figure 9.6).

Figure 9.6
Select or create a recipients list.

The options related to the recipient list are as follows:

- **Type a New List:** Use this option to create a new data source using the recipient list tools in Word. We will explore this option in more detail in a moment.

- **Use Existing List:** This option allows you to open an existing list created in Word or data sources created in Microsoft Access. The Select Data Source dialog box also provides options for connecting to shared data sources (on your corporate network) via a Microsoft Office Data Connection or a Microsoft SQL database server.

- **Select from Outlook Contacts:** This option enables you to select the names and addresses for the merge from your Outlook contacts. When you select the option on the Select Recipients menu, the Choose Profile dialog box opens, allowing you to choose the Outlook profile that provides the contacts for the merge. After selecting the profile, the Select Contacts dialog box opens to enable you to select an Outlook contact folder to import.

> *Outlook provides you with the ability to have multiple Outlook profiles on the same computer. For more about Outlook profiles, see the section "Understanding Outlook Profiles" in Chapter 22, "Requisite Outlook: Configuration and Essential Features."*

Obviously, using pre-existing lists or data sources that are shared on a network will make it easier for you to quickly access the records that you need to include in a merge. However, many of us are in the situation where we are required to create the recipient list (at least for our first merge) using the tools provided by Word. These tools, however, are certainly not lacking data-management tools that allow you to easily create, edit, and manipulate the records in the data source.

Creating a Recipient List

Creating a data source during the Mail Merge process is very straightforward. Word provides you with a form that you use to enter people's names, addresses, and other information. When you select Type New List on the Select Recipients command menu or in the Mail Merge task pane, the New Address List dialog box opens as shown in Figure 9.7.

Word provides a default set of fields for the recipient list. The field list includes files such as Title, First Name, Last Name, and so on. If you want to use the default fields (which also serve as the column headings in the New Address List dialog box), you can go ahead and enter the name, address, and other information that you want to place in the record for the first recipient. To move forward through the field columns, use the Tab key. To back up in a field or fields in a record, use the Shift+Tab keys. You would then create subsequent entries by selecting the New Entry button in the Address List dialog box. Each time you click New Entry, a new row is added to the address list.

If you want to modify the field list, it is important that you do so before you begin to enter field information into the address list. Select Customize Columns in the New Address List dialog box and the Customize Address List opens as shown in Figure 9.8.

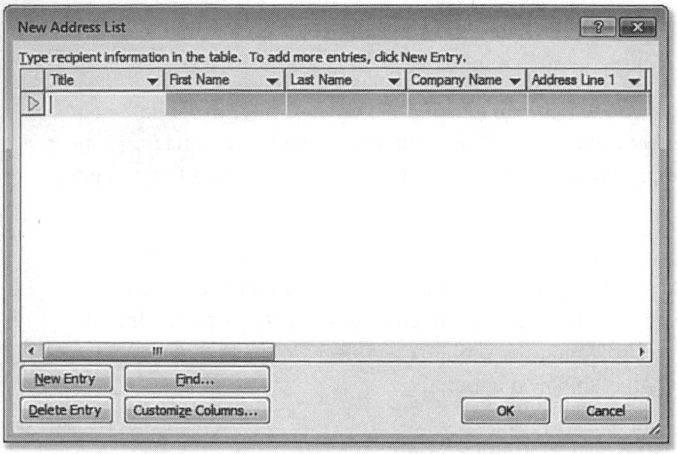

Figure 9.7
Create your records in the New Address List dialog box.

Figure 9.8
The Customize Address List dialog box.

You can add, delete, or rename field names in the list. You can also use the Move Up and Move Down buttons to change the relative position of the field columns. If you want to add a field, click the Add button. The Add Field dialog box opens. Enter the name for your new field and click OK. You can also use the Delete and Rename buttons as needed to modify the field list to your own particular needs. When you finish modifying the default field names, click OK to return to the New Address List dialog box.

Whether or not you modify the list's fields, enter your records as needed in the New Address List dialog box. If you want to delete a particular record, select that record and then click Delete Entry. When you finish entering your records, click the Close button on the New Address List dialog box.

The Save Address List dialog box opens (see Figure 9.9). By default your data sources are saved in the My Data Sources folder, which is a subfolder of your My Documents folder.

Figure 9.9
The Save Address
List dialog box.

Provide a name for the data source and specify a new location for the file if required. The file type for the new file is Microsoft Office Address Lists, which is actually saved with the .mdb extension (the same as Microsoft Access databases). To save the new data source, click the Save button.

Editing and Manipulating a Recipient List

After you create or select a recipient list for the merge, you will find that the Edit Recipient List command in the Start Mail Merge group activates. When you select it, the Mail Merge Recipients dialog box opens as shown in Figure 9.10.

This dialog box provides you with the ability to refine the recipient list using tools such as Sort, Filter, and Find Duplicates. You can also access the records in the data source and edit the records if needed.

You can sort the records in the recipients list by up to three sort criteria. Select Sort to open the Filter and Sort dialog box. You can use the Sort By drop-down list to specify the first field to sort by and then use the optional Then By drop-down lists (there are two) to specify a second and third field for the sort if necessary. You can also specify whether the sort should be ascending or descending using the supplied option buttons. When you are ready to perform the sort, click OK. The records in the Mail Merge Recipients dialog box sort according to your sort parameters.

note

The Mail Merge Recipients dialog box also provides you with the ability to validate addresses in the address list. To do this, you need validation add-on software. Visit www.microsoft.com to find more information about address validation options for Office.

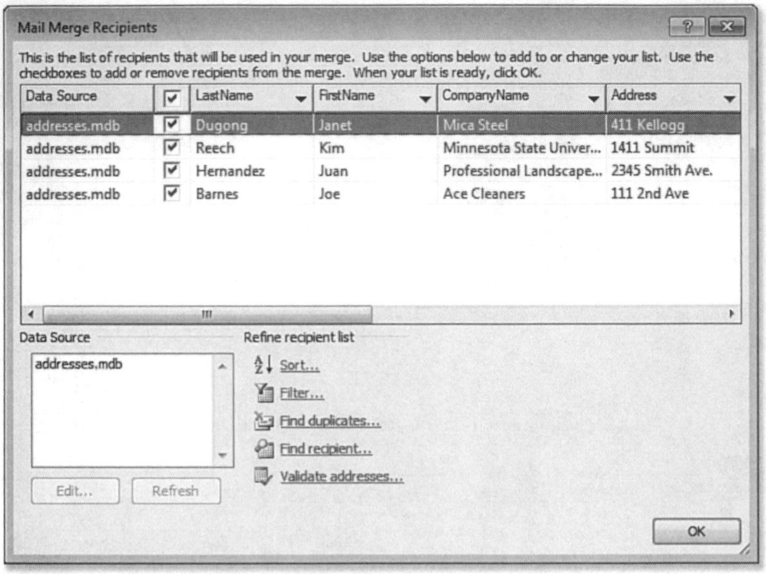

Figure 9.10
The Mail Merge Recipients dialog box.

If you want to preclude specific records from being included in the merge, deselect the check box for that record or records. This is a pretty quick fix for removing a recipient from the merge but keeping the record intact in the recipient's list.

You can also filter the records in the data source. This enables you to select a subset of recipients to include in the merge based on specific criteria related to a field or fields. You can filter by up to six fields.

To open the Filter and Sort dialog box with the Filter Records tab selected, select Filter. You then specify the field or fields by which you want to filter the data source by using the Field drop-down lists as shown in Figure 9.11.

After you select a field, you can then specify the type of comparison you want to make to that field's content. You can specify a number of comparisons including Equal To, Not equal To, Less Than, Is Blank, and Contains. After you select the Comparison Type (such as Equal To), you then type the actual text to be used by the comparison in the Compare To box for that particular field. For example, I might want to send my letters to people on my list in only a particular state, so I would select the State field, set the Comparison Type as Equal To and type the name of the state in the Compare To box.

> **note**
>
> You can actually set up conditional statements for your filters combining field criteria using AND, or you can set up a conditional OR statement where the field criteria can be equal to a particular field or another selected field. So, bottom line: You can do some very elegant filters using the tools provided on the Filter Records tab.

After you set your filter parameters, click OK. The records listed in the mail Merge Recipients dialog box are a subset of the original list based on the criteria you set for your filter.

Figure 9.11
The Filter Records tab.

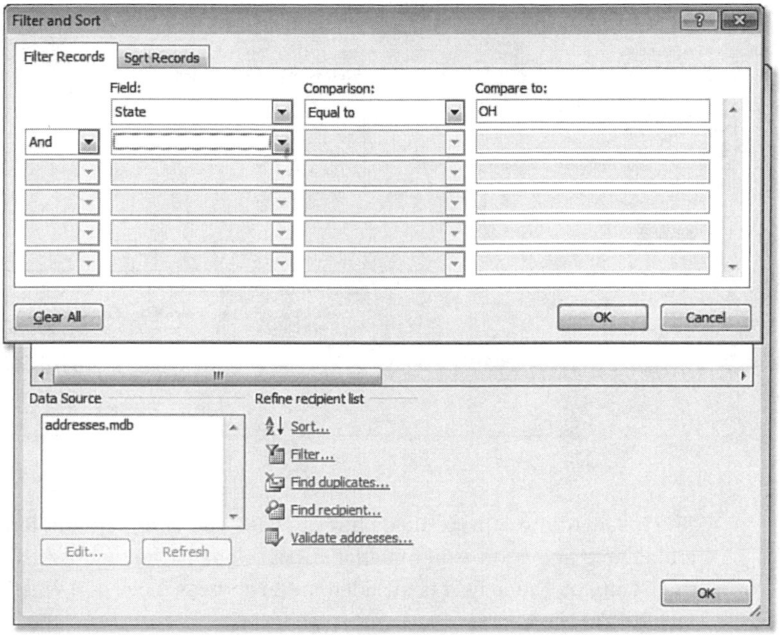

Filter and Sort

Filter Records | Sort Records

	Field:	Comparison:	Compare to:
	State	Equal to	OH
And			

Clear All | OK | Cancel

Data Source

addresses.mdb

Refine recipient list

- Sort...
- Filter...
- Find duplicates...
- Find recipient...
- Validate addresses...

Edit... | Refresh

OK

The Mail Merge Recipients dialog box also provides you with access to the Edit Data Source dialog box (which is very similar to the New Address List dialog box discussed earlier). In the Edit Data Source box, select the current data source and then click the Edit button. Use the Edit Data Source dialog box to edit records as needed. You can also add records in the Edit Data Source dialog box using the New Entry button.

Using Merge Fields

After you square away the data source, the next step in the merge process revolves around the merge fields to insert into the form letter or other merge document. The Field codes are inserted via the Write & Insert group on the Ribbon's Mailings tab.

If you are creating form letters, envelopes, or mailing labels, one of the most often used set of field codes will be the Address Block. The Address Block combines the name, company name, and address information including the state and ZIP code.

 tip

If your filter doesn't give you the expected results, click Filter to open the Filter and Sort dialog box and then edit the filter settings. If you want to completely clear the filter and return to your original list, click the Clear All command and then OK.

To insert the Address Block on a letter (typically three lines below the date) or an envelope, position the insertion point appropriately and then click the Address Block command. The Insert Address Block dialog box opens as shown in Figure 9.12.

Figure 9.12
The Insert Address Block dialog box.

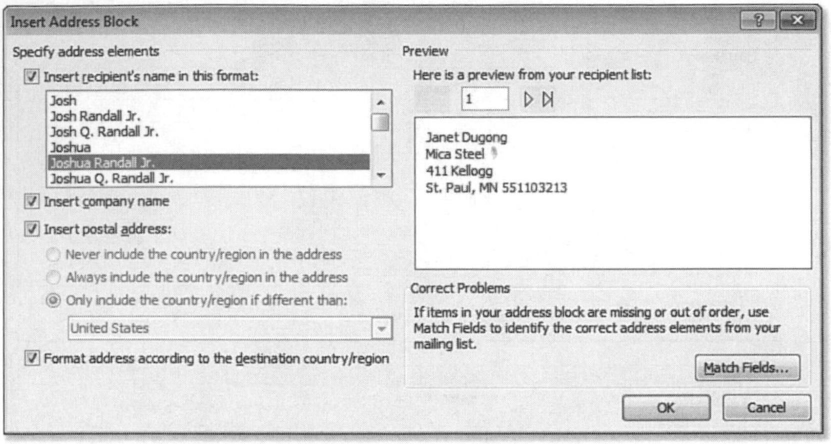

The Insert Address Block dialog box provides you with different formats for inserting the recipient's name and address information. Choose one of the formats listed. You can also specify whether the Company Name field is included in the address block and whether country/region should be included in the address.

After you completed configuring the address block, click OK to insert it into the merge document. The merge code <<AddressBlock>> is placed at the insertion point.

Another way to insert multiple merge codes into a merge document, such as a letter, is the Greeting Line command. It inserts a salutation such as Dear or To, and enables you to specify how the name field data is included with the greeting. You can also control the punctuation used after the greeting (comma, colon, or none—to punctuation). As with the Address Block, the Greeting Line has its own dialog box.

Be advised that the Address Block and Greeting Line are configured to use the default field names that Word supplies you when you create a recipients list (in Word). If your data source originated in another application, such as Microsoft Outlook, Microsoft Access, or an external SQL database, you must match the field names that you used to the typical Word merge fields that specify information such as the recipient's name or address. Click the Match Fields button in the Address Block or Greeting Line dialog box. This opens the Match Fields dialog box (see Figure 9.13).

The Word mail merge fields are listed on the left side of the dialog box. You use the drop-down boxes to specify the matching field from your data source. Each drop-down list shows all the field names for your recipients list that need to be reconciled with the field names that Word uses. For example, if you used the field name Address for the street and street number in your data source, you would match it to the Address 1 Word field. After you match all the fields, you can close the Match Fields dialog box by clicking OK.

> **tip**
>
> You can use the Preview pane in the Insert Address Block dialog box to preview all records in your recipient list. This allows you to catch any records that have blank address fields or other typos.

Figure 9.13
The Match Fields dialog box.

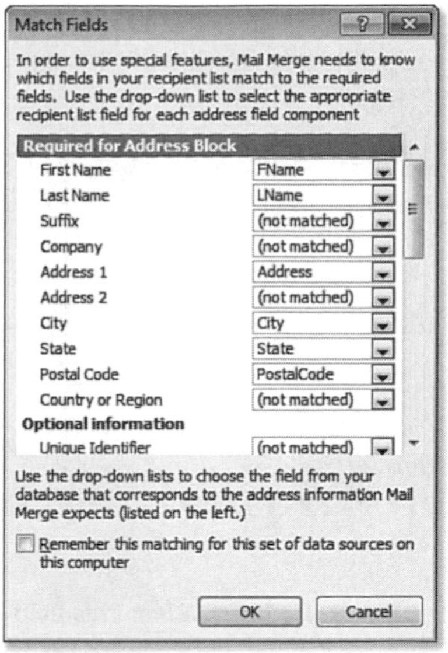

You can also insert individual field codes into a merge document if required. Place the insertion point in the merge document where you would like to insert the field code. Select the Insert Merge Field command on the Mailings tab and select a merge field from the list provided. Remember that merge field codes can relate to any data. So, you can set up a data source that includes information such as the names of your clients' spouses or their favorite sports, and then insert that information into an appropriately crafted merge letter. This allows you to personalize each of the form letters or other merge documents that you create.

> **tip**
>
> You can also reconcile your field names to the Word field names via the Match Fields command in the Write & Insert Fields group. This command opens the Match Fields dialog box. If you consistently used data sources that use the same field names, select the Remember This Matching for This Set of Data Sources on This Computer check box so that you won't have to match the fields each time you do a merge.

Using Merge Rules

One other merge tool that can help you personalize your merge documents and control the content of the documents created during the merge is the Rules command found in the Write & Insert Fields group. This command provides you with the ability to take advantage of several rules that actually allow you to control the content of merged documents during the actual merge process.

When you click the Rules command, the list of rules appears. The following rules, which are really special fields, are provided on the list:

- **Ask:** This field prompts you so that you can enter text during the merge. When you are creating an Ask field, you are creating a bookmark that can include a default response and the field appears as an empty bookmark in the merge document.

- **Fill-in:** This field prompts you to enter text that appears in place of the field when your merge is completed. The Fill-in can contain default text. Figure 9.14 shows the Insert Word Field: Fill-in box. You provide prompt text for the field and can provide default fill-in text.

Figure 9.14
The Insert Word Field: Fill-in box.

- **If...Then...Else:** This field enables you to enter two different text blocks into the merged documents depending on whether a condition is met. For example, if you have an actual storefront in a particular state for your business, this field can be used to insert a location (and address) for the store when the recipient's state matched the If statement.

- **Merge Record #:** You can use this field to provide a true count of the number of records in the data file even when you use fields such as Skip Record If to merge certain recipients into the same letter or other merged document.

- **Merge Sequence #:** This field counts the actual number of merged documents that result from your merge.

- **Next Record:** This field has Word insert the next data record into the current merged document without starting a new page. This field is used by default when you create mailing labels during a merge.

- **Next Record If:** This field enables you to set a conditional statement and if the statement is met, the next record will be merged into the current document without beginning a new document. This can be useful in cases where more than one recipient in your list works at the same company. You could send a single letter to all the recipients that meet the If condition of working at that particular company.

- **Set Bookmark:** This field can be used to control the text referred to by a bookmark such as the bookmark created by the Ask field. You can also use the Set Bookmark field with a conditional statement such as the If...Then...Else field.

> **tip**
>
> You can highlight the fields that you placed in the merge document when you are previewing the results of the merge. Select the Highlight Merge Fields command in the Write & Insert Fields group. Click the command again to turn the highlighting off.

- **Skip Record If:** You can use this field to set a conditional statement so that recipients that meet the condition are not included in the merge.

You will probably find some of these special fields useful and some you might not need to take advantage of. It definitely makes sense to experiment with these fields, particularly Fill-in and If... Then...Else because they can provide you with added ability in personalizing the letters that result from your merge.

Previewing Merge Results

After you have your merge document, recipient list, and merge field codes squared away, you can preview the merge results. Select the Preview Results command in the Preview Results group.

You can then use the Next Record and Previous Record buttons to preview each of the resulting merged documents. You can also use the Find Recipient command to open the Find Entry dialog box. You can then search for information in all the merge fields or a specific field. To toggle off the Preview Results feature, click Preview Results.

Another tool that you can use to check the merge results is the Auto Check for Errors command. When you select Auto Check for Errors, the Checking and Reporting Errors dialog box opens as shown in Figure 9.15.

Figure 9.15
The Checking and Reporting Errors dialog box.

The dialog box provides three options:

- **Simulate the Merge and Report Errors in a New Document**—This option performs the merge and then displays a message box detailing whether there were errors during the merge. When you click OK, you return to your merge document.

- **Complete the Merge, Pausing to Report Each Error as It Occurs**—This option pauses the merge each time an error is detected and then creates a merged document.

- **Complete the Merge Without Pausing, Report Errors in a New Document**—This option completes the merge and details any errors in the newly created merged document.

Any of these three options provides you with feedback in terms of whether there is an issue or issues with the merge. They are also useful in terms of saving paper because the merge doesn't go directly to the printer.

Completing the Merge

If you chose either of the complete the merge options in the Checking and Reporting Errors dialog box (the second and third options), you have, in effect, completed the merge. You can save the resulting merged document and then print the document as needed.

If you don't feel the need to check the merge for errors, you can complete the merge using the Finish & Merge command in the Finish group (it is the only command in this group). Select Finish & Merge and then select one of the following from the list provided:

- **Edit Individual Documents:** This creates a new merged document. Probably the best choice, it provides you with an opportunity to look through the results of the merge before printing.

- **Print Documents:** This sends the merge results to your printer.

- **Send E-mail Messages:** If you performed an email merge, this option sends the resulting emails through your Outlook email client.

After you make your selection, you are finished. You have completed the merge process.

Creating Merged Envelopes and Labels

The procedure for creating envelopes and mailing labels is very much the same as creating form letters. You can use the Mail Merge Wizard or you can cycle through the commands on the Mailings tab of the Ribbon.

For merged envelopes, a crucial step is selecting the appropriate envelope type. When you select Envelopes in either the Start Mail Merge list or the wizard's task pane, the Envelope Options dialog box opens. This dialog box allows you to select the envelope size and select the fonts for the delivery and return addresses. Figure 9.16 shows the Envelope Options dialog box.

Figure 9.16
The Envelope Options dialog box.

The dialog box also provides a Printing Options tab that allows you to specify the feed method and the orientation of the envelope in the printer. You can also select the printer tray that contains the envelopes.

After you select the envelope type, click OK to close the Envelope Options dialog box and the envelope appears in the Word workspace. You can then select or create your recipient list and insert the merge fields onto the envelope.

When you select labels for your merge document, the Label Options dialog box provides you with the ability to select the label vendor and product number and to specify the tray for the labels. Labels are a little tricky when inserting your merge fields (after you create or select your data source). Insert the merge field or fields (in most cases you will probably use the Address Block only) onto the first label.

Now here is the important step in terms of getting the labels to work: Click the Update Labels command in the Write & Insert Fields group. This places the entered field code, such as the Address Block, on all the labels. Note that each label (other than the first label) is automatically assigned the Next Record field, which keeps the labels on the same page when you complete the merge.

Understanding Word Fields

The mail merge process provides a good look at some of the possibilities that can be accomplished using fields. Merge fields pull data from a recipient list and place the data in the merged documents. You can use other fields, such as the Skip Record If field, to preclude certain recipients in your list from being included in the merge (based on a condition).

Word provides a variety of other field types that you can use to enhance your documents and to build online forms. For example, when you insert the current date into a document using the Date and Time dialog box, you have the option of selecting the Update Automatically check box. This option actually has Word insert a date field into your document. The field updates each time you open the document, and the current date is the result of the updated field. Page numbering in your document is controlled by a field when you insert the page number using the Page Number command on the Ribbon's Insert tab. So, you are actually using fields even in simple documents, although you might not be aware of it.

You can insert field codes into a document via the Field dialog box. To open this dialog box, access the Ribbon's Insert tab. Then select the Quick Parts command and select Field on the list provided. Figure 9.17 shows the Field dialog box.

tip

You can format field codes as if they are text. For example, select a field code such as the Address Block and then make it bold. The resulting merged information appears in bold in the merged documents.

tip

A very useful field is the FileName field, which you can use in conjunction with the path information. Place this information in the footer of a document and print a copy of the document. That way you have a hard copy of the document that also provides the file's name and where it is stored on your computer or the network. That information makes it easy to find the document when you need it at a later date.

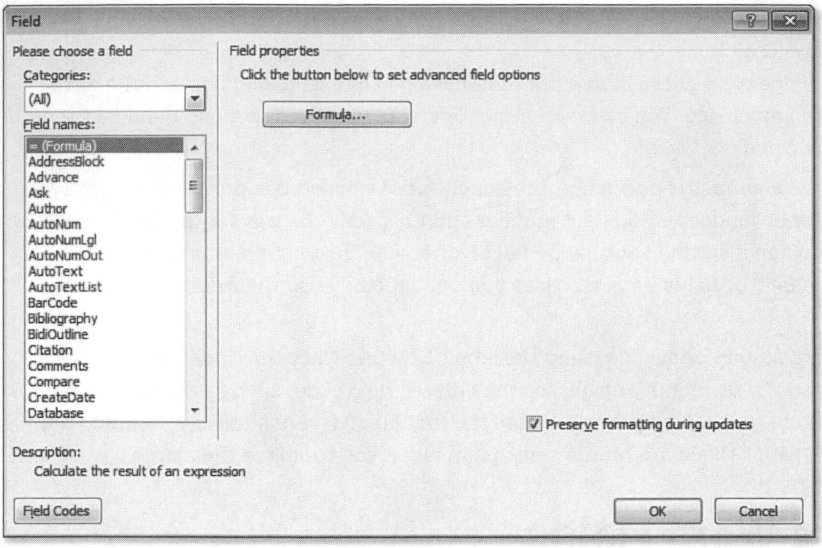

Figure 9.17
The Field dialog box.

A large number of fields are available in the Field Names list, particularly when you have the Categories selection set to All. You might want to concentrate on certain categories of fields that allow you to easily input information related to dates, document information, and user information. Many of these informational fields are best placed in the header or footer of a document, and are particularly useful in cases where users on a network share a document. The fields can serve a housekeeping function by specifying where the document is actually stored (the path) and which user actually saved the document in its current form.

For example, when you select the Document Information category, you will find that the available fields in the Field Names box include Author, FileName, LastSavedBy, NumPages, and other fields. These fields enable you to stamp a document with information that was stamped on the document at its creation (such as the author and the filename) as well as information that can change during the document's life (such as who last saved the document and the number of pages currently in the document).

You can view the actual field code for a selected field in the Field dialog box. Select a field and then click the Field Codes button. The field's code displays on the right of the dialog box. Click Hide Codes to return to the default field view.

To insert a field into a document, select the field in the Field Names list in the Field dialog box and then click OK. The field is inserted into the document at the insertion point.

note

You can use ActiveX controls to create a form that is then saved as an HTML document. It can then be used on a website as an online form.

When you insert the field, the results of the field (such as the date, page number, or filename) appear in the document. To actually view the field codes (which helps you manage the fields), you can press Alt+F9. To toggle back to the field results, press Alt+F9 again.

You can also change Word's options so that field codes are shown in a document: Select File to open the Backstage view and then select Options. In the Word Options window, select Advanced. In the Show Document Content area, select the Show Field Codes Instead of Their Values check box. You can also specify how fields should be shaded in the document when selected using the field shading options.

 note

By default field codes, meaning their result, are shaded with a gray background when you select the field text.

You can delete field codes as you would any Word text. You can also copy, cut, and paste fields as needed.

Building a Form with Form Controls

You can also build online forms using form fields, also referred to as form controls. The control is actually a placeholder for the text that will be input by the user of the form. Form controls can con-sist of text fields, check boxes, or drop-down lists. Your form controls can also include help text, which is very useful in terms of getting the appropriate type of response for a particular field on the form.

note

When designing your form layout, you might want to scratch it out on a piece of paper before creating it in Word. Remember that using various drop-down lists and check boxes on the form requires that the form have an easy-to-use layout. You might want to use a table to position the various form fields on the page.

The various form fields or controls are accessed via the Developer tab of the Ribbon. This tab is not included on the Ribbon by default, so you will need to enable it. Select File to go to Word's Backstage. Then click Options.

In the Word Options window, select Customize Ribbon in the Customize Ribbon list (on the right of the window). Select Developer in the Main Tab list. Then click OK. This puts the Developer tab on the Ribbon.

To create a form that any number of users can use (which is particularly useful in a setting where you work on a network), you need to create a template. Open a new blank document and then save the document in the Save As dialog box and make sure to change the Save as Type setting to Word Template.

After you have the new template ready to go, you can insert the various form fields that you want to use on the form. Follow these steps:

1. Select the Ribbon's Developer tab. In the Controls group, select Design Mode.

2. The Controls group provides all the control fields that you need. Click a control to insert it. The controls are as follows:

   - **Rich Text:** Provides a text block control and is typically used for text entry that you do not want changed or accessed.

   - **Text:** Provides a text block control.

   - **Picture Content Control:** Allows the user to select an image to insert into the form.

- **Building Block Gallery:** Allows the user to select text blocks from a building block gallery.

- **Combo Box:** Allows the user to select a response from a drop-down list or type in her own text response.

- **Drop-Down List:** Provides a list of responses for the user.

- **Date Picker:** Allows the user to select a date from an interactive calendar.

- **Check Box Content Control:** Provides a check box for user response.

- **Legacy Forms:** This form command supplies a list of legacy Word form controls and ActiveX controls such as the Option button and Toggle Button.

3. Insert all your form fields as needed to complete the form.

4. Save the template.

After you insert the form controls on the template page (or pages), you must go back and set the properties for the various controls (although you can set the properties for each field as you insert them). For example, if you have inserted a Drop-Down List field, you have to provide the list of responses that the field provides when selected by the user. Select the field control and then click the Properties command in the Controls group. The Content Control Properties dialog box opens as shown in Figure 9.18.

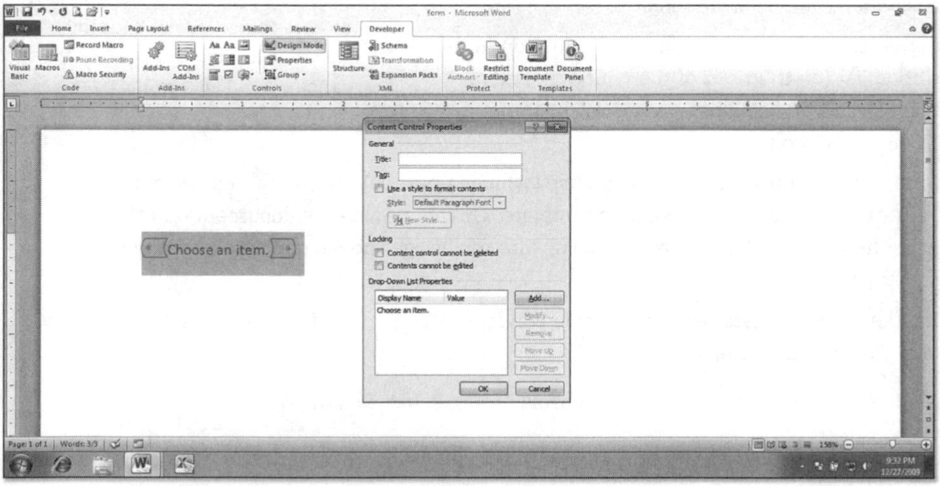

Figure 9.18
The Content Control Properties dialog box.

In the Content Control Properties dialog box, you can add an optional title and tag name for the control. You can lock the control using the Content Control Cannot Be Deleted and Contents Cannot Be Edited check boxes. To remove the default value (Choose an Item), select it in the Drop-Down List Properties. Then use the Add button to add the responses you want to include in the drop-down list.

You can change the order of the responses using the Move Up and Move Down buttons. After you edit the control's properties to suit your needs, click OK.

When you have the controls inserted and configured, you will want to restrict the editing on the template so that users cannot change it (other than allowing user response) when it is actually in use. Select the Restrict Editing command in the Protect group. The Restrict Formatting and Editing task pane opens. In the Editing Restrictions area of the task pane, select the Allow Only This Type of Editing in the Document check box. Then select Filling in Forms from the drop-down list. Then click Yes, Start Enforcing Protection to protect the template. You must enter a password (twice) in the Start Enforcing Protection dialog box. Save the template and it is ready for use.

10

CREATING SPECIAL DOCUMENTS

Word provides a number of features and tools that are designed for creating large and specialized documents. For example, if you create a document that requires a table of contents, Word has you covered. Word also enables you to easily divide a large document into different sections; each section can then have its own formatting including page layout attributes such as margins and even page orientation.

In this chapter we explore the creation of large and special documents. We take a look at creating a table of contents, adding sections to a document, and working with a table of figures. We also discuss how to create cross-references, indexes, citations, bibliographies, footnotes and endnotes and how to track the changes made by multiple authors.

Options for Large Documents

When you work with larger, more formal documents, they can typically have special parts such as a table of contents, table of figures, index, and/or bibliography. These documents might also require specialized notations such as cross-references and footnotes or endnotes.

To make it easier to work with large documents, you can use bookmarks to quickly navigate to a specific spot (or spots) in the document. You can also add nonprinting comments to the document to help you remember the status of a particular page or the need for a revision to particular content in the document.

> *When you work with larger documents, you typically will be using sections to break the document into different parts so that each section can have its own headers, footers, and page-numbering scheme. Sections are discussed in Chapter 8, "Working with Tables, Columns, and Sections," on page 219.*

If you are working with a very large document, you can keep the different parts of the document in separate files and then use the master document commands on the Outlining tab (available when you switch to the Outline view) to link other documents (such as the chapters of a document) to the current document.

In situations where you are collaborating with other users, you can take advantage of the Track Changes feature. Each user's changes are tracked in the document, and you can then accept or reject these changes as needed. You can also compare different versions of the same document. Let's begin our discussion of Word features for larger documents with an exploration of how to create a table of contents.

Creating a Table of Contents

If you want to make it easy for the reader of a large document to find specific parts or chapters of the document, you really need to include a table of contents. Creating a table of contents in Word relies on the use of specific styles to show the organizational structure of your document. As long as you do this, creating a table of contents is actually very straightforward.

For example, you can use either Word's built-in heading styles (Heading 1, Heading 2, Heading 3, and so forth; see Figure 10.1) to format the different levels of headings in the document, or you can create your own styles to do so. Using these headings requires you to use some methodology to break down the contents of your document, such as using section levels or chapter levels. The important thing is that you use them consistently to format the various headings that you use in the document.

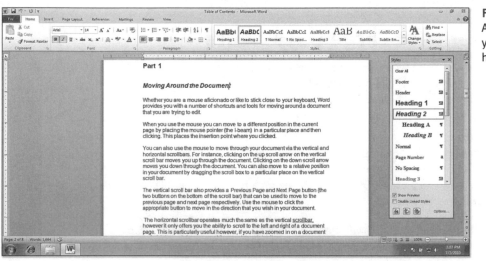

Figure 10.1
Assign styles to your document headings.

A good example is a document divided into parts and then further subdivided into chapters (each part contains several chapters). If you use Word's heading styles to format the different division levels in the document, you would use Heading 1 for the parts (Part I, Part II, and so forth) and Heading 2 for the chapter titles. By assigning these built-in styles (or your own) to your different headings, you can generate a table of contents that shows two levels: parts and chapters. This process works because Word can pinpoint a particular heading level by the style that you've assigned to it.

 tip

You can assign the built-in Word styles to your headings using the quick styles in the Styles group or by opening the Styles window and assigning the quick styles from the window.

When you create a table of contents, the page numbers generated will depend on the location of the headings that are formatted with the styles you have specified for the different levels of the table of contents. If you edit the document and move any of the headings, you will need to update the table of contents to reflect the new page references. You can regenerate an existing table of contents quickly by selecting the Update Table button that is placed at the top of your generated table of contents or by using the Update Table command in the Table of Contents group. We discuss options for updating a table of contents later in this chapter in the section: "Adding Entries and Updating the TOC."

➡ *For more about styles see page 195 in Chapter 7, "Enhancing Word Documents."*

So, the first step in the process of creating a table of contents is to use styles (either built-in or your own) to mark and format the various heading levels in the document. After you have the headings taken care of, you can generate the table of contents.

Creating a Table of Contents with Built-in Styles

If you use Word's built-in styles (Heading 1, Heading 2, and so on), you can quickly insert a table of contents into the document. However, before you actually insert the table of contents, I suggest that you create a blank page at the beginning of your document for your table of contents. Even a better idea would be to create a new section (a section break with a new page). That way you can assign different headers and footers to the table of contents section of the document and other headers and footers to the remainder of the document.

To insert the table of contents, follow these steps:

1. Park the insertion point where you want to insert the table of contents.

2. Select the Ribbon's References tab.

3. In the Table of Contents group, select the Table of Contents command.

4. From the Table of Contents gallery, choose one of the two built-in TOC styles provided that will format the different levels of the TOC as shown in Figure 10.2.

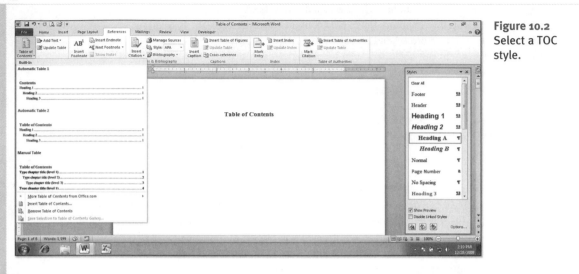

Figure 10.2
Select a TOC style.

The table of contents is inserted at the insertion point. The various levels of the table of contents are formatted by the TOC style that you selected in the Table of Contents gallery. When you select the table of contents (click within the table of contents area) a table toolbar actually appears at the top of the table. On the left of the toolbar is a button that provides access to the built-in table of contents styles and also a command that enables you to remove the table of contents. On the right is a button that enables you to update the table (Update Table) if you have edited the document or added additional items to the table of contents using styles.

Creating a Table of Contents with Your Own Styles

The alternative to creating a table of contents based on Word's built-in quick styles is to create your own styles and use them to designate the different heading levels for the table of contents. As with generating a table of contents with built-in styles, the first step in the process is to assign the appropriate level style to each level of headings in the document.

The trick with using your own styles is that you need to let Word know that these styles replace the heading styles that it normally uses to generate the table of contents. You do this in the Table of Contents dialog box.

Park your insertion point where you want to insert the table of contents and then select the Table of Contents command. On the Command gallery, select Insert Table of Contents. This opens the Table of Contents dialog box with the Table of Contents tab selected as shown in Figure 10.3.

> **tip**
> The entries in your table of contents are actually links to the headings in the document that you used to generate the TOC. You can use these TOC entries to quickly move to that part of the document. Press the Ctrl key and then click the mouse on an entry to move to that page in the document.

By default, the Table of Contents tab provides you with a preview of the table of contents hierarchy for Word's built-in heading styles. It also provides you with access to a number of options such as whether page numbers should be shown in the table of contents and the style of tab leader that should be used. You can also set the number of levels for the table of contents using the Show Levels spinner box.

To force Word to recognize your styles as the TOC levels, you must open the Table of Contents Options dialog box; click the Options button. Figure 10.4 shows the Table of Contents Options dialog box.

By default Heading 1 is marked as TOC level 1, Heading 2 is marked as TOC level 2, and so on. Individually select the numbers in the TOC level boxes for the default headings and delete them. This removes the check mark for each of the built-in headings. To specify one of your styles as a TOC hierarchical level, type the level number (1, 2, 3, and so on) into the appropriate style's TOC level box. After you have assigned the various TOC levels to your styles, click OK to return to the Table of Contents dialog box. Click OK and the table of contents (based on your styles) is inserted into the document.

Figure 10.3
The Table of Contents dialog box.

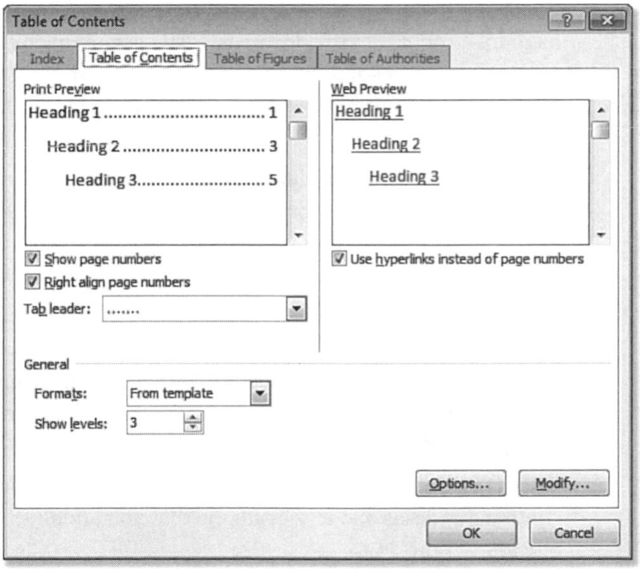

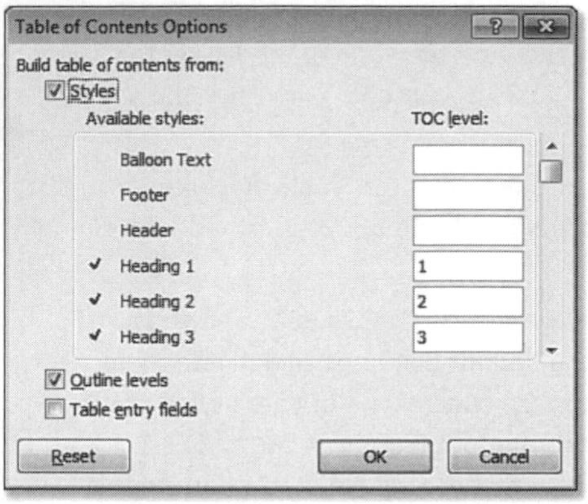

Figure 10.4
The Table of Contents Options dialog box.

Adding Entries and Updating the TOC

You can add entries to the table of contents even after you have inserted it into the document. This is very useful if you have missed a heading when assigning styles to the TOC levels and, as a result, the heading was not included in the table of contents.

Select the heading and then click the Add Text command in the Table of Contents group. On the Add Text list, select the TOC level that should be assigned to the selected heading (Level 1, Level 2, and so on). Note that the default is Do Not Show in Table of Contents.

> **⚠ caution**
>
> If the heading that you are adding to the TOC using the Add Text command is assigned a different style than the other headings at that level, it will not be reformatted with that level's assigned style. You should assign the style to the heading and then update the table rather than using the Add Text command.

Now that you have marked a new entry for the table of contents using the Add Text command, you need to update the TOC. Select the Update Table command in the Table of Contents group (or the Update Table button that appears at the top of your selected TOC). The Update Table of Contents dialog box opens as shown in Figure 10.5.

Select the Update Entire Table option button. Then click OK to close the dialog box. The table of contents updates and any headings that you added to the TOC using the Add Text command are included in the TOC.

If the situation arises where you need to delete a table of contents, you can select the table of contents and then press Delete. You can also delete the TOC from the Table of Contents (command) gallery. Select Remove Table of Contents.

Building a TOC with Field Codes

There is another option for building a table of contents in a document that uses the TC field code. This method identifies the heading and the TOC level for the heading using the TC, which will be placed to the right of the selected text. Because the code is nonprinting, its appearance in the document just serves as a marker. To view the TC field codes as you insert it in the document, click the Show/Hide command on the Ribbon's Home tab.

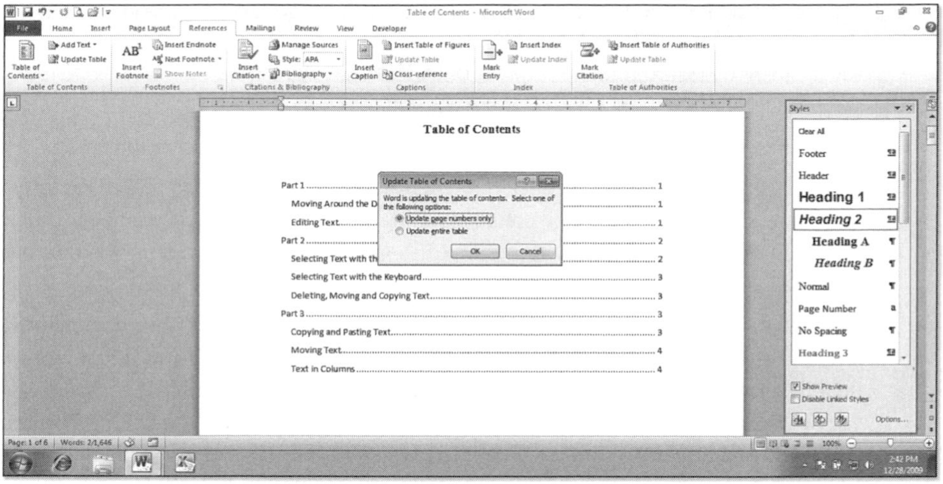

Figure 10.5
The Update
Table of
Contents dialog
box.

You can insert the TC field via the Field dialog box (as you can other field codes), but you must know some field switches and edit the field so that it provides the TOC level information for the entry. It is actually much easier to mark items for the table of contents with the TC field using the Mark Table of Contents Entry dialog box because it allows you to also select the level for the TOC entry.

Fields are also discussed in Chapter 9, "Managing Mailings and Forms," on page 239.

Select the text that you want to mark for the table of contents. Press Shift+Alt+O (the letter o). The Mark Table of Contents Entry dialog box opens as shown in Figure 10.6.

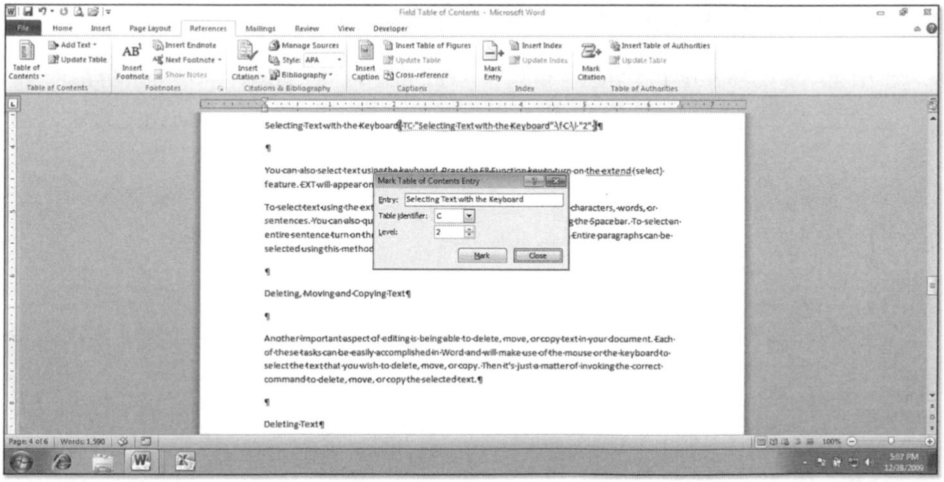

Figure 10.6
The Mark Table
of Contents
Entry dialog
box.

The text you have selected appears in the Entry box. The Table identifier is set to C by default and can remain as is. Use the Level spinner box to specify the level for the entry. Then click OK. Repeat the process as needed to mark all the headings with the TC field and the appropriate TOC level. Click Close to close the Mark Table of Contents Entry dialog box.

To generate the table of contents, select the Table of Contents command on the References tab and select Insert Table of Contents. Doing so opens the Table of Contents dialog box.

On the Table of Contents tab, click the Options button. In the Table of Contents Options dialog box, clear the Outline level check box and select the Table Entry Fields check box (because your TOC is based on field codes rather than styles). Click OK and then OK again to close the two dialog boxes. The TOC is inserted into the document.

Obviously, using styles to designate the TOC level for headings in your document is much more straightforward than using the TC field. However, you might find a situation where you want to generate two different TOCs in the same document. The Word table of contents feature provides you with the ability to create only one TOC per document. However, you can generate a second TOC in the document if you know how to mark TOC entries with the TC field (and a couple of other things that are discussed later).

The procedure for creating two TOCs in the same document is straightforward. Create the first TOC in the document using styles and then insert the TOC using the Table of Contents command.

Inserting the second TOC is a little trickier. Mark all the entries for the second TOC using the TC field (via the Mark Table of Contents Entry dialog box). Then place the insertion point where you want to insert the second TOC.

Now you need to insert a TOC field code at the insertion point, which will generate the second table of contents (using the entries marked with the TC code). Select the Quick Parts command (on the Ribbon's Insert tab) and then select Field. The Field dialog box opens.

In the Categories box, select Index and Tables. Then, in the Field Names box, select the TOC field. You have to edit the TOC field code with a switch, so select the Field Codes button. Then click Options.

In the Switches list, select the \f switch and then click Add to Field. Click in the Field codes box and type C. Remember that C was the table identifier designated in the Mark Table of Contents Entry dialog box. Figure 10.7 shows the Field Options dialog box with the edited field code.

Click OK to return to the Field dialog box. Click OK to close the Field dialog box. When you return to the document, the second table of contents appears at the insertion point.

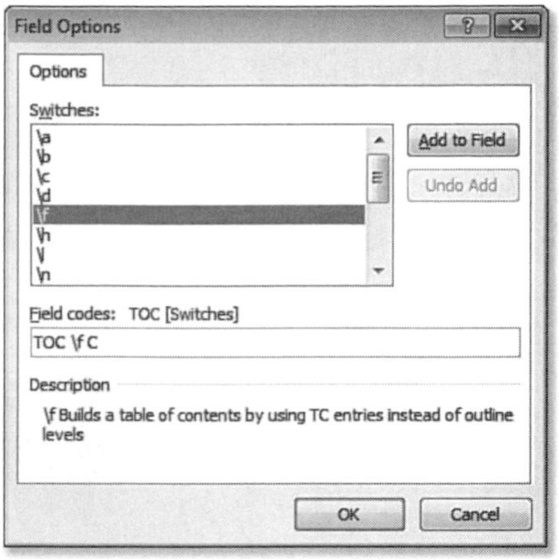

Figure 10.7
The Field Options dialog box.

Working with Captions and Tables of Figures

Business-related reports and articles for scholarly publications often contain tables, images, and other figures that provide supporting material for the text contained in the document. For example, a chart detailing quarterly sales data would typically accompany narrative text related to how the sales for the quarter actually went. You can add captions to your document figures and generate a table of figures, allowing the reader of the document with a reference for finding particular figures in the document.

Inserting a Caption

To add a caption to an image or table, select the Insert Caption command on the References tab or you can right-click on the item (such as a photo) and select Insert Caption from the shortcut menu that appears. The Caption dialog box opens as shown in Figure 10.8.

The figure numbers are assigned automatically to each subsequent figure. You can include additional text for the caption by typing it in the Caption text box. In the Options area of the dialog box, you can specify the label type for the figure: Figure, Table, or Equation. You can also use the Position drop-down list to specify the position for the caption. You can also modify the caption numbering for your figures if needed. Select the Numbering button in the Caption dialog box to access the Caption Numbering dialog box. This enables you to change the format for the numbering, and you can include the chapter number with the figure number by selecting the Include Chapter Number check box. You have to specify the style that you used for the heading that starts each chapter.

After you have configured the caption settings for the figure, click OK. This inserts the caption in the document.

> **tip**
>
> If you are going to insert into a document a number of figure objects, such as Excel charts, you can use the AutoCaption command to automatically add a caption when you are inserting a particular figure type. The figure types include Excel charts, PowerPoint slides, and Word tables.

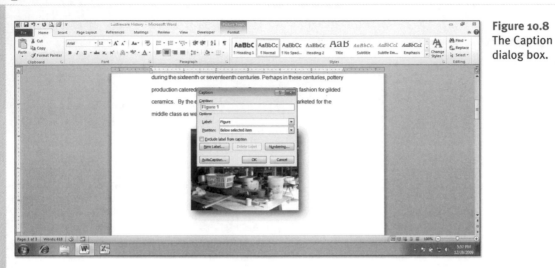

Figure 10.8
The Caption
dialog box.

Inserting a Table of Figures

Inserting a table of figures is extremely straightforward. The Table of Figures feature uses the figure style that you assigned to the figures via the captions that you inserted.

Park the insertion point where you want to insert the table of figures in the document. On the Ribbon's References tab, select Insert Table of Figures. This opens the Table of Figures dialog box as shown in Figure 10.9.

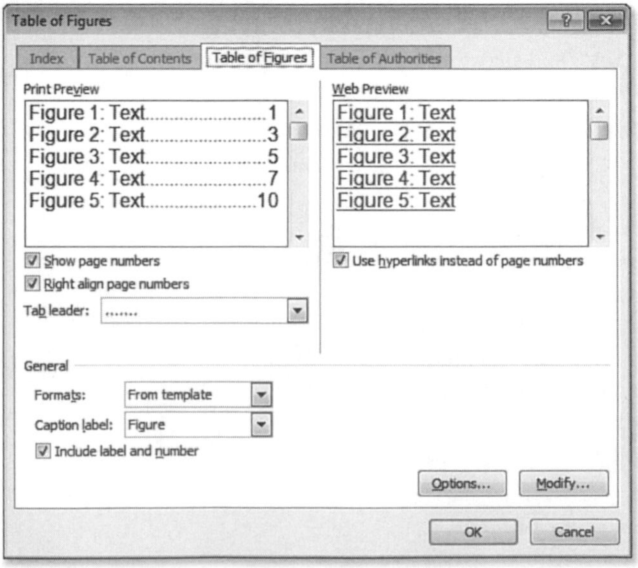

Figure 10.9
The Table of Figures dialog box.

You control whether page numbers are included in the table and the type of dot leader that is used to separate the figure caption from the page number. The most important setting in the Table of Figures dialog box is the Caption Label setting. Its options are none, Equation, Figure, and Table. If you are building a table of figures for items that you assigned the Figure caption label, make sure that it is selected in the Caption Label drop-down list.

When you are ready to generate the table of figures, click OK. The table of figures is inserted into the document. If you add additional figures (with captions) to the document, you can easily update the table of the figures.

Select the table of figures and then right-click. On the shortcut menu, select Update Field. This opens the Update Table of Figures dialog box. Select the Update Entire Table option button and then click OK. The table updates to include any additional figures you have added to the document.

Using Cross-References

Complex documents often require that you provide the reader with the ability to quickly reference other information in the document that is pertinent to text that they are currently reading. This is where cross-references come in. Cross-references are notations in the document that tell the reader where to find additional information on particular subject matter. Cross-references are, in effect, navigation mileposts within the document that make it easy for the reader to follow the information trail related to a particular topic that is referenced more than once in a document.

Word's cross-referencing capability is extremely flexible and you can create cross-references associated with a heading, figure, table, or any text in the document. The cross-reference can give you page number information or it can reference a particular table or figure number.

The great thing about cross-references is that they react to changes in the document. For example, if a figure noted by a cross-reference is moved to another location in the document and is renumbered, the cross-reference updates to provide the correct figure number. If text is rearranged in the document and headings associated with cross-references move, the cross-references update to provide the correct page numbers for the cited headings.

Creating a cross-reference is really a two-step process. First you need to supply the anchor for the cross-reference. As already mentioned, this can be a table, equation, or a figure that has been assigned a caption. Other possibilities are as follows:

- **Numbered Item:** Text in the document that has been numbered using the Numbering command.

- **Heading:** Text headings that have been assigned one of Word's built-in heading styles.

- **Bookmark:** Any text that has been assigned a bookmark (we discuss bookmarks later in this chapter).

- **Footnote:** Any footnote that you have placed in the document.

- **Endnote:** Any endnote that you have placed in the document.

> **⚠ caution**
>
> If you are going to create cross-references for tables, figures, or equations, you have to use the caption tool to assign captions to your tables, equations, or figures. The caption provides the cross-reference with the information that it needs to locate the figure or table and specify the figure or table number.

To create a cross-reference, place the insertion point in the document where you want to insert the cross-reference. Type the introductory text for the cross-reference, such as "For more information, see page".

Select the Ribbon's References tab and then click the Cross-Reference command in the Captions group. This will open the Cross-Reference dialog box.

Select the Reference type for the cross-reference (such as Heading, Bookmark, Figure, and so forth). The items available in the list box reflect the reference type that you selected. For example, if you select Heading as the reference type, all the headings (that have been assigned Heading quick styles) in your document will appear in the For Which Headings box as shown in Figure 10.10.

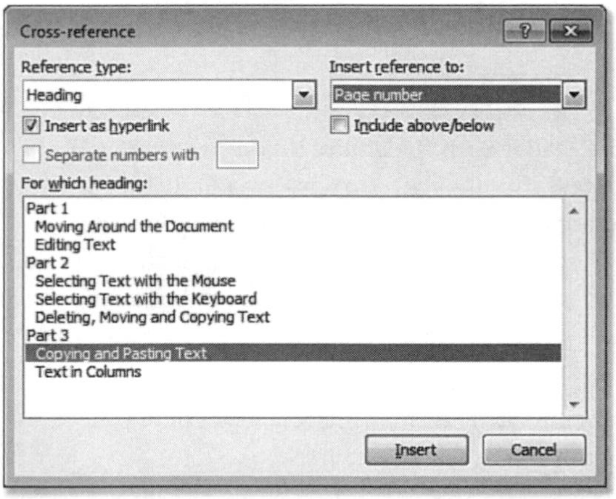

Figure 10.10
The Cross-reference dialog box.

After you select the reference type and the item in the document that will be connected to the cross-reference (such as a heading or bookmark), you need to determine what the cross-reference itself will consist of. For example, you can use a heading as the reference anchor and then select Page Number in the Insert Reference To drop-down list. This inserts the page number for the referenced heading into the document as your cross-reference.

 tip

To view the field codes placed in a document when you insert cross-references, press Alt+F9. Press Alt+F9 again to hide the cross-reference fields.

Each reference type has a number of choices in terms of what you insert into the document as the cross-reference. A figure reference type can provide the entire caption, the label and number, or the page number for a figure. A bookmark used as a cross-reference can include the bookmark text, the page number of the bookmark, or even the paragraph number. After you have selected your options for the cross-reference in the Cross-Reference dialog box, click Insert. You add additional cross-references as needed. When you are finished, click the Close button on the Cross-Reference dialog box.

Generating an Index

You might also want to include an index in a long or complex document. An index basically provides a list of important terms and other keywords from the document and provides a reference to the page number (or numbers) where the term appears. An index in a document is generated in a similar manner to creating a table of contents or a table of figures. To specify entries for the index, you mark the appropriate text items in the document.

The commands that you need to create your index are available in the Index group on the Ribbon's References tab. The first step in creating the index is to mark the index entries throughout the document.

> **note**
>
> Indexes are meant to contain key terms and major concepts in the document so that the reader of the document can quickly locate that information in the document; don't commit overkill when marking text entries for the index and don't completely skimp on entries for the index. It is a Goldilocks and the Three Bears dilemma. The index needs to be "just right."

Marking Index Entries

Select a text entry for the index, and then select Mark Entry to open the Mark Index Entry dialog box. The selected text appears in the main entry box of the Mark Index Entry dialog box as shown in Figure 10.11. You don't have to use the default text in the main entry box; you can type over the text to revise the main entry.

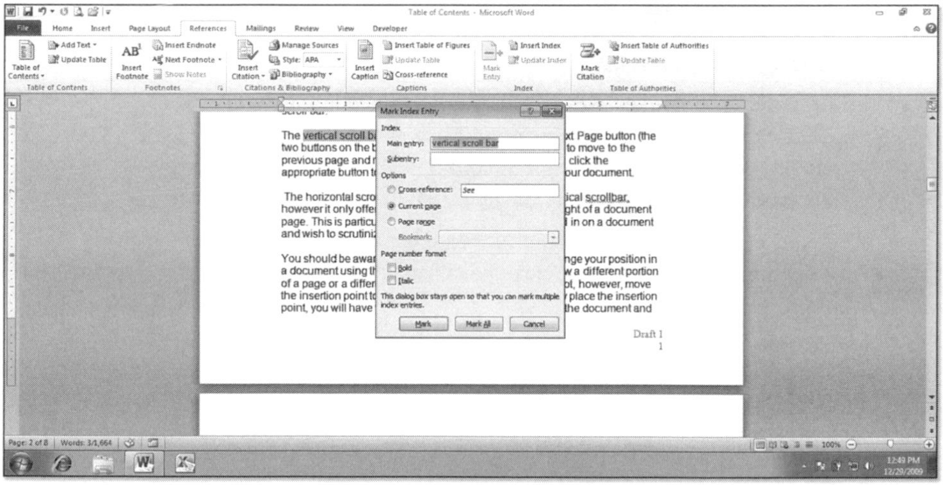

Figure 10.11
The Mark Index Entry dialog box.

If you want to create a subentry to accompany the main entry in the Index, type the text in the subentry. For example, if your index entry is footnotes but the index actually points to a passage that discusses converting footnotes to endnotes, you could add the subentry of "converting to endnotes." The index entry in the index would then contain "footnotes" followed by an indented "converting to endnotes" on the next line (which would also include the page number of the entry).

By default, the index entry includes the page number (the page where your index entry actually resides in the document). You can also specify a page range for the index entry by selecting the Page Range option button and supplying the name of a bookmark that you have created that includes the page range you want to assign to the index entry.

Bookmarks are discussed later in this chapter on page 270.

The Mark Index Entry dialog box also provides an option for creating a cross-reference for the index entry. For example, the main entry might be "data source" and you want to include a cross-reference in the index entry that states: "See mail merge." To use the cross-reference option, select the Cross-Reference option button and enter the required text. This type of entry will not include a page number reference but is designed to have the reader look elsewhere in the index to locate the document information that they require.

The Mark Index Entry also supplies two check boxes (Bold, Italic) that enable you to select formatting for the page numbers included with the index entries. After you have specified the parameters for your index entry, select Mark. Because the dialog box stays open as you mark the various index entries for the document, you can mark additional entries and then click Close when you finish marking all the index entries in the document.

Inserting the Index

After marking the index entries, you can insert the index. Park the insertion point in the document where you would like to insert the index. You might want to start a new page or even a new section in the document for the index.

To insert the index, click the Insert Index command in the Index group. The Index dialog box opens as shown in Figure 10.12.

By default, the index is set up indented in two columns. You can change the number of columns and other settings as needed. When you are ready to insert the index, select OK. The index is inserted into the document.

If you modify your document (meaning you move pages around, delete pages, or insert additional pages) and you mark additional entries for the index, you will need to update the index in your document. Select the Update Index command in the Index group to update the index.

 tip

If you want to go beyond the main entry and subentry levels and add a tertiary level entry to the index, type a colon (:) after the subentry text and enter text for the tertiary level index information.

note

There are a number of different style manuals for publications. Word actually provides citation and bibliography formatting for 10 different sets of style guidelines including the MLA, APA, and the *Chicago Manual of Style*.

Figure 10.12
The Index dialog box.

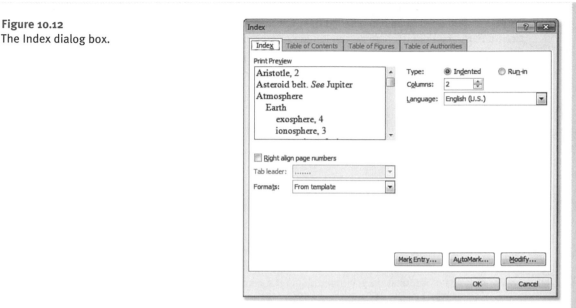

Working with Citations and Bibliographies

If you are working on a journal article, a paper for a conference proceedings, or some other document that requires a listing of your sources at the end of the document, you can take advantage of Word's citation and bibliography features. Citations are short references to articles, papers, books, or other material that you have consulted that appear directly in the text of your document. For example, if I need to cite an article that I read that was written by Jane Smith in 2009, the citation in the document would appear directly after any reference that I have made to Smith's article. A format that the citation might appear in would be (Smith, 2009).

The full reference for the article including the author's name, article title, publication date, and the publication that the article appeared in would then be provided in the bibliography itself. So, a bibliography is really a comprehensive list of all the source materials that you have referenced in your citations.

When you insert a citation (meaning when you create the citation) into the document, you actually provide all the information related to the article or book such as the title, author, date published, and so forth. When you generate the bibliography, the bibliography entries created for each of the publications cited is based on the information that you provided for each of your citations.

Before you begin to insert the citations into the document, you should specify the style guidelines that you use for your publications. Style guides supply the rules for citing the borrowing of other works in your own documents. For example, many educational institutions such as colleges and universities use the MLA style guidelines (MLA stands for the Modern Language Association) in the humanity disciplines and the APA (American Psychological Association) style guidelines for the social sciences. Other groups, such as book publishers, may use the *Chicago Manual of Style* as a resource for their writers.

So, step one in the citation to bibliography process is to choose the style guidelines that you will use for your citations and bibliography. All the commands that you will need in relation to creating citations and the bibliography are on the Ribbon's References tab in the Citations & Bibliography group.

To specify the style guidelines that you will use, select the Style drop-down box and select one of the listed styles. Now you can begin to create the citations for the document.

Creating Citations

Citations include all the information related to the publication that you are citing in your document. Park the insertion point at the end of a sentence where you want to insert the citation and then follow these steps:

1. Select the Insert Citation command in the Citations & Bibliography group.

2. On the Insert Citation gallery, select Add New Source. The Create Source dialog box opens.

3. Use the Type of Source drop-down list to select the type of publication you are citing (such as Book, Journal Article, Report, and so on.). The type of publication you select determines the number of fields of information you must fill in for a complete citation (see Figure 10.13).

4. Enter the appropriate information into each of the text boxes in the Create Source dialog box. A tag name is created for the citation based on the author's name and the year of publication.

5. When you have completed entering the data for the source, click OK.

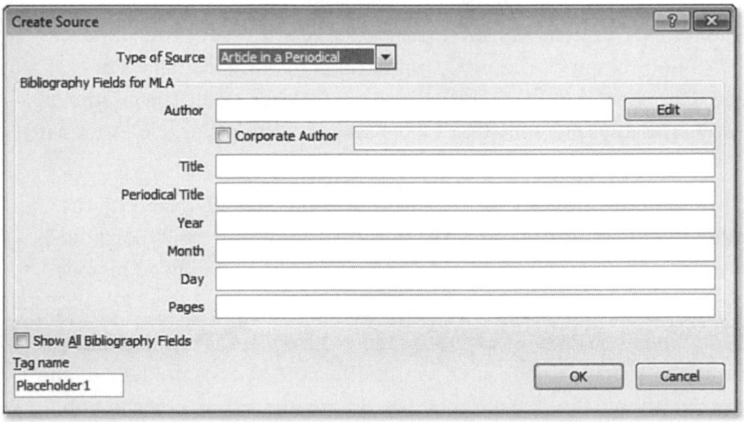

Figure 10.13
Enter the information for the publication in the Create Source dialog box.

The citation will be placed at the insertion point in parentheses. The appearance of the citation will depend on the style you are using. For example, the APA style will include the author's last name followed by the year of publication. The MLA style will use only the author's last name for the citation.

Repeat the insert citation process as needed to create all the citations for the document. If you need to edit a citation, click on it. A drop-down list arrow appears. Click Edit Source on the list and the Edit Source dialog box opens. Edit the citation source as needed.

Managing Citations

You can manage your citations or sources that you create using the Source Manager. The Source Manager actually provides a master list of citations compiled by Word (as an XML document) as you create the citations in your various documents. To open the Source Manager, select Manage Sources in the Citations & Bibliography group. Figure 10.14 shows the Source Manager.

 tip

You can save an inserted bibliography that you have modified or one that you have created from scratch to the Bibliography gallery, which is actually one of the building block galleries. Use the Save Selection to Bibliography Gallery command in the Bibliography command's gallery.

Figure 10.14
The Source Manager dialog box.

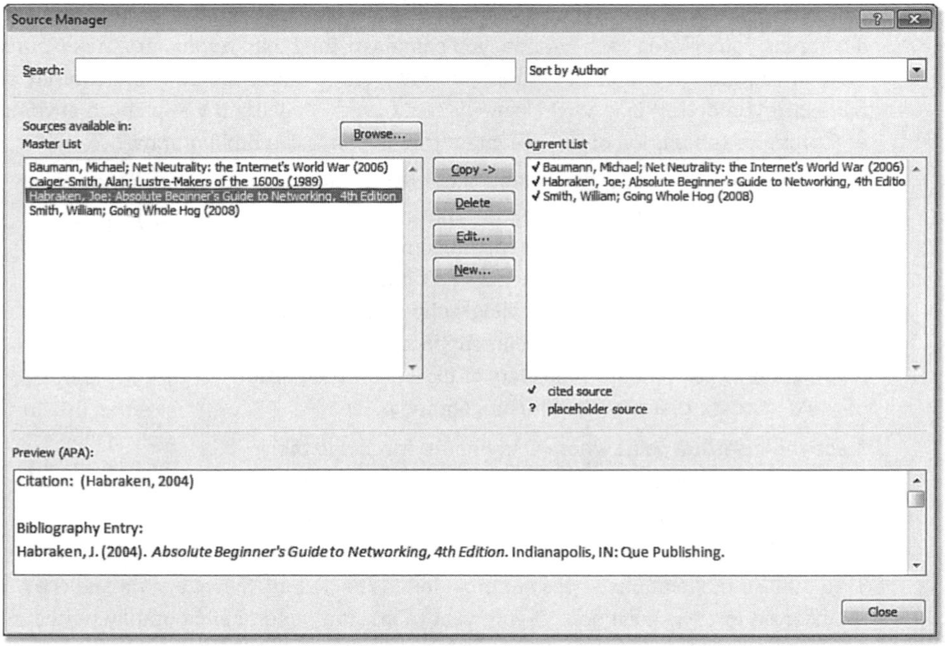

Source Manager	? x

Search: [   ]   Sort by Author [▼]

Sources available in:
Master List   Browse...   Current List

Master List		Current List
Baumann, Michael; Net Neutrality: the Internet's World War (2006)	**Copy ->**	✓ Baumann, Michael; Net Neutrality: the Internet's World War (2006)
Caiger-Smith, Alan; Lustre-Makers of the 1600s (1989)		✓ Habraken, Joe; Absolute Beginner's Guide to Networking, 4th Editio
Habraken, Joe; Absolute Beginner's Guide to Networking, 4th Edition	**Delete**	✓ Smith, William; Going Whole Hog (2008)
Smith, William; Going Whole Hog (2008)	**Edit...**	
	New...	

✓ cited source
? placeholder source

Preview (APA):

Citation: (Habraken, 2004)

Bibliography Entry:
Habraken, J. (2004). *Absolute Beginner's Guide to Networking, 4th Edition.* Indianapolis, IN: Que Publishing.

Close

The Source Manager provides two different lists. In the left pane is the master list, which is a compilation of all citations that you have created. In the right pane are the citations in the current document. You can select a citation in either the master list or the current list and copy it to the other list. For example, if the master list contains a citation that you want to include in the current list, select the citation and then click Copy.

When you close the Source Manager, you have to remember to actually insert that citation into the appropriate place in your document by using the Insert Citation command (all the citations in the document are listed on the Citation gallery). You can also copy citations from a document created on another computer into your master list using the Source Manager.

The Source Manager also provides you with the ability to edit existing citations (in either list) and create new citations (which, again, you will have to remember to insert into the document using the Insert Citation command). The Source Manager also makes it easy to view your source lists in a particular order; you can sort the lists by author, tag, title, or year.

If you want to see a subset of your source lists (meaning you would like to filter the lists by keywords), you can use the Search box. Type a keyword or keywords in the Search box and the lists filter using your terms.

Inserting the Bibliography

After you have inserted your citations into your document and entered the information for each publication as you created each citation, you can insert the bibliography into the document. As with a table of contents or a table of figures, you will want to insert the new bibliography on a new blank page or (even better) in a new document section—particularly if you want to have different headers or footers for the portion of the document that contains the bibliography.

After you have inserted your citations into your document (and entered the information for each publication as you created each citation), you can insert the bibliography into the document. As with a table of contents or a table of figures, you will want to insert the new bibliography on a new blank page or (even better) in a new document section, particularly if you want to have different headers or footers for the portion of the document that contains the bibliography.

 tip

You can save an inserted bibliography (that you have modified) or one that you have created from scratch to the Bibliography gallery, which is actually one of the Building Blocks galleries. Use the Save Selection to Bibliography Gallery command in the Bibliography command's gallery.

Place the insertion point where you want to insert the bibliography. Select the Bibliography command in the Citations & Bibliography group. The Bibliography gallery opens (see Figure 10.15).

Two built-in bibliography styles are provided in the gallery. Select a style and the bibliography will be inserted into the document. If you want to insert a generic bibliography (without a title), select Insert Bibliography.

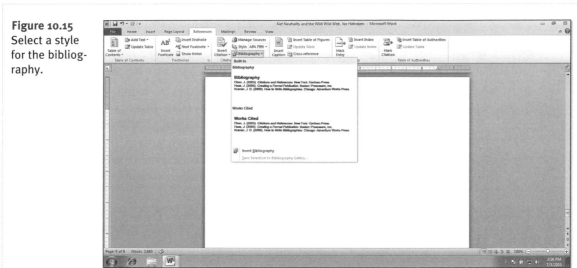

Figure 10.15
Select a style for the bibliography.

Inserting Footnotes and Endnotes

Footnotes and endnotes serve as explanatory additions to the text in your document. Both footnotes and endnotes, like citations, can also be used to reference published information that was consulted as you created your own work. Obviously, footnotes appear at the bottom of the page (in the footer area) and are included at the bottom of the same page that you inserted the footnote or footnotes on. Endnotes appear at the end of the document.

As you insert footnotes or endnotes into a document, they are numbered sequentially. If you delete a footnote or endnote, the remaining footnotes or endnotes renumber automatically. In addition, if you add footnotes or endnotes to the document, the existing footnotes or endnotes renumber as needed.

Place the insertion point where you want to insert the bibliography. Select the Bibliography command in the Citations & Bibliography group. The Bibliography gallery opens (see Figure 10.15). Two built-in bibliography styles are provided in the gallery. Select a style and the bibliography is inserted into the document. If you want to insert a generic bibliography (without a title), select Insert Bibliography.

Whether you use footnotes or endnotes depends on the type of document you are creating and also depends (somewhat) on the style manual that you are using as the guide for your document formatting and structure. The great thing about footnotes and endnotes is that footnotes can be converted to endnotes and endnotes can be converted to footnotes. So, if you start out using footnotes and determine that you should have been using endnotes, you can quickly remedy the problem.

> ## tip
>
> To view the text for the nearest footnote or endnote nearest to the insertion point, select the Show Notes command in the Footnotes group. It will either take you to the footer area to see the next footnote or to the last page of the document to view the current endnote.

The commands that you use to insert a footnote or an endnote are in the Footnotes group on the Ribbon's References tab. To insert a footnote or endnote, place the insertion point where you would like to place the footnote or endnote reference number in the document. To insert a footnote or an endnote, click the Insert Footnote or Insert Endnote command, respectively. Doing so places the note number into the text and also moves the insertion point to the appropriate place in the document for you to enter the note text.

When you insert a new footnote, your insertion point moves to the footer area of the current page. Type the text for the footnote. When you insert a new endnote, the insertion point moves to the last page of the current document. Enter the text for the endnote.

You can navigate from footnote to footnote (or endnote to endnote) using the Next Footnote command in the Footnotes group; its menu provides Next Footnote, Previous Footnote, Next Endnote, and Previous Endnote.

If need to modify the number format or other settings related to your footnotes or endnotes, you can do this in the Footnote and Endnote dialog box (see Figure 10.16). To open the dialog box, click the Footnote and Endnote handle on the Footnotes group.

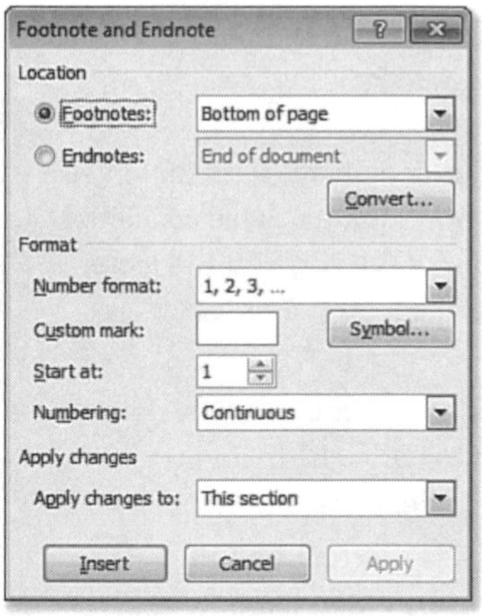

Figure 10.16
The Footnote and Endnote dialog box.

The Footnote and Endnote dialog box also provides you with the ability to convert your footnotes to endnotes and vice versa. Select the Convert button in the Footnote and Endnote dialog box. The Convert Notes dialog box opens and provides three options:

- **Convert all Footnotes to Endnotes:** Your footnotes become endnotes.

- **Convert all Endnotes to Footnotes:** Your endnotes become footnotes.

- **Swap Footnotes and Endnotes:** Any footnotes are converted to endnotes and any endnotes are converted to footnotes.

Select the appropriate option button and click OK. This returns you to the Footnote and Endnote dialog box, which you can then close.

Tracking Document Changes

If you work in an environment where you collaborate with others on Word documents such as reports, employee handbooks, or other materials, you can track the changes made by the various collaborators on the document. This enables you to keep track of changes made by each individual; in fact, each individual's changes are tagged with their username and shown in the document in a specific color. After all the changes have been made to a document by the various participants, you then have the ability to accept and reject changes as you review the edits made to the document.

The commands related to the Track Changes feature are located in the Tracking group on the Ribbon's Review tab. Before you begin tracking changes in the document, you might want to peruse and even change the various settings related to the tracking options. All these options are provided in the Track Changes Options dialog box.

Select the Track Changes command and then select Change Tracking Options. The Track Changes Options dialog box opens as shown in Figure 10.17.

In this dialog box, you can configure a number of different options related to how editing changes such as deletions and insertions are formatted and colored in the document. The Track Changes Options dialog box is broken down into category areas such as Markup, Moves, Table Cell Highlighting, and Formatting.

Each grouping, such as Markup, uses formatting attributes and color to specify a particular type of change. For example, the Markup group includes insertions, deletions, and changed lines. By default, insertions are formatted using an underline whereas deletions are formatted with a strikethrough.

You do have the ability to determine whether changes that do not actually remove or insert text, such as moves and formatting, are actually tracked (using the appropriate check box). This dialog box also provides settings related to balloons (we talk about balloons in the next section).

> **⚑ caution**
>
> Unless you have some really compelling reason to make a change, in most cases you can go with the default formatting and colors provided by the Track Changes Options dialog box.

You can also change color settings for the various markup items such as insertions or deletions. However, because the point of this feature is to be able to differentiate the changes made to the document by different individuals working on the document, I would suggest that you do not change any of the color settings for items that have the By Author selection by default. This includes items such as insertions, deletions, and formatting.

Options for Viewing Changes

To turn tracking on in the document, select the Track Changes command and then select Track Changes. As you edit, changes are marked in the document. When you share the document on a network or via email, any changes by subsequent collaborators are also marked in the document.

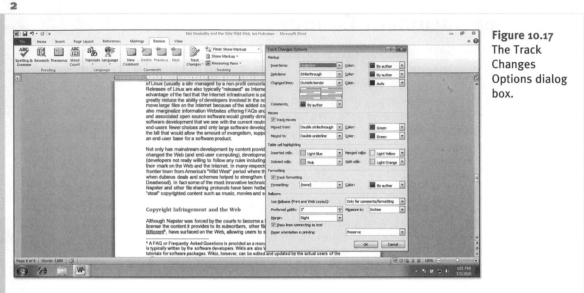

Figure 10.17
The Track Changes Options dialog box.

You do have some options in how changes made to the document display. First, you can choose whether comments, insertions, deletions, and formatting changes show in the document via the Show Markup menu (see Figure 10.18). Items such as comments and formatting have their own check box on the menu, which you can clear when you do not want to view that particular change type (select an option again to again display it in the document).

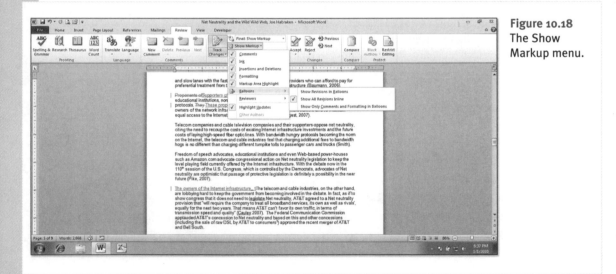

Figure 10.18
The Show Markup menu.

By default, all the various types of changes are shown inline; you can switch from this inline view to balloons using the Show Markup menu. Point at Balloons and then select Show Revisions in Balloons. Newly inserted text will still be displayed inline in the document, but deletions will be contained in the balloons in the right margin.

The Show Markup menu provides some other tricks such as giving you the ability to specify that only the changes made by certain reviewers (that's what Word calls your collaborators) are displayed in the document; point at Reviewers on the menu and the deselect the check boxes to hide the changes (in the document) made by specific reviewers. You can click All Reviewers at any time to return all the reviewer changes to the screen.

Reviewing Changes

When you have all the reviewers' changes marked in the document, you can review the document and determine which changes you want to accept and which you want to reject. The commands related to reviewing the document such as the Accept and Reject commands are in the Changes group on the Ribbon's Review tab.

To aid you in reviewing the various edits made throughout the document, you can open the reviewing pane. You can open the reviewing pane in a vertical or horizontal orientation. Select the Reviewing Pane command in the Tracking group and then select Reviewing Pane Vertical or Reviewing Pane Horizontal. Figure 10.19 shows the vertical reviewing pane.

To begin the process of reviewing the document changes, go to the top of the document (Ctrl+Home) and then click the Next command in the Changes group. You are taken to the first change in the document. At this point, you can take advantage of the Accept or Reject command and the choices on their menus.

note

On the Show Markup menu is an option named Ink. It refers to pen markup made to a document on a tablet PC.

note

You can control the type of changes and the level of access that reviewers have to a document. Use the Restrict Formatting and Editing pane (select Restrict Editing in the Protect group) to limit formatting and editing restrictions.

The Accept command and the Reject command provide you with the ability to accept or reject a change and then move to the next change—just accept or reject the change, or accept or reject all changes.

After you have accepted (or rejected) changes in the document, you can save the final version of the document. It makes sense to use Save As and save the document under a new filename detailing that the document review has taken place.

Comparing Documents

You might encounter a situation where you want to reconcile the text in two different drafts of a document or combine revisions from multiple authors (in different documents) to a single document. This is particularly useful if you did not circulate a single copy of a document with the Track Changes feature enabled among the various authors involved in the project. The Compare command has its own Compare group on the Ribbon's Review tab.

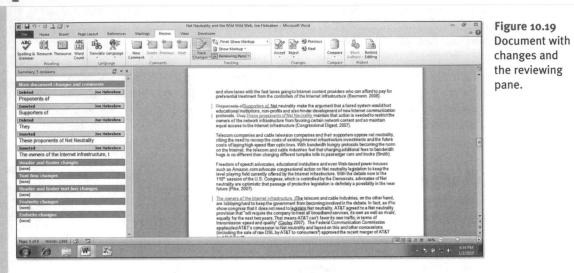

Figure 10.19
Document with changes and the reviewing pane.

To compare two versions of a document, select the Compare command and then select Compare on the Compare menu. Doing so opens the Compare Documents dialog box. To view all the settings available in this dialog box, click More (see Figure 10.20).

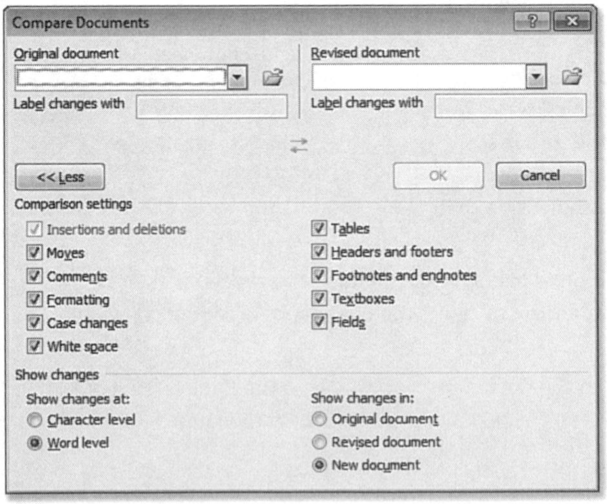

Figure 10.20
The Compare Documents dialog box.

Open the original document on the left side of the dialog box and the revised version of the document on the right side of the dialog box. The Label Changes boxes enable you to specify the author name used to label the changes found between the documents when the comparison is made.

You can select the various comparison settings in the Comparison Settings pane. This enables you to select specific actions for comparison such as moves, comments, formatting, and so forth.

You also have control over how Word displays the differences found in the two documents. You can choose to show the changes in the original document, the revised document, or a new document (with the latter being both the best option and the default).

After you specify the documents for comparison and set the various parameters in the dialog box, click the OK button. A document opens (a new document if you went with the default setting) in Word that has automatically marked changes to the original document based on the revised version you specified. The vertical reviewing pane also opens, detailing the changes that have been marked in the document. You can now review the changes in the document as if you had the Track Changes feature enabled during the entire editing process. Figure 10.21 shows the results of a comparison between two different versions of the same document. The Compared Document pane provides the results of the comparison between the original document and the revised document. The summary of revisions made is shown in the Reviewing pane on the left of the Word window. You can choose to accept or reject changes as you would any other document that you review for revisions.

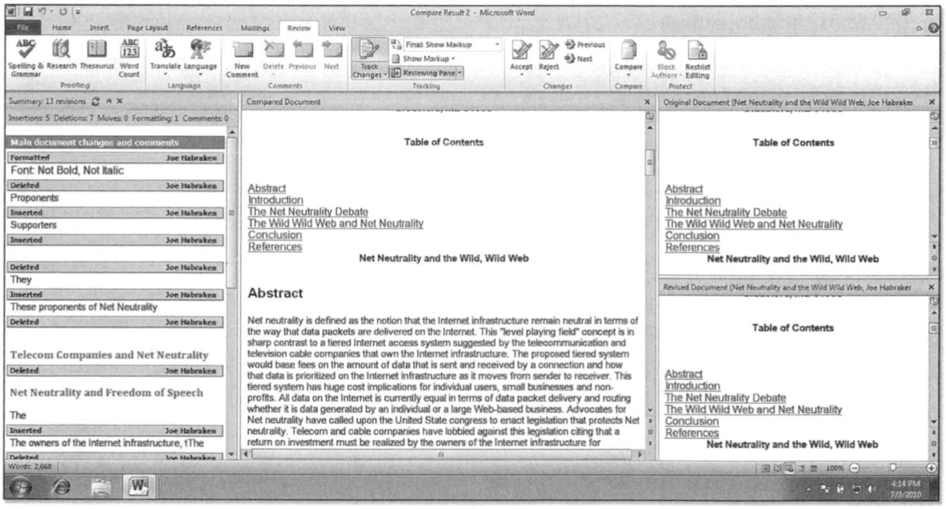

Figure 10.21
Review the changes resulting from the comparison of two versions of the same document.

The Compare command also provides the Combine command. This command opens the Combine Documents dialog box, which is structured the same as the Compare Documents dialog box. Use the Combine command and the Combine Documents dialog box when you want to reconcile the changes that have been marked in two different versions of the same document.

Building a Better "Big" Document

Much of this chapter related to creating larger documents and inserting special document parts, such as tables of contents, indexes, and bibliographies. It also provided some insight into features such as the Track Changes feature, which is useful when you are collaborating with others.

Larger documents can be a work in progress for an extended time, even in cases where one author is involved. In situations where multiple authors are responsible for different portions of a document, you might feel that you are sitting on your hands waiting for a collaborator to finish a portion of a document so that you can cut-and-paste the information into the final draft.

We have already discussed how the changes made by multiple reviewers can be viewed and accepted or rejected using the Track Changes feature. The other features that we discuss in this section are designed to make it easier to navigate, comment on, and build a bigger document both when you are the sole author and when you are collaborating with multiple authors.

Creating Bookmarks

Bookmarks mark the location of specific text blocks in a document. You can use bookmarks to generate cross-references in a document, and to create the page run for an index entry that encompasses multiple pages. In their simplest function, bookmarks are a good way to navigate a large document because they point to a specific place in the document.

The Bookmark command is in the Links group on the Ribbon's Insert tab. To create a bookmark, select text in the document or park the insertion point at a particular place in the document, and then click Bookmark. The Bookmark dialog box opens as shown in Figure 10.22.

Type a name for the new bookmark (no spaces are allowed). Then click the Add button to add the new bookmark to the list.

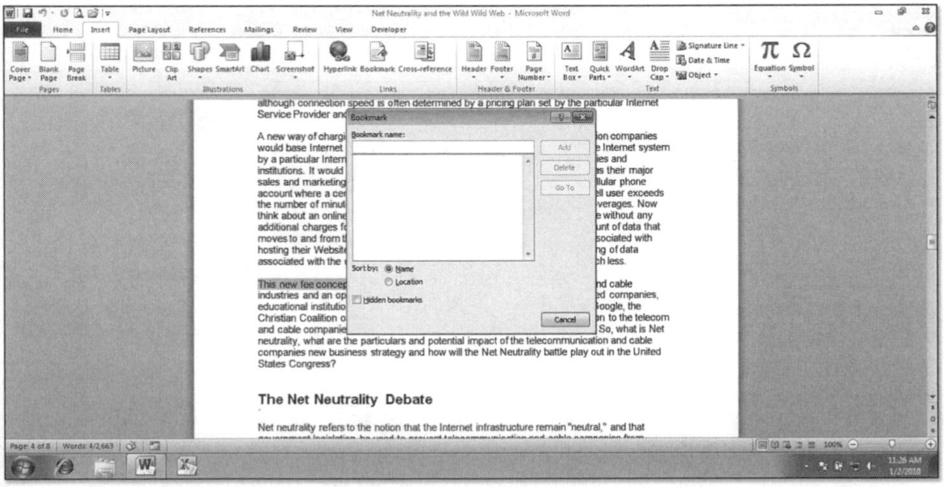

Figure 10.22
The Bookmark dialog box.

The Bookmark dialog box enables you to specify how the bookmark list is ordered; it can be sorted by name or location. Bookmarks can be deleted in the Bookmark dialog box (select a bookmark and click Delete) and you can use the Go To button to go to a selected bookmark.

After you have inserted a number of bookmarks into a document, you can move to a specific bookmark by using the Go To tab of the Find and Replace dialog box. You can open the dialog box with the Go To tab selected by using the Find command on the Ribbon's Home tab (click Find, and then click Go To).

On the Go To tab, select Bookmark in the Go to What list. Then select a specific bookmark from the Enter Bookmark Name drop-down list.

 tip

You can also delete comments from the reviewing pane. Select a comment and then right-click. Select Delete Comment from the shortcut menu.

Inserting Comments

You can insert nonprinting comments into your document. This enables you to leave a message (such as "Finish this chapter") in the document for yourself or for a collaborator or users who will be reviewing the document.

The Comments group is on the Ribbon's Review tab. To insert a new comment, select the New Comment command. The reviewing pane opens (the vertical pane opens by default). The new comment will be marked with your username and initials and numbered sequentially. Enter the new comment in the reviewing pane.

 tip

You can also get to Go To via the keyboard. Press Ctrl+G.

You can view a comment *in situ* by placing the mouse pointer on that particular comment. A preview box opens, showing the author of the comment, the date the comment was inserted, and the comment text. As already mentioned, you can view all the comments in the document using the reviewing pane. You can also move from comment to comment using the Go To tab of the Find and Replace dialog box (Find, and then Go To). Select Comment in the Go to What list and then use the Enter reviewer's name to go to a comment made by a specific reviewer.

The Comments group also provides two commands for moving to comments in the document: Previous and Next. The Delete command allows you to delete a selected comment, all comments shown, or all the comments in a document, as needed.

Creating a Master Document

An extremely useful feature when you are collaborating with multiple authors who are responsible for specific parts of a larger document (such as chapters) is the Master Document feature. The Master Document feature enables you to insert links to other documents. These links can be chapters or other document parts being written by other users. So, in my mind, the master document has one great and noble purpose: It allows you to create a master document outline of the entire document, even while the various parts of the document are still being created. When the various authors complete the linked subdocuments that make up the master document, your master document is also complete.

tip

Use a new blank document for the master document. Doing so provides you with complete flexibility in inserting and rearranging the subdocuments that will link to the master.

The Master Document feature provides an outline view of the entire document that you can expand and collapse using the Outlining tools. You can insert new document parts as links to other document files or you can create a new part for the master document from scratch. Global items, such as page numbering, can be created for the master document and then applied to the various linked documents as you add them to the master document. When you generate the table of contents for a master document, the "master" table of contents includes all the headings in the linked document. And, actually, when you are working with a master document in Word in the Print Layout or Draft view, it ends up looking like any other Word document, although it is a series of links to other documents.

Open a document that will serve as the master document. This can be a particular document that will appear in the master document (such as the first chapter of the master document) or a new blank document that will be used as the master document (a new blank document will include only links to external documents within it).

To enter the Outline view, click Outline on the ruler's View tab or take advantage of the Outline button in the Status bar. The Outline view provides commands (in the Outline Tools group) that enable you to promote and demote items in the outline to different levels. You can also select levels by using the Level drop-down list. Tools such as Move Up, Move Down, Expand, and Collapse enable you to move through the outline and expand or collapse outline parts, respectively.

While you're working with a master document, you can select Show Document to enable commands such as Create and Insert in the Master Document group. Other commands, such as Collapse Subdocuments, Merge, Split, and Unlink become available when you have inserted or created new subdocuments in the master document.

To create a new subdocument in the master document, all you need to do is make sure that you are at a heading level (such as Level 1, Level 2, and so on) in the outline. You can then select Create to add a new subdocument to the outline (at the insertion point). Type the text for the new subdocument and use the Level list to determine what level each text entry in the subdocument should be set at. For example, all regular text in the entry (excluding the headings) should be set as Body Text.

> **🔍 note**
>
> The Outline view uses the built-in Word heading styles to denote the different levels in the outline. For example, Level 1 in the level list is really the Heading 1 style. Regular text in the outline uses the Body Text designation, which is actually the Normal style.

Inserting subdocument links into the master document really takes advantage of the whole purpose of the master document feature, at least in my mind. The process is designed to pull together content from different Word files and combine it into one viewable, editable, and printable master document.

To insert a subdocument link into the master document, place the insertion point in the outline where you will make the insertion. Make sure that the line in the outline where it will insert the subdocument link is assigned the Body Text level. Select Insert in the Master Document group. The Insert Subdocument dialog box opens.

Select the file that will serve as the subdocument, and then click Open. Doing so inserts the subdocument into the outline of the master document. You can insert other subdocuments into the master document's outline as needed. If you want to view the outline as only the links that make up the various subdocuments, click the Collapse Subdocuments command (you will need to expand the subdocuments to insert additional links). Figure 10.23 shows a master document with the subdocuments collapsed to links.

Figure 10.23
A master document with linked subdocuments.

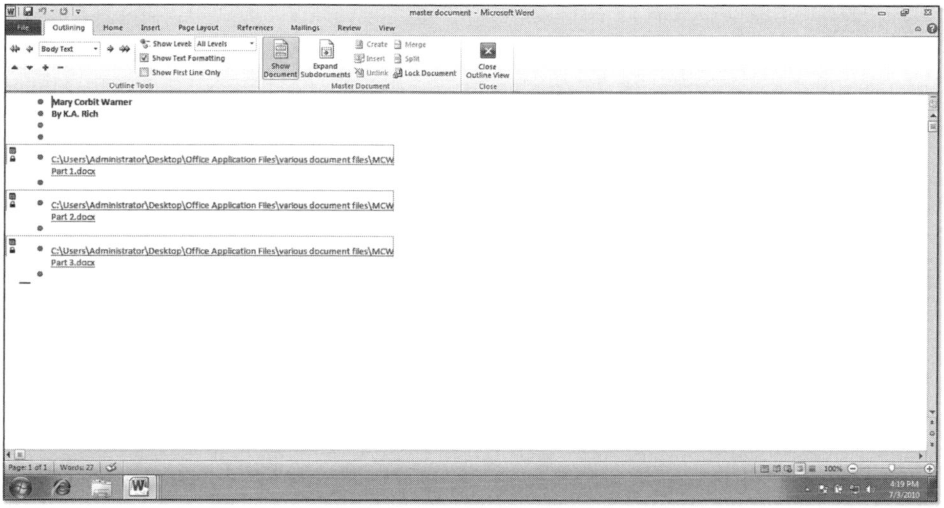

You can fine-tune your master document by using some of the other tools of the Master Document feature. For example, if you want to unlink a subdocument from the original file (meaning any changes made in the original file will no longer be linked into the master document), select a particular subdocument and select Unlink. You can use the Merge and Split commands to either merge two subdocuments in the outline or split a subdocument at a particular place (into two subdocuments). If you want to protect the actual files that make up the subdocuments, you can use the Lock Document command. This enables you to make global changes to the master document (such as styles, headers, footers[md]you name it) and not have them propagate back to the original subdocuments.

When you are finished working with the Outlining tools and the various tasks related to constructing the master document, click Close Outline View. In the other Word views, such as Print Layout or Draft, the master document appears like any other document that you work with, even though it consists of linked content.

REQUISITE EXCEL: ESSENTIAL FEATURES

Whether you create simple worksheets to track your small business income and expenses, or you do complex statistical analysis of migrating bird populations, Microsoft Excel provides you with all the tools and features you need to actually do the number crunching and analyze the results. Excel continues to be the gold standard for spreadsheet software and Excel 2010 provides you with all the possibilities provided by earlier versions of Excel along with a number of improvements and new features.

In this chapter, we take an introductory look at the new possibilities provided by Excel 2010. We also look at the process of building Excel worksheets, including entering data. We will also examine how to best navigate the Excel workspace and work with and manage Excel worksheets.

Introducing Excel 2010

When you first open the Excel 2010 application window (Start, All Programs, Microsoft Office, Microsoft Excel 2010), you will probably find the Excel workspace extremely similar to the environment provided by Excel 2007. If you used an Excel version that predates Excel 2007, just check the number of columns and rows available to see how the space available in a worksheet has changed. Excel 2010 provides 16,384 columns (as did its predecessor Excel 2007)) and more than a million rows (1,048,576 to be exact), so you should certainly not be limited by available space in an Excel worksheet. Other limits for Excel worksheets have also been increased. For example, the number of conditional formatting criteria is limited only by your computer's available memory. The number of unique colors in a worksheet has also been raised (to over four billion per sheet) and the size of pivot tables has been greatly increased (to one million rows and 16, 000 columns).

Excel 2010 has enhancements other than those related to feature limitations, however. There are improvements that are more under-the-hood enhancements that you won't really notice, but improve Excel's capabilities; for example, many of the Excel functions have been upgraded with new algorithms that make their results more accurate. In addition some functions have been added to Excel's large repertoire of built-in formulas.

There are other enhancements to Excel 2010 that will be readily noticeable and include features that you might find extremely useful. There are sparklines, (mini-charts that fit into worksheet cells), slicers (data filters for pivot tables and pivot charts), and a new version of the solver, which is used for what-if analysis. Let's take a quick look at each of these new features.

Sparklines

Sparklines are small charts that are embedded in cells and are designed to provide a handy visualization of data in a row or column, making the values easier to interpret. Sparklines are not meant to replace full-blown charts in Excel, but can be used to accompany data series in the worksheet. For example, if you have several rows of data, you can quickly insert a sparkline for each of the data rows, enabling you to readily see trends in the data points. Figure 11.1 shows a column of sparklines that visually summarizes the data in each of the worksheet's rows.

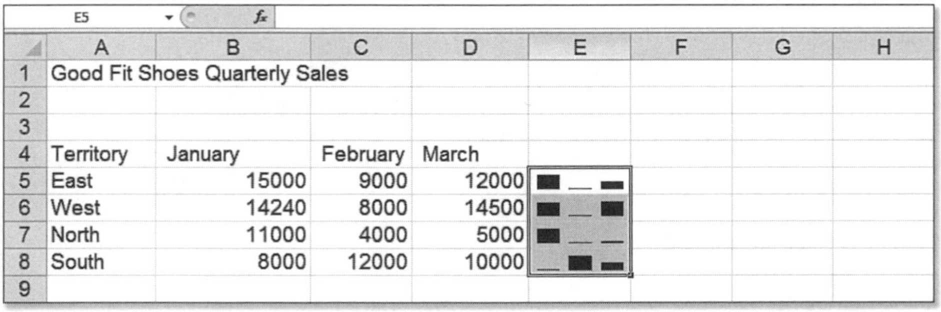

	A	B	C	D	E	F	G	H
1	Good Fit Shoes Quarterly Sales							
2								
3								
4	Territory	January	February	March				
5	East	15000	9000	12000				
6	West	14240	8000	14500				
7	North	11000	4000	5000				
8	South	8000	12000	10000				
9								

Figure 11.1
Sparklines can visually represent data in a worksheet.

A sparkline can take the form of a line, column, or win/loss chart. Sparklines can be inserted in a single cell or multiple cells (for multiple rows or columns of data). You can also insert a sparkline for a row or column of values and then drag the sparkline's fill handle to copy the sparkline to other rows or columns as you would an Excel formula or function. When you change the data in a row or column that has an associated sparkline, the sparkline chart will immediately be updated.

> **note**
>
> Sparklines might not be new to all Excel users. Several open source add-ins for Excel 2007 that provide sparkline capabilities have been available as downloads on the Web.

 For more information about using sparklines, see page 412 in Chapter 14, "Enhancing Worksheets with Charts."

Slicers

Another addition to Excel is the slicer. A slicer is a data-filtering tool that can be added to a pivot table or a pivot chart. A slicer floats in its own object box and can be used to quickly filter the data by a field or field contained in the pivot table or pivot chart. Figure 11.2 shows a slicer associated with a pivot table.

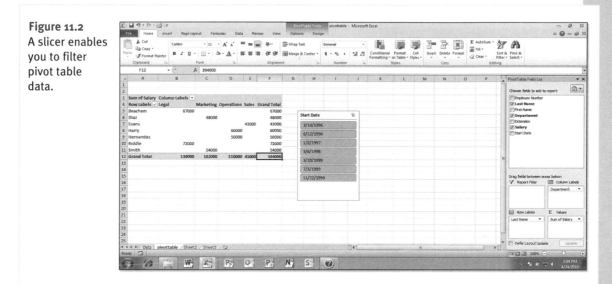

Figure 11.2
A slicer enables you to filter pivot table data.

You can set up your slicers to both sort and filter data in a pivot table. Excel also provides slider styles that you can use to dress up your slicers with border and color settings. Slicers provide you with one more option for interaction with data that you have configured for a pivot table or pivot chart. If you share pivot tables and other data on a network that provides a SharePoint site, your co-workers and colleagues can access your reports and take advantage of the slicers that you have configured.

➡ *For more information about using slicers, see page 448 in Chapter 15, "Using Excel Tables and PivotTables."*

The New Solver

The Solver add-in has been around for a number of Excel versions and has been updated for Excel 2010. The Solver is one of the what-if analysis tools that Excel provides and can be used to help you find an optimum value (either a maximum or minimum) in relation to limitations provided by the values in other cells in the worksheet. Figure 11.3 shows the new Solver Parameters dialog box.

As already mentioned, the Solver is an Excel add-in so you will need to make the Solver an active add-in and make sure that add-ins are included on the Excel Ribbon. We talk more about what-if analysis and tools such as the solver in Chapter 16, "Validating and Analyzing Worksheet Data."

➡ *For more information about the solver, see page 464 in Chapter 16.*

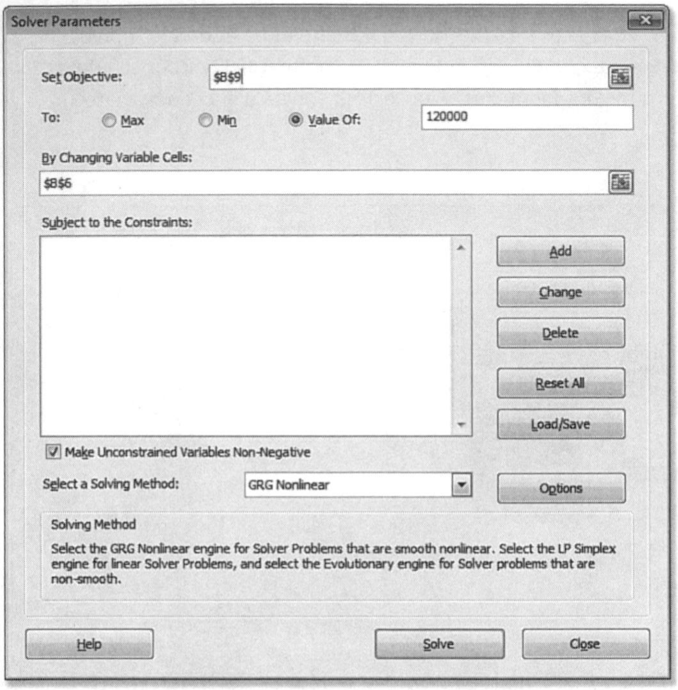

Figure 11.3
The Solver can be used for what-if analysis.

Navigating the Excel Workspace

When you open Excel, you will be greeted by the familiar columns and rows provided by a new worksheet. The actual file that contains the worksheet (and the other worksheets) is referred to as a workbook. Each workbook can contain multiple worksheets. You are provided three worksheets by default. You can add or remove worksheets as needed.

As already mentioned, each worksheet is divided into columns and rows. There are 16,000 columns. The column designation scheme uses the alphabet. The first 26 columns will be A through Z. The next column then begins with AA followed by AB and so on until you get to column XFD.

Excel 2010 provides you with more than a million rows. The last row in a worksheet is row 1,048,576. Obviously, the designation scheme for rows in a worksheet is a numbering system beginning with the number 1.

The intersection of a column and row is referred to as a cell. Cells are designed to hold information. So, the actual data that makes up your worksheet will be entered in the worksheet cells. Worksheets can also hold other objects such as charts and images.

In terms of selecting a cell, all you have to do is move to that particular cell. You can do it via the keyboard or you can move from cell to cell using the mouse. You can also select columns or rows. Click on a column indicator and the entire column is selected. The same goes for a row; click a row indicator to select that row.

The Excel Ribbon

At the top of the Excel application window is the Ribbon, which provides you with access to all the commands that you will use as you work on an Excel worksheet. The Excel Ribbon provides the following tabs by default:

- **Home:** This tab provides the Clipboard group and groups that are associated with formatting and editing the worksheet data. The tab provides font, paragraph, and number formatting, and provides styles for conditional formatting, tables, and cells. The Editing group provides quick access to functions such as AutoSum and provides the Fill, Sort & Filter, and Find & Select commands.

- **Insert:** This tab provides you with the ability to insert objects into an Excel worksheet including pivot tables, tables, illustrations, and charts. The Insert tab also provides access to new features, such as sparklines and slicers, and gives you access to the sheet header and footer. Figure 11.4 shows the Ribbon's Insert tab.

Figure 11.4
The Ribbon's Insert tab.

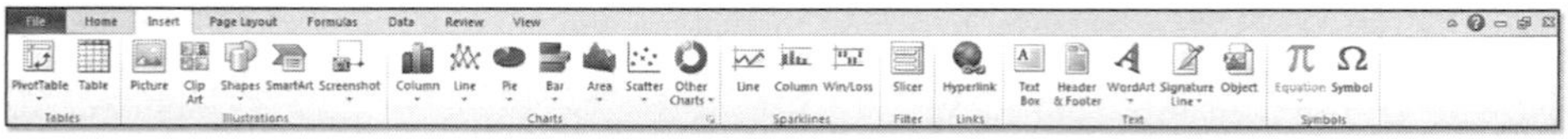

- **Page Layout:** This tab enables you to select a theme for your sheet and to manipulate the margins, orientation, and paper size for the sheet. The Page Setup group also provides you with the ability to place page breaks in a worksheet and select a background image for the sheet. Other commands available on this tab enable you to scale the worksheet for printing and to select sheet options such as gridlines and headings. The Arrange group enables you to manipulate and group multiple objects on a worksheet.

- **Formulas:** This tab provides easy access to the function library by function type and enables you to define names for cells and cell ranges in the worksheet. Commands are also provided for auditing formulas. The Watch Window command enables you to monitor specific cells (their results) as you add or manipulate the data in the worksheet. Figure 11.5 shows the Formulas tab.

Figure 11.5
The Ribbon's Formulas tab.

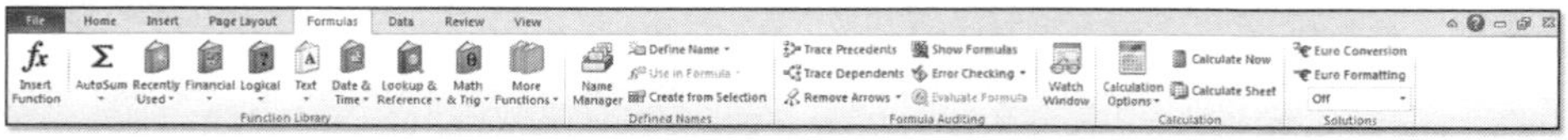

- **Data:** This tab makes it easy for you to import external data from other applications or the Web. Other commands available on this tab enable you to sort and filter data and specify data validation settings. The What-If Analysis command enables you to access tools for data analysis such as the Scenario Manager and Goal Seek.

- **Review:** This tab provides proofing tools such as the Spelling feature and enables you to manage comments added to cells in your worksheet. Commands are also available that enable you to protect a worksheet or the entire workbook. Commands related to sharing a workbook are also provided.

- **View:** This tab provides access to the various workbook views and also enables you to zoom in and out on the current worksheet. Other commands, such as Freeze Panes and View Side by Side, provide you with options for viewing a worksheet or multiple workbooks.

Below the Ribbon are a couple of other entities that you should become familiar with. The Name box, which is on the far left, shows the address of the currently selected cell in the worksheet. The Name box will also show the name of a range when a named range is selected (we talk about naming ranges in Chapter 12, "Worksheet Formatting and Management"). To the right of the Name Box is the formula bar. The formula bar does a couple of different things. As you enter information into a cell, it also appears in the formula bar. The formula bar will also show information that has been entered into the currently selected cell. You can also click in the formula bar to insert the insertion point and edit the cell entry. You will find that when you work with formulas or functions, the result of the formula or function is shown in the cell that contains it. To view the actual formula or function, select the cell and the formula bar will show you the formula or function as it was entered.

At the bottom of the Excel application window to the right of the vertical scrollbar, you will find sheet tabs that enable you to access the sheets in a particular workbook. Below the scrollbar is the Excel status bar, which includes the View shortcuts and the Zoom slider.

Moving Around a Worksheet

I've already mentioned that you can use the keyboard or the mouse to move within an Excel worksheet. It makes sense to use the keyboard for movement in the worksheet when you are actually entering data. Reaching out to grab the mouse every time you want to move to another cell will only slow down your data entry. A number of keyboard shortcuts make it easy to maneuver the worksheet geography. Obviously, the arrow keys will move you one cell in the direction specified by the key. Table 11.1 provides some of the other keyboard shortcuts available in Excel.

Table 11.1   Using the Keyboard to Move in a Worksheet

Key Combination	Result
Tab	One cell to the right
Shift+Tab	One cell to the left
Ctrl+Right arrow	Moves right to last occupied cell in the current row (before a blank cell)
Ctrl+Left arrow	Moves left to the first occupied cell in the current row (before a blank cell)
Ctrl+Up arrow	Move to topmost occupied cell in a column (before a blank cell)
Ctrl+Down arrow	Move to last occupied cell in a column (before a blank cell)
Ctrl+End	Move to first empty cell below the bottom most right occupied cell in sheet
Ctrl+Home	Move to cell A1 in the worksheet
Enter	Enters data into the cell and moves down one cell

The mouse also provides you with some possibilities in Excel other than the obvious such as clicking on a cell or manipulating the vertical or horizontal scrollbar. You can double-click in a cell to insert the insertion point and edit the data in that cell. The mouse can also be used to zoom in or out on the current worksheet. Hold down the Ctrl key and then use the mouse wheel to zoom in or out as needed.

 tip

Above the Ribbon is the Quick Access Toolbar, which provides the Save, Undo, and Redo commands. You can add other often-used commands to this toolbar.

Creating Workbooks and Worksheets

Workbooks are the container file that holds the worksheets and the data that you have entered on the worksheets. When you open the Excel application, a new blank workbook is created containing three sheets. Sheet 1 will be the active sheet and you can start entering information into the cells on the worksheet as soon as you get Excel up and running.

The empty workbook that appears when you start Excel is pretty much a blank canvas; you can enter data and format the worksheet as needed. Excel also enables you to create new workbooks based on a template, so you do have options for creating new Excel workbooks other than starting from scratch. These options are available in the Backstage view. To access the Excel Backstage, select File on the Ribbon.

In the Backstage, select New to open the Available Templates window (see Figure 11.6). This window provides access to a blank workbook template, any templates you have created, and a number of Excel templates available on Office.com.

Figure 11.6
The Available Templates window in the Backstage.

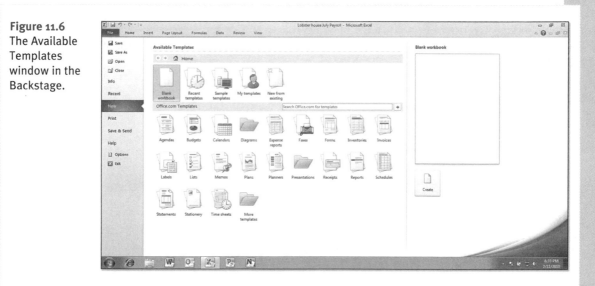

To create a new blank workbook, all you have to do is select the Blank Workbook template and then click Create. If you want to look at the sample templates installed on your computer when Office is installed, select the Sample templates icon. Several templates are provided such as a template for a billing statement, expense report, and time card.

Using Office.com Templates

Office.com provides a number of different types of templates. For example, there are budgets, calendars, invoices, plans and schedules that you can download. To view the templates available in one of the template groups, select a group such as Invoices. The number of templates available in a particular group will depend on the group you have selected. Each group provides a number of possibilities, however. In some cases, you might find that there are more templates of a particular type than you will ever need.

You can preview the templates by selecting a template in the list; the preview appears in the Preview pane of the Available Templates window. When you are ready to create a new workbook based on a particular template, make sure that the template is selected and then click either Create (for templates stored on your computer) or Download to download a template from Office.com. Figure 11.7 shows a new workbook based on an invoice template downloaded from Office.com.

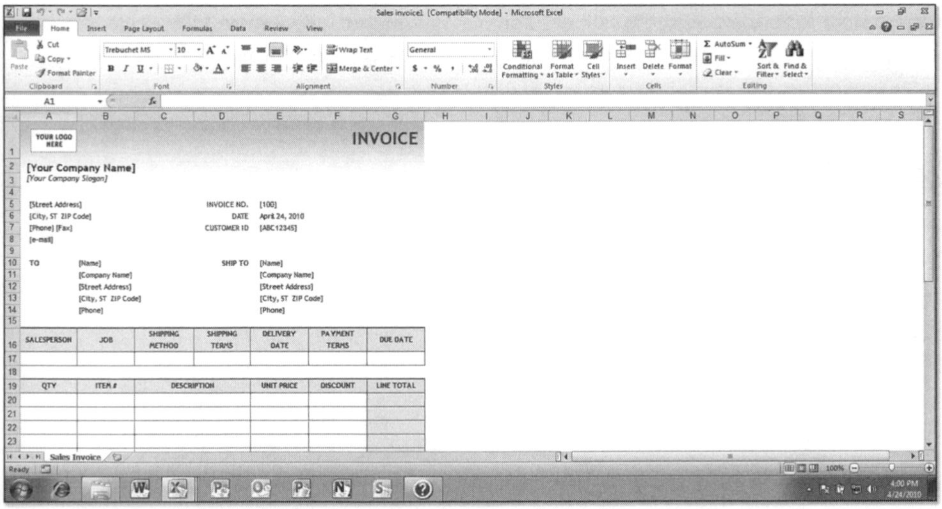

Figure 11.7
A new workbook based on an invoice template.

Although you are creating a new workbook with the template, the benefits you get from the template such as formatting, placeholder text, and specific formulas and functions are actually realized in a worksheet. A template such as the invoice template shown in Figure 11.7 creates a new workbook with one sheet named Sales Invoice.

Other templates, such as several of the report templates, will create multiple worksheets in the workbook. For example, the Budget Summary Report template creates a worksheet for the budget summary and two additional worksheets that hold a profit and loss chart and a balance sheet chart, respectively. So, you will find that some of the templates not only create multiple worksheets but also include ready-made charts on some worksheets in the new workbook. The great thing about templates is that even if you don't find a template that completely fits your needs, you can modify the worksheets provided by the template. You can also add additional worksheets as needed, which we discuss in the next section.

Inserting and Rearranging Worksheets

You can insert new worksheets into your workbook as needed. If you determine that you do not need particular worksheets, you can also remove them. Worksheets can be renamed and you can also rearrange the worksheets in a workbook.

The Insert command is in the Cells group on the Ribbon's Home tab. Select Insert then Insert Sheet. A new sheet will be inserted to the left of the currently selected sheet. You can grab the sheet tab with the mouse and then drag the worksheet to a new location in the sheet hierarchy. In terms of rearranging worksheets in a workbook, you can also take advantage of the Move or Copy dialog box, shown in Figure 11.8.

Figure 11.8
Rearrange worksheets using the Move or Copy dialog box.

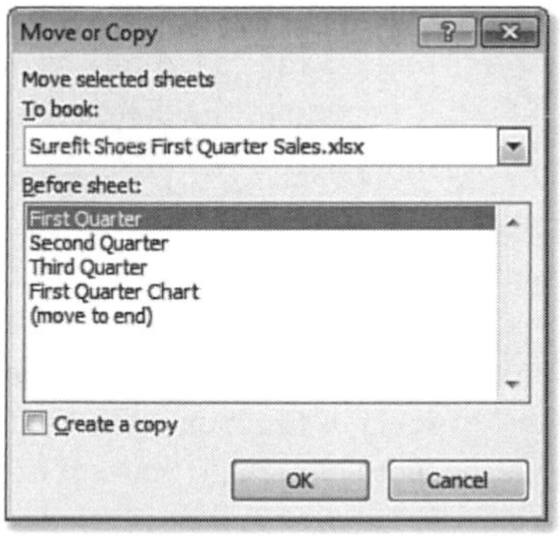

To open the Move or Copy dialog box, right-click on a sheet tab and then select Move or Copy. You can move the selected sheet before any of the listed sheets in the workbook. You can also use the Move or Copy dialog box to create a copy of a worksheet by selecting the Create a Copy check box.

The Move or Copy dialog box also provides you with the ability to move or copy the currently selected work-sheet or worksheets (hold down the Ctrl key to select multiple sheet tabs) to another workbook. The other workbook also needs to be currently active in Excel, so you will need to open it before accessing the Move or Copy dialog box. Use the To Book drop-down list to specify the work-book that will accept the move or copy and then click OK.

To rename a sheet, you can right-click on the worksheet tab and then select Rename from the short-cut menu. The current name will be selected (such as Sheet 1, Sheet 2, and so on). Type the new name for the sheet. You can also rename a sheet by right-clicking on a sheet tab and then selecting Rename from the shortcut menu. You can also delete a worksheet from the shortcut menu. Right click on any worksheet tab and then select Delete. If there is data on the worksheet, you will get a warning box alerting you to the fact that data might exist on the sheet you are deleting; select the Delete button in the warning box to continue. Be careful when deleting worksheets in a workbook. The Undo command on the Quick Access Toolbar won't undo a sheet deletion.

 tip

Double-click on a worksheet tab to select the current name if you want to rename the sheet.

Understanding Cell Addresses and Ranges

Before we get too far along in our discussion of working in the Excel application window and actually entering information into a worksheet, we should take a moment to discuss cell addressing. As already mentioned earlier in the chapter, cell addresses consist of two parts: the column designation and the row designation. When you select a cell in a worksheet, the cell address is shown in the Name box.

➡ *Relative references and absolute references are discussed in more detail starting on page 351 in Chapter 13, "Getting the Most from Formulas and Functions."*

Understanding cell addressing may seem like a no-brainer, however, when you start working with formulas and functions, particularly when you copy or move a formula or function, the perfect world of the Excel two-part address can actually get quite confusing. Excel actually uses a type of cell referencing called relative referencing. So, when a formula or function references a cell in a sheet, it is looking at the cell's relative position in the worksheet. If you move or copy a formula or function, this relative referencing can cause a problem.

Sometimes cells in a worksheet can be moved from their current position. This means that their cell addresses change. Any formulas or functions that refer to the previous addresses will no longer provide a correct calculation. One way around this is to name cells or cell ranges so that even if they are moved, a formula or function still sees that group of cells because you have configured the formula or function with the cell name rather than the cell address. Excel provides you with the capability of naming a cell or cell range (which we define in a moment).

➡ *Naming ranges is discussed beginning on page 345 in Chapter 12.*

Another worksheet entity that we should introduce at this point is the range. The concept of a cell range has been around since the days of DOS and early spreadsheet applications. A range was (and still is to some extent) defined as a group of contiguous (adjacent) cells. Figure 11.9 shows a selected contiguous range. Note that the range is not actually referred to in the Name box in Figure 11.9. Only the cell that is the start of the range will be specified. The selected range in Figure 11.9 would actually be referred to in a formula or function as B3:C16.

Although we typically think of a selected range of cells as a rectangular grouping of adjacent cells, ranges do not necessarily need to be contiguous, and you will find that when you are working with formulas, functions, and charts, you will also need to specify ranges of cells that are not contiguous. You can select a noncontiguous range by using the Ctrl key to specify nonadjacent cells. You can also specify cells in a formula or function by specifying a range of noncontiguous cells and setting the cell addresses apart by commas. For example, I might be using the Sum function to add a group of noncontiguous cells: G4, G6, and G9. The completed Sum function would look like this: =SUM (G4, G6, G9).

Figure 11.9
A selected
range of cells.

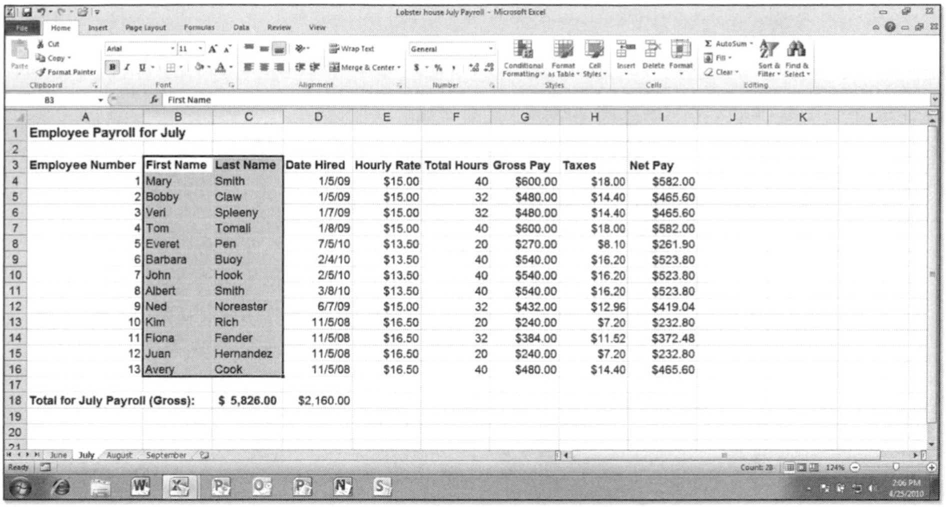

	A	B	C	D	E	F	G	H	I	J	K	L
1	Employee Payroll for July											
2												
3	Employee Number	First Name	Last Name	Date Hired	Hourly Rate	Total Hours	Gross Pay	Taxes	Net Pay			
4	1	Mary	Smith	1/5/09	$15.00	40	$600.00	$18.00	$582.00			
5	2	Bobby	Claw	1/5/09	$15.00	32	$480.00	$14.40	$465.60			
6	3	Veri	Spleeny	1/7/09	$15.00	32	$480.00	$14.40	$465.60			
7	4	Tom	Tomali	1/8/09	$15.00	40	$600.00	$18.00	$582.00			
8	5	Everet	Pen	7/5/10	$13.50	20	$270.00	$8.10	$261.90			
9	6	Barbara	Buoy	2/4/10	$13.50	40	$540.00	$16.20	$523.80			
10	7	John	Hook	2/5/10	$13.50	40	$540.00	$16.20	$523.80			
11	8	Albert	Smith	3/8/10	$13.50	40	$540.00	$16.20	$523.80			
12	9	Ned	Noreaster	6/7/09	$15.00	32	$432.00	$12.96	$419.04			
13	10	Kim	Rich	11/5/08	$16.50	20	$240.00	$7.20	$232.80			
14	11	Fiona	Fender	11/5/08	$16.50	32	$384.00	$11.52	$372.48			
15	12	Juan	Hernandez	11/5/08	$16.50	20	$240.00	$7.20	$232.80			
16	13	Avery	Cook	11/5/08	$16.50	40	$480.00	$14.40	$465.60			
17												
18	Total for July Payroll (Gross):		$ 5,826.00	$2,160.00								

Although it might sound a little patronizing, always look at the Name box to make sure where you are in a worksheet. Because most of the work that we do in Excel is based on cell addresses, you need to make sure that cell addresses are specified correctly, particularly when you are working with ranges of cells. Otherwise, the resulting calculations might not be providing the correct results.

Managing Excel Workbooks

When you save an Excel workbook, it is saved to the default file location, which is specified in the Excel Options. In most cases (unless your network administrator has configured Excel otherwise) that is \Users*Username*\Documents. So, any workbooks that you save should be located in your Documents folder. If you want to change the default file location, follow these steps:

1. Select File on the Ribbon to access the Backstage view.

2. Select Options to open the Excel Options window.

3. Select Save in the Excel Options window. Figure 11.10 shows the Save options.

4. Click in the Default File Location box and enter a new path for the file location.

5. Select the OK button to close the Excel Options window.

When you save an Excel workbook (click the Save button on the Quick Access Toolbar), it is saved in the .xlsx (XML file type) default file format. You can save your workbook in a number of other file formats, including Excel 97-2003 Workbook, Single File Web Page, or Excel Template. The different file types are found in the Save As Type drop-down list. If you have already saved a file and want to save it another format, use the Save As command in the Backstage.

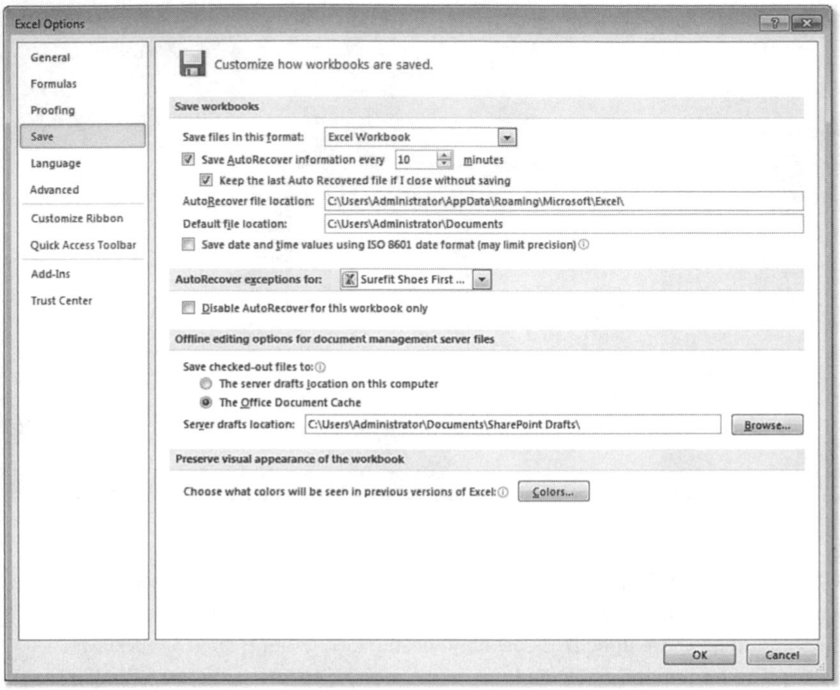

Figure 11.10
The Excel Save options.

The Backstage also provides you with other workbook management possibilities. When you select Info in the Backstage, you are provided access to the workbook permissions and settings related to sharing the workbook. You are also provided with access to the different versions of your workbook that have been created by the autosave feature. Figure 11.11 shows the Backstage Info view.

tip

You can access a workbook saved as a template from the My Templates icon in the Available Templates window.

As already mentioned, there are three distinct groupings of settings provided in the Info window: Permissions, Prepare for Sharing, and Versions. Let's look at each of these possibilities.

➡ *For more about Excel and other Office application file types, see page 51 in Chapter 3, "Managing and Sharing Office Files."*

Figure 11.11
The Backstage Info view.

Protecting Workbooks and Worksheets

You can configure the workbook so that changes made by other users you share the file with are limited. You can make the workbook read only or you can restrict permissions by individual users. The possibilities provided by the Protect Workbook command in the Info window are as follows:

- **Mark as Final:** This command marks the file as final and makes the file read-only. All editing commands for the file are disabled. This feature is primarily designed to keep users from inadvertently making changes to a file because a user can change the Mark as Final in the Backstage.

- **Encrypt with a Password:** The file will be encrypted and protected with a password. When you select this option, you will be required to enter a password for the workbook. Only users with the password will be able to open the workbook.

- **Protect Current Sheet:** This option opens the Protect Sheet dialog box. This dialog box enables you to password protect the sheet or you can specify individual sheet-related capabilities such as Format Cells, Insert Hyperlinks, and Delete Columns. Interaction with locked cells can also be configured in this dialog box. We discuss locked cells and sheet protection in more detail in a moment.

- **Protect Workbook Structure:** You can use this option to keep users from changing the number of sheets in the workbook. This means that worksheets cannot be deleted or added.

- **Restrict Permission by People:** This option enables you to take advantage of the Information Right Management Service. You can sign up for this free service from Microsoft using a Windows Live ID account. When the service is active on your computer via an installed certificate, you can assign users different permission levels using their Windows Live IDs for authentication.

- **Add a Digital Signature:** You can digitally sign a file to prove its authenticity. Signing a file digitally requires that you obtain a digital certificate. Digital certificates can be provided by a certifying authority.

You can see that the Backstage's Info window provides some protection schemes that are all-or-nothing propositions, such as Mark as Final and Encrypt with a Password, but in many cases, you might want to protect only certain cells on a particular worksheet when you share the workbook with other users. For example, you might want to lock cells that contain formulas and functions so that the person doing the data entry does not accidentally overwrite or delete the worksheet formulas or functions.

Locking Cells

Locking cells in a worksheet is a two-step process. You must first select and lock the cells. Then you must turn on protection on the entire worksheet for the lock to go into effect.

Select the cells in the worksheet that you want to lock. This may be cells containing formulas, functions, or column and row labels. Drag the mouse as needed to select the cells. If you need to select noncontiguous cells, hold down the Ctrl key and click on a cell to include it in the selected range of cells.

On the Home tab, select the Format command in the Cells group. Then select Format Cells. This will open the Format Cells dialog box with the Protection tab selected. Select the Locked check box as shown in Figure 11.12.

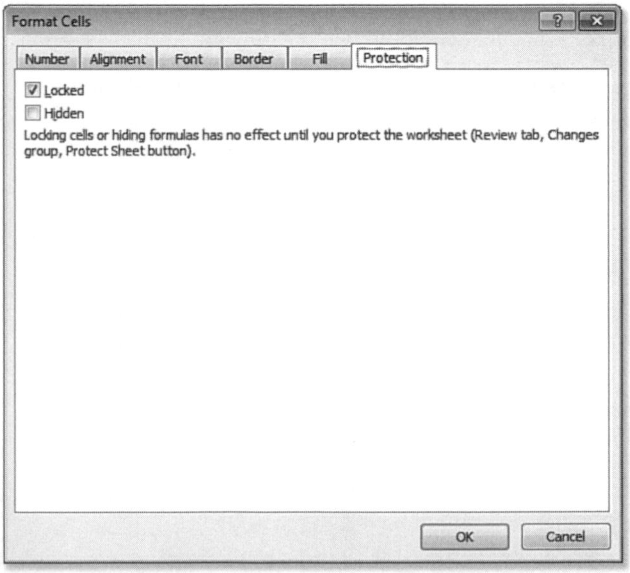

Figure 11.12
The Protection tab of the Format Cells dialog box.

After you have checked the Locked option, select OK to close the dialog box. Now you need to protect the worksheet. Select the Ribbon's Review tab and then select the Protect Sheet command in the Changes group. The Protect Sheet dialog box will open as shown in Figure 11.13.

Figure 11.13
The Protect Sheet dialog box.

You can enter a password to protect the sheet if you want. You can also select other options related to what users can do to the worksheet such as formatting cells, columns, or rows and inserting hyperlinks. To protect the locked cells on the sheet and allow data entry in other cells, you need not change any of the settings in the Protect Sheet dialog box. Even the password is optional. Select OK to close the dialog box.

When you (yes, you) or another user attempts to enter data into the locked cells on the worksheet, a message box will open to let you know that the cell is protected and is read-only. No data entry will be allowed in the cell.

Specifying Edit Ranges

There is actually a second way to specify groups of cells that can be edited by other users. This method actually seems easier to configure than the method discussed in the previous section, but specifying edit ranges is primarily designed for use in network environments. It works best when you use Excel on a Microsoft Windows Server network. Because users will be listed in a global catalog provided by the Active Directory (which is a catalog of all the objects on the network including users, computers, and networks), it is easy to set permissions for specific users or groups related to ranges that you password protect. This method certainly is not restricted to corporate networks because you can specify users that have been set up on your local computer using the Add or Remove User Accounts link in the Control Panel.

To specify the ranges that can be edited by users, you specify the ranges in the Allow Users to Edit Ranges dialog box. Each range can be protected by a different password so that you can provide access to some cells to certain users and other cells

> **tip**
>
> To unprotect a protected worksheet, select the Unprotect Sheet command on the Review tab.

> **caution**
>
> Working with Windows user accounts and permissions and using Windows 7 as a client on a Microsoft network can be a little tricky. If you need a complete reference to Windows 7, you may want to check out *Microsoft Windows 7 In Depth* by Robert Cowart and Brian Knittel.

to other users. This provides a little more fine-tuning in terms of cell access than the method that we looked at involving locking cells and then protecting the sheet. In the Changes group on the Ribbon's Review tab, select the Allow Users to Edit Ranges command. This will open the Allow Users to Edit Ranges as shown in Figure 11.14.

Figure 11.14
The Allow Users to Edit Ranges dialog box.

To specify an editable range, select the New button. This opens the New Range dialog box. Provide a title for the range. Click in the Refers to Cells box and you can then select the actual range of cells in the worksheet. You can select contiguous cells or noncontiguous cells as needed.

After specifying the range in the New Range dialog box, provide a password in the Range Password. You can also specify permissions related to the password protected range. Select the Permissions in the New Range dialog box and the Permissions dialog box for the range will open.

You can use the Add button to open the Select Users or Groups dialog box. You can then add users or groups to the list provided in the Users or Groups dialog box. User accounts or groups added to the list can be local accounts (accounts you have added to Windows 7) or can be user accounts and groups that are housed on your network server such as a domain controller in a Microsoft Windows Server network.

> **tip**
>
> Whenever you are working with passwords, you need to make sure you record the passwords and keep them in a safe place. Forgotten passwords don't really do anyone any good.

After specifying users and groups, click OK and you will be returned to the Permissions dialog box for the range. You can select a group or username in the Permissions dialog box and then specify whether you allow or deny access to the range without a password. The default setting is Allow, so you should change this because the whole point of this process to password protect a specific range.

When you have specified the individual permissions for each user or group, click OK. You will be returned to the New Range dialog box. You can click OK to close the dialog box. A Confirm Password dialog box will open, requiring that you re-enter the password you set for the range. Enter the password and then click OK. You will be returned to the Allow Users to Edit Ranges dialog box. The new range will appear in the range list. You can repeat the process to add other ranges to the Allow Users to Edit Ranges dialog box. When you are finished adding the ranges, click OK to close the Protect Sheet dialog box.

For this whole edit range thing to work, we still need to lock all the cells in the worksheet and then protect the sheet. Use the Sheet Selector button (the box just to the left of column A and above row 1) to select the entire worksheet. Then select the Format command on the Home tab and select Lock Cell on the menu provided. All the cells on the sheet are now locked.

Navigate to the Review tab of the Ribbon and select Protect Sheet. When the Protect Sheet dialog box opens, you can specify a password to unprotect the sheet or set other specific abilities for users of the worksheet such as the formatting of cells, columns, rows, and so on. Click OK to protect the sheet.

So, let's say you've shared the workbook with another user or users. When they attempt to access locked cells on the sheet, they will be greeted by a message box letting them know that the cell is locked and it is read only. When the user attempts to enter data in a cell that is in one of the edit ranges that you specified, the Unlock Range dialog box will open. The user will need to provide the password that unlocks the range. Using edit ranges is a good way to keep formulas and functions safe but allow an edit range for a user who is responsible for data entry. The user will need the password for the edit range to access any of the cells in it. All the other cells in the worksheet remain locked and protected.

Preparing a Workbook for Sharing

The Check for Issues button in the Backstage Info window provides you commands that enable you to check a workbook for hidden or personal information and for any accessibility or compatibility issues with your workbook. When you select the Inspect Document command, the Document Inspector opens as shown in Figure 11.15.

Figure 11.15
The Document Inspector.

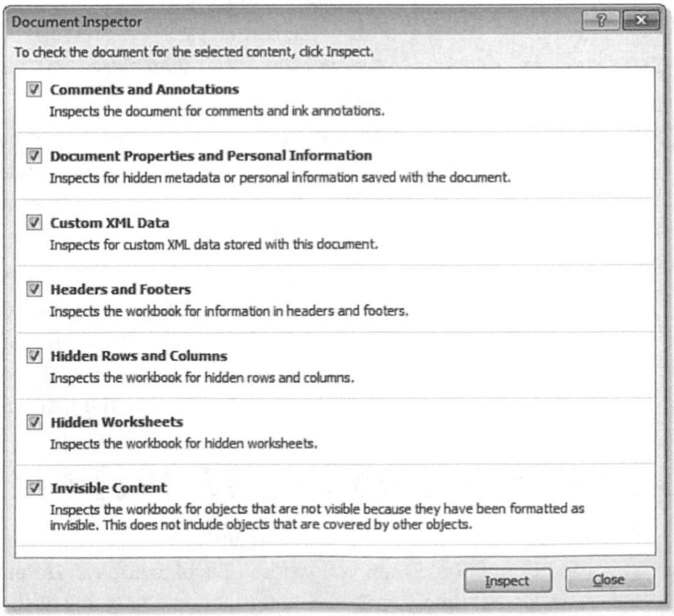

The primary job of the Document Inspector is to scour your workbook for any personal or sensitive information that you might not have realized is contained in the workbook. This includes information that you might have placed in comments or the headers and footers of the worksheets. The Inspector also checks for hidden items such as rows, columns, and sheets. When you select Inspect in the Document Inspector dialog box, an inspection will be run on the workbook.

> **tip**
>
> If you don't need any of the draft versions saved by Excel, select Manage Versions and then Delete All Draft Versions to remove them from your computer.

When the inspection has been completed, a list of results will appear in the Document Inspector. For example, personal information might have been included in the workbook properties and this will be flagged as a possible problem. As already mentioned, headers and footers might include information that you do not want to share with others, so if the workbook contains any headers or footers, they will be flagged as a potential problem.

The Document Inspector does provide remedies for these issues but they are pretty much the equivalent of blowing up your entire backyard to get rid of a few hungry moles. For example, if headers and footers are present, the Document Inspector's solution is Remove All, meaning all the information in the header or footer area will be removed. The same goes for information in the document properties.

Rather than going with the nuclear option provided by the Document Inspector, you might want to use the information provided in the Document Inspector as a checklist of things you need to actually look at before sharing the document.

Managing Versions

The options provided by the Versions area of the Info window relate to autosave copies of your workbook and any draft versions that have been created for the workbook in cases when you did not save changes to the workbook and then closed it. This would include situations where you lost power to your computer.

You can open any of the autosave versions of your workbook by clicking the link provided. The autosave versions are time stamped, so you will know when that particular version was created. Be advised that when you save and exit the current workbook, the various autosave versions of the workbook are deleted. So, you need to use these versions during your current editing session.

In the case of working with any saved draft versions, select the Manage Version button and then Recover Draft Versions. This will open the Open dialog box and any draft versions of the current workbook (or other workbooks) will be listed. All draft copies of workbooks have "UnSaved" included in the filename. Select a draft version and then click Open to open the draft in Excel. You can then use the Save As command to change the filename if you want to keep the draft.

Entering Data in a Worksheet

Entering data in a worksheet is really just a matter of clicking on a particular cell and then typing the information. When you work in Excel, you enter different types of information such as text, numbers, dates, times, formulas, and functions. In terms of the raw data that you enter (precluding the insertion of formulas or functions), you are really working with two different types of information: labels and values.

A label is typically descriptive information such as the name of a person, place, or thing or a time designation such as the day of the week or a month of the year. A label has no numerical significance in Excel; labels provide context for the values in the worksheet. Now, don't get me wrong, dates can actually have numerical significance and can be used in formulas and functions. For example, you can subtract today's date from the date of an upcoming holiday, such as Labor Day or Thanksgiving, and compute how many days remain until that particular holiday. Social Security numbers, on the other hand, are numbers, but they are descriptors and do not have numerical significance. We don't add or subtract Social Security numbers.

A value is data that does have numerical significance. Values can be numbers, dates, and even times. Values can be acted upon by formulas and functions. A value could be the monthly payment you have made on an automobile or it the water levels you have measured over the course of the year on a nearby lake. Values are the fuel that drive Excel's number-crunching engine.

Entering Labels

As already mentioned, text entries in the worksheet serve a descriptive purpose; they are labels. Text can be used as row and column headings and to describe particular cells. In fact, as soon as you press one of the letters of the alphabet, you will find that Excel aligns the text entry on the left side of the cell. Excel knows the basic difference between labels and values.

When you type a label into a particular cell, you need to seal the deal by pressing Enter, which actually enters the information into the cell. This will also move you one cell down. As you type, you will also find that your entry is shown in the formula bar.

You can also enter the typed data by advancing to another cell in the worksheet using a variety of methods. You can also use the arrow keys to complete a text entry and then move to an adjacent cell. For example, pressing the left-arrow key will enter a text entry and move you to the cell directly to the left of the cell that you entered the text in. You can also click in another cell to enter the data in the current cell.

In cases where you want to enter text in a cell and don't want to move from that cell, you can enter your data and then click the Enter icon (the check mark) to the left of the formula bar box.

In some cases, you might to enter numbers that will have no numerical significance. These can be formatted as text. In the good old days of primitive spreadsheet software (which weren't that good), numbers that served as labels were entered as text by preceding the number with an apostrophe. This was particularly useful in cases when you wanted a leading zero to show in the number (and not be removed by Excel) such as 003. You don't need to do this in Excel. You can select the cells that will contain the numerical labels and format the cells as text before entering the actual numbers. Follow these steps:

 tip

If you find that a text entry is cut off when you enter data in the next cell to the right, all you have to do is widen the column by dragging the column border to accommodate the entry in the cell.

1. Select the cells that will contain the numbers that will serve as labels.

2. On the Home tab, select the General command in the Number group.

3. In the Number format gallery that appears, scroll to the bottom and select text.

4. Enter the numbers in the formatted cells (including leading zeros).

You will find that the numbers entered into these formatted cells have been left-aligned in the cells as text entries are aligned. We discuss cell formatting in more detail in the next chapter.

➡ *For more about formatting cells see page 317 in Chapter 12.*

Entering Values

Values provide the raw data to be used in a calculation that is performed by a formula or function. You can enter values using the 0–9 keys on the keyboard or the numeric keypad. You are not required to enter commas, dollar signs, or percentage signs in the cell when you enter a value. The formatting of the value can be taken care after the fact using the number formats provided by Excel. You are required to place the decimal point in the correct place, however.

> **tip**
>
> To insert the current date into a cell press Ctrl + ; (semicolon).

You will find that Excel right-aligns values in the worksheet cells. Make sure that you check any values that you enter into your cells. Typing mistakes make up most of the errors typically found in a worksheet. Although a misspelled label might be embarrassing, an erroneous formula or function result due to incorrect data entry can be actually damaging to your credibility and business.

Dates and times that you enter into an Excel workbook can actually have numerical significance. Excel sees a date as a number that reflects the number of days that have elapsed since January 1, 1900. Even though you won't see this number (Excel displays your entry as a normal date), the number is used whenever you use the date in a calculation. Times are also considered values. Time is computed as a percentage of 24 hours. To you, 10:45 AM may be time for a coffee break, but to Excel it is actually the decimal value of .4479.

You can enter a date into a cell using more than one date shorthand or format. For example, you can use the MM/DD/YY or MM-DD-YY format. You can also enter a date in the format MONTH DAY, YEAR such as August 9, 2011. If you need to specify a year prior to 2000, include the entire year information such as "1954."

Dates entered will have the default date format applied to them. You can change the formatting for dates via the Number tab of the Format Cells dialog box, which can be opened using the dialog box launcher on the Font group on the Ribbon's Home tab. Formatting cell entries is discussed in Chapter 12.

> **tip**
>
> To quickly access the AutoComplete list in the current cell, press Alt+down arrow.

The format for entering time is HH:MM. You can specify AM or PM with a or p (following the time), respectively. You can also enter time using the 24-hour international time format.

Using AutoComplete

AutoComplete can take some of the drudgery out of entering the same label multiple times in a worksheet column. Excel keeps a list of all the labels that you enter in a worksheet column. For example, suppose you have a worksheet tracking sales in Europe and you are entering country

names, such as Germany, Italy, and so on, multiple times into
a particular column in the worksheet. After you enter Germany
the first time, it becomes part of the AutoComplete list for that
column. The next time you enter the letter G into a cell in that
column, Excel completes the entry as "Germany."

> ⦿ **tip**
>
> If you enter a value, particularly
> a date, and the entry is shown as
> #####, you need to widen the col-
> umn to accommodate the value.

AutoComplete works with text entries and entries that contain
a combination of text and numbers. Depending on the similarities of labels in a particular column, you might have to type
several characters before Excel provides you with the correct match. When the AutoComplete entry
appears in the cell, press Enter.

You can also choose to select an AutoComplete entry from a drop-down list. All the entries available
for a particular column will appear in the list. Right-click on a cell and then select Pick from Drop-
down List on the shortcut menu that appears. A drop-down list of AutoComplete entries will appear
as shown in Figure 11.16.

Figure 11.16
AutoComplete
drop-down list.

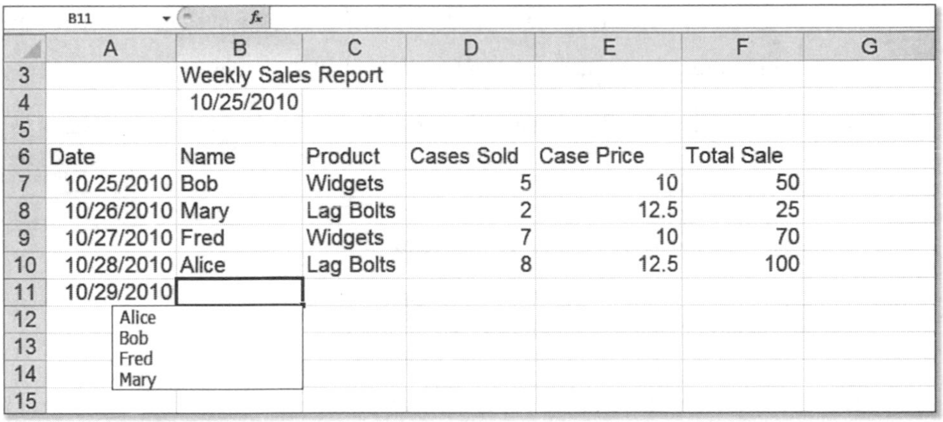

	A	B	C	D	E	F	G
3		Weekly Sales Report					
4		10/25/2010					
5							
6	Date	Name	Product	Cases Sold	Case Price	Total Sale	
7	10/25/2010	Bob	Widgets	5	10	50	
8	10/26/2010	Mary	Lag Bolts	2	12.5	25	
9	10/27/2010	Fred	Widgets	7	10	70	
10	10/28/2010	Alice	Lag Bolts	8	12.5	100	
11	10/29/2010						
12		Alice					
13		Bob					
14		Fred					
15		Mary					

Select an entry from the list. The entry will be entered in the cell. Using the list enables you to see
the available entries, which can be particularly useful in large worksheets that contain a large number of different labels in a particular column.

Filling and Entering Series

The ability to automatically fill cells with information is a useful and time-saving trick that can help
you avoid data entry drudgery and can also help you decrease the possibility of data entry errors in
your worksheets. There are a couple of different techniques for filling cells with information. You
can use the fill handle on a cell to extend a label or value series.

The Fill command in the Editing group of the Home tab can also be used to enter value series
where you can specify the type of series (such as linear or growth) and provide the step value for
the series. The step value serves as either the amount that the value in each subsequent cell is

increased (in a linear series) or as the multiple used to increase each subsequent entry in the series (in a growth series). Data series can also be created where the step value provides the increment for specifying each subsequent date in the series.

Using the Fill Handle

The fill handle can help you quickly create series for days of the week and months of the year. It can also provide a series for labels that contain a number. For example, if I divided my sales territory into regions specified as Region 1, Region 2, and so on, all I would have to do is enter the Region 1 label in a cell and then use the fill han-dle to drag the rest of the series into other adjacent cells as needed. The fill handle can create a series in a column or a row.

The fill handle is a small black box on the lower-right corner of a selected cell's border. The mouse pointer becomes a small + symbol when you are on the fill handle. To use the fill handle, you drag it in the direction that you want the fill to take place. For instance, if you are filling cells in a column, you can drag down or up (probably down) and if you are filling cells in a row, you can drag to the right or left.

To create a fill series such as the days of the week or months of the year, follow these steps:

1. Enter the first item in the series such as "Monday" or "January."

2. Grab the fill handle and drag in the appropriate direction to extend the series. ScreenTips will appear as you drag across the cells, showing a preview of each item that will be placed in each subsequent cell.

3. Release the mouse to enter the series items.

When you release the mouse, the series items will appear in the cells. The AutoFill Options button will also appear as shown in Figure 11.17.

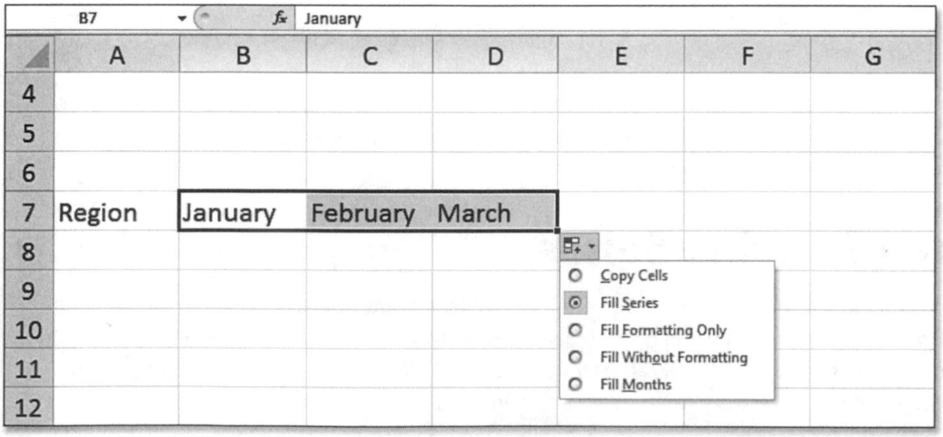

Figure 11.17
A filled month series and the AutoFill Options menu.

The AutoFill Options menu (accessed when you select the AutoFill Options button) provides a series of options related to your dragging of the fill handle. Although we are using the fill handle to extend a series, you can see from Figure 11.17 that other options are possible. These options will vary depending on whether you are using the fill handle to copy an item (such as a formula, function, or even a heading) or are creating a series such as we have discussed here. The possibilities provided by the AutoFill Options menu can include the following:

- **Copy Cells:** The fill handle might have created a series when you actually wanted to copy the entry in a cell to other cells using the fill handle. Select this option to copy rather than fill.

- **Fill Series:** If the fill handle has copied the entry in the cell, you can select this option to get an extended series.

- **Fill Formatting Only:** This option will fill the cells that you move across using the fill handle with the formatting provided by the selected cell. The actual contents of the cell will not be copied (or extended) into the subsequent cells in the fill range.

- **Fill Without Formatting:** This option will create a series but will not include any formatting that has been applied to the cell that you "extended" using the fill handle.

You can also use the fill handle to extend numerical series, date series, and time series. When you use the fill handle to extend a date series, the AutoFill Options menu will provide other options such as Fill Days, Fill Weekdays, Fill Months, and Fill Years. So, no matter what type of date series you are trying to create from a source date, the fill handle can create the series for you.

The fill handle can also be used to copy a cell's content, including formulas for functions, to a range of cells. Remember that if you don't get the result you are after, you might have to consult the AutoFill Options button's menu and select the option that provides the needed fill or copy.

 tip

You will find that when you are copying formulas and functions in a worksheet to multiple cells in a column or row, you will typically employ the fill handle rather than copy and paste.

In the case of numerical series, you can extend any series just as long as Excel knows what the step is between the numbers in the series. The step is the incremental difference between the numbers in the series, so when you enter 2 in a cell and then 4 in the cell below it, you are tipping off Excel that the step is 2. Select both of the cells containing the first two numbers in the series and then drag the fill handle on the second number to create the series as needed.

So, the fill handle can create a series, and it can quickly copy items to multiple cells. It does have a limitation, however, in terms of copying a cell's content in more than one direction (such as down and then to the right). You can only copy down or up in a single column or to the right or left in a single row. If you need to copy into multiple columns or rows, you will have to extend the series in one direction and then extend the series a second time in the second direction. This will make more sense when you attempt to copy formulas or functions to cells in a range that encompasses multiple columns or rows.

➡ *For more about copying formulas and functions, see page 367 in Chapter 13.*

Creating Custom Fill Lists

You can also create custom fill lists and then apply them using the fill handle. For example, you might have a group of employee names or location names that you always enter in the same order in different worksheets. When you create the custom fill list, all you have to do is enter the first item in the list in a cell and then use the fill handle to extend the rest of the custom fill list into the required cells.

note

The Fill command also provides a menu of commands for filling Down, Right, Up, or Left. You can use these commands to copy information from a cell to a group of selected cells.

A custom list can consist of text entries or text mixed with numbers. So, custom lists are reserved for series of labels. You can create a custom fill list from a range of cells that already exist in a worksheet or you can create a custom list by typing in the entries for the list manually. Custom fill lists are created in the Custom Lists dialog box, which is shown in Figure 11.18.

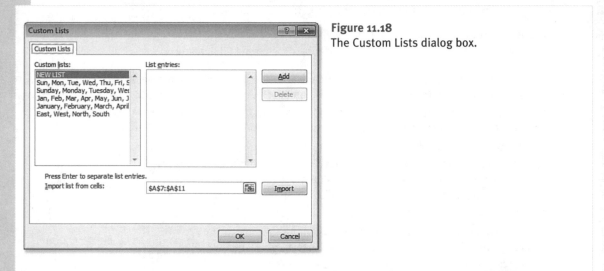

Figure 11.18
The Custom Lists dialog box.

To access the Custom Lists dialog box, select File on the Ribbon to enter the Backstage view and then select Options to open the Excel Options window. Select Advanced and then scroll down in the Advanced options; the Edit Custom Lists button is at the very bottom of the General category.

If you want to import a selected range of cells into a custom list, you can specify the range by selecting the Shrink button to the left of the Import button. This will provide you with access to the worksheet. Select the range and then click the Expand button to re-enter the Options dialog box. You can then click the Import button. The new list will be placed in the Custom Lists pane and the entries in the list will be shown in the List Entries pane.

If you want to create the custom list from scratch, select NEW LIST in the Custom Lists pane and then click Add. You can then type the entries in the List Entries pane. Press Enter after each entry. When you are ready to add the list, select the Add button in the Options dialog box.

You can now use the custom list or lists that you created in your worksheets. Type the first entry in a custom list in a cell and then use the fill handle to extend the range. The new range will consist of the entries you placed in the custom list.

> 🎵 **tip**
>
> To delete a custom list that you have created, select the list and then click the Delete button in the Options dialog box.

Creating Custom Series

Another option for creating a series (a series of values including dates) in a worksheet is to take advantage of the Series dialog box. The Series dialog box provides you with complete control over the series you want to create, including the step value (the increment between each subsequent cell and the cell before it) and the stop value. You can also create different types of series:

- **Linear:** This series type uses the starting value provided in the worksheet and then uses the step value to create a linear progression.

- **Growth:** This series type uses the starting value provided in the worksheet and then multiplies each value in the series by the step value to enter each subsequent value in the range. So, this type of series is really a geometric progression.

- **Date:** this series type allows you to specify a date Unit such as Day, Weekday, Month or Year. The step value is then added to each subsequent date in the series.

- **AutoFill:** This type of series mimics the use of the fill handle. You do not enter a step value for this type of series.

Enter the start value for the series you want to create in a cell in the worksheet. You can then select the cell and the range of cells that will be filled by the information you enter into the Series dialog box. To open the Series dialog box, select the Fill command on the Home tab and then select Series. The Series dialog box is shown in Figure 11.19.

Figure 11.19
The Series dialog box.

Select the appropriate option to specify whether the series will be in rows or columns. Select the type of series you want to create such as linear, growth, or date. Enter the step value for the series in the Step Value box. If you did not select the cells that you want to fill using the series, you can enter a step value for the series. This will specify the end of the series and will also dictate the number of cells that are filled by the series. When you are ready to create the series, select OK.

Copying, Moving, and Deleting Cell Contents

We have already discussed how the fill handle can be used to copy data (both labels and values) from one cell to a range of cells (or from a range to a range). You can also use the Copy command in the Clipboard group to copy a cell's content to another cell. Cell ranges can also be copied and then pasted and a single cell's content can be pasted to a range of cells. You can also move cell data using cut and paste, or drag and drop cells or cell ranges in new locations on a sheet.

Copy and paste and cut and paste are pretty familiar to even the most novice Office user, so there is no quantum physics involved in selecting a cell and then using Copy or Cut to place it on the Clipboard. It is the different possibilities provided by the Paste command that actually get a little confusing, but provide you with a lot of possibilities in terms of what is actually pasted from a selected cell or cell range to another cell or cell range. In terms of the possibilities provided by the Paste command, some of the options are related to information that you copy from another worksheet in your workbook or another workbook (you can open multiple workbooks and copy or cut and then paste cell information as needed). There will be times when you want only the cell contents and not the formatting found on the cells (such as borders or colors) or formatting used on the cell contents (such as the number format).

Select a cell or range of cells to be copied. Then select Copy or Cut as needed from the Clipboard group on the Ribbon's Home tab. When you select the Paste command, a gallery of different paste options appears as shown in Figure 11.20.

tip

You can use Ctrl+C to copy; Ctrl+X to cut and Ctrl+V to paste. When you use Ctrl+V, the Paste icon will appear below the pasted items, enabling you to adjust the type of paste you actually make.

Figure 11.20
The Paste gallery.

The Paste gallery divides the different paste options into categories. Each of the options found in the categories provides a ScreenTip when you place the mouse on a specific option icon. The options available will depend on what you have copied to the clipboard and the actual option you select will, obviously, depend on the results you require. The Paste gallery categories are as follows:

- **Paste:** This category provides, from left to right, the following options: Paste, Formulas, Formulas and Number Formatting, and Keep Source Formatting. The Paste option will paste the contents but they will be formatted according to the formatting that has been applied to the new location. If you want to keep the original formatting, use the Keep Source Formatting option. If you are pasting formulas or functions, you will want to take advantage of the Formulas option and if you want to keep the original formatting that was applied to the cells containing the formulas, use the Formulas and Number Formatting option.

- **Paste Values:** If you want to paste the values calculated by a formula or function, rather than pasting the formula or function itself, you can use the options provided in this category. Options are provided to paste the value only (Value), the value and its number formatting (Values & Number Formatting), and the value and the cell formatting (Values & Source Formatting).

- **Other Paste Options:** You can paste the formatting of the select cell (or cell range) using the Formatting option. If you want to link the copied data to the destination cell or cells, use the Paste Link option. Linked data will update automatically when you change the values (such as the results of a formula or function) in the source cell or cells.

When you select one of the options and actually paste the cell or range into a worksheet, the Paste Options button will appear just below the pasted content. You can access the same options that were available in the Paste gallery from this button. You will also find that the cell or range that you originally copied will still have a marquee (that sparkly rectangle thing) denoting that the cell or cells have been copied to the Clipboard. Press Esc to get rid of the marquee.

You can access the Office Clipboard to view cells or cell ranges that have been copied or cut to it. This allows you to reuse items on the Clipboard. For example, you can paste any of the items on the Clipboard, so if you have cut and then pasted a range, you can actually paste that same range again from the Clipboard to the current worksheet or another worksheet in the workbook.

To view the contents of the Clipboard, select the Clipboard launcher on the bottom right of the Clipboard group on the Ribbon's Home tab. The Clipboard appears as a pane on the left side of the Excel workspace, as shown in Figure 11.21.

The Office Clipboard can hold up to 24 items, so this makes it easy to paste data from worksheet to worksheet or even to another Excel workbook. When you place the mouse on an item stored in the Clipboard, a drop-down menu arrow appears. You can use the menu to paste the item. You can also remove it from the Clipboard by selecting Delete. You can also paste all the items on the Clipboard using the Paste All command. If you want to remove all the current items on the Clipboard, select the Clear All button.

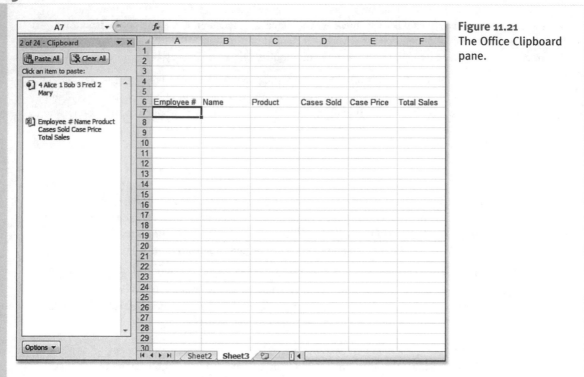

Figure 11.21
The Office Clipboard
pane.

Using the Paste Special Dialog Box

The Paste gallery provides a number of possibilities in terms of what is actually pasted after you copy or cut a cell's or range's data. The Paste Special dialog box provides even more possibilities. Many of the options provided in the Paste Special dialog box really relate to pasting cells from one worksheet to another worksheet (that have been copied or cut) or cells from one workbook to another. Because worksheets can be formatted differently, the options in the Paste Special dialog box are designed to enable you to fine-tune what is pasted and how it affects the worksheet where the cells are pasted. To open the Paste Special dialog box (once you have copied or cut a cell range), select Paste and then Paste Special. Figure 11.22 shows the Paste Special dialog box.

Most of the options provided in the Paste area of the Paste Special dialog box have names that provide you with a good idea of what the option does. Some of the options paste the contents of the cell or range in the worksheet. For example, Values converts formula and function results to the actual value calculated when the cells are pasted. The Formats option pastes the cell formatting. The Formulas option pastes the formulas or functions in the range but does not include any of the formatting provided by the source range. Some of the other options paste only formatting or other attributes. For example, the Formats option pastes only the cell formatting found in the range and any formatting that has been applied to the text or values found in the cells. Another example is the Column Width option, which pastes only the column width from the source range.

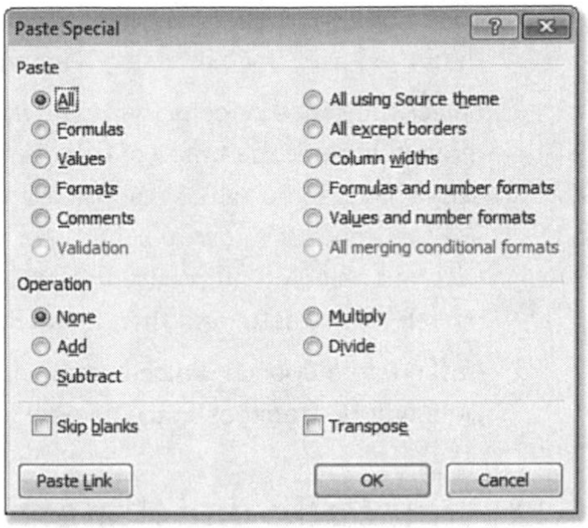

Figure 11.22
The Paste Special dialog box.

Using the Paste Special Operation Options

The Paste Special dialog box actually goes beyond the various options you might need for pasting cells and cell ranges into a worksheet. The Operation options enable you to perform an operation on a selected range of cells based on a value supplied in the copied cell. You don't actually paste a cell or range of cells for the operation to take place; the originally copied value is used by the Paste Special dialog box to adjust the values in a second range of cells. You can add, subtract, multiply, or divide the values in the range.

For example, you might have a list of products in a worksheet that is accompanied by a range of prices for the products. If your supplier raises your cost for each item by 2%, you can multiply the values in the range of prices by 1.02 to raise your prices by 2%. So, for lack of a better name, we can call the cell containing the 1.02 the "adjustment value." The cells that are adjusted using the adjustment value can be referred to as the "adjusted range."

 tip

The Skip Blanks check box in the Paste Special dialog box enables you to skip blank cells when pasting ranges in your worksheet.

To use the Operation option, enter a value in a cell that will serve as the adjustment value. Then copy the cell to the Clipboard using the Copy command (Ctrl + C). The marquee will appear around the cell. Now select the range of cells that you want to adjust. The marquee remains around the copied adjustment value even though the range of cells to be adjusted is currently selected. Select Paste and then Paste Special to open the Paste Special dialog box. In the Operation options area of the Paste Special dialog box, select the operation that you want to take place such as add, subtract, multiply, or divide. Then click OK. The selected range (the adjusted range) will be adjusted according to the operation you chose and the adjustment value you originally copied to the Clipboard.

Transposing a Cell Range

The Paste Special dialog box can also be used to transpose a range of cells that are currently in a row to a column or vice versa. This is particularly useful if you want to take the column headings that you have placed in the top row of your worksheet and change them to row headings. To transpose a range of cells, you typically use the Cut command (because you are moving the cells) and then the Paste Special dialog box, which provides the Transpose option.

Select the range of cells that you want to transpose, and then select Cut on the Home tab. The marquee will mark the range of cells that have been cut. Click in a cell that will be the first cell in the range where you will transpose the cut range. Make sure that there are empty cells below (if you are transposing a row to column) or to the right (if you are transposing a column to a row) of the cell that you selected after cutting the range to be transposed. Then open the Paste Special dialog box by selecting Paste, and then Paste Special.

In the Paste Special dialog box, select the Transpose check box and then click OK. The range of cut cells will be transposed to the new location.

Moving Cells and Ranges

For moving cell content from one place to another in a worksheet, you can use Cut and Paste if you choose; however, it is much easier to use drag and drop. You can drag cell content to a new location and you can drag the contents of a range of cells to a new location. If you drag and drop a range onto a cell or cells that already contain data, the data will be replaced by the data in the range that you are moving.

Select a cell or cell range to be moved and drag the border of the selected cell or cells to the new location. To insert the range between existing cells in a worksheet, hold down the Shift key as you drag. You can also move the data to another worksheet in the current workbook. To move the data to a different worksheet, press the Alt key and drag the selection to the worksheet's tab. You're switched to that sheet, where you can drop your selection at the appropriate location in the worksheet.

Clearing and Deleting Cells

A cell and its content are two different entities when you start looking at the possibilities for removing content from a worksheet. You can quickly remove a cell's content or the content of a number of cells in a selected range by pressing the Delete key on the keyboard. You can also use the Clear command to clear the contents of a cell, but it also provides you with some options for clearing formatting that has been applied to a cell or range of cells or comments that have been added to a cell. The Clear menu provides the following options:

 tip

If you want to copy a range using drag and drop, hold down the Ctrl key as you drag a copy of the range to a new location.

- **Clear All:** This option clears formatting, content, and comments.

- **Clear Formats:** This option clears the formatting that has been applied to the cell, including font, alignment, or number formatting. This option also clears any conditional formatting or cell styles that have been applied to the cell or cells.

- **Clear Comments:** A comment can be added to a cell to provide you with additional information about the cell's content. You can remove the comment from a cell or remove the comments on cells that are in a selected range by using this option on the Clear menu.

- **Clear Hyperlinks:** This option removes a hyperlink from the selected cell or range of cells.

- **Remove Hyperlinks:** This option deletes a hyperlink from a cell or cells and removes the formatting.

Clearing cells is pretty foolproof: You select the cell or a range of cells and then use the Delete key or one of the options on the Clear command's menu. If you want to actually remove cells from the worksheet, you need to determine how you want the cells around the deleted cells to be repositioned. Remove cells only if you want the other cells in the worksheet to shift to new positions. Otherwise, just delete the data in the cells or type new data into the cells.

To remove cells from a worksheet, select the cell or cell range and then select the Delete command in the Cells group of the Ribbon's Home tab. The Delete command provides a menu that enables you to delete cells, rows, columns, or an entire worksheet. Select Delete Cells; the Delete dialog box will open as shown in Figure 11.23.

Figure 11.23
The Delete dialog box.

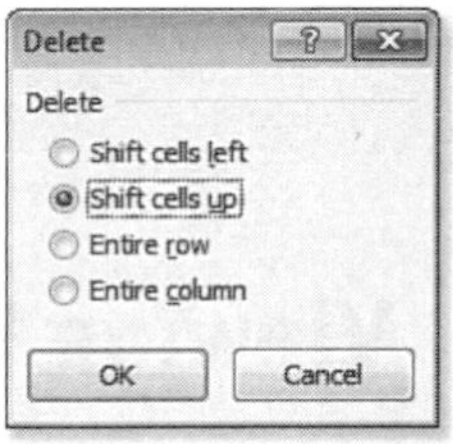

The Delete dialog box enables you to select whether the remaining cells shift left or up to fill the space left by the deleted cells. You can also choose to delete the entire row or column by selecting the appropriate option. When you are ready to delete the cells, click the OK button. The cells will be removed from the worksheet and the remaining cells will be moved to fill the gap left by the deleted cells.

> **tip**
> You can also check for typos using the Spelling feature. Select the Spelling command on the Review tab or press F7.

➡ *For information on inserting cells into a worksheet, see page 337 in Chapter 12.*

Editing Cell Content

Accurately entering information into the cells of your Excel worksheet is extremely important, particularly in the case of values. A worksheet boasting the most complex functions Excel can offer will still calculate incorrect results if you have made an error when entering the data onto the worksheet.

While entering text or values in a cell, you do have the ability to edit your work if you make a mistake. As you are entering data, you can quickly back up and delete a typo by using the Backspace key. If you've already entered the data and moved onto another cell before you noticed that it is incorrect, you have a couple of different options.

If the data entered is really a mess, click on the cell and retype the entire entry. When you press Enter or move to another cell, your new entry will replace the original data in the cell.

If the data contains only a one- or two-character mistake, you might want to edit the entry. Double-click on the cell with the error; the insertion point will appear on the far right of the cell. You can use the mouse or the keyboard to move the insertion point and correct the errors in the entry. Several keystrokes that are very useful when editing data directly in the cell follow:

- **Right or Left Arrow Keys:** Moves one character to the right or left

- **Home:** Moves to the beginning of the entry

- **End:** Moves to the end of the entry

- **Delete:** Deletes the character to the right of the insertion point

After editing the data in the cell, press Enter or click the Enter button on the formula bar to enter the changes to the data. You can also edit your cell data in the formula bar. Select a cell to edit and then use the mouse to place the insertion point in the formula bar. The various movement keystrokes listed earlier will also work in the formula bar. When you have finished editing the cell, select the Enter button in the formula bar or move to another cell.

Viewing Worksheets

Excel provides a number of different workbook views and makes it easy for you to zoom in and out on the current worksheet. Changing the view has no effect on how your worksheet looks when printed (unless you have hidden rows or columns, which are discussed in Chapter 12). The Ribbon's View tab, shown in Figure 11.24, provides the Workbook Views, Show, and Zoom groups, which enable you to manipulate the basic view of your worksheet and the Excel window.

Figure 11.24
The Ribbon's View tab.

The View tab also provides other commands for manipulating the worksheet and viewing multiple workbooks. Chapter 12 discusses the various commands found in the Window group.

➡ *For more information on manipulating the view of a worksheet or multiple workbooks, see page 343 in Chapter 12.*

The Workbook Views group provides you with different views of the current worksheet. The Normal view, which is the default view, provides the basic landscape that we use to enter values, labels, formulas, and functions in the worksheet. Because we spend most of our time working in the Normal view, we aren't always cognizant of where the page breaks are located in the worksheet and how the worksheet will translate to the printed page.

To get a better idea of the overall layout of the worksheet and to view any page breaks in the worksheet, select the Page Layout command. The amount of information that you can place on one Excel page will be based on the default paper size and page orientation that is configured for Excel. In most cases in the United States, the paper size will be letter (8.5 ×11) and the orientation will be portrait. So, page breaks will be automatically placed in the worksheet when you exceed the usable space on any page. Figure 11.25 shows a worksheet that has a page break between the last two columns of the sheet.

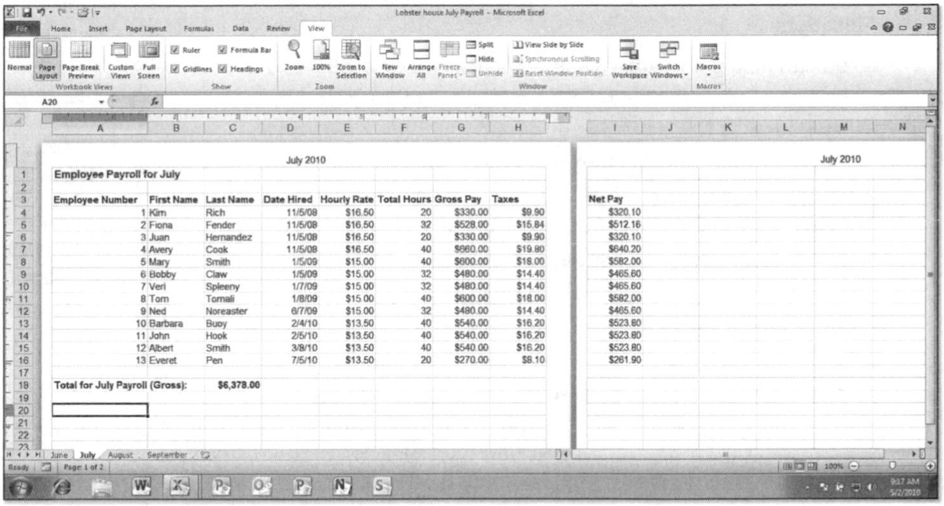

Figure 11.25
The Page
Layout view.

After you have an indication of the overall layout of the sheet, particularly in the case of the page breaks, you can attempt to remedy any issues before you print the worksheet. For example, the worksheet shown in Figure 11.25 would print out on two pages, in effect orphaning the last column of the worksheet. You do have options related to this problem. If the cell range that is pushed onto the second page (or any number of pages) is fairly small (such as a column or two or a row or two), you can have Excel scale the worksheet to fit on one page when you print the worksheet (which is discussed in the next section). However, doing so will reduce the font size on the printout and you don't want to end up with a printed page that requires a magnifying glass to read.

You will find that after you use the Page Layout view to take a look at your worksheet, dashed lines will appear on the worksheet in the Normal view. These are the page breaks present in the worksheet.

Another option would be to adjust the page orientation or the paper size, perhaps even the margins. For example, a worksheet with a lot of columns might print on one page if you switch the orientation from portrait to landscape using the Orientation command on the Page Setup tab (which is discussed in the next section of this chapter).

The Workbook Views group also provides a possibility for adjusting a page break or page breaks; you can use the Page Break Preview command. When you select Page Break Preview, Excel zooms out on the worksheet and shows the page breaks as dashed lines. The Welcome to Page Break Preview dialog box also appears, letting you know that you can drag page breaks to a new position in the worksheet as needed. Click on any of the page breaks and drag it to a new location.

You can also get a larger view of the current worksheet by using the Full Screen view. This command takes your current view (such as Normal or Page Layout) and blows it up on the screen by removing the title bar, Ribbon, and status bar from the Excel window. You can still access the worksheet tabs, however, at the bottom of the worksheet. To exit the Full Screen view, press the Esc key.

When you are working in the Normal view, Page Layout view, and the Page Break Preview, you can use the Zoom slider on the status bar to change the zoom level. You can also take advantage of the commands in the Zoom group on the View tab. To open the Zoom dialog box, select the Zoom command. The Zoom dialog box enables you to set a specific magnification from a range of options including 200%, 75%, and 25%. You can also choose to fit the current selection (a selected range) on the screen using the Fit Selection option. If you want to set a custom zoom level, use the Custom box in the Zoom dialog box.

You can quickly zoom to 100% using the 100% command. If you want to focus in on a particular range of cells, you can zoom to a particular selection. Select the range and then select the Zoom to Selection command. You can then use the Zoom slider as needed to zoom in or out on the current selection.

To finish of the first three groups on the View tab, we should probably take a quick look at the Show group. This group enables you to remove items from the Excel workspace such as the formula bar, the row and column headings, and the gridlines from the worksheet. This group provides four check boxes that toggle the feature on or off; these commands are Ruler, Gridlines, Formula Bar, and Headings. The Ruler command will be inactive in the Normal view and is available only in the Page Layout view. This makes sense because the Page Layout view shows you how your worksheet will appear on the printed page. You can use the ruler to align objects such as charts and images on a worksheet.

tip

If you don't want the Welcome to Page Break Preview dialog box to appear when you use the Page Break Preview, select Do Not Show This Dialog Again before you click OK to close the dialog box.

tip

You can also use the View shortcut icons on the status bar to switch between the Normal view, Page Layout view, and the Page Break Preview.

tip

You can also use the mouse wheel to zoom in and out on your worksheet. Hold down the Ctrl key and you are good to go.

Printing Worksheets

Printing worksheets is really a two-step process. As you enter information on a worksheet, you really don't need to worry about the overall layout of the sheet until you actually need a hard copy. The Page Layout tab of the Ribbon provides all the commands that you need to adjust the overall layout of the sheet including page orientation, margins, and page sizes. You can also scale the sheet and insert page breaks into the worksheet as needed.

After you have adjusted the various page layout settings using the Page Layout tab, you can open the Backstage Print window, which enables you to specify the printer for the printout and also to configure other print settings such as what is to be printed, how many copies should be printed, and how the printouts should be collated. Let's look at the Page Layout command and then the Print Window options.

Using the Page Layout Commands

The Ribbon's Page Layout tab provides several groups of commands that relate to getting the worksheet ready to print. The Page Setup, Scale to Fit, and Sheet Options groups enable you to control the size and orientation of the worksheet pages, scale the worksheet data to fit on a page, and to include gridlines or heading in the printout, respectively. The Page Setup tab, shown in Figure 11.26, also includes the Themes group and the Arrange group; Themes are discussed in Chapter 12.

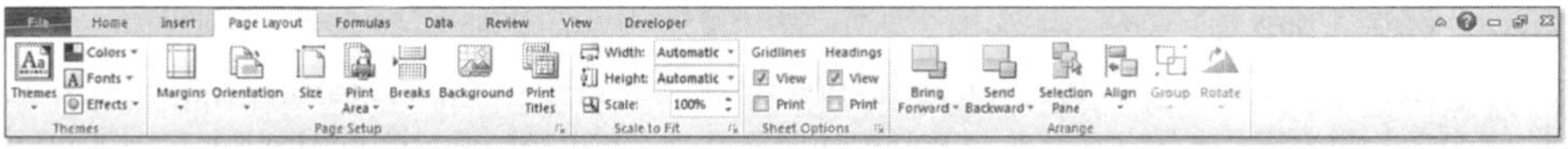

Figure 11.26
The Page Layout tab of the Ribbon.

➡ *For information on using themes in Excel, see page 326 in Chapter 12.*

The Page Setup group on the Page Layout tab provides commands that are important in terms of configuring the page settings for the worksheet. Commands are provided for setting everything from the margins to specifying print titles that consist of row or column headings that will be repeated on each page of the printout. The commands provided in the Page Setup group are as follows:

- **Margins:** The Margin command provides three different margin settings in a gallery: Normal (top and bottom .75 , left and right .7 ,) Wide (top, bottom, left, and right 1) and Narrow (top and bottom .75 , left and right .25). You can also access the Margins tab of the Page Setup dialog by selecting Custom Margins.

- **Orientation:** This command provides you with the ability to switch from portrait to landscape or vice versa.

- **Size:** This command provides a gallery of different page sizes such as Letter, Legal, Executive, and A3 through A5. Select More Paper Sizes to open the page tab of the Page Setup dialog box. You can use the Paper Size drop-down list to select other page sizes available on the default printer.

- **Print Area:** This command enables you to set a print area based on a selected range in the worksheet. You can also use this command to clear a print area that you have previously set.

- **Break:** This command provides a menu of commands that enable you to insert a page break, remove a page break, or reset all the page breaks in the worksheet.

- **Background:** This command enables you to select an image that will be used as a background for the worksheet.

- **Print Titles:** This command opens the Sheet tab of the Page Setup dialog box. Print titles are column or row headings that you want repeated on each page of the printout. This is an extremely useful feature when working with large worksheets that span multiple pages.

The Scale to Fit group on the Page Layout tab enables you to scale the worksheet by width, height, or scale. The scale is set by default to 100% and you can decrease or increase the scale as needed to either shrink or expand the size of the worksheet. The Width command can be used to shrink the width of the worksheet on a page or pages. The default width is set to Automatic and so the width of the actual sheet determines the number of pages to be used. If you want to shrink a worksheet that has a minimal number of columns that are outside the first page, you can select 1 on the Width menu to shrink the worksheet to fit on one page (by width). You can specify from one to nine pages on the Width menu.

The Height command also provides a menu of page number selections from 1 to 9. It is best used when you have a worksheet with a large number of rows and want to make a few errant rows fit onto a page.

Both the Width and the Height menus provide a More Pages selection that opens the Page tab of the Page Setup dialog box as shown in Figure 11.27. You can use the Fit To option and the accompanying spinner boxes for width and height to scale the worksheet to a specific number of pages wide and a specific number of pages tall.

The page tab of the Page Setup dialog box also provides an Adjust To option that enables you to scale the worksheet as a percentage of its normal size. This is the same setting as the Scale setting found in the Scale to Fit group on the Page Layout tab.

The Sheet Options group on the Page Layout tab provides check boxes related to gridlines and headings. If you want the gridlines on the worksheet to print, select the Print check box under Gridlines. You can also have the column and row headings print by selecting the Print check box under Headings.

 tip

You can remove a page break in the Page Break Preview by dragging the page break off of the worksheet.

Setting a Print Area

You do not always have to print an entire worksheet; instead, you can easily tell Excel what part of the worksheet you want to print by selecting the print area yourself. If the area you select is too large to fit on one page, no problem—Excel breaks it into multiple pages. Print areas are useful when you want to print only a portion of a worksheet.

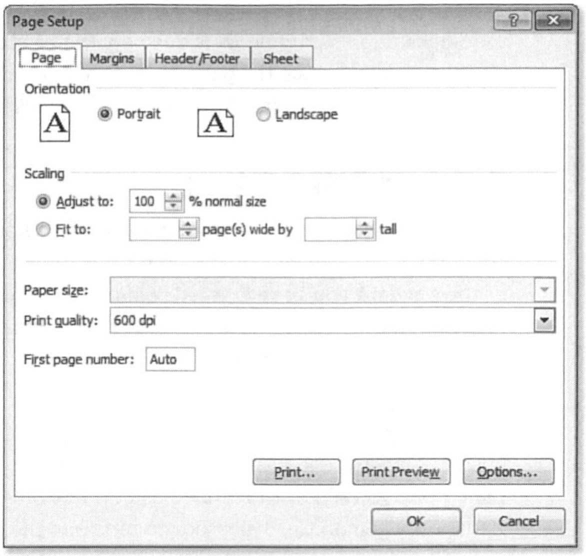

Figure 11.27
The Page tab of the Page Setup dialog box.

To set a print area, select the range in the worksheet that will serve as the print area. Select the Print Area command and then select Set Print Area. The print area will be denoted by a dashed-line frame. You will also find that when you open the Print window in the Backstage, only the print area will be previewed. You can also clear a print area if needed. Select the Print Area command and then select Clear Print Area.

Inserting Page Breaks

Excel determines the page breaks in the worksheet to be printed based on the paper size, the margins, and the print area (if one has been selected). Excel does not do any thinking when it places page breaks in your worksheet. It places them where they are needed, even if it breaks up the continuity of the data that you have entered in the sheet's columns and rows. To make the pages more presentable and understandable, and to break information in logical places, you can insert your own page breaks into the worksheet. You can insert page breaks into the worksheet in the Normal view, Page Layout view, or the page break preview.

To insert a page break to the left of a column, select the column in the worksheet (click on the column's heading). Select the Breaks command and then select Insert Page Break. You can also insert a page break, specifying a row as the break position. The page break will actually be inserted above the selected row.

You can also specify that a page break be inserted above and to the left of a cell in the worksheet, meaning you get two page breaks—one along the row and one along the column. This can be useful when you are working with a very large worksheet that might contain various sections such as four quarters worth of data positioned on the worksheet into obvious quadrants. All you have to do is select the cell that is below and to the right of where you want the page breaks to be inserted, select Breaks, and then select Insert Page Break.

After inserting page breaks, take the time to peruse your worksheet in the Page Layout view or the page break preview (particularly if you want to adjust the location of page breaks). You can also use the Backstage Print window to preview the printout of the worksheet. If you find that you want to start over and remove the page breaks that you have inserted in the worksheet, select the Breaks command and then select Reset All Page Breaks.

Setting Print Titles

If you are going to have a multiple-page worksheet where you have either a lot of rows or a lot of columns, it makes sense to set print titles for the worksheet. Print titles enable you to specify a rows or rows where you have entered column names or headings and repeat these on each sheet of the printout. You can also specify a column or columns that contain row headings and have these repeat on each page of the printout.

To access the Sheet tab of the Page Setup dialog box, select the Print Titles command. In the Print Titles area of the Sheet tab is a Rows to Repeat at Top box and a Columns to Repeat at Left box. To specify rows to repeat, select the Shrink button on the right of the Rows to Repeat at Top box. The dialog box will roll up or shrink. Select the row or rows to be repeated using the mouse. Click the Expand button on the dialog box to return to the Sheet tab. If you need to also include columns as print titles, select the Shrink button to the right of the Columns to Repeat at Left box and repeat the process by selecting the columns that will be printed. When you have completed the process, click OK to close the Page Setup dialog box.

Working in the Print Window

When you have the Page Layout settings the way that you want them, you can access the Backstage Print window to finalize settings for your worksheet printout. To access the Backstage, select File on the Ribbon. In the Backstage view, select Print to access the Print window. The Excel Print window is shown in Figure 11.28.

 tip

You can access the Page Setup dialog box by selecting the dialog box launcher on the Page Setup, Scale to Fit, or Sheet Options groups.

The Print window provides you with a preview of your printout. You can use the page indicators on the left of the preview to move through the pages of the printout. You can also use the Zoom to Page command to zoom in and out on the current page.

The Print window also provides you with the ability to set the number of copies that will be printed and also enables you to choose the printer for the printout. You can also adjust printer properties for the selected printer.

The Settings area of the preview window enables you to control a number of options related to the printout, including what is actually printed and how the printout and settings relate to page size, margins, and scaling. The options provided in the Print window as are follows:

- **Print Active Sheets:** By default, this menu is set to Print Active Sheets; it determines what you will actually print. You can also choose to print the entire workbook (all the sheets in the workbook) or only a selection in the current worksheet. To print only certain pages, enter the page numbers of the pages you want to print in the Pages boxes.

Figure 11.28
The Backstage
Print window.

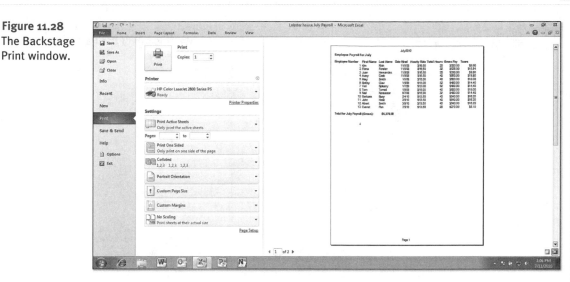

■ **Print One Sided:** Again, this is the default setting for this menu. You can also choose to print on both sides of the paper. Two settings for two-sided printing are supplied; one is for flipping pages on the long edge and the other is for flipping pages on the short edge.

■ **Orientation:** This menu enables you to switch between portrait and landscape orientation.

■ **Page Size:** The Page Size menu will be set to the page size you specified on the Page Layout tab of the ruler. You can change the page size via this menu.

■ **Margins:** This drop-down menu enables you to change the margin settings that you might have set via the Margins command on the Page Layout tab. You can choose from margins provided in the gallery or select Custom Margins to access the Margins tab of the Page Setup dialog box as shown in Figure 11.29. You can use the spinner boxes as needed to set the margins for the work-sheet. You can also specify a header or footer area using the appropriate spinner box.

■ **Custom Scaling:** You can scale the worksheet using the options provided on this menu. You can choose to have the sheet on one page or choose to fit either all the columns or all the rows on one page.

There is also a Page Setup link at the bottom of the various print options. This link opens the Page Setup dialog box. Before we end our discussion of worksheet printing (which is just a matter of clicking the Print button in the Print window), we need to look at how you specify headers and foot-ers for your worksheet printouts.

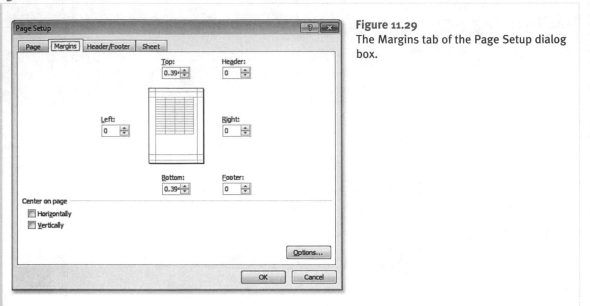

Figure 11.29
The Margins tab of the Page Setup dialog box.

Inserting Headers and Footers

To open the Page Setup dialog box, click Page Setup. To access the header/footer information for the worksheet, select the Header/Footer tab.

The Header/Footer tab provides a preview of the current header and footer (which means there is probably not a header or footer). The tab also provides check boxes that enable you to determine whether there are different headers and footers for odd and even pages and whether the first page is different (in terms of headers and footers) from the rest of the printout.

To specify a header for the worksheet, select the Custom Header button. This opens the Header dialog box as shown in Figure 11.30. You can specify a header for the left, center, and right sections of the worksheet.

For example, you might want to place your name in the left section of the header, the title of the worksheet in the center, and perhaps a draft number or the date in the right section. Enter the text for a header section. You can then select the text and use the Format Text button to open the Font dialog box and format the selected text.

A number of buttons are provided that insert information into the header such as the page number, date, file path, and sheet name. You can even insert and format a picture such as a logo into the header. When you have the information for the various sections of the header, click OK to return to the Header/Footer tab. A preview of the header will be provided.

Figure 11.30
The Header dialog box.

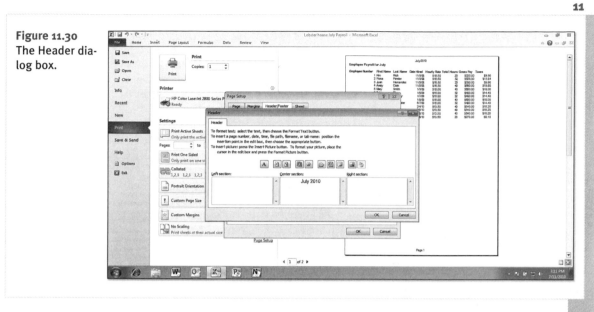

If you want to include a footer, select the Custom Footer button. The Footer dialog box will open. The Footer dialog box is basically a replica of the Header dialog box and provides you with the same three section panes and tools. Enter the footer information as needed in the three footer sections and then click OK to return to the Header/Footer tab of the Page Setup dialog box. When you have finished specifying the options for the header and/or footer, select OK to return to the Print window.

The header and/or footer information will appear in the preview provided by the Print window. When you are ready to print your worksheet, select the Print button.

WORKSHEET FORMATTING AND MANAGEMENT

Entering data into a worksheet, such as labels (text), values, formulas, and functions, is only one aspect of creating a worksheet. Formatting entries in cells so that certain information is highlighted or certain cells are emphasized can also be important. Creating a worksheet that has visual appeal as well as a sensible layout can help to make all those columns and rows of information easier to understand.

In this chapter we look at formatting cell entries. We look at how to format text labels, including how to wrap text in a cell or joined cells and also how to work with the formatting of values such as numbers and dates. Coverage is provided on manipulating cells and cell entries as well as columns, rows, and entire worksheets. We also discuss how to add graphics to Excel worksheets for more visual appeal.

Formatting Text Entries

Formatting text entries, or labels (as we like to call them in Excel worksheets), can be as simple as assigning different font or alignment attributes to a cell or a range of cells as you would text in Word or PowerPoint. For example, you can add bold or italic to the contents of a cell or cells. You can also change the font and font size used by a range. Excel, however, also provides some formatting features that are peculiar to Excel, such as cell alignment settings including the Orientation command, which enables you to rotate text in a cell or cell range. This can be particularly useful in cases when you want to create eye-catching row or column headings or are hampered by extremely narrow columns.

The Ribbon's Home tab provides all the commands for the basic formatting attributes. The Font group provides you with the ability to change the font and font size and to select font attributes such as bold, italic, underline, and font color. The Font group also includes the Border and Fill Color commands, which we discuss later in the chapter.

The Alignment group also includes a familiar group of commands. There are vertical alignment commands—Top Align, Middle Align and Bottom Align—that enable you to control the vertical alignment of text in a cell. The horizontal alignment tools are also present—Align Text Left, Center and Align Text Right—as are the Decrease Indent and Increase Indent commands.

To format labels in a cell or cell range, select the cells that are to be formatted. Then select the attributes that you want to apply to the text labels by using the commands in the Font and Alignment group.

Accessing the Format Cells Dialog Box

Font and alignment attributes can also be controlled via the Format Cells dialog box. Because all the information that we put into a worksheet is actually placed in cells, it makes sense that all the various formatting attributes we assign to worksheet labels would actually be considered cell formatting.

To format the text in a cell or cell range, select the range and then open the Format Cells Dialog box. You can open the Format Cells dialog box by selecting the dialog box launcher in the Font, Alignment, or Number groups. The group dialog box launcher that you use to open the dialog box will dictate the tab selected. For example, if you launch the Format Cells dialog box from the Font group, the Font tab will be selected when the dialog box opens.

You can also open the dialog box from the Format command in the Cells group; select Format then Format Cells. Figure 12.1 shows the Font tab of the Format Cells dialog box.

The Font tab of the Format Cells dialog box provides you with access to the same font attributes provided by the commands in the Font group. The Font tab, however, provides you with some additional font attributes such as the accounting underline styles (single and double accounting) and provides you with effects such as strikethrough and superscript and subscript.

Although font formatting is meant to make your worksheet look "better," you will find that too much font formatting can actually be distracting. You might want to limit yourself to only a font type or two and only use bold, italics, and other formatting attributes such as a font color when you are sure that they truly enhance the worksheet.

note

The Ribbon's Home tab is pretty consistent in Excel, Word, and PowerPoint. The Home tab always provides the Clipboard group and will also include Font and other attribute groups, such as Alignment or Paragraph, that are related to formatting or aligning the text that you type.

 tip

You can also use keyboard shortcuts to format cells such as Ctrl+B for bold, Ctrl+I for italic, Ctrl+U for single underline, and Ctrl+5 for strikethrough.

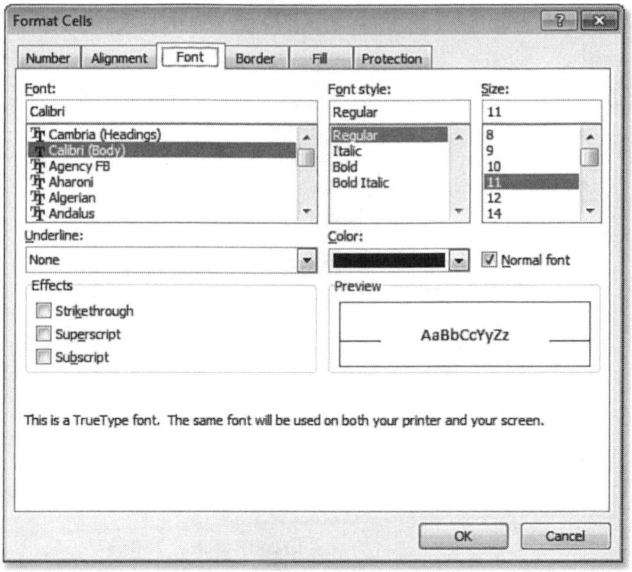

Figure 12.1
The Format Cells dialog box.

Changing Text Orientation

You can change the orientation of text in a range of cells by using the Orientation command in the alignment group. This is useful in cases where your labels must conform to very narrow columns or in cases where you want to align labels on the diagonal so that they are readily noticeable or you just want to add a little bit of design drama to the top of your worksheet.

Select the cell range that you want to format with the Orientation command. Then select Orientation in the Alignment group. The orientation possibilities are as follows:

- **Angle Counterclockwise:** This option tilts the text upward on the diagonal in a counterclockwise direction as shown in Figure 12.2.

- **Angle Clockwise:** This option titles the text onto the diagonal clockwise.

- **Vertical Text:** Aligns the text vertically in the cells expanding the row height as needed to accommodate the longest entry in the row.

- **Rotate Text Up:** Rotates the text up vertically.

- **Rotate Text Down:** Rotates the text down vertically.

- **Format Cell Alignment:** Opens the Format Cells dialog box with the Alignment tab selected.

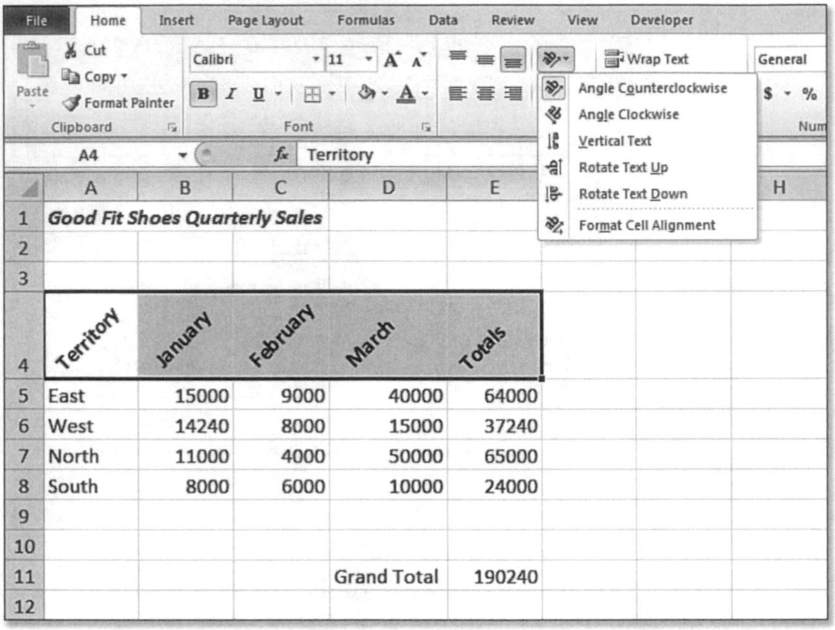

Figure 12.2
Rotate text labels using the Orientation command.

The options provided by the Orientation command are limited to five different orientations for the text. If you want to create a custom rotation, you can do so on the Alignment tab of the Format Cells dialog box. Drag the Orientation Degree dial to specify the orientation for the text visually. Or you can specify the orientation by specifying the actual degrees of the angle to be used using the Degrees spinner box. Positive angle values give you a text up rotation and negative angle values give you a text down rotation. When you have finished setting the orientation on the Alignment tab, select OK to close the Format Cells dialog box.

Formatting Values

The number formats provided by Excel for the numerical values in your worksheets are extremely useful for differentiating the different types of values present. You want to make it easy to for anyone viewing the worksheet to be able to distinguish between dollar amounts, percentages, and numbers of items. So, although you can format values as you format text with formatting attributes such as bold and italics or with a particular font color, it is the actual number formatting that provides the value with meaning.

Although you can enter numbers with formatting as you type such as $20.50 or 2,300 (Excel automatically recognizes this number formatting), it is much easier to enter the values and then format them after the fact. Excel provides you with more than one way to format the values in your worksheet.

The most obvious path for formatting numeric values in a worksheet is to take advantage of the commands in the Number group on the Ribbon's home tab. The Number group provides commands related to particular number formats, such as the percent style, and provides you with the ability to increase or decrease the decimal places in cell values. The Number group commands are as follows:

Accounting Number Format: This command provides different accounting or currency formats. The default is U.S. dollars. This command also includes other international accounting formats such as English pounds, the Chinese yuan (People's Republic of China), and the euro.

Percent Style: Displays the number as a percentage.

Comma Style: Displays the number with commas as the thousands separator.

Increase Decimal: Increases the number of decimal places.

Decrease Decimal: Decreases the number of decimal places and rounds the number as needed.

Number Format: This drop-down gallery, which is set to General by default, provides 11 different numeric formats such as Number, Currency, Fraction, Scientific, and Text.

Obviously, the Number Format command's gallery provides the greatest number of options in terms of formatting values in a worksheet. There are, however, more numeric formats available in Excel. To access all the available number formats, including options for creating custom number formats, you need to open the Format Cells dialog box and access the Number tab. This tab provides a Category list of different number formats as shown in Figure 12.3.

Figure 12.3
The Number tab of the Format Cells dialog box.

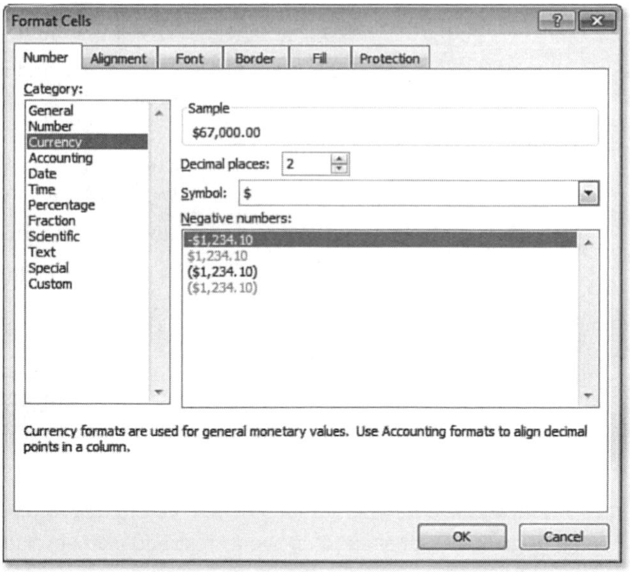

Using the Format Cells Dialog Box

The Format Cells dialog box can be opened using the More Number Formats option on the bottom of the Number Format gallery or you can access the dialog box by selecting the dialog box launcher in the Numbers group. Table 12.1 provides a list of the different number formats provided on the Number tab of the Format Cells dialog box and a short description of each.

Table 12.1 Excel Number Formats

Number Format	Examples	Description
General	10.6	No specific number format
Number	3,400.50	The default number format providing two decimal places and commas as separators. Negative numbers are shown in red.
Currency	$3,400.50	The default Currency format including the default symbol ($ for U.S.). Negative values are shown in red.
Accounting	$3,400.50	Aligns currency symbols and decimal points for values vertically (in a column).
Date	11/7/2010	The default Date format is the month, day, and year separated by a slash.
Time	10:30:45 PM	The default time format is the hour, minutes, and seconds separated by a colon; AM or PM is also designated.
Percentage	99.50%	The default percentage format has two decimal places.
Fraction	1/2	The default fraction format provides for up to one digit on either side of the solidus or fraction slash as the slash dividing the two numbers is also referred to.
Scientific	3.40E+03	The default scientific format has two decimal places and can be used to display extremely large numbers.
Text	123456	Use the text format to format numbers as text.
Special	44240	This format is designed to display ZIP codes, phone numbers, and Social Security numbers correctly so that you don't have to enter any special characters, such as hyphens or parentheses.
Custom	00.0%	Use this format to create custom number formats. You can edit any of the existing codes as you create your own custom formats.

Many of the number formats enable you to control the number of decimal places used by the format and also how negative numbers assigned the format will appear in the worksheet. Some formats also enable you to include or preclude the thousand separator—the comma. A sample of how the selected number format will look in your worksheet is provided on the right of the Number tab. After selecting a format (or designing

> **note**
>
> When you format Excel values, you are not changing or affecting the underlying value that you entered in the worksheet. Excel uses that original value when it includes the cell in a calculation.

your own format using the Custom category), click OK. The format will be assigned to the selected cell range in the worksheet.

Creating Custom Number Formats

Although there are probably more than enough built-in number formats for most Excel users, you might find yourself in a situation where you really need to create a custom format. To create a custom format, select the Custom Category on the Number tab as shown in Figure 12.4.

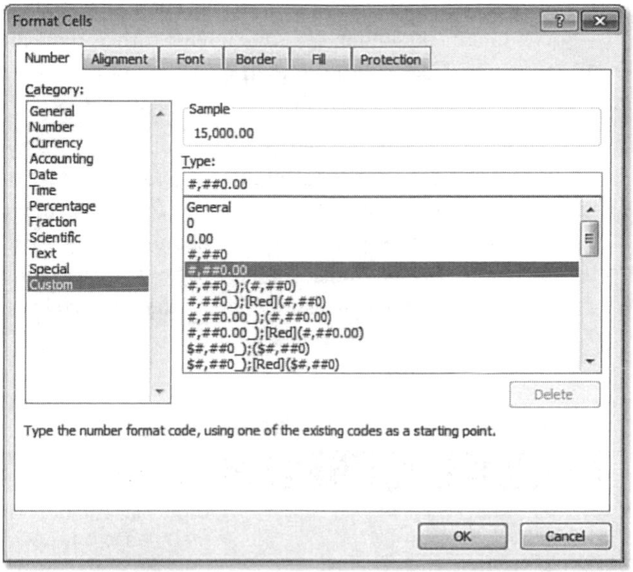

Figure 12.4
Creating a custom number format.

If you want to base your number format on an existing format, select that format. Then click Custom to view the codes for that format. You can then edit the existing number format and create your custom form in the Type box. As you specify the custom format, a sample will be provided above the Type box. Probably the best way to learn to create your own formats is to look at the format codes that have been created for the different numerical formats provided by Excel.

The rules for creating custom formats are pretty straightforward. Each custom format can consist of up to four sections. The sections are divided by semicolons. Each section has a specific purpose in terms of the state of the value to be formatted. The first section serves as the format for the number if it is positive; the second section provides the formatting if the number is negative; the third section provides the formatting for zero values, and the fourth section provides the formatting for text. So, a custom format would follow the pattern of POSITIVE; NEGATIVE; ZERO; TEXT. A sample format code with all four sections might look something like this:

#,##0.00;[Red] -#,##0.00;0.00;[Blue]"Replace with Value"

The number sign (#) serves as a digit placeholder and the zeros in the code pad the format with zeros when necessary to fill the format. The commas serve as thousand separators. The color codes, [Red] and [Blue], dictate the colors for those sections of the custom format. Note that the second section, which is used for negative numbers, also includes a hyphen (-) that serves as a minus sign.

Your custom format does not necessarily need to include all four sections. For example, you could create a custom format that includes only two sections such as #,##0.00;[Red] -#,##0.00;0.00, which specifies how to format the values when they are either positive (the first section) or negative (the second section).

After you have determined the number of sections you are going to create in the custom format, you can enter the codes that supply the formatting guidelines for each section. The actual codes that you use in the custom formats are straightforward. We have already looked at how you use the number sign (#) and zeros in a custom format. Table 12.2 provides a list of some of the other codes you can use in your custom formats and examples of how the code would be used.

> **🔍 note**
>
> The text formatting section of a custom number format might seem counterintuitive because we are talking about formatting numbers. You can actually use this section of the format code to let users who enter data in the worksheet know that they can't put text entries in cells formatted with the format. For example, you could set up the text section of the format as; [Blue]"Replace with Value" so that any text entered will be replaced with the text Replace with Value in blue.

Table 12.2 Excel Custom Format Codes

Code	Example	Usage
#	#,###	Digit placeholder; this particular example provides for no decimal places but does insert a comma at the thousands mark. The number of # placed in the code for your format does not limit the number of characters that you can type in a cell formatted with the code.
0	#,##0.00	Digit placeholder; use to pad format.
?	#0.0?	Digit placeholder for insignificant zeros. This code does not display the insignificant zeros but can be used to add spaces on either side of the decimal point to align numbers in a column by the decimal point.
.	#,##0.00	Specified the decimal place in the code.
%	0.000%	Formats the number as a percentage (meaning Excel multiplies the number by 100). This example includes three decimal places.
_	#,##0.00_	Creates a space in the format that is one character width.
" "	#,##0.00 "Profit"	The quotation marks can be used to include text in codes (with or without numbers). In this case, a positive number format includes the text "Profit."

Code	Example	Usage
$	$###.##	Designates that the numerical format following the $ code should be formatted as U.S. currency. Other codes that display without quotation marks include the /, &, -, and =.
m, d, y	m/dd/yy	The current month would be displayed (1–12) without leading zeros. The day would be displayed as two digits with leading zeros, as would the year.
h, m	hh:mm	The hour and minutes would be displayed as a double-digit number.

Table 12.2 provides only a subset of the different codes that you can use to create custom formats. As already mentioned earlier in this section, you can modify any of the format codes provided in the Format Cells dialog box to meet your needs. Just select a code such as a currency code and then click Custom to view the code and modify it as needed. Using the provided format codes as the starting point for your own custom number formats provides you with the basic design for custom formats for currency, dates, fractions, or scientific notation.

Adding Comments to Cells

Providing an explanation for the contents of a particular cell can be useful both to you and to others accessing your Excel workbooks. A comment enables you to include a brief text notation that describes what the content of a cell actually means or how you came up with a particular value. It can also be very useful for annotating complicated formulas or functions that are placed in a cell.

To add a comment to a cell, click on the cell to select it. You can then navigate to the Review tab of the Ribbon and select the Add Comment command. A new Comment box will open as shown in Figure 12.5.

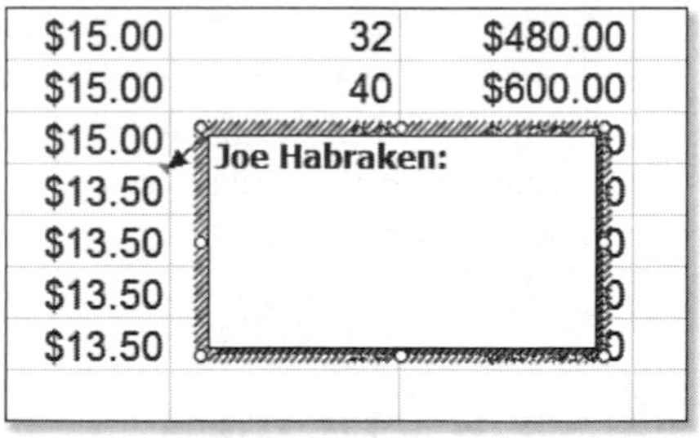

Figure 12.5
A new Comment box.

Type the comment text. When you have finished typing the comment, click elsewhere in the worksheet. The cell will not have a small red triangle in the upper-right corner of its border denoting that a comment has been added to the cell. To view a cell's comment, place the mouse on the cell. The comment box will open. If you want to edit the comment, you can select the cell containing the comment and then click the Edit Comment command in the Comments group. You can add or delete text as needed.

Formatting Comment Text

You can also modify the font attributes for the text in the Comment box using commands on the Home tab. Select the text when editing (or creating) a comment; the Font commands enable you to change the font size and type and also add other font attributes such as bold, italic, and underline. You can also use the various vertical and horizontal alignment commands such as Top Align and Middle Align or Center and Align Text Right, respectively.

If you wish to dramatically change the formatting of the comment text, you can right-click on the comment and select Format Comment. The Format Comment dialog box will open. In this dialog box, you can select the font, font style, and size for the comment and you can also change the color of the font. In addition, effects such as strikethrough, superscript, and subscript can be applied to the text if needed. When you select OK, the Format Comment dialog box closes and you return to the comment.

Deleting and Viewing Comments

The Comment group also provides you with the ability to delete comments—select the cell and then click the Delete command. If you want to cycle through the comments in a worksheet, you can use the Previous and the Next commands. To open a comment and leave it open in the worksheet (even if you click elsewhere in the worksheet), select a cell containing a comment and then click the Show/Hide Comment command. You can leave the comment open in the worksheet as needed and then select the cell and click Show/Hide Comment to hide the comment again.

 note

You can also add a comment to a cell by right-clicking on the cell and then selecting Insert Comment.

If you want to open all the comments in a worksheet, use the Show All Comments command. Click the Show All Comments command a second time to close the comments.

A couple of other things related to comments: When a comment is open, you can actually size the comment box, and you can drag the comment to a new position on the screen. This doesn't detach the comment from the cell, but it does enable you to get the comment off of other important data as you are perusing a particular area of the worksheet. You will be able to tell the cell that the comment is associated with because an arrow (think of it as a leash for the comment box) will be attached to the both the cell and comment with the actual arrow pointing at the cell. The comment will actually stay at the new position you have placed it in until you drag it back to the edge of the cell.

Using Themes

Excel provides you with more than one possibility for formatting cells with font attributes, cell borders, and cell colors. The most straightforward way to apply cell formatting and create a uniform-looking worksheet is to use a theme. A theme is a collection of colors, fonts, and text effects. Themes are consistent across the Office applications such as Excel, Word, and PowerPoint. This enables you to create a group of related Office suite files that have the same overall look.

You access the Themes gallery via the Themes command on the Ribbon's Page Layout tab. The Themes group also provides the Colors, Fonts, and Effects commands. Figure 12.6 shows the Themes gallery.

Figure 12.6
The Excel Themes gallery.

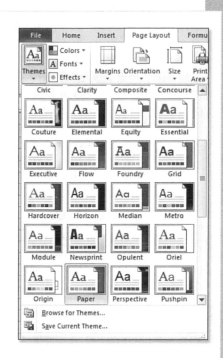

To preview a theme, place the mouse on that theme. When you have found the theme that you want to use for the worksheet, select the theme.

As already mentioned, themes control the colors, fonts, and effects used when formatting the worksheet. You can change each of these theme attributes using the Colors, Fonts, and Effects commands. If you adjust any of these theme attributes and want to save the result as a new theme, access the Themes gallery and then save the theme using the Save Current Theme command. You can then browse for saved themes using the Browse for Themes commands.

You can also create custom theme colors and theme fonts. To create custom theme colors, select Create New Theme Colors in the Colors gallery. This will open the Create New Theme Colors dialog box, which enables you to set the theme background color, accent colors, and hyperlink colors. In the case of theme fonts, select Create New Theme Fonts in the Fonts gallery and the Create New Theme Fonts dialog box will open, enabling you to specify the heading and the body font for your custom theme.

 For more information on working with themes, see page 512 in Chapter 18, "Advanced Presentation Formatting, Themes, and Masters."

Formatting Cells Using Borders and Color

The overall design of a worksheet is often dictated by the results that the worksheet is to produce. Data is often arranged in columns and rows so that formulas or functions can be strategically placed to do calculation on the data. This doesn't always result in a worksheet that provides visual cues that make it easy to see and understand the purpose of the worksheet. This is where cell borders and cell background or fill colors can be useful. You can use borders and colors to highlight certain areas of the sheet and draw attention to a specific cell or range of cells.

Cell formatting can make a worksheet look more visually appealing, but it can also emphasize cells or cell ranges, making it easier for anyone perusing the worksheet to have a more immediate understanding of how the results shown in the worksheet actually relate to the data that is used in the calculations. Borders can be used to group certain cells or highlight individual cells and you can use cell fill color to emphasize or group cells using color. The Borders command and the Fill Color command are both housed in the Font group on the Ribbon's Home tab.

Adding Cell Borders

The Borders command provides a gallery of different border types such a Bottom Border, Top Border, All Borders, and so on. Figure 12.7 shows the Borders gallery, which includes the Draw Borders tools at the bottom of the gallery.

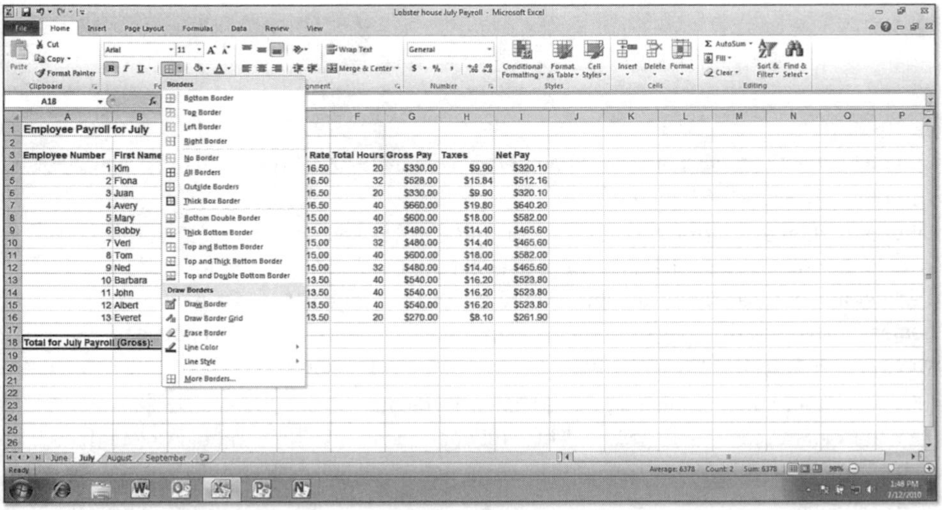

Figure 12.7
The Borders Gallery.

Select the cell or cell range to which you want to apply the border and then select a border from the Borders gallery (click the arrow to the right of the Borders command). The Borders gallery provides both single- and double-line border formats as well as thick border formats.

You can also choose to draw the border for a cell range. The Draw Borders area provides a drawing tool—Draw Border—and it also provides the Line Color and the Line Style menus that enable you to select the color for the border line and the line style such as a single line, dashed line, double line, or thick line.

To draw the border using the default line settings, select the Draw Border command and then use the pen mouse pointer to select the cells that you want to format. You can select the attributes for the line using the Line Color and Line Style menus. When you have finished working with the border drawing tool, press the Esc key or click the Draw Border Line command to turn off the feature (this is the Borders command in the Font group).

For maximum control over the borders you want to place on a selected range of cells, you can use the Border tab of the Format Cells dialog box. To access the dialog box, select More Borders in the Borders gallery. Figure 12.8 shows the Border tab of the Format Cells dialog box.

Figure 12.8
The Border tab of the Format Cells dialog box.

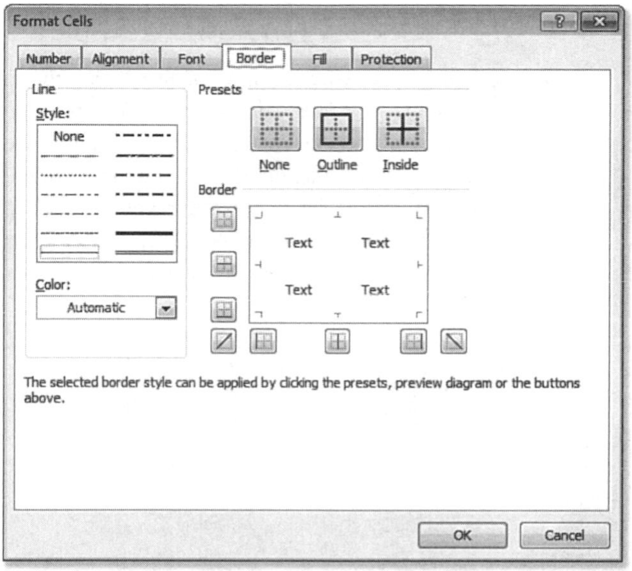

The Border tab provides you with border presets as well as all the tools that you need to create your own custom borders. You can use the Style box to select the line for the style and use the Color drop-down palette to specify the color for the line. You can use the various Border buttons provided adjacent to the border preview diagram to specify the borders that you want to apply to the cells. You can also click inside the preview diagram to place the borders. When you have completed specifying the options for your custom borders, select OK. The borders will be applied to the selected cell range in the worksheet.

> **note**
> The Draw Border Grid option on the Borders gallery enables you to draw both internal and external borders on a cell range.

Using Background Colors

Backgrounds or cell fill colors provide you with an excellent way to add color to your worksheets. The fill colors available will be based on the current theme that you have selected for your worksheet. You can quickly add a background color to a selected cell or cell range using the Fill Color command in the Font group.

Select the range of cells to which you want to add a fill color. Then select the drop-down arrow for the Fill Color command. The Color palette provided gives you access to the current theme colors and provides standard colors that you can apply to your cell range. If you want to select a custom color, you can click More Colors; this opens the Colors dialog box where you can specify a custom color for the range.

Using Cell Styles and the Format Painter

An extremely easy way to apply cell formatting to a range of cells that includes font, border, and fill attributes is to take advantage of the cell styles provided by Excel. These cell styles are more than just ways of adding color and formatting to a worksheet, however. Excel provides specific cell styles for helping you denote cells that need to be checked or results that should be considered bad or good. Other cell styles are provided specifically for headings and results, and there are also cell styles provided for number formatting. The Cell Styles command is in the Styles group on the Home tab. When you select the Cell Styles command, the Cell Styles gallery opens as shown in Figure 12.9.

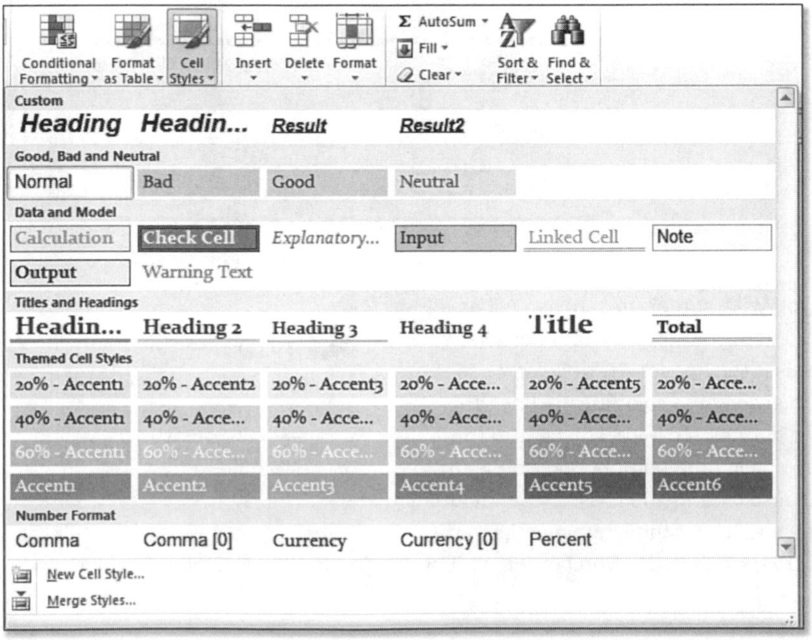

Figure 12.9
The Cell Styles gallery.

There are a number of useful cell styles in the Cell Styles gallery. There are Good, Bad, and Neutral categories of styles and also Data and Model styles. A number of themed cell styles are also provided based on the current worksheet's current theme.

The Cell Styles gallery is designed as a set of samples. As already mentioned, cell formatting can be used to differentiate cells that contain particular content; so, the cell styles provided are really to get you thinking about the possibilities for showing information more clearly in a worksheet by using cell styles. You can use the cell styles provided, but this feature becomes even more useful (and particular to your purposes) if you create your own cell styles.

Creating a Cell Style

You can create a cell style by example. Format a cell or range of cells with font and cell attributes (such as font settings and border and fill settings); you can also specify number formatting for the style by formatting the contents of the cell (or the cell range) with the different number formats provided in the Number group or the Number Format gallery.

When you are ready to create the cell style, select the Cell Styles command and then select New Cell Style in the Cell Styles gallery. The Style dialog box opens as shown in Figure 12.10.

Figure 12.10
The Style dialog box.

By default the style includes the number, alignment, font, border, fill, and any protection settings assigned to the cell. If you provided all these attributes by example, you can leave all the check boxes enabled. If there is a particular attribute that you do not want to include in the cell style, clear the appropriate check box.

If want to fine-tune any of the attributes that you have set for the cell style (your examples), select the Format button. This opens the Format Cells dialog box. Although we have discussed most of the tabs provided by this dialog box, it wouldn't hurt to provide a quick review in the list that follows.

- **Number:** This tab is where you set the number format for the values that will use the style. The formats include number, currency date, time, and percentage.

- **Alignment:** This tab enables you to specify the horizontal and vertical alignment of the cell content. You can also rotate text using the Orientation dial.

- **Font:** This tab provides all the font attributes such as the font, font style, size, underline, and color.

- **Border:** Use this tab to specify a border for the cell style including the line style and color.

- **Fill:** Select from a number of background colors and fill effects provided. You can also specify custom colors.

- **Protection:** You can lock cells that contain formulas or functions or data that you do not want others to be able to edit. Locking cells does not protect areas of the sheet until you choose to protect the sheet.

➡ *For more information on locking cells and protecting worksheets, see page 287 in Chapter 11, "Requisite Excel: Essential Features."*

When you have finished working with the various cell attributes for the style in the Format Cells dialog box, select OK to return to the Styles dialog box. Make sure that you provide a name for the style in the Style name box. When you click OK, the new cell style is created and is placed in the Custom category area in the Cell Styles gallery. You can now access your new cell style as needed.

Using the Format Painter

You can also copy the cell formatting from a cell to a cell or to a range of cells using the Format Painter. This is useful in cases where you just want to have consistent formatting in a worksheet but don't want to have to deal with cell styles.

Select a cell that has the formatting that you want to copy. Click the Format Painter command in the Clipboard group. You can then click on a single cell to paste the format or you can click and drag to format an entire range of cells. If you want to copy the formatting to multiple noncontiguous ranges or from a worksheet to two or more other worksheets, double-click the Format Painter. You can paste the format as many times as needed. When you have finished working with the Format Painter, click the Format Painter command to toggle it off.

Using Conditional Formatting

So far we have approached cell formatting from a static viewpoint; any formatting applied to cells was our job, even in cases where we wanted to highlight certain cells because of their contents using cell formatting. Conditional formatting provides a more dynamic (and often useful) way to use formatting to "point out" cells in a worksheet that meet certain conditions. For example, if you wanted to format all the monthly sales totals in a worksheet that fall below a certain conditional amount, you can use conditional formatting to do just that. The cells that meet the condition you set could be formatted with any of the cell-formatting attributes we have discussed. In the example we are discussing, a condition could state that all monthly sales figures that fall below 2500 are then formatted in red with a blue border. Both the condition that you set and the formatting that is applied is completely up to you. Just make sure that you select cell-formatting attributes for the conditional formatting that will stand out from the other formatted cells on the sheet. You are also not limited by the number of conditions that you can apply to a cell. The conditional formatting can actually be based on an unlimited set of conditions. Obviously, conditional formatting is an excellent tool to apply to cells that contain the results of formulas or functions.

When you select the Conditional Format command in the Styles group, the Conditional Formatting gallery opens. It actually provides you with several different options related to applying conditional formatting to the selected range of cells in the worksheet. Figure 12.11 shows the Conditional Formatting gallery with the Highlight Cells Rules command selected.

Figure 12.11
The Conditional Formatting gallery.

You will find that the conditional formatting feature provides you with more than just the ability to apply a condition or conditions to a cell range. Let's look at each of the options provided in the Conditional Formatting gallery and the possibilities that they present.

Using Highlight Cell Rules

When you select Highlight Cells Rules, you are provided with a list of conditions or rules such as Greater Than, Less Than, Between, and Duplicate Values. For example, if you select the Greater Than rule, the Greater Than dialog box opens as shown in Figure 12.12.

Figure 12.12
The Greater Than dialog box.

To take advantage of this prepackaged rule, specify a value on the left side of the dialog box that serves as the condition. You can type a value in the box or you can click the Shrink button and specify a value by selecting a cell in the worksheet. When you return to the Greater Than dialog box (after specifying a cell in the worksheet), you can fine-tune the formatting that is used by selecting the formatting drop-down arrow. A series of formatting attributes is supplied by default for the rule. You can specify a custom format for the rule by selecting Custom Format. This will open the Format Cells dialog box, which provides you with control over all the cell-formatting attributes applied by the rule.

tip

To clear the conditional formatting rules from a range, select Conditional Formatting, Clear Rules and then Clear Rules from Selected Cells. You can also clear all the rules on a worksheet by selecting Clear Rules from Entire Sheet.

When you are ready to apply the rule to the selected range, select OK. The conditional formatting will be applied to the cells that meet the conditions of the rule. You can apply additional rules to the range of cells as needed. Remember, you are not limited to the number of conditions that you apply to a cell or a range of cells. However, make sure that you keep track of the formatting that each rule applies to the range so that if a particular cell or cells meets more than one condition that is applied, you can tell by the formatting that the cell meets multiple conditions.

Using Top/Bottom Rules

The Top/Bottom rules enable you to quickly apply conditional formatting to cells in a range that fall into the top or bottom 10 items and the top or bottom 10% of the values in the range. You are not locked into the top or bottom 10 values in your range when you use the top or bottom 10 items rules. The dialog box for each of these rules provides spinner boxes that enable you to specify the number of items that are used by the rule. For example, if you want to see the bottom 5 items in the selected range, you can change the 10 in the Bottom 10 Items dialog box to 5 by using the spinner box (or by selecting the 10 and typing 5).

There are also two rules available in the top/bottom rules based on the average of the values in your selected range: Above Average and Below Average. You don't need to worry about calculating the highest 10 values or computing the average. The rule takes care of this and based on that computation, it applies the conditional formatting.

To apply one of the top/bottom rules, select Top/Bottom Rules in the Conditional Formatting gallery and then select one of the rules provided. When you select a rule such as Above Average, a dialog box specific to that rule appears. Select the formatting for the condition and then click OK.

Using Data Bars

If you like to visually compare data in a range of cells without resorting to a chart or sparklines, you can take advantage of the data bars provided in the Conditional Formatting gallery. The data bars are actually bar graphs that are placed in the cells of the selected range. This enables you to quickly see how the various values in the range compare to each other. Figure 12.13 shows a range of values that is formatted using data bars.

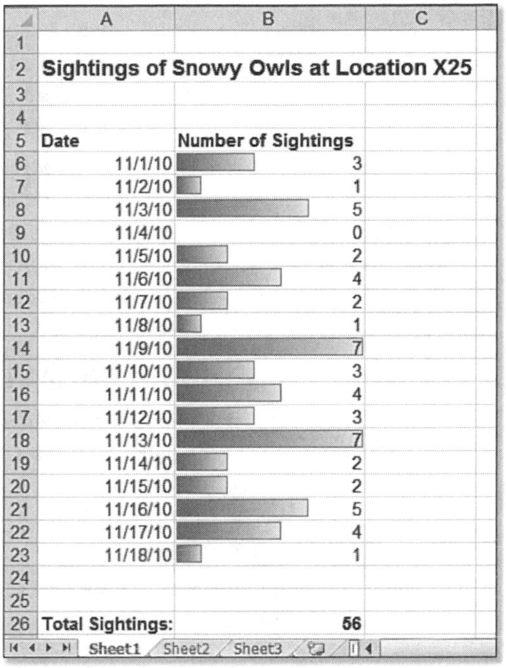

Figure 12.13
Data bars allow you to visually compare values in a range.

	A	B	C
1			
2	**Sightings of Snowy Owls at Location X25**		
3			
4			
5	Date	Number of Sightings	
6	11/1/10		3
7	11/2/10		1
8	11/3/10		5
9	11/4/10		0
10	11/5/10		2
11	11/6/10		4
12	11/7/10		2
13	11/8/10		1
14	11/9/10		7
15	11/10/10		3
16	11/11/10		4
17	11/12/10		3
18	11/13/10		7
19	11/14/10		2
20	11/15/10		2
21	11/16/10		5
22	11/17/10		4
23	11/18/10		1
24			
25			
26	**Total Sightings:**	56	

Sheet1 / Sheet2 / Sheet3

When you select Data Bars in the Conditional Formatting gallery, you can choose from bars that use a gradient fill or a solid fill. The data bars might skew the concept of how you think about conditional formatting but they do provide you with another option for quickly comparing worksheet values.

Using Color Scales

Another possibility provided by the Conditional Formatting gallery is the color scale. Each color scale consists of a set of colors. There are three-color scales and there are two-color scales.

When you apply a three-color scale to a range of cells—such as the Green-Yellow-Red Color Scale—you are actually separating the values into three subsets based on the values in the cell. The top third will be formatted with the first color (green), the middle third with the second color (yellow), and the bottom third with the third color (red). As already mentioned, there are also two-color scales, which divide the values in a top and bottom half using the two colors provided.

As with data bars, the color scales are used for relative comparison of the values in the cell range. They enable you to see by color the cells that fall in the same tier with the range. There are six preset three-color scales and six preset two-color scales available. Each scale uses a different set of colors.

Using Icon Sets

The Conditional Formatting gallery also provides you with icon sets that can be used to format the values in a selected range. The icon sets are somewhat similar to the color scales in that the icons are in groups that enable you to differentiate where the values in the range fall in relation to each other.

When you select Icon Sets in the Conditional Formatting gallery, you are provided different categories of icon sets such as Directional, Indicators, and Ratings. The number of icons in the set you select specifies how the values in the range are grouped. An icon set containing five icons will format the values in the range based on five groupings of the values (highest to lowest). A three-icon set will group the values in three different groupings (thirds).

Creating Conditional Formatting Rules

You are certainly not limited to the rules provided by the various rule categories provided in the Conditional Formatting gallery. You can create your own highlight cells rules, top/bottom rules, or other rule types as needed.

New rules are created in the New Formatting Rule dialog box. You can open this dialog box by selecting New Rule in the Conditional Formatting gallery or you can select More Rules when you have accessed a rule category such as Highlight Cells Rules or Color Scales. Figure 12.14 shows the New Formatting Rule dialog box.

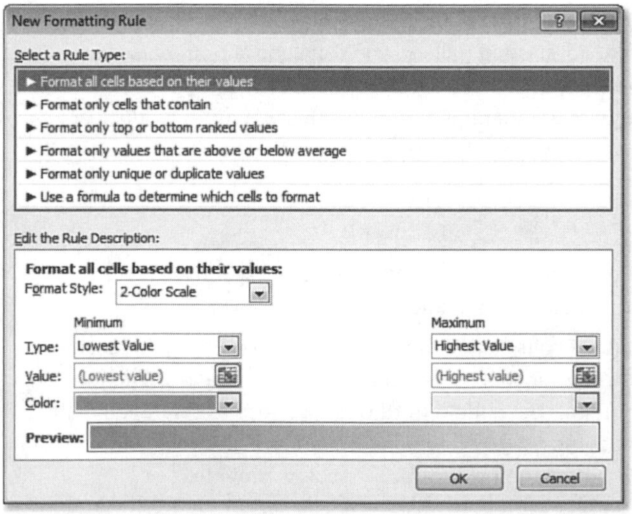

Figure 12.14
The New Formatting Rule dialog box.

Creating a new rule is really a two-part process. First you select the rule type in the Select a Rule Type list. For example if you wanted to create a rule that formatted cells in the worksheet that contained values that fell between two values, you would choose Format Only Cells That Contain in the Select a Rule Type box.

You would then select a condition for the new rule. For example, you might set the condition as Between. The rule also needs to know what two values specify the range that cell values would have to fall between to satisfy the rule. You can do this two ways: You can actually type the two values (the low and high value for the range) in the dialog box. The other possibility is to specify two cell addresses that contain the values that specify the range of values to be used by the rule.

As already mentioned, you can also create other rule types such as top or bottom rules or above or below average rules. To create a top or bottom rule, select Format Only Top or Bottom Ranked Values in the Select a Rule Type box. You can then specify whether you want to format the top or bottom of the values and specify the number of values you want the rule to format. The default number is 10 but you can specify any number you want. In the case of the above or below average rules, all you have to specify is whether the rule formats values above or below the average.

 tip

You can manage the rules that you create in the Conditional Formatting Rules Manager dialog box; select Manage Rules in the Conditional Formatting gallery. You can edit existing rules, delete rules, and create new rules from this dialog box.

The second part of the process of creating a new rule is specifying the formatting that will be applied to cells in the range that meets the condition of the rule. The New Formatting Rule dialog box provides a preview of the formatting for the new rule. However, it starts out as No Format Set, meaning you have to specify the formatting before the rule is ready to go.

Select the Format button in the New Formatting Rule dialog box. This opens the Format Cells dialog box. Use the tabs on the dialog box to specify the formatting for the new rule. You can work with any of the cell-formatting attributes including font, border, and fill. When you click OK in the Format Cells dialog box, you will be returned to the New Formatting Rule dialog box. Click OK and your rule will be applied to the selected range.

Manipulating Cells and Cell Content

As you enter data in Excel, you might find that you need to add additional cells to the worksheet to accommodate the information that you need to include in the worksheet. You might also find that there are occasions when you want to add long text entries or explanatory text, and want the information to span several cells and to wrap in the cells as text would in a paragraph. The solutions to these various minor issues are easy to come by in Excel.

You can easily insert cells and join cells, if necessary, and then wrap text in a cell or joined cells as needed. In cases where you have entered repeating labels or values into your worksheet and find that you need to either change the text entries or change the values, Excel also has you covered with the Replace feature, which shares the Find and Replace dialog box with the Find feature.

Inserting Cells

You can insert single or multiple cells into a worksheet. Inserting cells causes the data in the adjacent cells to shift down a row or over a column (to the right) to create a space for the new cells.

The number of cells inserted will depend on the number of cells that you select prior to inserting the new cells. To insert cells into a worksheet, follow these steps:

1. Select the cell range where you want the new cells to be inserted. Excel will insert the same number of cells as you select.

2. Select the Insert command on the Home tab and then select Insert Cells. The Insert dialog box appears as shown in Figure 12.15.

Figure 12.15
The Insert dialog box.

3. The Insert dialog box provides you with options for how the current cells will be affected by the insertion of the new cell. Select Shift Cells Right or Shift Cells Down. If you want to insert an entire row or column, select the appropriate option.

4. Select OK. Excel inserts the cells and shifts the adjacent cells according to the option you specified in the Insert dialog box.

You will find that inserting cells is useful if you have inadvertently mismatched data in your cells as you have entered it. For example, you might have entered an employee's name and then entered a portion of another employee's data. If you insert the required number of cells, you can fix the input problem by quickly adding the new data and editing the mismatched data without deleting a lot of information or messing around inserting new rows or other information. You can even drag the incorrect data to its appropriate location by dragging the information to the new cells.

Merging Cells and Wrapping Text

You can merge cells on a worksheet. This can be particularly useful when you want to add a large heading to a worksheet or need to add a paragraph or two of explanatory text and want it to appear directly on the worksheet. You can merge cells that are contiguous in a particular row (from left to right) or you can merge cells that are contiguous in a column (from top to bottom). You can also merge cells that are contiguous and span more than one row or column.

Excel provides you with options for merging cells. Select the cells you want to merge and then select the Merge & Center command in the Alignment group. The Merge & Center command provides four different options:

- **Merge & Center:** This option merges the cells and takes the content (such as a large heading) and centers it across the newly merged cells.

- **Merge Across:** Use this option to merge all the cells in a selected row or rows.

- **Merge Cells:** Use this option to merge contiguous selected cells in a single column or row or in multiple columns or rows. This option does not center the content across the merged cells.

- **Unmerge Cells:** This option enables you to unmerge cells that you have merged. All you have to do is select the merged cells and then use this option to put the cells back in their unmerged condition.

Selecting one of the merge options provided by the Merge & Center menu will merge the cells. When you have the cells merged, you can take advantage of the various alignment commands in the Alignment group to align the text in the merged cells as needed.

If you are working with a large block of text, you can wrap the text within the merged cells. As you type text, even in merged cells, you will find that the text will consist of a single line of text that bleeds over into the cells to the right of merged cells. As soon as you enter other data in the cells to the right of the merged cells, your large text entry will be truncated (as will any entry that is too large for a cell). To wrap the text within the merged cells, select the merged cell and then select the Wrap Text command in the Alignment group. The text will wrap in the merged cell, filling the cell much like a text box. The width of the cell that was created by merging the multiple cells will dictate the number of times your text needs to wrap.

 tip

You can find merged cells using the Find feature. You can search for merge cells when you use the Format option provided by Find.

Finding and Replacing Cell Items

Worksheets can become quite large (there are a lot of columns and rows that can be filled), so there might be occasions where you want to find specific cell content and the easiest way to find it quickly is using the Find and Replace feature. The Find and Replace feature is also useful in situations where you have entered a particular label or value into the worksheet and find that you have consistently entered it incorrectly. A great way to change multiple occurrences of a label or value is using Excel's Replace feature; you can locate data in the worksheet and replace it with new data as needed.

The Find and Replace feature can do more than just find text strings or values in cells and replace them with other information; it can also be used to search for cell formatting and optionally replace that formatting with formatting that you specify. To open the Find and Replace dialog box with the Find or the Replace tab active, select the Find & Select command in the Editing group and then select Find or Replace, respectively. Figure 12.16 shows the Replace tab of the Find and Replace dialog box with the options expanded.

The Find and Replace tabs function similarly. The only real difference is that the Replace tab also provides a Replace With box, enabling you to specify the content or formatting that you will replace the item or formatting that you find. If you want to match the case of your entry in the Find What box, select the Match Case check box. If you want to locate cells that contain exactly what you have entered into the Find What text box, select the Match Entire Cell Contents check box.

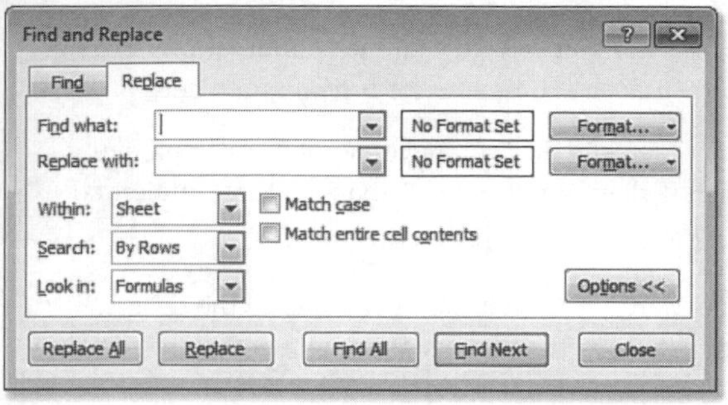

Figure 12.16
The Find and Replace dialog box.

You can use wildcards in the Find What box to aid in your searches. You can use the question mark (?) as a wildcard for a single character. The asterisk (*) can serve as a wildcard for any number of characters. Enter text in the Find What box (on either the Find or Replace tab) and then use the Format button to specify any formatting that you might want to include in the search; the Format button opens the Cell Formatting dialog box and provides you with access to all the cell-formatting possibilities.

If you want to provide the formatting by example, select the Format button's drop-down arrow and then select Choose Format from Cell. The mouse pointer becomes an eyedropper tool. Click it in a cell that contains the formatting that you want to find. You will be returned to the Find and Replace dialog box. After you specify formatting using either the Cell Format dialog box or the format eyedropper tool, the format will be previewed in the box that is to the right of the Find What or the Replace With dialog box.

So, let's look at what happens after you set up a search using the Find tab. When you are ready to conduct your search, you can use the Find Next button to find the next occurrence of the search string (or formatting). Click the Find Next button as needed to cycle through the found cells that match your search criteria. If you want to find all the cells that contain your search string, select the Find All button. A list of all the cells found by the search will be listed in the bottom of the Find and Replace dialog box. The sheet, cell address, and value found are supplied in the list. To navigate to a particular cell (that was found) click the cell reference in the list.

tip

You don't have to include a search string if you are searching for formatting only. Just specify the formatting and then run the search. You can also specify formatting only as the replace options for a find and replace.

When you are working on the Replace tab, you can replace each subsequent occurrence of the found string or form1atting using the Replace button. If you have set up your find and replace carefully and are sure that items will be replaced correctly, you can click Replace All and take care of all the replacements in one fell swoop.

The Go To feature is also accessed via the Find & Select menu, and specific items that you can go to are specified on the Find & Select menu such as Formulas, Comments, and Conditional Formatting. This provides a quick way to select occurrences of specific items or formatting in the worksheet. For example, if I select Formulas, the formulas in the worksheet are selected.

Working with Columns and Rows

Manipulating columns and rows in your worksheets is straightforward. You can easily change the column width for a column or columns and adjust row heights. You can also insert or delete columns and rows as needed. Inserting or deleting columns or rows doesn't actually change the number of columns or rows in the worksheet; they are fixed. In the case of inserting columns or rows, however, it does enable you to open up some white space in a worksheet when you need to add data.

You can also hide columns and rows in the worksheet. This is particularly useful in cases when you have data in the worksheet that you do not want prying eyes to see or information that you do not want to include in a printout. For example, you may want to print an employee list but do not want to include the columns that lists employee salaries.

Changing Column Width and Row Height

You have probably noticed that the default column width is not all that wide; it is 8.43 characters to be exact and it doesn't readily accommodate long text entries or values that have been formatted as currency or other numeric formats. You might have found entries in certain cells change to ########. This lets you know that you need to adjust the column width so that it can accommodate the entry and its formatting.

To adjust a column's width place, the mouse pointer on the column's right border. The mouse becomes a sizing tool. Drag the column border to the desired width. You can also change a column's width using AutoFit, which adjusts the column widths to accommodate the widest entry within the column; double-click the sizing tool on the column border. The column immediately adjusts to its widest entry.

If you want to adjust several columns at once, select the columns. Place the mouse on any of the column borders and drag to increase or decrease the width. Each selected column is adjusted to the width you select. You can also double-click to use AutoFit to adjust the width of the selected columns.

If you want to specify a more precise column width for a column or a number of selected columns, select the Format command and then select Column Width. The Column Width dialog box opens. Specify the width in the Column width box and then click OK.

> **tip**
>
> You can also access the Insert and the Delete commands from the shortcut menu. Right-click on selected columns or rows and then select Insert or Delete as needed.

> **tip**
>
> The Format command also provides an AutoFit Row Height and an AutoFit Column Width option.

You can also adjust row heights, if you want, using the mouse; just drag the bottom border of a row to adjust the height. However, your row heights will automatically adjust to any font size changes that you make to data held in a particular row. Row heights also adjust if you wrap text entries within them. You will probably find that you need to adjust column widths in your worksheets far more often than row heights.

You can adjust row heights using the Row Height dialog box. Select the Format command and then Row Height. Adjust the row height in the Row height box (the default is 15) and then click OK.

Inserting Columns and Rows

You can insert a single column or row or multiple columns or rows as needed. To insert a single column, click in the column that is to the right of where you want the new column to be inserted. Click the Insert command in the Cells group and then select Insert Sheet Columns. The new column is inserted to the left of the currently selected cell (and its column).

For inserting a single row, click in a cell in the row that you want to insert the new row below. Click the Insert command and select Insert Sheet Rows. The new row is inserted below the current row.

To insert multiple columns or rows, select the number of columns or rows you want to insert. In the case of columns, drag over the column headings; for rows, drag over the row numbers. Then use the Insert Sheet Columns or Insert Sheet Rows to insert the columns or rows specified. New columns are placed to the left of the selected columns and the selected columns are pushed to the right. The new rows are placed below the currently selected rows.

Deleting Columns and Rows

You can also delete a column or row from the sheet. In either case select either the column or row you want to remove by clicking on the appropriate column or row heading (drag to select multiple columns or rows).

Select the Delete command in the Cells group and then select Delete Sheet Columns or Delete Sheet Rows as needed. The columns or rows will be removed from the worksheet. Remember that any data that is included in the columns or rows that is delete is also deleted. It makes sense to make sure that you have laid out your worksheet in a way that is appropriate to your needs from the get go. This will save you a lot of time dragging information around on the worksheet and possibly negate the need for a lot of inserting new columns or rows or deleting columns and rows in the sheet.

Hiding Columns and Rows

As already mentioned, there might be occasions when you want to hide certain columns or rows in a worksheet both on the screen and when you print the worksheet. Hiding columns or rows is straightforward and the process is easy to reverse.

In the case of columns, select the columns you want to hide. Select the Format command and then point at the Hide & Unhide option. Select Hide Columns and the columns will be hidden.

The same process can be used for rows. Select the rows and then select Format, Hide & Unhide and then Hide Rows. The rows will be hidden.

Reversing the process is just a matter of accessing the Hide & Unhide options provided by the Format command. Select Unhide Columns to get your columns back and Unhide Rows to see those hidden rows.

Working with Worksheets

We had the opportunity to look at the various views that can be used when you are examining a worksheet in Chapter 11. There are also some other tricks related to viewing worksheets that can help you when you are working with large worksheets that contain many columns or rows or in cases when you want to see two disparate parts of the same large worksheet at the same time. As with columns and rows, you can also hide worksheets if needed.

➡️ *For more information about viewing Excel worksheets, see page 306 in Chapter 11.*

Freezing Rows and Columns

Adding data or just viewing the data can be problematic in a large worksheet that contains many columns, rows, or both. Because the column labels or row labels will not be visible when you scroll down or to the right, respectively, determining what you should type in a certain cell can be a mystery. For example, you might be entering employee information and the employee names are in the first and second columns of the worksheet. If you scroll to the right any distance (when you have a number of columns of data to work with), the names provided will no longer be visible in the Excel workspace. This makes it pretty difficult to add new data or even determine what the data in a particular cell actually represents.

You can freeze your column and row labels so that they remain on the screen no matter how far you scroll to the right or scroll down in the worksheet. The Freeze Panes command is in the Zoom group on the Ribbon's View tab. The Freeze Panes command enables you to freeze panes (both column and row labels), freeze the top row (the column labels), or freeze the first column (the row labels).

The Freeze Top Row and the Freeze First Column options on the Freeze Panes gallery are self-explanatory and require nothing from you other than just choosing one of these options after selecting the Freeze Panes drop-down arrow.

If you want to use the Freeze Panes option, you actually need to specify the rows and columns you want to freeze. This is accomplished by selecting the cell that is below the row you want to freeze and to the right of the column you want to freeze. Figure 12.17 shows a worksheet where the Freeze Panes command has been used to freeze rows 1 through 5 and to freeze column A. Notice that cell B6 was selected before the panes were frozen. This is because cell B6 is one cell below the last row to be frozen and one cell to the right of the column to be frozen.

When you have identified the cell you want to use to specify the rows and or columns to freeze, select the cell. Then all you have to do is select Freeze Panes to freeze the specified row and column in place. You can now scroll either down or to the right in the worksheet and the row and column labels should stay on the screen as you scroll.

When you have finished working with the frozen panes, you can easily remove them. Select the Freeze Panes drop-down arrow and then select Unfreeze Panes.

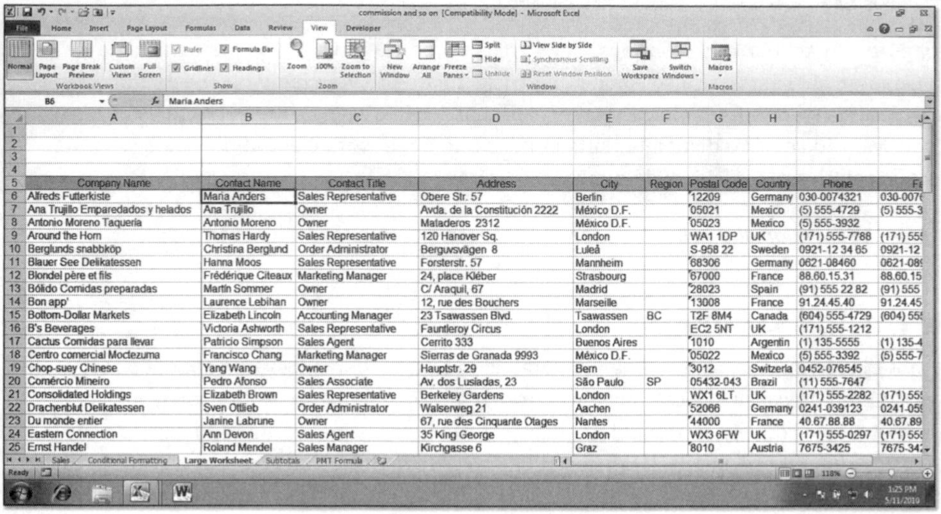

Figure 12.17
Freeze panes to keep column or row labels on the screen when you scroll.

Splitting Worksheets

Another useful trick for dealing with large worksheets is the Split command. You can split the current worksheet window into multiple panes. Doing so enables you to view different parts of the same large worksheet in different panes simultaneously. This is useful for looking at data or the results of calculations that are typically quite distant in the geography of a large worksheet.

To split the current worksheet into multiple panes, select the cell where you want the split to occur. When you specify a cell, the split will appear below the selected cell or to the right of the selected cell. After specifying the cell, select the Split command on the View tab. You can use the mouse to drag the split to a new location as needed.

You can also manually place splits in a worksheet. Just above the vertical scrollbar is a horizontal split box. Drag the horizontal split box onto the worksheet to create a horizontal split. There is also a vertical split box just to the left of the horizontal scroll bar. Drag the vertical split box onto the worksheet to create a vertical split.

After you have your splits on the Excel screen, you can scroll within each of the independent panes to locate certain parts of your worksheet. When you have finished working with the split panes, select the Split command to remove all the splits from the worksheet window.

Hiding Worksheets

We have already discussed hiding worksheet columns and rows, but you can also hide an entire worksheet in your Excel workbook. This enables you to hide sensitive information as you work on the other worksheets in the workbook.

The worksheet you want to hide should be the active worksheet. If it isn't, click the worksheet's tab to make it the active worksheet. Select the Format command on the Home tab; then point at the

Hide & Unhide option. Select Hide Sheet to hide the current worksheet. Other worksheets in the workbook will still be available. You can hide other worksheets in the workbook by repeating the process.

When you need to work on a worksheet that you have hidden, you are only a few mouse clicks away from unhiding it (yes, "unhiding" sounds wrong; I guess Microsoft didn't want to make "found" the opposite of "hidden"). Select Format and then point at the Hide & Unhide option. Select Unhide Sheet. The Unhide dialog box will open. The Unhide dialog box will list the sheets that you have hidden in the current workbook. Select the worksheet you want to unhide and then click OK.

Naming Ranges

When you work with values in an Excel worksheet, they typically make up a range of cells that contain like values. For example, all the cells containing employee salaries would typically be located in the same column and so would constitute a contiguous range of cells. You can then use this range for a number of calculations, such as total company salary, or compute the average or the mean for the salary range.

> **tip**
>
> You can hide an entire open workbook via the Ribbon's View tab. Use the Hide command to hide a workbook window and then use Unhide to unhide it.

You can actually select a range of values and give the range a range name. For example, the salary range that I discussed in the previous paragraph could be given the name "salary." The range name could then be used directly in formulas or functions as a substitute for the range, which is specified by the beginning and ending cell addresses in the range. Range names can actually be quite useful and remembering a range name is a lot easier than remembering the actual cell range in terms of the cell addresses.

You will find that you can use range names in calculations (in both your own formulas and Excel functions) to create charts and to move to a particular place in a worksheet using the Go To feature (press Ctrl+G to open the Go To dialog box).

Creating a range name for a selected range of cells is easy. There are some rules related to naming ranges, however. You are limited to 255 characters for a range name. You can't use spaces. You also cannot use most of the symbols on the keyboard. The underscore and the period are allowed.

You can use alphanumeric characters (A to Z and 0 to 9), so range names can consist of a combination of numbers and letters. You can also use the underscore in the place of a space where you want to create range names that describe the cell range, such as gross_income or taxable_income (these two types of income are actually the same if you don't have any tax_shelters).

There is actually more than one way to create range names. You can select a range of values and then define the name, or you can have Excel generate range names for the selected values using the column or row headings as the range names. To specify a range name for a selected range, select the range and then click the Define Name command in the Defined Names group of the Ribbon's Formulas tab. The New Name dialog box will open as shown in Figure 12.18.

Provide a name for the range in the Name box. By default the scope of the range name is at the workbook level, meaning you can specify this range anywhere in the workbook using the range name. You can change the scope to a specific sheet in the workbook. Select the Scope drop-down list and select a sheet from the provided list.

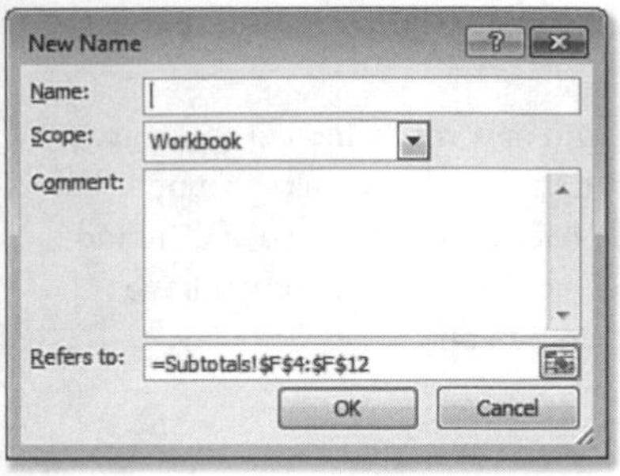

Figure 12.18
Create a range name for a selected range of cells.

You can also enter optional comments related to the range and its name in the Comment box. Before you create the new name, take a moment to check the range specified in the Refers To box. You can adjust the range if it is incorrect by selecting the Shrink button. You can then reselect the range in the worksheet and then click the Expand button to return to the New Name dialog box. Click OK to create the range name.

Creating Range Names from Selections

You can also create range names based on the column labels or row labels that you have created in the worksheet. For example, if you have several columns of numbers, such as sales figures for different regions by month (January, February, March), you can quickly create a range name for each of the columns using the column labels. To create range names from row or column labels, select the ranges (either in columns or rows) and make sure that you include the row or column containing the descriptive labels for the range. Then click the Create from Selection command in the Define Names groups. The Create Names from Selection dialog box will open as shown in Figure 12.19.

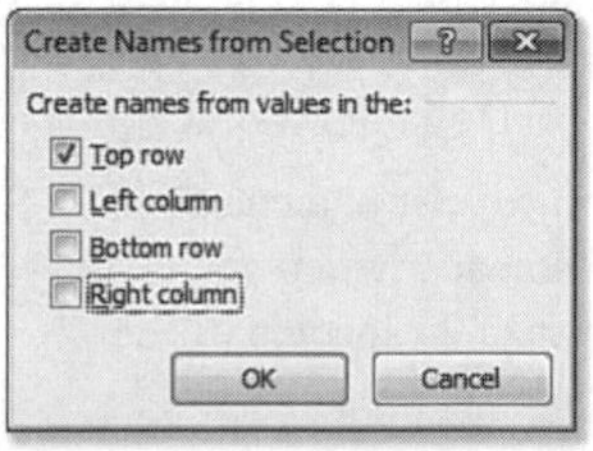

Figure 12.19
The Create Names from Selection dialog box.

Select the location of the labels that will be used as the range names using the check boxes provided: Top Row, Left Column, Bottom Row, or Right Column. If the labels are in the top row of the selected range and the values are arranged in columns, you would select Top Row. If the labels are in the first column (the left column) and the values are arranged in rows, select Left Column. When you are ready to generate the range names, select OK.

Managing Range Names

You can view and manage your range names in the Name Manager. The Name Manager enables you to create new range names, edit existing range names, and delete range names that you no longer want.

To open the Name Manager, select the Name Manager command in the Defined Names group. Figure 12.20 shows the Name Manager.

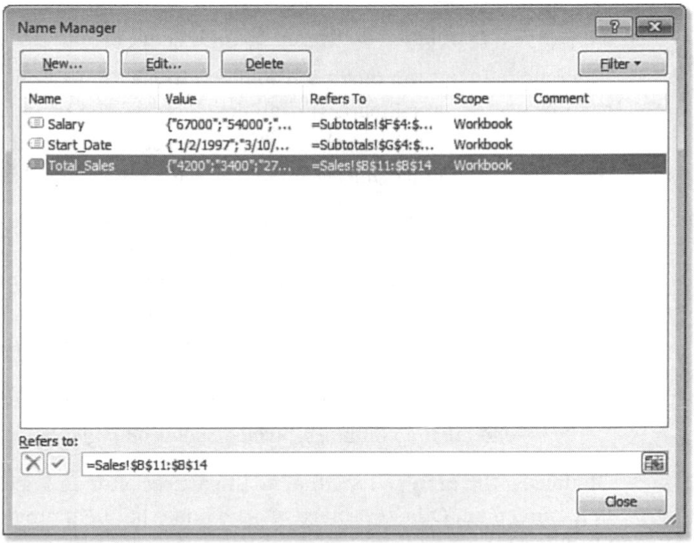

Figure 12.20
The Name Manager.

All the range names in the current workbook will be listed in the Name Manager. You can filter the list using the Filter drop-down button on the right side of the dialog box. You can filter by scope (worksheet or workbook) and filter for names that contain errors.

If you find that you need to edit a particular range name, select the name in the list and then select the Edit button. This will open the Edit Name dialog box, which enables you to modify the name, comments, or the range for that particular name.

To create a new range name, select the New dialog box. This will open the New Name dialog box. Specify a name, a cell range, and optional comments for the new range name. When you click OK to create the new name, you will be returned to the Name Manager.

You can also delete range names from the Name Manager. Select a name in the list and then click the Delete button. You will be asked if you are sure you want to delete the name. Click OK. The name will be removed from the list.

Remember that the main reason you create range names is to use them as a way to specify a range of values in a formula that you design or an Excel function that you use. Range names can be quickly inserted into a formula or function via the Use in Formula command, which provides a list of your range names.

➡ *For more information about using range names in formulas and functions, see page 363 in Chapter 13, "Getting the Most from Formulas and Functions."*

Adding Images and Graphics to Worksheets

You can add pictures, clip art, shapes, and SmartArt graphics to your Excel worksheets just as easily as you can add these items to Word documents or PowerPoint presentation slides. For example, you can quickly insert a company logo graphic or insert a picture of the salamander species that is the subject of a population study you have detailed in your Excel worksheet.

The Ruler's Insert tab provides the Illustrations group, which enables you to insert digital pictures, clip art, shapes, and SmartArt graphics. Pictures can be useful if the image directly relates to the subject matter of the worksheet. Clip art is less useful, and overly cute clip art can actually diminish the impact of the facts and figures that you have included in the worksheet.

SmartArt graphics actually provide you with the possibility of creating illustrative graphics that can help make sense out of the information in the worksheet. For example, if you have created a sales report that details the quarterly sales of your sales force by region, you can include an organizational chart showing the report structure for the regions. You can do this by creating an organizational chart using one of the SmartArt graphics provided in the Hierarchy category.

➡ *For an overview of using images and graphics in the Office applications see Chapter 4, "Using and Creating Graphics," which begins on page 77).*

Obviously, the graphic type that you use most often in Excel is going to be a chart based on the data in a worksheet. Other graphical possibilities that help provide meaning to data visually are sparklines and conditional formatting graphical options such as data bars, color scales, and icon sets.

➡ *For information on adding charts to your Excel worksheets, see Chapter 14, "Enhancing Worksheets with Charts," which begins on page 381.*

Excel differs from Word or PowerPoint in that Excel worksheets must be designed and formatted so that they can provide a meaningful snapshot of often complex numerical information. Use graphical elements such as pictures and graphics sparingly and only when they are an aid to understanding the data provided in the sheet.

GETTING THE MOST FROM FORMULAS AND FUNCTIONS

Excel's real power lies in its ability to do calculations. The whole point of entering values into Excel is to have these values acted on by formulas or functions; you are after what results from calculations, meaning answers. Whether you are a biologist using statistical functions to enumerate a population study of snowy egrets in the Hudson River valley or are a financial maven tracking your investments, Excel provides you with the all the tools that you need to do the math.

In this chapter, we look at the basics of building simple formulas and taking advantage of Excel's huge library of built-in formulas—functions—to do calculations. We explore a number of different function categories including statistical, logical, date, and financial functions. We also discuss best practices for entering, copying, moving, and proofing your formulas and functions.

Performing Calculations in Excel Worksheets

Excel provides you with two different possibilities for doing calculations in your worksheets: formulas and functions. Formulas are do-it-yourself math that require you to not only specify the cells referenced in the calculation, but you must also provide the operators specifying what type of calculation is to take place. Formulas are best reserved for simple calculations such as subtraction, multiplication, and division. Figure 13.1 shows a subtraction formula that subtracts the payment to the instructor (G10) from the Tuition Total for that class (D10).

Note that the formula (=D10-G10) is shown in H10 and in the formula bar. When you place the insertion point in the formula bar, the cells involved

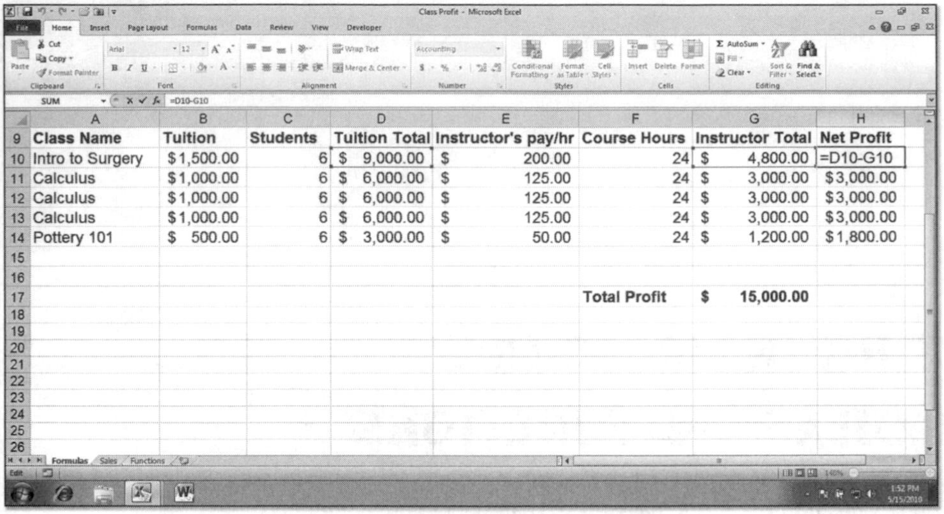

Figure 13.1
A subtraction formula.

in the formula are selected using a different color for each cell address included in the formula.

Functions, on the other hand, are built-in formulas provided by Excel. The Excel function library is huge; it provides more than 300 functions, grouped into categories that include date and time functions, engineering functions, financial functions, math and trigonometry functions, statistical functions, and even text functions. Figure 13.2 shows the PMT function, which is an Excel function used to determine the periodic payment on a loan that has a fixed interest.

note

The Show Formulas command on the Formulas menu has been used in these figures to show you what the formula or function actually looks like in the cell rather than showing the result of the formula or function.

Note that the function is designated by the function name (PMT). The cells that are to be acted on by the function are B7 (the interest rate), C7 (the term: 60 months), and D7 (the actual cost of the car or the principal). Note that the only operator you see in the function is the /. This is because I needed to divide the annual interest rate by 12 to get the monthly payment.

Creating your own formulas is best reserved for situations where Excel doesn't provide you with a function that will do the same job. As already mentioned, most of the formulas that you need to create will take care of simple math problems that are used to subtract or divide values (or results from other formulas or functions). Developing an awareness of what the Excel functions provide you in terms of doing complex calculations is time better spent than trying to create elaborate formulas of your own.

Figure 13.2
The PMT func-
tion.

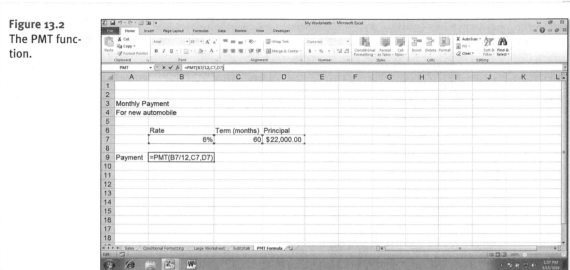

Relative Versus Absolute Referencing

One thing that you need to understand when working with both formulas and functions is how Excel references cells in your worksheets when you designate them in a formula or function. This is particularly important when you copy formulas and functions in the worksheet.

When you create a formula or function and designate cell references, Excel uses a form of referencing called relative referencing. When you copy a formula or a function from one cell to another cell, the cell references in the formula or function are rewritten to adjust to its new location. For example, Figure 13.3 shows a simple worksheet that uses the Sum function to add the January through March sales totals for each of the regions designated in column A. The Sum function was entered once in cell E4 and then copied (using the fill handle) to cells E5, E6, and E7.

Note that as the function was copied down into the other total cells, the function adjusted to its new location and specifies the correct range of cells to be acted on by the function. This is because of relative referencing. Although you specified a range of cells to be summed in cell E4, what Excel actually saw was that it was to take the three cells to the left of the cell containing the function (E4) and add them together. So, when you copy the function down to cells E5 through E7, Excel just takes the three cells to the left of the function and adds them together. This is what relative referencing is all about and why it is so easy to copy a formula and function in a worksheet and get the correct answer or answers.

> **note**
> When you select a cell containing a formula or function and place the insertion point in the Formula bar, the range finder will highlight the cells referenced in the formula or function.

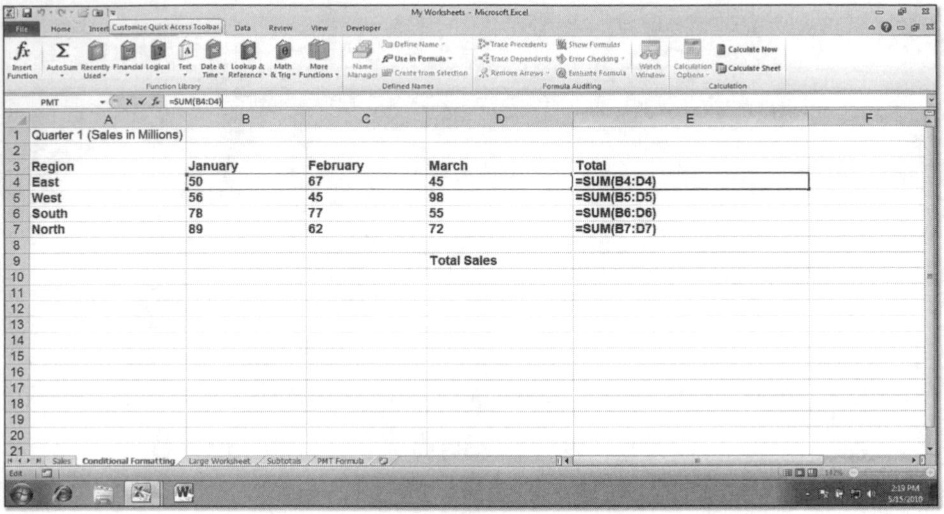

Figure 13.3
Relative referencing enables you to quickly copy a function to multiple cells.

In some situations, you will want to override Excel's relative referencing so that a formula or function does not change all the cell references when you copy it to a new location. This is where absolute referencing comes in. Suppose that you have a worksheet that computes the commission made on sales by each of your salespeople. The actual commission rate is specified in one cell. Figure 13.4 shows the simple multiplication formula that was created to multiply the total sales (in column B) by the commission percentage, which is located in cell D18. The formula was entered in cell C11 and then copied to cells C12 through C14.

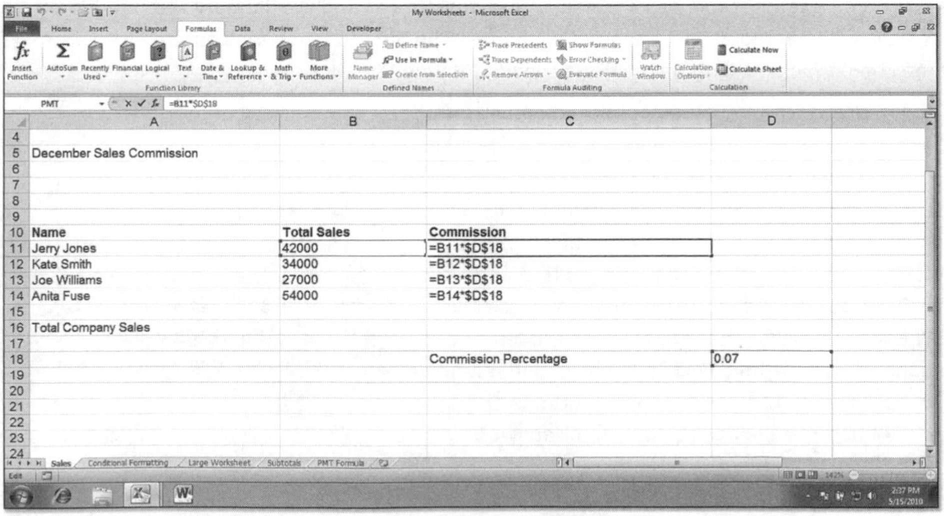

Figure 13.4
Absolute referencing is used to override relative referencing.

Note that the commission percentage (D18) is specified in the formula as D18. This is because you want the commission formula you created to always (absolutely) reference cell D18 even when you copy the formula to other cells. Note that cell B11 in the formula in cell C11 is a relative reference.

As the formula was copied down, B11 adjusted to the new location and was changed in each subsequent cell to B12, and then B13, and then B14. If cell D18 was not entered in the formula as an absolute reference, as soon as the formula was copied from C11 to C12, the formula would no longer work. That is because the formula would attempt to adjust the relative reference for D18 to D19, which on this particular worksheet does not contain any value at all.

note

In Figure 13.4, I used my own formula =B11*D18; I could have also used the Excel function: =PRODUCT(B11,D18).

To specify a cell reference as absolute, add a $ (dollar sign) before the column letter and before the row number that make up the cell address (such as our example of an absolute reference: D18). The easiest way to add the dollar signs to an absolute reference is to press F4 after you have specified the cell address in a formula or function.

In our example, we looked at a single cell as an absolute reference. You can, however, have situations where you need to designate the column or row in a cell address as absolute rather than making both the column and row designation in the address absolute. Remember that cell references are two parts: column designation and row designation. So, you can make a reference where only the column is absolute and the row reference is still relative. This is referred to as a mixed reference.

note

Using range names in formulas and functions can actually negate the need to use absolute references. We discuss using range names in formulas and functions later in this chapter.

Let's look at an example, using the PMT function as the function we want to copy in a worksheet. Figure 13.5 shows the PMT function as it was originally written in cell C7. A row of car amounts (principals) are listed in row 5 and different interest rates are listed in column B. Only one term (the number of monthly payments) is listed in cell C14.

When the function is copied across the columns, you always want the function to look for the rates in column B. So, column B is designated as absolute in the function ($B). You also want the function to continue to look in row 5 when it is copied down, so row 5 is designated as absolute in the function ($5). Finally, the term in C14 must always (absolutely) be referred to by the function, no matter where you copy it. So, it is designated as an absolute as C14. So, we have mixed references and one absolute reference in the same function.

Using absolute references and mixed references can be a little tricky. If you enter a formula or a function with incorrect absolute or mixed referencing, Excel will typically let you know. For example, if I neglect to make column B absolute in the example we looked at in Figure 13.5, as soon as I copy the function to the next column, I get the message #NUM in the cells. This is because there is a number error in the function. All I have to do is fix the function and then recopy it to the other cells in the sheet to fix the problem. Excel also offers a number of other tools for correcting formulas and functions including the ability to trace precedents and dependents and do error checking on formulas and functions. We look at some of these tools later in this chapter.

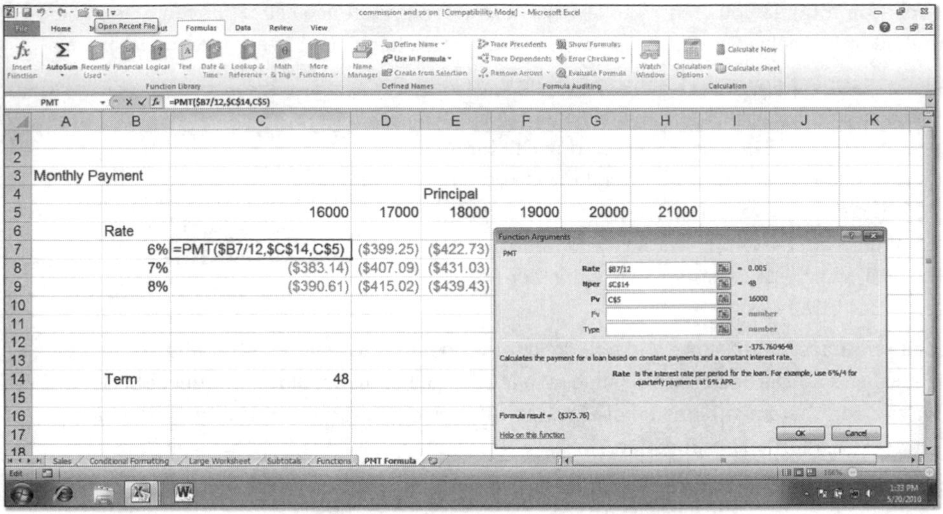

Figure 13.5
Mixed refer-
ences can be
used in cell
addresses.

Creating and Editing Formulas

Creating formulas in Excel is very straightforward. You can include cell addresses, values, and even functions in your formulas. The values in the formula (specified by cell addresses) are then acted on by an operator or operators that you specify in the formula. When you begin a new formula in a cell, you will start the formula's notation with the = sign. This lets Excel know that you are entering a formula. You can then specify the cell addresses for the formula and the required operators. For example, you might enter the formula:

=B6-C6

You are specifying that Excel should take the value in C6 and subtract it from the value in B6. The result will be placed in the cell where you entered the formula. Table 13.1 shows some of the common arithmetic operators used in Excel formulas.

Table 13.1 Arithmetic Operators

Operator	Performs	Examples
+	Addition	=A1+B1
−	Subtraction	=A1-B1
*	Multiplication	=A1*C12
/	Division	=A1/B3
∧	Exponentiation	=A1^2

Excel also provides other operators that are referred to as comparison operators. These operators can compare two cells and return one of two logical values: TRUE or FALSE. Table 13.2 provides a list of comparison operators.

Table 13.2 Comparison Operators

Operator	Comparison	Examples
=	Equal	=A1=B1
>	Greater than	=A1>B1
<	Less than	=A1<C12
>=	Greater than or equal to	=A1>=B3
<=	Less than or equal to	=A1<=2

Obviously, after you know what operator or operators you are going to use, the rest of the formula will typically consist of the cell addresses that are to be acted on by the formula. The values in those cell addresses that you reference are referred to as operands. Operands in a formula can actually consist of a cell range, single cell addresses, constants (values, dates, or text you actually enter as part of the formula), or range names.

Understanding Operator Precedence

An important aspect of creating formulas is understanding operator precedence. In simplest terms, operator precedence means that certain operations in a formula take precedence over (or take place before) other operations in a formula. For example, in the formula =B2+B3*C2, the multiplication of B3*C2 will take precedence, so B3 will be multiplied by C2 and then B2 will be added to that result. The order of operator precedence is as follows:

1. Parentheses ()

2. Exponent ^

3. Multiplication *, Division /

4. Addition +, Subtraction −

5. Equal to =, Less than <, Greater than >

In the case of the formula =B2+B3*C2, if you want the formula to add B2+B3 before multiplying the result by C2, you would have to write the formula as: =(B2+B3)*C2. Operations enclosed in parentheses take precedence over operations that are not in parentheses.

Entering Formulas

You can enter formulas in one of two ways: by typing the entire formula, including the cell addresses, or by typing the formula operators and selecting the cell references. Because many of the errors found in Excel typically relate to incorrectly entered information, it makes sense to point to the cells or cell ranges that are included in a formula. This makes it less likely for an incorrect cell address or range to be placed in the formula. Follow these steps to enter a formula:

1. Select the cell that will hold the formula. Type = to begin the formula.

2. Click on the first cell that will be referenced in the formula. The cell address will be entered in the formula in the formula bar.

3. Enter the appropriate arithmetic operator after the value to indicate the operation you want to perform.

4. Click on the next cell that will be referenced in the formula.

5. Repeat steps 3 and 4 if necessary. You can also enter constants into the formula as needed.

tip

If you are entering a formula and want to get rid of it and start again, press Esc.

6. When the formula is complete, click the Enter button on the Formula bar or press Enter. The formula is entered in the current cell.

After the formula has been entered in the cell, the result of the formula will appear in the cell. When you select the cell, you can view the formula in the formula bar. If you click in the formula bar, the range finder will highlight the cells that you specified in the formula.

Editing Formulas

Editing formulas in Excel is very straightforward. You can edit a formula in the formula bar or directly in the cell. To edit the formula in the formula bar, use the mouse to insert the insertion point into the formula and edit as needed. As soon as you place the insertion point in the formula bar, the range finder will highlight the cells referenced in the formula.

You can use the arrow keys to move within the formula bar. To go to the beginning of the formula in the formula bar, press the Home key; the End key will take you to the end of the formula. You can also do in-cell editing: Double-click on a cell to place the insertion point into the contents of the cell such as a formula.

When you need to edit an actual cell reference (or references) in a formula, it is probably easiest to do this on the formula bar. Select the cell address in the formula that you want to change. You can type the changes required; however, it is more foolproof to click on the cell and that cell's address will be inserted into the formula, replacing the selected cell reference. When you have finished editing the formula, click the Enter button in the formula bar or press the Enter key.

➡ *For more about editing a cell' s content, see page 275 in Chapter 11, "Requisite Excel: Essential Features."*

Working with Excel Functions

Formulas provide you with a way to do simple arithmetic and some logical expressions, but most of the heavy lifting you do in terms of calculations in Excel will be accomplished using functions. Functions can do everything from adding a range of numbers, to counting the number of entries in a range, to providing you with the return on an investment when you have a constant interest rate and consistent monthly deposits. And you can bank on the fact that my previous statement doesn't even scratch the surface of possibilities in terms of the different kinds of functions that Excel provides.

Functions consist of two parts: the function name and the cell addresses that are to be acted on. These cell ranges or individual cell addresses are also referred to as the function's arguments because they are used by the function to arrive at an answer. One of the most common functions used is the SUM function, which is also referred to as the AutoSum function because Excel has provided an AutoSum command in just about every version of Excel that I can remember. It is designed to quickly add a range of numbers. So, the SUM function might look like this in a worksheet: =SUM(B4:D4), where the argument is the range of cells B4 to D4, which will be added by the SUM function. The SUM function can also add cells that are not in a contiguous range using the syntax =SUM(B3, C6, D12); individual cell addresses serve as the arguments in the function and are separated by commas. The number of arguments (or cell addresses) that can be placed in the SUM function is endless, meaning that many functions do not control the number of legal arguments specified in the function.

Some functions actually do not have any arguments. For example, the =NOW() function, which is a date function, returns the current date and time formatted as a date and time. It does not require an argument in the parentheses to work.

The number of arguments allowed in Excel functions will vary, and some functions will allow optional arguments. For example, the FV function, which calculates the future value of an investment that has a constant interest rate and the same payment amount over the investment period. FV actually allows for an optional present value of the investment if you have rolled money over into a new money market account, certificate of deposit, or other investment instrument. Figure 13.6 shows a simple future value worksheet that includes an optional present value (the initial investment on the worksheet).

Figure 13.6 shows the Function Arguments dialog box, which is used to build a function. The future value function (FV), requires that a Rate (the interest rate divided by the number of payments in a year), the Nper (the total number of payment periods in the investment), and the Pmt (the actual payment) be supplied for the function to work. It also allows for an optional PV (or present value) to be included.

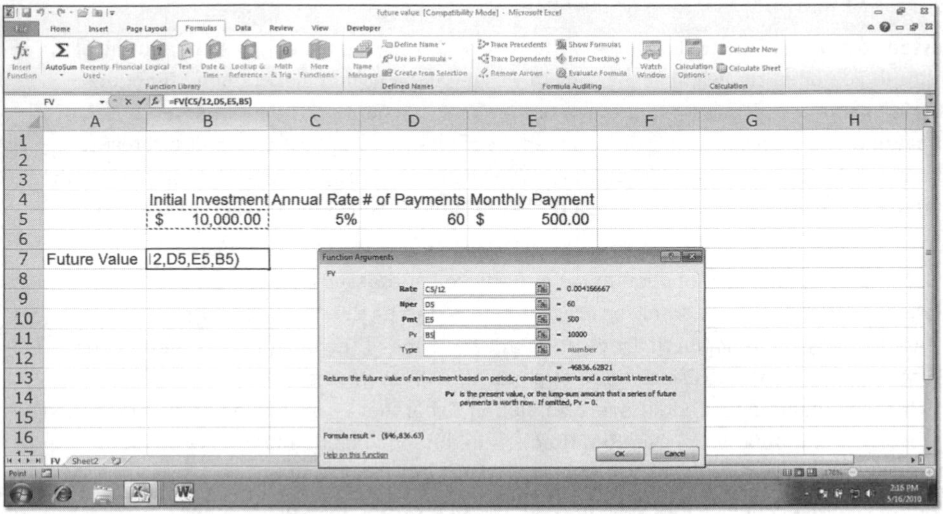

Figure 13.6 Supplying a Future Value function with arguments.

Entering a Function in a Cell

Excel offers you a choice of methods for inserting functions into your worksheet. You can type in a function (as you can a formula) by typing an equal sign (=) followed by the name of the function. The cell references for the function are then provided with the parentheses that follow the function name.

Typing functions can be just as fraught with potential errors as typing in formulas. Excel provides you with two methods for inserting functions: the Insert Function dialog box and the category commands provided in the Function library. Both of these avenues get you to the same place: the Function Arguments dialog box. The Function Arguments dialog box enables you to specify the arguments to be used by the function. This can require that you specify a range of cells or individual cell addresses. Because the Function Arguments dialog box breaks the required arguments for the function, you can use the mouse to easily specify the arguments directly on the worksheet. This can greatly cut down on the possibility of specifying the wrong range or cell address in the function.

> **tip**
>
> The Count Numbers or COUNT function does not count blank cells or cells containing text. If you want to count values, use COUNT. If you want to count the cells in the range no matter what is in the cells (excluding blank cells) use the COUNTA function.

Although using the Function Arguments dialog box is relatively straightforward, some of the more commonly used functions such as SUM, Average, and other statistical functions such as Max (maximum) and Min (minimum) can be inserted in a more direct way via the AutoSum command. Let's look at AutoSum and then we can return to our discussion of inserting functions using the Function Arguments dialog box.

Using AutoSum

As already mentioned, the SUM function is probably the most used function in Excel; we are always adding things together such as the total number of employees, the total number of widgets in our inventory, or the total amount of money in our bank account.

You can insert the SUM function into a worksheet using the AutoSum command on the Ribbon's Home tab or the AutoSum command in the Function library of the Ribbon's Formulas tab. Select the cell where you want to place the SUM function. Typically, you will choose a cell that is at the bottom of a column of values or at the end of a row of data. This makes it easy for AutoSum to figure out the range of cells that it should include in the SUM function.

When you select the AutoSum command, AutoSum inserts =SUM and selects the range of cells to be included in the function. The range is also specified in the function. Figure 13.7 shows the SUM function inserted by the AutoSum command and the range of cells that will be included in the function.

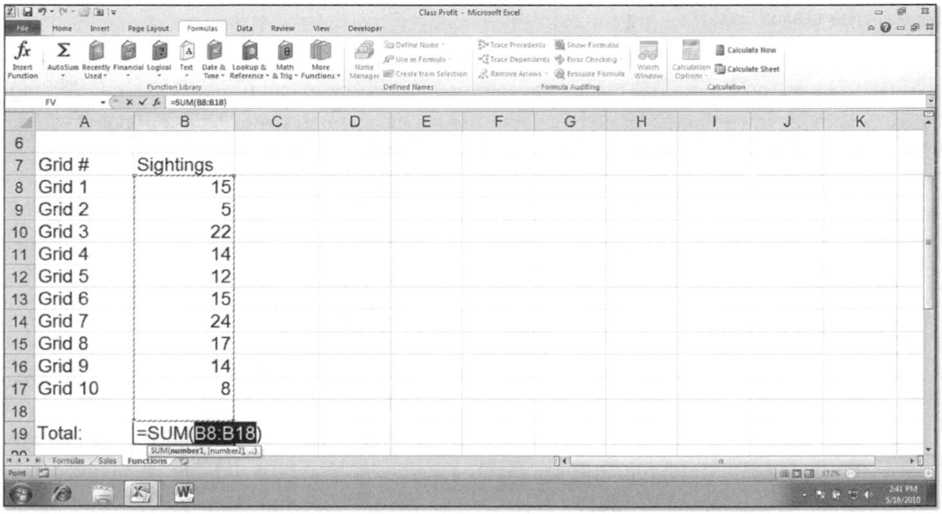

Figure 13.7
AutoSum attempts to select the range of cells to be added.

Note that the range of cells will be specified as B8:B18. The beginning and end of the range are separated by a colon (:). AutoSum does not always select the correct range of cells. When you insert the SUM function using AutoSum in a cell that is at the bottom of a column and at the end of a row, AutoSum will select the cells in the column. You will also find that blank cells within a range will stop AutoSum from selecting the entire range you might want to include in the function. You can change the range selected as needed. Use the mouse to extend or reduce the selection marquee or select an entirely new range of cells. After you have the correct range specified, click the Enter button in the formula bar or press the Enter key. The SUM function will be placed in the cell and return a result.

You can also insert other statistical functions from the AutoSum drop-down menu. These functions include Average (AVERAGE), Count Numbers (COUNT), Maximum (MAX), and Minimum (MIN). To enter one of these functions, such as AVERAGE, select the cell that will contain the function and then select the drop-down menu for the AutoSum command on the Home tab or the Formulas tab. The function will be entered in the cell. The function will attempt to select a range; however, how successful this is will depend on where you are placing the function and how the values that you want to be acted on are arranged in the worksheet. Use the mouse if you need to specify the range for the function and then press Enter. The result of the function will appear in the cell.

Using the Status Bar Statistical Functions

Because we are talking about some of the statistical functions, such as Average (AVERAGE), Count Numbers (COUNT), Maximum (MAX), and Minimum (MIN), and how to insert them, I want to take a short side trip and discuss the statistical counters or Autocalculate fields that are provided by the Excel status bar. When you select a range of cells, the status bar can automatically calculate such things as the average, count, minimum, maximum, and sum for the range. The result is shown in the status bar.

To activate these statistical counters, such as Average, Count, or Sum, right-click on the status bar to open the Customize Status Bar menu. Select a statistical function such as Average or Count. As soon as you select a range of cells in the sheet, you can view the results of these different statistical functions on the status bar. They can actually be a quick a way to check functions you might have inserted into the worksheet to compute the same result such as the Average or the Count for the range. If the result in the worksheet is different from the result on the status bar, you need to revisit the function you inserted into the worksheet.

Using the Insert Function Dialog Box

The Insert Function dialog box can be accessed via the AutoSum drop-down menu; select the AutoSum drop-down arrow on the Home tab of the Ribbon and then select More Functions. You can also access the Insert Function dialog box from the Insert Function command on the Ribbon's Formulas tab. In either case, the Insert Function dialog box will open as shown in Figure 13.8.

The Insert Function dialog box is designed to help you find a function in cases where you have a good idea of what you want to do in terms of a calculation in the worksheet but aren't sure which function to use or can't remember the name of a function that you use occasionally. To search for a particular function, type a brief description of what you want to do in the Search for a function box and then click Go. For example, you could type "investment value" and Excel would list financial functions (among other functions) that help you calculate the present or future value of an investment.

If you want to see functions that you have recently used you can use the Or Select a Category drop-down list to view the most recently used functions. You can also peruse the functions by category, such as Financial, Date & Time, Statistical, Logical, and so on, by selecting a particular category of functions via the Category drop-down box.

tip

If you need more help with a particular function, select the function in the list and then click Help on This Function to open the Excel Help window.

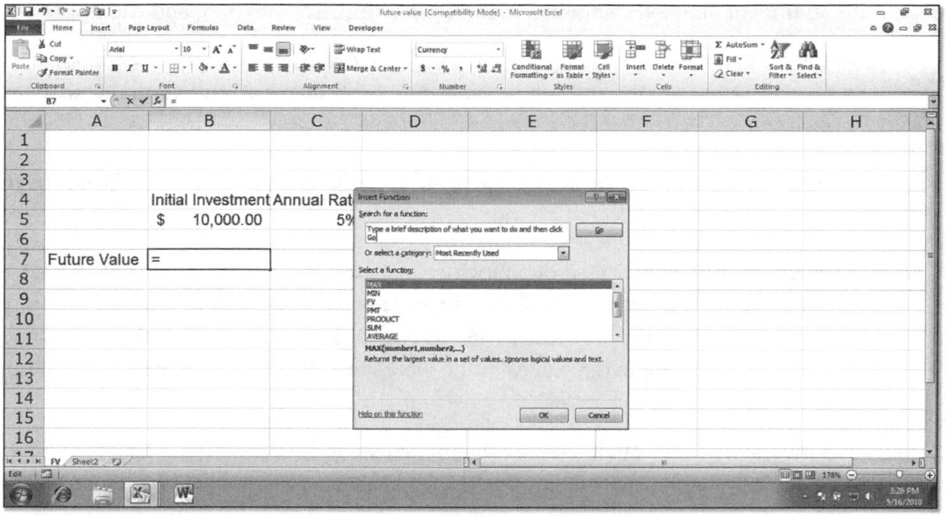

Figure 13.8
The Insert
Function dialog
box.

When you select a function in the Select a Function list box, the syntax for the function will appear below the function list. A definition of the function will also be provided.

After you have located the function that you want to place in the worksheet, make sure that the function is selected and then click OK. The Function Arguments dialog box will open. Provide the various arguments for the function as required by the function and then click OK. This will place the function in the worksheet and return your result.

Using the Function Library

An alternative to using the Insert Function dialog box is to use the various category commands provided on the Ribbon's Formulas tab. The Formulas tab provides more than just the Function library, however. Let's take a quick look at the geography of the Formulas tab, shown in Figure 13.9.

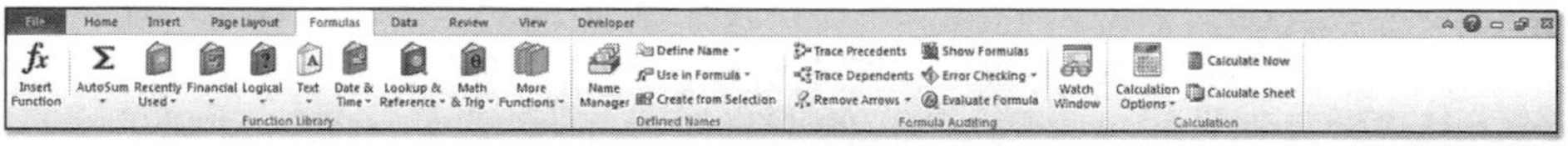

Figure 13.9
The Ribbon's
Formulas tab.

Although the Formulas tab is primarily dominated by the Function library, it also provides commands that are related to range names, auditing formulas and functions and determining when and how results should be calculated in the worksheet. The command groups on the Formulas tab are as follows:

- **Function Library:** This group provides function category commands that enable you to specify a function to be inserted into a worksheet. Commands include Insert Function, AutoSum, and Recently Used. Category commands, such as Financial, Logical, Text, and so on, enable you to access specific lists of commands by category. The More Functions command provides access to additional function categories such as Statistical, Engineering, and Cube.

- **Defined Names:** This group provides the commands for creating, accessing, and managing range names. Using range names in formulas and functions is discussed in the next section in this chapter.

  ➥ *For more about creating range names, see page 345 in Chapter 12, "Worksheet Formatting and Management."*

- **Formula Auditing:** This group provides tools that enable you to check formulas and functions for errors. It also enables you to show the formula and functions in a worksheet (rather than their results) and activate the Watch window, which is used to monitor the values in certain cells as changes are made to the values in the worksheet. Proofing your formulas and functions is discussed later in this chapter.

- **Calculation:** This group enables you to immediately calculate the results in a sheet (Excel automatically calculates results by default) and also change calculation options such as switching from automatic calculations to manual.

Using the Function library is really just a matter of selecting a particular category of functions such as Recently Used or Date & Time and then selecting a specific function from the list provided. When you place the mouse on a function listed in one of the category galleries, such as the Logical gallery, a screentip will appear providing you with a brief description of the function. For example, Figure 13.10 shows the Logical gallery with the screentip for the IF function.

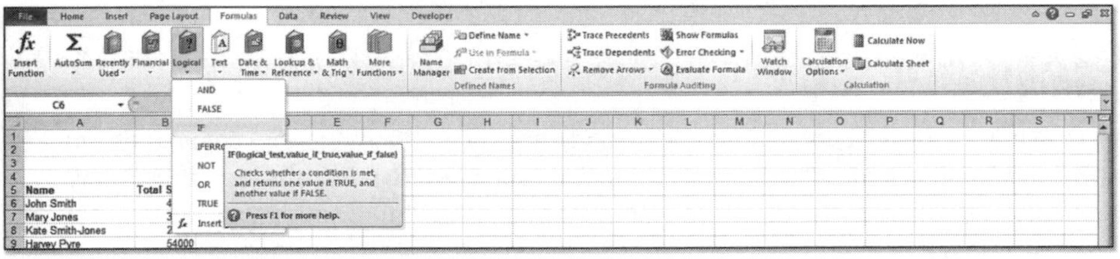

Figure 13.10
The Logical gallery and the screentip for the IF function.

After you have located the function that you want to insert into the worksheet, select the function in the gallery. The Function Arguments dialog box will open as shown in Figure 13.11.

The Function Arguments dialog box lists both the required (and in some cases optional) arguments for a function. In Figure 13.11 the IF function is shown, which requires that a logical test be provided along with a value if true and a value if false. The logical test can include cell addresses, operators, and a constant if needed. The value if true can be a calculation, a cell address, or a text string. Note that the value if false is specified as "No Commission." The text string "No Commission" will be placed in cells that do not meet the logical test (total sales greater than 27,000). When you include text strings in functions, you will need to place quotation marks around the text.

Figure 13.11
The Function Arguments dialog box for the IF function.

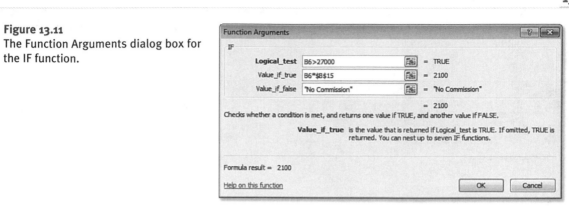

After you have provided the various arguments required by the function, you can select OK. This will close the Function Arguments dialog box; the function will be placed in the worksheet and provide you with a result.

Using Range Names in Formulas and Functions

Range names can be used in both your formulas and functions. Because range names are often descriptive in terms of the cell or cell range defined by the name, range names provide you with a more meaningful way to specify the arguments in a formula or function.

Using range names for cells that provide constants or other arguments for a formula or function can also negate the need to use absolute referencing in the formula or function. The range name is, in effect, an absolute reference of a specific cell or cell range by virtue of the range name itself. This can be particularly useful in cases when you are building formulas or functions that pull data from multiple worksheets in the same workbook. The range names help you differentiate arguments and can also cut down on the possibility of incorrectly specified cell addresses or ranges in a formula or function.

All the range names that you create can be accessed via the Use in Formula drop-down list. The Use in Formula command is housed in the Defined Names group on the Ribbon's Formulas bar. The Use in Formula drop-down list is available when you are typing a formula or function into a cell from the keyboard or inserting a function using the Function Arguments dialog box.

➡️ *For details on ways to create range names, see page 345 in Chapter 12.*

Inserting a Range Name into a Formula

You can insert range names into your formulas as you create them in a cell. Begin the formula by typing the equal sign (=); specify any cell addresses to be included in the formula by clicking on that cell or selecting the cell range. Add operators as needed to the formula. When you want to specify an argument by range name, select the Use in Formula command and select the range name from the list provided. Figure 13.12 shows a formula being created in cell C11. The Commission_ Percentage range name, which is the range name for cell F18 (the commission percentage value), will be pasted into the formula.

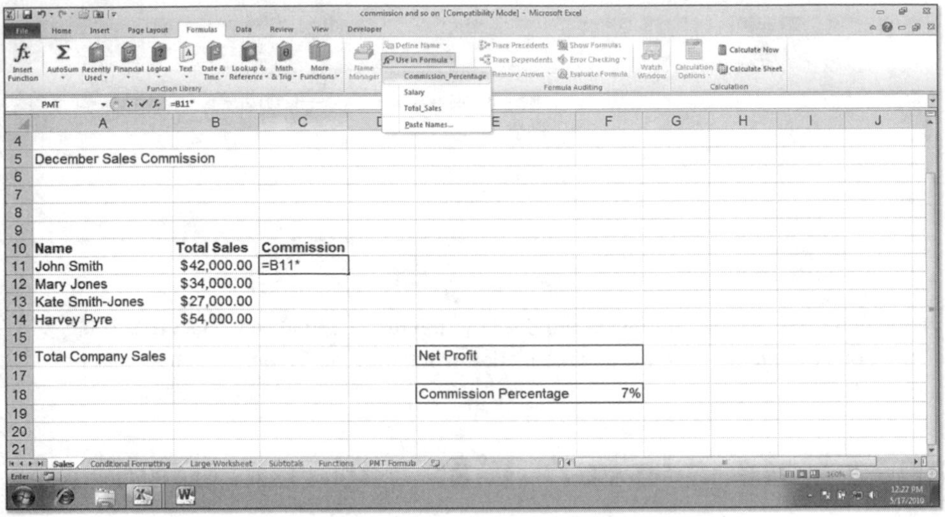

Figure 13.12
Insert range
names into a
formula.

When you have pasted the range name into the formula, you can complete the formula as needed. If you need to paste additional range names into the formula, repeat the process using the Use in Formula command. Press Enter when you have finished creating the formula.

Inserting a Range Name into a Function

You can also insert range names into the functions that you use in your worksheets. Select the function you want to use from the Function library category commands or the Insert Function dialog box. You will specify the range names to be used by the function in the appropriate argument box in the Function Arguments dialog box. Figure 13.13 shows the Function Arguments dialog box for the MAX function. The MAX function requires only one argument or range of cells to derive a result. Figure 13.13 also shows the Paste Name dialog box.

To insert a name in the Function Arguments dialog box, select the Use in Formula command and then insert the appropriate range name. If you want to view a list of the available range names, select the Use in Formula command and then select Paste Name. This will open the Paste Name dialog box as shown in Figure 13.13.

Locate the range name that you want to paste into the function in the Paste Name list and then click OK. The range name will be pasted into the Function Arguments dialog box. Enter other arguments into the Function Arguments dialog box as needed and then click OK. The function will be placed in the worksheet.

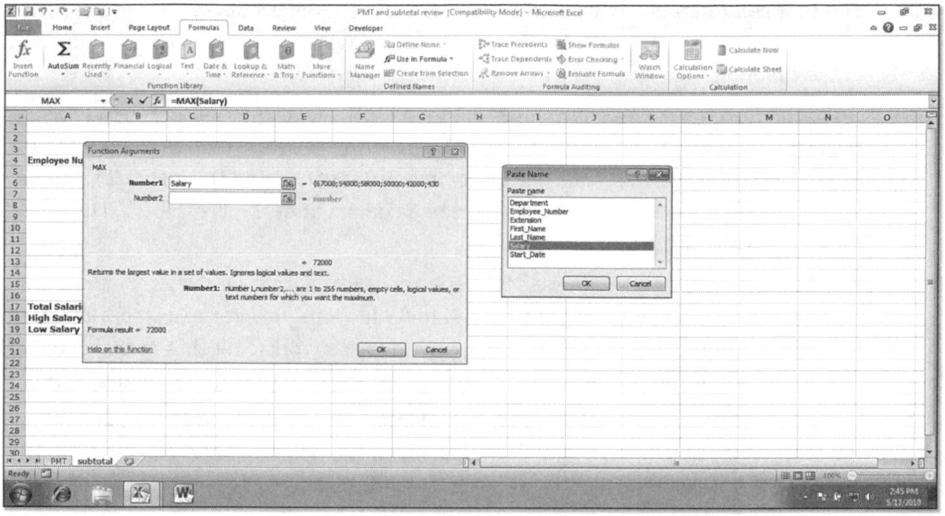

Figure 13.13
Insert range
names into
the Function
Arguments dia-
log box.

Referencing Cells or Ranges on Other Worksheets

When you are working in situations where data that spans more
than one worksheet in an Excel workbook must be summarized,
you will need to include cell references in a formula or function
that consist of cell addresses or ranges that are not on the current worksheet (the worksheet that will contain the formula or
function). For example, you might have created a different worksheet for each quarter of the year that details your sales figures
or expenditures, and you want to have a worksheet in the workbook that provides summary information for all four quarters.

The syntax for a cell reference on a worksheet that is in the
same workbook as the sheet you are working on is `'sheet
name'!cell address`. The single quotation marks are required
for the sheet name reference only if the sheet's name contains spaces.

> **tip**
>
> Range names make it very easy to
> refer to cells or ranges on a work-
> sheet in a workbook other than the
> worksheet that will contain the for-
> mula or function. Range names cre-
> ated in a workbook are, by default,
> available in all the worksheets in
> that workbook.

The best way to specify a cell address on another sheet in the same workbook, or a range of cells
in the same workbook, is to select the cell or range of cells as you create a formula or function that
includes this information as an argument. By pointing out the arguments contained on the other
worksheet or worksheets, you don't have to worry about the syntax related to how you refer to a
cell on another sheet; Excel will take care of that for you.

For example, let's say that you want to add your quarterly sales totals, each of which is on a separate quarterly worksheet in an Excel workbook. All you have to do is select the AutoSum command
to insert the SUM function in the cell. Now, you can show Excel the cells that are to be added. Click

on the worksheet tab that holds the first quarterly total. Then click on the cell containing that total. The first cell reference will be added to the function. Before navigating to the next worksheet, type a comma (,) after the first cell address entry. This will be used to separate each of the cell references in the function.

Go to the next worksheet and select the total for the next quarter and then type a comma. As you build the function, the cell references will appear on the formula bar. Repeat the process as needed, separating each cell reference with a comma. After specifying the last cell reference to be included in the function, press Enter (do not include a comma after the last entry). The SUM function will return the sum of the four quarter totals.

You can also insert cell addresses that specify cells on other worksheets into the Function Arguments dialog box, which is used to build functions. Select the appropriate argument box in the Function Arguments dialog and then navigate to the worksheet that contains the cell or cell range. Select the cell or range and it will be added to the Function Arguments dialog box.

Figure 13.14 shows a function and a formula that reference cell addresses on other worksheets in the workbook. Specifying these addresses using the point-and-click method is much easier than trying to type the cell references into the formula or function.

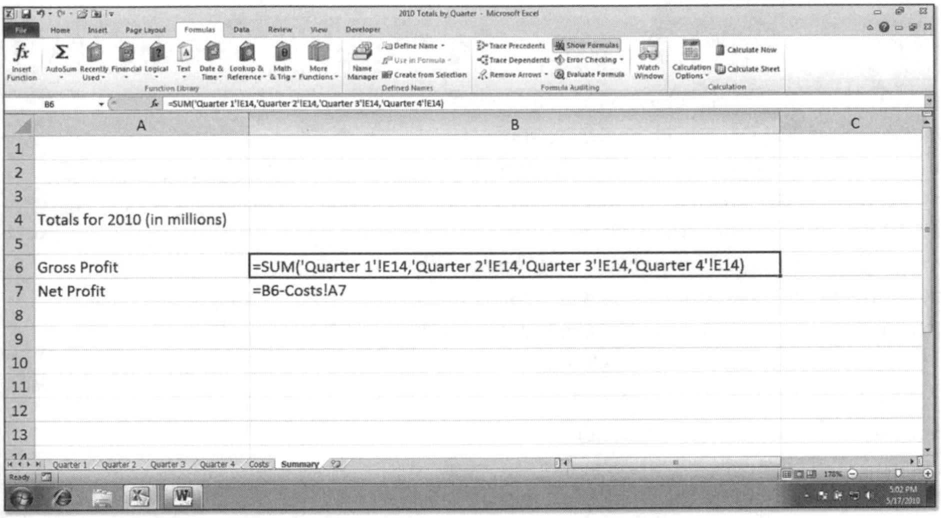

Figure 13.14
Functions and formulas can contain references to cell addresses outside the current worksheet.

You can also reference cell addresses that are in other workbooks (meaning a separate Excel file). The syntax for cell addresses referenced in other Excel workbook formulas or functions is as follows:

```
'[workbook name]sheet name'!cell address
```

tip
To view two open workbooks side by side, select the View Side By Side command on the Ribbon's View tab.

This is the syntax used when the other workbook is open. The syntax for a closed workbook is a little more involved:

```
'drive letter:\folder\[workbook name]sheet name'!cell address
```

The easiest way to reference cells or ranges in other workbooks is to open all the workbooks involved. You can then switch between the workbooks to specify the cell addresses used in a formula or function in much the same way that you can move from worksheet to worksheet in a single workbook and then select the cells to be used as operands or arguments.

Copying and Moving Formulas and Functions

Copying and moving formulas and functions is pretty straightforward as long as you remember the fact that Excel uses relative referencing by default. This makes it easy to copy a formula or function that will act on rows or columns that are similar to the row or column where you first inserted the formula or function. For example, if I have several rows of values that contain the same number of cells, I can use the SUM function to total the first row and then drag the SUM function down using the fill handle to copy it so that it totals each subsequent row in the worksheet. The cell references in the function change relative to its position because of relative referencing and so you get the correct total for each row.

You can copy formulas or functions using the fill handle (when appropriate) and you can also use the Copy and Paste commands. Remember that copying a formula or function can be tricky if you have not specified any absolute references that basically lock the address of certain values in the formula or function. If you get an error value such as #NUM, Excel's relative referencing is wreaking havoc with your copied formula or function.

➡️ *Check out more about relative and absolute referencing on page 351 in this chapter.*

Moving a formula or function can be accomplished by dragging the formula or function (actually the cell containing the formula or function) to a new location on the worksheet. You can also use Cut and Paste as needed. You will find that even if you move a formula or function, it will still return the original results, meaning it continues to reference the cell addresses originally specified when you built the formula or function.

Choosing the Right Function

Excel functions provide you with ready-made formulas for just about any type of calculation you want to undertake. Statistical, financial, and math and trig are all examples of function categories that supply functions that do calculations. Statistical functions such as COUNT and AVERAGE are designed for doing statistical analysis. Financial functions such as PMT and FV compute the monthly payment on a car or house or the return on an investment, respectively. Math and trig functions such as SINE and COS return the sine or cosine of an angle, respectively (sorry for dredging up any potential trigonometry nightmares).

There are also functions that do not actually do what we typically think of as calculations, meaning math. There are the lookup functions HLOOKUP and VLOOKUP, which are actually designed to look up information in a table and then return that value to a cell. The logical function IF provides you with the ability to set up a conditional statement and then have the IF function perform one action if the condition is true and another action if the condition is false. And I haven't even mentioned the text functions, which are designed to manipulate text strings in your worksheets.

It goes without saying (but obviously, I am going to say it), that there are a lot of different possibilities in Excel functions. Just take a tour of the possibilities by perusing through the different function categories provided in the Function library. An exhaustive listing of Excel functions and their uses are beyond the scope of this book. However, the information that follows is designed to provide you with some help in understanding some of the most often used functions in your worksheets.

Financial Functions

The financial functions provide you with the ability to do all sorts of different financial calculations; there are depreciation functions, financial functions (related to securities), and investment and annuities functions. Many of these functions are related to finance and accounting principles that require a solid knowledge base to use them correctly. However, there are other financial functions that just about anyone can take advantage of. For example, you can easily calculate monthly payments on loans, compute the present value of an investment, and determine the future value of an investment.

When you are working with financial functions, there is some basic terminology that you need to have under your belt, particularly if you want to take advantage of some of the financial functions that enable you to compute the return on an investment or the periodic payment on a loan. For example, to compute the current value of an investment, you need to know the rate, Nper, and the Pmt.

The rate (which is what Excel asks for in the Function Arguments dialog box when you are setting up a financial function such as PV or Present Value) or interest rate is straightforward. We have all at the very least had an interest-bearing checking account that is tied to a particular interest rate. The rate supplied to you for both investments and loans is typically the APR or the annual percentage rate. This means that when you provide the rate for a financial function such as PV, you need to divide the annual interest rate by the number of payments you make each year to provide the function with the interest rate per period.

Another piece of information that you need to supply to a financial function such as PV is the total number of payment periods in the investment or Nper; the Nper is based on the number of payments you make annually. So, if you make monthly payments on the investment for five years, the Nper is 60 (5*12).

The PV function also needs to know how much the payment was each period. For PV to work, the payment must be the same for each period during the life of the investment. Figure 13.15 shows a simple worksheet that uses PV to compute the value of a five-year investment.

You will find that if you understand one financial function such as PV that you can probably work your way through similar functions such as FV (future value), NPER (number of payment periods for a loan), and PMT (loan payment) because they use similar arguments such as the Nper and rate when you build the function. For example, the syntax for the PMT function is

```
=PMT(Rate, NPER, PV)
```

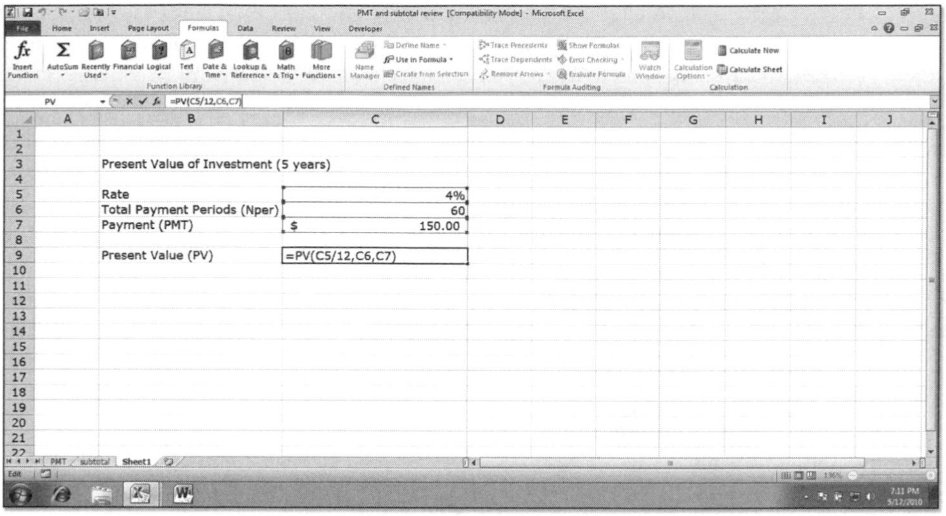

Figure 13.15
PV uses the rate, Nper, and PMT to calculate the value of an investment.

When using the PMT function and other financial functions that include the rate (interest rate), remember that it needs to be divided by the number of payments that you make in a year. For monthly payments, you would divide the rate by 12; for quarterly payments, you would divide by 4.

Logical Functions

Logical functions enable you to evaluate conditional statements. The IF function is probably the most used of the logical functions and provides you with the ability to include other formulas or functions as part of the true or false answer that is derived from your conditional statement. The syntax for the IF function is

```
=IF(logical_test, value_if_true,value_if_false)
```

The logical test can use operators such as less than (<), greater than (>), and equal to (=). The value_if_true or the value_if_false can consist of values, formulas, functions, or text strings. If you use text strings as the true or false values, the text must be enclosed within quotations marks such as "text".

In terms of providing an example to illustrate the use of the IF function, let's say that you have total sales figures for your sales personnel and you want to calculate the commission for each salesperson. You have two commission rates: a low commission rate and a high commission rate. Any sales person selling more than $28,000.00 of merchandise will receive the high commission rate. Those who fall below the $28,000.00 will receive the low commission rate. A breakdown of the IF function that I described would be as follows:

```
Logical_test: total sales > $28,000.00
Value_if_true: total sales*High Commission Rate
Value_if_false: total sales*Low Commission Rate
```

Figure 13.16 shows a sample worksheet that uses the IF function. The cells containing the low commission rate, high commission rate, and the threshold (B15, B16, and B17) have all been named using the row labels to the left. So, the range names have been used in the Function Arguments dialog box (which negates the need to use any absolute references, if you want to copy the function to other cells).

➡ *For details on ways to create range names, see page 345 in Chapter 12.*

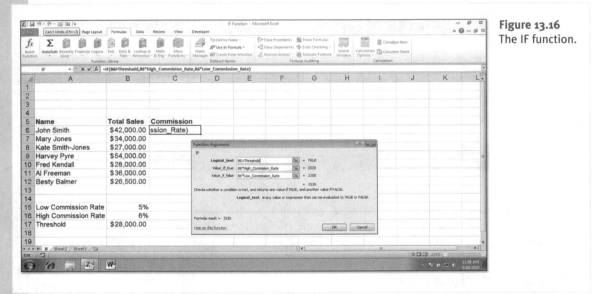

Figure 13.16
The IF function.

When you have finished entering the arguments for the IF function in the Function Arguments dialog box, select OK. You can then drag the fill handle down and copy the function to the other commission cells that are associated with each employee.

Statistical Functions

The statistical functions provide you with often-used functions such as SUM, AVERAGE, COUNT, MAX, and MIN. There are more complex statistical functions such as CORREL (correlate changes in compared variables), CHISQ.TEST (test how actual data compares to a random distribution), and FREQUENCY (used to analyze a series of values and group them in frequency ranges). So, whether you use basic statistical functions or perform fairly heavy-duty statistical analysis, the Excel Statistical functions provide you with all the analysis functions you need. Figure 13.17 shows the AVERAGE, COUNT, MAX, and MIN for a range of values.

Note that when you use the Show Formulas command on the Formulas tab to see the formulas rather than the results, the dates are changed to numerical values. The syntax is pretty consistent for the relatively simple statistical functions, such as AVERAGE and MAX, and some of the more esoteric statistical analysis functions, such as MEDIAN (computes the median for a range of cells) and STDEV.P (calculates the standard deviation of a range of values). The syntax for the AVERAGE function follows:

```
=AVERAGE(cell range)
```

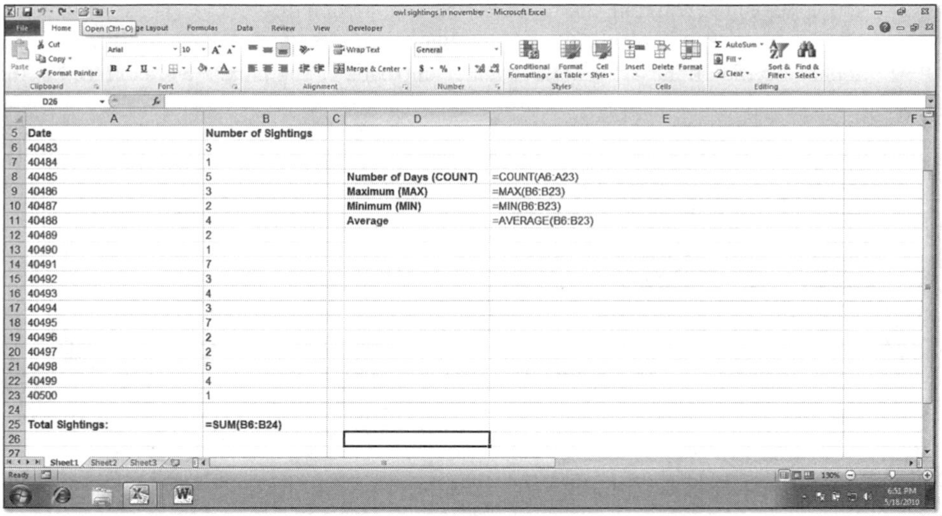

Figure 13.17
Many of the
Statistical func-
tions calculate
a result on a
range of cells.

The AVERAGE, COUNT (Count Numbers), MAX, and MIN functions can be quickly inserted into a function using the menu
provided by the AutoSum command on the Formulas tab and
the AutoSum command on the Home tab. For example, to insert
the AVERAGE function, select AutoSUM and then AVERAGE.
Use the mouse to specify the range for the function to act on
and then press Enter or click the Enter button on the formula bar.

> **tip**
>
> You can access all the Statistical
> functions by selecting the More
> Function command and then point-
> ing at Statistical.

Lookup & Reference Functions

The Lookup & Reference functions provide a number of different functions such as HYPERLINK
(enables you to specify a link to a local or remote file), TRANSPOSE (coverts a vertical range to a
horizontal range or vice versa), and the Lookup functions VLOOKUP and HLOOKUP. VLOOKUP and
HLOOKUP can be quite useful and they work in much the same fashion. They can look up values
from a table and place the value in the cell that holds the LOOKUP functions. Let's take a closer look
at VLOOKUP.

VLOOKUP does a vertical lookup and will return a value from an array (which is just another word
for a multicolumn lookup table) based on the search criterion. For example, you can create a four-
column array that contains employees' last names in the first column, the first name in the second
column, the department in the third column, and the phone extension of each employee in the in
fourth column. It is this fourth column that will serve as the information that VLOOKUP will insert
into the worksheet.

Place the VLOOKUP function in the Extension column of the sheet (directly to the right of the employee name column), the function will then automatically look up the phone extension based on the information in the employee name column. Figure 13.18 shows the VLOOKUP function that has looked up the phone extensions for each employee as the names were entered in the first column.

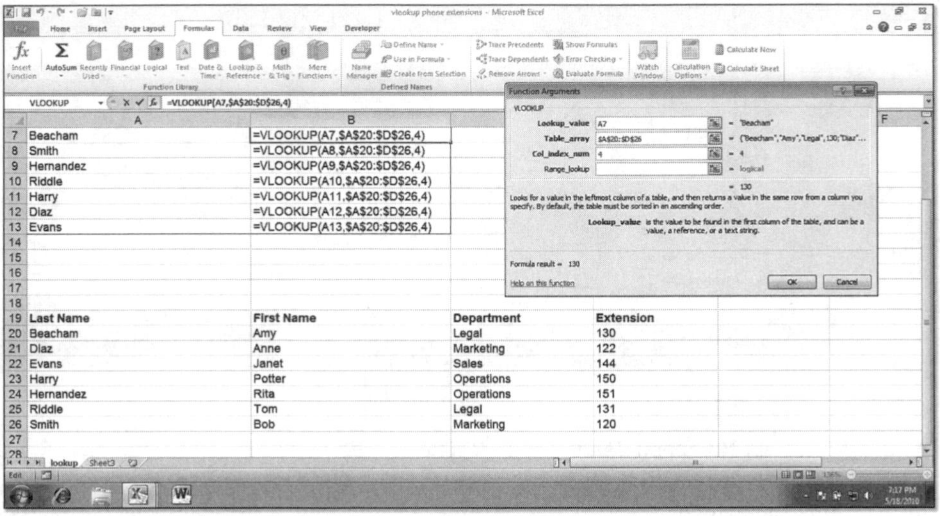

Figure 13.18
VLOOKUP can look up information in an array and insert it into a cell.

The syntax for VLOOKUP is

```
=VLOOKUP(Lookup_value,Table_array,Col_index_num
```

The Lookup_value is the cell that contains the information that the function will use to actually look up the information in the table array. So, the Table_array is the range or range name that specifies the table that contains the information. The Col_index_num tells VLOOKUP which of the columns in the table array should be placed in the cell that contains the VLOOKUP function. In Figure 13.17, the information is in column 4 of the table array.

When you create the VLOOKUP function, it makes sense to name the table array. If you don't name it, make sure that you specify the table array range as an absolute reference. That way the VLOOKUP function will always be looking in the correct place (the table array) when you copy the function to other cells. The VLOOKUP function can be accessed via the Lookup & Reference command on the Ribbon's Formulas bar. If your information is in rows rather than columns, you can use HLOOKUP, which is set up in a very similar manner to HLOOKUP.

The LOOKUP functions can do more than just return the extension numbers for employees. It can also be used for such things as price lists. You can create a worksheet using either VLOOKUP or HLOOKUP and when you enter the name of a product the price is returned by the LOOKUP function.

Date and Time Functions

Excel actually views dates and times as values. Dates are based on the starting point of January 1, 1900. So, if you enter this date in a worksheet and then format the date as a general number, the value shown will be 1.

Time is also perceived by Excel as a value. Times are seen as a fractional part of a day. For example, 12 PM is equivalent to 0.5; whereas 9 AM would be 0.375.

You don't typically have to convert dates or times to their actual value equivalents. The fact that dates and times are actually seen as numerical values means that you can include dates and times in your formulas and functions. In terms of date and time functions, Excel provides you with functions that enable you to quickly place the date and/or time into your worksheet or to calculate values related to date or time entries. For example, the NETWORKDAYS function can return the number of work days between two dates as long as you also supply the number of holidays that fall between the two dates. The NETWORKDAYS function uses the syntax:

```
=NETWORKDAYS(Start_date, End_date, Holidays)
```

The start and end dates are the beginning and end date for the time span. The holidays are also specific dates of when the holidays actually fall. The holidays (if there are multiple) can be entered as a range into the function. The NETWORKDAYS function would be an excellent way to determine how many working days there are during a particular project cycle.

The date and time functions are accessed via the gallery provided by the Date & Time command on the Formulas tab. Two simple-to-use functions that place the current date into a worksheet are NOW and TODAY. NOW enters the current date and the time. The TODAY function enters the current date only.

These two functions are dynamic and so they change to the current date and/or time when you open the workbook. If you want a static date on a worksheet that will serve as a timestamp of when you started the worksheet, enter the date and/or time manually.

Text Functions

You might find it odd that Excel also provides a number of functions designed to work with cells containing text entries or labels. As we discussed at the outset of the Excel section of this book, Excel knows when you have entered text in cells and it knows when you enter numbers—values— into cells. It automatically left aligns text and right aligns values because it knows which is which. The text functions provided by Excel enable you to split text entries in cells, combine text entries, manipulate the case of text, and convert numbers to text.

An easy way to join or concatenate text from multiple cells is to set up a simple formula that uses the ampersand (&) as the operator in the formula. For example, you could join the first name and last name of your employees into a single cell. The syntax for concatenation using the ampersand is

```
cell address&" "&cell address
```

Figure 13.19 shows the basic concatenation formula. The first name and last name of each employee was combined using the formula.

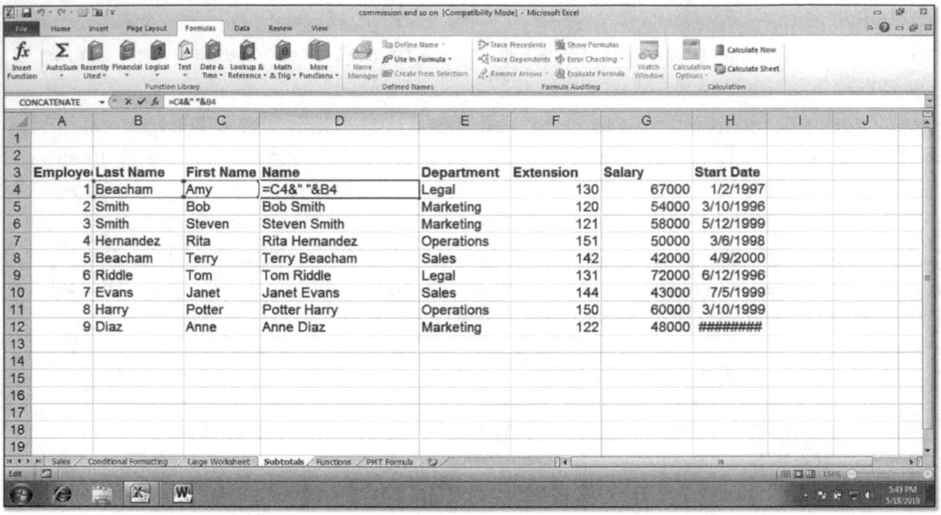

Figure 13.19
Create a simple formula to combine text entries into a cell.

The quotation marks are used in the formula to place a space (which is placed between the quotation marks) between the contents from the two different cells. As with any formula, after you create the formula in a cell, you can copy it to other cells as needed; in Figure 13.18, the formula was written in cell D4 and then copied to the other cells in column D.

In cases where you want to join a number of cells' text into one cell, you can use the CONCATENATE function. You can join the text from 255 different text strings into a single text string (in a single cell) using this function. The syntax for the CONCATENATE function is

```
= CONCATENATE (text1, text2, ...text255).
```

The cell addresses used by the CONCATENATE function are listed in the text boxes provided in its Function Arguments dialog box. Click in an argument box (such as Text1) and then click on the cell you want to reference. Then repeat this process placing the text string cell addresses in subsequent argument boxes. As already mentioned, you can specify 255 cell addresses.

Other useful text functions relate to problems you might have with information that you import into Excel, such as imported text that contains extra spaces or unprintable characters. The TRIM function can be used to remove extra spaces. If you want to remove any unprintable characters from imported text, use the CLEAN function. The TRIM and CLEAN function will actually make a copy of the text contained in the cell or cell ranges specified in the function (TRIM or CLEAN). So, you actually end

> **tip**
> You can actually type text in the argument boxes in the CONCATENATE function's Function Arguments dialog box. This enables you to add a text string to the text concatenated by the function that does not actually exist in a cell in the worksheet. This text must be placed between quotation marks.

up with multiple copies of the text string in your worksheet (the before and after). You can't delete the original text with too many spaces (or in the case of the CLEAN function, the unprintable characters) because the function will no longer have the original text to reference and provide you with the result.

You can actually convert the result of either the TRIM or CLEAN function to a value using Copy and Paste and then discard the original text that was imported. This will leave you with the trimmed or cleaned result.

Select the cell containing the TRIM or CLEAN function and then click Copy in the Clipboard group. Then select Paste. In the Paste gallery, select the Values option. Now when you select the cell or cells that originally contained the TRIM or CLEAN function, you will find that the function has been converted to a text string. You can go ahead and delete the original, imported text.

Other Function Categories

Excel also contains other function categories than those that we have discussed thus far. As already mentioned, there are more than 300 functions available in Excel. Many of the function categories relate to specific disciplines such as accounting, finance, statistical analysis, and engineering. When you select the More Functions command, several function categories are listed, such as Statistical, Engineering, and so on. We have already discussed the statistical functions. The list that follows provides a description of the other function categories found in the More Functions gallery:

- **Math & Trig:** This group provides a combination of useful mathematical and trigonometric functions. Functions such as COS (cosine), SIN (sine), and TAN (tangent) are used in computations related to a right-angled triangle. Another useful math function is ROUND, which enables you to specify the number of decimal places that a range of cell values should be rounded to. There are also the EVEN and ODD functions, which can be used to round values to even or odd numbers, respectively.

- **Engineering:** Excel provides a number of functions that are useful for various engineering-related applications. For example, there is CONVERT, which converts measurements from one system to another (such as miles to kilometers). Another conversion function provided in this category is the BIN2HEX function, which can be used to convert binary numbers to hexadecimal.

- **Cube:** The cube functions (all the cube functions are new to Excel 2010) are used to interact with external data that is derived from an analysis services cube. The data is actually served up from a Microsoft SQL Server that provides the analysis services.

- **Information:** These functions enable you to derive information concerning a cell, such as the content or formatting of a cell. For example, the ISERR function will return the statement TRUE if an error exists in a cell (meaning an incorrectly designed formula or function) or FALSE if there is no error in a cell. ISBLANK is similar in that it returns either TRUE or FALSE based on whether or not a cell is blank.

- **Compatibility:** This category consists of functions that were native to Excel 2007 and have been updated or replaced in Excel 2010. Use the compatibility functions only in cases where you will share your workbooks with coworkers or colleagues who still use Excel 2007.

Remember, you are not required to use every type of function provided by Excel. Make sure that you test functions that are new to you. Use sample data that enables you to easily determine whether you are getting the appropriate result when you plug the data into the function.

Proofing Your Formulas and Functions

Just because a formula or function returns a value, it doesn't necessarily mean that it's correct. Making sure that your formulas and functions are providing the correct results in your worksheets is incredibly fundamental; yet many Excel users figure that if Excel came up with that answer it has to be right. Fortunately, Excel provides tools that can help you proof your formulas and functions.

There can be different causes for formulas or functions to return an incorrect value. For example, you might have made a syntax error in actually creating the formula or function. You might not have included the appropriate operators for a formula or you did not provide a function's arguments in the correct order. This is why it makes sense to build functions using the Functions Argument dialog box rather than trying to type a function into a cell.

Errors can also result from incorrect cell references. You have the syntax for the formula or the function correct, but you did not reference the correct cells or range of cells.

Although Excel provides error messages in cases where a formula or function cannot calculate a return because of an obvious reason, the error messages will not save you when a formula or function contains an error that still allows it to return an answer—albeit an incorrect answer.

Excel provides a number of different error messages that can help you proof a problem formula or function. Other tools, such as the ability to view formulas in the worksheet and the fact you can also trace the cells related to a particular problem formula or function, can also help you fix issues related to calculations.

Common Error Messages

Excel seems to have an endless supply of error messages and it does have your back when a formula or function contains an egregious error. Excel will actually flag the problem formula or function with a specific error message. Some of the most common error messages are provided in Table 13.3.

Table 13.3   Common Error Messages

Error Message	Description
#REF	A cell referenced in the formula or function cannot be found. This can be the result of an incorrect range name or specifying a range that no longer exists.
#NAME?	Excel does not recognize text included in a formula or function such as a range name. This can be a syntax error (an incorrectly spelled function name) or a problem with a range name specified in the function.
#DIV/0!	The formula or functioning is attempting to divide by 0. This is typically due to an incorrectly referenced cell in the formula or function (a cell that does not contain a value).

Error Message	Description
#VALUE	An incorrect argument is present in the formula or function. This can be caused by referring to both text and value entries in the same formula or function. You can't add words to numbers.

These errors can often be easily corrected by carefully examining your formula or function. In the case of the #NAME? function, check to see whether you have misspelled the function name or have missing parentheses in a function. The #DIV/0! error can occur if you have copied a formula or function and have not taken into account cell referencing in the formula or function. You might have to use an absolute reference so that the cell you are dividing by is always referenced in the formula or function.

When an error message appears in a cell, a smart tag is provided for the error. When you select the smart tag, the menu provided will identify the error type and also provide you with access to help on the error. Other options provided enable you to view the calculation steps for the formula or function and an option to edit the function in the formula bar.

An error message that you want to definitely pay attention to is the Circular Reference Warning. When you attempt to create a formula or function that includes the formula or function within the range of cells that the formula or function will act on, you have a circular reference. Figure 13.20 shows the Circular Reference Warning dialog box.

Figure 13.20
The Circular Reference Warning dialog box.

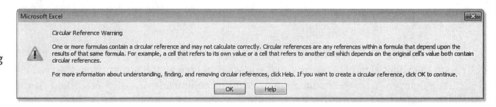

If you suspect that circular references are contained in workbooks that have been created by coworkers or colleagues, you can check them using the Circular References command in the Error Checking gallery. Any circular references in the worksheet will be listed. The Circular References check is just one of the possibilities provided by the Formula Auditing command group found on the Ribbon's Formulas tab. Let's look at some of the other tools.

Using the Auditing Tools

One of the easiest auditing tools to use is the Show Formulas Command. It shows you all the formulas and functions in a worksheet rather than their results. This enables you to peruse your formulas and functions for any possible issues that need to be addressed but were not of a nature that resulted in an error message being placed in the cell where the formula or function resides.

tip

You can configure the Error Checking settings such as background error checking and the error-checking rules that are enabled in the Excel Options window. Select File and then click Options in the Backstage. Select Formulas to view the error-checking settings.

Two extremely useful formula auditing commands are Trace Precedents and Trace Dependents. To display the cells that are referenced by a particular formula or function—the precedents—select a formula or function in the worksheet and then select the Trace Precedents command. Blue arrows will be drawn from the precedents for the currently selected function or formula as shown in Figure 13.21.

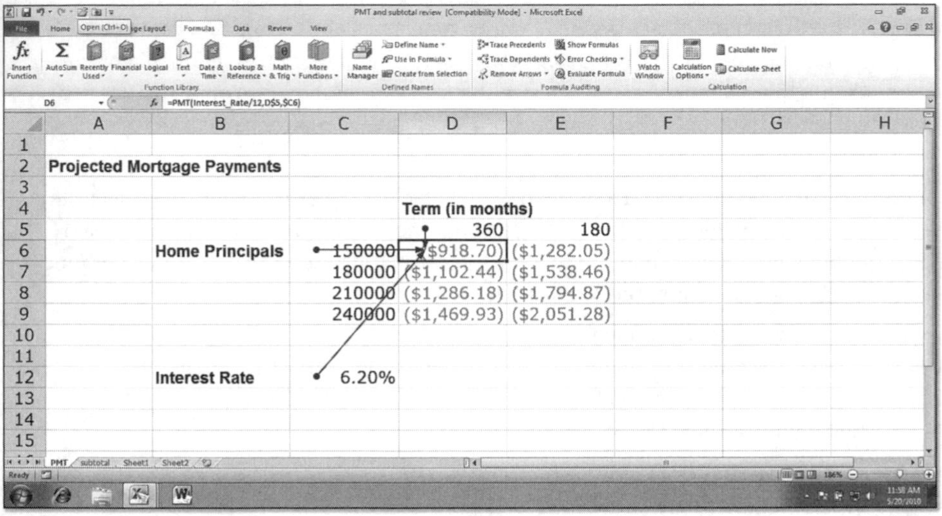

Figure 13.21 Trace precedents for a formula or function.

You can repeat the command as needed to view the precedents for other formulas or functions on the sheet simultaneously. When you want to remove the arrows from the worksheet, select the Remove Arrows command or one of its subcommands: Remove Precedent Arrows or Remove Dependent Arrows.

You can also trace the dependents for a particular value or range of cells. Select the cell or range of cells and then select the Trace Dependents command. Trace arrows will be drawn from the cell or cell range to any formulas or functions that depend on that value or values.

When an error message is shown in a cell, you can use the Trace Error command to show the cells or cell range involved in the bad formula or function. Select the cell containing the error message and select the Error Checking drop-down arrow; select Trace Error and the precedents for the cell will be shown.

Another very useful auditing command is the Error Checking command. It can be used when a cell contains an error message. The command opens the Error Checking dialog box as shown in Figure 13.22.

The Error Checking dialog box enables you to access help in the Excel Help window related to the type of error present in the cell. It also enables you to show the calculation steps and evaluate the formula. When you select Show Calculation Steps, the Evaluate Formula dialog box will open. Select Evaluate to begin evaluating the formula or function. You can also step in and out on the different portions of the formula or function until you find the portion of the formula or function that is causing the error.

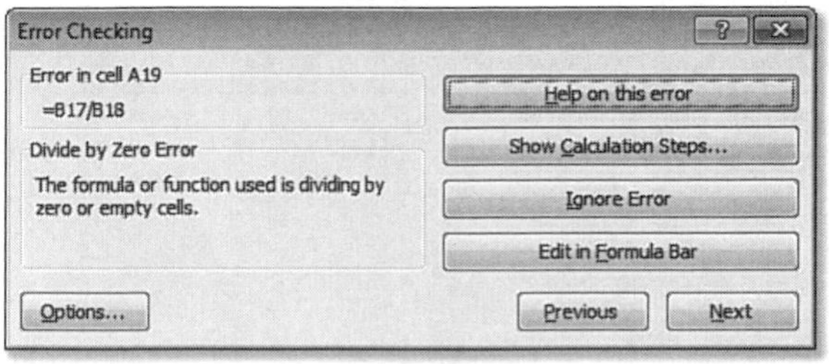

Figure 13.22
The Error Checking dialog box.

The Error Checking dialog box can also act as a sort of spell checker for errors. After you have dealt with one error in a worksheet, you can select Next in the Error Checking dialog box and proceed to the next error found in the sheet. After you have repaired that error (perhaps by viewing the calculation steps), you can then proceed to the next error and so on until you have dealt with any and all cells in the worksheet that contain errors.

Using the Watch Window

Although it is not an auditing tool per se, the Watch window can be a useful tool in monitoring certain cells in a worksheet in terms of how the entering of worksheet data or the editing of worksheet data affects those cells. The Watch window can be particularly useful in cases where you have formulas or functions that are dependent on cell addresses or ranges that span multiple worksheets in a workbook. For example, you might have a summary worksheet that summarizes data from other worksheets in the workbook that provide detailed information for each quarter of your fiscal year.

> 💡 **tip**
>
> You might want to name cells that you plan on watching in the Watch window. A descriptive range name will make it easier to differentiate from multiple cell references that you have placed in the Watch Window.

To open the Watch window, select the Watch Window command in the Formula Auditing group. Figure 13.23 shows the Watch window. The Watch window floats on top of your worksheets and remains in view even when you switch worksheets in a workbook. In fact the Watch window will also be visible even when you switch to a different Excel workbook. So, the Watch window is also very useful in cases where you have cells in other workbooks that provide precedents to the cell that you have included in the Watch window.

To add a cell to the Watch window, navigate to the sheet that contains the cell or a cell range and then select Add Watch in the Watch window. The Add Watch dialog box will open. Select the cell or cell range and the reference will be added to the Add Watch dialog box. When you click Add and return to the Watch window, the cell reference will be listed. It supplies the book, sheet, name, cell, and the current value of the cell as well as any formula or functions that reside in the cell. You can add additional cells to the Watch window as needed.

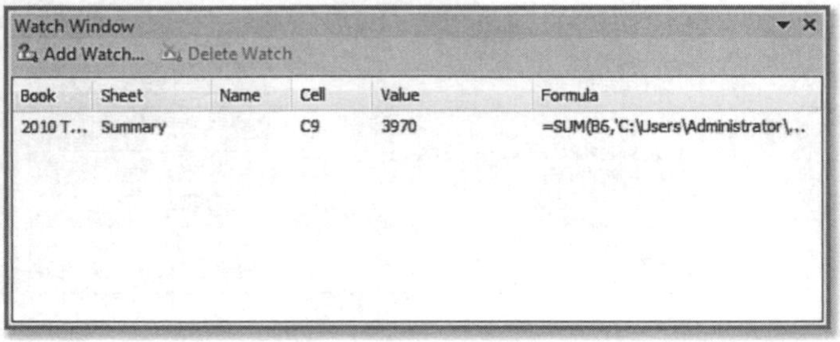

Figure 13.23
Keep an eye on specific workbook cells in the Watch window.

Any changes that you make to cells that are precedents for the cell or cells you are watching in the Watch window will be reflected in the Watch window. For example, if you entered data on a worksheet for first quarter sales and you are watching the yearly total SUM function on a summary sheet, the cell's value in the Watch window will reflect any data additions or changes.

To remove references from the Watch window, select a listed reference and then click the Delete Watch command. When you are finished using the Watch window, click its Close button. Even if you close the Watch window, it will retain the list of cell addresses that you have added to it.

ENHANCING WORKSHEETS WITH CHARTS

There is little doubt that Excel's incredible capabilities provide you with the tools to create complex and meaningful worksheets that serve all sorts of purposes from basic accounting to statistical analysis to complete mathematical mania. Excel has evolved far beyond the early spreadsheet programs that were first available for the personal computer. However, Excel still uses the very same classic spreadsheet geography of columns and rows of numbers used by these earlier programs. All those cells containing values, labels, formulas, and functions can be quite difficult for many people to readily understand. That is where charts come in. Charts provide you with the ability to take a visual snapshot of worksheet data and represent it as a graphic. Charts can greatly enhance the understanding of worksheet data and how the data is related.

In this chapter, we look at how to create charts in Excel. We also discuss what type of charts to use in particular situations and how you can modify and manipulate charts and chart elements. We also look at the new sparklines feature, which enables you to place inline mini-charts into the cells of a worksheet.

Understanding Excel Charts

Excel charts provide a pictorial representation of worksheet data. Charts not only provide a way for people to better grasp trends or relationships in the worksheet data but they can also add visual impact to your Excel worksheets. Charts are objects (just like an image or a SmartArt graphic) that can be included anywhere on a worksheet. Charts can also be created so that they reside on their own worksheet in a workbook. This is particularly useful for charts that contain a lot of detail and don't fit particularly well on a large worksheet that contains the data used to create the chart.

Chart Terminology

Working with charts is pretty straightforward. It does not hurt, however, to have a handle on some of the terminology you will run across when creating charts; a list of basic chart terms follows:

- **Chart Area:** The area inside the object frame that contains the chart, the axes, and the data point labels, the legend, the chart title, and other chart elements.

- **Plot Area:** The actual area of the chart between the chart axes. This is where the data points are plotted.

- **Data Series:** Related data points are referred to as a data series. A data series typically corresponds to a particular row or column of values in your worksheet (depending on how you have arranged your data in the worksheet). Each data series in a chart will have its own pattern or color. Single-line charts or pie charts are examples of charts that have only one data series. In bar charts, particularly in cases where you are comparing entities over time—such as the performance of sales regions over time—multiple data series will be present on the chart (one series for each region).

- **Categories:** Categories reflect the number of elements in a series. For example, on a chart that charts regional sales totals, the x-axis will consist of the names of the regions, which are the categories for the chart.

- **Axis:** A two-dimensional chart, such as a line chart, has an x-axis (horizontal) and a y-axis (vertical). The x-axis contains the data series and categories in the chart. If you have more than one category, the x-axis often contains labels that define what each category represents. The y-axis reflects the values of the bars, lines, or plot points. In a three-dimensional chart, the z-axis represents the vertical plane, and the x-axis (distance) and y-axis (width) represent the two sides on the floor of the chart.

- **Legend:** The legend provides the key for how color coding or patterns have been used to differentiate the different elements in a data series on the chart. For example, a pie chart will use a different color to show the various categories that appear as parts of the pie.

- **Data Labels:** Labels that appear on the chart denoting the value of the data points used to create the chart.

- **Gridlines:** Gridlines help visualize the actual value of a particular data point on the chart. Gridlines are typically used along the y-axis (where the value data points originate), but you can also include gridlines for the x-axis, which can be useful in situations where you have created a combination chart.

- **Background:** The background consists of the space behind and below the chart area. For example, the chart wall is the area directly behind the plot area and any gridlines shown on the chart. The chart floor of the chart is the bottommost part of the chart area.

Figure 14.1 shows a line chart embedded in a worksheet. This line chart contains one data series: the measured lake level for each month of the year. The x-axis consists of the labels associated with the data points; in this case, the months of the year, January through December. The y-axis consists of the scale for the values represented by the chart; in this case, a scale in feet. The x-axis lists the categories for the chart—each month is a specific category.

Figure 14.1
A line chart.

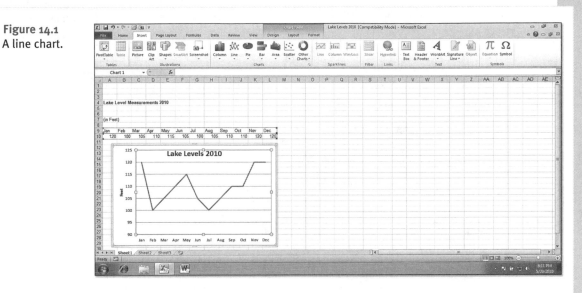

Notice that when a chart is selected in a worksheet (as it is in Figure 14.1), the contextual Chart Tools appear on the Ribbon and consist of Design, Layout, and Format tabs. Each of these tabs provides you with control over different aspects of a chart. We will be exploring the specific commands and tools provided by the Chart Tools as the chapter progresses.

Charts can also be created that have multiple data series. Figure 14.2 shows a bar chart that has four data series—one data series for each of the sales region's monthly totals. The chart in Figure 14.2 also includes a legend that shows the color coding for the different data series (each region's sales) displayed on the chart.

You can also build combination charts in Excel so that you can visualize the data series in a worksheet in a unique way that enables you to emphasize or differentiate different sets of data points. Figure 14.3 shows a combination chart that includes both a line chart and a column chart.

The columns in the chart show the sales for four regions—East, West, South, and North—over a three-month period (January through March). Total sales is also included in the chart and has been formatted as a line chart that shows the growth of overall sales during the three-month period. Combination charts provide you with the ability to have your chart emphasize more than one set of data points by combining two different chart types.

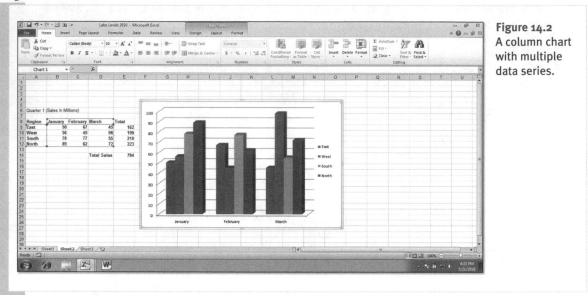

Figure 14.2
A column chart with multiple data series.

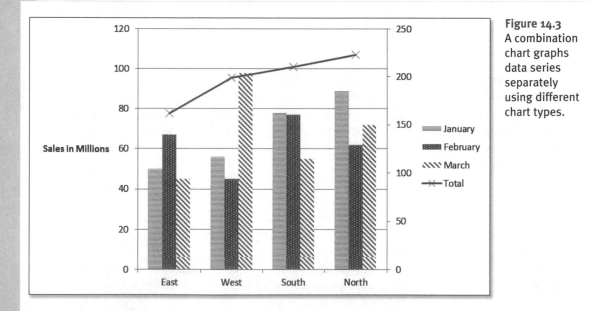

Figure 14.3
A combination chart graphs data series separately using different chart types.

Using Different Chart Types

Excel provides you with a number of different chart types. It is important that you develop an understanding of the purpose of each chart type and then use the appropriate chart type when charting your data. Using a chart type that isn't designed for your purpose won't really enhance anyone's understanding of the worksheet data and might actually misrepresent what is actually going on with the data.

For example, a line chart would do an excellent job of showing the change over time of the sales figures for a particular product or company. However, place that same data in a bar chart and the changes are less marked. Finally, throw that same data into a pie chart, which is completely wrong for showing change over time, and all of a sudden the sales figures (even poor sales figures) look relatively the same. This is not to say that people deliberately choose the wrong chart type to hide the true nature of worksheet data and any associated trends; however, Excel offers so many different chart types that it is easy to inadvertently select the wrong type of chart for a particular situation. Let's look at the different chart types that Excel provides.

Column Chart/Bar Chart

The column/bar chart is probably one of the most commonly used business chart types. These types of charts work very well in showing how different data series or groups of data points compare. Figure 14.4 shows a bar chart that displays the total sales for each salesperson listed in the worksheet.

Figure 14.4
A bar chart comparing total sales.

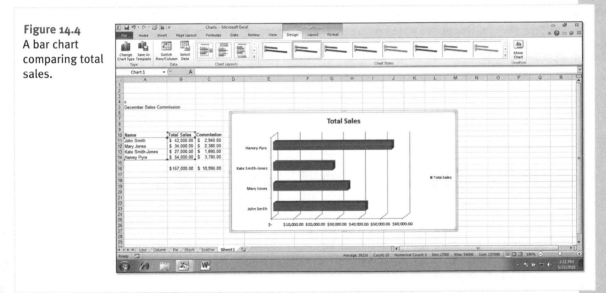

Column and bar charts make it relatively easy to quickly discern the highs and lows in terms of the data points charted. Column or bar charts are often used to show the relative success of salespeople or franchise locations, or can even be used to compare the number of home runs hit during a season by a group of baseball players. If you have totals you want to compare, column and bar charts are the route to go. Obviously, the tallest column in a column chart shows the highest data point; in a column chart, it will be the longest horizontal bar.

Line Chart

Line charts are perfect for showing change over time. Line charts are straightforward two-axis charts, with numerical values plotted on the y-axis in relation to labels provided on the x-axis that describe what is actually being measured. Line charts are often used to depict business growth or business decline.

For example, you might plot the monthly profits of your small company over the past 12 months. The y-axis would consist of the net profits for each month and the x-axis would consist of the months of the year, January through December. Line charts work very well when you want to discern the highs and lows in productivity or value. Line charts are not particularly good if you want to compare the relative success of one data series against another data series. Figure 14.5 shows a line chart that provides a separate line for each region's sales data points from January, February, and March.

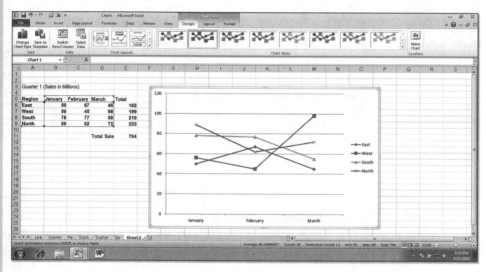

Figure 14.5
A line chart depicting different sets of data points.

Although the line chart does make it easy to track the changes over time for each of the regions in terms of their sales figures for the January through March timeframe, the lines do not provide a good way to compare the overall performance of each region. This would be accomplished better by using a column/bar chart.

Pie Chart

Pie charts enable you to show how the various parts relate to the whole. For example, you might be trying to keep track of your monthly expenses. A pie chart would enable you to visually represent the relative size of each of your monthly expenses as compared to your total expenses.

Pie charts are great for showing how costs, sales, or other data series for a group of categories relate to each other. Figure 14.6 shows a pie chart that has a single data series: the individual values for different monthly expense categories.

Figure 14.6
Pie charts show
how the parts
relate to the
whole.

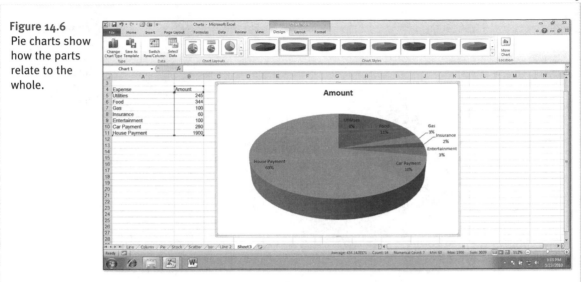

Pie charts can actually support only one data series and so differ from other chart types such as bar charts and line charts, which can show multiple data series on the same chart. If you need to show multiple data series in a pie chart–like format, you can use a doughnut chart.

In the case of the pie chart shown here, it is clear that the largest monthly expense is the house payment and expenses for items such as utilities, food, and car payment are fairly close in terms of their percentage of total expenses. Pie charts showing percentages make it even easier to determine the percentage of a particular item plotted on the chart in reference to the whole (meaning 100%).

Area Chart

Area charts enable you to show trends using cumulative totals over time. These types of charts emphasize the general direction of the data series up or down and show the magnitude of change. Area charts are somewhat similar to line charts; however, area charts show not only trends over time, but can also show how data series shown in the chart relate to the whole and each other. This enables you to view trends related to each data series and to compare data series. Figure 14.7 shows an area chart that tracks sales from different regions over 12 months of the year (January through December).

The chart uses the 3-D area chart type, which uses three axes, x, y, and z, to provide the vertical, horizontal, and depth aspects for the chart. The 3-D area chart shows the trends for the sales in each region and provides for a comparison of the regions. The 3D layout, however, can be problematic if you have a set of data points that are much smaller or larger than the other data sets depicted in the chart. You might want to go with a line chart that depicts each data series using a separate line rather than trying to use the area chart.

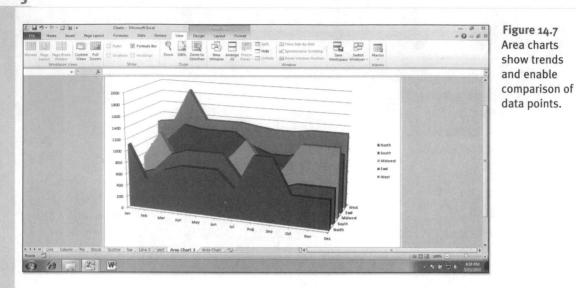

Figure 14.7
Area charts show trends and enable comparison of data points.

X Y (Scatter) Chart

Scatter charts enable you to determine whether the data points in a series fall on the chart in a pattern called a cluster. Scatter charts are used to see whether there is a correlation between values. One set of values is plotted on the x-axis and the other set of values is plotted along the y-axis. Figure 14.8 shows a scatter chart.

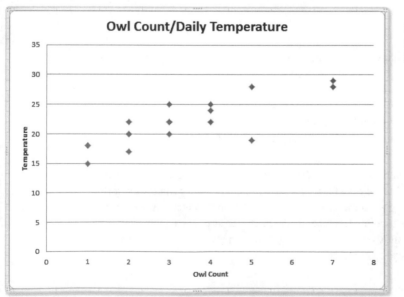

Figure 14.8
Scatter charts enable you to see the relationship between associated data series.

The scatter chart in Figure 14.8 plots owl count against the temperature taken each day the count was conducted. Let's say you want to see whether there is a correlation between owl activity and temperature. You could plot the daily count versus the daily temperature.

Because scatter charts are meant to determine the correlation between two different sets of values, you typically will need a large number of data points to actually get a discernable pattern on the chart. Remember that both the x-axis and y-axis on a scatter chart consist of values. If you have a situation where only one set of data is values, you should use a line chart.

> **note**
>
> Scatter charts use Cartesian coordinates (two different sets of values) to create the points that appear in the chart plane. René Descartes came up with the Cartesian coordinate system in the seventeenth century. Remember this the next time you get a Descartes question during trivia night.

Stock Chart

Stock charts (also known as box plots, box and whiskers plots, or candlestick plots) are particularly useful when you are tracking a particular stock that is in your stock portfolio or that you are considering making part of your portfolio. Stock charts can be created using three different data series, four different data series, or five different data series—all of which are related to the price of the stock. For example, the three data series stock chart uses the daily high, low, and close value of the stock. The four data series stock chart uses the open, high, low, and close price for the stock.

> **note**
>
> Finding stock information, such as the daily open, high, low, and close value of a particular stock on the Web is pretty easy. You can use the Microsoft MoneyCentral website, Yahoo! Finance, or Google Finance.

Figure 14.9 shows a stock chart tracking Microsoft stock from April 21 to May 21, 2010. Stock charts not only show you the range of a stock's price on a particular day, but the chart can also show trends over the timeframe that you have charted.

Figure 14.9
Stock charts provide trends while tracking multiple fluctuating data points.

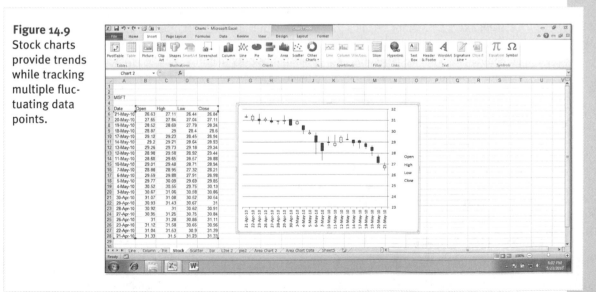

The stock chart can be used for data types other than stock prices. You can use it in any situation where you have a particular data point that will fluctuate during a specific timeframe. For example, you might want to chart data related to the daily change in water temperature of a vernal pool that you are using for a salamander population study.

Other Chart Types

We have already looked at the stock chart provided in the Other Charts command's drop-down gallery. There are four other chart types provided in this gallery. The list that follows provides a brief description of each chart type:

- **Surface Chart:** This type of chart is designed to group related values by color or pattern. A 3D surface chart will look a lot like a relief or topographic map and can be used to determine how one variable can be affected by two other variables. Surface charts are created using an x-axis data series, a y axis-data series, and a z-axis data series. There must also be a z-axis value for each x-axis and y-axis pair. So, basically, the surface chart shows how the z-axis data is affected by two variables: the x-axis data and the y-axis data.

- **Doughnut Chart:** This chart type is designed to show how the parts compare to the whole, much like a pie chart. A doughnut chart, however, can include more than one data series, which a pie chart cannot. You can use a doughnut to compare the sales of different regions over a specific timeframe or show your monthly expenses for more than one month for comparison.

- **Bubble Chart:** This chart type is similar to a scatter chart. However, a scatter chart can use only two sets of variables (one for the x-axis and one for y-axis); a bubble chart can work with three sets of values. The third value set will determine the size of the bubbles. So, the bubble chart will show related x and y data in clusters and show the relative value of each z-axis data point as a gradation of bubble sizes.

- **Radar Chart:** This chart type can plot multiple data sets. The values from each category are plotted along a separate axis line that radiates out from the chart's center point. The scale for each data set to be included on the chart must be the same. Radar charts can be used to show business performance measurements or compare safety features on different automobiles. These charts work best with a limited number of categories so that each data set is discernable on the chart.

Although each chart type has a somewhat specific purpose and requires that the appropriate data be supplied in your Excel worksheet, creating charts in Excel is straightforward. After you have created a particular chart type, the commands and tools available for changing the design, layout, and formatting of the chart and chart elements are a consistent proposition, no matter what chart type you are working with. Let's look at how to create a chart and then look at the options Excel provides for modifying the chart and chart elements.

Creating Charts

Charts reflect the data in a worksheet and so you need to make sure that the values and labels in the worksheet provide the information in a way that allows for charting. You should arrange the worksheet data in a consistent manner, either horizontally in rows or vertically in columns. Also avoid empty cells, rows, or columns within the areas of the worksheet that will serve as the data series for your chart or charts.

Although the actual values provide the numerical information for the chart, worksheet labels will provide the categories and information used as axis titles and legend information. It makes sense to try and make row and column headings, meaning labels, that are descriptive yet short enough to fit well on the chart as a chart element.

Another thing that you should keep in mind when building a worksheet that will also include a chart is to place the data on the sheet so that the sheet can also easily accommodate an inserted chart below or to the right of the data range. This enables you to easily view or print the worksheet data and the accompanying chart. Charts with a large amount of detail and those derived from large worksheets would probably best be created on their own worksheet.

Excel 2010 provides various commands for inserting the different chart types in the Charts group on the Ribbon's Insert tab. Figure 14.10 shows the Insert tab and the Charts group with the Pie command selected.

Figure 14.10
Create charts using the commands on the Insert tab.

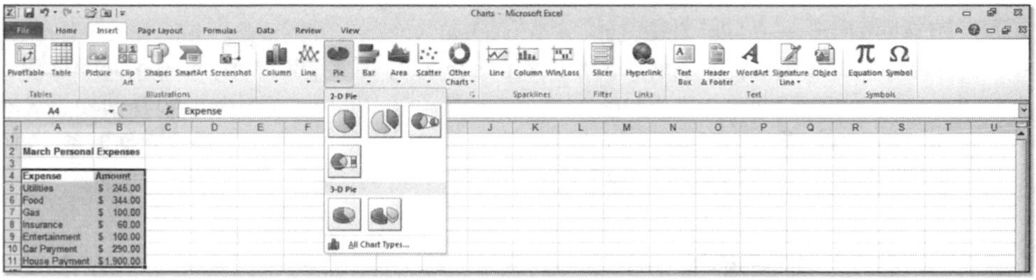

Each of the specific chart category commands, such as Column, Line, or Pie, offers a selection of different chart subtypes. Depending on the chart type, you will have a choice between a number of 2D and 3D subtypes. Chart types not provided a category command in the Charts group, such as the Stock, Surface, and Doughnut charts, can be accessed via the Other Charts command.

If you prefer to be able to view all the chart types and their associated chart subtypes when creating a new chart, you can open the Insert Chart dialog box. Figure 14.11 shows the Insert Chart dialog box. You can open the Insert Chart dialog box by selecting All Chart Types on the Other Charts command's gallery (or All Chart Types on the very bottom of any of the other chart galleries, such as the Column or Line gallery). You can also open the Insert Chart dialog box by clicking the dialog box launcher in the Charts group.

A chart type list enables you to select a particular type of chart in the dialog box. This will select the first subtype for that chart with other subtypes also shown in the subtype gallery provided. You can view the name of a particular subtype in the Insert Chart dialog box by placing the mouse on that subtype.

> **tip**
>
> When you place the mouse on a particular chart type in any of the chart galleries provided by the commands in the Charts group, a screentip appears, providing a brief explanation of the chart type.

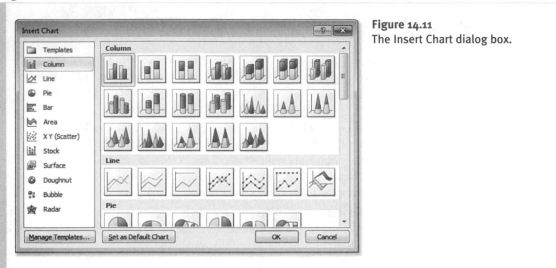

<figure>**Figure 14.11**
The Insert Chart dialog box.</figure>

If you use a particular chart type a great deal, you can select the chart in the Insert Chart dialog box and use the Set as Default Chart button to specify that chart type as the default. You can quickly create a chart using the default chart by selecting the range of data to be charted and then pressing the F11 key. This will immediately create a new chart sheet (a new worksheet) in the current workbook based on the default chart style you have selected.

Inserting a Chart

Inserting a new chart into the current worksheet involves specifying the data to be charted and the chart type to use. The new chart will then be inserted into the current worksheet. You can select the range to be charted using the mouse. If you are not selecting a contiguous range to be charted, select the first range of cells to be included in the chart and then hold down the Ctrl key to select other cells or ranges for the chart.

To choose the chart type, select one of the chart type commands on the Ribbon's Insert tab. Select the chart subtype you want to use and the chart will be inserted into the current worksheet.

You can also insert a chart from the Insert Chart dialog box. Select a chart type and a subtype; click OK to close the Insert Chart dialog box. The chart will be placed in the current worksheet.

Moving, Copying, or Deleting a Chart

If you want to place the chart on its own chart sheet (rather than as an object in the current worksheet), select the Move Chart command on the Chart Tools Design tab. (The Chart Tools should be available on the Ribbon when the chart is selected.) When you click Move Chart, the Move Chart dialog box opens as shown in Figure 14.12.

Figure 14.12
The Move Chart
dialog box.

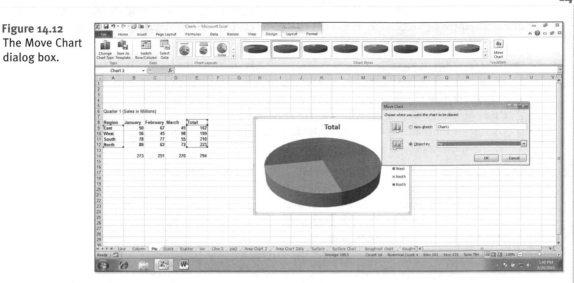

You can move the chart to a new sheet by selecting the New Sheet option button. You can also specify the name for the new sheet by typing the name in the appropriate text box. The Move Chart dialog box also provides you with the option of moving the chart to any of the worksheets in the current Excel workbook. Select the Object In drop-down list and then select the worksheet that will be home to the chart object. When you are ready to move the chart (to a new sheet or a different worksheet), click OK.

After a chart has been inserted into a worksheet, you can move the chart on the worksheet using the mouse. You can also select the chart and use the sizing handles provided to change the size of the chart.

Chart objects can be treated as any other object you place on an Excel worksheet such as an image, clip art, or a SmartArt graphic. You can use copy and paste to make copies of the chart and cut and paste to move the chart. You can also remove unwanted charts as needed. To remove an embedded chart in a worksheet, select the chart and then press the Delete key. If you want to delete a chart that is on its own worksheet (a chart sheet), right-click on the worksheet's name tab and then select Delete. The sheet will be removed from the workbook.

> **caution**
> When you delete a chart object on a worksheet, you can use Undo to get it back. When you delete a chart sheet in a workbook, Undo will not bring back the deleted sheet.

Modifying a Chart

After you have the chart embedded on the current worksheet (along with the worksheet data the chart uses) or have a chart in a new sheet, you can modify the chart's design, layout, and format. The Chart Tools, which are provided when the chart is selected, provide three different tabs:

Design, Layout, and Format. Each tab provides a set of command groups that enable you to modify and manipulate a particular aspect of the chart. The list that follows provides a description of the kind of commands found on each of the Chart Tools tabs:

- **Design:** This tab provides command groups related to the overall look of the chart. You can access commands on this tab that allow you to change the chart type and manipulate how the data is used by the chart, including the ability to change the data ranges used by the chart. Other groups on this tab provide you with the ability to change the current chart layout, select a chart style for the chart, and use the Move Chart command to place the chart in its own sheet or on another worksheet.

- **Layout:** This tab enables you to work with individual elements in the chart, such as the various labels, axes, gridlines, and backgrounds for specific chart types. An Analysis group provides commands that enable you to add different types of trendlines and drop lines to your chart and up/down bars or error bars. The commands on this tab provide the most possibilities in terms of fine-tuning the overall presentation that the chart makes in terms of readability and understandability.

- **Format:** This tab provides the command groups that you would find for modifying other graphic object types such as text boxes, images, and so on. These groups include the Shape Styles group and the WordArt Style group. The various commands in these groups can be applied to individual elements on a chart by using the Current Selection commands to specify the chart element to be modified.

> *For an overview on working with and formatting objects such as images and SmartArt graphics in the Office applications, see page 77 in Chapter 4, "Using and Creating Graphics."*

For modifying a chart, think of the Chart Tools Design tab as providing options that will most affect the chart in terms of how it plots the data (and what data it plots) and how it looks in terms of its overall layout. The Design tab is also the "decider" in terms of what chart type you ultimately settle on because the Change Chart Type command provided on the Design tab can be used to replace the current chart type with another chart type.

So, if the Design tab controls the gross anatomy of the chart, the Layout tab provides you with the commands that allow for a fine-tuning of the chart's presentation of information by enabling you to better label the data charted and to also work with axes, gridlines, backgrounds, and additions such as trendlines that make a chart more readable. The Chart Tools Format commands can then be used to make the chart's border and text, or the borders and text associated with other chart elements, look nicer (because these tools would be used on any graphical element placed in an a Microsoft Office application file). Let's look at some of the specifics for modifying a chart and then look at working with individual chart elements.

Changing Chart Type or Chart Data

As already discussed, the Chart Tools Design tab enables you to modify the chart type, manipulate the data used by the chart, and select a layout or style for the chart. If you find that you have created a chart that doesn't provide a proper picture of the data that you selected to include in the chart, you might want to rethink the chart type that you have selected. You might also need to change how the chart is looking at your data (in rows instead of columns) or you might even need to change the data selection that the chart is using.

Changing the chart type doesn't mean that you necessarily have to switch to a completely different chart type such as a line to bar—it also is a way to fine-tune the chart type you have currently selected by going with a different chart subtype. For example, you might be using the 3D pie chart type but want to switch to the exploded pie in 3D to better differentiate the parts of the pie.

To change the chart type, select the Change Chart Type command in the Type group. The Change Chart Type dialog box opens. This dialog box is the same as the Insert Chart dialog box. Select a chart type and/or subtype as needed to change the chart type of the currently selected chart. To apply the change in type or subtype, click OK.

> **tip**
>
> Right-click on a chart and then select Change Chart Type to open the Change Chart Type dialog box.

Another command that can be useful in cases where a chart doesn't look quite right is the Switch Row/Column command. This command can be used in cases where the chart has based the x-axis or y-axis on column data rather than row data and you want to swap the data on the x-axis with the y-axis or vice versa.

This command can also be used to manipulate a single axis, such as the x-axis, when you have labels at the top of your data columns and labels for each data row. A bar chart by default will chart the column labels along the x-axis. However, if you want the x-axis to show you data related to the row columns, such as the names of your salespeople or regions or the fruits and vegetables that you ate last week, you can use the Switch Rows/Columns command to switch the label data shown on the x-axis and the legend.

In cases where you have selected an incomplete or incorrect data range for a chart, you can modify the data selection used by the chart using the Select Data command. Click the Select Data command and the Select Data Source dialog box opens as shown in Figure 14.13.

Figure 14.13
The Select Data Source dialog box.

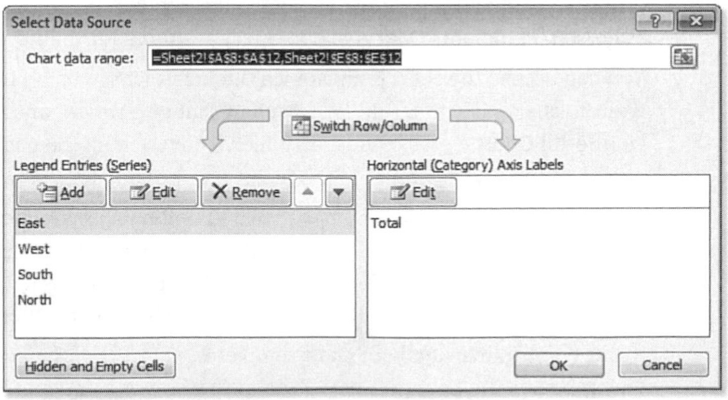

To change the data range for the chart, select the current data range in the Chart Data Range box and then use the Shrink button to access the worksheet data. Select the range to be used by the chart and return to the dialog box.

You can also use the Switch Row/Column button in the Select Data Source dialog box to swap the series or axis data. Using the Switch Row/Column command in the Select Data Source dialog box might actually make more sense to you because you see how the series and axis labels are swapped rather than how the chart itself is changed. You can add entries, such as legend entries, to the Select Data Source dialog box. You can also edit and remove labels as needed.

The Select Data Source dialog box also makes it easy to deal with hidden or empty cells that fall within the data range being used by the chart. Select the Hidden and Empty Cells button to open the Hidden and Empty Cells Settings dialog box. By default, empty cells are shown as gaps in the chart. You can also choose to have empty cells shown as zero or you can have the chart connect data points with a line so that gaps are effectively ignored. As for hidden rows or columns that fall into the chart data source range, you can choose to have the hidden data ignored or you can select the Show Data in Hidden Rows and Columns option button to have this data included in the chart. When you have finished working in the Hidden and Empty Cell Settings dialog box, click OK to return to the Select Data Source dialog box. To close the Select Data Source dialog box and return to the chart, click OK.

Creating and Using a Chart Template

Although we are probably getting ahead of ourselves in terms of the different modifications that can be made to a chart and its elements; the next command on the Design tab is Save as Template. You can take all the hard work that you have put into refining a particular chart, including chart settings and chart element changes, and then save the chart as a template. This enables you to use the various modifications that you have made to the chart and its elements in the future to create new charts without going through all the steps of changing the design and layout parameters for a particular chart that you create frequently.

To save the chart as a template, select the Save as Template command in the Design tab's Type group. The Save Chart dialog box will open. By default, chart templates are saved in the Roaming/Microsoft/Templates/Charts folder. Specify a name for the new chart template and then click Save.

You can access the chart template via the Insert Chart dialog box. Select the data range that you want to chart (as you would for any chart that you create) and then open the Insert Chart dialog box via the All Chart Types command, which is found in all the chart type galleries provided by the commands in the Charts group. In the Insert Chart dialog box, select Templates as shown in Figure 14.14.

Any chart templates that you have created will be shown when the Templates folder is selected in the Insert Chart dialog box. To use a template, select the template and then click OK. The new chart will be created using the settings provided by the chart template. You can modify a chart created with a template as you would any other chart that you have created.

If you want to manage your chart templates, select the Manage Templates button in the Insert Chart dialog box or the Change Chart Type dialog box. A Windows Explorer window will open. You can copy or move chart templates to other folders as renamed chart templates. You can also delete chart templates as needed. To return to the Excel window and the Insert Chart or Change Chart Type dialog box, close the Explorer window.

Figure 14.14
Selecting a chart template.

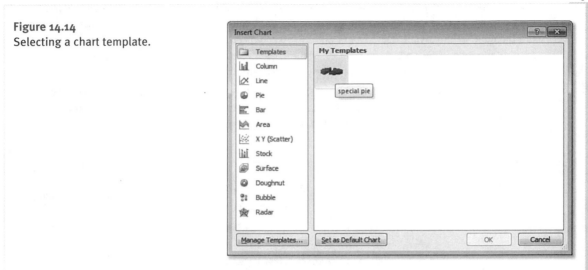

You can make a chart template your default chart type. This can be particularly useful when you create the same type of chart frequently and have taken the time to customize the chart, axes, labels, and other chart elements as you want them to be each time you create a chart using the template.

Selecting Chart Layouts and Styles

Each chart type will have a number of different chart layouts available. A chart layout will provide specific chart elements such as title, legend, and data labels. You can use a chart layout (also referred to as a quick layout) to quickly add needed chart elements to a chart and then you can further modify the layout as needed. Unfortunately, you cannot create custom chart layouts, but a chart layout can be saved as part of a template that you create from a specific chart type.

The entire Chart Layouts gallery can be accessed for a specific chart type by using the More button, which is just below the row scroll button for the layout gallery. Figure 14.15 shows the layout gallery for a 3D cluster column chart.

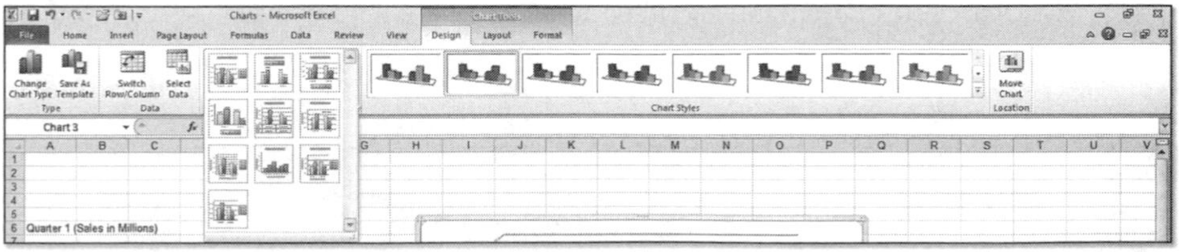

Figure 14.15
The chart layout gallery.

You will have to select a layout based on the thumbnail provided. Placing the mouse on a particular layout provides only the layout number rather than any information related to what chart elements are included in the layout. The layouts differ in the chart elements that they provide, such as the legend and axis titles, and in the position of these elements on the chart. Any of these elements can be fine-tuned using the commands provided by the Chart Tools Layout tab.

You can also modify the chart using one of the chart styles provided in the Chart Styles gallery. These styles are color schemes that affect the data series and the background of the chart (such as the back wall, floor, and so on). Figure 14.16 shows the Chart Styles gallery.

Figure 14.16
The Chart Styles gallery.

You will find that chart styles can be used to make the chart information more readable in certain situations. For example, a number of grayscale styles are provided if you plan on printing the chart on a grayscale printer such as a laser printer. Some of the styles, particularly those that provide a background color for the chart's back wall and floor, can be useful in cases where you will project the chart during a presentation using a video projector.

Working with Chart Elements

Although we think of a chart as a single object, it is actually made up of a number of different elements that can be manipulated individually. The Chart Tools Layout tab provides a number of commands that can be used to modify or enhance individual elements on the chart such as the title, the axis titles, the legend, the data labels, and even the background of the chart. The commands available on the Layout tab will depend on the type of chart that you have created. Figure 14.17 shows the Chart Tools Layout tab and the commands that it makes available when you are working with a line chart.

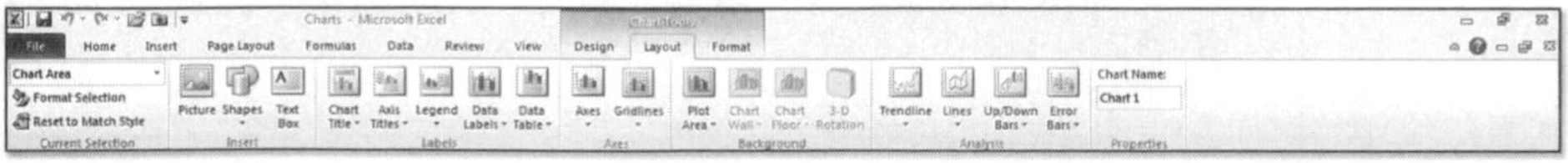

Figure 14.17
The Chart Tools Layout tab.

Many of the elements on a chart that contain text can be moved, sized, and formatted as needed. For example, the chart title can be dragged to a new position. You can also format the text within the chart title frame and size the element's frame if required.

The Chart Tools Layout tab also provides specific commands that make it easier to work with certain chart elements. The commands groups provided on the Layout tab are as follows:

- **Current Selection:** This group provides a drop-down list of all the elements in the chart. You can select a particular element and then open its Format dialog box by selecting Format Selection. If you want to reset a formatted element to the current chart style, select Reset to Match Style.

- **Insert:** This group enables you to add graphic elements to the chart, such as pictures, shapes, and text boxes.

- **Labels:** This group enables you to manipulate elements that provide text information in the chart. You can manipulate the chart title, axis titles, legend, and data labels. You can also use the Data Table command to add a data table directly to the chart.

- **Axes:** This group enables you to manipulate the scale and the direction of axes in the chart. You can also choose to turn labeling off on an axis and not to display the axis on the chart. This group provides a Gridlines command that enables you to determine the gridlines provided for both the horizontal and vertical axes. You can choose to show major gridlines, minor gridlines, or both.

- **Background:** This group provides commands that enable you to manipulate the plot area, chart wall, and chart floor. You can also rotate some 3D charts to change the viewpoint of the chart using the 3-D Rotation command. For example, you could change the rotation on the x-axis of a pie chart to rotate the pie pieces so that they are oriented more toward the front of the chart area.

- **Analysis:** This group enables you to add analysis markers to your chart. You can add trendlines such as linear and exponential trendlines to a chart and you can add drop and high-low lines. Error bars can also be added to charts. The availability of these different analysis additions will depend on the type of chart you have created. For example, all the Analysis options are available for line charts, whereas a column chart can be enhanced only with trendlines or error bars.

- **Properties:** This group provides the name of the current chart.

You will find that the command groups on the Chart Tools tab really provide only some of the possibilities for manipulating a particular chart element. The possibilities typically relate to the position of the element on the chart and whether the chart includes the element. For example, when you select the Chart Title command in the Labels group, you are provided with three options: None, Centered Overlay Title, and Above Chart.

In the case of the Data Labels command, you also have the choice of including data labels on the chart or turning data labels on the chart off. The other choices on the Data Labels gallery relate to the positioning of the data labels on the chart, including center, left, right, above, and below.

 tip

You can format text elements in a chart such as a label or text in the legend as you would any text in any of the Office applications. Select the text and use the formatting options provided on the Ribbon's Home tab.

Some of the element-related commands do provide greater capabilities and depth of choices but are still somewhat limited. The Axes command in the Labels group provides you with the ability to change settings related to the primary horizontal and vertical axes and a depth axis if the chart type you have created uses a third (or z) axis. If you look at the options provided by the Axes command for a primary vertical axis (which is typically a value axis), you will find that you can show the axis in thousands, millions, or billions or show the axis with a base 10 log scale.

 tip

You can double-click on a chart element's frame (the selectable elements) in the chart to open the Format dialog box for that chart element.

If you really want to manipulate a particular chart element, you will want to access the Format dialog box for that particular element. As already mentioned, you can select a chart element using the drop-down list provided in the Current Selection group. After selecting a chart element, you can then select Format Select to open that chart element's dialog box. Each command provided in the Labels, Axes, and Background groups also provides commands at the bottom of each gallery that will take you to a specific Format dialog box. For example, if you select the Data Labels command and then select More Data Label Options, the Format Data Labels dialog box will open as shown in Figure 14.18.

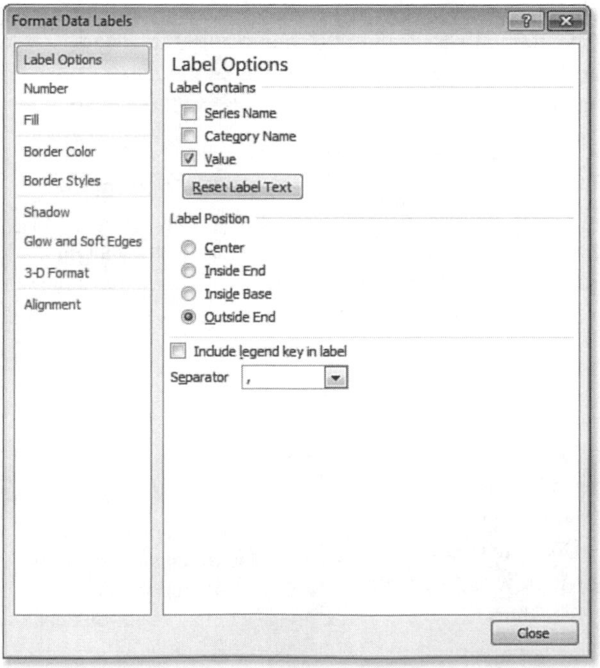

Figure 14.18
The Format Data Labels dialog box.

The options provided by various chart element format dialog boxes are relatively consistent. You can control a number of settings such as the fill, border color, border styles, and shadow for the element. Because each element is different, however, some elements will have additional settings available. For example, the Format Data Labels dialog box (shown in Figure 14.18) enables you to specify what the label contains: series name, category name, or value. Option buttons are also provided for the data labels' positions in relation to the chart, such as center, left, above, and below.

The other options provided by the Format Data Labels dialog box relate to the look of the specific chart element. The possibilities are similar to those that you find when formatting a shape, a SmartArt graphic, or other graphic element; you have control over the fill, border color, glow, and soft edges and in some cases even the 3D format of the specific chart element. So, in many respects, the various chart elements are really just graphic objects or text boxes, which happened to be associated with a larger graphical object—the chart.

 For an overview on working with and formatting objects such as images and SmartArt graphics in the Office applications, see page 77 in Chapter 4.

Modifying Titles and Data Labels

Titles on charts provide descriptive text for the chart and other elements such as the chart axes. Editing the chart title text or other text-based elements such as the axis titles can be done by using the mouse to place the insertion point in the text box that serves as a particular chart element such as the title. You can then edit the text as needed.

Data labels are different from the other text boxes on the chart in that the values shown for the data labels are derived from the worksheet data that you used to create the chart. So, you cannot edit a data label in situ. The value will change only if you edit the worksheet data related to the chart.

To change the position of a chart title or axis title, you can drag the selected title object to a new position on the chart. You can also take advantage of the commands in the Labels group of the Chart Tools Design tab to specify a position for an element such as the chart title or axis title. You can also position data labels using the Data Labels command as well as access the Format Data Label dialog box from this command.

Working with the Legend and Data Points

The legend for the chart is the color or pattern key for the data series represented on the chart. You can move and size the legend on the chart as needed. The Legend command on the labels provides a gallery of different legend positions and gives you with the option of turning off the legend.

You can format the legend's box by selecting the legend and then clicking on the Format Selection command in the Current Selection group. The Format Legend dialog box enables you to control the legend position and the fill, border color, border styles, and other options related to the overall look of the legend. You can also format each of the legend entries separately by double-clicking on a particular entry. This will open the Format Legend Entry dialog box, which enables you to control the fill, border color, and other graphic settings for the legend entry.

Although the legend shows the color scheme used to differentiate the different data points in a pie chart or a column chart, you actually change the data point colors by editing the data point chart element rather than the legend. You might have a case where you are going to print your chart using a grayscale printer rather than a color printer. You can replace the default colors used when you created the chart by using the different chart styles provided by the Design tab, however, you can also define your own custom color or fills for the different chart data points.

On a chart, double-click a data point such as a column on a column chart or a pie slice on a pie chart. The Format Data Point dialog box will open. The options available will depend on the type of chart. For example, series options for a pie chart enable you to rotate the angle of the first slice and to separate points using the Point Explosion slider.

In the case of the fill for the data point, you have a number of different choices as shown in Figure 14.19. You can set a solid fill, gradient fill, picture fill, texture fill, or pattern fill.

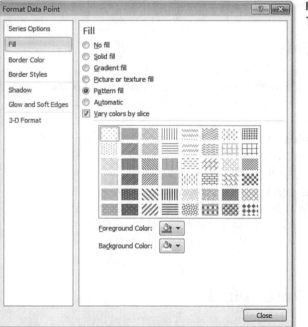

Figure 14.19
The Format Data Point dialog box.

For example, to use a pattern fill (as shown in Figure 14.19), select Pattern Fill in the dialog box. You can then pick a particular pattern and the foreground and background color to be used by the pattern. After you have set the fill options for the data point, you can also vary other options for the data point such as the border color, style, or shadow. Click Close when you have completed configuring the data point options.

You can then repeat the process for each data point on the chart. The format changes that you make to the data points will be reflected in the legend.

Manipulating Axes and Gridlines

If you are working with a chart type that shows the vertical and horizontal axes in the chart area, such as a line chart or a bar chart, you can manipulate the scale on the value axis. The Axes command in the Axes group enables you to manipulate both the primary horizontal and vertical axes for a chart and, in addition, to manipulate any secondary axes.

 tip

If you are going to use different patterns, textures, or gradients to differentiate data points on a chart, make sure that each data point can be readily identified—meaning don't select patterns for the different data points that are hard to tell apart.

In the case of axes that consist of text labels, you can choose to show the axis without the labels or change the axis so that it displays the labels from left to right or right to left. In the case of a value axis (such as the primary vertical or y-axis on many line and column charts), you can choose to display the axis using numbers represented in the thousands, millions, or billions. You can also choose to show the axis with a log 10–based scale. This is also known as a logarithmic scale because it uses a specific quantity to create the scale on the axis. In the case of the log 10–based scale, the scale would consist of 1 then 10 then 100 then 1000 and so on. This type of scale is extremely useful in cases where you have data that encompasses a very large range of values.

Gridlines make it easier for you to determine the values associated with a particular data point on a chart, particularly in cases where you have not included data labels. Depending on the chart layout that you select for your chart via the Chart Layouts gallery, your chart might already contain the major gridlines, which will be placed perpendicular to the value axis on your chart.

tip

Because some chart types include multiple value axes, you can use both horizontal and vertical gridlines as needed.

Because this is the y-axis in many chart types, the primary horizontal gridlines provide you with horizontal lines on the chart that serve as reference points for the value units placed on the y-axis itself. The Gridlines command in the Axes group can be used to turn gridlines on and off. You can also choose to add minor gridlines to a chart, which provide a greater number of reference points for reading the chart values.

Adding Trendlines, Drop Lines, and Bars to a Chart

You can use the commands in the Layout tab's Analysis group to add additional elements, such as trendlines, drop lines, and error bars, to your charts. A trendline provides the overall slope or trend of the data points and is based on the relationship between each set of x and y values shown on a chart. Figure 14.20 shows a linear trendline that has been added to a stock chart (which is also known as a candlestick or box plot). The trendline is based on the close value for the stock shown. The trendline provides an overall analysis of how the stock has done over the timeframe shown on the chart.

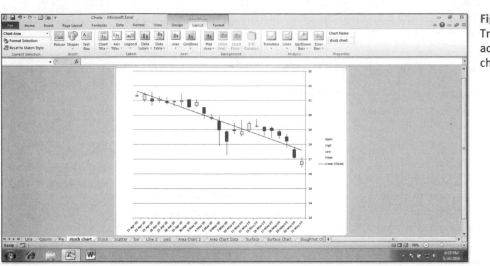

You can add trendlines to a number of Excel 2D chart types including line, column, bar, area, stock, scatter, and bubble charts. Excel provides a number of different trendline types via the Trendline command including linear, exponential, linear forecast, and moving average trendlines. Additional types of trendlines can be accessed via the Format Trendline dialog box. The type of trendline that you use will depend on the type of data that you are working with and the type of analysis you want to make with the trendline. The trendline possibilities are as follows:

- **Linear Trendline:** This type of trendline creates a best-fit straight line based on the data points in the series that you have specified for the trendline. This type of trendline is best used in cases where you want to see whether your data points are trending up or down; this trendline can be useful for a quick look at trends in sales figures.

- **Exponential Trendline:** This type of trendline will provide a best-fit curve that is best used in cases where the data points rise or fall in constantly increasing rates and then level off. For example, an exponential trendline could be used to analyze production data for a factory that has rapid growth in its production rate until it reaches maximum capacity and levels off.

- **Linear Forecast Trendline:** This trendline is similar to the linear trendline, however, it is used to forecast trends moving forward. The trendline is drawn to show a second timeframe based on the time scale on the chart, but one that has yet to occur and include data points.

> **note**
>
> When you are using trendlines on your charts, you are actually performing linear regression, which analyzes the relationship between data points on the x and y axes of your chart. The validity of a trendline is actually measured by determining the square of the correlation coefficient R, which is a fractional number between 0 and 1. The closer R^2 is to 1, the greater the correlation between the x and y variables; meaning as x changes, y also changes in a somewhat consistent manner.

- **Two-Period Moving Average:** This trendline averages the data points found in two periods and draws a trendline based on the averages. You can specify the period for a moving average trendline by formatting the trendline in the Format Trendline dialog box.

- **Polynomial Trendline:** This trendline type is basically a way to do linear regression on data that fluctuates greatly and where there is not necessarily a true linear relationship between the x and y variables.

- **Power Trendline:** This trendline is a curved line that can be used to show the relationship between two sets of values (x and y) when there is an increase or decrease at a specific rate.

 tip

You can also open the Format Trendline dialog box by clicking on a trendline on a chart.

The settings for any of the available trendline types can be fine-tuned via the Format Trendline dialog box. Select the trendline you want to modify, select Trendline, and then select More Trendline Options. Figure 14.21 shows the Format Trendline dialog box.

Figure 14.21
The Format Trendline dialog box.

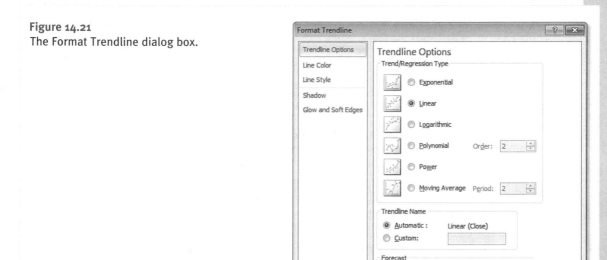

The Format Trendline dialog box enables you to modify the trend/regression type and set the order or period for polynomial and moving average charts, respectively. You can also set the forecast period for the trendline and display the linear regression equation (for the trendline) and/or the R2 value for the trendline (remember, the closer the R2 value is to 1, the stronger the correlation between the data sets).

You can also change other formatting options related to the trendline in the Format Trendline dialog box. You can change the line color, style, and other formatting attributes such as the shadow, glow, and soft edges settings.

Using Drop Lines and High-Low Lines

Drop lines are lines that extend from the data points on the chart down to the horizontal or x-axis. The drop lines are used to make the chart easier to read and the drop lines actually enable you to more easily determine the x-axis attributes of the data points used to create the chart. You can use drop lines on line and area charts. To add drop lines to a chart, select Lines and then Drop Lines.

You can also add high-low lines to your 2D charts. The high-low line extends from the highest to the lowest value in each chart category. For example, you might create a line chart that compares your actual monthly expenses (one data series for the chart) to a budget (another data series on the chart) that you create. The high-low lines will connect the high value in each category (say you have categories such as food, utilities, entertainment, rent, and so on) with the minimum value in each category.

You can format your drop-lines or high-low lines by double-clicking on a drop-line or high-low line on the chart. This will open the Format Drop Lines or the Format High-Low lines dialog box, respectively. You have control over the line color, line style, and other line attributes for both drop-lines and high-low lines.

Adding Up/Down and Error Bars to a Chart

The Analysis group also provides you with the ability to add up/down bars and error bars to your charts. You need multiple data series in a 2D line chart to use up/down bars. The up/down bars are used to show the difference between the first and the last data series on the chart. For example, if you are comparing two data series, you will get an up bar when the data point in the first series is less than the second series. You will get a down bar when a data point for the first series is greater than the second series.

To add up/down bars to a chart, select Up/Down Bars in the Analysis group and then select Up/Down Bars. You can format the bars if required; double-click on an up or down bar and the Format Up Bars or Format Down Bars dialog box will open.

Error bars can also be added to your charts. Error bars are used to reflect uncertainty or variability in the data that has been charted and can help show the potential amount of error relative to the data points in a chart data series. Error bars can be used in 2D area, bar, column, line, scatter, and bubble charts.

The error bars will be created on the chart based on an error amount. You can quickly create error bars that use the standard error, percentage, or standard deviation as the error amount using the choices provided by the Error Bars gallery. Other options are available in the Format Error Bars dialog box. The error amount can be set to one of the following:

- **Fixed Value:** You can specify a fixed amount as the error value.
- **Percentage:** A percentage can be specified as the error value.

- **Standard Deviation:** Excel computes the standard deviation for the chart data and uses it as the error amount for the error bars.

- **Standard Error:** Excel uses the standard error equation to compute the standard error for the chart data.

- **Custom:** You can specify the positive error value and the negative error value for the error bars. When you select Custom in the Format Error Bars dialog box, you must then specify the error values by clicking Specify Value. The error values (positive and negative) can be based on data ranges in the worksheet or you can specify them as a series of values separated by commas.

> **note**
>
> Scatter charts can have both vertical and horizontal error bars.

To quickly add error bars to your chart that use the standard error, percentage, or standard deviation as the error amount, select the appropriate error bar type from the Error Bars gallery using the Error Bar command in the Analysis group. To open the Format Error Bars dialog box, which provides both formatting options for the error bars and the full list of error amount options, select More Error Bars Options in the Error Bars gallery. Figure 14.22 shows the Format Error Bars dialog box.

Figure 14.22
The Format Error Bars dialog box.

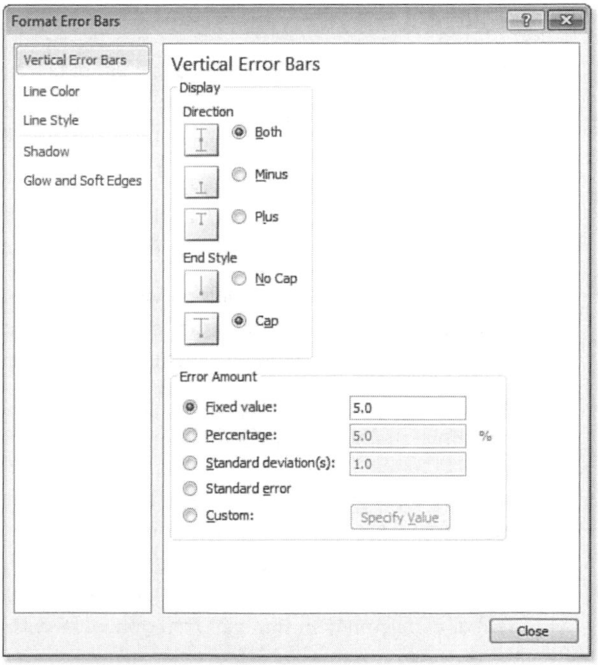

As already mentioned, the Format Error Bars dialog box enables you to specify the error amount for the error bars. It also enables you to set the direction and the end style for the error bars as well as the line attributes such as line color and line style.

Using the Chart Tools Format Tab

Although you have a great deal of control over individual chart elements by using the commands on the Chart Tools Layout tab, which also provides access to the Format dialog box for specific chart elements, the Chart Tools Format tab provides additional possibilities. Figure 14.23 shows the Chart Tools Format tab.

Figure 14.23
The Chart Tools Format tab.

The commands on the Format tab enable you to change the shape and text styles for the chart and for individual elements on the chart, such as the titles and the legend. Individual elements can be directly selected on the chart and then formatted as required. The command groups provided on the Chart Tools Format tab are as follows:

- **Current Selection:** This provides a list of chart elements, which shows the currently selected chart object. This group also provides access to the Format dialog box for the currently selected chart object and enables you to reset the formatting on the element to match the current style.

- **Shape Styles:** This group provides access to the Shape Styles gallery, which provides different border, fill, and font setting combinations that can be applied to the chart or other chart elements. This group also enables you to set the shape fill, outline, and effects independently.

- **WordArt Styles:** This group provides access to the WordArt Styles gallery. The group also provides access to commands that enable you to control the text fill, outline, and effects assigned to the text in the currently selected chart element.

- **Arrange:** This group provides commands that enable you to arrange, align, and rotate any shapes that you have added to the chart area.

When you have finished working with the Format tab commands, click outside the chart area anywhere in the worksheet. The contextual Chart Tools will "disappear" from the Ribbon and the Ribbon will again provide the default tabs. You will find that the Chart Tools Format tab is actually very similar to the Drawing Tools Shape tab. Excel and the other Office applications provide a great deal of consistency in terms of how you work with different objects and the commands provided by the Ribbon.

Creating a Combination Chart

Before we end our discussion of Excel charts, we should look at how you create a combination chart. A combination chart combines two or more chart types in a single chart. Excel provides premade combination charts such as pie of pie and bar of pie charts. A pie of pie chart is shown in Figure 14.24.

Figure 14.24
Pie of Pie chart.

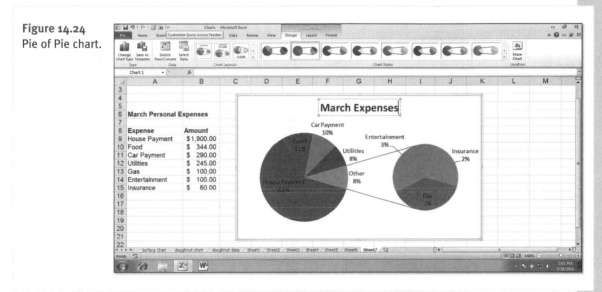

A pie of pie chart (or a bar of pie chart) enables you to separate out certain data points into the secondary chart, meaning the second pie. This can be extremely useful when you have a situation where a few large data points dominate the pie chart and you would like to make smaller slices of the pie more visible by moving data points that represent smaller values to the secondary pie.

Working with a Pie of Pie Chart

Because pie charts enable you to specify only a single data series, how the different data points end up in the primary and the secondary plot or pie depends on how you have the data series arranged in a column or row in your worksheet. By default, Excel actually uses the last third of the data points listed in the chart data range to create the secondary chart. Remember that this is the default setting for a pie of pie chart and you do have options regarding how the data series is split between the two charts in the combination chart. If you wanted to go with the default, you could arrange your data in the worksheet so that it is sorted from high to low based on the values you will chart (use the Sort & Filter command on the Home tab to quickly sort ascending or descending as needed). This means that the lower values, which would typically make up the smallest slices on the pie, will be placed at the bottom of your values and so will appear in the secondary pie when you are creating a pie of pie chart.

If you would like to customize how the series is split and the number of values contained in the secondary pie or plot, you can edit these settings in the Format Data Series dialog box. Select the data series using the drop-down list in the Layout tab's Current Selection group. Then select Format Selection. The Format Data Series dialog box will open as shown in Figure 14.25.

Figure 14.25
Format Data Series dialog box.

Use the Split Series By drop-down list to determine how you want to split the data series between the two charts (the primary pie and the secondary pie). You can split the series by position, value, and percentage value. You can also choose to customize how the data points are split between the charts using the Custom setting.

When you select Custom in the Split Series By drop-down list, you can then select individual data points on the chart and move them between the two plots. Keep the Format Data Series dialog box and then click on a particular data point (a piece of the pie) and then use the Point Belongs To drop-down list in the Format Data Series dialog box to specify that the point belongs to the first plot or the second plot. After you have sorted out the different data points in terms of the plot that they belong to, select the Close button to return to the chart.

Creating a Custom Combination Chart

You are certainly not limited to the combination chart types that Excel provides such as the pie of pie; charts are created by virtue of the fact that you supply a data series of values for the chart. If you have more than one data series in a chart, you can apply different chart types to the different data series, creating a combination chart that combines two or more of the different chart types supplied by Excel. This means that you can combine a line chart and a bar chart in the same combination chart or even have a combination chart that combines multiple chart types such as a line, bar, and pie. The possibilities are really dictated by your data and your need for showing the relationships between the various data series visually.

For example, you could easily create a column and line chart combination. Let's say that you have sales figures for each of your sales regions (East, West, South, and North) for the months January, February, and March. It certainly would not be difficult to calculate the quarter total for each region using the SUM function and to include this information in the worksheet.

You could then create a chart that places the sales figures for each region using the region names as the category names along the x-axis. The months (January through March) would serve as the data series for the chart (along with the values associated with the sales for each month by region), and so the legend would supply the color coding for each of the data point values by month.

The totals data series (the total sales for each region) would also be included on the chart. This data series could then be formatted as a line chart, providing you with a column chart that provides a comparison of the monthly sales of each region and a line chart that provides a look at the trend of your total sales for the quarter.

To create a combination chart, select all the data that you will include in the chart, including the data series that will serve as the secondary plot. Select the Insert menu, and then use the chart type commands to select the type of chart you want to specify as the primary plot or chart.

The chart will be placed on the worksheet. Now you need to select the series that you want to convert to a secondary chart. Use the drop-down list in the Current Selection group (on the Chart Tools Layout tab) to select the data series that will provide the values for the secondary plot.

Then select the Design tab and click the Change Chart Type command to open the Change Chart Type dialog box. Select the chart type that you will use as the secondary chart type. Remember that this chart type will be applied to only the data series that you selected. After the data series has been provided a chart type, it will appear in the chart area. Figure 14.26 shows a combination chart that combines a column chart and a line chart. Data labels and drop lines have been added to the line chart to make the combination chart easy to read.

note

The Format Data Series dialog box can also be used to set a number of options related to the data in a chart. In the case of pie charts, you can set the pie explosion percentage and the size of a secondary plot.

You can create a number of different combination charts including column/line, column/area, and even pie/area. Remember that each data series can be formatted separately, meaning that the attributes of each of the charts—the primary and secondary plots—can be modified as needed. This includes applying data labels to the different series and using things such as drop lines and other descriptive chart elements, such as axis titles and gridlines, to make the chart readily meaningful.

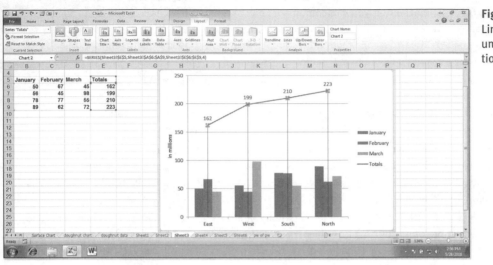

Figure 14.26
Line and column combination chart.

Using Sparklines

Sparklines are small charts that are embedded in worksheet cells and can be inserted in rows or columns. You can position sparklines so that they appear at the bottom of a column of values or at the end or a row of values (including formula or function results). This enables you to place the sparklines directly inline with the data that they visually represent.

> **note**
> Sparklines are a new addition to Excel 2010.

Sparklines are not meant to replace full-blown charts in Excel, but can be used to accompany data series in the worksheet.

A sparkline can take the form of a line, column, or win/loss chart. Sparklines can be inserted in a single cell or multiple cells (for multiple rows or columns of data). You can also insert a sparkline for a row or column of values and then drag the sparkline's fill handle to copy the sparkline to other rows or columns as you would an Excel formula or function. When you change the data in a row or column that has an associated sparkline, the sparkline chart will immediately be updated.

Creating Sparklines

As already mentioned, three different types of sparklines can be inserted in a worksheet: line, column, and win/loss. A line sparkline can be used to show a trend in the data. A column sparkline enables you to visually compare different data points. Win/loss sparklines can be used to show the win/loss trend over time for such things as investments or even the performance of a sports team.

You can insert a sparkline in a cell or a range of cells. The different types of sparklines are available in the Sparklines group on the Ribbon's Insert tab. To insert a sparkline, follow these steps:

1. Select the cell or cell range where you will insert the sparkline.

2. Select the sparkline type that you want to insert from the Sparklines group. The Create Sparklines dialog box will open as shown in Figure 14.27.

Figure 14.27
The Create Sparklines dialog box.

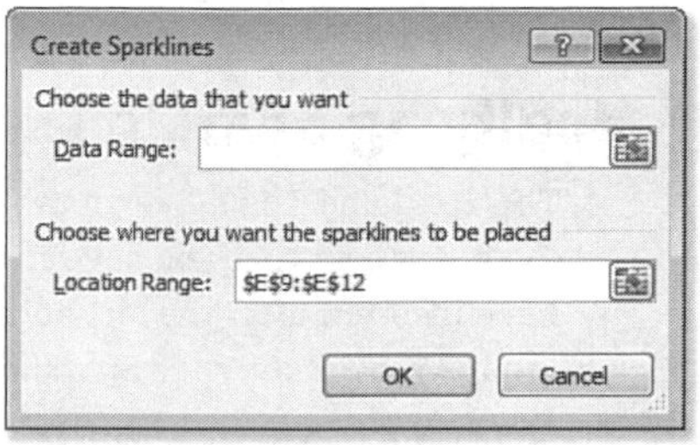

3. The Create Sparklines dialog box requires that you specify a data range and a location range. To specify the data range, click the Shrink button and select the cells that contain the values that will be used to create the sparklines. Do not include cells containing labels as you would for an Excel chart.

4. If you selected the cell range where the sparklines were to be inserted, a location range will already be shown in the Location Range box. If you need to specify the range or edit the current range, click the Shrink button and select the location range.

5. After the data range and the location range have been selected for the sparklines, click OK. The sparklines will appear in the location range cells. Figure 14.28 shows a range of cells containing sparklines that use values arranged in rows.

Figure 14.28
Sparklines in a worksheet.

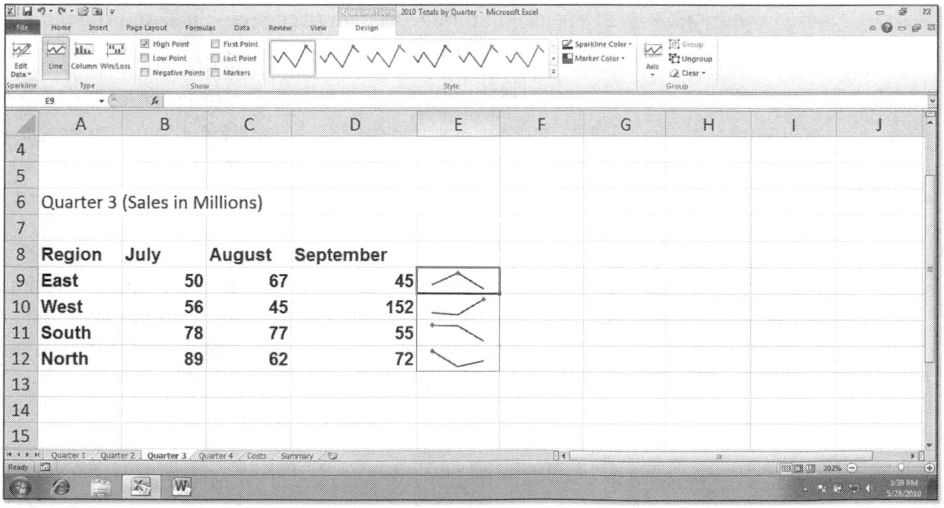

When you select a sparkline that is part of the same location range, you will find that the other sparklines in that range (meaning the cells in the range) are also selected. As with a number of other features in Excel, a specific set of contextual sparkline tools is provided when a cell containing a sparkline is selected. Let's look at the Sparkline Tools Design tab's commands.

Modifying Sparklines

The Sparkline Tools Design tab provides a number of different options for modifying and enhancing the sparklines that you have inserted into a worksheet. You can change the type of sparkline you have inserted after the fact and you can change the style assigned to the sparklines. The command groups provided by the Sparkline Tools Design tab are as follows:

- **Sparkline:** This group contains the Edit Data command. This command enables you to edit the group and data location for all the sparklines in a specific group. The Edit Single Sparkline's Data command enables you to edit a specific cell containing a sparkline without editing the values used by the other sparklines in the group. A Hidden and Empty Cells command enables you to specify whether hidden and empty cells should be treated as gaps or zeros and whether the data should be shown that is included in any hidden rows or columns included in the data range for the sparkline.

- **Type:** You can change the type of sparkline you have inserted using the Line, Column, or Win/Loss commands provided by this group.

- **Show:** You can highlight certain data points in the sparklines including the high point, low point, and negative points. You can also specify that markers are shown on the sparklines, which shows the number of data points used to create the sparkline.

- **Style:** The Style gallery provides you with a number of different sparkline styles for each sparkline type: line, column, or win/loss. Sparkline Color and Marker Color commands are also provided that enable you to select your own colors for the sparklines and the markers that you are including on the sparklines (selected via the Show group), respectively.

- **Group:** This group provides commands that can be used to group or ungroup sparklines. A Clear command is provided that enables you to clear the selected sparklines or selected sparkline groups. An Axis command enables you to modify the horizontal and vertical axis options. You can change the horizontal axis type, and specify minimum and maximum values for the vertical axis.

Sparklines provide you with another possibility for providing a visual representation of the data in a worksheet. And although sparklines do not provide the detail you find in an Excel chart, they can be useful in doing quick comparisons of a range of data values or to show a trend in the values.

USING EXCEL TABLES AND PIVOTTABLES

Although we primarily think of Excel as a number cruncher, it also provides a number of capabilities for working with collections of information—databases. Excel enables you to view and manipulate data records and field information in a database table. You can sort records in your table, filter the records, and import or connect to external data sources.

In this chapter, we look at Excel's database capabilities, including a number of different table manipulation tools and data tools. We also look at grouping and ungrouping ranges in a table and creating subtotals in a table. We wrap up this chapter with a discussion of PivotTables, which provide you with a dynamic way to view and analyze worksheet data.

Excel and Databases

A database is a collection of organized information. The basic container used to hold data in a database is the table, and complex databases can consist of many tables. Excel provides you with the ability to interact with and manipulate tables by using a number of different tools. You can create your own tables in Excel or import or connect to data provided by other databases external to Excel. The fact that database information is held in discrete tables means that you can interact with database information that lives in a number of different database platforms, including Microsoft Access, the Web, and server-based database systems such as those provided by Microsoft SQL Server (such as SQL Server 2008 R2). Excel tables can also be shared via a SharePoint Services server (such as a server running SharePoint 2010).

A table will look much like any other Excel worksheet, with the data arranged in columns and rows. However, it is important that a database table be structured correctly for you to take advantage of the commands and tools provided on the Ribbon's Data tab; a table must have the data arranged in records and fields.

Each column in the table is a field. Each field consists of a discrete piece of information such as an employee's phone number or department. The very first row in the table will actually consist of field names or headings, which define what is contained in each field. The field headings actually play an important role when you are filtering data in the table.

Each row in the table is a record. A record is all the information related to a particular person, place, or thing. The record comprises the field entries made for that particular record. For example, if you have a table of employees, each record in the table will be the record for a different employee.

You might be wondering why you would want to tackle database tables in Excel when there is more powerful relational database software such as Microsoft Access. The best answer is that when looking at individual tables, Excel provides a number of tools that enable you to view the data in different ways using sort and filter commands. Excel's ability to do calculations also enables you to use formulas, functions, and other Excel features to quickly go beyond the data analysis that you could do easily in a particular database software application. So, don't think of Excel as the database creation application as much as the analysis engine that can be used after the database has been created. Your Excel (database) tables will really look no different from other worksheets you create in Excel. The information will still appear in columns and rows.

> **🔍 note**
>
> Tables that you create in Excel are referred to as flat file databases because you cannot set up relationships between associated tables in Excel such as an employee table with an employee sales table. Relational databases created in Microsoft Access use related tables to create the structure and data relationships for the database. Tables in a relational database will each contain a primary key, which is a field (such as an employee number or invoice number) that discretely identifies each record in the table.

Defining a Table Range

To define a table in Excel, you will use the Format as Table command on the Ribbon's Home tab. Before you can define the table, you will need to create the table or import it from a source external to Excel. We look at working with external data later in the chapter, so let's concentrate on issues related to creating your own table directly in Excel.

Before you begin banging away on the keyboard, you might want to take a moment and do a little planning related to your table. It makes sense to determine the fields that you want to include in the table and that will make up each record. You also need to determine the purpose of the table; is it truly a data repository or is it a way to list some data and then manipulate it? If you are building the table for analysis purposes, you don't necessarily have to include all the information that you have collected for the database as you would if you are building a table that will serve primarily as an information resource.

> **〰️ tip**
>
> You might want to include a key field in your table. This provides a field column that contains a unique identifier for each record in the table, such as employee number or invoice number. You can then use the key field to quickly sort your records back into the original order. You can use the fill handle to quickly create a series and assign unique numbers in the key field column as needed.

For example, if you are working with employee salary data or sales information for your sales force and really want to be able to filter and sort the data to get a better picture of performance, do you need to include extraneous information in the table such as the employee's phone number or the names of a particular salesperson's children? So, the first thing you need to decide is what fields you will include in the table. After the fields are entered in the top row of the table, you can then enter each of the records that will make up the table.

🔍 **note**

Excel 2010 has a number of improvements related to tables. When you scroll down through a large table, you will find that the field headings now remain on the screen as you move down through the records in the table.

After you have the table in an Excel worksheet, defining the actual table range is very straightforward. Follow these steps:

1. Select the cell range for the table, including the field names in the top row of the table.

2. Select the Ribbon's Insert tab and then click the Table command in the Tables group. The Create Table dialog box will open as shown in Figure 15.1.

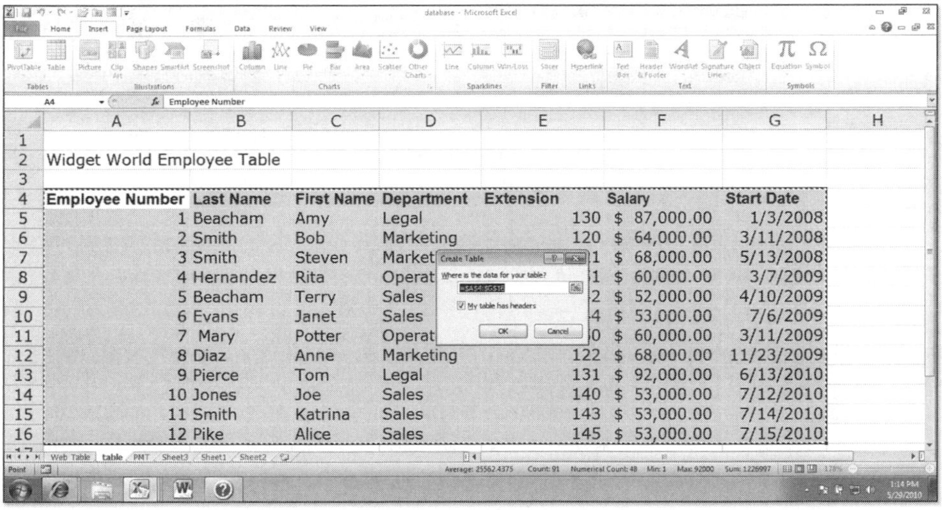

Figure 15.1
The Create Table dialog box.

3. Make sure that the range specified in the Create Table dialog box encompasses your entire table range. You can modify the range by clicking the Shrink button and then selecting a new range for the table.

4. Click OK. The range is now defined as a table.

As soon as you close the Create Table Dialog box, you will notice that the table will be formatted with the default table style and that drop-down lists appear on each field heading in the table. These are the AutoFilters for each field in the table. The AutoFilters enable you to sort and filter the records in the table by each field.

Creating a Table Using Styles

You can also create your database table by selecting a table style in the Table Styles gallery, which is accessed via the Format as Table command on the Ribbon's Home tab. This enables you to specify your table range and pick a table style—all pretty much at the same time.

Select the cell range for the table. Then select the Format as Table command in the Style group on the Ribbon's Home tab. The Table Styles gallery will appear as shown in Figure 15.2.

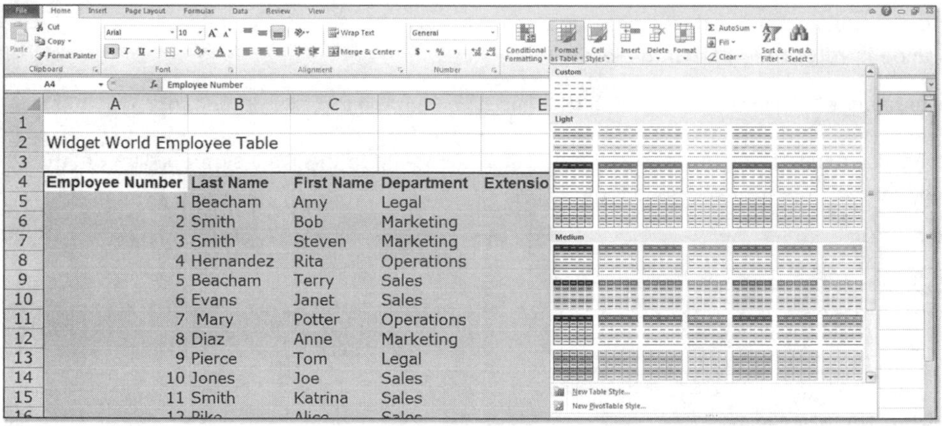

Figure 15.2
The Table Styles gallery.

Select one of the table styles in the gallery. When you select the style, the Table Styles gallery will close and the Format as Table dialog box will appear. Make sure that the data range for the table is correct and then click OK. The table will be created and assigned the table style you selected.

Database tables do not necessarily need to be discrete tables on their own worksheets. You can also create tables by selecting a subset range of the original worksheet. Think of the table feature as a way to access data analysis tools on the Data tab of the Ribbon. This enables you to use the table and accompanying tools as a way to work with existing data in large worksheets that contain information arranged in the appropriate table format of field columns and record rows.

You can also define multiple tables within a single worksheet, which enables you to group data in such a way that you can do some meaningful manipulations of the information by using the commands on the Data tab.

Using the Table Tools

After the table range has been specified, you can take advantage of the Table Tools to change the table style and other options related to the table style. You can also refresh data that comes from an external source, export the table to a SharePoint list, or convert the table back to a normal worksheet range. Figure 15.3 shows the Table Tools Design tab. It is another example of Excel's (and the Office applications') contextual tool sets.

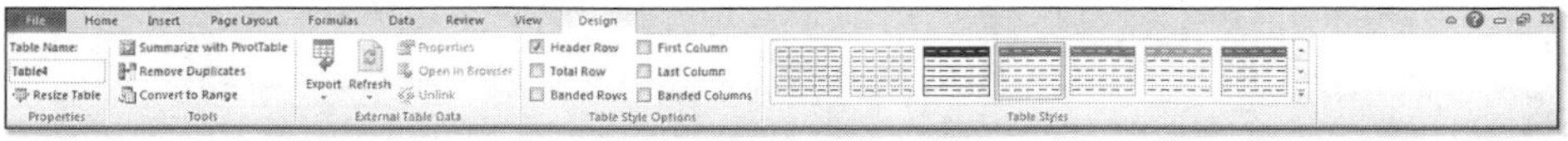

Figure 15.3
The Table Tools
Design tab.

Basic commands related to the table style and table options will be available to you whether the data is external or internal to Excel. The commands available in the External Table Data group will be limited to the Export command if you are working with a table created in Excel. The Table Tools Design tab command groups are as follows:

- **Properties:** This group provides the table name (which you can edit as needed) and also a Resize Table command. You can resize the table to include more or fewer rows and columns if required, meaning you are changing the table range.

- **Tools:** This group provides you with the ability to create a PivotTable from the current table (we discuss PivotTables later in the chapter). A Remove Duplicates command is also provided that enables you to specify a column that contains duplicate entries and delete them. This group also provides the Convert to Range command, which converts the table data range back to a regular worksheet data range.

- **External Table Data:** This group provides the Export command, which can be used to export your Excel table to a SharePoint list. Other commands in the group relate to external table data and enable you to refresh the data, view the data properties, and unlink from the external data source.

- **Table Style Options:** This group provides a series of check boxes that enable you to fine-tune the table. For example, you can include or preclude a header row or a total row. The Banded Rows formatting can also be turned on or off. You can also choose to format the first column or last column in the table and add banded columns to the table.

- **Table Styles:** This group provides access to the Table Styles gallery. Place the mouse on a style in the gallery to preview that particular style on your table. The More button enables you to view the entire gallery. Click a style to assign it to the current table.

Although the Table Tools Design tab becomes active when you select a cell range that falls in the table range, the commands that are the real meat and potatoes of table manipulation are provided by the AutoFilters placed on each of the table field headings and the commands provided on the Ribbon's data tab. Two of the most fundamental manipulations of table records are sorting and filtering.

Sorting Table Data

Sorting by the fields in a table enables you to quickly place the records in the table based on your sort criteria. You can sort data by using the sort commands on a field's AutoFilter menu or by selecting one of the Sort commands in the Sort & Filter group on the Ribbon's Data tab. To quickly sort the table by a particular field select that field's AutoFilter arrow as shown in Figure 15.4.

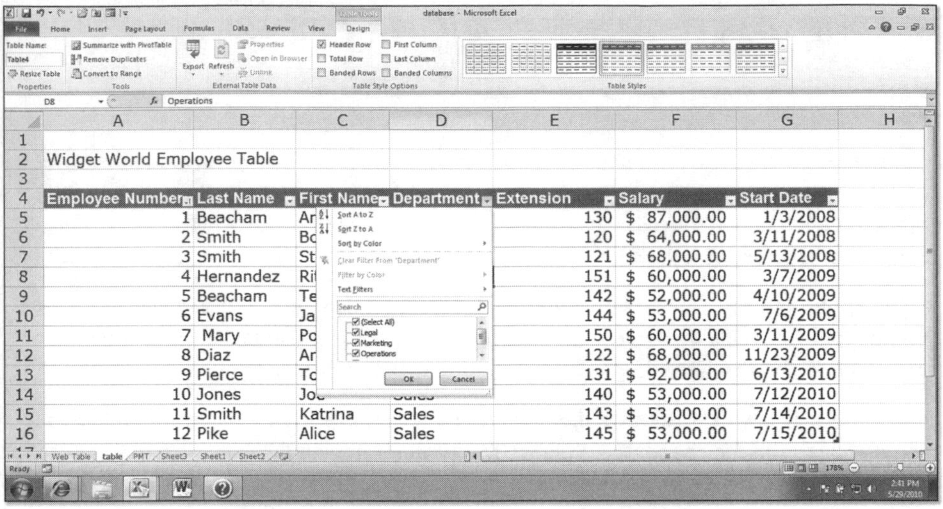

Figure 15.4
The AutoFilter menu for a table field.

You can then select Sort A to Z (ascending) or Sort Z to A (descending) as needed on the AutoFilter menu. The records in the table will be sorted by the field you selected in the direction you selected (ascending or descending). You can use the Sort commands in the Sort & Filter group. Click in the field column that you want to use as the sort field. Then select either the Sort A to Z or Sort Z to A command. The table records will be sorted by the field you specified.

You can also sort by multiple fields in the table. For example, assume that you have a table where the last name field column is followed by the first name field column. You can select any two cells in these two field columns and then select either the Sort A to Z or Sort Z to A command in the Sort & Filter group to sort the table by the last name field followed by the first name field.

This enables you to sort out all the Smiths and Jones that appear in your table. In terms of a more generic application of this multiple field sorting, Excel will sort by the first selected field column (starting on the left) and then move to the right, sorting by each subsequent field column that has been selected.

How Excel Sorts Data

When Excel sorts the records in a table, it follows rules for how the data is actually sorted. Numbers will appear first in a sort list and in the case of an ascending sort (A to Z) will be sorted from the smallest (negative numbers will qualify as small numbers) to the largest. Numbers (or values) include dates, which Excel perceives as values. Keep in mind that Excel looks at the content of the cell, not the formatting of the content. So, even a date that appears as January 1, 2011 is still a number to Excel.

In the case of text entries, the field column data will be sorted by punctuation and special characters such as #, &, *, and so on (in the order you find them on the keyboard) followed by the letters of the alphabet (A through Z). Text with numbers would follow regular text entries when doing a sort.

If you have a field column that contains numbers, text, and text with numbers, the ascending sort would use this sort order: numbers, followed by text, and then numbers with text.

Using the Sort Dialog Box

In cases where you cannot conveniently sort by multiple fields because of the location of the fields in the table and you would like more control over the number of levels in the sort, you can use the Sort dialog box. The Sort dialog box enables you to specify 64 levels for your sort.

To open the Sort dialog box, select Sort in the Sort & Filter group. Figure 15.5 shows the Sort dialog box.

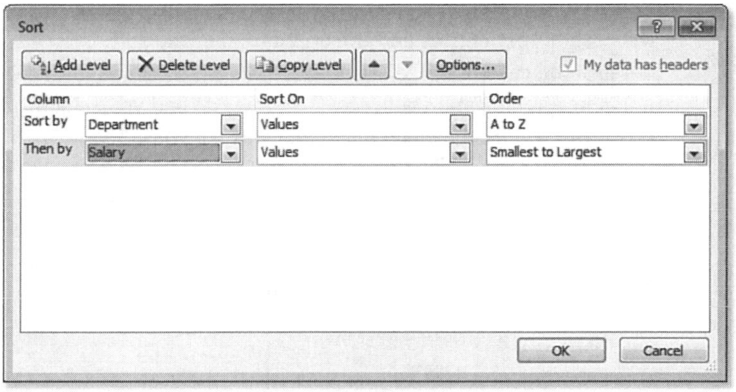

Figure 15.5
The Sort dialog box.

The first sort level is available when you open the Sort dialog box; specify the first field name in the first level's Sort By drop-down list, which will list all the fields in the table. By default, sort levels sort on the values that are in the field column you have specified in the primary sort level (or key, as sort levels are also known). You can choose to sort by values, cell color, font color, or cell icon. The cell and font color can be specified by cell attributes that you have manually assigned to cells. These attributes can also be the result of conditional formatting. This includes the possibilities of the field column's cells containing cell icons that have been inserted into cells that have met certain criteria related to conditional formatting that you have assigned to the table cells.

➡ *For information on using conditional formatting including icon sets, see page 322 in Chapter 12, "Worksheet Formatting and Management."*

After you have specified what column should be sorted and what the sort should be performed on (values, cell colors, and so on), you can specify the order of the sort level. For cells containing text, this will be A to Z or Z to A, and for numerical values, it will be smallest to largest or largest to smallest. Dates are oldest to newest or newest to oldest.

You can also create custom sort lists to determine the sort order. Select Custom List in the Order drop-down box and then create the custom list in the Custom Lists dialog box. Custom lists were discussed in Chapter 11, "Requisite Excel: Essential Features," in reference to creating custom series, but the lists can also be used to determine the sort order of information in a field column.

➡ *For information on creating custom lists, see page 299 in Chapter 11.*

After you have specified the parameters for the first sort level, click the Add Level button to add an additional level to the Sort dialog box. Configure the level by going through the same steps you used to configure the first level. You can also delete levels if needed and you can copy levels to hasten the configuration process for field columns that are similar in contents and how you want them to be sorted.

You also have the option of changing sort options related to the case of text entries and the orientation of the sort. By default, the case of the text is ignored during sorting and Excel assumes that you have placed your fields in columns and your records in rows. When you select the Options button in the Sort dialog box, the Sort Options dialog box opens as shown in Figure 15.6.

tip

If you don't see the AutoFilter arrows on the table field headings, make sure that you select a cell within the table range and then select the Filter command on the Ribbon's Data tab.

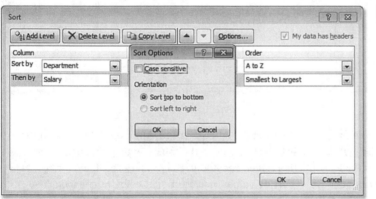

Figure 15.6
The Sort Options dialog box.

To specify that case be considered during the sort, select the Case Sensitive check box. Uppercase text will be sorted before lowercase text when this check box is enabled. As already mentioned, the sort takes place from top to bottom, meaning the rows are rearranged. If you have a situation where you want to sort the columns instead of the rows, you can switch the sort to Sort Left to Right (this would be useful in cases where you want to sort a worksheet arranged in columns rather than rows, such as a database table is). Click OK to close the Sort Options dialog box.

After you have specified your sort levels and the information for each level, you can run the sort. Click OK and the sort will take place in the table.

Filtering Table Data

Although sorting helps you arrange the records in the table in a particular order, filtering enables you to view subsets of the table records based on specific criteria. One option for filtering the data in the table is to use the AutoFilter lists on each of the table field headings. AutoFilter enables you to quickly filter the table in place.

When you select the AutoFilter arrow for a particular field, you will find that the AutoFilter menu provides a list of all the entries for that particular field. By default, all the values are selected, meaning there is no filtering currently applied to the table based on that field. Figure 15.7 shows the AutoFilter list for a table field.

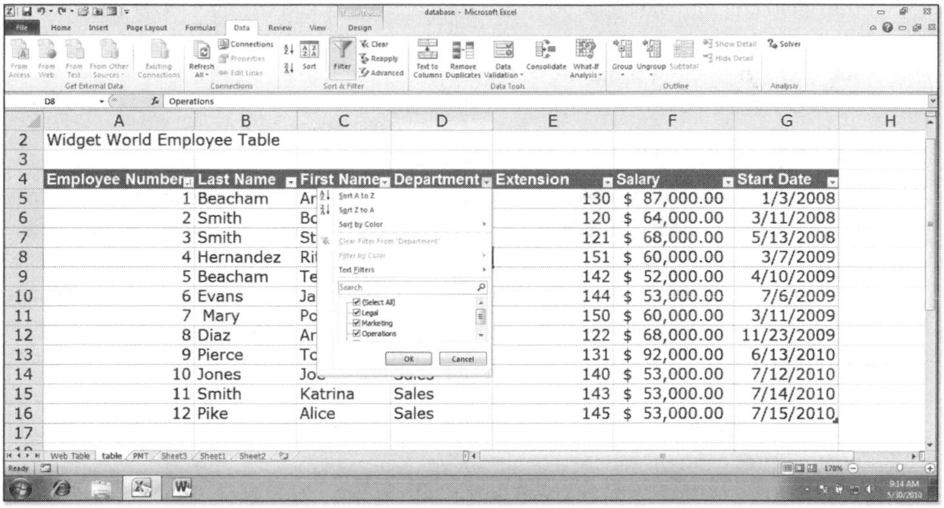

Figure 15.7
The AutoFilter drop-down menu.

The most straightforward method of filtering the table by a specific field is to deselect the Select All check box in the field list and then select the field value that you want to use to filter the table. You can select more than one value in the field data list. Remember that the purpose of the filter is to show a subset of the table records, so you can specify multiple criteria for a single field. When you are ready to run the filter based on actual field values, click OK. The table records will be filtered based on your selection or selections in the AutoFilter list.

AutoFilter enables you to filter by more than one field, so you can create filters based on criteria for more than one field in the table. Simply use the AutoFilter drop-down list to specify the filter criteria for each field. The field or fields that you have used to filter the table will have a small filter icon (it looks like a funnel) on the AutoFilter drop-down arrow. This serves as a reminder as to which fields in the table have been used to filter the data.

You can clear a filter that is specific to a field. Select the AutoFilter drop-down arrow and then select the Clear Filter From "field name" on the AutoFilter menu. Any other filters applied to the table will remain in force. If you want to clear all the filters that you have applied to the table, select the Clear command in the Sort & Filter group.

Using the AutoFilter Search Box

Excel 2010 provides a welcomed addition to the AutoFilter menu—a Search box. The Search box can be used to quickly search for data that appears in that field. This can be particularly useful when you are working with a database table that has a large number of records. The list of field values for each field will, obviously, be as numerous as the number of records in the table, so having a Search box that can be used to find a specific field value quickly can speed up the filtering of the table.

Select a field's AutoFilter arrow to access the AutoFilter menu. Click in the Search box. As you begin to type your search entry, matches will appear in the results list as you enter each character for a number (value) or a text entry. Continue to type the search parameter string until you have the desired results listed. For example, to view all the people with the last name of "Smith," you might need to type "smi" to view just the Smiths and not any Smythes. The data found by the search in that field column will be listed below the search box and the check box for matches to your search string will be selected. To run the AutoFilter based on the search results, click OK. If you need to fine-tune the search string, do so and then run the filter.

Creating Custom AutoFilters

So far we have looked at filtering tables as an all-or-nothing proposition. Either the records completely met the field parameters that were set via the AutoFilter menu on a field or fields or the records didn't. You can also create custom AutoFilters that provide you with the ability to create more robust filters based on conditional statements. These conditional statements enable you to filter the table records for a range of field values or text entries rather than an exact match to a particular criterion.

The AutoFilter menu provides number, date, and text filters that are designed to help you create more complex filters for each of these specific data types. For example, when working with a field column that contains numbers (values), you can specify filter criteria based on conditional statements such as equals, does not equal, is greater than, between, and so on. For text entries in a field column, you can also create conditional statements such as equals, begins with, ends with, and contains. In the case of dates, you can use conditional statements such as equals, before, and after, and you can also choose from a wide variety of data filters such as tomorrow, yesterday, next week, next quarter, and year to date. Figure 15.8 shows the different data filters provided for a field column that contains dates.

As already mentioned, each data type filter, such as those for numbers or for text, enables you to quickly create a custom AutoFilter based on a conditional statement that you select from a list. For example, if you wanted to see employee records that matched a salary range filter, you could select the Between filter on the Number Filters list. This would open the Custom AutoFilter dialog box as shown in Figure 15.9.

> ### 🔊 tip
> You can quickly filter a number field using the Top 10 number filter. The Top 10 AutoFilter enables you to quickly show the top or bottom items in a field column (10 is the default number but you can change it) based on the values in the field or a percent. For example, you could find the top 10 sales representatives based on the percent of sales.

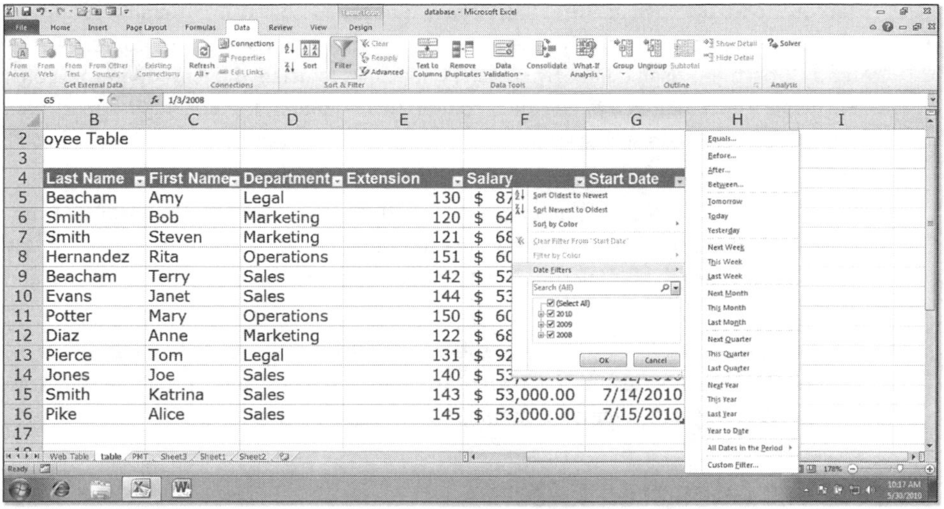

Figure 15.8
Custom
AutoFilters
such as Date
Filters enable
you to quickly
filter by a data
type.

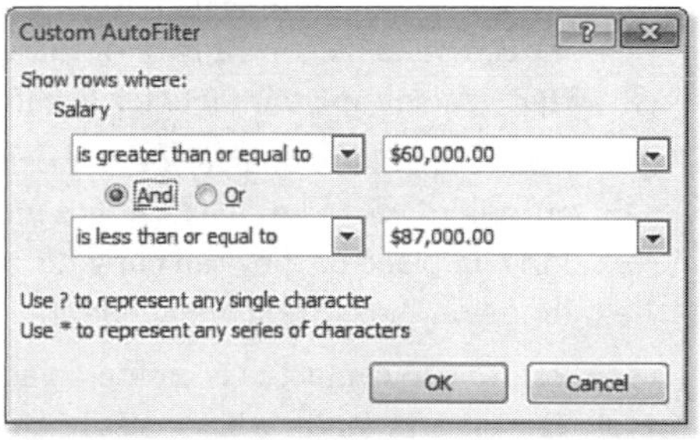

Figure 15.9
The Custom AutoFilter dialog box.

By selecting the Between filter, the Custom AutoFilter dialog box has automatically entered two criteria for the filter: is greater than or equal to and is less than or equal to. All you have to do is specify the two salary values that provide the beginning and end of the salary range that you want supplied by the filter.

When you use the Custom AutoFilter dialog box, you can modify the filter criteria by using the criteria drop-down lists. You specify the actual values, dates, or text entries for the AutoFilter by using the field content drop-down lists, which are to the right of the criteria lists. You can specify the specific value or text entry that should be used by the AutoFilter for each criteria by selecting an actual field column entry in the drop-down list. You can also type in filter parameters and use the question mark (?) to represent single characters and the asterisk (*) to represent a series of characters. These two wildcards will be most useful in situations where you are working with a field that contains text entries.

When you are ready to run the AutoFilter, click OK. The table will be filtered based on the criteria set for the field's custom AutoFilter. You can apply custom AutoFilters to multiple field columns to filter by more than one field in the table. For example, you could do a custom AutoFilter that will filter a Department Name field by specific departments using the And operator. You could then run a Between AutoFilter on a Salary field column to see who in the specified departments made a salary that fell in the range specified by the custom AutoFilter applied to the Salary field.

If you want to create a custom AutoFilter that isn't listed in the set of filters provided for a particular field, you can open the Custom AutoFilter dialog box and set up your filter from scratch. Select Custom Filter at the bottom of any of the different data types (numbers, text, or dates) filter lists. The Custom AutoFilter dialog box will open and you can set the filter operators and criteria as you require.

You can clear custom AutoFilters in the same way that the quick AutoFilters are cleared: by using the field's AutoFilter menu. If you want to clear all the custom AutoFilters that you have applied to a table, click the Clear command on the Sort & Filter group.

Creating Advanced Filters

You might find that even the custom AutoFilters are limiting in terms of the number of fields that you can use to filter the table and are rather cumbersome in terms of having to work in a different Custom AutoFilter dialog box for each field that you want to filter. Custom AutoFilters are best used for comparisons, and any filter that goes beyond a couple of comparison criteria is going to require that you set up your table for advanced filtering.

Advanced filters enable you to filter a database by as many fields as you like. Advanced filters use a criteria range to set the filter criteria (which we get to in a moment). Advanced filters can filter the table in place or they can copy the results of the advanced filter—the filtered records—to a specified range on the current worksheet.

Before you can actually create an advanced filter, you need to create a criteria range for the table. The criteria range will consist of an exact duplicate of the field headings found in the table. The criteria range will also consist of at least one empty row below the copied field headings. If you are going to use multiple criteria for a particular field, you will need multiple blank rows below field headings you designate as the criteria range. It is in the cells directly below each of the field heading copies that you will place the filter parameters for the advanced filter.

So, the first thing you need to do is copy the row that contains the field headings for the table. You can then paste these headings somewhere onto the worksheet so that there is at least one empty row below the copied field names. It makes sense, however, to have multiple empty rows available for multiple criteria for a single field.

You can place the copied field headings above or below the database table; it's up to you. Just make sure that there is clear separation between the table and the criteria range that you will specify when you run the advanced filter. Figure 15.10 shows a database table (A4:G16) and an accompanying criteria range (A20:A21).

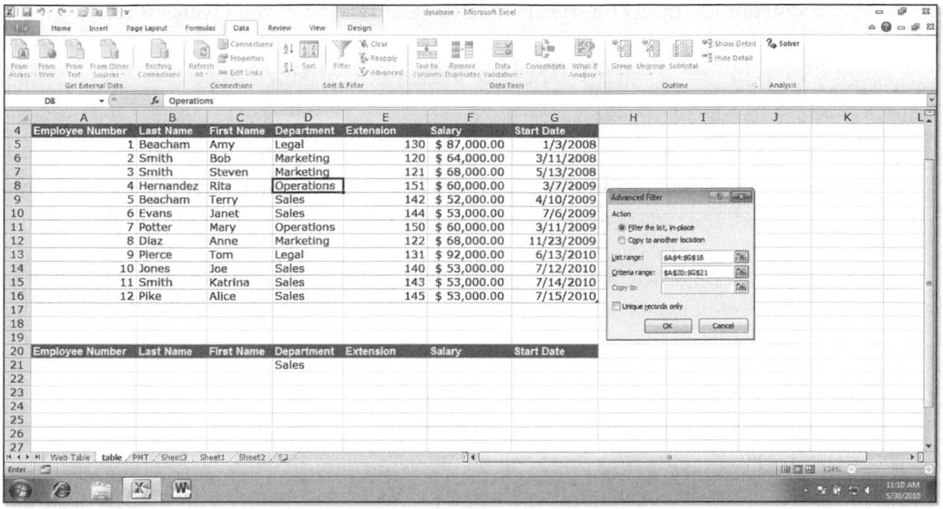

Figure 15.10
A table, criteria range, and Advanced Filter dialog box.

In this case, the criteria range consists of the cells containing the copied field headings and the row below the field headings. A criterion, Sales, has been typed below the Department field heading in the criteria range. The Advanced Filter dialog box is configured to filter the table in place. Both the List range (the table range) and the Criteria range are specified in the Advanced Filter dialog box.

It is the criteria that you place below the field names included in the criteria range that enables you to filter the table records. For example, in Figure 15.10, when OK is clicked in the Advanced Filter dialog box, the table will be filtered to show only the records that have Sales specified in the Department field column. This example shows only a single criterion, but you can specify multiple criteria and use different operators such as greater than (>) or less than (<) as part of the criteria.

In cases where you have criteria for more than one field column in the same criteria range row, you are actually creating an And statement. The advanced filter will base its results on the first criteria *And* the second criteria (and additional criteria if included). In cases where you are specifying multiple criteria for a single field column, you are actually creating an Or statement.

Although advanced filters might look like more trouble than they are worth, they are the only way to filter a table using a number and variety of criteria. Advanced filters can actually be used to copy records from a large table to a table that includes only a subset of records based on the filter. This makes it easier to work with subsets of the records provided by the table.

After you have copied the field headings for the advanced filter to an area that can serve as a criteria range, you are ready to create the advanced filter. Follow these steps:

1. Enter criteria for the filter under the criteria range field headings. You can enter filter criteria for more than one field (type the criteria below the field name) or you can enter multiple criteria for a single field: Type the multiple criteria in the required number of cells below the field name.

2. Click in the database table that you are filtering. Because you have defined this range as a table, it will automatically be specified as the List range for the advanced filter.

3. Select the Advanced command in the Sort & Filter group. The Advanced Filter dialog box will open.

4. Set the action for the filter. You can filter the list in place or copy the results of the filter to another location on the worksheet. If you are going to copy the results to another location, make sure that you give yourself plenty of open space (meaning empty cells) for the copied results.

5. The List range will be the range for the table. If you performed step 2, the range shown in the List range box should reflect the range for the table. If not, click in the worksheet and select the range for the table.

6. Click in the Criteria range box. Select the field headings and the number of rows below the field heading you have copied to provide the criteria range. If you are specifying criteria only in the row below the copied field headings, you only need to specify the field heading row and the row below it. If you are specifying multiple criteria for a single field (or fields), make sure that each row that contains a criterion statement is included in the criteria range.

 tip

You can use the question mark (?) and the asterisk (*) as wildcards when building filters for text fields. In cases where you want a filter criterion to find a specific occurrence of a specific text string when it is not part of a larger text string, use the format ="=text string".

7. (Optional) If you select the Copy to Another Location option button as the action for the filter, you need to specify where the filter should place its results. All you really need to do is click in the blank cell that will serve as the upper-left limit for the filter results. The results will then spill over into other cells as needed.

8. When you are ready to run the filter, click OK.

The results of the advanced filter will appear in the table if you filtered the table in place. If you chose to have the filter results copied to another area of the worksheet, the results will appear there. If you filtered the table in place, you can clear the advanced filter by selecting the Clear command in the Sort & Filter dialog box.

Each time you change the criteria in the criteria range, you will need to rerun the filter. Select Advanced in the Sort & Filter group and make sure the List range and Criteria range are correct for the filter you want to run. Then click OK to run the filter.

Using the Data Form

When Excel 2007 adopted the new Ribbon-based user interface, the data form lost its place as one of the readily accessible data tools on the Data menu. The form is not available via a command on the Ribbon's Data tab. This also holds true in Excel 2010 and so if you want to take advantage of the data

tip

If you want the results of the advanced filter to show only unique records, select the Unique Records Only in the Advanced Filter dialog box.

form to enter or find records in your database table, you will need to add the Form command to the Excel Quick Access Toolbar. The form can actually be quite useful when working with extremely large tables. Figure 15.11 shows the form containing a table record.

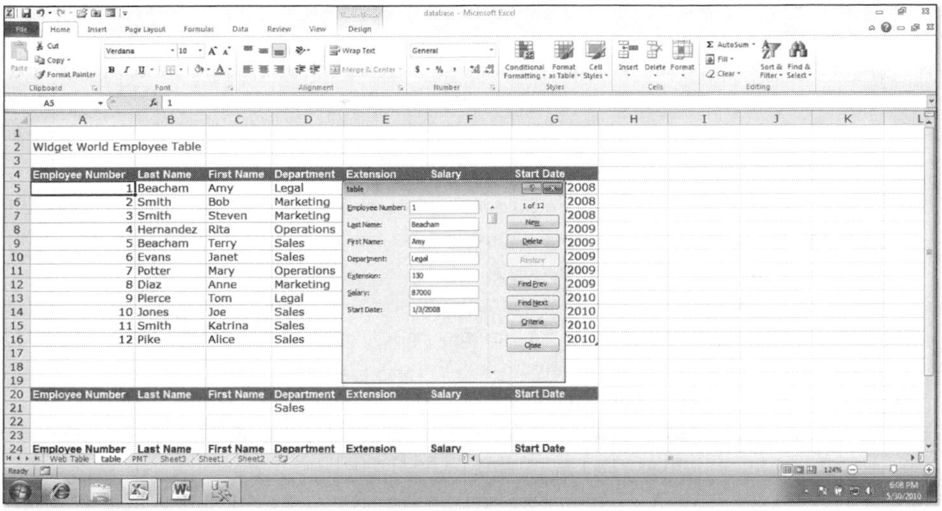

Figure 15.11
The data form can be used to view and edit individual records.

The form provides you with the ability to view, edit, and add records to the table individually. It also enables you to quickly search the database table to find records.

You can quickly add the Form command to the Excel Quick Access Toolbar from the Excel Options window. Follow these steps:

1. Select the Customize Quick Access Toolbar menu and then select More Commands. The Excel Options window will open with the Quick Access Toolbar settings selected.

2. In the Customize the Quick Access Toolbar pane of the Options window, select the Choose commands drop-down list and then select All Commands.

3. Scroll down through the commands listed in the Command pane and select Form.

4. Click the Add button to add the Form command to the Quick Access Toolbar. Then click OK to return to the Excel window.

Now you can open the form as needed when you are working with a table. Click in a record (a row in a table) and then click the Form command on the Quick Access Toolbar. The record will open in the Form window. You can edit a record or delete a record from the Form window. You can also enter new records to the table by selecting New. The new record will be inserted at the bottom of the table.

If you want to find a particular record or records, click the Criteria button. Enter criteria in a field or fields and then click the Find Next button. The first record that meets your criteria will be shown in the Form window. You can select Find Next to move to the next record that matches your criteria. When you have finished working with the form, select Close.

Creating Outlines and Subtotals

The Ribbon's Data tab also provides an Outline group that provides the Group, Ungroup, and Subtotal commands. The Group command enables you to create outline groups in a worksheet. The groups can then be individually expanded or collapsed, so you can hide information at a particular outline level and view only a summary of the data (such as sales totals by regions or salary data by department) rather than each individual row of data.

The purpose of an outline is to take advantage of a hierarchy that is already present in the worksheet. If you think about a text outline, it is made up of different levels of information such as primary levels, secondary levels, and so on. In Excel, the hierarchy is based on logical groupings of information. Typically the key to grouping several rows of information is that they are tied together by a summary row. This row can actually be above or below the detail rows, but it has to be in the same place for you to create an outline. For example, you might have a sales sheet that shows the monthly sales figures for each of your regions for an entire year. At the end of each quarter, a summary row provides a total for each region's sales for that quarter. Figure 15.12 shows a worksheet that has been formatted as an outline using the Group command.

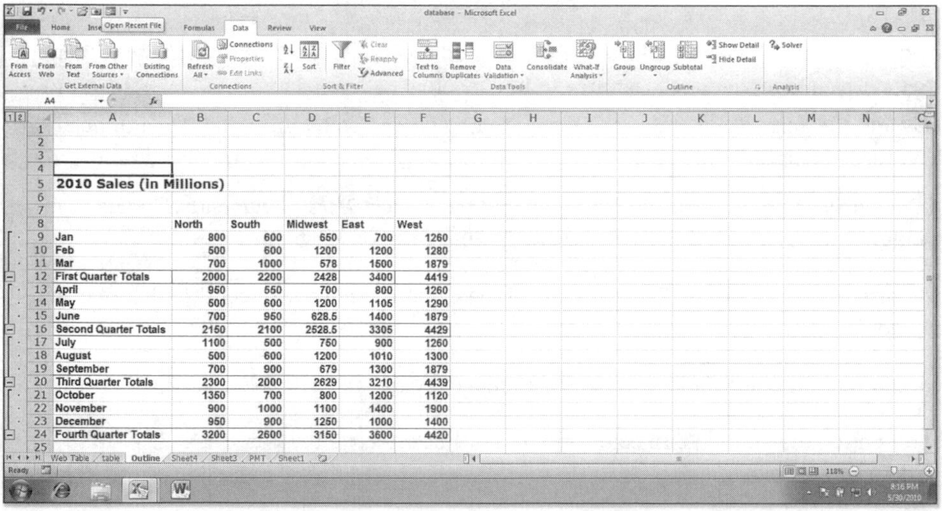

Figure 15.12
You can group related data into outlines.

Note that each group in the outline has a button that can be used to collapse grouped rows. You can collapse a particular quarter group and view the summary row for only that particular group. You can click the control for a collapsed group and expand the group to show all the data in a particular group. Level numbers are also provided at the top of the worksheet area just above the row numbers and to the left of the column letters. You can use these buttons to collapse the outline to level 1 or to expand the outline to level 2 as needed.

To create an outline, you have two choices: You can create the outline manually or you can allow Excel to create an auto outline. If you are working with a range of cells that has been formatted as a table, you can't use the auto outline possibility. So, you might want to use the Convert to Range command on the Table Tools Design tab to convert the table back to a regular worksheet. It definitely makes sense to try the auto outline scenario first because Excel is good at recognizing the groupings in a worksheet.

Select the worksheet and then click the Group command, and then select Auto Outline. If auto outline doesn't group the data in the worksheet as you anticipated, you can go the manual outline route. If you need to clear the outline grouping provided by auto outline, select the Ungroup command and then select Clear Outline.

To manually create the outline, select the worksheet data and then click the Group command. Select Group and the Group dialog box will open. This dialog box provides you with two options: Rows and Columns. Select the appropriate option button for grouping the data and then click OK. The worksheet will be converted to an outline. If you don't get a proper outline, you can clear the current outline and then rearrange the data as needed so that it can be placed in an outline. Remember it is all about establishing a hierarchy in the worksheet that is consistent throughout the worksheet.

> **tip**
> You can also collapse or expand the detail in your outline groups by using the Show Detail and Hide Detail commands in the Outline group, respectively.

Another possibility provided by the Outline group is the Subtotal command. The Subtotal command is actually easier to work with than the Group command because it will automatically insert subtotal rows for you in the worksheet and can also provide summary data. The trick with subtotals is that you need to have a data column that provides a way to group associated rows of data.

For example, an employee list that includes a Department column could be sorted by department, grouping all the employees in the worksheet in their respective departments. You can then have the Subtotal command act on other column data; for example, if a Salary column is also included in the worksheet, the Subtotal could group the employees by department and then provide a salary subtotal for each department. So, to use the Subtotal command to both group data rows and provide subtotals based on those groupings, you need one column of information that can provide the grouping and another column of information that provides the values that will be used to compute the subtotals for each group.

To apply the Subtotal command to a worksheet, sort the rows by the column data that provides the logical grouping of the row data. Then click the Subtotal command. The Subtotal dialog box will appear as shown in Figure 15.13.

> **note**
> You can't use the Subtotal command on a worksheet range that has been formatted as a table.

Use the At Each Change In drop-down list to specify the column title (or field name) that will serve as the grouping mechanism for the rows in the column (this would be the column that you used to sort the worksheet). In the Use Function drop-down list, select the function that you want to use for the subtotal rows in the worksheet. The default is Sum, but you can also use other statistical functions such as Count, Average, and Max.

In the Add Subtotal To box, select the check box for the column that contains the values you want to use in the subtotal calculation. This will be a column that contains numerical values.

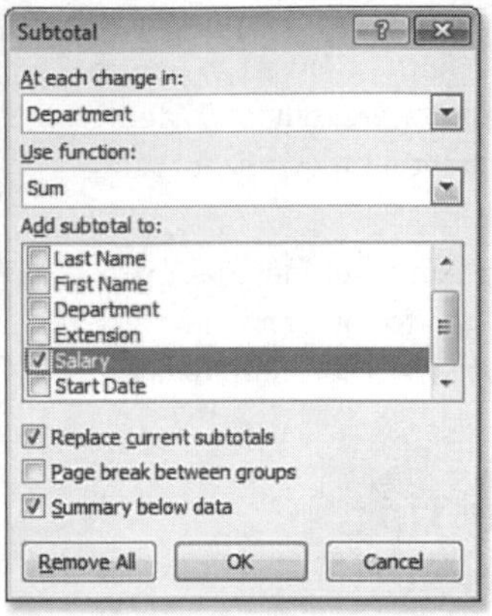

Figure 15.13
The Subtotal dialog box.

Other check boxes provided in the subtotal dialog box enable you to replace any current subtotals in the worksheet, or place page breaks between the groups, which can be useful on large worksheets that will then be printed. A check box is also provided that will include a summary including a grand total below the worksheet data. When you are ready to add the subtotals and groupings to the worksheet, click OK. Figure 15.14 shows a worksheet that has been grouped by department.

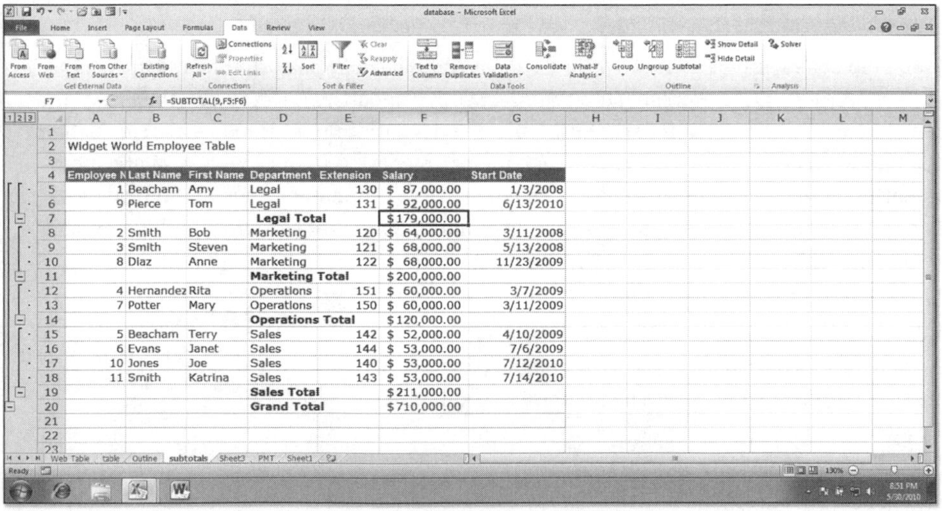

Figure 15.14
A worksheet configured with subtotals.

The Subtotal command placed a subtotal for each department in the Salary column. A grand total has also been placed at the bottom of the worksheet range. Controls are also provided that enable you to expand and collapse the different levels created in the worksheet by the Subtotal command, creating an outline in the worksheet.

Working with External Data

Excel provides you with a number of options for getting external data into a worksheet. After you import data from another source or connect to a data source such as a database server, you can then use Excel's wide variety of capabilities to work with the data. The fact that Excel is an extremely powerful number cruncher means that you can probably perform calculations and data analysis that would be extremely time-consuming or very labor intensive in another software application, such as Microsoft Access.

Excel makes it easy to import data from other applications or database servers. The Get External Data group commands on the Data tab enable you to import data from Access, web tables (on websites), text files, and other database sources such as a Microsoft SQL Server. Let's look at the possibilities.

Importing Data from Access

Access is a powerful desktop relational database application and it can also be used as the front-end client for databases hosted by a database server such as a server running Microsoft SQL Server. Access 2010 is the most recent version of the Access software and Access is one of the applications available in the Office 2010 suite.

Access uses the table as the data container for its database records. Most Access databases (of any complexity) will contain a number of related data tables.

Even though each database will contain multiple tables, it is not that difficult to specify a specific table in the Access database and import it into Excel. Follow these steps:

1. Select the cell in the current worksheet (an empty worksheet would be a good idea), which will serve as the upper-left corner of the imported table data.

2. Select the From Access command in the Get External Data group. The Select Data Source dialog box will open.

3. Navigate to the folder or the network drive that contains the Access database and then select it.

4. Select Open in the Select Data Source dialog box. The Select Table dialog box will open as shown in Figure 15.15.

Figure 15.15
The Select Table dialog box.

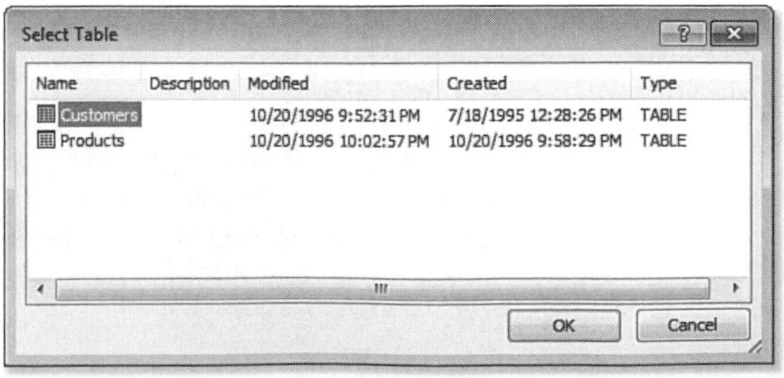

5. The Select Table dialog box lists the tables and the queries (queries look like tables and consist of columns and rows of data) in the database; select a specific table and then click OK. The Import Data dialog box will open.

6. The Import Data dialog box enables you to specify whether the data should be imported as a table, PivotTable report, or a PivotChart and PivotTable report. We talk about PivotTables later in the chapter, but because we are discussing importing tables in this section, we will import the Access data as a table. Select an option button in the dialog box (such as Table). You can also choose to have the data imported into the current worksheet (at a particular place) or you can specify that the imported data be placed on a new worksheet.

7. Click OK and the table will be imported.

The table will be imported as an Excel table, so it will be formatted as a table. You can use any of the Table Tools Design commands to change the look of the table. The Field heading drop-down lists will also be available on the imported table (as it would be for an Excel table), enabling you to sort and filter the table. The table you have imported is actually linked to the Excel worksheet, so changes made to the Access database will be reflected in the worksheet when you update the link between the external data and Excel. To refresh a link to an Access database or other external databases, select the Refresh All command on the Data tab. You can use the Refresh All command to refresh all the links to external data or refresh the data on the current worksheet by selecting Refresh.

Importing a Web Table

You can also import data from any table that appears on a web page. The New Web Query tool that is used to select a web table to be linked to an Excel worksheet is actually quite good at identifying table data on websites. You can import data from a table on the Web that is static; meaning the data in the table is not updated. You can also import data from a table that is dynamic; the data is updated in the table over time. For example, you might want to include stock data that is published in a table on the Web and that is periodically updated. Because Excel imports the external data as a link, the linked data can be refreshed in the Excel worksheet.

When you create a link to a web table, you must specify the site that contains the table. So, before opening the New Web Query window, you might want to use your web browser to navigate to the website. You can then select the website's URL and copy it so that you can paste it into the New Web Query's Address window.

To open the New Web Query window, select the From Web command in the Get External Data group. Figure 15.16 shows the New Web Query window.

You can type or copy and paste a URL into the Address box and then click Go to navigate to a specific website using the New Web Query window. It is basically a web browser with the ability to specify tables on a web page. All tables (the ones that can be identified as such) on the web page will be denoted by a yellow box containing an arrow. When you place the mouse on a specific table arrow, a blue border will appear, denoting the boundaries of that specific table.

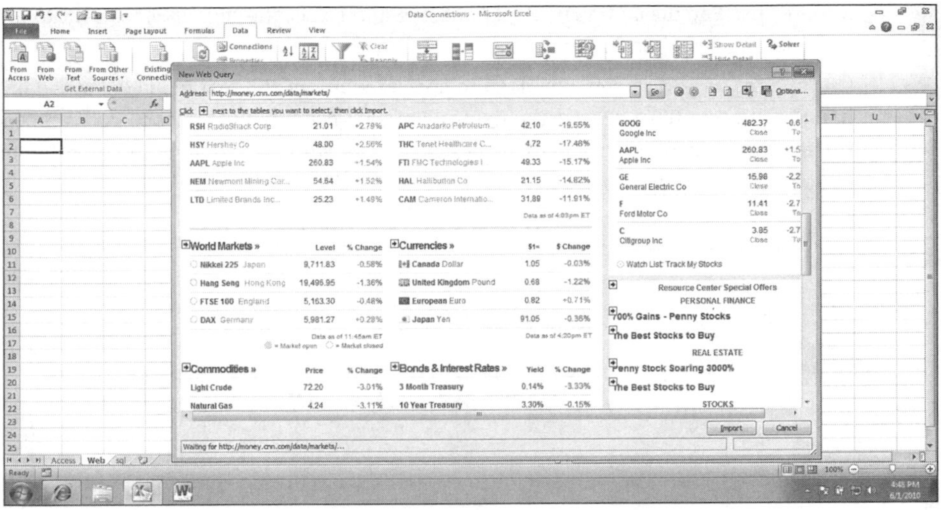

Figure 15.16
The New Web
Query window.

To import a particular table, select the arrow icon for that table. A check mark will appear in the box (that contained the arrow) and the table will be highlighted. Select the Import button in the bottom-right corner of the New Web Query window to import the current table.

The New Web Query window will close and the Import Data dialog box will open. You can specify that the imported data is placed in the current worksheet (or other worksheet in the workbook) or into a new worksheet. After specifying your preference, click OK to import the table. It might take a moment for the data to appear in the worksheet. Web table data imported into Excel is not automatically formatted as a table. You can select the imported data range and format it as a table if you choose. Even if you do not format the imported web table as a table, you can use many of the commands on the Data tab to manipulate the data, and you can add formulas and functions to the data for calculations or create a chart based on the data.

Importing Text Files

There are a lot of different database management software applications available; some are stand-alone and some use a server. For example, Outlook can be used as a standalone contact management application or it can be integrated into a Microsoft Exchange Server environment.

When users of one product attempt to share information with users of another product, they typically must resort to exporting data as delimited text files. These text files can then be imported into a product such as Excel. However, you will need to tell Excel what type of delimited text file it is dealing with—there are tab-delimited text files, comma-delimited text files, and other text files that use other characters to delimit its fields and records.

> **note**
>
> Many nonprofit corporations and government entities that provide data from various studies or government reports on their websites typically provide the data as a text-delimited file. This makes it usable because you can import the information into Excel.

To import a text file into Excel, select the From Text command in the Get External Data group. The Import Text File dialog box will open. Locate and select the text file you want to import and then click Import. The Text Import Wizard will open.

On the first wizard screen, you need to specify whether the text file is delimited or fixed width. A fixed-width text file will have the fields aligned in columns, with space between each field. Select Delimited or Fixed Width and then click Next. The Step 2 window of the Text Import Wizard will appear as shown in Figure 15.17.

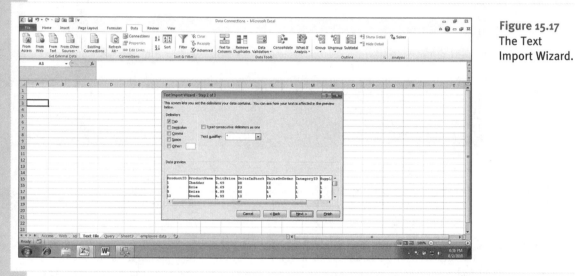

Figure 15.17
The Text
Import Wizard.

Specify the delimiter used for the text file such as tab, semicolon, comma, and so on. Then click Next to continue. The next wizard screen enables you to specify the date format in each columns shown in the bottom pane of the wizard screen. Select a column and then specify the data type for that column: General, Text, Date, or Do Not Import Column (skip). Repeat the process until you have formatted all the columns you will import.

When you are ready to import the text file, select Finish. The Import Data dialog box will open. Specify whether you want to import the data in the current worksheet or a new worksheet, and then click OK. The text file will be imported. You can format the imported data as a table or otherwise manipulate it using the various Excel commands and functions.

Connecting to a SQL Server

Microsoft SQL Server (SQL Server 2008 R2 was the most current version of SQL Server when this book was written) is a powerful network database platform. If you do a lot of work with information in a corporate or other large institution environment, chances are that you work with data that is stored on a SQL server or one of Microsoft's database platform competitors. Both Excel and Microsoft Access can be used to connect to a SQL server and work with the data on the server. Microsoft Access is often used in a SQL Server environment as the client for database end users. So, Excel doesn't have the capabilities that Access does in terms of working with SQL databases. However, that doesn't mean that table information can't be pulled off of the SQL database and then analyzed and manipulated in Excel.

To connect to a SQL Server database, select the From Other Sources command in the Get External Data group and then select From SQL Server. The Data Connection Wizard will open as shown in Figure 15.18.

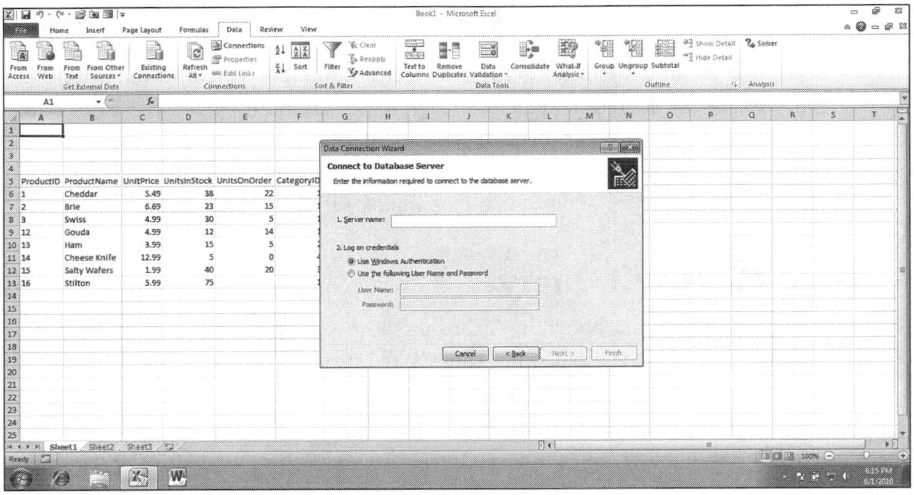

Figure 15.18
The Data Connection Wizard.

To log on to the server and import a data table, you need to know the server name and your logon credentials. In the case of SQL Server, you can log on in some situations using Windows authentication or you can logon using a username and password recognized by SQL Server. Enter the server name and then your logon information. Then click Next to continue.

The next screen provided by the Data Connection Wizard will request that you select a database provided by SQL Server and select a specific table in the database. Figure 15.19 shows the Select Database and Table screen of the Data Connection Wizard.

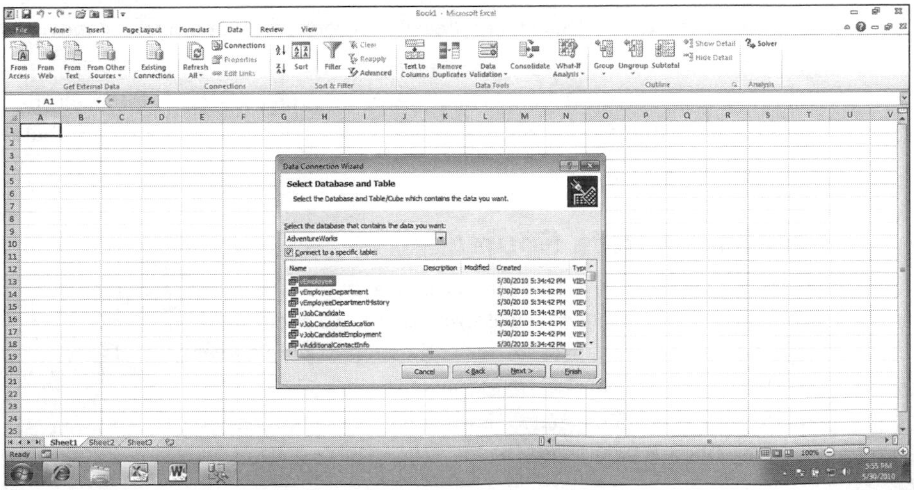

Figure 15.19
Select a database and table on the SQL Server.

Select the database by using the drop-down list and then select a table from the table list provided. After specifying the database and table, click Next. The Import Data dialog box will open; you can import the data as a table, PivotTable Report, or a PivotChart and PivotTable report. You can also specify that the imported data be placed starting at a particular cell in the current worksheet or a new worksheet. Click OK when you are ready to import the SQL data.

The Data Connection Wizard can also be used to connect to a number of different database server types and is not limited to a SQL Server connection. You can start the Data Connection Wizard from the From Other Sources command's gallery. Remember that the whole point of connecting to external data is so that you can use Excel's capabilities to analyze the data in a worksheet format. So, import tables that contain information that you can work with in Excel. Sales data, inventory data—any table with values—can then be manipulated, charted, and analyzed to your heart's content.

Using Microsoft Query

Although the Data Connection Wizard provides you with the ability to connect to a number of different database server platforms, there may be some occasions when you want to connect to a database source and actually run a query to select the data that you will import into Excel. A query is a really a question that you pose to a database. Queries enable you to extract data from more than one related table by specifying the field information that is to be included in the query. For example, you could design the query to extract data related to specific products that you sell from a products table and also extract data from a suppliers table that provides information about the suppliers that provide you with your products. For queries to work, there needs be a relationship between the tables that you will use in the query. So, you should have some familiarity with the database itself and how the database is structured before you attempt to create queries in Excel to access information in the database.

Microsoft Query enables you to connect to common data sources such as Access and Excel files and also dBASE files (dBASE was one of the first PC-based relational databases). You can also create queries to access data in a SQL Server database. After you create a query, you can then use the query in the future; the query can be used in other Excel worksheets and the query can be modified if needed. The data sources that you identify during the process of creating the query will also be available in the future. This makes it easy to reconnect to a particular database or database server from Excel.

When you create a new query, you must identify or create a data source for the query first. You can then create the query using the Query Wizard. Let's look at creating a new data source and then walk through creating a query with the Query Wizard.

Creating a Data Source

Creating a data source establishes a connection to the database you will use when you create your query. To open the Choose Data Source dialog box, select the From Other Sources command and then select From Microsoft Query.

The Choose Data Source dialog box will open. The Databases tab of the Choose Data Source dialog box provides a list of

note

You can also import XML files into Excel; the From Other Sources gallery provides the From XML Data Import command.

database file types such as dBASE file, Excel Files, and MS Access Database. You can select any of these file types and then create the query for a database in that format.

More importantly, the Choose Data Source dialog box enables you to create a query for a new data source such as a SQL, Oracle, or other network database platform. Select <New Data Source> and then click OK. The Create New Data Source dialog box will open. The New Data Source dialog box will actually walk you through the steps in creating the new data source.

The first step you must perform in the Create New Data Source dialog box is to enter a descriptive name for the data source. Create a name for the source that makes it apparent what database platform you are accessing and the database you will use in the query. After you have named the data source, select a driver for the type of database you will access.

You can choose a driver for a large number of different database types such as dBASE, Access, Paradox, Visual FoxPro, and database platforms such as SQL and Oracle.

After you have selected the driver for the data source, click the Connect button. What happens next will depend on the driver you selected for the database. If you select a driver for a database file type such as Access, dBASE, or Paradox, you will need to specify the location of the file on your computer or network. Figure 15.20 shows the ODBC Microsoft Access Setup dialog box, which is used to specify the Microsoft Access database to be used to create a query using Microsoft Query.

> **note**
>
> ODBC stands for Open Database Connectivity and is a standard (supported by Microsoft) for accessing different database file types and platforms. It is ODBC that allows Microsoft Query to connect to different types of databases.

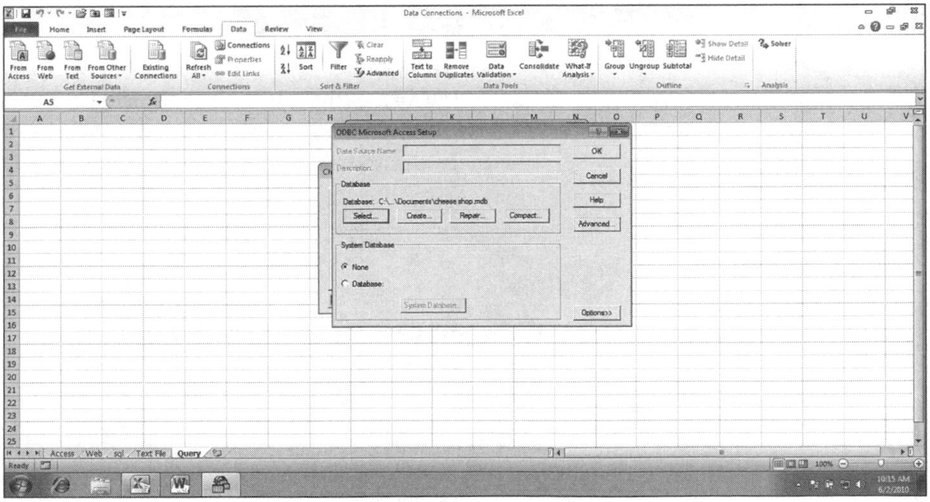

Figure 15.20
Use an ODBC driver to open a database file.

You can also connect to database tables that are in databases provided by database servers such as SQL or Oracle. All you have to do is select the appropriate driver and then log on to the server to access the table data.

Figure 15.21 shows the Create New Data Source dialog box and the SQL Server Login dialog box. In the Create New Data Source dialog box, the SQL Server driver has been selected.

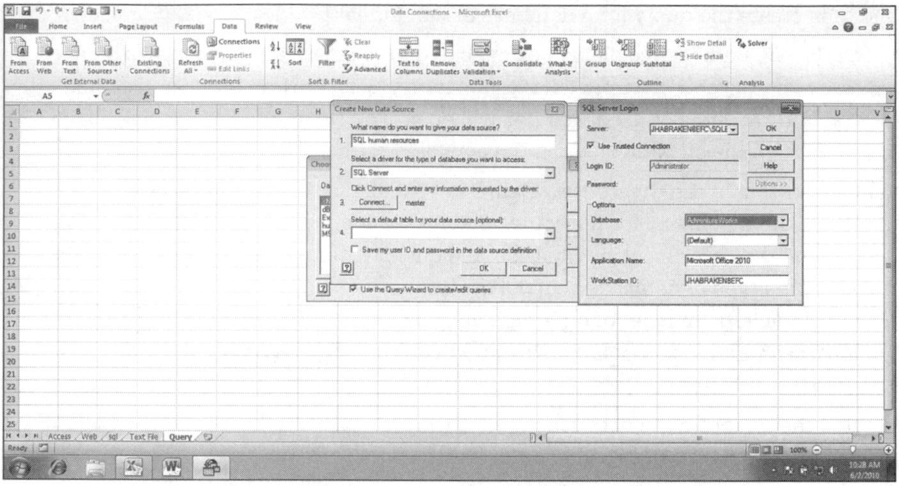

Figure 15.21
Specify the database to be used by Microsoft Query.

After the driver has been specified, you need to connect to the database server by clicking the Connect button in the Create New Data Source dialog box. Provide your logon credentials in the SQL Server Login dialog box. If the server provides more than one database, you will want to click the Options button and then use the Database drop-down list to specify the database you want to access on the server. Then click OK; you will be returned to the Create New Data Source dialog box. Click OK and you will be returned to the Choose Data Source dialog box.

Creating the Query

Now that you have identified the data source for the query, you can actually create the query using the Query Wizard. In the Choose Data Source dialog box, select the data source you want to use for the query and then click OK. The Query Wizard will open as shown in Figure 15.22.

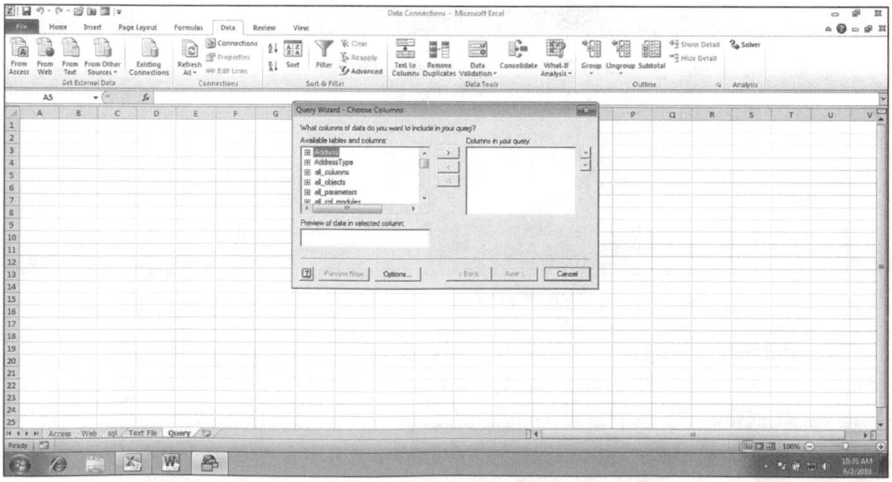

Figure 15.22
The Query Wizard.

On the left of the Query Wizard dialog box will be a list of the tables in the database. Expand a table and then choose specific fields that you want to serve as the columns in your query; select a field and then click the Add button to add it to the columns in your query list. You can use fields from multiple tables if required; it is important, however, that a relationship exist between the tables in the database.

If you attempt to create a query using fields from multiple tables that are not related, the Query Wizard will require that you create the joins between the tables. This would require that a key field in a table also exist as the foreign key in a second table for you to be able to create the relationship. This discussion is a little beyond the scope of this book, so I would say that if you are going to work with database tables in Excel, you should spend some time working with the databases in their native application (such as Access) to make sure you understand how relational databases actually work.

After you have specified the columns for your query, click the Next button. On the next screen, you can specify that the data be filtered by a particular field or fields, which establishes the row in the table that is created by the query. Set the filters for the query (if required) and then click Next. On the next screen, you can specify that the data be sorted by a field or fields. After specifying the sort fields and sort order, click Next.

The final Query Wizard screen enables you to save your query, so that it is available in the future in the Choose Data Source dialog box on the Query tab. Select Save Query and then use the Save As dialog box to name and save the query. You will then be returned to the Query Wizard's Finish screen; click Finish. The Import Data dialog box will appear as shown in Figure 15.23.

Figure 15.23
The Import Data
dialog box.

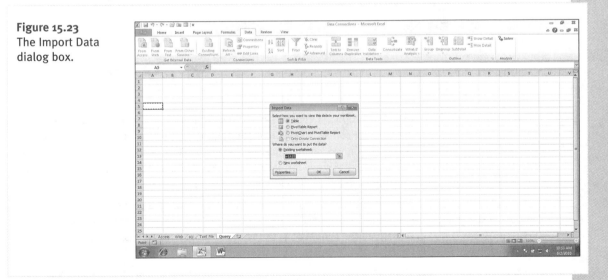

You can import the data as a table or as PivotTable (or as a PivotTable and PivotChart). The data can be imported into the current worksheet or a new worksheet. Specify the various options in the Import Data dialog box and then click OK. The date will be imported into an Excel table. You can manipulate the data as you would any Excel data, including sorting and filtering.

Viewing and Refreshing Connections

If you are working with external data in Excel tables, you might want to view the connections for your Excel workbook. You can also refresh connections to take advantage of the fact that when the data source is updated, this information will also be available in Excel after the link to the source has been refreshed.

To view the connection for the current Excel workbook, select the Connections command in the Connections group on the Ribbon's Data tab. The Workbook Connections dialog box will open as shown in Figure 15.24.

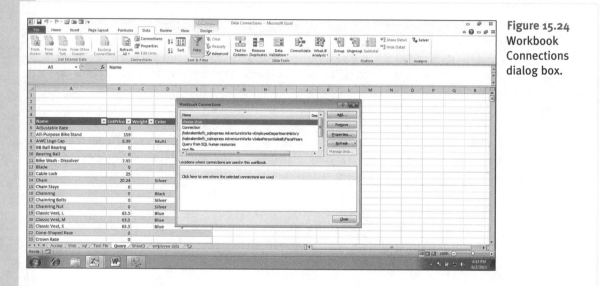

Figure 15.24
Workbook Connections dialog box.

You can refresh or remove a connection listed in the Workbook Connections dialog box. You can also set properties related to a particular connection such as the refresh properties for the source; select the Properties button to open the connection's Properties dialog box. The Usage tab enables you to specify refresh-related settings and also some formatting and drill-through (the number of records to retrieve) settings for OLAP (Online Analytical Processing) databases.

Although refresh options can be set for a data source using the connection's properties dialog box, you can also manually refresh the connections in the workbook or the current worksheet. Select the Refresh All command to refresh all the connections in the workbook or only connections on the current worksheet.

Additional options related to the data source in the current worksheet can also be controlled via the External Data Properties dialog box, which is opened using the Properties command in the Connections group. You can control data formatting and layout features such as preserving cell formatting and layouts. You can also specify what happens in the case of changes in data that affect the number of rows in the table (which typically relate to the adding or deleting of records in the data source).

Working with PivotTables

PivotTables enable you to analyze and summarize table data. You can use an Excel PivotTable to create a report for a table that you created in a worksheet and you can also create a PivotTable from data that you import into an Excel worksheet, such as an Access database table or a table from another data source. A PivotTable can even be used to analyze data that you imported into Excel using Microsoft Query.

An Excel PivotTable is called a pivot table because it enables you to arrange table data in a cross-tabulated report. You can pivot or rearrange the information in the PivotTable to analyze the data it contains. You not only determine which table fields are used as row and column headings in the PivotTable, you also specify fields that contain the values you want to analyze and summarize using the PivotTable. PivotTables can also specify fields that serve as filters for the data that is summarized in the PivotTable.

To take advantage of what a PivotTable can do with table data, you need a source table that has certain attributes. The table that you will specify as the data source for the PivotTable needs to contain at least one field in the table (meaning a column of data in the table) that contains repeating data. For example, you might have a table that shows the weekly sales for your sales force. A column in the table lists the product names that have been sold. Because your salespeople sell the same products, there will be repeated product names in the Product column.

Another requirement for a PivotTable is that the source table contains at least one field that consists of values. You need numerical data if the PivotTable is going to provide you with summary information such as subtotals and totals. Figure 15.25 shows a simple table that actually benefits from being analyzed using a PivotTable.

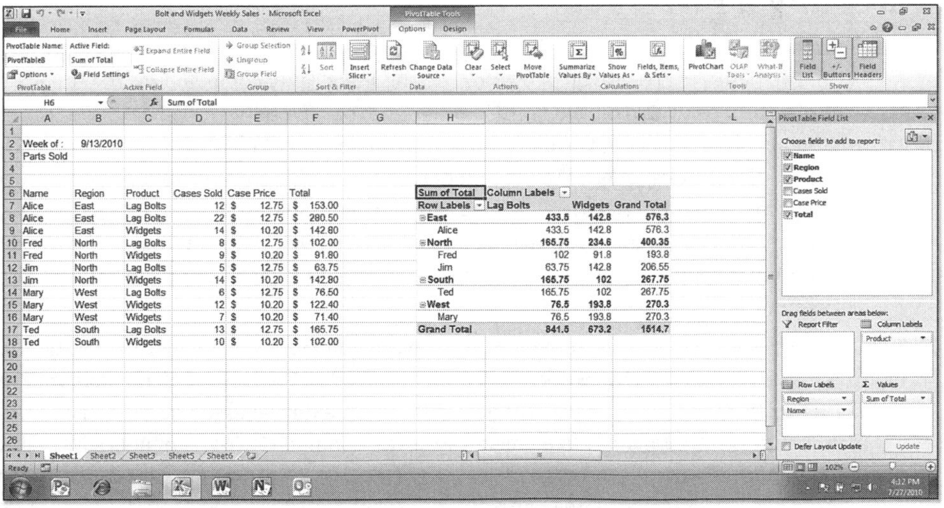

Figure 15.25
PivotTables enable you to analyze table data.

Figure 15.25 shows the source table on the left of the worksheet and the PivotTable is directly to the right of the source table. The PivotTable Field List (the task pane on the right side of the Excel window) provides the Field Section (a list of the fields in the source table) and the Areas Section, which provides the different areas of the PivotTable.

The row labels for the PivotTable, which are contained in the Row Labels section of the PivotTable task pane, are the Region entries followed by the Name column. The regions can then be expanded or collapsed to show or hide the name of the sales representatives in the region, respectively.

The column labels, which have been added to the Column Labels area, consist of the products listed in the source table's Product field. The Total field has been added to the Values area section. The fields placed in the Values area are automatically acted on by the PivotTable and by default sums are provided for the values. The subtotals provided by the PivotTable enable you to see how each salesperson did on each product item and the PivotTable can also be collapsed by region to view the region subtotals only.

> **🔍 note**
>
> Specifying row labels, column labels, and values is straightforward. Specifying a report filter can be a little confusing. Think of the report filter as a field or fields that you want to use to see a subset of the data. For example, if I have sales representatives names set as my row labels, I could then use a grouping field such as region to quickly filter the data by including the region field in the Report Filter area. Slicers also enable you to filter data, so you might find slicers even more useful than filters.

You can quickly rearrange the field information that you have placed into the various areas of the PivotTable task pane to quickly pivot the data shown in the PivotTable. You can also remove fields or add fields—whatever it takes to enable you to see the data in the PivotTable as you require.

Creating a PivotTable

Creating a PivotTable is really just a matter of inserting a new PivotTable using the Create PivotTable dialog box, which is opened via the PivotTable command on the Ruler's Insert tab . You can insert a PivotTable on the current worksheet or on a new worksheet. The PivotTable can use a table on a worksheet in the current Excel workbook as the data source or you can connect to an external data source. The real nuts and bolts portion of the PivotTable creation process relates to the field placement in the PivotTable. You will need to determine the fields that will serve as rows headings, column headings, and values to be acted on by the PivotTable. The great thing about the PivotTable is that you can quickly rearrange the field placement and look at the data in a number of different ways.

It makes sense to get your table in shape before you create the PivotTable, although you can edit a table and update the associated PivotTable or PivotTables (yes, you can have multiple PivotTables for a single data source). If you are going to use an external data source, use the Get External Data commands on the Data tab to connect to the data source. This will enable you to spend some time looking over the data before you create the PivotTable. You can create a PivotTable from any data source connection, even data connections in other workbooks. However, I think it is easier to create the PivotTable based on an actual table (external data or something you have input in Excel) that you can see on a worksheet in the current workbook. To insert a PivotTable, follow these steps:

1. On the Ribbon's Insert tab, select PivotTable and then click PivotTable on the gallery provided. The Create PivotTable dialog box will open as shown in Figure 15.26.

Figure 15.26
The Create PivotTable dialog box.

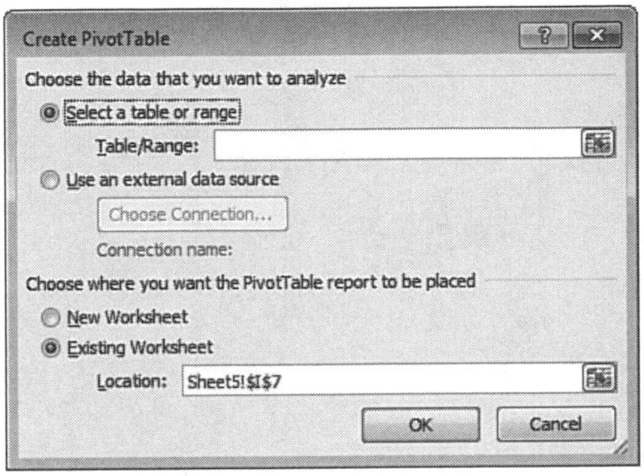

2. To create the PivotTable from a table or range on the current worksheet or in the current workbook, click on the Table/Range box and then select the range. If you are going to use an external data source, click the external data source option button and then select the Choose Connection button. In the Existing Connections dialog box, select a data source and then click Open.

3. After you have specified the range for the PivotTable or specified a connection, select either the New Worksheet or Existing Worksheet option button to specify where the PivotTable will be created. In the case of the Existing Worksheet option, also specify a location for the PivotTable. All you need to do is select the cell that will serve as the upper-left corner for the PivotTable.

4. Click OK and the new PivotTable's blank frame will be inserted into the current worksheet or a new worksheet. The PivotTable Field List will also open on the right of the Excel window as shown in Figure 15.27.

5. The PivotTable Field List is used to specify the data source table fields that will be used in the PivotTable. Select the fields that you want to add to the PivotTable report. You can drag the field names to the different report areas or you can click in an area and then select the check box next to a field. As you specify the fields for the PivotTable, the PivotTable will begin to appear on the worksheet.

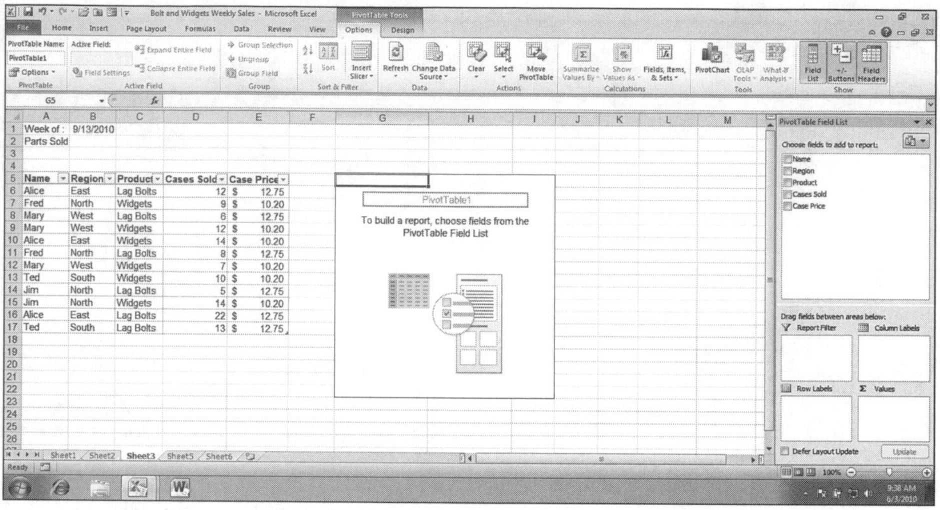

Figure 15.27
PivotTable Field List.

Remember that a PivotTable is meant to provide you with a dynamic report. If the field arrangement that you have specified for the PivotTable isn't working, or you want to rearrange the fields, you can do so in the PivotTable Field List. After you have a specific iteration of the PivotTable that you want to work with, you can close the PivotTable Field List.

The PivotTable will contain Expand and Shrink buttons as well as drop-down lists for the column and row labels. You can use the field drop-down lists to manipulate the data in the PivotTable. Figure 15.28 shows the list provided for row labels.

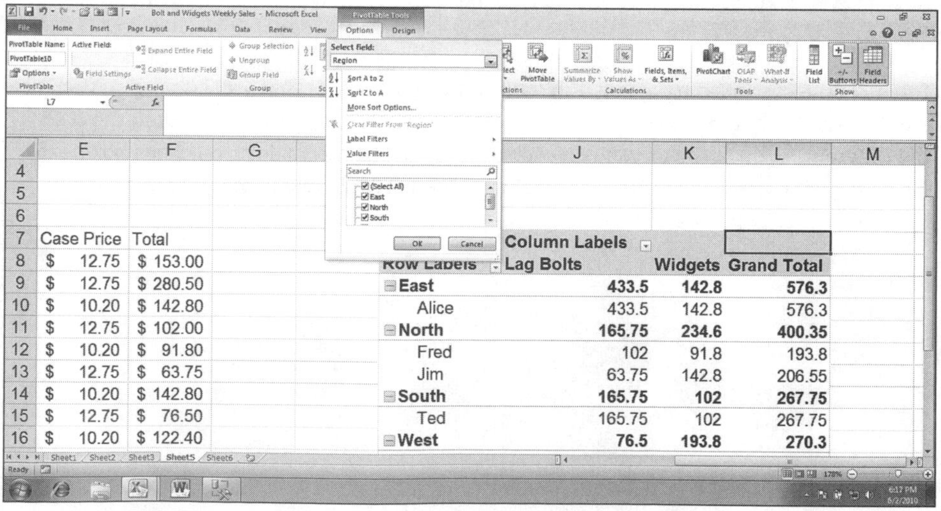

Figure 15.28
A field's drop-down list.

The list enables you to select the field that you want to use to manipulate the PivotTable (if you have more than one field specified for the row or column labels). You can then sort by specific entries in that field by using the filter check boxes provided for each field value. The sort order can also be controlled in the list as needed.

Working with the PivotTable Tools

When you select a cell in the PivotTable, the PivotTable Tools become available on the Ribbon. There is an Options tab and a Design tab. The Options tab enables you to specify PivotTable and field settings, and to specify how values are summarized and are shown. The Design tab is dedicated to the layout of the PivotTable and enables you to apply styles to your PivotTable.

The PivotTable Tools Option Tab

The Option tab enables you to manipulate the fields in the table and also sort or filter the data in the PivotTable. You can use the Expand Entire Field or Collapse Entire Field commands in the Active Field group to manipulate the currently selected field. Other commands available, such as the Sort & Filter commands, enable you to sort or filter the data in the table by a specific field. This group also provides the Insert Slicer command, which we talk about in a moment.

The Options tab also provides the Data group that supplies you with commands that enable you to refresh the data source for the PivotTable or to change the data source. The Show group enables you to toggle PivotChart items on or off, such as the Field List, buttons, and field headers on the PivotChart.

In terms of formatting fields containing values in the PivotTable, you can control how the values are summarized (the default calculation using the Sum function) and how the values are shown. Click in a value field and the commands available in the Calculations group will become active.

To change the type of summary calculation used in a field, select the Summarize Values By command. You can then change the function used to Count, Average, Max, Min, or Product by using the list provided. If you want to select an option other than those provided by the Summarize Values By command's list, select More Options. The Value Field Settings dialog box will open as shown in Figure 15.28.

You can choose a function for the value field summary by using the scroll box provided. Another option that the Value Field Settings dialog box provides, and which is extremely useful, is the Number Format button. By default, the values in the PivotTable are formatted as general numbers. You can click the Number Format button and then use the Format Cells dialog box to specify a different number format for the PivotTable such as Currency, Accounting, Percentage, and so on.

You can also manipulate how the values are shown in the PivotTable. The Show Values As command provides a list of different forms for the values such as % of Grand Total, % of Row Total, and Difference From. When you select a value form on the list that is followed by an ellipsis (...), an associated dialog box will open. For example, if you select Difference From, a dialog box opens that requires that you specify the base field base item for the value set. The values in the PivotChart will then appear as the difference between the original values (based on the worksheet data) and the value of the base field item that you specified. This would enable you to see how sales regions stacked up against a particular region sales region by specifying that region's sales as the base item.

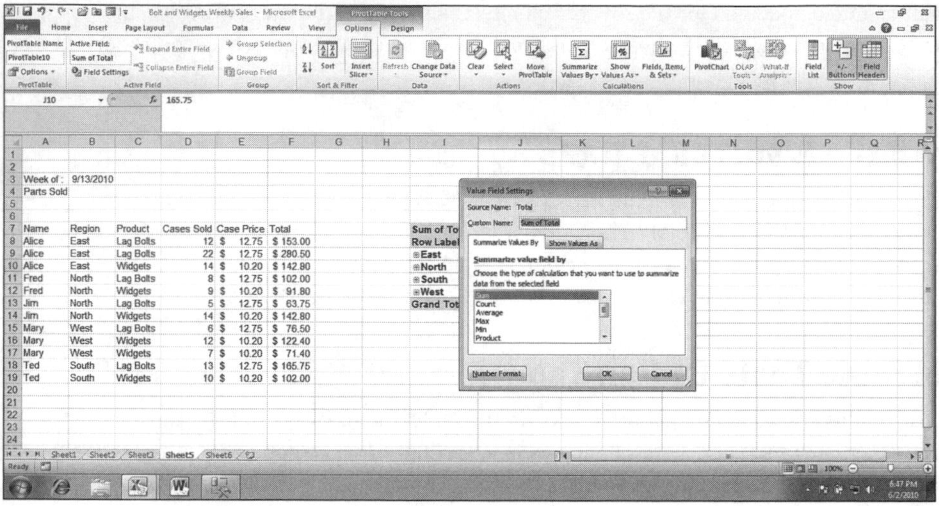

Figure 15.29
The Value Field Settings dialog box.

The PivotTable Tools Design Tab

The PivotTable Tools Option tab enables you to manipulate the layout of your calculated fields and to also assign styles to the PivotTable. The Layout group provides the Subtotals, Grand Totals, Report Layout, and Blank Rows commands.

The Subtotals command enables you to hide the subtotals or to specify that the subtotals appear at the bottom (the default) or top of a group in the PivotTable. The Grand Totals command enables you to turn the grand totals off or on for rows and columns or specify that grand totals are shown only for the rows or columns only in the PivotTable. The Report Layout command enables you to choose from a number of different formats for the PivotTable such as compact, outline, and tabular. The Blank Rows command is used to insert or remove blank lines after each item in the PivotTable.

The PivotTable Styles gallery provides a number of different styles that can be applied to the PivotTable. If you apply a particular style, you can then use the PivotTable Style Options check boxes to hide or show elements such as row headers, column headers, or banded rows and columns.

Using Slicers

The slicer is a new feature provided by Excel 2010. A slicer enables you to filter the data in a PivotTable. A slicer works in a very similar manner to a filter that you create by adding a field to the Report Filter area in the Field List, but slicers provide you with an easily accessible workspace object that makes it simple to apply a filter to a PivotTable. By default, a slicer will sort the data in ascending order and then filter the data.

> 🔍 **note**
>
> Slicers can also be used to filter data in a PivotChart. A PivotChart is a visualization of PivotTable data and be quickly be created via the PivotChart command on the PivotTable Tools Options tab.

You can create multiple slicers for a PivotTable. For example, you could create a slicer that filters row data and a slicer that filters column data. To create a new slicer, select the Insert Slicer command on the PivotTable Tools Options tab. The Insert Slicers dialog box will open as shown in Figure 15.30. The Insert Slicers dialog box will show all the fields available to your PivotTable.

Figure 15.30
The Insert Slicers dialog box.

A slicer can filter the data in the PivotTable by only a single field. However, you can create multiple slicers by selecting more than one field in the Insert Slicers dialog box. After selecting a field (for a single slicer) or multiple fields (for multiple slicers), click OK. The new slicer (or slicers) will appear on the current worksheet. The slicer will list the field values in the field that you selected in the Insert Slicers dialog box. Select a particular field value to filter the PivotTable by that value. To remove the filter, click the remove filter icon in the upper-right corner of the slicer's frame.

You will find that when you have a slicer selected, the Slicer Tools Options tab becomes available on the Ribbon. You can use the styles available and the size settings to format the slicer. If you have multiple PivotTables on a worksheet, you can associate the slicer with those PivotTables. This enables you to filter more than one PivotTable using a single slicer. Select the PivotTable Connections command and the PivotTables Connections dialog box will open. Select the PivotTables listed in the dialog box that you want to associate with the slicer. Then select OK to close the dialog box.

Slicers can be moved on the worksheet as needed and you can also delete a slicer that you no longer need. Make sure that the slicer is selected and then press Delete on the keyboard.

VALIDATING AND ANALYZING WORKSHEET DATA

Excel provides you with very powerful capabilities for analyzing worksheet data. Even the most elegant data analysis, however, won't mean much if you have incorrect data in a worksheet.

In this chapter we look at Excel's data validation features. You can create data validation rules that greatly cut down the possibility of data being entered into a worksheet incorrectly. We also discuss Excel's tools for analyzing worksheet data. We will look at the data table feature and the Scenario Manager, which both provide you with the ability to do a what-if analysis of your worksheet data. Coverage is also provided of Goal Seek and the Solver, both of which enable you to derive values based on a predefined goal. We wrap up this chapter with a look at the new Excel 2010 data connection and manipulation add-in PowerPivot for Excel.

Taking Advantage of Data Validation

Even a worksheet containing the best-built formulas and the most advanced functions possible can still end up providing you with invalid results for the various sheet calculations. This is due to the fact that people can make mistakes when entering data into the worksheet. No matter how well-designed the worksheet is, incorrect values in cells will still render invalid results when they are acted upon by formulas and functions in the worksheet.

A strategy for greatly reducing the possibility of an invalid entry in a cell or cell range or a field column in an Excel table is to use data validation rules. Data validation simply means that the data entered into a cell range that has a validation rule applied to it must meet the criteria specified by the validation rule. For example, the validation criteria for a data validation rule might specify that only a date can be entered into the cell range to which you have applied the rule. You can then specify a valid range of dates that can be entered. For example, you might be creating a quarterly expense report for your sales force and the only valid dates that can be entered into the range controlled by the validation rule are specified by a date range that you designate when you create the data validation rule.

note

You can create validation rules for any worksheet. This includes ranges in a worksheet that you have formatted as tables. When creating rules in tables, you need to select only a field column heading to apply the rule to all the cells in that particular column.

You can also create validation rules that control the number of characters that can be entered into the cells in a particular range. For example, you might create a validation rule for a cell range where a U.S. state must be entered and you want the state to always be entered using the two-character state abbreviation; the validation rule can limit the text length in the cell range to two text characters (such as IN or ME).

You can even take the state name validation rule a little farther. Let's say that you only do business in 15 states and you don't want someone to erroneously enter MA for Maine (rather than ME) and you don't want Mississippi (MS) to inadvertently be listed as Michigan (MI). You can actually have the validation rule allow only entries that are from a list of values that has been entered in a range elsewhere on the worksheet. The use of list values as the criteria for a validation rule can also be used in cases where you require that only specific values or dates be entered into a range of cells; the list defines the only valid entries.

Data validation rules can help you when you are inputting data into a worksheet that you use only occasionally or a large worksheet where it might be difficult to concentrate on what actually needs to be input into a particular range of cells. The validation rule can provide an input message that tells you fairly clearly what a valid entry would be for each cell in the range. In cases when incorrect data is entered into a cell in a range that is governed by a validation rule, the validation rule can also provide an incorrect data message that alerts you to the incorrect entry and provides help on the data that can be entered into the cell.

Data validation can also be extremely useful in situations where you design a worksheet that will be used by coworkers, colleagues, or subordinates. Creating data validation rules can help make sure that whoever ends up entering information into the worksheet does it correctly.

Specifying Validation Criteria

Creating a validation rule is very straightforward. You specify the criteria for the rule and then you have the option of also providing an input message and an error alert for the rule. The Data Validation command is in the Data Tools group on the Ribbon's Data tab.

To create a new data validation rule, select the cell range to which you will apply the rule. On the Ribbon's Data tab, select the Data Validation command and then select Data Validation. The Data Validation dialog box will open.

The criterion for the validation rule is specified on the Settings tab. The Allow drop-down box provides the following criteria:

- **Any Value:** The default setting has no restrictions. So, why is it even available? You can create a validation rule that doesn't restrict data input but provides an input message as a way to coach users to place certain data in a range of cells. Using this criterion will not restrict them from entering whatever they want in the cell, however.

- **Whole number:** Select this setting to restrict the data entry to numerical values with no decimals.

- **Decimal:** This setting restricts data entry to numerical values but allows decimals.

- **List:** This setting restricts the data entry to the entries that you have specified in a list that you have created elsewhere on the worksheet or workbook. Only the items in your list will be considered valid entries in the cell range.

- **Date:** This setting allows only calendar dates to be entered into the cell range validated by the rule.

- **Time:** This setting restricts the data entry to time values.

- **Text Length:** This setting enables you to restrict the entry of text in the cell range by a specific number of characters.

- **Custom:** This setting enables you to actually use a formula (or function) as the criterion for data validation. For example, you might have a total budget for a project of $5,000.00. You can specify that the sum of the range of individual expenses entered in the cell range do no exceed 5000; this would look something like =SUM(range of cells)<=5000. The cell range in the parentheses would have to be specified as absolute references for this scenario to work. You can also use other functions, such as the IF function, to validate whether an entry is true or false based on the condition set up in the IF function. Create the formula or function in a cell in the worksheet and then specify the cell's address when you specify the custom criterion.

> **tip**
>
> You can use the =TRIM function to keep users from inadvertently adding leading or trailing spaces to text entries in a cell. This is very useful when employee numbers (which are not values) or other identifying information needs to be entered in a cell range. The Custom criterion formula would be =cell range =TRIM (cell range). Both references to the cell range must be made absolute references for this to work.

Select the Allow criterion that you want to use for the validation rule. If you select Whole Number, Decimal, Date or Time, you will have the option of setting up a conditional statement for the rule. You can select from a number of different inequality statements including Between, Not Between, Equal To, Less Than and the like using the Data drop-down list.

For example, if you select Between, you will then need to provide the starting and ending value for the allowed range of data entries. Figure 16.1 shows the Data Validation dialog box with the Settings tab selected.

In Figure 16.1, the Allow setting is configured as Date. The Data option has been set to Between, which requires that a start date and end date be specified for the allowed data range.

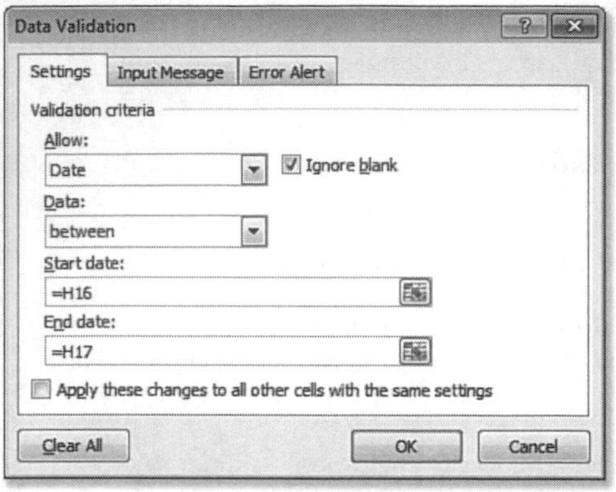

Figure 16.1
The Settings tab of the Data Validation dialog box.

When you use inequality statements such as between or greater than, you can specify the actual date, time, or numerical value by typing the value in the boxes provided at the bottom of the Data Validation dialog. For example, you could actually type the start date and end date for the allowed range.

You do have another alternative for providing the start and stop values of an allowed range when you use between or another inequality expression such as greater than; you can specify the start and stop values for the allowed range by specifying cell addresses in the worksheet that provide the values. For example, you might put the start date and end date in cells in the worksheet and then specify these values by entering the appropriate cell address in the Start Date and End Date boxes.

Configuring Input Messages and Error Alerts

After you have configured the validation criteria for the data validation rule, you can configure an optional input message and error alert for the rule. The input message is specified on the Input Message tab of the Data Validation dialog box.

The input message is made up of a title and an input message. Figure 16.2 shows the Input Message tab of the Data Validation dialog box.

The input message is designed so that it appears when you or another user click on a cell that has been assigned the data validation rule. The more specific you are when entering the input message, the easier it will be for users to comply with the validation rule as they enter data.

You can also configure an error alert for the validation rule. The purpose of the error alert is to give the user some sort of direction in terms of correcting the entry of invalid data. Figure 16.3 shows the Error Alert tab of the Data Validation dialog box.

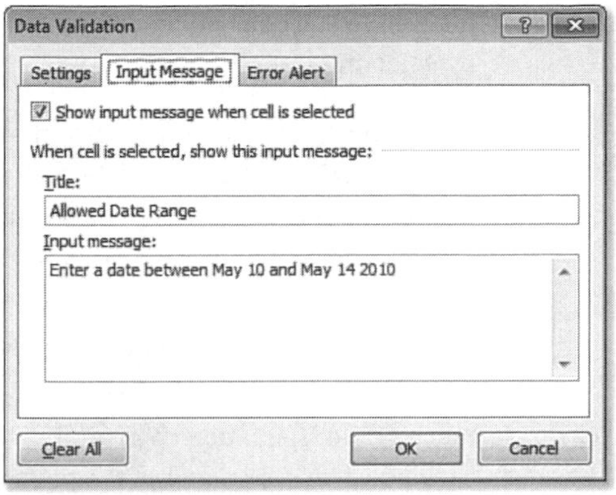

Figure 16.2
Enter an input message for the validation rule.

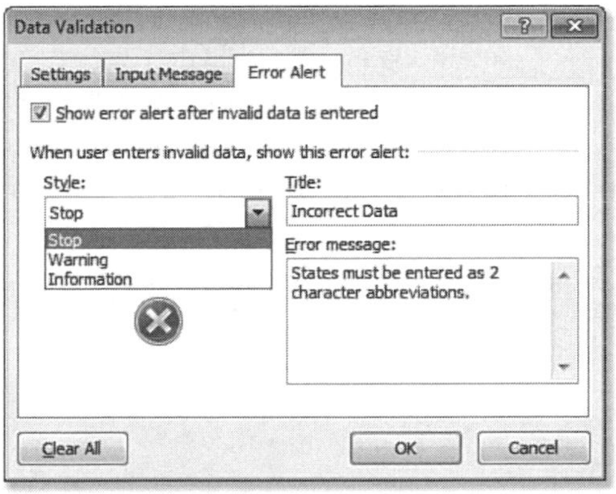

Figure 16.3
Create an error alert for the validation rule.

Error alerts can be configured so that they provide different levels of protection in terms of whether invalid data is even allowed to be entered into the cell. Three different error alert styles are provided as follows:

- **Stop:** This error message style will provide an error message dialog box that enables you to retry or to cancel the entry. Data that violates the rule cannot be entered into the cell range assigned this rule.

- **Warning:** This error message style provides a warning dialog box. The user has the option to continue by selecting Yes. This means that incorrect data can be entered in the cell range. The user is also provided the option of selecting No or Cancel in the warning dialog box, which removes the entry from the cell.

- **Information:** This error message style provides an informational dialog box. Incorrect data can be entered in the cell and all you have to do is select OK in the message box. You can retry the entry by selecting Cancel.

It makes sense to use the Stop error message style when it is imperative that data entered in a cell range be completely valid as dictated by the validation rule. You can make use of the Warning and Information styles when you want to suggest how data be entered in a cell range but it isn't crucial that data be entered in a form other than that dictated by the validation rule.

When you have completed configuring the validation rule, click OK to close the Data Validation dialog box. You can now enter data into the range governed by the validation rule.

If you decide that you want to remove a validation rule from a cell range, select the range and then select the Data Validation command to open the Data Validation dialog box. You can clear the rule by clicking Clear All on any of the dialog box tabs.

Circling Invalid Data

If you create validation rules that use the Warning and Information error message styles, users can potentially insert invalid data into the range where you have applied the validation rule. Users can also use the Clipboard to paste information into a cell bypassing a validation rule.

You can circle the invalid data that appears in a cell range where a validation rule has been applied. Figure 16.4 shows invalid data that has been circled in a worksheet.

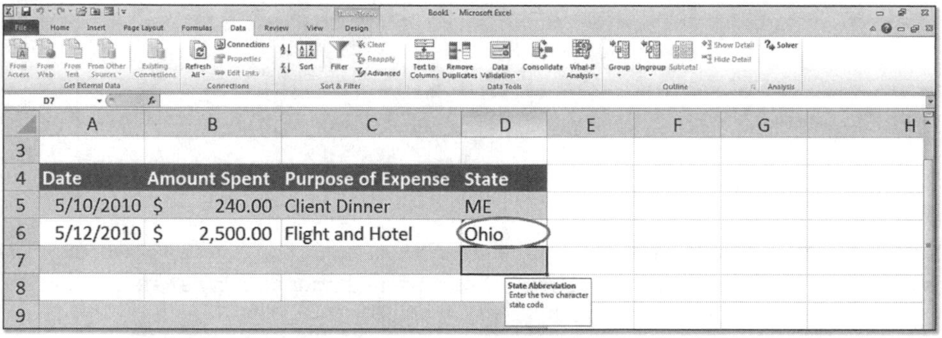

Figure 16.4
Circle invalid data in a worksheet.

To circle invalid data, select the Data Validation command and then select Circle Invalid Data. Any cells that contain invalid data and are governed by a validation rule will be circled. You can correct the cell entries as needed. To remove the validation circles from the worksheet, select the Data Validation command and then select Clear Validation Circles.

You can also do error checking related to your validation rules via the Error Checking command in the Formula Auditing command group on the Formulas tab. The Error Checking dialog box will flag validation errors as you use it to move through a worksheet. More about the auditing tools is discussed in Chapter 13, "Getting the Most from Formulas and Functions."

 For information on error checking, see page 377 in Chapter 13.

Performing a What-If Analysis

Excel provides you with the ability to perform a what-if analysis on worksheet data. An analysis of the data in a worksheet can really be approached in two different ways: manipulating values to affect outcomes or specifying an outcome such as a required net profit and allowing Excel to determine the values required to give you the desired outcome.

As already mentioned, the first possibility for conducting a what-if analysis consists of varying key values in a worksheet, which enables you to see how these changes to the key values affect the result of a particular formula or function. For example, you might want to analyze how different variable costs such as marketing and supplies affect your net profits.

There are two different ways to perform a what-if analysis where you specify changes to key values to affect the results of formulas or functions (meaning the outcomes). A data table enables you to vary one or two input values. The changes in input are then reflected in the results of formulas or functions also included in the table.

The other possibility for performing a what-if analysis where key values are varied to provide different calculated outcomes is the scenario. Scenarios enable you to create different versions of the same worksheet where certain values in the worksheet are changed. Each scenario will then provide a different outcome. For example, you might be selling your house and the only variables that are fluid are the actual sale price that you will get and the real-estate broker's fee. You can create different scenarios that show different sale prices and broker's fees to see the different possible profits you might make on your home sale.

The other approach to analyzing data is to specify an outcome and then work backward (sort of a reverse what-if analysis) to see what key values must be in the worksheet to get the desired outcome. For example, you might want to save 200 dollars a month in an IRA. You can do a worksheet that shows your monthly income and fixed monthly expenses (such as your mortgage). You can also include expenses that are not fixed, such as entertainment and travel, and allow Excel to determine how much you can spend on these variable costs and still sock the desired amount of money away in your retirement fund each month.

There are actually two different tools that enable you to start with an outcome value (actually the result of a formula or function) and then work backward to determine what key values must actually be to get the desired results. Goal Seek enables you to determine the value that you need in an input cell to get a desired result. The other tool is the Solver add-in, which can be used to help you find an optimum value in relation to limitations that are provided by the values in other cells in the worksheet such as the fixed and variable expenses that we discussed in relation to specifying a monthly contribution to your IRA account.

The Goal Seek tool is limited to determining one key value. The Solver can help you determine the value for more than one variable based on a desired result.

Let's look at working with data tables and the Scenario Manager to determine how changes in values affect outcomes. We can then look at how you can work backward from a particular outcome and determine the values necessary to reach your specified goal.

Creating a Data Table

Creating a data table is actually a straightforward way to vary one or two values involved in a work-sheet calculation or calculations and then view the results based on the changes that were made to the value or values. Data tables are actually a quick way to quickly see how a single varied input cell affects calculations performed by formulas or functions. If you are going to tackle multiple variables for a what-if analysis, it probably makes more sense to use the Scenario Manager, which we discuss in the next section. So, the discussion that follows looks at how to create a one-value data table.

The data table is really an addition to your worksheet. The first thing that you need to do is go ahead and create the worksheet that contains the values, formulas, and functions that provide you with results based on a set of values required by the formula or function.

For example, let's say that you want to see how different automobile values (ranging from $14,000.00 to $25,000.00) will affect your monthly payment when you have a four-year loan (48 months) with a fixed interest rate of 6%. You can use the PMT function to quickly calculate the monthly payment at $14,000.00 by using the Functions Arguments dialog to specify the cell location for the Rate (divided by 12 for monthly payments), Nper (the term in months), and Pv (the present value or cost of the car).

When you have your simple worksheet complete and it is returning results from the formulas or functions you placed in the worksheet, you can build the data table as an accessory to the work-sheet. Placement of the data table isn't really crucial, but the layout of the data table certainly is. Figure 16.5 shows a simple car loan worksheet that uses the PMT function in cell D9.

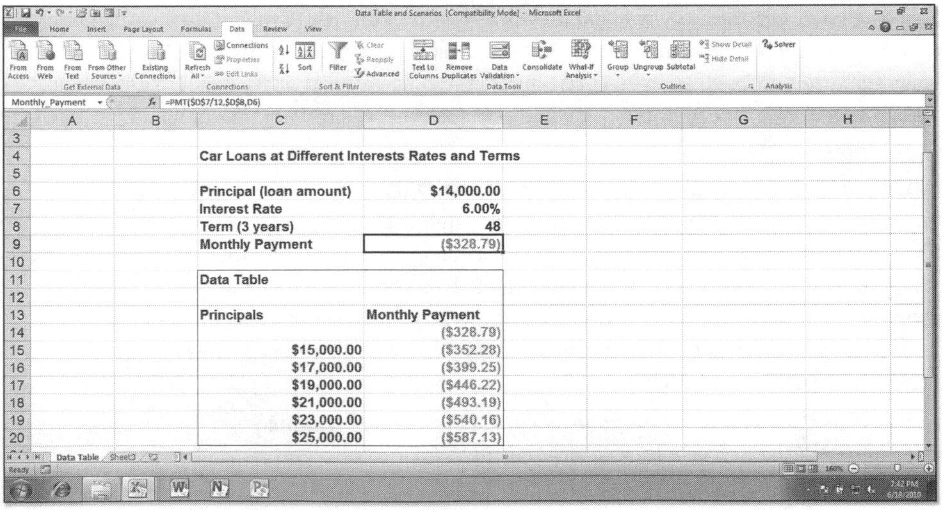

Figure 16.5
Create a data table for your what-if analysis.

The leftmost column of the data table is where you can place range of values that will serve as the values that will replace the original input cell in your worksheet. In our example, the input cell is actually the principal for the loan, which is in cell D6 of the worksheet. The values in the data table that will be used to replace the input value are in the range C15:C20.

Leave a blank cell between the first value in the leftmost column of the data table and the heading for that column. In Figure 16.5, the blank cell is C14.

The top row of the data table is where you reference any formulas or functions in your worksheet that you want to calculate different results based on the range of possibilities provided in the first column of the data table. In our example, the worksheet contains only one function in cell D9. I reference this function in the top row of the data table (Row 14) by typing an equal sign in cell D14 and then clicking on cell D9. This places =D9 in cell D14 and is basically a pointer to cell D9, which contains the PMT function.

After you have the data table set up, you can have Excel work its magic and calculate the different monthly payments for each of the principal values that you have input in the data table. Select the empty cell above your range of different principals (input values) and make sure that the selection range includes all the cells to the right of the input values, including the cell that references the function (or functions) back in the worksheet. In our example shown (see Figure 16.6), the data table range would be C14:D20. After you have selected the cells in the data table, select the What-If Analysis command on the Data tab and then select Data Table. The Data Table dialog box will open as shown in Figure 16.6.

> **🔍 note**
>
> Think of the data as a cross-tabulated report. The range of different values is placed in the first column of the table and, in the case of a two varied inputs table, also in the first row of the table. The results in the table will then relate to the formulas or functions that act on the variable data ranges.

> **🔍 note**
>
> You can specify up to 32 changing cells for a scenario, meaning you can vary the values in 32 different cells in a worksheet for your what-if analysis.

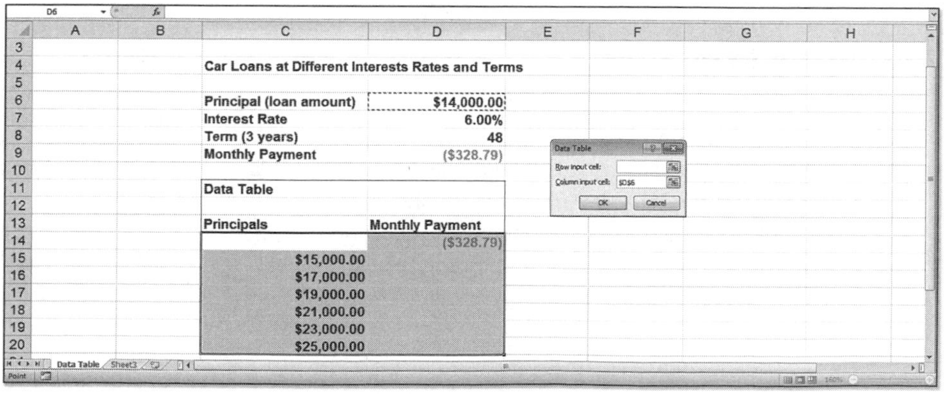

Figure 16.6
The Data Table dialog box.

In the Data Table dialog box, you specify the row input cell and/or the column input cell. When you are using only one variable for the data table, as we have in the example provided here, only the Column Input cell needs to be specified. This would be cell D6 where the principal for the loan was specified in the worksheet.

After specifying the input cell addresses, click OK. The values will appear in the data table. After you get a feel for the general layout of a data table, you can use it with worksheets that contain more than one formula or function. The great thing about a data table is it provides you with a whole range of possible values based on the varied input values.

The Scenario Manager enables you to create different scenarios or models of what the results might be in a worksheet when different values are placed in key cells in the worksheet. For example, you might be selling your house and want to calculate different scenarios related to the profit that you will make. Two key values related to calculating your net profit that might be variable are the real estate broker's commission and the actual sale price of the home.

You can put your data (and appropriate formulas and/or functions) in a worksheet that provides baseline calculations. For example, in the case of the home sale, you would create a worksheet that calculates your net profit on the sale based on your costs related to the sale and a specific sale price for the house. The worksheet can be structured to provide the most realistic calculation of the net profit for the sale.

You can then create different scenarios that enable you to see how changes in the sale price and brokerage fees (let's say you are talking to different agents that charge different percentages) affect the amount of money you will walk away with at closing. For example, you could create a scenario that provides the best case scenario where you are paying the lowest brokerage fee but selling your house for the highest possible price. You might also create a worst case scenario that shows your net profit when you sell your house for a lower sale price and pay a higher agent commission.

Each scenario created provides you with a different potential outcome. When you create scenarios, you can vary a number of data values in a worksheet to view different potential outcomes for the formulas and functions that will be affected by the changing cells you specify for the worksheet's scenarios.

Creating Scenarios

To create scenarios for a worksheet, build a worksheet as you would any other worksheet. Enter your data, formulas, and functions. When you are ready to begin the scenario creation process, select the What-If Analysis command on the Data tab and then select Scenario Manager—the Scenario Manager dialog box will open. Select the Add button to create a new scenario. The Add Scenario dialog box will appear as shown in Figure 16.7.

 tip

If you are working with a large number of changing cells for your scenario, you might want to name those cells and then specify the Changing Cells addresses using the cell names rather than the cell addresses. This will help you keep the different values you're working with straight as you specify the different values for each scenario.

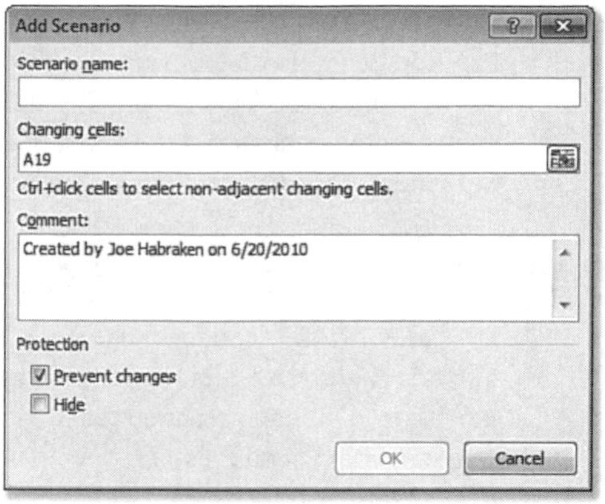

Figure 16.7
The Add Scenario dialog box.

Enter a name for the scenario in the Scenario name box. Use a descriptive name for the scenario because you will be creating multiple scenarios for the worksheet. For example, you might name the scenario "best case" if you will provide values for the changing cells that are optimum values. You might also name the scenario "most likely" or "reality" and provide values for the changing cells that are extremely realistic.

The most important aspect of creating the new scenario is to specify the cells in the worksheet that will serve as the changing cells for the scenario. The changing cells are the cells in the worksheet that can be varied. In our home sale example, the sale price of the house and the broker's fee were both considered values that could be changed and so the cells in the worksheet that contain these values would be listed in the Changing Cells box.

Select the changing cells as needed. To select a contiguous range, drag with the mouse. You can select nonadjacent cells by selecting the first cell and then holding down the Ctrl key as you select other cells. Cell addresses inserted into the Changing Cells box will be specified as absolute references.

When you have provided the name and changing cells (there is also an optional Comment box), click OK. The Scenario Values dialog box will open as shown in Figure 16.8.

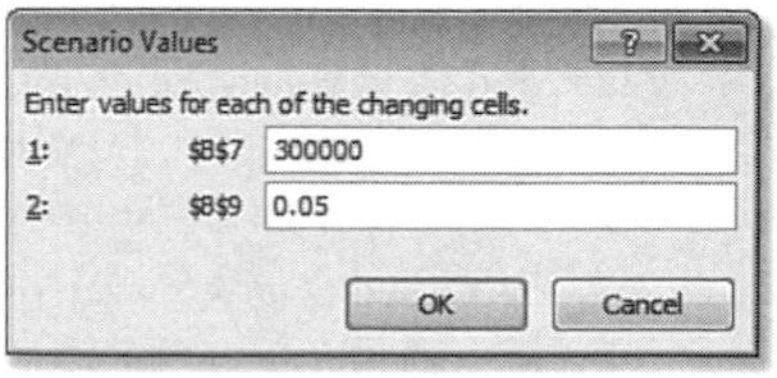

Figure 16.8
The Scenario Values dialog box.

Enter a value for each of the changing cells that you specified in the Add Scenario box in the Scenario Values dialog box. When you have completed entering the values, click OK.

The Add Scenario dialog box will open; you can create another scenario; create your next scenario for the worksheet. This cycle will continue (Add Scenario dialog box to Scenario Values dialog box) as you create each additional scenario. When you have finished creating all the scenarios for the worksheet, click Cancel to close the Add Scenario dialog box.

Viewing Scenarios and Creating Reports

You can view the scenarios that you create for your worksheet by using the Scenario Manager. The Scenario Manager not only enables you to quickly plug the changing cells values into your worksheet based on each scenario that you created, but you can also add additional scenarios or edit or delete existing scenarios.

To open the Scenario Manager, select the What-If Analysis command and then select Scenario Manager. The Scenario Manager will list all the scenarios that you have created for the worksheet as shown in Figure 16.9.

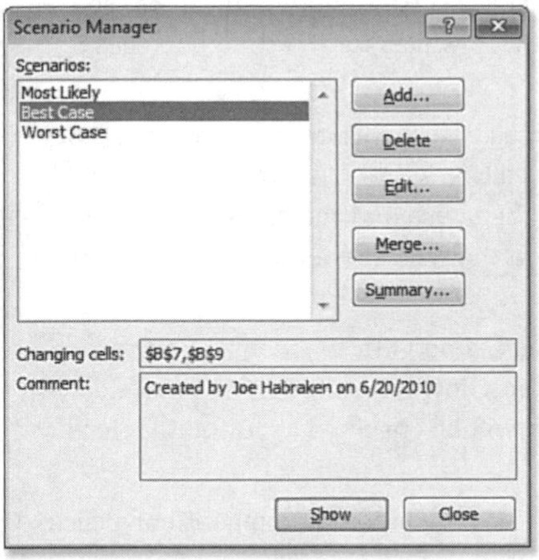

Figure 16.9
The Scenario Manager dialog box.

To view the results of a particular scenario in your worksheet, select the scenario in the Scenarios list and then select the Show button. The results of formulas and functions in the worksheet will be recalculated based on the values for changing cells specified in the scenario. You can select any of the scenarios and quickly view the outcomes provided by that specific scenario.

The Scenario Manager dialog box not only provides you with the ability to view the results provided by each scenario and manage your scenarios (such as edit or delete scenarios), it also provides you with the ability to create reports or summaries of the scenarios that you have created for a worksheet.

The summary of the worksheet scenarios that you have built can take the form of a scenario summary that lists each scenario and the changing values provided by the scenario. Summary information includes the results of formulas or functions in the worksheet that were affected by the changing cells specified for the scenarios. Figure 16.10 shows a scenario summary for a worksheet that had three different scenarios.

Figure 16.10
A scenario summary for a worksheet with multiple scenarios.

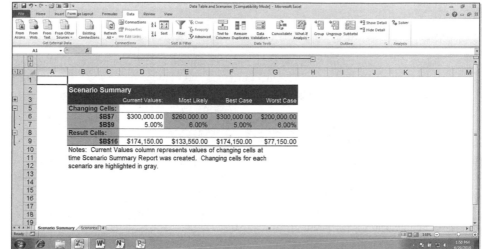

The summary lists the changing cells and specifies how result cells were affected by the changing cells in each scenario. The result cells are the cell addresses for the cells that contain the formulas or functions affected by the changing cells.

Your scenario summary can also take the form of a PivotTable report. The PivotTable report enables you to sort and filter the data provided in the report as you would data in any Excel PivotTable. You will find that the PivotTable report can be very useful when you have a large number of different changing cells in your worksheet scenarios and the changing cells affect a number of different cells containing the results of formulas or functions.

➥ *For information on using PivotTables, see page 443 in Chapter 15, "Using Excel Tables and PivotTables."*

To create a new scenario summary from the Scenario Manager dialog box, select the Summary button. The Scenario Summary dialog box will open as shown in Figure 16.11.

> **note**
>
> If multiple copies of a particular worksheet exist (in different workbooks) and different users have created scenarios for that worksheet, you can merge the scenarios into a single worksheet using the Merge command in the Scenario Manager dialog box.

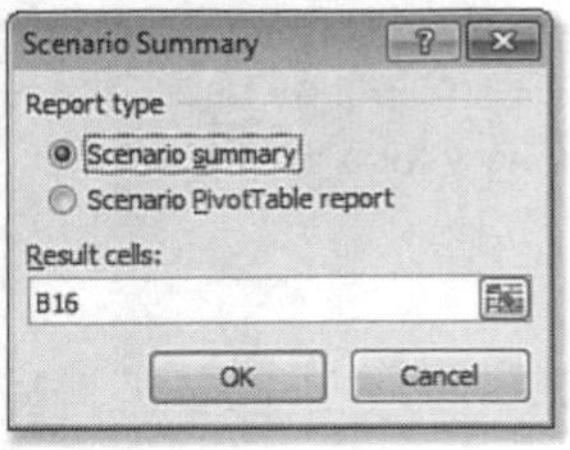

Figure 16.11
The Scenario Summary dialog box.

Select the report type: Scenario Summary or Scenario PivotTable Report. In the Result Cells box, specify the cells that contain results (formulas and functions) that are affected by changing cells in your scenarios. When you click OK, the report is created on a new worksheet.

Using Goal Seek and Solver

As mentioned earlier in this chapter, Excel also provides two other analysis tools: Goal Seek and the Solver. Goal Seek is designed to work backward from a desired outcome. Goal Seek determines that value that is required for a particular input cell to get a specific result in a dependent formula or function. Goal Seek is designed to help you determine the value of only one input cell involved in the calculation, so although it can be extremely useful, it is also fairly limited.

The Solver, which is an Excel add-in, provides you with the ability to find the required value for a number of input cells involved in a pre-determined calculation result. So, the Solver can be used in situations where you want to determine the value for more than one input cell involved in the calculation result provided by a dependent formula or function.

Working with Goal Seek

To use Goal Seek, create your worksheet including the formula or function that will be dependent on the input value that Goal Seek will determine for you. For example, let's say that you put together a worksheet that uses the FV (Future Value) financial function to determine how much you need to put into an investment account each month over a 10-year period to end up with 20,000 dollars in the account when you are getting a 3% annual interest rate.

The FV function uses the format =FV(Rate, NPER, PMT) where the rate is the interest rate, the NPER is the total number of payments, and PMT is the payment made each period. You want Goal Seek to determine the PMT because you already know the interest rate (3%) and the number of payments, which would be 120 (12 monthly payments × 10 years).

➡ *For more information on using financial functions, see page 368 in Chapter 13.*

After you have your worksheet set up, all you will need to do is tell Goal Seek three things: the cell address and desired goal amount for the dependent, and the cell address for the cell that is the changing cell that Goal Seek will figure out a value for. Select the What-If Analysis command and then select Goal Seek. The Goal Seek dialog box will appear as shown in Figure 16.12.

Figure 16.12
The Goal Seek dialog box.

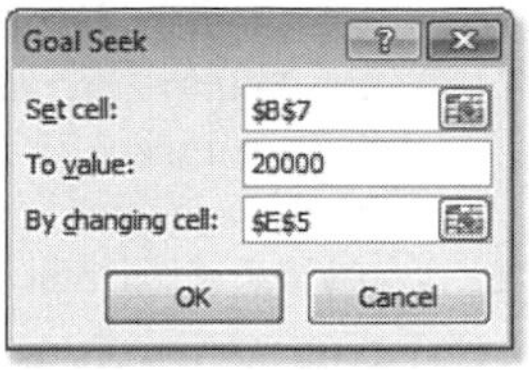

Goal Seek	?	✕
Set cell:	B7	
To value:	20000	
By changing cell:	E5	
	OK	Cancel

Specify the Set Cell address, which is the cell containing the formula or function. Enter the desired goal for the value in the To Value box. Specify the address of the cell for which Goal Seek will determine a value in the By Changing Cell box. Click OK and Goal Seek will determine the changing cell value and show your goal value in the cell containing the formula or function.

The target value and found value (in the changing cell) will be inserted into the worksheet. The Goal Seek Status dialog box will open, letting you know that Goal Seek found a solution. Select OK to close the Goal Seek Status box.

In some cases, Goal Seek might not be able to find a value that provides you with the goal that you have specified. You can use the Goal Seek Status dialog box to step through the calculations to see where the problem might be or why Goal Seek was not able to arrive at a solution. If you are using Goal Seek in relatively simple worksheets that do not use a long change of calculations to arrive at a particular specified goal, Goal Seek will be able to provide a solution in most cases.

Working with the Solver

If you need to determine the values for multiple adjustable or changing cells based on a desired outcome, you can take advantage of the Solver. The Solver not only provides for multiple changing cells, but it also enables you to set constraints on the value that a changing cell can have to satisfy the desired outcome. This means that you could specify a value that a particular changing cell must be above or below when the Solver determines the value for that cell based on the outcome value. The Solver (as is Goal Seek) is really an optimization tool and enables you to find the best solution in a worksheet that has obvious constraints on certain values. This can be useful when you want to optimize sales or production or find the best mix of variable values related to a particular outcome.

Before you take advantage of the Solver, which is an Excel add-in, you will need to enable it. Open the Excel Options window in the Backstage by selecting Options. In the Excel Options window, select Add-Ins. At the bottom of the Add-ins settings, select Excel Add-ins in the Manage drop-down list and then click Go. The Add-Ins dialog box will appear, listing a selection of available add-ins, which includes the Solver. Select the Solver Add-in check box and then click OK. The Solver will be added to an Analysis group available on the Ribbon's Data tab.

As with the other analysis tools that we have discussed, such as scenarios and Goal Seek, build your worksheet including the formulas and functions required. You can put values in the cells that will serve as changing cells when you configure the Solver.

As already mentioned, the Solver enables you to place constraints on the values allowed in a changing cell. For example, you might be looking at how you want to allocate your small business's monthly budget dollars based on the total budget and certain limitations you have set for budget line items such as marketing or travel. Let's say that you would rather see more money go toward marketing in a particular month, so you are setting a ceiling on travel (which is also a changing cell). You can place the constraints amounts directly on the worksheet (in an area near the actual monthly budget worksheet that you have created) or you can specify the constraint amount when you specify the constraint in the Add Constraint dialog box (which is accessed via the Solver).

Placing the constraint amounts on the worksheet itself means that you can always go back and change those amounts and then rerun the Solver to see how changed constraints have affected the changing cell values that were used by the Solver to adhere to your specified outcome. The Solver can actually save its findings as scenarios, which you can then access as needed using the Scenario Manager.

To configure the Solver, click the Solver command in the Analysis group. The Solver Parameters dialog box will open as shown in Figure 16.13.

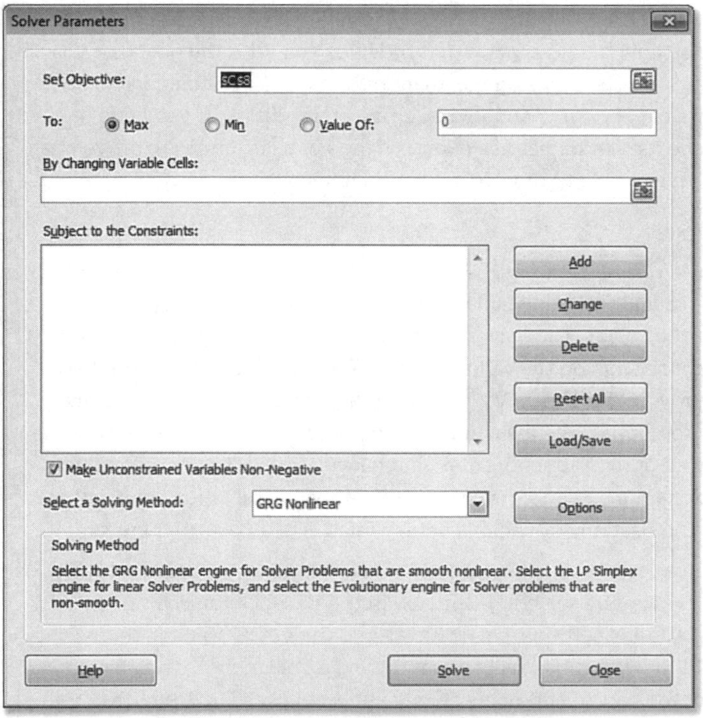

Figure 16.13
The Solver Parameters dialog box.

Click in the Set Objective box and then click on the cell that will provide the outcome for the Solver to use to calculate the values of changing cells. If you want to maximize the set objective (such as maximize your profits), select the Max option in the To: area of the dialog box. You can also select Min to minimize the value. If you want the set objective to be a specific amount, click the Value Of option button and specify the actual value for the Solver to use as a goal.

In the By Changing Variable Cells box, specify the cells that the Solver can change as it attempts to reach your set objective. You can select a range of cells or select multiple noncontiguous cells by holding down the Ctrl key as you select each cell.

After you have the variable cells specified, you can set any constraints that should be applied to changing cells as the Solver works to set values for your specified goal. To add a constraint, click the Add button. The Add Constraint dialog box will open. Specify the changing cell's address in the Cell Reference box; you can then specify that the cell reference be less than equal to, equal to, or adhere to another constraint parameter provided by the drop-down list.

In the Constraint box, specify the value that should be used to constrain the changing cell. You can type the value in the Constraint box or specify a cell address in the worksheet that contains the constraint value. For example, Figure 16.14 shows a constraint that specifies that the value in the changing cell B6 just be greater than or equal to a constraint value specified in cell B15.

Figure 16.14
Create a Solver constraint in the Add Constraint dialog box.

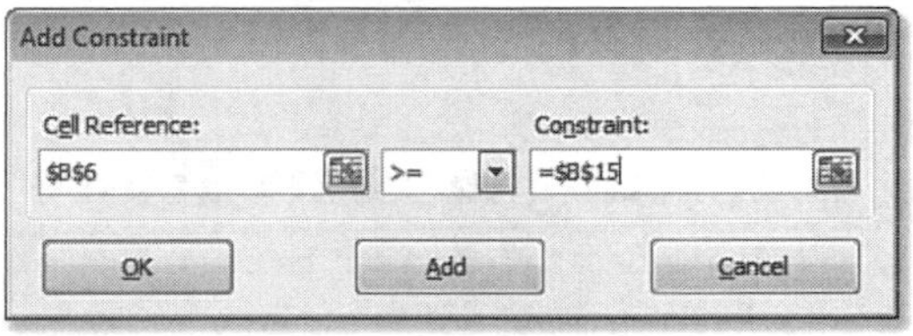

You can add as many constraints as needed. All the constraints will be listed in the Subject to the Constraints list in the Solver Parameters dialog box. Your constraints can be changed and deleted as needed using the Change and Delete buttons, respectively.

If you are working with some functions that use payments (which are considered negative numbers) or you want the Solver to be able to make certain variables negative numbers, deselect the Make Unconstrained Variable Non-Negative option. The Solver also provides you with different solving algorithms such as the GRG nonlinear, LOM simplex, and Evolutionary engines. For most financial and statistical functions, you can use the GRG nonlinear default setting.

When you are ready to run the Solver, click the Solve button. The Solver Results dialog box will open. It lets you know whether the Solver was able to find a solution. If you want to save a solution as a scenario, select the Save Scenario button. To keep the Solver solution and exit the Solver Results dialog box, select the Keep Solver Solution option button and then click OK.

Using PowerPivot

Microsoft has developed a new data analysis tool for Excel 2010: PowerPivot. Although PowerPivot is primarily designed for analyzing data that is pulled from a SQL Server database, it can also be useful for analysis of Access database tables or data from other sources including SharePoint Server sites. PowerPivot provides a very impressive array of capabilities that build on Excel's capabilities for working with external database tables and manipulating table data. PowerPivot also makes it easy for you to create a PivotTable from external data.

A number of the capabilities provided by PowerPivot, particularly those related to creating and managing table relationships, are beyond the scope of this book. However, if after digesting the information covered in Chapter 15, you find that you need more possibilities for working with database tables, PowerPivot will provide you with an excellent addition to Excel's other data manipulation commands and tools. Microsoft provides a number of resources for learning all the ins and outs of PowerPivot on the PowerPivot website.

You can download the PowerPivot add-in from the PowerPivot website at http://www.powerpivot.com. Download the .msi installation file for PowerPivot to your Windows desktop. There is both a 32-bit and a 64-bit version of PowerPivot, so download the appropriate version for your version of Office 2010 (Office 2010 comes in both 32-bit and 64-bit versions as does Windows 7). After the file has downloaded, you can run it. The PowerPivot for Excel Installation Wizard will open. Use the wizard to install PowerPivot. When the installation is complete, select Finish to close the wizard.

When you open Excel, the Microsoft Office Customization Installer will open. The Installer will add PowerPivot to Excel; click the Install button. After PowerPivot has been added to your Excel installation, you will find that a PowerPivot tab has been added to the Excel Ribbon.

Connecting to a Data Source

To connect to a data source using PowerPivot, you have to launch the PowerPivot window. Select the PowerPivot tab on the Ribbon. Then select the PowerPivot Window command in the Launch group. You can expand the PowerPivot window to use the entire desktop as needed.

To connect to a database source, select the From Database command on the PowerPivot Home tab. You can connect to a database on SQL Server or Access, or from an analysis service. When you select one of the database sources, such as SQL Server, the Table Import Wizard will open. You use the Table Import Wizard to specify the SQL Server name, the database name (in the case of an Access database), or the server name providing the analysis services (if you selected to connect to SQL Server providing the analysis services).

The possibilities for importing data into PowerPivot are very similar to those available for retrieving external data using the commands in Excel's Get External Data group, which is available on the Excel Ribbon's Data tab.

For more information on using Excel's data import commands, see page 433 in Chapter 15.

If you are connecting to a database server, such as SQL Server (which PowerPivot can search for), you will also need to provide the database name that you want to use. Figure 16.15 shows a connection being created to a SQL Server database.

The Table Import Wizard also enables you to select from a list of tables in a database that will be imported into PowerPivot. Whereas Excel's external data commands really enable you to connect to only a single external database table, PowerPivot enables you to connect to multiple tables in the database. You can select a table in the database and then use the Select Related Tables button to also select tables that are related to the table that you selected. All these tables will then be imported into PowerPivot.

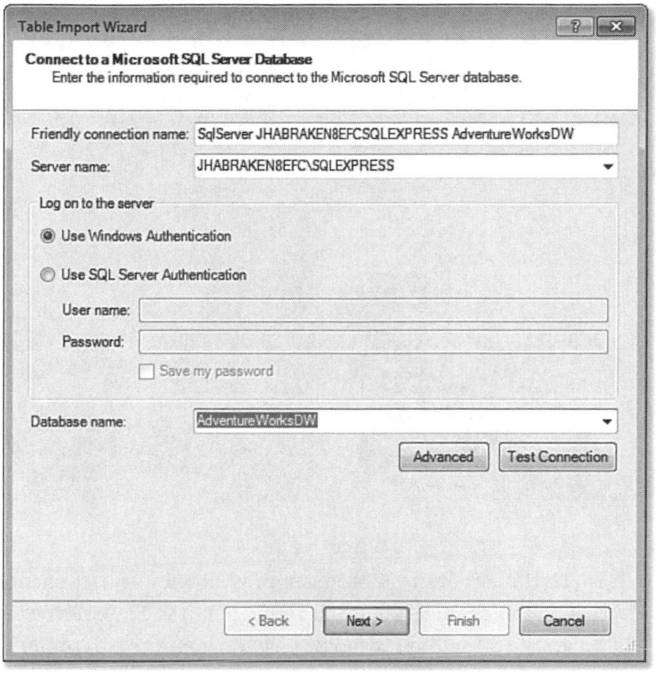

Figure 16.15
Create a connection to a server and database.

You can also preview or filter selected tables as needed via the Table Import Wizard. After you have specified the tables for import, you can click the Finish button in the Table Import Wizard. An Importing screen will appear, letting you know the status of the import. When the import is complete, you can click the Close button to close the Table Import Wizard.

Manipulating Data in PowerPivot

PowerPivot runs in its own application window. It uses the same overall geography and Fluent User Interface that is used by the other Office 2010 applications. Figure 16.16 shows the PowerPivot application window.

The PowerPivot Ribbon consists of two tabs: Home and Design. The Home tab provides command groups such as the Clipboard, Get External Data, Reports, and Formatting groups. The Home tab commands are primarily dedicated to using the Clipboard, getting external data into PowerPivot, building a PivotTable from the table data, and formatting and manipulating the data in a table.

The Design group provides access to the commands that enable you to work with columns in the table (columns are fields in a table) and also create and manage relationships between associated tables. The Design group also provides the Table Properties command, which enables you to quickly view a table's name and connection source information.

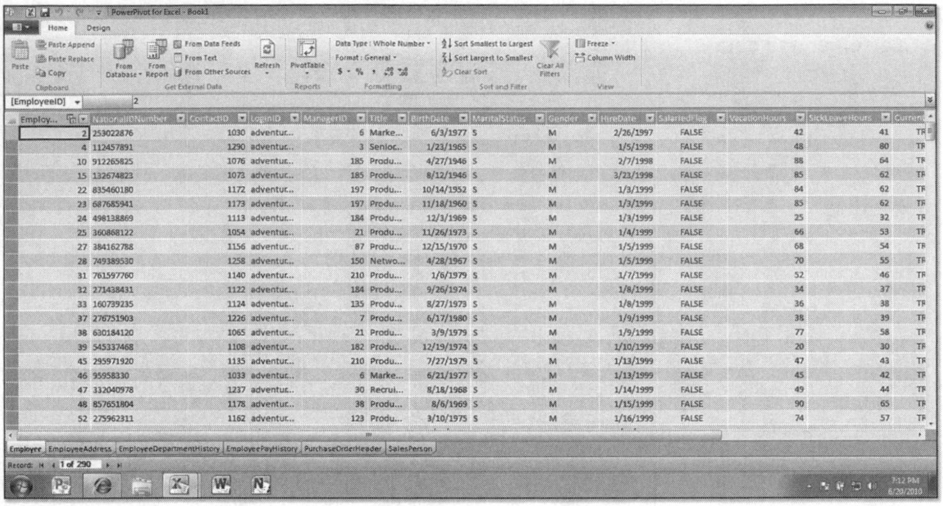

Figure 16.16
The PowerPivot
for Excel appli-
cation window.

To the left of the Ribbon is a drop-down menu. It enables you to save or publish (to another location) the tables that you are currently using in PowerPivot. A Close button is also provided that enables you to close the PowerPivot window and return to the Excel window.

After you have imported table data into PowerPivot, you can use the commands on the PowerPivot Ribbon to manipulate the data. When you import multiple tables into PowerPivot, each table will be placed on its own PowerPivot sheet. The selection tabs for the individual table sheets are at the bottom of the PowerPivot window (as Excel sheet tabs are). Below the table tabs is a set of controls that enable you to move through the records in the currently selected table.

Because you are working with tables in PowerPivot, each table has a drop-down arrow to the right of the field headings (the column labels). You can use the drop-down arrows next to each table field heading to sort the records in the table by that field. You can also use the filter list provided on the field drop-down menu to filter the table by specific field parameters. Sorts can also be accomplished using the commands in the Sort and Filter group. You can clear any filters that you have set by using the Clear All Filters command.

If you want to create a PivotTable from the records in the tables that you imported into PowerPivot, you can select the PivotTable command on the Home tab. You will be returned to the Excel application window and the Create PivotTable dialog box will open. You can create the PivotTable in a new worksheet or existing worksheet. The PowerPivot Field List, shown in Figure 16.17, provides you with access to the fields in each of the tables.

The PowerPivot Field list is very similar to the PivotTable Field list that you use to create a PivotTable in Excel. You can drag fields to the different areas provided, such as Report Filter, Column Labels, Row Labels, and Values, to build your PowerPivot PivotTable. The PowerPivot Field list provides you with the ability to quickly add vertical and horizontal slicers to the PivotTable. Figure 16.17 shows a vertical slicer that can be used to filter the PivotTable data by Territory ID.

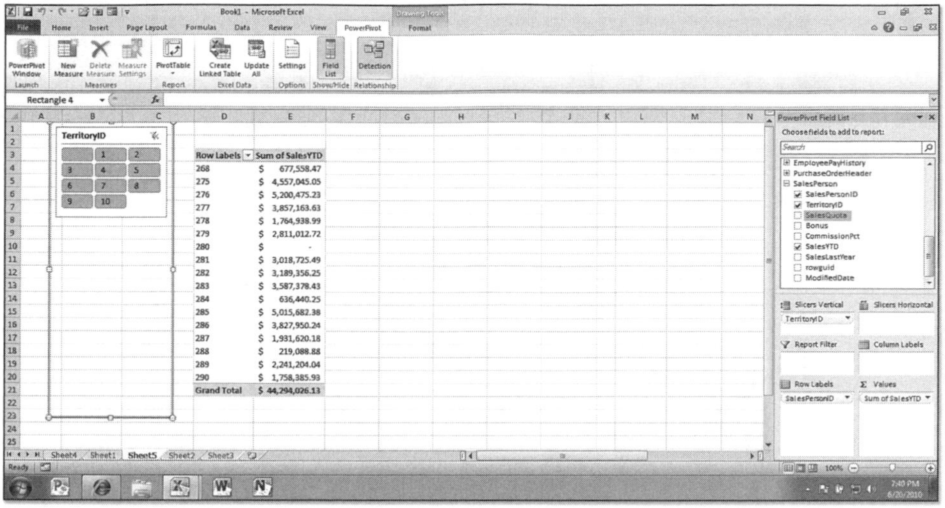

Figure 16.17
The PowerPivot
field list and
associated
PivotTable.

If you want to return to the PowerPivot window after creating your PivotTable, which is in your Excel workbook (remember to save it), select the PowerPivot Window command. This will enable you to work with the imported table data as needed. You can refresh the external data in the PowerPivot window by selecting the Refresh command on the PowerPivot Ribbon's Home tab.

PowerPivot's greatest asset is that it enables you to work with related database tables, meaning you are working with relational database records without actually using a database front-end such as Access. The Excel built-in data manipulation features are all geared toward individual flat file database tables. This is why PowerPivot's capabilities are a real addition to Excel.

For more about creating PivotTables, see page 443 in Chapter 15.

17

REQUISITE POWERPOINT: ESSENTIAL FEATURES

When we consider any type of live business presentation, we always think of PowerPoint. Microsoft PowerPoint is the standard "visual aid" software application for providing informative presentations. Whether you are giving a presentation as an important business meeting or showing pictures of your latest journey to a group of travel enthusiasts, PowerPoint provides an easy-to-use yet powerful presentation platform. It is used not only by many speakers but it is also often used at demonstration tables and kiosks as a method of playing a self-running presentation.

In this chapter, we look at the improvements and enhancements that you will find in PowerPoint 2010. As you get familiar with the PowerPoint 2010 interface and workspace, we will also look at the basics of constructing a PowerPoint presentation including the options provided for creating a new presentation. We also spend time looking at how to best create and manipulate your presentation slides.

Introducing PowerPoint 2010

Microsoft PowerPoint 2010 builds on the changes and functional improvements that were part of the PowerPoint 2007 release. PowerPoint 2010 uses the Office Fluent User Interface dominated by the Ribbon as did its predecessor, PowerPoint 2007. PowerPoint 2010 does provide some improvements to the overall interface, however, that are worth noting.

First, PowerPoint 2010 also takes advantage of the Backstage, as do the other Office 2010 application suite members. This makes it easy to access the Info, Print, Share, and PowerPoint Options windows. The Backstage also provides easy access to file-related commands such as Save As, Open, and Close.

You will also find that PowerPoint 2010 has fine-tuned the PowerPoint Ribbon. Transitions and Animations shared a common Ribbon tab in PowerPoint 2007. These two similar but different sets of slide special effects have now been broken out into separate Ribbon tabs: Transitions and Animation.

You will find that other enhancements to PowerPoint 2010 are more in the nature of under-the-hood improvements rather than changes that are immediately identifiable. Some of these additions and fine-tunings of PowerPoint are as follows:

- **Slide Sections:** You can now organize related slides in a presentation into sections. So, a section is typically related slides like chapters in a book. Figure 17.1 shows Hardware and Router Configuration sections that have been added to a slide presentation to keep slides covering like information grouped together in a slide presentation. The presentation is displayed in the Slide Sorter view. Sections can be collapsed for easy viewing of the overall content structure of your presentation. You can also move sections to rearrange the parts of a presentation as needed.

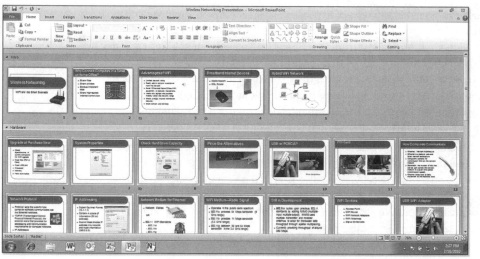

Figure 17.1
Divide presentations into sections.

- **New Animations:** You will find that new animations have been added to the Animation gallery. There is also a new Animation Painter tool that can be used to copy the animation settings from one object to another object or objects.

- **New Transitions:** A number of new transitions have been added to the Transitions gallery, which now has its own home on the new Transitions tab. These new transitions include new 3D transitions such as Flip, Gallery, and Cubes.

- **Video Enhancements:** PowerPoint 2010 provides new video-editing capabilities, including the trimming of video clips and the adding of borders and effects to your videos. This includes a gallery of video styles (much like a picture style) that you can apply to your videos. You will also find that PowerPoint 2010 makes it much easier to embed HTML code on a slide that links to video content on websites such as YouTube.com. You also now have the capability to save your PowerPoint presentations as .wmv video files, making it very easy to share your presentations online or as content for smart phones and other devices.

This is just a subset of some of the improvements that you will run into as you work with PowerPoint 2010. We will explore other new additions to PowerPoint within the context of specific features as we work with Microsoft's powerful presentation application in the PowerPoint section of this book.

The PowerPoint Workspace

The first thing you see when you start PowerPoint (Start, All Programs, Microsoft Office, Microsoft PowerPoint 2010) is that it opens to a new presentation and a blank title slide. The application window is divided into different areas and the default view for PowerPoint is the Normal view. Figure 17.2 shows the PowerPoint workspace in the Normal view.

Figure 17.2
The PowerPoint workspace.

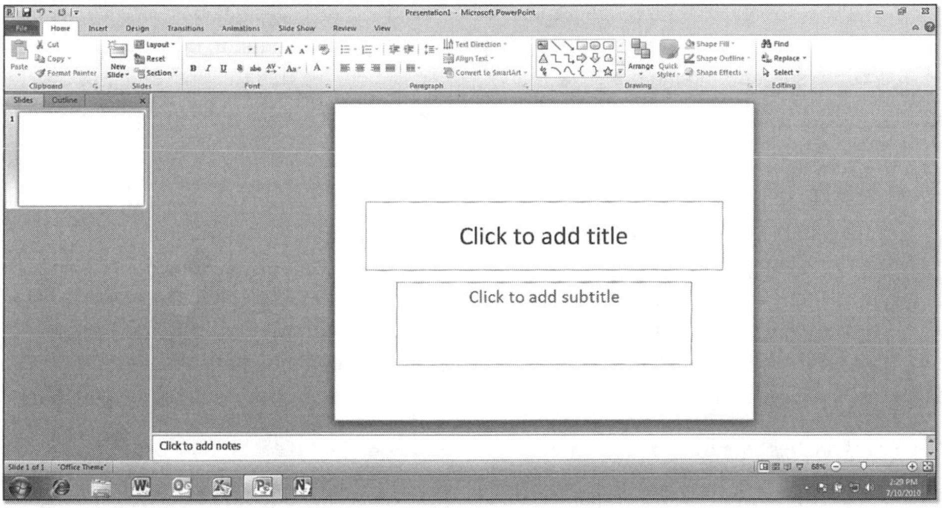

At the top of the workspace is the Ribbon, which provides all the commands for working with presentation slides and the objects that you will place on your slides. On the left of the screen is a pane that you can use to switch between the Slides and Outline tab for the current presentation. In the center of the PowerPoint application window is the Slide pane; this is where you work individually on each slide in the presentation.

Below the Slide pane is also a Notes pane, which enables you to add notes to the presentation for each slide. By default, the Notes pane doesn't appear in the Normal view; however, if you drag the Notes pane border upward (it is just above the Status bar), you will be able to see the Notes pane and enter text into it as you create each of your presentation slides.

Options for Creating a New Presentation

PowerPoint provides different options for creating a new presentation. One possibility is starting a new blank presentation, which is just a matter of starting PowerPoint. A default title slide is provided and you can add other slides to this blank presentation as needed. You can then determine the layout of each slide and the theme that is applied to the presentation.

There are other options for creating a new presentation. You can create a new presentation based on a template. A template is a presentation blueprint that provides an overall slide theme, individual slides with specific slide layouts, and, in a number of cases, placeholder text and other design objects already on the individual slides. Templates provide the greatest amount of handholding in terms of placing content on the presentation slides and determining the type of information that should be available on each individual slide.

note

There are presentation templates available that have been designed for specific types of presentations such as training, reports, evaluations, and proposals.

You can also create new presentations based on an existing presentation. This option actually opens a copy of an existing presentation, including the theme, slide layout, and slide content from the presentation. You can then edit the presentation copy as needed to create a new presentation. Creating a presentation using the New from Existing option negates the possibility of overwriting the slides and other settings of an existing presentation by not using the Save As option.

Using Templates

A number of presentation templates are installed on your computer or available from Office.com. You can even create your own templates and then use them as starting material to create new presentations. The templates provided by PowerPoint (both the sample templates installed on your computer and the Office.com online templates) vary in the amount of prepackaged design elements and placeholder text, both of which can help you get a jumpstart on creating your presentation.

To create a new presentation based on a template, follow these steps:

1. Select File to open the PowerPoint Backstage.

2. Select New. The Available Templates and Themes window will open as shown in Figure 17.3.

3. Select a template category such as Sample Templates, My Templates, or any of the Office.com template categories. If the category provides additional categories, open a category as needed to view individual templates.

4. Select a template. A preview of the presentation will be shown in the preview pane of the Available Templates and Themes window.

5. You can now use the template. In the case of templates stored on your computer, such as the sample templates, select Create in the Preview pane. In the case of templates on Office.com, select Download.

Figure 17.3
The Available Templates and Themes window.

After you select Create or Download (depending on whether the template is on your computer or Office.com), you will be switched to the PowerPoint workspace. The first slide provided by the template will be shown in the Slide pane and the other slides will be listed in the Slides/Outline pane. Figure 17.4 shows a downloaded training presentation template.

tip

If you prefer creating presentations from scratch, use the Blank presentation template.

Figure 17.4
Edit the template placeholder content.

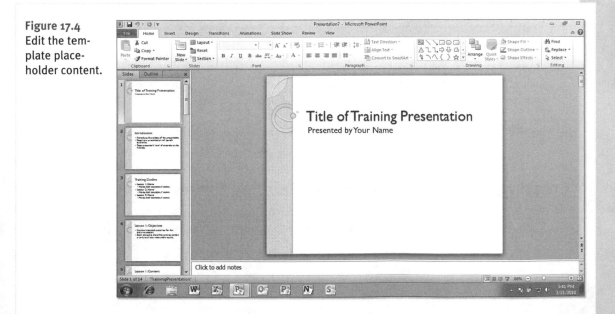

You can edit the slides as needed to complete your presentation. You can also insert additional slides and add objects to slides as needed.

Using a Theme to Create a New Presentation

If you want to specify the overall look of a new presentation, but don't want to have to edit a lot of placeholder text and other objects that are provided by a presentation template, you can specify a theme for the new presentation. A theme is a collection of colors, fonts, and text effects. The Available Templates and Themes window provides a collection of themes. Select Themes to view the available themes as shown in Figure 17.5.

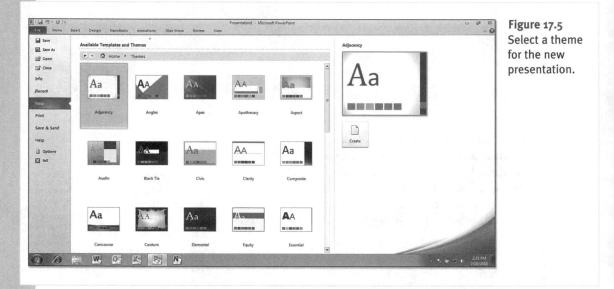

Figure 17.5
Select a theme for the new presentation.

Select a specific theme in the Themes gallery to view a preview of that theme. When you have found the theme that you want to use for the new presentation, select Create. A new title slide will open in the PowerPoint workspace using the theme that you selected.

 We will be discussing changing themes in a presentation in Chapter 18, "Advanced Presentation Formatting, Themes, and Masters," on page 512.

Creating a Presentation from an Existing Presentation

You can also create a presentation based on any existing presentation. This enables you to make a copy of the existing presentation and then edit it as needed to create a whole new presentation. Follow these steps:

1. Select File to open the Backstage.

2. Select New to open the Available Templates and Themes window.

3. Select New from Existing. The New from Existing Presentation dialog box will open as shown in Figure 17.6.

Figure 17.6
The New from Existing Presentation dialog box.

4. Select an existing presentation in the New from Existing Presentation dialog box.

5. Select Create New.

A new presentation based on the existing presentation will open in the PowerPoint workspace. The new presentation will include all the slides from the existing presentation and use the theme and other settings that were part of the original presentation. You can click Save to save the new presentation. You will not overwrite the existing presentation that you, in effect, used as the template for the new presentation.

Creating Individual Slides Using Slide Templates

You can also create complex or content-specific slides using slide templates provided in the Available Templates and Themes window. For example, you can create timer slides such as 1-minute or 10-minute timer slides that can be used as transitional slides in a presentation such as a slide that gives your audience a 10-minute break (visually as a slide). You can also create a special slide such as a process diagram slide or a seating chart. These special slide templates are found in the Content Slides group of the Office.com presentation templates.

To create a slide from one of the content slide templates, select the Content Slides category in the Available Templates and Themes window. Select a content slide template to preview it. When you are ready to create a new slide based on the content slide template, select Download.

A new presentation will be created with the special content slide as the only slide in the presentation. Now you might be saying, "I have this special slide now but I want it to be part of a presentation that I've already created." No problem. You have a couple of options related to this new presentation and its one special slide. First, you can copy the slide (right-click on the slide in the Slides tab and select Copy) and then switch to the other presentation and paste the slide into that presentation. Or if you already have slides in another presentation that you would like to insert into the new presentation, you can do that.

The Reuse Slides task pane enables you to use any or all slides in an existing presentation and easily place them into a new presentation. You use only the slides that you need; follow these steps:

1. On the Ribbon's Home tab, select the New Slide command, and then select Reuse Slides. The Reuse Slides task pane will appear as shown in Figure 17.7.

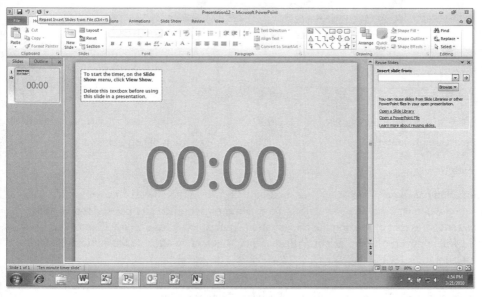

Figure 17.7
The Reuse Slides task pane and a special content timer slide.

2. In the Reuse Slides task pane, select the Open a PowerPoint File link. The Browse window will open.

3. Locate the PowerPoint presentation that will supply the slides for this new presentation (which includes the special slide). Then select Open. When you select Open, the slides in the presentation will be listed in the Reuse Slides task pane.

4. To add a slide from the Reuse Slides task pane to the current presentation, select a slide. By default, it will be formatted using the theme that has been set for the new (current) presentation. Add other slides as needed to build the new presentation.

Obviously, the reverse of this discussion is also another possibility for getting a special slide, such as a timer slide, into a new or existing presentation. After you have created the new presentation containing the special slide, such as the timer slide shown in Figure 17.7, save the new presentation. You can then use the Reuse Slides task pane to paste the special slide into any presentation that you are working on (at any time). The presentation containing the special slide, such as a timer slide, becomes a resource for all future presentations you create.

Creating a Template

You can create your own templates from your PowerPoint presentations. This can be useful in cases where you want a team of coworkers to create different portions of a presentation that you will then collate and you want everyone to use the same theme and overall look for their presentation parts. Or if you do a particular presentation on a regular basis that requires new content, you can create the template with some slide content and then add slides as needed to the new presentation created using your template.

Any presentation can be saved as a template. To create your own template, follow these steps:

1. Select File to open the PowerPoint Backstage.

2. Select Save As. The Save As dialog box will open.

3. In the Save as Type drop-down box, select PowerPoint Template. When you select the template file type, the folder location will default to your Templates folder (AppData\Roaming\Microsoft\Templates).

4. Specify a name for the template.

5. Select Save.

The new template will be saved to your Templates folder. The new template will be available via the Available Templates and Themes window when you want to use it to create a new presentation. Select My Templates and the New Presentation dialog box will open as shown in Figure 17.8.

Figure 17.8
Select one of your templates from the New Presentation dialog box.

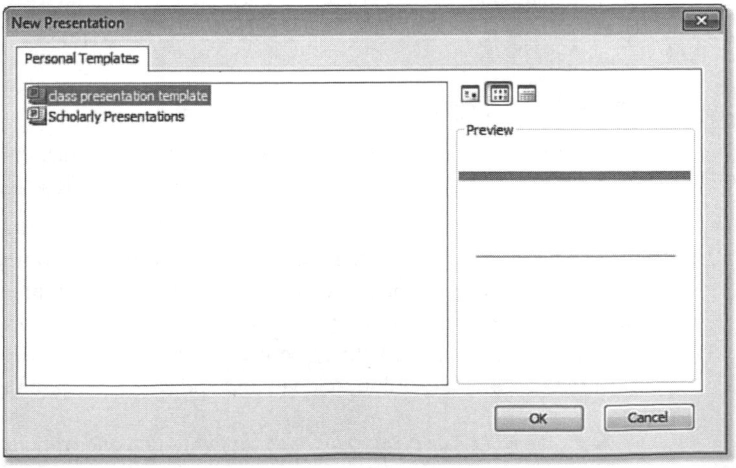

The New Presentation dialog box will list templates that you have downloaded (including slide templates) from Office.com. It will also list any templates that you have created. You will find that when you select a template that you have created, there is not a preview available. To start a new presentation based on template, select the template and then click OK. A new presentation based on the template will open in the PowerPoint workspace.

Inserting Slides

When you create a new presentation using a template (even the Blank presentation template), you are provided a title slide. The title slide contains two text boxes: one for the title and one for a subtitle. All text on your slides will reside in text boxes or table boxes (all objects appear on a slide in their own frames for easy manipulation). To enter text on a slide, such as the title text box, click in the text box and type the required text.

After you fill the text box or boxes on a slide, you will probably be ready to insert another slide into the presentation. When you add a new slide, you will also want to select the layout for that slide. The new Slide command is in the Slide group, which resides on the Ribbon's Home tab. Other slide-related commands such as the Layout, Reset, and Section commands are also in the Slides group.

Inserting a New Slide

When you select the New Slide command, a gallery of slide layouts is provided for common slide types such as Title Slide, Title and Content, and Blank. Figure 17.9 shows the Slide gallery. The slides available in the gallery will be based on the currently selected presentation theme (which is listed at the top of the gallery).

 tip

Use the new Presentation dialog box to use templates that you have previously downloaded from Office.com. You can even access them when you are not online.

To insert a particular slide layout type, select it in the gallery. The new slide will open in the Slide pane and be added to the list of slides on the Slides tab. You can click in the provided text boxes, such as the slide title, and add text as needed. Many of the slide layouts include a content area that can contain text or another object such as a table picture or clip art.

Entering Text

If you want the content area to contain text, select the Click to Add Text placeholder and type the text for the slide. The default formatting for content text is a bulleted list.

If you don't like entering text directly onto the slides, the Outline tab provides another way to edit text in a slide. To switch to the Outline view on the Slides/Outline pane, click the Outline tab. You simply click to move the insertion point where you want it (or select the range of text you want to replace) in the outline, and then type your text. Working on the Outline tab might make it easier for you to concentrate on the actual text and the sequencing of your text to build an informative presentation with a clear beginning, middle, and end (Aristotle came up with this concept, not me).

➡ *We will be discussing more about formatting and working with slide text in Chapter 18, on page 498.*

Figure 17.9
Insert a new slide into the presentation.

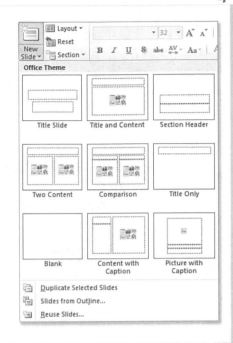

You will also find that it is easier to rearrange text on your slides using the Outline tab. You can select an entire bulleted list and drag it to another slide. This is more efficient than cutting and pasting information from slide to slide in the Slide pane.

Inserting Object Content

If you want an object other than text in a slide's content pane, you can use the icons provided in the content pane to select the type of object that should be inserted. We discuss working with tables, graphics, and media such as sound and movies in subsequent chapters, but the basics of inserting an object other than a text box is very straightforward.

Select an object icon such as the Insert Picture from File icon. The Insert Picture dialog box will open as shown in Figure 17.10.

All you have to do to insert a picture is select the picture file in the Insert Picture dialog box and then click Insert. The picture will be sized to the object content frame that was contained on the slide. The process is very similar for inserting any of the object types in the content pane; just select the appropriate icon and then select the object from the object-related dialog box that opens.

Figure 17.10
The Insert Picture dialog box.

Inserting Slides from Another Presentation

As already mentioned earlier in the chapter, you can insert slides into the current presentation from any of your other saved presentations. The Reuse Slides command is available on the New Slide command's gallery. Follow these steps:

1. Select the slide in the Slides/Outline pane (or in another view such as the Slide Sorter) where you would like the new slide or slides to be inserted into the current presentation.

2. Select New Slide on the Home tab and then Reuse Slides. The Reuse Slides task pane appears.

3. Select the Open a PowerPoint File link in the task pane; the Browse dialog box will open.

4. Specify the presentation file in the Browse dialog box that will provide slides for the current presentation. Then click Open. The slides in the presentation will be listed in the Reuse Slides task pane.

5. Click on a slide in the Reuse Slides task pane to add it to the current presentation. Repeat as necessary.

When you have finished working with the Reuse Slides task pane, you can close it. Make sure that you save the changes that you have made to the current presentation by selecting the Save button on the Quick Access Toolbar.

Inserting Slides from an Outline

Another option for creating a presentation is to create slides based on an outline created in another program. This option quickly creates new slides that will contain slide titles and accompanying slide text based on the text in the outline. You can insert as many slides as the outline provides; inserting outlines from Microsoft Word works particularly well.

> 🢂 *You will find that outlines created in Word using the Outline view translate the best to slides in PowerPoint. See page 271 in Chapter 10, "Creating Special Documents."*

To insert a Word outline into PowerPoint as presentation slides, select the New Slide command on the Home tab and then select Slides from Outline. The Insert Outline dialog box will open.

Select the outline document and then click Insert. The new slides (based on the outline) will be inserted into the current presentation. You can access the slides in the Slides/Outline pane tabs as needed. You can edit the new slides as you would any other slide, including adding objects to the slides as needed.

Modifying a Slide's Layout

You might find that the initial slide layout you selected for a slide needs to be modified. For example, you might want to take a slide that has a title text box and single content pane and make it a slide with two content panes. You can then have one pane with bulleted text and another pane with an object such as a picture. You can change the layout for any slide in the presentation. Even if you have already entered text or other objects on the slide, you can modify the layout.

Select a slide or slides in the Slides/Outline pane. Then select the Layout command on the Home tab. The Layout gallery will open. Select a new layout from the gallery. The new layout will be applied to the currently selected slide or slides.

Working with Slides in Different Views

PowerPoint can display your presentation in different views. Each view is designed for you to perform certain types of tasks as you create and edit a presentation.

For example, the Normal view contains the Slide pane, the Slides/Outline pane, and (potentially) the Notes pane. The Normal view is the ideal view for working on each slide in the presentation, and you can use the Slides/Outline pane as a tool for organizing the slides themselves and their content. You can even enter your speaker notes in the Notes pane as you create each of your slides.

> 🔍 **note**
>
> Creating an outline of your presentation in Word enables you to concentrate on the text in the presentation and makes it easy to arrange your thoughts. You can add pictures and other objects after you insert the outline into PowerPoint.

The Slide Sorter view, on the other hand, is designed for arranging your presentation slides into the proper order. You can also create presentation sections in the Slide Sorter view that enable you to group related slides. The available views in the PowerPoint workspace are as follows:

- **Normal:** The default view, which includes the Slide pane, Slides/Outline pane, and the Notes pane.

- **Slide Sorter:** This view shows all the slides as thumbnails so that you can easily rearrange them by dragging slides to new positions in the presentation. Figure 17.11 shows the Slide Sorter view.

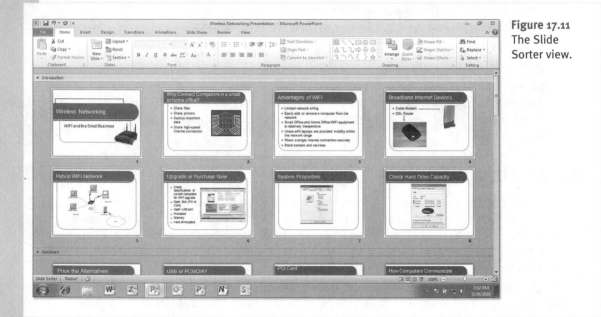

Figure 17.11
The Slide
Sorter view.

- **Reading View:** This view actually plays the presentation as a slide show. However, it shows the slide show so that it fits within the current PowerPoint window, even when the window is not maximized. This enables you to view the presentation and work with another application on the Windows desktop.

- **Slide Show:** This view plays the presentation as a slide show in the fullscreen mode. Click to progress through the slides in the presentation. You can press Escape on the keyboard to exit the Slide Show view at any time.

- **Notes Page:** This view enables you to see the current slide and its accompanying notes page. This view is designed for you to enter and review the speaker notes that you are creating to go with each slide in the presentation. Figure 17.12 shows the Notes Page view.

You have options in terms of switching from view to view in the PowerPoint workspace. You can take advantage of the view shortcuts on the PowerPoint status bar. Icons are provided on the right side of the taskbar for the Normal, Slide Sorter, Reading, and Slide Show views. The Slide Show icon plays the slide show beginning with the current slide.

Figure 17.12
The Notes Page view.

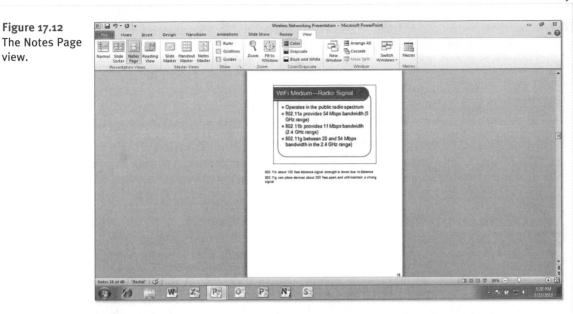

You can also change the view for the PowerPoint workspace by using the commands in the Presentation View group on the Ribbon's view tab. Commands are provided for the Normal, Slide Sorter, Notes Page, and Reading views. Figure 17.13 shows the View tab and its associated command groups.

As already mentioned, the View tab provides different commands for changing the current presentation view. This tab also includes groups that house other view-related commands such as the Master Views group, Zoom group, and Color/Grayscale group.

> ⚠ **caution**
>
> You can't edit the slide content when you are in the Slide Sorter or Notes Page views. However, double-click on the slide and you will be returned to the Normal view.

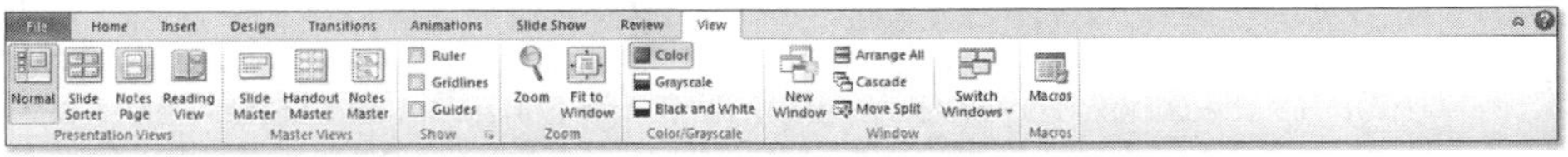

Figure 17.13
The Ribbon's View tab.

➥ *We will be discussing the slide master and other presentation masters in Chapter 18, "Advanced Presentation Formatting, Themes, and Masters," on page 517.*

Zooming in and Out

As you work on the content of individual slides, you might want to zoom in or out on a slide. You might also find it useful to be able to zoom in and out as you work with your slides in the Slide

Sorter view. You can use the Zoom slider to zoom in and out on presentation slides or slide content when you are in the Normal, Slide Sorter, or Notes Page view.

You can also change the zoom level using the commands in the Zoom group on the View tab. When you select Zoom, the Zoom dialog box opens as shown in Figure 17.14.

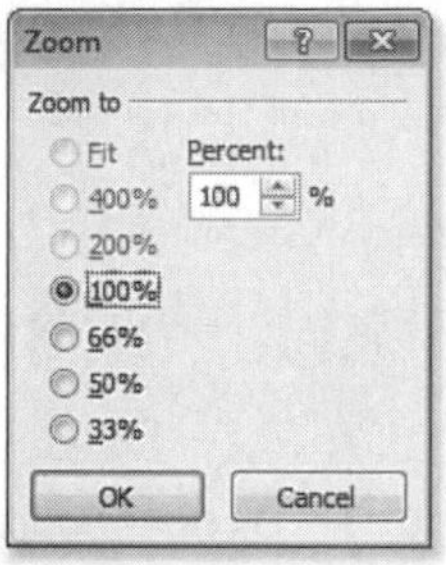

Figure 17.14
The Zoom dialog box.

You can select any of the available presets in the Zoom dialog box by selecting the appropriate option button. You can also use the percent spinner box to specify an actual percentage as needed. The Zoom group also provides the Fit to Window command. Select this command in either the Normal view or Slide Sorter view; the zoom percentage will be adjusted so that the slide or slides fill the window. In the Normal view, this will set the zoom percentage to 70%. In the Slide Sorter view, the zoom percentage will be adjusted to 50%.

Rulers, Gridlines, and Guides

The View tab also provides other commands that are view related. The Show group provides the Ruler, Gridlines, and Guides commands. These commands are designed to provide you with features that will help you place and align objects on your slides.

To view the horizontal and the vertical rulers, select the Ruler check box. When the rulers (horizontal and vertical) are placed in the workspace, you will find that as you move the mouse on the slide, the horizontal and vertical positions of the mouse pointer are shown as tick marks on the horizontal and vertical rulers.

If you want more help in aligning objects on the slide, you can turn on the gridlines; select the Gridlines check box. The gridlines are nonprinting horizontal and vertical lines. For even more precision, you can use the guides. When you select the Guides check box, a horizontal and a vertical guide line appear on the slide. You can move either of these guide lines as needed on the slide's surface. You can then use either guide to help you more accurately align objects on the slide. Clearing any of these command check boxes will remove those particular items from the workspace.

If you want to specify settings related to the gridlines and the guides, you can open the Grid and Guides dialog box. Select the dialog box launcher at the bottom of the Show group. Figure 17.15 shows the Grid and Guides dialog box.

Figure 17.15
The Grid and Guides dialog box.

By default, the Snap To setting is Snap Objects to Grid. If you also want objects to snap to other objects, select the Snap Object to Other Objects check box. You can also change the default spacing for the grid using the Spacing box. Check boxes are also provided that can be enabled to show the grids on screen and the drawing guides on screen. You can select these options and then use the Set as Default button so that your settings in the Grid and Guides dialog box become the default for all your presentations. When you have finished working in the Grid and Guides dialog box, select OK.

Color/Grayscale Commands

By default, your presentation slides are shown in color. You will find that the Color command is selected (by default) in the Color Grayscale group. You can view your presentation in grayscale or black-and-white and then customize how the various colors are translated to grayscale or black-and-white. This translation can be done on an object-by-object basis. So, you have complete control on how a particular object, such as a clip art image or table, will look in grayscale or black-and-white. This is extremely useful in cases where you will be providing your audience with grayscale or black-and-white handouts.

To view the slides in grayscale or black-and-white, select either the Grayscale or Black and White command. You will be switched to the Grayscale or Black and White view and the Ribbon will show the Grayscale or Black and White tab. This tab provides a series of commands that enable you to change the grayscale or black-and-white characteristics of a selected object on the slide. Figure 17.16 shows the grayscale view of a slide and the Grayscale tab on the Ribbon.

> **note**
>
> If you still create black-and-white overhead projector transparencies from your presentation slides, you will find the grayscale and black-and-white possibilities useful.

Figure 17.16
The Grayscale tab and associated commands.

The commands provided by the Grayscale or Black and White tabs are extremely straightforward. For example, if you want an object to be rendered to grayscale or black-and-white automatically (based on its actual color), select the object and then select the Automatic command. The other commands provide more definitive options for the grayscale or black-and-white rendering of an object. For example, if you select an object and then select the Black command, the object will be black when printed on a black-and-white printer. You can select multiple objects and then assign the same grayscale or black-and-white attribute to several objects at once.

tip

If you don't want an object to be included in a black-and-white printout of the slide, select the object and then select the Don't Show command.

When you have completed working with the Grayscale or Black and White commands, select the Back to Color View command. This actually returns you to the Ribbon's Home tab rather than the View tab.

Opening a New Presentation Window

You can open a second presentation window of the current presentation. This enables you to view a presentation in two different views at the same time. For example, one window could use the Normal view and the other window could use the Slide Sorter view. This enables you to manipulate the same presentation in different ways. For example, you could cut and paste or copy and paste an object from slides in one of the windows to the other window. Changes that you make to the presentation in either window are reflected in both of the windows.

To open a second presentation window, select the New Window command. A second window containing the current presentation will open on the Windows desktop. To arrange the two open presentation windows side by side, select the Arrange All command. Figure 17.17 shows two windows containing the same presentation. The Normal view is used on the left window and the Slide Sorter view is used in the right window.

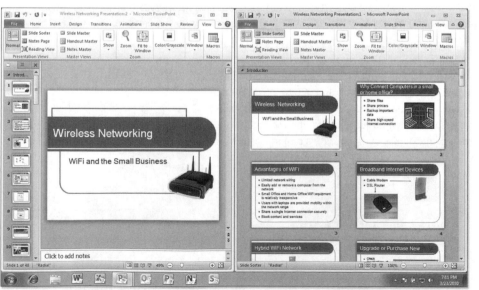

Figure 17.17
Multiple windows containing the same presentation can be opened.

You can close either window at any time. When you close one of the windows, you will want to maximize the remaining window so that PowerPoint takes full advantage of the space available on the Windows desktop.

Rearranging and Deleting Slides

Once you have a few slides in a presentation, you may have the need to rearrange them. Although you can reorder slides using both the Slides and Outline tabs in the Slides/Outline pane (which we discuss in a moment), the Slide Sorter view probably provides the best view for moving slides in the presentation because it provides thumbnails of your slides. Depending on the size of the presentation, you might be able to view many if not all the slides in the presentation when you are in the Slide Sorter view; this makes it easy to rearrange the slide order.

To switch to the Slide Sorter view, select Slide Sorter on the View shortcuts or select Slide Sorter on the View tab. Drag the slide to its new location; a vertical line shows the position of the slide as you drag it in the presentation. If you need to drag the slide to a location that is not in the Slide Sorter view, drag the slide downward and you will scroll through the slides in the presentation.

You can also copy a slide in the Slide Sorter view as easily as you can move a slide. Simply hold down the Ctrl key while you drag the slide. When you release the mouse, PowerPoint inserts a copy of the selected slide into the presentation.

> **🔍 note**
>
> The Slides tab in the Normal view probably works best for moving slides when you have only a few slides in a presentation. When you have a large number of slides, you might want to switch to the Slide Sorter view.

Although the Slides tab of the Slides/Outline pane available in the Normal view doesn't provide a view of as many slides as the Slide Sorter view does, you can also drag slides to new locations as needed. Drag up or down in the Slides tab to scroll up or down in the slides list. Release the mouse when you reach the position in the presentation that you want to place the slide.

You can also rearrange slides in the Outline tab of the Slides/Outline tab. Click the slide number you want to move. This highlights the contents of the entire slide. Drag the slide up or down within the presentation (by its slide icon), and then release the mouse.

You can delete a slide easily by selecting a slide (or slides) in either of the Slides/Outline pane tabs or in the Slide Sorter view. After you have the slide or slides selected that you want to delete, press the Delete key.

Modifying Bulleted Lists

When you enter new slides into a presentation, most of the slide layouts provide some combination of a title and content. There is a title and content layout, a title and two contents layout, a title and text layout, and so on. As soon as you enter text into a content box, it becomes a text box and provides you with a simple bulleted list. Each time you press Enter, a new bulleted item can be created in the list.

Because presentations are really a collection of topics and points that you want to bring to your audience's attention, most of your presentation slides will probably contain bulleted lists. Again, by default, typing in any content box or text box provided by the new Slide gallery will produce a bulleted list. You do have control over the bullet styles these lists.

You can modify bulleted lists quickly using the Bullets gallery. In cases where you want to specify a custom bullet for a list, you can access the Bullets and Numbering dialog box.

To modify a bulleted list on a slide, select the bulleted text. Select the Bullets command arrow to access the Bullets gallery. Select one of the bullet styles provided in the gallery. To specify a custom bullet shape for a bulleted list, you need to access the Bullets and Numbering dialog box. Select the Bullets command arrow and then select Bullets and Numbering in the Bullets gallery. The Bullets and Numbering dialog box will open with the Bulleted tab selected, as shown in Figure 17.18.

 note

If you insert a text box, you will need turn on bulleting by selecting the Bullets command. You can then type your bulleted list.

tip

You can insert picture bullets that you have created using picture-editing software by selecting the Import Button button. Make sure that the file size for the picture is 15×15 pixels.

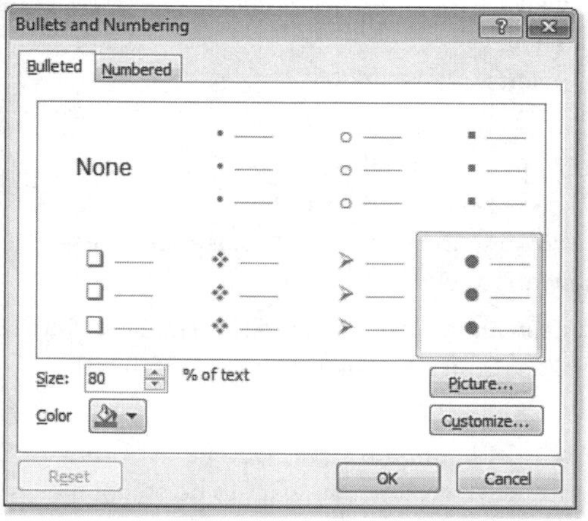

Figure 17.18
The Bullets and Numbering dialog box.

You can (obviously) select the bullet shapes provided on the Bulleted tab. In terms of custom bullets, you can use pictures or you can select a bullet from one of the symbol sets provided by the font families installed in Windows.

Picture Bullets

If you want to specify a picture as the bullet shape, select the Picture button in the Bullets and Numbering dialog box. The Picture Bullet dialog box will open. By default, the Picture Bullet dialog box will list any installed picture bullets and picture bullets available on Office.com.

You can scroll through the bullet gallery to locate a new bullet or you can search for a particular bullet type by typing search criteria in the Search text box. For example, if you want to view only square picture bullets, type **square** in the Search text box.

After you have located the picture bullet you want to use, you can select it and then click OK to return to the slide. The picture bullet will be assigned to the bulleted list.

Symbol Bullets

You can also specify a new bullet type based on a large number of symbols that are installed with the fonts on your computer. Select the bulleted list on the slide and then open the Bullets and Numbering dialog box (Bullets arrow, Bullets and Numbering).

On the Bulleted tab, select the Customize button. The Symbol dialog box will open as shown in Figure 17.19.

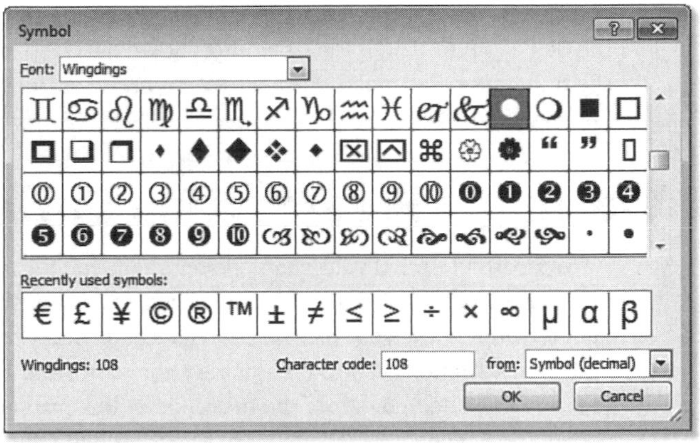

Figure 17.19
The Symbol dialog box.

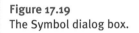

You can use the Font drop-down list to select different font symbol sets. Some of the most interesting symbols are found in the Wingdings and Webdings font sets, but there are symbols provided by all the font families you have available.

To select a particular symbol, select the symbol in the list provided. Then click OK. You will be returned to the Bullets and Numbering dialog box and the new bullet symbol will be added to the list of bullets provided on the Bulleted tab. You can change the size or color of the new bullet symbol (which is selected) by using the Size spinner box or the Color drop-down list, respectively.

When you have finished making modifications to the new bullet symbol, select OK. You will be returned to the current slide and the new bullet will be applied to your selected bulleted list.

Using Numbered Lists

Because your presentation might also serve the purpose of providing the audience with step-by-step procedures or a sequence of topics, you will also probably work with numbered lists on some of your presentation slides. Numbered lists are like bulleted lists, except they have sequential numbers instead of symbols. You can convert any selected text list to a numbered list by selecting the Numbering command on the Home tab.

If you want to select a particular numbering style, select the Numbering command arrow and the Numbering gallery will open. Select a number style from the gallery.

You can modify size and color settings for a numbered list and specify the number for the list to start at. This is useful if you have two associated slides and you want to the list on the second slide to pick up where the numbering on the previous slide's numbered list left off.

To open the Bullets and Numbering dialog box, select the Numbering command arrow and then select Bullets and Numbering in the Numbering gallery. When the Bullets and Numbering dialog box opens, the Numbered tab will be selected. You can choose from any of the numbering styles provided on the tab, but you will find, however, that they are the same styles provided in the Numbering style gallery.

If you want to change the starting number for the numbered list, use the Start At spinner box to specify the "start at number." You can also change the size or color of the numbering by using the Size spinner box or the Color drop-down list, respectively. When you have finished modifying the numbering settings, select OK. You will be returned to your slide and the new settings will be applied to the numbered list.

Viewing a Presentation During Editing

As you begin to build your slide presentation, you will want to check to see how slides will actually look when displayed in a slide show. The Slide Show tab of the Ribbon provides commands that enable you to view your presentation as a slide show and you will find these commands in the Start Slide Show group. The From Beginning command and From the Current Slide command can be used to start the Slide Show from the first slide or the currently selected slide, respectively. Figure 17.20 shows the Ribbon's Slide Show tab. The Start Slide Show commands are on the far left of the tab.

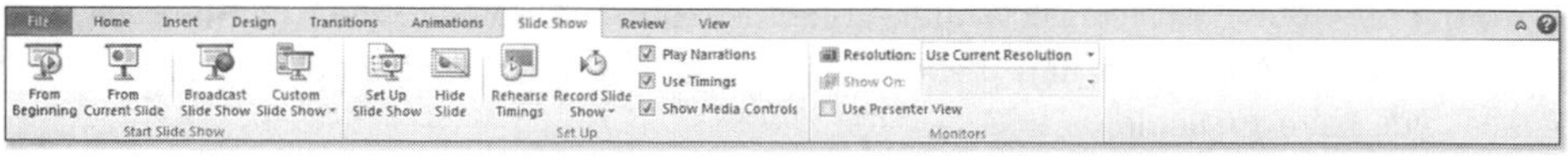

Figure 17.20
The Slide Show tab of the Ribbon.

When you select either the From Beginning or Current Slide command, the appropriate slide will appear full screen in the Slide Show view. You can advance to the next slide by clicking the mouse. You can also press the Page Down key, the right-arrow key, or down-arrow key to navigate to the next slide in the slide show.

If you want to back up a slide, press the Page Up key (you can also use the up-arrow or left-arrow key as well). You can also back up a slide by right-clicking the mouse and selecting Previous from the shortcut menu that appears.

tip
You can also start the slide show from the current slide by clicking the Slide Show button in the View shortcuts area.

When you have completed viewing the slide show, you can end the slide show and return to the PowerPoint workspace; press the Esc key or right-click the mouse and select End Show. You will be returned to the slide that was last viewed in the slide show.

 tip

Move back and forth in the slide show using the wheel on your mouse.

This short discussion of previewing a slide show as you begin to piece together your presentation is provided only to get you in the habit of previewing your slides in the format that they will typically be seen in: a slide show. We look at issues and PowerPoint features related to planning and preparing a professional presentation in Chapter 21, "Delivering a Presentation and Creating Support Materials."

 For a more complete look at the Slide Show commands and finalizing a presentation, see page 578 in Chapter 21.

18

ADVANCED PRESENTATION FORMATTING, THEMES, AND MASTERS

Creating PowerPoint presentations that are both informative and visually appealing means you must walk a fine line between the purpose of your presentation and its overall design. To get your message across, you must create slides that are both easy to read and easy to understand. PowerPoint slides are meant to hit the high points related to your subject matter and provide a guide to both you and the audience as you walk them through the information.

Even the most informative and easy-to-understand presentation, however, can be plagued by visually unappealing slides or slides that are not uniform in fonts, colors, and design elements. In this chapter, we look at options for formatting slide text and arranging text in both text boxes and tables. We also discuss the possibilities for manipulating slide color and other attributes using themes and background styles.

We also look at the possibilities for inserting repeating information or elements in slides using headers and footers. Our look at overall design considerations and repeating objects also includes a discussion of slide masters. In terms of organizing the overall presentation into subgroups of information, we look at the new sections feature.

Working with Text Boxes and Formatting

Most of the text found on your presentation slides is typically held in a frame called a text box (although tables can also hold text as can other objects). When you insert a new slide into a presentation, you are provided several layout options for that slide. The new slide can use such layouts as "title and content" or "two content." All you have to do to enter text into a title or content box is click in the box to place the insertion point and then enter the text. By default, the text is formatted as a bulleted list.

For editing the text in a text box, all you have to do is select the current text and then edit the text as needed. The only time that you will need to create a new text box is when you want to place text on the slide in a position other than what is provided by the default text box or text boxes on the slide.

> **note**
>
> You can add text to nearly any inserted shape. Select the shape and then select the Text Box command on the Drawing Tools Format tab.

Inserting a Text Box

Text boxes are drawn onto a slide using the Text Box command in the Text group of the Ribbon's Insert tab. You will find that not only do you have control over the format of the text within the box, including the text direction and special text effects, but there are also options for formatting the text box itself, including outside borders and fill color.

To create a new text box on a slide, follow these steps:

1. Select the Text Box command on the Insert menu.

2. Place the mouse pointer on the page and drag diagonally to create the text box.

3. Release the mouse button and the insertion point appears in the text box.

Figure 18.1 shows a new text box on a presentation slide. To enter text in a text box, type the text as required.

You can type the text and then format the text after the fact or you can immediately take advantage of the various font and paragraph-formatting tools provided on the Home tab to apply basic formatting attributes before you type. These attributes include options such as bold, italic, and bulleted or numbered lists.

You will find (in the next section) that the possibilities for formatting the text in the text box are not limited to the various font and paragraph commands on the Home tab. Other tools that provide you with the ability to add text effects and WordArt styles to your text are provided by the Drawing Tools.

> **note**
>
> The text you enter into a text box you have created will use the default font and font size for body text, which is Calibri, 18 point.

Figure 18.1
A new text box.

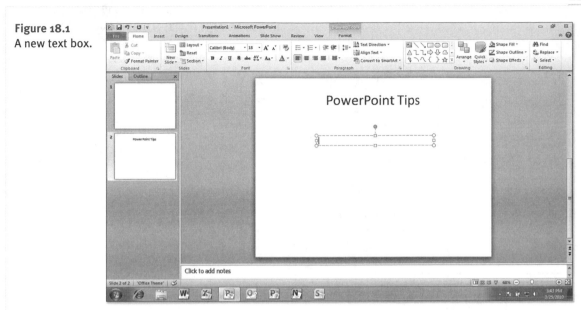

Basic Text Formatting

The typical formatting commands for both the font and paragraph attributes of the text in a text box are provided in the Font and Paragraph groups on the Home tab. The Font group provides control over such things as the font type, size, color, and other attributes such as bold, italics, and underline. The Paragraph group enables you to change the horizontal alignment of the text, create bulleted and numbered lists, change the line spacing, and indent text. Figure 18.2 shows the Home tab, including the Font and Paragraph groups.

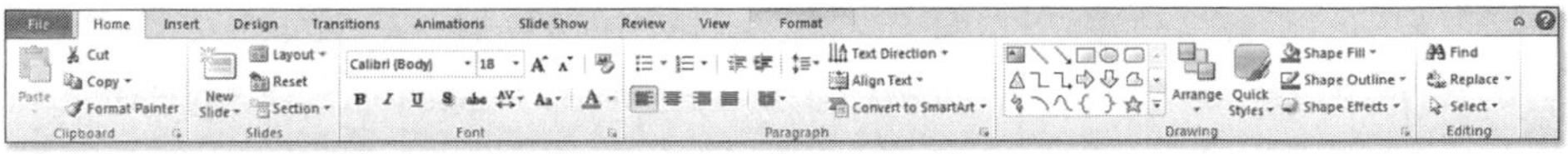

Figure 18.2
The Ribbon's
Home tab.

Changing Font Attributes

To change the font attributes of selected text, select the text attribute by clicking the appropriate command (or commands) in the Font group. If you find that you want to remove the text formatting that you have applied to text in a text box, you can select the Clear All Formatting command and it will remove all the formatting from the selected text.

🔍 note

You can select text in a text box and change font and paragraph attributes, or select the text box itself and then change attributes for all the text in the text box.

You can also access additional font attributes such as strikethrough, superscript, and small caps by using the Font dialog box. To open the Font dialog box, select the dialog box launcher on the Font group. Figure 18.3 shows the Font dialog box.

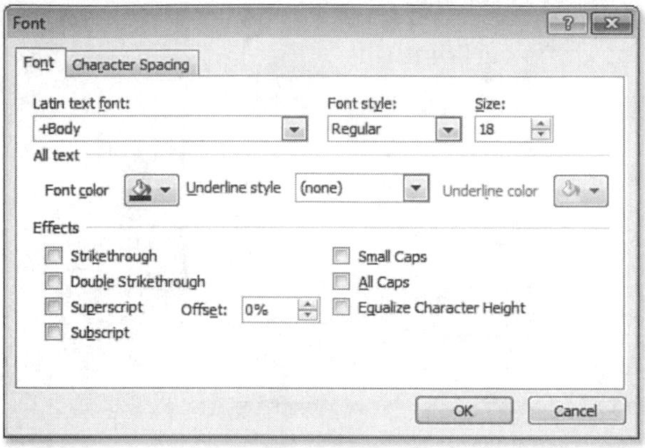

Figure 18.3
The Font dialog box.

The Font dialog box offers you control over the same font attributes available in the Font group on the Home tab. However, other font-formatting possibilities, such as strikethrough, superscript, subscript, and small caps, are also available as check boxes in this dialog box.

tip

You can copy and paste text formats using the Format Painter on the Home tab.

Changing Paragraph Attributes

Paragraph attributes include settings such as paragraph alignment (left, center, right, and justify), indents, columns, bulleted and numbered lists, and line spacing. You can assign any of these paragraph settings to selected text (including an entire selected text box) by using a specific command or commands and also turn on the settings and then type new text as needed.

The Paragraph group also offers three additional commands that go beyond the typical paragraph formatting. These commands are as follows:

- **Text Direction:** This command provides a gallery of text orientations including Horizontal, Rotate All Text 90°, and Stacked. Hover the mouse over a text direction setting in the gallery to preview the setting on the currently selected text box.

- **Align Text:** This command provides a gallery of settings that change how the text is aligned within the text box. Settings provided for Align Text are Top, Middle, and Bottom. You can access more alignment settings by selecting More Options; this opens the Format Text Effects dialog box, which provides a larger list of alignment possibilities in the Vertical Alignment drop-down list.

- **Convert to SmartArt:** This command provides a gallery of SmartArt shapes. You can convert the text box to any of the shapes provided. Place a mouse on a SmartArt shape in the gallery to preview the shape on the currently selected text box.

> *We will be discussing SmartArt in more detail in Chapter 19, "Better Slides with Clip Art, Pictures, and SmartArt," on page 525.*

You can also access the more basic paragraph settings for selected text or a text box via the Paragraph dialog box. Select the dialog box launcher in the Paragraph group. The Paragraph dialog box provides more precise setting possibilities for indents and line spacing, including spinner boxes for Before and After, which enable you to set the amount of white space before and after a text line, respectively. The Paragraph dialog box also provides access to the Tabs dialog box, which you can use to set tab stops for a selected text box.

> *Setting tabs in PowerPoint, both in the Tabs dialog box and directly on the ruler, is very similar to creating tab settings in Word. See Chapter 6, "Requisite Word: Essential Features," on page 158.*

Formatting a Text Box with the Drawing Tools

Possibilities for formatting a text box and its contents way beyond the more basic settings found on the Home tab are provided by the Ribbon's Drawing Tools. When you select a text box on a slide, the contextual Drawing Tools Format tab appears on the Ribbon. Select Format and the various Drawing Tools command groups are made available. These commands are used to format a PowerPoint object that you add to a slide, which includes AutoShapes and text boxes. The Drawing Tools Format tab and its various command groups are shown in Figure 18.4.

Figure 18.4
The Drawing Tools Format tab.

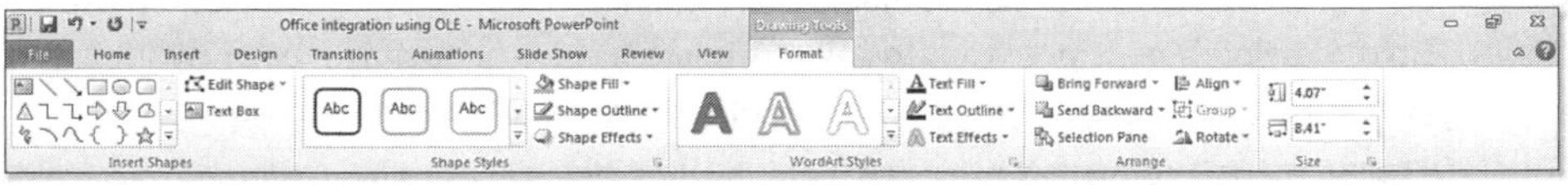

The commands directly associated with the changes that you can make to the text box and the text within the text box are primarily housed in the Shape Styles and WordArt Styles command groups. The Shape Styles commands are used to apply formatting to the text box. The WordArt Styles group enables you to apply special text effects and control the text fill and outline.

Selecting Quick Styles and Shape Attributes

Shape styles or quick styles, as they are also referred to, are sets of formatting attributes that affect the text box border, font color (and bullet color if applicable), and text box background (fill) color. The shape styles are housed in the Shape Styles gallery. You can use the scroll arrows to scroll through the styles provided or you can select the More button to view the entire gallery as shown in Figure 18.5.

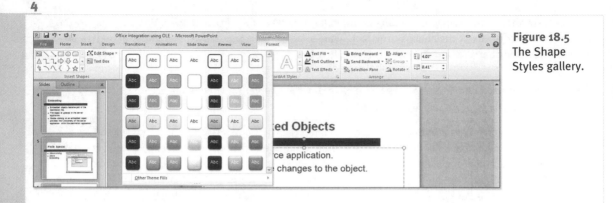

Figure 18.5
The Shape
Styles gallery.

The fills (text box background) and styles provided are based on the current theme. You can view additional theme fills by selecting Other Theme Fills at the bottom of the gallery. These fills do not provide changes in the font color, however, you can easily change that font attribute by using the Font Color command on the Home tab.

> **tip**
>
> You can also assign quick styles to text boxes and other shapes from the Quick Styles command on the Home tab.

Shape Fill, Outline, and Effects

The alternative to selecting one of the quick styles is to change the shape fill, outline, and effects manually. The Shape Fill, Shape Outline, and Shape Effects commands are also available in the Shape Styles group.

To change the text box (or other shape) fill, select the Shape Fill command and select a color from the theme colors provided. You can also choose from standard colors or select More Fill Colors to choose a color from the Colors dialog box. Standard colors can be selected on the Standard tab of the Colors dialog box. If you want to select a custom color or specify a color by its RGB (Red, Green, and Blue) designation, you can use the Custom tab of the Colors dialog box.

The Shape Fill command provides more options for a text box background than colors. You can select Picture to specify a picture as the background; all you have to do is specify the picture file in the Insert Picture dialog box. When the picture appears in the text box, you can use the Picture Tools to customize the image so that it works well as a background for the accompanying text in the text box.

➡️ *Editing pictures in the Office applications, including PowerPoint, is discussed in Chapter 4, "Using and Creating Graphics," on page 86.*

The Shape Fill command does not limit you to color and pictures as a text box background. You are also provided with gradients and textures. When you select the Gradient command, a gallery of gradients appears. Point at a gradient to preview it on the text box.

Textures are also an option as the fill for the text box. Select Texture on the Shape Fill menu and a gallery of textures will appear as shown. Preview a texture or textures by moving the mouse over the possibilities in the gallery.

After you have selected a fill for the text box, you can use the Shape Outline command to specify the color for the text box border. You can select from theme or standard colors or use the Color dialog box to specify a custom color. The Shape Outline command also enables you to specify the weight for the text box border and the dash style for the line. The default is a solid line.

To put the finishing touches on the text box, you can add an effect using the Shape Effects command. This command provides a number of different effects that are grouped in galleries under a particular effect category. These categories include preset, Shadow, Reflection, Glow, and 3-D Rotation. Select any of the specific shape effects in the category galleries to preview the effect on the text box.

Fine-Tuning Shape Formatting

Although the Shape Styles group commands take care of most of the possibilities in formatting the appearance of a text box (or other shape), you can fine-tune these settings using the Format Shape dialog box. The Format Shape dialog box is shown in Figure 18.6 and is opened using the dialog box launcher on the Shape Styles group.

Figure 18.6
The Format Shape dialog box.

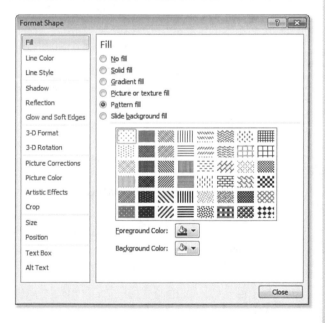

The settings provided in the Format Shape dialog box that are roughly equivalent to the settings provided by the Shape Styles group commands are Fill, Line Color, Line Style, Shadow, Reflection, Glob and Soft Edges, 3-D Format, and 3-D Rotation. When setting these different attributes via the dialog box, you still get a preview of an attribute, so you might want to move the dialog box off of the current slide so that you can see how the setting changes affect the text box.

The advantage of using the Format Shape dialog box for setting text box and other shape attributes is that you have greater control over the settings than is provided by the presets that you get when you use the commands in the Shape Styles group. The Format Shape dialog box settings relevant to text box formatting are defined in the list that follows:

- **Fill:** Use this setting to specify the fill for the text box. You can select from a variety of possibilities including solid fill, gradient fill, pattern fill, and slide background fill (the text box picks up the fill color from the slide). When you specify a fill type such as solid fill, you will specify the fill color in the dialog box. The gradient fill provides you with a slide to specify gradient stops and you can also set the brightness and transparency for the selected fill color.

- **Line Color:** This setting enables you to specify the line type (solid or gradient) and the line color. A Transparency slider enables you to specify the transparency of the text box border.

- **Line Style:** Use this setting to set the width and compound and/or dash type for the text box border. You can also specify the cap and join type for the text box.

- **Shadow:** This is a shape effect that can be used to specify a shadow type for the text box using a gallery of presets. Additional settings including Transparency, Size, Blur, Angle, and Distance enable you to fine-tune the overall look and size of the shadow.

- **Reflection:** Another of the shape effects; select a preset from the provided gallery. You can then fine-tune the reflection using the Transparency, Size, Distance, and Blur settings.

- **Glow and Soft Edges:** This shape effect can be specified by selecting a preset for both the glow and the soft edges. You can then control the color, size, and transparency of the glow and the size of the soft edges.

- **3-D Format:** You can specify a 3D bevel effect for the text box (or other shape) based on the bevel, depth, contour, and surface settings for the object. Galleries are provided by both top and bottom bevels and you have control over the depth and contour by selecting a color and adjusting the setting using the accompanying spinner box. Figure 18.7 shows the various settings provided by the Format Shape dialog box for 3D custom formatting of a text box.

- **3-D Rotation:** This shape effect allows you to rotate a 3D version of the text box or shape by selecting from a gallery of presets. You can then customize the rotation axes by specifying the X, Y, and Z settings using the provided spinner boxes or a direction button such as Left, Right, Up, or Down. You can also choose to keep the text flat in the 3D object.

As you work with the 3-D Format and the 3-D Rotation settings, you might need to take advantage of the Reset button that both of these rather complex formatting options provide for your convenience. After you have specified the settings for in the Format Shape dialog box, select Close. You will be returned to the PowerPoint workspace.

Figure 18.7
The 3-D Format settings in the Format Shape dialog box.

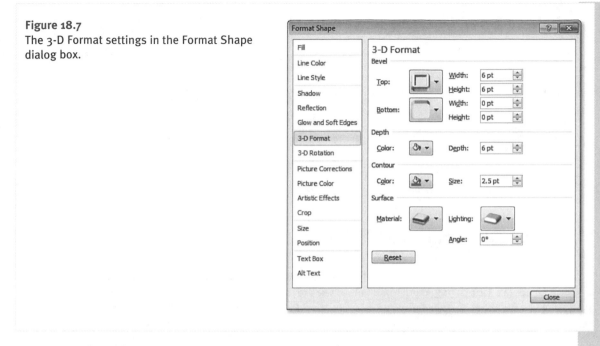

Using WordArt Styles and Text Settings

The Drawing Tools Format tab also provides you with special settings for the text that is contained in a text box or other shape. You can assign WordArt styles to the text, which provides text effects that greatly surpass the possibilities supplied by the regular text-formatting possibilities provided on the Ribbon's Home tab.

The WordArt styles provide a gallery of different effect styles that can be directly assigned to the text. If you want to have greater control over the customization of the text box in a text box or other shape, you can set your own text fill, outline, and effects as required.

To take advantage of the WordArt Styles gallery, scroll through the possibilities provided in the gallery. If you want to see the entire gallery, select the More button. The WordArt Styles gallery is shown in Figure 18.8.

Place the mouse on a style to preview the style on the text in the text box. Select a style to assign it to the text in the text box (or other shape). You can clear a previously assigned WordArt style from the text by using the Clear WordArt selection in the WordArt Styles gallery.

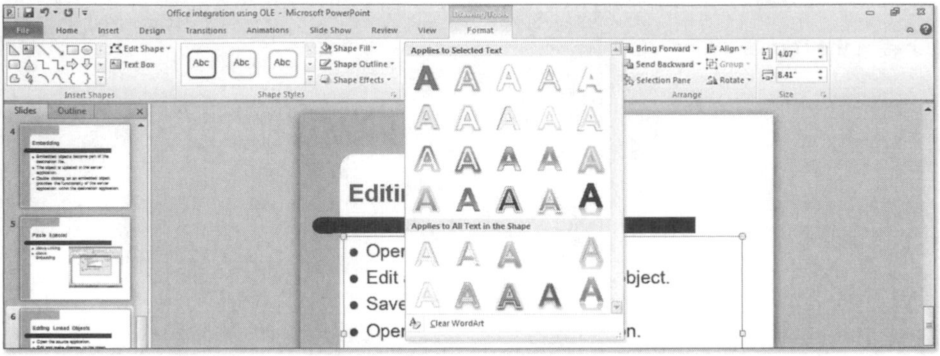

Figure 18.8
The WordArt
Styles gallery.

Text Fill, Outline, and Effects

If you don't want to use a WordArt style provided in the gallery, you can customize the text by assigning your own fill, outline, and effects settings to the text. The Text Fill command enables you to apply a text color, picture, gradient, or texture to the text in the text box. You can select a color from the colors provided or you can select More Fill Colors to access the Color dialog box.

You can also use a picture as the fill for text in a text box; select Picture and then specify and insert the picture file from the Insert Picture dialog box. You might wonder why you would want to use a picture to provide the fill for text given that you won't actually see the entire picture, but think of this possibility in terms of the colors provided by the picture rather than the picture itself. Assigning the background colors to the text using the Text Fill command would enable you to match the text nicely with the accompanying picture on the same slide. Both would use the same color palette, making you look like a design guru. The text fill can also consist of a gradient or texture. Either of these possibilities can be selected from the Text Fill command.

In terms of the text outline, you can use the Text Outline command to select from a variety of colors or you can use a color you select from the Color dialog box (use the More Outline Colors setting). The Text Outline command also enables you to set the weight and dash style used by the text outline color you select.

The Text Effects command enables you to select from a number of different effects galleries including Shadow, Reflection, Glow, and Transform. Select a category such as Transform and then preview the possibilities provided in a specific gallery by mousing over a choice or choices. Figure 18.9 shows the Transform gallery provided by the Text Effects command.

Although the various text effects are certainly more exciting than what we typically think of as text formatting, I suggest that you use these possibilities judiciously. Cramming a slide with text that has had different effects applied to it might be hard to read or just might be jarring in terms of design sensibility. Use the effects to best effect, which means use them sparingly and appropriately. The effects should add to the slide's appeal, not take away from its ability to communicate.

Figure 18.9
Use the Text Effects command to assign special effects to your text.

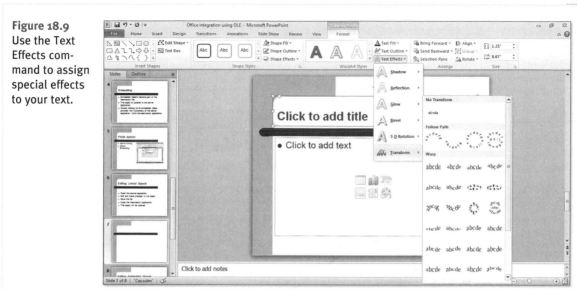

Using the Format Text Effects Dialog Box

You can configure and fine-tune text effect settings in the Format Text Effects dialog box. This dialog box provides greater control over settings related to the text fill, text outline, and text effects. To open the Format Text Effects dialog box, select the dialog box launcher on the WordArt Styles group.

Figure 18.10 shows the Format Text Effects dialog box. The Text Fill settings are selected in the dialog box, which shows the Gradient Fill setting tools.

The settings available in the Text Effects dialog box are accessed via a series of categories on the left side of the dialog box. The categories and the settings that they provide are as follows:

- **Text Fill:** The Text Fill can consist of no fill, solid fill, gradient, picture, texture, or pattern. When working with the Solid Fill option, you can select a color and transparency level for the text. The Gradient option provides you with the ability to set the color, direction, type, and angle of the gradient. You can then use the Gradient Stops slider to set the stops for the gradient. The Picture or Texture Fill option enables you to select from provided textures or use a picture or clip art as the fill for the text. The last of the fill options, the Pattern Fill, enables you to select a pattern and foreground and background color.

- **Text Outline:** The Text Outline (meaning the text border) can be a solid line or a gradient line. When you select the Gradient Line option, you can set the preset colors, type (linear, radial, rectangular, or path), the gradient stops for the gradient, and the brightness and transparency of the gradient (refer to Figure 18.10).

- **Outline Style:** The Outline Style options for the text characters consists of the width, compound type, dash type, cap type, and join type.

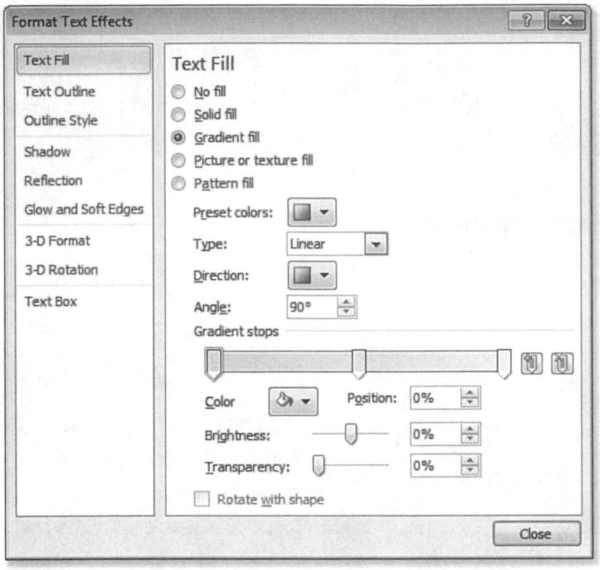

Figure 18.10
The Format Text Effects dialog box.

- **Shadow:** Select a shadow type from the presets provided. You can then edit the color and other settings for the shadow such as transparency, size, blur, angle, and distance (from the text).

- **Reflection:** Preset reflections are provided in the Presets gallery. You can then modify the transparency, size, distance, and blur for the reflection as needed.

- **Glow and Soft Edges:** These settings enable you to select a glow from a gallery of presets. You can then modify the color, size and transparency of the glow as needed. You can also change the format for soft edges by using the Soft Edges Presets gallery. Once a preset is selected, you can change the size using the Soft Edges slider provided.

- **3-D Format:** These options enable you to specify the top and boot bevel for the text and also control the depth, contour, and surface of the text. The Surface settings are provided by presets listed in the Material and Lighting galleries.

- **3-D Rotation:** You can choose from a gallery of 3D rotation presets. You can then modify any of the presets using the Rotation spinner boxes for the axes (X, Y, and Z).

After you have modified the settings in the Format Text Effects dialog box, select Close. You will be returned to the PowerPoint workspace.

Arranging Text in Tables

An alternative to the text box is the table. Tables are very useful when you want to display numerical information in an easy-to-read format or want to arrange information in columns or rows. The intersection of a table column and row is referred to as a cell.

The easiest way to create a table on a slide is to create a new slide that uses the Title and Content layout; insert the new slide using the New Slide command on the Home tab. In the content area of the slide, select the Insert Table icon. The Insert Table dialog box will appear as shown in Figure 18.11.

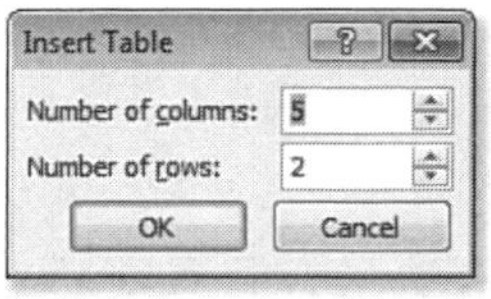

Figure 18.11
The Insert Table dialog box.

Specify the number of columns and the number of rows for the new table using the spinner boxes provided. When you are ready to place the table on the slide, select OK. The table will be placed on the slide.

Insert a Table on an Existing Slide

You can also insert a table onto an existing slide. This enables you to include a table on a slide in cases where you don't want to change the slide's layout (particularly in cases where the slide already contains content) or just want to place the table on the slide as an object.

Switch to the Ruler's Insert tab and then select the Table command; you can select the columns and rows for the table by using the table grid provided by the Table command. When you release the mouse, the table will be placed on the slide. You can drag the table to the appropriate position on the slide as needed. You can also use any of the sizing handles to size the table so that it is appropriate for your purposes.

Formatting a Table

After you have the table on the slide, you can enter text into the cells provided by the table. The easiest way to move forward from cell to cell in the table is the Tab key. Shift+Tab will move you backward from cell to cell. As you type text in a cell and exceed the width of the column, the cell's height will grow as needed to accommodate your entered text. You can widen columns as needed by dragging the border of a particular column.

PowerPoint also provides specific tools for working with both the layout and design of a table. When you select a table (as an object) or place the insertion point in a cell, the Table Tools appear on the Ribbon.

The Layout commands appear on the Table Tools Layout tab. These tools range from commands that enable you to insert columns and rows, merge and split cells, and change the text alignment in a cell or cells. The Design commands, which appear on the Table Tools Design tab, control the overall look of

> **🔍 note**
>
> You can draw a new table on a slide. Select the Table command on the Insert tab and then select Draw Table. You can then use the mouse to draw the outside borders of the table and the interior row and column borders. If the columns and rows are uneven, use the Distribute Columns or Distribute Rows commands on the Table Tools Layout tab as needed.

the table by providing table styles and commands that enable you to configure the shading, border, and effects for the table.

Table Layout Commands

The Layout tab houses several command groups that enable you to manipulate your rows, columns, and cells and also work with the text alignment within the cell. Figure 18.12 shows the Table Tools Layout commands.

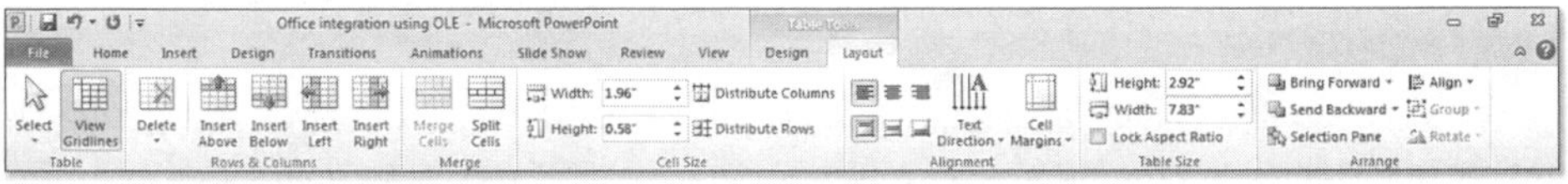

Figure 18.12
The Table Tools Layout commands.

The Layout command groups are as follows:

- **Table:** This group provides the Select, View Gridlines, and Delete commands. The Select command provides you with the ability to select the table, the current column, or the current row. The Delete command enables you to delete selected columns, rows, or the entire table.

- **Rows & Columns:** These commands enable you to insert rows and columns into the table. You can insert rows above or below a selected row or rows. You can also insert columns to the left or right of the selected column or columns. If you select multiple rows or columns, that is the number of new rows or columns that will be inserted into the table.

- **Merge:** You can select cells and then merge these cells into a single, larger cell using the Merge Cells command. If you want to split a cell (a regular cell or a merged cell) into two or more cells use the Split Cells command. You specify the number of columns and rows created when the cell is split by using the Split Cells dialog box as shown in Figure 18.13.

Figure 18.13
The Split Cells dialog box.

- **Cell Size:** You can change the width or height of the current row or column (or a selected rows or columns) by using the Width and Height spinner boxes, respectively. If you want to evenly distribute the columns or rows in the table, use the Distribute Columns or Distribute Rows command, respectively. Using both of these commands makes all the cells in the table the same size.

- **Alignment:** This group provides commands such as the Align Text Left and the Center command that can be used to specify the horizontal alignment of the text within a cell or cells. If you want to specify the vertical alignment of text in a cell or cells, use the Align Top, Align Center, or Align

Bottom commands. This group also provides commands for specifying the text direction in a cell or cells and internal cell margins for a cell or cells.

- **Table Size:** This group contains the Height and Width spinner boxes, which can be used to adjust the size of the table. If you want the height and width ratio to remain the same when you change the height or width of the table, select the Lock Aspect Ratio check box.

As already mentioned, many of the command options provided on the Layout tab can be used on an individual cell or a group of selected cells. The easiest way to select entire columns or rows is to place the mouse at either the top of a column or on the left of a row until the mouse pointer becomes an arrow. Then use the arrow to drag and select multiple columns or rows as needed.

Table Design Commands

The Table Tools Design tab provides commands that enable you to quickly format the table's shading and borders. Commands are also available that enable you to apply quick styles and other WordArt formatting to the text within the table cells.

The first set of commands on the Design tab is housed in the Table Style Options group. Because tables often contain headings in the top row or can contain important information in the first column, the Table Style Options group provides check box commands that enable you to emphasize certain rows and columns in the table. For example, you can emphasize your column headings (which appear in the first row) by selecting the Header Row check box. If you are planning on having totals or other summary information in the last row of the table, you can use the Total Row check box to emphasize the last row of the table. The colors used by the Table Style Options command are based on the table style currently assigned to your table.

You can choose an alternative table style by selecting a style from the Table Styles gallery. You can scroll through the table styles available in the gallery or you can select the More button to view the entire gallery as shown in Figure 18.14.

Figure 18.14
The Table
Styles gallery.

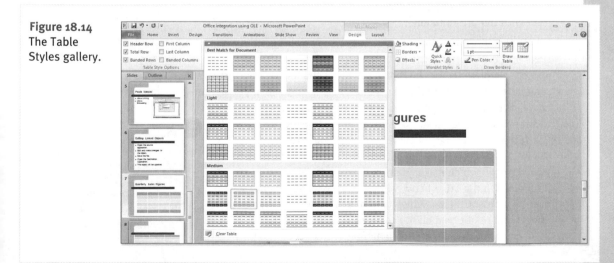

In cases where you want to specify shading for the table that is not available in one of the table styles provided in the gallery, you can use the Shading command to select a color, picture, gradient, or texture for the fill. You can specify the external and internal borders for the table using the Borders command and its accompanying gallery. You can even specify Diagonal Down and Diagonal Up borders for table cells.

If you would like to add 3D effects to table cells, the Effects command enables you to select bevels, shadows, and reflections for a cell or cells. The effect choices are very similar to the effect possibilities that we discussed earlier in the chapter when we looked at the Drawing Tools shape effects provided in the WordArt Styles group. And as with text in a text box, you can choose to format the text in your table with WordArt Styles or specify text fill, lines, and effects using the commands available in the WordArt Styles group.

> **🔍 note**
>
> Themes are now also available in the other Office applications such as Word and Excel, and provide you with a uniform design for a document or Excel worksheet.

Working with Themes

PowerPoint pioneered the concept of the theme, which is best described as a unified collection of font and design attributes that can be applied to all the slides in a presentation. This provides an overall look of uniformity for the slides in the presentation, even when the slides use different layouts or contain different types of objects. PowerPoint provides a number of different themes and you can modify these themes to create your own custom themes.

In PowerPoint, a theme controls the slide colors (the fill or background), the fonts, and the effects. It will also control the layout of the title and content areas on a slide (depending on the slide layout you chose for the slide). So, a theme will also affect how information is laid out on each slide.

You already know that you can base a new presentation on a template by selecting a presentation template in the Available Templates and Themes window in the Backstage. Each template has its own theme and the theme provides the slide background, fonts, and other design elements associated with the presentation.

Whether you use templates that already have an assigned theme or prefer to create blank presentations and then assign a theme to the presentation, you need to keep in mind how the colors, fonts, and effects provided by the theme can affect the tone of your presentation. You always need to remember the purpose of the presentation. For example, if you are presenting information on major cost-cutting measures that will be taken at your company to keep it afloat, you want to select a theme appropriate for the subject matter. I don't think you would want to use a theme such as the Black Tie because it uses a lot of back and muted grays, which makes it seem like you are presenting at a funeral. On the other hand, you probably wouldn't want to use the Opulent theme, which uses a lot of violet and gradient effects and might be a bit too cheery and contrast with the seriousness of the information being presented.

> **🔍 note**
>
> There is actually a Communicating Bad News presentation template available on Office.com. Open the Presentations category in the Available Templates and Themes window to locate this template.

As already mentioned, the theme will also control the position and orientation of title and content boxes on the slide, meaning it controls the layout of each of the different slide layouts that you select when you insert a new slide into the presentation. If a particular theme doesn't provide slide layouts that you find appropriate for the type of content you are presenting, you can go with another theme or adjust how the theme affects the different layout masters for the presentation. We discuss the slide master and the layout masters later in this chapter.

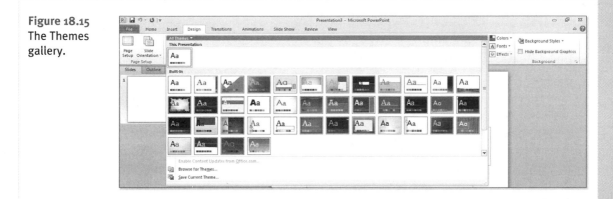 Presentation templates are discussed in Chapter 17, "Requisite PowerPoint: Essential Features," on page 476.

Applying Themes

It probably makes sense to choose a theme for a presentation before you add a lot of slides and slide content. This enables you to work within the slide layouts provided by the theme's layout masters; meaning you won't have to go back and rearrange text and other content boxes when they are adjusted by the new layouts provided by the theme.

You access the Themes gallery on the Ribbon's Design tab. Figure 18.15 shows the Themes gallery.

Figure 18.15
The Themes gallery.

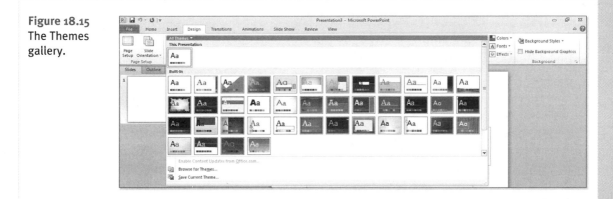

To preview a theme on the current presentation, place the mouse on a particular theme. When you have found the theme that you want to use for the presentation, select the theme. It will be applied to all the slides in the presentation.

Adjusting Colors, Fonts, and Effects

As already mentioned, themes control the colors, fonts, and effects used on the slides in the presentation. You can adjust each of these theme elements using the commands provided in the Themes group. These commands are the Colors, Fonts, and Effects commands.

There are two possibilities for saving your changes when you adjust the colors, fonts, and/or effects for a theme. You can adjust each of these theme attributes and the changes will be applied to the current theme. If you like the changes and want to be able to access this customized theme in the future, you can create a custom theme. All you have to do is select Save Current Theme in the Themes gallery and then provide a name for the theme. The theme is then saved to a default location of Templates\Document Themes. You can open saved themes using the Browse for Themes command in the Themes gallery. So, you certainly are not limited to the built-in themes provided by PowerPoint.

In some cases, you might not want to save the modified theme as a new theme but prefer to create custom theme colors or fonts that can be accessed when needed. You can create custom sets for each of these theme attributes.

Theme Colors

Each theme has a set of colors referred to as the theme colors. You can adjust the color set used by the current theme via the Colors command in the Themes group. The Colors command provides a gallery of different built-in theme colors. You can preview the colors on the current slide by placing the mouse on one of the theme color sets.

If you want to create your own theme colors, you can do so in the Create New Theme Colors dialog box. You have control over the text and background colors and the various accent and hyperlink colors. Select Create New Theme Colors in the Colors command gallery and the Create New Theme Colors dialog box will appear as shown in Figure 18.16.

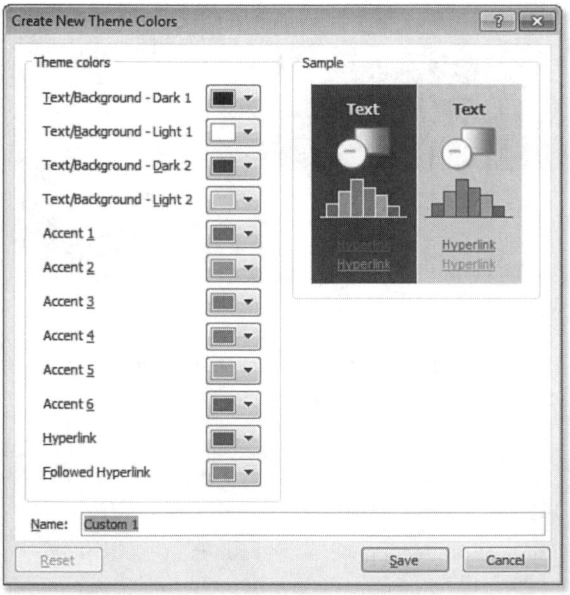

Figure 18.16
The Create New Theme Colors dialog box.

Use the various color drop-down palettes to select the specific colors for the theme color set. When selecting a color, you can use theme colors or standard colors. To access more colors (more than the theme and standard colors), select More Colors and the Color dialog box will appear.

When you have selected the colors for the new theme colors, provide a name in the Name box. When you click save, the color theme is added to the Colors command gallery under the Custom heading.

Theme Fonts

You can also adjust the fonts used by the current theme. Select the Fonts command and a gallery of different font sets will be provided. Each font set provides the appropriate font sizes for the different title and text boxes that will appear when you use different slide layouts.

If you want to create your own theme fonts, you can select Create New Theme Fonts in the Fonts gallery and the Create New Theme Fonts dialog box will open. All you have to do is provide the font to be used as the heading font (via the Heading font drop-down list) and the font to be used as the body font (via the Body font drop-down box). Specify a name for the new theme fonts and then select Save. The new theme fonts will appear on the Fonts commands gallery under the Custom heading.

Theme Effects

Theme effects can be modified for the current theme by selecting a built-in effects set from the Effects gallery. Select the Effects command and the Effects gallery will appear as shown in Figure 18.17.

Figure 18.17
The Effects gallery.

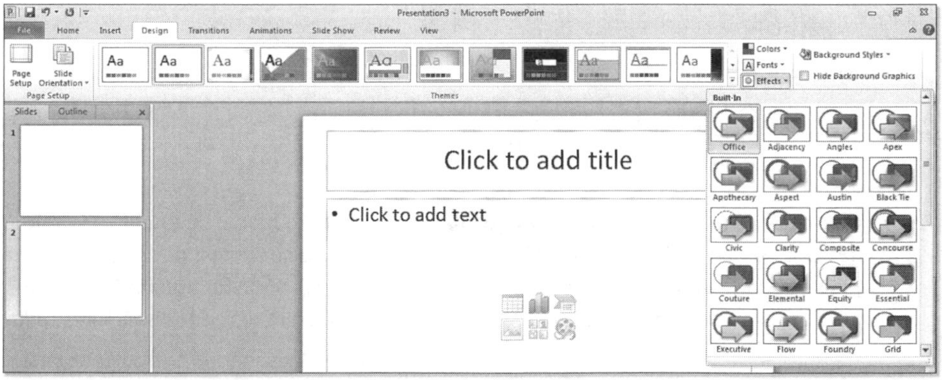

You won't see dramatic changes to your slides when you change the theme effects. Think of the effects as theme design refinements. You also can't create your own effects sets, but you can save effects changes that you have made to the current theme by saving a custom theme.

Using Headers and Footers

You might want to add repeating information to the slides in your presentation. For example, you might want to include the date or slide number at the bottom of every slide. And in cases where others might use your PowerPoint slides to give a presentation, you might want to place your name on each slide—I mean, it's a case of credit where credit is due.

You can easily add footer information to the slides in your presentation. The footer information can appear on all the slides or you can choose to have the footer omitted from the title slide.

Not only do you have control over the footer on your slides, but you also have control over the headers and footers that appear on your note pages and handouts. The settings for slide footers and the notes and handouts headers and footers are located in the Header and Footer dialog box. A tab is provided for slides and a tab is provided for notes and handouts.

To open the Header and Footer dialog box, navigate to the Ribbon's Insert tab. Then select Header & Footer in the Text group. Figure 18.18 shows the Header and Footer dialog box with the Slide tab selected.

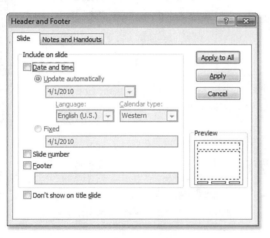

Figure 18.18
The Header and Footer dialog box.

On the Slide tab, you can specify that that date and time be included in the footer and whether the date should be updated automatically. A check box is also provided for the slide number, which will place a slide number in the footer. If you also want to include additional footer information, such as your name, select the Footer check box and then enter the text into the Footer text box provided.

If you want to apply the footer settings you set on the Slide tab to the current slide only (or a group of selected slides in the Slide Sorter or on the Slide tab), select the Apply button. If you want to apply the footer settings to all the slides in the presentation, select the Apply to All button. If you apply the footer settings to all slides, you might want to take advantage of the Don't Show on Title Slide check box because footer information is typically not included on the presentation's title slide.

> *Headers and footers can also be set for your presentation notes and handouts. For information on working with the notes and handout masters, see page 591 in Chapter 21, "Delivering a Presentation and Creating Support Materials."*

Understanding Masters

When you assign a theme to a presentation or add footers to the presentation slides, you are actually manipulating the master slide for the presentation. The master slide isn't actually a slide, but is the design blueprint for all the slides including the background fill, colors, fonts, and effects provided by the current theme. The master slide also provides the positioning and the size of the content placeholders—the title text box and the bulleted list text box—which are present on most slides.

Whatever you do to the master slide is inherited by the slides in the presentation. For example, if you place a company logo graphic on the slide master, the log will appear on all the slides in the presentation. Or if you change the background style for the master slide, the background style will be changed on all the presentation slides.

This ability to modify the master slide goes beyond broad changes such as applying a background style or placing an image on the master slide. If you change the bullet character or change the indents for the different levels of the default bulleted list in the bulleted list placeholder on the master slide, these changes will propagate to all slides in the presentation, including slides that you add to the presentation.

To view the slide master for your presentation, select the Ribbon's View tab. Select the Slide Master command in the Master Views command group. The slide master and its accompanying layout masters will appear on Slide Master pane, which looks very much like the Slide tab of the Slides/Outline pane. Select the slide master (the first slide on the Slide tab) and the slide master will appear in the Slide pane as shown in Figure 18.19.

Figure 18.19
The Master view.

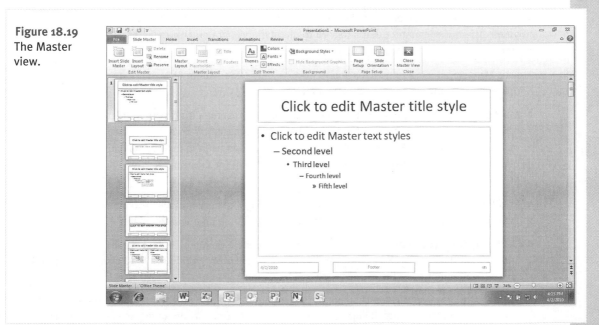

You will find that what appear to be additional slides accompanying the master slide in the Slide Master pane (they are smaller than the master slide). These are the layout masters. Note that a dotted line connects each of the layout masters with the slide master. The layout masters provide the different slide layouts provided by both the Insert Slide command and the Layout command on the Ribbon's Home tab. Each slide you insert into your presentation is associated with a particular layout master.

note

When you switch to the Master view, the layout master associated with the slide you were working on will be selected in the Slide Master pane.

Changes that you make on the master slide are inherited by the slide masters; the dotted connection line that runs from the master slide to the layout masters illustrates the fact that thematic changes (colors, fonts, and so on) will propagate to the layout masters. The opposite is not true, however. If you make changes directly on a layout master, these changes will not propagate back to the slide master.

So, in cases where you want a unified, consistent look for a presentation, you will want to edit the master slide. You might be tempted to edit individual layout masters to suit a particular purpose, but it is probably a better idea to create a new layout master that is specific to your purpose. This gets you your special layout without changing any of the default layouts provided. The next section discusses altering and creating master slides and is followed by a section that discusses working with layout masters.

Altering and Creating Master Slides

When you are in the Master view, the Slide Master tab appears on the Ribbon. The Slide Master tab provides different command groups related to modifying and/or creating master slides and layout masters. These command groups are as follows:

- **Edit Master:** This group enables you to insert a new slide master or layout master. Commands are also providing for deleting and renaming masters.

- **Master Layout:** This group enables you to specify the master slide layout's default placeholders (title, text, date, and so on) via the Master Layout command. By default, all placeholders are present on a master slide. The Insert Placeholder command is used to insert placeholders on layout masters and check boxes are also provided in this group for including a title and footers on layout masters.

- **Edit Theme:** This group provides access to the Themes gallery and also the Colors, Fonts, and Effects commands, which can be used to modify the theme on a master slide.

- **Background:** If you want to change the background style on a master slide or layout master, you can use the Background Style command. A check box is also provided to hide background graphics that you might have inserted onto the slide master.

- **Page Setup:** You can change the default page setup for the slide master by using the Page Setup command. The Page Setup dialog box (see Figure 18.20) provides you with the ability to change the slide size and to change the orientation of the presentation slides (as well as the notes, hand-outs, and outline). The Slide Orientation command in the Page Setup group can also be used to switch the slide orientation for the slide master to either portrait or landscape as needed.

Figure 18.20
The Page Setup dialog box.

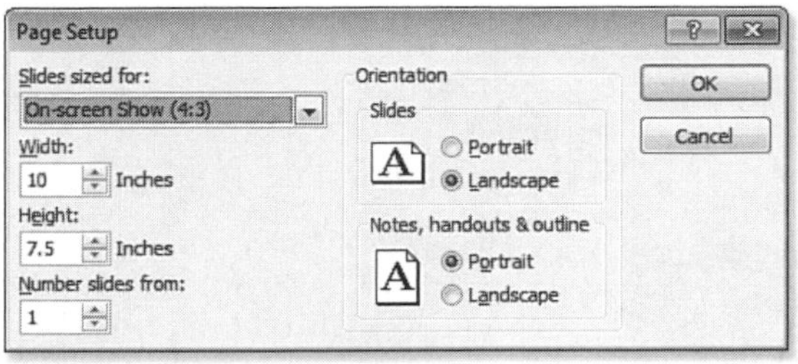

Altering the Slide Master

You can change the slide master as you require. This includes rearranging and sizing the content placeholders on the master slide. You also have control over any of the theme-related settings (colors, fonts, and effects) and background styles for the slide master using the Edit Theme and/or Background group commands.

When altering the slide master, you should be aware of a couple of things. If you radically change the location of the title or content placeholders provided on the master slide, or move the footer content boxes to another location on the slide, this can negatively affect the layout masters. For example, if you move the default title placeholder down on the master slide, it might overlay other content placeholders that are on individual layout masters. This means slides that you base on particular placeholders might look really messed up because of changes that were made to the slide master.

Create a New Slide Master

In situations where you feel that you need a slide master with a dramatically different look, it makes better sense to create a new slide master. You can then apply the new slide master to only the slides that require this dramatically different look.

To create a new slide master, select the Insert Slide Master command in the Edit Master group. The new slide master will be inserted into the Slide Master pane. You will also find that a default set of layout masters will also be created and associated with the new slide master. You can modify the new slide master as needed. Creating a second slide master is the easiest way to employ two different themes in the same presentation. The first slide master can be formatted with one theme and the second slide master can be formatted with a second theme.

When you use two or more slide masters, you will find that the number of layouts available for a new slide will multiply (in the case of two slide masters, you will double the number of layouts available). Figure 18.21 shows the New Slide gallery, which is opened via the New Slide command on the Home tab (when you

 tip

You can delete a slide master by selecting it and then selecting the Delete command in the Edit Master group.

are working in the Normal view). Note that two different sets of slide layouts are provided; one set has not been assigned a theme and the second set has been assigned the Angles theme.

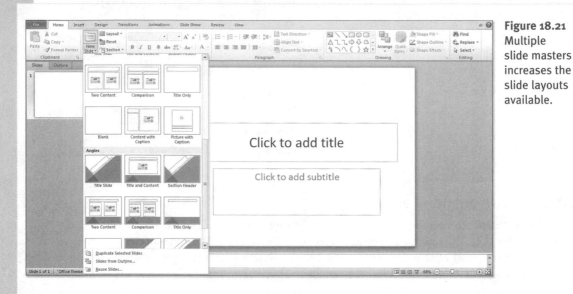

Figure 18.21
Multiple slide masters increases the slide layouts available.

The changes that you make to your second slide master are not limited to theme formatting. As with any other slide master, you can add graphics and rearrange the content placeholders on the slide master as needed.

When you are in the Master view, you can check which slides have been assigned a particular slide master or a particular layout master. Place the mouse on the slide master or the layout master and a message box will appear, detailing which slides are associated with the master.

If you create additional slide masters and then find that you don't actually use them, you can delete them from the Side Master pane. By default new slide masters are preserved in the Slide Master pane, whether or not you use them. This isn't a bad thing, it just keeps your added slide masters as part of the presentation regardless of whether you use them. If you are uneasy about having slide masters that you do not use still hanging around, deselect the Preserve command after you create a new slide master. If you don't use the slide master, it will not be preserved.

Creating Layout Masters

You also have the ability to create new layout masters. You can create a new layout master for the default slide master or you can create a new layout master for a slide master that you have added to the presentation.

Creating your own layout masters enables you to specify layouts for special slides. This negates the need for radically changing the layout of individual slides in the presentation. You can probably create a new layout faster than you can edit an existing slide in the presentation.

To create a new layout master, select the last layout master associated with the slide master that will be associated with the new layout master. Then select the Insert Layout command in the Edit Master group. The new layout master will be added to the Slide Master pane and appear in the Slide pane. By default, a title placeholder and footers will be added to the layout master. You can remove the title or the footers by deselecting the Title or Footers check boxes in the Master Layout group.

To add placeholders to the new layout master, select the Insert Placeholder command in the Master Layout group. Figure 18.22 shows the different placeholder types provided by the Insert Placeholder command.

Figure 18.22
Insert a place-holder on the new layout master.

You can add content, text, picture, and chart (just to name a few) placeholders to the new layout master. Then when you use the layout master to create a new slide, the content specified on the layout master will be provided in the new slide.

For example, to place a content box on the layout master, select Content on the Insert Placeholder gallery. You then use the mouse to draw the content placeholder box. You can size the placeholder and arrange the placeholder on the layout master as needed. Arranging and sizing placeholders is no different from working with content boxes on a regular slide—it is all mouse work.

As already mentioned at the beginning of our discussion related to slide master and layout masters, I think it is better to create custom slide masters and layout masters rather than radically changing the default slide master and its associated layout masters. In most cases, radically different slide looks and layouts are used minimally in a presentation. So, create your own masters for these exceptions and rely on the default masters for the more typical slides in your presentation.

 tip
You can change the background style for a layout master. This change will not affect the other layout masters associated with the slide master.

tip
When you have finished working in the master view, select the Close Master View command to return to your presentation.

Using Slide Sections

A new feature provided by PowerPoint 2010 is the slide section. Slide sections do not affect the layout or look of slides but provide you with an organizational tool for grouping associated slides in a presentation into a specific section. Having the slides in a presentation grouped by sections makes it easy for you to arrange large parts of your presentation without dragging individual slides around. This is particularly useful when you are fine-tuning the sequence of slides in your presentation. Sections can be collapsed, which enables you to focus on the section itself. This makes it even easier to move a section within the presentation.

The best view to work in when you are creating and rearranging sections is the Slide Sorter. You can switch to the Slide Sorter by using the Slide Sorter button on the PowerPoint status bar or by switching to the View tab on the Ribbon and then selecting Slide Sorter.

The Section command is on the Ribbon's Home tab in the Slides group. The easiest way to create a new section is to select the first slide that will appear in the section. Then select Section and then Add Section. A new section will be placed between the selected slide and the slides that precede the selected slide in the presentation. You can then navigate to the next slide that starts a new section in the presentation and create a new section at that point. Repeat the process until you have grouped all the slides into the presentation into specific sections.

 note

If you create a new section in the presentation in a place other than the very beginning of the presentation, the slides that precede the new section will automatically be placed in a section titled Default Section.

When you insert the section into the presentation, the section will be listed as "Untitled Section." If you select the section, you can then rename it by clicking the Section command and then selecting Rename Section. The Rename Section dialog box will appear as shown in Figure 18.23.

Figure 18.23
The Rename Section dialog box.

You can rename any section that you create, and rename the Default Section if it is created automatically for you by PowerPoint. If you are working on a Ribbon tab other than the Home tab, right-click on a section and then select Rename Section to access the Rename Section dialog box. This forgoes the necessity of switching back to the Home tab.

When you have the presentation divided into sections, you can easily rearrange the presentation. Each section has a collapse/expand button on the left side of the section bar. You can collapse a section or sections as needed. If you want to collapse all the sections in the presentation, right-click on any section and then select Collapse All from the shortcut menu provided. Figure 18.24 shows a presentation with five sections; four of the sections have been collapsed and one section shows thumbnails of the slides in that section.

Figure 18.24
Collapsed sections in the Slide Sorter.

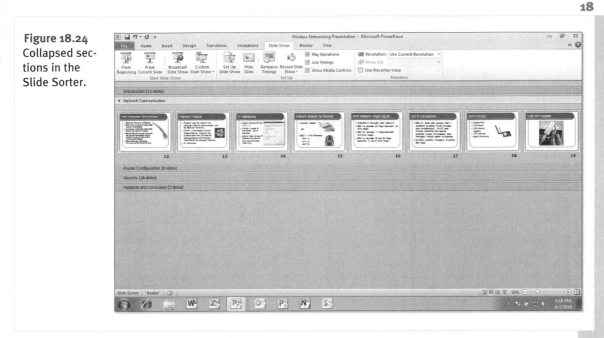

You can drag a section to a new position in the presentation to rearrange the presentation as needed. The number of slides in a collapsed presentation will be noted to the right of the section title.

You can also copy all the slides in a section and paste the entire section into another presentation. Select a section and then select Copy on the Home tab. You can then open an existing presentation or start a new presentation and paste the slides into the presentation. You can also cut and paste slide sections from one presentation to another.

You will also find that sections provide markers in your presentation that make it easy to jump to a particular part of the presentation when you are running a slide show. More about running a slide show is discussed in Chapter 21.

For more about showing presentations as a slide show, see page 578 in Chapter 21.

BETTER SLIDES WITH CLIP ART, PICTURES, AND SMARTART

PowerPoint presentations are meant to tell a story. Whether you are providing an update on your company's quarterly sales goals or sharing your latest vacation with your travel club, a presentation needs to succinctly and completely provide its intended information. Much of the information can be shared as text, but images and other graphics can greatly enhance the audience's understanding of the presented material. Clip art, pictures, and SmartArt can also make slides more visually interesting and appealing.

In this chapter, we look at adding graphics such as clip art, pictures, and SmartArt to your PowerPoint slides. We will explore how graphics can serve as informational objects, such as pictures and charts, and how objects such as clip art and SmartArt can be used as design elements on your slides. We will also discuss working with object layers and how to group related objects. Our discussion will include the addition of hyperlinks to slides and how hyperlinks can be used to access external information on the Web and be used to point to information in a presentation.

Using Graphics to Enhance Slides

The graphics on your PowerPoint slides can serve as information or as design elements (or both). In terms of information, a chart or picture can often be more effective in getting an idea or concept across than text. For example, a chart of recent sales figures will provide the audience with a better feel for recent sales trends than a table of numbers. Graphics can be also used just to add visual interest to your slides. Microsoft Office and Office.com provide you with enough clip art images to add visual objects to your slides that often match the theme of that slide. For example, if you are talking about the need for a new playground in the city, you can do a search for *playground* in the clip art gallery. You can then select from a number of playground-related clip art images for your slide or slides.

PowerPoint enables you to insert a number of different visual objects onto a slide. Several of the possibilities are as follows:

- **Picture:** You can insert your digital picture files directly onto your presentation slides. PowerPoint supports a number of digital picture file formats. PowerPoint also provides tools that enable you to modify inserted pictures. You can crop, correct, and add effects to your images.

- **Clip Art:** PowerPoint and Microsoft.com provide you with a seemingly unending library of clip art images. Static clip art is referred to as an illustration. The Clip Art library also provides animated GIF images, which are referred to as videos; however, GIF images are just a layering of static images that provide the appearance of motion. The Clip Art gallery also includes photographs and audio files.

- **Screenshot:** You can actually capture the Windows desktop and specific windows using the Screenshot command. You can then add these screenshots directly to a slide. This is extremely useful in situations where you are using PowerPoint to discuss how to use a particular software package.

- **Shapes:** You can insert many different shapes onto your slides (or onto the master slide) to add visual appeal to a slide or slide. PowerPoint provides a Shapes gallery that provides an enormous number of different shapes including lines, rectangles, block arrows, flowcharts, banners, and callouts.

- **SmartArt:** SmartArt provides you with all sorts of diagrams that enable you to create block diagrams, flow charts, organizational charts, and even pyramid diagrams. If you've ever had to place an inverted pyramid on a slide and tried to draw it in another software package or construct it from shapes, you understand how useful SmartArt can be.

- **Charts:** You can add column, line, pie, bar and a number of other chart types to your PowerPoint slides. The chart data is entered into an Excel worksheet, making it easy to provide the information that will make the chart a reality. You can edit the chart data at any time.

> *You can also link Excel worksheet data and Excel charts to PowerPoint slides. See page 868 in Appendix A, "Office Application Integration," for more information.*

There are other objects provided by PowerPoint that can also be considered graphics or design elements. For example, you can insert WordArt text boxes. These special text boxes can be used to add interesting text elements to a slide. You can also add equations to your slides. PowerPoint provides a gallery of equations, including the area of a circle, the binomial theorem (one of my favorites), and the Pythagorean theorem (okay, this is my favorite). You can also insert new equations that you create.

> *Video and sound can also be used to enhance your slides. For more about adding video and sounds to your PowerPoint presentations, see the information that begins on page 568 in Chapter 20, "Enhancing Slides with Animation, Transitions, and Multimedia."*

There is more than one way to insert a graphic such as a picture or clip art onto your slides. When you insert a new slide into a presentation, most slides have content areas that provide you with icons for inserting a chart, SmartArt graphic, picture, or clip art image. When you select one of these graphic options, the graphic will be inserted onto the slide, replacing the content frame.

You can also insert graphics as objects within their own frame. The Ribbon's Insert tab, shown in Figure 19.1, provides the commands for inserting the various graphic object types onto your slides.

Figure 19.1
The Ribbon's
Insert tab.

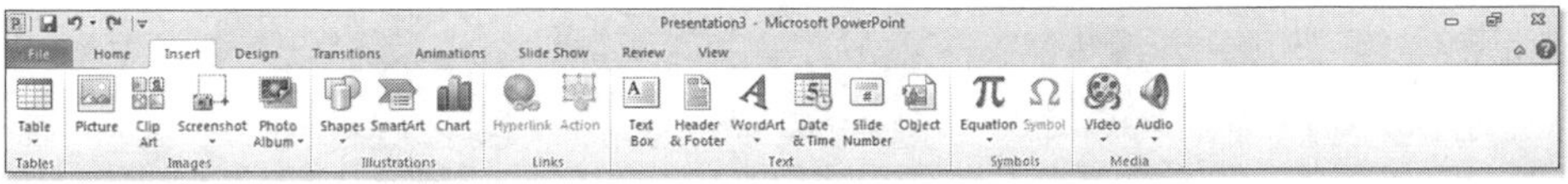

After you insert a graphic on a slide, you will find that contextual tools will be provided on the Ribbon that related to the particular graphic type. For example, when you insert a picture, the Picture Tools Format tab appears on the Ribbon. When you insert a SmartArt Graphic, the SmartArt tools become available on the Ribbon. PowerPoint 2010 actually makes it easier to insert and then manipulate graphics on your slides than previous versions of PowerPoint.

➡ *For an overview of working with graphics in Office 2010, look in Chapter 4, "Using and Creating Graphics," on page 77.*

Inserting a Picture

Inserting a picture file onto a slide is really just a matter of selecting a picture file from the Insert Picture dialog box. PowerPoint supports a number of popular picture file formats including Windows Bitmap (.bmp), Graphics Interchange Format (.gif), Joint Photographics Expert Group (.jpg), Portable Network Graphics (.png), and TIFF, Tagged Image File Format (.tif).

You can open the Insert Picture dialog box via the Picture command on the Insert tab or the Insert Picture from File icon in a slide's content box. Figure 19.2 shows the Insert Picture dialog box.

The default location for the Insert Picture dialog box is the Pictures library. If you need to navigate to another location on your computer or computer network, do so. After you have located the picture you want to insert, select the picture and then click Insert. The picture will be inserted onto the current slide.

When the picture is selected on the slide, the Picture Tools Format tab appears on the Ribbon. Figure 19.3 shows the Picture Tools Format tab.

The picture tools provide you with the ability to adjust the picture (such as brightness and contrast), select a picture style, arrange multiple pictures on the page, and crop and size the selected picture. The Picture Tools groups are as follows:

- **Remove Background:** This command enables you to remove the background from the picture. This is a new tool in PowerPoint 2010 (and other Office applications such as Word and Excel). When you select the Remove Background command, the Background Removal tab appears on the Ribbon. You can mark areas to keep in the picture or mark areas to remove from the picture.

Figure 19.2
The Insert Picture dialog box.

Figure 19.3
The Picture Tools Format tab.

Figure 19.4 shows a picture with the background to be removed and the Ribbon's Background Removal commands used to fine-tune the removal of the picture's background.

- **Adjust:** This group provides commands that enable you to adjust the sharpness, brightness, and contrast, and to make color corrections to the picture, including saturation and tone. You can also add artistic effects to the picture and reset the picture settings if needed.

- **Picture Styles:** Picture styles provide you with different frame formats, which include frame shapes and frame border styles. You can preview a style on the selected picture by placing the mouse on any of the styles in the gallery.

- **Arrange:** This group enables you to layer multiple images (using commands such as Bring Forward and Send Backward). It also enables you to group graphics and align images (left, center, right, top middle, bottom), and provides you with the ability to rotate and flip pictures.

- **Size:** This group provides Height and Width spinner boxes for sizing a picture. You can also use the Crop command to crop the image as needed.

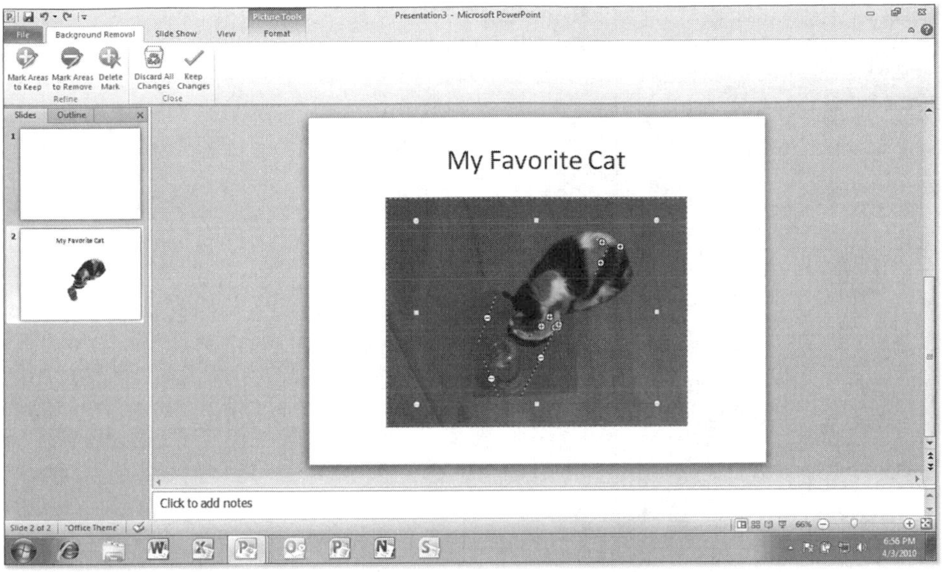

Figure 19.4
Remove the background from a picture.

When you have finished manipulating the picture, click outside the picture frame to deselect it. The picture tools will also be removed from the Ribbon.

➡ *For detailed information on working with pictures in the Office applications, see page 86 in Chapter 4.*

Adding Clip Art to Slides

PowerPoint and Office.com provide you with an extremely large library of clip art possibilities. Clip art can add visual interest to slides and can (at the right time) even add a little humor to your presentation. The clip art library consists of photos in the jpeg format (.jpg), illustrations and cartoons in the Windows media file format (.wmf), and animated GIFs or videos in the GIF format (.gif).

tip

If you are working offline, deselect the Include Office.com Content check box. The clip art search will be limited to the clip art installed on your computer.

You can open the Clip Art task pane by selecting the Clip Art command on the Insert tab or by clicking the Clip Art icon in a content box. To search for clip art, enter a search string in the Search for box and then select Go. You can also specify the type of media files that the search will include by selecting the Results Should Be drop-down list. The list provides the following media types: Illustration, Photographs, Videos, and Audio. Figure 19.5 shows the Clip Art Task Pane with a completed search using the search string "bird."

Figure 19.5
The Clip Art task pane.

When you have completed a search for a particular search string, you can peruse the results of the search. If you place the mouse on a clip art image that appears in the task pane gallery, the name and type of the file will be provided. This is particularly useful when you are trying to sort whether the image is a static .wmf or .jpg image file or an animated GIF with the .gif extension.

In the case of animated GIFs, you can preview the GIF before you insert it onto the slide. Select the drop-down arrow next to the clip art image and select Preview/Properties. The Preview/Properties dialog box will open for the clip art image as shown in Figure 19.6.

In the Preview/Properties dialog box you are provided a preview of the animated GIF. This dialog box also provides you with the option of adding a caption to the GIF (and any clip art image) by entering the caption text in the Caption area. The Preview/Properties dialog box also lists the keywords that have been assigned to the clip art for searches performed in the Clip Art task pane.

If you want to edit the keywords and add or remove keywords from the list, select the Edit Keywords button. The Keywords dialog box will open. You can add or remove keywords only from clip art that is part of the clip art collection installed on your computer. You will find that much of the clip art available to you is actually provided by Office.com.

Figure 19.6
The Clip Art Preview/Properties dialog box.

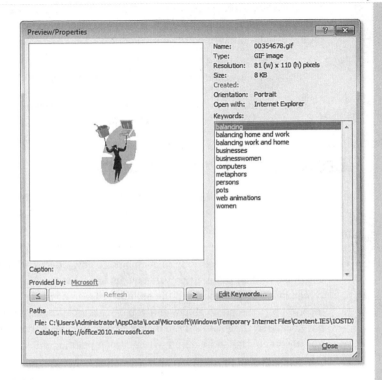

So, before you can edit keywords for a clip art image, you must copy the temporary file provided by Office.com to your permanent collection. This is accomplished by selecting Copy to Collection on the shortcut menu that appears when you select the drop-down arrow to the right of the clip art in the Clip Art task pane's clip art gallery. You will find that copying clip art images from Office.com to your clip art collection will not only place these images at the top of the clip art gallery when you run a search that includes keywords for that particular image, but you will also have access to the clip art when you are not connected to the Internet.

Inserting clip art onto the slide is just a matter of clicking on the image in the Clip Art task pane (or selecting Insert from the drop-down menu for that clip art image). The currently selected content box will be replaced by the image when you open the Clip Art task pane using the Clip Art icon in a content box. If you insert clip art via the task pane when a content box or other object is not selected on the slide, the clip art will be inserted in its own frame.

> **tip**
>
> If you want clip art or a picture to repeat on every slide, say a logo for instance, you should place the image on the presentation's master slide.

As soon as you insert clip art onto the slide, the Picture Tools Format tab will appear on the Ribbon. You can adjust the clip art's settings using the Adjust tool and assign picture styles to the clip art as needed. The same command groups are provided by working with clip art as discussed in the previous section related to pictures. You will find, however, that the Remove Background tool is not available for clip art files that have the .wmf or .gif file extensions. You can remove the background from any of the stock photos provided by the Clip Art task pane that have the .jpg extension. They are, in effect, no different from picture files that you have on your computer that have been taken with your digital camera or scanned to your computer.

You can size and move the clip art image on the slide as you would any other object box. When you deselect a clip art image, the picture tools will no longer be available on the Ribbon.

➡ *For more information on working with clip art in the Office applications, including adding clip art to your collection and working with clip art offline, see page 99 in Chapter 4.*

Creating a Photo Album

Although a PowerPoint photo album is not an object that you can insert on a slide, such as a picture or clip art, it is a very quick way to place digital photos on presentation slides. The Photo Album tool is perfect for placing your digital vacation photos on a series of slides with a minimum of effort. The Photo Album command is on the Insert tab in the Images group.

When you use the Photo Album command, a new presentation is created, including a title slide for the presentation. Different picture layouts are provided that enable you to specify the number of pictures placed on each slide on the album. You also have control over the frame shape for each picture inserted into the photo album and you can assign a theme to the photo album. All these settings are housed in the Photo Album dialog box, so you can specify the pictures for the album and then quickly create the entire album without manipulating individual slides or pictures.

You can start your new photo album when you are already working on a presentation or you can start the new photo album on starting PowerPoint. It doesn't matter what you are currently doing in PowerPoint because the Photo Album command creates an entirely new presentation file.

To create a new photo album, select Photo Album on the Insert tab and then select New Photo Album. The Photo Album dialog box will open. The first step in the process of creating the photo album is to specify the pictures that will be included in the album. Select the File/Disk command and the Insert New Pictures dialog box will open. This dialog box opens to the Pictures library by default. Locate the pictures that you want to use for the photo album. It makes sense to select as many of the pictures as you can at this point. Select the first picture and then select subsequent picture files by holding down the Ctrl key. When the pictures are selected, click the Insert button in the dialog box.

You will be returned to the Photo Album dialog box as shown in Figure 19.7. You can now manipulate the picture order in the album, choose picture options, and specify the layout for the album.

If you need to change the order of the pictures in the album, select a picture and then use the Move Up or Move Down button to change the position of the picture in the album list. If you decide you don't want a particular picture in the album, select the file name and then click the Remove button.

 tip

If you need to add additional pictures to the photo album that are in a different location from the pictures already inserted, select File/Disk and use the Insert Picture dialog box to locate and add the pictures to the Photo Album dialog box.

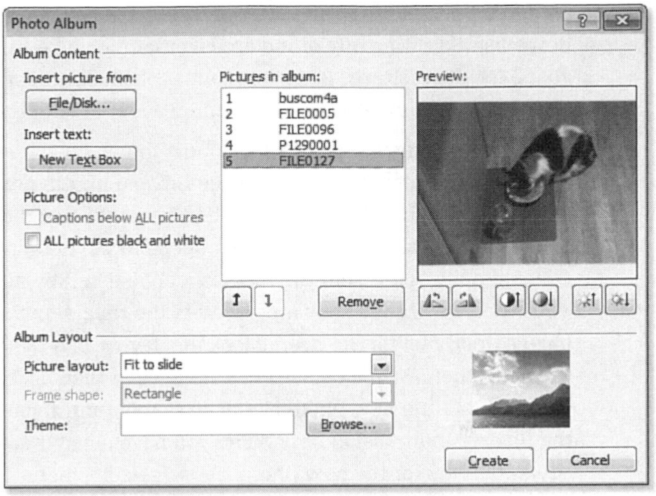

Figure 19.7
The Photo Album dialog box.

Adjusting Picture Settings

The Photo Album dialog box also provides a series of buttons that enable you to adjust settings for each individual picture. You can use the Rotate Left or Rotate Right buttons to rotate the currently selected picture 90 degrees to either left or right, respectively. You can also adjust the contrast or brightness of the selected picture up or down as needed using the appropriate buttons. You can adjust other picture options, such as selecting to have all the pictures changed to black-and-white.

If you want to include a text box on each slide that is created in the photo album, select the New Text Box. The text box is added to the Pictures in Album list. The text box will appear on each slide; after the photo album has been created, you can add text to the text box to describe the picture on the slide or provide other ancillary information related to each picture.

➥ *For more about adjusting and formatting digital pictures, see page 86 in Chapter 4.*

Setting Album Layout Settings

By default, each picture listed in the Photo Album dialog box will be placed on a separate slide and will be fitted to the slide, so you don't have to worry about the potentially different sizes of the pictures that you want to add to the photo album. The Fit to Slide option does not provide you with the ability to select the frame shape for the inserted pictures.

The Picture Layout drop-down list does provide you with other options for how the pictures appear on the slides. The one picture, two pictures, or four pictures options place the specified number of pictures on each slide. These settings also enable you to specify the frame shape for the picture by selecting a shape from the Frame Shape drop-down list. A number of frame shapes are available including Rounded Rectangle, Simple Frame, White, Center Shadow Rectangle, and Soft Edge Rectangle.

If you want to include a title text box on each slide, you can select the one picture with title picture layout. Options for two and four pictures with title are also included in the Picture Layout drop-down list. Selecting any of the options that include a title also enables you to specify the frame shape for the pictures. Both the number of slides you specify in the layout and the frame shape you select will be previewed in the Album Layout area of the Photo Album dialog box.

You also have the option of specifying a theme for the new photo album presentation. Select the Browse button next to the Theme box. This will open the Choose Theme dialog box. The Choose Theme dialog box opens to the default Office themes folder and the themes will be listed by name. You won't be able to view a preview of the theme, but if you have a good feel for the overall look and layout of a particular theme or themes, you can select a theme and then click Open to apply it to the new photo album. This will return you to the Photo Album dialog box. When you have all your settings squared away for the new photo album, select Create. The photo album will open in the PowerPoint workspace with the title slide selected. Figure 19.8 shows a photo album in the Normal view.

> **⚠ caution**
>
> If you aren't all that familiar with the frame shapes and presentation themes available in PowerPoint, you might want to wait and adjust these settings on the photo album after the album has been created. You can then take advantage of the Themes gallery and the Pictures Style gallery, which both provide visual examples of the themes and styles.

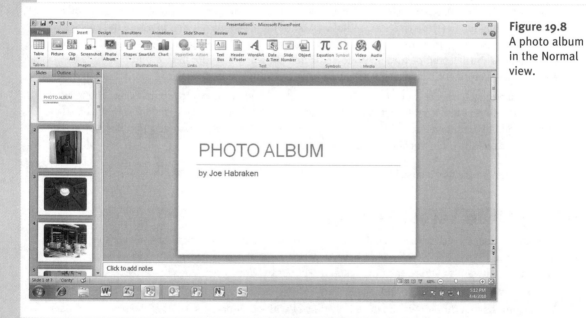

Figure 19.8
A photo album in the Normal view.

Because the photo album is no different from any other PowerPoint presentation, you can modify presentation settings such as the theme for the presentation. You can also edit each slide in the presentation, which will be required if you specified that a text box or title box be included on each slide when you configured the settings for the photo album in the Photo Album dialog box.

If you want to add additional photos to the photo album or change any of the settings related to the photo album, you can do so in the Edit Photo Album dialog box. Select the Photo Album command and then select Edit Photo Album. The Edit Photo Album dialog box provides all the settings that were available in the Photo Album dialog box. You can insert additional pictures, modify picture settings, or change the picture layout and frame shape as needed.

Interestingly, the Edit Photo Album dialog box provides a command that was grayed out in the Photo Album dialog box. If you want to include a caption below all the pictures, you can select the Captions Below All Pictures check box in the Picture Options area of the dialog box. This will place the filename of each picture under the image. You can edit this text as needed on each slide.

When you have completed making changes to the album settings, click the Update button. This will return you to the photo album. Remember that the photo album is a new presentation, so click on the Save button on the Quick Access Toolbar and specify a name and location for the photo album in the Save As dialog box.

Working with Shapes

Shapes can be added to your slides to add visual interest. Many shapes can also function as text boxes. When you work with shapes, remember that less is always better, so don't crowd your slides with a lot of rectangles and circles. Proper slide design relates to balance, and emphasis is not on the quantity of shapes and other graphic elements crammed on each slide.

To insert a shape, select the Shapes command on the Ribbon's Insert tab. The Shapes gallery will appear as shown in Figure 19.9.

Figure 19.9
The Shapes gallery.

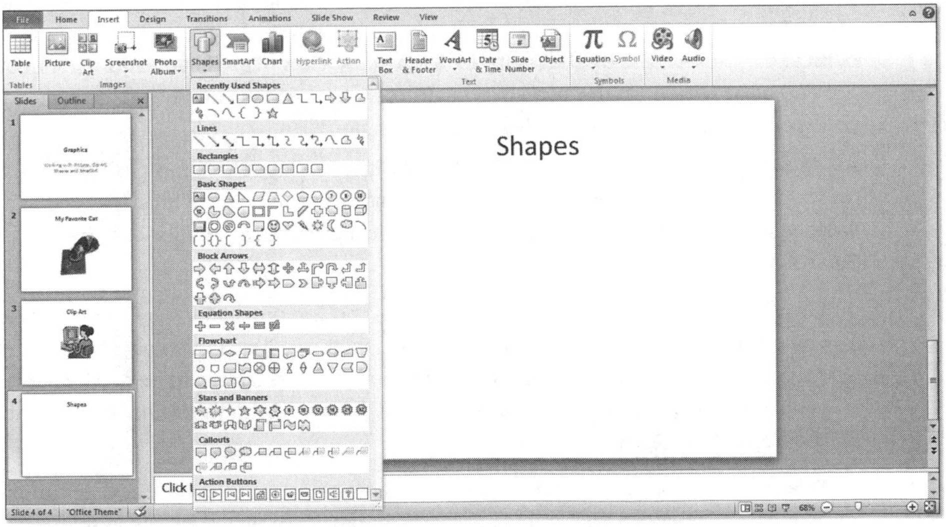

The shapes provided in the gallery are divided into different categories. There are lines, rectangles, block arrows, and callouts just to name a few. When you have located the shape that you want to use, click it. A drawing tool will replace the mouse pointer. Drag on the slide to draw the shape. You can size and position the shape on the page as needed.

When the shape is selected, the drawing tools are available on the Ribbon. Shape styles are provided in the Shapes Style gallery and you can also change the shape fill, outline, and effects as needed using the appropriate command in the Shape Style group.

If you would like to place text in a shape, select the Text Box command in the Insert Shapes group, and then click in the shape to place the insertion point. You can type your text as needed. You can then use the WordArt Style gallery to format the text. Individual WordArt text settings can be configured using the Text Fill, Text Outline, and Text Effects commands.

 Working with shapes and the drawing tools are discussed in greater detail starting on page 92 in Chapter 4.

Using SmartArt Graphics

SmartArt graphics provide you with a number of different diagram types that you can use to visually illustrate information on a slide; SmartArt isn't just a series of design elements or shapes, however. You can use SmartArt to show relationships between text entries, providing you with slides that make important concepts easy for your audience to understand. And bottom line: SmartArt graphics look professional and are impressive additions to your slides in both visual and informational terms.

PowerPoint provides different types or categories of SmartArt, each type having a particular purpose. For example, the Cycle category of SmartArt graphics enables you to create diagrams that represent sequential cycles or a process that takes place in a circular flow. Figure 19.10 shows a cyclical diagram on a slide that is in the Slide Show view. The SmartArt diagram not only provides the audience with a picture of an overall process, it provides you with the outline for your talking points related to the subject of that particular slide.

As already mentioned, there are a number of different SmartArt graphics categories. Because SmartArt is designed to enable you to communicate visually, each SmartArt type or category provides you with SmartArt slanted toward a particular purpose. The list that follows describes the SmartArt categories:

- **List:** The SmartArt lists enable you to go beyond the typical PowerPoint bulleted list and provide you with the ability to better show the relationship of items in a list. You can arrange text in both vertical and horizontal lists that include shapes to emphasize the text. The list SmartArt graphics can also provide insight into the relative importance of the list items or the sequence in which the listed items occur.

- **Process:** This group of SmartArt graphics shows a progression of items. It can provide the sequential steps in a task or process and can provide a visual representation of linear workflow or display how parts of an information sequence relate to the whole.

Figure 19.10
A cyclical
SmartArt
graphic.

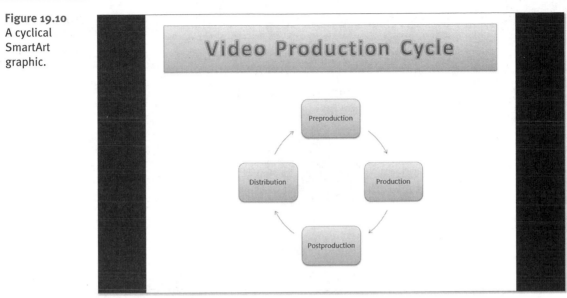

- **Cycle:** This category provides a number of different graphics related to process cycle and the circular flow of events or steps. Diagrams are available that emphasize the steps in the process cycle, whereas others enable you to better describe the overall process and the relationship of the various segments to each other.

- **Hierarchy:** These SmartArt graphics provide you with diagrams such as the classic organizational chart in a branching tree format, and enable you to emphasize the hierarchical relationship of items listed in a diagram. There is even a Picture Organization Chart SmartArt graphic that makes it easy to construct an organizational chart that includes photos of the individuals listed in the chart. Other diagrams in this category provide you with the ability to show how items in the diagram build upon each other.

- **Relationship:** This category provides relationship diagrams that enable you to show the hierarchy of related items and how concepts or ideas relate to a central theme. This group also includes the basic Venn and radial Venn diagrams. Venn diagrams provide you with the ability to show the possible or logical relationship between different items. Figure 19.11 shows an example of a basic Venn diagram.

- **Matrix:** The matrix SmartArt graphics are designed to show the relationship of different items or quadrants to the whole. These graphics enable you to create affinity diagrams, which are designed to organize information based on natural relationships. A cycle matrix is included that enables you to show how items are related to a central cyclical process. A good example of this is the basic communication process, which requires listening, interpreting, and responding.

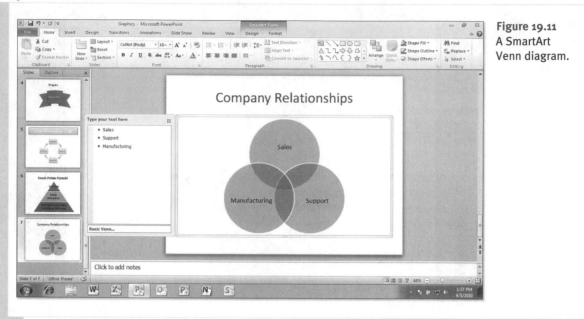

Figure 19.11
A SmartArt
Venn diagram.

- **Pyramid:** This group provides both a basic pyramid and inverted pyramid diagram. Pyramids show both hierarchical relationships and the proportional importance of items in the hierarchy. Maslow's hierarchy of needs uses a classic pyramid diagram, showing the basic human needs from physiological needs such as food and water to the more creative aspects of self actualization. Figure 19.12 shows a basic pyramid diagram.

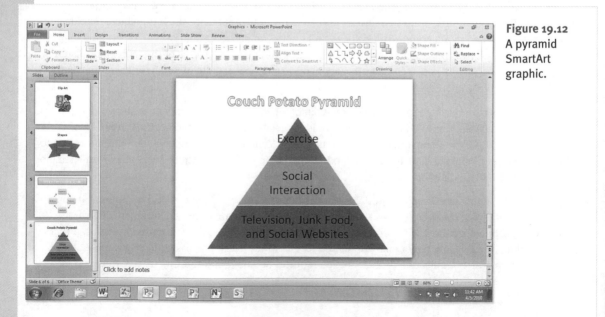

Figure 19.12
A pyramid
SmartArt
graphic.

- **Picture:** This group pulls all the SmartArt graphics from the other categories that provide you with the ability to incorporate pictures into the diagram. These possibilities include the continuous picture list, the captioned pictures diagram, which provides multiple levels of pictures, and the hexagon cluster, which provides a grouping of clustered images with minimal accompanying text.

- **Office.com:** This group provides additional SmartArt graphics provided online via the Office.com website.

note

You can add animation schemes to your SmartArt graphics to create slides with even more visual impact. See Chapter 20, "Enhancing Slides with Animation, Transitions, and Multimedia."

You can add a SmartArt graphic to a slide and then enter the accompanying text and pictures or you can format existing text on a slide, such as a bulleted list, with any of the SmartArt graphics provided in the SmartArt Graphic gallery. When you insert a SmartArt graphic on a slide or convert existing text to a SmartArt graphic, you are provided with the SmartArt tools, which provide both a Design tab and a Format tab. So, even after you insert a SmartArt graphic onto a slide, you are provided with a number of possibilities for enhancing the graphic in terms of its layout, style, and overall formatting including the text that the SmartArt graphic contains.

Inserting a SmartArt Graphic

You can insert a new SmartArt graphic on a slide via the Insert SmartArt Graphic icon in a slide content box or you can select the SmartArt command on the Ribbon's Insert tab. In both cases, the Choose a SmartArt Graphic dialog box opens as shown in Figure 19.13.

Figure 19.13
The Choose a SmartArt Graphic dialog box.

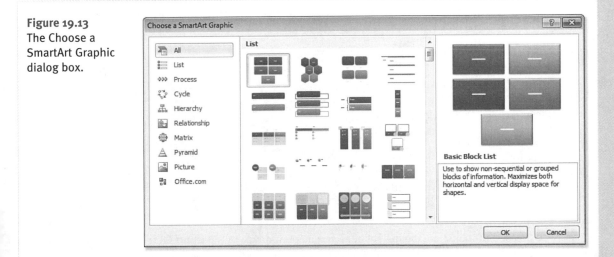

The graphic categories are located on the left side of the dialog box. All is selected by default. Select the category of SmartArt graphic you want to create. The graphics in the category will be listed. To preview an individual SmartArt graphic, select the graphic and a preview and description of the graphic will appear on the right slide of the dialog box.

After you have located the diagram that you want to use, make sure that the graphic is selected and then click OK. The SmartArt graphic will be placed on the current slide.

You can enter the text for the diagram directly on the diagram parts itself (such as the item boxes in a cyclical diagram). Just place select any of the [TEXT] placeholders in the diagram and type the required text. You can also add the text for the diagram using the Text pane that accompanies the SmartArt graphic (to the left of the slide). Replace the [TEXT] placeholders in the list provided with your text. The Text pane can be collapsed by clicking the pane's Close button and then expanded when needed by using the expand button on the left side of the graphic. Remember that diagrams visually communicate an idea, process, or relationship, so the diagram should not require much text; in fact your text entries should be considered the labels for the diagram parts—that's it.

Converting Text to a SmartArt Graphic

You can also convert existing text in a text box to a SmartArt graphic. This enables you to quickly take a bulleted list on a slide (or other text) and convert it to an appropriate diagram. To convert text to a SmartArt graphic, follow these steps:

1. Select the text box that contains the text you want to convert. This can be any text box on a slide, including bulleted lists.

2. On the Home tab, select the Convert to SmartArt command in the Paragraph group. The SmartArt gallery will open, providing a subset of the available SmartArt graphics as shown in Figure 19.14.

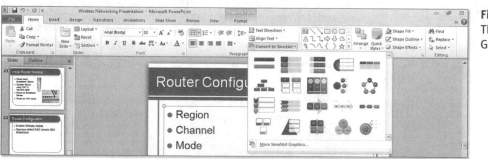

Figure 19.14
The SmartArt Graphic gallery.

3. Select a graphic from the gallery or access more graphics by selecting More SmartArt Graphics and selecting a graphic. This will open the Choose SmartArt Graphic dialog box.

4. If you select a diagram in the gallery, the text in the text box will immediately be converted. To do the conversion from the Choose SmartArt Graphic dialog box, select a graph and then click OK.

The existing text will be placed in the text placeholders on the SmartArt diagram. The diagram will replace the original text box. You can edit the text as needed on the diagram or using the SmartArt's accompanying text pane.

Using the SmartArt Tools

Whether you create a SmartArt graphic from scratch or convert existing text to a SmartArt graphic, after the diagram is on the slide and is selected, the SmartArt tools will appear on the Ribbon. There are two different tabs of SmartArt tools: Design and Format.

The SmartArt Tools Design Tab

The Design tab provides commands that enable you to manipulate the number and position of individual graphics in the diagram and to change the layout and style of the SmartArt graphic. Figure 19.15 shows a Vertical Box List SmartArt graphic and the Design tab commands.

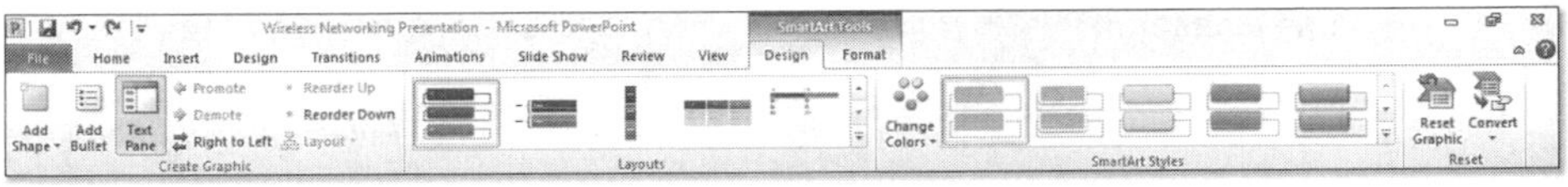

Figure 19.15
The SmartArt
Tools Design
tab.

The commands groups on the Design tab are as follows:

- **Create Graphic:** This group enables you to add elements (shapes) to the diagram and change the positioning of the shape. For example if you have a box list graphic, you can add another shape (a box) before or after the currently selected shape by using the Add Shape command. You can also reorder the shapes in the list using the Reorder Up and the Reorder Down commands, and change the positioning of the diagram from Right to Left or vice versa using the Right to Left command. The commands available in this group will depend on the type of SmartArt graphic you inserted onto the slide.

- **Layouts:** The layouts available in the Layouts gallery will be specific for the type of SmartArt graphic that you placed on the slide. For example, if you inserted a basic cycle diagram onto the slide, you can change the layout from the Basic Cycle to the Block Cycle or Radio Cycle by selecting a new layout in the Layouts gallery. More layouts are provided in the Choose a SmartArt Graphic dialog box, which is also accessible from the Layouts gallery.

- **SmartArt Styles:** This command group provides the Change Colors command, which can be used to specify a new color scheme for the SmartArt graphic. The schemes available will be specific to the type of diagram that you placed on the slide. You can also change the style for the diagram by selecting one of the styles from the SmartArt Styles gallery. These styles will be specific to the type of diagram that you inserted and will include 3D possibilities.

- **Reset:** If you don't like the changes that you have made to the SmartArt graphic, you can select the Reset Graphic command. The Convert command enables you to convert the SmartArt graphic to text or convert the diagram to a group of shapes.

When you have finished working with the Design tab commands, deselect the SmartArt graphic's frame. This will remove the SmartArt tools from the Ribbon.

The SmartArt Tools Format Tab

SmartArt Tools also has a Format tab. This tab provides commands related to the formatting of the SmartArt graphic frame (not the individual items) and the text within the various shapes that populate the diagram.

You can use the Shape Fill, Shape Outline, and Shape Effects to format the SmartArt graphic's outside frame. This enables you to select a fill color for the SmartArt background (this will not fill the individual shapes in the diagram) and format the SmartArt graphic with different effects such as the Shadow, Reflection, and 3D Rotation settings.

The WordArt Styles gallery and the Text Fill, Text Outline, and Text Effects commands in the WordArt Styles group can be used to change the formatting of the text that has been entered on the various shapes in the diagram. When you use these commands to format the text, it is a one-size-fits-all scenario. All the text on the various shapes that make up the diagram will be formatted in the same manner.

 More information related to working with SmartArt graphics can be found on page 79 in Chapter 4.

Adding Charts to Slides

Charts can be used to great effect on your slides to visually represent important data. Because many people do not immediately relate to tables full of numbers, an accompanying chart provides your audience with a better understanding of everything from sales trends to population figures to quarterly earnings. Charts take all those numbers and digest them, providing you with a much more meaningful pictorial view.

PowerPoint now provides a much more practical approach to inserting charts on your slides, and many improvements were added to this feature in PowerPoint 2010's predecessor, PowerPoint 2007. When you insert a chart, you will actually use an Excel worksheet to enter the data for that chart. You are also using the Excel chart feature, so many of the considerations that go into creating a chart in Excel are applicable when you insert a chart onto a PowerPoint slide.

You are also provided a number of tools for working with charts on your PowerPoint slides, which come in the form of the chart tools. The Chart Tools contextual Ribbon addition provides three different tabs of commands: Design, Layout, and Format.

 Charts are covered in detail in the Excel section of this book. See the information that begins on page 381 in Chapter 14, "Enhancing Worksheets with Charts."

Inserting a Chart onto a Slide

You can insert a chart using the Chart command on the Ribbon's Insert tab or you can select the Insert Chart icon in a content box. Both scenarios open the Insert Chart dialog box, which is shown in Figure 19.16.

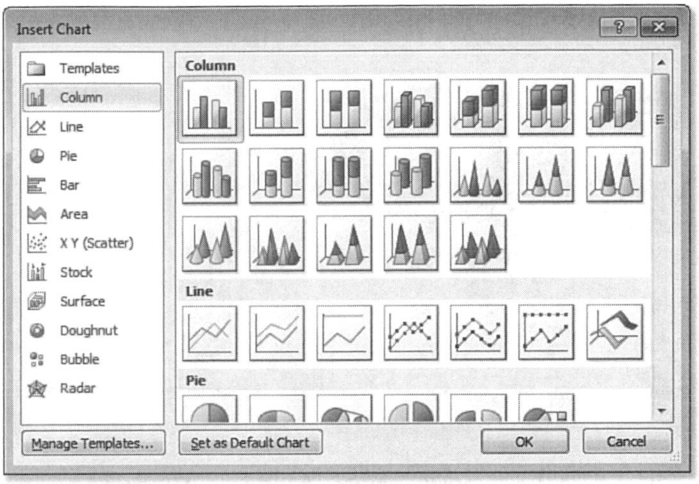

Figure 19.16
The Insert Chart dialog box.

The different chart types are listed on the left side of the Insert Chart dialog box. Select a particular chart type such as Column or Pie. You will find that each chart type also provides different formats. For example, the column chart type can be inserted in a number of different formats, including a clustered column, stacked column, or clustered cylinder. The pie chart formats include a 3D pie and an exploded pie. Select the format type for the particular chart type and then click OK.

The chart will be inserted on the slide and an Excel window will open, containing the labels and data points for the chart on a worksheet. Figure 19.17 shows a pie chart on a PowerPoint slide and the data range for the chart in an accompanying Excel worksheet.

At this point your chart is just a generic chart and is certainly not based on your data. You need to modify the labels (text entries) and the numerical data on the worksheet. When you do so, the chart will immediately reflect the new data. Click in the appropriate cells on the Excel worksheet and enter your text labels and data as needed. If you need to add more data points than those provided, you can drag the data range border (the lower-right corner) to extend the data range and enter more labels and numerical information.

> **⚠ caution**
>
> You must enter your data and text labels within the data range provided on the Excel worksheet for the chart to reflect the modifications that you make.

After you have finished editing the data on the Excel worksheet, you can close the worksheet. You don't need to save the worksheet; the data that you entered in the sheet remains linked to the chart on the PowerPoint slide. If you do need to reopen the Excel worksheet, you can do so by selecting the Edit Data command on the Chart Tools Design tab.

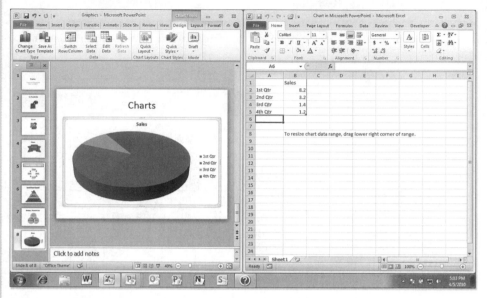

Figure 19.17
An inserted chart and the associated Excel work-sheet.

Modifying and Formatting a Chart

When the chart is selected on a slide, the chart tools are available on the Ribbon. You can use the various chart tools to modify the chart layout and style, edit the chart title, legend, and data labels, and format the chart's frame and text using the shape styles and WordArt styles. Although the chart is based on data that was entered in an Excel worksheet, the chart itself is very much like any other object that you place on a slide such as SmartArt or a picture. You can size and move the chart on the slide as needed.

As already mentioned, the chart tools provide you with a great deal of control over the chart and the frame that holds the chart. The three Chart Tools tabs are described in the list that follows:

- **Design Tab:** The Design tab provides you with commands related to the chart's type and layout, and provides you with the ability to edit the data used to create the chart. The Change Chart Type command enables you to change the current chart to another type. If you then need to edit the data for the chart, select the Edit Data command. This tab also provides a Chart Layouts gallery, which enables you to adjust the overall layout of the chart. Each chart type will have specific layouts available. You can also change the style of the chart by taking advantage of the Chart Styles gallery. Figure 19.18 shows the Design tab on the Ribbon.

- **Layout Tab:** This tab enables you to insert other objects onto the slide, including pictures, shapes, and text boxes. More importantly in regard to your chart, the Labels group on this tab provides commands for configuring the chart title, legend, and data labels. The choices provided by the Chart Title and Legend commands revolve around the positioning of the title and legend, respectively. The Data Labels command enables you to turn on data labels so that the values that built the chart are included with the data points. This tab also provides a 3-D Rotation command and commands for adding trendlines and drop-lines to line charts and up/down bars to bar charts.

Figure 19.18
Modify the
chart's design
using the
Design tab
commands.

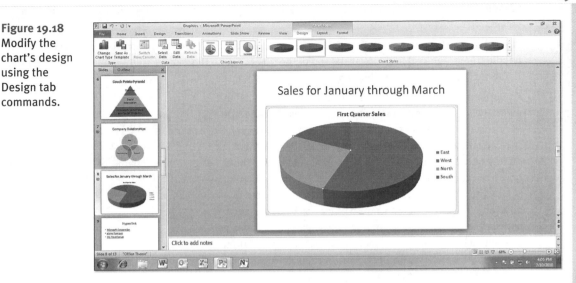

- **Format Tab:** This tab is almost the same as the Drawing Tools Format tab and the SmartArt Tools Format tab. Shape styles are provided to modify the frame of the chart and you can also change the fill, outline, and effects for the chart frame. When you select text objects on the chart, such as the title or legend, you can take advantage of the WordArt Styles gallery and the other text settings provided on this tab.

Although I have stressed the construction and the formatting of a chart, you also need to use the charts appropriately, meaning the chart type that you select should match the purpose of using the chart in the first place—to show data pictorially. This means choosing the right chart type for the situation. If you are showing the relationship of parts to a whole, such as how your individual monthly expenses relate to your total monthly expenses, you would use a pie chart. If you want to show change over time, such as changes in your retirement account, you would use a line chart (avert your eyes, please). Make sure that you understand how the chart type you pick translates the numerical data into a visual representation. Selecting the wrong chart type for the situation and the data will provide useless information to your audience.

➡ *More about choosing the right chart type is covered beginning on page 381 in Chapter 14.*

Working with Slide Objects

An object can be anything you place on the slide, and in this chapter we looked at a number of object types including pictures, clip art, shapes, and Smart Art. Text boxes qualify as objects as well. Resizing and rotating objects is very straightforward. To resize an object, drag the sizing handles on the object's frame as needed. If you are working in a situation where you want to maintain the height/width ratio of an object, drag the lower-right corner sizing handle diagonally to size the object.

You can also easily rotate a selected object such as a shape. When you select the object, the rotation handle (the green dot) appears at the top of the object. Place the mouse on the handle and when the Rotation icon appears, drag the rotation handle to rotate the object.

PowerPoint makes it simple to position multiple objects and even deal with layered objects on a slide. If you need to be very accurate in placing items on a slide, you might want to take advantage of the ruler, gridlines, or guides. You can turn on any of these items by using the commands in the Show group on the Ruler's view tab. By default, objects are snapped to the grid. If you are placing objects very close together, you can also have objects snap to other objects. You can specify the grid and guide settings by selecting the dialog box launcher on the Show group. This will open the Grid and Guides dialog box, which provides the snap, grid, and guide settings for the presentation.

 note

When you align two or more objects on a slide (vertically or horizontally), you will find that smart guides appear automatically. This enables you to align objects in relation to each other without using the gridlines or guides.

Grouping Objects

Grouping objects enables you to fine-tune the positioning of any number of objects on slide. You might have already placed the objects exactly the way you want them in terms of their positioning to each other. You then might need to adjust the overall positioning of all the objects in relation to the top or bottom of the slide or the slide title.

You can group the objects on the slide and then move them as a group. Select all the objects on the slide by using the mouse to drag a selection box around the objects. You can also click to select an object and then hold down the Ctrl key to select subsequent objects as needed.

When the objects are selected, click the Format tab of the drawing tools. Use the Group command in the Arrange group to group the objects. A frame will appear around the grouped objects. You can now position or rotate the grouped objects as if they were a single object. If you need to ungroup the select the group's frame; select Group and then select Ungroup. The objects will become individual items with their own frames.

Layering Objects

In some cases, you might end up with fairly complex slides that contain a number of objects. You might have even deliberately layered objects on a slide. For instance, you might be using a combination of shapes, text boxes, and pictures to build a custom logo or other layered item. Or you might overlap adjacent objects using layering to provide the slide with additional visual interest.

You can use the Bring Forward command to bring an object forward in the stack (one object) or to bring it to the front of the stack (it will be on top). The Send Backward command enables you to send a selected object backward (one layer) or to send it to the bottom of the object pile using the Send to Back option. After you have the objects layered correctly, select the entire stack (drag the mouse around the object stack). You can then group the layered objects using the Group command. This will enable you to move the stack without messing up the layers.

Adding Hyperlinks to Slides

You can add hyperlinks to your PowerPoint slides. Hyperlinks enable you to jump to external information such as web pages or even files on your computer. For example, you could use a hyperlink to open an Excel worksheet that is associated with a chart that you have copied and pasted onto a slide. Hyperlinks can also be used to jump to a bookmark, which can point to a slide in the current presentation. This is useful in cases where you anticipate that a slide shown later in the presentation will elicit requests from the audience to see the earlier slide. You can be ready for the question by placing a hyperlink to the slide on the current slide.

Hyperlinks are added to a text box on a slide using the Insert Hyperlink dialog box, which is shown in Figure 19.19. You open the Hyperlinks dialog box using the Hyperlink command on the Insert tab.

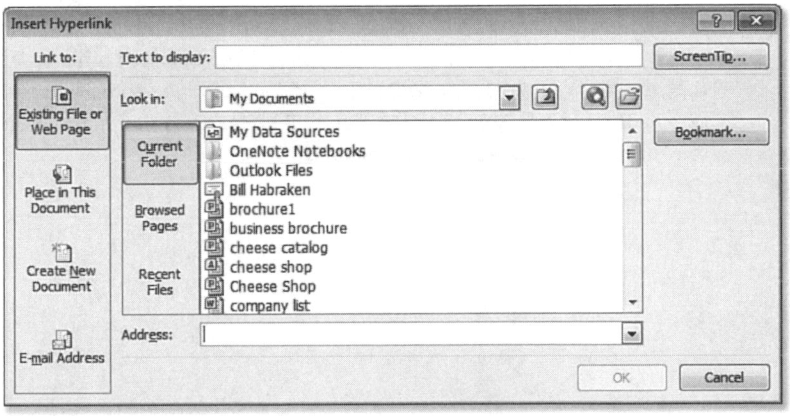

Figure 19.19
Insert a hyperlink onto the current slide.

By default the Existing File or Web Page setting is selected in the Link To box. This setting enables you to create a hyperlink to a file on your computer or a web page. Also by default the contents of the My Documents folder are displayed in the Insert Hyperlink dialog box. If the hyperlink is to an existing file, you can select any document in the folder or navigate to another folder to specify an existing file. You can also select Recent Files to view a list of files that you have recently opened. This provides another option for specifying an existing file as the destination for the hyperlink.

If you want to create a hyperlink to a web page, you can type the URL for the site in the Address box. If you select Browsed Pages, you will be provided a list of recently browsed web pages. You can select from this list to specify the web address for the hyperlink.

There is also another alternative for specifying the web address (URL) for a website. Open Internet Explorer or your default web browser and navigate to the website. When you return to PowerPoint, the address of the website that you navigated to in your web browser will appear in the Address box.

In cases where you want to specify a slide as the destination for the hyperlink, select Place in This Document in the Link To box. A list of slides in the presentation will appear in the Insert Hyperlink dialog box. Select the appropriate slide in the list.

Before you click OK, which closes the Insert Hyperlink dialog box and creates your hyperlink on the slide, there is one more thing that you need to take care of. Enter the text that you want to display on the slide when the hyperlink is inserted. The text can be any text you choose. It won't affect the hyperlink's ability to navigate to the destination. For example, the hyperlink text displayed on the slide does not have to be the URL for the website that they hyperlink takes you to. When you have finished configuring the hyperlink, click OK to return to the slide.

The hyperlink won't be active on the slide when you are in Normal view. You need to run the slide in a slide show to test your hyperlink. Select the Slide Show shortcut on the right side of the PowerPoint status bar. The slide show will begin from the current slide, which is the slide that contains the hyperlink to be tested. Click on the hyperlink. If the hyperlink is to a website, your web browser will open and navigate to the site. If you selected a file as the destination, the application that the file was created in will open and load the file. And if you specified a slide in the presentation as the hyperlink destination, you will be taken to that slide in the slide show. You can press Esc to return to the PowerPoint workspace.

> **note**
> You can also create a screen tip for the hyperlink. Select ScreenTip in the Insert Hyperlink dialog box and then specify the ScreenTip text in the Set Hyperlink Screen Tip dialog box.

20

ENHANCING SLIDES WITH ANIMATION, TRANSITIONS, AND MULTIMEDIA

As Microsoft PowerPoint has become more sophisticated over the years in terms of the enhancements that you can apply to your presentation slides, people have come to expect flashier and more graphically rich presentations. Whether you regularly give PowerPoint presentations as part of your profession or just use PowerPoint for your travel club or to show family pictures at a get-together, your audience expects a visually compelling slide show. You just can't click through a static series of slides without any special effects or multimedia.

In this chapter, we look at animation effects and how you can apply them to slide objects and how to customize these animations. We will also discuss the use of slide transitions and the addition of sound and video to a presentation.

Animations Versus Transitions

Before we dive into working with animation effects and slide transitions, a few things should be said about each of these different special effect options with regard to what they do to a slide and its content and how they differ. Animations are special effects that are added to an object or objects on the slide. Animations can be applied to text boxes, pictures, clip art, SmartArt graphics—any object type.

Animations are designed to emphasize objects on a slide and can also be used to control the entrance or exit of objects as the slide is viewed during the slide show. Animations affect objects such as clip art and SmartArt a little differently than text boxes. For example, if you assign an animation to a clip art object such as the Fly In animation, the clip art will fly onto the slide when you click the mouse or when a delay timer has expired (we talk more about setting timers for animations later in this chapter).

In the case of text boxes that include bulleted lists or text in paragraphs, each paragraph is animated by the animation effect. So, if I have a text box that includes four items in a bulleted list (each item in the list is considered a separate paragraph), I will (by default) have to click the mouse four times to get the entire bulleted list to appear on the slide. Each bulleted item will fly in separately upon each subsequent click of the mouse.

> **note**
>
> You will find that you have complete control over how and when objects assigned animation effects appear on or exit the screen. We discuss this in detail in the sections of this chapter that cover animation effects.

You are not limited to one animation per slide and can apply an animation effect to each object on a slide if you choose. You can also apply multiple animations to a particular object. For example, you could apply an entrance effect for a bulleted list and then assign a secondary animation to the bulleted list that emphasizes each item in the list.

When you assign animation effects to objects, a number is placed to the left of the object to show that an effect has been applied. The number also tells you the sequence that the effects will be applied to the objects when you run the slide show. Figure 20.1 shows a slide with multiple objects. An animation effect has been applied to the clip art on the right of the slide and this animation is the first effect in the animation sequence (and so is assigned the number 1).

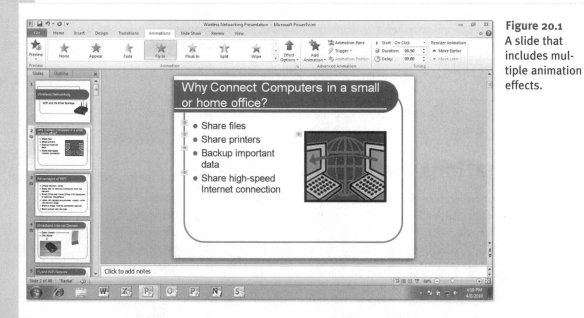

Figure 20.1
A slide that includes multiple animation effects.

The slide also includes a bulleted list consisting of four bulleted items. An animation effect has also been applied to the text box that contains the bulleted list. Notice that the individual bulleted items have been numbered in a sequence from 2 through 4.

When this slide is viewed during a slide show, only the title of the slide will appear when you switch to the slide. On the first click of the mouse, the clip art will appear. On subsequence clicks of the mouse, each of the bulleted list items will appear in sequence. So, animation effects are designed to add effects to the objects on the slide.

Transitions, which are also referred to as transition effects, can also provide you with a way to add special effects to a presentation. Transitions are assigned to slides. A transition will go into effect or "play" during the slide's entrance in the slide show. So, transitions are more of an all-or-nothing proposition. You can't have the transition affect apply to only certain objects on the slide; it is applied to the entire slide.

PowerPoint provides a number of different transition effects. Some of the transition effects are based on film and video transitions, which are used to switch between scenes in a film or television program; these effects include the fade, wipe, and dissolve. Other transitions such as shred, vortex, and ripple provide extremely visually exciting transitions that will wow your audience.

When using animation effects and transitions in your slide presentations, there are some things that you should keep in mind. The list that follows provides some tips for using these special effects appropriately and judicially.

- **Less Is Better:** Remember that your presentation is meant to convey information, not hypnotize the audience (or make their eyes hurt). You don't have to animate every object on every slide or necessarily assign transitions to every slide. Use these features sparingly to get the most bang out of them when you do use them.

- **Give the Audience a Rest:** There is no crime in showing slides that do not have animations or transitions. After animating several slides in a row or having slide transitions for several slides in a row, put a slide or two in the mix that are just regular slides with no effects. This is particularly useful when you are showing a slide that contains very important information. You are stressing the information by not dressing it up with an animation or transition.

- **Use Effects to Best Effect:** Both the animations and transitions provide effects that can be of thematic value to your presentation. For example, if you are discussing issues related to the proper disposal of hard copy proprietary information, what better slide transition to use than the shred transition? Or if you are emphasizing the spiraling value of a company's stock using a chart, why not animate that chart with the spin animation?

The use of special effects such as animations and transitions should be something that you think about when you are developing the overall design plan for your presentation. How you present the information can be as important as the information itself. You can take advantage of special effects to add interest to your presentation, but don't let them take over your presentation or obscure the information you want to provide your audience.

Assigning Animation to a Slide Object

PowerPoint 2010 has separated the animation effect commands and the transition commands onto separate tabs of the Ribbon. This makes it easy to focus on a particular type of special effect such as animation. The Animations tab of the Ribbon provides all the commands related to the application and modification of animation effects. PowerPoint 2010 also makes it much easier (easier than its predecessor, PowerPoint 2007) to select animation effects by providing the Animation gallery, which is shown in Figure 20.2.

Figure 20.2
The Animation gallery.

The Animation gallery groups the animation effects into four categories: Entrance, Emphasis, Exit, and Motion Paths. The first three categories—Entrance, Emphasis, and Exit—are self-explanatory. Let's look at these standard animation effects and we will pick up motion paths in their own section of the chapter.

The Entrance category provides animations that dictate how the object will enter the slide when the animation plays. The Emphasis group provides animations that enable you to emphasize objects such as the items in a bulleted list. For example, as you talk about a particular item in the list, you can click the mouse so that the bulleted item is emphasized with a pulse or spin. The Exit category provides animations that remove items from the slide. For example, if you assign an exit animation such as the Fade effect, the items in the bulleted list will fade (sequentially) each time you click the mouse.

To assign an animation effect to an object or objects on a slide, follow these steps:

1. Select the object or objects on the slide. You can select multiple objects by clicking on the first object and then holding down the Ctrl key as you click on subsequent objects.

2. Select the Animations tab on the Ribbon.

3. Place the mouse on an animation in the Animation gallery to preview an animation on the slide object. If you want to access the entire gallery, select the More button.

4. Select the animation you want to use to close the gallery and assign the animation to the slide object.

You can repeat this process as needed to apply other animation effects to other objects on the slide. When you want to preview the animation effects assigned to the objects on a slide, select the Preview button on the Animations tab. This will provide you with a preview of the animation effect or effects in the Normal view.

Accessing Additional Animation Effects

The Animations gallery provides only a subset of the animation effects available. You can access additional animation effects via a set of dialog boxes that open via the Animations gallery. Each animation effect type—entrance, emphasis, and exit—has a separate dialog box. For example, the Change Entrance Effect dialog box, shown in Figure 20.3, provides you with a large number of different entrance effects.

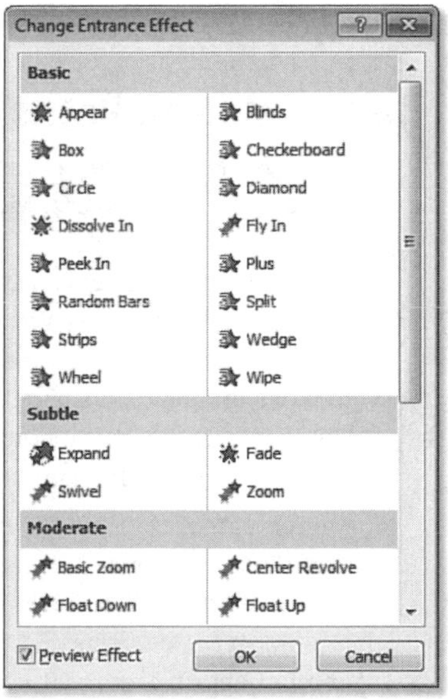

Figure 20.3
The Change Entrance Effect dialog box.

The entrance effects provided by the Entrance Effect dialog box are grouped into categories. These categories are Basic, Subtle, Moderate, and Exciting.

The categories are based on the "specialness" of the effects they include. The Exciting category provides more elaborate animation effects than the Basic category. For example, a basic entrance effect such as Fade will fade the object or object elements, such as a bulleted list, onto the slide. In contrast, an entrance effect in the Exciting category, such as Pinwheel, will spin the object elements onto the slide, providing a much more exciting and elaborate entrance for the object. It's kind of like the difference between a magician walking onto the stage from behind the curtain or appearing on the stage in a flash of light of smoke.

To access the dialog box for a specific effect type, click the More button on the Animation gallery. You can then use the More Entrance Effects, More Emphasis Effects, and the More Exit Effects commands at the bottom of the gallery to open the Change Entrance Effects dialog box, the Change Emphasis Effects dialog box, or the Change Exit Effects dialog box, respectively.

By default, each dialog box will provide a preview of the effect you select and the effect is previewed on the selected object or objects. You might want to drag the dialog box off of the Slide pane so that you can see the preview of the effect on the slide. The selected effect is not actually assigned to the object until you click the OK button in the dialog box and return to the PowerPoint workspace.

If you would like to preview the animation after you have closed the dialog box, select the Preview command on the Animations tab. You can also open the slide show at the current slide by selecting the Slide Show button on the status bar. This enables you to view the animation as it will appear during the slide show. When you want to stop the slide show and return to the Normal view, press the Esc key on the keyboard.

Using Motion Paths

There is another type of animation effect type that you can add to your slide objects. Motion paths are effects that enable you to move an object on a slide in a prescribed path. Motion paths can emphasize objects in much the same way that you use the emphasis animation effects such as the Spin or Underline effects. Motion paths are provided that enable you to move an object in a circular, octagonal, or trapezoidal path. There is even a vertical figure eight motion path that moves an object in a figure eight pattern.

> **note**
>
> If you do not want to preview an effect selected in one of the Change Effects dialog boxes, clear the Preview Effect check box at the bottom of the dialog box.

Motion paths, however, do not necessarily have to move only objects in place on the slide. You can actually use a custom motion path to relocate an object on a slide. For example, you might want to have a chart and a text box switch positions on the slide to get your audience to concentrate more closely on the chart itself. Or you might want to use a motion path to have an object interact with another object. Figure 20.4 shows a clip art image of a cow that has been assigned a custom motion path that allows the cow to jump over the clip art moon.

The path for the clip art image is shown in Figure 20.4 by a dotted line that appears on the slide. A green triangle shows the beginning of the motion path and a red arrow designates the end point for the motion path.

Applying a Motion Path

To apply a motion path to a selected object or objects, scroll through the Animations gallery until you can access the Motion Paths category area provided in the gallery. You can also open the entire gallery by clicking the More button (you still might have to scroll down to see the available motion paths).

Figure 20.4
A custom
motion path
assigned to a
clip art object.

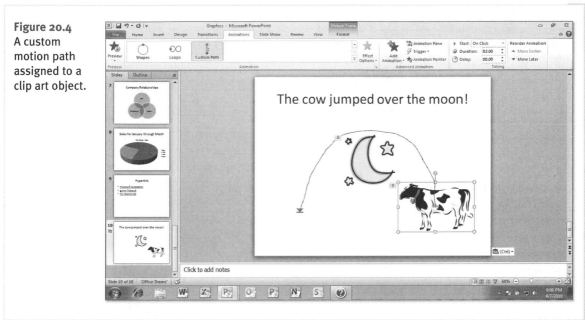

The available motion paths in the Animation gallery might appear on first inspection to be rather meager. The motion paths are a little different, however, from the other animation effects available in the gallery. Although you can change some options related to the entrance, emphasis, and exit animation effects, such as the direction and whether or not a compound object (such as a SmartArt Venn diagram) is animated as a whole or as parts, you will find that motion paths provide you with more customization possibilities. For example, you can control the length of the path, the position of the path, and other path attributes such as the shape of the path and the path direction. So, think of the motion paths available in the Animations gallery as just types of motion paths that can then be highly customized; this provides you with more options than you might at first expect.

To assign a motion path to an object on a slide, select the object. Then select a motion path in the Animation gallery such as Lines, Arcs, or Loops. If you want to access additional motion path animations, select the More Motion Paths command at the bottom of the gallery. The Change Motion Path dialog box will open as shown in Figure 20.5.

The Motion Path dialog box is divided into different categories of paths. These categories are as follows:

- **Basic:** This category provides different path shapes including circle, hexagon, and square paths as well as a number of star paths.

- **Lines & Curves:** This category provides different arc, line, and curve paths, and includes a number of special paths such as funnel, heartbeat, and spring.

- **Special:** This category provides unique paths such as bean, loop de loop, peanut, and neutron. It also includes different figure eight paths.

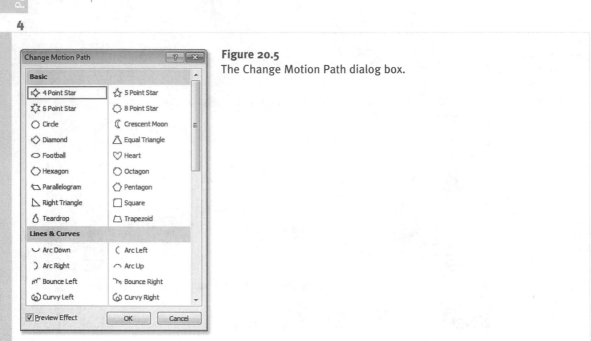

Figure 20.5
The Change Motion Path dialog box.

When you select a motion path in the Change Motion Path dialog box, it will be previewed on the selected object. To assign the motion path to the object, click OK to close the Change Motion Path dialog box.

Editing a Motion Path

After the path has been assigned to the object, you will find that the path itself is represented by a dotted line (when the Animations tab is selected on the Ribbon). The beginning of the path is designated by a green triangle and the end of the path is designated by a red triangle. The path will also have its own sizing handles.

Some of the motion path's attributes, such as its size and its location in relation to the object, can be changed using the mouse. The path's start point will begin at the center of the object assigned the motion path and the object will move through the path to the end point, which will also occur when the center of the object reaches the red triangle (in the case of loops and circular paths, the start point and end point are the same). You can change the position of the start and end points and change the relative positioning of the path itself in relation to the object.

> **note**
>
> Fine-tuning a motion path can be a little tricky. After each change made to the motion path, use the Preview command. If you don't like a particular change, take advantage of Undo.

Additional motion path settings can be accessed via the Effect Options command. The options available in the Effect Options gallery, which are shown in Figure 20.6 for a horizontal figure eight effect, will depend on the motion path that you have selected. Some motion paths have alternative motion paths such as the horizontal and vertical figure eight. You can switch between these two orientations via the Effect Options gallery.

Figure 20.6
Change the
motion path
options.

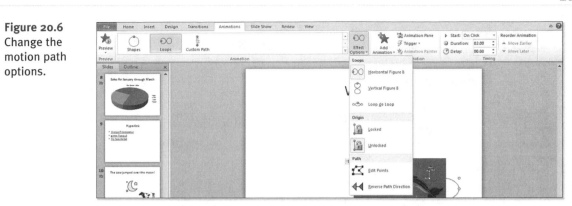

The options typically available on the Effect Options gallery will provide you with the ability to reverse the path direction and edit individual points in the path. When you select the Edit Points command, a series of point handles will become visible on the motion path. You can drag any of these handles to change the path. For example, on a figure eight motion path, I could stretch the size of the ovals that make up either oval that makes up the 8 or change the ovals into pretty much any shape desired.

You will also find in the Effect Options gallery that there are two commands grouped in an Origin category: Locked and Unlocked. These options do not dictate whether you can make changes to the motion path animation (such as locking the settings for a motion path) but relate to what happens when you move the motion path or the object that has been assigned the motion path.

By default the motion path is unlocked. This means that when you move the object on the slide, the motion path moves with it. If you select Locked, the path does not move when you move the object. So, in a sense, these two options are a little counterintuitive. You would probably think that Locked setting would keep the object and the motion path locked, but the reality is just the opposite.

You will also find that the locked and unlocked options do not differ when you move the motion path itself. In both cases, moving the motion path does not also move the object that the path has been assigned to.

Although the Effect Options gallery is rather limited in terms of the different possibilities for modifying a motion path, you can access additional options in a dialog box that is specific to the motion path that you have selected. All you have to do is select the dialog box launcher under the Effect Options command. Figure 20.7 shows the Horizontal Figure 8 dialog box.

The dialog box provides you with an Effect tab and a Timing tab. The Effect tab enables you to set the path for the animation to Locked or Unlocked (the default). You can also use the available sliders to change the start, end, and bounce intervals for the animation. For example to lengthen the duration of the start, move the Smooth Start slider bar to the right. You will find that this takes duration time away from the Smooth End setting (and the Bounce End setting if there is a bounce at the end of the animation). By default animations are provided a duration of 2 seconds. You can modify the duration on the Timing tab using the Duration drop-down list.

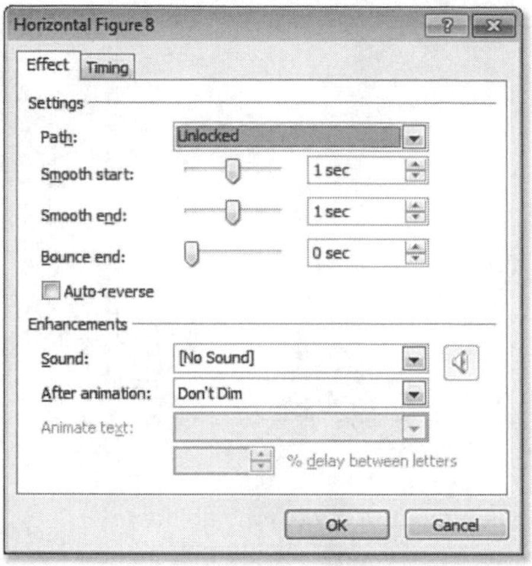

Figure 20.7
A motion path's dialog box.

The Effect tab also enables you to include enhancements to the animation, such as sounds, and specify what happens after the animation ends, including settings such as Hide After Animation or Hide on Next Mouse Click (we talk more about animation and sound later in this chapter). Colors are also provided in the After Animation drop-down list to enable you to change the fill color for the object upon the completion of the animation. If you choose the same fill color as that used by the slide, the object will actually disappear after the animation plays.

I've already mentioned that the motion path animation's duration can be set on the Timing tab of the dialog box. This tab also enables you to set the Start parameter for the animation by selecting On Click, With Previous, or After Previous. You can also set a delay for the animation or choose to have the animation repeat.

The Timing tab also enables you to specify the trigger for the animation. A trigger can be any object on the slide. For example, you can specify the title text box as a trigger for an animation. When you click the title on the slide, the animation plays. Triggers can also be related to the playing of other animations or events on the slide. For example, if you have a video or sound file on the slide, the animation can be triggered to play upon the playing of that other object (the video).

When you have completed editing the settings for the motion path, click OK. This will enable your new settings on the motion path animation and return you to the Normal view.

Creating a Custom Motion Path

You can also create a custom motion path. This is easier than it sounds and really is just a matter of recording the path of the object as you drag it with the mouse. Because most of the motion paths provided by PowerPoint are designed to move an object in place, the creation of a custom motion path for an object enables you to dictate the final position of the object on the slide after the motion effect animation plays.

To create a custom path, follow these steps:

1. Select the object you will assign the custom path.

2. Navigate to the Animations tab and open the Animations gallery.

3. In the Motion Paths category of the gallery, select Custom Path.

4. Place the mouse pointer on the center of the object that you will assign the custom path.

5. Hold down the left mouse button; the mouse pointer will become a drawing tool. Draw the custom path on the slide.

6. When you reach the end point for the custom motion path, double-click the mouse.

A preview of the custom path will be played. The path itself will be represented on the slide as a dotted line.

As with any motion path, you can change the settings for the path using the mouse (and the sizing handles) or the options in the Effect Options gallery. You can also access a Custom Path dialog box by selecting the dialog box launcher under the Effect Options command. This enables you to change the effect settings (including the addition of a sound), timing, and triggers for the custom path as discussed in the previous section. You can preview any of the changes that you make to the custom path by selecting the Preview command.

Advanced Animation Techniques

PowerPoint provides you with additional tools and options for fine-tuning animation effects. We have already looked at effect options related to motion paths. You will find, however, that even simple entrance effects can be modified, particularly in cases where you are assigning an animation to a bulleted list, a SmartArt graphic, or chart that contains multiple items in a sequence.

PowerPoint also provides you with the ability to add more than one animation effect to an object. Although restraint is in order with regard to piling animation effects onto your objects, this option enables you to add a entrance effect to an object such as a bulleted list and then also assign an emphasis effect, which enables you to revisit each bullet point on the slide to emphasize and review important information before changing to the next slide.

PowerPoint also provides a new Animation Painter, which is a tool much in the same vein as the Format Painter, which enables you to copy text and paragraph formatting from formatted text and apply it to other text. The Animation Painter enables you to copy the animation effects assigned to an object (including any effect options that you have fine-tuned) to another object.

The Advanced Animation group provides access to the Add Animation, Animation Pane, Trigger, and Animation Painter commands. We will discuss all these commands in later sections, including how to set triggers for an animation, which is considered one of the options when you set the Timing options for an effect in that effect's dialog box. The dialog box associated with a selected animation can be opened using the dialog box launcher that is available below the Effect Options command in the Animation group.

The Trigger command enables you to specify how a particular animation is triggered or started. You can specify the trigger on the click of a particular object on the slide. For example, you can specify the title text box as a trigger for an animation. When you click the title on the slide, the animation plays. You can specify any object on the slide as the trigger for an animation. The animation does not have to be applied to the trigger object, so you could click a clip art image or picture on a slide and an animation on another object will be triggered by this action. The trigger can also be set so that an animation begins after a particular bookmark is reached in a sound or video object on the slide.

Changing Effect Options

To modify the effect options for an animation assigned to an object, select the object and navigate to the Ribbon's Animations tab if necessary. The Effect Options command provides a gallery of options that relate to the type of animation effect, meaning whether you have assigned an entrance, emphasis, or exit animation. The options available in the Effect Options gallery will also be specific to the type of object assigned the animation. For example, text boxes will have different options available than a clip art image or a SmartArt graphic that has been assigned an animation effect. You will find that objects made of multiple paragraphs, such as a text box or a SmartArt graphic that includes a number of shapes in the graphic, are provided options for animating all the object parts one by one or all at once.

To change the options for an animation effect, select the object assigned the animation. Then select the Effect Option command to access the options available for that effect and object type. Figure 20.8 shows the Effect Options gallery for a bulleted list assigned an entrance animation.

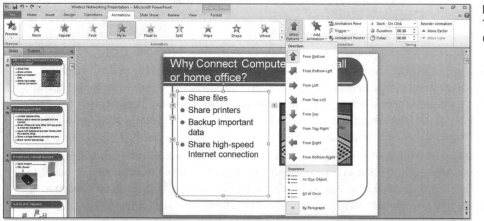

Figure 20.8
The Effect Options gallery.

Both entrance and exit animations provide effect options that enable you to specify the direction of the object's entrance or exit, such as to bottom, to left, to top, and so on. Emphasis animations will have effect options that relate to the color or the level of the animation effect. For example, if you use the Fill Color animation, the effect options provided include a color palette that enables you to select the fill color to be used by the animation. In the case of the Transparency animation, you select the level of transparency assigned the objects in the Effect Options gallery.

As already mentioned, the type of object will also have a bearing on the effect options available for a particular animation. You will find that when you access the effect options for an object that has multiple parts, such as a bulleted list, you are provided sequence options that enable you to determine whether the object should be animated all at once or if the individual parts should be animated separately.

In cases where you would like to fine-tune the options for an animation, you can open the animation effects dialog box. Select the dialog box launcher below the Effect Options command. The dialog box for a particular animation type will provide you with options related to the effect itself and provide you with enhancement possibilities such as whether a sound plays with the animation effect. The dialog box for an animation will also provide a Timing tab that enables you to set options related to the start, delay, and duration of the animation. We discuss animation sound and timing options later in the chapter.

Because the dialog box is specific to a particular type of animation, the settings available will vary in the dialog box, as do the options that are available for that animation type in the Effect Options gallery. For example, the dialog box for an entrance or an exit animation will have options for setting the direction of the effect and will also provide slider bars that enable you to specify the duration of the "smooth start" or "smooth end" for the animation. In contrast, the dialog box for an emphasis animation would include only options for the inclusion of a sound with the animation and timing settings related to the animation effect.

Adding Additional Animations

The Advanced Animation command group on the Animations tab provides you with the Add Animation command. This command opens the Add Animation gallery, which is really a duplicate of the Animation gallery provided in the Animation group. You can add any of the available animation effects to the current object. The added effect will be numbered sequentially in relation to the other animations that have been already added to the slide.

> **note**
>
> The default animation setting for text boxes is to animate the object by paragraph. This is what allows you to bring in each item in a bulleted list separately when you use an entrance animation.

The added animation will occur after the primary animation that you have added to the object. So, if you plan on using both an entrance and an exit animation on a particular object, make sure that the entrance animation occurs in the animation sequence before the exit animation. It would make sense to assign the entrance animation to the object via the Animation gallery and assign the exit animation, which is really the secondary animation for the object, using the Add Animation command.

As already mentioned, the Add Animation gallery is much the same as the Animation gallery. At the bottom of the Add Animation gallery is a series of commands such as More Entrance Effects, More Emphasis Effects, and so on. Use any of these commands to open the corresponding dialog box for that type of animation. You can then select from the larger library of animation effects (by type) provided in the specific dialog boxes.

Using the Animation Painter

The Animation Painter enables you to copy the animations that have been applied to an object and "paint" these animation settings onto another object or objects. This enables you to fine-tune animations on a particular object and then apply the animation or animations to other objects on the same slide or other slides in the presentation. This can be particularly useful if you want to have an overall scheme related to the animations that you use and you want particular animations to be repeated on like objects that appear throughout the presentation.

To use the Animation Painter, select an object that has been assigned the animation or animations you want to copy. Then select the Animation Painter in the Advanced Animation command group. The mouse pointer will include a paintbrush, letting you know that the Animation Painter is active. Navigate to the slide that contains the object that you want to assign the animations that have been copied from the previous object. Click the object and the animations will be assigned to the object. A preview of the pasted animations will be played as soon as you click the Animation Painter on the object.

One click on the Animation Painter command enables you to apply the copied animations to one object. As soon as you click on that object, the Animation Painter applies the animations and then becomes inactive. You can use the Animation Painter to apply copied animations to multiple objects in the presentation by double-clicking on the Animation Painter command. When you have finished assigning the animation or animations to objects in your presentation, select the Animation Painter command again to deactivate the tool.

Including Sound Effects with Animations

You can enhance your animations by adding sound effects to them. When the animation plays, the accompanying sound also plays. PowerPoint (and the other Office applications) support a number of popular sound file formats. The supported sound file extensions include the following:

- **Wave:** The .wav format stores sound as a waveform files. These files are relatively small in terms of file size when compared to some of the other sound file formats.

- **MIDI:** The MIDI or Musical Instrument Digital Interface file format (.mid) contains a series of control information that can be played back on a MIDI-enabled device such as a computer.

- **MP3:** The MPEG 3 (.mp3) audio file format is a popular compressed file format.

> **tip**
>
> You can also active the Animation Painter by pressing Alt+Shift+C on the keyboard.

- **WMA:** The Windows Media Audio (.wma) file format is a compressed music file format developed by Microsoft.

- **AIFF:** The Audio Interchange (.aiff) file format is an uncompressed waveform sound file type originally used by Apple computers.

To specify a sound for an animation, select the object assigned the animation and then click the dialog box launcher under the Effect Options command. This will open a dialog box for the animation effect assigned to the object. Figure 20.9 shows the dialog box for a Fly In animation applied to a bulleted list.

Figure 20.9
The Fly In dialog box.

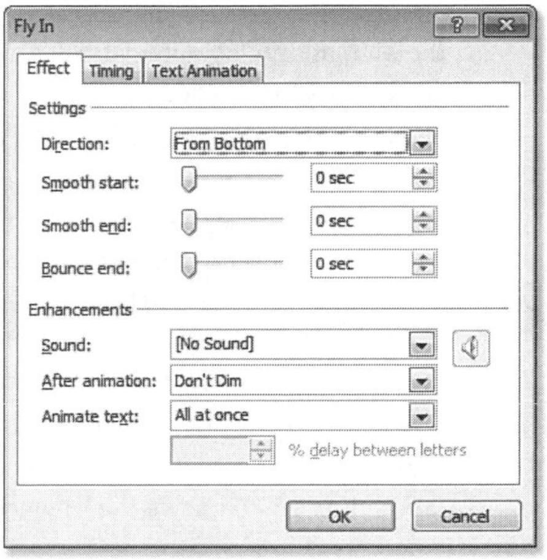

The Effect tab of the dialog box enables you to control settings related to the direction and start and end of the animation. More importantly to our discussion of sound, the Enhancements area of the Effect tab enables you to specify a sound file to be played with the animation.

The default sound setting for all animations that you have assigned to slide objects is No Sound. When you select the Sound drop-down list, you are presented with a list of sound files that can be applied to the animation. These sounds include applause, camera, chime, and window. Select a sound provided in the list (these sounds consist of .wav files). Click the Sound icon to set the volume level for the sound.

> **tip**
>
> If you have assigned multiple animations to an object, the easiest way to open the options for a specific effect is to use the Effect Options command that is available for each animation listed in the animation pane.

If you want to use a sound file other than the ones provided by PowerPoint, you can access these sounds via the Other Sound option in the Sound drop-down list. Selecting the Other Sound option opens the Add Audio dialog box. You can take advantage of any sound files that you have created or downloaded to your computer. However, to use the sound file, it must be in one of the supported file formats discussed earlier in this section.

When you have added the sound to the animation, you can click OK to close the animation's dialog box. Select the preview button on the Animations tab to preview the animation with the assigned sound.

Setting Timings for Animations

You can set the timing for an animation using the commands available in the Timing group on the Animations tab. The Start command enables you to set how the animation will be started. The default setting is On Click, but you can also specify that the animation start with the previous animation (With Previous) or after the previous animation has ended (After Previous).

The Duration command provides a spinner box that enables you to set the actual duration of the animation. This enables you to speed up or slow down animations as you require. If you want to have the animation play automatically after a specified delay, use the Delay spinner box to specify the actual time for the delay.

Although it is not included in the Timing group, the Trigger command in the Advanced Animation group also has some bearing on the mechanism for actually starting an animation. The Trigger command enables you to specify how a particular animation is triggered or started. You can specify the trigger on the click of a particular object on the slide. For example, you can specify the title text box as a trigger for an animation. When you click the title on the slide, the animation plays. You can specify any object on the slide as the trigger for an animation. The animation does not have to be applied to the trigger object, so you could click a clip art image or picture on a slide and an animation on another object will be triggered by this action.

The timing settings for an animation can also be set in the animation's dialog box on the Timing tab. Figure 20.10 shows the Timing tab of the Fly In animation's dialog box.

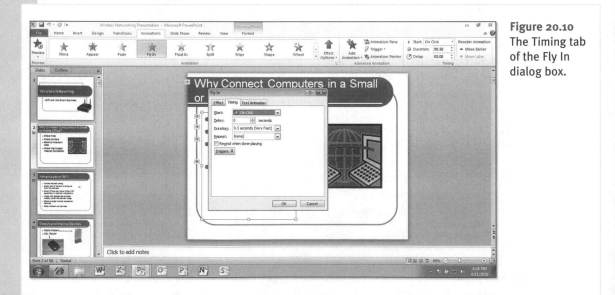

Figure 20.10
The Timing tab of the Fly In dialog box.

The Timing tab provides you with the ability to set the start, delay, and duration settings for the animation. The dialog box also provides you with the ability to configure the animation to repeat using the Repeat drop-down list. If you want the animation to rewind when it is done playing (which is useful if you have used an animation such as a motion path that moves an object on the slide), you can select the Rewind When Done Playing check box. The trigger options can also be set for the animation via the Triggers drop-down command provided on the Timing tab. You can specify any object on the slide as the trigger for the animation.

When you have finished setting the timing-related settings for the animation in the dialog box, click OK. You will be returned to the PowerPoint workspace. Take advantage of the Preview command to preview the settings that you have configured for the animation.

Managing Slide Animations

An extremely useful tool for managing reordering and fine-tuning the animations that you have assigned to your slide objects is the Animation pane. The Animation pane will list all the animations that have been assigned to objects on the current slide. Figure 20.11 shows a presentation in the Normal view with the Slide pane present on the right side of the PowerPoint workspace.

Figure 20.11
Slide with assigned animations and the Animation pane.

You can use the Slide pane to accomplish a variety of different animation management tasks, including the reordering, deletion, and modification of animations. To reorder the animations in the Animation pane, you have a couple of options. You can select an animation and then move it up or down in the Animation pane using the Move Earlier or Move Later arrows provided at the bottom of the Animation pane. You can also drag an animation to a new position in the Animation pane to reorder the sequence of the animations.

 tip

You can also reorder animations on a slide without using the animation pane. Use the Reorder Animation commands on the Animations tab.

The bottom of the Animation pane provides delay and duration information for the animation. You can use the Seconds drop-down button to zoom in or out on the advanced timeline information provided to the right of each of the animations. This provides you the relative timing of the animation as it compares to the other animations placed on the slide.

If you want to delete an animation from the slide, select the animation in the Animation pane and then press the Delete key on the keyboard or select Remove from the drop-down list to the right of the animation. This drop-down list also provides you with the ability to set the start for the animation and access the timing settings for the animation.

The Slide pane is particularly useful in sorting out multiple animations that you might have added to an object. For example, you might have assigned both an entrance and exit animation to an object. Both these animations will be listed separately in the Animation pane. This makes it easy to access the dialog box for an animation by selecting the drop-down list next to the animation and then selecting Effect Options.

When you have finished working with the Animation pane, you can close it using its Close button. This will free up more of the PowerPoint workspace for working with your slides in the Normal view.

Adding Transitions to Slides

Transitions provide you with another effect type that you can use to add visual interest and perhaps even a little bit of excitement to your PowerPoint presentations. When you show a slide show of a presentation that does not contain any slide transitions, you are in effect doing what is called a straight cut in film terminology. The change from the current slide to the next slide is abrupt and can be jarring to the audience. There is no visual buffer between the content of the two adjacent slides. A transition is a special effect that provides a visual shift between slides rather than an abrupt cut or switch. The transition between the slides is actually triggered when you navigate from the current slide to the next slide (either by a click of the mouse or based on a timing) and that next slide has been configured with the transition. So, if you want a transition between slide A and slide B, you assign the transition to slide B.

PowerPoint 2010 has uncoupled animations and transitions (PowerPoint 2007 grouped these effects on the same Ruler tab), so these different effect types have their own tabs on the Ribbon. The Transitions tab provides command groups that enable you to select a transition, configure transition options, and configure sound and timing settings for the transition. Figure 20.12 shows the Transitions tab of the Ribbon.

Figure 20.12
The Ribbon's
Transitions tab.

The Transitions tab also provides a Preview command, making it easy for you to preview a transition assigned to a slide. The Preview command is greatly improved in PowerPoint 2010 in that it shows the actual transition as the changeover is made between the two slides. PowerPoint 2007 allowed you to preview only the transition itself and the slide content on the slide that you assigned the transition.

PowerPoint provides a number of different transitions, including the wipe, split, dissolve, checkerboard, and blinds. The Transitions gallery groups the transitions into three categories: subtle, exciting, and dynamic content.

Before we review how to assign a transition to a slide or slides, let me say a couple things about transitions in general. Remember that these are special effects just like the animation effects. They should be used to add visual interest to the presentation, not make the audience feel like they are sitting in front of a strobe light at a 1970s disco. Also take into account the additive effect of animations and transitions. If you use a slide transition to get to a slide, is it really necessary to also load up the slide with animations? For example, if you use the Glitter transition, followed by objects on the slide configured with the Grow and Turn animation effect, you might have too much going on in terms of visual interest. That is not to say that transitions and animations can't be used together; you can, but just don't randomly mix different type of effects. Plan the actual look that you want for the slide, taking into consideration your purpose and the presentation's topic and then planning out your use of transitions and animations appropriately.

You can assign transitions to your slides when you are working in the Normal view or the Slide Sorter. If you want to apply the same transition to a number of slides, you can easily do this in the Slide Sorter view by selecting multiple slides. And although the preview will obviously be smaller in the Slide Sorter view, you can get previews of all the selected slides and the assigned transition by selecting the Preview command.

To assign a transition to a slide, select the slide. You can then scroll through the Transition gallery (which is in the Transition to This Slide group) to select a transition. Or you can click the More button to view the entire gallery. When you place the mouse on a specific transition, it will be previewed on the selected slide or slides. To assign a transition, select the transition in the gallery.

Modifying Transitions

After you have assigned a particular transition in the gallery to a slide, you can then modify the transition. The Effect Options command will provide a gallery of options related to the transition that you have selected. Figure 20.13 shows the Effect Options gallery for the Wipe transition.

tip
If you want to apply a selected transition to all the slides in the presentation, select the Apply to All Command on the Transitions tab.

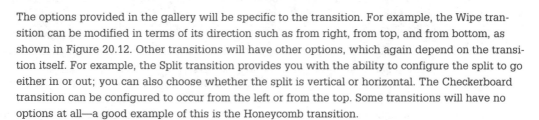

Figure 20.13
Effect Options gallery for a Wipe transition.

The options provided in the gallery will be specific to the transition. For example, the Wipe transition can be modified in terms of its direction such as from right, from top, and from bottom, as shown in Figure 20.12. Other transitions will have other options, which again depend on the transition itself. For example, the Split transition provides you with the ability to configure the split to go either in or out; you can also choose whether the split is vertical or horizontal. The Checkerboard transition can be configured to occur from the left or from the top. Some transitions will have no options at all—a good example of this is the Honeycomb transition.

Not only do you have control over transition options (if available), but you can also control the duration of the transition and whether a sound plays when the transition plays. To set the duration of the transition, use the Duration spinner box in the Timing group of the Transitions tab.

If you want to have a sound play with the transition, select the Sound drop-down list in the Timing group. A number of sound files are provided, such as Applause, Chime, and Voltage. If you want to use a sound that you have recorded or downloaded to your computer, you can select the Other Sound command in the Sound drop-down list. This will open the Add Audio dialog box. Navigate to the folder that holds the sound file and then select the appropriate file; click OK and the sound file will be assigned to the transition.

You can also specify how the slide is advanced. By default, slides are advanced by a click of the mouse. You can specify a time in the After spinner box. The slide will automatically advance based on that setting. You can then clear the On Mouse Click check box in the Timing group if you plan on using the timing to advance the slide or you can leave the option selected. Doing so enables you to advance the slide before the timing that you have set. It's always good to have options.

 Working with slide timings and recorded slide shows is discussed in Chapter 21, "Delivering a Presentation and Creating Support Materials" on page 583.

Adding Sound to a Slide

Sounds can add emphasis to information on slides or add some auditory interest to your presentation. The sound can consist of a sound effect or narration. You can insert a sound clip as an object onto a slide. When you click the image that represents the sound object during a slide show, the sound will play. PowerPoint provides you with the ability to insert clip art sound files and sound files that you have created or downloaded to your computer. You can also record sound, such as narration, using the Record Sound utility and place that sound on a slide. After you have inserted a sound on file on a slide, PowerPoint provides a number of formatting options and playback tools in the form of audio tools.

The Insert tab of the Ribbon includes the Media group, which provides commands for inserting video and audio onto your presentation slides. When you select the Audio command, you are provided with three options:

- **Audio from File:** Enables you to insert a sound file saved on your computer (or computer network). File formats supported included wave, MIDI, MP3, WMA, and AIFF. Only supported sound file types will be shown in the Insert Audio dialog box, which opens when you select this command.

- **Clip Art Audio:** This command opens the Clip Art task pane and enables you to do a search for audio files. The selected media file type is set to Audio in the task pane so that your search results only include audio files. When you have found a sound file, you add it to the slide as you would any clip art. If you want to preview the audio file before inserting it onto the slide, select the drop-down arrow for the audio file and then select Preview/Properties.

- **Record Audio:** This command opens the Record Sound utility. If you have a microphone connected to your computer, you can record sound effects and narration.

You will find that all three of these options produce the same result; an image is placed on the slide that represents the associated sound file. You can then edit options related to the sound file using the contextual audio tools, which appear when the image representing the sound file is selected on the slide.

Editing Sound Options

After you have added an audio file to a slide, you have a great deal of control over both the graphic that represents the sound file and the actual audio file embedded onto the slide. When you insert the audio onto the slide, it is represented by a sound image and has a control bar that enables you to play the sound, rewind the sound, and adjust the sound volume. Figure 20.14 shows a sound file that has been inserted onto a slide.

You might want to replace the standard sound icon picture that is inserted onto the slide. The Format tab of the audio tools (shown in Figure 20.13) provides the same type of tools used to adjust the settings of a picture, including a Picture Styles gallery and tools for cropping and sizing the image.

You can easily replace the sound image with any picture you like. Select the Change Sound image on the slide and then select the Change Picture command in the Adjust group. Use the Insert Picture dialog box to insert a new picture. After the picture has been inserted, you can use any of the various Format tab commands to change the picture style and to adjust picture attributes such as brightness, contrast, and color.

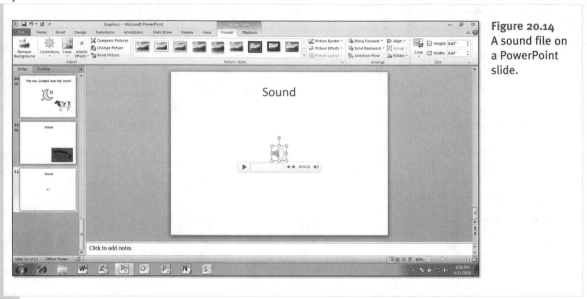

Figure 20.14
A sound file on a PowerPoint slide.

> For detailed information on working with pictures in the Office applications, see page 86 in Chapter 4, "Using and Creating Graphics."

The Playback tab provided by the audio tools enables you to trim your audio clip, apply fades to the audio, and adjust how the audio clip is started during the slide show. A Play command is also provided on the Playback tab, enabling you to preview any changes that you make to the audio clip.

If you want to trim the audio, you can select the Trim Audio command, which opens the Trim Audio dialog box shown in Figure 20.15. The timeline provided in the Trim Audio command has both a start marker (green) and an end marker (red).

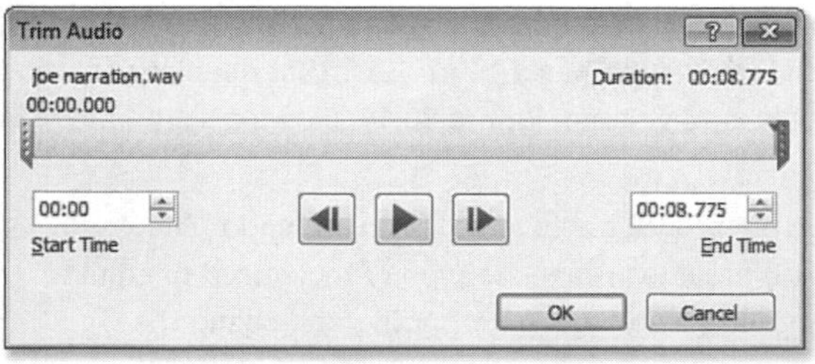

Figure 20.15
The Trim Audio dialog box.

You can trim the clip from the beginning using the start marker. This enables you to cue up the audio to start at a particular point. If you want the clip to end before it plays in its entirety, you can move the end marker to establish a new end time for the marker. Spinner boxes are also provided for the start and end times, and can also be used to set the starting and ending point of the clip. When you have finished working in the Trim Audio dialog box, click OK.

You can also add a fade to either the beginning or the end of the audio clip. Specify the Fade In or the Fade Out duration using the appropriate spinner box. The fades enable you to put a little bit of dead air at the beginning or end of a clip so that they do not seem to start or end abruptly when you play them during your presentation.

 tip

If you want to loop a sound so that it repeats until you stop it, select the Loop until Stopped check box on the Playback tab.

In situations where you would like a slide animation to play when a sound object file reaches a certain point during play-back, you can add a bookmark to the sound object. Play the audio file to the point where you want to place the bookmark. Then, on the Audio Tools Playback tab, select the Add Bookmark command. This will place the bookmark in the sound file. If you need to remove a bookmark in a sound file, select the bookmark on the sound object's playback bar and then select the Remove Bookmark command.

Adding Video to a Slide

You can also add video files to your PowerPoint slides. You can add a video file that you have created or downloaded to your computer or you can include a video from a website. The Clip Art library also includes a number of animated GIF files, which provide you with motions on a slide, although these clip art files are not truly video files.

➡ *For more information about animated GIFs, see page 529 in Chapter 19, "Better Slides with Clip Art, Pictures, and SmartArt."*

So, when adding true video to your PowerPoint slides you have two options. You can place a video file on the slide (in much the same way you place an audio file) or you can embed a video from an online video site such as YouTube.

Inserting a Video File

When inserting video files that are stored on your computer, your video file must be in a file format that PowerPoint can use. The file types supported are as follows:

- **Windows Video File:** The audio video interleave or .avi file type is a commonly used video format, and has been the standard for Microsoft Windows for a number of years. It uses the Microsoft Resource Interchange file format to store compressed audio and video information.

- **Movie File:** The Moving Picture Experts Group file format (.mpg or .mpeg) has been around for a number of years and was one of the first standards for video and audio compression.

- **Windows Media Video:** The .wmv file format provides highly compressed video and audio in a file that requires minimal space when stored on a computer.

- **Windows Media Streaming File:** Yet another Microsoft media file type, the .asf file format is used to stream video and audio over a network.

There are two options for inserting a video file onto a slide. You can select the Insert Media Clip icon in a slide content box or you can use the Video command on the Insert menu (select Video and then Video from File). Both possibilities will open the Insert Video dialog box. Navigate to the folder that holds your video file. Select the file and then click Insert. The video will be inserted onto the slide. Accompanying the video will be a control bar that enables you to play the video, rewind or fast-forward the video, and change the sound level for the clip. You can size the video frame if required, and move the video on the slide as you would any other slide object.

> **⚙ tip**
>
> If you are working with a very large video file, you can link it to the PowerPoint slide rather then embedding it. Select the Insert drop-down arrow in the in the Insert Video dialog box and select Link to File.

Modifying Video Clips

When the video is selected on the slide, the video tools become available on the Ribbon. The video tools provide two tabs: Format and Playback. The Format tab is shown in Figure 20.16. It has a number of similarities to the Format tab of the picture tools.

Figure 20.16
The Video Tools Format tab.

The Format tab enables you to make adjustments to the video, such as brightness and color corrections. You can also select a style for the video frame from the Video Styles gallery. Commands are also provided that enable you to change the video frame shape's and border settings. The command groups provided on the Video Tools Format tab are as follows:

- **Preview:** This group contains the Play command.

- **Adjust:** The Corrections command enables you to manipulate the brightness and contrast of the video. The Color command actually enables you to recolor the video, so you could create a black-and-white or sepia tone video from your original color video. The Poster Frame command enables you to use a picture file as the "poster" for the video clip so that the audience will see only the poster until you actually play the video. A Reset Design command is also provided in this group for those of you who are overzealous when making adjustments to the video.

- **Video Styles:** This group provides the Video Styles gallery, which provides a number of styles for the video's frame. You can also use the Video Shape, Video Border, and Video Effects to customize the shape, border, and effect settings (such as shadow, glow, and bevel) for the video frame.

- **Arrange:** This group enables you to align or rotate your video and arrange it in a stack with other objects.

- **Size:** The Size group enables you to modify the size of the video box on the slide. More importantly, you can actually crop the video frame (just like a picture) using the Crop command.

PowerPoint provides some powerful capabilities on the Video Tools Format tab, particularly in terms of the adjustments that you can make to the video clip image and the different styles that you can apply to the video framer. The Crop command is pretty much off the charts as far as providing you with a capability that many video-editing software packages don't provide.

 The Video Tools Format tab provides a lot of commands that are very similar to those found on the Picture Tools Format tab. Check out the information beginning on page 527 in Chapter 19 to get more insight into how the Format tab tools are used.

The Video Tools contextual addition to the Ribbon also has a Playback tab. The commands on the Playback tab are related to the actual manipulation of the video itself. You can use the Trim Video command to trim the beginning or end of the video. This enables you to specify a new start or stop point in the video so that you show only the portion of the video clip that is important to your presentation.

The Playback tab also provides the Bookmarks group. You can use the Add Bookmark command to insert bookmarks into the video object. Bookmarks in a video file can be used to trigger animation effects that you have configured on other objects on the slide. For more about triggering animations see "Advanced Animation Techniques" earlier in this chapter.

> **tip**
>
> If you think your audience might want to see the video a second time, select the Rewind After Playing check box in the Video Options group so that the video will be ready to go when you need it.

You can also set fades at both the beginning and the end of the clip using the Fade In and Fade Out commands, respectively. You can also specify that the video be played in full screen mode when you play the presentation as a slide show. Select the Play Full Screen check box in the Video Options group.

You can test any of the playback changes that you make to the video. Use the Play button as needed. If you want to get a better idea of how the changes you have made will appear in an actual slide show, select the Slide Show icon on the PowerPoint status bar to start a slide show from the current slide.

Embedding Web Video Clips

You can also embed video clips onto your PowerPoint slides from popular video websites such as YouTube, Veoh, Yahoo! Video, and LiveLeak. This gives you an incredible number of videos to include on your PowerPoint slides. If you decide to use embedded web video clips, you will need to make sure that you have an Internet connection on the computer that you use to show your PowerPoint presentation as a slide show. Also be aware of the fact that websites can be down and video websites sometimes remove videos from their site. So, although this is a great way to include video in your presentation, there is a chance that it might not work. Certainly don't make it the center of your presentation.

Before you attempt to embed Web video on a slide, make sure that you have the most recent version of Adobe Flash and the Windows Media Player installed on your computer. You can get the Flash player at www.adobe.com and the Windows Media Player from www.microsoft.com.

To embed video from the Web on a PowerPoint slide, you first need to locate the video on a website such as YouTube. You then need to copy the video's embed code to the clipboard. On YouTube videos, the embed code is accessed by selecting the Embed button just below and to the right of the clip's video window. You can use the Copy command on your web browser's edit menu or use Ctrl+C to copy the selected embed code using the keyboard.

After you have the embed code for the video, you can select the Video command on the Insert tab and then select Video from Web Site. This will open the Insert Video from Web Site dialog box as shown in Figure 20.17.

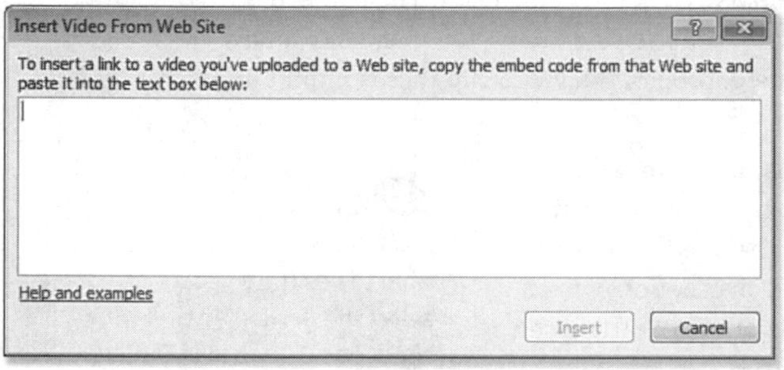

Figure 20.17
The Insert Video from Web Site dialog box.

Paste the video's embed code into the Insert Video from Web Site dialog box by pressing Ctrl+V on the keyboard. You can then click the Insert button to insert the web video onto the slide.

When you select an embedded web video, you will find that all the commands available on the Video Tools Format tab will be available to modify the video frame. You can adjust the video using the Adjust group commands and apply a style to the video frame. You can also crop the video, as needed using the Crop command.

You will probably be disappointed when you switch to the video tools Playback tab; most of the commands available on the tab will be grayed out and are not available when you are working with an embedded web video. You can, however modify the start trigger for the video using the Start command.

DELIVERING A PRESENTATION AND CREATING SUPPORT MATERIALS

After you have created and fine-tuned your presentation, you are ready to show it to your audience. Traditionally, the slide show is a speaker's aid and provides the audience with important points and visuals related to the presentation. PowerPoint, however, also provides you with other possibilities for sharing a presentation with an audience. You can create a self-running presentation, which allows individuals or small groups to view the presentation at a conference booth or in a kiosk setting. PowerPoint also provides you with the ability to show a presentation on the Web, making it easy for anyone who has the URL for the presentation to view it.

There is often more to a presentation than just the slide show itself. It is often expected (by the audience) that you will provide handouts or other supporting material related to the presentation. PowerPoint makes it easy to print handouts and speaker notes for your presentation.

In this chapter, we look at the different ways for showing your presentation to others. We discuss finalizing the presentation and using how to create self-running presentations and presentations for viewing on the Web. We will also look at how to create ancillary materials such as handouts.

Planning Your Presentation

Before we look at some of the aspects of getting a PowerPoint presentation finalized and ready to deliver as a slide show, I wanted to say a few words about planning your presentation. This isn't related to actually planning the presentation outline and the content but is about preplanning involved in the actual delivery of the presentation.

Even if you have created the most incredible PowerPoint presentation ever seen, you still need to do some planning related to the actual carrying out of your presentation. PowerPoint provides you with a technological edge when you are speaking to your audience, but it won't save you if you don't know some basic facts related to the actual event that will be the occasion for your presentation. I'm talking about the who (or is that whom), what, and where aspects of the event, and so you should probably know the following before finalizing your presentation:

- **Audience:** You need to have a very good idea of who will be in the audience when you give your presentation. This will affect not only the level of the information you are providing but will also, to some degree, dictate the tone of the presentation including your use of slide styles, animations, transitions, and multimedia. For example, if you are a sophisticated engineering project to a neighborhood association, keep the technical aspects of the presentation simple. Likewise consider your audience's visual literacy. A presentation using a lot of bells and whistles, such as animations and multimedia, will be easier to digest for a crowd that is technically attuned to graphics and special effects.

- **Purpose:** You need to have a very good feel for why you are actually giving the presentation. If you are trying to drum up investors for a construction project, the slide show must help sell the need for the project and make it clear to the audience that you have the expertise to execute the project. Remember that most people can remember only a few major points from even a short presentation, so hit the most important information more than once, and provide a solid conclusion that pulls the major concepts together for the audience.

- **Place:** You really need to know some things about the venue where you will give your presentation. If you have included a lot of web hyperlinks and perhaps web videos in your presentation and there is no Internet connection at the site, you are going to have to do a lot of dancing to make up for all that missing information. You really need to be ready for anything; always consider bringing your own laptop. You might also want to have hard copies of the presentation ready in case there is no video projector available or the bulb blew before just you were to take the stage. Oh, and don't count on there being any kind of speaker system that you can tie in to take advantage of sound during your presentation.

So, your presentation has to be tailored for the audience and the venue. It also needs to have an extremely clear purpose (clear to the audience, not just you). Remember that you can hope to make only a few main points; any more than that and the audience will be bordering on overload. Reaffirm your main points in the conclusion of the presentation.

As both a speaker and attendee at a multitude of educational and technical conferences, I have seen a nearly endless list of things that can go wrong with a presentation actually go wrong, so it is important that you be ready for any eventuality. Spend some time both planning the delivery of your presentation and trying to anticipate some of the potential problems you might face. Doing so will make the actual presentation go so much more smoothly.

Checking the Presentation for Spelling and Grammar Errors

Making sure that your presentation slides are free of spelling and grammatical errors is important in terms of protecting the veracity of the information in the presentation. If you have obvious spelling errors, for example, it is going to be hard for the audience to take you seriously. You are probably familiar with the Spelling and Grammar features in Microsoft Word and the fact that they flag spelling and grammar errors automatically: red wavy lines for spelling errors, green wavy lines for grammar errors.

PowerPoint does provide the Spelling feature but doesn't provide the Grammar checking that you would find in Word. So, spelling errors will be flagged in PowerPoint (the red wavy line) but errors of a grammatical nature will not.

> **note**
>
> Use the thesaurus to find synonyms for specific words on your slides. You can also translate slide text using the Translate command in the Language group.

So, you might be thinking that the fact that PowerPoint doesn't check for grammar errors is no big deal because most text on PowerPoint slides is either titles or bulleted items, which might actually consist of sentence fragments (that would be flagged by the Grammar feature if PowerPoint had one). And you would probably be right in most cases. However, if you are going to have any lengthy text paragraphs on your PowerPoint slides, I suggest that you type these text items in Word and then copy and paste the information onto the PowerPoint slide. This allows Word to check the copy for any grammar issues.

In terms of spelling errors, you might also be rather complacent because PowerPoint (by default) flags misspellings. However, due to the fact that each slide is a separate entity and visually checking slides is a little different from checking pages in a Word document, I would suggest that you run the Spelling feature when you are finishing up the presentation. The Spelling command is on the ruler's Review tab.

In terms of using the Spelling feature to greatest effect, you might want to enable contextual spelling in the PowerPoint proofing options. Contextual spelling will flag errors such as when you use the word *there* and should have used the word *their*. Because PowerPoint text is usually short bulleted fragments, it can be fairly easy to make a contextual error, which will not normally be flagged by the Spelling feature.

To enable contextual spelling, select File on the Ribbon to enter the PowerPoint Backstage. Then select Options. Doing so will open the PowerPoint Options window. Select Proofing to view the various proofing settings. Figure 21.1 shows the PowerPoint Options window and the various proofing settings.

In the bottom of the proofing options are three check boxes related to spelling in PowerPoint. Make sure that the Check Spelling as You Type check box is enabled. Then click the Use Contextual Spelling check box to enable it. The Spelling feature will now flag contextual spelling problems as you type. Right-click on a spelling error to view a list of possible solutions (as you would for any misspelled word).

 For more general information about the Spelling feature in Office applications, see page 188 in Chapter 7, "Enhancing Word Documents."

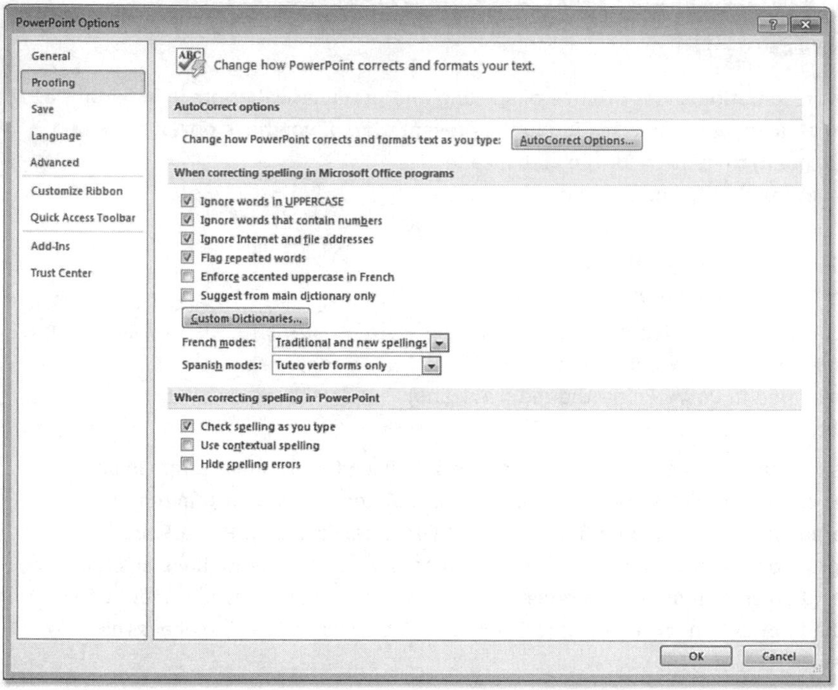

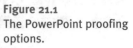

Figure 21.1
The PowerPoint proofing options.

Running Through a Completed Presentation

Before you show your presentation to an audience, you should run through it several times, checking that the slides are in the right order and that the animations that you have added to objects and the transitions you have assigned to slides work correctly (particularly in cases where you have assigned triggers or timings to animations or transitions). Running through the presentation also enables you to practice the speech that you will give as you show the slides.

The Slide Show tab of the Ribbon provides all the commands you will need to run through your presentation; there are even options for the use of multiple monitors and a command for setting the resolution of the slide show. If you know that you are going to be using a large screen or a video projector that has a specific resolution (particularly when it is other than your computer's monitor), you might want to specify the resolution using the Resolution command on the Slide Show tab. This enables you to view the slide show at the resolution that will be available when you show it to your audience.

The Slide Show tab also provides commands that you can use to create custom slide shows, hide slides in a presentation, and record slide show timings for a self-running show. We discuss a number of these possibilities later in this chapter. Figure 21.2 shows the Slide Show tab.

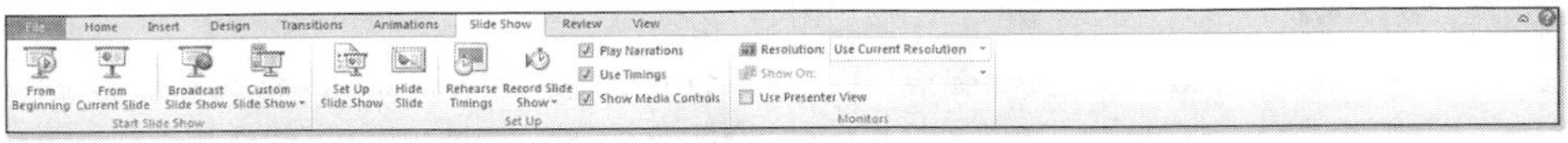

Figure 21.2
The Slide Show tab.

The Start Slide Show group on the Slide Show tab provides you with two commands for starting the slide show. The From Beginning command and the From Current Slide command operate exactly as advertised. You can use either command to fire up your slide show depending on whether you want to start from the beginning or the slide you are currently editing.

After you start the slide show (from the commands on the Slide Show tab or the Slide Show button provided in the View shortcuts on the status bar), you typically click the mouse as needed to advance through the slides. If you have set timings for slides via slide transitions, you can sit back and practice your narration as the slides change automatically (we talk more about setting slide timings later in the chapter).

> **tip**
>
> To access a "laser pointer" during the slide show, hold down the Ctrl key and press the left mouse button.

In terms of navigating the slide show itself, PowerPoint also provides you with some easy-to-access tools when you are in the Slide Show view. When you move the mouse over the bottom left area of the current slide, you will find a collection of four tools. From left to right, these tools are as follows:

- **Previous:** The Previous arrow can be used to quickly return to the previous slide.

- **Pointer Menu:** A Pen icon is provided that enables you to change the mouse pointer into a pen or highlighter. You can use it to write on a slide or highlight information on a slide.

- **Menu:** A Menu icon provides you with a menu that enables you to move between the slides using commands such as Next, Previous, and Last Viewed. Commands are also provided that enable you to go to a specific slide or section in the presentation. You can use the Screen submenu to "black" or "white" the screen—doing so enables you to hide the current slide while you answer a question or make other comments.

- **Next:** The Next arrow can be used to advance to the next slide in the presentation.

You can also access all these different command options from a shortcut menu that is provided when you right-click on a slide. This is the same menu that you can activate from the Menu icon provided with the Slide Show tools except that it includes the pointer options, including the pen and highlighter. So, you might find that shortcut menu even more convenient than the Slide Show tools.

You can stop the slide show at any time by pressing the Esc key or by selecting End Show on either the shortcut menu or the Slide Show menu that you can access when in the Slide Show view. When you have completed the slide show, a black screen will appear. Click the mouse to exit the screen and return to the PowerPoint workspace.

Using Hidden Slides

At the outset of this chapter we discussed the fact that you need to anticipate potential problems when you actually deliver your presentation. You also need to anticipate, as much as possible, what type of additional information your audience might request during your presentation. For example, if you show a chart on a slide, someone in the audience might ask you about the raw data that the chat is based on. Even though you didn't originally plan on showing the actual data during the presentation, wouldn't it be great if you already had the data arranged in an easy-to-read table on an available slide? This is where hidden slides come in. These are slides that you prepare in anticipation of audience questions or follow up that you might want to make on your topic if you have extra time at the end of your presentation. The sides are saved in the presentation but are hidden, however, and aren't shown when you run the presentation as a slide show.

 tip

To unhide a slide or slides, select the slide or slides and then click the Hide Slide command a second time.

The Hide Slide command is housed on the Ribbon's Slide Show tab in the Set Up group. You can hide a slide or slides when you are working in the Normal view or in the Slide Sorter. To hide slides in either the Slides tab of the Slides/Outline pane or in the Slide Sorter, select the slide or slides (select the first slide and then hold down the Ctrl key to select subsequent slides). Select the Hide Slide command to hide the slide or slides.

A hidden slide is marked as hidden by a box with a diagonal slash through it on the slide's number (which you can see in both the Normal view and the Slide Sorter). The slide or slides will still remain in the presentation; however, hidden slides are not shown during a slide show. Figure 21.3 shows a presentation in the Slide Sorter. Slides 11 through 15 are marked as hidden.

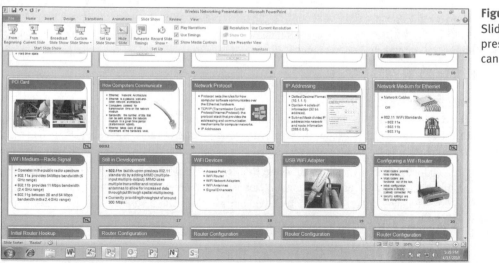

Figure 21.3
Slides in the presentation can be hidden.

Hidden slides can be anywhere in the presentation. You don't necessarily have to group them. You might like to keep them in sequence with slides that cover similar information. However, just to keep your presentation slides organized, particularly in cases where you have a lot of slides in the presentation, you might want to create a section in your presentation that houses all the hidden slides that you might take advantage of during your slide show. That way the hidden slides aren't mixed in with the rest of the slides.

To access a hidden slide during a slide show, right-click on the current slide in the show. A shortcut menu will appear. On the shortcut menu, point at Go to Slide. A list of all the slides in the presentation will appear, including the hidden slides. Figure 21.4 shows the slide list available during the slide show.

Figure 21.4
The Slide Show shortcut menu provides a list of all the presentation slides.

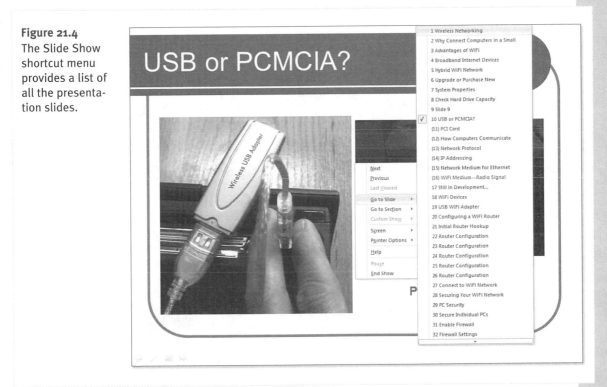

Hidden slides will have parentheses around the slide number. To access a particular hidden slide, select the slide in the list.

Note that the shortcut menu available during a slide show also provides a Go to Section choice. This would enable you to go to a section of hidden slides, if you happened to have placed all the hidden slides in the same section. This is just food for thought, but keeping all the hidden slides in the same section enables you to more easily access and show these slides when required.

Creating a Custom Slide Show

There is an option on the Slide Show tab for creating a custom slide show. The Custom Slide Show command enables you to take a subset of your current presentation and designate it as a custom show. This would enable you to take a lengthy presentation that you have created and create shorter presentations from the contents. For example, you might have given a two-hour presentation at a conference and now want to break the presentation into two one-hour custom shows that you can give as lunch-time seminars. You can create any number of custom shows from a PowerPoint presentation.

To create a custom slide show, select Custom Slide Show on the Slide Show tab and then select Custom Shows. The Custom Shows dialog box will open as shown in Figure 21.5.

Figure 21.5
The Custom Shows dialog box.

The Custom Shows dialog box enables you to create new custom shows and to modify existing custom shows, which will appear in the Custom Shows list after you create them. To create a new custom show, select the New button. The Define Custom Show dialog box will appear as shown in Figure 21.6.

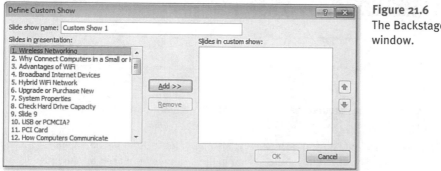

Figure 21.6
The Backstage Save and Send window.

All the slides in the presentation are listed in the Sides in Presentation list. To add a slide to the custom show, select the slide and then click the Add button. You can select multiple slides by using the Ctrl key or the Shift key (to select a series of slides) and the mouse. Slides added to the custom show will be listed in the Slides in Custom Show list.

When you have specified the slides for the custom show, click in the Slide Show Name text box and type a name for the custom show. To create the custom show and return to the Custom Shows dialog box, select OK. The new custom show will be listed in the Custom Shows dialog box.

You can edit a custom show by selecting the show in the Custom Shows dialog box and then clicking Edit. This will open the Define Custom Show dialog box and you can use the Add and/or Remove buttons to add additional slides to the custom show or remove slides from the show. You can also use the Move Up or Move Down arrows to reorder the slides in the Slides in Custom Show list.

The Custom Shows dialog box also provides you with the ability to remove a custom show or copy a custom show. Making a copy of a custom show enables you to add or remove slides from the copy and specify a new name for the copy. This provides a very quick way to take an existing custom show and repurpose it.

When you are finished working in the Custom Shows dialog box, select Close. You will be returned to the PowerPoint workspace.

 tip

You can also run a custom show as a slide show from the Custom Shows dialog box. Select the show in the Custom Shows list and then select Show.

You will find that the custom show or shows that you create for a presentation will be listed on the menu that is provided when you select the Custom Slide Show command. To show a custom show as a slide show, select the custom show's name on the menu. The custom show will begin to play. The custom show performs in the Slide Show view the same as any other PowerPoint presentation; any settings that you assigned to the slides in the original presentation that are part of the custom show, including animations and transitions, will be in force during the showing of the custom show.

Creating a Self-Running Presentation

A self-running presentation means different things to different people. For example, you might want to create a self-running slide show that advances each slide after a specified period. You, however, plan to provide the narration that accompanies the slides in person. So, you are configuring the slides with timings because you want to concentrate on your speech rather than changing the slides in the slide show. This scenario requires that you spend time practicing the presentation so that the slides don't get ahead of you or you don't get ahead of your slides as you deliver the narrative.

Another type of self-running presentation is a presentation that will run at a tradeshow booth or in a kiosk. A live speaker does not accompany this type of self-running show, so you will want to record the narration that go with the slides as part of the presentation. There are also options for this unaccompanied self-running show; you might allow a user (such as an interested customer) to browse the presentation interactively (which we discuss in the next section) or the presentation can loop continuously. The Ribbon's Slide Show tab provides you with the commands that you can use to set up the type of show you are running and to add timings. There is also an option for recording the entire slide show, which will create the timings and can also record narration. This option can also record your use of the mouse pointer during the recorded slide show.

Setting Up the Slide Show

You can specify settings for the slide show including the show type, the slides shown during the slide show, the selection of a custom show, and other options related to the slide show, such as how the slides are advanced and the pen and/or laser pointer color you want to use. The Set Up Show dialog box is opened by selecting the Set Up Slide Show command in the Set Up group. Figure 21.7 shows the Set Up Slide Show dialog box.

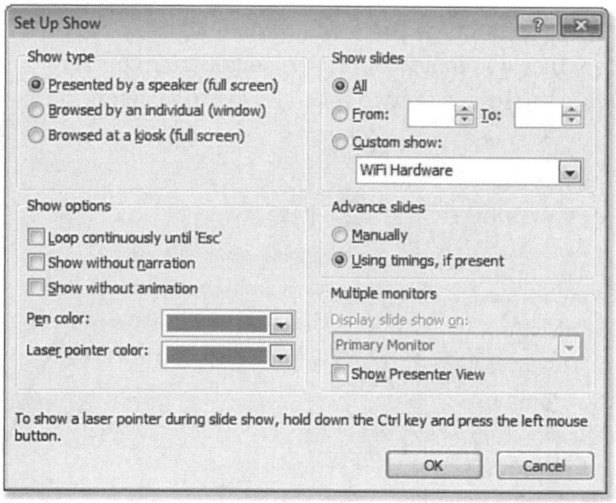

Figure 21.7
The Set Up Show dialog box.

Specify the show type by selecting one of the type option buttons provided. The default show type is Presented by a Speaker (Full Screen). If you are setting up a self-running show, you can specify either the Browsed by an Individual (Window) or Browsed at a Kiosk (Full Screen) option.

Show options are also provided and enable you to loop the show continuously, turn off the animation, or turn off any animation in the presentation. When you select Browsed at a Kiosk (Full Screen) as your show type, the Loop Continuously Until "Esc" option is automatically selected. Options are also provided for the pen and laser pointer color (hold down the Ctrl key and press the left mouse button during the slide show to access the laser pointer). The Pen Color option is available only when you are setting up a show that is to be presented by a speaker. Other settings provided in the Set Up Show dialog box enable you to specify the slides to be shown or you can choose from a list of custom shows. You can also specify how the slides should be advanced in the presentation. Using Timings, If Present, is the default setting. This option makes the best sense for self-running presentations unless you want to include action buttons on slides that allow users to interact with the presentation.

 tip

If you are configuring a slide show that you will present and you will have access to multiple monitors, you can select the Presenter View option. This enables you to show the slide show on a specified monitor and view speaker notes and timings on another monitor. This option can be set from the Slide Show tab.

The Set Up Show dialog box also provides you with the ability to specify the monitor to use when you have multiple monitors available (including video projectors). When you have finished setting the options for the slide show, select OK. You will be returned to the PowerPoint workspace.

Rehearsing Timings

If you want to set the timings for a self-running presentation that will not include narration, you can use the Rehearse Timings command on the Slide Show tab. This scenario will work when you want to set the timings for a self-running show that will run in a kiosk or in a case where you want the slides to advance automatically when you are presenting and narrating the slide show. Remember that setting up the timings will not only involve the moving from slide to slide but will also include the timing of animations that you have set for the various objects on the slides. For example, if you have entrance animations configured for objects, particularly bulleted lists, you will need to step through the animation to set the appropriate timing for the animation.

When you are ready to rehearse the timings for the slide show, select the Rehearse Timings command. The slide show will begin. A Recording toolbar will be present in the upper left of the show window as shown in Figure 21.8.

Figure 21.8
The Slide Show window with Recording toolbar.

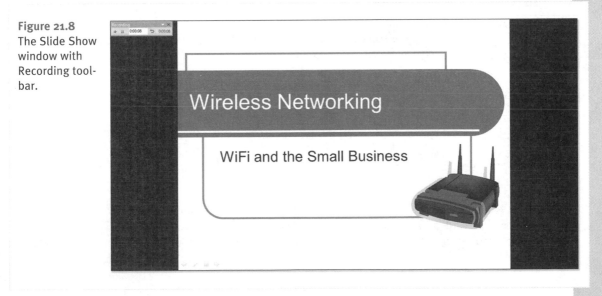

It includes a timing counter that will be timing the slide show. The Recording toolbar also provides a Next button, which works the same as a mouse click in terms of advancing to the next slide or stepping through an animation sequence. A Pause button is also provided that allows you to pause the timer as needed. If you want to reset the timer for a particular slide and start the timing for that slide over, you can click the Repeat button on the Recording toolbar.

After you select the Rehearse Timings command, the clock is ticking, so be ready. Work through the slides as you give your narration if you are setting up timings for a slide show that you will present. When you have completed the slide show, a message box will open providing the total time for the slide show. If you want to keep the slide timings for the show, select Yes; click No if you want to dump the timings and try again.

Recording a Slide Show

You can also record a slide show that has the timings for the slides and animations and includes recorded narration and laser pointer actions. The Record Slide Show command provides you with the ability to record the slide show from the beginning or from the current slide.

The actual recording process is very similar to the process discussed for rehearsing timings as discussed in the previous section. The big difference is that you will be able to record audio (meaning your narration) and record your mouse laser pointer actions as if you were giving the slide show. The recorded show can then be played back as a self-running show. You can use the Set Up Slide Show dialog to configure the slide show to loop continuously.

To start the slide show recording, select the Record Slide Show command and then select Start Recording from Beginning or Start Recording from Current Slide. In both cases the Record Slide Show dialog box will open as shown in Figure 21.9.

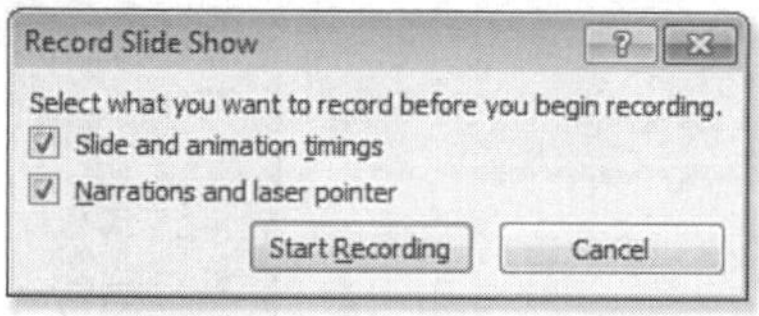

Figure 21.9
The Record Slide Show dialog box.

In this dialog box, you can select options related to what is recorded. By default slide and animation timings are recorded, as are narration and your use of the laser pointer. You can deselect options such as Narrations and Laser Pointer as needed. If you don't record the narration, you are basically doing the same thing that the Rehearse Timings command provided: You are recording the timing for the slide changes and the animation effects on the slides.

When you are ready to begin, select the Start Recording button in the Record Slide Show dialog box. The slide show will start and the Recording toolbar will be present in the upper-left corner of the slide show window. As already mentioned, you can use it to pause the recording or to restart the recording for the current slide as needed.

When you have completed recording the timings, the presentation will open in the Slide Sorter view (the timings are saved automatically, unlike the Rehearse Timings command). The timing for each of the slides will appear just to the left and below each slide in the presentation.

You can clear the timing and/or narration for the currently selected slide or all the slides in the presentation. Select the Record Slide Show command and then point at Clear. Select the appropriate option from the menu provided (such as Clear Timing on Current Slide). If you clear timings and/or narrations on a particular slide, you can then go back to that slide and do the recording over. With the slide selected in the Slide Sorter, select Record Slide Show and then select Start Recording from Current Slide. Select the Start Recording button in the Record Slide Show dialog box.

Record your timing and narration for the slide (including the timing for any animations on the slide). When you have finished with that slide, immediately click the Close button on the Recording toolbar. You will be returned to the Slide Sorter and the new timing will be shown for the slide.

To play your automated slide show, select the From Beginning button on the Slide Show tab. The slide show will play using the timings that you set and will include recorded narration (if you recorded the narration).

Creating an Interactive Presentation

If you are considering creating a slide show for a trade show booth or some other venue where the audience for the show will consist of only one or two people at a time, you might want to provide your audience with the ability to control the show rather than create a self-running show. Obviously, turning control over to your audience is fraught with danger, but you might find that more people are likely to avail themselves of the information in the presentation if they can interact with it rather than just passively standing by and watching it.

You can use action buttons to place different controls on the slides, meaning you place the action button on a slide and a particular action takes place when it is clicked. Action buttons can perform all sorts of different actions. PowerPoint provides a number of premade controls, including buttons that enable you to go back or forward and buttons that enable you to play a movie or a sound. There is also a custom action button that can be configured to meet your particular needs, such as moving to a particular slide in the slide show, running an application, or running a macro that you have recorded.

> *Macros are discussed in Appendix B, "Office Macros." For more information about enabling and recording macros see page 881.*

The use of action buttons on slides is certainly not limited to slide shows where you want to provide the audience interactive capabilities. You can use action buttons on slide shows that you will actually present. They can make it convenient for you to go back to a particular slide or open another application as you show your slides.

The action buttons are actually part of the shape library provided by the Shape gallery on the Ribbon's Insert tab. To insert an action button, follow these steps:

1. In the Normal view, navigate to the slide that will hold the action button.

2. Select the Ribbon's Insert tab.

3. Select the Shapes command in the Illustrations group. The Shapes gallery will open as shown in Figure 21.10.

Figure 21.10
The Shapes gallery, including the action buttons.

4. Select an action button from the Action Buttons section of the Shapes gallery. The mouse pointer will become a drawing tool.

5. Drag the drawing tool on the slide to create the action button shape. The Action Settings dialog box will appear.

6. You can set up the action settings for the action button so that a mouse click or a mouse over activates them. A single action button can actually do one action on a mouse click and then do a second action on a mouse over. Select the dialog box tab you want to configure based on how you want the action to be activated (the settings on the Mouse Click and Mouse Over tabs of the dialog box are the same).

7. Specify the action for the action button by using the option buttons on the dialog box tab that you selected.

8. When you have finished setting the options for the action button, select OK. You will be returned to the slide in the Normal view.

> 🔍 **note**
>
> Action buttons are just like any other shape or object you place on a slide. You can move them, size them, or delete them as necessary.

To test your action button, select the Slide Show shortcut on the status bar to start the slide show from the current slide. Click on the action button to see whether you get the expected results. You can add multiple action buttons to a particular slide if needed. In cases where you want to set up the same action buttons on all your slides, such as Backward and Forward Action buttons for navigation of the slide show, you will want to place the action buttons on the slide master for the presentation.

➡ *The slide master is discussed in Chapter 18, "Advanced Presentation Formatting, Themes, and Masters." See page 517 for more information.*

Broadcasting a Slide Show on the Web

When we think of content for the Web, we typically think of HTML and the fact that we will have to either convert whatever type of content that we are working with to HTML or otherwise format the content so that it can be viewed on a web page. PowerPoint 2010 makes it extremely easy for you to stream a slide show to a web URL, which any number of online participants can access. Your audience does not require any special software but can view the slide show in a web browser.

The broadcast of your slide show is handled by the PowerPoint Broadcast Service, which is a service provided by Microsoft to users of PowerPoint 2010. For you to take advantage of the service, you will need to have a Windows Live ID (meaning an MSN or Hotmail account).

To open the Broadcast Slide Show dialog box, select the Broadcast Slide Show command on the Ribbon's Slide Show tab. The Broadcast Slide Show dialog box provides you with information related to the broadcast service, which you can read if you choose. To start the broadcast, click the Start Broadcast button.

You will be connected to the broadcast service and the slide show will be prepared for broadcast. A link will appear in the Broadcast Slide Show dialog box as shown in Figure 21.11.

Figure 21.11
A web link will be created for the slide show broadcast.

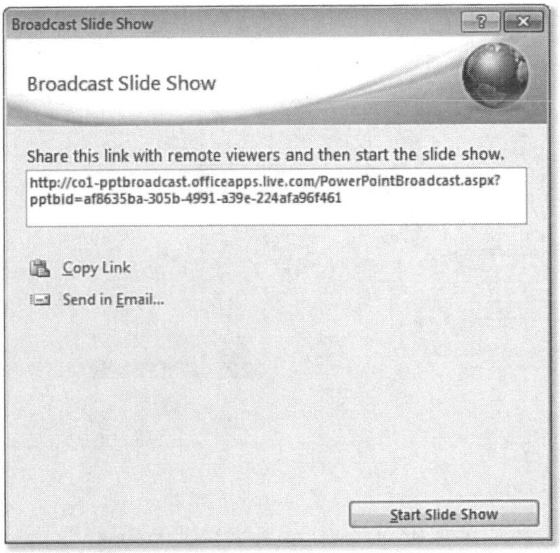

Broadcast Slide Show

Broadcast Slide Show

Share this link with remote viewers and then start the slide show.

http://co1-pptbroadcast.officeapps.live.com/PowerPointBroadcast.aspx?
pptbid=af8635ba-305b-4991-a39e-224afa96f461

Copy Link
Send in Email...

Start Slide Show

You need to share that link with your audience. You can copy the link and then paste it in an email or onto a page that you place on a website (which you can create in Word or other web design tool). The dialog box also provides a command to send the link via your default email client. When you click Send in Email, a new email message will open (in Outlook if it is your default email client). The subject for the message will be "View my PowerPoint Broadcast" and the link will be provided in the body of the email message. You can add the email addresses of the audience to the message as needed.

One other thing that you should consider related to the slide show broadcast: You probably don't want to broadcast the slide show forever. So, you should make it clear in the invitation message when you will begin broadcasting and when you will end broadcasting. It does make sense to loop the presentation and run it as an automated slide show at least a few times during the scheduled broadcast. This should allow most of your invitees to view the content.

After you have sent the web link for the broadcast, you can start the slide show. Click the Start Slide Show button in the Broadcast Slide show dialog box. The presentation will open in the Slide Show view. You can show your presentation and your online audience can follow along. The slide show can be a manual slide show (where you advance the slides) or you can set up an automated slide show that loops.

When you end the slide show, you will find that you are still in the Broadcast view and that a Broadcast tab is available on the Ribbon, as shown in Figure 21.12. There is also a Broadcast View message at the top of the slide pane that lets you know that you cannot make changes to the presentation while you are in Broadcast view.

Figure 21.12
The Broadcast view and the Ribbon's Broadcast tab.

The Broadcast tab provides commands for starting the slide show and changing the resolution of the slide show. A Send Invitations command is also provided so that you can send additional invitations to the broadcast.

When you have finished broadcasting the slide show, select the End Broadcast command on the Ribbon. A message box will open, letting you know that remote viewers will be disconnected if you end the broadcast. Select End Broadcast in the message box. You will be returned to the Normal view.

Working with the Notes and Handouts Masters

Although we typically think of PowerPoint presentations as slide shows, there are ancillary printed materials that can be created from your PowerPoint presentations: notes and handouts. Notes are basically the script that you create to go with the slide show. You might create notes that provide only a very general framework of information that helps you remember facts or other key points that you have not included as content on the slides, or you might create very detailed notes for some presentations. For example, you might be creating training materials that include a PowerPoint presentation and you want to include a detailed script for use by the trainers who will actually give the presentation to your employees or clients.

Handouts, on the other hand, are for the audience. Handouts make it easier for your audience to follow the presentation and perhaps take notes of their own. You can print out handouts to provide a hard copy of each slide, and the number of slides printed on each page of the handout can range from one to nine slides.

PowerPoint provides masters for both your notes and your handouts. The master enables you to determine whether header or footer information is included on the handout or note pages. Additional options are also provided for the handouts and notes, such as the slides per page (in the case of handouts) and the size of the slides or notes area (on the note pages).

> **🔍 note**
>
> It is always hard to determine whether you should distribute your presentation handouts before or after the presentation. Sometimes handouts can be a distraction and you will find that the audience is more absorbed with reading the handouts than watching your presentation. You will have to decide what works best for you.

You can access the master for either your handouts or notes on the Ribbon's view tab. The Handout Master and the Notes Master commands are in the Master Views group.

Setting Handout Master Options

To access the handout master, select the Handout Master command on the View tab. The Handout Master tab will appear on the Ribbon as shown in Figure 21.13.

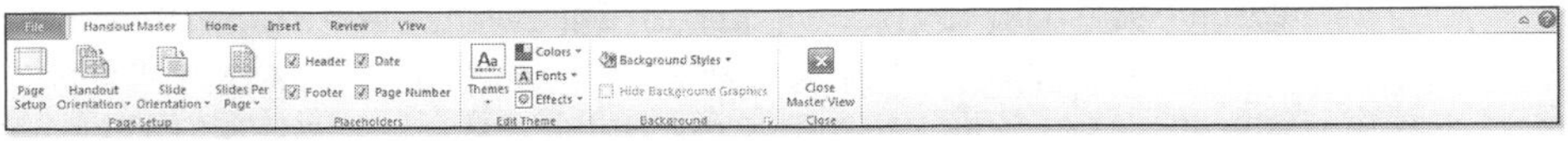

Figure 21.13
The Handout Master tab.

You can configure page settings, determine the placeholders on the handout master, and set a theme or background for the handouts. The Handout Master tab provides the following groups:

- **Page Setup:** This group provides commands that enable you to set up the page size using the Page Setup dialog box. It also provides commands for changing the handout orientation from portrait to landscape. You can also change the slide orientation on the page and select the number of slides to show on each page. You can select from one to nine slides per page or provide an outline view of the slides on the page.

- **Placeholders:** This group is a set of check boxes that enable you to determine whether a header or footer appears on the page. Options are also provided for the inclusion of the date and page numbering.

- **Edit Theme:** You will find that the choices in the Theme gallery are grayed. Because the actual design of the slides printed in the handout depends on the theme you set for the presentation, you won't have access to these commands when working on the handout master.

- **Background:** You can specific a background for the handout pages by using the Background Styles gallery.

- **Close:** This group provides one command: Close Master View. Click this view when you want to return to the Normal view.

For the header and the footer text, placeholder text is provided. You can select this text and then replace it as needed to insert header and footer information onto the handout master. When you finish working with the master, select Close Master View.

Setting Notes Master Options

To access the Notes Master from the View tab, select Notes Master. The Notes Master tab will appear on the Ribbon. The Notes Master tab provides the same command groups provided by the Handout Master tab.

You can use the Page Setup commands to change the page setup and also to change the page and slide orientation as needed. The Placeholders group holds a number of check boxes that enable you to determine what appears in the header and footer areas on the page such as the date and page number.

 note

If you are creating printed notes for yourself, you might not even want to bother fiddling with the Notes Master. Notes, after all, are just notes. In cases where you are distributing the notes to other speakers, you might want to take the time to make the notes look a little more formal.

The slide and notes text box on the Notes Master can also be manipulated. For example, if you want the slide to take up less space on the master, you can select the slide box and size or move the slide as needed. You can then expand the notes area as needed.

By default the master text box is configured to include a five-level outline. You can select the text in the master text box and then change it using the various font and paragraph commands available on the Home tab. You can also select the Format tab of the drawing tools (which appears when you select the text box) and change settings as needed. When you have completed setting the options for the notes master, select Close Master View on the Notes Master tab.

Printing Presentations, Notes, and Handouts

You can print the slides in your presentation as needed. You can also print your speaker notes and print handouts for your audience. The printing of these various items is accomplished from the PowerPoint Backstage. To access the Backstage, select File on the Ribbon. To access the Print window, select Print. The Print window will open as shown in Figure 21.14.

Figure 21.14
The Backstage
Print window.

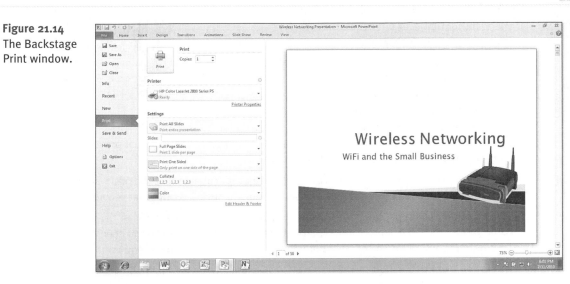

You can specify the number of copies you want to print, and specify the printer and its properties for the print job. The Settings area of the window lists the various options related to printing your presentation slides.

By default all sides will be printed. You can change this setting to print the current slide or you can specify a custom range in the Slides box. For example, you can specify a range such as 1–23 or specify slides that are not in a range by using commas—for example, 2, 5, 8, and so forth.

By default full page slides print with one slide per page. This is unfortunate because this is the last thing that you would probably want to print. To change this setting, select the arrow to the right of the Full Page Slides setting. The Print Layout gallery will appear as shown in Figure 21.15.

Figure 21.15
The Print
Layout gallery.

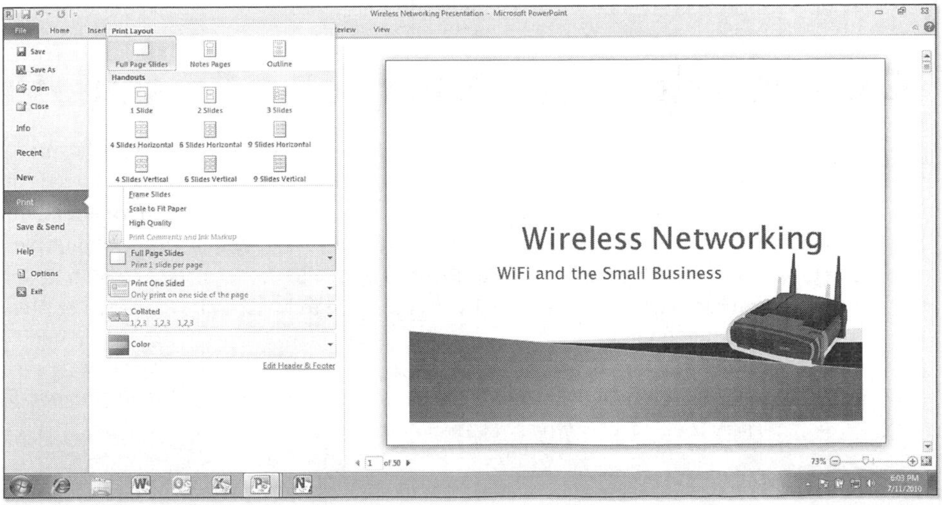

You can choose a number of different layouts for the printout. If you want to print your notes, select the Notes Page layout. There is also an Outline layout provided for printing the presentation as an outline.

When printing out handouts, you are provided with a number of different layouts, which enable you to specify the number of slides that are printed on each page. You can also select special options related to the printout, such as Frame Slides (a frame prints around each slide), Scale to Fit Paper, and High Quality (which provides a printout of the highest quality provided by your printer).

> **tip**
>
> Select the Edit Header & Footer link at the bottom of the Print window if you want to edit the header and/or footer for the printout.

After you determine the layout for the printout, you can specify whether the printout should be printed one sided or on both sides of the paper (when you have a printer that provides this option).

If you are printing multiple copies of the printout, you can also specify whether the print job should be collated or uncollated. An orientation drop-down menu also enables you to specify the orientation for the printout. Portrait is the default, but you can switch to landscape if required.

There is one more option that you might want to take advantage of depending on the printer you are using and whether you are going to make grayscale copies of your printout. The Color menu enables you to specify Color, Grayscale, or Pure Black and White for your printout. The Color setting is pretty straightforward. There are some differences between the Grayscale and Pure Black and White settings, however.

These two noncolor settings print text, fill, lines, clip art, and slide backgrounds exactly the same. In terms of shadows and charts, however, the Grayscale setting will use grayscale to print these items whereas the Black and White setting will use black for the shadows and white for charts. So, in most cases, particularly when you have a laser printer that provides excellent print density, you might want to go with a grayscale printout. You can always print a slide page as a test using the Grayscale setting and then the Pure Black and White setting to determine the best setting for your particular printer.

When you have finished setting the options for your printout, click the Print button in the Print window. Your printout will be sent to your printer.

Collaborating with Others on a Presentation

You can also collaborate with colleagues and co-workers as you build your PowerPoint presentations. If you work on a corporate network that provides network shares, a PowerPoint presentation can be edited as needed by different users on the network. An even more effective sharing strategy is sharing a presentation via a Microsoft SharePoint server, which enables multiple users to work on the presentation at the same time. For those of you who do not have access to a SharePoint server, presentation files can also be shared by saving a file to Microsoft's SkyDrive or files can be shared via email as attachments.

 An overview related to sharing files is provided in Chapter 3, "Managing and Sharing Office Files." See page 71 for more information.

The Save & Send window in the PowerPoint Backstage provides you with different strategies for sharing your presentation files with other users. To access the Backstage, select File on the Ribbon and then select Save & Send. Figure 21.16 shows the Save & Send window.

Figure 21.16
The Backstage Share window.

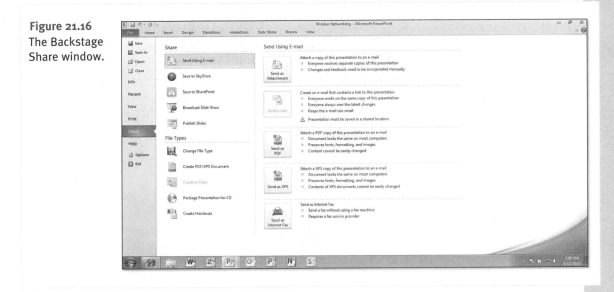

Options for pretty much any network or connectivity scenario are provided in the Save & Send window. The options are as follows:

- **Send Using E-mail:** You can send the presentation file as an attachment or send it as a noneditable PDF or XPS file. If you send the presentation as an attachment, other users can make changes to the presentation. You can then compare the different versions to your original file using the Compare command (and accompanying commands in the Compare group) on the Review tab of the Ribbon. This would enable you to accept or reject changes based on the comparison.

- **Save to Web:** You can save the presentation to a shared folder on your SkyDrive, such as the Public share, so that other users can access the presentation file online.

- **Save to SharePoint:** You can save the presentation to a SharePoint server deployed on your network. Multiple users can edit the presentation simultaneously and you can actually retrieve previous versions of the presentation if necessary. Files saved to a SharePoint server can also be edited using Microsoft web apps when the actual application (such as PowerPoint) is not installed on a user's computer.

- **Broadcast Slide Show:** You can broadcast the slide show via the Web to anyone who has an Internet connection and a web browser. Broadcasting slide shows was discussed earlier in this chapter.

- **Publish Slides:** This option enables you to publish your slides to a shared location such as a SharePoint site. This allows multiple users to use and edit the slides. When you choose to publish slides in the presentation, the Publish Slides dialog box enables you to specify the slides that should be shared.

The Save & Send window also provides you with the ability to change the file type for your current presentation, quickly create handouts and package a presentation on a CD. When you create the CD, any linked or embedded object such as videos or sounds will be included on the CD. So, this option provides you with the ability to get the whole presentation on a CD and either mail it to a recipient or use it when you are traveling.

REQUISITE OUTLOOK: CONFIGURATION AND ESSENTIAL FEATURES

Outlook has been the Office suite's personal information manager for many years. It provides you with the ability to communicate with others and also to catalog appointments, tasks, and other information that helps you to stay organized and productive.

Outlook has gone through quite a transformation in the last couple of versions of Office and is now better than ever. In this chapter we look at some of the new enhancements found in Outlook 2010. We also look at the configuration of Outlook, including information on profiles and data files.

As the introductory material to the Outlook section of this book, we also get you up to speed with navigating the Outlook application environment. How to organize Outlook items using categories, importing/exporting data, and the use of the new Backstage Print window are also discussed.

Introducing Outlook 2010

Microsoft Outlook differs from the other standard Microsoft Office 2010 member applications, such as Word and Excel, in that does not create a single type of file such as a Word document or an Excel workbook. Outlook is actually multifaceted in terms of the different types of information it can manage. Although many of us think of Outlook as our email client, it really is so much more; it can serve as a multipurpose management tool where you can work with all sorts of information. Outlook enables you to create and manage a number of different items, such as emails, appointments, meetings, tasks, and contacts.

Outlook 2010 has a number of new enhancements that make it an even better personal information manager. One of the major changes in Outlook 2010 is that it completely adopts the Office Fluent user interface. The Ribbon now serves as the command interface in the Outlook window no matter what type of Outlook items you are working with. This change standardizes the overall layout of the Outlook window with the other Office 2010 applications. The logical grouping of commands on Ribbon tabs also makes it easier for you to find commands when you need them.

You will find that the Outlook Ribbon behaves exactly as the Ribbon does in other Office applications, such as Word or Excel. You can minimize and restore the Ribbon using the buttons on its right side (next to the Help button). You might find it useful to minimize the Ribbon in Outlook to free up workspace in the application window; you can still select a Ribbon tab, such as Home, and the Home tab and its associated command groups will appear in the Outlook window. When you click anywhere else (other than the Ribbon) in the Outlook window, such as the Mail pane or the Reading pane, the Ribbon will minimize again.

Outlook 2010 provides a number of other minor (and one or two major) improvements. A number of these enhancements related to managing email messages, whereas others improve Outlook's overall functionality. The list that follows highlights some of these changes and improvements:

note

Outlook 2010 also takes advantage of changes that were made to Outlook 2007. You will be able to take advantage of the Instant Search box that allows you to quickly search a folder such as your Inbox or Sent Items; you can use color-coded categories to help you manage Outlook items; and can immediately access your to do list in the To Do bar without opening the Tasks pane.

tip

If you don't like using the minimized Ribbon and want the Ribbon tab commands to show in the Outlook window as you work, select the Pin button on the right of the Ribbon to pin the Ribbon to the application window.

- **Conversation View:** Outlook 2007 first introduced the concept of viewing email messages by conversation. A conversation includes all messages with the same subject. Outlook 2010 enhances the conversation view by enabling you to see an entire conversation no matter what folders contain the messages that are part of it. This makes it possible for you to more easily view your responses that are part of the conversation.

- **Ignore Command:** This command, which is in the Home tab's Delete group, is used to ignore the conversation that includes the currently selected message, meaning that the selected message and all current and future messages in the same conversation will be moved to the Deleted Items folder.

- **Clean Up Command:** This command can clean up a conversation by moving older messages in the conversation to the Deleted Items folder. You can also use the Clean Up command to clean up a folder of messages and a folder including subfolders.

- **Forgotten Subjects:** When you attempt to send a message that does not include a subject, a message box opens, offering you the option of not sending this message. This gives you a second chance to add a subject to the message. Subjects are important if you want to be able to manage the email as part of a particular conversation.

- **Multiple Exchange Accounts:** You can configure Outlook to use multiple Exchange accounts. You will be able to access these accounts from a single Outlook profile. In the past, a different profile was required for each Exchange account.

- **IMAP Improvements:** Outlook 2010 makes it easier for you to set up IMAP (Internet Message Access Protocol) email such as Google Gmail. IMAP email accounts also now have a separate Deleted Items folder.

Our coverage of Outlook will explore other improvements. This will enable you to see these Outlook additions and enhancements within the context of their associated Outlook feature or task.

Quick Steps

One of Outlook's newest features, Quick Steps, is worth exploring in more detail. Figure 22.1 shows the Outlook Ribbon with the Home tab selected. The Quick Steps commands are in the Quick Steps group on the Home tab.

Figure 22.1
Quick Steps are housed on the Home tab.

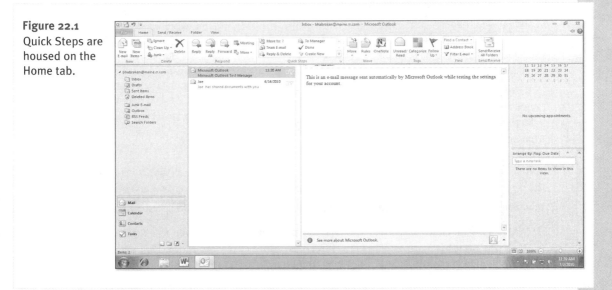

So, the question is this: What are Quick Steps? Quick Steps are commands that combine multiple actions into one click; a Quick Step can be created that will do several things to an item, such as the steps required to complete a particular series of commands, in one click. For example, the Move To: Quick Step (one of the default Quick Steps) enables you to mark an email as read and move it into a particular folder. The Reply & Delete Quick Step opens a reply message for a selected message and, after you have completed and sent your reply, the Quick Step deletes the original message.

Some of the default Quick Steps, such as the Move To and the Done commands, require a brief set up the first time that you select them. For example, if you select a message or messages and then select the Move to Quick Step, the First Time Setup dialog box opens as shown in Figure 22.2.

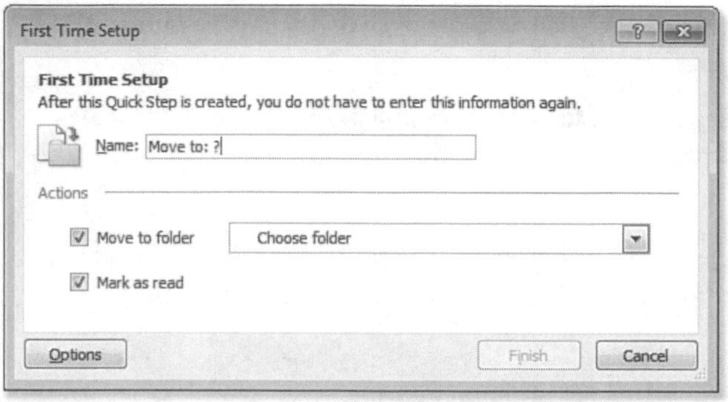

Figure 22.2
A Quick Step's First Time Setup dialog box.

By default this Quick Step moves items to the specified folder and marks them as read. Use the Choose Folder drop-down to specify the folder that the Quick Step should use. The name of the Quick Step changes to the name of the folder that you select. You can, however, change the name as needed in the Name box. When you have finished setting up the Quick Step, click Save.

You aren't limited to the default Quick Steps provided in the Quick Steps group. You can create additional Quick Steps by selecting the dialog box launcher in the Quick Steps group. This opens the Manage Quick Steps dialog box. You can use the dialog box to edit, duplicate, and delete existing Quick Steps. You can also change the order in which the Quick Steps appear in the Quick Steps group. Use the Move Up and Move Down buttons in the Manage Quick Steps dialog box as needed.

You can create your own custom Quick Steps. To create a new Quick Step, follow these steps:

> **tip**
>
> You can add additional actions to a Quick Step. Right-click on the Quick Step on the Ribbon and then select Edit Quick Step. In the Edit Quick Step dialog box use the Add Action button to select an additional action for the Quick Step. You can also assign the Quick Step a shortcut key.

1. In the Manage Quick Steps dialog box, click the New button and then select the type of Quick Step you want to create, such as Move to Folder, Categorize and Move, Flag and Move, and so on. When you select the Quick Step type, the First Time Setup dialog box will appear.

2. Click the Options button in the First Time Setup dialog box to expand the dialog box. This enables you to see the current actions for the Quick Step and provides you the ability to add actions if needed. Figure 22.3 shows the expanded Edit Quick Step dialog box (which is actually the expanded First Time Setup dialog box).

3. Specify options related to the actions. For example, if the action is Move to Folder, select the folder that the mail should move to.

4. If you want to add an action to the Quick Step, click the Add Action button. Then select the action you want to take place (such as Categorize Message or Flag Message) from the Choose an Action drop-down list for the new action.

Figure 22.3
The Edit Quick Step dialog box.

5. (Optional) Select a shortcut key for the Quick Step from the Shortcut key drop-down list.

6. (Optional) Type text in the ToolTip text box (which appears when you hover the mouse over the Quick Step).

7. Type a name for the Quick Step in the Name box.

8. Click the Save button.

Outlook adds the Quick Step to the Quick Step group on the Ribbon's Home tab. You can also edit, duplicate, and delete Quick Steps in the Manage Quick Steps dialog box as needed.

Outlook and Email Accounts

Outlook supports different types of email accounts; you can use Outlook as your email client for an Internet email account from your Internet Service Provider, a Web-based email account such as Microsoft's Hotmail, or a Microsoft Exchange mail account hosted by an Exchange server on your corporate network. In fact, you can configure Outlook to manage multiple (and different types of) email accounts at the same time.

Outlook actually considers email accounts, text messaging, and other communication options such as fax mail as services—and new services can be added to the Outlook configuration at any time. During the initial configuration of Outlook (discussed later in this chapter), you are provided with the opportunity to configure an email account—it's more than an opportunity; Outlook pretty much demands that you set up the account.

 tip

You can delete actions from the Quick Step by clicking the Delete button to the right of the action.

Outlook divides the different email account types into two categories: Internet email and Microsoft Exchange. Figure 22.4 shows the Add New Account window. The email account possibilities include the two Internet email types, POP3 and IMAPand Microsoft Exchange or compatible service.

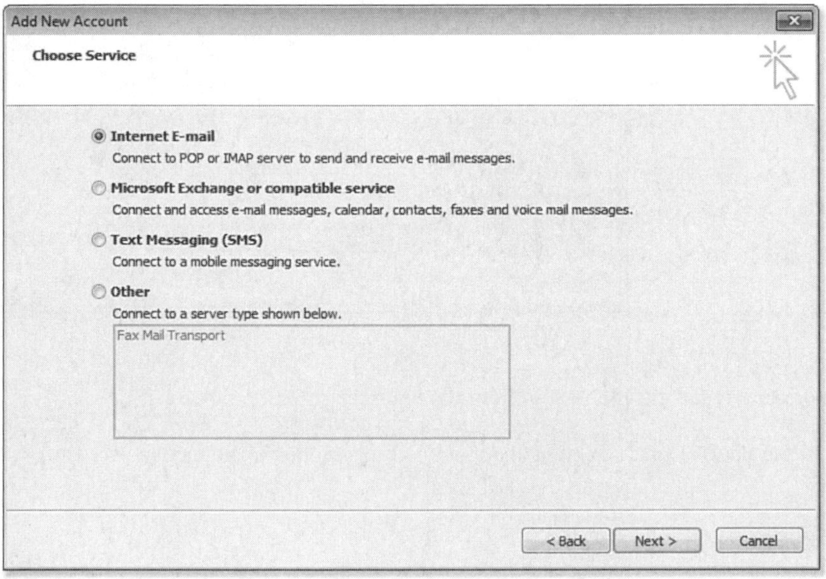

Figure 22.4

Add an email account using the Add New Account window.

The information that follows discusses these two categories of email accounts (Internet and Exchange Server) in more detail. We also look at the Microsoft Outlook Hotmail connector and issues related to adding a Hotmail account to Outlook.

note

You might wonder why I'm not including Web-based, HTTP (Hyper Text Transport Protocol) email accounts such as Microsoft's Hotmail as a type of Internet email account. Outlook 2010 actually uses an add-on service called the Microsoft Outlook Hotmail Connector for your Hotmail accounts. We will discuss the connector later in this section.

Internet Email

Internet email accounts can be either of two different types of email retrieval systems. These email types are based on the protocol used by the email server: POP3 (Post Office Protocol version 3) and IMAP (Internet Message Access Protocol). Outlook supports both of these mail retrieval protocols.

POP3 has been the standard protocol for Internet email for years and Internet Service Providers typically use POP3 on their mail servers. A POP3 email server really functions as a mail drop, meaning that your email is forwarded to the POP3 server and sits there until you connect with your email client (Outlook) and download the mail to your computer. The great thing about POP3 accounts, at least for Internet Service Providers, is that you download your email from their server, meaning you get it off their server and they don't have to store it for you.

If you are using a POP3 account, the Post Office Protocol handles only the receive part of the send-and-receive process for your email. Your ISP will also provide an SMTP (Simple Mail Transport Protocol) server. This server handles the email that you send from Outlook, over the Internet, to a final destination. That destination is typically the POP3 server that serves as the mail drop for the person to whom you are sending the Internet email.

IMAP is a protocol that allows an email client to download email from an IMAP mail server. IMAP differs from POP3 in that connecting to the server with your email client (Outlook) does not remove your email from the mail server. Instead, you receive a list of saved and new messages, which you can then open and read. You can, however, delete messages from the IMAP server.

IMAP is particularly useful when you access one email account on more than one computer or other device (such as a mobile phone or 3G-enabled device). Because the email is not downloaded to the email client as POP3 email is, you can access it on the IMAP sever as needed from different devices.

Email accounts supplied by ISPs and by the popular webmail from Google (Gmail) use IMAP. Although many people access their webmail accounts from a client that functions within their web browser, Outlook's capabilities as an email manager might make it worth your while to add your Gmail account to Outlook's configuration. Obviously, having an email client such as Outlook that can access and manage Internet email accounts using either POP3 or IMAP provides you with a single resource for managing multiple and different types of email accounts.

Exchange Server

No one would deny that Outlook was originally conceived as the client software for Exchange Server accounts. And Outlook really shines when you are connected to an Exchange Server; you can easily share calendars, tasks, meetings, and all sorts of information with other Exchange users.

> **note**
>
> When configuring an IMAP email account you will need to know the incoming mail server and outgoing mail server names.

If you are using Outlook on a corporate network that deploys an Exchange Server, the network administrator will typically set up your account on your computer (this also establishes your profile for you). The name of the Exchange Server and your network username are required to complete the configuration. An Exchange Server network provides several email features that are not available when you use Outlook for Internet email, such as for a POP3 account. For example, you can redirect replies, set message expirations, and even grant privileges to other users who can then monitor your email, calendar, contacts, and tasks.

Configuring different types of email accounts, including Exchange Server accounts, is discussed in Chapter 23, "Managing Email in Outlook," on page 656.

Windows Live Hotmail

When you choose to add an email account to Outlook, you might be surprised to find that Outlook lists Microsoft Exchange, POP3, and IMAP as the three types of email accounts that you can add. What happened to the HTTP email type provided in Outlook 2007 and earlier versions of Outlook? Well, the HTTP mail type was actually limited to Microsoft Webmail products such as Hotmail, so it wasn't like you were going to be able to configure Outlook to serve as the client for just any old Web-based HTTP email account.

Microsoft has dropped that conceit and now configures Hotmail accounts through a separate add-on service called the Microsoft Outlook Hotmail Connector. When you specify that you want to add a Hotmail account to Outlook's configuration, the connector automatically downloads and installs.

Configuring Outlook at First Start

When you run Outlook for the first time, you have the opportunity to configure your email account. When configuring your email account, Outlook also creates a profile that contains your email account information, the location of your data files, and the location where your emails reside. We discuss Outlook profiles in the next section, but it should be made clear at this point that the profile created will be closely associated with the first email account that you create in Outlook. So, if you use Outlook primarily as an Exchange Server client, you will want to configure your Exchange email account as the initial account in Outlook. If you use Outlook as an Internet email client only, configure Outlook at first start for Internet email.

To get this show on the road, select Start, All Programs, Microsoft Office, and then Microsoft Outlook 2010. The Outlook 2010 Startup Wizard opens. The first wizard screen explains that the wizard will guide you through the process of configuring Outlook; this means that it will walk you through the steps of setting up Outlook's initial email account. Click Next to begin the process.

note

You can actually create more than one profile for Outlook. This makes it easy to create one profile for an Exchange Server account and one for Internet email. More about profiles is discussed in the section that follows.

The next wizard screen, the E-Mail Accounts screen, asks whether you would like to configure an email account. This can be an Internet email account, Microsoft Exchange account, or other email account such as a Hotmail account. This screen requests only a yes or no answer. Let's assume that you will configure an email account. Select the Yes option button and then click the Next button.

You can use the next wizard screen, Auto Account Setup, to automatically configure your email account by providing a minimal amount of information. Figure 22.5 shows the Auto Account Setup screen.

On the Auto Account Setup screen, you enter your email account information including your name, email address, and password (twice). Outlook refers to this method of configuring your email account as "Auto" because it relies on Outlook's capability to search the network, including the Internet, for your account information. This allows Outlook to configure the email server settings for your account based on your email address. When you have entered the required information, click the Next button to continue.

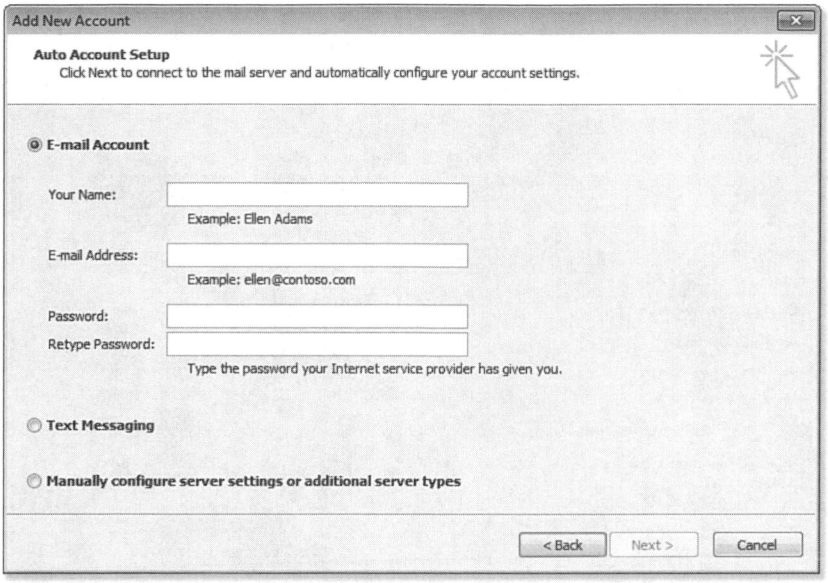

Figure 22.5
Outlook can attempt to automatically set up your email account.

Add New Account

Auto Account Setup
Click Next to connect to the mail server and automatically configure your account settings.

◉ **E-mail Account**

Your Name: [   ]
Example: Ellen Adams

E-mail Address: [   ]
Example: ellen@contoso.com

Password: [   ]
Retype Password: [   ]
Type the password your Internet service provider has given you.

◯ **Text Messaging**

◯ **Manually configure server settings or additional server types**

[< Back] [Next >] [Cancel]

Outlook will establish a network connection and search for the email account's server settings. If you are on a network that has its own Microsoft Exchange Server, the Auto Account Setup will typically be successful. However, in most Exchange Server environments, the network administrator will have set up your Outlook client, profile, and email accounts, so you would not be responsible for Outlook's configuration at first start.

In situations involving Internet email accounts, this online search for your server settings might not work. Outlook is attempting to make an encrypted connection to your mail server to verify your email account. Your ISP's mail server might not be able to deal with the encrypted connection or to verify your server settings based on your email account. Other reasons for this search failing may be due to firewall settings or other connectivity issues.

So, if the Auto Account Setup fails, the wizard will ask you to make sure that you entered the email account information correctly. If you want to take a second shot at communicating with the server, you can have Outlook do another online search (by clicking Next) without trying to establish an encrypted connection to the server. If the unencrypted attempt fails, you need to go to plan B, which is to manually configure the account settings. Select the Manually Configure Server Settings check box in the bottom left of the wizard screen (the screen notes that the online search failed) and then click Next.

The next wizard screen, the Choose Service screen, asks you to select one of the following: Internet E-Mail, Microsoft Exchange, or Text Messaging. Because you are trying to configure an email account that couldn't be automatically set up, let's assume that you are going to select the Internet E-Mail option and then click Next.

Figure 22.6 shows the next wizard screen, Internet E-mail Settings. It requires that you supply user, server, and logon information to configure the account.

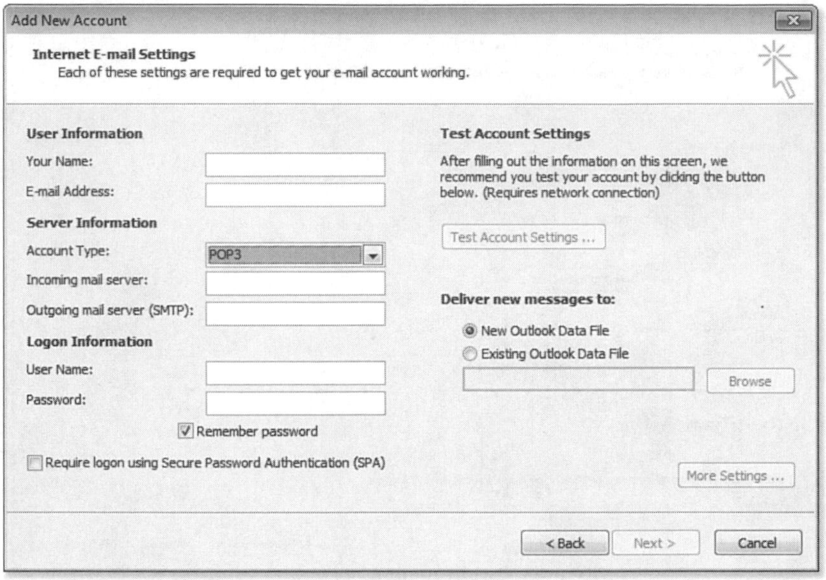

Figure 22.6
You can manually configure your Internet email account.

Add New Account

Internet E-mail Settings
Each of these settings are required to get your e-mail account working.

User Information

Your Name:

E-mail Address:

Server Information

Account Type: POP3

Incoming mail server:

Outgoing mail server (SMTP):

Logon Information

User Name:

Password:

☑ Remember password

☐ Require logon using Secure Password Authentication (SPA)

Test Account Settings

After filling out the information on this screen, we recommend you test your account by clicking the button below. (Requires network connection)

Test Account Settings ...

Deliver new messages to:

◉ New Outlook Data File

○ Existing Outlook Data File

Browse

More Settings ...

< Back   Next >   Cancel

Enter your name, your email address, your username, and your password. Select either POP3 or IMAP as the account type. You also must provide the name of your ISP's POP3 or IMAP server (incoming server) and SMTP server (outgoing server) in the appropriate box.

If your ISP uses Secure Password Authentication, which provides a second layer of authentication for its mail servers, click the Log On Using Secure Password Authentication (SPA). If SPA is used, you receive a second username and password, other than your email username, to log on to the servers. Most ISPs do not use SPA.

You can test your new account settings to make sure that they work. A Test Account Settings dialog box appears. Click Close to close the dialog box.

> ⚠ **caution**
>
> Attempting to configure Internet email accounts using the Auto Account Setup may be a non-starter for you. You might find it easier to just manually configure an Internet email account. All you need to know to manually configure the account are the server names (such as the POP3 and SMTP server names), which are provided to you by your Internet Service Provider.

When you have tested the account settings and are ready to complete the email account creation process, click the Next button. A final screen appears, letting you know that you have provided all the necessary information. Click Finish to end the process. Outlook will start and open to your email inbox.

After configuring the first account, you can begin to use Outlook. You can add additional email accounts as needed or change the configuration information for existing accounts. The next chapter discusses more information related to working with email accounts.

 For more about working with Outlook email accounts, including Hotmail accounts, see Chapter 23, "Managing Email in Outlook," on page 656.

Understanding Outlook Profiles

Outlook creates an Outlook profile, on initial start, when you configure an email account in Outlook. That profile is loaded every time you start Outlook. It provides information to Outlook related to your email account (or accounts) configuration. You can use different types of email accounts in Outlook and have only one Outlook profile. However, multiple profiles can help sequester settings for different types of email accounts in their own related profiles.

Email accounts are contained in profiles. An email profile comprises email accounts, data files, and information about where your email is stored. Outlook automatically creates a new profile when you run Outlook for the first time. After that, the profile is loaded every time that you start Outlook.

> **tip**
>
> If multiple people use the same computer to access their email accounts in Outlook, you would want each person's email account kept in their own specific profile. This is actually a case where multiple profiles would be a necessity to provide anytime of privacy and security.

Most users need only a single profile, even in cases where you have configured Outlook for multiple email accounts. However, you might find it advantageous to create more than one profile for yourself. This would allow you to have one profile related to your Internet email account, meaning your personal email, and another profile for your Exchange email account. This would be useful in a case where you want to use Outlook on your home computer for Internet email, but you can also connect to your Exchange server and network via a secure connection (such as a virtual private network connection over the Internet) and like to check your Exchange email as well. The two different profiles would keep the two different types of email accounts separate and sequestered from each other.

Creating a New Profile

As already mentioned earlier, as soon as you configure an email account in Outlook, you have also created a profile. If you need to create a new profile or manage existing profiles, you use the Mail Setup dialog box, which you access via the Windows Control Panel.

In Windows 7, select Start, and then Control Panel to open the Control Panel. In the Control Panel, select User Accounts and Family Safety. In the Accounts and Family Safety pane, select Mail. The Mail Setup dialog box will open as shown in Figure 22.7.

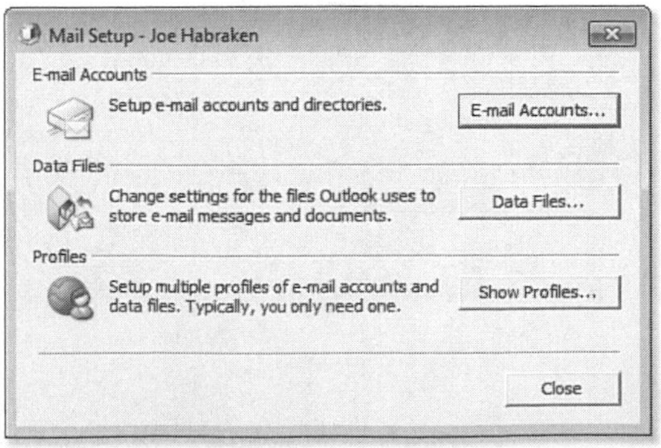

Figure 22.7
The Mail Setup dialog box.

The Mail Setup dialog box enables you to manipulate Outlook settings without actually being in Outlook. You can create email accounts; change data file settings; and also create and manage profiles. Because you can't actually create a profile from within Outlook, you do it outside Outlook.

To create a new profile, follow these steps:

1. In the Mail Setup dialog box, click Show Profiles. The Mail dialog box will open with the General tab selected (it is the only tab).

2. Select Add. The New Profile dialog box will open.

3. Type a name for the new profile. Then click OK.

As soon as you click OK, the Add New Account wizard will open. This same wizard opens at Outlook's first start, which we discussed in the previous section. To summarize: You can enter your name, email address, and password, and then Outlook will attempt to connect with your mail server and automatically configure your account. Or you can manually configure the server settings for the account.

When you click Finish on the last screen of the Add New Account Wizard (after configuring the email account), you return to the Mail dialog box. The dialog box will list your new profile.

Managing Profiles

The Mail dialog box not only lists the profiles set up on your computer but it also provides you with the ability to manage them. You can remove a profile if you no longer need it; select the profile and then select Remove.

You can also edit the properties of a profile. In editing the properties of a profile, there are two possibilities: the email accounts associated with the profile and the data files used to store documents. Select a profile in the Mail dialog box and then select Properties. This opens the Mail Setup dialog box for the selected profile, as shown in Figure 22.8 (this is not the same as the Mail Setup dialog box shown in Figure 22.7).

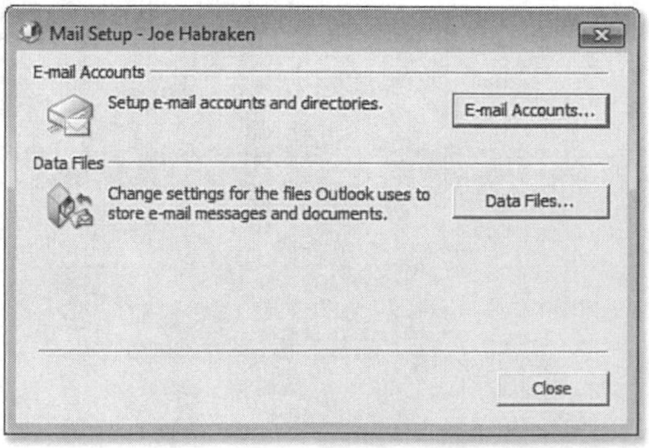

Figure 22.8
The Mail Setup dialog box.

If you want to change the email account settings in the profile, select the E-mail Accounts button. This opens the Account Settings dialog box. This dialog box, which you can also access directly from Outlook via the Backstage Info window, provides access to many Outlook settings. For example you can edit data file settings on the Data Files tab. You can also edit other settings, including the RSS feeds, calendars, and address books. Figure 22.9 shows the Account Settings dialog box with the E-mail tab selected.

Figure 22.9
You can change email and data file settings in the Account Settings dialog box.

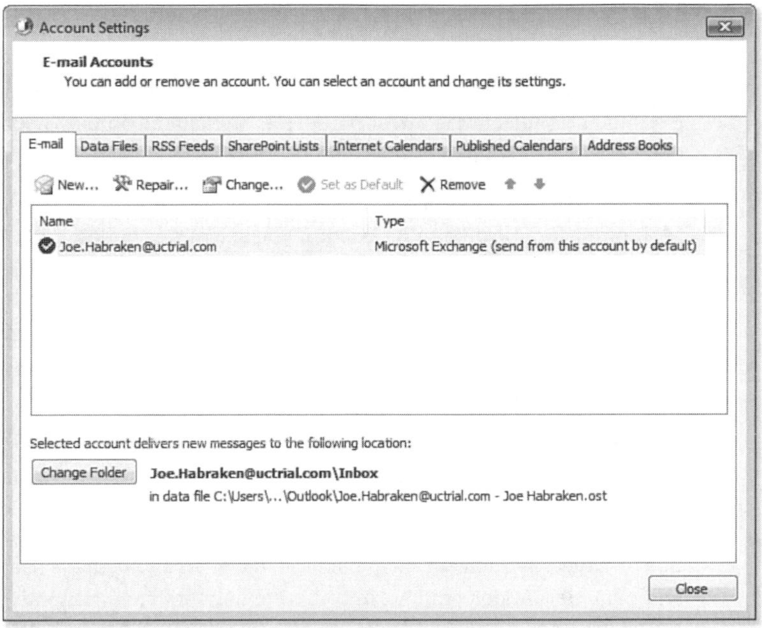

In changing the email settings for the current profile, you can add an email account, repair an existing email account, or remove an account. You also can change the folder used by the account when new messages arrive.

The Data Files tab of the Account Settings dialog box enables you to view the location of the Outlook data files associated with the current profile. We discuss managing Outlook data files in the next section of this chapter, "Understanding Outlook Data Files." When you click Close in the Account Settings dialog box, you return to the Mail Setup dialog box. Click the Close button again and you return to the Mail dialog box and your list of profiles.

Because you can manage both the email accounts and data files from inside Outlook, we will be working with these different settings in the appropriate context in other chapters found in the Outlook section of this book. However, it is important to understand that you can access profile-related setting issues via the Mail dialog box, which you reach using the Windows Control Panel. You will find that, in some situations, you have to change settings related to a profile from the Mail dialog box. For example, let's say you want to add an Exchange Server email account to your current Outlook profile. Let's also assume that the email account that you configured on Outlook's first start (using the Startup Wizard) was an Internet email account.

You won't be able to add the Exchange Server email account to the Outlook profile while Outlook is running the profile. This means that you have to close Outlook and then add the email account to the profile using the Mail Setup dialog box for that profile.

 For information about adding and editing email accounts in Outlook, see Chapter 23, "Managing Email in Outlook," on page 656.

Loading Profiles

One other issue that we should discuss about multiple Outlook profiles relates to which profile should be loaded when you start Outlook. The Mail dialog box provides option buttons related to the loading of profiles in the lower portion of the Mail dialog box. Look for the When Starting Microsoft Outlook, Use This Profile statement in the lower part of the Mail dialog box. You have two different options, which are as follows:

- **Prompt for a Profile to Be Used:** If you select this option button, a Choose Profile dialog box will open when you start Outlook, providing you with the ability to select the profile that will be loaded from a drop-down list. This is useful if you have multiple profiles for different types of email accounts; say, Internet email versus Exchange Server email. This setting would be a necessity in cases where you have multiple users accessing their Outlook email accounts on the same computer. The user can select his or her specific profile.

- **Always Use This Profile:** Select this option if you want to specify a default profile to be loaded when Outlook starts. Use the drop-down list to select the profile name.

Whether you will need to deal with multiple profiles and profile settings will depend on your particular work environment. If you are a home or small business user, you might have a need to create and manage Outlook profiles. In corporate network environments, particularly those that use an Exchange Server for email accounts, you will have a network administrator who takes care of email account configurations and profile settings. So, even though you might feel empowered after reading this material on profiles, I suggest that you leave the profile and email settings completely alone. You might also find that the Control Panel doesn't even provide you with an icon that gets you to the Mail dialog box—network administrators can also control what icons show up in the Control Panel when you log on to your computer.

Understanding Outlook Data Files

When you work in Outlook, you are managing and manipulating different types of items such as email, appointments, contacts, and tasks. These different items have their own homes in Outlook. For example, new email messages are in the Inbox, whereas the To Do bar or the To Do list displays tasks. You might find it odd to learn that these different Outlook items are actually stored in a single Outlook data file.

I need to say up front that we are talking about a data file that stores your data locally on your computer; we are ignoring how Outlook stores data when it serves as an Exchange Server client. So, we are assuming, at least in the next paragraph or so, that you configured the first email account on

Outlook as a POP3 or IMAP account. When you configure the first email account for Outlook, it creates the default profile and your Outlook data file. By default, the profile's name will be Outlook. The data file's name will be *"your email account"* .pst, meaning the .pst file is named after the first email account you configured in Outlook. The .pst file is often referred to as the personal folders file.

When you consider how important the personal folders file is to Outlook and to you (in terms of all those emails that you have in Outlook), you will understand that in most cases, you should not play around with this file. That is not to say that you shouldn't back up the personal folders file, which we discuss in a moment. But you should have a compelling reason for other manipulations of the personal folders file, such as changing the file's location or renaming the file—both of which you can do.

Configuring Outlook as an email client for Microsoft Exchange Server does not create a personal folders file. In the Exchange Server environment, your email and other items are stored on the server running Exchange Server. Outlook does create a local data file, however, so that you can use your Exchange account offline. This data file will have the extension .ost; it contains a copy of the items stored on the Exchange server. This file is referred to as the offline Outlook data file.

note

Depending on how Outlook was initially configured (and by whom), your profile may not be named Outlook. The name of your Personal Folders file may also vary. Remember it has the extension .pst, no matter what the name.

To view the default personal folders file, or the offline Outlook data file, or both, select the Outlook Ribbon's File tab to access the Outlook Backstage. Select Info, and then click the Account Settings button. Select Account Settings on the button's menu to open the Account Settings dialog box.

The Account Settings dialog box will open to the E-mail tab by default. Select an email account from the Settings list and the Outlook data file for that account (either a .pst or .ost file) appears in the lower pane of the dialog box. You can select the Data Files tab to view the Outlook data files associated with the current Outlook profile. Figure 22.10 shows the Accounts Settings dialog box with the Data Files tab selected. Two email accounts are associated with the profile.

note

When you create a Hotmail account using the Outlook Connector, an offline Outlook data file will also be created on your computer.

The type of data files shown in the Account Settings dialog box will depend on the type of email accounts you have configured. Any POP3 or MAPI email account will have an associated personal folders file, and an Exchange account will have an offline Outlook data file.

The Account Settings dialog box provides you with the ability to change the default data file for the Outlook profile. You can also open the file location for a selected data file. There is also a Remove command that you can use to remove an unneeded data file.

You can view the settings for a personal folders file or an offline Outlook data file. Select the data file in the list and then select Settings on the Account Settings toolbar. This opens the Outlook Data File dialog box.

For personal folders files, the Outlook Data File dialog box will provide the alias or name of the data file and the actual file name and path for the data file. You have two options related to a personal folders file. You can use the Change Password button to assign a password to the Outlook data file.

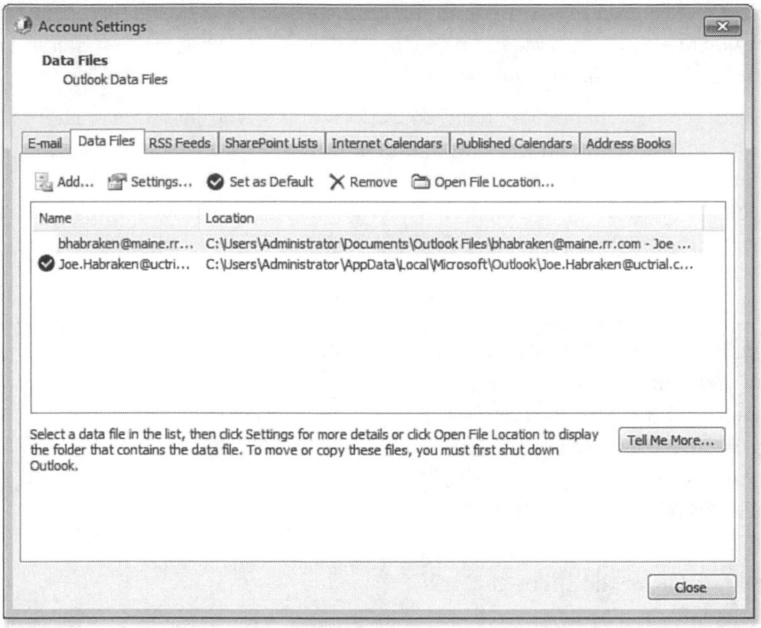

Figure 22.10
You can view the data files associated with the current profile.

This is useful if multiple users share the same computer. You can also use the Compact Now button to compact the data file. This reduces the size of the file.

If you open the settings for an offline Outlook data file (.ost) associated with your Exchange Server account, the Microsoft Exchange dialog box opens. This dialog box provides four different tabs of settings. Remember that your network administrator probably configured your Exchange server account for you. So, I would not suggest that you change any of the settings provided by the Microsoft Exchange dialog box. Consider the explanation of the dialog box tabs that follows purely informational:

- **General:** This tab specifies the name of the Exchange server and the account mailbox name.

- **Advanced:** This tab allows you to add additional mailboxes that should be open when Outlook connects to the Exchange server. You also have the option of using the cached exchange mode (which places the .ost file on your computer) so that you can work offline. The default setting enables the cached exchange mode.

- **Security:** This tab provides options related to encryption and user identification. By default, Outlook and Microsoft Exchange trade encrypted data. You can also choose to have user identification required at logon. The type of authentication used is another selection you can make on this tab.

- **Connection:** This tab allows you to select the connection type that you use to reconnect to Exchange when you have been working offline. You can connect to Exchange via your local area network or phone line, or via HTTP by using Outlook Anywhere.

When you close either the Outlook Data File dialog box or the Microsoft Exchange dialog box, you return to the Account Settings dialog box. Click Close to close this dialog box and return to the Outlook application window.

Protecting and Creating Personal Folders Files

One thing that you can do to help protect your personal folders file and the information that it contains is to periodically back up your computer files. Windows 7 provides the Office Backup, which you can use to back up computer data to writeable CDs or DVDs, an external drive, or a USB flash drive. You can access the Windows Backup utility via the System and Security group in the Windows Control Panel.

Outlook provides you with the ability to create new personal folders files. This can be useful if you want to create a personal folders file for a particular project, and then place items from your current Outlook Inbox or other email folders into the new personal folders file. This is useful in that it removes the emails from your default personal folders file and cleans up your Outlook folders. It also creates an archive of the project. Obviously, if you have used earlier versions of Outlook, you are already aware of Outlook's capability to archive older emails. So, if you are good about archiving Outlook items, you might not feel a huge need to be moving things into secondary .pst files that you create. Think of the use of secondary .pst files as a potential convenience, not something that you have to do.

➡ *Outlook provides you with the ability to archive old email messages and items. Outlook actually saves these items in another personal folders file. See Chapter 27, "Securing Outlook," on page 752.*

You can create a new Outlook personal folders file from the Account Settings dialog box (with the Data Files tab selected) or the Outlook application window. From the Outlook window, follow these steps:

1. Select the Ribbon's Home tab.

2. Select the New Items command in the New group.

3. Point at More Items and select Outlook Data File. The Create or Open Outlook Data File dialog box will open.

4. The Data File dialog box will show the default Outlook data file and any other created data files. Type a name for a new data file in the File Name box and then click OK.

The new data file will appear in the Outlook Navigation Pane below your email account's Inbox and other mail folders. You can create folders in the new data file and then copy or move email messages to the data file. So, you can use the secondary data file to back up specific items or to group items related to a specific project that you no longer need to keep in your current Inbox or other folders.

Repairing Outlook Data Files

Personal folders files can become damaged. A sure sign that your default personal folders file is corrupt is that Outlook is unable to open it when you start Outlook.

You can use the inbox repair tool (scanpst.exe) to try and correct problems with a personal folders file. You must exit Outlook to run the tool, which the installer placed in the \Program Files\ Microsoft Office\Office14 folder when you installed Microsoft Office 2010.

When you have exited Outlook, use the Windows Explorer to locate the scanpst.exe program file. Double-click the scanpst.exe file and the Microsoft Outlook Inbox Repair Tool dialog box will open as shown in Figure 22.11.

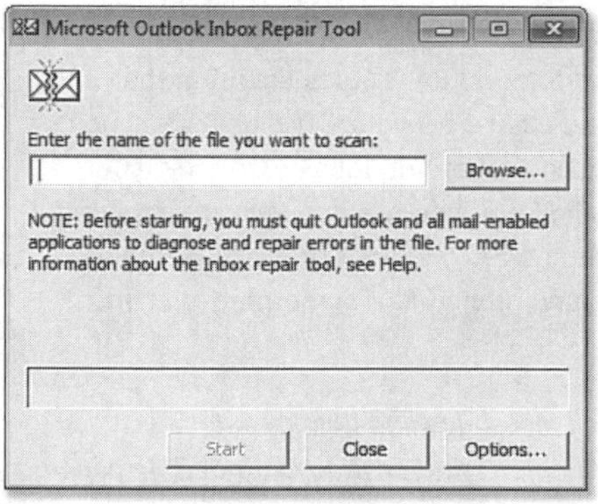

Figure 22.11
Use the inbox repair tool on damaged personal folders files.

Enter the name of the file you want to scan or use the Browse button to locate the file. The default folder for your personal folders file is Documents\Outlook Files. After entering the filename, click the Start button. The inbox repair tool checks the file and a message box will open, letting you know the level of the problems identified during the scan.

You can have the inbox repair tool make a backup copy of the file before repairing it. This is the default setting and a good idea, particularly if the repair process further damages an already corrupted file. The inbox repair tool will place the backup copy in your Outlook Files folder with the extension .bak.

Click the Repair button and the inbox repair tool will attempt to repair the file. When the process is complete, the Repair Complete message appears; click OK to close it. You can now open Outlook with the repaired .pst file.

If the inbox repair tool recovered folders and items, you will find a Lost and Found folder in your folder list (in the Navigation pane). At this point you should probably create a new Outlook personal files folder (using the method we discussed in the previous section). You can then drag the items in the Lost and Found folder to the new .pst file. You can drag additional items to the new personal folders file, and then make the new .pst file the default personal folders file for Outlook by using the Accounts Settings dialog box (accessed via the Backstage). You can then restart Outlook and it will load the new .pst file. You can then delete the old personal folders file using the Account Settings dialog box.

Offline Outlook data files (.ost files) can also become damaged. However, these are easier to re-create because the Exchange server contains the working copies of all your email and other items. Open the Mail Setup dialog box from the Control Panel (select Mail in the User Accounts and Family Safety group). Select Show Profiles, select the Exchange Server profile in the profile list, and then select Properties. This opens the Account Settings dialog box with the E-mail tab selected. Select the Exchange Server email account in the list of email accounts and then select Change. The Change Account dialog box will open. Right below the Microsoft Exchange server name box is the Use Cached Exchange Mode check box. Clear this check box.

Now we need to open the Microsoft Exchange dialog box; select More Settings in the Change Account dialog box (on the lower right). In the Microsoft Exchange dialog box, select the Advanced tab. On the Advanced tab, select the Outlook Data File Settings button to open the Outlook Data File Settings. Select Disable Offline Use and then click OK. Click Yes to verify the change. You have turned off the offline use feature, which synchronizes your Exchange Server folders with the .ost file. Now all you have to do is turn this feature back on to create a new .ost file (replacing the dam-aged file).

You should still be in the Microsoft Exchange dialog box, on the Advanced tab. Select the Use Cached Exchange Mode check box. Then click OK. This closes the Microsoft Exchange dialog box and returns you to the Change Account dialog box. You can click the Next button and then Finish to close this dialog box. Now all you have to do is close the Account Settings, Mail Setup, and Mail dia-log boxes. You can return to Outlook and your Exchange folders should replicate with the .ost file.

Importing and Exporting Data

You can import and export information to and from Outlook. The types of information that can be imported include RSS feeds, mail account settings, Internet email, addresses, calendars (.ics and .vcs), and Outlook personal folders files (.pst). For example, you might be migrating from another personal information man-ager or email client to Outlook and want to import your address book or contacts list; Outlook can import this type of informa-tion in a number of different file formats, including comma sepa-rated values (.csv) and vCards (.vcf).

You might also have a need to export data from Outlook to another application. You can export Outlook data to Excel and Access, and in several different file types, including comma separated values, tab-separated files, and as Outlook data files (.pst).

> **tip**
>
> Importing data into Outlook may take some prep work in the applica-tion that contains the original data. For example, to import Google Gmail contacts, you will need to export the contacts to a CSV file (the actual export file type in Gmail is Outlook CSV (for import into Outlook clients). Once you have the CSV file, you can import it into Outlook using the Import and Export Wizard.

The Backstage Open window handles both the importing and exporting of data. This is where you can access the Open Calendar command to open a calendar file, and this is also where you access the Import and Export Wizard, which takes care of both the importing and exporting of a number of different data types.

Importing Data

To import data into Outlook, open the Backstage by selecting File on the Ribbon. Then select Open. The Open window provides two commands that are useful for importing data into Outlook: Open Calendar and Import. The Open Calendar command enables you to open a calendar file in Outlook, such as an iCalendar file. Select Open Calendar. The Open Calendar dialog box will open. Navigate to the path that contains the calendar file. Then click OK. The calendar will be added to your my Calendars list under Other Calendars.

If you want to import contacts or emails, you will use the Import command, which opens the Import and Export Wizard. Follow these steps:

1. Select Import; the Import and Export Wizard opens (see Figure 22.12).

Figure 22.12
The Import and Export Wizard.

2. Select the type of data you want to import or select Import from Another Program or File for a data type not shown. Then click Next.

3. On the next wizard screen, select the file type to import from the list. Then click Next.

4. On the next wizard screen, use the Browse button to select the file to import. You can also select options related to the import, such as replace duplicates with items imported, allow duplicates to be created, and do not import duplicate items. Click Next.

5. On the next screen, select the destination folder, such as Calendar or Contacts. Then click Next.

6. The next screen lists the file to be imported and the folder that Outlook will import it into. At this point, you can choose to map custom fields. This allows you to match up the field names used in the import file with the field names used in Outlook, such as the field names used in the Contacts folder. Select Map Custom Fields.

7. (Optional) Drag the field names from the source file on the left of the Map Custom Fields box to the Outlook field names on the right (see Figure 22.13). When you have completed mapping the fields, click OK.

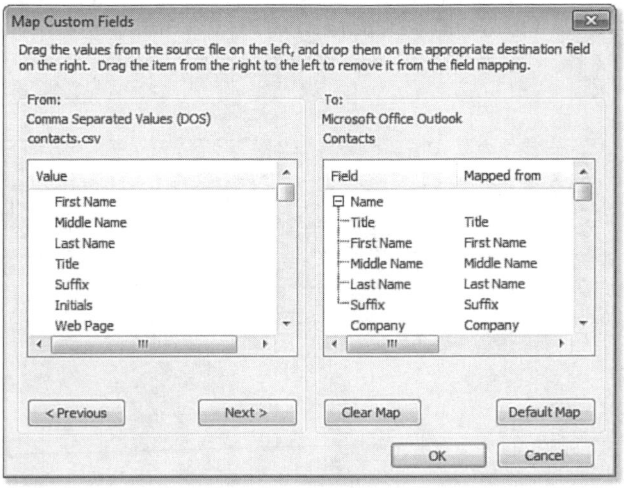

Figure 22.13
Map the fields from the import file to the Outlook fields.

8. Click Finish.

Outlook will place the imported data in the Outlook folder that you selected during the import procedure. For example, if you imported contacts, select Contacts in the Navigation pane and the imported contacts will display.

Exporting Data

You can also use the Import and Export Wizard to export Outlook data into a variety of file formats. Open the Import and Export Wizard from the Backstage Open window. On the first wizard screen, select Export to a File and then click Next.

On the next wizard screen, you can select the file format for the export. File types include tab-and comma-separated values. You can also import to Access and Excel file formats or export the data as an Outlook data file. When you have selected the export file type, all you have to do is select the Outlook folder that contains the data that you want to export. Specify an export file name and a location and you can then export the data.

> **note**
>
> The steps involved in exporting data from Outlook are pretty much the same as the steps for importing data. You specify the file type, the Outlook folder involved and the location of the file that is to be created. I guess that isn't exactly the same, but you get the picture.

Navigating the New Outlook Interface

Outlook is all about accessing and managing different types of items. So, the Outlook application window makes it easy for you to access and manage your emails, contacts, calendar, and tasks. We have already discussed the fact that Outlook 2010 also completely embraces the Office Fluent Ribbon-based interface, which also makes it more consistent with the other Office applications. Figure 22.14 shows the default Outlook application window.

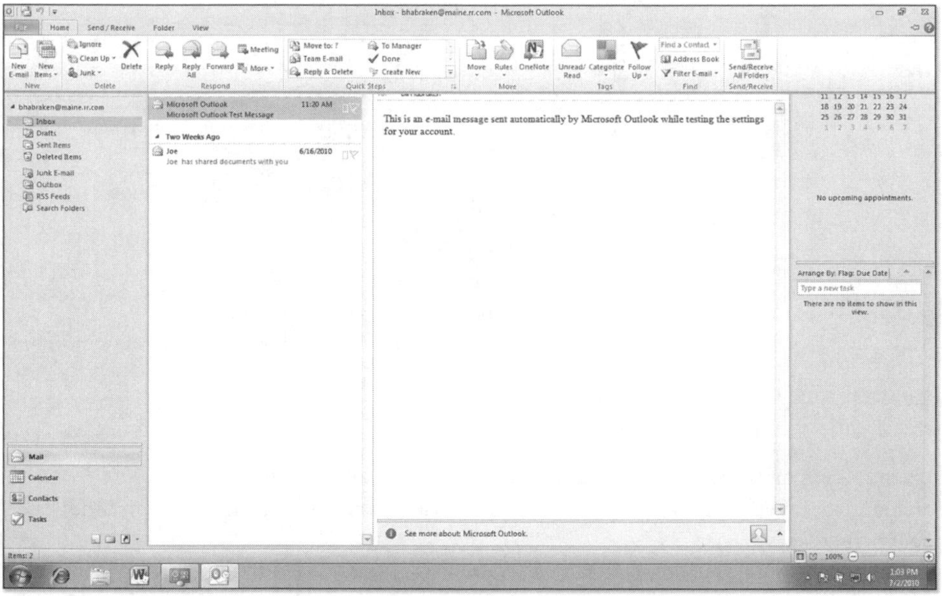

Figure 22.14 Outlook gives you easy access to different types of items.

The various parts of the Outlook application window are as follows:

- **Navigation Pane:** Serves as the main navigational tool for Outlook; it enables you to navigate individual folders and views for the currently selected item, such as email or contacts. The Navigation pane also provides a button for each of the Outlook folders (Mail, Calendar, Contacts, and so on).

- **Reading Pane:** Enables you to view (and read) the currently selected email or task.

- **Details Pane:** This pane provides a list of available items in a folder such as your emails or tasks.

- **To Do Bar:** Provides a calendar and a list of appointments for the currently selected date (which by default would be the current date). The To Do bar also provides a list of tasks for the day and provides you with the ability to quickly add new tasks.

> **tip**
>
> You can grab the top of the Navigation pane's button area and drag it upward to view more Outlook item buttons such as the Notes and the Folder list.

- **People Pane:** Provides you with the ability to connect Outlook to online social networks and then communicate with your peeps. At the time of this book's writing, Microsoft had plans for a number of social network add-ins that would allow you to connect to your various social networking accounts.

 tip

Place the mouse on the edge of any of the panes or the To Do bar to access the resize tool. You can then drag to change the size of a pane as needed.

- **Status Bar:** Provides the View shortcuts, Zoom and Zoom Slider. You can add other information, such as quota information, to the status bar as needed via the Customize Status Bar menu.

You can minimize and expand all the various Outlook panes such as the Navigation pane and the To Do bar as needed. For example, you can minimize the To Do bar by clicking the minimize button on the upper right of the bar.

You can also manipulate the panes and the To Do bar on the Ribbon's View tab. The Navigation pane, Reading pane, and To Do bar have drop-down menus that allow you to view the pane in the Normal or Minimized view. You can also choose to turn off a particular pane by selecting Off on the pane's menu.

Accessing Outlook Items Using the Navigation Pane

The Navigation pane provides access to the different Outlook folder buttons. When you select a button such as Mail, the Navigation pane also provides a list of folders associated with that item. In the case of Mail, you can access the Inbox, Drafts, Junk E-mail, and other associated mail folders.

By default, the Navigation pane shows the Mail, Calendar, Contacts, and Tasks folder buttons. At the bottom of the Navigation pane there is another grouping of four buttons. The first button on the left is the Notes button, which enables you to access notes that you have created.

The next button, the Folder List button, will open a list of all your Outlook folders in the Navigation pane including the Calendar, Contacts, Journal, and Notes. This makes it easy to access these various items.

The Shortcuts button allows you to access special shortcut icons such as those for Outlook Today (which provides an overview of your current Calendar, mail, and tasks) and Microsoft Office Online, which allows you to access Office support and updates.

The Configure Buttons menu provides access to a shortcut menu that enables you to show more or fewer buttons and to add or remove buttons from the Navigation pane. The Configure Buttons menu also provides access to the Navigation pane options.

Customizing the Navigation Pane

You can use the Navigation pane options dialog box to change the order in which buttons display and determine the buttons actually shown. You access the Navigation pane options by using the Configure Buttons menu or by selecting Navigation Pane, and then Options on the Ribbon's View tab (in the Layout group). Figure 22.15 shows the Navigation Pane Options.

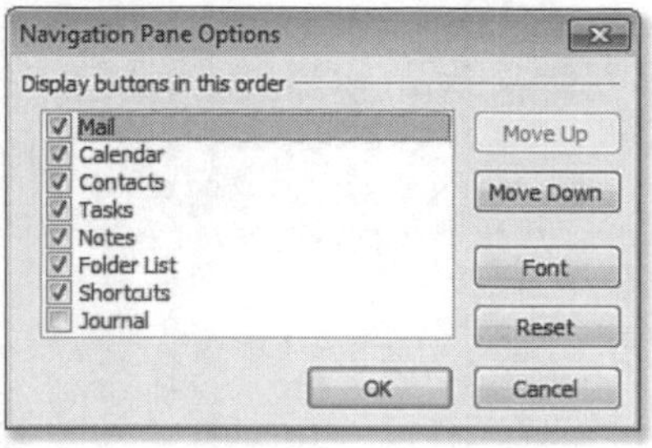

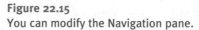

Figure 22.15
You can modify the Navigation pane.

You can deselect or select buttons as needed. You can also use the Move Up and Move Down buttons to change the button order in the pane. You can also change the font used for the buttons. And if you want to return to the default settings for the Navigation pane, you can select Reset.

We will be working extensively with the Navigation pane and the other areas of the Outlook application window, including the Ribbon, as we work with specific items in Outlook in the chapters found in this section of the book.

Working with Views in Outlook

As you work with the different items in Outlook, the Outlook panes provide you with a default view for each item type. For example, Outlook uses the Compact view to display mail, by default. Emails sort by conversation in the details pane, with each email's subject line showing in the email list.

When you work with your Contacts folder, the default view is Business Card. You can select from alternative views related to each of the Outlook items (such as mail, contacts, and the calendars). The Change View command is on the View tab in the Current View group. You can select Change View and then select one of the other view possibilities provided. Figure 22.16 shows the view choices for the Contacts folder (Business Card, Card, Phone, and List).

 tip
If you change the current view using the Advanced View Settings, you can then save the "changed" view as a new view. Select Save Current View As a New View on the Change View command.

You can actually change the settings for the current view. Select View Settings in the Current View group. The Advanced View Settings dialog box will open for the current view (such as the Business Card view for Contacts). You can change settings related to the view, such as the sort order for the view (using the Sort button). And you can also use the Filter button to modify the current view so that it filters the item list using keywords, categories, or by other parameters such as whether the item is unread or has an attachment (in the case of emails). Other settings that you can change for the current view are such things as the font and the size of the items in the view.

Figure 22.16
Change the
view for the
current folder.

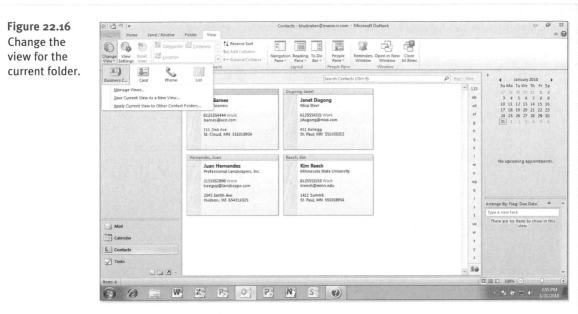

In addition to Outlook's many supplied views (for each folder type), you can also create custom views for the information in your Outlook folders. Select Change View on the View tab and then select Manage Views. This will open the Manage All Views dialog box. The dialog box will show the preconfigured views for the current folder (such as Mail or Contacts). You can use commands in this dialog box to copy, modify, and rename views. You can also use the Reset button to change a view back to its default settings, which is useful in cases where you have modified a view and want to put it back to the way it was by default.

To create a new view, select the New button to open the Create New View dialog box. In this dialog box, you supply the name for the new view, the type of view, and the folders on which Outlook can use the view. In terms of the type of view you select for the new view, you have several options:

- **Table:** Presents items in a grid of n rows and columns. Use this view type to view mail messages, tasks, and details about any item.

- **Timeline:** Displays items as icons arranged in chronological order from left to right on a time scale. Use this to examine journal entries and other items in this type of view.

- **Card:** Presents items such as cards in a card file. Use this to view contacts.

- **Business Card:** Presents items in a business card format that provides details for the contact such as name, email, address, and so on.

- **Day/Week/Month:** Displays items in a calendar view in blocks of time. Use this type for meetings and scheduled tasks.

- **Icon:** Provides graphical icons to represent tasks, notes, calendars, and so on.

Use the Advanced View Settings dialog box to configure the new view settings. Although not all the settings will be available for each type of view, you can specify the columns to be included in the view (for a table view). These columns or fields (as they are also referred to) can be such things as importance, subject, size, created, due data, follow up flag, as well as many others.

Obviously most of the view types relate to a particular Outlook folder. For example, Business Card relates to contacts, whereas the Day/Week/Month type would be for your calendars.

You can specify additional options related to the view, such as whether the view is used on the current folder and visible to everyone or visible only to you. Another option allows Outlook to use the view on all mail and post folders. When you have provided the information required by the Create New View dialog box, select OK. This will open the Advanced View Settings dialog box for the new view. Figure 22.17 shows the Advanced View Settings dialog box.

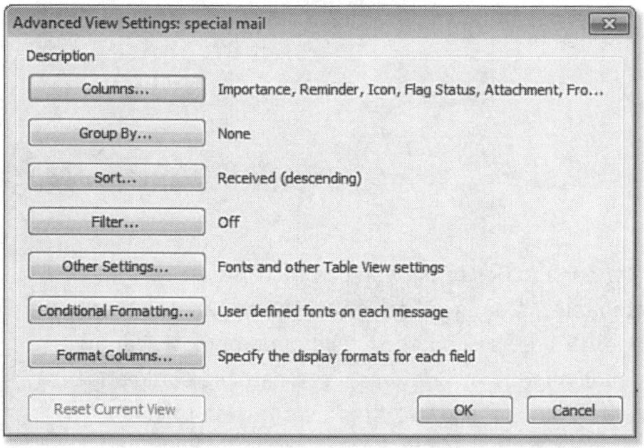

Figure 22.17
Advanced View Settings dialog box.

You can also specify whether the view should group information in a particular way, sort the information, or filter the information. For example, you could group email items in a table view that you create so that Outlook groups them by their creation date or by the categories assigned to the messages.

After you configure the new view and click OK, you return to the Manage All Views dialog box. If you need to change a view that you have created, select the view and then select

> **tip**
> If you decide you don't want a view that you have created, you can delete it in the Manage All Views dialog box

Modify. You can then modify the view as needed. When you close the Manage All Views dialog box, you will find that Outlook added your new view to the Change View menu. You can select it when needed, as you do with the default views provided.

Categorizing Outlook Items

You can use categories to Outlook items to aid you in locating and organizing information in Outlook. You can assign a category or categories to an Outlook item. You can then have Outlook organize items in a particular view by category. You can also use Search to locate items assigned to a particular category, and you can create Search folders that also find items based on category.

By default, each Outlook category is color coded. The categories have names such as Blue Category, Green Category, and so on. The Color Categories dialog box shown in Figure 22.18 shows the color categories.

Figure 22.18
The Color Categories dialog box.

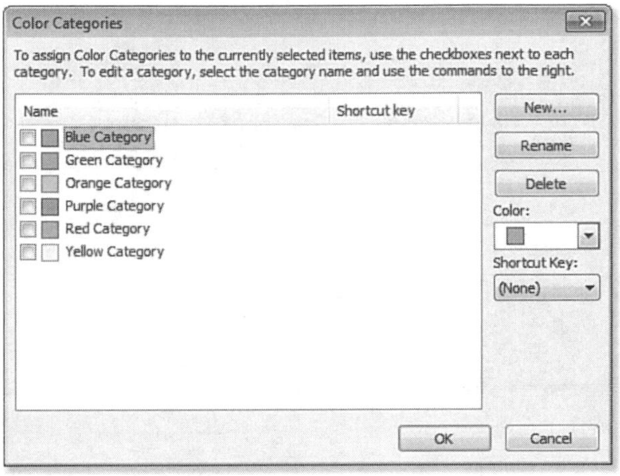

You will want to rename the various color categories to assemble your own list of categories that you can then assign to your Outlook items. If you exhaust the default categories, you can create new categories in the Color Categories dialog box. You can open this dialog box from the Ribbon provided for each Outlook item. For example, when you open a mail message, you can access the Categorize command on the Message tab. For contacts, the Categorize command is on the Contact tab.

The first time that you assign one of the color categories to an Outlook item, the Rename Category dialog box will open. You can quickly rename the category by typing a new name in the Name box.

When you have renamed categories, you can assign them to your Outlook items as needed. Then when you select the Ribbon's View tab in one of the Outlook folders, you can use the Categories command to arrange the items in the current folder by category. You can filter items in a particular view by using the Search box. Click in the Search box and then select the Categorized command provided by the contextual search tools that appear. Select a category and the list of items filters by that category.

Searching for Outlook Items

Outlook provides you with some different possibilities for finding items in your various Outlook folders. The simplest way to search for items in the current folder is to click in the Search box. When you place the insertion point in the Search box, the search tools will appear on the Ribbon with the Search tab selected. Figure 22.19 shows the search tools on the Ribbon.

Figure 22.19
The search
tools.

The Search tools provide a number of options. You can specify the scope for the search, such as the current folder, all subfolders, or all Outlook items. You can also use commands in the Refine group to search for items that have attachments, a particular subject, or the flag or importance level assigned to the item.

After you have specified the various options for the search, type your search terms in the Search box and Outlook provides the results of the search. You can actually modify the search on the fly and enable or disable search parameters on the Ribbon as needed. When you have finished the search, click the Close Search command to return to the current folder view.

Using Advanced Find

If you prefer, you can use the Advanced Find dialog box to conduct your search. Click in the Search box; the search tools will appear on the Ribbon. Select the Search Tools command and then select Advanced Find. This will open the Advanced Find dialog box.

The Advanced Find dialog box allows you to specify the type of item that you want to find and the location that you want to search. You can also specify parameters such as who a message is from or its recipients. Advanced Find enables you to specify keywords for different fields, such as the subject field. Additional search parameters on the More Choices tab enable you to specify categories to be used in the search ad other parameters, such items that are unread or have a particular importance. The Advanced tab enables you to specify parameters by field, such as address fields, date/time field, and so on.

When you have specified the parameters for the search, select Find Now. Outlook will list the items found by the search.

Using Search Folders

Search folders are containers that you can use to locate mail items in your email accounts. The Search folders don't really contain mail items, but they provide you a listing of email items that meet your search criteria. For example, you could search for all unread emails or all emails from a particular person. Then when you access the search folder in the Navigation pane, you will have access to the emails that meet your search criteria.

To create a new search folder for an account, select Search Folder in the Navigation pane; then select New Search Folder. The New Search Folder dialog box will open as shown in Figure 22.20.

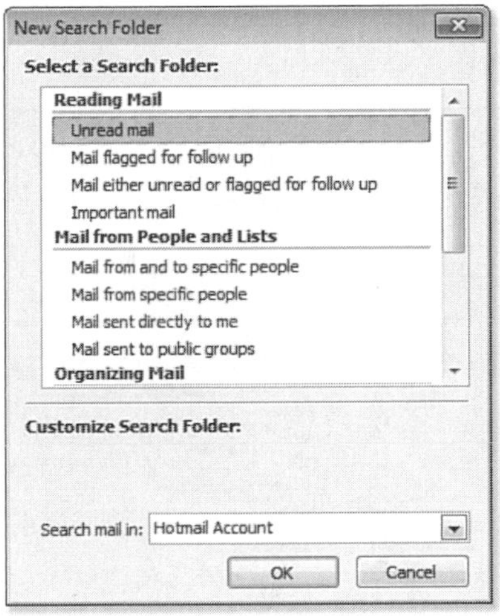

Figure 22.20
The New Search Folder dialog box.

You can select a search folder provided by the New Search Folder dialog box. Different categories, such as Reading Mail, Mail from People, and Lists and Organizing Mail provide specific types of searches that you can assign to the folder. For example, to create a search folder for unread mail, select Unread Mail in the Reading Mail category. If you select a search folder such as Mail from Specific People, you must use the Customize Search Folder option to specify the person or persons you are talking about (you can select the contact or contacts from your Contacts folder by using the Choose button).

> **tip**
>
> You can create custom search folders by selecting Create a Custom Search Folder in the New Search Folder dialog box. This opens the Custom Search Folder dialog box, which can be used to specify custom criteria for the search folder.

When you have selected the type of search folder and supplied the additional information needed, click OK. The new search folder will appear in your email folder list. Select the search folder to view the mail items that meet the folder's search criteria.

Printing Outlook Items

Printing Outlook items is easier than ever in Outlook 2010. The Backstage houses the Print command. You can access the Backstage from the Ribbon. The Outlook window has a Ribbon, as do the individual windows that you use to view specific items such as an email, contact, or appointment. So, you can quickly print any Outlook item. You can also print the entire contents of an Outlook folder such as Contacts. Because the Print window combines print settings, such as the selection of the print style, and print preview, you can fine-tune your print job before actually printing.

Open a specific Outlook item or open an Outlook folder such as your mail or tasks. To access the Backstage, select File on the Ribbon. Select Print to open the Print window. Figure 22.21 shows the Print window.

Figure 22.21
The Print window.

You can select the printer for the print job by using the Printer drop-down menu. The Print What area of the window provides a list of the different styles available for the current item type that you want to print. The styles will vary depending on the type of item you are printing; so, for example, an email will use the Memo Style by default and all the emails in a folder will print using the Table Style. For contacts, individual contacts print by using the Memo Style but entire contacts list print using the Card Style, Small Booklet Style, or Phone Directory Style. Because you are provided a preview of your printout after you select a style, you can try out different styles until you find the one most appropriate for the printout you want to create.

If you want to control the number of copies, how the copies are collaged, or other print parameters such as the page range, select the Print Options button on the Print window. This will open the Print dialog box.

You access print settings via the Print dialog box that provides access to all the print options, including the fonts used in the print out and the paper type. You can even specify a header or footer to print on each page of the printout. Click the Page Setup button to set the format, paper, and Header/Footer settings in the Page Setup dialog box.

When you change options in the Print dialog box, it makes sense to click the Preview button to return to the Print window. This provides a print preview using the settings you configured in the Print dialog box. You can use the various preview buttons such as Actual Size, One Page, and Multiple Pages to preview your printout. When you are ready to send the print job to the printer, click the Print button on the window.

MANAGING EMAIL IN OUTLOOK

Although Outlook is a multitasker's dream in terms of its different functions, one of its primary purposes is that of email client. Considering that most of us (no matter what our vocation) send and receive large volumes of email, you will find that Outlook takes the "mess" out of messages (as opposed to putting the "fun" in dysfunctional) and enables you to communicate with others in an organized and effective manner.

Outlook's mail client supports a number of email account types such as Internet email, Microsoft Exchange Server mail, and other mail account types, such as Microsoft Hotmail. In this chapter, we look at Outlook's email management tools and features starting with basic concepts related to creating and sending and receiving emails. We also look at Outlook's capabilities for managing and organizing emails and setting email account configurations and other email settings.

Working in the Mail Folder

Once you have configured the initial email account on Outlook's first start (as discussed in Chapter 22, "Requisite Outlook: Configuration and Essential Features"), you are ready to begin creating, sending, and receiving e-mails. Remember that you are not limited to a single email account in Outlook, and can configure multiple email accounts (and different types of email accounts) as discussed later in this chapter.

> ➡ *For information about configuring an Outlook profile and email account the first time you run Outlook, see Chapter 22, "Requisite Outlook: Configuration and Essential Features," on page 604.*

The Outlook Mail folder provides access to the specific email folders that hold different types of messages, such as received and sent messages.

Select the Mail folder in the Navigation pane to view the default email folders, as shown in Figure 23.1.

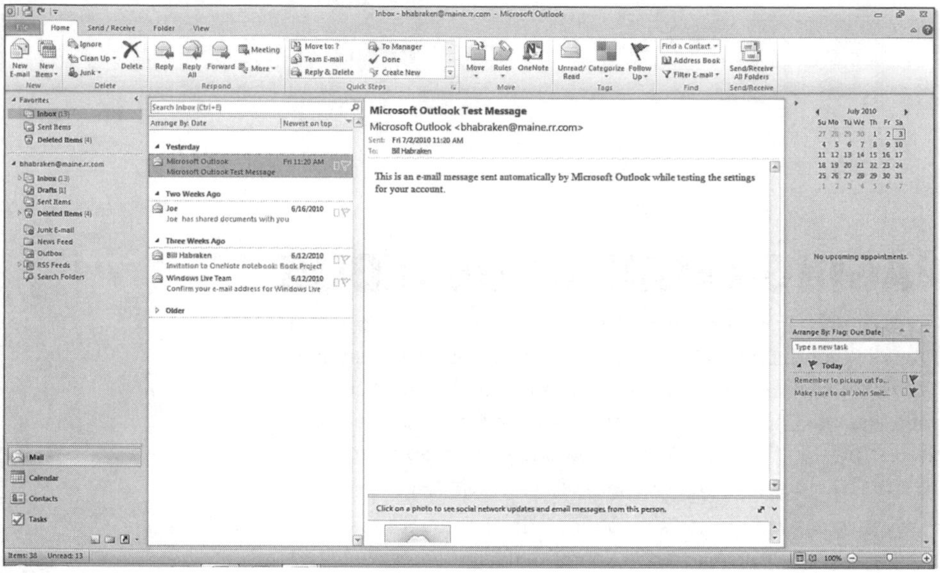

Figure 23.1
The Outlook Mail folder.

When you select the Inbox folder, the Details pane lists the emails in the Inbox. The Reading pane shows currently selected email.

At the top of the Navigation pane you will see Favorites, which provides shortcuts to the Inbox, Sent Items, and the Deleted Items folders by default. You can add folders to the Favorites list as required. Select any folder in the email folder list, and then select the Ribbon's Folder tab. To add the selected folder to Favorites, select the Show in Favorites command.

> **tip**
>
> Drag a folder from the email folders list to Favorites to add it to the Favorites list.

You also have the option of closing the Favorites list if you find it distracting or would like more room in the Navigation pane for multiple email accounts and their associated folders. On the Ribbon's View tab, select Navigation Pane and then clear the check box for Favorites.

Each Outlook email account has its own set of associated mail folders such as an Inbox, Drafts, and Sent Items. You can collapse an email account in the Navigation pane to hide the folders associated with the account; click the Collapse button for the account. A second click will expand the account, showing the associated folders. The default folders for your primary or default email account are as follows:

- **Inbox:** Outlook places received mail in the Inbox by default. When you select the Inbox, the Details pane lists emails by date order in conversations.

- **Drafts:** The Drafts folder can potentially contain any email that you compose and then close without sending. When you close an unsent email message, Outlook prompts you to save the email as a draft.

- **Sent Items:** Emails that you send from the email account are stored in this folder. Sent emails display in date order.

- **Deleted Items:** Outlook places deleted emails in this folder. You have the option of letting Outlook empty the Deleted Items folder when you exit the application.

- **Junk E-Mail:** This folder sequesters emails flagged as junk email by Outlook.

- **Outbox:** When you send a message, Outlook places it in the Outbox folder until sending the email by connecting to the outgoing email server.

- **RSS Feeds:** This folder is not a mail related, but provides you with a way to access Really Simple Syndication (RSS) news feeds in Outlook. You can read content from an RSS feed in the Outlook window in much the same way that you read an email. We discuss RSS feeds at the end of this chapter.

- **Search Folders:** A search folder isn't really an actual folder. Rather it comprises search parameters you can set so that emails meeting your conditions display in the search folder.

As already mentioned, Outlook arranges email in your Inbox folder by date in conversations. This means that even messages contained in other folders, such as the Sent Items folder, will appear in the Inbox because of the default Conversations view. This makes it easy for you to view associated messages that relate to a particular mail message subject. We discuss the other views available for emails later in this chapter.

Creating an Email Message

You can send an email message to anyone for whom you have an email address, whether that address is in your list of contacts or scribbled on a scrap of paper. You can even email groups of people listed in your various distribution lists.

You can attach Outlook items and other files to your emails. Because Word is the default email editor for Outlook, you can use all of Word's capabilities to create emails that include formatted text, charts, and SmartArt. You can use the Review tab's tools to check the spelling and grammar in the message or to open the Research pane to find information important to your message.

When you are in the Mail folder, you can quickly open a new email message; select the New E-mail command on the Ribbon's Home tab. If you happen to be in one of the other Outlook folders, select the New Items command and then select E-Mail Message. Whichever route you take (there are actually more possibilities than the two mentioned, which we discuss in a moment), a new message window will open as shown in Figure 23.2.

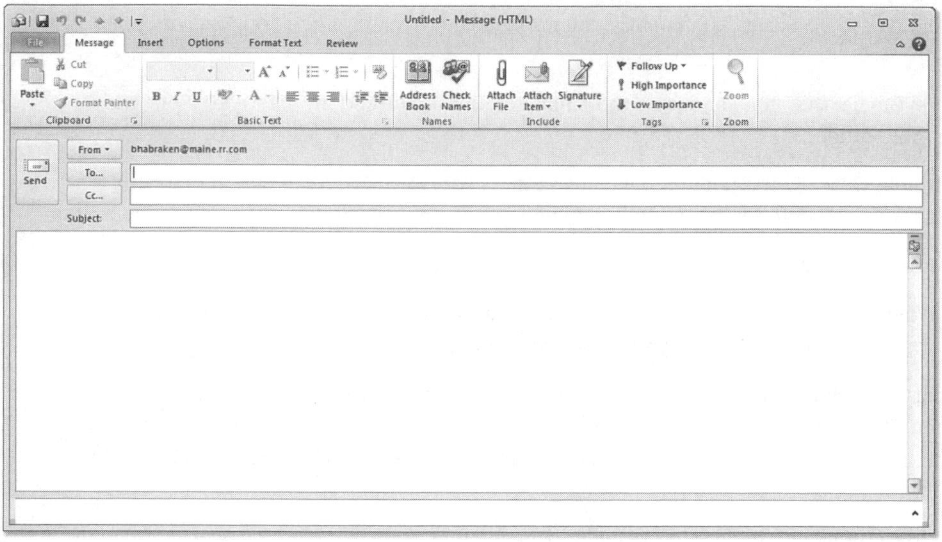

Figure 23.2
A new message window.

If you have not changed the message type for Outlook, the new message will be in the HTML format; Outlook will send the message from your default email account. You can change both of these settings via commands provided by the message Ribbon. The list that follows provides a brief description of the command sets found on each of the message Ribbon's tabs:

- **File:** Provides access to the Backstage view. You can set permissions for the mail message, and set properties such as the importance, sensitivity, and delivery options.

- **Message:** Provides access to the Clipboard commands, basic text formatting, and the Outlook Address Book. Other commands include attachment commands and tags.

- **Insert:** Provides options for attachments. This tab also includes a variety of commands for inserting different items into the body of the message, such as illustrations, links, and text objects.

- **Options:** Enables you to assign a theme to the message. Other options available include additional fields for the message (BCC), voting buttons, delivery and received receipts, and options related to saving and delivery of the message.

- **Format Text:** Enables you to change the format of the message (from HTML to plain text, for example). The various text formatting options provided by Word, such as font, paragraph, and style settings, are also available.

- **Review:** Provides proofing aids such as the Spelling & Grammar tool, and language options such as Translate.

> **tip**
>
> You can create a new message as plain text, rich text, or HTML. Select New Items, point at E-mail Message Using, and then select Plain Text, Rich Text, or HTML for the message format.

No matter what enhancements or options you select for your message, you will still need to supply the body of the message, a subject for the message, and the email address of the recipient (or addresses of the recipients). Obviously, you can type an email address in the To: box to specify the recipient. You can also enter multiple email addresses by separating the addresses with a semicolon. A better way to address mail messages, however, is by using the Outlook Address Book.

Using the Outlook Address Book

Outlook has the capability to access different stores or lists of information that can provide you with people's email addresses and other contact information, such as phone numbers and addresses. The Address Book is a catchall repository for address lists and can be used to access your Outlook Contacts list, contacts associated with a particular email account (such as your Microsoft Hotmail account), and other directory lists, such as mobile lists and lists provided by other email and communication servers. For example, in a corporate network, a Microsoft Exchange Server provides a global address list shared by all users on the Exchange network.

Where your email addresses and other contact information are stored depends on whether you are using Outlook on a corporate network that uses Active Directory (a network that deploys Microsoft Windows network servers), a network that uses Exchange Server, or as a standalone product where you use an Internet email account. However, no matter where your contact information is, the Address Book can open the different address lists that you can access.

When you are composing a new message in the message window, you can open the Address Book by selecting To: in the message window or by selecting Address Book on the Ribbon's Message tab. Figure 23.3 shows the Address Book dialog box.

Figure 23.3
The Address Book dialog box.

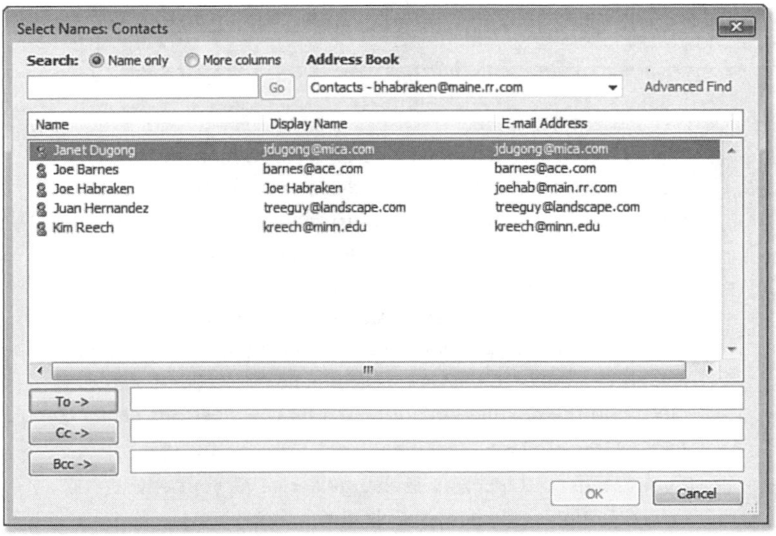

The Address Book drop-down list in the Address Book dialog box enables you to select the list you want to access to address the email, such as your contacts or the Exchange global address list. You can also search the address list using the Search box. By default, the Search feature is set to search the selected address list by name only. Enter a name and then click Go. Outlook highlights the first record in the current address list that matches the search term (such as the first or last name of a contact).

You can also search the address list by selecting the More Columns option button. This enables you to enter a search string and have the Search feature look in all the fields contained in the records in the address list. This would make it possible for you to search for people in the list from a particular state or with a particular company name.

If you would like to view the fields (individual pieces of information such as names, addresses, or company names) available in a particular list such as your Contacts list or the global address list, select the More Columns option button and then select the Advanced Find link. This will open the Find dialog box as shown in Figure 23.4.

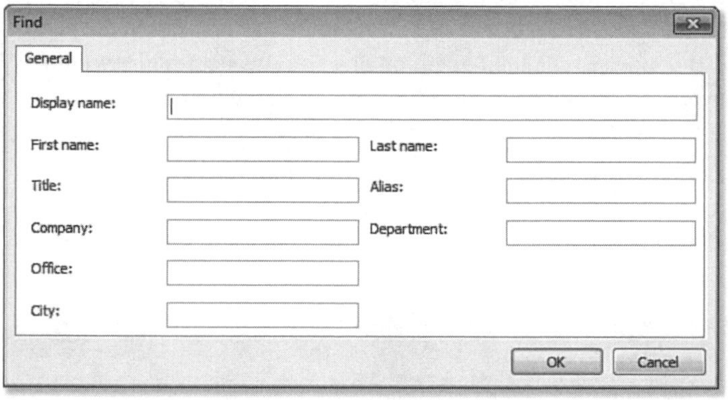

Figure 23.4
The Find dialog box.

The Find dialog box enables you to devise a more complex search than the Search box. You can specify information in different fields and then click OK to search the address list. After you have located the email address you want to use to address the message, select an address and then click the To button in the lower part of the Address Book dialog box. Repeat as necessary to add additional email address. You can also add contacts to the Cc box or Bcc box as needed. After specifying the destination addresses for the message, click OK to close the Address Book dialog box.

If you are using Microsoft Exchange server as your email server, Outlook will immediately check the validity of the email addresses that you have entered in the To Cc and Bcc boxes. If you have entered an invalid address because of a typo or have entered an e-mail address that is no longer on the Exchange server, Outlook will let you know. It places a message below the

> **note**
>
> After you address the mail message, you will find that the People pane appears at the bottom of the message window, listing the recipients. If the recipient is one of your contacts, you can use the information provided in the People pane to view different interactions you have had with the contact, such as mail, meetings, and so on.

Ribbon in the message window saying that the email message cannot be delivered to the email address you have supplied because it is no longer valid. You will also be notified by Outlook if any of the email addresses entered in the To, Cc, or Bcc boxes are Internet email addresses rather than Exchange addresses. The message "The following recipient is outside your organization" will appear, letting you know that the address is not in the Exchange global address list.

Even if you do not use Exchange Server as your email server, you can check the email addresses that you have added to the address boxes in the message, such as To and Cc, to see whether you entered them correctly. Select Check Names on the Ribbon's Message tab. This process will check Internet email addresses for proper email format (*name@something.com*), and will check the email address against those that you have listed in your Contacts folder. If an incorrect or incomplete email address is entered in a To, Cc, or Bcc box, the Check Names dialog box will open. It will attempt to provide you a suggestion as to what the email address should be. The Check Names dialog box also provides you access to the Address Book so that you can check the email address manually and provide the correct address.

When you have the message addressed correctly, you can move on to the subject of the email and the actual body of the message. If you find that you want to put the message aside for the moment and are not ready to actually complete and send the message, you can save it as a draft.

Click the Close button in the Message window. A message box will open asking you whether you want to save changes to the email; click Yes. Outlook will place the message in the Drafts folder. To access the message later, open the Drafts folder and then double-click the message to open it in its window. You can then complete the message and send it.

Setting Message Options

Outlook provides options that enable you to configure the email format, importance, sensitivity, and security settings for a message. You can also specify voting and tracking options for the message, and specify delivery options, such as the email address to use when recipients send replies to the message. Other options relate to the format for the email and policies for the message with regard to archiving and retention.

In accessing these various message options, you will find that they are not on a single Ribbon tab but somewhat dispersed among the tabs. A Properties dialog box for the message provides the greatest aggregate of the different settings. We will look at this dialog box in a moment.

Specifying Email Format

When you create a new email message using the New E-mail Message command, Outlook creates a new message in your default message type, which is HTML if you haven't changed the Outlook settings. You might have some mail recipients that prefer to receive email messages in a particular format, such as, plain text, because of the email client that they are using. As already mentioned, you can select the email format when you use the New Items command to create new email. Select the E-mail Message Using submenu; the different email formats—HTML, plain text, and rich text—are then available for selection.

You can change the email type of an already existing new message. Select the message Ribbon's Format Text tab. The different email format commands are located in the Format group. Outlook highlights the current format for the message in the group. To change the format of the message, select one of the other formats provided. If you select Plain Text as the message type, you will find that the most of the Font and Paragraph commands on the Format Text tab will not be available, nor will the Basic Text group commands on the Message tab.

Setting Message Importance, Flags, and Policies

You can add flags to a message that serve as reminders to you or the message recipient for follow up. You can also assign an importance level to the message so that the recipient knows if the message is of high or low importance.

The message flag assigned to a message will appear at the top of the message window. Messages that you have flagged and then sent will appear marked by a flag in your Sent Items folder. If the recipient also uses Outlook, any messages sent with flags display as tagged with the flag in the recipient's Inbox folder.

To assign a follow-up flag for you on the current message, select Follow Up on the Ribbon's Message tab and then select one of the flags from the flag list, such as Today, Tomorrow, This Week, and so on. Outlook places the flag information at the top of the message window below the Ribbon.

If you want to set a custom flag for you or the recipient of the message, select the Follow Up command in the Tags group and then select Custom. The Custom dialog box will open. You can use the dialog box to set a flag for yourself (me) and a flag for the recipients. Figure 23.5 shows the Custom dialog box with both the Flag for Me and the Flag for Recipients check boxes selected.

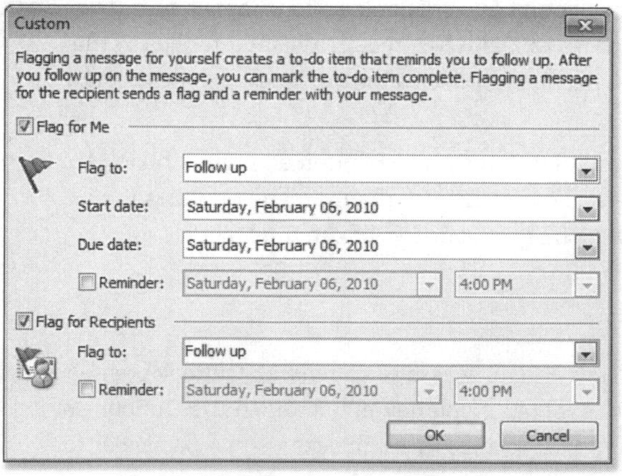

Figure 23.5
The Custom dialog box enables you to select flags for the message.

Use the Flag To: drop-down list to select the flag type, such as Call, Do Not Forward, Follow Up, For Your Information, and so forth. You can also specify a start date and a due date for the flag. If you want to set a reminder for the flag, select the Reminder check box and specify a date and time for the reminder.

To set a flag for the recipient or recipients, select the Flag for Recipients check box. Then use the Flag To: drop-down list to specify the flag type. You can also set reminders for recipient flags: Select the Reminder check box and specify the date and time for the reminder.

Importance Level

There are three importance levels for Outlook messages: low, normal, and high. By default, Outlook assigns all messages the normal importance level. You can change the importance level to high or low importance as needed.

Assigning an importance level to a message is a one-click endeavor. Select either High Importance or Low Importance on the Ribbon's Message tab. If you assigned high importance, you can toggle the setting off by clicking it a second time. This resets the importance level to normal.

Assigning Policies

If you are using Outlook on an Exchange Server network, you will find that the Tags group on the Message tab also includes an Assign Policy command. This command enables you to control both the archive policy and the retention policy for the message. Figure 23.6 shows the policy choices on the Assign Policy menu.

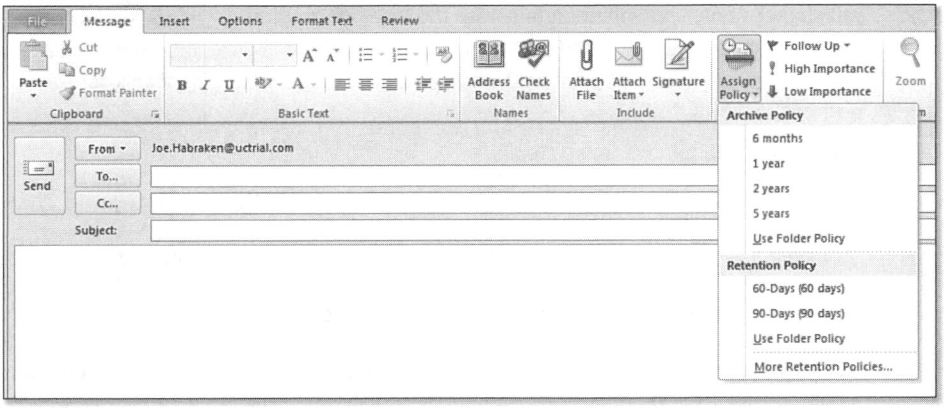

Figure 23.6
The Assign Policy command menu.

The archive policy settings enable you to determine how long Outlook should keep the message in a mail folder, such as the Sent Items folder, before moving it to the Archives folder. The retention policy relates to how long Outlook retains the message in a folder, such as the Sent Items folder, before acting on it. Your Exchange Server administrator typically sets archive and retention policies. The Assign Policy menus are supplied to help you override policies that have been set for you (as an Exchange user) and for your mail folders, which are synchronized with folders found on the Exchange server. Before assigning your own policies to mail items, you should confer with your network administrator.

Setting Permissions and Tracking Options

You can specify permissions for a message that enable you to set an expiration date for the message and control whether a recipient can forward a message. You can also configure the Information Rights Management (IRM) service that makes it possible for you to authenticate the credentials of recipients to whom you send messages that have restricted permissions. IRM is discussed in the next section.

The Tracking options enable you to insert voting buttons on an email that allow the recipients to respond with a click of the mouse. Voting buttons can include items such as approve and reject or yes and no options. The Tracking options also include commands that enable you to receive notification that the recipient of the message has received the message or opened and read it, respectively. The Permission and the Tracking groups are on the Ribbon's Options tab.

Installing the Information Rights Management Service

If you are going to use the permission options, you must have access to a rights management service. If you are on a corporate network, particularly a network that deploys Exchange Server, a network service will manage rights management. If you use Internet-mail and do not have access to an information rights management service, but still want to use the permission options, you will need to set up the free Information Right Management Service (IRMS) provided by Microsoft. You can configure it using a Windows Live ID (a Hotmail email address).

> **⚠ caution**
>
> If you use Outlook primarily for personal email, you may find that there is not a compelling reason to add the IRMS service to your computer because your use of permissions would be more of a novelty rather than a necessity.

To set up IRMS follows these steps:

1. Select Permission and then Manage Credentials. The IRMS Service Sign-Up Wizard will open.

2. Select Yes, I Want to Sign Up for This Free Service from Microsoft and click Next.

3. On the next screen, select Yes, I Have a Windows Live ID and click Next.

4. On the next screen, enter your Windows Live ID (your Hotmail address) and your password. Then click Sign In.

5. On the next screen, select I Accept. The wizard will configure the IRMS feature on your computer.

6. Click Finish to close the wizard.

7. The Select User dialog box will open. Select your Hotmail account and then select OK.

Emails sent from your Outlook email accounts actually have their permissions assigned by the Hotmail account you used to configure the IRMS on your computer. You do not have to actually add the Hotmail account to Outlook as one of the configured email accounts.

When you have the IRMS configured, you can set permissions for a message; select the Permissions command. You can select from the following permissions: Do Not Forward and Set Expiration Date. When you select the Set Expiration Date permission, the Properties dialog box will open for the message. You can set the date and time in the Expires After area of the dialog box. Permissions that you assign to the message, such as the do not forward permission or the message expiration date, display at the top.

Configuring Voting Buttons and Receipts

Voting buttons enable you to make it easy for a recipient or recipients to respond to your email content, such as a question that requires a yes or no answer or a suggestion for either approval or rejection. To add voting buttons to a message, select the Use Voting Buttons command in the Tracking group as shown in Figure 23.7.

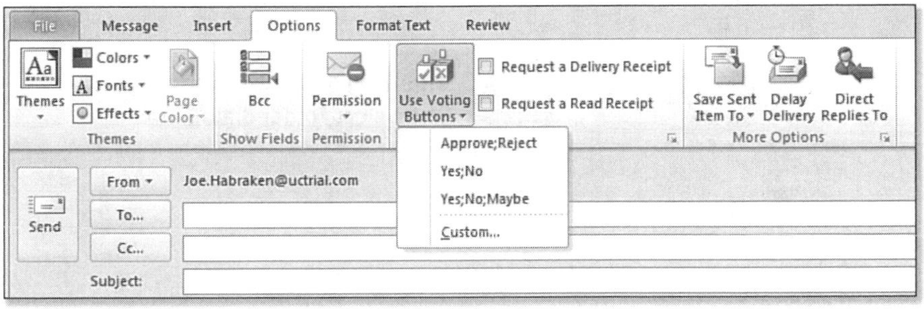

Figure 23.7
The Use Voting
Buttons command
menu.

Select any of the following: Approve, Reject; Yes, No; Yes, No, Maybe. If you want to create a custom set of voting buttons, select Custom. This opens the Properties dialog box for the message. You can type possible responses for the voting buttons in the Use Voting Buttons text box. Separate the selections using a semicolon.

When the recipient votes using the vote buttons on the received message, a message box will open asking whether Outlook should send the vote response immediately or whether to allow the recipient to edit the message before sending. If the recipient closes the email without sending his or her vote, you won't get that vote even if the recipient used the voting buttons.

Requesting Receipts

You can request receipts for your mail messages using the receipt commands in the Tracking group. Outlook provides two possibilities via check boxes. Select Request a Delivery Receipt to receive an email notification that the intended recipient has received the message. Select Request a Read Receipt to receive email confirmation that the recipient has opened the message.

Even if you select either of these options, the recipient can choose not to send the receipt. The dialog box that opens when the recipient opens the message will provide the opportunity for the recipient to say no to sending the receipt.

Setting Delivery Options

You can set certain delivery options, such as where a sent message is saved (the folder that is used when it is saved upon sending), when the message is actually sent (delay delivery), and the email address that replies should be directed to. These options can be useful in cases where you want certain emails placed directly in a folder related to a particular project. They are also handy in the case when you are sending an email and you want all the replies to the email to go to a third party, such as the person who will track who is going to attend a particular event detailed in the message. These delivery options are in the More Options group on the Ribbon's Options tab.

note

If you don't want to save a copy of a sent message (for some reason), select Do Not Save on the Save Sent Item To menu.

To specify a folder as the location for a saved sent item, select the Save Sent Item To command. By default, the message is saved to the default folder, which is the Sent Items folder. Select Other Folder. The Select Folder dialog box will open as shown in Figure 23.8.

Figure 23.8
The Select Folder dialog box.

Select a folder in the list. If you want to create a new folder, click the New button. The Create New Folder dialog box will open. Type the name of the new folder and select where you want to place the new folder in the folder list; then click OK. After you have specified the folder (or created a new folder), select OK to close the Select Folder dialog box.

If you want to specify a delivery date for the message, select the Delay Delivery command. The Properties dialog box for the message will open. By default, Outlook selects the Do Not Deliver Before check box in the Delivery Options area of the Properties dialog box. Specify a date and time for the delivery. Then click Close to close the dialog box.

The Message Properties Dialog Box

Several of the commands that we have discussed in this section have required access to the new message's Properties dialog box. If you are going to set a number of options related to a message, it makes sense to select your settings in the dialog box. Select the dialog box launcher in the Tracking group or More Options group of the Options tab. Figure 23.9 shows the Properties dialog box for a message.

Figure 23.9
The Properties dialog box for a message.

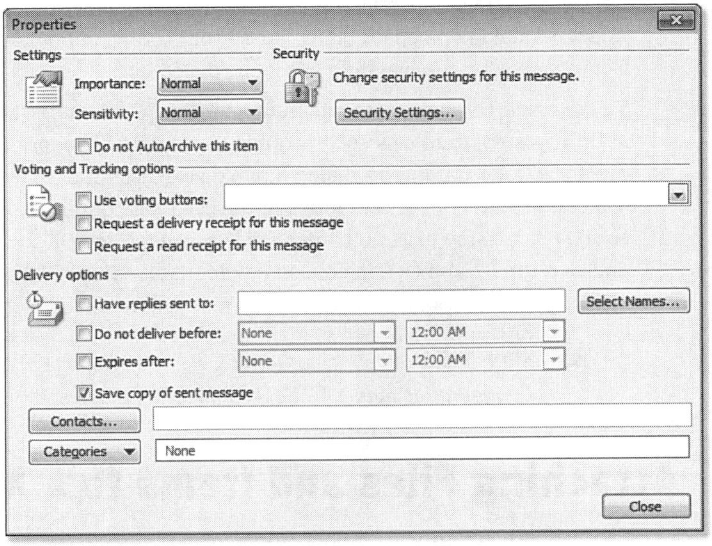

In the Settings area of the Properties dialog box, you can set the importance (which we already discussed) and the sensitivity of the message. The sensitivity settings include Normal, Personal, Private, and Confidential. Marking the message with a sensitivity level, such as Confidential, is only to suggest how the recipient should handle the contents of the message. The sensitivity setting does not preclude the recipient from forwarding the message, for instance.

You can also configure the Voting and Tracking options in the Properties dialog box as you can delivery options. All these options are also accessible via the various Ribbon groups we have discussed in previous sections of this chapter.

> *Security settings can also be set in the Properties dialog box, see Chapter 27, "Securing and Maintaining Outlook," on page 737.*

The Message Options dialog box also enables you to link a contact or contacts to a message and assign categories to a message. Linking a contact to a message enables you to view the message on that contact's Activities page when you are viewing that particular contact's record in the Contacts folder.

When you associate contacts and categories to messages, you are actually just applying organizational tags to the emails. You can then view all the email sent to a particular contact in

tip

If you only occasionally set properties related to your email messages and are not consistently using the same settings, you can use the various commands on the Ribbon or the Options dialog box. If you find that you always use the same options for your mail (other than the defaults), change the Mail Options in the Outlook Options window. This chapter discusses mail options a little later.

the Contacts folder or sort sent email by a particular category. The recipient of email that you have tagged in this manner does not know that you have assigned the contact or the category to the message.

To assign a contact to a message, click the Contacts button in the Options dialog box. The Select Contacts dialog box opens, showing all your contacts. Double-click a contact to add it to the Contacts box on the message's Options dialog box.

You can add categories to a message in a similar manner. Click the Categories drop-down list to assign a category to a message. You can select All Categories on the Categories drop-down list to open the Color Categories dialog box. You can assign a category (or categories) to the message by selecting a category or categories in the color Categories dialog box. You can also create new categories or rename existing categories if needed. Click OK to close the Color Categories dialog box and to return to the Options dialog box for the message. When you have completed setting options related to the message, select Close to exit the Options dialog box.

 More about categorizing Outlook items is available in Chapter 22, "Requisite Outlook: Configuration and Essential Features," on page 622.

Attaching Files and Items to a Message

You can attach files and Outlook items to your email messages. You can send Word documents, Excel workbooks, a family photo, or any other file you want, including a collection of files in various archive formats such as Zip. You can also send Outlook items, such as business cards of your contacts. Commands for attaching files and Outlook items are available on the Message tab and the Insert tab of the message window's Ribbon.

When you attach a file, it appears as an icon in an attachment box that resides in the message window right below the Subject box. If you want to view an attachment in the parent application (such as an Excel workbook in Excel), double-click the attachment in the message and the attached file will open in the appropriate application.

> ⚠ **caution**
>
> The number and overall size of attachments can be problematic, particularly in cases where you have an Internet email account that limits the size of attachments. The size allowed can vary from provider to provider, so you should read the provider's FAQ or call your provider to determine attachment limits before you try to send all your family reunion photos attached to a single email message.

You can attach multiple files to an email as needed. To attach a file to a message, select the Attach File command on the Ribbon's Message tab in the message window. The Insert File dialog box will open as shown in Figure 23.10. By default, your Documents library folder will open.

Select the file (or files) that you want to attach to the message and then click Insert. The Attached box will list the attached file or files. If you attach a file and then decide that you don't want it attached to the message, select the attachment in the Attached box and delete it by pressing the Delete key.

Figure 23.10
The Insert File dialog
box.

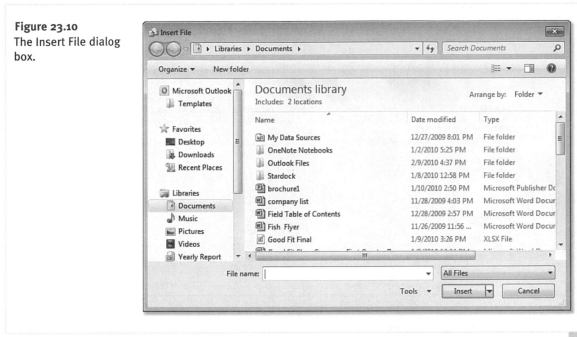

If you are working in Windows Explorer and want to send a file listed, right-click on the file and the select Send from the shortcut menu. This will open a new message in Outlook with the file attached.

In addition to attaching files from other programs, you can also attach an Outlook item to a message. An Outlook item can be any item saved in one of your personal folders, including an appointment, a contact, a note, and so on. Outlook actually makes it very easy for you to attach business cards of your Outlook contacts and calendars. The recipient can view calendar items even if she does not use Outlook.

To attach an item, select the Attach Item command on the Message tab. This command provides a menu of three possibilities: Business Card, Calendar, and Outlook Item.

Attaching a Business Card

To attach a business card of one of your contacts, select Attach Item, Business Card. The submenu will list any contact cards that you have recently attached to messages. To view a list of all your contacts, select Other Business Cards to open the Insert Business Card dialog box.

Use the Look In: drop-down list to select the Contacts list that you want to view in the dialog box. To preview a contact as a business card, select the contact. When you are ready to attach the business card, select OK. Outlook will attach the card to the message, and the card will be inserted into the body of the message as shown in Figure 23.11.

If you don't want to include the business card in the body of the message, select the business card and then press Delete. The card itself will remain as an attachment in the Attached box. You can also delete it from the Attached box if you decide not to send the business card: Select the card in the Attached box and press Delete.

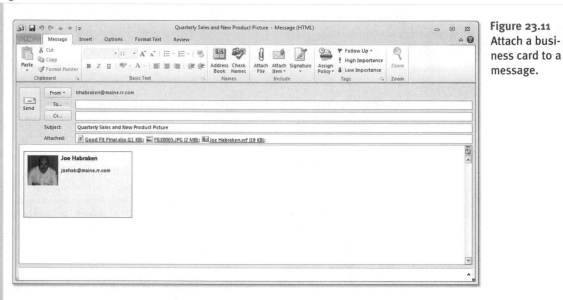

Figure 23.11
Attach a business card to a message.

Attaching a Calendar

You can attach a calendar as an item to your mail message. The recipient need not use Outlook to view the calendar information. The attached calendar can consist of the current date (Today) or a range of dates. You also have control over the level of detail provided in the calendar.

To send a calendar via the message, select Attach Item and then Calendar. The Send a Calendar via E-mail dialog box will open as shown in Figure 23.12.

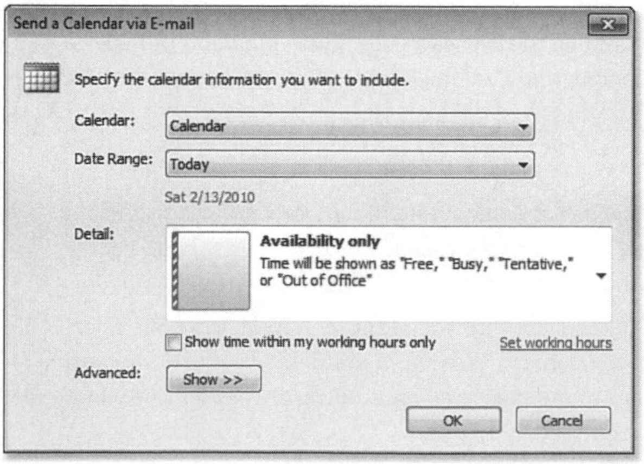

Figure 23.12
Attach a calendar to the message.

Use the Calendar drop-down list to select the calendar that will supply the information for the attachment (if you have multiple calendars in your Calendar folder). Select the Date Range drop-down list to select the range of dates for the calendar. You can select set ranges, such as Tomorrow and Next 7 Days, or you can click the Specify Dates button and provide the start and end dates for the range.

The Detail settings for the calendar relate to the amount of detail you want to provide the recipient. By default the detail level is set to Availability only, which will show time as free, busy, tentative, and so on. If you want to include the availability and the subjects of your calendar items (within the date range), select the Limited Details setting. For full disclosure, you can select the Full Details setting.

 tip

You can select the Show Time Within My Working Hours Only check box and then set your working hours in the Send a Calendar via E-mail dialog box. This precludes any appointments or items in the calendar from the attached calendar that fall outside your working day.

If you select either the Limited Details or the Full Details setting, Outlook gives you additional options in the Advanced area of the dialog box. You can choose to include the details of items marked private and in the case of the Full Details setting, you can also include items attached to calendar items within the date range that you have selected.

You can also specify the format of the attached calendar. Select the Show button to view the advanced settings. Select E-mail Layout to choose the layout for the calendar; you can select from Daily Schedule (the default) or List of Events. When you have completed your selection related to the attached calendar, select OK to close the dialog box. Outlook inserts the calendar in the Attached box and the details of the calendar into the body of the message. Users of Outlook can open the attached Calendar (.ics) file in Outlook. If you are going to send the calendar to someone who does not use Outlook, you might want to delete the calendar file in the Attached box and leave the calendar embedded in the body of the message. The calendar will actually provide links from a calendar to a list of specific appointments it includes.

Using Themes and Email Stationery

If you use the HTML or the rich text message format, you can use themes for your mail messages. A theme provides formatting attributes for the colors, fonts, and effects used in the message. Because you are using Word as your message editor, you are, in effect, applying a Word theme to the body text of the message. Themes are useful because they enable you to have a consistent look across a family of associated items such as mail messages, Word documents, or Excel worksheets.

➡ *For information on using themes in Word, see Chapter 7, "Enhancing Word Documents," on page 171.*

Email stationery has been available in the last few versions of Outlook. Stationery provides you with an overall look for the message's text and includes backgrounds for the body of the message. You can use stationery when you compose HTML emails. Let's look at assigning a theme to a message and then we can discuss creating a message using stationery.

To select a theme for the message, follow these steps:

1. Type the body of your message or make sure that the insertion point is in the body of the message.

2. Select the Options tab of the Ribbon.

3. Select the Themes command. You can preview any of the themes in the gallery by placing the mouse on a particular theme.

4. When you have decided on the theme you will use, click the theme to assign it to the message.

You can fine-tune the themes by using the Colors, Fonts, and Effects command as needed to adjust settings for the current theme. If you want to add a background color to the body of the message, use the Page Color command to select from the various theme colors. You can preview the colors by placing the mouse on a color.

If you want to use stationery, you must select the stationery as you create the new message. On the Home tab of any of the Outlook folders, select the New Items command, point at E-Mail Message Using, and then select More Stationery. The Theme or Stationery dialog box will open as shown in Figure 23.13.

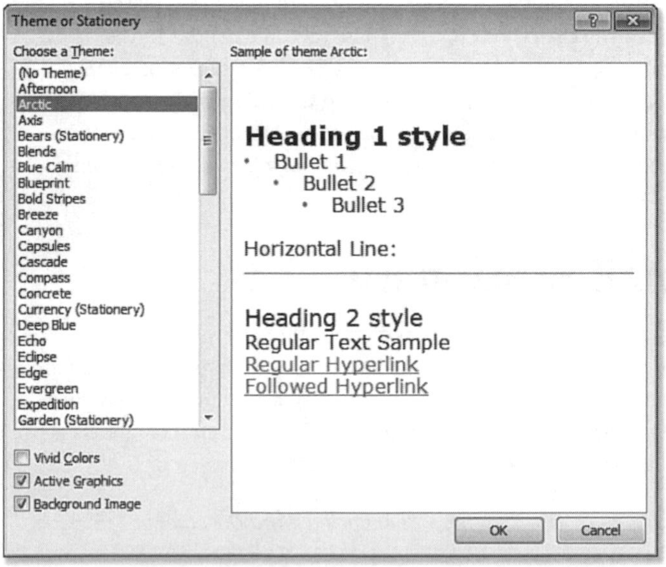

Figure 23.13
Select stationery for the new message.

This dialog box provides a list of available themes and installed stationery. The stationery is marked with the parenthetical tag (Stationery). Select stationery (such as Bears, Currency, or Garden) and a preview of the stationery will display in the dialog box. When you have found the stationery that you want to use, select OK to apply the stationery to the new message and return to the message window.

Adding a Signature

You can further personalize your emails by adding a signature to the message. A signature can be as simple as just your name, or a signature can include your phone number, extension, or other information. Some people even add a favorite quote to their signature. If you use HTML as your message format, you can even include signature files that contain graphics. Plain-text signatures (for use with plain-text messages) will consist of text characters only.

You can create more than one signature for your mail messages. This enables you to have a different signature for your business emails and personal emails. You can also create signatures for your plain-text messages and HTML messages.

> ### 🔍 note
> Signatures for your emails are not the same thing as digital signatures. Digital signatures ensure that a mail message is from a trusted source. Chapter 27, "Securing and Maintaining Outlook," discusses digital signatures.

To create a signature, select the Signature command on the message Ribbon's Message tab and then select Signature again. The Signatures and Stationery dialog box will open. The E-Mail Signature tab of the dialog box will contain a list of your signatures in the Select Signature to Edit box. If you haven't created any signatures, there obviously won't be any signatures in the list.

To create a new signature, click the New button. The New Signature dialog box will open. Type a name for the new signature and click OK. The signature will appear in the signature list. Now you can edit the signature using the various tools shown in the Edit Signature pane (see Figure 23.14).

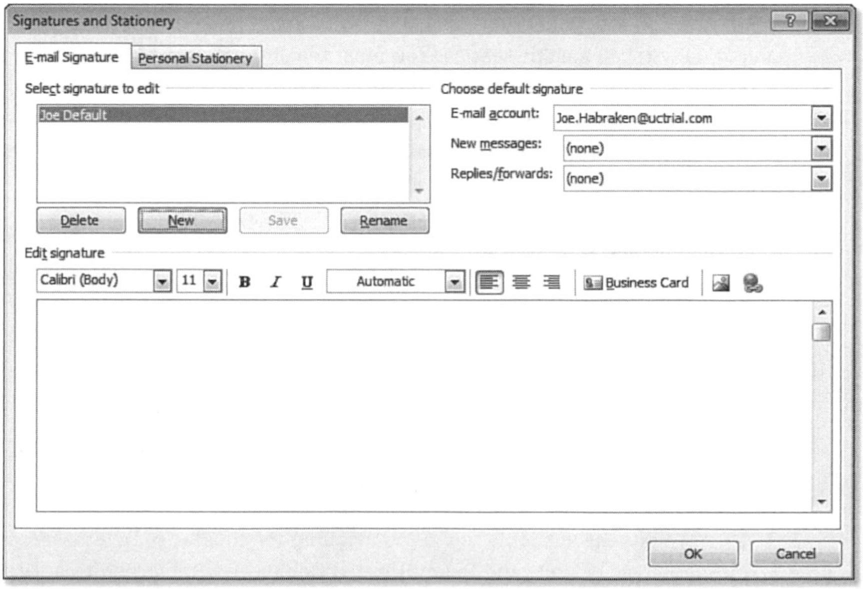

Figure 23.14
Create signatures in the Signatures and Stationery dialog box.

Type the text for the signature and use the various drop-down formatting lists to format the text. You can also insert a business card or pictures and links in the signature. When you are finished creating the signature, you can repeat the process to create other signatures as needed. When you click OK, the Signatures and Stationery dialog box will close. You can now use the Signature command to select from the list of the signatures that you have created and add them to the email.

Sending Mail

When you have completed your email message, you can send it. You can click Send and Outlook will place the message in your Outbox folder. If you have a persistent connection to your outgoing mail server, Outlook sends the message immediately and places a copy of the message in your Sent Items folder.

If you are working offline, Outlook places the message in your Outbox folder. The message will remain in the Outbox until you connect to your network (or the Internet, if you are using Internet email) and use the Send and Receive command. If you configured the message with delivery options that specified a delivery date, the message will stay in the Outbox until the delivery date arrives.

> **tip**
>
> You can also send an email by pressing Ctrl+Enter. The first time you press this key combination, Outlook will ask that you verify it as a shortcut for sending email. Click Yes.

Recalling a Message

If you work on a network that uses Microsoft Exchange Server as your email messaging server, you can actually recall sent messages. You must recall the message before the recipient opens, deletes, or moves it to another folder. This feature is useful if you have inadvertently sent an incomplete message or have forgotten to include an important attachment with the message. The recall feature actually provides you with two possibilities. You can recall the message and delete unread copies of the message. Or you can recall the message and replace it with a new message, such as a message that actually includes the attachment you wanted to send.

To recall a message, follow these steps:

1. With the Mail folder selected, select the Sent Items folder.

2. Double-click the message that you want to recall to open it.

> **note**
>
> By default, Outlook will provide information on whether the recall succeeds for each of the message recipients.

3. On the Ribbon's Message tab, select Actions, and then Recall This Message. The Recall This Message dialog box will open as shown in Figure 23.15.

4. Two options are available related to recalling the message: Delete Unread Copies of This Message (the default) and Delete Unread Copies and Replace with a New Message. Select the option that you want to use.

Figure 23.15
Recall a message.

5. If you go with the default option to recall the message, select OK and the Recall Message dialog box will close. If you select the replace with a new message option, a new message will open. Create the message that will replace the recalled message and then click Send.

You eventually receive a notification in your Inbox folder (as new mail) notifying you whether the recall was successful. Remember that this feature is for Exchange Server mail accounts. It does not provide you with the ability to recall messages sent via Internet email accounts.

Although you can't recall Internet email messages, you can use this feature to notify the recipients of a particular email message that you want them to ignore the message. Use the message recall feature as detailed in the steps in this section. When you "recall" the message, Outlook sends a new message that states you would like to recall the previous message to the original recipients. This doesn't remove the original message from the recipients' inboxes, but it at least provides them with a follow-up message that the original message is essentially invalid.

Working with Received Email

New email is downloaded when you open Outlook and connect to your mail server; this is either accomplished automatically if you have a persistent connection to the mail server (such as through network, DSL [designated service line], or cable modem connections) or when you connect to your Internet Service Provider via a modem.

By default, when Outlook opens, it selects your email inbox and lists new emails in the Details pane. Outlook groups email in your Inbox folder by date and arranges it in conversations. This means that even messages that are contained in other folders, such as the Sent Items folder, will appear in the Inbox folder because of the Conversations view. This makes it easy for you to view associated messages that relate to a particular mail message subject. You can expand conversations as needed to view all the messages in a particular conversation.

As already mentioned, the conversations are listed by date and convenient date groupings, such as Today, Last Week, Two Weeks Ago, and Older, enabling you to quickly locate messages that relate to a particular time period. You can collapse and expand a time period group, such as Last Week, to make it easier to concentrate on other date groupings of email conversations listed in the Inbox folder.

Reading mail is really just a matter of selecting the message that you want to read; the message will appear in the Reading pane. You can also open a message in a separate window. Double-click the message in the Details pane.

After you read a particular message, you will typically answer it, forward it, or delete it. Outlook tracks each of these actions. For example, when you reply to a message, the original message in the Inbox folder is marked with a Replied symbol. Outlook saves the actual reply message in the Sent Items folder. You will find that, if you are in the Conversations view, the reply will also appear in the Inbox folder as part of the conversation. The same is true for forwarded email, which will be marked with a Forwarded symbol in the Inbox folder.

Deleted items generate the least amount of electronic redundancy (in terms of saving and listing copies). When you delete a message, Outlook moves it to the Deleted Items folder. When you empty the Deleted Items folder, that message is gone.

Managing Email

Managing email is really just a matter of determining what to do with your received email messages, although you can manage the Sent Items folder and messages that you save in other folders for later consideration. Whether you read your messages in the Reading pane or prefer to open them in a separate window, all the commands that you need to manage individual messages are easily accessible via the Ribbon. If you are working in the Inbox folder, the Mail Ribbon provides most of the message management commands on the Home tab. If you are working with a received message that you have opened in its own window, the message management commands are on the Ribbon's Message tab (which is the only tab available other the File tab that takes you to the Backstage). You will find that more commands related to dealing with a message are on the Message tab of the message window's Ribbon. So, you might want to open a message if you want to quickly perform an action related to that message. Figure 23.16 shows the message window's Ribbon with the Message tab selected.

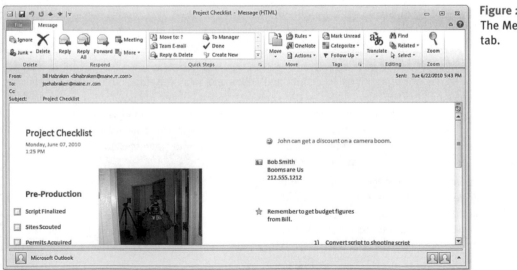

Figure 23.16
The Message tab.

Outlook dedicates most of the command groups on the Message tab to managing received messages. For example, the Delete group provides options for dealing with messages that you no longer want, whereas the Respond group provides different commands for replying to or forwarding a message. The Quick Steps group provides access to Quick Steps, which are commands that combine multiple actions into one click; you can create a Quick Step that does several things to a received message. For example, the Reply & Delete Quick Step will open a reply message to the current message and delete the message itself from the Inbox folder.

 For more about the basics of Quick Steps, see Chapter 22, "Requisite Outlook: Configuration and Essential Features," on page 599.

Answering a Message

Answering or replying to a message can take the form of a simple reply to the sender of the message or can encompass a reply that goes to everyone who received the original message and the sender of that message.

To reply to the sender of the message, select the Reply command in the Respond group. A new message window will open containing the original message text. Type your response to the message and then select Send.

If you want to reply to the sender and all the recipients of the original message, select Reply All. This will open a new message window addressed to the sender and all recipients, including those listed in the Cc or Bcc address boxes.

The next time you open a message to which you've replied, there is a reminder at the top of the message window telling you the date and time you sent your reply. Don't forget that the Replied To arrow next to a message in the Inbox window also shows that you have responded to the message.

Forwarding a Message

You can forward received mail as needed to coworkers or other concerned parties. When you forward a message, you can add additional text to the email and include new attachments to the message, if you so choose. Forwarded mail will include any attachments that were part of the originally received message.

Open the message that you want to forward or select the message in the Inbox folder. Select the Forward command in the Respond group. A new message window will open. Provide the addresses of the individuals that you want to receive the forwarded message. Select Send to send the forwarded message. Outlook places a copy of the forwarded message in your Sent Items folder and tags the original message as forwarded.

> **note**
>
> Attachments are not included with your response to the message, so if you add recipient addresses to an email reply, they are not going to receive any attachments related to the original message.

> **tip**
>
> You can right-click a message and then select Reply or Reply All from the shortcut menu that appears.

> **caution**
>
> Attachments can pose a security hazard. Do not open attachments from unknown e-mail senders. Even email from known parties merits at least some scrutiny. Save attachments to your computer and then scan them with anti-virus software before opening.

Saving an Attachment

When you receive messages with attachments, it makes sense that you will want to save those attachments to folders on your computer for later examination or reference, or even for editing. You can pick out messages with attachments in your inbox because a paper clip icon beside the message subject represents a message attachment.

Select (in the Inbox) or open the message that contains the attachment that you want to save. The attachment appears as an icon above the message area. To save the attachment, select the attachment icon. Outlook previews the attached item in the message window or Reading pane as shown in Figure 23.17 (which shows the attachment in the Reading pane). The Attachment Tools contextual tab for the Ribbon will also appear.

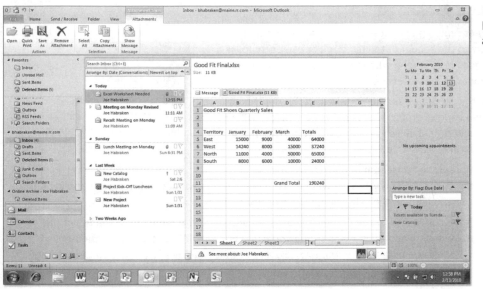

Figure 23.17
Preview the attachment.

The Actions group on the Attachment Tools tab provides you with the ability to open, print, save, and remove the attachment. To save the attachment to your computer, select the Save As command. The Save Attachment dialog box will open. Navigate to the folder where you want to save the attachment. You can also change the filename of the saved version of the attachment if needed. Select Save to save the attachment.

You can toggle between the message and the attachment preview using the Message and attachment icons provided above the message text. If you do not want to preview the attachment before saving it, right-click the Attachment icon and select Save As from the shortcut menu. You can then save the file via the Save Attachment dialog box as previously discussed.

If a message contains multiple attachments and you would like to save them without previewing or opening them, select File to open the Backstage and then select Save Attachments. The Save All Attachments dialog box will open. You can specify which attachments to save in the dialog box.

When you are ready to save the attachments, click OK. The Save All Attachments dialog box will open. Specify the folder where Outlook should save the attachments and then select OK.

 For more about attachments and Outlook security settings, see Chapter 27, "Securing and Maintaining Outlook," on page 740.

Deleting Messages

You actually have options related to the deletion of messages in your Inbox folder (or other mail folders). As already mentioned, the commands related to deleting mail messages are in the Delete group. The most straightforward way to deal with a selected message or group of selected messages that you no longer want is to click the Delete command. The message or messages will move to your Deleted items folder. Outlook provides three other possibilities in the Delete group. These commands are as follows:

- **Ignore:** This command will move the currently selected message and any future messages in the conversation (based on the subject) to the Delete Items folder.

- **Clean Up:** This command actually provides a list of three related commands: Clean Up Conversation, Clean Up Folder, and Clean Up Folder & Subfolders. If you select Clean Up Conversation, Outlook moves redundant messages in the conversation to the Deleted Items folder. Remember that the Conversation view can include messages that are present in other Mail folders not just the Inbox folder. The Clean Up Folder and Clean Up Folder & Subfolders commands will remove redundant messages in the current folder or the current folder and its subfolders, respectively.

- **Junk:** This command provides an options list that enables you to block the sender or to never block the sender or the sender's domain (such as *@whatever.com*). This command also provides you with the ability to access the Junk E-Mail Options dialog box for your email account.

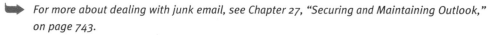 *For more about dealing with junk email, see Chapter 27, "Securing and Maintaining Outlook," on page 743.*

The various commands provided in the Delete group make removing items from the Inbox folder or another mail folder a more constructive process in terms of keeping the Inbox free of unwanted, redundant, and spam email. Email messages can also be managed using rules, which are discussed later in the book.

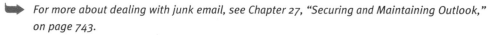 *For more about using message rules, see Chapter 27, "Securing and Maintaining Outlook," on page 746.*

When your emails are in the Deleted Items folder, they are destined for oblivion (although you can move a message in the folder to another folder if you decide you want to keep it). To permanently delete a message in the Delete Items folder, select the message (you can select multiple messages) and then click the Delete command. A message will appear asking whether you want to delete the selected item or items permanently. Click Yes to permanently delete the message or messages.

If you typically are confident about the status of messages that you delete (you know that you won't want to undelete them), you can empty all the messages in the Deleted Items folder rather than emptying it piecemeal, message by message. Right-click the Deleted Items folder and select Empty Folder. Click Yes to verify the permanent deletion of the items in the Deleted Items folder.

You can also configure Outlook so that your Deleted Items folder empties when you exit Outlook. Select File to open the Backstage and then select Options. In the Outlook Options window, select Advanced and navigate to the Outlook Start and Exit settings. Select the Empty Deleted Items Folders When Exiting Outlook check box. Now Outlook will empty your Deleted Items folder (or folders, if you have multiple email accounts) when you exit.

Printing Mail

You can print your email messages in multiple ways. To send a message to the printer without previewing it, right-click the message and select Quick Print from the shortcut menu. This will send the message directly to your default printer.

If you want to specify the printer, the print options, or the print style for the printout, select File and then Print. The Print window will open and provide a preview of the message. You can change the settings related to the print job, such as the printer and the print style.

Organizing Messages

Organizing messages can relate to how you fine-tune your view of the Inbox folder (particularly the Details pane), and it can relate to sorting and filtering messages in the Inbox or other mail folder. You can use the Ribbon's View tab to change the view of your email in the Inbox (or any email folder, for that matter). The view tab provides the Arrangement group that enables you to change the way Outlook arranges messages in the Inbox folder (or other mail folder). Figure 23.18 shows the expanded Arrangement group on the View tab.

Figure 23.18
The Arrangement group on the View tab.

You can arrange the messages shown in the Inbox folder by using the various commands in the Arrangement group. By default, Outlook arranges the messages by date, in groups. You can specify that Outlook arrange the messages by sender, whether a message has an attachment, or by importance level or category.

You can also change the sort order of the message list. Select the Reverse Sort command to change the order of the message list. By default, Outlook lists messages newest to oldest; reversing this order would show the message oldest to newest.

Filtering Email

The Arrangement commands change how Outlook arranges the messages in a folder such as the Inbox, but you might also want to view a subset of the messages in the Inbox folder based on certain criteria, such as only messages flagged as high importance or only emails that have attachments. You can filter email using the Filter E-mail command on the Ribbon's Home tab. The command actually uses the Outlook Search feature to filter the messages in the Inbox folder.

> ### tip
> You can create your own filters directly in the Search box. Type search criteria to view the messages that match the criteria.

Select Filter E-Mail and then select one of the available filters such as Unread, Has Attachments, or Flagged. The list will filter based on your selection and the Search Tools tab will appear on the Ribbon. This tab provides you with the ability to set the scope for the filter, such as the current folder or all subfolders, and refine the search. Search refinements enable you to add additional criteria to the search. For example, if you filtered your Inbox folder by Has Attachments, you could then select the Categorized command to add a category to your search filter. You could add another refinement such as importance, for example, by selecting the Important command.

Several filter refinement commands (which add criteria to the search filter) are available in the Refine group of the Search Tools tab, including Categorized, Sent To, and Flagged. You can access additional refinement criteria by selecting the More command, which provides the Common Properties list. This list enables you to refine the search by all sorts of criteria, including Bcc, Cc, Due Date, From, and Received.

When you have completed work with the Search Tools and want to remove the filter that you have placed on the current folder, select the Close Search command. Outlook returns you to the folder such as the Inbox and removes the filter, showing the entire contents of the folder.

Moving Email

You can also organize your mail messages by moving the messages from your Inbox folder to other folders. You can use the Move command on the Home tab of the Ribbon to move and copy messages from one folder to another. This provides you with alternative places to store items, and can make finding them in the future easier rather than just having all your messages languish in the Inbox folder in one huge mess.

> ### tip
> If you have a lot of messages in the Inbox, you might want to filter the messages using particular criteria and then move those messages *en masse* to another folder.

To move a message, select the message in the Details pane. Then select the Move command on the Ribbon's Home tab. If you want to move the selected messages to another folder, select Other Folder. The Move Items dialog box will open as shown in Figure 23.19.

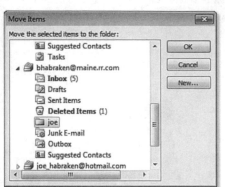

Figure 23.19
Move messages to another folder.

Specify the folder that you want to move the items to. If you need to create a new folder, select the New button. The Create New Folder dialog box will open. Type a name for the new folder and then select the location in the folder list where you want to place the new folder. Click OK to close the Create New Folder dialog box—you return to the Move Items dialog box. Click OK to move the items and to close the Move Items dialog box.

If you don't like working with the Move Items dialog box, you can also create folders directly in the Navigation pane's folder list and then drag items from the current folder, such as the Inbox, to another folder. Right-click on a particular email account and then select new Folder from the shortcut menu. Provide a name for the folder and it's ready to go. You can then select items in the current mail folder in the Details pane and then drag them to the new folder.

> **note**
>
> An excellent way to keep your mail messages organized is to use rules that automatically determine what happens to an email message or messages that meet particular conditions. These rules will move or delete messages depending on the rule actions. See Chapter 27 for more about rules.

Managing Email Accounts

As we discussed in Chapter 22, Outlook makes it easy for you to configure your default email account the first time you run Outlook. You can add or delete email accounts as needed. You can also change the configuration settings for any existing email accounts. Outlook supports four different types of email accounts:

- **Exchange Server:** This type of account makes Outlook an Exchange Server client; mailboxes and other resources, such as shared public folders, are managed on the Exchange Server on your network. Your network system administrator will typically configure or provide you with the settings for an Exchange account.

- **POP3 Account:** POP3 (Post Office Protocol 3) is a protocol that most ISPs use, which allows a POP3 email server to function as a mail drop. This means that your incoming email arrives at the POP3 server and sits there until you connect with your email client (Outlook) and download the mail to your computer.

- **IMAP Account:** IMAP (Internet Message Access Protocol) is a protocol that allows Outlook to download email from an IMAP mail server. IMAP differs from POP3 in that your email is not removed from the mail server when you connect to the server with Outlook. Instead, Outlook provides you with a list of saved and new messages, which you can then open and read. IMAP is particularly useful when more than one device, such as your computer and a smart phone or other mobile device, may access a single email account.

> **🔍 note**
> You must configure both POP3 and IMAP accounts for the outgoing mail server, which is the SMTP server. SMTP is the Simple Mail Transport Protocol and is used to get your mail from your computer to your provider's SMTP mail server and then on to the Internet for delivery.

- **HTTP Account:** Hypertext Transfer Protocol (HTTP) is the protocol that enables you to browse websites using a web browser. Typically you access HTTP email through a website such as Microsoft's Hotmail website. You can configure Microsoft Hotmail as an Outlook email account using the Outlook Connector, which is a free download provided by Microsoft—you download it when you add a Hotmail account to your Outlook email configuration. You can add other HTTP email accounts to the Outlook configuration, however, Hotmail is the only one really supported by Microsoft. Downloads are available on the Web that can help you configure a Yahoo! account, for example.

To access your Outlook account settings, select File and then Info. On the Backstage Account Information window, select Account Settings. If you are using Outlook for Internet email only, only one command will be available on the Account Settings menu: Account Settings. If you use Outlook as an Exchange Server client, you also receive the Delegate Access, Download Address Book, and Manage Mobile Notifications commands. Select Account Settings on the menu. The Account Settings dialog box will open. The E-mail tab of the Account Settings dialog box will list your currently installed email accounts, as shown in Figure 23.20.

Editing Email Account Settings

To view the current settings for an email account, double-click the account. The Change Account dialog box will open (which you can also open by selecting the account and then clicking the Change icon on the toolbar). You can view the user information, server information, and logon information for the account. You can edit account settings, if necessary, and then use the Test Account Settings button to see whether the new account settings work correctly. You would need to change account settings only if your ISP sent you a notice to change settings or if the account was not working correctly.

If an account is not working correctly, you can also use the Repair command to open the Auto Account Setup Wizard. The wizard will walk you through all the steps of setting up the account, so

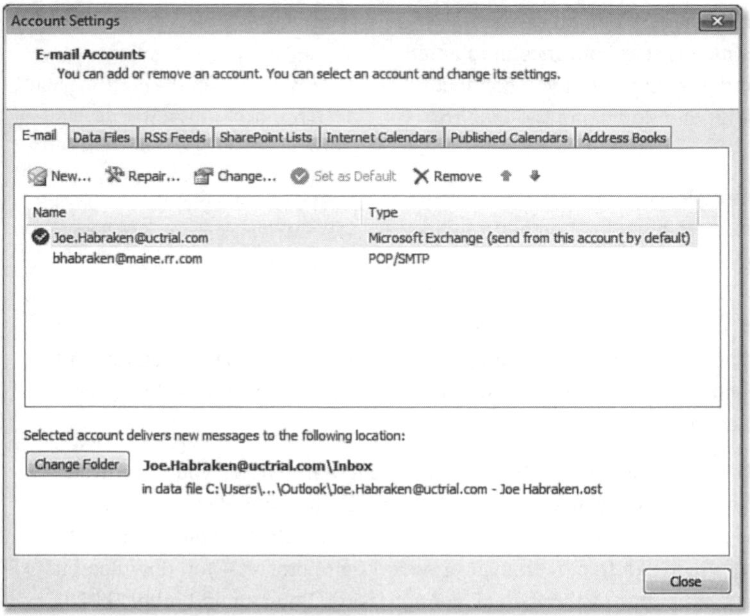

Figure 23.20
The Account Settings dialog box.

it might be your best bet to find a typo or other incorrectly entered information that is not allowing the account to operate in Outlook.

If an email account is listed in the Account Settings dialog box that you no longer have or use (for instance, you have changed ISPs), you can delete an account from the list. Select the account and then click the Remove button. Outlook will ask you to verify the removal. If you truly want to remove the account, select Yes.

You have control over the email account considered the default account for Outlook. Typically you will send new mail messages from the default account. Select an account in the account list and then click the Set as Default button. Outlook designates the account as the default with the default icon (a circle with a checkmark). This change will not take place until you close the Account Settings dialog box and restart Outlook.

Adding an Email Account

You can add email accounts to the Outlook configuration; you should know a couple of things first, however. If you configured an ISP (Internet) email account as your first email account, you won't be able to add an Exchange Server account via Outlook. You will have to close Outlook and add the Exchange account using the Mail Setup dialog box in the Windows Control Panel, which you reach via the Mail icon in the User Accounts and Family Safety group. You can select the E-Mail Accounts button on the Mail Setup dialog box, and the Account Settings dialog box will open—this is the same dialog box that you can open from within Outlook. You can then add the account as detailed next.

Whether you are in Outlook or have opened the Account Settings dialog box via the Control Panel's Mail Setup dialog box, select New in the Account Settings dialog box. The Add New Account dialog box will open. You must choose a service to add, and because we are adding an email account, the Microsoft Exchange, POP3, or IMAP option button will be selected. That's what we want, so click Next to continue.

The next screen requests that you enter your name, email address, and password (twice). You can enter this information and Outlook will attempt to search your network (in the case of an Exchange account) or search the Internet to verify the account settings.

> ### ⚓ caution
> Outlook email accounts and Outlook profiles are closely wound entities. I suggest that you look at Chapter 22, and read the sections "Configuring Outlook at First Start" and "Understanding Outlook Profiles" before adding additional email accounts to Outlook's configuration.

I suggest that you forgo the auto setup and manually configure your account. Here is why: If you have an Exchange Server account, typically your network administrator set it up for you unless he or she likes living dangerously. I have never worked in an environment where Exchange users set up their own accounts other than downloading a configuration file that set up the account automatically.

If you get your email from an ISP, the ISP will supply you with the POP3, MAPI (Messaging Application Programming Interface), and SMTP (Simple Mail Transfer Protocol) server names. With these types of email accounts, your ISP typically provides you with a master logon name and password and you can then specify the username and password for email accounts associated with your ISP account. You typically do this on the ISP's website.

So, to correctly configure the email account settings, you need to know the incoming mail server name (POP3 or IMAP), the outgoing mail SMTP server name, your account name, and your password. Now back to the Add New Account dialog box.

Select the Manually Configure Server Settings or Additional Server Types option button at the bottom of the Add New Account dialog box. Then click Next. The next screen will ask you to select the type of service you want to add (yes, I know we already did this once). For POP or IMAP accounts, select Internet E-mail. If you are configuring a Microsoft Exchange account, which is unlikely, you would select Microsoft Exchange. Let's assume that you are adding Internet E-Mail. Select Next. The Add New Account dialog box, which provides the Internet E-mail Settings screen, will appear as shown in Figure 23.21.

Enter your name, the server information, and the logon information for the account. Use the Test Account Settings button to make sure that the settings work as you have entered them. If you entered all the information correctly, the account should work. Select Next and then Finish. When you return to the Account Settings dialog box, it will list the new email account.

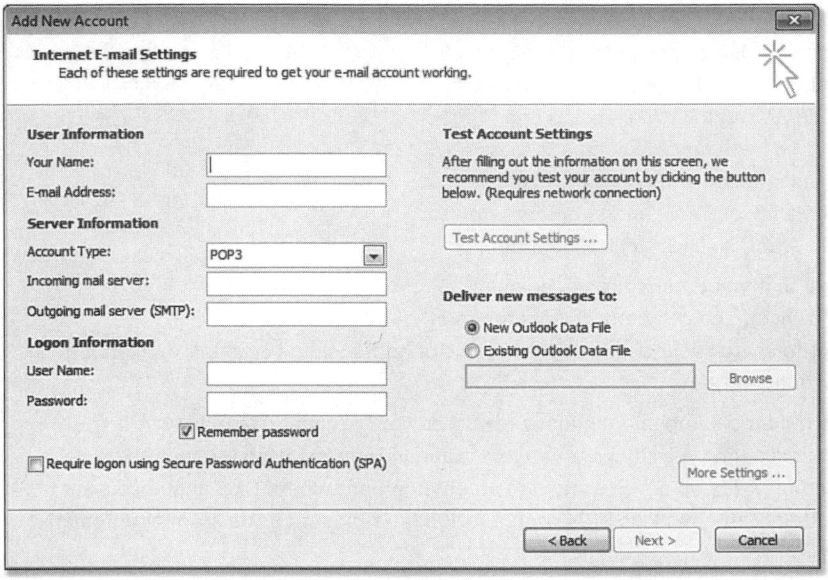

Figure 23.21
The Internet E-mail Settings screen.

Adding a Hotmail Account

As already mentioned, you can add a Microsoft Hotmail account to your Outlook configuration. You can quickly add Hotmail accounts to Outlook with the help of the Outlook Connector—a free download provided by Microsoft.

In the Account Settings dialog box, select New to open the Add New Account Wizard. Make sure the Microsoft Exchange, POP3, or IMAP option button is selected and click Next. On the next screen, enter your name, the Hotmail account email address, and the password (twice). Then click Next. When you click, a message box will open that recommends that you download and install the Microsoft Outlook Connector to manage the Hotmail account. Select Install Now.

A file download box will open, detailing the filename: OutlookConnector.exe. Click Run. The file will download. A second security box will open asking whether you want to run the software; select Run. The Microsoft Outlook Hotmail Connector Setup dialog box will open (watch for it on the Windows taskbar, you might have to select it to bring it to the top of the currently open windows). Accept the terms of the license agreement and then click Install. When the installation is complete, you can select Finish to close the installation window.

Now, you actually need to cancel out of the current Outlook dialog boxes that you have opened and then restart Outlook. This might seem counterintuitive, but that is what is required. When you restart Outlook, a message box will ask whether you would like to add a Hotmail account; select Yes. The Windows Live Hotmail Settings dialog box will open. Enter your name, Hotmail email address, and password. Click OK.

Outlook adds mail folders (Inbox, Sent Items, and Deleted Items) for the Hotmail account. You can now send and receive emails using the Hotmail account and manage the emails in the account Inbox folder.

Setting Outlook Mail Options

We have already discussed options that can be set for individual Outlook mail messages, such as tracking options and delivery options. You can also configure a number of Outlook options related to mail messages. You access the Outlook options via the Backstage.

Select File and then Options; the Outlook Options window will open. Select Mail to access the mail-related options as shown in Figure 23.22.

Figure 23.22
Outlook mail Options.

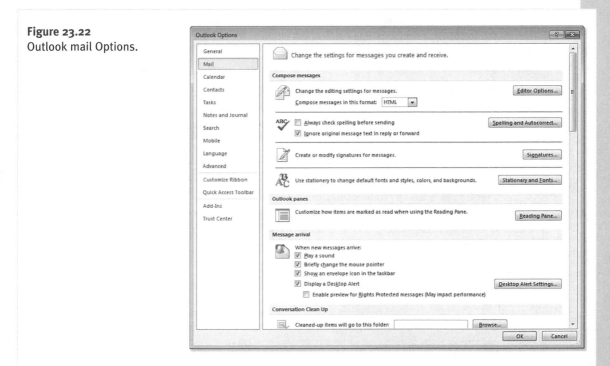

The Mail options window provides a number of categories of options. They are as follows:

- **Compose Messages:** These settings include the default message format (HTML, rich text, or plain text) and whether messages are spellchecked before Outlook sends them. Other options include the creation and modification of signatures and whether Outlook uses personal stationery when creating new messages.

- **Outlook Panes:** This group provides access to the Reading pane dialog box. You can select options such as when items are marked as read and whether to enable single key reading using the spacebar.

- **Message Arrival:** These options relate to what happens when a new message arrives in the Inbox folder. Options include the playing of a sound, changing of the mouse pointer, and displaying an envelope icon in the taskbar. You can also enable an automatic preview for messages that have been assigned rights protection.

- **Conversation Clean Up:** These options related to how Outlook cleans up the Inbox folder when you select the Clean Up command. You can specify the folder that clean-up items move to, and you can specify that Outlook not move messages meeting certain criteria, such as unread, categorized, or flagged messages.

- **Replies and Forwards:** These options include one for automatically closing the original message window when you reply to or forward the message. You can also specify whether the original message text is included in your replies or forwarded messages.

- **Save Messages:** These options relate to saving drafts and whether Outlook saves forwarded messages in the Sent Items folder. You can set when a draft of a message should be saved based on the minutes it has been opened and not yet sent. You can also determine whether forwarded messages should be saved if copies of sent messages are being placed in the Sent Items folder.

- **Send Messages:** These options enable you to specify the default importance and sensitivity levels and to specify an expiration date for messages. Other settings include automatic name checking (of email addresses), and whether Outlook should delete meeting requests and notifications from your mailbox as you respond.

- **MailTips:** These options enable you to specify when MailTips display. You make settings in the MailTips options dialog box and can assign them to specific email accounts. MailTips options include messages, such as recipient address is not valid, message is too large to send, and the recipient is external to your network (in the case of an Exchange server environment). You might want to leave all these settings alone because these tips can actually help you avoid issues with messages, particularly those related to mail addressing.

- **Tracking:** These options enable you to require delivery and read receipts for all your messages, and always to send a read receipt when you receive a message with Read Receipt Required specified.

- **Message Format:** These options primarily relate to HTML emails. You can send HTML messages using cascading style sheets and reduce message size by removing unnecessary formatting that is not essential to display the message properly.

- **Other:** These options include shading message headers when you are reading messages, and whether Outlook shows the Paste Options button when you paste content into a message.

There are two additional options related to the Inbox and the Deleted Items folders that we should also look at before closing out this discussion of Outlook mail-related settings. When you select Advanced in the Outlook options window, look at the Outlook Start and Exit options. By default, Outlook starts with the Inbox folder selected. You can change this to one of the other Outlook folders if you want, such as the Calendar or Contacts. However, because email seems important to everyone, why not leave it set to the Inbox folder? A check box related to the Deleted Items folder is also available in this set of options. If you want to empty your Deleted items folder, select the Empty Deleted Items Folders When Exiting Outlook. Then click OK to close the Outlook Options window.

USING THE CALENDAR FOR APPOINTMENTS AND TASKS

We all strive to keep our busy schedules organized. A variety of different types of events have to be managed including appointments, meetings and tasks. Outlook's calendar provides a complete environment for managing your schedule. You can keep track of one-time appointments and other events and also easily schedule recurring appointments and tasks.

Outlook can manage multiple calendars. For example, you can have a calendar associated with each email account you manage using Outlook. You can also create calendars that allow you to manage different types of events. You could have a calendar for work-related events and a calendar for personal appointments and events.

The importance of the Calendar and your list of to dos is evident in the fact that default Outlook Mail view includes the To Do bar, which provides a view of your calendar and a list of upcoming appointments and current tasks. In this chapter we look at navigating the calendar and working with multiple calendars including shared calendars. We will also look at working with appointments and tasks; setting Calendar and tasks options will also be explored.

Navigating the Calendar

To access the Outlook Calendar folder, select Calendar in the Navigation Pane. By default the Calendar shows the current day in the Reading Pane. Figure 24.1 shows the Calendar folder.

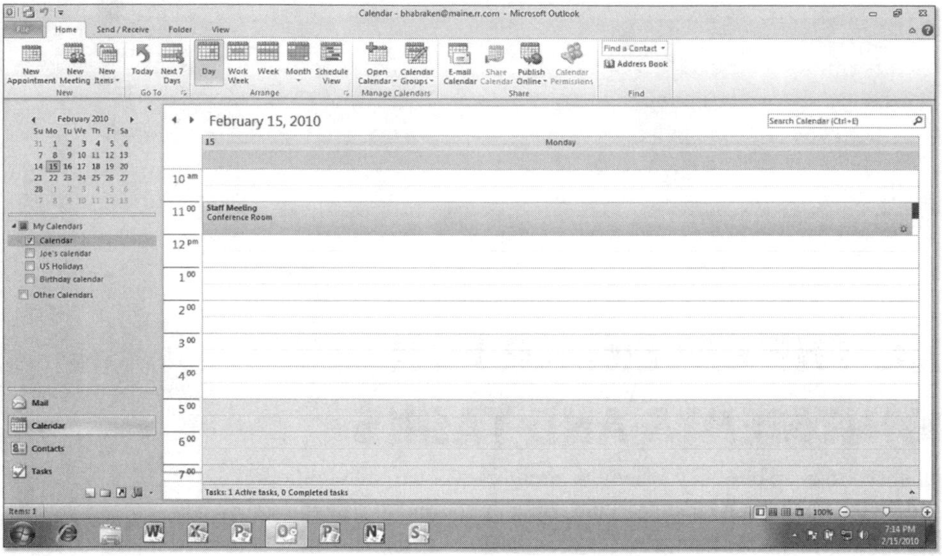

Figure 24.1
The Calendar
Folder.

The calendar will list all the appointments and events that you have scheduled for the day. You can scroll through the hours of the day to view scheduled appointments. Once you place appointments or other events on the calendar, you will also find that Previous Appointment (on the left) and Next Appointment (on the right) appear on the calendar making it easy for you to view either recent or future appointments.

On the Navigation Pane, a small version of current month is shown. This is the Date Navigator. The current date (when you are in the Day view) will be identified on the Date Navigator by a box around the date. Any dates in the current month that have scheduled appointments or events will be shown in bold.

The Navigation Pane will also provide a list of your calendars under the My Calendars group. You may have only one calendar listed in the Navigation Pane (Calendar) but this will depend on your Outlook configuration (Internet-email versus Exchange client) and if you have added an email account for a Microsoft Hotmail account, which will also have its own calendar.

To navigate the current view, such as the Default Day view, use the Back and Forward buttons on the left corner of the Calendar. You can also navigate your Calendar using the Date Navigator; select a date on the Navigator to go to the date. The Calendar Navigator also provides Back and Forward buttons that allow you to change the month shown.

> **tip**
> To view more months in the Date Navigator drag the border between the navigator and the calendar list downward in the Navigation Pane to expand the navigator area.

> **note**
> The To Do Bar is an obvious presence when you are in the Mail or Contacts folders. The To Do Bar is turned off by default when you are in the Calendar folder. You can use the To Do Bar command on the View tab if you wish to have it available when you are in the Calendar folder.

The Daily Task List is also available at the bottom of the Calendar and is minimized by default. You can use the Minimize/Expand button on the right of the Daily Task List to expand or minimize the list as needed.

Changing the Calendar View

You can quickly change your view of the Calendar information by using the commands in the Arrange group. These commands are available on both the Ribbon's Home tab and the View tab. The Calendar views are as follows:

- **Day:** This shows the current day. You can use the Calendar Navigator to quickly change the current day shown in0 the Reading Pane.

- **Work Week:** shows the current work week of Monday through Friday. Select any date on the Calendar Navigator to view a different work week.

- **Week:** shows the current week. Use the Calendar Navigator to specify a different week for this view.

- **Month:** shows the current month. When you change the month in the Calendar Navigator that particular month will be shown in the Reading Pane.

- **Schedule View:** This a new view provided by Outlook 2010. This view provides a horizontal layout (the time scale is across the top of the calendar) that consists of a seven day (calendar week) range. Use the Horizontal scroll bar along the bottom of the Reading Pane to scroll through the hours and days provided in the range on the calendar.

The Back and Forward buttons provided at the top left of the Reading Pane can be used to navigate backward and forward in the view you currently have selected. To change to one of the other views such as Work Week or Month select the appropriate command. Figure 24.2 shows the Month view.

You can change the level of detail shown when you select the Month view. By default, the detail level is set to High, which shows all appointments and events for reach day. You can also choose Low or Medium Detail using the menu provided by the Month command. The Medium detail level will show all day events and free/busy information for each day. The Low detail level shows all day events only.

The Calendar folder's Ribbon also provides a Go To group on the Home tab that can be useful for going to a particular day or range of days. To return to the current day, (no matter which of the views you are currently using), select the Today command. If you wish to view the next seven days, which uses a format similar to the Work Week and Week views, select the Next 7 Days command in the Go To group.

If you select the Dialog Box Launcher on the bottom right of the Go To group, the Go To Date dialog box opens. This dialog box allows you to specify both a date and a view. You can use the Date drop-down button to open a Calendar Navigator and then specify the date that you want to go to. You can then use the Show in drop-down list to specify the view that you want to use, such as Week Calendar, Day Calendar Month Calendar, and so on.

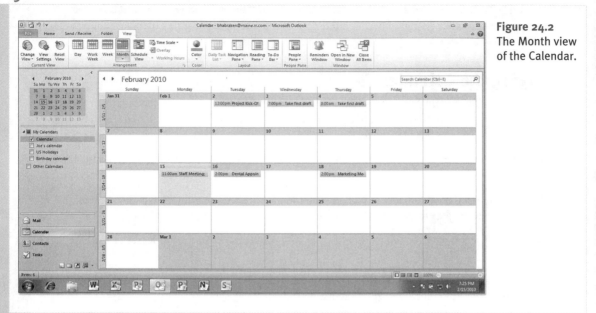

Figure 24.2
The Month view of the Calendar.

Change the Time Scale and Time Zone

When you are working in a particular view, you may want to change the time scale that is currently being used in that view. By default the time scale is set to 30 minutes. You can change the time scale using the Time Scale command in the Arrangement group on the View tab (the Time Scale command is not available on the Home tab).

If you decrease the time scale you have more space for viewing the details related to your various scheduled appointments and events. If you increase the time scale, you will have less space to view the details related to your appointments but will be able to condense the time line for that particular view and see a greater range of time.

You can change the time scale in the following views: Day, Work Week, Week and Schedule View. To change the time scale, select the Time Scale command and then select a different time scale interval such as 60 Minutes, 15 minutes, and so on.

You can also use the Time Scale command to change the current time zone. This is particularly useful when you are on the road and are operating in a different time zone. Changing the time zone will make sure that any appointment or task alarms that have been set will be operating in the correct time zone. The default time zone set for Outlook will be based on the time zone that you selected for your Windows installation. The time zone information is located in the Outlook options for the Calendar, which is typically accessed via Options command the Backstage.

 Changing Calendar options are discussed later in this chapter on page 678.

You can, however, quickly access the Calendar options via the Time Scale command. To change the current time zone select the Time Scale command and then select Change Time Zone. The Outlook Options window will open with Calendar selected as shown in Figure 24.3.

Figure 24.3
The Outlook Options window.

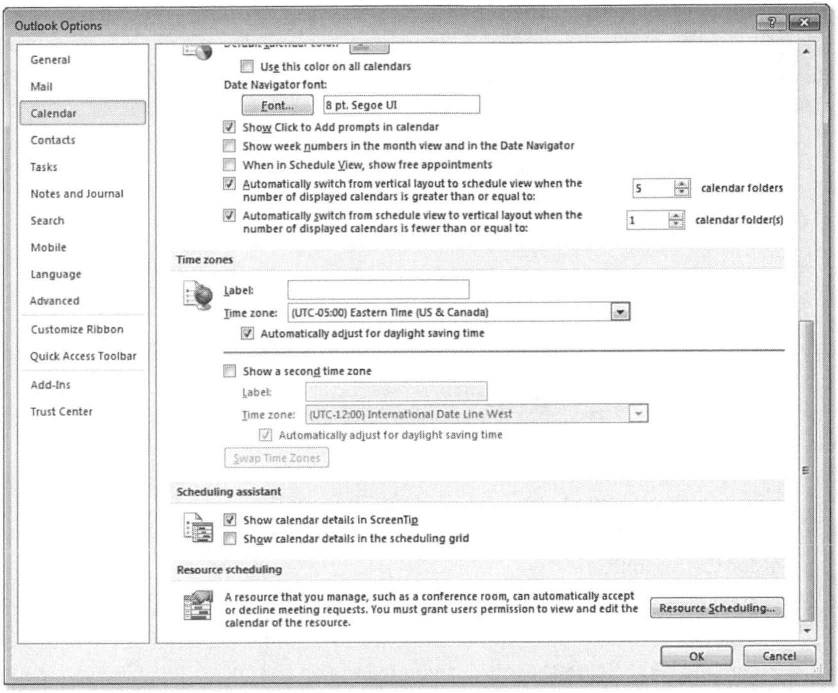

Select the Time zone drop-down list and select a new time zone for Outlook. Then click OK. This will close the Outlook Options window and return you to the calendar.

Scheduling an Appointment

You can quickly create appointments in any Calendar view and you actually have options for creating a new appointment. Two possibilities are the New Appointment command on the Ribbon's Home tab or just double-clicking on a specific day and time in the Reading Pane. Either option opens the Appointment dialog box as shown in Figure 24.4.

Enter a subject for the appointment in the Subject box. You can also enter a location as needed. You will want to make sure the appropriate date and start time are entered in the Start time box. You can use the Start Time drop-down box to access a Calendar Navigator and then specify the date that you want for the appointment. You can also set the time as needed. If you double-clicked on a particular time in the Calendar in the Reading Pane, the date should be correctly specified when the Appointment dialog box opens.

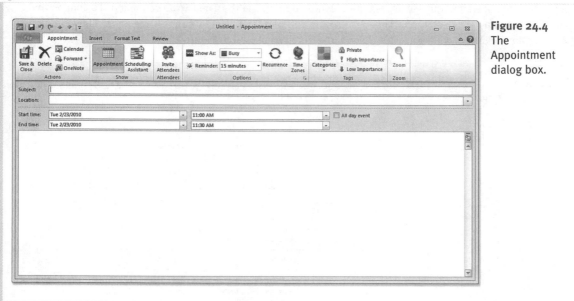

Figure 24.4
The Appointment dialog box.

You may also want to adjust the End Time for the meeting. By default, Outlook schedules each appointment for one half hour. Use the End Time box's time drop-down list to specify the end time for the appointment.

Each appointment has a body text area that allows you to add notes related to the appointment. You can also insert Business Cards, Outlook items, pictures or other items that are related to the appointment using the various commands on the Insert tab. You can also attach files to an appointment if needed.

If you want to specify a time zone for the Start Time or End Time, which can be extremely useful if you are traveling between time zones, select the Time Zones command on the Ribbon's Appointment tab. This places Time Zone drop-down lists to the right of the Start Time and End Time boxes. You can select a time zone from the time zone drop-down list.

When you create an appointment, you also have control over how the appointment is shown on the calendar and have the option of setting a reminder for the appointment. Appointments are shown on the calendar as "Busy" by default but you can use the Show As list on the Options tab to change the show as option to other possibilities such as Tentative and Out of Office.

In terms of a reminder for the appointment, Outlook specifies a 15-minute reminder by default. You can select the Reminder command to select from a list of different time increments (5 minutes, 10 minutes, 1 hour, 1 day, and so on). By default a reminder sound is also played when the Reminder box opens for the appointment. You can select the Sound command at the bottom of the Reminder list to open the Reminder Sound dialog box. Use the Browse button to locate a different sound file, if you wish to use a sound other than the default. If you do not wish a sound to play when the reminder opens, deselect the Play This Sound check box in the Reminder Sound dialog box.

You can also tag an appointment with categories, importance levels or mark the appointment as private using the commands available in the Tags group (on the appointment tab). When you mark an appointment as private it, the details of the appointment will not be shown to other users who you may have shared your calendar with.

Once you have specified the various parameters and options for your new appointment, select the Save & Close command on the Appointment tab. The appointment will be added to the calendar.

Scheduling a Recurring Appointment

You can create recurring appointments. This allows you to quickly schedule an appointment that recurs at a specific time interval such as once a week, once a month and so on. To create a recurring appointment from the Calendar folder select the New Items command on the Home tab, point at More Items and then select Recurring Appointment. The Appointment Recurrence dialog box will open as shown in Figure 24.5.

In the Appointment Time area, enter the Start and End times for the appointment. Outlook calculates the duration of the appointment for you. In the Recurrence Pattern area, indicate the frequency of the appointment: Daily, Weekly, Monthly, or Yearly. After you select the recurrence pattern, you will be provided with options, such as days of the week for a weekly recurring appointment or day-of-the-month options for a monthly recurring appointment. Specify how often the appointment recurs and the time period (such as a day of the week) that the appointment recurs on.

In the Range of Recurrence area, enter appropriate time limits using the following guidelines:

- **Start:** select the date on which the recurring appointments begin.

- **No End Date:** select this option if the recurring appointments are not on a limited schedule.

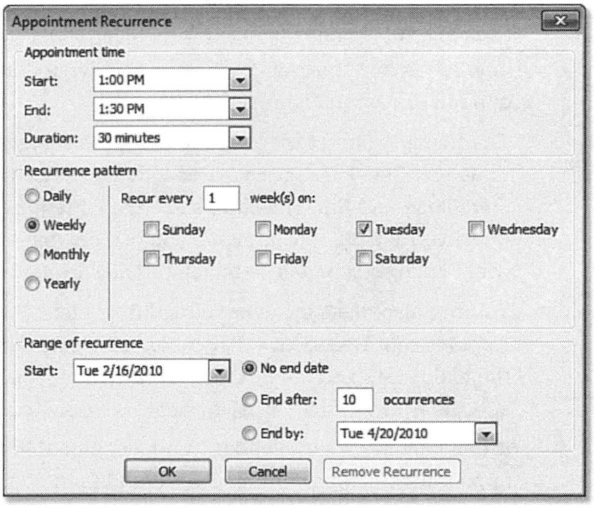

Figure 24.5
The Appointment Recurrence dialog box.

- **End After:** select this option and enter the number of appointments if there is a specific limit to the recurring appointments.

- **End By:** select this option and enter an ending date to limit the number of recurring appointments.

Once you have set all the recurrence options for the appointment, select OK to close the Appointment Recurrence dialog box. This will take you to the Appointment dialog box for the recurring appointment. You will find that the start and stop options for the appointment have been replaced by recurrence information, which specifies when the appointment recurs, when it starts (an effective date) and the time for the recurring appointment.

Enter a subject for the appointment and you can also add a location and other information in the appointment body. You can also specify the reminder settings for the appointment and tag the appointment as you would any other appointment. When you are ready to place the recurring appointment on the calendar, select Save & Close.

Scheduling an Event

An event is really just an appointment that lasts an entire day (24 hours or longer actually). You can use events to block of larger blocks of times than you would for normal appointments. As with appointments, you can also schedule recurring events such as a monthly seminar you attend that lasts an entire day.

To quickly create a new event, select a time slot in the Calendar (to specify the date for the event) and then select new Items and then All Day Event. The Event dialog box will open as shown in Figure 24.6.

 tip

You can make any appointment (new or existing) a recurring appointment. Select the Recurrence command on the Appointment tab to open the Appointment Recurrence dialog box.

The Event dialog box is almost exactly the same as the Appointment dialog box, however the Start Time and End Time boxes are deactivated since the event lasts all day. You can edit the date for the Start Time and End Time (the same day) if required. Specify a subject for the event and an optional location. As with appointments you can set reminder options for the event and assign tags to the event such as categories and importance levels.

You can also make the event a recurring event. Select the Recurrence command and the Appointment Recurrence dialog box will open. Set the recurrence parameters and click OK to close the dialog box and return to the event. When you are ready to add the event to the Calendar, select Save & Close.

When viewing your Calendar, you have probably noticed that appointments appear in the Calendar in their specific time slots. Events are listed just below the day designation in Calendar when you are using the Day, Work Week, or Week view. When you use the Month view, you can tell events from appointments because events will be shown in bold on the calendar day.

tip

Any appointment can become an event. In the Appointment dialog box select the All Day Event check box.

Figure 24.6
The Event dialog box.

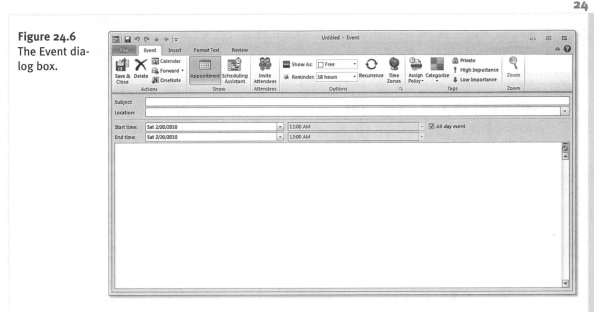

Editing and Managing Appointments

You can edit appointments (or events) in the Calendar as you require. Double-click on an appointment in the Calendar and the appointment's dialog box will open. You can change the subject, location, date and time for the appointment. You can also add additional information to the appointment body or change other settings related to the appointment using the various commands on the Ribbon. After making changes to an appointment, recurring appointment or event, select the Save & Close command.

You can also manage appointments directly on the Calendar. To change the appointment subject select the appointment on the Calendar and then click inside the subject text. You can edit the text as needed.

You can also move an appointment to a different time or day on the calendar to change either of these appointment parameters; drag the appointment to a new location (location in terms of date and time). If you want to change the time for the appointment by dragging make sure that you are in the Day, Work Week, or Week view. You can also drag appointments to a different date in the Month view, but you cannot change the time of the appointment. You can quickly edit the time, however, by double-clicking the appointment and then editing the time in the Appointment dialog box. You can view the time range for an appointment in any of the Calendar views; hover the mouse over the appointment.

When you do select an appointment in the Calendar, the Calendar Tools will appear with the Appointment tab. Options such as the reminder settings and tags can be quickly selected for the appointment.

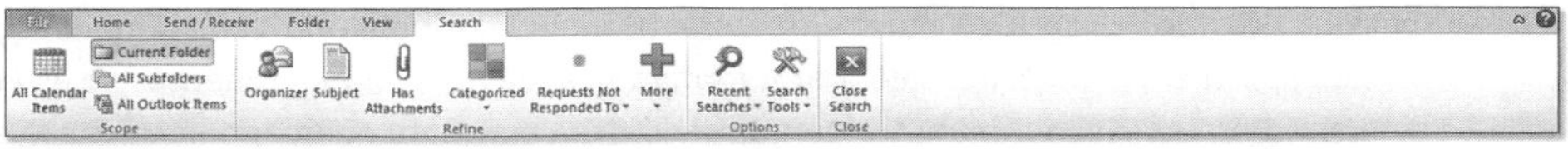

Figure 24.7
The Ribbon's
Search Tools.

You can also delete unneeded appointments from the Calendar. Select the appointment. Then press the Delete key. You can also delete a selected appointment or event from the Calendar using the Delete command in the Action group on the Ribbon. In either case, the appointment will be removed from the Calendar.

Searching the Calendar

Outlook 2010 provides you with a great deal of flexibility and control when you search your Calendar (or shared calendars). When you click in the Search box, the Search Tools appear on the Ribbon as shown in Figure 24.7.

One way to search the Calendar is to type keywords into the Search box. The appointments and events that match the search terms will be displayed in the Reading Pane sorted by date. Appointments will be listed in a tabular format that provides the field names such as Subject, Location, Start and End as the field column headings. You can re-order the list of appointments found by the search by clicking on any of the field headings. To clear the search, click the X to the right of the Search box.

As already mentioned, a number of commands are provided to you by the Search Tools tab that appears on the Ribbon when you click in the Search box. You can use commands in the Refine group to conduct a new search or refine a search that was based on keywords. For example, you can view appointments that have file attachments, by selecting the Has Attachments command. If you have categorized appointments or events, you can use the Categorized command to select a specific category and only those messages that have been assigned that category will appear in the search results.

To access additional properties for your search criteria, you can select the More command. This will provide you with a list of Common Properties such as Attachments, Categories, Importance and Recurring (select Recurring and then Yes in the Recurring box to quickly find recurring appointments). It also allows you to specify more exacting parameters for your search. For example, you can select Body in the Common Properties list and a Body box will appear below the Search box. You can type text in the Body box (yes, that sounds scary) and the search will list appointments that have the search text in their appointment bodies.

You can also use the common Properties to search for appointments that have a particular start or end time using the Start and End properties respectively. For example, you can select Start and the Start box will appear below the Search box. Click the Start box to select Start criteria such as Today, Tomorrow, Next Week, and so on. When you have finished working with the Search feature, you can quickly return to the Calendar by selecting the Close Search command.

> *An overview of the Outlook Search feature is provided in Chapter 22, "Requisite Outlook: Configuration and Essential Features," on page 623.*

Sharing Calendars

Outlook provides you with a number of different options for sharing your calendar information. One of the easiest ways to share Calendar information such as an appointment is to use the Forward command on the Appointment tab to quickly send a currently open appointment to a co-worker or colleague. In terms of other options for sharing your calendar, the possibilities will depend on whether or not you use Outlook as an Exchange Server client. The Exchange environment allows you to share your calendar and also allows others to share their calendars with you.

Even if you use Outlook as an Internet email client, you are provided with capabilities for sharing your calendar information. These possibilities include emailing calendar information and publishing calendars online.

Sharing Your Calendar

If you are using Outlook as an Exchange Server client, your Calendar is stored on the Exchange server, making it very easy to share your calendar with other users on the Exchange network.

note

Calendars can also be shared by users on a Microsoft SharePoint Server.

To share your Calendar, select the Share Calendar command on the Home tab. A Sharing invitation will open as shown in Figure 24.8.

To address the Sharing invitation, select the To button (or select the Address Book command on the Ribbon). The Global Address List will open in the Address Book dialog box. Add a recipient or recipients as needed using the list (select a recipient or recipients and then click the To button). You can also add recipients from your Contacts list if the recipient is an Exchange Server client.

The invitation also provides several settings. By default the Allow Recipient to View Your Calendar check box is selected. If you want to be able to view the calendar of the invitation recipient, select the Request Permission to View Recipient's Calendar check box.

Figure 24.8
A sharing invitation for your Calendar.

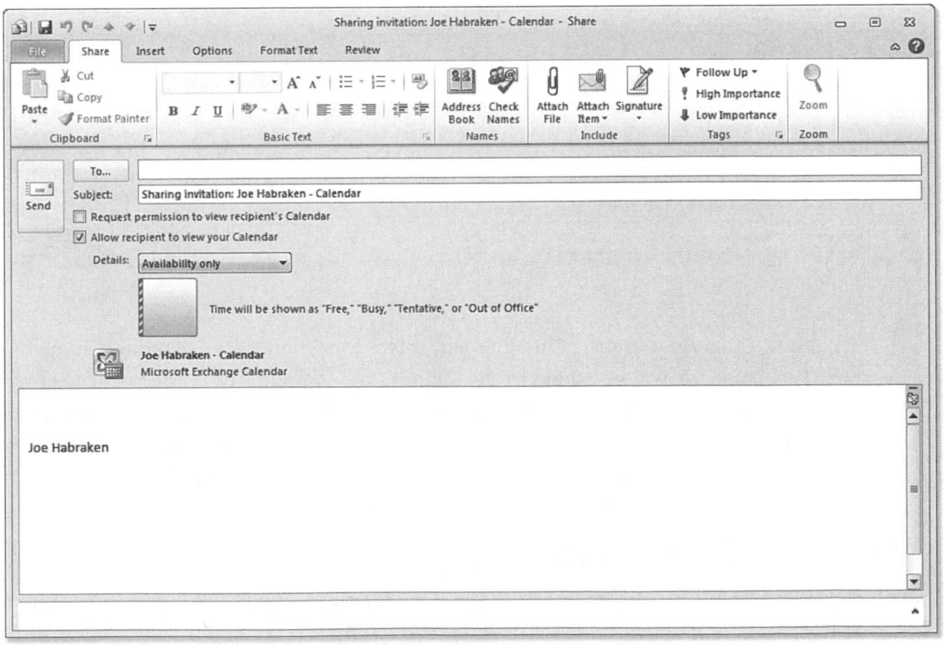

![Screenshot of the Sharing invitation window for Joe Habraken - Calendar - Share, showing the Share ribbon tab with Clipboard, Basic Text, Names, Include, Tags, and Zoom groups. The message area shows To, Subject fields with "Sharing Invitation: Joe Habraken - Calendar", checkboxes for "Request permission to view recipient's Calendar" and "Allow recipient to view your Calendar", Details set to "Availability only", with note "Time will be shown as 'Free,' 'Busy,' 'Tentative,' or 'Out of Office'", and "Joe Habraken - Calendar / Microsoft Exchange Calendar".]

You can also control the amount of detail that is shown when the recipient views your Calendar. Select the Details drop-down list; the default setting is Availability Only but you can also select Limited Details and Full Details. Obviously, Full Details will share all the information on the Calendar including appointment body notes.

Once you have addressed the Sharing invitation and set the other options, select Send. The invitation will be sent to the recipient or recipients.

Opening a Shared Calendar

If co-workers or colleagues share a Calendar with you, you will receive a Sharing invitation. The invitation is an email as shown in Figure 24.9.

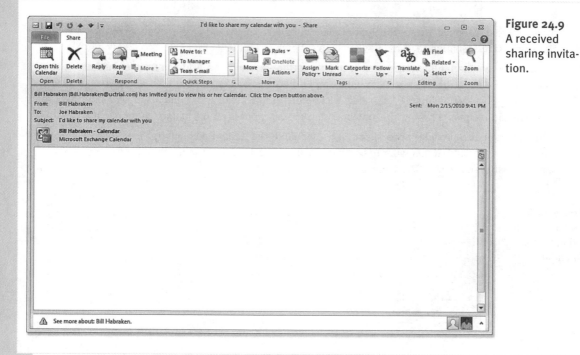

Figure 24.9
A received sharing invitation.

To add the Calendar to your Calendar list, select the Open This Calendar command on the Share tab. The Calendar will be added to the Shared Calendars group in the Navigation Pane. The level of detail that you can view in the Calendar will depend on the detail setting that was selected by the user who is sharing the calendar. You can view the shared Calendar as you would your own calendar using the various Arrange and View commands provided on the Ribbon.

Viewing Multiple Calendars

Multiple calendars can be opened in the Reading Pane. Select the check box for each calendar that you wish to view. Each calendar is in its own pane in the Reading Pane. When you are working with multiple and shared calendars, Outlook provides you two very useful tools that allow you to compare your appointments and events with another user's Calendar. These two tools are overlays and Calendar groups.

The overlay feature allows you to superimpose calendars. This can be very useful in detecting overlapping or conflicting appointments. To overlay multiple calendars, select the calendars in the Navigation Pane. On the Ribbon's View tab select the Overlay command. The calendars will be superimposed as shown in Figure 24.10.

The calendar that is in the front of the overlay will have its appointments shown in bold. You can click the tab for a calendar to bring it to the forefront. If you wish to close a calendar, select the Close Calendar button (X) on the calendar.

If you view multiple Exchange (or SharePoint) calendars in Outlook often, you may want to create calendar groups. A calendar group is really just a listing of multiple calendars. You can quickly open these calendars by selecting the group that contains the calendars.

Figure 24.10
Calendars in the overlay view.

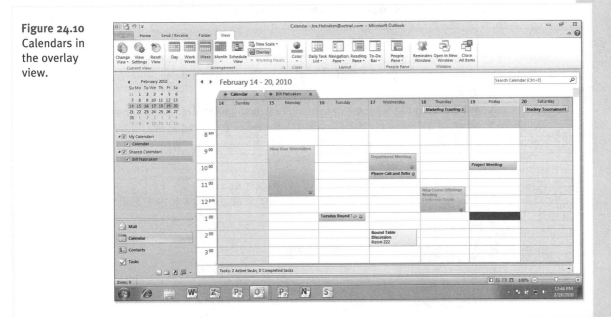

The easiest way to create a new calendar group is to open the calendars you wish to include in the group in the Reading Pane; select each calendar in the Navigation Pane. On the Home tab, select Calendar Groups and then select Save a New Calendar Group. The Create New Calendar Group dialog box will open. Provide a name for the new group and then click OK. In the future, you can quickly open all the calendars in the group by selecting the group in the Navigation Pane.

Emailing a Calendar

Even if you don't have the calendar sharing capabilities provided by Exchange Server, you can email content from your Calendar to others. The E-Mail Calendar command is in the Share group on Ribbon's Home tab (when you are in the Calendar folder).

With your Calendar open in the Reading Pane, select the E-mail Calendar command. The Send a Calendar via E-mail dialog box will open as shown in Figure 24.11.

In the Date Range drop-down list select the calendar range that you wish to include in the email message. You choose details such as Today, Tomorrow, and Whole Calendar. You can also specify a range of dates.

note

You can also publish calendars to custom servers (other than Office. com). For example you can publish calendars to SharePoint servers.

note

You can also set permissions for calendars shared on an Exchange network. Use the Calendar Properties dialog box to set permissions for your shared calendar.

Use the Detail drop-down list to specify the level of detail that you wish to provide in the Calendar information: Availability Only, Limited Details or Full Details. You can also choose to only show time within your working hours by selecting the Show Time Within My Working Hours Only. Select the Show button to set advanced parameters related to the Calendar such as the layout in the e-mail: Daily Schedule or List of Events.

When you have specified the settings for the email calendar, select OK. The Calendar information will be embedded in the email message and also attached to the email as an .ics calendar file. Click Send to send the Calendar information to the recipient or recipients.

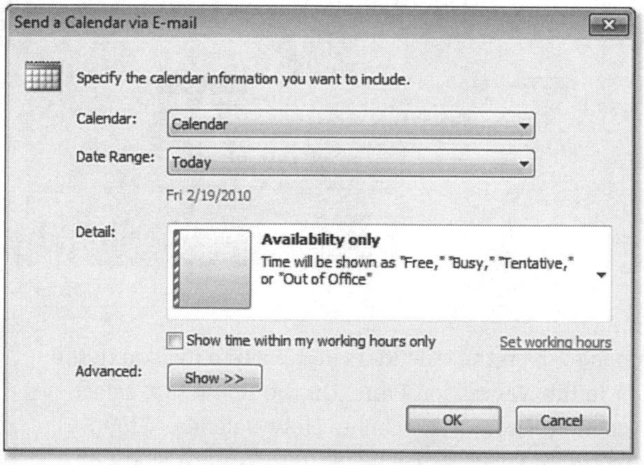

Figure 24.11
The Send a Calendar via E-mail dialog box.

Publishing a Calendar Online

Even Outlook users who use Outlook as an Internet email client can publish calendars online. Microsoft provides this service and the calendar is published to Office.com. To publish a calendar to Office.com, you will need a Microsoft Windows Live ID (meaning a Microsoft Hotmail account).

Assuming that you have signed up for your Windows Live ID, select the Publish Online command on the Home tab and then select Publish to Office.com. The Microsoft Outlook Calendar Sharing Service dialog box will open. Select the Sign in button and enter your Windows Live ID email address. Select I Accept and then on the next screen Finish to continue. The Publish Calendar to Office.com dialog box opens as shown in Figure 24.12.

 tip

If you no longer need a shared calendar, you can remove it from the Navigation Pane. Right-click the calendar and select Delete Calendar. This will remove the calendar from your Outlook account.

Use the Time Span drop-down lists to set the range of days to be published in the online calendar. You can also choose to show only time within your working hours. By default only invited users will be able to subscribe to the calendar. If you wish to allow anyone to subscribe to the calendar, select the Anyone Can Subscribe to This Calendar option button.

If you wish to set the upload method for the calendar, select the Advanced button. The Published Calendar Settings dialog box will open. The default setting in this dialog box allows the calendar to be updated directly. If you only wish to upload current appointments and events in the calendar range, select the Single Upload: Updates Will Not Be Updated option button. Select OK to return to the Published Calendar Settings dialog box. Select OK and the calendar will be uploaded to the Web and then the Send a Sharing Invitation dialog box will open. Select Yes (to send an invitation) and a new Sharing invitation email will open. Address the email as needed to share the calendar with other users. Then click Send. The invitation will be sent to the recipients.

When the recipient opens the email invitation for the calendar they can select Subscribe to This Calendar on the Ribbon. They can then add the calendar to Outlook and subscribe to updates of the calendar. The calendar will be added to the list of calendars available in the Navigation Pane. You can also use the information discussed in this paragraph to subscribe to any Web published calendars that are shared with you.

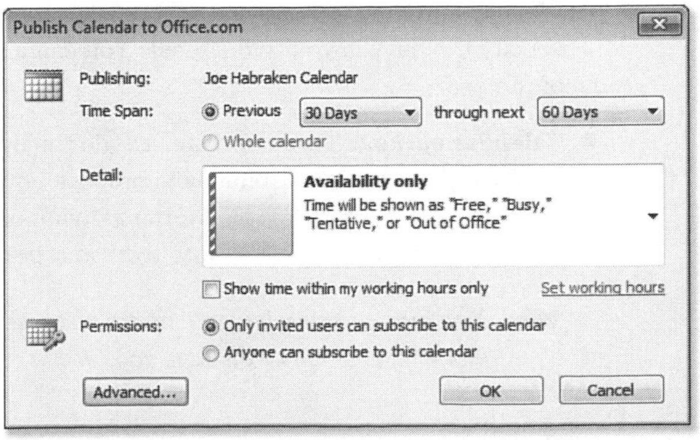

Figure 24.12
Share the calendar online.

Setting Calendar Options

The Calendar options can be accessed via the Outlook Options window. Select File to access the Backstage and then select Options. The Outlook Options window will open. Select Calendar in the options list to access the Calendar options. Figure 24.13 shows the Outlook Options dialog box with Calendar selected.

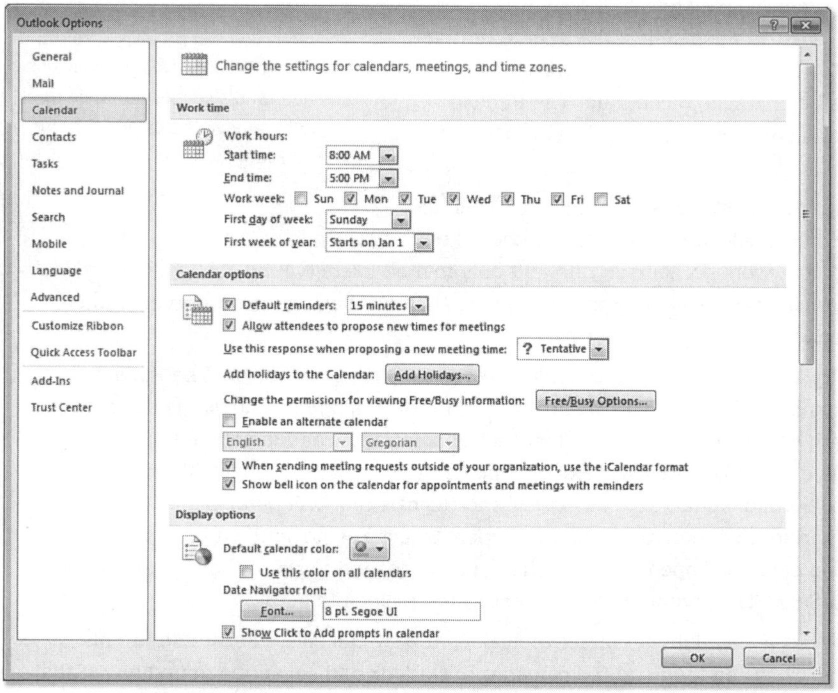

Figure 24.13
The Calendar options.

The Calendar options allow you to set your work time, reminder defaults and other options such as the current time zone. The Calendar options categories are as follows:

- **Work time:** These options allow you to set the start and end time for your work hours and also to specify the days in your work week. You can also set the first day of the week and the first week of the year.

- **Calendar options:** These options include the default reminder time and settings related to meetings such as allowing attendees to propose new times for meetings. You can also add holidays to the calendar, set permissions for the viewing of Free/Busy times and enable an alternative calendar (useful if you keep a separate work and personal calendars.

    ➡ *Meetings and meeting options are discussed in Chapter 25, "Working with Contacts and Planning Meetings," on page 709.*

- **Display options:** These options allow you to control the default calendar color and also specify the Date Navigator prompt. Other settings include the switching from vertical layout to schedule view based on the number of opened calendars.

- **Time zones:** These options allow you to set and able the current time zone. Options are also available for showing a second time zone.

- **Scheduling assistant:** These options allow you to show calendar details in a ScreenTip when using the Scheduling assistant and also whether or not calendar details are shown in the scheduling grid.

- **Resource scheduling:** You can manage resources such as conference rooms, overhead projectors and other items by creating calendars for that resource. The resource can then accept or decline meeting requests based on its calendar. Options available allow you to set permissions related to the resource calendar. This setting is primarily used in Exchange Server environments where a resource calendar can easily be shared on the network.

When you have finished setting the various Calendar options, select OK. This will close the Outlook Options window and return you to Outlook.

Working with Tasks

All of us have a task list. It may be scribbled on scraps of paper or on a calendar but we all need to manage and complete tasks on a daily basis. Outlook makes it easy for you to create and manage tasks. Task properties can include reminders and you can also assign tasks to co-workers and colleagues (and you can be assigned tasks as well).

When you open Outlook, the default view (if you haven't changed it) consists of the Navigation Pane, the Details Pane (showing your email in the Inbox) and the Reading Pane. More importantly this view also includes the To Do Bar.

You can quickly create a task via the To Do Bar. Double-click in the Task list at the bottom of the To Do Bar and a new Task dialog box will open as shown in Figure 24.14.

Follow these steps to create the new task:

1. Enter the subject of the task into the Subject box.

2. Enter a date on which the task should be complete, or click the Due Fate list arrow to open the Date Navigator, and then choose a due date.

3. Enter a start date, or use the Date Navigator to select a start date.

4. From the Status drop-down list, choose the current status of the project: Not Started, In Progress, Completed, Waiting on Someone Else, or Deferred.

5. Enter any comments, descriptions, or other information related to the task in the body of the task.

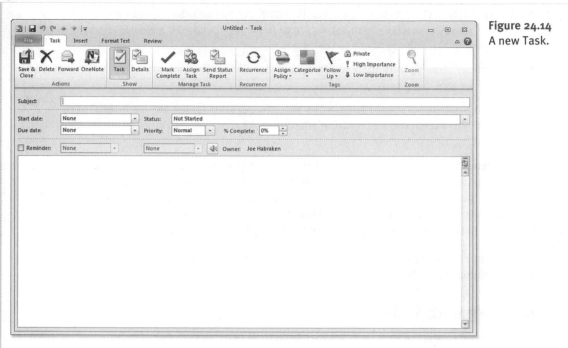

Figure 24.14
A new Task.

You can use the Task tab of the Ribbon to set other attributes related to the task (much in the same way that you assign options to an appointment). You can use the Categorize command to assign a category or categories to the task. You can also tag the task with a flag using the Follow Up command. If the task is private, high importance or low importance, use the appropriate command in the Tabs group to set options for the task. When you are ready to place the task on the Task list, click Save & Close. The task will be listed in the Task list on the To Do Bar.

Using the Task Folder

You can also create, view and manage tasks from the Task folder. Select Tasks in the Navigation Pane. Your list of tasks (grouped by date ranges such as Today, Next Week, and so on) will be listed in the Details Pane in a To Do list. Select a task to view the details related to that task in the Reading Pane. When you use the Task folder, the To Do Bar will also be displayed in the Outlook window and it provides a Date Navigator, a list of your appointments and a list of tasks. Figure 24.15 shows the Task folder.

Creating a New Task from the Task Folder

You can also create task from the Task folder. Select the New Task command and a new Task dialog box will open. Enter the necessary and information for the task and then click the Save & Close command. The new task will appear in the Task list and on the To Do Bar.

Figure 24.15
The Task folder.

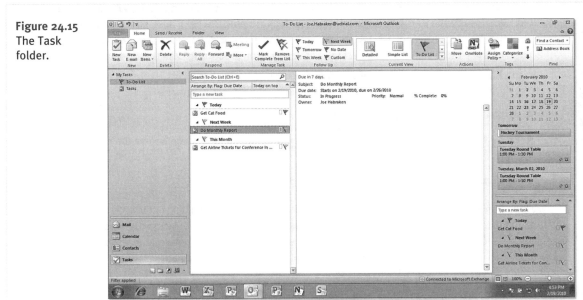

Creating a Recurring Task

You can create recurring tasks. For example, you may always have to provide a weekly report each Friday and so it makes sense to schedule a recurring task that reminds you to get that weekly job done. Recurring tasks can easily be created to recur daily, weekly, monthly or yearly.

You can create a recurring task from an existing task or by creating a new recurring task. To create a recurring task from any Outlook folder, select the New Items command on the Home tab and then select Task. A new Task dialog box will open. Type a subject for the task. Then select the Recurrence command on the Task's Ribbon. The Task Recurrence dialog box opens as shown in Figure 24.16.

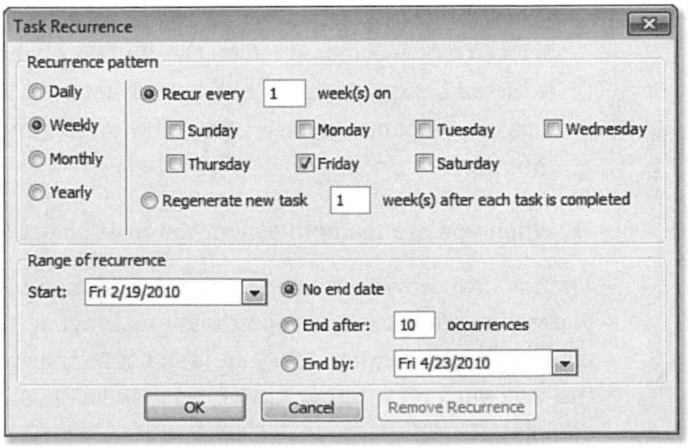

Figure 24.16
The Task Recurrence dialog box.

In the Task Recurrence dialog box set the Recurrence patter by selecting Daily, Weekly, and so on and then specify the Recur Every increment (such as 1 week, 2 week). Also specify the day that the recurring task recurs using the day checkboxes (Sunday through Saturday). You can also specify when a new task should be "regenerated" as the previous recurring task has been completed.

In the Range of Recurrence area of the Task Recurrence dialog specify the start date for the task. You can then specify the end date for the task using the following options:

- **No End Date:** No end date is specified for the recurring task.

- **End After:** Specify the number of occurrences that should take place before the recurring task is ended.

- **End By:** Specify an end date for the recurring task.

When you have completed setting the options for the recurring task, select OK to return to the Task dialog box. The recurrence information for the task (and the next due date) will appear above the subject of the task. You can assign policies (on an Exchange Server network), categories and other tags such as follow up flags to the recurring task as needed. When you have completed setting the options for the task select Save & Close.

Assigning and Accepting Tasks

There is probably no greater joy in the workplace than being able to pass off your tasks to other people. You can assign tasks to co-workers or subordinates. Assigned tasks will appear in your Task list and on the To Do Bar. It will also appear on the Task list of any person you assign to the task.

To assign a task to a co-worker or colleague follow these steps:

1. Select the New Task command or double-click on the To Do list in the To Do Bar. A new Task dialog box will open.

2. Enter the subject and other details for the task.

3. Set options for the task using the appropriate commands on the Ribbon.

4. Select Assign Task. A To box will appear above the Subject box so that you can address the task.

5. Select To or Address Book on the Ribbon to open the Address Book. You can use the Global Address List on an Exchange Server network to add the recipient or recipients of the assigned task or you can switch to your Contacts list and select the names as needed. Select OK to close the Address Book.

6. When you are ready to assign the task, select Save & Close.

The task can now be managed by the assignee of the task (although you can view it). By default, you will receive a status report (via email) when the task is complete. Also by default, an updated copy of this task is kept on your task list so that you can view any changes that have been made to the task such as whether or not the task has been started and the percent of the task that has been completed.

Paybacks can be nasty and in the case of tasks there is no doubt that those who give shall also receive. When a co-worker or manager assigns you a task, the assigned task will be sent as a mail message. Double-click the message to open the task. The Respond group on the Ribbon provides the necessary commands for you to respond to the assigned task. You can click the Accept command to accept the task. If you select Accept, an Accepting Task message box will open. You can immediately send a response that you are accepting the task and the task will be moved to your Tasks folder. If you wish to edit your response to the task before sending it, select the Edit the Response Before Sending option button. Then click OK.

If you wish to decline the task, select Decline. The Declining Task dialog box will open. When you decline a task a message is sent to the originator of the task and the task is moved to your deleted Items folder. You do have the option of editing your response (that you are declining the task) before sending it.

 note

You can reply to a task "invitation" before accepting it. Use the Reply command in the Respond group.

Viewing and Managing Tasks

Outlook provides you with different options for viewing your tasks. When you select the To Do List in the Navigation Pane, the tasks are listed in the details pane and individual task properties can be viewed in the Reading Pane when that task is selected. You can manipulate the view of tasks on the To Do list using the various commands provided on the Ribbon's View tab.

The Arrangement group on the View tab provides commands that allow you to arrange the Task list by categories, start date, due date and importance. The Reverse Sort command can be used to quickly reverse the sort order of the To Do List.

Viewing the Tasks List

You can also view a list of tasks by selecting Tasks in the Navigation Pane. Tasks will be listed in a tabular format, which includes field columns for Subject, Due Date and Categories. The tasks are listed by due date in ascending order. You can use the column heading to quickly sort the list by subject or category and change whether the tasks are listed in ascending or descending order by that field. In this view each task will have the default Simple List view of the Task list provides each task with a check box that makes it easy to select a task or tasks.

Figure 24.17
The Current View gallery.

The Home tab of the Ribbon makes it easy for you to change the Simple List view of the Tasks list to a different view using the Current View group commands. Figure 24.17 shows the different views available in the Current View gallery.

Each view provides a different tabular view of the tasks including different fields. The different views available on the Current View gallery are as follows:

- **Detailed:** Displays the subject, status, modified, date completed, in folder and categories.

- **Simple List:** Shows the subject, due date and categories.

- **To Do List:** Changes to the To Do List view (which can also be accessed via the Navigation Pane).

- **Prioritized:** This view groups the tasks by priority.

- **Active:** This view shows the active tasks including the status, due date, % complete and categories.

- **Completed:** Filters the list to show completed tasks only.

- **Today:** Lists the tasks with "today" as the due date.

- **Next 7 Days:** Lists the tasks with a due date that falls in the next seven days and includes the status, % complete and categories.

- **Overdue:** Filters the task list and lists overdue tasks only.

- **Assigned:** Filters the task list to show tasks that have been assigned to you by others.

- **Server Tasks:** This view lists tasks stored on the Exchange server (which will be all tasks that you have created and have been assigned from other users on the Exchange server network). This view will not be available when you use Outlook as an Internet e-mail client only.

You can add columns to any of the tabular views (other than the Simple List views) as needed. Select the View tab and then select Add Columns. The Show Columns dialog box will open as shown in Figure 24.18.

Select a column in the Available columns list and then click the Add button to add the column to the current view. By default, frequently used fields are shown in the list but you can use the drop-down list to select other field categories such as Info/Status fields, Date/Time fields or All Task Fields.

When you click OK the Show Columns dialog box will close and you will be returned to the Tasks list. The column or columns that you added using the Show Columns dialog box will appear in your current view of the tasks.

 tip

When you view other items such as emails or contacts in a tabular view, you can use the Add Columns command to get more information about a particular item. Just add columns as required.

Figure 24.18
The Show Columns dialog box.

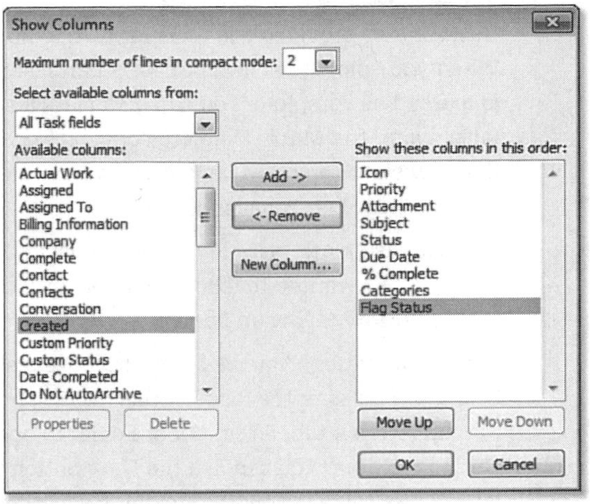

Editing Tasks

You can edit any task in the Tasks list or the To Do List. Double-click on the on the task and the task's dialog box will open. You can edit any of the fields related to the task and you can also tag the task with categories, follow up flags and set the level of importance.

> **note**
> By default, assigned tasks generate a status report when they are completed. The report is forwarded to the assignor of the task.

In cases where you wish to add additional information to a task, particularly information related to the number of hours required to complete the task or other information such as mileage or the company that you did the work for, select the Details command on the Task tab. Fields are provided for total work, actual work, mileage and billing information. Enter the information as needed and make sure to select Save & Close when you have finished editing the task's details.

In the case of tasks that you have assigned to others, you can rescind the task. Open the task and then on the Task tab of the Ribbon, select Cancel Assignment. The name of the assignee or assignees will be removed from the task. The task will still exist; however, it is now your task and is no longer assigned to a co-worker or subordinate. To save changes that you have made to a task in the task's dialog box, select Save & Close.

You can generate a status report for your tasks and then send the report to a co-worker or colleague. This is particularly useful in situations where you are working with a task that has been assigned to you and you want to provide an update to the assigner of the task. In the task's dialog box select the Send Status Report command (on the Task tab). A new email message will appear including the status of the task in the body of the message. Address the message as needed and then click the Send button to send the status report to a recipient or recipients.

Managing Tasks

Outlook also provides you tools for managing your tasks.
When you select the checkbox for a particular task that task
is marked as complete. You can also mark a selected task or
tasks using the Mark Complete command on the Home tab.
If you wish to remove a task or tasks from the list, select the
Remove from List command.

 tip

You can copy tasks from your Tasks
list to another folder using the Copy
to Folder option on the Move command's menu.

You can also mark tasks for follow up using the various flags provided in the Follow Up group. For
example, if I wanted to follow up on a particular task in my task list tomorrow, I could mark it with
the Tomorrow follow up flag.

In some situations you may want to move tasks from the Tasks folder to another Outlook folder.
Select the tasks in the task list that you wish to move and then select the Move command on the
Ribbon's Home tab. Select Other Folder to open The Move Items dialog box, which will list your
Outlook folders. You can use the New button to create a new folder if necessary. To move tasks from
your Tasks folder to another folder, select the folder in the Move Items dialog box and then click OK.
The dialog box will close and the task or tasks will be moved to the folder that you selected.

Setting Tasks Options

The Tasks options can be accessed via the Outlook Options window. Select File to open the Outlook
Backstage. Then click Options to open the Outlook Options window.

When you select Tasks in the Outlook Options window, you will find that there are a limited number
of options specifically related to tasks. In fact there are only two groups of options: Task options and
Work hours. Figure 24.19 shows the Tasks options.

The Task options include settings related to task reminders, reports and task flags. You can choose
to have reminders set for all tasks with due dates and set a default reminder time. In relation to
tasks that you assign to other people or are assigned to you, you can choose to keep updated copies of tasks you assign in your Tasks list and also have a status report sent automatically when you
complete an assigned task. Both of these settings are enabled by default.

You also have control over the color of overdue and completed tasks. Select the Overdue task color
or the Completed task color to change the default color for either of these task types. You can also
set a Quick Click flag for flagging tasks with a particular flag type. What this feature actually does is
allows you to add a flag to a task in the Task list with a single click. To specify the flag type for the
Quick Click feature, select Quick Click and then use the Set Quick Click dialog box to choose the flag
type, such as Today, Tomorrow, Complete.

The other options group for Tasks is the Work hours group. There are two possible settings: Task
working hours per day and Task working hours per week. The default settings for these two options
are 8 hours per day and 40 hours per week. You can use the spinner boxes for either of these settings to change the defaults if required.

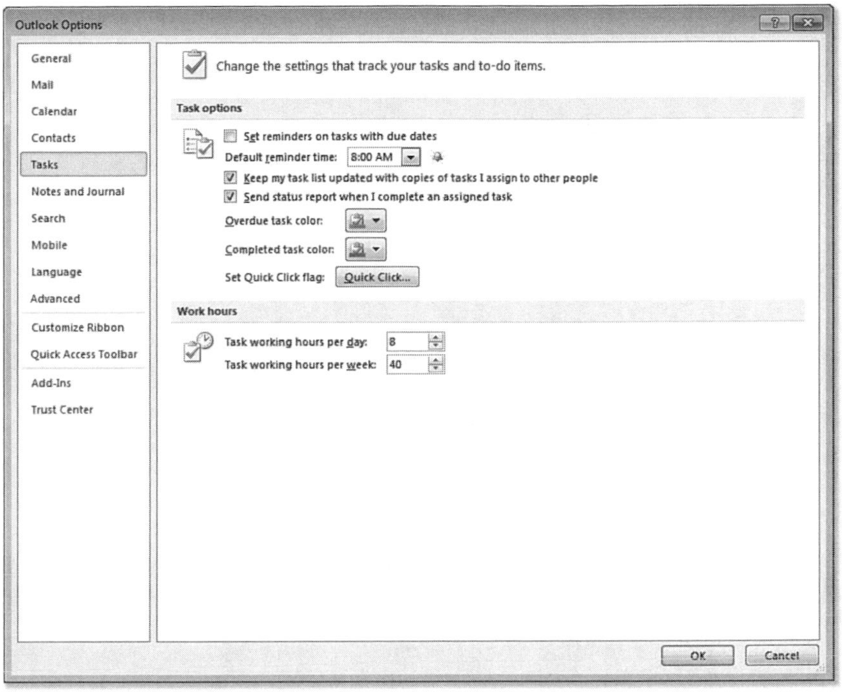

Figure 24.19
The option settings for
Outlook tasks.

WORKING WITH CONTACTS AND PLANNING MEETINGS

Any user of Outlook when asked about Outlook's primary function would probably say that it is an email application. However, when you think about how important it is to manage and communicate with your contacts, whether you are sending out a group email invitation to a party or mining your Outlook Contacts list for customers, Outlook really shines in terms of its capabilities for working with contact information.

In this chapter we take a look at the possibilities for creating and managing contact data in Outlook and how the Contacts folder's data becomes a key part of using Outlook to communicate with others. Outlook also provides a number of tools related to scheduling meetings with your contacts and we will look at how meetings are scheduled and managed.

Navigating the Contacts List

The Outlook Contacts folder is accessed via the Navigation Pane. Select Contacts and the Contacts folder will open in the Outlook window as shown in Figure 25.1

The contacts in your Contacts folder are listed in the Reading Pane. By default the contacts are listed as business cards. You can quickly change the view using the commands in the Current View group on the Ribbon's Home tab. These views are:

- **Business Card:** This view provides the name, phone number, title, company, and address of the contact and can include a photo of the contact. This is the default Contact view.

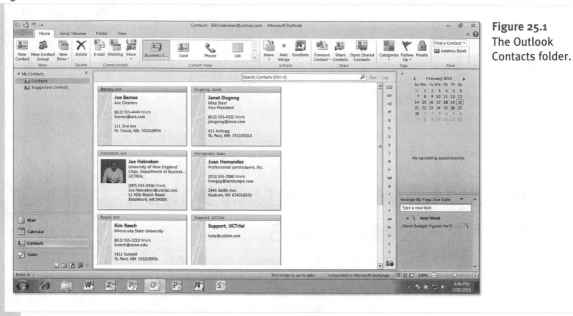

Figure 25.1
The Outlook
Contacts folder.

- **Card:** This view provides more detail than the business card view and includes more field information including assigned categories and notes. This view does not show photos of contacts (when you have inserted a digital photo of the contact in the Contact information).

- **Phone:** This view provides a tabular view of your contacts and includes filed columns for the business phone, business fax, home phone and mobile phone. It is extremely useful for making phone calls to your contacts.

- **List:** This view provides a tabular format for the contacts and includes a number of field columns for Full Name, Job Title, Company, Department and Business Phone.

You can further manipulate the views provided in the Current View by switching to the Ribbon's View tab. On the View tab you can use the commands in the Arrangement group to fine-tune the current view. These commands include the grouping commands such as Company, Categories and Location and there are commands for reversing the current sort direction and adding columns to the current view. You will find that the Arrangement commands such as Company and Location are not available when you are using the Business Card or Card views. So, don't worry, you didn't break Outlook. These commands only work in the tabular view layouts such as Phone and List. Figure 25.2 shows the commands available on the View tab in the Arrangement group.

When you are in a tabular view such as the List view, you can also use the field column headings (such as Full Name or Department) to sort the list by that particular field. The Reverse Sort command in the Arrangement group can then be used to re-order the sort based on the selected field column.

 tip

You can switch the current view using the view shortcuts on the status bar. You can also use the Zoom slider to zoom in and out on items as needed.

Figure 25.2
The Contacts folder Ribbon's View tab.

Creating a New Contact

You can create a new contact in more than one way. One possibility is to create a new contact from scratch using the New Contact command on the Home tab of the Contacts folder's Ribbon. You can also create a new contact from any of the Outlook folders using the New Items command (and then selecting Contact).

Other possibilities for adding a contact to the Contacts folder are related to other Outlook items. For example, you can right click on an email address in the From, Cc or BCc of a received message and select Add to Outlook Contacts; this will open a new Contact dialog box and the name and email information will already be entered for the contact. All you have to do is supply other pertinent information.

Other means of sharing contacts are also possible, particularly in situations where you use Outlook as an Exchange Server client. We will discuss possibilities for sharing contacts with others later in this chapter.

Let's take a look at creating a new contact from scratch. In the Contact folder, select the New Contact on the Home tab. A new Contact dialog box will open as shown in Figure 25.3.

A wide-variety of information can be added for the contact. You don't have to use all the fields provided in the dialog box, but it does make sense to enter the information that makes new contact that you are creating useful to you in terms of communicating with the contact and also accessing information about the contact. In terms of basic information you need for your contacts (to make the Contacts folder more than just a glorified email address list), the following field information should be entered:

- Name

- Company

- Job title

- E-mail address

- Web page address

- IM address

- Phone numbers (business, home, business fax, mobile)

- Address (street, city, state, ZIP Code, and country)

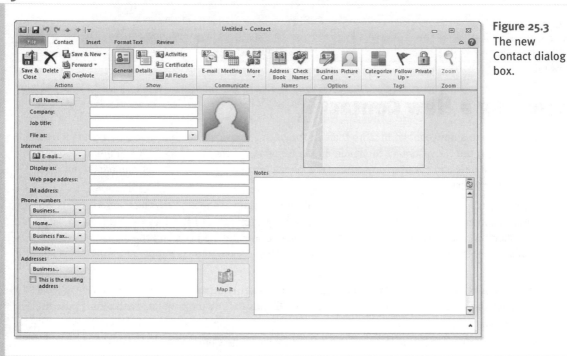

Figure 25.3
The new
Contact dialog
box.

When you are working in the various fields in the Contact dialog box, you can use the Tab key to quickly navigate from field
to field (or Shift + Tab) to move backward from field to field).
Some fields, such as Full Name and the Addresses fields, provide you with dialog boxes that make it easy for you to enter
(and check) all the information possible for that particular
field. For example, select the Full Name field and the Check
Full Name dialog box opens as shown in Figure 25.4.

This dialog box allows you to enter a contact's title such as
Miss, Ms., Dr., or Mr. and also first, middle and last name
including a suffix such as Jr. When you have entered the information in one of the "Check" dialog boxes, click OK to return
to the Contact dialog box.

As you enter the information for the contact, you will find that a business card is being built for the
contact on the right side of the dialog box. Depending on the purpose of your Contact list, you may
want to include images of your contacts, which will then appear in the Contacts folder when you
use the Business Card view. This can be particularly useful in cases where you have clients or customers in your Contacts folder who you really don't see that often and need a reminder related to
their appearance (you can't remember everyone's face).

To add a digital image of the contact to the Contact dialog box, select the Add Contact Picture box (it is a silhouette of a person). The Add Contact Picture dialog box will open. Navigate to the folder that contains the picture and then select the picture. Click OK to add the picture to the contact's information. You will be returned to the Contact dialog box.

Figure 25.4
The Check Full Name dialog box.

Entering Details Fields Information

As already mentioned the level of detail you provide for a particular contact is up to you but the more information you enter for a contact the more useful the contact listing is. You can also enter information related to a contact such as their department, office, manager's name. You can even enter personal information such as the contact's spouse/partner or birthday. To enter additional information related to a contact, select the Details command (in the Show group) on the Contact tab. Figure 25.5 shows the details fields.

⬤ tip

You don't necessarily have to worry about the file size of the picture that you use for a client; it will be sized appropriately to appear in the Contact dialog box. If you want to change the picture once you have inserted it, use the Picture command in the Options group.

Adding Fields for a Contact

You also have the option of adding information in additional fields to provide you with more complete information related to a particular contact (or contacts) This can be useful if you want to include the contact's children's names, a field to enter the name of the person who referred the contact to you or you want to be able to enter the contact's assistant's phone number. To use additional fields, follow these steps:

1. Select the All Fields command in the Show group. A blank field pane will open in the Contact dialog box.

2. Use the Select from drop-down list to select a field category such as Frequently-used fields, Miscellaneous fields or Personal fields. When you select one of the field groups, a list of specific fields will be listed in the field pane. For example, the Personal fields supply fields such as Birthday, Children, Hobbies and Language.

   Enter the information as needed in the details fields. You can return to the "main" fields for the contact by selecting the General command in the Show group.

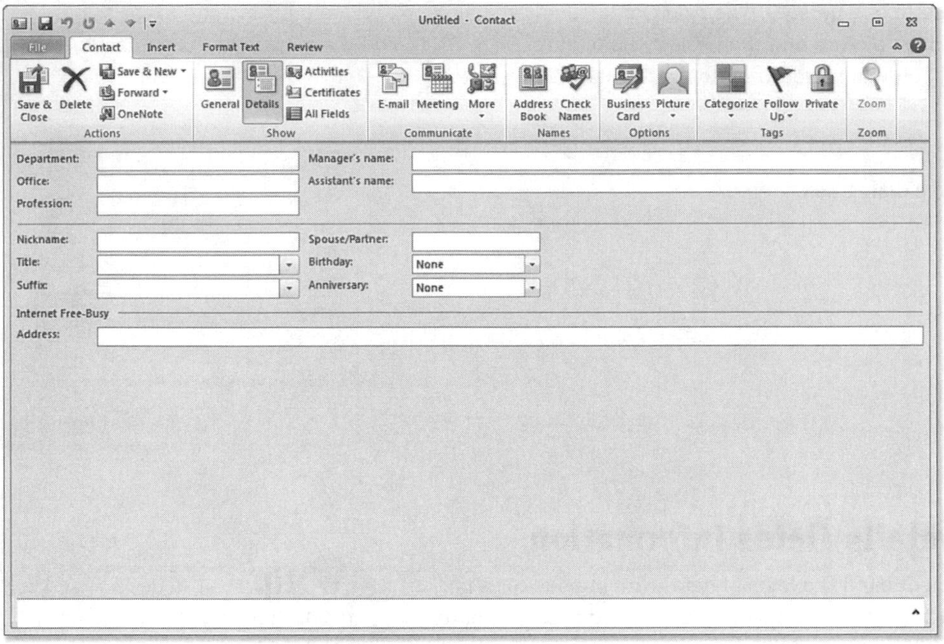

Figure 25.5
The new contact's details fields.

3. Enter the information as needed in the fields provided. You can return to the Select from drop-down list to view other fields and enter information in those fields.

4. When you have completed working with the additional fields, you can return to the general contact information for the contact by selecting General.

Adding additional field data only strengthens your informational IQ for the contacts you place in your Contacts folder. Be advised that viewing the information that you place in these additional fields will require that you use the All Fields command and then select the group of fields that you used for the additional information via the Select from drop-down list.

When you have completed entering information for a new contact, select Save & Close. This will place the contact in the Contacts list and return you to the Contacts folder.

Taking Advantage of Suggested Contacts

You might have noticed the Suggested Contacts icon in the Navigation Pane. It resides below the icon for your default Contacts list. When you send an email to a recipient who is not one of your contacts or is not listed in your Address Book (in lists such as the Global Address List), Outlook will create a suggested contact using the email address.

You can then view any suggested contacts that Outlook has created by selecting Suggested Contacts in the Navigation Pane. These suggested contacts will appear in the Reading Pane. To add a suggested contact or contacts to your Contacts list, drag the suggested contact or contacts from the Reading Pane onto the Contacts icon in the Navigation Pane. The suggested contact will be moved to your Contacts list.

You can then open the contact and enter the contact's information such as name, company, address and so on. The email address will have been entered for you by Outlook automatically.

When viewing the Suggested Contacts list, you also have the option of deleting any and all the contacts that Outlook places in this list. Select the suggested contact or contacts and then select the Delete command on the Home tab.

Editing Contact Information

You can open a contact's dialog box to access field data and add additional information or edit specific fields. In the Contacts folder, double-click the contact. Add and edit field information for the contact as needed.

Using the Notes box located in the Contact dialog box effectively allows you to enter narrative text related to that particular contact. You can enter any type of information in the Notes box such as notes on a conversation that you had with the contact or the fact that the contact is not very good at golf (no golf invitation for that contact). Editing contacts may primarily relate to making sure that the contact's information is accurate but it also pertains to having any and all information that you can accumulate for that contact.

You are not limited to editing contact information in the Contact dialog box. You can also edit certain fields directly in the Reading Pane. Select the List view in the Current View group (this view shows the most fields). Using the field column names as a reference, click in one of the field positions in a Contact's record (each row of information in the list is the record for a specific contact) and then enter the information for that field. Figure 25.6 shows department information being added directly to a contact in the List view.

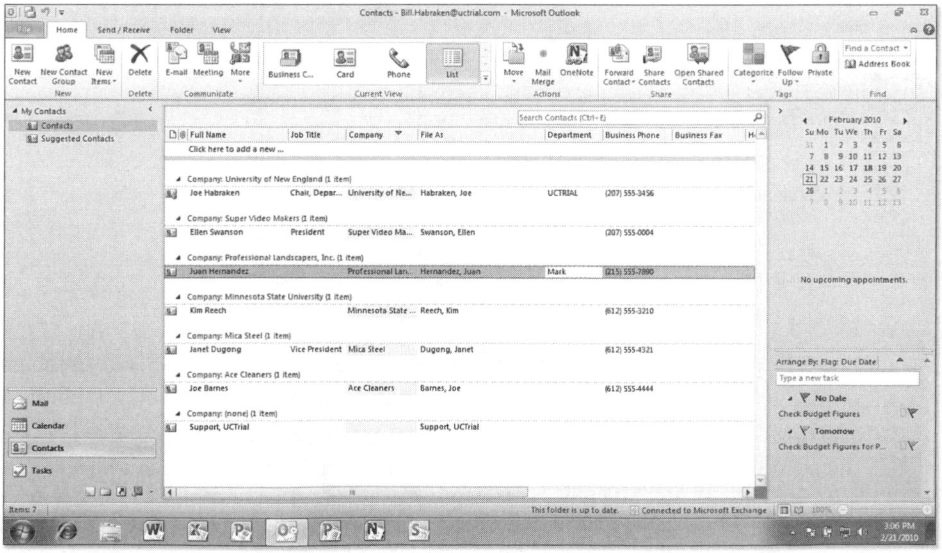

Figure 25.6
Enter information for your contacts in the List view.

Editing a contact's information might also relate to the format of the electronic business card that is created when you create a new contact. The use of flags and categories can also be used both in an informational sense and as a way to sort and filter the Contacts list.

Editing a Business Card

When you enter the information for a contact a default business card is created. You can edit the layout and fine-tune the field information in the business card. Creating a more custom layout for contact business cards can be very useful if you have a Contact listing for each of your employees and colleagues. When you provide their information to a potential customer or client, you will be providing an electronic business card that can be extremely informational and also visually appealing. It makes sense to create your own Contact entry and then build your own electronic business card for inclusion in your own emails.

To edit the business card for a contact, double-click the contact in the Contacts list to open the contact's dialog box. Then select the Business Card command in the Options group. The Edit Business Card dialog box will open as shown in Figure 25.7.

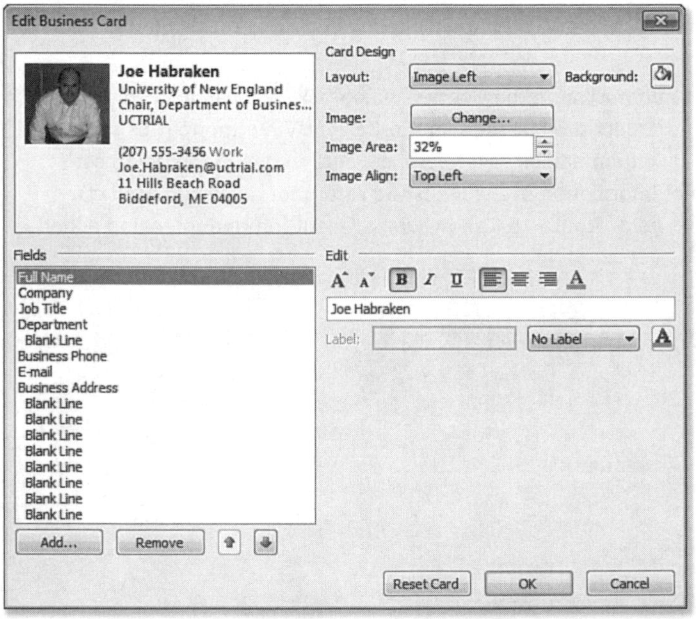

Figure 25.7
The Edit Business Card dialog box.

The Edit Business Card dialog box gives you control over the fields shown on the business card, the position of the image, and the fonts used on the business card. Let's start with the fields.

The fields currently used on the business card are listed in the Fields box. You can select a field and then use the Remove button to remove the field from the card. You can also add fields to the business card. Select the Add button. A menu will appear providing categories of fields that you can add to the card. For example, the Organization group provides the Company, Department and Job Title fields. The Address group lists the Business Address, Home Address and Other Address fields.

Use the Add field menu to add fields to the business card as needed. This menu also provides you with a Blank Line options and a Custom field category. Once you have removed or added fields, you can use the Move Field Up or the Move Field Down buttons to rearrange the fields on the business card.

If you have not added an image to the business card or wish to change the image on the business card, select the Change button. This will open the Add Card Picture dialog box. Locate the image and select it and then click Open.

You also have control over the layout of the business card in terms of where the image is positioned and whether or not you use a background color. You can use the Layout drop-down list to position the image as follows: Image Left (the default), Image Right, Image Top, Image Bottom, Text Only or Background Image. If you wish to add a background color to the card, select the Background button and select a color from the Color dialog box.

Depending on the layout setting that you select for the image in the Layout drop-down list, you can select the actual alignment of the image using the Image Align drop-down list. For example, if I choose the Image Bottom Layout setting, I can then align the image on the bottom of the card using the Bottom Right alignment setting.

You can use the various font and alignment settings in the Edit area of the dialog box to change the various attributes for the text on the business card. For example, you may want the company name to be in italics or use a bold, red font for your name. Having options related to text color and appearance can be particularly useful if you have used a background color or used the image as a background (not unlike a watermark). You can make sure that you use a text color and size that is readable on the background.

When you have finished editing the business card, click OK. This will return you to the contact's dialog box. The new layout for the business card will appear in the business card preview that is provided to the right of the various contact fields in the contact's dialog box.

 tip

You can also open the Edit Business Card dialog box by double-clicking the business card preview in the contact's dialog box.

 tip

You can also open the Edit Business Card dialog box by double-If you don't like the changes that you have made to the card, you can use the Reset Card button in the Edit Business Card dialog box to reset the card to the Outlook defaults.

Tagging Contacts with Flags and Categories

Although you are not actually editing information in the various contact fields, you can also modify a contact's listing using tags such as categories and follow up flags. The tag commands are provided in the Tags group on the Contact tab of the Ribbon. To add a category to a contact, select the Categorize command and select a category from the list provided.

 note

Using follow up flags is just one way to tag a contact for follow up. You can also create a task or a specific appointment in the Calendar, which would serve the same purpose of making sure that you follow up with that contact.

You can also flag contacts for follow up. For example, you may have had an appointment with a contact recently and want to follow up with that contact sometime this week. You could flag the contact with the This Week flag. To select a flag for a contact select the Follow Up command.

Although the follow up flag itself may serve as a visual reminder that you are going to follow up with the contact, you may want to create a reminder to go with the flag. That way Outlook will alert you to the fact that you want to follow up with the contact. Select Follow Up and the Add Reminder. The Custom dialog box will appear as shown in 25.8.

Specify the flag type in the Flag to: drop-down list. You can also specify a start date and a due date for the follow up. Use the reminder date and time settings to specify when you will receive the reminder related to the flag. Select OK to return to the contact's dialog box.

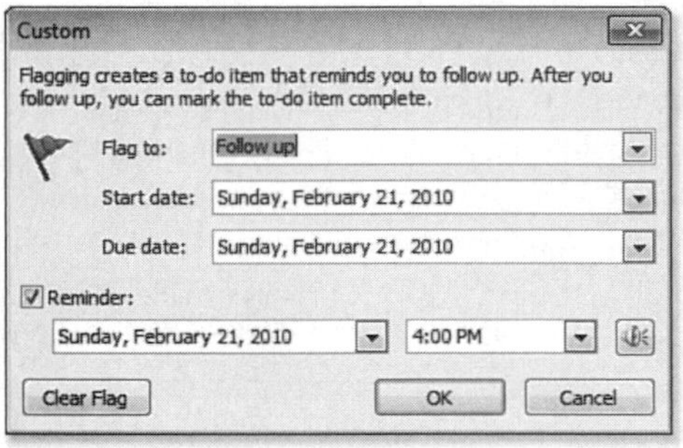

Figure 25.8
The Custom dialog box.

Mapping a Contact's Address

Despite all the possibilities for electronic communication that a software tool such as Outlook provides us, there may be times when you need to meet with a contact face to face. So, before you go on the road, you may want to map the contact's address.

In the contact's dialog box, select Map It. Your default Web browser will open up a map of the address using Bing.com. You can Select the Directions link on the left side of the Website and then enter your location to get direction to the contact's address. After you have printed the directions, you can close your Web browser to return to Outlook.

Finding Contacts

Once your Contacts folder reaches a critical mass, you will need some tools that help you locate a particular contact quickly. As already mentioned, you can jump alphabetically around your Contacts list using the Index buttons on the right side of the Reading Pane. In terms of finding specific contacts or contacts that meet certain criteria, you can use the Search Contacts box at the top of the Reading Pane.

You can search by keywords by entering a text search string in the Search Contact box. For example, you can type in a portion of a last name to filter the Contacts list by that particular text string.

When you click in the Search box, a number of commands are provided to you by the Search Tools tab that appears on the Ribbon. You can use the commands in the Refine group to conduct a new search or refine a search that was based on keywords. Figure 25.9 shows the Refine group commands.

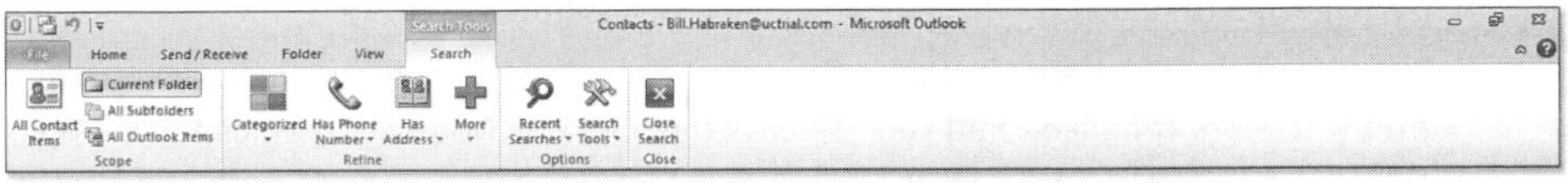

Figure 25.9
The Search Tools' Refine Group.

The Refine commands provided for searches in the Contacts folder are as follows:

- **Categorized:** This command allows you to search for contacts by category.

- **Has Phone Number:** This command allows you to filter the Contacts list by the phone fields: business phone, home phone or mobile phone. For example, if you select Has Business Phone only the contacts who have a business phone listed will be shown in the Reading Pane.

- **Has Address:** This command filters the Contacts list based on whether or not specific address fields contain information. The possibilities are: Has E-Mail Address, Has IM Address, Has Business Address or Has Home Address.

- **More:** This command provides access to additional properties for your search criteria via a list of Common Properties. These properties include Business Phone, Company, Home Address, and Street Address.

You can also access recent searches and other search tools via the Search Tools command groups. To access recent searches that you have used, select the Recent Searches command and select a search from the list provided.

If you wish to access advanced search tools, select the Search Tools command. A particularly useful search tool in relation to a large Contacts list is the Indexing Status command. Select this command to have Outlook index your contact entries. This will make your searches faster and more efficient. When you have finished working with the Search feature, you can quickly return to the Calendar by selecting the Close Search command.

 An overview of the Outlook Search feature is provided in Chapter 22, "Requisite Outlook: Configuration and Essential Features," on page 623.

Organizing Contacts with Groups

We have already discussed ways to "visually" organize your Contacts folder using different views and the Search box. You can also quickly sort contacts in the Phone or List view using the field headings to sort the list by things such as name, company or category.

> **note**
> In Outlook 2010 contact groups replace distribution lists found in earlier versions of Outlook.

Another way to organize your contacts is to use contact groups. By default the Contacts list is one big list with no real subdivisions. You can use contact groups to group contacts by such things as company or location. You could also create a personal group and a business group to provide some functional division between the types of contacts you store in your Contacts folder.

To create a new contact group, select the new Contact Group on the Ribbon's Home tab. The new Contact Group dialog box will open as shown in Figure 25.10.

Type a name for the new group in the Name box. You can then add contacts to the group. Select the Add Members command and then select From Outlook Contacts (you can also add contacts from the Address Book). The Select members: Contacts dialog box will open with your Contacts list selected.

Select a contact or contacts in the list and then click the Members button. When you have finished adding members to the new group, click OK to close the Select members: Contacts dialog box. You will be returned to the Group dialog box and the new members will be listed. If you want to remove a member or members, select the member (or members) and then select the Remove Member command.

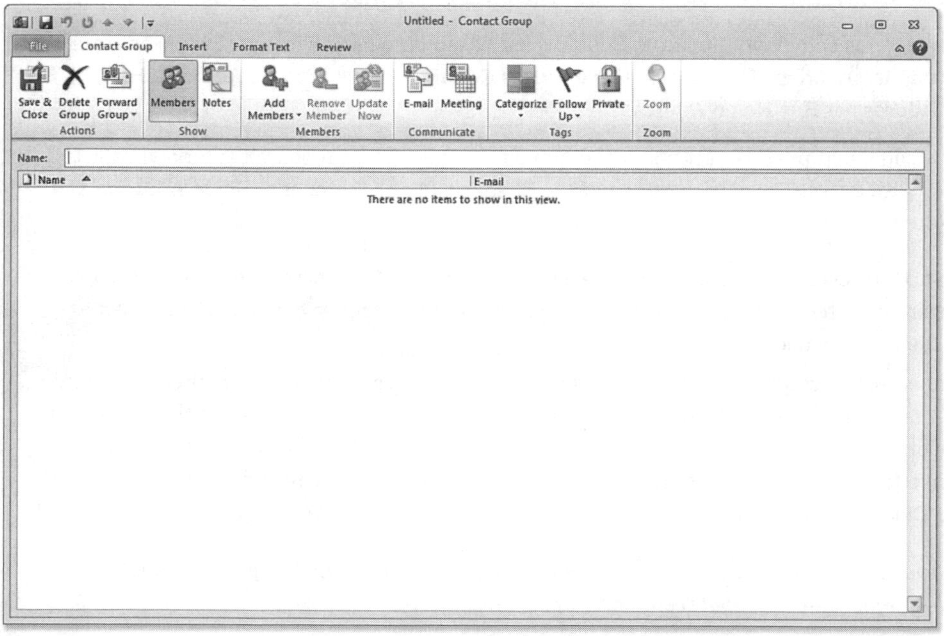

Figure 25.10
The Contact Group dialog box.

To close the new Contact Group dialog box, select Save & Close. The new contact group will appear in your Contacts folder, meaning in the Reading Pane with your contacts. To view the contacts in a contact group, open the contact group. You can open a specific contact in the group by double-clicking on the contact.

Including a contact in a contact group does not remove the contact from your Contact list. It basically creates a shortcut to the contact. So, if you remove a contact from a contact group you are not removing the contact from the Contacts folder.

The great thing about contact groups is that you can basically treat them like a contact. If you find that you are sending email messages or assigning tasks to the same group of recipients, create a contact group and then address the email to the contact group. Contact groups can also be used to send multiple meeting invitations (scheduling meetings is discussed later in this chapter).

Forwarding and Sharing Contacts

You can share your Outlook contacts with co-workers and colleagues. Whether you use Outlook as an Internet email client or use Outlook in an Exchange Server environment, you can quickly forward contact information to anyone with an email address. In Exchange Server environments, you can share your Contacts folder with other network users and these users can share their Contacts folder with you.

Figure 25.11 shows the Share group on the Contacts folder Ribbon's Home tab. This group provides the Forward Contact, Share Contacts and Open Shared Contacts commands.

These commands can also be accessed via the Ribbon when you are working in the dialog box for a particular contact. The Share group is located on the Contact tab.

Figure 25.11
The Share group commands.

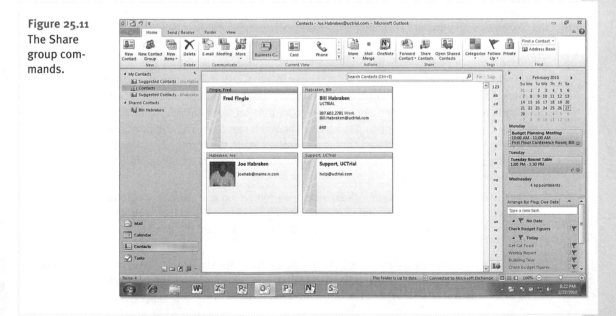

Forwarding Contacts

When you forward a contact or contacts to other people, the contact information comes in the form of an email attachment. The actual contact information can be attached to a message in two different formats:

- **Business Card:** This format is also known as a vCard and uses the VCard file extension .vcf. The vCard is considered the standard for electronic business cards and can be interpreted by most email and contact management software packages.

- **Outlook Contact:** You can also attach a contact or contacts to a message as an Outlook Contact item. Obviously, contacts attached as an Outlook Contact item can be opened by recipients who use Outlook and can also be used by recipients that use an email client that supports the Outlook Contact file format.

You can also forward contacts group via a mail message. However, contacts groups can only be sent as Outlook Contact items. You cannot send an Outlook contacts group as a vCard attachment.

There is also an additional possibility for forwarding contact information. You can forward contact information as a text message (you know, those messages you create on your cell phone with your thumbs). If you are using Outlook in an Exchange Server environment that provides a text messaging service, your network administrator will set you up with a Text Messaging account. Even if you don't work in a corporate environment you can sign up for a third-party service (someone other than Microsoft) who provides you with an account for the text messaging service.

You can set up the text messaging feature by selecting the Forward Contact command and then the Forward as Text Message choice on the menu provided. The Configure a Text Messaging (SMS) account dialog box will open. Click Next and you will be walked through the process of entering your provider information and your username and password for the text messaging account. Once the text messaging account is configured, a new text message will open, allowing you to enter the mobile phone number of the recipient you wish to text with the contact information. You can also use this service to send text messages from Outlook.

To forward a contact or contacts from the Contacts folder, select the contact or contacts in the Contacts list. Select the Forward Contact command in the Share group and then select one of the commands on the menu provided: As a Business Card, As an Outlook Contact, or Forward as Text Message. A new message will open. Figure 25.12 shows a message with a contact's business card that will be forwarded. The business card is also embedded in the body of the message. When you forward the contact information as an Outlook Contact item, the contact information is not embedded in the body of the message.

Specify the recipient or recipients for the message as you would any other email message. You can also include explanatory or other text in the body of the message. You can also choose to attach other files to the message as needed. When you are ready to forward the contact information, select Send.

If you happen to be the recipient of contact information as a business card (vCard) or as an Outlook item, double-click the attachment in the received message. This will open the forwarded contact's dialog box. Select Save & Close and the contact will be added to your Contacts list.

Figure 25.12
Mail message
with attached
contact infor-
mation.

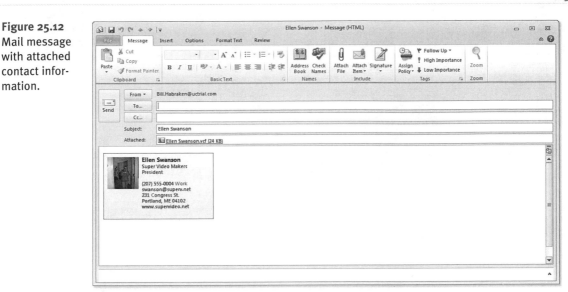

Sharing Contacts

If you are working in an Exchange Server environment, you can share all your contacts with other
users on your network. And when I say all of your contacts, I mean all of your contacts in the
"main" Contacts list. So, you may want to consider a couple of possibilities for protecting contact
information that you don't really want to share. One possibility is to tag specific contacts as private.
Users who you share your Contacts list with will not be able to view the details for any contacts
you have tagged as private. So, select those contacts in the Contacts list and then select the Private
command on the Home tab.

Another possibility is to create a new folder in your Contacts folder and move contacts you don't
want to share to this new folder. In the Navigation Pane right click on the Contacts icon and then
select New Folder. Use the Create New Folder dialog box to specify a name for the new folder and
click OK. Drag contacts you do not wish to share from your Contacts list to this new folder.

Now we can share the Contacts list. Select Share Contacts on the Home tab. A Sharing invitation
message will open as shown in Figure 25.13.

Specify the recipients for the sharing invitation by addressing the message as you would any other
email message. You can also add text to the body of the message if needed. A check box in the message specifies that you will allow the recipient (or recipients) of the invitation to view your Contacts
folder. You can also select the Request permission to view recipient's Contacts folder check box if
you would like to be able to view the recipient's Contacts folder. Click Send. A message box will
open asking you to verify that the Contacts folder will be shared as read only (which is a good
thing). Click Yes and the invitation is on its way.

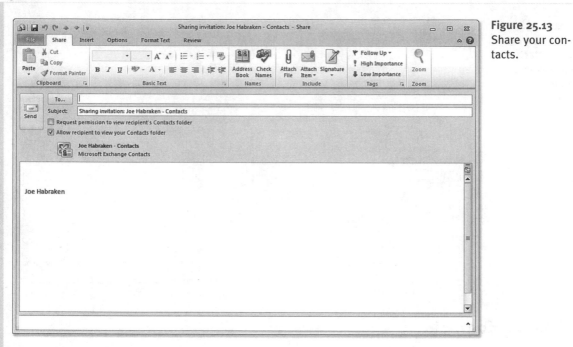

Figure 25.13
Share your con-
tacts.

When the recipient receives the sharing invitation and opens it, all they have to do is select the Open This Contacts Folder command on the Share tab. This will place your Contacts list on the Navigation Pane in a Shared Contact group folder. Figure 25.14 shows a shared Contacts list in the Contacts folder.

If you also requested that the recipient share contacts with you, the recipient will need to select the Allow command on the Share message's Ribbon. An Outlook message box will open asking if the user wants to share the contact folder with you (a read-only version). When they click Yes, a sharing message will be sent to you. All you have to do is use the Open this contacts folder command when you open the message and you can view the shared contacts. Now everybody is happy.

Figure 25.14
Shared contacts can be accessed via the Navigation Pane.

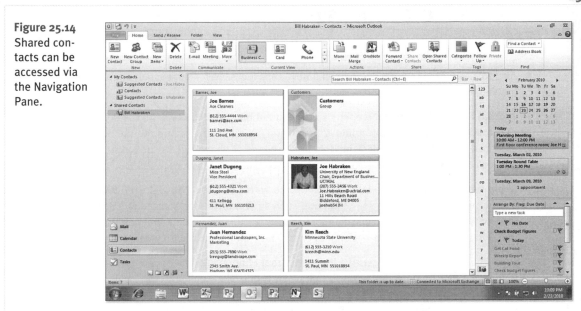

Contact Communication and Action Options

The whole point of accumulating a Contacts list is so that you can communicate efficiently with your contacts. You can quickly communicate with your contacts directly from the Contacts folder. The Communicate group commands on the Home tab allow you to quickly send email, meeting requests or assign tasks to a contact or contacts. Figure 25.15 shows the Communicate group commands.

For example, to email a contact or contacts, select the contact or contacts in the Contact list. You need not open specific contact dialog boxes. Select the E-Mail command in the Communicate group; a new email will open addressed to the selected contact or contacts. You will experience the same scenario when creating a new meeting using the Meeting command (which is discussed later in this chapter). A meeting request will open with the selected contact or contacts listed in the To box.

Figure 25.15
Communicate with contacts directly from the Contacts folder.

Other Communication Options

There are additional options for communicating with contacts other than emails or meeting invitations. The More command provides you with following possibilities:

- **Assign Task:** This command will open a new Task message for the contact or contacts. Provide the subject and other particulars for the task and then click Send.

- **Journal Entry:** This command opens a new Journal Entry dialog box with the selected contact or contacts listed in the Subject line. You can add additional information to the entry as needed or start a timer if you are using the default entry type of Phone call for the journal entry. This is particularly useful if you are also going to use the Call command described below.

- **Reply with IM:** You can use IM to communicate with a contact. You will need to install an instant messaging client on your computer such as Windows Live Messenger. You will also need to specify the IM address for the contact in the contact's information. You can then use this command to initiate your instant messaging client and communicate with a contact

- **Call:** You can have Outlook (with a little help from Windows) dial a phone number for a client if you have a modem on your computer that can dial out. This command can be used to dial any of the phone numbers listed for a particular contact. When you select this command, the New Call dialog box will open (see Figure 25.16). Options are provided for dialing properties and dialing options. You can begin the call by selecting Start Call.

The Assign Task and Journal Entry commands allow you to work with multiple selected contacts in the Contacts list. The IM and Call commands are designed for individual communication with a particular contact.

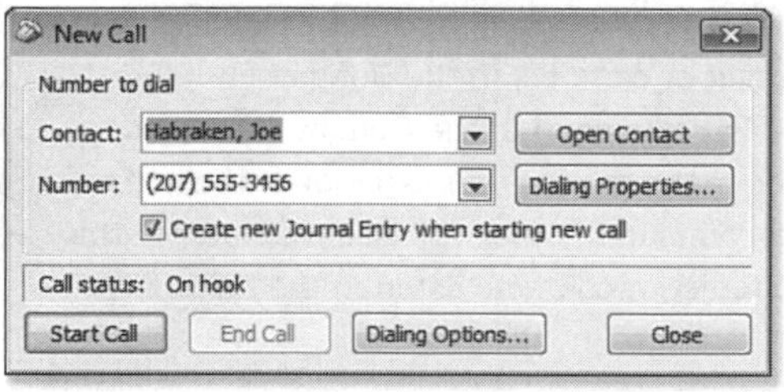

Figure 25.16
Call a contact from Outlook.

➡ *For more about assigning Outlook tasks see Chapter 26, "Using the Calendar for Appointments and Tasks," page 683.*

➡ *For more about using the Outlook Journal see Chapter 24, "Using the Journal and Notes," page 722.*

Contact Actions

There are also additional actions that you can take related to the contacts in your Contacts list. The Actions group provides the Move, Mail Merge and OneNote command.

The Move command is self-explanatory. You can use it to move contacts from the primary Contacts list to other folders within the main Contacts folder. When you select Move, a list of your Contacts folder will be listed. You also have the option of moving contacts to other folders or copying selected contacts to a folder.

The Mail Merge command allows you to merge all your contacts or selected contacts to a Word document. Figure 25.17 shows the Mail Merge Contacts dialog box, which opens when the Mail Merge command is selected.

The Mail Merge Contacts dialog box provides options for merging the contact date to a new or existing document. You can also specify that the contact data be saved as a Word data source. You can then use the data source for future merges by selecting the file when using Microsoft Word.

Figure 25.17
Create a Mail Merge using your contacts.

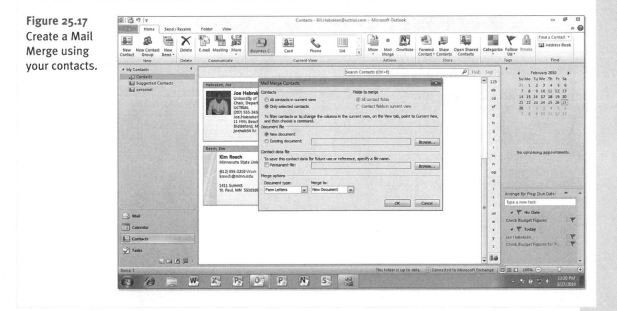

When you select OK, the Outlook data is provided to Word and a new or existing document (depending on the option you selected in the Mail Merge Contacts dialog box) will open in the Word application window. You can use the Mailings tab to enter the merge fields into the new letter as needed and then complete the merge.

> For a discussion of the Word mail merge feature, see Chapter 9, "Managing Mailings and Forms," page 225.

Checking Contact Activities

Since there are a variety of ways to communicate with contacts, it is particularly useful to be able to view all the various activities that have taken place related to a particular contact. You can view items such as emails (sent and received) tasks (assigned to the contact and assigned by the contact) and other Outlook items such as meetings and journal entries.

To view the activities for a particular contact, open the contact's dialog box. Then select the Activities command in the Show group. A list of all the activities for that contact will be listed as shown in Figure 25.18.

You can use the Show drop-down list in the Contact Activities window to view specific types of activities. For example, you can choose to view only email related to the contact. Or you may wish to view upcoming tasks/appointments related to that contact. You can return to the entry fields for the contact by selecting the General command in the Show group.

> *The Show group also provides a Certificates command that can be used to show the digital ID certificates related to a particular contact. For more information see Chapter 27, "Securing and Maintaining Outlook," on page 737.*

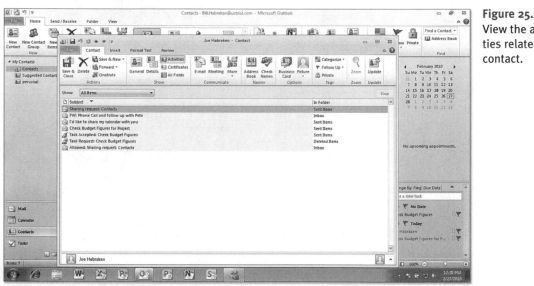

Figure 25.18
View the activities related to a contact.

Printing Contact Information

You can print your contact information in a variety of formats. These formats include an alphabetical card style, memo style and a phone directory style.

To print the current Contacts list (this can be the main Contacts list or any lists that you have created in separate folders), select File to access the Outlook Backstage. Then select Print. The Print window will open with a preview of the default print style. You can specify the printer for the print job and also set print options as needed. When you are ready to print the Contacts list, select the Print button.

Setting Contact Options

The Outlook options related to the Contacts folder are accessed via the Outlook Backstage (select File) In the Backstage select options and then Contacts to view the Contacts options. The Contacts options are as follows:

- **Names and Filing:** These options include the default formatting for new contacts and the format that contacts are filed under. Use the Order of New Contacts drop-down list to specify the formatting for new contacts, which is set to First (Middle) Last by default. To specify the format for filing contacts use the Order tThat Contacts Are Saved drop-down list. The default is Last, First. The Names and filing options also include a checkbox that has Outlook check for duplicates when saving new contacts.

- **Linking:** Disabled by default, this option will require Outlook to display all Contacts that are linked to a current item such as a task.

- **Contacts Index:** You can specify that an additional index be shown for the Contacts in a language other than the default language set for Outlook.

- **Online Status and Photographs:** If you are using instant messaging and wish to see the online status of contacts, select the Display online status next to name checkbox. You can also specify that user photographs are shown when available.

- **Suggested Contacts:** Enabled by default, this option will place a suggested contact listing in the Suggested Contacts folder for any contact (such as the recipient of a new e-mail) who is not currently in your Contacts list or your Outlook Address Book.

When you have finished working with the Contacts options, click OK. You will be returned to the Outlook application window.

Scheduling Meetings

Once you have your contacts in place in your Contacts folder, there are a variety of actions that you can take related to those contacts. We have already discussed sending messages to contacts and using other methods of communicating with your contacts such as task assignments and phone calls. You can also schedule meetings quickly and efficiently using the information in your Contacts folder. Since the scheduling of meetings also relates to the Outlook Calendar, you can sort out who is available for a particular meeting using the Scheduling Assistant. In environments where you are able to share calendars on the network, such as an Exchange Server environment, you will be able to accurately tell when a contact is available and when a contact is busy.

 For more about the Outlook Calendar, see Chapter 24, "Using the Calendar for Appointments and Tasks," on page 663.

When you create a new meeting, Outlook enables you to plan the time and date of the meeting, identify the subject and location of the meeting, invite contacts to attend the meeting, and identify resources that will be needed for the meeting.

You can create a new meeting from any of the Outlook folders. When you create a new meeting from the Contacts folder, you can select the contacts you wish to invite to the meeting in the Contacts list before you actually invoke the Meeting command.

After selecting the contacts for the meeting, select the Meeting command on the Ribbon's Home tab. The Meeting dialog box will open as shown in Figure 25.19.

The contacts you selected in your Contacts list will appear in the To box. You can add additional contacts using the Address Book command in the Attendees group. This allows you to invite attendees to the meeting who are not in your Contacts list but are in other lists in the Address Book such as the Global Address List that is provided to you when you use Outlook as an Exchange Server client. You may also have lists in your Address Book that you imported from other software applications that can be accessed to building the list of attendees for the meeting. When you use the Address Book dialog box to specify attendees for the meeting you can specify both required and optional attendees and specify any resources that are needed for the meeting.

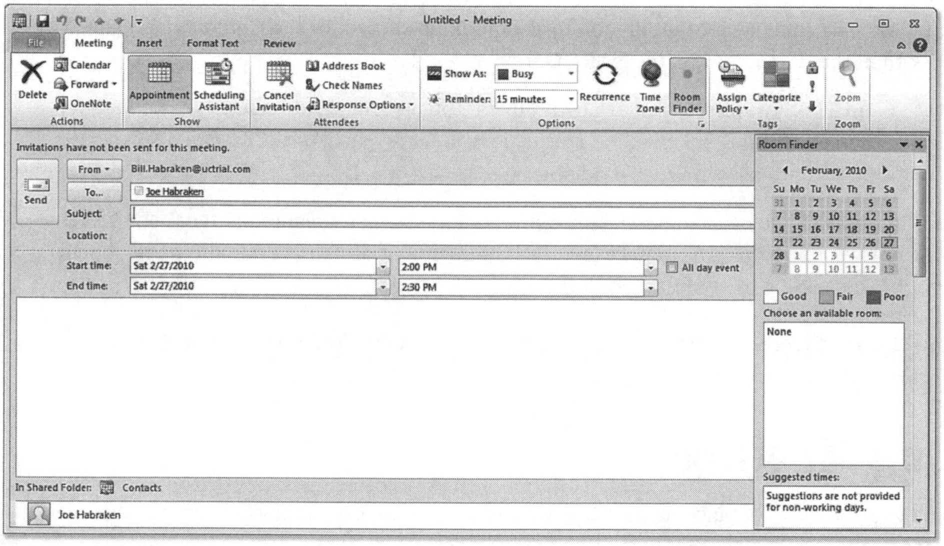

Figure 25.19
Create a new meeting.

You will also want to enter a subject for the meeting in the Subject box. You can also type a location for the meeting into the Location box such as a particular conference room, building location or site external to your company or institution (say a local coffee or doughnut shop). You can also specify the start and end time for the meeting (including the date and the time). If you are scheduling an all day event, select the All Day Event check box.

As with any Outlook item, you can use the Options and Tags group commands to specify options related to the meeting. For example, you can specify when the reminder for the meeting should be provided, if the meeting is recurring (use the Recurrence command) and you can also specify multiple time zones for the meeting (particularly if it is a video conference or an online meeting). You can also tag the meeting as necessary with categories and importance level flags.

Since the meeting information is sent out to the potential attendees as an email message (these are invitations after all), you will want to provide additional information regarding the meeting in the message body box. You can tell attendees more about what the meeting will entail and if they should bring anything to the meeting.

> **🔍 note**
>
> Online services are available that enable you to share your Outlook calendar with other users. This is a possible alternative to being on an Exchange Server or SharePoint network. Do a search for Outlook free/busy service on the Web.

Selecting the Meeting Location

If you are using Outlook as an Exchange Server client, you can select the Rooms button to the right of the Location box. The Address Book will open, showing the Global Address List for your Exchange Server network, which may also include a listing of meeting rooms for your corporation or institution. You can select any room listed in the address list and specify it as the location for the meeting by selecting Rooms. Select OK to return to the Meeting dialog box. The meeting room will actually be listed in the Location box and the To box since the room itself becomes a participant (albeit a location) for the meeting.

The big problem with scheduling a meeting relates to making sure that your contacts can attend the meeting at the scheduled time and that you are sure that the room you are going to use for the meeting is actually available. We will get to subject of attendee scheduling conflicts in a moment, but a few words should be said related to the Room Finder provided by Outlook 2010.

I've already mentioned that you may be able to specify a location for the meeting using the Global Address List if you use Outlook as an Exchange Server client. You can also use the Room Finder to see when a location (or locations) may be available.

Select the Room Finder command in the Options group. The Room Finder Task Pane will appear on the right of the Meeting dialog box. The Room Finder provides a list of rooms that you manage (as resources) and also provides a list of suggested times (each time block is one-half hour). Each time block will either let you know that a room is available or that there is a time conflict with the room. You can select a time block to specify the start time for a meeting if you wish. When you have finished working with the Room Finder task pane, close it.

> **📡 caution**
>
> Many people use Outlook as an Internet email client but do not get to take advantage of all of Outlook's bells and whistles that are provided to users who use Outlook on an Exchange Server networ . So, don't be disheartened when you can't take advantage of absolutely every Outlook feature. It is a very powerful piece of software no matter what type of environment you use it in. You can still schedule meetings, specify the meeting location and invite attendees.

Using the Scheduling Assistant

Although scheduling a room might be a bit of a trial, finding a meeting time that accommodates the schedules of all the meeting participants can even be more frustrating. The Scheduling Assistant can help you ferret out potential conflicts and schedule your meeting when most, if not all, participants are available.

To open the Scheduling Assistant, select the Scheduling Assistant command in the Show group on the Meeting tab. The Scheduling Assistant will open including the Room Finder Task Pane as shown in Figure 25.20.

The Scheduling Assistant will list the participants (and resources and rooms if you have added them) in the All Attendees List. The date (the meeting date) will be broken down in a tabular format with the column headings defined by hours. Each attendee's free/busy time for the date will be shown on the time line.

A green vertical line will show the start time for the meeting. A red vertical line will show the end time for the meeting. You can drag the start and end time lines on the time grid to specify a meeting time that does not have any conflicts. You can also cross-reference information provided in the Room Finder Task Pane to make sure that there is not a room conflict at the newly specified room time.

The Scheduling assistant also provides you with the ability to add attendees and rooms, so you can build a meeting directly from the Scheduling Assistant before you add an attendee or other information to the meeting. When you have completed fine-tuning the meeting time and other settings in the Scheduling Assistant, select the Appointment command in the show group. This will return you to the meeting dialog box.

Before you send the meeting invitations, you may want to alter the Response options available on the Response Options command in the Attendees group. By default a response is requested to the invitation and attendees are provided the option of proposing a new time for the meeting. If you do not wish to allow new time proposals, deselect the Allow New Time Proposals option.

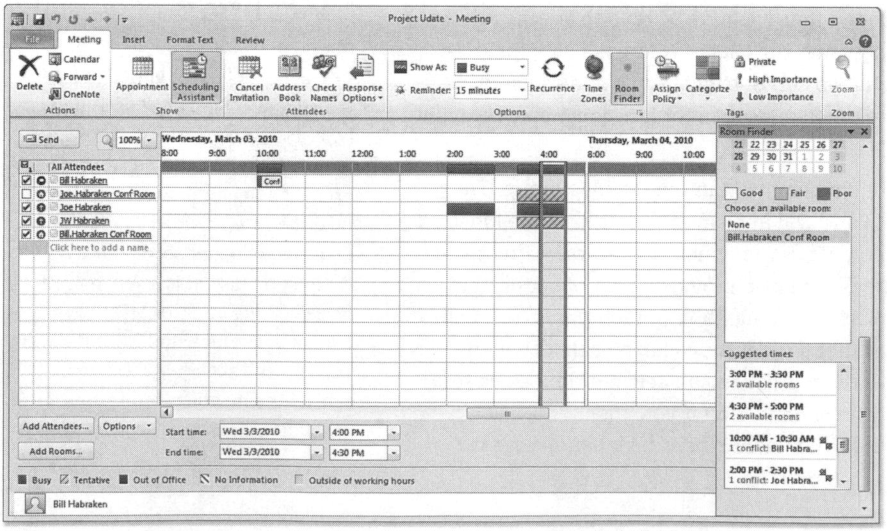

Figure 25.20
The Scheduling Assistant and Room Finder.

If you are sending the invitation to possible attendees where you manually entered the email address or in cases where you are not sure if an email address is valid, select the Check Names command. If there is a problem with an address or name, Outlook will provide a message box detailing the problem.

When you are ready to send the meeting, click Send. The meeting invitations will be sent to the attendees. The meeting will also be added to your Outlook Calendar as an appointment.

Viewing and Editing Meeting Information

You can open a meeting on your Calendar and view or edit the meeting details as needed. Double-click the meeting in the Calendar (which appears as an appointment) and the Meeting dialog box will open.

If you want to quickly track responses for the meeting invitations that were sent, select the Tracking command in the Show group (the Tracking command is only available for sent meetings) and then select View Tracking Status.

You will see a list of the attendees and the status of their responses. If an attendee has not responded, the Response will be labeled as None. Attendees can also respond to the invitation using Accept, Tentative or Decline.

You can also edit the meeting parameters. You can change the time and date of the meeting and you can also edit the list of attendees for the meeting. If necessary, you can use the Scheduling Assistant to reschedule the meeting and specify a new location for the meeting. You can even use the Cancel Meeting command to cancel the meeting.

If you make substantive changes to the meeting, you will want to send these changes to the attendees. When you have completed making your changes, select the Send Update button. Updated invitations will be sent to the attendees. If you have changed the date or time for the meeting, the meeting will also be moved on your Calendar.

When you do receive meeting response messages from attendees, the message will detail whether or not a specific attendee has accepted, tentatively accepted or declined the invitation. The email will also provide tracking information related to the number of accepted, tentative and declined responses you have received related to the meeting.

Responding to Meeting Requests

When you are a potential attendee for a meeting, you will receive a meeting invitation from the meeting organizer. The invitation comes in the form of an email. The invitation will provide the details of the meeting and also provides you with the ability to accept or decline the meeting invitation. If you accept the meeting invitation, the meeting will automatically be added to your Outlook Calendar.

Double-click a meeting invitation in your Inbox to open it. Figure 25.21 shows a meeting invitation message.

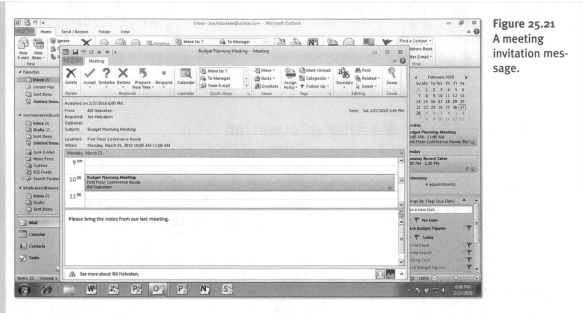

Figure 25.21
A meeting invitation message.

You are provided with four alternatives for the meeting: Accept, Tentative (accept tentatively), Decline and Propose New Time. The Propose New Time command allows you to either accept tentatively and propose a new time or decline and propose a new time.

When you select the Accept, Tentative or Decline commands, you are provided with three options related to your response to the originator of the meeting:

- **Edit the Response before Sending:** this command allows you to include additional comments with your response message. Selecting this command will open a new message and you can add text to the body of the message, attach files or do anything that you can normally do to an email message such as address or copy the message to other recipients.

- **Send the Response Now:** this command sends a response immediately without additional comments or information.

- **Do Not Send a Response:** this command will add the meeting to your Calendar in the case of an acceptance or tentative acceptance response from you but will not provide a response to the meeting planner. If you Decline the meeting and use this option, the originator will be able to track your response in the meeting's tracking information.

As already mentioned you can also propose a new time and accept tentatively or decline the message. When you select the Propose New Time command you have two options: Tentative and Propose New Time or Decline and Propose New Time. When you select either of these possibilities, the Propose new time dialog box will open (see Figure 25.22).

Figure 25.22
You can propose a new time for the meeting.

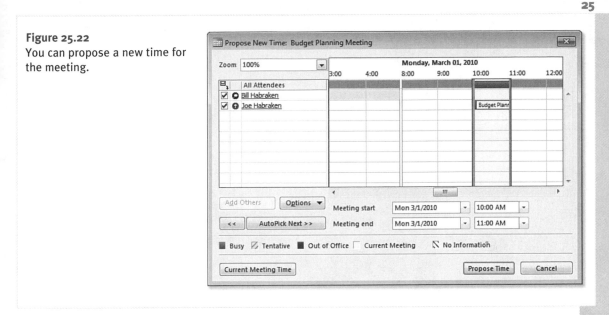

This dialog box is basically a compact version of the Scheduling Assistant. You can use the Start and End lines (drag them to a new position on the timeline) to propose a new start and end time for the meeting. You can also use the AutoPick Next button to find the next available time slot for all the participants. AutoPick Next allows you to search forward in the timeline. The Back button to the left of the AutoPick Next button allows you to search backward in the timeline.

Once you have specified your proposed time for the meeting, select the Propose Time button. A new message opens with both the current and proposed time for the meeting detailed. You can add information to the body of the message as needed. When you are ready to send the message, select Send.

USING THE JOURNAL AND NOTES

Outlook not only helps you manage emails, contacts, and tasks, it can also assist you in developing an "informational trail" related to your interactions with your contacts as well as work that you do in the other Office applications, such as Word or Excel. The Journal can help record a timeline of important interactions with your contacts including emails, assigned tasks, or meeting requests related to contacts. It can also help you keep track of when you created documents or other files in your Office applications. In this chapter, we look at how you can record information in the Outlook Journal both automatically and manually.

There are also times when you just want to get some information onto a piece of paper for later reference. It always seems that those sticky notes are buried somewhere under a pile of papers or are being used as a coaster for your coffee cup. Outlook has you covered: You can create electronic notes in Outlook. You can then use the information on those notes as you create other Outlook items, such as emails, or enter information for a new contact. This chapter covers notes in addition to covering the Journal.

Using the Outlook Journal

You can create a record of various actions so that you can track your work, communications, meetings, and so on using the Outlook Journal. In the Journal, you can manually record any activities, items, or tasks you want. For example, you might want to record the results of a telephone conversation or other communication.

You also can automatically record items in the Journal, such as email messages, meeting requests, meeting responses, task requests, and task responses. In addition, you can automatically record activity related to documents created in the other Office applications: Excel, PowerPoint, and Word.

The Navigation pane does not include the Journal by default. So, the first thing that you will need to do is add the Journal button. At the bottom of the Task pane, select Configure Buttons. On the menu that appears, point at Add or Remove Buttons and then select the Journal. Doing so adds the Journal button to the button array at the bottom of the Task pane. You can drag the Task pane sizing bar (if you like) to show more buttons on the Task pane to include the Journal.

Enabling Automatic Journaling

The first time you select the Journal button in the Navigation pane, a Microsoft Outlook message box will open. This box details that the Journal can track Office documents and emails associated with a contact by the Activities page. Because the Journal can log a variety of information, it makes sense to turn it on. Click Yes. This will open the Journal Options dialog box as shown in Figure 26.1.

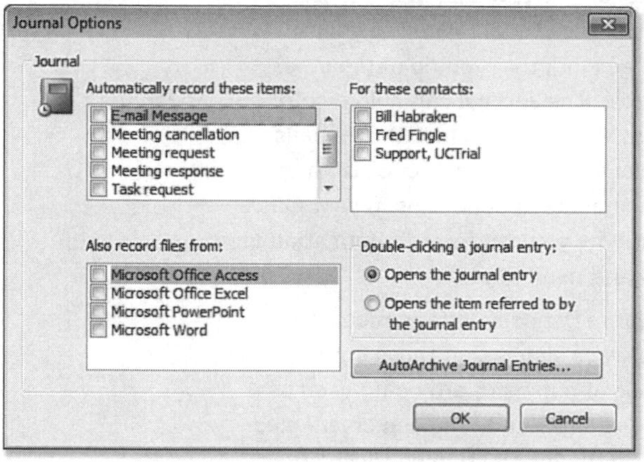

Figure 26.1
The Journal Options dialog box.

In this dialog box, you can specify what type of events you want to have automatically recorded in the Journal. Outlook provides check boxes to include email messages, meeting requests, and other events received from people in your Contacts folder. To specify the items that you want automatically recorded, follow these steps:

1. In the Automatically Record These Items list, check those items you want Outlook to automatically record in your Journal. (The items recorded correspond with the people selected in the list of contacts in step 2.)

2. In the For These Contacts list, check any contacts you want automatically recorded in the Journal. Outlook records any items selected in step 1 that apply to the selected contacts.

3. In the Also Record Files From list, check the applications for which you want to record Journal entries. Outlook records the date and time you create or modify files in the selected programs.

4. Outlook also provides options related to what happens when you double-click a Journal entry. The default setting is Opens the Journal Entry. You have the option of selecting Opens the Item Referred To by the Journal Entry. In most cases, it makes sense to go with the default.

5. When you have completed your selections, click the OK button.

The Journal opens. It is now ready to automatically record the items that you chose in the Journal Options dialog box.

Viewing the Journal

By default, the Journal provides a timeline view by week. It categorizes the entry types recorded. For example, any emails from contacts that you specified in the Journal Options dialog box will appear under the E-mail Message entry type. The same goes for meeting responses or other items that you specified to record for specific contacts. The Journal will also track files that you create in other Office applications, such as Excel and Word, if you specified those settings when you configured the Journal's options. Figure 26.2 shows the Journal's timeline containing email, meeting response, and Excel application items.

Figure 26.2
The Journal timeline with automatically recorded items.

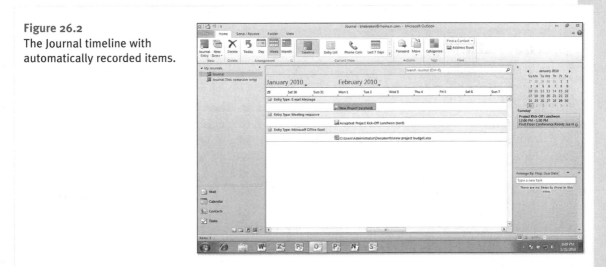

You can use the commands in the Arrangement and Current View groups on the Ribbon's Home tab to manipulate your view of the Journal. The Arrangement group enables you to view the timeline by day, week (the default), and month. The Current View group provides different views of the Journal; the views are as follows:

- **Timeline:** The default view for the Journal, this view groups entries by type and enables you to change the interval for the timeline (day, week, or month).

- **Entry List:** This view displays the entries in a columnar arrangement that includes column headings such as Entry Type, Subject, Start (the date and time you placed the item in the Journal), Duration, and Contact. By default, Outlook lists the items in order by start date, with the newest item listed first.

- **Phone Calls:** This view lists only phone calls in a tabular format much the same as the Entry List view. So, this view is really a filter for phone call entries.

- **Last 7 Days:** This view arranges the item in the same columnar format as the Entry List, but shows only items logged in the Journal during the last seven days.

> **tip**
>
> In the Timeline view, the Journal provides a banner at the top of the Journal window that lists the months. Click below a month heading to open a calendar box showing the entire month.

You can manipulate the items in a particular view. For example, in the Timeline view, you can collapse or expand the entry type listings; doing so enables you to focus on the entries of a particular type by collapsing all the other entries in the different types. When you are using the Entry List view (or the Phone Calls or Last 7 Days view, which also use a columnar format), you can click on a column heading to order the items by the heading. For example, you could list the items by contact (click the Contact column heading) in either an ascending or descending order.

Journal Actions

You can also perform actions related to specific items listed in the Journal. The Action group of the Ribbon's Home tab provides two commands: Forward and Move.

If you want to forward an item to another contact, select the item's icon in the Journal, such as an email, file, or other item. Select the Forward command. A new email message will appear with the Journal item as an attachment (see Figure 26.3).

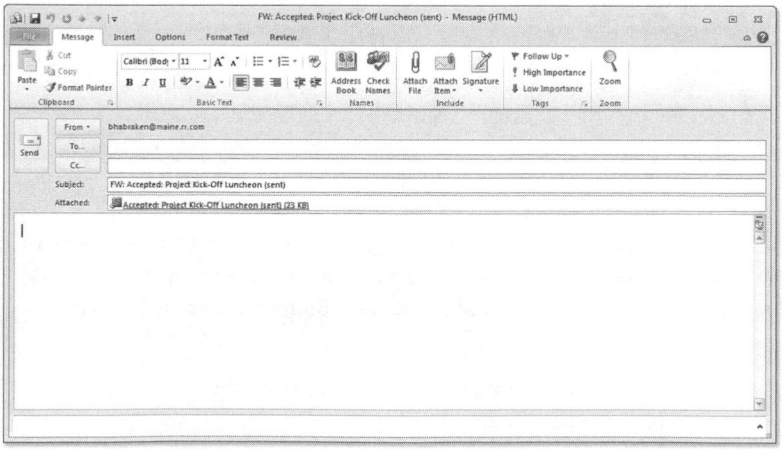

Figure 26.3
You can forward a Journal item.

You can manipulate this email as you do any other email, such as adding a flag to the email or specifying an importance level for the message. Remember that you are attaching a Journal item, which will open in the recipient's Journal. You are not attaching the original item itself, such as an email or a logged application file (such as a Word document logged in the Journal).

The Move command enables you to move items in the Journal to other folders and locations. Select an item or items in the Journal and then select Move in the Actions group on the Journal Ribbon. The Move menu provides destination options for the move, such as the Deleted Items folder and the Inbox. It will also list any secondary data files that you have created. So, your options for moving the item include Outlook folders and data files. Moving Journal items to other Outlook folders helps you keep your various items organized, whereas moving items to secondary data files is a way to store information in a backup data file.

➡ *Working with Outlook data files is discussed in Chapter 22, "Requisite Outlook: Configuration and Essential Features," on page 610.*

To access an Outlook folder not listed on the Move menu (such as the Inbox), select Other Folder on the menu to open the Move Items dialog box. Figure 26.4 shows the Move Items dialog box.

Figure 26.4
Use the Move Items dialog box to specify a destination folder.

Select a folder from the list provided (the dialog box lists all your Outlook folders). If you want to create a new folder, click the New button to create a new Outlook folder using the Create New Folder dialog box. When you have specified a folder (or a new folder), select OK to close the Move Items dialog box.

If you want to copy the selected Journal item to a folder rather than moving it, select the Copy to Folder command on the Move menu. The Copy Items dialog box will open. Select the destination folder for the copy or create a new folder as needed.

Viewing a Journal Entry

You can view entries in the Journal; double-click on an entry to open it in a Journal window. Figure 26.5 shows a Journal entry containing a logged Excel workbook.

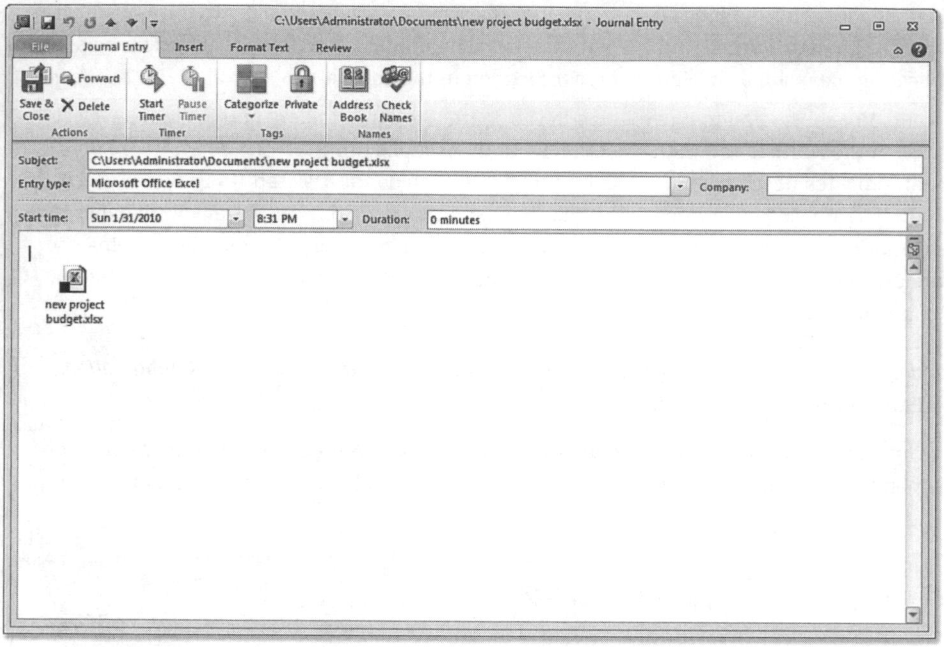

Figure 26.5
Open Journal items in their own window.

The Journal Entry window provides information related to the Journal entry, such as the subject, the entry type, and the date and start time for the entry. The actual items such as an application file, email, or meeting invitation that are the subject of the entry will be attached to the entry and appear in the entry body as icons. You can open the actual items by double-clicking the icons.

You can add information to the body of the Journal entry as needed, and categorize the entry or mark it as private using the commands in the Journal Entry tab's Tags group. Because Journal entries, by definition, are a log of your activities, it makes sense to add explanatory text and other information to the Journal item. This can include additional attachments in the form of files or emails (inserted via the Insert tab); you can add pictures and other graphics as needed. When you add additional information to a Journal item (such as a duration or explanatory text) or edit the item, select Save and Close on the Ribbon's Journal Entry tab to exit the item's window and return to the Journal.

> **tip**
>
> In the Timeline view, you can open the actual item (such as an email or a file) attached to a Journal entry. Right-click on the Journal entry and then select Open Item Referred To.

Manually Adding Journal Items

You can also add items to the Journal that Outlook does not log automatically based on the Journal options that you configured. You can add any Outlook items such as emails, contacts, and tasks quickly to the Journal using drag and drop. You can also create new Journal items that enable you to log items such as phone calls, which you can also conveniently time so that you have an accurate duration for the item (particularly useful if you do your billing based on time).

To drag an Outlook to the Journal, select the Folder List button at the bottom of the Navigation pane. This will show the Folder list in the Navigation pane, including the Journal as one of the folders. With any of the other folders selected, such as Inbox, Tasks, or Contacts, drag an item from the Details pane onto the Journal folder icon. A New Journal Entry window will open with the Outlook item attached to the Journal entry. You can edit the subject add information to the body of the entry as needed. Select Save & Close to add the new entry to the Journal.

Creating New Journal Entries

If you want to create a new Journal entry, but you don't have a contact, a task, an email, or other item that you want to use to create the entry, you can create a Journal entry from scratch, meaning it is not associated with any existing Outlook item. For example, you might want to create a Journal entry that holds information related to a phone call. You can actually use the Journal entry to record notes as you make the phone.

To create a new Journal entry from scratch, follow these steps:

1. From any of the Outlook folders (Mail, Contacts, and so on), select the Ribbon's Home tab.

2. In the New group, select New Items, point at More Items and then select Journal Entry. A new Journal entry will open.

3. Enter the subject for the new entry.

4. To specify the entry type for the new entry, use the Entry Type drop-down list as shown in Figure 26.6. Outlook provides a number of possibilities, including Conversations, Letter, Meeting, Note, and Task. The Phone Call type displays in the Entry type box by default.

5. Enter other information for the entry as needed including text in the body of the entry.

6. Select Save & Close to add the new entry to the Journal.

Using the Timer

You can use the Journal entry timer for existing Journal entries or Journal entries that you have just created. The timer provides you with the ability to record an accurate timing of a task, such as a phone call, while performing the actual task.

To use the timer to create a new Journal entry or open an existing entry, on the Ribbon's Journal Entry tab, select Start Timer. The timer will begin running. The timer uses minutes as the base time increment (it doesn't provide the time down to the second). As the minutes pass, the duration will provide the running time for the entry.

Because you are pausing the timer (not resetting it) when you complete your timing, you can return to the Journal entry when needed and time the performance of additional work or tasks related to the particular Journal entry. The timer keeps a running total of the duration rather than the timer resetting itself each time you close the Journal entry.

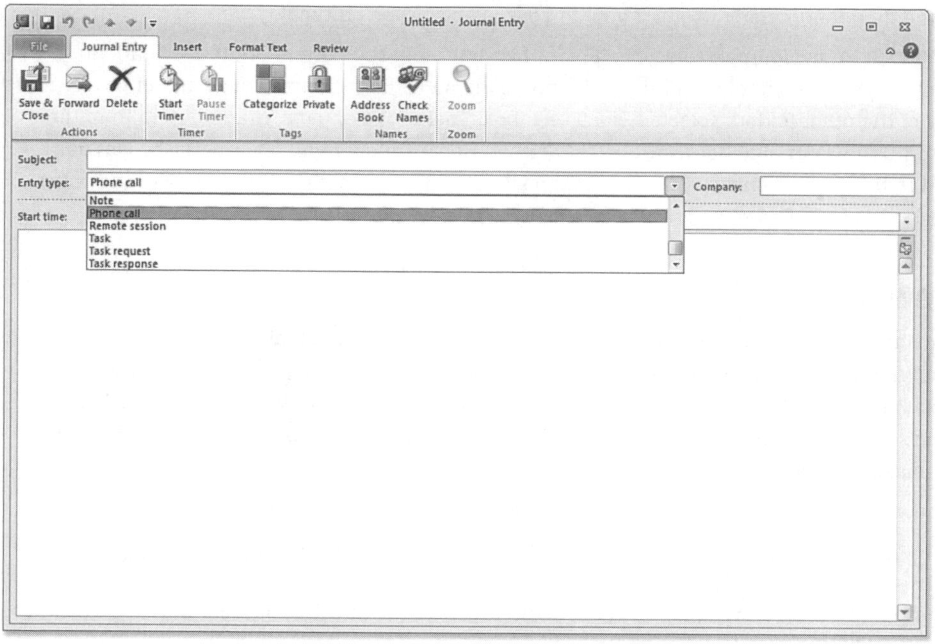

Figure 26.6
Specify an entry type for the new Journal entry.

Changing Journal Options

You might find that the initial Journal options you configured the first time you started the Journal are not recording all the events that you would like automatically included. You can modify the Journal settings in the Outlook Options window, which you access via the Backstage.

Select File on the Ribbon to open the Backstage and then select Options to open the Outlook Options window. To access settings related to the Journal, select Notes and Journal. To open the Journal Options dialog box, select Journal Options.

The Journal Options dialog box is the same dialog box that opened the first time you started the Journal. Your original settings for the Journal will appear in the dialog box. You can use the various check boxes and option buttons to edit your Journal settings as required.

> **tip**
>
> The timer feature provided by the Journal isn't just for timing phone calls or meetings. You can use it to determine the amount of time (duration) that it took you to create a Word report, an Excel workbook, and so on. Create the new Journal entry when you first start the new project. Then start the timer to record the duration.

The Journal Options dialog box also provides access to settings related to the autoarchiving of Journal entries. When you select AutoArchive Journal Entries in the dialog box, the Journal properties dialog box opens with the AutoArchive tab selected, as shown in Figure 26.7.

The default setting for the autoarchiving of Journal items is to archive items using the Outlook default archive settings. We discuss autoarchiving in Outlook in Chapter 27.

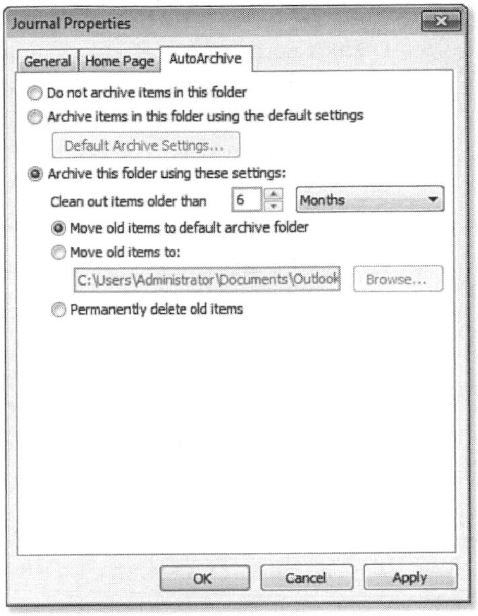

Figure 26.7
Set archiving options for Journal items.

> *Outlook archiving is discussed in Chapter 27, "Securing Outlook," on page 752.*

You can choose not to archive Journal items by selecting the Do Not Archive Items in This Folder option button.

If you do want to autoarchive Journal items but do not want to use the default Outlook autoarchive settings, you can select the Archive This Folder Using These Settings option button. After selecting this option button, you can set the following settings, which will be specific to the archiving of Journal items:

- **Clean Out Items Older Than:** Use this option to specify the number of months, weeks, or days that should be set as the threshold age for the archiving of Journal items.

- **Move Old Items To:** This option enables you to specify the data file used for the archiving of old Journal items. The default is the archive data file. You can specify any other data file that you have created as the destination for archived Journal items.

- **Permanently Delete Old Items:** The Journal will delete old items rather than archiving them to the archive data file.

Remember that these settings for the Journal will override the default Outlook autoarchive settings that have been configured. When you have completed changing your archive settings for the Journal items, click OK to return to the Journal Options dialog box.

Working with Notes

Outlook notes are the electronic equivalent of all those scraps of paper in and around your desk that you've used for a quickly scrawled notes. Creating notes in Outlook really doesn't take any more time than handwriting a note, but you will find that Outlook notes are easier to access and use than the paper equivalent. You can use Outlook notes to write down reminders, names, phone numbers, directions, or anything else you need for later reference.

You can quickly create a note from any of the Outlook folders. On the Ribbon's Home tab, select New Items, point at More Items, and then select Note. A new note will appear in the Outlook application window. All you have to do is type the information that you want to appear on the note and then close it. You don't have to actually save the note; Outlook automatically saves it to the Notes folder.

Notes are simple when you compare them to the other Outlook items such as emails and contacts. Figure 26.8 shows a note.

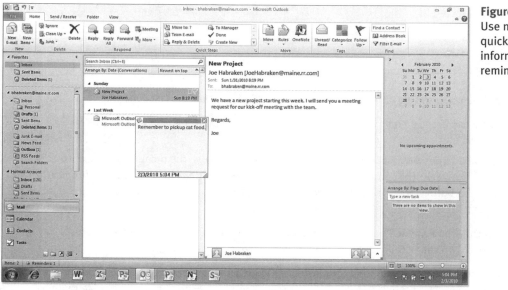

Figure 26.8
Use notes to quickly record information or reminders.

A note consists of your typed text. You can type as much text as required for the note; however, remember that Microsoft designed notes to be quick reminders. Outlook notes automatically record the time and date of their creation.

In terms of the note's window, it includes a Close button on the right and a menu button on the left. You can use the menu to save the note in a variety of formats, including text. You can also categorize the note or associate the note with a particular contact. If you have a lot of text on a note, you can enlarge the note by using the sizing handle on the bottom right.

As already mentioned, you can create a note from any Outlook folder by using the New Items command. If you are working in an email window or with a particular contact or appointment, you can open a new note by using the shortcut keys Shift+Ctrl+N.

Viewing and Managing Notes

Outlook keeps all your notes in the Notes folder. To open the Notes folder, select the Notes button in the Navigation pane. You can also open the Notes folder via the Folder list.

The default Notes folder view shows the notes as icons. You can drag the notes within the Notes folder and order them as you like in this view. There are also two alternative views: Notes List and Last 7 Days. The Notes List view provides you with a columnar format that includes a Subject column, a Created column and a Categories column. Figure 26.9 shows the Notes List view of the Notes folder.

> 🔵 **tip**
>
> You can drag a note icon from Outlook onto the Windows desktop. Doing so places a copy of the note on the desktop. The copy functions as any other note would even if Outlook is not running.

Figure 26.9
Inspect your notes using different views.

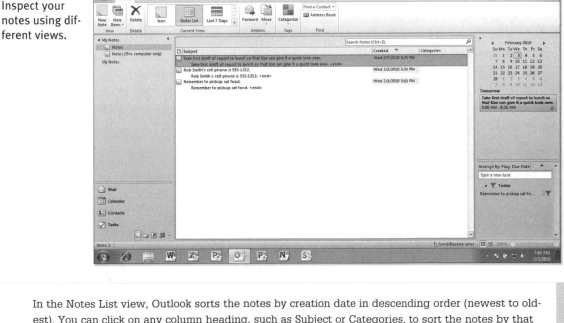

In the Notes List view, Outlook sorts the notes by creation date in descending order (newest to oldest). You can click on any column heading, such as Subject or Categories, to sort the notes by that particular column. A second click on a column will reverse the order of the sort. The Last 7 Days view will filter the list of notes and show only the notes from the last seven days. You can also use the column headings to sort the notes when you are in this view.

 You can create your own views for the Notes folder. See Chapter 22, "Requisite Outlook: Configuration and Essential Features," on page 597.

If your Notes folder is out of control in terms of the number of notes that currently populate it, you can find individual notes using the Search Notes box. Type a search term in the box and only the notes that meet the search criteria will appear in the Notes folder.

When you are in the Notes folder, you can quickly create a new note using the New Note on the Ribbon's Home tab. The Home tab also provides commands in the Actions group that enable you to forward notes to your contacts or to move notes to other folders, such as the Journal and Deleted Items folder. You can also move notes to secondary data files that you have created to back up Outlook items.

To open an existing note, double-click that note in the Notes folder. You can edit the text in the open note as needed. If you want to copy, print out, or delete a note, right-click on the Note. The shortcut menu that appears provides a Copy, Quick Print, and Delete command (among others).

Creating Appointments and Tasks from Notes

Because notes often contain information that would be better placed in another Outlook item, such as an appointment or a task, you might want to create other Outlook items using your notes. For example, I might have a note that reminds me to take a report with me when I meet a colleague for lunch, and I want to make sure that I create a lunch appointment in my calendar that includes this information.

You can quickly create a new appointment by dragging a note onto the calendar provided in the To Do bar. Drag the note from the Notes folder and drop it on the calendar date you want to specify for the new appointment. A new appointment will open as shown in Figure 26.10.

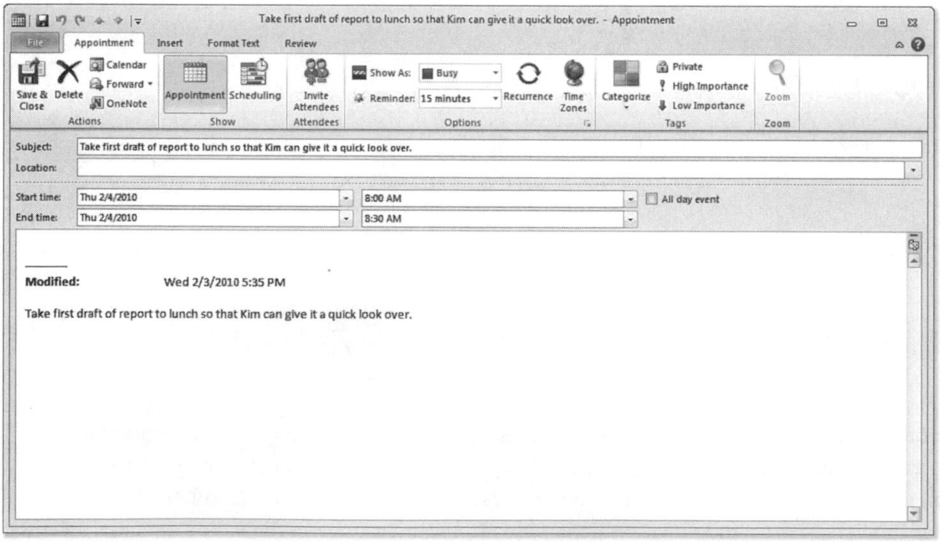

Figure 26.10
Create a new appointment by dragging a note onto the calendar.

A new appointment window will open in Outlook. The subject of the appointment will contain the text from the note. The note's time and date of creation and the note text will also appear in the body of the appointment. You can modify the subject and body of the appointment as needed. You can also enter the location and the start and end times for the appointment. When you select Save & Close, Outlook adds the new appointment to your calendar.

tip

If the To Do Bar is not available in the Outlook window, select the Ruler's View tab and then select To Do Bar. Make sure that the To Do Bar menu is set to Normal and that the Date Navigator, Appointments, and Task List are selected.

You can also quickly create tasks from your notes. Simply drag the note onto the task list at the bottom of the To Do bar. Outlook creates the new task, using the note's text as the task's subject. You can double-click the new task in the task list and modify the task as needed, including the subject, start date, due date, status, and priority. When you select Save & Close, Outlook saves the changes to the task and returns you to the Notes folder.

Configuring Notes Options

Because notes are a simple Outlook item, the options available related to configuring the Notes feature are simple as well. You can control the color, size, and font of your notes.

You access Outlook's options via the Backstage. Select File, and then Options to open the Outlook Options window. For the options related to notes, select Notes and Journal. The Notes options appear as shown in Figure 26.11.

The options available consist of two drop-down lists, a dialog box, and a check box. The Notes options are as follows:

- **Default Color:** Use the drop-down list to choose the note color from the gallery provided. You have five color possibilities to choose from.

- **Default Size:** The default size is Medium, You can use the Size drop-down list to change the size to either Small or Large.

- **Font:** The default font is Calibri 11 point. Select the Font button to open the Font dialog box. You can change the font, font style (such as bold or italic), font size, and font color.

- **Show Date and Time That the Note Was Last Modified:** Outlook enables this check box by default. When you edit a note, the date and time stamped on the note will change to the new date and time. If you want the date and time to remain the date and time placed on the note when you first created it, you can clear this check box.

When you have finished configuring the Notes options, click OK. This will close the Outlook Options window and return you to Outlook.

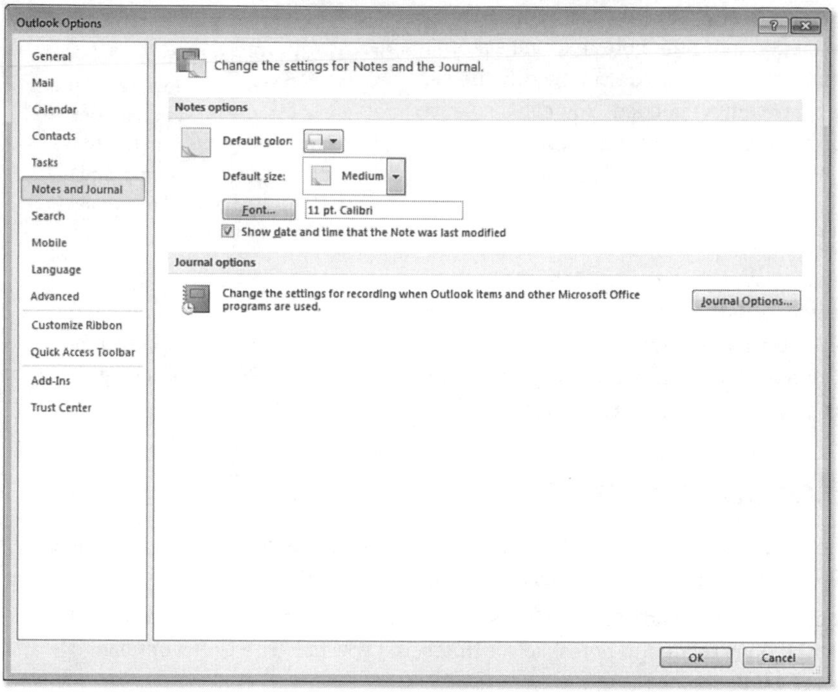

Figure 26.11
The Notes options.

SECURING AND MAINTAINING OUTLOOK

Outlook's capabilities for communication are based on the fact that Outlook is connected to a data network. While some Outlook users take advantage of Outlook's features in controlled and secure corporate network environments, many of us use Outlook as a tool for communicating over the Internet. This potentially opens up our computers to outside attack by viruses and other malware. Even the most secure network environments fail to completely protect Outlook users from malicious email file attachments or junk email.

In this chapter we take a look at some of the ways to secure Outlook. This chapter also discusses some of the maintenance tools that you can use to keep your Outlook environment more organized such as email rules and the Outlook archiving feature. We even look at how to configure Outlook to auto-reply to messages that you receive when you are out of the office.

Security Overview

The fact that Outlook receives data from other people, in some cases people unknown to you, makes Outlook a potential source of attacks on your computer. These attacks can include the appropriation of information that you store in Outlook such as your Contacts list. There is nothing more embarrassing (and potentially damaging) than having an infected file attachment "take over" Outlook and send copies of itself to everyone in your Address Book.

> **tip**
>
> A complete discussion of computer and network security is beyond the scope of this book. For more information on securing Windows 7 checkout Que's *Microsoft Windows 7 in Depth* by Robert Cowart and Brian Knittel.

Attacks on your computer are not limited to email attachments and code embedded in HTML messages (which we discuss later in this chapter). Hackers have been known to exploit imperfections in software packages such as Microsoft Outlook and the other Office applications. Operating systems (such as Windows) and applications use TCP/IP ports for communication between your computer and the Internet. Remember that most of us now use persistent Internet connections, such as broad band and DSL, which means our computers are constantly connected to a public network. This provides hackers with the ability to potentially invade our computers.

 note

The TCP/IP (Transport Control Protocol/Internet Protocol) protocol stack is the protocol that your computer uses to communicate on IP networks such as the Internet.

Protecting your computer will potentially involve a number of different measures. Attacks via TCP/IP port exploits can be countermanded by using a firewall such as the Windows firewall or the firewall capabilities of your WiFi router. A firewall is software or a device that sits between your computer (or computer network) and the Internet. A firewall examines data coming into the computer network or network and can filter out data that does not adhere to the firewall's rules.

Although this chapter primarily looks at what Outlook has to offer in terms of security features, it's not a bad idea to have a good feel for the type of threats you may face. We have already briefly discussed IP port exploits and how a firewall can help protect your computer. Let's discuss viruses and other malware a little more closely and also look at some basic things over and above the Outlook security settings that you can do to protect your computer.

Malware and Anti-Virus Software

It seems that malware, software designed to do your computer harm, such as viruses, has been around as long as personal computing. All of us who use Windows as our computer operating system know that we must install some sort of anti-virus and anti-malware software that helps defend our computer and the information stored on our computer from attack.

Malware (or "bad" software) comes in a variety of flavors. There are self-replicating viruses, which can easily be spread from computer to computer via infected email attachments. Viruses typically require that you activate them. So, don't open attachments in emails that are from senders who you don't know. However, even a friend can inadvertently send you an infected file.

There are also worms that can infect your computer and do not require you to activate them. They can quickly spread to computers on the same network (yes, even a home or small business network). Trojan horses are malware programs that are disguised as something else. For example, you may receive a file that claims it is a slideshow of firework displays from around the world. Well, if the file is a Trojan horse there will be fireworks but just in terms of the havoc that will be wreaked on your PC.

note

Outlook automatically blocks a lot of file extensions that prevent you from receiving malware attachments. For example, program files such as .exe, .com and .app files are blocked as are active server pages (.asp) and basic source code (.bas).

The best way to protect against viruses and other malware is to use an anti-virus program. There are ample choices. Some of these products also provide functions that become integrated within Outlook. For example, a number of anti-virus programs also provide you with a spam filter that helps identify spam and junk email that has been received in Outlook. You may notice that there is a spam or anti-spam folder (in addition to the Outlook default Junk E-mail folder) in your Mail folder. This folder is placed there by the anti-virus program.

The anti-spam filter provided by your anti-virus software will typically scan new emails when they are received using its own criteria for determining what constitutes spam email. Some anti-spam filters can be reconfigured to use an Outlook rule (rules are discussed later in this chapter) for dealing with spam email.

Some anti-virus programs may also add additional commands to the Outlook Ribbon. Check to see if the Add-Ins tab has been added to your Ribbon after you have installed Office or after you have installed a new anti-virus software package. For example, you may find commands on the Add-Ins tab related to marking messages as spam (or not spam). You may also find commands for the immediate scanning of email items or attachments. Some anti-virus programs may also provide a command on the Add-ins tab that allows you to access the configuration or properties of the anti-virus scanner from within Outlook.

It makes sense for you to spend a little time getting to know your anti-virus program and how it operates. If the anti-virus program also provides integrated functionality with Outlook, it also makes sense to take advantage of the spam filters and file attachment scans that it may provide.

Strong Password Protection

Not all attacks on your computer are related to nefarious and complex viruses infiltrating Outlook. If you password protect your computer with a weak, easily guessed password (or no password at all), pretty much anyone could log onto your computer and access your data including personal and professional information. So to negate this type of threat, you need to protect the account with a strong password.

> **⚑ caution**
>
> If you don't share your computer with other users, there is no real advantage to password protecting your Outlook date file. And if you forget the password it is a real disadvantage.

A strong password (as defined by Microsoft) is a password with at least seven characters. The strong password also uses a combination of numeric and alphanumeric characters and does not include easy to guess or personal information. For example, if I use the password "joseph" as my Windows account password, I'm making it pretty easy for someone else to guess my password. Create a more complex, strong password, but make sure that you remember the password. However, remember that scribbling passwords on scraps of paper that lie around your office and are easily accessible by anyone walking in the door doesn't set up a very secure environment either even if you have created the strongest of passwords.

Another way to keep other users (even friends and family) out of your Outlook information to password protect your Outlook data file (.pst file). You have probably noticed that Outlook does not require a logon password when you start Outlook. So, if you computer is running and you are away from the computer, anyone can start up Outlook and poke around in your Mail, Contacts or Calendar folders.

You can password protect your Outlook data file, which will then require that you provide the password for the data file when you start Outlook. You can also save this password in your password list, which is a part of the configuration for your Windows user account. To password protect your Outlook data file follow these steps:

1. Select File to open the Backstage.

2. With Info selected in the Backstage, select Account Settings and then select Account Settings (again). The Account Settings dialog box will open.

3. Select the Data Files tab in the Account Settings dialog box.

4. Select a data file in the list provided by the Data Files tab.

5. Click Settings. The Outlook Date File dialog box will open for the selected data file.

6. Select Change Password. The Change Password dialog box will open as shown in Figure 27.1.

7. Enter a new password and then verify the new password. To save the password in your Windows password list, select the Save This Password in Your Password List check box.

8. Click OK.

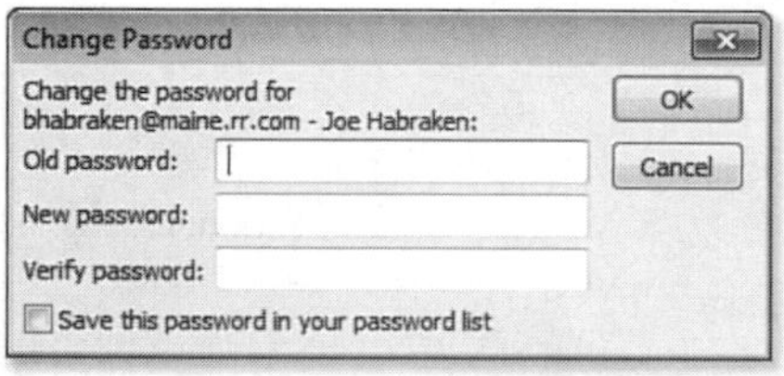

Figure 27.1
The Change Password dialog box.

The data file is now password protected. The next time you start Outlook, you will be asked to provide the Outlook data file password. Enter the password and then click OK to open Outlook.

Keeping Office and Windows Up to Date

We have already mentioned IP port exploits. These types of attacks are often related to flaws in your operating system or application software. While you may think that keeping your Windows operating system and your Office application up to date is more about usability, it can also relate to security. Many of the updates for these products are meant to plug security holes.

It is important that you update Windows and your Office applications. Windows will typically alert you when updates are available. You should take the time to install these updates as soon as possible. Office updates can also easily be installed on your computer without a lot of effort on your part.

To keep your Office applications up to date select File on the Ribbon (such as the Outlook Ribbon). Once in the Backstage, select Help to open the Support window as shown in Figure 27.2.

To check for Office updates, select the Check for Updates button. Your Web browser will open to the Microsoft Update Website. Install new updates when available to keep your Microsoft Office applications (and Windows) up to date.

Figure 27.2
Keep Office up to date.

Configuring Outlook Security Settings

Microsoft Office 2010 has bundled the security settings for each of the member applications in the Trust Center. Each application, such as Outlook, will have its own Trust Center where you can view and configure the various security settings.

➡ *For an overview of the Trust Center, see Chapter 2, "Navigating and Customizing the Office Interface," page 47.*

To access the Outlook Trust Center follow these steps:

1. Select File to open the Outlook Backstage.

2. In the Backstage select Options. The Outlook Options window will open.

3. Select Trust Center; an Options window will open and provide a series of links that include access to Microsoft's privacy statement for the Outlook and Office. A link will also be provided for Microsoft Trustworthy Computing. A recommendation is provided by Microsoft that you should not change the settings in the Trust Center, if you wish to keep your computer secure.

4. To access the Trust Center settings, select the Trust Center Settings button. The Trust Center will open as shown in Figure 27.3.

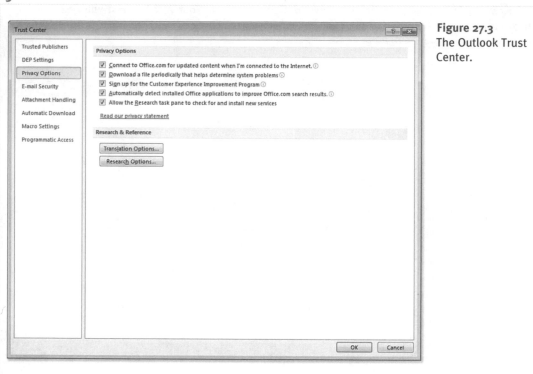

Figure 27.3
The Outlook Trust Center.

The Trust Center provides different categories of privacy and security settings. Figure 27.3 shows the Privacy Options. Categories such as Trusted Publishers and Macro Settings will be found in the Trust Center of other Office applications such as Word and Excel. Trusted Publishers are discussed in Chapter 2 and the Macro Settings options are discussed in Appendix B, "Office Macros."

For an overview of the macro related Trust Center settings, see Appendix B, "Office Macros," page 883.

The Trust Center categories that are directly related to the Outlook application environment are as follows:

- **DEP Settings:** Data Execution Protection or DEP is a strategy for keeping malicious code from executing. If malware attempts to run on a system with DEP enabled, Windows will shut down the problem application (such as Outlook) that is being misappropriated by the malware. This prevents the malware from gaining a foothold on your computer. The Enable Data Execution Prevention mode is selected by default. You should leave this feature enabled.

- **Privacy Options:** The actual privacy options are all check boxes related to connecting to Office. com for such things as content update, the Microsoft Customer Experience Improvement program and the installation of new services for the Research task pane. It is up to you in terms of the privacy options that you disable. The options for updating content should remain updated. The Privacy Options window also provides settings for research and reference. You have the option of selecting language pairs for translation (Translation options) and you can select the reference books and research sites used by the Reference task pane using the Research options.

- **E-mail Security:** The security options provide encrypted mail settings and the ability to manage Digital IDs for the sending of encrypted and secure mail. You can also choose to read all your standard mail in plain text. We talk about encrypted email options in the next section.

- **Attachment Handling:** These options relate to the inclusion of personal information when sending Office documents as attachments and attachment preview for received emails. These options are discussed in more detail in the Dealing with Message Attachments section in this chapter.

- **Automatic Download:** These options are related to the download and display of pictures in email messages. Pictures in HTML messages can actually be used by junk email senders to increase the number of junk emails you receive. For more about these settings see "The Perils of HTML E-Mail" in this chapter.

- **Programmatic Access:** These settings allow you to enable warnings that will alert you when the Outlook address book is accessed by another program. For example, you may use a smart phone or smart device that syncs your contacts, calendar or email with the device. This is considered access by another program but is OK. Other access may be the work of a virus or other malware. You can also set a warning for your anti-virus program; Outlook can let you know if it is inactive or out of date.

Many of these Trust Center options can be left with the default options enabled. Only change the security settings if you have a compelling reason to do so. In some networking environments the network administrator will determine the settings for your Outlook mail client.

Encrypting Email and Using Digital Signatures

You can choose to raise the bar for email security by choosing to encrypt your email. Encrypted email is mail that has been transformed using a mathematical algorithm. The only way to read encrypted mail is to decrypt the mail. Outlook uses digital certificates to verify the sender of encrypted email. If you don't want to encrypt your emails you can also use a digital certificate (also known as a digital ID) to verify the authenticity of the email that you send.

To send encrypted email you must obtain a digital certificate. If you work at a company that wishes you to be able to encrypt your email, they will provide you with a digital certificate. If you run your own small business or work at home and feel the need to encrypt messages, you will need to obtain your own digital certificate from a certifying authority. A number of certificate authorities are available online such as A-Trust (http:// www.a-trust.at), CertPlus (http://certplus.com), VeriSign (http://digitalid.verisign.com).

> **⚠ caution**
>
> If you are going to send encrypted email to another user, that user will also need to have a Digital ID. Then you and the other party must exchange emails that are digitally signed. When you add that person to your contacts (or update the contact information) the digital certificate is added to the Contact information. The person on the other end must also add you to the Contacts folder in the same manner.

The settings related to encrypted email and digital certificates are in the Outlook Trust Center's E-mail Security options. Figure 27.4 shows the E-mail Security options.

Before you use the Encrypted email settings, you need to either import an existing Digital ID or get a Digital ID online. If you need a Digital ID, select the Get a Digital ID button. This will open your Web browser and open a Microsoft sponsored Web page that provides a list of certificate authorities. Select a certificate authority and you will be walked through the process of obtaining (meaning paying for) a digital certificate.

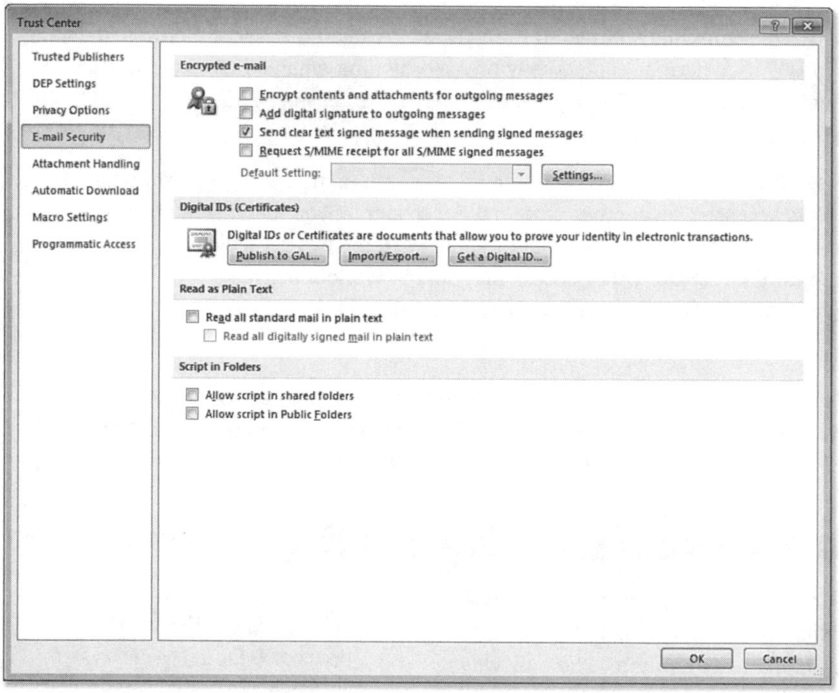

Figure 27.4
E-Mail Security Options.

If you have a Digital ID that has been provided to you by your company it may have already been configured on your computer. If a digital certificate has been exported from another computer you can import the ID into the Trust Center. Select the Import/Export button and then use the Import/Export Digital ID dialog box to specify the file name, password and Digital ID Name for the certificate. Then select OK.

If you have purchased your own Digital ID, you will need to install it on your computer. The certificate installation process will typically be provided to you in an email from the certifying authority. Many certifying authorities provide a link that takes you to an installation Web page.

Encrypted email uses a private and a public key. The email is encrypted by the public key associated with your Digital ID. The private key, which is then used on the receiving end to decrypt the message, will be stored in the recipient's Contacts folder in your contact entry. Anyone intercepting or otherwise pirating the message will not be able to decrypt the message content or attachments.

Options for Encrypting Email

You actually have options for encrypting your e-mail. If you want to encrypt all outgoing email and attachments you can specify that fact in the Encrypted E-mail section of the E-mail Security options. Select the Encrypt Contents and Attachments for Outgoing Messages check box.

You can also choose to encrypt individual emails. This makes more sense than sending all your email encrypted, particularly if you only need to share encrypted messages with one or two recipients. Remember that you and the recipient must share Digital ID information before you can send encrypted emails.

> **tip**
>
> You can check to see if a digital certificate is installed and available to Outlook. In the E-Mail Security options window select the Settings button. The Change Security Settings dialog box should list your digital ID in the Signing Certificate and the Encryption Certificate boxes.

When you have a new message open that you wish to encrypt, select the Ribbon's Options tab. In the Permissions group select the Encrypt command. Prepare your mail message including attaching files or items as needed. You can then send the message.

If you send an encrypted message to an individual who does not have a digital signature (or if you haven't added the individual to your Contacts folder), Outlook will open an Encryption Problems dialog box and list recipient of the email. You can click the Send Unencrypted button to send the email as a regular message. Otherwise, click Cancel and make sure that the recipient is in your Contacts folder. Then attempt to send the message again.

Digitally Signing Emails

You can also use your Digital ID to digitally sign email. This does not encrypt the message content or attachments but it does verify you as the sender. You can choose to send a digital signature with all your outgoing messages by selecting the Add Digital Signature to Outgoing Messages check box in the Encrypted E-mail section of the E-mail Security options.

> **note**
>
> If you don't have a digital ID the Encrypt and Sign commands will not be listed on the Options tab.

Since you are using a digital signature as a security measure, it makes sense to receive confirmation that your digital signature is validated by the recipients and that messages are received unaltered. This notification sent to you related to your digitally signed messages can also tell you when a message was opened and by whom. In the Encrypted E-mail section of the E-mail Security options select the Request S/MIME receipt for all S/MIME messages.

You can also choose to digitally sign specific messages (rather than signing all messages). With a new message open, navigate to the Ribbon's Options tab. Then select the Sign command in the Permission Group. When you send the email, a message box will open asking you to grant permission to use the key (associated with the digital ID) to sign the message; click Grant permission and then select OK to send the message. When the recipient receives the email it will provide a Signed By statement and include a digital certificate image in the header of the message. The recipient can click the digital certificate to view details related to the digital ID.

The Perils of HTML Email

Believe it or not HTML email can pose a threat to your computer. HTML email can actually include active content such as Active X controls and scripts and these can potentially be malware. HTML email can also include graphic images. These images can include a Web beacon.

A Web beacon is basically HTML code that is typically used on sebsites to count the number of people that access the website. However Web beacons can also be used to send information to a website. So, Web beacons in HTML emails can verify that your email address is valid (you activate the Web beacon when you open or view the email). The verification of your email address is sent to the "owner" of the Web beacon. This will result in you actually receiving much more junk email.

To "turn off" HTML email as the format for received messages, select the Read All Standard Mail in Plain Text check box in the Read As Plain Text section of the E-Mail Security options. Even if you choose to receive plain text messages, you can quickly switch a message from plain text to HTML when viewing the message. In the message Infobar it will say: "This message was converted to plain text. Select the message and then select Display as HTML."

If you still decide to receive messages as HTML email (I mean, who really wants to receive text only email messages), you will be happy to hear that Outlook blocks automatic picture downloads for external sources by default. And since many Web beacons are associated with images, you are protected to a certain extent. The settings related to picture download and other download-related options (such as RSS item downloads are in the Automatic Download options of the Outlook Trust Center. Since you can specify safe senders and save recipients in the Junk e-mail filter (which we discuss later in this chapter), you can leave the Don't Download Pictures Automatically in HTML E-mail Message or RSS Items setting enabled. You can then place friends and family members (or other trusted individuals) in the Safe Senders and Safe Recipients lists (as discussed in "Coping with Junk Email").

Dealing with Message Attachments

Outlook blocks many file types as mail attachments. When a blocked file type is included in a message that you receive, Outlook will provide a message that a potentially unsafe file type was blocked. Message attachments can certainly contain malware, so blocking file types that are programs or executable files does make sense. Table 27.1 lists some of the blocked file types.

Table 27.1 A Subset of Blocked File Types

File Extension	Description
.app	Executable application file
.asp	Active Server Page
.bat	Batch processing file
.chm	HTML help file
.com	Command file
.crt	Certificate file
.hlp	Windows Help file
.js	JavaScript source code
.jse	JScript encoded script file
.msh	Microsoft Shell
.prf	Windows System file
.prg	Program file
.scf	Windows Explorer command
.scr	Windows Screen Saver
.vbp	Visual Basic project file
.vbs	Microsoft Visual Basic for Applications script (or Visual Basic script)

These (and a number of other) file types are blocked because they are considered potential vehicles for malware. If you glance at the subset of blocked files listed in Table 27.1, you can see why these file types are on the blocked list. Malware masquerading in any of these file types could do a lot of bad things to your computer.

There are no configuration settings in Outlook that can be adjusted to allow blocked file types. You will also find that if you attempt to send one of these file types as an email attachment, Outlook alerts you to the fact that the recipient will not be able to receive the attachment (this is definite if they use Outlook). If you have to send a blocked file type, there is a way around this.

The first possibility for sending a blocked file type to an Outlook user is to change the file extension on the file. For example, you can change a blocked extension to .txt or .blk (for blocked). When you send the attachment to the recipient, make sure you direct them in the message to rename the file and change the extension back to the original (such as .chm or .js).

> ⚠ **caution**
>
> In an Exchange Server environment, your administrator can tweak the blocked file list. If you are using Outlook for Internet email, you can change settings in the system registry to unblock specific file types. I don't think this is a good idea unless you are very familiar with editing the Windows registry. The Microsoft Support website (support.microsoft.com) provides the steps for editing the registry. Do a search for "Outlook blocked unsafe attachments."

There is a second possibility for sending blocked file types, which is probably easier and a little more fool proof than messing around with the file name and the default extension. You can place the file in a zipped folder (archive) and then send the zipped file as the attachment. The recipient can "unzip" the file and access the original file. Right-click on any file in Windows 7 and on the shortcut menu select Send To. You can then select Compressed (zipped) folder from the submenu that appears.

Before we end our discussion of attachments and Outlook, we should take one more look at the Trust Center. There are two settings in the Attachment Handling options of Outlook's Trust Center that need to be addressed. Figure 27.5 shows the Attachment Handling options.

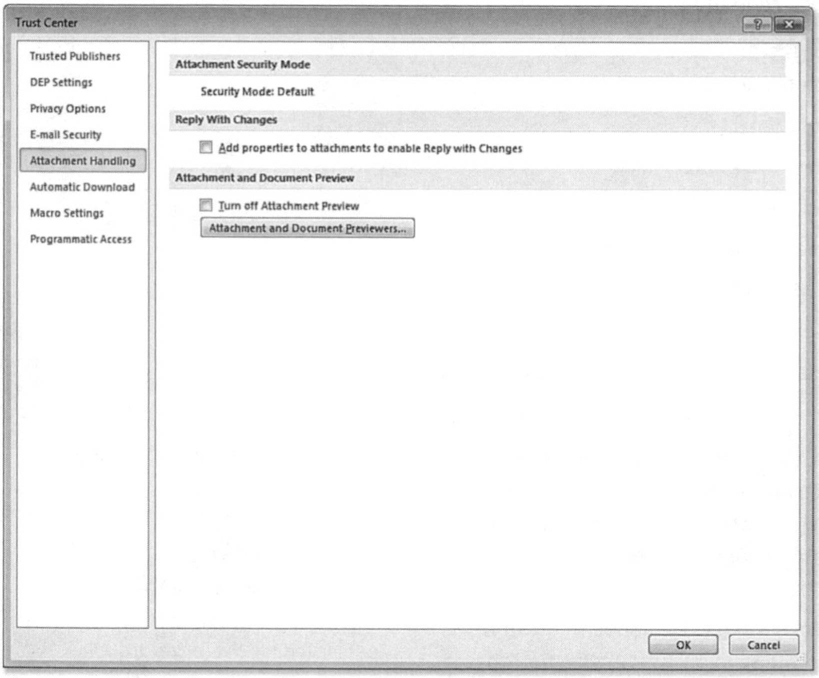

Figure 27.5
Attachment Handling Options.

When you select the Add Properties to Attachments to Enable Reply with Changed check box you are allowing Outlook to send personal information that has been placed in a document that you have edited using the Track Changes feature. Information such as your name or email address can easily end up in the properties of an Office file that you have worked with.

If you don't want Outlook to "share" this personal information in the file's properties, clear the Add Properties to Attachments to Enable Reply with Changed check box. This will keep your personal information out of the attached document. However, this will make it impossible for you to track changes that others may make to a document that you send them. So, you have to decide if you need to track changes or need to protect your personal information.

One other setting that can help protect you from security issues with attachments is the Turn Off Attachment Preview check box. If you wish to negate a preview of attached files, make sure that the check box has been cleared.

Coping with Junk Email

Junk Email is certainly a scourge. It fills up your Inbox with a lot of spam that you just don't want or need. Junk email can also potentially serve as part of a Phishing scam. This is where you receive what appears to be a legitimate email message from a business that you frequent on the Web (Amazon, eBay, i.e. any website where you might buy stuff or do financial transactions). These businesses typically keep your personal information on file including credit card numbers. The Phishing email asks you to update personal information or provides a link that takes you to a fake website that asks you to supply your password or other personal information. Once the Phisher has the info, all sorts of bad things can happen.

Outlook's junk email filtering relies on message content including keywords and phrases to determine if a message is junk. Sometimes it will place a legitimate message in the Junk E-mail folder.

The Junk E-mail Filter can also block senders that are contained in your blocked sender list. So, while Outlook tries its best to ferret out junk email, you can help it out by providing information such as safe senders, safe recipients and blocked senders to make the junk email filter more efficient.

The Junk E-Mail Filter can provide different levels of protection from junk email. By default the filter is set to low, which only moves messages received in the Inbox to the Junk E-Mail folder if they are obvious junk email messages (at least obvious to Outlook in terms of content and overall structure). You can change the level of protection using the Junk E-Mail Options dialog box (which we discuss in a moment).

Working with the Junk E-mail Commands

The commands for dealing with individual messages in terms of their junk email status (whether they are or aren't) are in the Delete group of the Ribbon's Home tab (when the Mail folder is selected in the Navigation pane). Figure 27.6 shows the Junk command and its menu of associated commands.

Figure 27.6
The Junk commands.

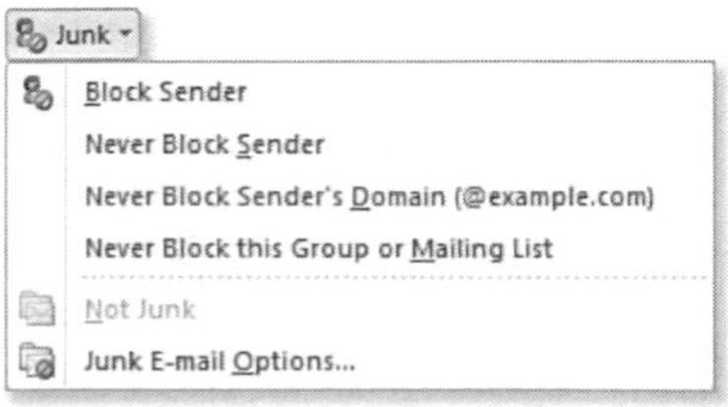

You can use the commands found on the Junk command's menu to specify the "junk" status of a message no matter the mail folder you are working in (meaning the Inbox or the Junk E-mail folders). First let's look at options related to messages marked as junk and placed in the Junk E-Mail folder that are actually legitimate.

As you receive email the Junk E-mail Filter will move any email to the Junk E-Mail folder that it considers junk. You can view mail that has been placed in the Junk E-Mail folder by selecting Junk E-Mail in Navigation pane (when the Mail folder is selected).

If you find a message listed in the Junk E-Mail folder that is not junk, you can mark it as "not junk" and have it moved to the Inbox. Select the message in the Junk E-Mail folder and then select Junk and then Not Junk. The Mark as Not Junk dialog box will open, letting you know that the message will be moved back into the Inbox folder. Select OK.

If you are finding that the emails from a particular sender (or senders) always seem to end up in your Junk E-Mail folder, you can specify that the sender be added to the Safe Sender List. Select the message and then select Never Block Sender on the Junk command's menu. A message box will open letting you know that the sender has been added to your Safe Senders List. You can also place a sender's entire domain on the Safe Sender List by using the Never Block Sender's Domain. These two commands do not move the email from your Junk E-Mail folder to the Inbox. You will need to drag it to the Inbox or use the Not Junk command as discussed earlier.

When you are working in the Inbox, you can specify a message or messages as junk. Select the message or message and then select Block Sender. The sender of the message (or messages) will be added to the Block Sender List. The message will also be moved to the Junk E-Mail folder.

Setting Junk E-Mail Options

You can set the level of protection that the Junk E-Mail Filter provides and also work with your safe senders, safe recipients and blocked senders lists. Select the Junk command and then select Junk E-Mail Options. The Junk E-Mail Options dialog box will open as shown in Figure 27.7.

The dialog box provides five tabs. These are as follows:

- **Options:** The Junk E-mail options are a series of option buttons and check boxes (see Figure 27.7. The Low, High, and Safe Lists Only option buttons determine the level of protection. Low, obviously, is the lowest setting with Safe Lists Only as the highest level. The higher the protection level settings the greater the number of received messages that will end up in your Junk E-Mail folder. The Options tab also allows you to specify if junk email should be deleted rather than moved to the junk email folder. By default, links are disabled in phishing messages and you are also warned when a suspicious domain name appears in an e-mail address. By default, your sent emails are postmarked to help the receiver distinguish it as a regular e-mail.

- **Safe Senders:** This tab provides a list of safe senders that you may have created using the "never block" commands on the Junk menu. You can also add, edit or remove senders from the Safe Senders list on this tab. You can also import a list of safe senders from a delimited text file or export your list to a text file. Two other options provided by this tab are two check boxes: Also Trust E-mail from My Contacts and Automatically Add People I E-mail to the Safe Senders List. Both of these check boxes are designed to keep your frequent contacts' and e-mail recipients' messages out of the Junk E-Mail folder.

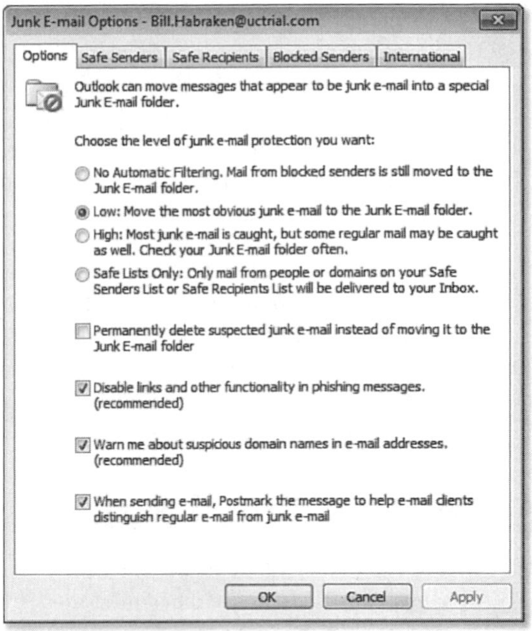

Figure 27.7
The Junk E-Mail Options dialog box.

> **Junk E-mail Options - Bill.Habraken@uctrial.com**
>
> Options | Safe Senders | Safe Recipients | Blocked Senders | International
>
> Outlook can move messages that appear to be junk e-mail into a special Junk E-mail folder.
>
> Choose the level of junk e-mail protection you want:
>
> ○ No Automatic Filtering. Mail from blocked senders is still moved to the Junk E-mail folder.
>
> ⦿ Low: Move the most obvious junk e-mail to the Junk E-mail folder.
>
> ○ High: Most junk e-mail is caught, but some regular mail may be caught as well. Check your Junk E-mail folder often.
>
> ○ Safe Lists Only: Only mail from people or domains on your Safe Senders List or Safe Recipients List will be delivered to your Inbox.
>
> ☐ Permanently delete suspected junk e-mail instead of moving it to the Junk E-mail folder
>
> ☑ Disable links and other functionality in phishing messages. (recommended)
>
> ☑ Warn me about suspicious domain names in e-mail addresses. (recommended)
>
> ☑ When sending e-mail, Postmark the message to help e-mail clients distinguish regular e-mail from junk e-mail
>
> [OK]   [Cancel]   [Apply]

- **Safe Recipients:** This list may seem a little odd since you are receiving the message that must be either marked as junk (or not). If you receive emails from people that include other recipients (such as the recipients in a particular Contact group that they have created), you can specify any or all these recipients in the Safe Recipients list. This provides Outlook another parameter in determining a received message's junk status. You can Add, Edit or Remove safe recipients as needed. You can also import a list from a file. This tab works in much the same way as the Safe Senders tab.

🔍 note

When a message is postmarked it is tagged with unique information related to that message such as the list of recipients and the time the message was sent. The postmark is only valid for that message. Postmarking a message means that the message will take a little longer to be processed and leave your Outlook Outbox. Postmarked emails are not viewed as junk by Outlook. Postmarks are good because it would be a burden on spammers to postmark all their messages; sending tons of spam requires a lot of computing power and postmarking all spam would take increased computing power. This means that postmarking spam would cost spammers money.

- **Blocked Senders:** This is your rogues' gallery of blocked senders. You can Add, Edit or Remove blocked senders on this tab. You can also import a list of blocked senders or export your list. Remember any messages from an address or domain name on the Blocked Senders list will be treated as junk email.

- **International:** This tab allows you to block top-level domains, meaning you can block emails from senders who are from specific countries or regions. Countries have their own top level domain designation such as .aq (Antarctica), .ba (Brazil) and .nz (New Zealand)—all places that I want to go. To block all emails ending in a specific top-level domain, select the Blocked Top-Level Domain List button. Select from the list provided and then click OK. You can also blocked emails that are encoded in a particular character set; this means that you can block email sent in specific languages. Select the Blocked Encodings List button and then specify by language the mail you wish to block.

The strength of the Junk E-mail filter will be directly related to the time you take to fine-tune the various options provided in the Junk E-mail Options dialog box. If you are fairly diligent about specifying safe senders and blocked senders and up the level of junk email protection on the Options tab, you should see a decrease in junk email. However, remember that spam email is actually an industry and they are constantly looking for ways to get around junk email filters and other types of spam protection. So, I doubt if any of us will ever be completely free from spam.

Creating Email Rules

You can automate the management of your Mail folder using Outlook rules. A Rule can delete messages, flag messages or move messages. For example, a rule can be used to automatically move messages in the Inbox from a particular sender to a particular mail related folder. This can help you keep organized; particularly if you have a need to place mail from a particular sender in a folder other than the Inbox. Although rules can't necessarily be considered a security feature they do give you control over the disposition of the email messages that you receive.

Outlook rules are basically a set of conditions. When the conditions of the rule are met by an email message, the message will be acted upon by the rule. Rules can take all sorts of things into account such as sender, message subject and message body content. Rules can be simple or they can be complex; it all depends on what you want the rule to do.

Create a Quick Rule for a Specific Sender

Outlook makes it very easy for you to create rules based on the properties of a selected email. For example, you can quickly create a simple rule that moves email from a particular sender from your Inbox to another specified location. Follow these steps:

1. Select a message from the sender in your Inbox.

2. Select the Rules command in the Move group.

3. Then select Always Move Messages From: name of sender. The Rules and Alerts dialog box will appear as shown in Figure 27.8.

4. Select a folder in the Rules and Alerts dialog box or use the New button to create a new folder using the Create New Folder dialog box (then select the new folder).

5. Click OK.

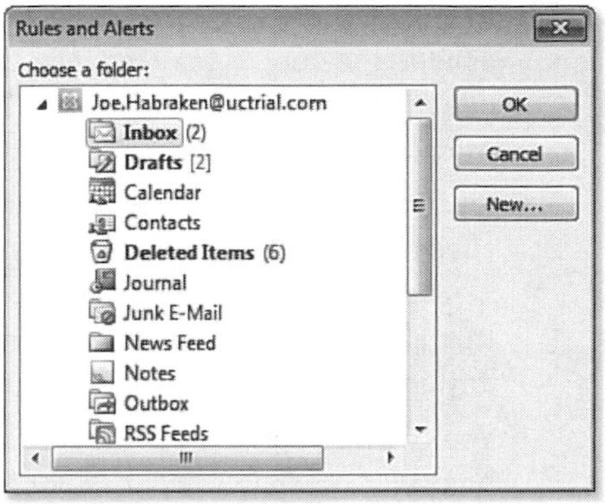

Figure 27.8
The Rules and Alerts dialog box.

The new rule will be created. The Selected message will be moved to the folder that you specified when you created the rule. Messages in the Inbox that also meet the conditions of the rule (actually the one condition of a specific sender) will also be moved to the specified folder.

Creating Complex Rules

You can also create rules that are more complex. Rules can require multiple criteria and can perform multiple actions. Outlook provides a Rules Wizard that makes it a fairly straightforward process to create rules with multiple criteria and multiple actions.

If you have an email message that meets the criteria (or some of the criteria) that you will include in a rule, you can speed up the actual creation of the rule by selecting that message. To open the Create Rule dialog box select the Rules command and then select Create Rule. Figure 27.9 shows the Create Rule dialog box.

Figure 27.9
The Create Rule dialog box.

The Create Rule dialog provides a number of check boxes and other selection tools that allow you to create a rule based on the currently selected message. The criteria for the rule can consist of the sender, the subject text and who the message was sent to (if the message was sent to more than one recipient). To set the criteria or conditions for the rule select the appropriate check boxes and provide additional information as required (such as Subject text).

Since rules will need to actually "do something" based on your conditions, you are provided several check boxes in the Do the Following area of the dialog box. You can have the rule provide a new alert window when a message is received that meets the conditions of the rule. You can also choose that a sound be played when the rule's conditions are met. You can use the Browse button to use any .wav sound file on your computer for this purpose.

You can also specify that the rule move the item to a particular folder. The Select Folder button can be used to specify a folder as needed.

So, the Create Rule dialog box limits you to three different conditions (sender, subject and receiver) and can open an alert window, play a sound and/or move the message to a specified folder. This doesn't seem all that complex nor much better than the rule we quickly created in the previous section based on the sender of the email. What do we need to do to beef up a rule with more conditions and multiple actions?

The Rule Wizard

Complexity and functionality can be added to a rule using the Rule Wizard. With the Create Rule dialog box open, select the Advanced Options button in the lower-right corner. The Rules Wizard opens as shown in Figure 27.10.

The first wizard screen asks you to select all the conditions that are to be used by the new rule. These conditions can be related to: sender, subject, message importance, specific words in the body, flags, categories and messages with an attachment. Many of conditions that you select in the conditions list will require you to provide additional information in the Edit the Rule description box of the Rules Wizard to flesh out that particular condition. So, select conditions using the check boxes provided in the Step 1 Select Conditions Box.

note

Rules can actually be created for your RSS feeds. See the RSS feed conditions provided by the Rules Wizard on the condition screen.

In the Step 2: Edit the Rule Description box, select any underlined items associated with the conditions you select in the Step 1 box. You will have to provide the information required by each condition. For example, the Specific Words in the Body Condition requires that you click the specific words link and provide a list of words to be used by the rule. At this point in the process, you are only provided the conditions for the rules, not what the rule will do. After providing and fine-tuning your conditions, click Next.

The next wizard screen is used to specify the actions that the rule will perform. Figure 27.11 shows the What Do You Want to Do with the message screen.

Select an action or actions in the Step 1: Select Action (s) box. If you select an action that contains a link, you will need to provide the details for the action in the Step 2: Edit the Rule description box. For example, if you select the Forward It to People or Public Group action in Step 1 you would need to specify the people or public group in Step 2 (you would specify the people using the Address Book).

Figure 27.10
The Rules Wizard.

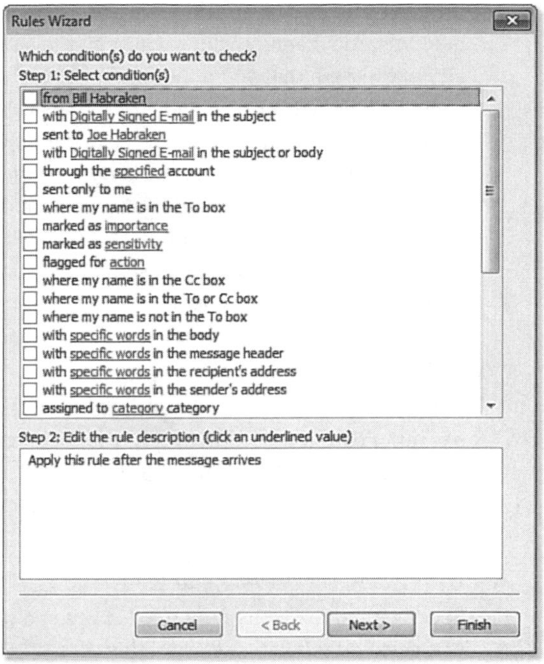

Figure 27.11
Specify the actions for the rule.

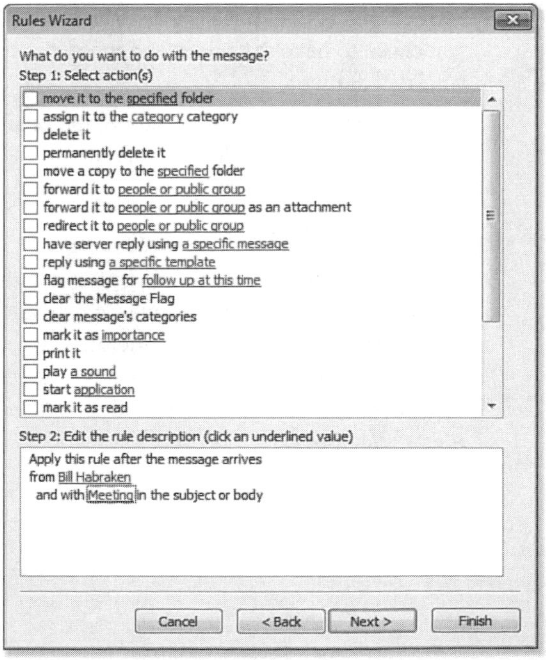

Once you have specified the action or actions for the rule and provided the details for the action, you can click Next. The next wizard screen provides you with the ability to configure any exceptions that you may want to have for the rule. These exceptions could relate to mail from specific people, messages that are flagged for a particular action or messages with specific words in the subject or body. Use the check boxes in the Step 1 box to select individual exceptions to the rule. For example, if you create a rule that moves messages to a particular folder (the action) based on the subject line or keywords in the body (the condition), you can set an exception for the rule such as ignoring the rule if the message is from a particular person.

> **note**
>
> Although the Rule Wizard provides a separate screen for the rule's conditions, actions and exceptions, configuring each of these items for a rule are similar. You specify a condition, action or exception on the appropriate wizard screen (Step 1) using a check box. Then you provide the details for the condition, action or exception in the Step 2 box. diff the conditions, actions and exceptions for a rule.

You are certainly not required to specify an exception or exceptions for a rule. However, if there are exceptions, use the exceptions check boxes in the Step 1 box to specify them. Then provide the underlined value information for any exception you may have selected for the rule in the Step 2 box.

When you are ready to continue the rule creation process, click Next. The Finish rule setup screen will appear as shown in Figure 27.12.

Specify a name for the new rule (or you can go with the default, which is based on the first action you selected when you started this process). The Turn on This Rule check box is selected by default, so the rule is enabled. You can choose to run the rule on messages already in the Inbox by selecting the appropriate check box. This screen also provides you with the ability to review your rule including the conditions, actions and exceptions. Once you are sure that everything is configured correctly, click the Finish button. The Rule will be created and added to your Rules and Alerts list. If you chose to have the rule act on messages already in the Inbox, the rule will do its stuff based on your rule settings.

You can run rules that you have created at any time via the Ribbon's Folder tab. Select the Run Rule Now command in the Clean Up group.

Managing Rules

You can manage your rules via the Rules and Alerts dialog box. This dialog box allows you to edit existing rule settings, delete rules, create new rules and run rules in the Rule list. It also allows you to determine the specific order that rules will run in, which is important if the rule sequence is of consequence to your overall plan related to using rules. To open the Rules and Alerts dialog box select the Rules command and then Manage Rules & Alerts. Figure 27.13 shows the Rules and Alerts dialog box.

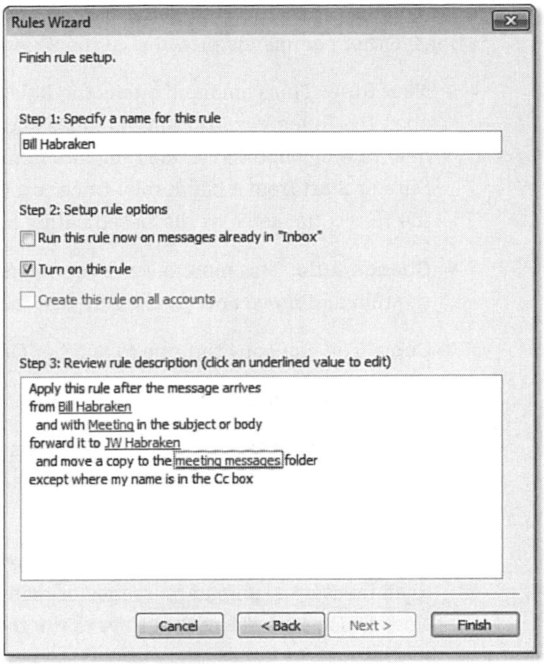

Figure 27.12
Name and review the rule.

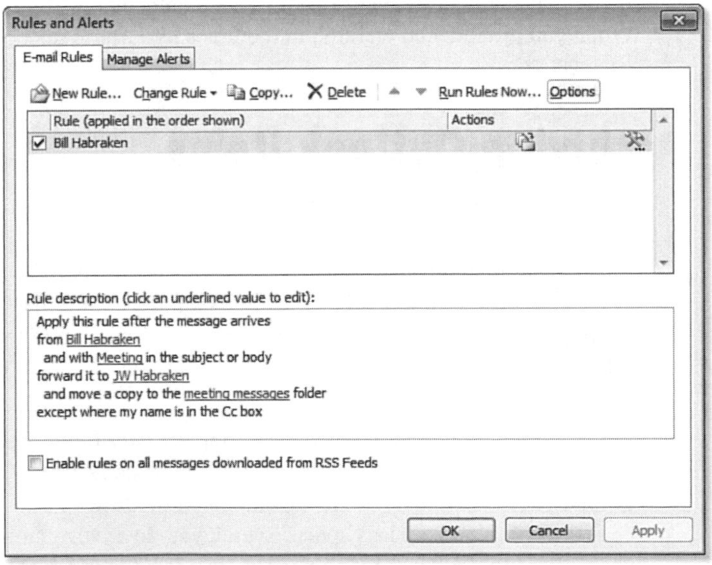

Rules Wizard

Finish rule setup.

Step 1: Specify a name for this rule

Bill Habraken

Step 2: Setup rule options

☐ Run this rule now on messages already in "Inbox"

☑ Turn on this rule

☐ Create this rule on all accounts

Step 3: Review rule description (click an underlined value to edit)

Apply this rule after the message arrives
from Bill Habraken
  and with Meeting in the subject or body
forward it to JW Habraken
  and move a copy to the meeting messages folder
except where my name is in the Cc box

Cancel   < Back   Next >   Finish

Figure 27.13
The Rules and Alerts dialog box.

Rules and Alerts

E-mail Rules | Manage Alerts

New Rule... Change Rule ▾ Copy... ✕ Delete ▲ ▼ Run Rules Now... Options

Rule (applied in the order shown) | Actions
☑ Bill Habraken |

Rule description (click an underlined value to edit):

Apply this rule after the message arrives
from Bill Habraken
  and with Meeting in the subject or body
forward it to JW Habraken
  and move a copy to the meeting messages folder
except where my name is in the Cc box

☐ Enable rules on all messages downloaded from RSS Feeds

OK   Cancel   Apply

The rules will be listed on the E-mail Rules tab. You can select a message in the dialog box and then use the Rule description area to actually edit the values for the rule's conditions, actions, or exceptions. Other commands provided in the Rules and Alerts dialog box are as follows:

- **New Rule:** This command opens the Rules Wizard so that you can create a new rule. When you open the Rules Wizard from the Rules and Alerts dialog box, you have the option of starting the new rule by choosing a rule template from three different categories: Stay Organized, Stay Up to Date or Start from a blank rule. Once you have selected a rule template the process for creating the rule is the same as discussed earlier in this chapter.

- **Change Rule:** This menu allows you to edit a rule's settings, rename a rule, change the alert for the rule and move or copy the rule to a folder.

- **Copy:** You can copy the rule to another Outlook message folder.

- **Delete:** You can delete the selected Rule.

- **Move Up/Move Down:** Use these buttons to change the order of the rules. Remember that the rules perform their actions in the order that they are listed in the Rules list.

- **Run Rule Now:** This command opens the Run Rule Now dialog box. You can select a rule or rules in the dialog box and specify a folder in which the rules will run. You can apply the rule (or rules) to all messages, unread messages or read messages. After making your choices in the Run Rules Now dialog box, select Run Now to run the rules.

- **Options:** This command opens the Options dialog. You can use the commands in this dialog box to export or import Outlook rules.

If you make changes to your rules, you can immediately apply the changes by selecting Apply. When you are finished working in the Rules and Alerts dialog box and wish to close the dialog box, click OK.

Archiving Outlook Items

Another Outlook management tool is the AutoArchive feature. Older mail messages can be periodically and automatically archived in an archival Outlook data file. This "archive.pst" file is kept in the same location on your computer's hard disk as the Outlook data source file that holds your Outlook profile information. You can archive mail messages, calendar items such as appointments and tasks.

The point of archiving is to save messages, for later reference, but also to remove some of the older items that are floating around your mail folders. Items autoarchived by Outlook are compressed to take up less space. Even if you do archive messages, you can access them as needed from the Archive folders that are made available in the Navigation pane once you enable the AutoArchive feature. You actually have a couple

> **note**
>
> If you use Outlook as an Exchange client, you won't find the AutoArchive command on the Outlook Ruler's Folder tab or in the Outlook Advanced options in the Backdtage. Exchange and your network administrator handle the backup of your data files. You can, however, use the Cleanup Tools on the Info window of the Backdtage to manage your Exchange mailbox.

of options for archiving information in an Outlook mail related folder. You can use the AutoArchive feature or you can manually archive specific folders.

The great thing about using the AutoArchive feature is that you can specify global archiving settings that will affect all your Outlook mail folders. For those of you who don't like "a one size fits all" approach to folder archiving can breathe a sigh of relief because you can also set the AutoArchive settings for individual folders if required.

Configuring AutoArchive Settings

The AutoArchive feature is configured in the AutoArchive dialog box. You can open this dialog box from the Outlook Advanced options window (in the Backdtage) using the AutoArchive Settings button. Figure 27.14 shows the AutoArchive dialog box.

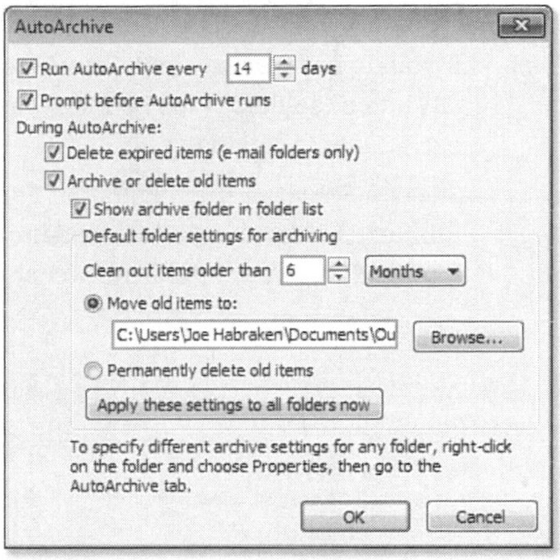

Figure 27.14
The AutoArchive dialog box.

By default, the AutoArchive feature is disabled. To enable the feature select the Run AutoArchive Every 14 Days check box. This means that every 14th day the AutoArchive feature will automatically archive the contents of the Inbox and other e-mail folders. You can use the day spinner box to specify a different interval for running the AutoArchive feature if you wish. You have probably noticed that there are a lot of settings crammed into the AutoArchive dialog box; they are as follows:

- **Prompt before AutoArchive runs:** If this item is enabled, Outlook displays a dialog box each time it is about to perform the AutoArchive; you can click OK to continue or Cancel to stop the operation.

- **Delete expired items (e-mail folders only):** Check this box to have Outlook delete messages from the Inbox after archiving them.

- **Show archive folder in folder list:** This option makes the archive folder available from the Mail Folder List, making it easier to access archived files.

- **Clean out items older than:** Use this spinner box to specify the increment and then the drop-down list to specify Months, Weeks or Days. The default age for older items is 6 months.

- **Move old items to:** This setting provides the path and file name for the archive file. The default name is "archive.pst" and the location is My Documents\Outlook Files. You can use the Browse button to specify another location (or file name) if needed.

- **Permanently delete old items:** Select this option if you want old items to be deleted rather than archived.

When you have specified the settings for the AutoArchive feature, you can apply these to the Outlook folders (those that can be archived such as the Inbox, Tasks and Calendar). Select the Apply these settings to all folders now. Then click OK to close the dialog box.

Setting AutoArchive Options for a Folder

If you do not want to apply the AutoArchive options that you set in the AutoArchive dialog box to all Outlook folders (such as Mail, Tasks and Calendar folders), you can set AutoArchive options for each folder individually.

Select a Folder in the Navigation Pane and then select the Folder Properties command on the Ribbon's Folder tab. Select the AutoArchive tab to view the archive settings for the selected folder. Figure 27.15 shows the AutoArchive tab of the Inbox Properties dialog box.

Figure 27.15
The AutoArchive tab of the Inbox Properties dialog box.

To set custom archiving options for the folder, select the Archive This Folder Using These Settings option button. You can then set the increment and time frame (months, weeks, or years) for the age of items to be archived. By default the Move old items to default archive folder is selected. You can choose to use the Move old items to option button to specify another archive file and/or path or you can choose the Permanently Delete Old Items option button to delete the old items rather than archive them. Click OK to close the dialog box.

Archiving Manually

If you don't want to use the AutoArchive feature or feel the need to archive a folder outside the archiving cycle that you have established in the settings for the AutoArchive feature, you can choose to archive folder items manually. This feature allows you to archive one folder at a time (and any subfolders it might hold). The manual archive can be run using the current AutoArchive settings for a folder (such as the age of items that should be archived), or you can select new age parameters while doing the manual archive.

To open the Archive dialog box, select File on the Ribbon and then select Info in the Backstage. On the Info window select the Cleanup Tools button and then select Archive. The Archive dialog box will appear as shown in Figure 27.16.

Figure 27.16
The Archive dialog box.

Choose one of the following options in the Archive dialog box:

- Archive all folders according to their AutoArchive settings: use this option to manually archive all the Outlook folders using their individual AutoArchive settings. Using this option is no different from running an AutoArchive, except that you are prompting Outlook to archive the folders immediately.

- Archive this folder and all subfolders: select this option to archive the selected folder. Using this option requires that you provide an age date for items to be archived, and you can also specify the path for the archive to be created.

> **note**
>
> Another tool that you might find useful is the Mailbox Cleanup tool, which is also available in the Backstage Cleanup Tools. Use it to find old and large items and manage the size of your mailbox.

If you selected to archive the folder selected in the Folder list, provide an item age (Archive items older than) using the drop-down list. You are specifying the age by an actual date. You can also choose to include items that have been flagged as do not AutoArchive (in their own Properties dialog boxes). You can also specify an archive file other than the default using the Browse button. When you have completed specifying your settings for the manual archive, select OK.

Whether you use autoarchiving or manual archiving is up to you. Once you archive items in Outlook, an Archive group will appear in the Navigation Pane. It will provide a list of folders that have been archived. You can access archived items by selecting the appropriate archived folder and selecting the item.

Configuring an Automatic Reply Message

You can use an Outlook rule and template to create an automatic reply system for when you are out of the office. This may help keep your Inbox from being crammed to the max upon your return since senders of messages to you will receive a reply message that you are out of the office. This may make them hold back any additional messages until your return (or so we can hope).

> **note**
>
> If you use Outlook as an Exchange Server client you can use the Automatic Replies command on the Info window of the Backstage to configure an out of office reply.

The first thing that you should do to create your automatic reply is to open a new mail message. Since you want the reply to reach everyone who sends you a message, it makes sense to create the email as a plain text message. On the Ribbon select new Items and then point at E-mail Message Using. Select Plain Text.

Type a subject for the new message such as "Out of Office" or "On Vacation" or any subject that works best for you in terms of letting recipients of the reply know that you are currently unavailable. Also enter body text for the message that provides any other information that you feel is required for the automatic reply that is being created.

Once you have the subject and the message body text entered, you will need to save the message as an Outlook template. Select File to open the Backstage. Then select Save As. In the Save As dialog box change the Save as type to Outlook Template. Supply a file name and path for the message and then select Save. You can then close the message without saving it.

Now you can create the rule, which will use the template as the automatic reply message. Select Rules and then Create Rule. In the Create Rule dialog box select Advanced Options. The Rules Wizard will open. In the condition box select the sent only to me check box. Then select Next.

On the Action screen, select the reply using specific template check box. In the Step 2 box of the Action screen, select the specific template value to open the Select a Reply Template dialog box. In the Look In box select User Templates in File System. Select the template that you created in the template list (use the Browse button if you saved your template to a folder other than the default path for user templates). Figure 27.17 shows the Select a Reply Template with a user created template selected.

Once you have selected the template, click Open. The Select a Reply Template dialog box will close and you will be returned to the Rules Wizard. The path and template name will now appear in the Step 2 box with the Reply Using action. Click Next. You can add any exceptions to the auto reply rule on this wizard screen. Then click Next.

Figure 27.17
The Select a Reply Template dialog box.

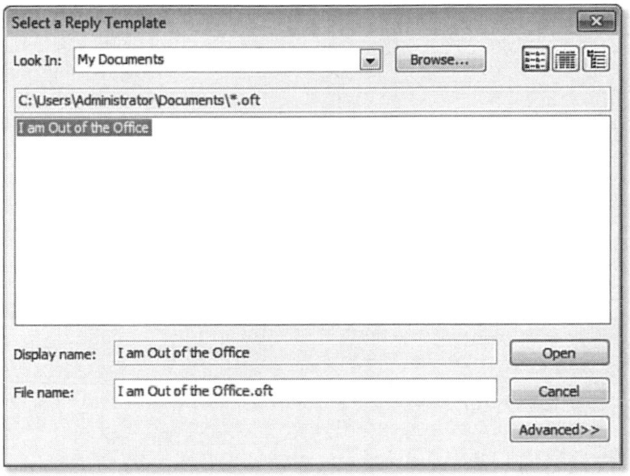

We are almost finished; provide a name for the rule. By default, the Turn on This Rule check box is selected. All you have to do is click Finish. Now when you receive a message in your Inbox, your auto reply rule will send a response to the sender using your mail template.

REQUISITE PUBLISHER: ESSENTIAL FEATURES

Desktop publishing applications have typically been intended for well-schooled designers who create complex publications. These applications were not for the typical user and required a very steep learning curve to really take advantage of the tools provided by the software. Microsoft introduced Publisher a number of years ago as a publication design application that made it easy for just about anyone to create a wide variety of publication types.

Microsoft Publisher has evolved over the years. It has gone from a somewhat basic application for creating simple publications into a fairly powerful desktop publishing tool. Publisher also stood apart from the other Office applications in terms of its user interface, but now is an integrated part of the Office application suite. In this chapter, we look at the features you need to know to begin creating your own publications in Microsoft Publisher 2010.

Introducing Publisher 2010

Publisher 2010 takes full advantage of the Office Fluent User Interface. As with the other members of the Office 2010 application suite, you will access the commands that you use from the various tabs provided on the Ribbon. Publisher also takes advantage of the Backstage, which makes it easy to access the Info, Print, Share, and Publisher Options windows. The Backstage also provides easy access to file-related commands such as Save As, Open, and Close.

As you work with Publisher 2010, you will find new features and improvements to features found in earlier versions of Publisher that make it easier to create professional-grade publications. Some of these features are as follows:

- **Contextual Tabs on Ribbon:** I've already mentioned that Publisher 2010 has adopted the Ribbon as its command interface; however, this fact is particularly important in Publisher where you work with a number of different object types on a publication. You will find that selecting an object on a publication page will immediately provide object-related tools such as the Drawing tools, Text Box tools, and Picture tools.

- **Less Hectic Workspace:** The Publisher 2010 workspace provides a cleaner, less hectic workspace so that you can concentrate on your publication's content. For example, the Format Publication pane (which was crowded with options related to the publication's template and pages) has been replaced by a more streamlined Page pane, which provides a preview of each page in the publication (and you can use it to go to the page). Publisher 2010 also keeps the publication page cleaner by hiding object boundaries and alignment guides until you need them. Select or hover the mouse over an object to see the boundaries; when you drag an object on a publication, alignment guides will appear to help you align the object.

 note

Publisher now provides you with the ability to add captions to your pictures. You can actually choose from different caption designs using the Caption gallery.

- **Working with Pictures:** Publisher 2010 provides a number of improvements related to the use of pictures and images in your publications. You can now crop images into nonrectangular shapes, and preview the images while keeping the picture in the desired size, shape, and location. You can also replace pictures in a publication using drag and drop or paste pictures from other applications into a picture placeholder. If you paste a picture that is too large or small for the picture placeholder, the picture itself resizes to fit the placeholder.

- **Building Blocks:** Publisher 2010 provides document building blocks such as page parts, calendars, borders, and advertisements. For example, the Building Block command provides a gallery of headings, pull quotes, sidebars, and other items that you can quickly add to your document. You can even add modified building blocks or your own building blocks to the gallery. Advertisements are special graphic elements, such as attention-getters and coupons.

- **Save File as PDF or XPS:** You can save your publications directly to two of the most popular electronic paper document formats PDF (Adobe Acrobat file) or XPS (a document using the XPS page description language, which is Microsoft's new electronic paper format).

This is just a subset of some of the new features and improvements that you will run into as you work with Publisher 2010. The Publisher chapters of this book will highlight other new features as they are covered.

You also should be aware of a change that actually removes features rather than adding them: The Web mode and features related to creating new websites and web publications have been removed from Publisher 2010. You can still edit websites that you created in Publisher 2007 or earlier, but you won't be able to access web templates or features to create new web publications. You can still save a publication as an HTML file, but think of Publisher as a desktop publishing package for creating either print publications or publications saved as PDF or XPS files.

Planning Your Publication

Although Publisher makes it easy for you to create a variety of publication types, you should still spend some time planning a new publication before you actually assemble it in Publisher. If you are poised to create a business card, newsletter, or flyer, you have already established that you have a need for a particular publication type. You should, however, also look at the core purpose of the publication and determine how you will approach the overall look, feel, and theme of the publication. For example, a newsletter for your book club might have a playful, friendly look and differ decidedly in layout, tone, and the type of graphics used from a flyer or other publication that will go out to your business clients.

Another important aspect of planning a new publication is assembling all the different objects and the text that will go into making up the publication. Because Publisher is a design and layout tool, it makes sense to have a folder on your computer that contains all the pictures, images, and perhaps even the pretyped text blocks that you will use as you create the layout for the publication. Of course you can create these items on the fly, particularly the text, as you assemble the publication, but doing so takes some of your concentration away from the focus of creating a professional and eye-catching publication.

Here are some other things that you should keep in mind as you get ready to create a new publication in Publisher:

- **Know Your Printer:** Printers differ in the amount of white space they require on the outside edge of a page when they print. Inkjet and laser printers have different requirements. If you plan on doing bleeds off the page for brochures or flyers, you need to know whether your printer can even do it before setting up the publication with that particular design feature. If you need professional-looking results for your finished publication and your printer isn't really up to the task, consider using the Save for a Commercial Printer settings on the Backstage Share window and let a printer with the proper equipment print out your publication for you.

- **Print Publications Versus Electronic Paper Publications:** As already mentioned, Publisher publications that are printed will have their overall quality affected by the printer that you use. You might consider creating publications for online viewing, such as PDF/XPS documents. These electronic paper versions of your publications can actually look better when viewed on a computer than your hard copy ever could. Consider using PDF or XPS files to create electronic paper versions of your publications when it is not necessary to supply your publication to the recipients as a printed hard copy.

- **Balance Objects on the Page:** Using the white space on a page effectively is an important aspect of creating an eye-catching layout. Consider balancing the layout of a page on the diagonal (the upper-left part of the page should balance with the lower-right part of the page) and align items in respect to the outside borders of the page rather than the center of the page. A publication with everything centered on the page looks unprofessional and doesn't use the page space effectively. The best way to get a feel for balanced publications is to examine flyers, brochures, or ads that you feel are designed well and then adapt these overall layout concepts to your own Publisher publications.

- **Size Items According to Their Importance:** The relative size of an item on the publication page reflects the importance of that item. Make sure that the objects on the page that are important to the overall theme or message of the publication are sized to have maximum impact.

These are just a few of the things that you should keep in mind when designing a new publication. Ultimately, you must remember the importance of emphasizing the purpose of a particular publication while also exercising your artistic sensibilities. Even the most eye-catching publication will ultimately fail if it doesn't get its message across.

Working with Publication Templates

As with earlier versions of Publisher, you will base most of the publications you create on Publisher templates. Publisher 2010 provides a wide variety of template categories that enables you to create very professional-looking publications without requiring you to be a polished graphic designer. You will find that additional templates available online from Office.com augment a large number of the installed templates.

Publisher 2010 actually makes it easier to access both local templates (those stored on your computer) and templates available online. When you start the Publisher application, it provides you with only two options related to working on a publication. You can select Open and open an existing publication or you can open an application that you worked on recently by selecting Recent in the Backstage. Your only other option is to select a template and start a new publication. By default the Available Templates window opens in the Backstage (New is selected automatically). You will also find that Publisher selects the Installed and Online Templates option in the Templates drop-down list at the top of the template window, as shown in Figure 28.1.

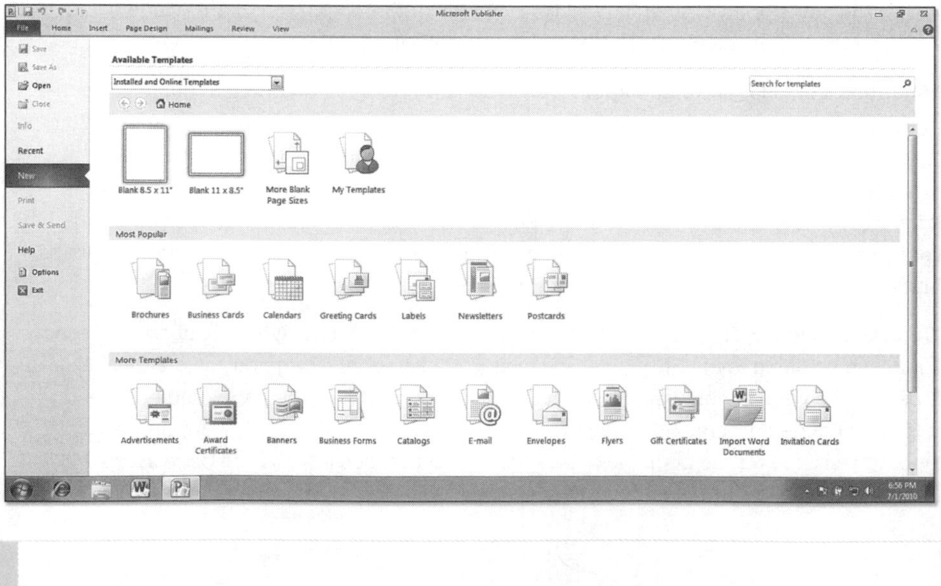

Figure 28.1
The Available Templates window.

The Available Templates window enables you to select from different categories of templates. At the top of the window, you have easy access to blank templates and any templates that you have created and saved. You can access your saved templates by selecting My Templates.

If you would like to search for a particular template, use the Search for Templates box in the upper right of the template window. You can focus on either online or installed templates by selecting Online Templates or Installed Templates in the Template drop-down list, respectively.

The template categories consist of Most Popular and More Templates. When you select a particular template category, such as Business Cards, a list of installed templates will appear in the Available Templates window. Depending on the type of template you select, there may be a Manufacturers list for that template type. For example, a number of companies sell sheets of blank business cards. If you want to build your business cards based on a particular manufacturer's business card sheet, you can select from the sheets provided by each manufacturer listed in the Manufacturers section of the template list.

You will find that most publication types provide you with blank templates and a number of prede-signed templates. So, it is up to you whether you want to use a preformatted template or start from scratch when you create a new publication.

If you select to use a preformatted template, you still have con-trol over options related to the template's color scheme, font scheme, and page size. When you select a particular template, a Customize pane appears on the right side of the Available Templates window and provides you with a preview of the business card, for example. It also provides a Color Scheme drop-down list, Font Scheme drop-down list, and a Page Size drop-down list. You can use any of these options to modify the default settings for the publication. Figure 28.2 shows the Customize pane and a preview of the selected business card template.

 tip

If you select an option in the Available Templates window, such as a Manufacturer, and want to return to the available templates, use the Back button. If you want to return to the main Available Templates list, click the Home but-ton.

Any changes that you make to the template will appear in the preview provided. By default the template preview uses your default business information set, which is information such as your name, title, business name, address, and phone number.

You can create a number of business information sets. This enables you to change the information that Publisher will place in the publication template. You can use the Business Information drop-down list to select the information set (the default is Custom 1) that you want to use for the publica-tion.

➥ *Creating and editing business information sets is discussed later in this chapter on page 771.*

You can also customize blank templates. The color scheme, font scheme, and business information set can be changed for a blank template. Because blank templates do not provide placeholder text or default design elements and graphics, however, you won't see a preview of the publication in the Customize pane. You receive a description of the template and dimensions for the publication, such as the page size and the sheet size.

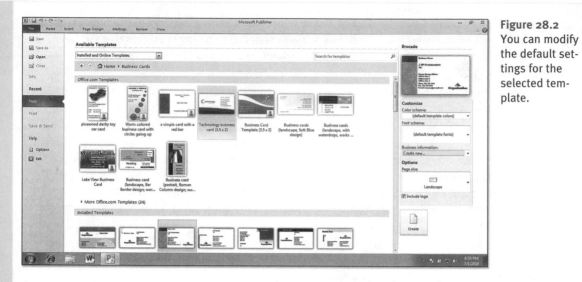

Figure 28.2
You can modify the default settings for the selected template.

Before we look at actually creating a new publication using a template (preformatted versus blank), an explanation of the difference between a page and a sheet is in order. A page is exactly what you think a page would be; a page is represented in the Publisher Workspace as a white space (in the dimensions you selected, when you selected the template), and this is where you place the objects that will appear in the publication. You can navigate from page to page in the publication by using the Page pane.

A publication can have multiple pages. You can modify page dimensions by using the Page Setup commands on the Page Design tab and the Page Setup dialog box.

A sheet is the actual piece of paper that you will use when you print the publication. You can specify the sheet size, orientation, and other settings for the sheet in the Backstage Print window. If you use a template based on a paper size, the paper and the sheet would be the same. In some cases, the sheet size can be bigger than the actual publication. For example, when you create a business card, the page is the size of one business card, with the understanding that you will print multiple pages on a single (and larger) sheet.

Creating a New Publication

As far as selecting a route for creating your new publication, that will depend on your experience with Publisher and the particular design requirements of your publication. The various document templates provide you with a lot of help as you initially design your publication. They create placeholder objects in your new publication that you can replace with your own pictures or design elements.

Creating a new publication using a blank template requires more initial layout and design work, but depending on your desktop publishing abilities, you might find that creating your own publications from scratch gives you the product that you desire. In the final analysis, your only option for creating custom publications that really stand out from all the publications made by other people using Publisher is to start from scratch and develop your own unique look and layout for your publications.

Using a Template

We have already discussed the overall geography of the Available Templates window in the Backstage. You have the option of using an installed template or an Office.com template to create your new publication with a preformatted template.

If you select an installed template, you can customize the settings for the template such as the color scheme, font scheme, and business information set. Select Create when you are ready to create the publication. The new publication will open in the Publisher workspace.

If you select an online template that is on Office.com, you will need to download the template before you can begin editing your new publication. Select the online template; a preview of the template will appear in the Customize pane (but you will not be provided the customize options provided for an installed template). Select the Download button. The Downloading Template dialog box will open, letting you know that that the template is on its way. When the download is completed, the new publication will open in the Publisher workspace.

Using Blank Sizes

In terms of creating a publication from scratch based on sheet size and orientation, you have a couple of options. When you start Publisher, the Available Templates window provides the template icons for the various publication categories. Even if you have already been working on a publication, you can get to the Available Templates window by selecting File, and then New.

At the very top of the Available Templates window, blank options are provided for 8.5 × 11 sheets in both portrait and landscape orientation. If you want to select from more blank page sizes (which relate directly to sheet sizes that would go in your printer), select the More Blank Page Sizes icon. You receive a number of standard blank page sizes in the Available Templates window as shown in Figure 28.3.

You can select any of the page sizes provided. If you scroll down through the list of blank templates, you will find a Publication Types category that provides blank templates for specific publication types such as booklets, greeting cards, and posters. Select a publication type such as Business Cards and a number of blank standard business card sizes display in the Available Templates window.

You can also select a blank template based on a manufacturer. In the Manufacturers area of the Available Templates list, select a manufacturer such as Ace Label, Avery US Letter, or Office Depot. A number of different blank templates for different types of publications display when you select a particular manufacturer, such as Office Depot. You can choose from such things as binder divider tab, business card, mailing label, and postcards (depending on the manufacturer).

When you have found the blank template you want to use, select the template. You receive a preview of the template, and you can customize the template as needed in the Customize pane. When you select Create, the new publication (based on the template) will open in the Publisher workspace.

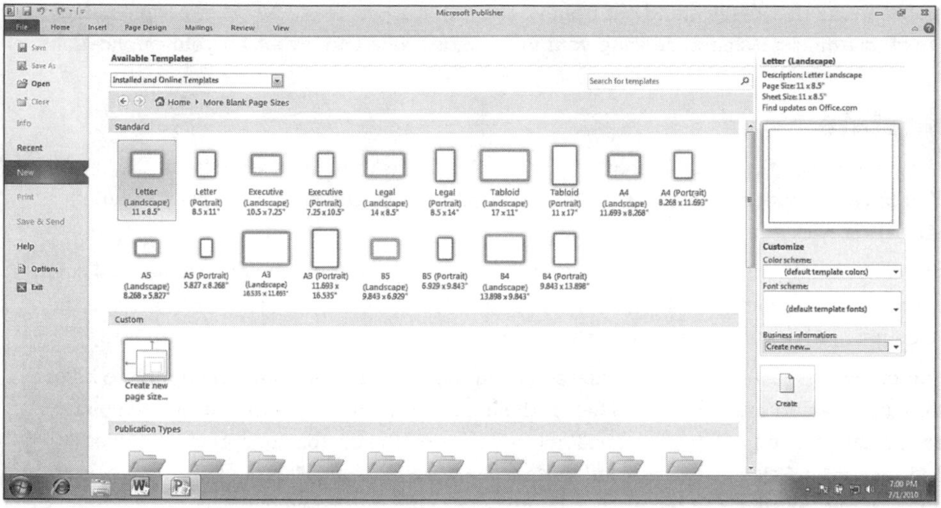

Figure 28.3
You can select from a number of blank page sizes.

Creating a New Template

Although this is a little bit like putting the cart before the horse because we haven't discussed all the ins and outs of the various Publisher commands and tools, you do have the option of creating your own templates and then saving them for future use. Follow these steps to create and then save your own template:

1. Start a new publication or open an existing publication.

2. In the Publisher workspace, modify the current publication as needed. You can insert objects including pictures, page parts, and so on. You can also modify the page setup and color scheme settings on the Paper Design tab.

3. When you have modified the publication to meet your needs, select File to access the Backstage.

4. In the Backstage, select Save As. The Save As dialog box will open.

5. Provide a filename for the new template in the File Name box.

6. Select the Save as Type drop-down list and select Publisher Template as shown in Figure 28.4.

7. Click Save to save the template.

The new template will save to the default template folder. When you select New in the Backstage and then select My Templates, your new template will be among those listed. If you want to use the template to create a new publication, select it and then click Create.

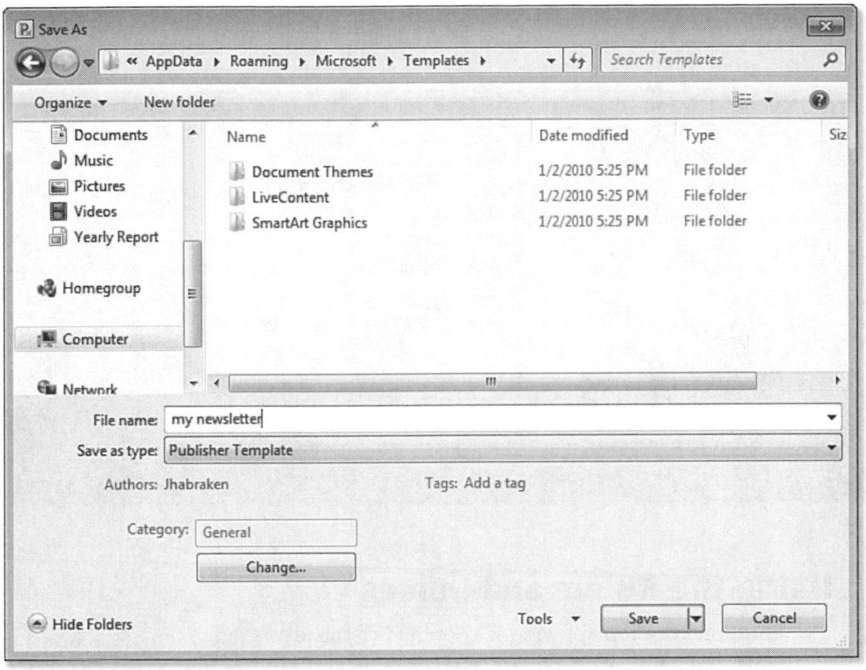

Figure 28.4
Save a template.

Navigating the Publisher Workspace

Whether you use a preformatted template, a blank template, or your own template to create a new publication, the publication will open in the Publisher workspace. The Ribbon on the top and the status bar on the bottom form the border of the workspace. On the right side of the status bar are the View shortcuts and the Zoom slider, which make it easy to change the current view of the publication and to zoom in and out of the publication page. Figure 28.5 shows the Publisher workspace.

On the left side of the workspace is the Page pane, which you use to navigate the various pages in the publication. A thumbnail displays for each page in the publication. The gray area surrounding the current publication page is the Scratch area. You can drag items from a publication page and place them on the Scratch area. You will find that objects in the Scratch area will be available even when you switch between pages in the publication or open a different publication. Think of the Scratch area as a place to leave logos, headings, or other items that you will use as you work on a particular publication. It is also the easiest way to move an object from one page to another.

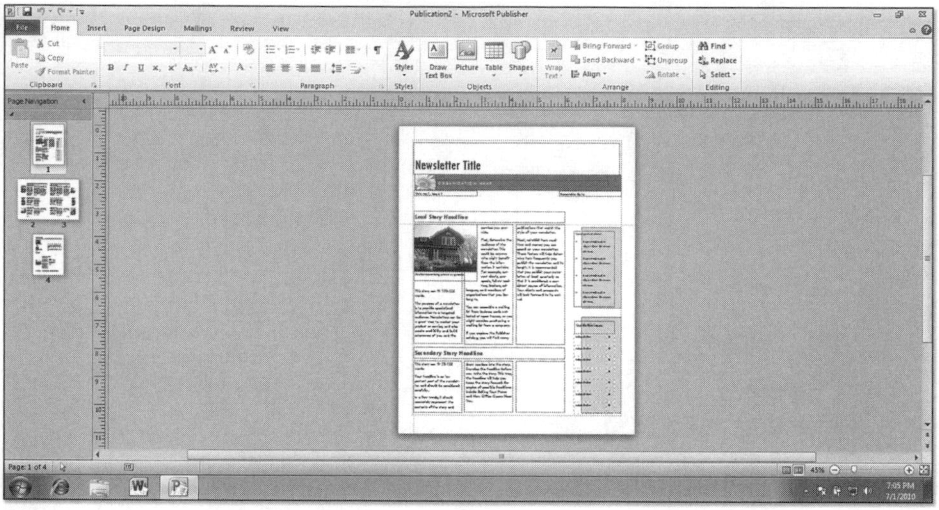

Figure 28.5
The Publisher workspace.

Using the Rulers and Guides

Bordering the top and left sides of the Scratch area are the horizontal and vertical rulers, respectively. You can use the rulers to help you place objects on a publication page. When you move the mouse on the page, you will notice that the vertical and horizontal positions of the mouse pointer are shown as tick marks on the vertical and horizontal rulers. When you drag an object on the publication page, the actual position (horizontal and vertical) of the mouse pointer also displays on the Publisher task bar. This allows you to precisely place objects on a page.

> **tip**
>
> If you don't like using guides, you can move either of the rulers onto the publication page. Hold down the Shift key and drag a ruler (vertical or horizontal) onto the publication. Repeat the process to place the ruler back in its original position adjacent to the Scratch area.

You can also drag horizontal or vertical guides from the rulers onto the publication page. Place the mouse on the horizontal or vertical ruler edge, and drag the guide onto the publication when you see the guide mouse pointer. The guides are nonprinting, and you can use them to align objects on the publication more precisely. Placing guides on the page enables you to actually place an object on the guide. When you move the object near the guide, it snaps onto the guide, precisely aligning the object.

If you want to remove a guide, drag it off of the publication page. You will find that it is easiest to grab a guide if you select it in one of the page margins. That way you aren't inadvertently selecting objects that are within the confines of the page itself.

If you find that you like using guides but don't like creating and positioning them with the mouse, you can choose to have a series of horizontal and vertical guides created for you automatically. This forms a grid pattern on the publication, providing you with a sort of topography that you can use to align your publication items appropriately.

Select the Ribbon's Page Design tab, and then select the Guides command in the Layout group. The Guides gallery will open as shown in Figure 28.6.

Figure 28.6
The Guides gallery.

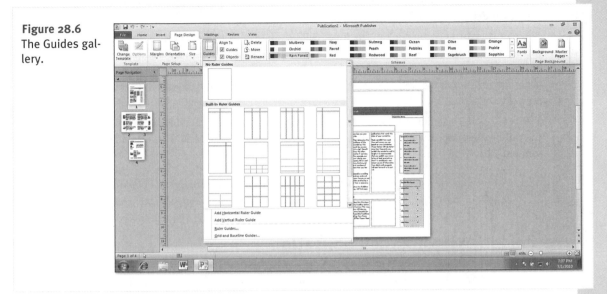

You can choose from any of the built-in ruler guides provided in the Guides gallery. If you want to add a single horizontal or vertical ruler guide, use the Add Horizontal Ruler Guide or Add Vertical Ruler Guide, respectively.

If you find that the built-in ruler guides don't provide you with the guide layout that you want, you can create your own custom ruler guides. Select Ruler Guides in the Guides gallery to open the Ruler Guides dialog box as shown in Figure 28.7.

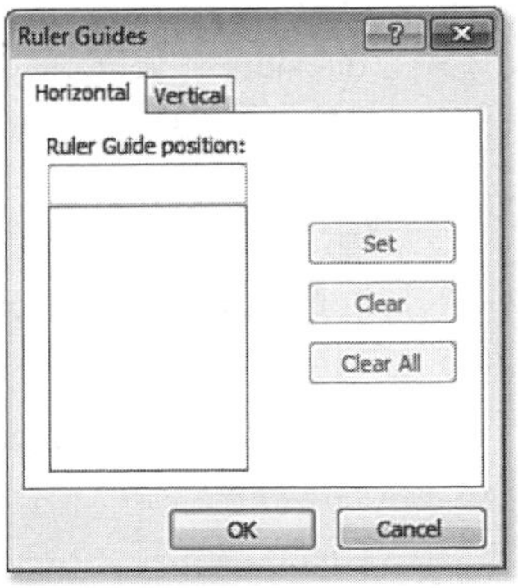

Figure 28.7
The Ruler Guides dialog box.

The Ruler Guides dialog box provides both a Horizontal and a Vertical tab. To set the guide position on the Horizontal tab, specify a position in the position box (such as 4 for 4 inches) and then click the Set button. Each time you specify a position and click the Set button, Publisher adds a guide to the guide list.

You can select the Vertical tab of the Ruler Guides dialog box and set vertical guides as needed by providing a position and then clicking the Set button. You can clear individual guide positions on either tab by selecting a position and then clicking the Clear button (Clear All clears all the guides). When you click OK, the Ruler Guides dialog box will close and the guides you specified will appear on the publication.

You can quickly clear all the guides (those selected from the gallery or those that you created) on the publication page by using the Guides command. Select Guides and then select No Ruler Guides in the gallery.

 You can use layout grids on master pages to help you align objects in a publication. For more about master pages and layout grids see Chapter 29, "Advanced Publisher Features," page 794.

Options for Viewing the Publication

As already mentioned, the Page pane provides a thumbnail of each page in your publication. You can use the Page pane to quickly move from page to page in your publication. You can also collapse or expand the Page pane by using the button at the top of the pane. If you want to increase the size of the page thumbnails on the Page pane, you can drag its border (on the left side of the vertical ruler) toward the scratch area as needed.

Because the Publisher workspace contains both your actual publication and a number of other tools such as the rulers, Page pane, and (potentially) guides, you might want to manipulate the view of the publication and the items actually shown in the workspace. The Ribbon's View tab provides command groups for changing the view and the items shown in the workspace, and for manipulating the current zoom level for the publication. Figure 28.8 shows the Ribbon's View tab.

The Views group on the View tab provides you with the ability to switch between the Normal view (the view of your publication pages) and the Master Page view (we talk about master pages in the next chapter). The Layout group enables you to view a single page or view two facing pages using the Two-Page Spread Command. The Show group has a number of check boxes that enable you to view different items in the workspace. These commands are as follows:

- **Boundaries:** This command enables you to view the boundaries for the objects on the page, such as images, text boxes, and shapes.

- **Guides:** To view guides on your publication, this command must be enabled (it is enabled by default).

- **Fields:** Select this command to show fields in the publication. The mail merge process uses fields as placeholders for names and addresses in your recipient list.

- **Rulers:** Enabled by default, this command shows or hides the rulers.

Figure 28.8
The Ribbon's
View tab.

- **Page Navigation:** When you select this command, the Page pane displays on the left side of the Publisher workspace. Clear the Page Navigation check box to hide the Page pane.

- **Scratch Area:** Enabled by default, this command shows the Scratch area and any objects you might have dragged to the Scratch area.

- **Graphics Manager:** This command opens the Graphics Manager task pane. The Graphics Manager provides a list of pictures on the publication. You can select from the picture list to select a picture in the publication.

- **Baselines:** Shows the baseline guides set for the publication. You can use baseline guides to align text to the guides, which will control the spacing between text lines in a story (we discuss text and stories later in this chapter).

The other command groups on the View tab include the Zoom commands and the Window group. The Zoom commands include the 100%, Whole Page (the default), and other zoom settings. If you want to change the zoom on a particular item, select the item and then click the Select Objects command.

You use the Window commands to arrange open publication windows. You can tile (Arrange All) or cascade (Cascade) the open publication windows, which is particularly useful if you want to drag an object from one publication to another or do a copy and paste between publications.

Creating a Business Information Set

Before you get too far into the publication creation process, you might want to create one or more business information sets. A business information set is a collection of information about you (and your company) for use by Publisher templates such as business cards, brochures, and envelopes.

The information in the business information set is automatically inserted into the appropriate fields in the template.

The best thing about a business information set is that you enter the information once and can use it again and again as you create your various publications. Publisher even provides you with the ability to create multiple business information sets, which is extremely useful if more than one person is using Publisher on the computer or if you create publications for both personal and business uses on the same computer.

Creating a New Business Information Set

You can create a new business information set or edit an existing business information set from the Publisher Backstage or as you work on a publication in the Publisher workspace. The first time you select the Edit Business Information button in the Publisher Info window in the Backstage, the Create New Business Information dialog box will open. The dialog box is shown in Figure 28.9. Use the Create New Business Information dialog box to create your default business information set.

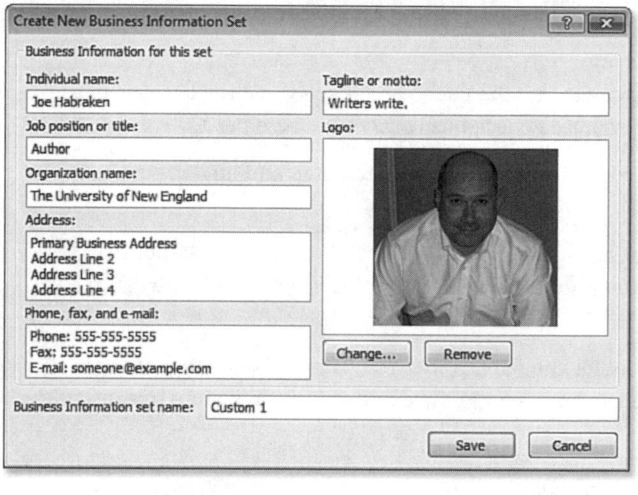

Figure 28.9
The Create New Business Information Set dialog box

Provide the information required in each of the fields provided by Create New Business Information Set dialog box such as Individual Name, Tagline or Motto, Address, and so on. You can also specify a logo for your company, which will replace the default placeholder logo. Select the Change button. Use the Insert Picture dialog box to specify the new logo for your company—select a new image file and then select Insert. Publisher places the new logo in the Logo box. When you have finished editing the information set, you can type a new name for the set in the Business Information Set Name box (the default is Custom 1). Then click Save to save the information.

After you have created the initial business information set, you can create additional business information sets as needed. To access your default business information set in the Backstage, select Edit Business Information. The Business Information dialog box will open. Use the drop-down list to select a business information set and then select Edit. Editing of the business information set takes place in the Edit Business Information Set dialog box, which is basically the same as the Create New Information Set dialog box. After you have edited the business information set, you can select the Save button. This will save your changes and close the Edit Business Information Set dialog. You will be returned to the Business Information dialog box. If you want to update the information used in the current publication, select the Update Publication button; otherwise, click Close.

Creating Additional Business Information Sets

If you use Publisher to create publications for both personal and business use, or if multiple people use the same computer (and Publisher), you might want to create multiple business information sets. You can open the Business Information dialog box from the Backstage by clicking the Edit Business Information button in the Info window. You can also open the Business Information dialog box as you work on a publication. Select the Business Information command on the Ribbon's Insert tab and then select Edit Business Information. Figure 28.10 shows the Business Information dialog box.

Figure 28.10
The Business Information dialog box.

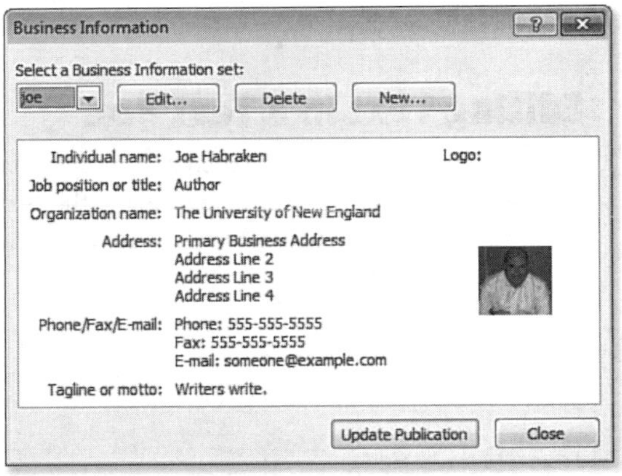

To create a new business set, select New and the Create New Business Information Set dialog box will open (refer to Figure 28.9) Supply the information for the set using the various field boxes. You can also specify a logo for the new information set. Type a new name for the set in the Business Information Set Name box. You can then click the Save button to save the new information set.

When you open the Business Information dialog box in the future, you will be able to specify the business information set to use. Use the drop-down box to select a specific information set. You can actually change the information set for the current publication. Select an information set from the list and then select Update Publication.

You can also edit the current Business Information set, create a new set, or select a different information set for the current publication from the Publisher workspace. Select the Ribbon's Insert tab. In the Text Group, select the Business Information command.

You can use the Business Information Fields list to insert any of the field information in the information set directly into the publication. If you want to edit the business information set or to create a new set, select the Edit Business Information command on the Fields list. The Business Information dialog box will open. Use the Edit or New commands in the dialog box as needed. You can delete an information set by selecting the set in the drop-down list and then clicking the Delete button.

Working with Text

When you work with text in Publisher, a text box called an object frame holds the text inside. You will find that Publisher provides you with complete control over the look and formatting of text in the box, including the font style, font size, font attributes (such as bold and italic), and the color of your font. You can edit any or all of these font parameters for a particular text box.

Working with text in Publisher is more than just typing inside boxes. You have control not only over the format of the text within the box, including the text direction and special text effects, but there are also options for formatting the text box itself, including outside borders and fill color. You can create text boxes as space holders as you design your publication and then add the text to the box at your convenience. You can even insert text files into your publication.

Editing Text in a Text Box

If you use a template that contained text boxes with placeholder text, you will need to edit the text in each of the text boxes. Select the text in a specific text box and then type the text that will replace the placeholder text. Figure 28.11 shows selected placeholder text in a template text box.

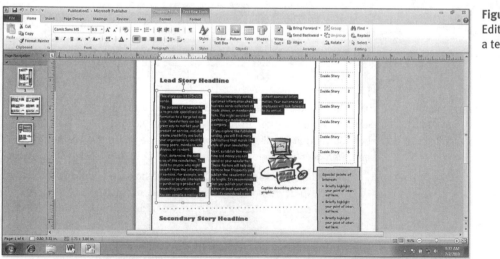

Figure 28.11
Edit the text in a text box.

The new text will use the same font attributes as the placeholder text. If you want to change the font or paragraph attributes for text, select the text that you want to format (in the text box) and then use the Font and Paragraph commands on the Home tab as needed. You can also create bulleted and numbered lists inside a text box by using the Bullets and Numbering commands in the Paragraph group.

When you use templates to create your publications, you might also find two or more text boxes linked together. That is, clicking on the text in one of the text boxes on the publication page selects the text in more than one text box. This means that the text actually flows from one text box to the other (it can flow through several text boxes). The text in a text box or linked text boxes is also referred to as a story. We look at creating linked text boxes in a moment.

Creating Your Own Text Boxes

You can insert a new text box on any publication page as needed. The Draw Text Box command is on the Ribbon's Insert tab. Follow these steps:

> **🔍 note**
>
> You can also format the text in text boxes using styles. Publisher provides a number of different style formats in the Styles gallery (click the Styles command).

1. Select the Draw Text Box command.

2. Place the mouse pointer on the page and drag diagonally to create the text box (in the required dimensions).

3. Release the mouse button and the insertion point appears in the text box.

4. Use the Font commands on the text box tools Format tab to set the font size and attributes for the font such as font color or switch to the Home tab to use the font, paragraph, and styles commands that it provides.

5. After specifying your font attributes, type the text that you want to place in the box.

When you have completed entering the text into the text box, click outside the text box to deselect it. You might find that it makes sense to zoom in on the text box when you are entering the text. This is particularly true if you are looking at a large publication page in the Whole Page view.

Formatting Text Boxes

As already mentioned in our discussion of text boxes, you have control over the text inside the box as well as the text box itself. When you click inside a text box to select text, you will find that two sets of contextual tools appear on the Ribbon: drawing tools and text box tools. You use the drawing tools (available when you select Format under the Drawing Tools tab) to format the text box itself, including the shape style, fill, outline, and special effects.

The text box tools (available when you select Format under the Text Box Tools tab) enable you to change text, font, and alignment settings. This set of tools also provides the commands for linking text boxes and adding effects to your text. Typography settings are also available that enable you to use the Drop Cap feature and special typographic features, such as ligatures.

Using the Drawing Tools

To format the text box itself, select the text box and then click Format under the Drawing Tools tab to access the various tools for formatting an object (remember that text boxes, pictures and clip art are all Publisher objects). Figure 28.12 shows a selected text box and the Drawing Tools Format tab on the Ribbon.

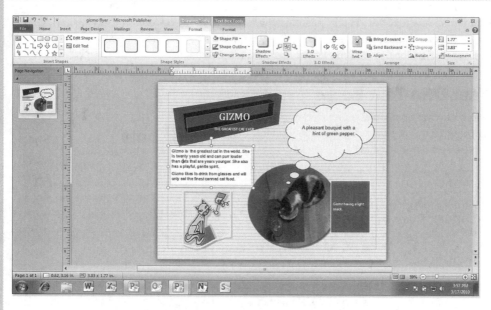

Figure 28.12
Use the Drawing Tools to enhance the text box.

Because you are working with an existing object, you will find that only a subset of the commands available on the Drawing Tools tab will be useful. The command groups that you might want to take advantage of are as follows:

- **Shape Styles:** This group includes the Shape Styles gallery. You can point at a particular shape style in the gallery to preview that style on the text box. This group also includes the Shape Fill command, which you use to select a fill color, gradient, texture, or pattern. You can also specify a picture as the fill element. The Shape Outline command enables you to select a border color and also the weight and type of line to use. The Change Shape command enables you to change the shape of the text box to any of the shapes provided in the shape gallery.

- **Shadow Effects:** This command group includes the Shadow Effects command and the Nudge commands. Select Shadow Effects to select a shadow type from the gallery. You can then use the Nudge command to nudge the shadow in a particular direction (left, right, up, or down).

- **3-D Effects:** The 3-D Effects command allows you to select a 3D effect and also edit the effect setting's color, depth, direction, lighting, and surface. When you have selected a 3D effect, you can use the Tilt buttons to tilt the shape in a particular direction (left, right, up, or down).

- **Size:** This command group provides measurement spinner boxes that allow you to adjust the height and width of the text box. You can also access the Format Text Box dialog box by selecting the dialog box launcher at the bottom of this command group.

All the commands that we have discussed related to a text box are also applicable to another Publisher object: shapes. You have probably noticed that we skipped the Arrange group. We will discuss the arrange group in the next chapter when we look at working with multiple objects on a page.

 Aligning and layering multiple objects can be tricky. See Chapter 29, "Advanced Publisher Features," on page 799.

Using the Text Box Tools

As already discussed, you can use any of the font and paragraph attributes to format the text in a text box using the commands on the Home tab. If you want to use special formatting attributes, you will want to use the text box tools. The text box tools go beyond the settings for basic font attributes and enable you to specify the text's direction and how it fits in the box (including special alignment commands). You can also add effects and special typography settings to the text. Figure 28.13 shows the Text Box Tools tab.

Figure 28.13
Format the text in the text box using the Text Box Tools.

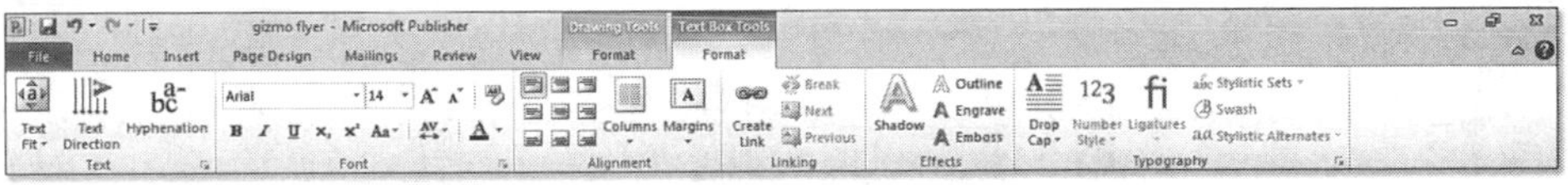

The command groups provided on the Text Box Tools tab are as follows:

- **Text:** These commands fit text in the box, change the text directions, and set the hyphenation for the text. The Text Fit command enables you to use best fit to change the size of the text so that it will fit in the box. You can also choose to grow the text box or shrink text on overflow. The Text Direction command enables you to rotate the text from the horizontal to the vertical. The Hyphenation command opens the Hyphenation dialog box and enables you to change the hyphenation zone or manually hyphenate the text.

- **Font:** This command group provides font attribute settings (such as size, bold, italics, and font color) and enables you to adjust the character spacing (normal, tight, loose, and so on). A Clear Formatting command is also available that allows you to clear all formatting on the selected text.

- **Alignment:** These commands enable you to align the text in reference to the borders of the text box. For example, the Align Top Left command moves the text to the top-left corner of the text box. There are nine different alignment options. The Columns command enables you to create columns in the text box. You can select from one to three columns on the Columns menu or select More Columns to open the Columns dialog box. The Margins command enables you to set the margins for the text (the margins in the box) using presets such as Narrow, Moderate, and Wide. You can select the Custom Margins command to open the Format Text Box dialog box and set custom margins for the text box.

- **Linking:** The Create Link command links two or more selected text boxes. We look at linking text boxes in the next section.

- **Effects:** These commands enable you to add special effects to selected text. The commands are Shadow, Outline, Engrave, and Emboss.

- **Typography:** These commands add items such as a drop cap to text, set the number style, or add special typography formatting, such as ligatures and stylistic sets. Ligatures are text characters tied together using a common design element (common to the text characters). The Drop Cap command provides a gallery of different types of drop caps as shown in Figure 28.14. You can preview any of the drop cap styles provided in the gallery or use the Custom Drop Cap command to set your own drop cap in the Drop Cap dialog box. The stylistic sets provide alternative character shapes for the selected text. Not all font families provide this option. Some font families also enable you to turn on flourishes using the Swash command.

Figure 28.14
Select a drop cap style.

If you would like additional control over settings related to the text box and the text inside the text box, you can go old school and open the Format Text dialog box. On the Text Box Tools tab, select the dialog box launcher at the bottom of the Text group. Figure 28.15 shows the Format Text Box dialog box.

The Format Text Box dialog box provides six tabs that provide control over such things as the text box lines and fill, size, layout, alignment, and margins. The Color and Lines tab enables you to set the fill color and level of transparency as well as the line color, style, and weight. You can use presets or set your own borders. You can even use the Border Art button to select from a list of available borders with titles such as Apple, Baby Pacifier, and Cake Slice.

 note

Because you can add text to any shape you insert into a publication, both the Drawing Tools and Text Box tools discussed in this chapter are applicable to any shapes you place.

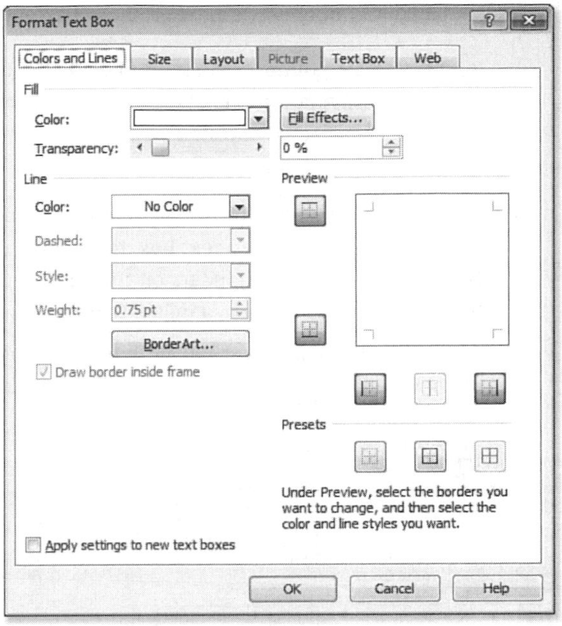

Figure 28.15
Set text box options in the Format Text Box dialog box.

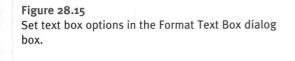

The Size tab provides settings for the size and rotation of the text box. It also provides scale settings for the height and width and enables you to lock the aspect ratio. The Layout tab provides settings for the position of the text box on the page and the wrapping style if an image is included in the text box. The Text Box tab is where you set the margins for the text box and specify the vertical alignment of the text in the box.

Linking Text Boxes

If you want text to flow from one text box to another text box, you can link the text boxes. Publisher then considers the text that fills the text boxes to be a single story. You will find many linked text boxes in the flyer, brochure, and a number of the other Publisher preformatted templates.

To create your own linked text boxes, follow these steps:

1. Use the Draw Text Box command to create a new text box and enter text into that text box as needed.

2. Create a second text box using the Draw Text Box command.

3. Select the first text box.

4. Select the Text Box Tools tab on the Ribbon.

5. Select the Create Link command in the Linking group. An ellipsis symbol will appear on the selected text box.

6. The mouse pointer becomes a pitcher (like a pitcher of water). Navigate to the text box that you will link to the currently selected text box and then click the mouse. The text boxes will link.

note

If you don't like typing text in the text boxes, create your text in Word and then copy and paste the text into your Publisher text boxes.

You can tell when two (or more) text boxes are linked because when you select a linked text box, the Next symbol (a right-pointing arrow) or the Previous symbol (a left-pointing arrow) appears on the edge of the text box frame. You can use these buttons on the text box frame to move to a linked text box from its partner.

After you fill the first text box with text (either by typing the text or inserting a text file as discussed in a moment), the text will flow into the next text box. Figure 28.16 shows two linked text boxes.

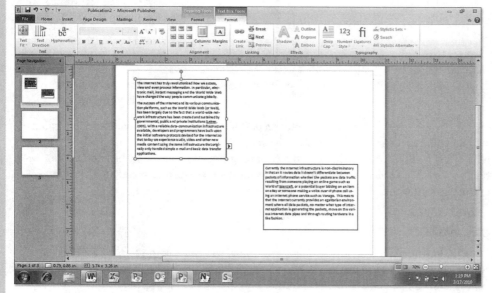

Figure 28.16
Link text boxes.

Note the Next button on the text box on the upper right of the page. One thing to keep in mind is that as you size either of the boxes, the amount of text in the boxes will shift from one box to the other, particularly if you make the primary box in the linked pair larger or smaller.

In cases where you enter more text into a text box than it can hold (or copy and paste more than it can hold), you will find that an ellipsis (...) button appears on the text box frame. This means that the text box contains more text than it can accommodate. This also means that you have the Do Not Autofit command selected on the Text Fit command menu. You can fix this problem by creating another text box, and then clicking on the ellipsis button. The mouse pointer will show the Create Link icon (the pitcher); click it on a text box to link the boxes. The overflow text (the text that you can't see) will flow into the second text box.

Inserting a Text File

You can insert text files directly onto a publication page. This is extremely useful in cases where someone is creating the publication copy (the text) as you design the publication in Publisher. You can easily insert files created in Word. The Word document can even have images and other objects embedded in the text (such as pictures or even Excel worksheets). In cases where you are using some other word processor, you should save the text document as plain text (.txt) or rich text format (.rtf).

You can actually insert a Word document or text file directly onto a publication page and the Insert feature will create its own text boxes to accommodate the text as needed. You will find, however, that you have greater control over the process if you create your own text box and then insert the file text directly into the text box. If you know that the text file is going to require more than one text box, create the text boxes and then link them. You can then have the story flow from the initial text box into the other text box (or boxes). To insert a text file into your publication, follow these steps:

 note

If you misjudge the size of your text box (or linked text boxes) to accommodate all the text in an inserted text file, Publisher will create an additional linked text box to make sure that all the imported text is taken care of. Resize your original text boxes and then delete the added text box.

1. Draw a text box (or linked text boxes) on the publication page.

2. Click inside the text box (or in the first of the linked text boxes).

3. Select the Insert tab on the Ribbon.

4. In the Text group, select the Insert File command. The Insert Text dialog box will open.

5. Locate the file using the Insert Text dialog box and then select the file you will insert.

6. Select OK.

Publisher will insert the text into the text box (or linked text boxes). You can modify the formatting for the text as needed by using the font and paragraph formatting attributes on the Home tab or the additional text formatting tools on the Text Box Tools tab.

Inserting Illustrations

Publisher provides you with a lot of flexibility as to the types of illustrations that you can add to your publication pages. You can add a picture file in any number of image file formats, and you can add a clip art image installed on your computer or from the extensive clip art library on Office.com. You can also add a variety of shapes to your publication pages using the Shapes gallery.

Images on a publication page not only add interest to the publication but also can greatly enhance the probability that your publication will get its intended purpose across to the reader. Although it is fun to add a lot of graphic elements to a publication, make sure to place and size key graphics, particularly important pictures, for maximum visual impact.

Options for Inserting Pictures

Publisher supports a wide variety of picture file formats that you can insert into a publication. File formats that do not require you to add a graphics filter are as follows:

- Windows Bitmap (.bmp)

- Graphics Interchange Format (.gif)

- Joint Photographic Expert Group (.jpg)

- Portable Network Graphics (.png)

- TIFF, Tagged Image File Format (.tif)

- Windows Metafile (.wmf)

Some older file formats might require you to add a graphics filter to insert the file type directly into a publication. These file types include CorelDraw (.cdr), Encapsulated PostScript (.eps), and WordPerfect graphics (.wpg). You can add these graphics filters using your Microsoft Office installation DVD.

> *Installing the Office applications is discussed in Chapter 1, "Getting Oriented to the Office 2010 Applications" on page 15.*

When inserting an image into your publication, you can insert the picture directly onto the publication page or you can insert a picture placeholder. Inserting a large image onto a page will require that you size and/or crop the image to get it into a manageable size. Of course, the size of the image on the page will depend on the size of the image file. I think it is preferable to use the picture placeholder because the image will then have to conform to the size of the placeholder. This enables you to position the placeholder on the page and make sure that its alignment and adjustment appropriately suit the other objects on the page. Let's look at both possibilities.

Insert a Picture

Inserting a picture is really just a matter of selecting a picture file and having Publisher plop it on the current publication page. To insert a picture, follow these steps:

1. Navigate to the page where you will insert the picture.

2. Select the Insert tab of the Ribbon.

3. Select the Picture command. The Insert Picture dialog box will open.

4. Locate the picture using the Insert Picture dialog box and then select the file.

5. Click Insert.

Publisher will place the picture on the publication page. The picture tools will become available on the Ribbon. You can size the picture as needed and position the image on the page.

Insert a Picture Placeholder

The alternative to inserting the picture directly is to insert a picture placeholder. You can then specify that the picture file be placed in the placeholder frame. This enables you to size the picture by specifying the picture placeholder size.

On the Insert tab, select the Picture Placeholder command and then size and position the picture placeholder as needed. When you click on the picture icon in the middle of the picture placeholder, the Insert Picture dialog box will open. Locate your picture file, select it, and then click Insert. Figure 28.17 shows an inserted picture on the left and the same picture placed directly into a picture placeholder.

Figure 28.17
Inserted picture versus picture in a placeholder.

Notice that Publisher sized the picture in the placeholder appropriately for the publication page. The picture on the left was from a somewhat small (in size) picture file. You can see why I suggest that you place pictures in placeholders rather than just dropping them on a page.

You can replace a picture on a publication page by using the Change Picture command on the Picture Tools tab. The new picture will conform to the frame that contains the current picture.

Formatting a Picture

After you have a picture on a publication page, you have a number of tools that you can use to modify and stylize the picture. When you select a picture, the contextual picture tools become available on the Ribbon. Figure 28.18 shows the picture tools.

Figure 28.18
The picture
tools.

You can use the various commands provided by the picture tools to adjust the picture itself or to change the formatting for the frame (or box) that surrounds the picture. The Adjust group of commands, which includes Brightness, Contrast, and Recolor, can enhance the image itself.

The Picture Styles and Shadow Effects groups provide commands that enable you to change the shape of the picture frame and add shadows to its edge. You can use the Picture Styles gallery to create a number of different picture frame shapes. Place the mouse on a style to preview its effect on the picture. The Picture Styles group also provides a picture Border command for specifying a border color and type for the picture. You can also use the Caption command to specify a number of different styles of captions for the image.

> **tip**
>
> If you aren't satisfied with the picture shapes provided by the Picture Styles gallery, you can use any of the shapes provided by the Picture Shape command.

> ➡ *For an overview of working with graphics in Office 2010, look in Chapter 4, "Using and Creating Graphics," on page 77.*

Inserting Clip Art

Another way to add pictures to your publication pages is to use clip art. When you install Microsoft Office on your computer, you automatically install a number of clip art images that you can use in any of the Office applications, including Publisher. Office.com also provides a seemingly unending supply of additional clip art files, if you need more.

When the urge to use clip art comes over you, take a moment and determine whether cutesy clip art will negatively affect the publication that you are creating. I suggest that you reserve clip art for personal publications and use it extremely sparingly on any publications that you are creating for use in a professional context.

To insert clip art onto the current publication page, select the Ribbon's Insert tab. Then click the Clip Art command in the Illustrations group. The Clip Art task pane will open. Use the Search For box to specify search criteria for the type of clip art you want to use. Select the clip art image that you want to use in the clip art list. Then select the clip art image to insert it in the publication. When you select the clip art image, the picture tools will become available on the Ribbon.

Inserting Shapes

You can insert any of the autoshapes available in the Shapes gallery. These shapes include lines, arrows, flowchart items, and a number of other shapes.

To insert a shape, select the Shapes command. When you have located the shape that you want to use, click the Shape. A drawing tool will replace the mouse pointer. Drag on the page to create the shape. You can size and position the shape on the page as needed.

When you select the shape, the drawing tools become available on the Ribbon. These same tools are available when you select a text box on the page. We discussed formatting text boxes earlier in this chapter. If you want to place text in an autoshape, select the shape on the page and then select the Edit Text command in the Insert Shapes group.

Using Building Blocks

Believe it or not, we have not exhausted the possibilities for adding graphic elements to a Publisher publication. The Building Blocks group on the Insert menu provides a number of other premade graphics that you can use to enhance your pages. These items range from headings and pull quotes to calendars and advertisements. The commands in the Building Blocks group are as follows:

- **Page Parts:** The page parts are a gallery of items that include ready-made headings, sidebars, and stories. The stories are preformatted text boxes, placeholder text, and an image that you can replace with your own text and picture file. The great things about the various page parts is that they are well designed and save you the time it takes to create these types of items from scratch.

- **Calendars:** This command provides a gallery of calendars that you can insert into your publication. Calendars are available for the current month (This Month) and the next month (Next Month).

- **Borders & Accents:** This command provides a gallery of different box frames and accents that you can use to enhance your publication.

- **Advertisements:** The advertisements range from simple graphic elements, such as attention getters, to more complex advertisements that are predesigned text boxes containing pictures, text, and other graphic elements. You can modify the text in even the simplest of the attention getters, if required.

tip

Don't forget to take advantage of the Spelling feature on the ruler's Review tab before printing your publication.

Inserting a building block is just a matter of selecting one of the building block commands, such as Page Parts or Advertisements, and then selecting a particular item provided in that command's gallery.

Printing Publications

When you are working in Publisher, you are, in effect, always seeing each page as it will print. This means that objects, pictures, and text boxes appear on the Publisher pages as they will on printed pages.

The best strategy for previewing your publication is to go from the general to the specific. Zoom in and make sure that individual objects are correctly set up and that text boxes do not contain typos.

When you zoom out on the publication, you can check placement of objects, the overall design of the publication, and the use of color.

When you are ready to print your publication, select File to open the Backstage. In the Backstage, select Print. The Print window will open as shown in Figure 28.19.

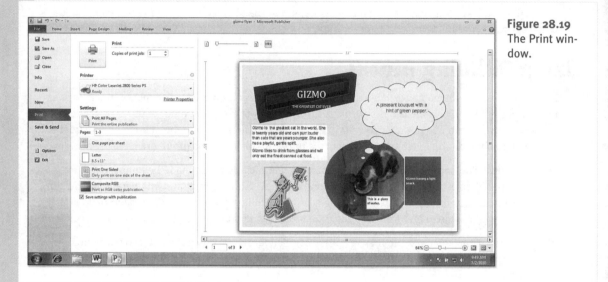

Figure 28.19
The Print window.

As with any of the other Office applications, you can use the printer settings to specify the printer for the print job and specify properties for your printer. The actual settings for the publication specified in the Settings area will depend on the type of publication you are printing. For example, if you are printing a flyer, the one page per sheet setting makes sense. However, if you want to print multiple business cards to a blank sheet of perforated business cards, you will want to select multiple copies per sheet and then specify the number of items that should print on each sheet.

For double-sided printing, you have the option of flipping the page on the long edge or on the short edge. Select the option that makes it easiest for the recipient of your publication to read the front side and then the flip side without having to rotate the page.

In most cases, it is assumed that you will print your publication to a color printer. However, if you are going to print to a black-and-white printer, you will want to switch the publication color from composite RGB (red, green, blue) to composite grayscale. This will provide you with a more readable product than just sending the RGB print job to a black-and-white printer.

When you are ready to print your publication, click the Print button. This will close the Print window and send your publication to the specified printer.

ADVANCED PUBLISHER FEATURES

When creating a Microsoft Publisher publication, it is extremely tempting to take advantage of one of the many provided preformatted templates. Whether you are creating a business card, brochure, or flyer, Publisher makes it easy to create many different types of publications. However, this reliance on templates keeps many Publisher users from exploring more advanced Publisher tools and features that could greatly enhance even the simplest of publications.

In this chapter, we look at some of the more advanced features of Microsoft Publisher. We start with an exploration of features related to the pages in a publication, including master pages. Master pages make it easy to include design elements and ensure consistent layout options across the pages of a publication. We will also look at using tables in a publication and manipulating multiple objects on a page. We will close out the chapter with a look at merging information into a publication and fine-tuning your publications.

Adding Pages to a Publication

Whether you are working on a publication you have created from scratch using a blank template or have created using a preformatted template, you might need to add pages to your publication. You might be thinking that adding pages to a publication created with a blank template is risk-free because you are doing most of the layout and formatting work on the pages, and that adding pages to a publication based on a preformatted template might be a rather scary experience. Not so. You will find that there are different options for inserting new pages, and whether or not you are using a fancy template, you will be able to add usable new pages.

The Page command is on the Ribbon's Insert tab in the Pages group. You will find that the Pages group contains only two commands: Page and Catalog Pages. We discuss the Catalog Pages command later in this chapter.

 tip

To delete a page from a publication, right-click on the page in the Page pane and select Delete from the shortcut menu.

When you select the Page command, you receive three possibilities: Insert Blank Page, Insert Duplicate Page, and Insert Page. The Insert Blank Page command inserts a blank page after the currently selected page. The page will be the same size and have the same orientation as the page selected (before adding the new page). It will also have the same margins. So, other than the fact that page is blank; it is close to the original page in terms of page setup.

The page is the same because Publisher bases it on the same master page as the other pages in the publication. We talk more about master pages later in this chapter. For now, you just need to know that the master page contains the page layout information for the publication pages, and can contain other elements you want on every page such as logos or information in headers and footers. Each publication has a single master page by default (although you can create additional master pages for a more complex publication).

If you are using a template that provides objects that you don't feel you can duplicate, you can choose the Insert Duplicate Page option on the Page command to create a duplicate of the currently selected page. You can then remove the objects that you don't need or rearrange the objects to create your new page.

In cases where you would like to add multiple pages before or after the current page and have options related to the objects placed on the new page, you need to use the Insert Page command on the Page gallery. This will open the Insert Page dialog box as shown in Figure 29.1.

Figure 29.1
The Insert Page dialog box.

Specify the number of new pages needed and specify whether you want the new pages before or after the currently selected page. You have three options for the new page or pages: You can insert blank pages, create one text box on each new page, or duplicate all the objects on a specified page in the publication. After setting the options in the Insert Page dialog box, click OK. Publisher will add the pages (based on the options you chose) to the publication.

You will find that when you use the Insert Page command in a publication that is based on one of the Publisher newsletter templates that the Insert Newsletter Pages dialog box opens rather than the Insert Page dialog box. The Insert Newsletter Pages dialog box enables you to insert a two-page spread of facing pages into the newsletter. This spread will duplicate the stories and graphics found in the default two-page spread for the newsletter. You can use the drop-down list at the top of the Left-hand page pane or Right-hand page pane in the Insert Newsletter Pages dialog box to specify that items such as a calendar order form or response form be inserted in place of the default story for the new page. You can also access the Insert Page dialog box from the Insert Newsletter Pages dialog box; select the More button.

Configuring Page Settings

The commands related to managing and formatting pages are found on the Ribbon's Page Design tab. Command groups such as Template, Page Setup, Pages, Schemes, and Page Background populate this tab. In regard to margins, page orientation, and the size of the pages in the publication, the Page Setup commands enable you to quickly and easily change page attributes. For example, the Orientation command has two possibilities: Portrait and Landscape. You will find, however, that if you have a publication in landscape and you want to change the orientation of a single page (the currently selected page) to portrait, all the pages will change orientation when you select Portrait on the Orientation gallery.

> **note**
>
> You can have more than one master page for a publication. This enables you to mix pages that use different page setup attributes in the same publication. We discuss master pages later in this chapter.

So, using the term "Page Setup" as the name for this command group might be a little misleading because you are actually changing the settings for the master page that your document pages are based on. Be advised that Publisher will apply any changes you make using the Page Setup commands to all the pages in your publication.

The Margins and the Size commands both provide a number of presets. For example, the Margins command provides a gallery of margin possibilities as shown in Figure 29.2.

Figure 29.2
Select from a gallery of margin presets.

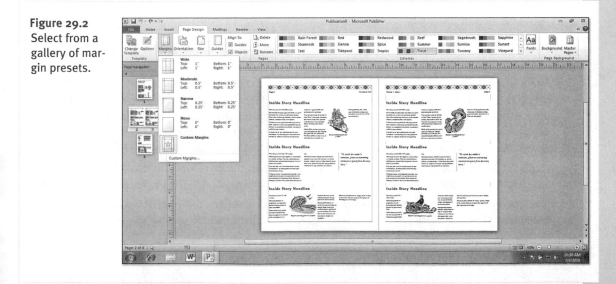

You can select from the margin presets: Wide, Moderate Narrow, or None. There is no preview for the margin changes, so you will need to select one of the presets to actually see how it affects the objects currently on the page. If you want to set custom margins, select the Custom Margins command in the Margins gallery. The Layout Guides dialog opens as shown in Figure 29.3.

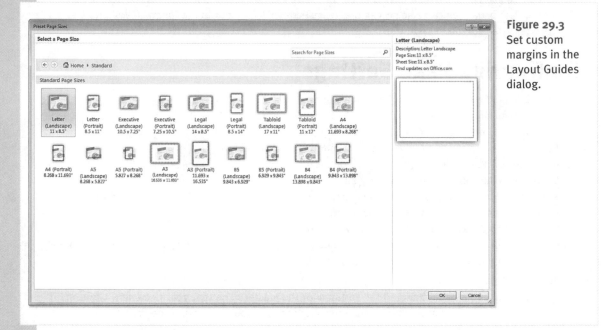

Figure 29.3
Set custom margins in the Layout Guides dialog.

Use the margin spinner boxes to set the margin guides for the pages in the publication. Remember, you are actually setting the margins for the master page for the publication. When you have finished configuring the margin guides, click OK. The new margin guides will appear on the pages of the publication.

The Size command also provides a list of preset page sizes such as A5 (Landscape), Letter (Landscape), and Tabloid (Landscape). The preset page sizes available will depend on the template you have used for your publication.

Again, any selection in the Size gallery is going to change the size of all the pages in the publication. If you select More Preset Page Sizes, you go to the Preset Page Sizes window, which is actually a list of the different publication types and manufacturers that you would find in the Available Templates window. To view the page sizes provided by a particular page size group, select that group. Figure 29.4 shows the page sizes available when you select the Standard group.

When you have found the page size you want to use, select the page size and then click OK. You return to the Publisher workspace, and the page size will be applied to the pages in the publication.

The Size gallery also provides a Page Setup command, which opens the Page Setup dialog box. This dialog box, shown in Figure 29.5, provides you with settings for all the various page options.

Figure 29.4
Select a page size.

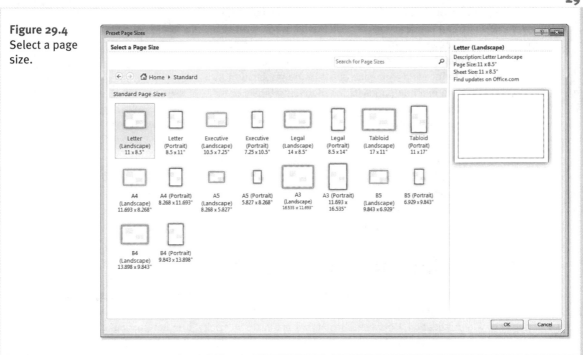

Figure 29.5
Set the page configuration options in the Page Setup dialog box.

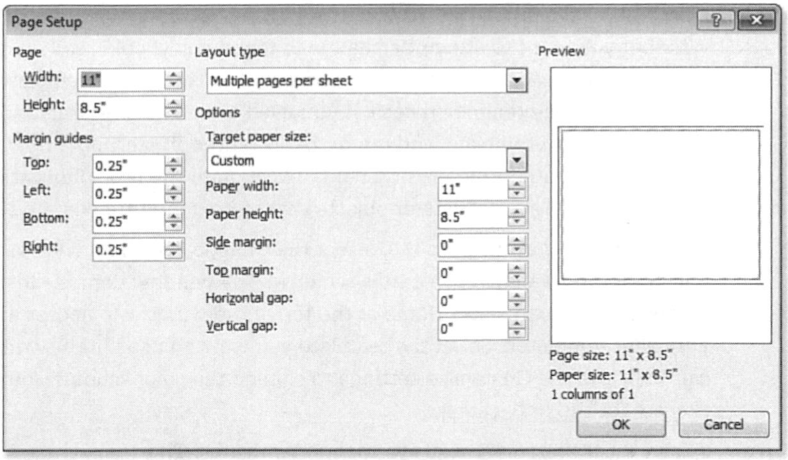

The Page Setup dialog box provides you with access to page size and margin guides settings. It also provides you with settings for the number of pages per sheet and the settings for the target paper. Remember that sheets are what the printer will actually produce and that each sheet in the publication can actually have multiple pages (think of mailing labels or business cards). To set the number of pages per sheet, use the Layout Type drop-down list.

To set the options for the actual printer paper that will be used, select a target paper size in the drop-down list or select Custom and then use the page option spinner boxes to set the width, height, margins, and so on for the target paper. As you change the settings in the Page Setup dialog box, the results display in the preview pane. When you have finished setting the page setup options, click OK to apply the settings and close the Page Setup dialog box.

 tip

You can create your own custom page sizes. Select Create New Page Size on the Size gallery. The Create New Page Size dialog box is almost identical to the Page Setup dialog box. Specify your page settings, name the new page size, and then click OK.

Changing the Current Template

You can actually change the template used by a publication. This can be a little tricky, particularly because you probably have already established objects such as text boxes and pictures on the pages of the publication. However, although it is a little bit tricky, it is not particularly risky. You can choose to apply a new template to the current publication and have Publisher create a new publication as the result rather than changing (or perhaps destroying) the current publication. You can then decide whether you want to save the new publication and continue to edit it, or discard it and return to your original publication.

Whether you want to attempt a change in templates should really depend on the number of changes that you have made to the current document and the type of template you used when you began your publication-creation process. If you used one of the preformatted templates, such as a brochure or business card template, you are probably better off starting a new publication and copying the objects you created from the original publication to the new publication. The preformatted templates actually contain a lot of default objects that often do not translate well to a different template.

To change the current template, select the Change Template command on the Page Design tab. This will open the Available Templates window. The window defaults to a listing of various flyer templates, but you can select Home at the top of the window to access any of the installed or Office.com Publisher templates. Select the template you want to use in the Available Templates window. You can then use the Customize settings to change the color scheme, font scheme, or business information set for the publication.

Click OK when you are ready to change templates. The Change Template dialog box will appear as shown in Figure 29.6.

caution

Apply the template to your current publication only if you are sure that it will not negatively affect the publication layout. It makes more sense to create a copy; you can always discard it later.

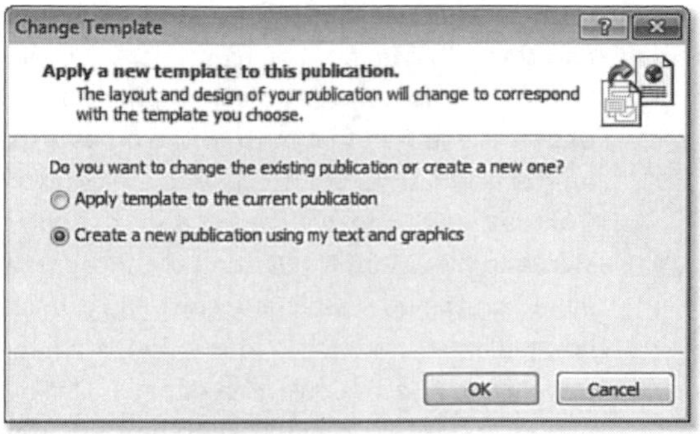

Figure 29.6
The Change
Template dia-
log box.

> **Change Template**   ? ✕
>
> **Apply a new template to this publication.**
> The layout and design of your publication will change to correspond
> with the template you choose.
>
> Do you want to change the existing publication or create a new one?
> ○ Apply template to the current publication
> ◉ Create a new publication using my text and graphics
>
> OK   Cancel

By default the Change Template dialog box will specify that
a new publication be created using the new template. This is
probably the best way to proceed. When you are ready to create
the copy of the current publication based on the new template,
click OK. It might take a moment, but the new publication will
display in the Publisher workspace.

How successful the template change was in the layout and look
of the new publication is really a matter of how well the new
template was able to "digest" the objects that you placed in the original publication. If Publisher was
unable to place objects on the pages (mainly due to available space or page formatting), the Extra
Content task pane will appear as shown in Figure 29.7.

The Extra Content task pane will list all the objects that did not fit into the changed publication. You
can choose to view subsets of different object types not placed using the Show check boxes: Text
and Tables, Images or Shapes, and WordArt.

Figure 29.7
The Extra Content task pane.

To place an object in the new publication from the Extra Content task pane, select the arrow to the right of the object and then click Insert. You can repeat this process as needed to place all the unused objects on the publication page or pages. If you find that most of the objects that you inserted on the original publication pages are showing up in the Extra Content task pane, you might want to abort this entire mission and try again. If you don't want the new publication based on the new template, close the publication. A message box will open letting you know that you have not used all the items in the Extra Content task pane. Click OK to close the message box. Another message box will appear alerting you to the fact that you have not saved changes to the publication (meaning the new publication); select Don't Save and the publication will close.

 note

Although many of the commands on the Ribbon's Page Design tab affect all the publication pages because they change the master page settings, the Background command in the Page Background group changes only the background on the selected page.

Working with Master Pages

Master pages have already cropped up in our discussion of page setup attributes such as margins and page orientation. When you create a new publication, whether based on a blank template or a preformatted template, Publisher creates a master page that supplies basic page-formatting attributes to the pages in the publication. If you are creating a simple publication that consists of pages with the same formatting, this single-master-page approach will probably work for you just fine. You already know that Publisher applies page setup changes to the master page.

Master pages can also include information and objects that you want repeated on every page of the publication. For example, if you want to include a logo on the top-right corner of every page, it makes sense to place that logo on the master page. You can also place header and footer items on the master page, which can include page numbering and other information, such as a draft number or date.

Believe it or not, you do not have to apply the master page to a page in your publication. By default, Publisher assigns the default master page to the pages. If you have pages that you do not want affected by changes in the master page, you can select those pages and then choose None on the Master Pages gallery (select Master Pages on the Page Design tab). This breaks the tie between the page and the master page. You can always associate the page with the master page as needed by selecting the master page in the Master Pages gallery.

Even though you have the option of applying or not applying master page settings to the pages in the publication (by virtue of the fact that you can specify None as the master page setting for a page), you might still find the need to create multiple master pages. This is useful in cases where you are working with a more complex publication that required different page setup values (such as page orientation) in the same publication because you can create additional master pages. Each master page can have its own settings and objects, which will repeat on the pages assigned that master page. You can even create a two-page master for publications that contain facing pages (such as a booklet).

Placing Objects on the Master Page

You can place objects on a master page that you want to have repeated on all the pages assigned that master page. This means that in cases where you are using a single, default master page, any object you place on the master page will be placed on all the publication pages.

To edit a master page, select the Master Pages command on the Page Design tab and then select Edit Master Pages. This will switch you to the Master Page view. Publisher will list the master page (or pages) for the publication in the Page pane and the Master Page tab will appear on the Ribbon. The current master page displays in the Publisher workspace. Figure 28.8 shows the Master Page view.

Figure 29.8
The Master
Page view.

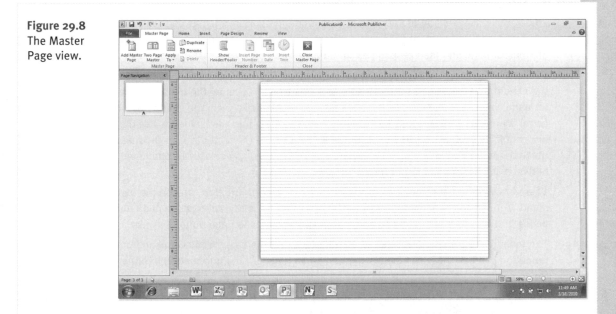

Letters of the alphabet specify the master pages in a publication, beginning with A. You can change the name or ID of a master page using the Rename command, however, Publisher provides only a one-character ID.

In some respects, a master page is no different from a publication page. You can use the various tools on the Ribbon's Insert tab to add objects to the master page. These objects, such as a text box or a logo, will display on each page in the publication.

Select the Insert tab and add objects to the master page as needed. If you want to have repeating page parts, borders, accents, or advertisements in the publication use the Building Blocks group commands to insert items. You can also insert pictures, clip art, and shapes as needed.

The Apply To command on the Master Page tab provides you with the ability to apply the master page (and the changes you have made to the master) to all the pages in the publication, the current page, or a specific range of pages. Use the Apply to All Pages to assign the change to all pages in the publication. Apply to Current Page will affect only the page that was selected when you switched to the Master Page view.

To specify a range of pages, select Apply Master Page; the Apply Master page dialog box will open. It has options for all pages, a range of pages, or the current page. To set a range of pages, select the Pages option button and then use the From and To boxes to specify the page range. When you have finished working in the dialog box, click OK.

When you have finished working with the master page (or pages), select the Close Master Page command on the Master Page tab. This will return you to your publication.

Inserting Headers and Footers

You can use headers and footers to add repeating information, such as page numbers, dates, or any other information you want to repeat, to the pages in a publication. The header or footer resides in the master page and then propagates to the pages assigned the master page.

You add headers and footers to a master page in the Master Page view. The commands related to the header and footers are in the Header & Footer group. To show the header in the selected master page, select the Show Head/Footer command. Publisher selects the header area on the master page; it appears as a selected text box. You can type text into the header or use the Insert tab to insert objects such as pictures or other items. To move to the footer area of the master page, select the Show Head/Footer command a second time. Each time you select this command, you will toggle between the header and footer (or vice versa).

There are three other commands in the Header & Footer group. You can use the Insert Page command to insert the page number symbol (#). This will place the appropriate page number on the pages in the publication. You can add text before or after the page number symbol.

The Insert Date command enters the current date, and the Insert Time command enters the current time. You can use these commands to place page, date, or time information in either the header or the footer.

You can apply the header and footer to all the pages in the document or to specific pages using the Apply To command. When you have finished working in the header or footer of a master page, click in the body of the master page to deselect the header or footer.

Creating Master Pages

You can add additional master pages to your publication in the Master Page view. You can also rename and/or delete master pages if required. One option for adding a new master page is the Add Master Page command. When you select the Add Master Page command, the New Master Page dialog box opens as shown in Figure 29.9.

 note

If you want to create a new master page that is a duplicate of an existing master page, you can use the Duplicate command in the Master Page group. This creates a new master page with a new ID that is a duplicate of the currently selected master. You can then edit the duplicate master as needed and assign it to pages in the publication.

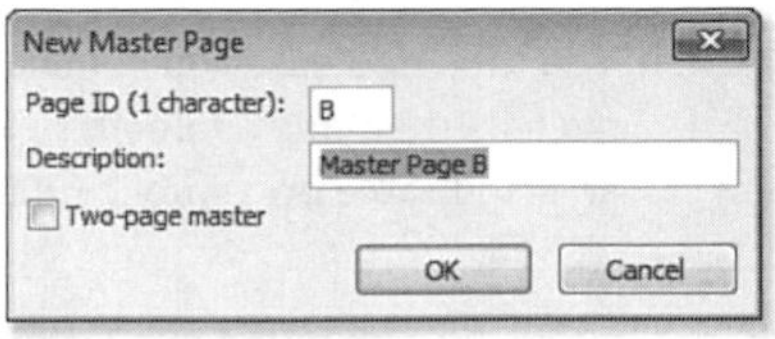

Figure 29.9
The New Master Page dialog box.

New Master Page	
Page ID (1 character):	B
Description:	Master Page B
☐ Two-page master	
	OK Cancel

By default, Publisher sets the page ID to B (which you might as well leave as is). If you choose to do so, you can add a description for the new master page. When you click OK, Publisher adds a new master page to the Page pane. The new master page is also selected so that it is the active page in the Publisher workspace. You can modify the master page as already discussed and then use the Apply To command to apply the new master page to specific pages in the publication.

Having more than one master page allows you to mix different pages with different layouts and default objects in the same publication. For example, you could have a master page that does not include a header or footer and a master page that does include a header or footer. Assigning the master page without a header or footer to the first page in the publication enables you to follow the general rule that page numbers and header/footer information is not typically included on the first page of a publication, but is included on subsequent pages in the publication. Remember that you can assign master pages to selected publication pages when you are working on the pages in the workspace. Use the Master Pages command on the Page Design tab to assign a master page to the current publication page by selecting from the master page gallery.

Using Tables in Publications

You can use tables on your publication pages to arrange objects on the page. When you place a table on a page, you are inserting a Publisher object, just like a text box or picture. So, you can size and move the table on the page as needed. You can place text in the table cells or you can place other objects, such as pictures, in the cells. Although you might think of a table as columns and rows that enable you to enter text information into a cell, you should also consider a table as a potential layout tool for positioning objects on the page.

You can insert a table into a page using the Table command on the Ribbon's Insert tab. You have two options for creating the table. You can select the Table command and then use the table grid to specify the number of columns and rows for the table using the mouse. When you release the mouse button, Publisher inserts the table into the publication.

Or, if you would like to specify the number of rows and columns for the dialog box without having to drag the mouse on the table grid, you can select the Insert Table command, which is below the table grid. Selecting Insert Table opens the Create Table dialog box. It provides a spinner box for both the number of rows and the number of columns. Specify the number of columns and rows as needed and then click OK.

When you insert the new table, the table will be the selected object on the page. The table tools will appear on the Ribbon. The table tools consist of two different tabs: Design and Layout.

Table Design Commands

The table tools Design commands consist of commands related to the overall look of the table, such as the table's format, or the fill color, or border parameters for the table. Figure 29.10 shows a selected table on a publication page and the table tools Design commands on the Ribbon.

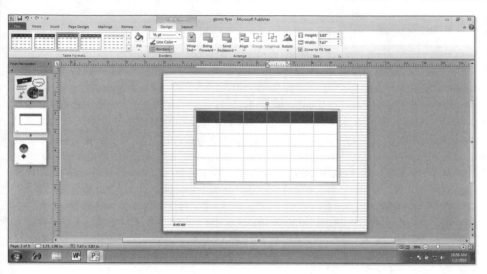

Figure 29.10
The table tools Design commands.

You can use the Table Formats gallery to select a format for the table from the supplied gallery. Place the mouse on a format in the gallery to preview the format on your table. If you do not want to use a table format, you can use the Fill command to select a fill color for the table. The commands in the Borders group enable you to select a line weight and color and to specify the location of the border in the table.

Because you are working with a table that consists of separate cells, you can format the entire table by selecting the table frame. If you want to format specific cells or ranges of cells in the table, select those cells and then use the commands provided in the various Design groups.

Table Layout Commands

Publisher also provides a number of commands related to the layout of the table, which include commands for inserting rows and columns and aligning text (or other objects) within the table cells. To access the Layout commands for a table, select the table and then click the Layout tab under Table Tools. The table tools Layout command groups are as follows:

- **Table:** This group provides the Select command. You can use the options on the Select command menu to select a cell, column, or row, or the entire table.

- **Rows & Columns:** This group provides insertion commands for rows and columns. You can insert above or below a row and to the left or right of a column. Select multiple rows or columns to add a like number using these commands.

- **Merge:** The Merge Cells command will merge selected cells. If you want to split merged cells, use the Split Cells commands. The Diagonals command enables you to divide a cell or cells on the diagonal either downward (Divide Down) or upward (Divide Up).

- **Alignment:** These commands enable you to control how text characters or other objects align within cells, the text direction in a cell, or merged cells and cell margins. Use any of the alignment commands, such as Align Center, to align the contents in the cell. You can change the text direction of text in cells using the Text Direction command, which rotates the text from the horizontal to the vertical. The Cell Margins command enables you to set cell margins from a gallery or you can use the Custom Margins command, which opens the Cell Properties tab of the Format Table dialog box. The Hyphenation button will automatically hyphenate any text in a cell or selected cells.

- **Typography:** These commands add items such as a drop cap to text, set the number style, or add special typography formatting such as ligatures and stylistic sets. Ligatures are text characters tied together using a common design element (common, that is, to the text characters involved). The Drop Cap command provides a gallery of different types of drop caps for your text blocks in cells.

These layout commands provide basic table construction tools such as inserting rows and columns and merging cells. You can enhance the overall look of a table by taking advantage of text alignment in cells and special typography features such as drop caps. Remember that a table is more than just a container for text. You could use a table to lay out the entire page of a publication.

Manipulating Publication Objects

Publisher provides you with the ability to manipulate the objects on a page. You can group objects, layer objects on a page, and even swap images between two picture frames and maintain the size settings for each of the picture placeholders involved in the swap.

Grouping Objects

Grouping objects allows you to fine-tune the positioning of any number of objects on the page. For example, after you have objects placed on a page, you might want to adjust the overall positioning of all the objects in relation to the top or bottom of the page or some other special element on the page (such as a large heading). Moving each object individually can be time-consuming and frustrating, especially if you have the objects currently positioned exactly where you would like them to be in relation to each other.

To group objects, select the first object. Select subsequent objects by holding down the Control key as you select the objects. After you select all the objects that you want to include in the group, select the Group command on the Home tab. Figure 29.11 shows a group of objects on a page.

A group will have its own frame. You can now move the entire group of objects by placing the mouse on the group frame and dragging it to a new position. You can also use the group frame to size the entire group of objects at the same time.

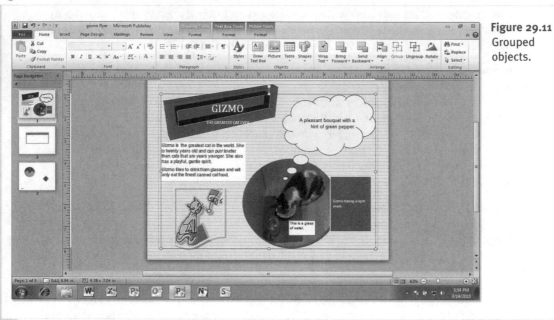

Figure 29.11
Grouped
objects.

You can delete a group and all the objects in the group at once, or copy the objects and then paste them on another page in your publication. When you finish manipulating the grouped objects, click anywhere outside the group to deselect it.

Layering Objects

You might find occasion to layer several objects on top of each other in a stack. For instance, you might be using a combination of shapes, text boxes, and pictures to build a custom logo or other layered item. You can also overlap adjacent objects by layering to provide the page with more visual interest.

> **note**
>
> Use the Ungroup command to separate the objects in a selected group.

Layering objects is just a matter of dragging the objects onto each other and then sorting out the layers using the commands in the Arrange group. You can use the Bring Forward command to bring an object forward in the stack (one object) or to bring it to the front of the stack (it will be on top). The Send Backward command enables you to send a selected object backward (one layer) or to send it to the bottom of the object pile using the Send to Back option.

When you have the objects layered correctly, select the entire stack (drag the mouse around the object stack). You can then group the layered objects using the Group command. This will enable you to move the stack without messing up the layers.

Swapping Images

A nice addition to Publisher's overall capabilities for working with pictures is the Swap command on the picture tools Format tab. It enables you to swap the pictures in two selected picture frames or swap the formatting of two selected picture frames.

Select a picture on a page, and then hold down the Ctrl key and select a second picture. You will find that the Swap command becomes active on the Ribbon as soon as you select the second picture. Select the Swap command. On the menu provided by the Swap command select Swap.

This will swap the two pictures but keep the formatting of the picture frame the same. In fact, the pictures will adapt to the size of the frame. For example, if you swap a larger picture with a small picture (in terms of the picture frame size), the large picture will take the place of the smaller picture and, in effect, become the smaller picture. The real value of being able to swap the pictures without disturbing the placement and the formatting of the picture frame is that you don't disrupt the overall balance of your publication page.

In cases where you want to swap the formatting of the picture frames between the two selected pictures, select Swap Formatting Only on the Swap command menu. This will swap the formatting of the frames but will not change the size, content, or placement of either frame.

Merging Data into a Publication

You can perform a variety of data merges into Publisher publications. You can do a mail merge to envelopes or mailing labels as well as addressable brochures or other publications. You can also perform email merges to an email publication. A catalog merge enables you to merge text or picture entries into a publication. For example, you might want to generate a product list using a data file that contains the name and perhaps even pictures of your products. Publisher will merge each product and any accompanying information related to the product to a new publication page.

 note

The data file that is used for a merge in Publisher can be created in Microsoft Excel, Microsoft Word or directly in Publisher as you perform the merge.

When you conduct a merge, be it a mail merge or catalog merge, you need two items: the publication containing the merge codes that will identify the information that is to be placed on the page or pages, and the data file that contains the information to be used in the merge.

Publisher actually inserts the information in the data file, known as the data source, into the form letter, envelope, or mailing label using placeholder codes called merge fields. Each merge field in the merge publication relates to a piece of information in the data source, such as first name, last name, or street address.

The publication that you use as the destination for the merged information can be any publication that you create in Publisher. For example, you might want to use an envelope template if you want to do a merge of client name and address information to envelopes that you can then print out. The merge publication is only the model for the merge, and Publisher will create multiple copies of the merge publication (such as an envelope or a catalog page)—one for each record (meaning each person, in the case of clients) in the data file.

Performing a Mail Merge

To perform a mail merge, create a new publication. For example, you could create a new postcard using one of the postcard templates. Most of the envelope, postcard, and other mail-related templates have reserved areas on them for the recipient's address. It is in that area of the publication that you will want to place the merge codes for data source information. Delete the text box text reserved for the address information on the publication. The commands that you will use to perform the merge are on the Mailings tab.

After beginning the merge, the first thing that you have to do is supply an address list, meaning a data source, for the merge. You can create it or use an existing list. Publisher actually saves the data source in the Microsoft Access database format with the extension .mdb.

To begin the merge and create a new address list, follow these steps:

1. Select the Mail Merge command and then select Mail Merge. The Select Recipients command in the Start group will become active.

2. Click the Select Recipients command. You can specify the recipients for the merged publication in either a new list or an existing list.

3. Let's assume that you need to create a new list; select Type New List. The New Address List will open as shown in Figure 29.12.

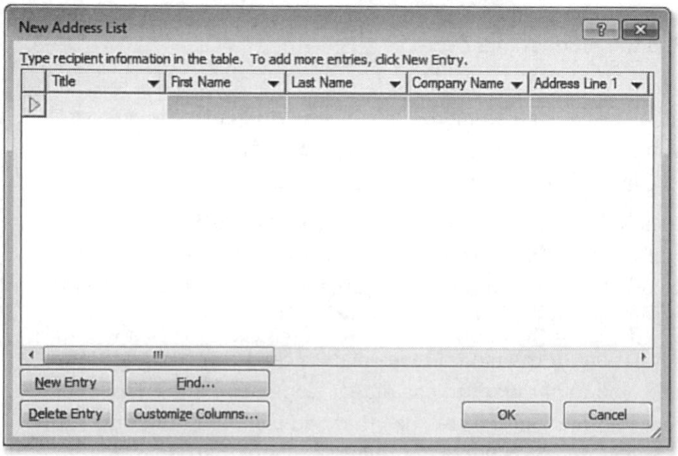

🌊 **tip**

If you are entering individual fields using the Insert Merge Field command, you can put spaces or blank lines between fields as needed. Line up the fields as you would the address information on an envelope or other publication to be mailed.

🌊 **tip**

Use the Tab key to move forward a field and Shift+Tab to move back.

Figure 29.12
The New Address List dialog box.

4. Each column in the address list is a different field. Each row will be a different record. Type the field entries for the first recipient (that is, first name, last name, and so on).

5. To enter additional records, select the New Entry button as needed.

6. When you have finished entering the recipients in the address list, click OK. The Save Address List dialog box will open.

> **note**
>
> The Mail Merge Wizard can walk you through the steps of the merge. I think it is more trouble than just using the commands supplied on the Mailings tab and your own common sense.

7. Specify a name and location for the list and then click Save. The Mail Merge Recipients dialog box will open. You can clear recipient check boxes so that those people are not included in the merge.

8. Click OK to close the dialog box.

When you have specified the recipient list for the merge, you will find that commands in the Write & Insert Fields group, such as Insert Merge Field, Address Block, and Greeting Line, become active. This is because you have provided the merge fields for the merge by creating the recipient list. You can enter individual field names from the Insert Merge Field command. It provides a list of all the field names in the recipient list.

If you are creating envelopes or mailing labels, the easiest way to get the name and address on the envelope or label publication is to use the Address Block command. Position the insertion point on the publication where you want the recipients' names and addresses to reside. For example, in a text box on an envelope. Then select the Address Block command. The Insert Address Block dialog box will open as shown in Figure 29.13.

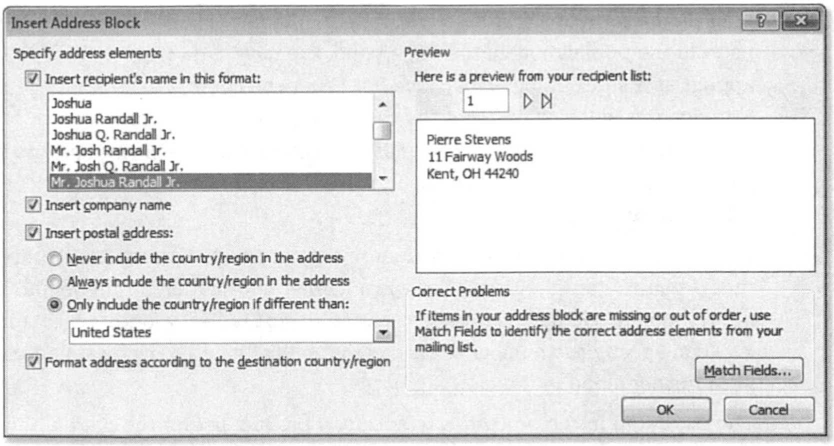

Figure 29.13
The Insert Address Block dialog box.

Select a recipient's name format and then deselect items that you do not want in the address block, such as Insert Company Name. You can also specify that the country/region not be included in the address. A preview will appear on the right side of the dialog box. When you are ready to return to your publication, click OK. The address block field will appear on the publication page as <<AddressBlock>>.

After the merge fields are on the publication, you are ready to perform the merge. You can select the Preview Results command and then preview each of the merged publications (such as individual envelopes) if you are unsure of what the results of the merge will look like. When you are ready to complete the merge, select the Finish & Merge command.

The Finish & Merge command provides three options: Merge to Printer, Merge to New Publication, and Add to Existing Publication (in the case of an email merge, it will supply Send E-mail Messages). I suggest you merge to a new publication, which allows you to closely examine the results of the merge before you print the merged publication pages. When you complete the merge and create a new publication, a multipage publication will open in Publisher. There will be a copy of the publication created for each of the recipients. For example, if I used a two-page postcard publication as my starting material, there will be a two-page postcard created for each recipient.

Performing a Catalog Merge

Another Publisher tool that allows you to merge date into a publication is the Catalog Merge feature. This merge tool creates product lists in catalogs. The data placed into the catalog comes from a data source of products. You can use an existing list or you can create the list when you create the catalog pages.

To begin a catalog merge into the current publication, select the Insert tab and then select Catalog Pages. A catalog merge area (in the form of a text box) will appear on a new blank page in the publication. In the Page pane, the new page will appear as a stack of pages because Publisher considers it a catalog. You will also find that the catalog tools become available on the Ribbon. These commands will actually walk you through the process if you start on the left (with the Start group) and then take advantage of the subsequent commands as they become active on the Ribbon.

 tip

To specify pictures for the product list, you need to type the picture filename in the Picture field including the file extension for the picture (such as .jpg, .png, and so on). You also need to specify the folder that will hold the picture files, but that happens later in the process.

You can size or move the catalog merge area as needed on the blank publication page. Remember that it will contain the fields that specify what information to merge into the catalog pages using the information in the data source. You cannot insert tables or other objects in the catalog merge area. You can specify the number of entries that will appear on each catalog page, but not until you get a little further along in the merge process.

The next step in the process is to specify a product list for the merge. This will serve as the data source. Select the Add List command. You can type a new list or use an existing list. Again, let's assume that you need a new list. Select Type New List. The New Product List dialog box will open as shown in Figure 29.14.

Figure 29.14
The New Product List dialog box.

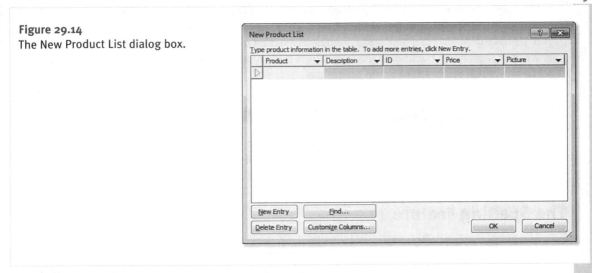

Enter the field information into each of the fields for your first product. Repeat as needed to build your product list. If you want to add additional fields to the product information, select the Customize Columns button. The Customize Product List dialog box will open. You can add fields, rename fields, or delete fields as needed. When you click OK, you return to the New Product List dialog box.

When you have completed your data entry, click OK. The Save Address List dialog box will open. Specify a name and location for the list and click Save. Publisher will save the file and the Catalog Merge Product List will open. You can deselect records that you do not want to include in the merge by deselecting the check box for that item. Then click OK to close the dialog box.

After you have specified the data source for the catalog merge (or created it), you will find that many of the catalog tools become active on the Ribbon. You can use the various layout commands, such as the Layout gallery, to specify how you want the catalog entries to appear on the page, including the number of entries per page. You can also use the Rows and Columns command to manually set the number of columns and rows in the catalog merge area if you do not like any of the presets in the Layout gallery.

When you have a layout selected, you can insert the merge field codes into the catalog merge area. When you select the layout, Publisher inserts placeholder text into the catalog merge area; you can replace this text with merge fields. Select the appropriate placeholder text and then use the Text Field command to enter the field name. Repeat this process as necessary to add all the field codes to the catalog merge area.

You will find that if you included a picture field in the product list, a picture placeholder will appear in the catalog merge area. Click the picture placeholder. The Insert Picture Field dialog box will open. Select the Picture field and then click the Specify Folders button. You can specify the folder that holds your pictures by using the Add button. This will open the Browse dialog box; use it to specify the folder that contains the pictures (such as the My Pictures folder), and then click OK.

We are almost finished; you can use the Preview Results command to preview the results of the merge. When you are satisfied with the results, use the Merge to New or Add to Existing commands to merge the catalog to a new publication or an existing publication document as needed. I suggest you merge to a new publication. After you are sure that the catalog data has merged correctly into the new publication, you can print the results.

Fine-Tuning Your Publications

After you spend a lot of time designing a publication, you will want to print a hard copy of the final product. But first you will want to make sure to correct all the errors in the publication and to check the overall design. Publisher offers several tools that enable you to fine-tune your publication.

The Spelling Feature

The Spelling feature checks your documents for misspellings and typos. It is available in the Proofing group of the Ribbon's Review tab. The Proofing group also provides access to the Research task pane and the Thesaurus, which you can use as resources for finalizing text in your publication.

You can set spelling options for Publisher in the Publisher Options window. Select File to open the Backstage and then select Options. Select Proofing to select (or deselect) settings related to spelling, such as Flag Repeated Words and Ignore Words That Contain Numbers.

Hyphenation

Another element of fine-tuning a publication is determining where words hyphenate in your text boxes. You can have Publisher automatically hyphenate the text in your text frames, which means it determines where to break words with a hyphen and continue the remaining portion of the word on the next line. Because Publisher enables automatic hyphenation by default, it places hyphens only as needed. The great thing about the feature is that if you edit the text, Publisher automatically removes unnecessary hyphens and places new hyphens as needed.

You can also specify the hyphenation zone for new text boxes in the Publisher Options window. Select Advanced and the hyphenation-related settings display in the Editing Options area. By default, Publisher automatically hyphenates text. You can set the hyphenation zone as needed.

You can manually hyphenate text in a text box by selecting the Hyphenation command in the Text group of the text box tools. When you select Hyphenation, the Hyphenation text box appears. You can clear the Automatically Hyphenate This Story check box and then change the hyphenation zone. To manually hyphenate the story, click Manual.

Design Checker

The Design Checker is another great tool for helping you fine-tune your publication. The Design Checker actually looks at the design elements and objects in your publication and helps you find empty frames, improperly proportioned pictures, font problems (such as too many fonts), and other design problems. The Design Checker also offers you help when it identifies a potential design problem.

To run the Design Checker on the current publication, select File to access the Backstage. Select Info. In the Info window, select the Run Design Checker button. The Design Checker will review your publication. When it is finished, you return to the Publisher workspace. The Design Checker task pane will appear on the right side of the workspace as shown in Figure 29.15.

Figure 29.15
The Design Checker task pane.

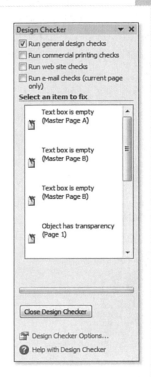

By default the Design Checker runs a general design check. Any problems unearthed by the Design Checker display in the Select an Item to Fix list. The Design Checker will flag problems on publication pages as well as master pages associated with the publication. You can quickly go to a flagged item in the publication by selecting the item in the list. As soon as you fix the problem, such as placing text in an empty text box or deleting the empty text box, Publisher removes the item from the Design Checker list.

If you want to run additional tests, such as check for commercial printing of the publication, select the appropriate check boxes in the Design Checker task pane. When you select one of the additional test possibilities, the Design Checker will immediately begin inspecting the publication. Be advised that the commercial printing check will take a while.

If you want to fine-tune the type of problems that the Design Checker flags, you can open the Design Checker Options dialog box; click the Design Checker Options link in the task pane. The Design Checker Options dialog has two tabs: General and Checks. The General tab enables you to specify the display options for the list of problems and the page range to examine when you run the Design Checker (you can select all pages or the current page).

The Checks tab lists the actual items that the Design Checker uses when it checks the publication. It looks for problems such as Picture Is Missing, Object Is Overlapping Text, and Text Is Too Big to Fit in the Frame. You can clear any of the check boxes if necessary. The Design Checker will no longer flag items that meet that particular condition as items to fix. When you have finished with the Design Checker Options dialog box, click OK. You can close the Design Checker task pane by clicking its Close button.

REQUISITE ONENOTE: ESSENTIAL FEATURES

Keeping information organized can be a constant battle. Contact information can end up on a scrap of paper or a sticky note stuck on your monitor. Notes for a presentation or project might end up buried in a pile of papers on your desk.

Microsoft OneNote 2010 provides a place for your ideas, notes, and other important information that is easy to access and easy to use. Each OneNote notebook can contain a variety of information including your notes, digital pictures, screen clips from other applications, and even drawings that you create using the tools provided on the OneNote Ribbon's Draw tab. You can even keep track of important files created in the other Office applications that play a part in a project or presentation; all the information can be part of a OneNote notebook.

In this chapter we look at how to navigate the OneNote application workspace. We also discuss the basics of creating OneNote notebooks and how to add sections and pages to them. We also examine how to add tables, notes, and tag notes to a notebook page. This chapter also covers sharing notebooks and syncing notebooks accessed by multiple users.

Introducing OneNote 2010

OneNote 2010 provides you with digital notebooks that can keep your projects organized whether you are using OneNote at work or at home. For example, at work you might be working on an important presentation to a group of investors; OneNote enables you to organize your thoughts, important project files, and digital content such as pictures, audio, and video; any information related to your presentation can be contained in or linked to a OneNote notebook that is specific to the presentation.

At home you might be planning a graduation party or adding an addition to your home. OneNote can keep track of lists of party supplies and guests or information on building subcontractors and scanned images of building plans. So, bottom line: Use OneNote any time you need to keep a lot of information organized, and a OneNote notebook can contain or reference just about any type of information that you need.

> **🔍 note**
>
> OneNote can be particularly useful on a tablet PC where you can write directly on OneNote pages and use the Draw tab commands to create your own drawings. You can also convert OneNote "ink" to text and convert handwritten math equations to text.

New Features in OneNote 2010

OneNote 2010 incorporates a number of changes and improvements added to this information organizer since the OneNote 2007 release. One of the most noticeable changes is the OneNote 2010 application window is consistent with the other Office 2010 applications in using the Microsoft Office Fluent Interface that uses the Ribbon as the command center for the application. Some of the other changes you will find in OneNote 2010 are as follows:

- **More Possibilities for Sharing Notebooks:** OneNote notebooks could always be shared on a shared network folder or on a share in a home or small office workgroup. OneNote 2010 enables you to share notebooks on the Windows Live SkyDrive and Microsoft SharePoint sites. In addition, new users can now edit shared notebooks simultaneously.

- **Retrieve Deleted Items from the Notebook Recycle Bin:** Each notebook has its own recycle bin, which stores deleted notebook sections and pages for 60 days. You can easily retrieve items from the recycle bin, which is very useful when you are sharing a notebook with others and decide to place something back into the notebook that another user has deleted.

- **New OneNote File Format Allows New Features:** The OneNote 2010 file format not only allows for notebook sharing on the Web, but it also enables you to insert mathematical equations, take advantage of linked note taking (when using other applications), and access different versions of the same notebook using the versioning feature.

You will also find other improvements and changes in OneNote 2010 (if you were a OneNote 2007 user). In terms of text formatting, OneNote 2010 provides you with quick styles and makes available more formatting options for numbered and bulleted lists. Many of the new features in OneNote relate to the sharing of notebooks with other users. When you share a notebook, new content added will be highlighted automatically and the versioning support enables you to view who changed items in a notebook and when.

Although it is not actually an improvement to the OneNote 2010 application, Microsoft also now provides a OneNote web app. You can use the OneNote web app to access your notebooks stored on the Windows Live SkyDrive or a SharePoint site directly in your web browser.

How OneNote Notebooks Are Organized

OneNote notebooks are actually a lot like outlines; they provide a hierarchy that enables you to organize information at different levels. As you drill down through each level in a OneNote notebook, you are able to access information that is more specific. In OneNote you are using different containers to define the hierarchical levels, with the top-level container being the notebook. The following list describes each of the different types of OneNote "information containers":

- **Notebook:** This is the container file for OneNote. The notebook will contain all the sections, pages, and information that you place on the pages.

- **Section Group:** A group enables you to place associated sections together. This is particularly useful when a notebook contains many sections. Section groups are optional.

- **Section:** A tabbed divider that enables you to group pages related to a particular topic or project phase. Each section provides delineation in the notebook and serves as the main topical level in the notebook's hierarchy.

- **Page:** You place your notes and other items on the notebook pages. The Page Tabs pane lists pages in a selected section.

- **Subpage:** Subpages enable you to break up information normally placed on a single page. The subpage serves as the lowest level in the notebook's structure. Subpages are listed below the page that they are associated with in the Page Tabs pane.

It really makes sense to think of a OneNote notebook in the same way you would a three-ring binder. The different sections in a OneNote notebook would be synonymous with the colored tabs you place in a regular binder. Each binder tab (or section in OneNote) would serve to organize pages of information into logical groupings. You would then place individual pieces of information on the pages. In cases where you need a way to manage a notebook that contains a lot of sections, you can add another level of organization to the notebook by creating section groups and placing related sections in a particular group.

Although you can think of a OneNote notebook as the same thing as a physical three-ring binder, after you start working with OneNote and experience how easy it is to organize information and quickly insert all sorts of text and digital content onto a notebook's pages, you might rethink ever using a three-ring binder again.

Navigating the OneNote Workspace

When you open OneNote 2010 for the first time (select Start, All Programs, Microsoft Office, and then Microsoft OneNote 2010), you will be asked if you want to save your notebooks on your computer or sync with the Web. If you have a Windows Live ID (such as a Hotmail email account), you can actually save your notebooks to the Microsoft SkyDrive. This will allow you to access your notebooks from any computer using the OneNote Web app.

After you get through the screens related to saving your notebooks locally or on the Web, you will find that the OneNote workspace already contains a Personal notebook. This notebook provides a General tab and an Unfiled Notes tab. The Personal notebook provides an overview of OneNote, and the General

> ⚕ **tip**
>
> To actually delete a notebook after closing it, use the Windows Explorer to navigate to your Libraries\Documents\OneNote Notebooks folder. Select the notebook and press the Delete key to remove it from your computer.

section includes several pages related to working in OneNote and a list of new features found in OneNote 2010. If you find this default notebook distracting, you can close it: Right-click on the notebook and then select Close This Notebook. That will remove the notebook from the navigation bar. It does not delete the notebook, however. You can reopen it at any time via the OneNote Backstage.

The OneNote application workspace is unique in terms of the specific tools provided, such as the Sections tabs and the navigation bar, but it is still similar to the other Office 2010 applications and provides the same overall geography that you would find in another Office application such as Outlook or Word. At the top of the application window (on the left) is the Quick Access Toolbar. Just below the Quick Access Toolbar is the Ribbon, which is actually hidden by default in OneNote so that you can see the sections in the currently selected notebook. Figure 30.1 shows the OneNote application window.

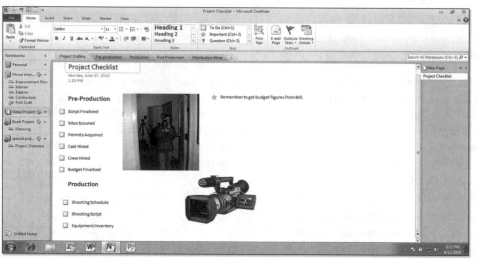

Figure 30.1
The OneNote workspace.

To access the Ribbon commands, click any of the Ribbon tab names such as Home or Insert. The Ribbon will appear and you can then use any of the commands available on that tab. As soon as you click on the current page in the selected section or move to a different page or subpage using the Page Tabs pane (on the right of the application window), the Ribbon will be hidden again. Directly below the Ribbon is a list of the sections in the currently selected notebook.

The OneNote Ribbon

The OneNote Ribbon provides seven different tabs; each tab contains a number of different command groups. The OneNote Ribbon tabs are as follows:

- **File:** This tab provides access to the OneNote Backstage. The Backstage provides access to information on your notebooks and enables you to access sharing settings for the current workbook. The Backstage also provides access to the Save As dialog box and the Print window and enables you to access configuration options for OneNote.

- **Home:** This tab provides the Clipboard group and three groups designed for working with the text on your notebook pages. The Basic Text and Styles groups provide you with the ability to change text formatting attributes and assign styles to text, respectively. The Tags group enables you to assign tags to page notes and provides a tool for locating tags in notebooks. The Outlook groups provide commands that enable you to interact with Microsoft Outlook. You can email a notebook page in an Outlook email as well as insert Outlook tasks directly onto your notebook pages. Meeting details from Outlook can also be inserted onto a page and include the meeting subject, date, and attendee information. You can add additional notes to the inserted meeting note box.

- **Insert:** This tab provides you with the ability to insert different objects onto a page such as tables, pictures, and links. It also enables you to use to insert printouts of files or scanned items from your scanner. The Insert tab also provides commands for recording audio and video directly onto a page and adding time stamps, equations, and symbols.

- **Share:** This tab provides commands for emailing notebook pages and marking unread pages (in a shared notebook) as read. The Shared Notebook group enables you to create a new shared notebook and change the share settings for the current notebook. You can also view recent edits and find information by author. The History group enables you to view different versions of notebook pages and to open the notebook's recycle bin.

- **Draw:** This tab provides you with tools and shapes for creating your own drawings on your notebook pages. It also provides commands for highlighting information on a page and arranging multiple objects that you have stacked or overlapped.

- **Review:** This tab provides access to the Spelling and Research features and the Language group, which provides the Translate and Language commands. The Linked Notes command on this tab enables you to take linked notes in a docked window. The note you create actually links to the information you are looking at, such as a PowerPoint presentation or a particular Web page.

- **View:** This tab provides access to the different OneNote views, such as Normal View and Full Page View, and enables you to change page setup parameters such as the page color. The Rule Lines command enables you to place horizontal or grid lines on a page. The View tab also provides the various zoom commands, and enables you to open a new OneNote window or a new docked window for taking notes as you work in other applications.

OneNote is a little different from the other Office 2010 applications in that it doesn't provide quite the level of redundancy you find in Word or Excel in terms of having a number of different ways to access a particular command or feature. In fact, there are commands that you can access via other areas of the OneNote workspace or via shortcut menus that aren't even available on the Ribbon. For example, you insert a new section using the Create a New Section command, which is just to the right of the last section in the notebook. You add pages by clicking the New Page command in the Page Tabs task pane.

Shortcut menus also provide some commands that you won't find anywhere else. For example, when you right-click on a section tab, you will find commands specific to sections, such as the Merge into Another Section command and the Password Protect This Section command. Although the two commands noted are for somewhat more advanced manipulations of a section, even the Section Color command is available only on the shortcut menu and is not included on the Ribbon.

The OneNote Navigation Bar

Your notebooks will be listed in the navigation bar on the left of the OneNote window. The navigation bar is collapsed by default and so shows only the icon and name of the available notebooks. You can expand the navigation bar by selecting the Expand Navigation Bar arrow at the top of the navigation bar. When you expand the navigation bar, you will still see the notebook names and a list of all the sections in each notebook. This makes it extremely easy to jump from section to section in the current notebook or to another section in a different notebook with a single click.

You can collapse or expand the section lists below each notebook name as needed. You can also switch notebooks by using the navigation bar. This might make you cringe a little bit because you probably have an urge to save changes you have made to the current notebook before switching to another notebook; there is no need to worry. OneNote automatically saves additions and changes that you make to your notebooks.

Creating a Notebook

You can create a new notebook for any project, plan, or other endeavor. It makes sense to create a new workbook for each of the different projects or major tasks you want to undertake, whether you are using OneNote at work or at home. For example, having one notebook named Work is probably only going to get you a big mishmash of information stored together with no obvious relationship even though you can use sections to divide an even poorly conceived notebook (for more about modifying a notebook, see "Modifying a Notebook" later in this chapter).

> ### tip
>
> If you end up with pages in a notebook that really belong in a new or different notebook, it is easy to copy or move notebook pages as needed.

Try to plan ahead in terms of what should go in a particular notebook and what should not; you really should think of the notebook as a container for just the information related to one thing or project. There is certainly no penalty for having a lot of very specific OneNote notebooks. For example, you could have a notebook related to every report or project assigned to you. Your notebooks should not become like that miscellaneous drawer you have in your filing cabinet that contains everything from old reports and project files to loose paperclips and rubber bands to a dirty coffee mug and spoon.

You create new notebooks in OneNote via the Backstage. Select File on the Ribbon and then New. The New Notebook window appears in the Backstage as shown in Figure 30.2.

You are actually provided with different options for where the new notebook will be stored. You can use the Web option to store the new notebook on the Web via Windows Live SkyDrive. This enables you access to the notebook from any computer with an Internet connection. You can access it using the OneNote web app when you are working on a computer that does not have OneNote installed.

 For information on using SkyDrive and the OneNote web app, see page 127 in Chapter 5, "Working with the Office Web Apps."

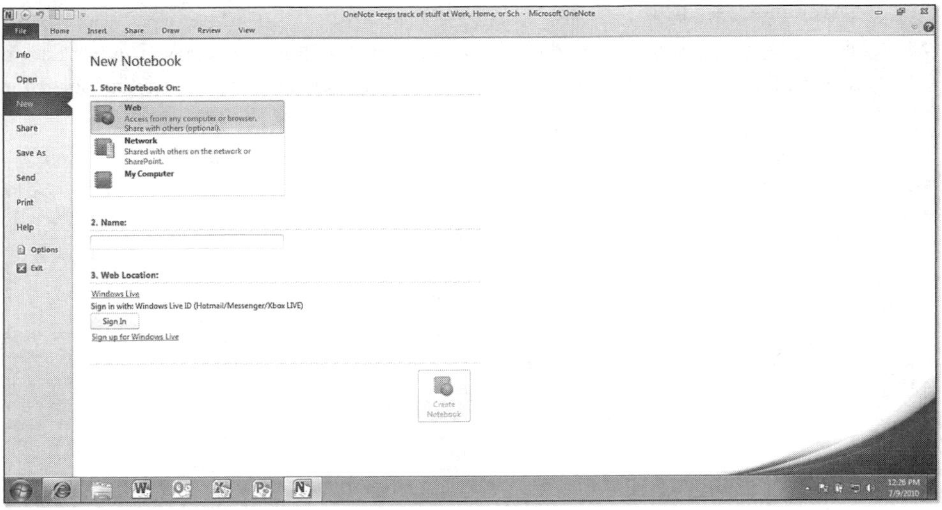

**Figure 30.2
The Backstage
New Notebook
window.**

You can also choose to save the notebook on your local network or on a SharePoint site by using the Network option. Storing the file on the SharePoint site will also provide you with access to the OneNote web app when you require it. Notebooks can also be saved to your computer. Even notebooks saved to your computer can be easily shared on the Web or your network after the fact.

Select one of the storage options: Web, Network, or My Computer. Each option requires that you provide a name for the notebook. The Web option will also require you to log on to Windows Live. The Network option enables you to browse for a network folder or specify the address for a SharePoint site. In the case of the My Computer option, the \Users*username*\Documents\OneNote Notebooks path is the default location for new notebooks stored on your computer. You can use this default location or specify another location by using the Browse button.

After you have specified the platform (Web, Network, or My Computer), the name, and the location for the notebook, click the Create Notebook button. The new notebook will open in the OneNote workspace. The icon for the notebook will also be available in the navigation bar.

Modifying a Notebook

When you create a new workbook it will contain a single section (New Section 1), which contains a single untitled page. Although a lot of white space is staring you in the face at the outset, it is not that difficult to immediately begin building an organizational structure in your notebook using sections. You can then create pages in the sections and actually insert the notes and other information that will make up the content of the notebook. We discuss working with sections and pages later in this chapter.

You can make some modifications to the notebook itself. You can change the Share settings for a notebook and share the notebook on the Web or your network (including SharePoint sites). You can also modify the display name for the notebook, change the notebook's icon color, and convert a

OneNote 2010 notebook to a 2007 notebook so that co-workers or colleagues who are using OneNote 2007 can access it.

To access these notebook options, select File on the Ribbon to access the Backstage. When you select Info in the Backstage, the Notebook Information window appears as shown in Figure 30.3.

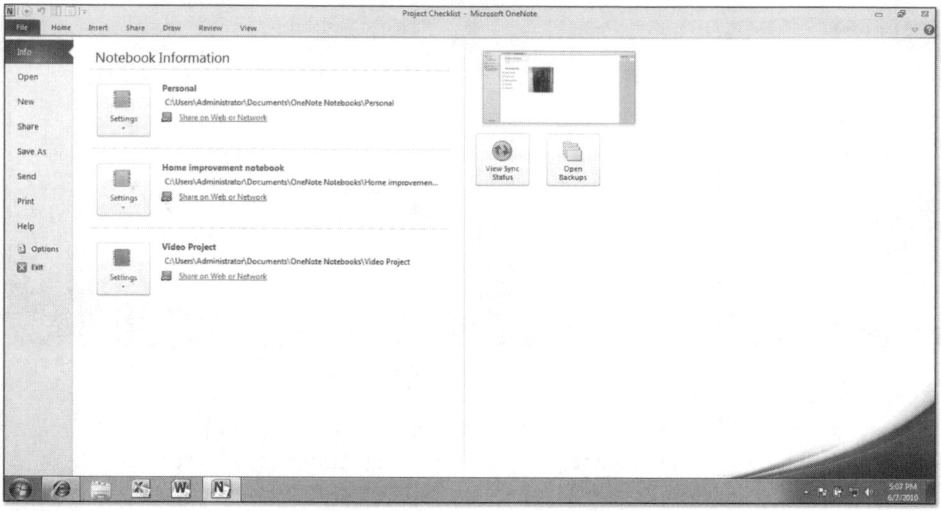

Figure 30.3
The Backstage
Notebook
Information
window.

The Notebook Information window provides a list of notebooks that are currently available on the taskbar. Each notebook will have a Settings button that you use to access the share settings for the notebook and other notebook properties.

Sharing a Notebook

You can share a notebook to the Web (SkyDrive) or on your network. The Network option can include share folders on your local area network or a SharePoint site. If you initially saved a new document to a Web or network location, that notebook is already shared and so you do not have to go through the steps to initiate the sharing process.

To share a specific notebook, select the notebook's Settings button and then select Share, or you can click the Share on Web or Network link under the project name. The Share Notebook window will open. If you want to share the notebook on SkyDrive, select the Web icon in the Share On area of the window and then provide your SkyDrive credentials. You can then specify the folder that will be used as the destination for the shared notebook.

> **note**
>
> Specifying the share location information in the Share Notebook window is very similar to specifying the initial storage location for a new OneNote notebook in the New Notebook window. If you specified a web or network location for the notebook when you first created it, the notebook is already shared.

If you want to share the notebook on your local area network, you can specify a network path in the Network Location box or choose from a list of recent locations. If you are sharing the notebook on a SharePoint site, provide the URL for your SharePoint site and then click Browse. (If this is the first time you have accessed the SharePoint site, you might have to select a valid digital certificate on your computer that validates you as a trusted user.) Enter your logon credentials for the site in the Windows Security window and then click OK. You will be provided with the workspace provided by the SharePoint site and you can save the notebook to that space. Figure 30.4 shows the Share Notebook window. A local network share path has been entered in the Network Location box.

Figure 30.4
The Backstage Share Notebook window.

After you have specified the location for the shared notebook, select the Share Notebook button. A Microsoft OneNote message box will open, letting you know that the notebook is now accessible to anyone who has permissions to the network location that you specified in the Network Location box. The message box also provides you with the ability to email other users and provide them with a link to the shared notebook.

When you select E-mail a Link in the message box, a new Outlook email message window opens. The message serves as an invitation to the OneNote notebook and provides a link to the notebook on the network. Use your Outlook Contacts list or other address book to provide the destination email address in the To box. When you are ready to send the email, click Send.

> **tip**
> You can send email invitations to shared notebooks even after sharing it. Select Share in the Backstage and then select the E-mail Others About the Notebook link.

After you have shared the notebook on the Web or on your network, you can invite other people to access the notebook. In the Notebook Information window (select Info in the Backstage), select the Invite People to This Notebook link under the shared notebook's name. This will take you to the Share Notebook window. Select the E-Mail Others About the Notebook link to send an invitation and link to the notebook.

Viewing the Sync Status

After you have shared a notebook, that notebook will be synchronized with a cached copy of the notebook. You set the synchronization settings for a shared notebook so that the sync occurs automatically or occurs only when you manually sync the notebook.

To view the sync status for the workbook you currently have open in OneNote, select File and then Info. A preview of the currently active notebook page is provided—select the View Synch Status button. The Shared Notebook Synchronization dialog box will appear as shown in Figure 30.5.

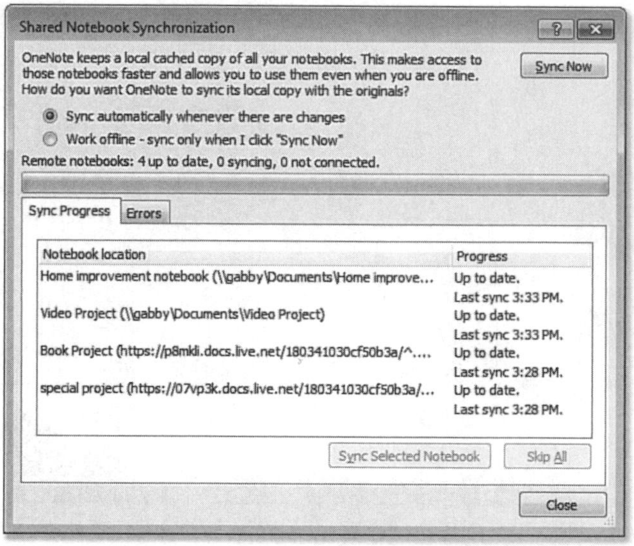

Figure 30.5
The Shared Notebook Synchronization dialog box.

The Shared Notebook Synchronization dialog box provides you with the sync progress for the notebook as well as its location. If there have been errors during synchronization, you can view them by selecting the Errors tab.

By default the sync option is set to Sync automatically whenever there are changes. If you want to work offline or sync the notebook only at certain times, select the Work Offline – Sync Only When I Click "Sync Now" option button. If you select this option, you will have to access the Shared Notebook Synchronization dialog box whenever you want to sync the shared notebook via the Sync Now command. When you are ready to exit the Shared Notebook Synchronization dialog box, select Close. You will be returned to the active notebook in the OneNote workspace.

> **tip**
>
> You can access the Share Notebook Synchronization dialog box for a shared notebook via the expanded navigation bar. To open the dialog box, click the sync status icon for a specific notebook.

Changing Other Notebook Properties

You can also modify other notebook properties. You can change the display name for the notebook, the color of the notebook (the color used in the Navigation Pane for the notebook's icon), the location of the notebook, and even the file format.

To access the Notebook Properties dialog box for a notebook, select File to access the Backstage and then click Info. The Notebook Information window provides a list of all your current notebooks. Select the Settings button for a specific notebook and then select Properties. The Notebook Properties dialog box will appear as shown in Figure 30.6.

Figure 30.6
The Notebook Properties dialog box.

You can edit the display name as needed. This does not change the notebook folder name created when you originally created the notebook. This is a necessity of shared notebooks because a change in the name of the actual notebook folder would change the path for the shared notebook.

You can also use the change color drop-down box of the notebook icon that represents the notebook in the navigation pane. Select the Color drop-down box and select a new color. The Color palette provided contains 16 different notebook color possibilities.

You can also choose a new sync location for a notebook. This is particularly useful for notebooks shared on a local area network. When you select the Change Location button, the Choose a Sync Location for This Remote Notebook dialog box opens. You can use it to browse your network to find a specific share or network folder that will serve as the new location.

Because a local cache keeps track of changes that you make to a shared notebook and syncs them with the remote notebook folder (as it does for other users who access to the notebook), you can change the location of a shared notebook. However, it probably makes more sense to establish the permanent path for the notebook when you first create it. This is particularly true for notebooks that you are sharing via Microsoft's SkyDrive service.

The Notebook Properties dialog box also provides you with the ability to convert a notebook to a different format. The default format for OneNote 2010 notebooks is the 2010 format. OneNote was also a member of the Office 2007 application suite, so you might need to share notebooks with users who are still working with OneNote 2007.

If the notebook is in the 2010 format, you can change it to the 2007 format using the Convert to 2007 button. Doing so will negate your use of some of the OneNote 2010 features, however.

If you have notebooks that you created in OneNote 2007, you can also convert them to the 2010 format, which enables you to take advantage of all the features provided in OneNote 2010 such as linked notes, math equations, and notebook history. You would accomplish this by selecting the Convert to 2010 button.

 tip

If you find that converting a notebook's format has caused problems for other users (or yourself), you can always convert the notebook back to its original format via the Notebook Properties dialog box.

In either case, a Convert dialog box opens and provides a warning related to the type of conversion that you are making. If you want to continue, click OK and OneNote will convert the notebook.

Remember that if you convert a shared OneNote 2007 notebook to the 2010 format, it will be problematic for users of earlier OneNote versions. Also, if you convert a 2010 notebook to the 2007 format, users of OneNote 2010 (including yourself) will lose some functionality. Change the format of a notebook only if there is a compelling reason to do so.

Working with Sections

Sections provide you with important organizational containers for your notebooks. Sections are not unlike the file folders that you use in a file cabinet drawer; sections provide you with the ability to group related pages for easy access and are designed to help you keep like information together.

In cases where you end up with a lot of sections in a notebook, you might decide that you need to collate related sections into a higher-level storage container. You can create a section group or groups and then move associated sections into the appropriate group. This creates a structure in the notebook where the section group is akin to a hanging file folder and the section becomes the manila file folders that you use to divide information in each hanging file folder. You certainly are not required to use section groups, particularly in cases where a notebook contains only a few sections. Section groups, however, are available if needed to increase the notebook's overall organization.

Creating or Deleting a Section

You can quickly add a new section to the current notebook. Select the Create a New Section tab to the right of any existing sections. A new section will be added to the notebook. The new section will contain a new untitled page as shown in Figure 30.7.

To name the section, double-click the New Section 1 placeholder text on the section's tab. Type the name for the section. You can add additional sections to the notebook as they are needed.

If you end up with a section that you don't need, you can quickly remove it. Right-click on the section's tab and then select Delete. A message box will open asking you if you want to move the section to the notebook's recycle bin; click Yes to confirm the deletion. Deleted sections and pages are actually stored in the notebook's recycle bin for 60 days and can be restored to a notebook if needed; we discuss the recycle bin later in this chapter.

Figure 30.7
A new section containing an untitled page.

Modifying Sections

There are modifications that you can make to a section. You can change its name and the color of its tab. You can also move or copy a section within a notebook or to another notebook. You can password protect a section and merge a section into another section to combine two sections.

To change the name of a section, double-click the current name on a section's tab and then type a new name. To change the color of the section's tab, right-click on the section and then point at Section Color on the shortcut menu. A color palette will open; select a new color on the palette.

Copy, Move, or Merge Sections

You can quickly rearrange the sections in a notebook. Drag a section to a new location in the notebook by grabbing its tab with the mouse. You can also drag a section from one notebook to another notebook. This will move the section—this action cannot be reversed using the Undo command on the Quick Access Toolbar. Drag a section from the current notebook into one of the other notebooks listed on the navigation pane.

You can also move or copy a section in the current workbook by using the Move or Copy Section dialog box. Using the Move or Copy Section dialog box enables you to specify the position that the moved or copied section should take in relation to the other sections that already exist in the destination notebook to which the section will be moved or copied.

Right-click on a section's tab and then select Move or Copy. The Move or Copy Section dialog box will appear as shown in Figure 30.8.

> **tip**
> You can also rearrange sections in a notebook or move sections between notebooks using the expanded navigation pane.

Figure 30.8
The Move or Copy Section dialog box.

You can expand any of the projects listed in the All Notebooks list to view the sections in a particular project. Select the section in a project to which you would like to move or copy the current section. The current section will be copied or moved to a position after the selected section. After you have provided the positioning for the moved or copied section, select the Move or Copy button at the bottom of the dialog box. The section will be moved or copied, depending on your choice in the dialog box.

Password Protect a Section

If you have a section in a notebook that contains private or proprietary information and you share the notebook online or on your network, you might want to password protect that section. When you password protect a section only users who have the password can access that section.

To password protect the current section, right-click on the section's tab and select Password Protect This Section on the shortcut menu. The Password Protection pane will appear on the right side of the OneNote window as shown in Figure 30.9.

Click the Set Password button and the Password Protection dialog box will open. Enter the password for the section and then confirm the password. Click OK to set the password for the section.

Password protect only those sections that truly contain highly sensitive information. If you forget the password, OneNote does not have any method of recovering the password. So, use the password protection feature only for sections when it is absolutely necessary.

After you have set the password for the section, you can lock the section and any other sections that you have password protected. Click the Lock All button in the Password Protection pane.

Figure 30.9
The Password Protection pane.

When any user attempts to access the password protected section, a message will appear on the section to let the user know that it is locked. Click on the section or press Enter to access the Protected Section dialog box. Provide the password for the section and then click OK.

If you decide that the section doesn't actually need to be password protected, right-click on the section's tab and select Password Protect This Section on the shortcut menu. You can use the Remove Password button to remove the protection from the section. Enter the password in the Remove Password dialog box and then click OK.

Merging a Section

You can merge a section in a notebook into another section. This enables you to do away with a redundant section and combine the pages in that section with those of another section. You can merge the current section into a section in the current notebook or any of the other notebooks listed in the navigation pane.

The merge feature is actually a way to move all the pages in a section to another section. When you complete the section merge, you are provided with the choice of keeping the section that you merge, which will be emptied of all its pages.

Right-click on the tab of the section you want to merge and then select Merge into Another Section. The Merge Section dialog box will open as shown in Figure 30.10. Expand the notebooks listed as needed to locate the section that will serve as the destination for the merge.

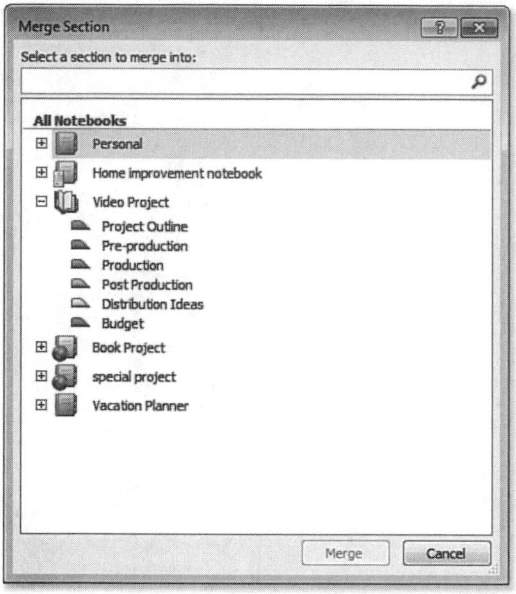

Figure 30.10
The Merge Section dialog box.

Select the destination section for the merge in the current notebook or other notebook, and then select Merge. A OneNote message box will open, asking you if you are sure that you want to merge the sections. The merge cannot be undone after you perform it. Click Merge Sections to complete the merge. A second dialog box will open, allowing you to delete or keep the section that you merged. The only thing that you would be keeping is the empty section because its pages have been moved into the other section you specified.

Creating a Section Group

A section group is actually a higher-level organizational container than a section and can be used to group sections in a notebook. Section groups are useful when you have a large number of sections in a notebook and want to further organize a more complex notebook.

After you create a section group, you can move existing sections into the group or you can create new sections in the section group. To create a new section group, right-click on any of the section tabs in the current notebook and then select New Section Group. The new section group will appear to the right of the section tabs in the notebook (just below the Ribbon). The icon for a section group consists of several section tables. You can type a name for the section group in its name box.

After you create the section group, you can drag sections into the group. A Create New Section tab is also provided in the group to enable you to quickly create new sections within the section group. Figure 30.11 shows a section group and the sections that it contains.

**Figure 30.11
A section
group.**

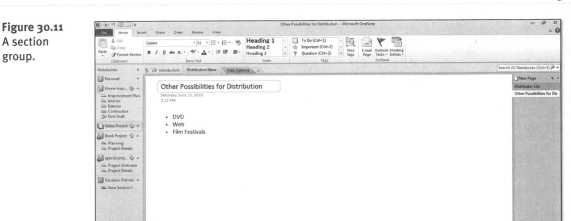

You can also rearrange sections in a group as needed. To close a group and return to the main section tabs in a notebook, select the Navigate to Parent Section Group button to the left of the section name.

Working with Pages

The pages in the various sections of your notebook will actually hold the notebook's content such as notes, pictures, links, and drawings. You can add pages to the current section by selecting New Page in the Page Tabs pane. A new page will appear in the section. Type a title for the page above the page time stamp. The title will also appear on the tab that represents the page in the Page Tabs pane.

You can delete a page if it is no longer needed: Right-click on the page in the Page Tabs pane and then select Delete. You don't get to confirm the deletion; the page is immediately removed. You can use the Undo button to reverse a page deletion. You can also restore pages from the notebook recycle bin if necessary, which is discussed later in this chapter.

Creating Pages Using Templates

You can also create new pages based on templates. OneNote provides a number of different page templates. There are different academic page templates for lecture notes and business page templates for meeting notes. There are also decorative and planner page templates; the planner templates make it easy to create a new page containing a ready-made simple or prioritized to-do list.

To create a new page based on a template, select the New Page drop-down arrow in the Page Tabs pane and then select Page Templates. The Templates pane will appear on the far right of the OneNote workspace as shown in Figure 30.12.

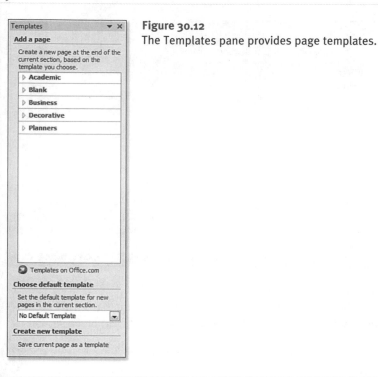

Figure 30.12
The Templates pane provides page templates.

Expand one of the template categories, such as Academic, Business, or Decorative. Select the template that you want to use to create the new page. The new page will appear in the Page Tabs pane. You can edit the title of the new page to fit your needs. You can also add additional pages based on other templates. When you have finished working with the Templates pane, click its Close button.

> **tip**
>
> You can promote a subpage to a "regular" page. Right-click on the subpage in the Page Tabs pane and select Promote Subpage.

You will find that the page templates can help you quickly put together a page that will hold information of a particular type. For instance, the meeting note templates (such as the Detailed Meeting Notes template) set up the new page with different headings, such as Meeting Details, Attendees, and Summary. All you have to do is provide the specific information for the meeting under the appropriate note heading on the page.

Creating Subpages

You can also create subpages in a OneNote notebook. A subpage is subordinate to an existing page in a notebook section. Not unlike subordinate items in an outline, a main page can have several subpages. The whole point of the subpage is to add another level to the organizational structure of the notebook. For example, you might have a meeting page that has subpages that provide details of each meeting listed on the meeting page. A subpage appears as its own separate page when you select it in the Page Tabs pane, but it will be listed under the page to which it is subordinate.

To create a new subpage for a page, select the page in the Page Tabs pane. Select the New Page drop-down arrow and then select New Subpage. The new subpage will appear under the currently selected page. As with any new page, you can type the page name in the header area of the page above the time stamp.

You can collapse or expand the subpages for a particular page. A collapse/expand button will be available to the right of a page that has subordinate subpages in the Page Tabs pane. Subpages can be rearranged, if necessary, by dragging a particular subpage to a new position under the main page in the Page Tabs pane.

Restoring Sections and Pages from the Notebook Recycle Bin

If you inadvertently delete a section or page from a notebook, you can go to the notebook's recycle bin and restore that section or page. As mentioned earlier in the chapter, the recycle bin is a new feature in OneNote 2010. It retains deleted sections and pages for 60 days.

You can undelete a section or page that you have deleted or that has been deleted by another user who has access to a shared notebook. The Notebook Recycle Bin command is on the Ribbon's Share tab in the History group.

When you select the Notebook Recycle Bin command, it actually provides a menu that enables you to access the recycle bin, empty the recycle bin, or disable the history feature for the current notebook. If you disable the history feature, you will neither be able to restore deleted sections or pages nor view different page versions, which are accessed via the Page Versions command.

When you open the recycle bin for the current notebook, you will find that it is arranged as a notebook. Figure 30.13 shows the recycle bin for a notebook.

Figure 30.13
A notebook's recycle bin.

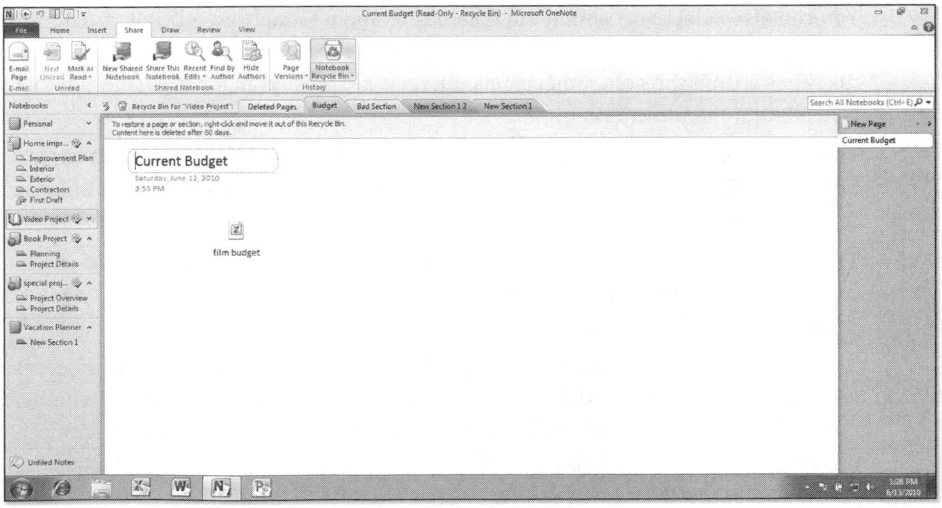

The easiest way to move a section from the recycle bin is to expand a notebook in the navigation pane so that you can see all the sections in that notebook (this can include the current notebook). Then drag the deleted section from the recycle bin to the notebook in the navigation pane.

You can also drag pages from the recycle bin to restore them to a notebook. When viewing the recycle bin, drag a page from the Page Tabs pane to a section that is listed in a project on the navigation pane.

When you have finished working in the notebook's recycle bin, click the Notebook Recycle Bin command to deactivate the recycle bin and return to the current notebook. You can also exit the recycle bin by clicking the Navigate to Parent section group on the right side of the Recycle Bin icon in the sections area at the top of the workspace.

Inserting and Formatting Notes

Notes are the primary informational object on a notebook page. Notes provide you with a container for your thoughts, ideas, lists—any text entry that you need to make. You can click anywhere on a page and quickly insert a note. As you type, the note box will size itself to accommodate the text that you enter. To place blank lines in a note, press the Enter key.

You can move a note on a page as needed; just drag it to a new location. You can also resize notes to any dimensions that you require. If you need to delete a note, select the note and then press the Delete key.

 note

If you are using a tablet PC, you can write your notes directly on a page.

You can format the text in your notes using the commands provided on the Home tab's Basic Text group. This group provides commands for font attributes, such as font size and color, and provides paragraph attributes, such as indents and text alignment. To format all the text in a note, select the note's frame. You can then apply formatting attributes as needed by selecting a specific command or commands.

You can also select text within the note box to apply formatting attributes. This enables you to do such things as place a bold title at the top of the text box or assign different font colors to different text lines within the note. You can clear formatting for text in a note using the Clear Formatting command in the Basic Text group.

The Basic Text group also provides you with the ability to create notes that contain bulleted or numbered lists. Click on a page to place the insertion point and then select the Bullets or Numbering command to create the list.

The Bullets command provides a drop-down arrow that allows you to access the Bullet Library. You can specify the bullet style that you want to use by selecting a particular style in the library. Figure 30.14 shows the Bullet Library.

The Numbering command also provides a Numbering Library, which you can access via the drop-down area on the right of the Numbering command. The library provides a number of different numbering formats that use numeric, alphanumeric, and Roman numerals. You can customize the numbers for a list by selecting the Customize Numbers command in the Numbering Library. This will open the Customize Numbering pane as shown in Figure 30.15.

Figure 30.14
The Bullet Library.

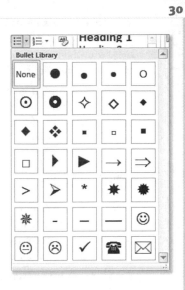

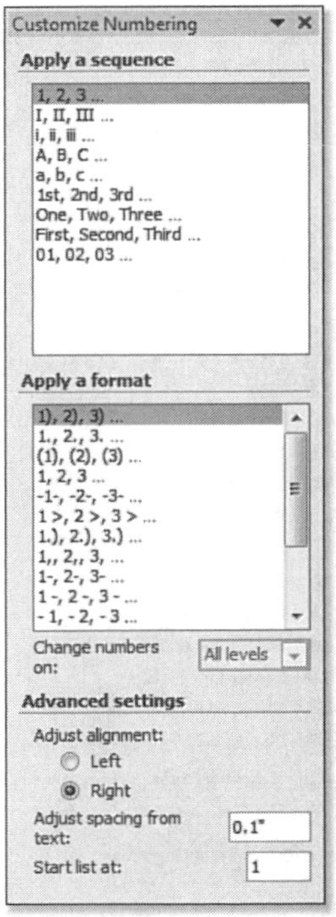

Figure 30.15
The Customize Numbering pane.

You can specify a particular sequence type for the custom list, and you can apply a specific format to the sequence. You can also adjust advanced settings for the numbered list such as the alignment and the spacing of the number from the text. When you have built your list, you can close the Customize Numbering pane by clicking its Close button.

You can also format note text using the Styles gallery. The Styles gallery can be accessed via the Styles group provided on the Ribbon's Home tab. You can apply a style to all the text or to selected text in a note. To view the entire Styles gallery, click the More button on the right of the Styles gallery.

Using Tags

Another way to differentiate the notes on your notebook pages is to use tags. A tag is a way to assign a category to a note. Each tag category also assigns a distinct icon to the note. For example, there is an Important tag, a Question tag, a Contact tag, and all sorts of other tags. You can tag existing notes or you can create a new note by selecting the tag first and then typing the note.

You can access the Tags gallery via the Tags group on the Ribbon's Home tab. Figure 30.16 shows the Tags gallery.

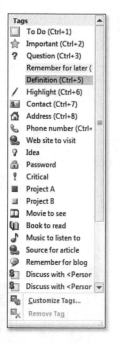

Figure 30.16
The Tags gallery.

Click a tag in the gallery to start a new tagged note or select an existing note and apply a tag to it. You can apply multiple tags to a note. If you want to remove a tag from a note, right-click on the tag and select Remove Tag. The text in the note is not affected.

You can modify existing tags and create new tags in the Customize Tags dialog box. Select Customize Tags in the Tags gallery to open the Customize Tags dialog box. You can reorder the existing tags in the gallery by using the Move Tag Up and the Move Tag Down buttons. To modify an existing tag, select Modify Tag. This opens the Modify Tag dialog box, which enables you to specify the name, symbol, font color, and highlight color for a tag.

Rather than spending a lot of time customizing existing tags, it might make more sense to create your own tags. This enables you to create tags that you use a lot. You can then move your custom tags to the top of the Tags gallery to make them easily accessible.

> 🔍 **note**
>
> Customizing a tag will not affect notes that have been previously tagged with that tag.

To create a custom tag, select the New Tag button in the Customize Tags dialog box. The New Tag dialog box will appear as shown in Figure 30.17.

Figure 30.17
The New Tag dialog box.

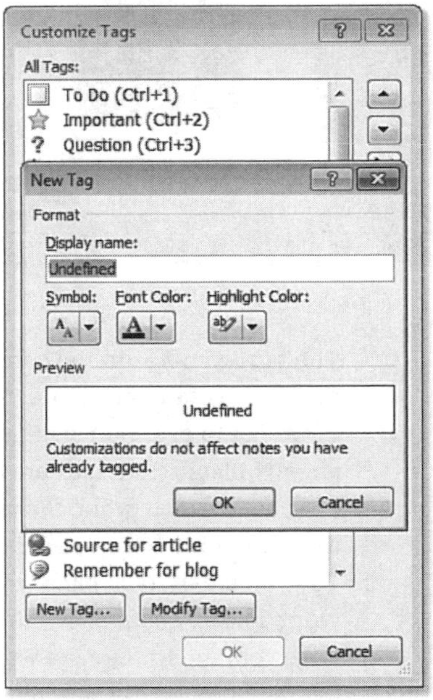

Specify a display name for the tag. You can then specify a symbol for the tag and also specify an optional font color and/or highlight color for the tag. The tag settings that you specify for the new tag will be previewed in the New Tag dialog box. When you have completed creating the new tag, click OK. The tag will be listed in the Customize Tags dialog box. Click OK to return to the OneNote workspace. You will now be able to access your custom tag directly from the Tags gallery.

Finding Tagged Notes

You can use the Tags Summary pane to quickly list the tags that you have used in a notebook or notebooks. This enables you to view tagged notes by the tag type you assigned to a note or notes. It also enables you to use a tagged note listed in the Tags Summary pane to immediately move to the page that contains that particular tagged note.

To open the Tags Summary pane select the Find Tags command in the Tags group on the Ribbon's Home tab. The Tags Summary pane will open as shown in Figure 30.18.

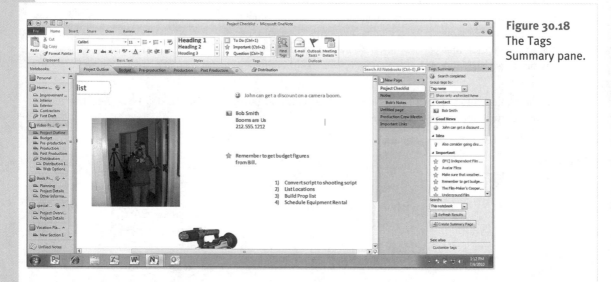

Figure 30.18
The Tags Summary pane.

The tagged notes in the current notebook will be listed and grouped by tag name. You can use the Group tags by drop-down list to change how the tagged notes are grouped. As already mentioned, tags are grouped by tag name by default but you can also group the tagged notes by section, title, date, and note text. You can use the listed tagged notes in the Tags Summary task pane to actually navigate to a particular tagged note; select the note in the Tags Summary pane. The page containing the note will become the active page and the tagged note will be selected.

> **tip**
>
> If you want to create a summary page that lists all the tagged notes in the Tags Summary pane, select the Create Summary Page button. The summary page is added to the current section.

The Tags Summary pane also provides a Search drop-down box at the bottom of the pane. By default the Tags Summary pane only searches for tagged notes in the current notebook. However, you can use the Search drop-down box to search for notes in the current section, section group. You can also search the current notebook or all your notebooks. You can also search for notes by the time frame in which they were inserted. For example, you can search for notes you added today (Today's Notes), or you can use other time-related options such as Yesterday's notes or This Week's notes.

Using Tables to Store Information

Another way to organize text or other objects on a notebook page is to use a table. A table enables you to arrange text and other objects in a tabular format using rows and columns. Each intersection of a row and a column is referred to as a cell. You can type text in a cell, insert a picture into a cell, or place a link in a cell. You can show the borders on the table or you can turn the borders off so that only the contents of the various cells are shown.

When you insert a table onto a notebook page, you are actually creating a note. The table will reside in a note box just like any text note that you place on a page. You can move the table to a different location on the page and, in addition, you can size the frame around the table to change its dimensions. To insert a table follow these steps:

1. Click on the page to place the insertion point where you would like to insert the table.

2. Select the Insert tab on the Ribbon.

3. Click the table command and then use the Insert Table grid to specify the number of rows and columns in the table using the mouse.

4. When you release the mouse, the table is inserted onto the page.

When you are entering text in the table, you can move forward through the table from cell to cell by pressing the Tab key. If you need to move backward from cell to cell, use Shift+Tab.

When the table is selected, the Table Tools Layout tab becomes available on the Ribbon. Figure 30.19 shows the Table Tools Layout tab.

Figure 30.19
The Table Tools Layout tab.

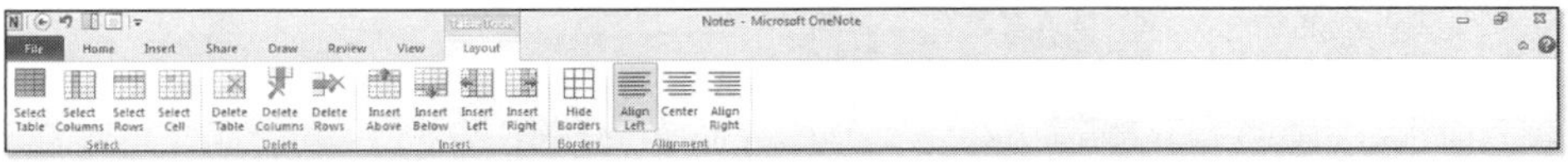

The Table Tools Layout tab provides you with all the commands that you need to modify the table. The Table Tools Layout tab's command groups are as follows:

- **Select:** This group provides commands for selecting the table, columns, rows, or a cell. Selecting the table, columns, rows, or a cell enables you to then apply text -formatting attributes to the selected area of the table using the text-formatting commands on the Home tab. You can also select a column or row by placing the mouse at the top of a column or the left of a row and then clicking when the selection arrow appears. You can also click and drag to select a group of cells.

- **Delete:** This group provides commands for deleting the table or deleting a column or a row. You can also select multiple columns or rows and then delete them.

- **Insert:** This group provides commands that enable you to insert rows or columns into the table. For example, if you click in a row, you can then use the Insert Above command to place a new row above the current row. If you select multiple rows, you can insert that number of rows above or below the selected rows. Single or multiple columns can also be inserted using the Insert Left or Insert Right commands.

- **Borders:** This group provides the Hide Borders command. It removes the borders from the table but not the row and column boundaries that create the cells in the table. Removing the borders enables you to align items in the table and then have them seemingly floating on the page because the table borders cannot be seen.

- **Alignment:** This group provides you with commands for changing the horizontal alignment of text or other objects within a cell or selected cells. These commands are Align Left, Center, and Align Right.

You can apply tags to text in your tables and quick styles to text entries in cells. As already mentioned, you are not limited to text entries in the table's cells. You can also insert pictures, links, file attachments, and other items, such as time stamps and symbols from the Ribbon's Insert tab.

 For information on adding links or file attachments to OneNote pages, check out the information that begins on page 856 in Chapter 32, "Integrating OneNote with Other Office Applications."

WORKING WITH NOTEBOOK PAGES

OneNote notebooks provide a convenient organizational container that can be subdivided using section groups and sections. The actual information that you work with will be located on the notebook pages. OneNote provides you with the ability to easily manage pages in a notebook and copy, move, or delete pages as needed. You can also view different versions of a page, which can be particularly useful in situations where multiple users are contributing to a shared notebook.

In this chapter, we look at managing and configuring pages and discuss the different ways to search for information in a notebook. We also discuss page versions and the possibilities for viewing recent edits and changes on notebook pages. Adding items such as time stamps, pictures, and clip art is also discussed, as is the direct recording of audio and video onto a notebook page.

Managing Pages

Organizing your notebooks is really all about managing the notebook pages, which, after all, contain the actual information in the notebook. Sections might provide structure to the notebook, but the page sequence in a section provides a chronological structure for the information—from beginning to end. Most projects are executed according to a schedule or a logical sequence of steps, and the pages in each section should relate this chronology when viewed.

This means that keeping a notebook in proper shape might require the rearranging of pages. Pages can easily be copied, moved, or deleted. You can copy or move a page or pages within a notebook or between notebooks.

To move a page from one section to another section in the notebook, select the page in the Page Tabs pane and then drag it to any of the section tabs at the top of the current notebook. You can also drag a page from the Page Tabs pane to a section in another notebook. Drag the page to a section in a notebook that is displayed in the expanded navigation pane.

You can also drag pages within a section as needed. Drag a page to a new location in a section via the Page Tabs pane.

 tip

You can rename a page by changing the page name in the page's name area, which is right above the date stamp on the page.

Using the Move Copy Dialog Box

You can also move or copy pages to another section of a notebook or to another current notebook in OneNote using the Move or Copy Pages dialog box. This enables you to easily expand notebooks to view the sections that they contain and it gives you easy access to other notebooks listed in the OneNote navigation pane.

Select the page or pages (hold down the Ctrl key when selecting multiple pages) in the Pages Tabs pane, and then right-click on the selected page or pages and select Move or Copy. The Move or Copy Pages dialog box will open as shown in Figure 31.1.

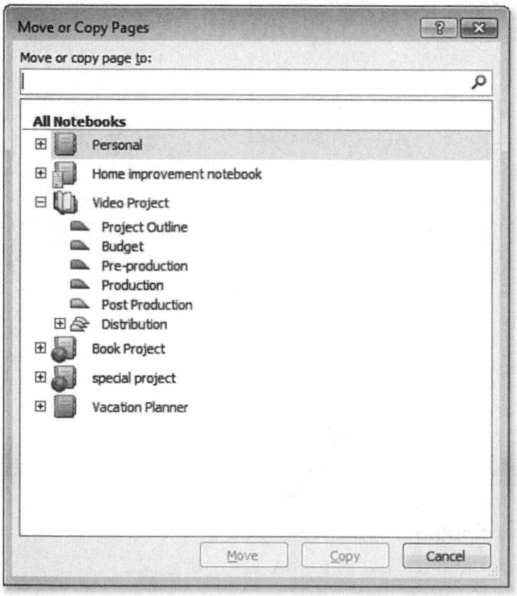

Figure 31.1
The Move or Copy Pages dialog box.

You can type a search string in the Search box to show any sections in all current notebooks that match the string. For example, you could type **pro** and any sections with "pro" in their name, such as production or project, will be listed in the Move or Copy Pages dialog box. The Search box provides you with a quick way to filter all the sections available in your notebooks into a specific subset. You can also expand any of the notebooks listed to view the sections in the notebook if you want to locate the destination section manually.

After you have specified the destination section, click Move to move the pages from their current location to the destination section or select Copy to make a copy of the pages. The Move or Copy Pages dialog box will close and your pages will be moved or copied depending on your selection.

Making More Space Available on a Page

If you are adding a lot of notes and other objects to a particular page, you might fill up the space provided on a page. You can insert additional space on a page, enabling you to continue to add information as needed. This can be particularly useful if you are inserting large pictures or potentially large objects such as the file printout or scanner printout objects on a page. The file printout and the scanner printout objects are actually printed copies of a file that is rendered onto the notebook page using the File Printout command or the Scanner Printout command, respectively. (We discuss the File Printout command in Chapter 32, "Integrating OneNote with Other Office Applications.")

Either of these printout objects can consist of multiple pages if you are inserting or scanning a multiple-page file such as a Word document or Excel worksheet that consists of a number of pages. So, if you need additional space on a particular page, you can expand the page using the Insert Space command on the Ribbon's Insert tab. This provides you with more writing space on a page.

Select the Insert Space command on the Ribbon's Insert tab. The mouse pointer will become a sizing tool. Drag down on the bottom of the page; an expanding arrow will appear showing the amount of space you have added to the page as shown in Figure 31.2.

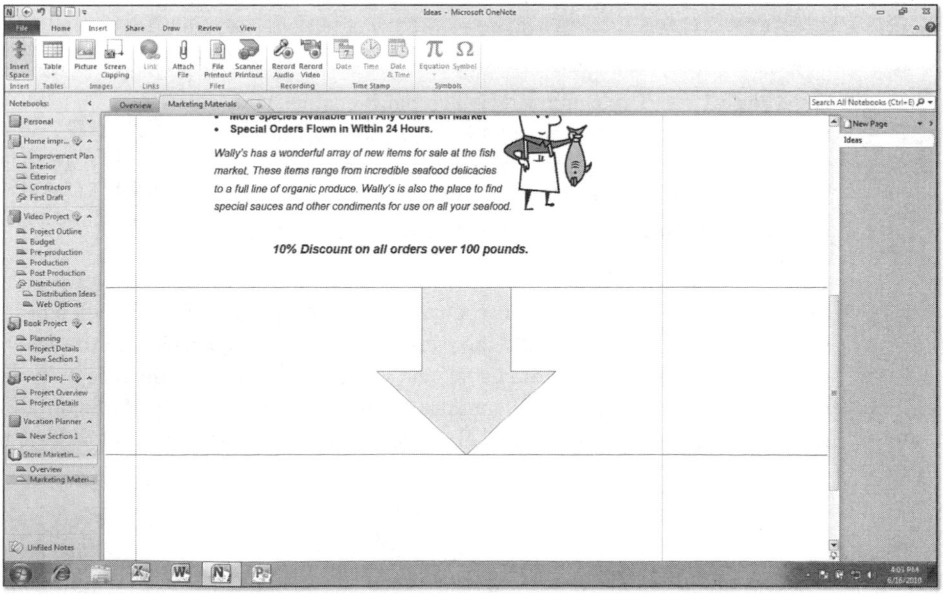

Figure 31.2
Use the Insert Space command to add space to a page.

When you have added the required space, release the mouse button. You can also use the Insert Space command to decrease the amount of space available on a page if required.

➤ *For information on using the File Printout command in OneNote, see page 854 in Chapter 32.*

Modifying the Page Setup and View

You have control over a number of different page configuration options, such as the page background color, rule lines on the page, and the paper size and margins for a page. The Page Setup group, which contains the commands for modifying page settings, is located on the Ribbon's View menu. The commands in the Page Setup group are as follows:

- **Page Color:** This command provides a color palette that contains a number of different colors. Select a color to change the page background.

- **Rule Lines:** This command provides a gallery of both rule lines and grid lines as shown in Figure 31.3. When you add rule lines or grid lines to the page, you can then use the Rule Line Color command in the Rule Lines gallery to specify a color for the rule or grid lines on the page.

Figure 31.3
The Rule Lines gallery.

- **Hide Page Title:** This command claims that it enables you to hide the page title, but it actually will delete the title and date stamp on the page. Use this only if you intend to remove the header area of the page that contains the name and default time stamp. A message box will appear, requiring you to confirm the deletion.

> **⦿ tip**
> You can toggle in and out of the Dock to Desktop view using the keyboard shortcut Ctrl+Alt+D.

- **Paper Size:** When you select this command, the Paper Size pane will open on the right side of the OneNote workspace. By default, the page size is Auto. You can change the size to a number of different sizes including Letter, Legal, and Postcard by selecting the Size drop-down arrow. If you select a specific page size, you can then control the orientation, width, height, and margins for the page. Figure 31.4 shows the Paper Size task pane with the selected size set to Letter.

Figure 31.4
The Paper Size pane.

The View tab also provides you with the Zoom group. This group provides commands that enable you to zoom in and out on the current page and specify different zoom levels. OneNote does not provide a Zoom slider as do the other Office applications such as Word or Excel. In fact, OneNote does not have a status bar, which is where the Zoom slider is located in the other applications. So, the Zoom group is really your only recourse for changing the zoom settings as you work in OneNote.

The View tab also provides access to the Views group, which provides the Normal View, Full Page View, and Dock to Desktop options. The Normal view is the default view and provides you with a view of the current page, the navigation pane and the Page Tabs pane.

When you select Full Page View or press F11, you get a view of the current page using the entire screen. This enables you to better see the various objects on the page. You can continue to work on the current page in the Full Page view. When you are ready to return to the Normal view, press F11 or deselect the Full Page View icon on the Quick Access Toolbar.

The Dock to Desktop view pushes the OneNote window against the right side of the Windows desktop and greatly reduces the width of the application window (which you can change if needed by dragging the left border). This view is designed for when you want to take notes in OneNote as you work in another Office application or surf the Web. You can return to the Normal view by selecting the Dock to Desktop icon in the OneNote Quick Access Toolbar.

Viewing Page Versions

You can view the different versions of the pages in your OneNote notebooks. This is extremely useful when you share a notebook with other users. Page versions are listed by date and author. You can actually go through the different versions of a page and restore a particular version if necessary.

The Page Versions command is in the History group on the Ruler's Share tab. The Page Versions command enables you to view the versions of a page (if any exist) and to delete versions in a section, section group, or a notebook. To view the versions of a page follow these steps:

1. Navigate to the appropriate notebook section and use the Page Tabs pane to select the page you want to check for page versions.

2. Select Share on the Ribbon.

3. Select the Page Versions command. The command's menu will open.

4. Select Page Versions.

The page versions for the selected page will appear. The page versions will be listed below the page in the Page Tabs pane and ordered by date. Figure 31.5 shows the Page Tabs pane and a number of different versions for a page.

Figure 31.5
The Page Tabs pane.

To view a particular page version, select the version in the Page Tabs pane. Remember that OneNote saves a page version for 60 days—after that, the page version is deleted.

You have three options when you are viewing a page version. You can do nothing and let the page version be deleted after 60 days. You can delete the page version immediately. Or you can restore the page version replacing the current version of the page.

To delete a page version, right-click on the page version in the Page Tabs pane and then select Delete Version. The page version will be deleted; there is no warning message, it is just gone. It cannot be retrieved from the Notebook Recycle Bin as can regular pages that have been deleted.

 tip

You can view all the notes that have been tagged in a notebook via the Tags Summary pane, which shows all tagged notes grouped by tag name. Select the Find Tags command on the Home Tab to open the Tags Summary pane.

If you have determined that a particular page version should actually be the current version of the page, you can restore the page version. This will replace the current version of the page with the page version that you restore: Right-click on the page version and select Restore Version.

Fortunately, this action is reversible. The page version that you replaced when you restored one of the page versions is actually added to the list of page versions for that page. It will be the most recent version of the page. You can always restore it if you need to get things back the way they were before you started playing with the different page versions.

Viewing Recent Edits

You can view a list of pages that have been changed in a notebook based on a particular timeframe. For example, you can view recent edits to pages that have been made today, since yesterday, in the last 7 days, or the last 6 months; a number of other different timeframes are provided from which you can select. You can also choose to view a list of all the pages in a notebook, which will group the pages according to when they were last edited using timeframes such as yesterday, this week, and last week.

Recent edits can be viewed using the Recent Edits command, which is in the Shared Notebook group on the Ribbon's Share tab. Viewing the recent edits in a shared notebook enables you to keep track of the individual page changes made by all the users who have access to the shared notebook. The ability to view recent edits can also be useful even in cases where you have not shared a notebook. It enables you to track changes that you have made and quickly navigate to pages in the notebook that have been changed most recently.

When you select the Recent Edits command on the Share tab, you are provided a menu with different timeframes: Today, Since Yesterday, Last 6 Months, and so on. As previously mentioned, you are also provided an All Pages Sorted by Date option.

Select the timeframe that you want to use for the viewing of recent edits on the Recent Edits menu. The Search Results task pane will open as shown in Figure 31.6. The figure shows the pages in a notebook that have changed when Last 7 Days was selected on the Recent Edits menu.

Figure 31.6
View recently edited pages in a notebook.

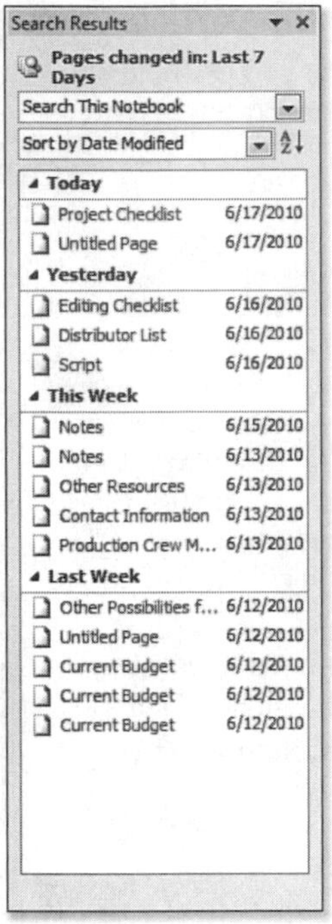

You can navigate to a specific page by clicking a page link provided in the Search Results task pane. You can also use the Search This Notebook box to search the current workbook by keywords if you want to find pages containing a specific search string.

By default the pages are sorted by Date Modified. You can use the Sort By box to change how the pages are sorted and you can list them in the Search Results pane by section, title, or author. When you have finished working with the Search Results task pane, you can close it by clicking its Close button.

Viewing Changes by Author

When you work on a shared notebook, you will find that the notes and other items added to the notebook pages by other authors are tagged with an author icon and the authors' initials. So, it is easy to keep track of who has added what to the pages in a shared notebook. Figure 31.7 shows a notebook page containing an author icon and the initials of one of the authors sharing the notebook.

> **tip**
> Insert a time stamp and author name directly into a note by right-clicking on an author icon associated with that note.

You can view the name of the author and the date that the change was made. Place the mouse on the author code. You can toggle the various author codes off so that they are not shown on the notebook pages. Select the Hide Authors command on the Ribbon's Share tab. You can toggle the author information back on by clicking the Hide Authors command again.

Figure 31.7
Additions and changes made by other authors are shown by default on notebook pages.

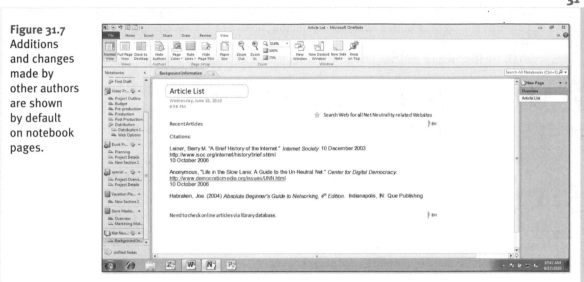

You can also search in a notebook for notes based on author. When you select the Find by Author command in the Share Notebook group on the Share tab, the Search Results pane opens on the right of the OneNote window as shown in Figure 31.8 and provides the Changes by Author information.

Figure 31.8
View changes by each author of a shared notebook.

Each author for the shared notebook will be listed in the Search Results pane. Click the expand button to the left of an author name to view all the pages that contain changes contributed by that author. By default the Changes by Author list is sorted by author name. You can also change the list so that it is sorted by date modified if you want.

Adding Objects to Notebook Pages

You can add a number of different object types to your notebook pages. The Ribbon's Insert tab provides you with options for adding tables, images, links, files, recordings, time stamps, and symbols. All these different objects are intended to provide with options for adding important information to your pages that goes way beyond what you can place in a note. Figure 31.9 shows the Ribbon's Insert tab.

Figure 31.9
The OneNote Ribbon's Insert tab.

For example, you can attach an Excel workbook to a page that contains information related to the budget for a project. Or you can include pictures of new appliances that you want to order as you plan a kitchen renovation using a OneNote notebook.

Each of the command groups on the Insert tab provides you with the ability to place different types of objects onto a page. The Ribbon's Insert tab command groups are as follows:

- **Insert:** This group provides the Insert Space command, which is used to add more space to a page.

- **Table:** Insert a table using this command. Tables are discussed in Chapter 30, "Requisite OneNote: Essential Features."

- **Images:** This group enables you to insert pictures and screen clippings.

- **Links:** You can insert links to web pages and files that are on your computer or on your network.

- **Files:** This group provides access to the Attach File, File Printout, and Scanner Printout commands. You can attach any file type to a OneNote page. You can also print a file onto the page using the File Printout command. If you have a scanner and want to scan pages directly into notebook pages as objects, use the Scanner Printout command.

- **Recording:** This group provides access to the Record Audio and Record Video commands. If your computer has a built-in microphone and camera or you have attached an external microphone or camera to the computer, you can record audio and video directly into your notebook pages.

- **Time Stamp:** This group provides different time stamp commands that can be used to add the date and/or the time to a page. This enables you to time stamp particular items that are placed on the page, such as notes or other objects.

■ **Symbols:** You can use the commands in this group to add equations or symbols to your notebook pages.

Many of the options provided by the Insert tab enable you to take information that already exists in pictures, files, or web pages and make it part of a OneNote page. This makes your notebook pages not unlike the pages of a scrapbook where you can glue just about any type of information or item onto a page. Let's look at some of the object types that can be inserted into a notebook page. We look at some of the other options provided by the Insert tab in Chapter 32.

 For information on integrating items from other Office applications into a notebook, see page 854 in Chapter 32.

Adding Pictures

You can insert pictures into your notebook pages. This enables you to add visuals that complement other information on the page such as notes or tables of text. The options for working with a picture in OneNote are much more limited than the possibilities provided by Word or PowerPoint, which enable you to adjust and correct a picture, apply styles to a picture, and remove the picture's background.

You can move and size a picture that you insert onto a OneNote page. The Ribbon's Draw tab also provides an Edit group that contains commands that enable you to rotate or flip a picture or arrange several pictures that are layered.

To add a picture to a page, click on the page and then select the Picture command on the Insert tab. The Insert Picture dialog box will open. Locate the picture you want to insert and then click Open. The picture will be inserted onto the page as shown in Figure 31.10.

Figure 31.10
Insert a picture
on a page.

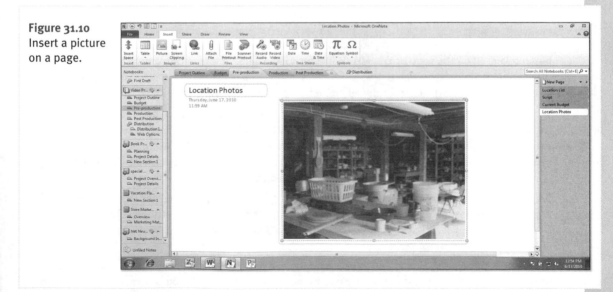

You can drag the picture to any location on the page. When the picture is selected, you can use the sizing handles to size the picture as needed.

Recording Audio

If you have either a built-in or externally attached microphone on your computer, you can add audio notes to your notebook pages. This enables you to add audio messages to other users of a shared notebook or just add ideas or other thoughts to a notebook page in the form of a recorded audio file.

To take advantage of audio recording (and video recording) in OneNote you must have DirectX version 8 (or later) and Windows Media Player (version 8 or later) installed on your computer. If you are using certain versions of Windows 7, such as Windows 7 Professional N, DirectX and the Windows Media Player were not installed on your computer when Windows was installed. You can go to the Microsoft Download Center (http://www.microsoft.com/downloads) and download the media feature pack. When you install the media feature pack, the DirectX and Media Player files are added to your Windows installation.

Recording audio onto a notebook page is extremely straightforward. Click on the page where you would like to insert the recorded audio. Then click the Record Audio command on the Insert tab; speak into your microphone and record your audio.

The Audio & Video tab will appear on the Ribbon as shown in Figure 31.11. You can pause your recording by selecting the Pause button. You can then click the Pause button again to continue recording.

Figure 31.11
The Audio & Video controls on the Ribbon.

When you have finished recording your audio, select Stop on the Ribbon. The audio recording will be represented on the page by a WMA (Windows Media Audio file) file box that uses the page's title as the name for the audio placeholder. The WMA icon will actually be located in a note box and a time stamp detailing the start time and date for the recording will also be inserted into the note.

When you select an audio recording on a page, the audio and video controls become available on the Ribbon. You can play a previously recorded audio file and you can use the controls provided to rewind or fast forward the audio recording as needed. Because the audio recording is in a note, you can drag the audio note anywhere on the notebook page as you would any other note. To delete an audio note, select the note box and then press Delete on the keyboard.

If you find that the recording level was low or that you need to fine-tune the settings related to making an audio recording directly from OneNote, you might have to change settings in the Windows Control Panel. The settings for audio recording can be accessed via the Hardware and Sound group in the Windows 7 Control Panel.

Other settings related to audio and video recording can also be set in the OneNote Options window; select the Audio & Video Settings command on the Audio & Video tab. You can specify the device to be used for recording and the codec used for the audio recording, which will be one of the Windows

Media codecs installed on your computer. (A codec is software used to compress and decompress recorded media such as audio or video.)

Recording Video

Recording video directly into OneNote is very similar to recording audio. After you are ready to record, select the Record Video command on the Insert tab. A video window will open showing the live feed that your video camera is recording; so it's "lights, camera, action" within a split second. Figure 31.12 shows the Video window and the Audio & Video commands available on the Ribbon as you record your video.

Figure 31.12
Record video onto a notebook page.

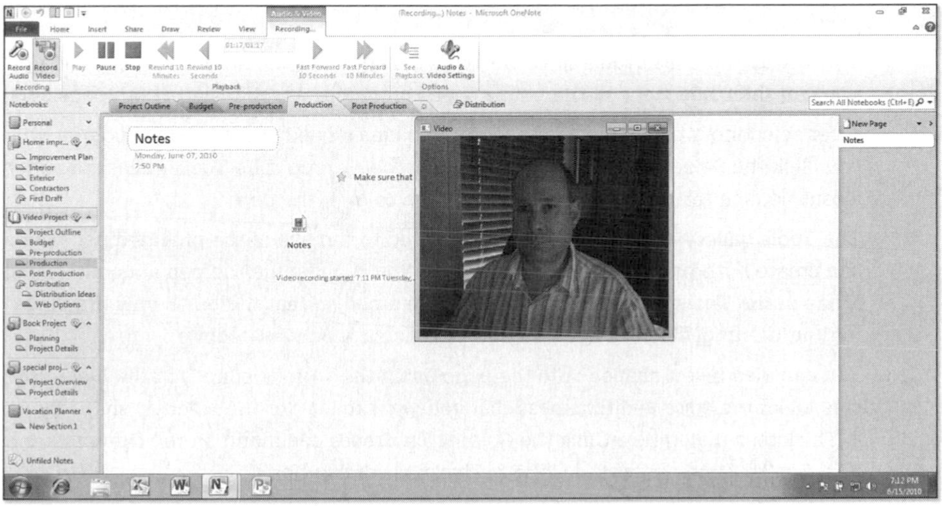

As you record your video, the Audio & Video tab is available on the Ribbon. You can pause the recording as needed using the Pause button. When you have finished making the video recording, click the Stop button.

As with an audio recording, you can use the Audio & Video commands to play back any selected video note that you have inserted onto a notebook page. You can move the video recording on the page and you can cut, copy, and paste the video note as needed.

note

If you are using OneNote on a tablet PC, the drawing tools will even be more useful because you can draw objects freehand using the PC's pen.

Adding Drawings to OneNote Pages

Other possibilities for adding visuals to your notebook pages are the various drawing tools provided on the Ribbon's Draw tab. You can draw freehand using pens that come in a variety of color and sizes. You can also choose from a number of different highlighters. The Draw tab also provides a Shapes gallery that enables you to insert a number of shape types, including squares, circles, and lines.

You can use these tools to create diagrams or other freehand drawings on a page. You can layer different drawn objects and then use the Arrange command to specify where a particular object is in a series of layered drawn objects. Figure 31.13 shows the Ribbon's Draw tab. Most of the tools that you use to create drawings or shapes are found in the Tools command group and the Insert Shapes command group.

Figure 31.13
Create your own drawings on notebook pages.

To view all the pens available in the Tools gallery, click the More button on the right of the gallery. You can then select one of the built-in pens provided, which include both pens and highlighters.

After selecting a pen, you can draw on the page as needed. The mouse pointer will stay a pen until you click the Select & Type command in the Tools group. The Tools gallery provides a number of different pens in terms of both pen size and the color of the pen.

The Tools gallery also provides options related to the use of the provided pens. By default the pens can create both handwriting and drawings. You can change the pen's function by selecting Pen Mode in the Tools gallery. You can configure a pen so that it creates only drawings or is used only for handwriting. There is even an option to use the pen as a pointer.

You can also insert shapes onto the page using the various shapes in the Insert Shapes gallery. You can select the color and thickness that you want to use for the inserted shape by using the Color & Thickness dialog box. Click the Color & Thickness command on the Draw tab to open this dialog box. Figure 31.14 shows the Color & Thickness dialog box.

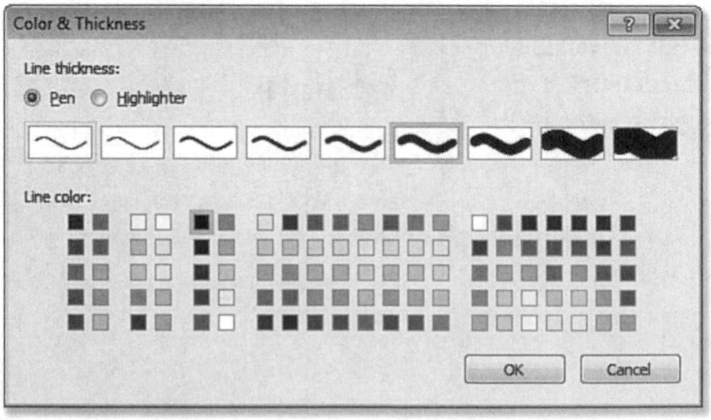

Figure 31.14
The Color & Thickness dialog box.

Specify a thickness and color for the pen and then click OK. You can now select a shape from the Insert Shapes gallery and use the mouse (or a pen on a tablet PC) to draw the shape on the page.

When you draw shapes, the mouse pointer returns to the I-beam as soon as you complete the shape by releasing the mouse. You do not have to click the Select & Type command to return to the typing mode as you do when you use one of the pens in the Tools gallery.

In terms of selecting drawn objects or shapes on the page, you can use the I-beam as you would to select a note box or picture. You can also use the Lasso Select tool provided on the Draw tab to select items by drawing a lasso around the drawings or shapes that you want to select. When you create drawings and shapes, they are contained in a box much like a note. You can drag the drawing or shape to any position on the page as needed and also size the drawing or shape using the sizing handles provided when the object is selected.

> **tip**
>
> You can select any pen drawing or shape and then change its color and thickness using the Color & Thickness dialog box.

Printing Notebook Pages

Although OneNote is designed for creating electronic notebooks, you can print pages in a notebook if required. You can print a specific page, a group of pages, or all the pages in a particular section.

The Print command and print preview are accessed via the OneNote Backstage. To access the Backstage, select File on the Ribbon. When you select Print in the Backstage, the Print window for OneNote contains two possibilities: Print and Print Preview.

When you select Print, the Print dialog box opens as shown in Figure 31.15. The Print dialog box enables you to specify the printer to be used for the print job and you can specify preferences related to the selected printer.

In terms of the actual printout, you can specify that all pages be printed, the current selection be printed, or a particular range of pages (in the current section) be printed. When you are ready to print the page or pages, select the Print button.

Figure 31.15
The Print dialog box.

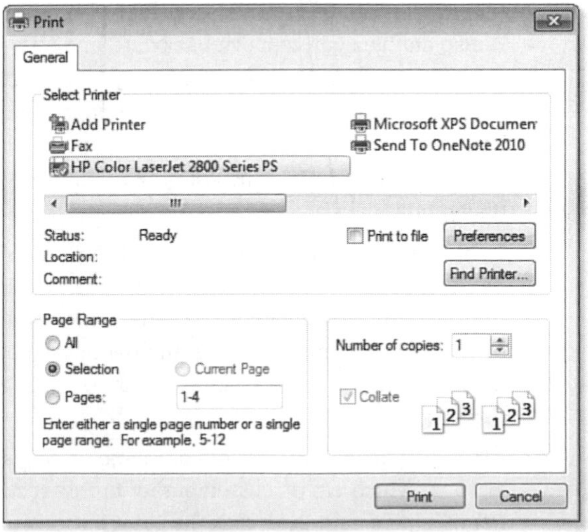

You might find it a little more comforting to have a preview of the print job before you send it to the printer. This is where the Print Preview command available in the Backstage Print window comes in. When you select Print Preview, the Print Preview and Settings dialog box opens as shown in Figure 31.16.

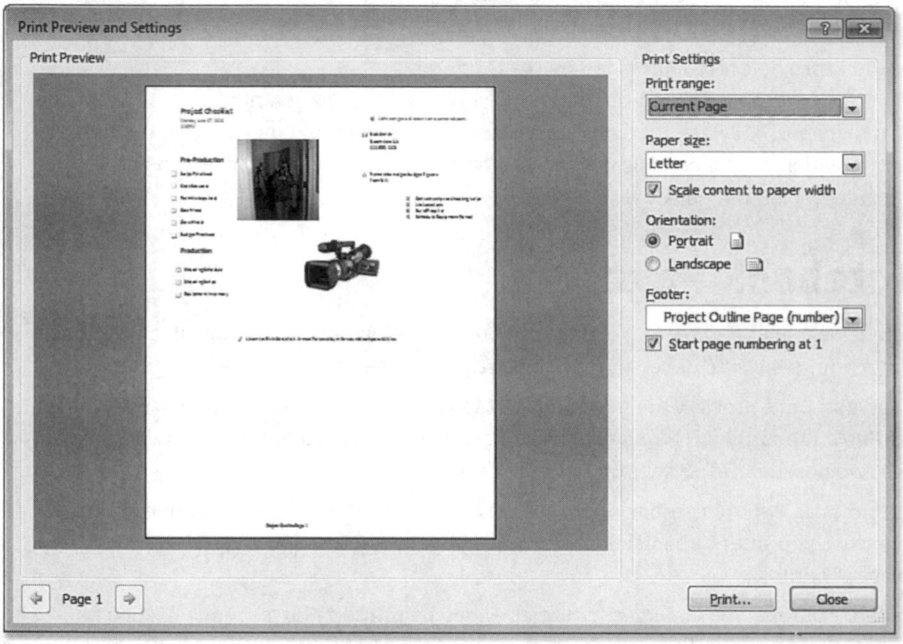

Figure 31.16
The Print Preview and Settings dialog box.

The Print Preview and Settings dialog box provides you with more options for the print job than are provided in the Print dialog box. More importantly, it provides you with a preview of your printout. It also enables you to move backward and forward if you select multiple pages for the print job (just select more than one page in the Page Tabs pane before opening the Print Preview and Settings dialog box) or if you are going to print a page group, which consists of a main page and subpages. You can cycle through the pages when you have selected multiple pages or you are printing a page that contains subpages by using the Next Page and Previous Page buttons on the lower left of the dialog box.

Print settings provided by the Print Preview and Settings dialog box include the print range, the paper size, and the orientation of the printout. By default, a footer will also be included on the printed page that includes the page name and the page number. You can change the footer setting so that it prints only the page number or the page title rather than both as the default setting will do. If you do not want a footer to print on the page or pages printed, select None in the Footer drop-down box.

When you are ready to print your page or pages, click the Print button. This will open the Print dialog box, which we discussed earlier in this section. Select the printer, printer preferences, and number of copies, and then click the Print button to send the printout to your printer.

INTEGRATING ONENOTE WITH OTHER OFFICE APPLICATIONS

OneNote notebooks can hold information in a number of different forms. There are, of course, notes, pictures, and tables; however, OneNote also makes it very easy for you to insert a link that points to a file on your computer or to the URL of a website. OneNote also enables you to include file attachments on notebook pages and insert screen clips of other application windows.

OneNote makes it easy for you to quickly get information that was created in one of the other Office applications into a notebook. This includes the ability to take notes as you work in another application such as Word or Excel, and to insert information that has already been recorded in Microsoft Outlook onto a page.

In this chapter, we look at OneNote tools that enable you to better integrate information from the other Office applications into your OneNote notebooks. We will look at how to include Office file information on a notebook page using the File Printout feature, links, and file attachments. We will also look at how to integrate Outlook and OneNote information.

Taking Linked Notes

OneNote provides you with the ability to take linked notes. This is extremely useful when you are working in one of the other Office applications such as Word or PowerPoint, and you would like to take notes as you work. The Linked Notes feature takes advantage of a docked window. The OneNote window will be relocated to the far right of the Windows desktop with just enough room available to record notes as you use the remainder of the Windows desktop to work in the other application.

The OneNote Linked Notes mode can be used to take notes no matter what application you are working with as you take your notes. However, it is really helpful when you are working in Word, PowerPoint, or Internet Explorer. The notes you create are automatically linked to the application that you are using.

As you take notes in the OneNote docked window and work in Word or PowerPoint, the notes that you create are actually tagged with an application icon. When you place the mouse on the icon, you are provided with a thumbnail of the page or slide that you were working with (in the other Office application) when you created the note. For example, if you are working on a PowerPoint slide presentation and take a linked note related to the current slide, the note will be tagged with the PowerPoint icon. When you place the mouse on the icon, a thumbnail of that slide appears. This enables you not only to immediately determine the application that the linked note was created for, but it also provides you with a visual of the actual slide that the linked note pertains to.

When you open the notebook later, you can use the application icon to quickly launch PowerPoint, which will load the presentation that contains the slide referred to in the linked note.

When you are working in Word, the thumbnail will be a representation of the current page in the Word document. You can use the linked icon to quickly open the Word document that contains the page associated with the linked note.

Linked notes are also created when you use Internet Explorer and take notes in the OneNote docked window. An Internet Explorer icon will be used to tag the note and a thumbnail is created that provides a preview of the web page associated with the linked note. The URL (web address) is also provided for the web page on the thumbnail. You can quickly navigate to the page in your web browser by selecting the thumbnail provided by the linked note.

 note

You can also create manual links to files, so any notes related to another application file that you are working with can include a link to that file. Creating links is discussed later in the chapter.

To take advantage of the OneNote docked window and linked notes, open OneNote and the other applications that you will be using such as Word or PowerPoint. In OneNote, navigate to the Ribbon's Review tab and then click the Linked Notes command. The Select Location in OneNote dialog box will open as shown in Figure 32.1.

The Select Location in OneNote dialog box will list sections and pages you have recently accessed in the Recent Picks list. All your current notebooks will be available in the All Notebooks list. Expand a notebook to select a section and then the page that you want to use as you take the linked notes. After you have selected the page, click OK in the dialog box.

You can now use the Windows taskbar to navigate to the application that you want to use as you take your linked notes. If you haven't opened the application, use the Windows Start menu and open the application. As you work in the application window, the OneNote Linked Notes pane remains on the right side of the Windows desktop. Figure 32.2 shows the PowerPoint application window and the OneNote Linked Notes pane on the Windows desktop.

Figure 32.1
The Select Location in OneNote dialog box.

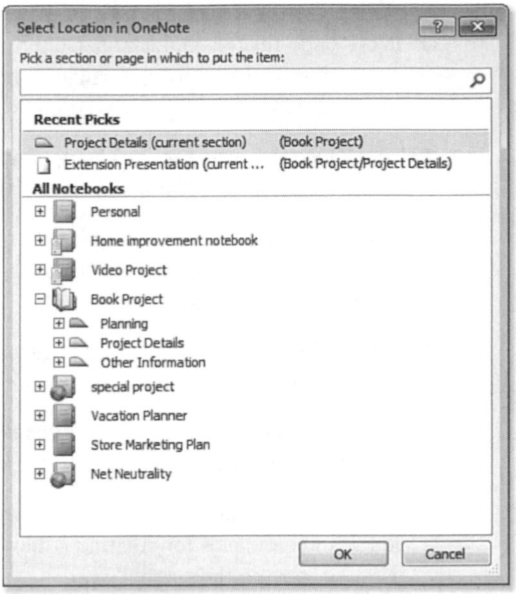

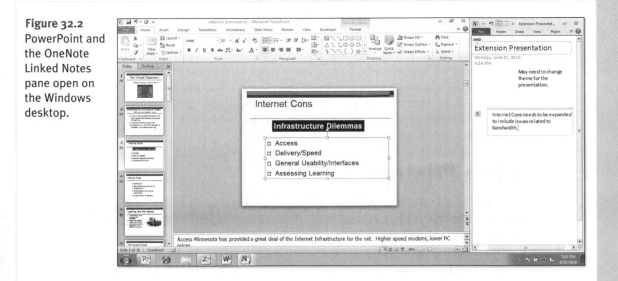

Figure 32.2
PowerPoint and the OneNote Linked Notes pane open on the Windows desktop.

The OneNote Linked Notes pane (or docked OneNote window if you prefer) can do more than just take notes related to the other application that you are using. You can also take advantage of OneNote page-related commands. Options and commands related to notebook pages are provided on the Ribbon at the top of the Linked Notes pane. The tabs provided on the Linked Notes Ribbon are as follows:

- **File:** This tab opens the Backstage. It is the same Backstage that you open by selecting File when OneNote is in Normal mode. All the Backstage commands are available.

- **Home:** Because you are working with notes on a page, the Home tab provides the Basic Text commands for formatting text. This tab also includes commands for adding screen clips and audio and video clips to the page.

- **Draw:** This tab provides access to the different pen tools and enables you to switch between the Select & Type mode and the Drawing mode.

- **View:** This tab enables you to switch back to Normal view (you are currently in the Dock to Desktop view) and access page colors, rule line settings, and different zoom commands.

- **Pages:** This tab provides page navigation commands and the Search command. It also provides you with commands for creating a new page, deleting a page, or moving the current page.

When you have finished working with the OneNote docked window, you can close the window or you can toggle off the Dock to Desktop icon at the top of the Linked Notes pane.

> **tip**
>
> You can press Ctrl+Alt+D to toggle off the Linked Notes mode.

When you return to the OneNote application window in the Normal view, you can access the page that contains the linked notes as you would any other page in a notebook section. You can use any of the linked notes to quickly open Word, PowerPoint, or the website associated with the linked notes. Using linked notes saves you time in that you do not have to create a link to the Word or PowerPoint file; it is created for you automatically. It also negates the need to add a lot of file attachments to your notebook pages, which will slow down the synchronization of a notebook stored online or on a network server.

Using File Printout

Another useful tool for placing information from other applications onto a notebook page is the File Printout command. The File Printout command actually creates a printed version of a file and places each page in the printout on the current notebook page. This feature is very useful if you want to place a printout of a short Word document or other file on a notebook page rather than creating a link or inserting a file attachment.

For example, if you use File Printout to insert a two-page Word document onto a notebook page, the pages will appear the same as they would on the printed page—including the size of the printed page. Each page in the printout can be sized or deleted as needed. You can search the text contained in File Printout pages using the OneNote Search feature as you would text on your notebook pages. Figure 32.3 shows a Word document (a single-page flyer) that has been inserted onto a notebook page using File Printout.

Figure 32.3
Insert file printouts onto your notebook pages.

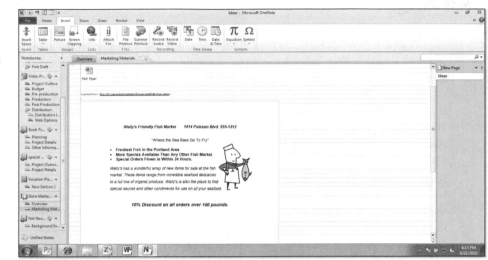

When you insert a file printout, an application icon and a file link are also created for the file represented in the printout. The printout gives you a look at the contents of the document or other file, and you can double-click the file icon or click the link provided (yes, both are provided) to quickly open the original file if you need to access it.

Although the printout pages look a lot like pictures, you can actually copy and paste information from the printout to OneNote notes. Right-click on a printout page and you can then use the shortcut menu commands to copy the text from the current page of the printout or all the pages of the printout. You can the paste this text onto a notebook page as you require.

To insert a file printout using the File Printout command, follow these steps:

1. Navigate to the page that will contain the file printout.

2. Select the File Printout command. The Choose Document to Insert dialog box will open.

3. Locate the file you want to insert and select it.

4. Click the Insert button in the Choose Document to Insert dialog box.

Inserting the printout might take a moment depending on the size of the document. You can use the Insert Space command on the Insert menu to lengthen the current page or remove unneeded white space before the printout. You can also delete an individual printout page by selecting a specific page and then pressing Delete. Each printout page is similar to a picture of a page, although, as mentioned previously, you can search and copy the text from a printout page. You can size and arrange the pages using the commands available on the shortcut menu that appears when you right-click on a printout page.

> ▲ **caution**
>
> If you attempt to use File Printout on a document that contains a large number of pages, you might get a message at the top of the notebook page that not all the pages were able to fit on the page. If you want to include a Word document or other file with a lot of pages in it, you might be better off creating a link or attaching the file.

Adding Links

You can access files, content on websites, email addresses, or pages in the current or other OneNote notebook by taking advantage of links. Links are exactly as advertised; they are pointers to a file location, a website URL, an email address, or a page in a notebook. When you select a link, the appropriate application will open to provide you with the linked item. For example, in the case of a linked Word document, Word would open and load the file referenced in the link. If the link is a web page URL, your web browser will open and load the page. For an email address, your default email client (probably Outlook because you are using Office) will start and open a new email for the contact referenced in the email link. For a page link in a OneNote notebook, the link will take you to that notebook page.

Links are extremely useful in OneNote notebooks because they point to files or other items but don't really add any appreciable size to your OneNote notebook as file attachments do. It makes sense to take advantage of links when you are using a shared notebook that is stored on a file server or the Web and you don't want to extend the time it takes to synchronize the notebook by adding a lot of file attachments or file printouts to the notebook pages.

The Link command is located in the Links group of the Ribbon's Insert tab. To insert a new link, click on the current notebook page to begin a new note and then click the Link command. The Link dialog box will open as shown in Figure 32.4.

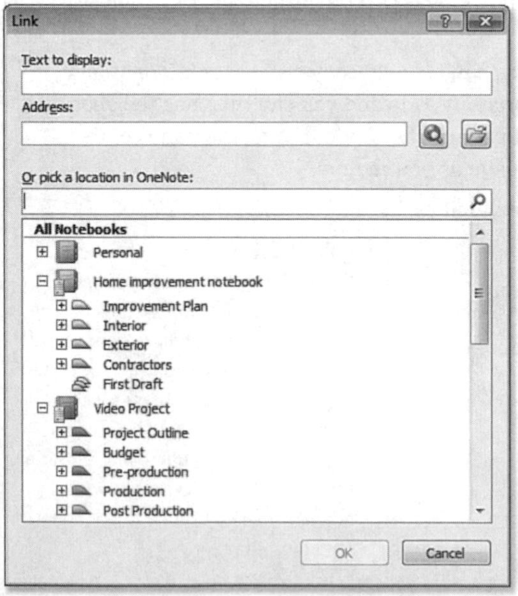

Figure 32.4
The Link dialog box.

Enter the text for the link in the Text display box. The text you enter will actually be the link and appear in a note. The link will be formatted with a blue font color and underlining (as most text links are formatted on web pages). After entering the text, you need to specify the address or path of the link.

To create a link to a website, click the Browse the Web button. Your web browser will open. Navigate to the site that you want to use for the link. Select the website's URL (address) in your web browser's address box and then use Ctrl+C to copy the address. Return to the Link dialog box and paste the address into the address box using Ctrl+V.

If the link is for a file on your computer or your network, use the Browse for File button in the Link dialog box to open the Link to File dialog box. Locate and select the file and then click Open. The path to the file will appear in the Address box.

You can also create a link to a location in another OneNote notebook. Use the All Notebooks list to specify a page (in a notebook) that will serve as the link. An address to the page will be inserted into the address box.

After you have provided the text for the link and the source for the link (web page, file, or OneNote page), click OK. The link will appear on the page in the note. You can use the link to quickly open the web page, file, or OneNote page that you specified as the address for the link.

You can copy or move links on your notebook pages. If you need to delete a link, select the note containing the link and press the Delete key.

Attaching Files

Another way to add information to a OneNote notebook is to attach files to notebook pages. This enables you to quickly access a file such as an Excel workbook, PowerPoint presentation, or Word document. Any file type can be attached to a notebook page. If you have the application used to create the file installed on your computer, you can quickly open the file in that application.

Attaching files to a shared notebook is an easy way to share files with other users who have access to the shared notebook. It also provides you another way to make readily available information that should be included in a notebook. The downside of file attachments is that they increase the overall size of the OneNote notebook. This can be an issue in cases where a shared notebook is synchronized over a slow network or Internet connection. It might take a fair amount of time to totally sync up a notebook with a lot of file attachments.

To attach a file to a page, click on the page to start a new note. Then select the Attach File command on the Ribbon's Insert tab. The Choose a File or a Set of Files to Insert dialog box will appear. You can select one file to attach or you can select multiple files in the same folder location. To select multiple files, click the first file and then hold down the Ctrl key as you click subsequent files. You can select a contiguous series of files by clicking the first file in the folder list and then holding down the Shift key when you click the last file in the series.

> **⚠ caution**
>
> When you attempt to open an attached file, a warning box will open, letting you know that file attachments can harm your computer. File attachments opened from a shared notebook could possibly consist of harmful malware, although the risk is pretty minimal if you share notebooks with only people you are familiar with.

When you are ready to attach the selected files, click the Insert button. The files will be attached to the current page. The attached files are represented on the page by an application icon that denotes the application that was used to create them. The names of the files will inserted be below the application icon.

After you attach a file, you can access the file whenever required. This will also be true for other users who have access to the shared notebook. Double-click on an attached file icon to open that file in the source application. For example, if you double-click on an Excel icon that represents an Excel workbook, Excel will open and load the workbook.

When you attach a file to the OneNote notebook, you are actually creating a copy of the file. If the original file on your computer or the network is moved or inadvertently deleted, the file attached to the notebook page is not affected (as a link would be) and you can still open the file when needed.

Inserting Screen Clips

Another way that you can insert information created in other applications is the Screen Clipping command. This command is housed in the Images command group on the Ribbon's Insert tab. You can capture a screen clip of any application window by using the mouse. This means that you can include a screen clip of a web page or a portion of an Excel worksheet. Anything you can open on your computer screen is fair game for creating a screen clip using the Screen Clipping command. Figure 32.5 shows a screen clip of an Excel PivotTable that has been inserted into a notebook page.

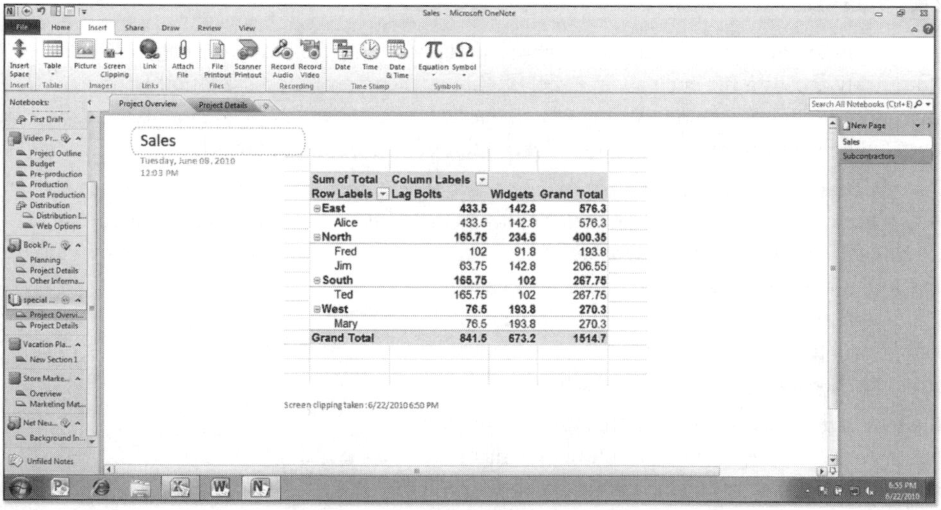

Figure 32.5
Insert screen clips into your notebook pages.

This feature is similar to the Screenshot command provided in the other Office applications such as Word, Excel, and PowerPoint. However, the Screen Clipping command in OneNote has one huge advantage over the Screenshot command found in Word or Excel. When you insert a screen clip into OneNote, any of the text contained in the screen clip picture can be searched using the OneNote Search feature.

To insert a screen clip, follow these steps:

1. Open the application that contains the information that you want to capture as the screen clip. This can be an Office application such as Word or Excel, your web browser, or any other application.

2. On the OneNote Ribbon's Insert tab, click the Screen Clipping command. You will be immediately switched to the other open application window.

3. Use the mouse pointer to select the area of the application screen that you want to capture as the screen clip.

4. When you release the mouse, the screen clip will be inserted onto the notebook page in OneNote.

The screen clip will be automatically time and date stamped. You can drag the screen clip to relocate it on the page if necessary. Screen clips can also be copied or moved (using the Copy, Cut, and Paste commands) using the command available on the shortcut menu when you right-click on the screen clip. Screen clips cannot be resized as pictures can be on your notebook pages.

➡️ *For more information on using the Screenshot feature in the other Office applications such as Word or PowerPoint,* see page 97 in Chapter 4, "Using and Creating Graphics."

Integrating OneNote and Outlook

OneNote provides you with a command group on the Ribbon's Home tab that enables you to quickly interact with Outlook as you work in OneNote. The Outlook group on the Home tab provides the following commands:

- **E-mail Page:** This command enables you to email the current OneNote page to a recipient or recipients.

- **Outlook Tasks:** This command enables you to insert a new task into a note on the current notebook page. The task, which can be time stamped using a number of time frames such as Today, Tomorrow, Next Week, or No Date, will be replicated to your Outlook Tasks list. When you open the task in Outlook, a link is provided that makes it easy to open the associated OneNote notebook directly from Outlook.

- **Meeting Details:** This command enables you to insert meeting details from your Outlook calendar. After you insert the meeting information into OneNote, you can add additional notes to the OneNote page related to the meeting.

The Outlook group commands in OneNote are another example of how OneNote has been tightly integrated with the other applications in the Office 2010 suite. Let's look at how to take advantage of each of these commands.

Emailing a Notebook Page

You can quickly email the current notebook page to coworkers or colleagues. This can be useful in situations where you want to share information from a OneNote notebook but the notebook itself is not shared with other users.

To email the current page, select the E-mail Page command on the Home tab. A new Outlook email message will open as shown in Figure 32.6.

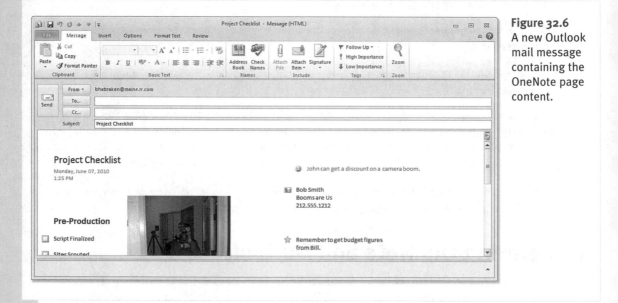

Figure 32.6
A new Outlook mail message containing the OneNote page content.

The subject of the mail message will be the title of the page that you are emailing. You can edit the subject line if you choose. The content of the web page will appear in the body of the mail message.

Address the message to the recipients and then click Send. You will be returned to the OneNote application window.

When the message is received by a recipient, the notebook page will appear as a picture. The recipient will be able to view all the information on the page, such as the notes or other items, but will not be able to interact with the objects on the page or open it in OneNote. When viewing emailed notebook pages, you will get a bigger view of the page if you open the email in its own window.

Adding Outlook Tasks

As you work in OneNote adding notes and other items to a page, you will probably list tasks or To Do items. Although there are tags that you can use to arrange tasks in a list with check boxes or mark the note item as important, it makes sense to create tasks in OneNote that can also be tracked along with the other tasks that you are compiling in your Outlook Tasks list.

To insert an Outlook task into a note, click on the page where you want to place the new task. Then select the Outlook Tasks command in the Outlook command group. The Outlook Tasks command provides a gallery of different time stamps that can be used for the task, such as Today, Tomorrow, and so on, as shown in Figure 32.7.

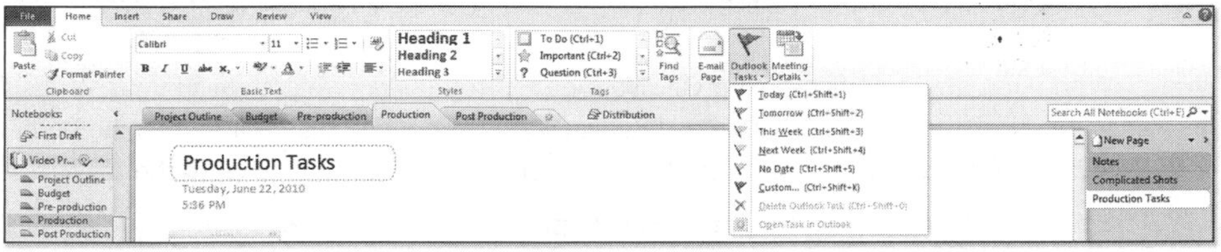

Figure 32.7
The Outlook Tasks gallery.

Select one of the time stamp options provided. This will insert a Task icon into the current note. Enter explanatory text for the task in the note.

If you want to create a custom task, where you specify the subject, date, and other settings related to the task, select the Custom option. A new Outlook Task window will appear as shown in Figure 32.8.

tip

You can delete a task from the page and the Outlook Tasks list by pressing Ctrl+Shift+0 on the keyboard.

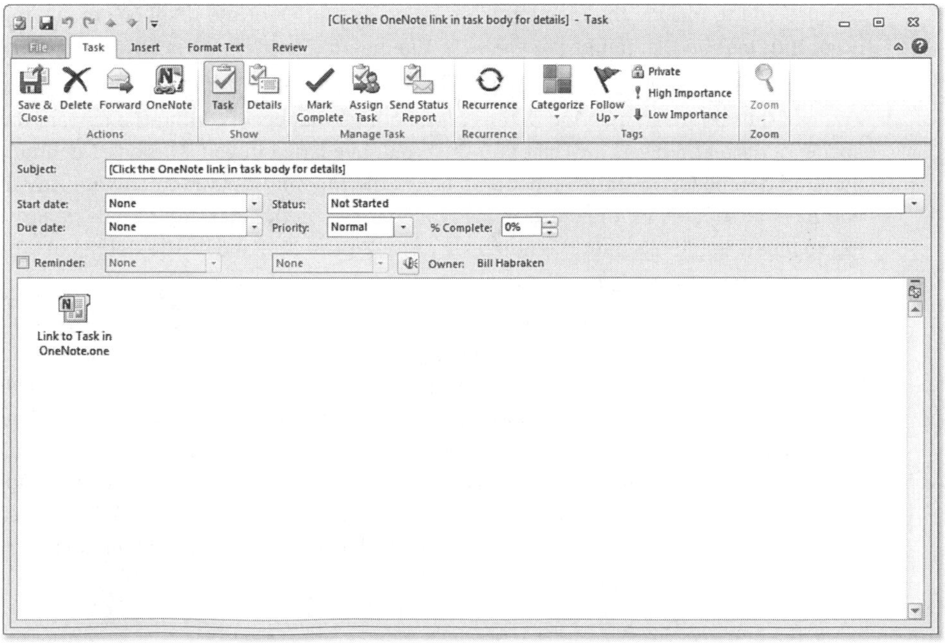

Figure 32.8
The Custom task option opens a new Outlook Task window.

Provide the information for the task such as start date, due date, and priority. When you have completed configuring the task, select Save & Close. You will be returned to the OneNote application window.

An inserted Outlook task can be opened in Outlook. In OneNote, select the note containing the task or place the insertion point in the text you entered for the task's text. Select the Outlook Tasks command and then select Open Task in Outlook. The task's window will open. You can add information to the task's body, change the start or due date, or mark the task as complete. Anything that you would do to an Outlook task created in Outlook can be done to an Outlook task that is generated from OneNote.

When you are in Outlook, your OneNote-generated tasks will appear in your Tasks list (as would any task you created in Outlook). The OneNote tasks will include a link in the body of the task that enables you to quickly open the OneNote notebook page that contains the task.

You can delete a task from a notebook page by selecting the note containing the task and then pressing Delete. This does not remove the task from Outlook, however. If you want to delete a task that you have inserted onto a notebook page and want to delete the task from Outlook, you will need to click in the task's note box and then select Delete Outlook Task from the Outlook Tasks command's gallery.

➡ *For more information on working with Outlook tasks, see page 683 in Chapter 24, "Using the Calendar for Appointments and Tasks."*

Inserting Meeting Details

You can also insert information from an Outlook meeting into a note on a notebook page. This enables you to include the meeting information in your OneNote notebook on a page that contains other information that might be related to the meeting, and it also enables you to record additional notes or add links and file attachments that were related to the meeting's discussion.

You can quickly insert meeting details for meetings that occur during the current day. You can also specify a date and insert any meeting that you have listed in your Outlook calendar. To insert the meeting details for an Outlook meeting, select the Meeting Details command. Any meetings that you have scheduled for the current day will be listed on the Meeting Details gallery. Select a meeting to insert its details onto the notebook page. Figure 32.9 shows the details of a meeting that has been inserted onto a page.

If the meeting details you want to insert into your page are for a meeting that does not occur on the current day, you can easily select a meeting from another date. Select the Choose a Meeting from Another Day option from the Meeting Details gallery. This opens the Insert Outlook Meeting Details dialog box. The dialog box will show the current date. You can use the Previous Day and Next Day buttons to move backward and forward in your calendar to find the day when the meeting was or is scheduled. If you want to view a calendar and specify the date when the meeting is scheduled, select the Calendar icon on the right side of the Insert Outlook Meeting Details dialog box. Figure 32.10 shows the Insert Outlook Meeting Details dialog box and the accompanying calendar.

Figure 32.9
Insert Outlook meeting details into your notebook pages.

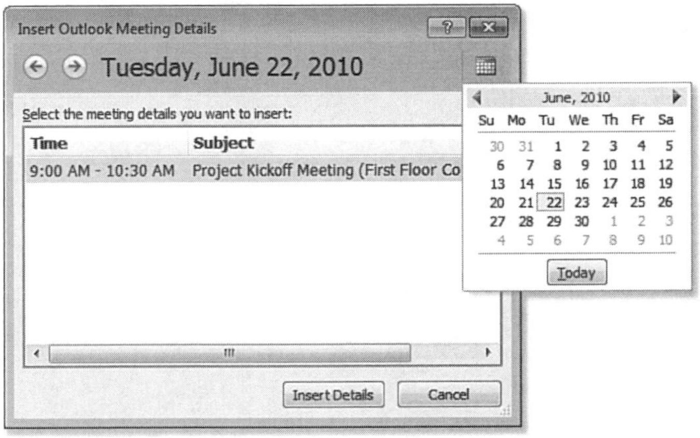

Figure 32.10
Specify the meeting's date in the Insert Outlook Meeting Details dialog box.

When you select a date on the calendar, the meetings scheduled for the day will be listed in the dialog box. Select the meeting from the list and then click the Insert Details button.

After you have inserted meeting details onto the page, you can add additional notes related to the meeting using the Notes area that is provided in the Notes box that holds the meeting details. As with other page notes, you can move the meeting details note box on the page and you can size the note box if needed. If you want to delete the meeting details, select the note box and the press Delete or right-click on the meeting details and select Delete from the shortcut menu.

> **note**
>
> Meeting details are inserted in a table. You can use the Table Tools Layout commands to format the table and align the text in the table if needed.

A

OFFICE APPLICATION INTEGRATION

The Office 2010 application suite provides specific software applications for specific jobs: Word for documents, Excel for spreadsheets, PowerPoint for presentations and Outlook for email management. However, Office isn't just a collection of unrelated software tools; it is actually a suite of well-integrated applications.

In this appendix we take a look at how you can integrate information from an Office application into another application. For example, you might want to insert an Excel workbook into a Word document. We will look at the two different ways of sharing data between applications: linking and embedding.

Sharing Application Data

Many of us share information on corporate networks via network shares and file servers. Users not attached to a corporate network can take advantage of file-sharing capabilities provided by Microsoft's SkyDrive on the Web. And all of us use emails with file attachments as our fallback plan for sharing files with others; email attachments still provide a way to get a file from your computer to the computer of another user.

 Microsoft's SkyDrive and the Office Web apps are discussed in Chapter 5, "Working with the Microsoft Office Web Apps."

Microsoft Office 2010 provides two more possibilities for sharing information with other users beyond the typical network share environment that we see at businesses and institutions: SharePoint Workspace and OneNote. You can take advantage of SharePoint Workspace without access to a SharePoint site (on a SharePoint server). The SharePoint

Workspace application provides you with the ability to create and share workspaces and Windows folders. It also provides tools for communicating with users who have access to your shared workspaces and folders. SharePoint Workspace is for collaborating with others and functions to a certain degree even on a home network.

➡ *SharePoint Workspace is discussed in Chapter 3, "Managing and Sharing Office Files," on page 72.*

Microsoft OneNote is designed to help you stay organized and keep track of projects, notes, and even ideas. Notebooks created in OneNote can contain attached files and you can share these notebooks with other users. As you stay organized with OneNote, you can allow collaborators access to the materials that you are collating in the OneNote notebook.

➡ *Microsoft OneNote is discussed in Part VII, "OneNote," beginning on page 809.*

Sharing files is certainly not rocket science, considering advancements in computer networking and the possibilities provided by SharePoint Workspace, OneNote, and SkyDrive. However, all these shared files are still not worth a lot if we cannot take all that information and massage it into some kind of meaningful output.

Almost more important than file-sharing capabilities (at least in my mind) is the capability of the Microsoft Office suite to share information from one member application to another. Being able to take information that resides in different applications and then pull that information together into a report or a presentation without converting any of the data is virtually priceless. For example, you can perform a mail merge in Microsoft Word, which uses recipient information contained in your Contact folder in Outlook to generate form letters.

➡ *Mail merges are discussed in Chapter 9, "Managing Mailings and Forms," on page 225.*

There are other examples of Word's and Outlook's cooperative abilities. Word functions as the Outlook email editor (providing you with all of Word's features when composing emails), and Smart Tags in Word documents can be used to automatically input information into Outlook. Word and Outlook are truly integrated their capability to work together.

These collaborative abilities found in Word and Outlook are certainly not the exception. As already mentioned, the ability to seamlessly share information between the applications is a huge benefit and you can share information in Excel with Word (or vice versa) and application data with PowerPoint or Publisher. All the Office applications provide a platform for comingling data from the various suite members. The basis for much of this data sharing is called object linking and embedding.

Understanding Object Linking and Embedding

Microsoft's object linking and embedding or OLE has been around since the early 1990s, and enables you to create "compound" documents that consist of data from more than one application. Breaking down the name (object linking and embedding) into its component parts is the easiest way to define what OLE actually is. An object can be anything from worksheet data or a chart in Excel, to a slide in PowerPoint, to an image in a Word document, to pretty much any selectable entity in any of the Office applications. So, OLE works with application objects.

Now let's tackle linking. When you link an object to a document or other application file, you are creating a connection between the source file and your current document, the container file. The object does not reside in the container; it is represented there by a linking code. When you update the object, the update occurs in the original source application, and the results of the update are seen in the container. For example, you can link a Microsoft Excel workbook to a Word document. When you activate the workbook with a double-click, its source application is started (Microsoft Excel), and the linked workbook is opened in it. Figure A.1 shows a linked workbook in Word that has been opened in Excel.

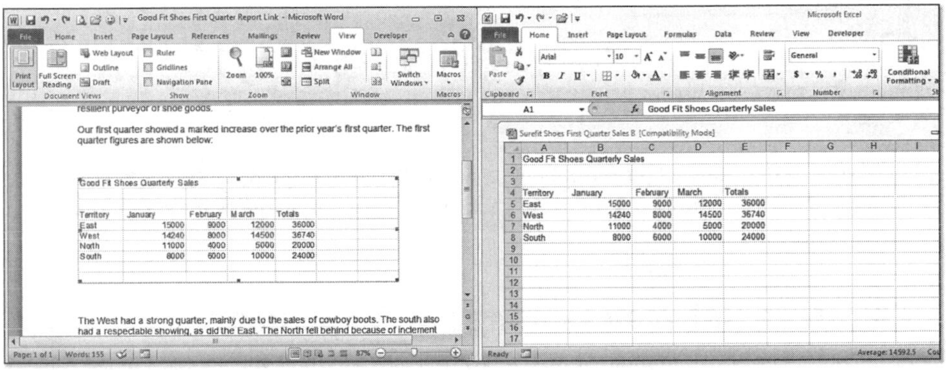

Figure A.1
A linked worksheet in a Word document with the Excel Source data.

Embedding gets the data into a document or presentation, but the information is no longer linked to the original source information in the other application such as an Excel worksheet or chart. An embedded object becomes part of the destination file and increases that file's size. It is basically a transplanted copy of the original data. Because the embedded file resides in the destination file, updating the original file in the original application does not update the embedded copy; there is no link between the two.

Embedded objects are dynamic, meaning that you can edit them. However, because they now reside in a destination application such as Word or PowerPoint, the information would be edited or manipulated within that particular destination application, but in a rather unusual way. When you activate an embedded object (double-click it), the server application opens inside the current application. For example, if you activate an Excel object such as an embedded worksheet in Word, the Word Ribbon is replaced by the Excel Ribbon while the worksheet object is activated. So, in essence, you are running the server application (Excel) from inside the application (Word) that holds the embedded object.

An example of an embedded object is an Excel workbook (such as sales figures for your company) embedded in an Outlook appointment. Double-click the embedded image to activate it. Figure A.2 shows an embedded Excel workbook in an activated appointment.

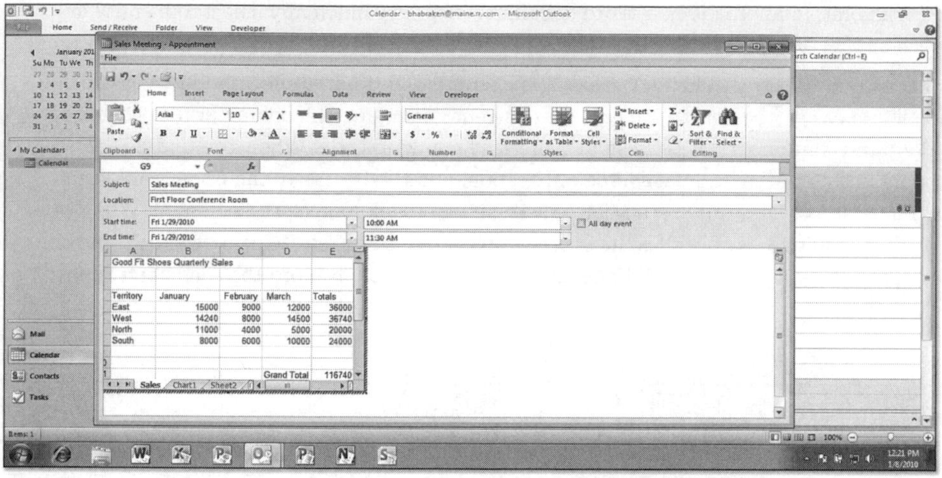

Figure A.2
An embedded Excel workbook that has been activated in an Outlook appointment.

Note in Figure A.2 that the Ribbon typically found in the Appointment widow has been replaced with the Excel Ribbon. When you click outside the embedded worksheet, the Appointment commands return.

Choosing Between Linking and Embedding

You might be wondering when it's best to link and when you should embed. This really depends on the type of information that you want to place in a particular file. Objects, such as worksheets built in Excel or reports written in Word, that are dynamic (the information in them updates continually) are best linked to your container file. This enables you to update the object in the application you created it in and still have the current results linked to several containers. For example, the same Excel worksheet (which is being updated weekly) could be linked to a Word report (container one) and a slide in a PowerPoint presentation (container two).

Objects, such as Excel worksheets containing information from past quarters or a completed PowerPoint presentation attached to an upcoming meeting appointment in Outlook—any items that are static and will not be updated over time—can be embedded into your application files, making them part of the file rather than linked content.

Linking Objects

There are actually different possibilities for linking objects from one application to another. One option uses Copy and Paste Special, a tried and true method of quickly linking data.

Another possibility takes advantage of the new Paste Options gallery, which is a new addition to the Office 2010 paste feature. Interestingly, a link created by using one of the new Paste Options does create a link to external content but does not create the same kind of link that Paste Special does (we will look at the differences in a moment).

The third possibility for creating a link to external data is to use the Object command on the Ribbon's Insert tab. This allows you to specify a filename (you can actually browse to locate the file) that should be linked to the current document or other application file type. Let's look at the mechanics of each of these linking possibilities.

Linking with Paste Special

When an object copied in an application is pasted into a document or other file type with the regular Paste command, the data is dropped in with no information about its origin. In contrast, when an object is pasted into a document using Paste Special options such as Paste Link, several pieces of information about the object are stored in the container file, including the source file's name and location, the server application, and the location of the object within the source file. This extra information is what makes it possible for the linked object to update whenever the source file updates.

Open the application that serves as the destination (container file) for the linked information. Then to link with Paste Special, follow these steps:

1. Open the application that contains the information that you want to link (such as an Excel workbook).

2. Select the information that will serve as the object.

3. Select the Copy command on the Ribbon's Home tab.

4. Return to the application (click the Application's icon on the taskbar) that will receive the linked information.

5. Select the Paste command (in the Clipboard group) and then select Paste Special. This opens the Paste Special dialog box as shown in Figure A.3.

6. In the dialog box, select the object that you want to place into the current application (Figure A.3 shows a Microsoft Excel Worksheet Object).

7. Select the Paste Link option button.

8. Click OK.

The object is pasted into the application file (such as a Word document). The object that you have linked really looks no different from any information that you have pasted into a document or other file. However, the information is actually linked into the file and you can view the link at any time by pressing Alt+F9, which allows you to view field codes in a document or other file. Figure A.4 shows the linking field code that was inserted into a Word document using the steps discussed in this section.

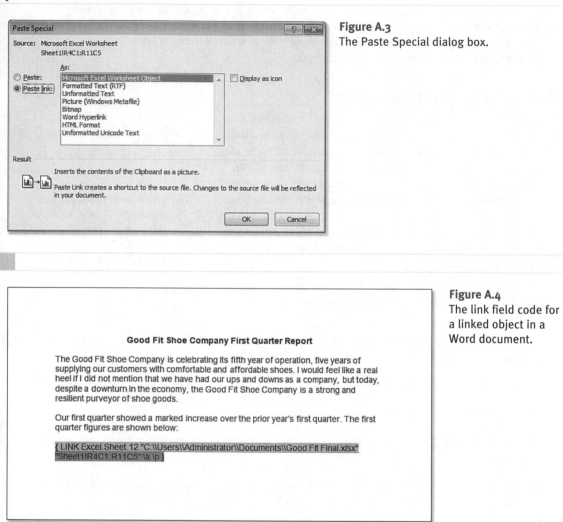

Figure A.3
The Paste Special dialog box.

Figure A.4
The link field code for a linked object in a Word document.

You can toggle the field view off by pressing Alt+F9. Linked content differs from information that you've pasted in that you can select it (when you click on it) only as a complete object. For example, clicking on linked Excel worksheet data selects all the data; you don't have the option of changing individual cells in the container application.

Linking with the Paste Options Gallery

You can also paste a link using two of the commands in the Paste Options gallery. After you select and copy the object to be inserted as a link (in the source file), return to the application and the file that will serve as the linking container.

In the container application, select Paste (on the Home tab) and the Paste Options gallery opens as shown in Figure A.5. The two option commands of interest in the gallery are the third and fourth commands from the left.

The third Paste Options command is Link and Keep Source Formatting. If you hover over this command with the mouse, you see what the pasted link will look like in the container file. Select this option if you want to have the link created and keep the formatting for the object that was assigned to it in the source file.

If you want to create the link but take advantage of styles in the destination file (the container file), select the fourth command: Link and Use Destination Styles. For example, if you are pasting a link for Excel worksheet data into Word, the pasted information will be formatted using the default table style for the current document.

Either of these Paste Options commands inserts the link into the document. You can view the link code by pressing Alt+F9. These links, however, are different from the link that you get when you use the Paste Special dialog box as discussed in the previous section.

When you double-click the link created using the Paste Special dialog box, the source application opens and you can update the data as needed. When you use the Paste Options commands, double-clicking on the linked information does not open the source application. However, when you update the information in the source file, the linked information is still updated. This might seem odd, but this is the way that these two different linking techniques work.

You can, however, still open the source file for a link even if you have used the Paste Options command. Right-click on the linked object and then point at the object name (such as Linked Worksheet Object) on the shortcut menu. Then select Links; the Links dialog box opens. Select the link in the Links list. Then click the Open Source button to open the source file for that particular link.

Linking Using the Object Command

There is a third option for creating links. You can also create a link using the Object command on the Ribbon's Insert tab. This option enables you to link an entire file to the container (destination) file. Because Word is often used as a container file, let's look at how you would link into a Word document. Follow these steps:

1. Place the insertion point where you will place the linked object.

2. Select the Insert tab.

3. Select the Object command (in the Text group), and then select Object. The Object dialog box opens.

4. Select the Create from File tab in the Object dialog box as shown in Figure A.6.

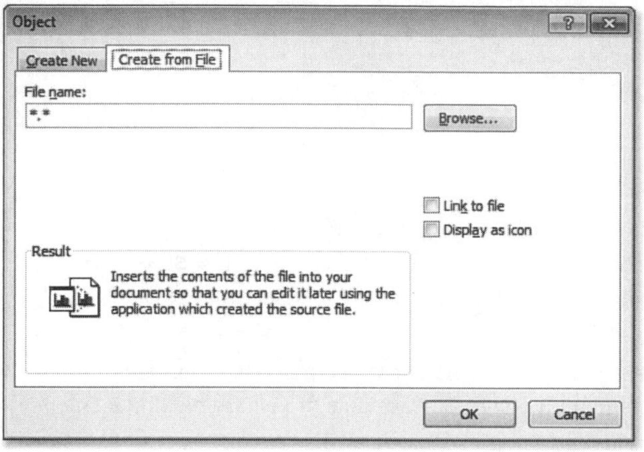

Figure A.6
Create the link using the Create from File tab.

5. Use the Browse button to locate the file that you want to link into the current document. In the Browse dialog box, select the file and then click Insert.

6. Select the Link to File check box on the Create from File dialog box.

7. Click the OK button.

The information links into the current document. When you double-click the linked object, the source application opens, showing the linked file data.

Updating and Breaking Links

When you link objects to a file, you have complete control over that link; you can configure how the link data should update and you can break the link while retaining the currently shown information from the data source in your container file. Links (by default) update when you open the container file; any changes made in the source file should be present in the linked content when you open it. For example, if an Excel worksheet links into a Word document, any changes made to the Excel data since the last time you opened the Word document update when you open the Word document.

You have control, however, over whether the link updates when you open the document. A Microsoft Word information box opens (see Figure A.7) asking you whether you want to update the links in the document. Click Yes or No depending on whether you want the links update. Not updating the links does not forgo you the opportunity of updating the links manually or updating the links the next time you open the container file.

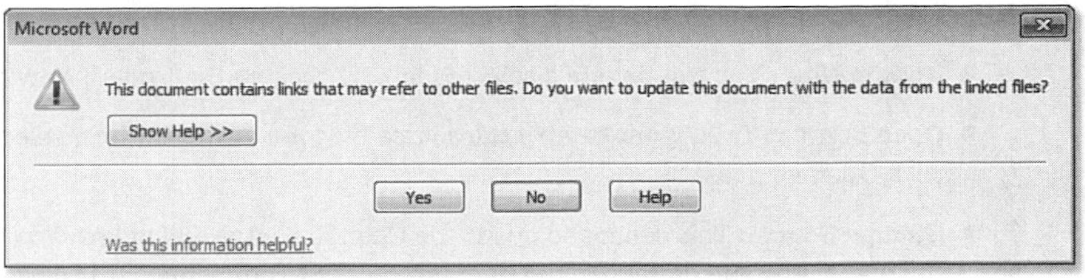

Figure A.7
You determine
whether links should
update.

In some cases, you might want to configure a link so that it is updated only when you want (and need) to see the updated content. This is particularly useful when you have linked source files that may be updated by a number of users. You can wait until you are sure that the source data is in its final form before you manually update a link.

You can specify the update settings for links in a file in the file's Info window. Let's look at a Word document containing links as an example. Select File to open the Backstage. Then click Info.

The Info window provides access to settings related to permissions and sharing settings for the current document. To access the Links dialog box, select the Edit Links to Files command in the Related Documents area of the window (the bottom right). Figure A.8 shows the Links dialog box.

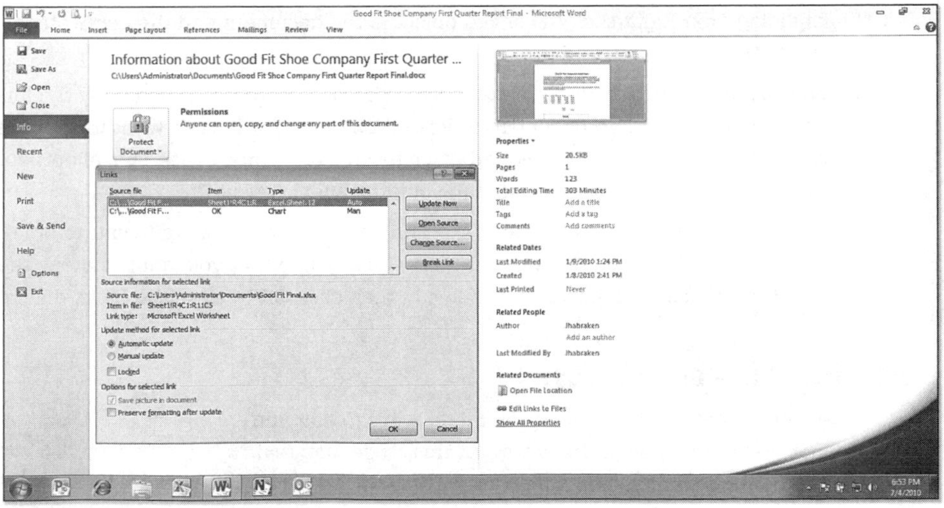

> ### note
> You can actually prevent a link from updating (automatically or manually) in a document by locking the link. This can be useful in cases where you are not sure about the linked content and whether it originates with a trusted source. Select the link and click the Locked check box in the Links dialog box.

Figure A.8
The Links
dialog box.

The Links dialog box provides you with complete control over the links in your document or other file. Four buttons in the dialog box provide commands related to your links as follows:

- **Update Now:** You can update a selected link by clicking the Update Now button.

- **Open Source:** If you want to view the source file for a particular link, select the link and then click Open source.

- **Change Source:** This command opens the Change Source dialog box. You can browse for a file in the dialog box and then open the file to replace the source file in the currently selected link.

- **Break Link:** You can break the current link to the source file. This allows you to retain the current content in the source file in your container document but it no longer updates when the source file is edited.

For our discussion in this section relating to automatic versus manual updates, two option buttons provided in the Links dialog box are important: Automatic Update and Manual Update. By default the Automatic Update option button is selected for each link. If you want to change a link to manual updating, select the link and then click Manual Update. When you finish working in the Links dialog box, click OK.

In the future, you can update links manually from the Links dialog box (select a link and then click Update Now). You can open the Links dialog box from the Backstage as previously discussed or you can right-click an object in the container file and point at the object name on the shortcut menu (such as a linked Worksheet object) and then click Links on the shortcut menu.

You can also update a link within the container file, such as a Word document, without opening the Links dialog box: Right-click the linked object in the document and then click Update Link on the shortcut menu.

When breaking links, you might want to keep the data currently provided by the link in your container file (such as a Word document or PowerPoint slide) and don't want to allow the object to be updated when the source file is edited (such as an Excel worksheet). This allows you to take a snapshot of the current data and include it in your document.

To break a link, open the Links dialog box and select the link that you want to break. Click Break Link. A message box opens, asking whether you are sure that you want to break the selected link (or links); click Yes to break the link. You can then click OK to close the Links dialog box.

 tip

You can select multiple links in the Links dialog box if you want to change multiple link settings such as configuring the links for manual update. Select the first link and then hold down the Ctrl key to select other links as needed.

Editing Linked Objects

After you create a linked object, you might want to edit and update the information in the object. At this stage, you realize the full benefit of an OLE link because you can edit the object one time, and it updates in every document to which it is linked.

note

Linked objects provide a great way to get multiple sources of information from different users into a particular destination application.

You can edit a linked object in two ways. The first is to start at the source file, using the server application to make changes to the object. The second is to start at the container file and let the link information lead you to the correct source file and server application. With the second method, you do not have to remember the name of the source file or even which server application created it.

To edit a linked object starting from the source file, start the server application, and then open the source file that contains the object you want to edit. Edit and make changes to the object as needed. When you open the container file containing the linked object, the link updates (or you can update it manually) and the most current version of the data's object is provided in the container file.

Editing from the container file is quick and easy because you do not have to find and open the server application manually. To edit a linked object from the container file, double-click the linked object you want to update. The server application starts and displays the source file. If double-clicking the object does not start the server application, right-click on the object and point at the object name on the shortcut menu. Then select Links to open the Links dialog box. Select the link you want to edit and click the Open Source button. The server application starts.

Edit the information in the server application and then save the changes that you have made. You can then close the server application. When you return to the container application, the data should have updated in the linked object.

Embedding Objects

If you want to embed data into a destination file, you can embed with the Paste Special dialog box or using the Object command on the Insert tab. Remember that embedding places the information into the destination file. However, it does not create a link to the source, so editing embedded objects is a different process from editing links. After you embed information, it becomes a part of the destination file.

Embedding with Paste Special

Embedding information from one application into another application using Paste Special is similar to linking an object. However, no actual link is created. Only a copy of the information in the source file is placed into your destination file. Follow these steps to embed information using Paste Special:

1. Open the application that contains the information that you want to embed.

2. Select the data, text, or other item that will serve as the object.

3. Select the Copy command in the Clipboard group or press Ctrl+C.

4. Open (or navigate to) the application that provides the file that will serve as the destination for the embedded object. If necessary, open the specific file.

5. In the destination file, select the Paste command and then select Paste Special. The Paste Special dialog box opens.

6. Select the object type in the As box (such as Microsoft Excel Worksheet Object).

7. Select OK.

The Paste Special dialog box closes and the object is embedded into the current document. Note that when you click on the object, particularly if the object is Excel worksheet data, you cannot actually place the insertion point in any of the sheet cells. You can select only the entire object.

Embedding Using the Object Command

If you want to embed an entire file as an object, or create a new object, you can use the Object command. For example, let's say that you want to insert an Excel worksheet into a PowerPoint slide. You can use the Object command to do this.

You might wonder why you might want to create a new object in a destination file. If you look back at the description of embedding, it creates an object in a destination file that is then edited using the server application. So, if you want to put a very complex table in a PowerPoint slide or Word document and want to have the capabilities of Excel (in terms of Excel functions) available when you edit the object, it would make sense to embed an Excel object. The real power of embedded objects is that they are edited using all the capabilities of the server application without leaving the destination application.

 note

In Word, the Object command opens the Object dialog box as opposed to the Insert Object dialog box found in PowerPoint.

To embed an existing file as an object into a destination file, open the destination file. Let's say that you are going to place an Excel object into a PowerPoint slide. Then select the Object command on the Ribbon's Insert tab. The Insert Object dialog box opens. Select the Create from File option button (in PowerPoint) and then use the Browse button to locate the file you want to embed.

After you locate the file in the Browse dialog box, select the file and then click OK. The filename appears in the File box on the Insert Object dialog box as shown in Figure A.9.

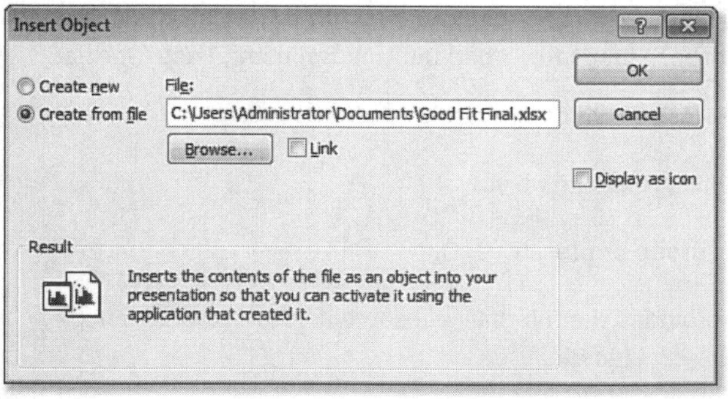

Figure A.9
The Insert Object dialog box in PowerPoint.

To embed the object and close the Insert Object dialog box, click OK. The object appears in the container file (a document, slide, or other file type). You can relocate the object as needed. For example, on a PowerPoint slide, the object can repositioned as any other object—such as an image or chart that can be dragged and sized.

Embedding New Objects

You can also embed new objects in a destination application file such as a document or presentation. Use the Object command to open the Object (Word) or Insert Object (PowerPoint) dialog box. In PowerPoint, select the Create New option and then select an object type in the Object Type list. Then click OK to insert the object. In Word, use the Object Type list on the Create New tab of the Object dialog box to select an object type and then click OK.

In either case (PowerPoint or Word), a new object is placed in the file. The server application's Ribbon (an application such as Excel) replaces the destination application's Ribbon. Edit the new object as needed. To return to the destination application's Ribbon, click outside the object.

Editing Embedded Objects

Editing embedded objects is extremely straightforward. Remember that although the object doesn't have any association with specific content in a source file, it is a copy of that source file and is still tied to the server application that was used to create it.

To edit an embedded object, double-click the object. This action actually evokes the server application and provides you with the Ribbon and commands found in that application. For example, when you double-click an Excel object in a PowerPoint slide, Excel basically takes over the PowerPoint application window. You are still in PowerPoint, but you now have all the capabilities of Excel to edit the object. Figure A.10 shows an activated Excel object embedded in PowerPoint.

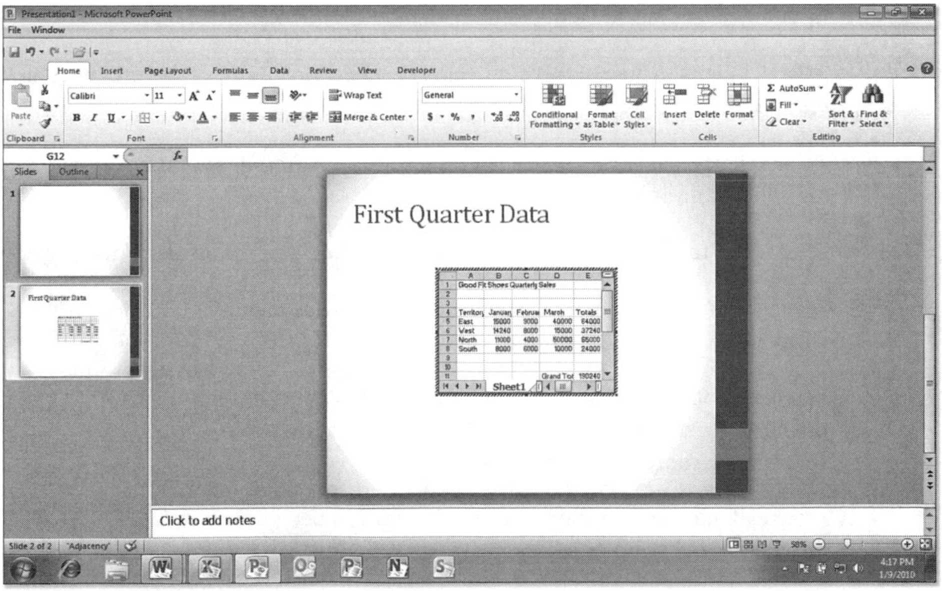

Figure A.10
An Excel Object embedded on a PowerPoint slide.

When you complete editing the object using the server application tools, you can return to the destination application. Click outside (anywhere outside) the object. The Ribbon for the destination application returns and you can continue to work in the application as needed.

Sharing Data with Outlook Using Actions

Previous versions of Microsoft Word used smart tags to take name, address and date information and share it with Microsoft Outlook. Smart tags are actually absent from Word 2010 (just search for smart tag using the Word Help); they have been replaced by actions. Several actions are available in Word such as the Date, Person Name and Telephone Number actions. Actions do similar things to what smart tags did in previous versions of Word but they require more interaction. A smart tag would place a purple dotted underline under text such as a date or name. An action, such as the Date action or Person Name action requires that you right-click on a text item to complete the action. There is no visual cue (the purple underline) as was provided by a smart tag.

 tip

If you inserted a new embedded object, you edit it just like an existing object that was embedded. Double-click the object to edit it.

 tip

You can also use smart tags on dates to create meetings or appointments in Outlook.

To take advantage of the actions provided in Word, you will need to enable them. This is accomplished via the AutoCorrect dialog box, which is accessed via the Word Options window. To enable actions in Word follow these steps:

1. In Word, select File to open the Backstage.

2. Select Options to open the Word Options window and then select Add-Ins. The Word Add-ins options will be listed.

3. To enable the available actions, select the Manage drop-down list at the very bottom of the Add-ins window and select Actions from the list.

4. Click Go to the right of the Manage drop-down list. The AutoCorrect dialog box will open.

5. Select the Enable additional actions in the right-click menu check box as shown in Figure A.11.

6. You can enable any of the available actions listed such as the Date, Person Name, Place and Telephone number by selecting the appropriate check boxes.

 note

Smart tags have been around since Office XP. In Office 2010, the smart tags are turned off by default, so you will have to enable them.

7. After making your selections, select OK. You will be returned to the Word application window.

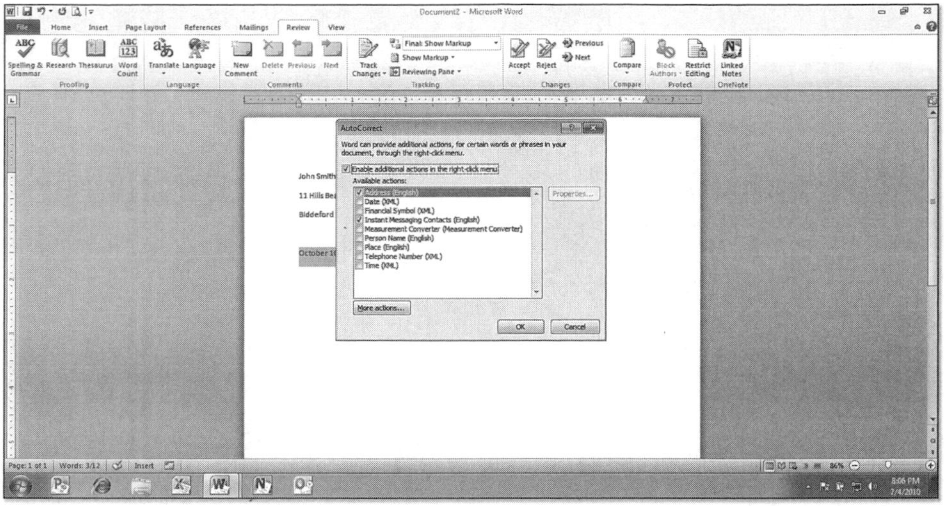

Figure A.11
Enable actions in the AutoCorrect dialog box.

To use an action to place information in Outlook, place the mouse on an item, such as name or date and then right-click. On the shortcut menu point at Additonal Actions. The Additonal Actions submenu will provide you with choices related to placing the information into Outlook or allowing Outlook to use the information to perform a particular action. For example, in the case of right-clicking on a name (the Person Name action) you will be provided with choices such as send mail, schedule a meeting, open contact or add to contacts. All of the choices request that Outlook perform an action based on the text in the Word document.

You will find that is probably worth your while to enable the Word AutoCorrect actions. It is just another possibility for quickly taking information in a Word document and using it to interact with another Office application: Outlook.

B

OFFICE MACROS

The Office applications provide extremely easy access to commands and features via the Office Fluent user interface's Ribbon. Many other file management commands including printing have been nested in the new Office BackStage. Even though working in the Office applications has never been easier or more intuitive, you may find occasions when you would like to automate a particular series of command by recording a macro.

In this appendix we take a basic look at the process of recording your keystrokes and mouse clicks as part of a macro script. This macro primer includes information on how to add the Developer tab to the Ribbon and enable macros in the Office Trust Center.

Macros and Office 2010

The ability to record software commands via keystrokes (and eventually mouse clicks) and save them in the form of a short script or mini-program has been available in the Office applications for years. This series of recorded commands that is saved as a short script or routine is called a macro. The great thing about macros is that they can help you to automate repetitive tasks.

Another great thing about macros is that you don't really have to be a programmer to create some very useful macros. You don't write the code for the macro, you record it.

Each of the Office applications, Word, Excel, PowerPoint, Outlook, and Publisher, provides you with the ability to create your own macros. Even simple macros can reduce the drudgery associated with certain tasks. For example, you might create a macro in an Excel worksheet that helps you insert a new row into a spreadsheet and then copies the necessary formatting and formulas into the new row from the previous row in the sheet. This is a simple macro; however, having this macro available would make this routine Excel task much more efficient. Or let's say that in Word you create a macro that saves and prints a form based on a template that you created. This type of macro would greatly simplify the completion of an online survey by your network users.

In terms of creating macros, you can write the code for a macro or you can record a macro (depending on the application you are working with). Word and Excel provide you with the ability to actually record macros. PowerPoint, Publisher, and Outlook require that you actually write the macro. So, you might find that you will want to start exploring macros in Word and Excel because you can record the macros, which doesn't require a great deal of knowledge of the coding language (Visual Basic for Applications) that you use to make macros.

The types and complexity of macros that you ultimately create will be up to you. Macros provide you with a great deal of flexibility in terms of automating routine tasks in the Office applications; you should definitely consider them as a resource in reducing the number of steps typically required to do often-required tasks.

Adding the Developer Tab to the Ribbon

In Office 2007, the change in the Office applications' user interface to an environment that centered on the use of the Ribbon and its tabs to access commands relocated many commands based on function. The various macro commands were also affected and were placed on the Ribbon's Develop tab. This is also true in Office 2010. However, by default, the Developer tab is not included as one of the Ribbon's tabs such as Home and Insert (this is true for all the Office applications).

So, if you are going to record a macro in a particular application, such as Word or Excel, you will need to add the Developer tab to that application's Ribbon. For example, in Excel, follow these steps to add the Developer tab to the ribbon:

1. On the Ribbon, select File to open the Backstage.

2. Select Options to open the Options window for the application.

3. In the application's Options window, select Customize Ribbon. Figure B.1 shows the Excel Options window with the Customize the Ribbon pane open.

4. Make sure that Main Tabs is selected in the Customize the Ribbon drop-down box (on the right of the pane).

5. In the Main Tabs list, select the Developer check box.

6. Click OK to close the application's Options window.

You will be returned to the application window. The Developer tab will now be included on the Ribbon.

Figure B.1
Use Excel's Options window to access the Customize the Ribbon settings.

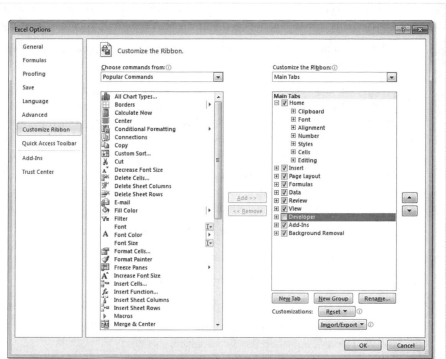

Enabling Macros in the Trust Center

Macros are actually a security risk; remember that macros are, in effect, programs. That means a macro can contain all sorts of things, including code that can do bad things to your Office applications and potentially your computer. And antivirus software isn't always able to catch malware (meaning malicious software) that comes in the form of a macro.

Because macros pose a potential security risk to your computer, macros are disabled in your Office applications by default. The default setting in the Trust Center is actually Disable All Macros with Notification. This means that you are notified by a security box if you open a file that contains macros. You are given the opportunity to keep the macros disabled or allow them to be enabled in the file. This enables you complete control whether the macros remain disabled when you open a particular document, presentation, or workbook.

Depending on the environment that you work in, the macro settings in the Trust Center might have been changed from the default to protect the computers on the network. For example, if you work on a corporate network, the setting in the Trust Center might

> 🔍 **note**
>
> Macro viruses, such as the Melissa virus that spread like wildfire a decade or so ago, can be potentially easy to catch and easy to spread. You should be very careful opening emails in Outlook with unknown attachments, which can contain macros. You should also be very careful about opening Office files that contain macros that you have downloaded from the Web. Remember that macro viruses were the first cross-platform viruses and even spread between computers running Windows and the Mac OS.

have been changed (by your network administrator) to Disable All Macros Except Digitally Signed Macros. This would require you to digitally sign your macros before using them.

➥ *For information on digitally signing macros, see "Digitally Signing Macros" on page 894 in this appendix.*

If you work in a home office environment and plan on using only macros that you create, you might want to change the macro setting in a particular Office application to the Enable All Macros (Not Recommended; Potentially Dangerous Code Can Run) option. This provides you with the most flexibility in running your own macros but it can potentially open up your computer to attack via a macro virus if you run macros in other files, particularly those that you download from the Web.

How you approach your application security is up to you. If you are going to be working with your own macros in an application, you might want to edit the macros using the Trust Center. To access the Trust Center for an application, follow these steps:

1. On the application's Ribbon, select File to open the Backstage.

2. Select Options to open the Options window for the application.

3. In the application's Options window, select Trust Center.

4. In the Trust Center pane, select Trust Center Settings. This will open the application's Trust Center.

5. To change the macro settings for the application, select Macro Settings. Figure B.2 shows the Word Trust Center and the default macro settings.

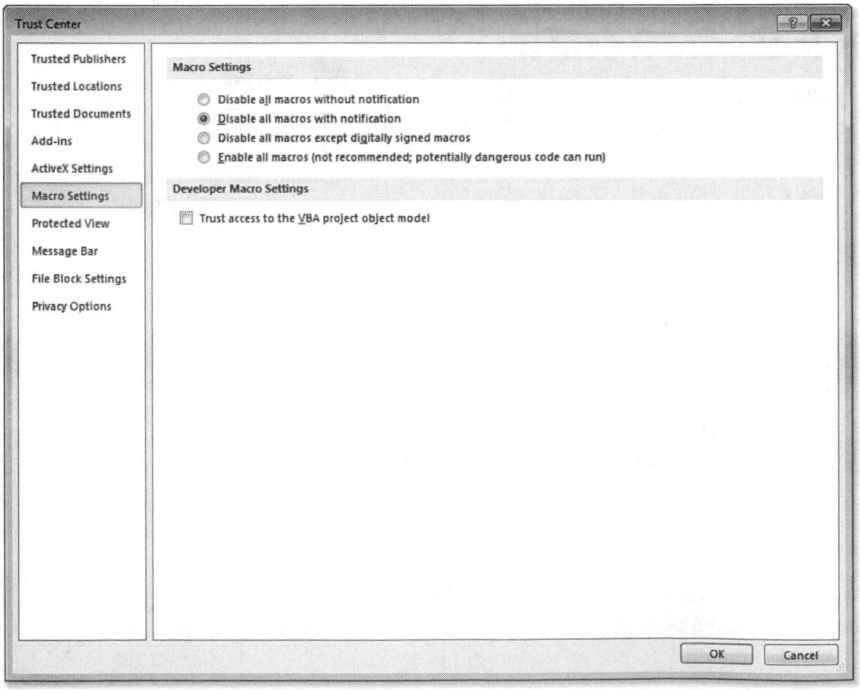

Figure B.2
The Word macro settings in the Trust Center.

6. Select the macro setting that you want to use for the application and then click OK.

The Trust Center will close and you will be returned to the application's Options. Click OK to return to the application window.

➡ *For more about the Trust Center, see Chapter 2, "Navigating and Customizing the Office Interface," on page 41.*

Creating Macro-Enabled Office Files

An alternative to adjusting the macro settings in the Trust Center is to save your Word document or Excel workbook in a file format that enables the macros that you have created and stored in the file. Each of the Office applications, precluding Microsoft Outlook, provides you with this ability. This approach to enabling macros in a file does not put you at the level of risk that allowing an application to enable all macros via the Trust Center macro settings would.

So, let's say that you want to save a PowerPoint presentation as a PowerPoint macro-enabled presentation. You can create a new presentation and save it in the macro-enabled file format or you can use the Save As command to save a macro-enabled copy of any presentation that you have previously created.

Whether you are saving a presentation for the first time (with Save) or using Save As to create a macro-enabled version of the presentation, the Save As dialog box will open. In the Save as Type drop-down list, select PowerPoint Macro-Enabled Presentation as shown in Figure B.3.

Figure B.3
Saving a macro-enabled presentation.

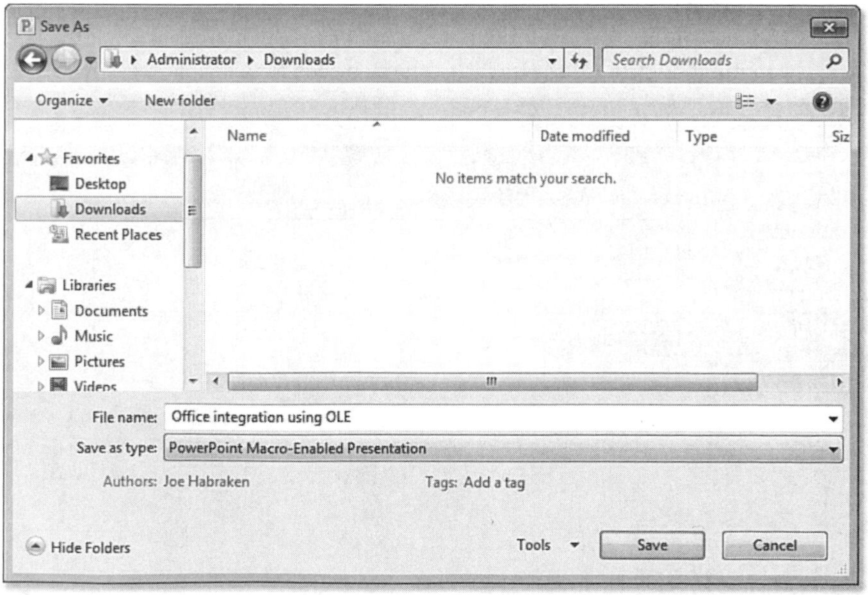

Then all you have to do is supply a filename (if you are saving the presentation for the first time) and a location for the saved file. Then click Save. Now you can create macros as needed in this presentation and they will be enabled.

Understanding Macros

Macros created in the Office applications are saved in a scripting language called Microsoft Visual Basic for Applications or VBA. Creating macros in VBA really only scratches the surface of what can be accomplished using the VBA scripting language. Developers use VBA to create add-ons and other special tools for the various Office applications. VBA can enhance the user interface for an Office application by creating new Ribbon tabs and commands for those tabs.

VBA is an object-oriented programming language. This means that it is designed to manipulate different classes of objects, which is exactly what is necessary for a programming language to work in an environment such as Office where many different object types are found in the different Office applications. In fact, VBA is designed so that developers can create new object classes, if necessary, as they design and code tools and application add-ons.

When you record VBA code for a macro, the code is actually contained in what is referred to as a module. Each application will have its own module for the macros that you create for that application.

 note

A complete discussion of VBA as a programming tool and language is far beyond the scope of this appendix and this book. If you want to delve further into VBA programming, I suggest you acquire a book on VBA, such as Que's *VBA for the 2007 Microsoft Office System* by Paul McFedries.

Each individual macro will consist of a subroutine that dictates what the macro actually does when you run it. Figure B.4 shows the subroutine code for a simple Excel macro.

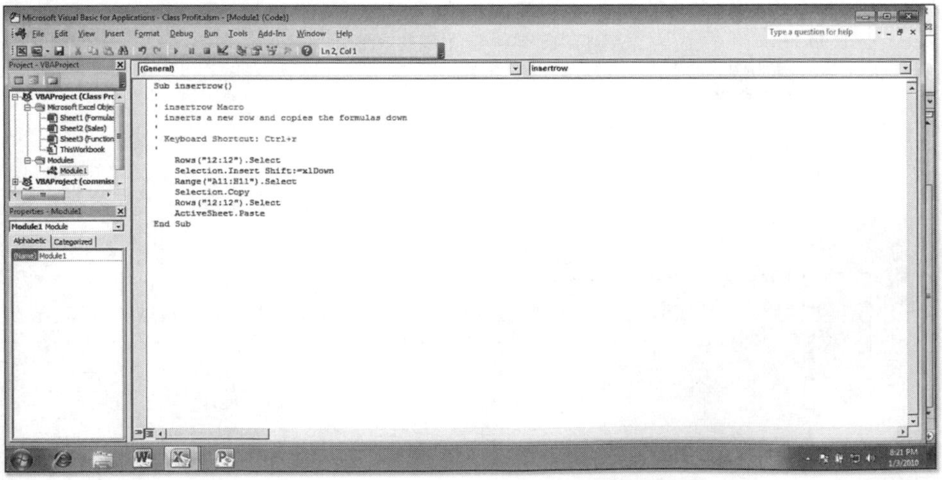

Figure B.4
Macros consist of VBA code subroutines.

Because we are primarily exploring the recording of macros (rather than writing code), you won't have to worry too much about the actual code created during the process, although you can edit the code in the Microsoft VBA editor (which we touch on later in this appendix). You have only to turn on the macro recorder and then perform the actual steps that will make up the macro's routine.

Another subject area that you should have an understanding of before you begin to create your macros relates to where your macros are saved after you create them. Each Office application offers slightly different options in this respect. The list that follows provides the options for each member of the Office suite discussed in this book (precluding OneNote as already mentioned):

- **Word:** Macros recorded in Word can be saved to the Normal template (Normal.dotm), which makes the macros available to all documents based on that template. You can also save macros to a specific template or to the current document.

- **Excel:** Macros recorded in Excel can be stored in the current workbook, a new workbook, or in a macro catch-all workbook called the Personal Macro workbook. Macros stored in the Personal Macro workbook are available globally, meaning in all your Excel worksheets.

- **PowerPoint:** Macros in PowerPoint can be saved in the current presentation or all currently open presentations (when you use the macro recorder). You can also use the Save as Type list to save presentations, templates, and even shows (meaning the macros can be run while you show the presentation) using the macro-enabled file types.

- **Outlook:** Outlook saves macros with the application's dataset so that you can access any macros you create in Outlook anytime you need them.

- **Publisher:** Macros in Publisher are stored in the Publisher publication that is open when you record the macro. You can also use the Save As command to save a Publisher file as a Word document containing the recorded macros using the Word 2010 Macro-Enabled Document file type.

There is one other thing related to macros that you should also understand: They can require a great deal of trial and error on your part because they do not always work as intended. For example, sometimes the VBA code that you create when you record a macro doesn't define an object correctly (such as a range you selected in an Excel worksheet) or the macro (when played) has a problem actually relocating a particular object.

You will find that simple, well thought-out macros will typically work as you intended. More complex macros might require more research into VBA on your part if you want to create them.

Creating a Macro

The macro-related commands are in the Developers tab's Code group. To record a new macro in Word or Excel, you use the Record Macro command. Other macro-related commands included in this group are (in Word and Excel) are as follows:

- **Visual Basic:** This command opens the Visual Basic editor. The editor has its own toolbar that you can use to create VBA modules and subroutines from scratch.

- **Macros:** This command opens the Macros dialog box. It enables you to view the list of macros. Commands are available for editing, deleting, and running macros in the list. The Macros dialog box also provides access to the Organizer, which you can use to copy macros from one file to another.

- **Record Macro:** This command starts the macro recording process.

- **Pause Recording:** In Word and Excel, you can pause the macro recording process and then restart it as needed.

- **Macro Security:** This command opens the Trust Center's macro settings.

Before actually recording steps in the macro, you must supply a name for the macro, and you have the option of specifying a shortcut key for the macro. Keyboard shortcuts for macros can include the use of the Ctrl, Alt, and Shift keys as well as the function keys and the alphanumeric keys on the keyboard. As already discussed in the previous section, you might also have the ability to choose where the macro is stored, depending on the specific Office application you are using (you definitely have options in Word and Excel).

In terms of naming conventions for macros, there are some rules. First, the macro can be up to 80 characters and must begin with a letter or an underscore. The remaining characters in the macro name can be letters, numbers, or the underscore symbol. You cannot use spaces in your macro names or special characters such as *, /, :, and the like. Finally, your macro name cannot be a duplicate of an Excel built-in name or an object that already exists in the workbook. If you do violate any of these rules, a warning box will open to let you know that the name that you have entered is not valid. This is no big deal because you can close the box and re-enter a name for the macro (a name that follows all the rules).

One other aspect of creating your macro that you should take into account before you turn on the macro recorder relates to planning. It makes sense to plan a macro in terms of the series of commands and actions that you will record. Definitely consider practicing or even writing down the steps that will be included in the macro before you actually record it.

If you create a macro that doesn't function correctly, it is certainly no big deal. You can easily delete a macro that doesn't operate properly. You also have the option of editing a macro, which we discuss later in this appendix, but you might find that deleting a bad macro and attempting to record it again is as easy (particularly for short macros) as trying to debug and edit your problem child macro.

> **note**
>
> When the macro recorder is running, you will find that you lose some functionality normally attributed to the mouse; for example, you will not be able to select text in a Word document. Use keyboard shortcuts as much as possible when you are recording your macros.

> **note**
>
> The Record Macro dialog box in Word provides a Button command that enables you to assign the macro you are recording to a button, which can then be placed on a toolbar such as the Quick Access Toolbar. You are also provided the option of assigning a keyboard shortcut to the macro (using the Keyboard button).

Recording a Macro

The macro recording process is pretty much the same for the various Office applications, although you will find slight differences; it is definitely the same for Excel and Word, which are two of the most often-used Office applications. So, let's walk though how you record a macro in Excel. We will then look at creating a macro in Word and assigning it to the Quick Access Toolbar as a button. Follow these steps:

1. In the Developer's tab's Code group, select Record Macro. This will open the Record Macro dialog box as shown in Figure B.5.

Figure B.5
Excel's Record Macro dialog box.

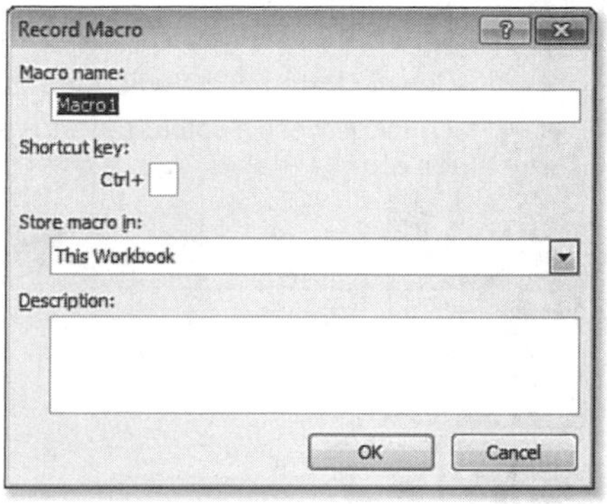

2. Enter a name for the macro in the Macro name box.

3. Set the shortcut key for the macro.

4. Use the Store Macro In drop-down box to select where you would like to store the macro.

5. Provide an optional description for the macro in the Description box and then click OK.

6. Perform the various actions that will be recorded in the macro. You can access the various Ribbon tabs as needed to access commands and you can use the keyboard or mouse to move in the worksheet.

7. When you have completed recording the macro, click Stop Recording.

> **tip**
>
> If you are creating a macro in Excel that is used to move a certain number of cells from a cell of origin (but is to be used with a variable starting cell), select the Use Relative References command in the Code group before recording the macro.

The macro will be stored as you specified in step 4. You can view the list of macros available including the new macro that you have recorded—select Macros in the Code group.

Assigning a Macro Button to the Quick Access Toolbar

Word makes it very easy for you to create a new macro and assign it to the Quick Access Toolbar. This is extremely useful if you create a macro that opens a weekly report form or an invoice that you use frequently. You can use the macro to open a new document based on a template that you have created (such as an invoice template).

> *For more about creating forms using form controls see Chapter 9, "Managing Mailings and Forms" on page 241.*

To create a macro in Word and assign it to a button the Quick Access Toolbar, follow these steps:

1. In the Developer's tab's Code group, select Record Macro. This will open the Record Macro dialog box.

2. Enter a name for the macro and provide an optional description.

3. Select Button. This will open the Word Options with the Quick Access Toolbar settings selected as shown in Figure B.6.

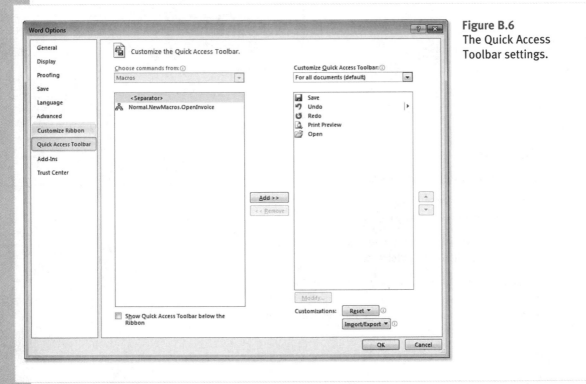

Figure B.6
The Quick Access Toolbar settings.

4. In the Command pane, choose the icon that represents your new macro.

5. Click Add to add the macro button to the Quick Access Toolbar pane, and then click OK.

6. Perform the actions that will be included in the macro. Then click Stop Recording.

The new macro will be stored in the Normal template. The button for the new macro will be included on the Quick Access Toolbar. You can run the macro using the button.

You can also add macros to the Quick Access Toolbar in the other Office applications, such as Excel, Outlook, and PowerPoint. Open the Backstage (select File, and then Options) in the application and then select Quick Access Toolbar. In the Choose Commands From drop-down list, select Macros.

You can add any of the macros listed to the Quick Access Toolbar. Select a macro and then click the Add button.

Running Macros

Macros can be run in a variety of ways. You can run a macro using the shortcut key that you have assigned to that macro. You can also run a macro from an assigned button on the application's Quick Access Toolbar.

Before you run a macro, you need to make sure that you provide the appropriate conditions in your application required by the macro. For example, if the macro performs a particular task in an Excel worksheet, you need to be in the correct cell so that the macro navigates the sheet correctly as it performs its tasks.

You can also run macros from the Macros dialog box. To view available macros, select the Macros command. The Macros dialog box will open as shown in Figure B.7.

 tip

You can specify a Quick Access Toolbar button for your macro other than the default in the Quick Access Toolbar settings (in Options). Select the macro in the Quick Access Toolbar list and then click Modify. Select a new button and then click OK.

 tip

You can open the Macros dialog box at any time by pressing Alt + F8.

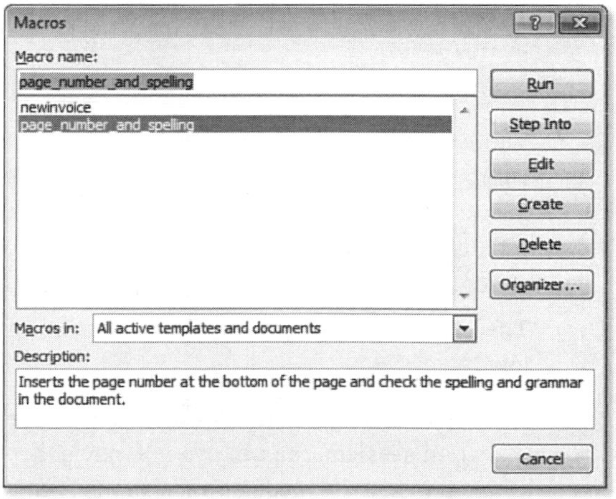

Figure B.7
The Macros dialog box.

Macros	
Macro name:	
page_number_and_spelling	**Run**
newinvoice	**Step Into**
page_number_and_spelling	**Edit**
	Create
	Delete
	Organizer...
Macros in: All active templates and documents	
Description:	
Inserts the page number at the bottom of the page and check the spelling and grammar in the document.	
	Cancel

To run a macro from the Macros dialog box, select the macro. Then all you have to do is select the Run button. The macro will run.

Editing Recorded Macros

As already mentioned in the previous section, macros can be accessed via the Macros dialog box. The Macros dialog box also provides you with the ability to open a macro in the VBA editor.

Although it isn't exactly editing, you can delete unwanted macros from the list. To delete a macro from the Macros dialog box, select a macro and then click Delete. A message box will open asking you if you want to remove the selected macro; click Yes to confirm the deletion.

Exploring the VBA Editor

To actually view the VBA code in a macro and edit it, you need to open the VBA editor. Select a macro in the Macros dialog box and then click Edit. The VBA Editor will open as shown in Figure B.8.

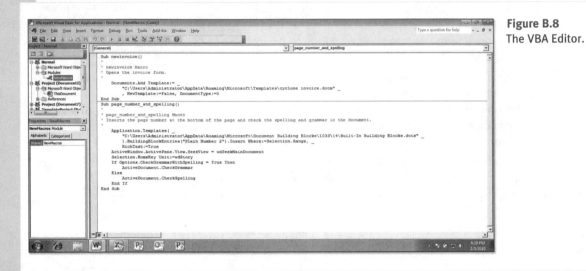

Figure B.8
The VBA Editor.

The VBA editor window shown in Figure B.8 shows the NewMacros module, which contains the subroutines for two different macros: newinvoice and page_number_and_spelling (note that neither macro name uses special characters or spaces). The editor is really a standalone application (for all intents and purposes) and provides a menu system and command toolbar structure much like the Office application interfaces were prior to Office 2007.

The VBA Editor window is actually broken up into three different panes. These panes are as follows:

- **Project Explorer:** Provides a list and is used to access the projects available in the current application session. You can use it to navigate (and select) available objects in the projects. These objects include modules such as the NewMacros module and other objects, including the current document (or worksheet) and references to other objects such as templates.

- **Properties:** This pane provides a list of the properties for the object currently selected in the Project Explorer.

- **Code Window:** This is the largest pane of the editor's pane and contains the actual VBA code for the selected module.

The actual geography of the VBA code in the macro is straightforward; each subroutine (for a macro) begins with the Sub line followed by the name of the macro. Directly under the Sub line, the name of the macro will be repeated (followed by the word *Macro*). The next line will consist of the description that you provided for the macro.

Below the macro's name and description (which typically appear in a green font), the actual lines of code that make up the macro (and relate to the actual actions that you performed) will be listed. The macro subroutine end with the code line End Sub.

In terms of editing the code lines, one of the simplest possibilities is changing references to specific files or objects specified in the macro. For example, if the macro opens a new file from a template named cyclone.dotm and you have modified the template and renamed it newcyclone.dotm, you can change the reference within the specific code line that refers to the template. Or, let's say that you have a macro that inserts a particular building block into an Excel worksheet. You can edit the actual name of the building block in the macro to refer to any building block in your building block galleries just as long as you only edit the name and do not delete or disturb any of the other text in the code line.

Any addition of code lines to a macro will require that you enter the VBA code in the correct syntax and in the appropriate context. For example, the Selection code is used to specify a command from the keyboard. If I wanted to specify that selected text be cut by the macro, I would add a code line: Selection.Cut.

Obviously, I would have had to specify the text to be selected in a code line that comes before Selection.Cut. To specify the text selection, I would use the code line Selection.Extend followed by Selection.MoveDown Unit:=wdLine, Count:=3. This means that I am turning on the Extend feature (which is F8; you can't drag with the mouse to select text when the Macro Recorder is on) and then using the down arrow key to move down three text lines to select that text. You can see that VBA code lines can be read and understood (by you). As you add more code vocabulary to your repertoire, you will have more confidence in editing macros and potentially writing your own VBA code.

Stepping Through a Macro

A very good way to troubleshoot a macro that is not working correctly is to step through the macro. This process enables you to go through the code lines one at a time. The best way to perform a step debugging is to open the VBA Editor window and then rearrange the open windows so that you can see the editor and the application window (such as Word) either side-by-side or top and bottom. This enables you to actually see what happens in the application window as you execute each line of code.

Open the Macros dialog box and then select the macro that you want to step through. Then click Edit to open the VBA Editor. When you have the editor and the application arranged on your screen so that you can see them both, follow these steps to step through the macro:

1. Place the insertion point in the macro subroutine where you would to begin the step through.

2. Press F8 to execute that line of code. The code will be highlighted yellow.

3. To step to the next line of code, press F8.

4. Continue to press F8 to execute each line of code until you come to the End Sub line.

5. To end the debugging process, click the Reset button on the editor's toolbar.

As you step through each line of code, you will want to take note of what is actually happening in the application window as each code line executes. This enables you to find the actual line of code that is misbehaving in a macro that does not work correctly.

Digitally Signing Macros

We have already discussed the fact the macros can be a security risk and that the security settings for the Office applications are geared toward not allowing macros to run by default. So, another alternative for verifying that your macros are not malware is to digitally sign the macro project (which can contain a number of macros). This enables you to use and share the macros without enabling macros in the Security Center and so lessening the possibility of executing a "bad" macro.

After you digitally sign your macro projects, you can change the macro settings in the Trust Center to use the Disable All Macros Except Digitally Signed Macros option. Collaborators and other users that might use your templates or other files that contain macros can also use this setting, which enables you to share the macros but doesn't open up any of your colleagues to a macro attack.

Digitally signing a macro project requires that you obtain a digital certificate. Digital certificates can be provided by a certifying authority. For example, you can obtain digital certificates from online certifying authorities such as A-Trust (http://www.a-trust.at), VeriSign (http://digitalid.verisign.com), and a whole host of other certifying authorities (just do a search at microsoft.com for Microsoft Root Certificate program members). Some companies might also have their own in-house certifying authority.

> **⊛ tip**
>
> If the Digital Certificate for VBA Projects utility is not available in the Microsoft Office 2010 Tools group, you can reinsert your Office 2010 DVD and add this and other uninstalled Office components as needed.

So, you can purchase a digital certificate from a certifying authority for your VBA code or you can ask your digital certificate overlord (a network administrator or CIO perhaps) at your company for a digital certificate for your VBA projects. If neither of these options is open to you, you can still create your own digital certificate using an Office 2010 utility program named Digital Certificate for VBA Projects. To create a digital certificate using the Digital Certificate for VBA Projects utility, follow these steps:

1. On the Start menu, select All Programs, Microsoft Office and then Microsoft Office 2010 Tools.

2. In the Microsoft Office 2010 Tools group, select Digital Certificate for VBA Projects to open the Create Digital Certificate window.

3. Type a name for the new digital certificate.

4. A dialog box will open telling you that your certificate was successfully created. Click OK to close the message box.

After you have a digital certificate (self-generated or provided by a certificate authority), you can use it to digitally sign your macro projects. This process takes place in the VBA Editor. Follow these steps:

1. On the Developer's tab, click the Macros command to open the Macro dialog box.

2. Select a macro in the Macro Name list and then click Edit to open the VBA editor.

3. In the Project Explorer, select the name of the VBA project (the name will begin with VBAProject) that you want to digitally sign.

4. Select the editor's Tools menu and then select Digital Signature. This will open the Digital Signature dialog box as shown in Figure B.9.

Figure B.9
The Digital Signature dialog box.

5. Select the Choose button in the Digital Signature dialog box. A Windows Security box opens showing the certificate that you created.

6. Click OK and you will be returned to the Digital Signature dialog box. The name of your certificate will now be listed as the certificate name in the dialog box.

7. Click OK.

You can now close the VBA editor. The Project module (and all the macros that it contains) is now digitally signed.

You probably have digitally signed the macro project so that it is easy for others to use your macros in templates or other documents, worksheets, and so on. You plan on sharing it on the network or emailing it to another user. There is a problem, however.

Because you generated the digital signature certificate, it is not considered a certificate from a trusted source. When a user on another computer attempts to open the document or use the template, the Office application being used will actually check the certificate to see if it is from a certifying authority on the trusted list. Because you aren't really a certifying authority, any user opening your document or template containing the macros will be visited by a security message in the application (just below the Ribbon) detailing that the macros have been disabled.

There is a quick workaround to remedy this problem. Users can add your certificate to their trusted root certificate authorities store. The macros can then be enabled. So, this set of tasks should be performed on the computer of the other users.

Select the Options button in the security warning that has appeared in the application. This will open the Security Alert-Macros dialog box. At this point, there is no way to activate the macros. In the dialog box, click the Show Signature Details link. This will open the Digital Signature Details dialog box, which shows the details related to your digital certificate. To view the certificate, select the View Certificate button.

The Certificate dialog box doesn't really provide any more information than the digital Signature Details dialog box, but it does provide access to the Certificate Import Wizard, which is where we need to end up to add the certificate to the trusted store.

Select the Install Certificate button in the Certificate dialog box. The Certificate Import Wizard will open. Click Next to bypass the initial wizard window. On the next wizard window, select the Place All Certificates in the Following Store option button, and then click Next. On the next screen, select the Browse button and the Select Certificate Store dialog box will open as shown in Figure B.10.

Figure B.10
The Select Certificate Store dialog box.

In the certificate store list, select the Trusted Root Certification Authorities folder. Then click OK. Now you can click Next. The final wizard screen will appear showing the settings that you have selected, such as the certificate store. Click Finish.

A security warning dialog box will open detailing that you are about to install a certificate and Windows cannot validate that the certificate is authenticate. Select Yes to install the certificate. A Certificate Import Wizard message box will open letting you know that the import was successful. Click OK. And then click OK two more times to return to the Microsoft Office Security Options dialog box, which is where we started this entire process.

As you can see from Figure B.11, the macro-related options available have been expanded because the digital certificate was added to the store.

The possibilities are as follows:

- **Help Protect Me from Unknown Content (Recommended):** This option was initially the only possibility in the dialog box. It is still the default but can be changed to allow the macro to run in the application.

- **Enable Content for This Session:** This option enables the macros for this session. When you open the file in the future, the macros will be disabled and a warning will be provided by the application. However, you can use this same option (each time) to enable the macros.

Figure B.11
The options for enabling your macros.

- **Trust All Documents from Publisher:** This option will enable the user to open files with the macros enabled and no macro-related warning will be provided when you open the file in an application.

After you have changed the security settings related to the macros in the document or file, you can click OK. If you have selected the second or third possibility, the security warning will close in the application. Now the macros can be run in the application as needed.

INDEX

Symbols

+ (addition) operator, 354

/ (division) operator, 354

= (equal) operator, 355

^ (exponentiation) operator, 354

> (greater than) operator, 355

>= (greater than or equal to) operator, 355

< (less than) operator, 355

<= (less than or equal to) operator, 355

* (multiplication) operator, 354

- (subtraction) operator, 354

1.5 line spacing, 155

3D effects
  PowerPoint text boxes, 504
  Publisher, 776
  slides, 504

3D SmartArt, 84

A

absolute referencing, 352-353

Access data, importing, 433-434

Accessibility Checker, 71

accessing
  Backstage, 30
  business information sets, 773
  Calendar (Outlook), 659-664
  email accounts, 657
  hidden slides, 581

homegroup settings, 65
  Publisher templates, 762-763
  Ribbon, 29-30
  Word document properties, 177

Account Configuration Wizard, 72

accounting format, 322

Acrobat Reader, 54

actions (data sharing), 878-879

Add a Digital Signature option, 68

Add Animation gallery, 561-562

Add Constraint dialog box, 467

Add Files dialog box, 74

Add Scenario dialog box, 461

add-ins, 45-47
  activating, 46-47
  viewing, 45

Add-Ins dialog box, 46

addition (+) operator, 354

Address Block field, 233-234

Address Book (Outlook), 633-635
  dialog box, 633
  email addresses, adding, 634
  opening, 633
  searching, 634
  validity of email address, 635

Advanced Filter dialog box, 427

advanced filtering, 426-428

Advanced Find dialog box, 624

Advanced options, 43-45

alignment. *See also* tabs
  paragraphs, 154-155
  Publisher text boxes, 778
  slide objects, 546
  text
    PowerPoint, 500
    shapes, 95
    SmartArt, 85-86

Allow Users to Edit Ranges dialog box, 290

analyzing data (Excel)
  Goal Seek, 464-465
  PowerPivot, 467-471
    benefits, 471
    data, editing, 470
    data sources, connecting, 468-469
    downloading, 468
    drop-down menu, 470
    external data, refreshing, 471
    PivotTables, creating, 470
    Ribbon, 469
    website, 468
    window, 469
  Solver, 465-467
    configuring, 466-467
    constraints, 466, 467
    enabling, 465
    running, 467
  what-if analysis, 457-464
    creating scenarios, 460-462
    data tables, creating, 458-460
    scenario summaries, 463-464
    viewing scenarios, 462

B

Background Removal tool, 10, 91-92

backgrounds
Excel
cells, 330
charts, 382
master slides, 518
pictures
editing, 88
removing, 528

backing up data files (Outlook), 613

Backstage
accessing, 30
commands, 31
Info, 31-32
Print, 32
Save & Send, 32-33
Excel, 7
Print Window, 312-313
templates, 281
help, 18
new documents,
creating, 137
New Notebook window, 815
Notebook Information
window, 816
overview, 7-8, 30
Print Window
PowerPoint, 592
Word, 163-164
printing, 8
Save & Send options, 7, 595

bar charts, 385

bar tabs, 159

basic motion paths, 555

bibliographies, 259
inserting, 262
style guidelines, 259-260

Bibliography gallery, 262

blocked file types, 740-741

bold text keyboard shortcut, 151

Bookmark dialog box, 270

bookmarks, 270-271

borders
Excel, 328-329
PowerPoint
tables, 512
text boxes, 503, 504
Publisher, 785
Word
colors, 170
formatting, 170
pages, 171
paragraphs, 170
tables, 214

Borders and Shading dialog box, 170-171

Borders Gallery, 328

breaking object links, 874

Broadcast Slide Show dialog box, 589

broadcasting slide shows, 589-590

bubble charts, 390

Building Block Gallery form control, 242

building blocks
Publisher, 785
Word
creating, 192
defined, 191
galleries, 191
headers and footers, 177
inserting, 193-194

bulleted lists
OneNote notes, 828-830
PowerPoint, 492
animating, 550
editing, 492
picture bullets, 492-493
symbol bullets, 493
Word, 166-167

Bullets and Numbering dialog box, 492

business card attachments, 643

Business Information dialog box, 773

business information sets, 772
accessing, 773
creating, 772-773
editing, 773
multiple, creating, 773-774

C

Calendar (Outlook)
accessing, 659-664
appointments
creating, 667-669, 728-729
deleting, 672
editing, 671
managing, 671
moving, 671
recurring, 669-670
viewing, 664
Daily Task List, 665
Date Navigator, 664
emailing, 676
events, scheduling, 670
months, viewing, 664
multiple, viewing, 674-675
opening shared, 674
publishing online, 677-680
options, 678-679
tasks, 679-680
searching, 672
sharing, 672-674
tasks
accepting/declining, 683
arranging, 683
assigning, 682
creating, 680
deleting, 686
editing, 685
managing, 686
marking for follow up, 686
moving, 686
options, 686
recurring, 681-682
Task folder, 680
task list, viewing, 683-684
viewing, 649
time scale, 666
time zones, 666-667

How can we make this index more useful? Email us at indexes@quepublishing.com

P

page breaks
- Excel
  - *printing, 311-312*
  - *viewing, 307-308*
- Word, 156, 163

page layout. *See* layouts

Page Layout tab (Excel Ribbon), 279, 309

Page Number Format dialog box, 178

page numbering
- table of contents, 247
- Word, 178-179

Page pane (Publisher), 770

Page Setup dialog box
- margins, 161-162
- master slides, 519
- page orientation, 162
- publication pages, 792

Page Tabs pane, 840

pages (OneNote), 811, 825. *See also* notebooks; OneNote
- audio, recording, 846-847
- colors, 838
- copying and pasting, 836-837
- creating with templates, 825-826
- drawings, inserting, 847-849
- files, attaching, 857-858
- managing, 832-838
- moving between sections, 836-837
- multiple authors, 842-844
- objects, inserting, 844-845
- paper sizes, 838
- pictures, adding, 845-846
- printing, 849-850
- recent edits, viewing, 841-842
- renaming, 836
- rule lines/grid lines, 838
- screen clips, 858-859
- space, inserting, 837-838
- subpages, creating, 826-827
- titles, hiding, 838

undeleting, 827-828
versions, viewing, 840-841
video, recording, 847
viewing, 839
zooming in/out, 839

pages (Publisher)
- commands, 789
- defined, 764
- deleting, 788
- inserting, 785-789
  - *blank, 788*
  - *duplicate, 788*
  - *multiple, 788*
- margins, 789-790
- master, 794
  - *applying, 796*
  - *creating, 796-797*
  - *headers and footers, 796*
  - *multiple, 797*
  - *names, 795*
  - *objects, placing, 795-796*
  - *viewing, 795*
- Page Setup dialog box, 792
- sizes, 790-792
- viewing, 770

paper sizes
- OneNote, 838
- Word, 162

Paragraph dialog box, 153

paragraphs (Word)
- alignment, 154-155
- formatting, 153-154
- hyphenation, 156
- indenting, 157-158
- line spacing, 155-156
- line/page breaks, 156
- widows/orphans, 156

Password Protection dialog box, 822

Password Protection pane, 823

passwords
- notebook sections, 822-823
- Outlook, 733-734

Paste gallery, 300-301

Paste Options gallery, 870-871

paste preview, 11

Paste Special dialog box
- cell contents (Excel), 302-304
  - *Operation options, 303*
  - *transposing cell ranges, 303-304*
- object embedding, 875-876
- object linking, 869-870

PDF file format, 53-54

People pane (Outlook), 619

percentage format, 322

Permission dialog box, 70

permissions, 68
- Add a Digital Signature, 68
- digital signatures, 70-71
- email messages, 638
- Encrypt with a Password, 68
- Excel workbooks/ worksheets, 287-288
- Mark as Final, 68
- Restrict Editing, 68
- Restrict Permission by People, 68
- restricting by people, 69-70
- viewing, 68

Phishing scams, 743

Photo Album dialog box, 533

photo albums (PowerPoint), 532
- captions, 535
- creating, 532
- layouts, 533-535
- pictures, editing, 533
- themes, 534

Picture Bullet dialog box, 492

Picture Content Control form control, 241

picture diagrams, 81

Picture Tools, 528

pictures, 78
- Background Removal tool, 91-92
- captions, adding, 88
- catalog merges, 805
- compression, 86
- Contacts, 692-693
- cropping, 90

How can we make this index more useful? Email us at indexes@quepublishing.com

How can we make this index more useful? Email us at indexes@quepublishing.com

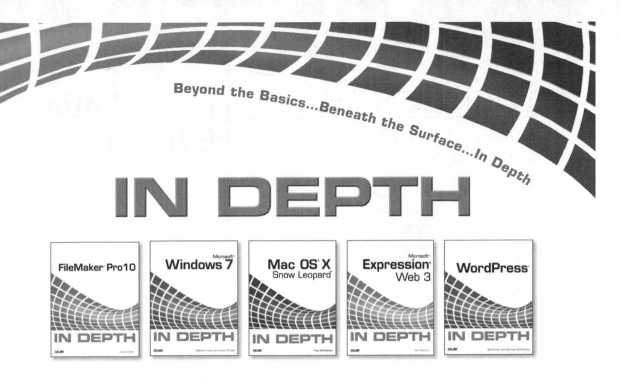

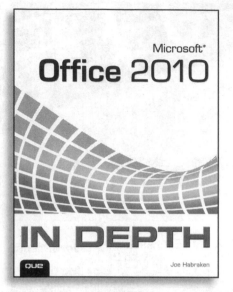